St. Thomas Aquinas

Aquinas

Summa Theologica

St. Thomas Aquinas
Summa Theologica

COMPLETE ENGLISH EDITION

IN FIVE VOLUMES

Translated by
Fathers of the English Dominican Province

VOLUME TWO

1ª IIᵃᵉQQ. 1–114

WITH SYNOPTICAL CHARTS

Christian Classics ✠ *Notre Dame, Indiana*

NIHIL OBSTAT:

RT. REV. MSGR. JOHN M. FEARNS, S.T.D.,
Censor Depvtatvs

IMPRIMATUR:

FRANCIS CARDINAL SPELLMAN,
Archbishop of New York

New York, 1946 & 1947

Approbatio Ordinis

NIHIL OBSTAT:

F. RAPHAEL MOSS, O.P., S.T.L.
F. LEO MOORE, O.P., S.T.L.

IMPRIMATUR:

F. BEDA JARRETT, O.P., S.T.L., A.M.
Prior Provincialis Angliae

1920

Founded in 1865, Ave Maria Press is a ministry of the United States Province of Holy Cross.

www.christian-classics.com

ISBN-10	CLOTH EDITION	PAPERBACK EDITION
Volume I	0-87061-064-3	0-87061-070-8
Volume II	0-87061-065-1	0-87061-071-6
Volume III	0-87061-066-X	0-87061-072-4
Volume IV	0-87061-067-8	0-87061-073-2
Volume V	0-87061-068-6	0-87061-074-0
Complete Set	0-87061-063-5	0-87061-069-4

ISBN-13	CLOTH EDITION	PAPERBACK EDITION
Volume I	978-0-87061-064-6	978-0-87061-070-7
Volume II	978-0-87061-065-3	978-0-87061-071-4
Volume III	978-0-87061-066-0	978-0-87061-072-1
Volume IV	978-0-87061-067-7	978-0-87061-073-8
Volume V	978-0-87061-068-4	978-0-87061-074-5
Complete Set	978-0-87061-063-9	978-0-87061-069-1

LIBRARY OF CONGRESS CATALOG CARD NUMBER: 81-68580

PRINTED IN THE UNITED STATES OF AMERICA

CONTENTS

FIRST PART OF THE SECOND PART

HUMAN ACTS

581

TREATISE ON THE LAST END

Prologue

SINCE, as Damascene states (*De Fide Orthod.* ii. 12), man is said to be made to God's image, in so far as the image implies *an intelligent being endowed with free-will and self-movement*: now that we have treated of the exemplar, *i.e.*, God, and of those things which came forth from the power of God in accordance with His will; it remains for us to treat of His image, *i.e.*, man, inasmuch as he too is the principle of his actions, as having free-will and control of his actions.

QUESTION 1

Of Man's Last End

(In Eight Articles)

IN this matter we shall consider first the last end of human life; and secondly, those things by means of which man may advance towards this end, or stray from the path: for the end is the rule of whatever is ordained to the end. And since the last end of human life is stated to be happiness, we must consider (1) the last end in general; (2) Happiness.

Under the first head there are eight points of inquiry: (1) Whether it belongs to man to act for an end? (2) Whether this is proper to the rational nature? (3) Whether a man's actions are specified by their end? (4) Whether there is any last end of human life? (5) Whether one man can have several last ends? (6) Whether man ordains all to the last end? (7) Whether all men have the same last end? (8) Whether all other creatures concur with man in that last end?

FIRST ARTICLE

Whether It Belongs to Man to Act for an End?

We proceed thus to the First Article:—

Objection 1. It would seem that it does not belong to man to act for an end. For a cause is naturally first. But an end, in its very name, implies something that is last. Therefore an end is not a cause. But that for which a man acts, is the cause of his action; since this preposition *for* indicates a relation of causality. Therefore it does not belong to man to act for an end.

Obj. 2. Further, that which is itself the last end is not for an end. But in some cases the last end is an action, as the Philosopher states (*Ethic.* i. 1). Therefore man does not do everything for an end.

Obj. 3. Further, then does a man seem to act for an end, when he acts deliberately. But man does many things without deliberation, sometimes not even thinking of what he is doing; for instance when one moves one's foot or hand, or scratches one's beard, while intent on something else. Therefore man does not do everything for an end.

On the contrary, All things contained in a genus are derived from the principle of that genus. Now the end is the principle in human operations, as the Philosopher states (*Phys.* ii. 9). Therefore it belongs to man to do everything for an end.

I answer that, Of actions done by man those alone are properly called *human*, which are proper to man as man. Now man differs from irrational animals in this, that he is master of his actions. Wherefore those actions alone are properly called human, of which man is master. Now man is master of his actions through his reason and will; whence, too, the free-will is defined as *the faculty and will of reason*. Therefore those actions are properly called human which proceed from a deliberate will. And if any other actions are found in man, they can be called actions *of a man*, but not properly *human* actions, since they are not proper to man as man.—Now it is clear that whatever actions proceed from a power, are caused by that power in accordance with the nature of its object. But the object of the will is the end and the good. Therefore all human actions must be for an end.

Reply Obj. 1. Although the end be last in the order of execution, yet it is first in the order of the agent's intention. And it is this way that it is a cause.

Reply Obj. 2. If any human action be the last end, it must be voluntary, else it would not be human, as stated above. Now an action is voluntary in one of two ways: first, because it is commanded by the will, *e.g.,* to walk, or to speak; secondly, because it is elicited by the will, for instance the very act of willing. Now it is impossible for the very act elicited by the will to be the last end. For the object of the will is the end, just as the object of sight is color: wherefore just as the first visible cannot be the act of seeing, because every act of seeing is directed to a visible object; so the first appetible, *i.e.,* the end, cannot be the very act of willing. Consequently it follows that if a human action be the last end, it must be an action commanded by the will: so that there, some action of man, at least the act of willing, is for the end. Therefore whatever a man does, it is true to say that man acts for an end, even when he does that action in which the last end consists.

Reply Obj. 3. Such like actions are not properly human actions; since they do not proceed from deliberation of the reason, which is the proper principle of human actions. Therefore they have indeed an imaginary end, but not one that is fixed by reason.

SECOND ARTICLE

Whether It Is Proper to the Rational Nature to Act for an End?

We proceed thus to the Second Article:—

Objection 1. It would seem that it is proper to the rational nature to act for an end. For man, to whom it belongs to act for an end, never acts for an unknown end. On the other hand, there are many things that have no knowledge of an end; either because they are altogether without knowledge, as insensible creatures: or because they do not apprehend the idea of an end as such, as irrational animals. Therefore it seems proper to the rational nature to act for an end.

Obj. 2. Further, to act for an end is to order one's action to an end. But this is the work of reason. Therefore it does not belong to things that lack reason.

Obj. 3. Further, the good and the end is the object of the will. But *the will is in the reason* (*De Anima* iii. 9). Therefore to act for an end belongs to none but a rational nature.

On the contrary, The Philosopher proves (*Phys.* ii. 5) that *not only mind but also nature acts for an end.*

I answer that, Every agent, of necessity, acts for an end. For if, in a number of causes ordained to one another, the first be removed, the others must, of necessity, be removed also. Now the first of all causes is the final cause. The reason of which is that matter does not receive form, save in so far as it is moved by an agent; for nothing reduces itself from potentiality to act. But an agent does not move except out of intention for an end. For if the agent were not determinate to some particular effect, it would not do one thing rather than another: consequently in order that it produce a determinate effect, it must, of necessity, be determined to some certain one, which has the nature of an end. And just as this determination is effected, in the rational nature, by the *rational appetite,* which is called the will; so, in other things, it is caused by their natural inclination, which is called the *natural appetite.*

Nevertheless it must be observed that a thing tends to an end, by its action or movement, in two ways:—first, as a thing, moving itself to the end,—as man; secondly, as a thing moved by another to the end, as an arrow tends to a determinate end through being moved by the archer, who directs his action to the end. Therefore those things that are possessed of reason, move themselves to an end; because they have dominion over their actions through their free-will, which is the *faculty of will and reason.* But those things that lack reason tend to an end, by natural inclination, as being moved by another and not by themselves; since they do not know the nature of an end as such, and consequently cannot ordain anything to an end, but can be ordained to an end only by another. For the entire irrational nature is in comparison to God as an instrument to the principal agent, as stated above (I. Q. 22, A. 2 *ad* 4: Q. 103, A. 1 *ad* 3). Consequently it is proper to the rational nature to tend to an end, as directing (*agens*) and leading itself to the end; whereas it is proper to the irrational nature to tend to an end, as directed or led by another, whether it apprehend the end, as do irrational animals, or do not apprehend it, as is the case of those things which are altogether void of knowledge.

Reply Obj. 1. When a man of himself acts for an end, he knows the end: but when he is directed or led by another, for instance, when he acts at another's command, or when he is moved under another's compulsion, it is not necessary that he should know the end. And it is thus with irrational creatures.

Reply Obj. 2. To ordain towards an end belongs to that which directs itself to an end: whereas to be ordained to an end belongs to that which is directed by another to an end. And this can belong to an irrational nature, but owing to some one possessed of reason.

Reply Obj. 3. The object of the will is the end and the good in universal. Consequently there can be no will in those things that lack reason and intellect, since they cannot apprehend the universal; but they have a natural appetite or a sensitive appetite, determinate to some particular good. Now it is clear that particular causes are moved by a universal cause: thus the governor of a city, who intends the common good, moves, by his command, all the particular departments of the city. Consequently all things that lack reason are, of necessity, moved to their particular ends by some rational will which extends to the universal good, namely by the Divine will.

THIRD ARTICLE

Whether Human Acts Are Specified by Their End?

We proceed thus to the Third Article:—

Objection 1. It would seem that human acts are not specified by their end. For the end is an extrinsic cause. But everything is specified by an intrinsic principle. Therefore human acts are not specified by their end.

Obj. 2. Further, that which gives a thing its species should exist before it. But the end comes into existence afterwards. Therefore a human act does not derive its species from the end.

Obj. 3. Further, one thing cannot be in more than one species. But one and the same act may happen to be ordained to various ends. Therefore the end does not give the species to human acts.

On the contrary, Augustine says (*De Mor. Eccl. et Manich.* ii. 13): *According as their end is worthy of blame or praise so are our deeds worthy of blame or praise.*

I answer that Each thing receives its species in respect of an act and not in respect of potentiality; wherefore things composed of matter and form are established in their respective species by their own forms. And this is also to be observed in proper movements. For since movements are, in a way, divided into action and passion, each of these receives its species from an act; action indeed from the act which is the principle of acting, and passion from the act which is the terminus of the movement. Wherefore heating, as an action, is nothing else than a certain movement proceeding from heat, while heating as a passion is nothing else than a movement towards heat: and it is the definition that shows the specific nature. And either way, human acts, whether they be considered as actions, or as passions, receive their species from the end. For human acts can be considered in both ways, since man moves himself, and is moved by himself. Now it has been stated above (A. 1) that acts are called human, inasmuch as they proceed from a deliberate will. Now the object of the will is the good and the end. And hence it is clear that the principle of human acts, in so far as they are human, is the end. In like manner it is their terminus: for the human act terminates at that which the will intends as the

end; thus in natural agents the form of the thing generated is conformed to the form of the generator. And since, as Ambrose says (*Prolog. super Luc.*) *morality is said properly of man,* moral acts properly speaking receive their species from the end, for moral acts are the same as human acts.

Reply Obj. 1. The end is not altogether extrinsic to the act, because it is related to the act as principle or terminus; and it is just this that is essential to an act, viz., to proceed from something, considered as action, and to proceed towards something, considered as passion.

Reply Obj. 2. The end, in so far as it pre-exists in the intention, pertains to the will, as stated above (A. 1 *ad* 1). And it is thus that it gives the species to the human or moral act.

Reply Obj. 3. One and the same act, in so far as it proceeds once from the agent, is ordained to but one proximate end, from which it has its species: but it can be ordained to several remote ends, of which one is the end of the other. It is possible, however, that an act which is one in respect of its natural species, be ordained to several ends of the will: thus this act *to kill a man,* which is but one act in respect of its natural species, can be ordained, as to an end, to the safeguarding of justice, and to the satisfying of anger: the result being that there would be several acts in different species of morality: since in one way there will be an act of virtue, in another, an act of vice. For a movement does not receive its species from that which is its terminus accidentally, but only from that which is its *per se* terminus. Now moral ends are accidental to a natural thing, and conversely the relation to a natural end is accidental to morality. Consequently there is no reason why acts which are the same considered in their natural species, should not be diverse, considered in their moral species, and conversely.

FOURTH ARTICLE

Whether There Is One Last End of Human Life?

We proceed thus to the Fourth Article:—

Objection 1. It would seem that there is no last end of human life, but that we proceed to infinity. For good is essentially diffusive, as Dionysius states (*Div. Nom.* iv). Consequently if that which proceeds from good is itself good, the latter must needs diffuse some other good: so that the diffusion of good goes on indefinitely. But good has the nature of an end. Therefore there is an indefinite series of ends.

Obj. 2. Further, things pertaining to the reason can be multiplied to infinity: thus mathematical quantities have no limit. For the same reason the species of numbers are infinite, since, given any number, the reason can think of one yet greater. But desire of the end is consequent on the apprehension of the reason. Therefore it seems that there is also an infinite series of ends.

Obj. 3. Further, the good and the end is the object of the will. But the will can react on itself an infinite number of times: for I can will something, and will to will it, and so on indefinitely. Therefore there is an infinite series of ends of the human will, and there is no last end of the human will.

On the contrary, The Philosopher says (*Metaph.* ii. 2) that *to suppose a thing to be indefinite is to deny that it is good.* But the good is that which has the nature of an end. Therefore it is contrary to the nature of an end to proceed indefinitely. Therefore it is necessary to fix one last end.

I answer that, Absolutely speaking, it is not possible to proceed indefinitely in the matter of ends, from any point of view. For in whatsoever things there is an essential order of one to another, if the first be removed, those that are ordained to the first, must of necessity be removed also. Wherefore the Philosopher proves (*Phys.* viii. 5) that we cannot proceed to infinitude in causes of movement, because then there would be no first mover, without which neither can the others move, since they move only through being moved by the first mover. Now there is to be observed a twofold order in ends,—the order of intention, and the order of execution: and in either of these orders there must be something first. For that which is first in the order of intention, is the principle, as it were, moving the appetite, consequently, if you remove this principle, there will be nothing to move the appetite. On the other hand, the principle in execution is that wherein operation has its beginning; and if this principle be taken away, no one will begin to work. Now the principle in the intention is the last end; while the principle in execution is the first of the things which are ordained to the end. Consequently, on neither side is it possible to go on to infinity; since if there were no last end, nothing would be desired, nor would any action have its term, nor would the intention of the agent be at rest; while if there is no first thing among those that are ordained to the end, none would begin to work at anything, and counsel would have no term, but would continue indefinitely.

On the other hand, nothing hinders infinity from being in things that are ordained to one another not essentially but accidentally; for accidental causes are indeterminate. And in this way it happens that there is an accidental infinity of ends, and of things ordained to the end.

Reply Obj. 1. The very nature of good is that something flows from it, but not that it flows from something else. Since, therefore, good has the nature of end, and the first good is the last end, this argument does not prove that there is no last end; but that from the end, already supposed, we may proceed downwards indefinitely towards those things that are ordained to the end. And this would be true if we considered but the power of the First Good, which is infinite. But, since the First Good diffuses itself according to the intellect, to which it is proper to flow forth into its effects according to a certain fixed form; it follows that there is a certain measure to the flow of good things from the First Good from Which all other goods share the power of diffusion. Consequently the diffusion of goods does not proceed indefinitely, but, as it is written (Wisd. xi. 21), God disposes all things *in number, weight and measure.*

Reply Obj. 2. In things which are of themselves, reason begins from principles that are known naturally, and advances to some term. Wherefore the Philosopher proves (*Poster.* i. 3) that there is no infinite process in demonstrations, because there we find a process of things having an essential, not an accidental, connection with one another. But in those things which are accidentally connected, nothing hinders the reason from proceeding indefinitely. Now it is accidental to a stated quantity or number, as such, that quantity or unity be added to it. Wherefore in such like things nothing hinders the reason from an indefinite process.

Reply Obj. 3. This multiplication of acts of the will reacting on itself, is accidental to the order of ends. This is clear from the fact that in regard to one and the same end, the will reacts on itself indifferently once or several times.

FIFTH ARTICLE

Whether One Man Can Have Several Last Ends?

We proceed thus to the Fifth Article:—

Objection 1. It would seem possible for one man's will to be directed at the same time to several things, as last ends. For Augustine says (*De Civ. Dei* xix. 1) that some held man's last end to consist in four things, viz., *in pleasure, repose, the gifts of nature, and virtue.* But these are clearly more than one thing. Therefore one man can place the last end of his will in many things.

Obj. 2. Further, things not in opposition to one another do not exclude one another. Now there are many things which are not in opposition to one another. Therefore the supposition that one thing is the last end of the will does not exclude others.

Obj. 3. Further, by the fact that it places its last end in one thing, the will does not lose its freedom. But before it placed its last end in that thing, *e.g.*, pleasure, it could place it in something else, *e.g.*, riches. Therefore even after having placed his last end in pleasure, a man can at the same time place his last end in riches. Therefore it is possible for one man's will to be directed at the same time to several things, as last ends.

On the contrary, That in which a man rests as in his last end, is master of his affections, since he takes therefrom his entire rule of life. Hence of gluttons it is written (Phil. iii. 19): *Whose god is their belly:* viz., because they place their last end in the pleasures of the belly. Now according to Matth. vi. 24, *No man can serve two masters,* such, namely, as are not ordained to one another. Therefore it is impossible for one man to have several last ends not ordained to one another.

I answer that, It is impossible for one man's will to be directed at the same time to diverse things, as last ends. Three reasons may be assigned for this. First, because, since everything desires its own perfection, a man desires for his ultimate end, that which he desires as his perfect and crowning good. Hence Augustine (*De Civ. Dei* xix. 1): *In speaking of the end of good we mean now, not that it passes away so as to be no more, but that it is perfected so as to be complete.* It is therefore necessary for the last end so to fill man's appetite, that nothing is left besides it for man to desire. Which is not possible, if something else be required for his perfection. Consequently it is not possible for the appetite so to tend to two things, as though each were its perfect good.

The second reason is because, just as in the process of reasoning, the principle is that which is naturally known, so in the process of the rational appetite, *i.e.*, the will, the principle needs to be that which is naturally desired. Now this must needs be one: since nature tends to one thing only. But the principle in the process of the rational appetite is the last end. Therefore that to which the will tends, as to its last end, is one.

The third reason is because, since voluntary actions receive their species from the end, as stated above (A. 3), they must needs receive their genus from the last end, which is common to them all: just as natural things are placed in a genus according to a common form. Since, then, all things that can be desired by the will, belong, as such, to one genus, the last end must needs be one. And all the more because in every genus there is one first principle; and the last end has the nature of a first principle, as stated above. Now as the last end of man, simply as man, is to the whole

human race, so is the last end of any individual man to that individual. Therefore, just as of all men there is naturally one last end, so the will of an individual man must be fixed on one last end.

Reply Obj. 1. All these several objects were considered as one perfect good resulting therefrom, by those who placed in them the last end.

Reply Obj. 2. Although it is possible to find several things which are not in opposition to one another, yet it is contrary to a thing's perfect good, that anything besides be required for that thing's perfection.

Reply Obj. 3. The power of the will does not extend to making opposites exist at the same time. Which would be the case were it to tend to several diverse objects as last ends, as has been shown above (*ad* 2).

SIXTH ARTICLE

Whether Man Wills All, Whatsoever He Wills, for the Last End?

We proceed thus to the Sixth Article:—

Objection 1. It would seem that man does not will all, whatsoever he wills, for the last end. For things ordained to the last end are said to be serious matter, as being useful. But jests are foreign to serious matter. Therefore what man does in jest, he ordains not to the last end.

Obj. 2. Further, the Philosopher says at the beginning of his *Metaphysics* (i. 2) that speculative science is sought for its own sake. Now it cannot be said that each speculative science is the last end. Therefore man does not desire all, whatsoever he desires, for the last end.

Obj. 3. Further, whoever ordains something to an end, thinks of that end. But man does not always think of the last end in all that he desires or does. Therefore man neither desires nor does all for the last end.

On the contrary, Augustine says (*De Civ. Dei* xix. 1): *That is the end of our good, for the sake of which we love other things, whereas we love it for its own sake.*

I answer that, Man must, of necessity, desire all, whatsoever he desires, for the last end. This is evident for two reasons. First, because whatever man desires, he desires it under the aspect of good. And if he desire it, not as his perfect good, which is the last end, he must, of necessity, desire it as tending to the perfect good, because the beginning of anything is always ordained to its completion; as is clearly the case in effects both of nature and of art. Wherefore every beginning of perfection is ordained to complete perfection which is achieved through the last end. Secondly, because the last end stands in the same relation in moving the appetite, as the first mover in other movements. Now it is clear that secondary moving causes do not move save inasmuch as they are moved by the first mover. Therefore secondary objects of the appetite do not move the appetite, except as ordained to the first object of the appetite, which is the last end.

Reply Obj. 1. Actions done jestingly are not directed to any external end; but merely to the good of the jester, in so far as they afford him pleasure or relaxation. But man's consummate good is his last end.

Reply Obj. 2. The same applies to speculative science; which is desired as the scientist's good, included in complete and perfect good, which is the ultimate end.

Reply Obj. 3. One need not always be thinking of the last end, whenever one desires or does something: but the virtue of the first intention, which was in respect of the last end, remains in every desire directed to any object whatever, even though one's thoughts be not actually directed to the last end. Thus while walking along the road one needs not to be thinking of the end at every step.

SEVENTH ARTICLE

Whether All Men Have the Same Last End?

We proceed thus to the Seventh Article:—

Objection 1. It would seem that all men have not the same last end. For before all else the unchangeable good seems to be the last end of man. But some turn away from the unchangeable good, by sinning. Therefore all men have not the same last end.

Obj. 2. Further, man's entire life is ruled according to his last end. If, therefore, all men had the same last end, they would not have various pursuits in life. Which is evidently false.

Obj. 3. Further, the end is the term of action. But actions are of individuals. Now although men agree in their specific nature, yet they differ in things pertaining to individuals. Therefore all men have not the same last end.

On the contrary, Augustine says (*De Trin.* xiii. 3) that all men agree in desiring the last end, which is happiness.

I answer that, We can speak of the last end in two ways: first, considering only the aspect of last end; secondly, considering the thing in which the aspect of last end is realized. So, then, as to the aspect of last end, all agree in desiring the last end: since all desire the fulfilment of their perfection, and it is precisely this fulfilment in which the last end consists, as stated above (A. 5). But as to the thing in which this aspect is realized, all men are not agreed as to their last end: since some desire riches, as

their consummate good; some, pleasure; others, something else. Thus to every taste the sweet is pleasant; but to some, the sweetness of wine is most pleasant, to others, the sweetness of honey, or of something similar. Yet that sweet is absolutely the best of all pleasant things, in which he who has the best taste takes most pleasure. In like manner that good is most complete which the man with well-disposed affections desires for his last end.

Reply Obj. 1. Those who sin turn from that in which their last end really consists: but they do not turn away from the intention of the last end, which intention they mistakenly seek in other things.

Reply Obj. 2. Various pursuits in life are found among men by reason of the various things in which men seek to find their last end.

Reply Obj. 3. Although actions are of individuals, yet their first principle of action is nature, which tends to one thing, as stated above (A. 5).

EIGHTH ARTICLE

Whether Other Creatures Concur in That Last End?

We proceed thus to the Eighth Article:—

Objection 1. It would seem that all other creatures concur in man's last end. For the end corresponds to the beginning. But man's beginning—i.e., God—is also the beginning of all else. Therefore all other things concur in man's last end.

Obj. 2. Further, Dionysius says (*Div. Nom.* iv) that *God turns all things to Himself as to their last end.* But He is also man's last end; because He alone is to be enjoyed by man, as Augustine says (*De Doctr. Christ.* i. 5, 22). Therefore other things, too, concur in man's last end.

Obj. 3. Further, man's last end is the object of the will. But the object of the will is the universal good, which is the end of all. Therefore all must needs concur in man's last end.

On the contrary, man's last end is happiness; which all men desire, as Augustine says (*De Trin.* xiii. 3, 4). But *happiness is not possible for animals bereft of reason,* as Augustine says (QQ. 83, qu. 5). Therefore other things do not concur in man's last end.

I answer that, As the Philosopher says (*Phys.* ii. 2), the end is twofold,—the end *for which* and the end *by which;* viz., the thing itself in which is found the aspect of good, and the use or acquisition of that thing. Thus we say that the end of the movement of a weighty body is either a lower place as *thing,* or to be in a lower place, as *use;* and the end of the miser is money as *thing,* or possession of money as *use.*

If, therefore, we speak of man's last end as of the thing which is the end, thus all other things concur in man's last end, since God is the last end of man and of all other things.— If, however, we speak of man's last end, as of the acquisition of the end, then irrational creatures do not concur with man in this end. For man and other rational creatures attain to their last end by knowing and loving God: this is not possible to other creatures, which acquire their last end, in so far as they share in the Divine likeness, inasmuch as they are, or live, or even know.

Hence it is evident how the objections are solved: since happiness means the acquisition of the last end.

QUESTION 2

Of Those Things in Which Man's Happiness Consists

(In Eight Articles)

WE have now to consider happiness: and (1) in what it consists; (2) what it is; (3) how we can obtain it.

Concerning the first there are eight points of inquiry: (1) Whether happiness consists in wealth? (2) Whether in honor? (3) Whether in fame or glory? (4) Whether in power? (5) Whether in any good of the body? (6) Whether in pleasure? (7) Whether in any good of the soul? (8) Whether in any created good?

FIRST ARTICLE

Whether Man's Happiness Consists in Wealth?

We proceed thus to the First Article:—

Objection 1. It would seem that man's happiness consists in wealth. For since happiness is man's last end, it must consist in that which has the greatest hold on man's affections. Now this is wealth: for it is written (Eccles. x. 19): *All things obey money.* Therefore man's happiness consists in wealth.

Obj. 2. Further, according to Boëthius (*De Consol.* iii), happiness is *a state of life made perfect by the aggregate of all good things.* Now money seems to be the means of possessing all things: for, as the Philosopher says (*Ethic.* v. 5), money was invented, that it might be a sort of guarantee for the acquisition of whatever man desires. Therefore happiness consists in wealth.

Obj. 3. Further, since the desire for the sovereign good never fails, it seems to be infinite. But this is the case with riches more than anything else; since *a covetous man shall not be satisfied with riches* (Eccles. v. 9). Therefore happiness consists in wealth.

On the contrary, Man's good consists in retaining happiness rather than in spreading it. But as Boëthius says (*De Consol.* ii), *wealth shines in giving rather than in hoarding: for the miser is hateful, whereas the generous man is applauded.* Therefore man's happiness does not consist in wealth.

I answer that, It is impossible for man's happiness to consist in wealth. For wealth is twofold, as the Philosopher says (*Polit.* i. 3), viz., natural and artificial. Natural wealth is that which serves man as a remedy for his natural wants: such as food, drink, clothing, cars, dwellings, and such like, while artificial wealth is that which is not a direct help to nature, as money, but is invented by the art of man, for the convenience of exchange, and as a measure of things salable.

Now it is evident that man's happiness cannot consist in natural wealth. For wealth of this kind is sought for the sake of something else, viz., as a support of human nature: consequently it cannot be man's last end, rather is it ordained to man as to its end. Wherefore in the order of nature, all such things are below man, and made for him, according to Ps. viii. 8: *Thou hast subjected all things under his feet.*

And as to artificial wealth, it is not sought save for the sake of natural wealth; since man would not seek it except because, by its means, he procures for himself the necessaries of life. Consequently much less can it be considered in the light of the last end. Therefore it is impossible for happiness, which is the last end of man, to consist in wealth.

Reply Obj. 1. All material things obey money, so far as the multitude of fools is concerned, who know no other than material goods, which can be obtained for money. But we should take our estimation of human goods not from the foolish but from the wise: just as it is for a person, whose sense of taste is in good order, to judge whether a thing is palatable.

Reply Obj. 2. All things salable can be had for money: not so spiritual things, which cannot be sold. Hence it is written (Prov. xvii. 16): *What doth it avail a fool to have riches, seeing he cannot buy wisdom.*

Reply Obj. 3. The desire for natural riches is not infinite: because they suffice for nature in a certain measure. But the desire for artificial wealth is infinite, for it is the servant of disordered concupiscence, which is not curbed,

as the Philosopher makes clear (*Polit.* i. 3).
Yet this desire for wealth is infinite otherwise
than the desire for the sovereign good. For the
more perfectly the sovereign good is possessed,
the more it is loved, and other things despised:
because the more we possess it, the more we
know it. Hence it is written, Ecclus. xxiv. 29):
They that eat me shall yet hunger. Whereas
in the desire for wealth and for whatsoever
temporal goods, the contrary is the case: for
when we already possess them, we despise
them, and seek others: which is the sense of
Our Lord's words (Jo. iv. 13): *Whosoever
drinketh of this water,* by which temporal
goods are signified, *shall thirst again.* The reason of this is that we realize more their insufficiency when we possess them: and this
very fact shows that they are imperfect, and
that the sovereign good does not consist
therein.

SECOND ARTICLE

Whether Man's Happiness Consists in Honors?

We proceed thus to the Second Article:—

Objection 1. It would seem that man's happiness consists in honors. For happiness or
bliss is *the reward of virtue,* as the Philosopher
says (*Ethic.* i. 9). But honor more than anything else seems to be that by which virtue is
rewarded, as the Philosopher says (*Ethic.*
iv. 3). Therefore happiness consists especially
in honor.

Obj. 2. Further, that which belongs to God
and to persons of great excellence seems especially to be happiness, which is the perfect
good. But that is honor, as the Philosopher
says (*Ethic.* iv. 3). Moreover, the Apostle
says (1 Tim. i. 17): *To . . . the only God be
honor and glory.* Therefore happiness consists
in honor.

Obj. 3. Further, that which man desires
above all is happiness. But nothing seems more
desirable to man than honor: since man suffers loss in all other things, lest he should suffer loss of honor. Therefore happiness consists
in honor.

On the contrary, Happiness is in the happy.
But honor is not in the honored, but rather
in him who honors, and who offers deference
to the person honored, as the Philosopher says
(*Ethic.* i. 5). Therefore happiness does not
consist in honor.

I answer that, It is impossible for happiness
to consist in honor. For honor is given to a
man on account of some excellence in him;
and consequently it is a sign and attestation
of the excellence that is in the person honored.
Now a man's excellence is in proportion, especially, to his happiness, which is man's perfect
good; and to its parts, *i.e.,* those goods by

---

* Augustine,—*Contra Maxim. Arian.* ii. 13.

---

which he has a certain share of happiness. And
therefore honor can result from happiness, but
happiness cannot principally consist therein.

Reply Obj. 1. As the Philosopher says
(*ibid.*), honor is not that reward of virtue, for
which the virtuous work: but they receive
honor from men by way of reward, *as from
those who have nothing greater to offer.* But
virtue's true reward is happiness itself, for
which the virtuous work: whereas if they
worked for honor, it would no longer be a virtue, but ambition.

Reply Obj. 2. Honor is due to God and to
persons of great excellence as a sign of attestation of excellence already existing: not that
honor makes them excellent.

Reply Obj. 3. That man desires honor above
all else, arises from his natural desire for happiness, from which honor results, as stated
above. Wherefore man seeks to be honored
especially by the wise, on whose judgment he
believes himself to be excellent or happy.

THIRD ARTICLE

Whether Man's Happiness Consists in Fame or Glory?

We proceed thus to the Third Article:—

Objection 1. It would seem that man's happiness consists in glory. For happiness seems
to consist in that which is paid to the saints
for the trials they have undergone in the world.
But this is glory: for the Apostle says (Rom.
viii. 18) *The sufferings of this time are not
worthy to be compared with the glory to come,
that shall be revealed in us.* Therefore happiness consists in glory.

Obj. 2. Further, good is diffusive of itself,
as stated by Dionysius (*Div. Nom.* iv.). But
man's good is spread abroad in the knowledge
of others by glory more than by anything else:
since, according to Ambrose,* glory consists
in being well known and praised. Therefore
man's happiness consists in glory.

Obj. 3. Further, happiness is the most enduring good. Now this seems to be fame or
glory; because by this men attain to eternity
after a fashion. Hence Boëthius says (*De
Consol.* ii): *You seem to beget unto yourselves
eternity, when you think of your fame in future time.* Therefore man's happiness consists
in fame or glory.

On the contrary, Happiness is man's true
good. But it happens that fame or glory is
false: for as Boëthius says (*De Consol.* iii),
*many owe their renown to the lying reports
spread among the people. Can anything be
more shameful? For those who receive false
fame, must needs blush at their own praise.*
Therefore man's happiness does not consist in
fame or glory.

I answer that, Man's happiness cannot consist in human fame or glory. For glory consists *in being well known and praised,* as Ambrose* says. Now the thing known is related to human knowledge otherwise than to God's knowledge: for human knowledge is caused by the things known, whereas God's knowledge is the cause of the things known. Wherefore the perfection of human good, which is called happiness, cannot be caused by human knowledge: but rather human knowledge of another's happiness proceeds from, and, in a fashion, is caused by, human happiness itself, inchoate or perfect. Consequently man's happiness cannot consist in fame or glory. On the other hand, man's good depends on God's knowledge as its cause. And therefore man's beatitude depends, as on its cause, on the glory which man has with God; according to Ps. xc. 15, 16: *I will deliver him, and I will glorify him; I will fill him with length of days, and I will show him my salvation.*

Furthermore, we must observe that human knowledge often fails, especially in contingent singulars, such as are human acts. For this reason human glory is frequently deceptive. But since God cannot be deceived, His glory is always true; hence it is written (2 Cor. x. 18): *He . . . is approved . . . whom God commendeth.*

Reply Obj. 1. The Apostle speaks, then, not of the glory which is with men, but of the glory which is from God, with His Angels. Hence it is written (Mark viii. 38): *The Son of Man shall confess him in the glory of His Father, before His angels.*†

Reply Obj. 2. A man's good which, through fame or glory, is in the knowledge of many, if this knowledge be true, must needs be derived from good existing in the man himself: and hence it presupposes perfect or inchoate happiness. But if the knowledge be false, it does not harmonize with the thing: and thus good does not exist in him who is looked upon as famous. Hence it follows that fame can nowise make man happy.

Reply Obj. 3. Fame has no stability; in fact, it is easily ruined by false report. And if sometimes it endures, this is by accident. But happiness endures of itself, and for ever.

FOURTH ARTICLE

Whether Man's Happiness Consists in Power?

We proceed thus to the Fourth Article:—

Objection 1. It would seem that happiness consists in power. For all things desire to become like to God, as to their last end and first beginning. But men who are in power, seem,

* Augustine,—*Contra Maxim. Arian.* ii. 13.

on account of the similarity of power, to be most like to God: hence also in Scripture they are called *gods* (Exod. xxii. 28),—*Thou shalt not speak ill of the gods.* Therefore happiness consists in power.

Obj. 2. Further, happiness is the perfect good. But the highest perfection for man is to be able to rule others; which belongs to those who are in power. Therefore happiness consists in power.

Obj. 3. Further, since happiness is supremely desirable, it is contrary to that which is before all to be shunned. But, more than aught else, men shun servitude, which is contrary to power. Therefore happiness consists in power.

On the contrary, Happiness is the perfect good. But power is most imperfect. For as Boëthius says (*De Consol.* iii), *the power of man cannot relieve the gnawings of care, nor can it avoid the thorny path of anxiety:* and further on: *Think you a man is powerful who is surrounded by attendants, whom he inspires with fear indeed, but whom he fears still more?* Therefore happiness does not consist in power.

I answer that, It is impossible for happiness to consist in power; and this for two reasons. First because power has the nature of principle, as is stated in *Metaph.* v. 12, whereas happiness has the nature of last end.—Secondly, because power has relation to good and evil: whereas happiness is man's proper and perfect good. Wherefore some happiness might consist in the good use of power, which is by virtue, rather than in power itself.

Now four general reasons may be given to prove that happiness consists in none of the foregoing external goods. First, because, since happiness is man's supreme good, it is incompatible with any evil. Now all the foregoing can be found both in good and in evil men.—Secondly, because, since it is the nature of happiness to *satisfy of itself,* as stated in *Ethic.* i. 7, having gained happiness, man cannot lack any needful good. But after acquiring any one of the foregoing, man may still lack many goods that are necessary to him; for instance, wisdom, bodily health, and such like.—Thirdly, because, since happiness is the perfect good, no evil can accrue to anyone therefrom. This cannot be said of the foregoing: for it is written (Eccles. v. 12) that *riches* are sometimes *kept to the hurt of the owner;* and the same may be said of the other three.—Fourthly, because man is ordained to happiness through principles that are in him; since he is ordained thereto naturally. Now the four goods mentioned above are due rather to external causes, and in most cases to fortune; for which reason they are called goods of for-

† St. Thomas joins Mark viii. 38 with Luke xii. 8, owing to a possible variant in his text, or to the fact that he was quoting from memory.

tune. Therefore it is evident that happiness nowise consists in the foregoing.

Reply Obj. 1. God's power is His goodness: hence He cannot use His power otherwise than well. But it is not so with men. Consequently it is not enough for man's happiness, that he become like God in power, unless he become like Him in goodness also.

Reply Obj. 2. Just as it is a very good thing for a man to make good use of power in ruling many, so is it a very bad thing if he makes a bad use of it. And so it is that power is towards good and evil.

Reply Obj. 3. Servitude is a hindrance to the good use of power: therefore is it that men naturally shun it; not because man's supreme good consists in power.

FIFTH ARTICLE

Whether Man's Happiness Consists in Any Bodily Good?

We proceed thus to the Fifth Article:—

Objection 1. It would seem that man's happiness consists in bodily goods. For it is written (Ecclus. xxx. 16): *There is no riches above the riches of the health of the body.* But happiness consists in that which is best. Therefore it consists in the health of the body.

Obj. 2. Further, Dionysius says (*Div. Nom.* v), that *to be* is better than *to live,* and *to live* is better than all that follows. But for man's being and living, the health of the body is necessary. Since, therefore, happiness is man's supreme good, it seems that health of the body belongs more than anything else to happiness.

Obj. 3. Further, the more universal a thing is, the higher the principle from which it depends; because the higher a cause is, the greater the scope of its power. Now just as the causality of the efficient cause consists in its flowing into something, so the causality of the end consists in its drawing the appetite. Therefore, just as the First Cause is that which flows into all things, so the last end is that which attracts the desire of all. But being itself is that which is most desired by all. Therefore man's happiness consists most of all in things pertaining to his being, such as the health of the body.

On the contrary, Man surpasses all other animals in regard to happiness. But in bodily goods he is surpassed by many animals; for instance, by the elephant in longevity, by the lion in strength, by the stag in fleetness. Therefore man's happiness does not consist in goods of the body.

I answer that, It is impossible for man's happiness to consist in the goods of the body;

and this for two reasons. First, because, if a thing be ordained to another as to its end, its last end cannot consist in the preservation of its being. Hence a captain does not intend as a last end, the preservation of the ship entrusted to him, since a ship is ordained to something else as its end, viz., to navigation. Now just as the ship is entrusted to the captain that he may steer its course, so man is given over to his will and reason; according to Ecclus. xv. 14; *God made man from the beginning and left him in the hand of his own counsel.* Now it is evident that man is ordained to something as his end: since man is not the supreme good. Therefore the last end of man's reason and will cannot be the preservation of man's being.

Secondly, because, granted that the end of man's will and reason be the preservation of man's being, it could not be said that the end of man is some good of the body. For man's being consists in soul and body; and though the being of the body depends on the soul, yet the being of the human soul depends not on the body, as shown above (I, Q. 75, A. 2); and the very body is for the soul, as matter for its form, and the instruments for the man that puts them into motion, that by their means he may do his work. Wherefore all goods of the body are ordained to the goods of the soul, as to their end. Consequently happiness, which is man's last end, cannot consist in goods of the body.

Reply Obj. 1. Just as the body is ordained to the soul, as its end, so are external goods ordained to the body itself. And therefore it is with reason that the good of the body is preferred to external goods, which are signified by *riches,* just as the good of the soul is preferred to all bodily goods.

Reply Obj. 2. Being taken simply, as including all perfection of being, surpasses life and all that follows it; for thus being itself includes all these. And in this sense Dionysius speaks. But if we consider being itself as participated in this or that thing, which does not possess the whole perfection of being, but has imperfect being, such as the being of any creature; then it is evident that being itself together with an additional perfection is more excellent. Hence in the same passage Dionysius says that things that live are better than things that exist, and intelligent better than living things.

Reply Obj. 3. Since the end corresponds to the beginning; this argument proves that the last end is the first beginning of being, in Whom every perfection of being is: Whose likeness, according to their proportion, some desire as to being only, some as to living being, some as to being which is living, intelligent and happy. And this belongs to few.

SIXTH ARTICLE

Whether Man's Happiness Consists in Pleasure?

We proceed thus to the Sixth Article:—

Objection 1. It would seem that man's happiness consists in pleasure. For since happiness is the last end, it is not desired for something else, but other things for it. But this answers to pleasure more than to anything else: *for it is absurd to ask anyone what is his motive in wishing to be pleased* (*Ethic.* x. 2). Therefore happiness consists principally in pleasure and delight.

Obj. 2. Further, *the first cause goes more deeply into the effect than the second cause* (*De Causis* 1). Now the causality of the end consists in its attracting the appetite. Therefore, seemingly that which moves most the appetite, answers to the notion of the last end. Now this is pleasure: and a sign of this is that delight so far absorbs man's will and reason, that it causes him to despise other goods. Therefore it seems that man's last end, which is happiness, consists principally in pleasure.

Obj. 3. Further, since desire is for good, it seems that what all desire is best. But all desire delight; both wise and foolish, and even irrational creatures. Therefore delight is the best of all. Therefore happiness, which is the supreme good, consists in pleasure.

On the contrary, Boëthius says (*De Consol.* iii): *Any one that chooses to look back on his past excesses, will perceive that pleasures have a sad ending: and if they can render a man happy, there is no reason why we should not say that the very beasts are happy too.*

I answer that, Because bodily delights are more generally known, *the name of pleasure has been appropriated to them* (*Ethic.* vii. 13), although other delights excel them: and yet happiness does not consist in them. Because in every thing, that which pertains to its essence is distinct from its proper accident: thus in man it is one thing that he is a mortal rational animal, and another that he is a risible animal. We must therefore consider that every delight is a proper accident resulting from happiness, or from some part of happiness; since the reason that a man is delighted is that he has some fitting good, either in reality, or in hope, or at least in memory. Now a fitting good, if indeed it be the perfect good, is precisely man's happiness: and if it is imperfect, it is a share of happiness, either proximate, or remote, or at least apparent. Therefore it is evident that neither is delight, which results from the perfect good, the very essence of happiness, but something resulting therefrom as its proper accident.

But bodily pleasure cannot result from the perfect good even in that way. For it results from a good apprehended by sense, which is a power of the soul, which power makes use of the body. Now good pertaining to the body, and apprehended by sense, cannot be man's perfect good. For since the rational soul excels the capacity of corporeal matter, that part of the soul which is independent of a corporeal organ, has a certain infinity in regard to the body and those parts of the soul which are tied down to the body: just as immaterial things are in a way infinite as compared to material things, since a form is, after a fashion, contracted and bounded by matter, so that a form which is independent of matter is, in a way, infinite. Therefore sense, which is a power of the body, knows the singular, which is determinate through matter: whereas the intellect, which is a power independent of matter, knows the universal, which is abstracted from matter, and contains an infinite number of singulars. Consequently it is evident that good which is fitting to the body, and which causes bodily delight through being apprehended by sense, is not man's perfect good, but is quite a trifle as compared with the good of the soul. Hence it is written (Wisd. vii. 9) that *all gold in comparison of her, is as a little sand*. And therefore bodily pleasure is neither happiness itself, nor a proper accident of happiness.

Reply Obj. 1. It comes to the same whether we desire good, or desire delight, which is nothing else than the appetite's rest in good: thus it is owing to the same natural force that a weighty body is borne downwards and that it rests there. Consequently just as good is desired for itself, so delight is desired for itself and not for anything else, if the preposition *for* denote the final cause. But if it denote the formal or rather the motive cause, thus delight is desirable for something else, *i.e.*, for the good, which is the object of that delight, and consequently is its principle, and gives it its form: for the reason that delight is desired is that it is rest in the thing desired.

Reply Obj. 2. The vehemence of desire for sensible delight arises from the fact that operations of the senses, through being the principles of our knowledge, are more perceptible. And so it is that sensible pleasures are desired by the majority.

Repy Obj. 3. All desire delight in the same way as they desire good: and yet they desire delight by reason of the good and not conversely, as stated above (*ad* 1). Consequently it does not follow that delight is the supreme and essential good, but that every delight results from some good, and that some delight results from that which is the essential and supreme good.

SEVENTH ARTICLE

Whether Some Good of the Soul Constitutes Man's Happiness?

We proceed thus to the Seventh Article:—

Objection 1. It would seem that some good of the soul constitutes man's happiness. For happiness is man's good. Now this is three-fold, external goods, goods of the body, and goods of the soul. But happiness does not consist in external goods, nor in goods of the body, as shown above (AA. 4, 5). Therefore it consists in goods of the soul.

Obj. 2. Further, we love that for which we desire good, more than the good that we desire for it: thus we love a friend for whom we desire money, more than we love money. But whatever good a man desires, he desires it for himself. Therefore he loves himself more than all other goods. Now happiness is what is loved above all: which is evident from the fact that for its sake all else is loved and desired. Therefore happiness consists in some good of man himself: not, however, in goods of the body; therefore, in goods of the soul.

Obj. 3. Further, perfection is something belonging to that which is perfected. But happiness is a perfection of man. Therefore happiness is something belonging to man. But it is not something belonging to the body, as shown above (A. 5). Therefore it is something belonging to the soul; and thus it consists in goods of the soul.

On the contrary, As Augustine says (*De Doctr. Christ.* i. 22), *that which constitutes the life of happiness is to be loved for its own sake.* But man is not to be loved for his own sake, but whatever is in man is to be loved for God's sake. Therefore happiness consists in no good of the soul.

I answer that, As stated above (Q. 1, A. 8), the end is twofold: namely, the thing itself, which we desire to attain, and the use, namely, the attainment or possession of that thing. If, then, we speak of man's last end, as to the thing itself which we desire as last end, it is impossible for man's last end to be the soul itself or something belonging to it. Because the soul, considered in itself, is as something existing in potentiality: for it becomes knowing actually, from being potentially knowing; and actually virtuous, from being potentially virtuous. Now since potentiality is for the sake of act as for its fulfilment, that which in itself is in potentiality cannot be the last end. Therefore the soul itself cannot be its own last end.

In like manner neither can anything belonging to it, whether power, habit, or act. For that good which is the last end, is the perfect good fulfilling the desire. Now man's appetite, otherwise the will, is for the universal good.

And any good inherent to the soul is a participated good, and consequently a portioned good. Therefore none of them can be man's last end.

But if we speak of man's last end, as to the attainment or possession thereof, or as to any use whatever of the thing itself desired as an end, thus does something of man, in respect of his soul, belong to his last end: since man attains happiness through his soul. Therefore the thing itself which is desired as end, is that which constitutes happiness, and makes man happy; but the attainment of this thing is called happiness. Consequently we must say that happiness is something belonging to the soul; but that which constitutes happiness is something outside the soul.

Reply Obj. 1. Inasmuch as this division includes all goods that man can desire, thus the good of the soul is not only power, habit, or act, but also the object of these, which is something outside. And in this way nothing hinders us from saying that what constitutes happiness is a good of the soul.

Reply Obj. 2. As far as the proposed objection is concerned, happiness is loved above all, as the good desired; whereas a friend is loved as that for which good is desired; and thus, too, man loves himself. Consequently it is not the same kind of love in both cases. As to whether man loves anything more than himself with the love of friendship, there will be occasion to inquire when we treat of Charity.

Reply Obj. 3. Happiness itself, since it is a perfection of the soul, is an inherent good of the soul; but that which constitutes happiness, viz., which makes man happy, is something outside his soul, as stated above.

EIGHTH ARTICLE

Whether Any Created Good Constitutes Man's Happiness?

We proceed thus to the Eighth Article:—

Objection 1. It would seem that some created good constitutes man's happiness. For Dionysius says (*Div. Nom.* vii) that Divine wisdom *unites the ends of first things to the beginnings of second things,* from which we may gather that the summit of a lower nature touches the base of the higher nature. But man's highest good is happiness. Since then the angel is above man in the order of nature, as stated in the First Part (Q. 111, A. 1), it seems that man's happiness consists in man somehow reaching the angel.

Obj. 2. Further, the last end of each thing is that which, in relation to it, is perfect: hence the part is for the whole, as for its end. But the universe of creatures which is called the macrocosm, is compared to man who is called the microcosm (*Phys.* viii. 2), as perfect to imperfect. Therefore man's happiness consists in the whole universe of creatures.

Obj. 3. Further, man is made happy by that which lulls his natural desire. But man's natural desire does not reach out to a good surpassing his capacity. Since then man's capacity does not include that good which surpasses the limits of all creation, it seems that man can be made happy by some created good. Consequently some created good constitutes man's happiness.

On the contrary, Augustine says (*De Civ. Dei* xix. 26): *As the soul is the life of the body, so God is man's life of happiness: of Whom it is written: "Happy is that people whose God is the Lord"* (Ps. cxliii. 15).

I answer that, It is impossible for any created good to constitute man's happiness. For happiness is the perfect good, which lulls the appetite altogether; else it would not be the last end, if something yet remained to be desired. Now the object of the will, *i.e.,* of man's appetite, is the universal good; just as the object of the intellect is the universal true. Hence it is evident that naught can lull man's will, save the universal good. This is to be found, not in any creature, but in God alone; because every creature has goodness by participation. Wherefore God alone can satisfy the will of man, according to the words of Ps. cii. 5: *Who satisfieth thy desire with good things.* Therefore God alone constitutes man's happiness.

Reply Obj. 1. The summit of man does indeed touch the base of the angelic nature, by a kind of likeness; but man does not rest there as in his last end, but reaches out to the universal fount itself of good, which is the common object of happiness of all the blessed, as being the infinite and perfect good.

Reply Obj. 2. If a whole be not the last end, but ordained to a further end, then the last end of a part thereof is not the whole itself, but something else. Now the universe of creatures, to which man is compared as part to whole, is not the last end, but is ordained to God, as to its last end. Therefore the last end of man is not the good of the universe, but God himself.

Reply Obj. 3. Created good is not less than that good of which man is capable, as of something intrinsic and inherent to him: but it is less than the good of which he is capable, as of an object, and which is infinite. And the participated good which is in an angel, and in the whole universe, is a finite and restricted good.

QUESTION 3

What Is Happiness

(In Eight Articles)

WE have now to consider (1) what happiness is, and (2) what things are required for it.

Concerning the first there are eight points of inquiry: (1) Whether happiness is something uncreated? (2) If it be something created, whether it is an operation? (3) Whether it is an operation of the sensitive, or only of the intellectual part? (4) If it be an operation of the intellectual part, whether it is an operation of the intellect, or of the will? (5) If it be an operation of the intellect, whether it is an operation of the speculative or of the practical intellect? (6) If it be an operation of the speculative intellect, whether it consists in the consideration of speculative sciences? (7) Whether it consists in the consideration of separate substances, viz., angels? (8) Whether it consists in the sole contemplation of God seen in His Essence?

FIRST ARTICLE

Whether Happiness Is Something Uncreated?

We proceed thus to the First Article:—

Objection 1. It would seem that happiness is something uncreated. For Boëthius says (*De Consol.* iii): *We must needs confess that God is happiness itself.*

Obj. 2. Further, happiness is the supreme good. But it belongs to God to be the supreme good. Since, then, there are not several supreme goods, it seems that happiness is the same as God.

Obj. 3. Further, happiness is the last end, to which man's will tends naturally. But man's will should tend to nothing else as an end, but to God, Who alone is to be enjoyed, as Augustine says (*De Doctr. Christ.* i. 5, 22). Therefore happiness is the same as God.

On the contrary, Nothing made is uncreated. But man's happiness is something made; because according to Augustine (*De Doctr. Christ.* i. 3): *Those things are to be enjoyed, which make us happy.* Therefore happiness is not something uncreated.

I answer that, As stated above (Q. 1, A. 8; Q. 2, A. 7), our end is twofold. First, there is the thing itself which we desire to attain: thus for the miser, the end is money. Secondly there is the attainment or possession, the use or enjoyment of the thing desired; thus we may say that the end of the miser is the possession of money; and the end of the intemperate man is to enjoy something pleasurable. In the first sense, then, man's last end is the uncreated good, namely, God, Who alone by His infinite goodness can perfectly satisfy man's will. But in the second way, man's last end is something created, existing in him, and this is nothing else than the attainment or enjoyment of the last end. Now the last end is called happiness. If, therefore, we consider man's happiness in its cause or object, then it is something uncreated; but if we consider it as to the very essence of happiness, then it is something created.

Reply Obj. 1. God is happiness by His Essence: for He is happy not by acquisition or participation of something else, but by His Essence. On the other hand, men are happy, as Boëthius says (*loc. cit.*), by participation; just as they are called *gods*, by participation. And this participation of happiness, in respect of which man is said to be happy, is something created.

Reply Obj. 2. Happiness is called man's supreme good, because it is the attainment or enjoyment of the supreme good.

Reply Obj. 3. Happiness is said to be the last end, in the same way as the attainment of the end is called the end.

SECOND ARTICLE

Whether Happiness Is an Operation?

We proceed thus to the Second Article:—

Objection 1. It would seem that happiness is not an operation. For the Apostle says (Rom. vi. 22): *You have your fruit unto sanctification, and the end, life everlasting.* But life is not an operation, but the very being of living things. Therefore the last end, which is happiness, is not an operation.

Obj. 2. Further, Boëthius says (*De Consol.* iii) that happiness is *a state made perfect by the aggregate of all good things.* But state does not indicate operation. Therefore happiness is not an operation.

Obj. 3. Further, happiness signifies something existing in the happy one: since it is man's final perfection. But the meaning of operation does not imply anything existing in the operator, but rather something proceeding therefrom. Therefore happiness is not an operation.

Obj. 4. Further, happiness remains in the happy one. Now operation does not remain, but passes. Therefore happiness is not an operation.

Obj. 5. Further, to one man there is one happiness. But operations are many. Therefore happiness is not an operation.

Obj. 6. Further, happiness is in the happy one uninterruptedly. But human operation is often interrupted; for instance, by sleep, or some other occupation, or by cessation. Therefore happiness is not an operation.

On the contrary, The Philosopher says (*Ethic.* i. 13) that *happiness is an operation according to perfect virtue.*

I answer that, In so far as man's happiness is something created, existing in him, we must needs say that it is an operation. For happiness is man's supreme perfection. Now each thing is perfect in so far as it is actual; since potentiality without act is imperfect. Consequently happiness must consist in man's last act. But it is evident that operation is the last act of the operator, wherefore the Philosopher calls it *second act* (*De Anima* ii. 1): because that which has a form can be potentially operating, just as he who knows is potentially considering. And hence it is that in other things, too, each one is said to be *for its operation* (*De Cælo* ii. 3). Therefore man's happiness must of necessity consist in an operation.

Reply Obj. 1. Life is taken in two senses. First for the very being of the living. And thus happiness is not life: since it has been shown (Q. 2, A. 5) that the being of a man, no matter in what it may consist, is not that man's happiness; for of God alone is it true that His Being is His Happiness. Secondly, life means the operation of the living, by which operation the principle of life is made actual. thus we speak of active and contemplative life, or of a life of pleasure. And in this sense eternal life is said to be the last end, as is clear from Jo. xvii. 3: *This is eternal life, that they may know Thee, the only true God.*

Reply Obj. 2. Boëthius, in defining happiness, considered happiness in general: for considered thus it is the perfect common good; and he signified this by saying that happiness is *a state made perfect by the aggregate of all good things,* thus implying that the state of a happy man consists in possessing the perfect good. But Aristotle expressed the very essence of happiness, showing by what man is established in this state, and that it is by some kind of operation. And so it is that he proves happiness to be *the perfect good* (*Ethic.* 1. 7).

Reply Obj. 3. As stated in *Metaph.* ix. 7 action is twofold. One proceeds from the agent into outward matter, such as *to burn* and *to cut.* And such an operation cannot be happiness: for such an operation is an action and a perfection, not of the agent, but rather of the patient, as is stated in the same passage. The other is an action that remains in the agent, such as *to feel,* *to understand,* and to will: and such an action is a perfection and an act of the agent. And such an operation can be happiness.

Reply Obj. 4. Since happiness signifies some final perfection; according as various things capable of happiness can attain to various degrees of perfection, so must there be various meanings applied to happiness. For in God there is happiness essentially; since His very Being is His operation, whereby He enjoys no other than Himself. In the happy angels, the final perfection is in respect of some operation, by which they are united to the Uncreated Good: and this operation of theirs is one only and everlasting. But in men, according to their present state of life, the final perfection is in respect of an operation whereby man is united to God: but this operation neither can be continual, nor, consequently, is it one only, because operation is multiplied by being discontinued. And for this reason in the present state of life, perfect happiness cannot be attained by man. Wherefore the Philosopher, in placing man's happiness in this life (*Ethic.* i. 10), says that it is imperfect, and after a long discussion, concludes: *We call men happy, but only as men.* But God has promised us perfect happiness, when we shall be *as the angels ... in heaven* (*Matth.* xxii. 30).

Consequently in regard to this perfect happiness, the objection fails: because in that state of happiness, man's mind will be united to God by one, continual, everlasting operation. But in the present life, in as far as we fall short of the unity and continuity of that operation, so do we fall short of perfect happiness. Nevertheless it is a participation of happiness: and so much the greater, as the operation can be more continuous and more one. Consequently the active life, which is busy with many things, has less of happiness than the contemplative life, which is busied with one thing, *i.e.,* the contemplation of truth. And if at any time man is not actually engaged in this operation, yet since he can always easily turn to it, and since he ordains the very cessation, by sleeping or occupying himself otherwise, to the aforesaid occupation, the latter seems, as it were, continuous. From these remarks the replies to Objections 5 and 6 are evident.

THIRD ARTICLE

Whether Happiness Is an Operation of the Sensitive Part, or of the Intellective Part Only?

We proceed thus to the Third Article:—

Objection 1. It would seem that happiness consists in an operation of the senses also. For there is no more excellent operation in man than that of the senses, except the intellective operation. But in us the intellective operation

depends on the sensitive: since *we cannot understand without a phantasm* (*De Anima* iii. 7). Therefore happiness consists in an operation of the senses also.

Obj. 2. Further, Boëthius says (*De Consol.* iii) that happiness is *a state made perfect by the aggregate of all good things.* But some goods are sensible, which we attain by the operation of the senses. Therefore it seems that the operation of the senses is needed for happiness.

Obj. 3. Further, happiness is the perfect good, as we find proved in *Ethic.* i. 7: which would not be true, were not man perfected thereby in all his parts. But some parts of the soul are perfected by sensitive operations. Therefore sensitive operation is required for happiness.

On the contrary, Irrational animals have the sensitive operation in common with us: but they have not happiness in common with us. Therefore happiness does not consist in a sensitive operation.

I answer that, A thing may belong to happiness in three ways: (1) essentially, (2) antecedently, (3) consequently. Now the operation of sense cannot belong to happiness essentially. For man's happiness consists essentially in his being united to the Uncreated Good, Which is his last end, as shown above (A. 1): to Which man cannot be united by an operation of his senses. Again, in like manner, because, as shown above (Q. 2, A. 5), man's happiness does not consist in goods of the body, which goods alone, however, we attain through the operation of the senses.

Nevertheless the operations of the senses can belong to happiness, both antecedently and consequently: antecedently, in respect of imperfect happiness, such as can be had in this life, since the operation of the intellect demands a previous operation of the sense;— consequently, in that perfect happiness which we await in heaven; because at the resurrection, *from the very happiness of the soul,* as Augustine says (*Ep. ad Dioscor.*) *the body and the bodily senses will receive a certain overflow, so as to be perfected in their operations;* a point which will be explained further on when we treat of the resurrection (Suppl. QQ. 82-85). But then the operation whereby man's mind is united to God will not depend on the senses.

Reply Obj. 1. This objection proves that the operation of the senses is required antecedently for imperfect happiness, such as can be had in this life.

Reply Obj. 2. Perfect happiness, such as the angels have, includes the aggregate of all good things, by being united to the universal source of all good; not that it requires each individual good. But in this imperfect happiness, we need the aggregate of those goods that suffice for the most perfect operation of this life.

Reply Obj. 3. In perfect happiness the entire man is perfected, in the lower part of his nature, by an overflow from the higher. But in the imperfect happiness of this life, it is otherwise; we advance from the perfection of the lower part to the perfection of the higher part.

FOURTH ARTICLE

Whether, If Happiness Is in the Intellective Part, It Is an Operation of the Intellect or of the Will?

We proceed thus to the Fourth Article:—

Objection 1. It would seem that happiness consists in an act of the will. For Augustine says (*De Civ. Dei* xix. 10, 11), that man's happiness consists in peace; wherefore it is written (Ps. cxlvii. 3): *Who hath placed peace in thy end* (Douay,—*borders*). But peace pertains to the will. Therefore man's happiness is in the will.

Obj. 2. Further, happiness is the supreme good. But good is the object of the will. Therefore happiness consists in an operation of the will.

Obj. 3. Further, the last end corresponds to the first mover: thus the last end of the whole army is victory, which is the end of the general, who moves all the men. But the first mover in regard to operations is the will: because it moves the other powers, as we shall state further on (Q. 9, AA. 1, 3). Therefore happiness regards the will.

Obj. 4. Further, if happiness be an operation, it must needs be man's most excellent operation. But the love of God, which is an act of the will, is a more excellent operation than knowledge, which is an operation of the intellect, as the Apostle declares (1 Cor. xiii). Therefore it seems that happiness consists in an act of the will.

Obj. 5. Further, Augustine says (*De Trin.* xiii. 5) that *happy is he who has whatever he desires, and desires nothing amiss.* And a little further on (6) he adds: *He is almost happy who desires well, whatever he desires: for good things make a man happy, and such a man already possesses some good—i.e., a good will.* Therefore happiness consists in an act of the will.

On the contrary, Our Lord said (Jo. xvii. 3: *This is eternal life: that they may know Thee, the only true God.* Now eternal life is the last end, as stated above (A. 2 *ad* 1). Therefore man's happiness consists in the knowledge of God, which is an act of the intellect.

I answer that, As stated above (Q. 2, A. 6) two things are needed for happiness: one, which

is the essence of happiness: the other, that is, as it were, its proper accident, *i.e.*, the delight connected with it. I say, then, that as to the very essence of happiness, it is impossible for it to consist in an act of the will. For it is evident from what has been said (AA. 1, 2; Q. 2, A. 7) that happiness is the attainment of the last end. But the attainment of the end does not consist in the very act of the will. For the will is directed to the end, both absent, when it desires it; and present, when it is delighted by resting therein. Now it is evident that the desire itself of the end is not the attainment of the end, but is a movement towards the end: while delight comes to the will from the end being present; and not conversely, is a thing made present, by the fact that the will delights in it. Therefore, that the end be present to him who desires it, must be due to something else than an act of the will.

This is evidently the case in regard to sensible ends. For if the acquisition of money were through an act of the will, the covetous man would have it from the very moment that he wished for it. But at that moment it is far from him; and he attains it, by grasping it in his hand, or in some like manner; and then he delights in the money got. And so it is with an intelligible end. For at first we desire to attain an intelligible end; we attain it, through its being made present to us by an act of the intellect; and then the delighted will rests in the end when attained.

So, therefore, the essence of happiness consists in an act of the intellect; but the delight that results from happiness pertains to the will. In this sense Augustine says (*Conf.* x. 23) that happiness is *joy in truth,* because, to wit, joy itself is the consummation of happiness.

Reply Obj. 1. Peace pertains to man's last end, not as though it were the very essence of happiness; but because it is antecedent and consequent thereto: antecedent, in so far as all those things are removed which disturb and hinder man in attaining the last end: consequent, inasmuch as, when man has attained his last end, he remains at peace, his desire being at rest.

Reply Obj. 2. The will's first object is not its act: just as neither is the first object of the sight, vision, but a visible thing. Wherefore, from the very fact that happiness belongs to the will, as the will's first object, it follows that it does not belong to it as its act.

Reply Obj. 3. The intellect apprehends the end before the will does: yet motion towards the end begins in the will. And therefore to the will belongs that which last of all follows the attainment of the end, viz., delight or enjoyment.

Reply Obj. 4. Love ranks above knowledge

in moving, but knowledge precedes love in attaining: for *naught is loved save what is known*, as Augustine says (*De Trin.* x. 1). Consequently we first attain an intelligible end by an act of the intellect; just as we first attain a sensible end by an act of sense.

Reply Obj. 5. He who has whatever he desires, is happy, because he has what he desires: and this indeed is by something other than the act of his will. But to desire nothing amiss is needed for happiness, as a necessary disposition thereto. And a good will is reckoned among the good things which make a man happy, forasmuch as it is an inclination of the will: just as a movement is reduced to the genus of its terminus, for instance, *alteration* to the genus *quality*.

FIFTH ARTICLE

Whether Happiness Is an Operation of the Speculative, or of the Practical Intellect?

We proceed thus to the Fifth Article:—

Objection 1. It would seem that happiness is an operation of the practical intellect. For the end of every creature consists in becoming like God. But man is like God, by his practical intellect, which is the cause of things understood, rather than by his speculative intellect, which derives its knowledge from things. Therefore man's happiness consists in an operation of the practical intellect rather than of the speculative.

Obj. 2. Further, happiness is man's perfect good. But the practical intellect is ordained to the good rather than the speculative intellect, which is ordained to the true. Hence we are said to be good, in reference to the perfection of the practical intellect, but not in reference to the perfection of the speculative intellect, according to which we are said to be knowing or understanding. Therefore man's happiness consists in an act of the practical intellect rather than of the speculative.

Obj. 3. Further, happiness is a good of man himself. But the speculative intellect is more concerned with things outside man; whereas the practical intellect is concerned with things belonging to man himself, viz., his operations and passions. Therefore man's happiness consists in an operation of the practical intellect rather than of the speculative.

On the contrary, Augustine says (*De Trin.* i. 8) that *contemplation is promised us, as being the goal of all our actions, and the everlasting perfection of our joys.*

I answer that, Happiness consists in an operation of the speculative rather than of the practical intellect. This is evident for three reasons. First because if man's happiness is an operation, it must needs be man's highest operation. Now man's highest operation is that of his highest power in respect of its highest object: and his highest power is the intellect, whose highest object is the Divine Good, which is the object, not of the practical, but of the speculative intellect. Consequently happiness consists principally in such an operation, viz., in the contemplation of Divine things. And since that *seems to be each man's self, which is best in him,* according to *Ethic.* ix. 8, and x. 7, therefore such an operation is most proper to man and most delightful to him.

Secondly, it is evident from the fact that contemplation is sought principally for its own sake. But the act of the practical intellect is not sought for its own sake but for the sake of action: and these very actions are ordained to some end. Consequently it is evident that the last end cannot consist in the active life, which pertains to the practical intellect.

Thirdly, it is again evident, from the fact that in the contemplative life man has something in common with things above him, viz., with God and the angels, to whom he is made like by happiness. But in things pertaining to the active life, other animals also have something in common with man, although imperfectly.

Therefore the last and perfect happiness, which we await in the life to come, consists entirely in contemplation. But imperfect happiness, such as can be had here, consists first and principally in contemplation, but secondarily, in an operation of the practical intellect directing human actions and passions, as stated in *Ethic.* x. 7, 8.

Reply Obj. 1. The asserted likeness of the practical intellect to God is one of proportion; that is to say, by reason of its standing in relation to what it knows, as God does to what He knows. But the likeness of the speculative intellect to God is one of union and *information;* which is a much greater likeness.—And yet it may be answered that, in regard to the principal thing known, which is His Essence, God has not practical but merely speculative knowledge.

Reply Obj. 2. The practical intellect is ordained to good which is outside of it: but the speculative intellect has good within it, viz., the contemplation of truth. And if this good be perfect, the whole man is perfected and made good thereby: such a good the practical intellect has not; but it directs man thereto.

Reply Obj. 3. This argument would hold, if man himself were his own last end; for then the consideration and direction of his actions and passions would be his happiness. But since man's last end is something outside of him, to wit, God, to Whom we reach out by an operation of the speculative intellect; therefore man's happiness consists in an operation of the speculative intellect rather than of the practical intellect.

SIXTH ARTICLE

Whether Happiness Consists in the Consideration of Speculative Sciences?

We proceed thus to the Sixth Article:—

Objection 1. It would seem that man's happiness consists in the consideration of speculative sciences. For the Philosopher says (*Ethic.* i. 13) that *happiness is an operation according to perfect virtue.* And in distinguishing the virtues, he gives no more than three speculative virtues—*knowledge, wisdom* and *understanding,* which all belong to the consideration of speculative sciences. Therefore man's final happiness consists in the consideration of speculative sciences.

Obj. 2. Further, that which all desire for its own sake, seems to be man's final happiness. Now such is the consideration of speculative sciences; because, as stated in *Metaph.* i. 1, *all men naturally desire to know;* and, a little farther on (2), it is stated that speculative sciences are sought for their own sakes. Therefore happiness consists in the consideration of speculative sciences.

Obj. 3. Further, happiness is man's final perfection. Now everything is perfected, according as it is reduced from potentiality to act. But the human intellect is reduced to act by the consideration of speculative sciences. Therefore it seems that in the consideration of these sciences, man's final happiness consists.

On the contrary, It is written (Jer. ix. 23): *Let not the wise man glory in his wisdom:* and this is said in reference to speculative sciences. Therefore man's final happiness does not consist in the consideration of these.

I answer that, As stated above (A. 2 *ad* 4), man's happiness is twofold, one perfect, the other imperfect. And by perfect happiness we are to understand that which attains to the true notion of happiness; and by imperfect happiness that which does not attain thereto, but partakes of some particular likeness of happiness. Thus perfect prudence is in man, with whom is the idea of things to be done; while imperfect prudence is in certain irrational animals, who are possessed of certain particular instincts in respect of works similar to works of prudence.

Accordingly perfect happiness cannot consist essentially in the consideration of speculative sciences. To prove this, we must observe that the consideration of a speculative science does not extend beyond the scope of the principles of that science: since the entire science is virtually contained in its principles. Now the first principles of speculative sciences are received through the senses, as the Philosopher clearly states at the beginning of the *Metaphysics* (i. 1), and at the end of the *Posterior Analytics* (ii. 15). Wherefore the entire consideration of speculative sciences cannot extend farther than knowledge of sensibles can lead. Now man's final happiness, which is his final perfection, cannot consist in the knowledge of sensibles. For a thing is not perfected by something lower, except in so far as the lower partakes of something higher. Now it is evident that the form of a stone or of any sensible, is lower than man. Consequently the intellect is not perfected by the form of a stone, as such, but inasmuch as it partakes of a certain likeness to that which is above the human intellect, viz., the intelligible light, or something of the kind. Now whatever is by something else is reduced to that which is of itself. Therefore man's final perfection must needs be through knowledge of something above the human intellect. But it has been shown (Part 1, Q. 88, A. 2), that man cannot acquire through sensibles, the knowledge of separate substances, which are above the human intellect. Consequently it follows that man's happiness cannot consist in the consideration of speculative sciences. However, just as in sensible forms there is a participation of the higher substances, so the consideration of speculative sciences is a certain participation of true and perfect happiness.

Reply Obj. 1. In his book on *Ethics* the Philosopher treats of imperfect happiness, such as can be had in this life, as stated above (A. 2 and 4).

Reply Obj. 2. Not only is perfect happiness naturally desired, but also any likeness or participation thereof.

Reply Obj. 3. Our intellect is reduced to act, in a fashion, by the consideration of speculative sciences, but not to its final and perfect act.

SEVENTH ARTICLE

Whether Happiness Consists in the Knowledge of Separate Substances, Namely, Angels?

We proceed thus to the Seventh Article:—

Objection 1. It would seem that man's happiness consists in the knowledge of separate substances, namely, angels. For Gregory says in a homily (xxvi. *in Ev.*): *It avails nothing to take part in the feasts of men, if we fail to take part in the feasts of angels;* by which he means final happiness. But we can take part in the feasts of the angels by contemplating them. Therefore it seems that man's final happiness consists in contemplating the angels.

Obj. 2. Further, the final perfection of each thing is for it to be united to its principle:

wherefore a circle is said to be a perfect figure, because its beginning and end coincide. But the beginning of human knowledge is from the angels, by whom men are enlightened, as Dionysius says (*Cœl. Hier.* iv). Therefore the perfection of the human intellect consists in contemplating the angels.

Obj. 3. Further, each nature is perfect, when united to a higher nature; just as the final perfection of a body is to be united to the spiritual nature. But above the human intellect, in the natural order, are the angels. Therefore the final perfection of the human intellect is to be united to the angels by contemplation.

On the contrary, It is written (Jerem. ix. 24): *Let him that glorieth, glory in this, that he understandeth and knoweth Me.* Therefore man's final glory or happiness consists only in the knowledge of God.

I answer that, As stated above (A. 6), man's perfect happiness consists not in that which perfects the intellect by some participation, but in that which is so by its essence. Now it is evident that whatever is the perfection of a power is so in so far as the proper formal object of that power belongs to it. Now the proper object of the intellect is the true. Therefore the contemplation of whatever has participated truth, does not perfect the intellect with its final perfection. Since, therefore, the order of things is the same in being and in truth (*Metaph.* ii. 1); whatever are beings by participation, are true by participation. Now angels have being by participation: because in God alone is His Being His Essence, as shown in the First Part. (Q. 44, A. 1). It follows that God alone is truth by His Essence, and that contemplation of Him makes man perfectly happy. However, there is no reason why we should not admit a certain imperfect happiness in the contemplation of the angels; and higher indeed than in the consideration of speculative science.

Reply Obj. 1. We shall take part in the feasts of the angels, by contemplating not only the angels, but, together with them, also God Himself.

Reply Obj. 2. According to those that hold human souls to be created by the angels, it seems fitting enough, that man's happiness should consist in the contemplation of the angels, in the union, as it were, of man with his beginning. But this is erroneous, as stated in the First Part (Q. 90, A. 3). Wherefore the final perfection of the human intellect is by union with God, Who is the first principle both of the creation of the soul and of its enlightenment. Whereas the angel enlightens as a minister, as stated in the First Part (Q. 111, A. 2 *ad* 2). Consequently, by his ministration he

helps man to attain to happiness; but he is not the object of man's happiness.

Reply Obj. 3. The lower nature may reach the higher in two ways. First, according to a degree of the participating power: and thus man's final perfection will consist in his attaining to a contemplation such as that of the angels. Secondly, as the object is attained by the power: and thus the final perfection of each power is to attain that in which is found the fulness of its formal object.

EIGHTH ARTICLE

Whether Man's Happiness Consists in the Vision of the Divine Essence?

We proceed thus to the Eighth Article:—

Objection 1. It would seem that man's happiness does not consist in the vision of the Divine Essence. For Dionysius says (*Myst. Theol.* i) that by that which is highest in his intellect, man is united to God as to something altogether unknown. But that which is seen in its essence is not altogether unknown. Therefore the final perfection of the intellect, namely, happiness, does not consist in God being seen in His Essence.

Obj. 2. Further, the higher perfection belongs to the higher nature. But to see His own Essence is the perfection proper to the Divine intellect. Therefore the final perfection of the human intellect does not reach to this, but consists in something less.

On the contrary, It is written (1 Jo. iii. 2): *When He shall appear, we shall be like to Him; and* (Vulg., *because*) *we shall see Him as He is.*

I answer that, Final and perfect happiness can consist in nothing else than the vision of the Divine Essence. To make this clear, two points must be observed. First, that man is not perfectly happy, so long as something remains for him to desire and seek: secondly, that the perfection of any power is determined by the nature of its object. Now the object of the intellect is *what a thing is, i.e.,* the essence of a thing, according to *De Anima* iii. 6. Wherefore the intellect attains perfection, in so far as it knows the essence of a thing. If therefore an intellect know the essence of some effect, whereby it is not possible to know the essence of the cause, *i.e.* to know of the cause *what it is;* that intellect cannot be said to reach that cause simply, although it may be able to gather from the effect the knowledge that the cause is. Consequently, when man knows an effect, and knows that it has a cause, there naturally remains in man the desire to know about that cause, *what it is.* And this desire is one of wonder, and causes inquiry, as is stated in the beginning of the *Metaphysics* (i. 2). For instance, if a man, knowing the eclipse of the sun, consider that it must be due to some cause, and know not what that cause is, he wonders about it, and from wondering proceeds to inquire. Nor does this inquiry cease until he arrive at a knowledge of the essence of the cause.

If therefore the human intellect, knowing the essence of some created effect, knows no more of God than *that He is;* the perfection of that intellect does not yet reach simply the First Cause, but there remains in it the natural desire to seek the cause. Wherefore it is not yet perfectly happy. Consequently, for perfect happiness the intellect needs to reach the very Essence of the First Cause. And thus it will have its perfection through union with God as with that object, in which alone man's

happiness consists, as stated above (AA. 1, 7; Q. 2, A. 8).

Reply Obj. 1. Dionysius speaks of the knowledge of wayfarers journeying towards happiness.

Reply Obj. 2. As stated above (Q. 1, A. 8), the end has a twofold acceptation. First, as to the thing itself which is desired: and in this way, the same thing is the end of the higher and of the lower nature, and indeed of all things, as stated above (*ibid.*). Secondly, as to the attainment of this thing; and thus the end of the higher nature is different from that of the lower, according to their respective habitudes to that thing. So then the happiness of God, Who, in understanding his Essence, comprehends It, is higher than that of a man or angel who sees It indeed, but comprehends It not.

QUESTION 4

Of Those Things That Are Required for Happiness

(In Eight Articles)

WE have now to consider those things that are required for happiness: and concerning this there are eight points of inquiry: (1) Whether delight is required for happiness? (2) Which is of greater account in happiness, delight or vision? (3) Whether comprehension is required? (4) Whether rectitude of the will is required? (5) Whether the body is necessary for man's happiness? (6) Whether any perfection of the body is necessary? (7) Whether any external goods are necessary? (8) Whether the fellowship of friends is necessary?

FIRST ARTICLE

Whether Delight Is Required for Happiness?

We proceed thus to the First Article:—

Objection 1. It would seem that delight is not required for happiness. For Augustine says (*De Trin.* i. 8) that *vision is the entire reward of faith.* But the prize or reward of virtue is happiness, as the Philosopher clearly states (*Ethic.* i. 9). Therefore nothing besides vision is required for happiness.

Obj. 2. Further, happiness is *the most self-sufficient of all goods,* as the Philosopher declares (*Ethic.* i. 7). But that which needs something else is not self-sufficient. Since then the essence of happiness consists in seeing God, as stated above (Q. 3, A. 8); it seems that delight is not necessary for happiness.

Obj. 3. Further, the *operation of bliss or happiness should be unhindered* (*Ethic.* vii. 13). But delight hinders the operation of

the intellect: since it destroys the estimate of prudence (*Ethic.* vi. 5). Therefore delight is not necessary for happiness.

On the contrary, Augustine says (*Conf.* x. 23) that happiness is *joy in truth.*

I answer that, One thing may be necessary for another in four ways. First, as a preamble and preparation to it: thus instruction is necessary for science. Secondly, as perfecting It: thus the soul is necessary for the life of the body. Thirdly, as helping it from without: thus friends are necessary for some undertaking. Fourthly, as something attendant on it: thus we might say that heat is necessary for fire. And in this way delight is necessary for happiness. For it is caused by the appetite being at rest in the good attained. Wherefore, since happiness is nothing else but the attainment of the Sovereign Good, it cannot be without concomitant delight.

Reply Obj. 1. From the very fact that a reward is given to anyone, the will of him who deserves it is at rest, and in this consists delight. Consequently, delight is included in the very notion of reward.

Reply Obj. 2. The very sight of God causes delight. Consequently, he who sees God cannot need delight.

Reply Obj. 3. Delight that is attendant upon the operation of the intellect does not hinder it, rather does it perfect it, as stated in *Ethic.* x. 4: since what we do with delight, we do with greater care and perseverance. On the other hand, delight which is extraneous to the operation is a hindrance thereto:—sometimes by distracting the attention; because, as already observed, we are more attentive to those things that delight us; and when we are very attentive to one thing, we must needs be less attentive to another:—sometimes on account of opposition; thus a sensual delight that is contrary to reason, hinders the estimate of prudence more than it hinders the estimate of the speculative intellect.

SECOND ARTICLE

Whether in Happiness Vision Ranks before Delight?

We proceed thus to the Second Article:—

Objection 1. It would seem that in happiness, delight ranks before vision. For *delight is the perfection of operation* (*Ethic.* x. 4). But perfection ranks before the thing perfected. Therefore delight ranks before the operation of the intellect, *i.e.*, vision.

Obj. 2. Further, that by reason of which a thing is desirable, is yet more desirable. But operations are desired on account of the delight they afford: hence, too, nature has adjusted delight to those operations which are necessary for the preservation of the individual and of the species, lest animals should disregard such operations. Therefore, in happiness, delight ranks before the operation of the intellect, which is vision.

Obj. 3. Further, vision corresponds to faith; while delight or enjoyment corresponds to charity. But charity ranks before faith, as the Apostle says (1 Cor. xiii. 13). Therefore delight or enjoyment ranks before vision.

On the contrary, The cause is greater than its effect. But vision is the cause of delight. Therefore vision ranks before delight.

I answer that, The Philosopher discusses this question (*Ethic.* x. 4), and leaves it unsolved. But if one consider the matter carefully, the operation of the intellect which is vision, must needs rank before delight. For delight consists in a certain repose of the will. Now that the will finds rest in anything, can only be on account of the goodness of that thing in which it reposes. If therefore the will reposes in an operation, the will's repose is caused by the goodness of the operation. Nor does the will seek good for the sake of repose; for thus the very act of the will would be the end, which has been disproved above (Q. 1, A. 1 *ad* 2; Q. 3, A. 4): but it seeks to be at rest in the operation, because that operation is its good. Consequently it is evident that the operation in which the will reposes ranks before the resting of the will therein.

Reply Obj. 1. As the Philosopher says (*ibid.*) *delight perfects operation as vigor perfects youth,* because it is a result of youth. Consequently delight is a perfection attendant upon vision; but not a perfection whereby vision is made perfect in its own species.

Reply Obj. 2. The apprehension of the senses does not attain to the universal good, but to some particular good which is delightful. And consequently, according to the sensitive appetite which is in animals, operations are sought for the sake of delight. But the intellect apprehends the universal good, the attainment of which results in delight: wherefore its purpose is directed to good rather than to delight. Hence it is that the Divine intellect, which is the Author of nature, adjusted delights to operations on account of the operations. And we should form our estimate of things not simply acording to the order of the sensitive appetite, but rather according to the order of the intellectual appetite.

Reply Obj. 3. Charity does not seek the beloved good for the sake of delight: it is for charity a consequence that it delights in the good gained which it loves. Thus delight does not answer to charity as its end, but vision does, whereby the end is first made present to charity.

THIRD ARTICLE

Whether Comprehension Is Necessary for Happiness?

We proceed thus to the Third Article:—

Objection 1. It would seem that comprehension is not necessary for happiness. For Augustine says (*Ad Paulinam de Videndo Deum*):* *To reach God with the mind is happiness, to comprehend Him is impossible.* Therefore happiness is without comprehension.

Obj. 2. Further, happiness is the perfection of man as to his intellective part, wherein there are no other powers than the intellect and will, as stated in the First Part (QQ. 79, *and foll.*). But the intellect is sufficiently perfected by seeing God, and the will by enjoying Him. Therefore there is no need for comprehension as a third.

Obj. 3. Further, happiness consists in an operation. But operations are determined by their objects: and there are two universal objects, the true and the good: of which the true corresponds to vision, and good to delight. Therefore there is no need for comprehension as a third.

On the contrary, The Apostle says (1 Cor. ix. 24): *So run that you may comprehend* (Douay,—*obtain*). But happiness is the goal of the spiritual race: hence he says (2 Tim. iv. 7, 8): *I have fought a good fight, I have finished my course, I have kept the faith; as to the rest there is laid up for me a crown of*

* Cf. *Serm.* xxxviii. *de Verb. Dom.*

justice. Therefore comprehension is necessary for Happiness.

I answer that, Since Happiness consists in gaining the last end, those things that are required for Happiness must be gathered from the way in which man is ordered to an end. Now man is ordered to an intelligible end partly through his intellect, and partly through his will:—through his intellect, in so far as a certain imperfect knowledge of the end pre-exists in the intellect:—through the will, first by love which is the will's first movement towards anything; secondly, by a real relation of the lover to the thing beloved, which relation may be threefold. For sometimes the thing beloved is present to the lover: and then it is no longer sought for. Sometimes it is not present, and it is impossible to attain it: and then, too, it is not sought for. But sometimes it is possible to attain it, yet it is raised above the capability of the attainer, so that he cannot have it forthwith; and this is the relation of one that hopes, to that which he hopes for, and this relation alone causes a search for the end. To these three, there are a corresponding three in Happiness itself. For perfect knowledge of the end corresponds to imperfect knowledge; presence of the end corresponds to the relation of hope; but delight in the end now present results from love, as already stated (A. 2 *ad* 3). And therefore these three must concur in Happiness; to wit, vision, which is perfect knowledge of the intelligible end; comprehension, which implies presence of the end; and delight or enjoyment, which implies repose of the lover in the object beloved.

Reply Obj. 1. Comprehension is twofold. First, inclusion of the comprehended in the comprehensor; and thus whatever is comprehended by the finite, is itself finite. Wherefore God cannot be thus comprehended by a created intellect. Secondly, comprehension means nothing but the holding of something already present and possessed: thus one who runs after another is said to comprehend* him when he lays hold on him. And in this sense comprehension is necessary for Happiness.

Reply Obj. 2. Just as hope and love pertain to the will, because it is the same one that loves a thing, and that tends towards it while not possessed, so, too, comprehension and delight belong to the will, since it is the same that possesses a thing and reposes therein.

Reply Obj. 3. Comprehension is not a distinct operation from vision; but a certain relation to the end already gained. Wherefore even vision itself, or the thing seen, inasmuch as it is present, is the object of comprehension.

* In English we should say "*catch.*"

Whether Rectitude of the Will Is Necessary for Happiness?

We proceed thus to the Fourth Article:—

Objection 1. It would seem that rectitude of the will is not necessary for Happiness. For Happiness consists essentially in an operation of the intellect, as stated above (Q. 3, A. 4). But rectitude of the will, by reason of which men are said to be clean of heart, is not necessary for the perfect operation of the intellect: for Augustine says (*Retract.* i. 4): *I do not approve of what I said in a prayer: O God, Who didst will none but the clean of heart to know the truth. For it can be answered that many who are not clean of heart, know many truths.* Therefore rectitude of the will is not necessary for Happiness.

Obj. 2. Further, what precedes does not depend on what follows. But the operation of the intellect precedes the operation of the will. Therefore Happiness, which is the perfect operation of the intellect, does not depend on rectitude of the will.

Obj. 3. Further, that which is ordained to another as its end, is not necessary, when the end is already gained; as a ship, for instance, after arrival in port. But rectitude of the will, which is by reason of virtue, is ordained to Happiness as its end. Therefore, Happiness once obtained, rectitude of the will is no longer necessary.

On the contrary, It is written (Matth. v. 8): *Blessed are the clean of heart; for they shall see God.* and (Heb. xii. 14): *Follow peace with all men, and holiness; without which no man shall see God.*

I answer that, Rectitude of the will is necessary for Happiness both antecedently and concomitantly. Antecedently, because rectitude of the will consists in being duly ordered to the last end. Now the end in comparison to what is ordained to the end is as form compared to matter. Wherefore, just as matter cannot receive a form, unless it be duly disposed thereto, so nothing gains an end, except it be duly ordained thereto. And therefore none can obtain Happiness, without rectitude of the will. Concomitantly, because as stated above (Q. 3, A. 8), final Happiness consists in the vision of the Divine Essence, Which is the very essence of goodness. So that the will of him who sees the Essence of God, of necessity, loves, whatever he loves, in subordination to God; just as the will of him who sees not God's Essence, of necessity, loves whatever he loves, under that common notion of good which he knows. And this is precisely what makes the will right. Wherefore it is evident that Happiness cannot be without a right will.

Reply Obj. 2. Every act of the will is preceded by an act of the intellect: but a certain act of the will precedes a certain act of the intellect. For the will tends to the final act of the intellect which is happiness. And consequently right inclination of the will is required antecedently for happiness, just as the arrow must take a right course in order to strike the target.

Reply Obj. 3. Not everything that is ordained to the end, ceases with the getting of the end: but only that which involves imperfection, such as movement. Hence the instruments of movement are no longer necessary, when the end has been gained: but the due order to the end is necessary.

FIFTH ARTICLE

Whether the Body Is Necessary for Man's Happiness?

We proceed thus to the Fifth Article:—

Objection 1. It would seem that the body is necessary for Happiness. For the perfection of virtue and grace presupposes the perfection of nature. But Happiness is the perfection of virtue and grace. Now the soul, without the body, has not the perfection of nature; since it is naturally a part of human nature, and every part is imperfect while separated from its whole. Therefore the soul cannot be happy without the body.

Obj. 2. Further, Happiness is a perfect operation, as stated above (Q. 3, AA. 2, 5). But perfect operation follows perfect being: since nothing operates except in so far as it is an actual being. Since, therefore, the soul has not perfect being, while it is separated from the body, just as neither has a part, while separate from its whole; it seems that the soul cannot be happy without the body.

Obj. 3. Further, Happiness is the perfection of man. But the soul, without the body, is not man. Therefore Happiness cannot be in the soul separated from the body.

Obj. 4. Further, according to the Philosopher (*Ethic.* vii. 13) *the operation of bliss*, in which operation happiness consists, is *not hindered.* But the operation of the separate soul is hindered; because, as Augustine says (*Gen. ad lit.,* xii. 35), the soul *has a natural desire to rule the body, the result of which is that it is held back, so to speak, from tending with all its might to the heavenward journey,* i.e., to the vision of the Divine Essence. Therefore the soul cannot be happy without the body.

Obj. 5. Further, Happiness is the sufficient good and lulls desire. But this cannot be said of the separated soul; for it yet desires to be united to the body, as Augustine says (*ibid.*).

Therefore the soul is not happy while separated from the body.

Obj. 6. Further, in Happiness man is equal to the angels. But the soul without the body is not equal to the angels, as Augustine says (*ibid.*). Therefore it is not happy.

On the contrary, It is written (Apoc. xiv. 13): *Happy* (Douay,—*blessed*) *are the dead who die in the Lord.*

I answer that, Happiness is twofold; the one is imperfect and is had in this life; the other is perfect, consisting in the vision of God. Now it is evident that the body is necessary for the happiness of this life. For the happiness of this life consists in an operation of the intellect, either speculative or practical. And the operation of the intellect in this life cannot be without a phantasm, which is only in a bodily organ, as was shown in the First Part (Q. 84, AA. 6, 7). Consequently that happiness which can be had in this life, depends, in a way, on the body.

But as to perfect Happiness, which consists in the vision of God, some have maintained that it is not possible to the soul separated from the body; and have said that the souls of saints, when separated from their bodies, do not attain to that Happiness until the Day of Judgment, when they will receive their bodies back again. And this is shown to be false, both by authority and by reason. By authority, since the Apostle says (2 Cor. v. 6): *While we are in the body, we are absent from the Lord;* and he points out the reason of this absence, saying: *For we walk by faith and not by sight.* Now from this it is clear that so long as we walk by faith and not by sight, bereft of the vision of the Divine Essence, we are not present to the Lord. But the souls of the saints, separated from their bodies, are in God's presence; wherefore the text continues: *But we are confident and have a good will to be absent ... from the body, and to be present with the Lord.* Whence it is evident that the souls of the saints, separated from their bodies, *walk by sight,* seeing the Essence of God, wherein is true Happiness.

Again this is made clear by reason. For the intellect needs not the body, for its operation, save on account of the phantasms, wherein it looks on the intelligible truth, as stated in the First Part (Q. 84, A. 7). Now it is evident that the Divine Essence cannot be seen by means of phantasms, as stated in the First Part (Q. 12, A. 3). Wherefore, since man's perfect Happiness consists in the vision of the Divine Essence, it does not depend on the body. Consequently, without the body the soul can be happy.

We must, however, notice that something may belong to a thing's perfection in two ways.

First, as constituting the essence thereof; thus the soul is necessary for man's perfection. Secondly, as necessary for its well-being: thus, beauty of body and keenness of perfection belong to man's perfection. Wherefore though the body does not belong in the first way to the perfection of human Happiness, yet it does in the second way. For since operation depends on a thing's nature, the more perfect is the soul in its nature, the more perfectly it has its proper operation, wherein its happiness consists. Hence Augustine, after inquiring (*Gen. ad lit.* xii. 35) *whether that perfect Happiness can be ascribed to the souls of the dead separated from their bodies,* answers *that they cannot see the Unchangeable Substance, as the blessed angels see It; either for some other more hidden reason, or because they have a natural desire to rule the body.*

Reply Obj. 1. Happiness is the perfection of the soul on the part of the intellect, in respect of which the soul transcends the organs of the body; but not according as the soul is the natural form of the body. Wherefore the soul retains that natural perfection in respect of which happiness is due to it, though it does not retain that natural perfection in respect of which it is the form of the body.

Reply Obj. 2. The relation of the soul to being is not the same as that of other parts: for the being of the whole is not that of any individual part: wherefore, either the part ceases altogether to be, when the whole is destroyed, just as the parts of an animal, when the animal is destroyed; or, if they remain, they have another actual being, just as a part of a line has another being from that of the whole line. But the human soul retains the being of the composite after the destruction of the body: and this because the being of the form is the same as that of its matter, and this is the being of the composite. Now the soul subsists in its own being, as stated in the First Part (Q. 75, A. 2). It follows, therefore, that after being separated from the body it has perfect being, and that consequently it can have a perfect operation; although it has not the perfect specific nature.

Reply Obj. 3. Happiness belongs to man in respect of his intellect: and, therefore, since the intellect remains, it can have Happiness. Thus the teeth of an Ethiopian, in respect of which he is said to be white, can retain their whiteness, even after extraction.

Reply Obj. 4. One thing is hindered by another in two ways. First, by way of opposition; thus cold hinders the action of heat: and such a hindrance to operation is repugnant to Happiness. Secondly, by way of some kind of defect, because, to wit, that which is hindered has not all that is necessary to make it

perfect in every way: and such a hindrance to operation is not incompatible with Happiness, but prevents it from being perfect in every way. And thus it is that separation from the body is said to hold the soul back from tending with all its might to the vision of the Divine Essence. For the soul desires to enjoy God in such a way that the enjoyment also may overflow into the body, as far as possible. And therefore, as long as it enjoys God, without the fellowship of the body, its appetite is at rest in that which it has, in such a way, that it would still wish the body to attain to its share.

Reply Obj. 5. The desire of the separated soul is entirely at rest, as regards the thing desired; since, to wit, it has that which suffices its appetite. But it is not wholly at rest, as regards the desirer, since it does not possess that good in every way that it would wish to possess it. Consequently, after the body has been resumed, Happiness increases not in intensity, but in extent.

Reply Obj. 6. The statement made (*ibid.*) to the effect that *the souls of the departed see not God as the angels do,* is not to be understood as referring to inequality of quantity; because even now some souls of the Blessed are raised to the higher orders of angels, thus seeing God more clearly than the lower angels. But it refers to inequality of proportion: because the angels, even the lowest, have every perfection of Happiness that they ever will have, whereas the separated souls of the saints have not.

SIXTH ARTICLE

Whether Perfection of the Body Is Necessary for Happiness?

We proceed thus to the Sixth Article:—

Objection 1. It would seem that perfection of the body is not necessary for man's perfect Happiness. For perfection of the body is a bodily good. But it has been shown above (Q. 2) that Happiness does not consist in bodily goods. Therefore no perfect disposition of the body is necessary for man's Happiness.

Obj. 2. Further, man's Happiness consists in the vision of the Divine Essence, as shown above (Q. 3, A. 8). But the body has no part in this operation, as shown above (A. 5). Therefore no disposition of the body is necessary for Happiness.

Obj. 3. Further, the more the intellect is abstracted from the body, the more perfectly it understands. But Happiness consists in the most perfect operation of the intellect. Therefore the soul should be abstracted from the body in every way. Therefore, in no way is a disposition of the body necessary for Happiness.

On the contrary, Happiness is the reward of virtue; wherefore it is written (Jo. xiii. 17): *You shall be blessed, if you do them.* But the reward promised to the saints is not only that they shall see and enjoy God, but also that their bodies shall be well-disposed; for it is written (Isa. lxvi. 14): *You shall see and your heart shall rejoice, and your bones shall flourish like a herb.* Therefore good disposition of the body is necessary for Happiness.

I answer that, If we speak of that happiness which man can acquire in this life, it is evident that a well-disposed body is of necessity required for it. For this happiness consists, according to the Philosopher (*Ethic.* i. 13) in *an operation according to perfect virtue;* and it is clear that man can be hindered, by indisposition of the body, from every operation of virtue.

But speaking of perfect Happiness, some have maintained that no disposition of body is necessary for Happiness; indeed, that it is necessary for the soul to be entirely separated from the body. Hence Augustine (*De Civ. Dei.* xxii. 26) quotes the words of Porphyry who said that *for the soul to be happy, it must be severed from everything corporeal.* But this is unreasonable. For since it is natural to the soul to be united to the body; it is not possible for the perfection of the soul to exclude its natural perfection.

Consequently, we must say that perfect disposition of the body is necessary, both antecedently and consequently, for that Happiness which is in all ways perfect.—Antecedently, because, as Augustine says (*Gen. ad lit.* xii. 35), *if the body be such, that the governance thereof is difficult and burdensome, like unto flesh which is corruptible and weighs upon the soul, the mind is turned away from that vision of the highest heaven.* Whence he concludes that, *when this body will no longer be "natural," but "spiritual," then will it be equalled to the angels, and that will be its glory, which erstwhile was its burden.*—Consequently, because from the Happiness of the soul there will be an overflow on to the body, so that this too will obtain its perfection. Hence Augustine says (*Ep. ad Dioscor.*) that *God gave the soul such a powerful nature that from its exceeding fulness of happiness the vigor of incorruption overflows into the lower nature.*

Reply Obj. 1. Happiness does not consist in bodily good as its object: but bodily good can add a certain charm and perfection to Happiness.

Reply Obj. 2. Although the body has no part in that operation of the intellect whereby the Essence of God is seen, yet it might prove a hindrance thereto. Consequently, perfection of the body is necessary, lest it hinder the mind from being lifted up.

Reply Obj. 3. The perfect operation of the intellect requires indeed that the intellect be abstracted from this corruptible body which weighs upon the soul; but not from the spiritual body, which will be wholly subject to the spirit. On this point we shall treat in the Third Part of this work (Suppl., Q. 82, *seqq.*).

SEVENTH ARTICLE

Whether Any External Goods Are Necessary for Happiness?

We proceed thus to the Seventh Article—

Objection 1. It would seem that external goods also are necessary for Happiness. For that which is promised the saints for reward, belongs to Happiness. But external goods are promised the saints; for instance, food and drink, wealth and a kingdom: for it is said (Luke xxii. 30): *That you may eat and drink at My table in My kingdom:* and (Matth. vi. 20): *Lay up to yourselves treasures in heaven:* and (Matth. xxv. 34): *Come, ye blessed of My Father, possess you the kingdom.* Therefore external goods are necessary for Happiness.

Obj. 2. Further, according to Boëthius (*De Consol.* iii): happiness is *a state made perfect by the aggregate of all good things.* But some of man's goods are external, although they be of least account, as Augustine says (*De Lib. Arb.* ii. 19). Therefore they too are necessary for Happiness.

Obj. 3. Further, Our Lord said (Matth. v. 12): *Your reward is very great in heaven.* But to be in heaven implies being in a place. Therefore at least external place is necessary for Happiness.

On the contrary, It is written (Ps. lxxii. 25): *For what have I in heaven? and besides Thee what do I desire upon earth?* As though to say: "I desire nothing but this,—*It is good for me to adhere to my God.*" Therefore nothing further external is necessary for Happiness.

I answer that, For imperfect happiness, such as can be had in this life, external goods are necessary, not as belonging to the essence of happiness, but by serving as instruments to happiness, which consists in an operation of virtue, as stated in *Ethic.* i. 13. For man needs in this life, the necessaries of the body, both for the operation of contemplative virtue, and for the operation of active virtue, for which latter he needs also many other things by means of which to perform its operations.

On the other hand, such goods as these are nowise necessary for perfect Happiness, which consists in seeing God. The reason of this is that all suchlike external goods are requisite either for the support of the animal body; or for certain operations which belong to human life, which we perform by means of the animal body: whereas that perfect Happiness which consists in seeing God, will be either in the soul separated from the body, or in the soul united to the body then no longer animal but spiritual. Consequently these external goods are nowise necessary for that Happiness, since they are ordained to the animal life.—And since, in this life, the felicity of contemplation, as being more God-like, approaches nearer than that of action to the likeness of that perfect Happiness, therefore it stands in less need of these goods of the body as stated in *Ethic* x. 8.

Reply Obj. 1. All those material promises contained in Holy Scripture, are to be understood metaphorically, inasmuch as Scripture is wont to express spiritual things under the form of things corporeal, in order *that from things we know, we may rise to the desire of things unknown,* as Gregory says (*Hom.* xi. *in Ev.*). Thus food and drink signify the delight of Happiness: wealth, the sufficiency of God for man; the kingdom, the lifting up of man to union with God.

Reply Obj. 2. These goods that serve for the animal life, are incompatible with that spiritual life wherein perfect Happiness consists. Nevertheless in that Happiness there will be the aggregate of all good things, because whatever good there be in these things, we shall possess it all in the Supreme Fount of goodness.

Reply Obj. 3. According to Augustine (*De Serm. Dom. in Monte* i. 5), it is not a material heaven that is described as the reward of the saints, but a heaven raised on the height of spiritual goods. Nevertheless a bodily place, viz., the empyrean heaven, will be appointed to the Blessed, not as a need of Happiness, but by reason of a certain fitness and adornment.

EIGHTH ARTICLE

Whether the Fellowship of Friends Is Necessary for Happiness?

We proceed thus to the Eighth Article:—

Objection 1. It would seem that friends are necessary for Happiness. For future Happiness is frequently designated by Scripture under the name of *glory.* But glory consists in man's good being brought to the notice of

* Seneca, *Ep.* 6.

many. Therefore the fellowship of friends is necessary for Happiness.

Obj. 2. Further, Boëthius* says that *there is no delight in possessing any good whatever, without someone to share it with us.* But delight is necessary for Happiness. Therefore fellowship of friends is also necessary.

Obj. 3. Further, charity is perfected in Happiness. But charity includes the love of God and of our neighbor. Therefore it seems that fellowship of friends is necessary for Happiness.

On the contrary, It is written (Wisd. vii. 11): *All good things came to me together with her, i.e.,* with divine wisdom, which consists in contemplating God. Consequently nothing else is necessary for Happiness.

I answer that, If we speak of the happiness of this life, the happy man needs friends, as the Philosopher says (*Ethic.* ix. 9), not, indeed, to make use of them, since he suffices himself; nor to delight in them, since he possesses perfect delight in the operation of virtue; but for the purpose of a good operation, viz., that he may do good to them; that he may delight in seeing them do good; and again that he may be helped by them in his good work. For in order that man may do well, whether in the works of the active life, or in those of the contemplative life, he needs the fellowship of friends.

But if we speak of perfect Happiness which will be in our heavenly Fatherland, the fellowship of friends is not essential to Happiness; since man has the entire fulness of his perfection in God. But the fellowship of friends conduces to the well-being of Happiness. Hence Augustine says (*Gen. ad lit.* viii. 25) that *the spiritual creatures receive no other interior aid to happiness than the eternity, truth, and charity of the Creator. But if they can be said to be helped from without, perhaps it is only by this that they see one another and rejoice in God, at their fellowship.*

Reply Obj. 1. That glory which is essential to Happiness, is that which man has, not with man but with God.

Reply Obj. 2. This saying is to be understood of the possession of good that does not fully satisfy. This does not apply to the question under consideration; because man possesses in God a sufficiency of every good.

Reply Obj. 3. Perfection of charity is essential to Happiness, as to the love of God, but not as to the love of our neighbor. Wherefore if there were but one soul enjoying God, it would be happy, though having no neighbor to love. But supposing one neighbor to be there, love of him results from perfect love of God. Consequently, friendship is, as it were, concomitant with perfect Happiness.

QUESTION 5

Of the Attainment of Happiness

(In Eight Articles)

WE must now consider the attainment of Happiness. Under this heading there are eight points of inquiry: (1) Whether man can attain Happiness? (2) Whether one man can be happier than another? (3) Whether any man can be happy in this life? (4) Whether Happiness once had can be lost? (5) Whether man can attain Happiness by means of his natural powers? (6) Whether man attains Happiness through the action of some higher creature? (7) Whether any actions of man are necessary in order that man may obtain Happiness of God? (8) Whether every man desires Happiness?

FIRST ARTICLE

Whether Man Can Attain Happiness?

We proceed thus to the First Article:—

Objection 1. It would seem that man cannot attain happiness. For just as the rational is above the sensible nature, so the intellectual is above the rational, as Dionysius declares (*Div. Nom.* iv, vi, vii) in several passages. But irrational animals that have the sensitive nature only, cannot attain the end of the rational nature. Therefore neither can man, who is of rational nature, attain the end of the intellectual nature, which is Happiness.

Obj. 2. Further, True Happiness consists in seeing God, Who is pure Truth. But from his very nature, man considers truth in material things: wherefore *he understands the intelligible species in the phantasm* (*De Anima* iii. 7). Therefore he cannot attain Happiness.

Obj. 3. Further, Happiness consists in attaining the Sovereign Good. But we cannot arrive at the top without surmounting the middle. Since, therefore, the angelic nature through which man cannot mount is midway between God and human nature; it seems that he cannot attain Happiness.

On the contrary, It is written (Ps. xciii. 12): *Blessed is the man whom Thou shalt instruct, O Lord.*

I answer that, Happiness is the attainment of the Perfect Good. Whoever, therefore, is capable of the Perfect Good can attain Happiness. Now, that man is capable of the Perfect Good, is proved both because his intellect can apprehend the universal and perfect good, and because his will can desire it. And therefore man can attain Happiness.—This can be proved again from the fact that man is capable of seeing God, as stated in the First Part (Q. 12,

A. 1): in which vision, as we stated above (Q. 3, A. 8) man's perfect Happiness consists.

Reply Obj. 1. The rational exceeds the sensitive nature, otherwise than the intellectual surpasses the rational. For the rational exceeds the sensitive nature in respect of the object of its knowledge: since the senses have no knowledge whatever of the universal, whereas the reason has knowledge thereof. But the intellectual surpasses the rational nature, as to the mode of knowing the same intelligible truth: for the intellectual nature grasps forthwith the truth which the rational nature reaches by the inquiry of reason, as was made clear in the First Part (Q. 58, A. 3; Q. 79, A. 8). Therefore reason arrives by a kind of movement at that which the intellect grasps. Consequently the rational nature can attain Happiness, which is the perfection of the intellectual nature: but otherwise than the angels. Because the angels attained it forthwith after the beginning of their creation: whereas man attains it after a time. But the sensitive nature can nowise attain this end.

Reply Obj. 2. To man in the present state of life the natural way of knowing intelligible truth is by means of phantasms. But after this state of life, he has another natural way, as was stated in the First Part (Q. 84, A. 7; Q. 89, A. 1).

Reply Obj. 3. Man cannot surmount the angels in the degree of nature, so as to be above them naturally. But he can surmount them by an operation of the intellect, by understanding that there is above the angels something that makes men happy; and when he has attained it, he will be perfectly happy.

SECOND ARTICLE

Whether One Man Can Be Happier Than Another?

We proceed thus to the Second Article:—

Objection 1. It would seem that one man cannot be happier than another. For Happiness is *the reward of virtue,* as the Philosopher says (*Ethic.* i. 9). But equal reward is given for all the works of virtue; because it is written (Matth. xx. 10) that all who labor in the vineyard *received every man a penny;* for, as Gregory says (*Hom.* xix. *in Evang.*), *each was equally rewarded with eternal life.* Therefore one man cannot be happier than another.

Obj. 2. Further, Happiness is the supreme good. But nothing can surpass the supreme.

Therefore one man's Happiness cannot be surpassed by another's.

Obj. 3. Further, since Happiness is *the perfect and sufficient good* (*Ethic.* i. 7) it brings rest to man's desire. But his desire is not at rest, if he yet lacks some good that can be got. And if he lack nothing that he can get, there can be no still greater good. Therefore either man is not happy; or, if he be happy, no other Happiness can be greater.

On the contrary, It is written (Jo. xiv. 2): *In My Father's house there are many mansions;* which, according to Augustine (*Tract.* lxvii. *in Joan.*) signify *the diverse dignities of merits in the one eternal life.* But the dignity of eternal life which is given according to merit, is Happiness itself. Therefore there are diverse degrees of Happiness, and Happiness is not equally in all.

I answer that, As stated above (Q. 1, A. 8; Q. 2, A. 7), Happiness implies two things, to wit, the last end itself, *i.e.,* the Sovereign Good; and the attainment or enjoyment of that same Good. As to that Good itself, Which is the object and cause of Happiness, one Happiness cannot be greater than another, since there is but one Sovereign Good, namely, God, by enjoying Whom, men are made happy.—But as to the attainment or enjoyment of this Good, one man can be happier than another; because the more a man enjoys this Good the happier he is. Now, that one man enjoys God more than another, happens through his being better disposed or ordered to the enjoyment of Him. And in this sense one man can be happier than another.

Reply Obj. 1. The one penny signifies that Happiness is one in its object. But the many mansions signify the manifold Happiness in the divers degrees of enjoyment.

Reply Obj. 2. Happiness is said to be the supreme good, inasmuch as it is the perfect possession or enjoyment of the Supreme Good.

Reply Obj. 3. None of the Blessed lacks any desirable good; since they have the Infinite Good Itself, Which is *the good of all good,* as Augustine says (*Enarr. in* Ps. cxxxiv). But one is said to be happier than another, by reason of diverse participation of the same good. And the addition of other goods does not increase Happiness, hence Augustine says (*Conf.* v. 4): *He who knows Thee, and others besides, is not the happier for knowing them, but is happy for knowing Thee alone.*

THIRD ARTICLE

Whether One Can Be Happy in This Life?

We proceed thus to the Third Article:—

Objection 1. It would seem that Happiness can be had in this life. For it is written (Ps. cxviii. 1): *Blessed are the undefiled in the way, who walk in the law of the Lord.* But this happens in this life. Therefore one can be happy in this life.

Obj. 2. Further, imperfect participation in the Sovereign Good does not destroy the nature of Happiness, otherwise one would not be happier than another. But men can participate in the Sovereign Good in this life, by knowing and loving God, albeit imperfectly. Therefore man can be happy in this life.

Obj. 3. Further, what is said by many cannot be altogether false: since what is in many, comes, apparently, from nature; and nature does not fail altogether. Now many say that Happiness can be had in this life, as appears from Ps. cxliii. 15: *They have called the people happy that hath these things,* to wit, the good things of this life. Therefore one can be happy in this life.

On the contrary, It is written (Job xiv. 1): *Man born of a woman, living for a short time, is filled with many miseries.* But Happiness excludes misery. Therefore man cannot be happy in this life.

I answer that, A certain participation of Happiness can be had in this life: but perfect and true Happiness cannot be had in this life. This may be seen from a twofold consideration.

First, from the general notion of happiness. For since happiness is a *perfect and sufficient good,* it excludes every evil, and fulfils every desire. But in this life every evil cannot be excluded. For this present life is subject to many unavoidable evils; to ignorance on the part of the intellect; to inordinate affection on the part of the appetite, and to many penalties on the part of the body; as Augustine sets forth in *De Civ. Dei* xix. 4. Likewise neither can the desire for good be satiated in this life. For man naturally desires the good, which he has, to be abiding. Now the goods of the present life pass away; since life itself passes away, which we naturally desire to have, and would wish to hold abidingly, for man naturally shrinks from death. Wherefore it is impossible to have true Happiness in this life.

Secondly, from a consideration of the specific nature of Happiness, viz., the vision of the Divine Essence, which man cannot obtain in this life, as was shown in the First Part (Q. 12, A. 11). Hence it is evident that none can attain true and perfect Happiness in this life.

Reply Obj. 1. Some are said to be happy in this life, either on account of the hope of obtaining Happiness in the life to come, according to Rom. viii. 24: *We are saved by hope;* or on account of a certain participation of

Happiness, by reason of a kind of enjoyment of the Sovereign Good.

Reply Obj. 2. The imperfection of participated Happiness is due to one of two causes. First, on the part of the object of Happiness, which is not seen in Its Essence: and this imperfection destroys the nature of true Happiness. Secondly, the imperfection may be on the part of the participator, who indeed attains the object of Happiness, in itself, namely, God: imperfectly, however, in comparison with the way in which God enjoys Himself. This imperfection does not destroy the true nature of Happiness; because since Happiness is an operation, as stated above (Q. 3, A. 2), the true nature of Happiness is taken from the object, which specifies the act, and not from the subject.

Reply Obj. 3. Men esteem that there is some kind of happiness to be had in this life, on account of a certain likeness to true Happiness. And thus they do not fail altogether in their estimate.

FOURTH ARTICLE

Whether Happiness Once Had Can Be Lost?

We proceed thus to the Fourth Article:—

Objection 1. It would seem that Happiness can be lost. For Happiness is a perfection. But every perfection is in the thing perfected according to the mode of the latter. Since then man is, by his nature, changeable, it seems that Happiness is participated by man in a changeable manner. And consequently it seems that man can lose Happiness.

Obj. 2. Further, Happiness consists in an act of the intellect; and the intellect is subject to the will. But the will can be directed to opposites. Therefore it seems that it can desist from the operation whereby man is made happy: and thus man will cease to be happy.

Obj. 3. Further, the end corresponds to the beginning. But man's Happiness has a beginning, since man was not always happy. Therefore it seems that it has an end.

On the contrary, It is written (Matth. xxv. 46) of the righteous that *they shall go . . . into life everlasting,* which, as above stated (A. 2), is the Happiness of the saints. Now what is eternal ceases not. Therefore Happiness cannot be lost.

I answer that, If we speak of imperfect happiness, such as can be had in this life, in this sense it can be lost. This is clear of contemplative happiness, which is lost either by forgetfulness, for instance, when knowledge is lost through sickness; or again by certain occupations, whereby a man is altogether withdrawn from contemplation.

This is also clear of active happiness: since

man's will can be changed so as to fall to vice from the virtue, in whose act that happiness principally consists. If, however, the virtue remain unimpaired, outward changes can indeed disturb such like happiness, in so far as they hinder many acts of virtue; but they cannot take it away altogether, because there still remains an act of virtue, whereby man bears these trials in a praiseworthy manner.— And since the happiness of this life can be lost, a circumstance that appears to be contrary to the nature of happiness, therefore did the Philosopher state (*Ethic.* i. 10) that some are happy in this life, not simply, but *as men,* whose nature is subject to change.

But if we speak of that perfect Happiness which we await after this life, it must be observed that Origen (*Peri Archon.* ii 3), following the error of certain Platonists, held that man can become unhappy after the final Happiness.

This, however, is evidently false, for two reasons. First, from the general notion of happiness. For since happiness is the *perfect and sufficient good,* it must needs set man's desire at rest and exclude every evil. Now man naturally desires to hold to the good that he has, and to have the surety of his holding: else he must of necessity be troubled with the fear of losing it, or with the sorrow of knowing that he will lose it. Therefore it is necessary for true Happiness that man have the assured opinion of never losing the good that he possesses. If this opinion be true, it follows that he never will lose happiness: but if it be false, it is in itself an evil that he should have a false opinion: because the false is the evil of the intellect, just as the true is its good, as stated in *Ethic.* vi. 2. Consequently he will no longer be truly happy, if evil be in him.

Secondly, it is again evident if we consider the specific nature of Happiness. For it has been shown above (Q. 3, A. 8) that man's perfect Happiness consists in the vision of the Divine Essence. Now it is impossible for anyone seeing the Divine Essence, to wish not to see It. Because every good that one possesses and yet wishes to be without, is either insufficient, something more sufficing being desired in its stead; or else has some inconvenience attached to it, by reason of which it becomes wearisome. But the vision of the Divine Essence fills the soul with all good things, since it unites it to the source of all goodness; hence it is written (Ps. xvi. 15): *I shall be satisfied when Thy glory shall appear;* and (Wisd. vii. 11): *All good things came to me together with her, i.e.,* with the contemplation of wisdom. In like manner neither has it any inconvenience attached to it; because it is written of the contemplation of wisdom (Wisd.

viii. 16)): *Her conversation hath no bitterness, nor her company any tediousness.* It is thus evident that the happy man cannot forsake Happiness of his own accord. Moreover, neither can he lose Happiness, through God taking it away from him. Because, since the withdrawal of Happiness is a punishment, it cannot be enforced by God, the just Judge, except for some fault; and he that sees God cannot fall into a fault, since rectitude of the will, of necessity, results from that vision as was shown above (Q. 4, A. 4).—Nor again can it be withdrawn by any other agent. Because the mind that is united to God is raised above all other things: and consequently no other agent can sever the mind from that union. Therefore it seems unreasonable that as time goes on, man should pass from happiness to misery, and *vice versa;* because such like viscissitudes of time can only be for such things as are subject to time and movement.

Reply Obj. 1. Happiness is consummate perfection, which excludes every defect from the happy. And therefore whoever has happiness has it altogether unchangeably: this is done by the Divine power, which raises man to the participation of eternity which transcends all change.

Reply Obj. 2. The will can be directed to opposites, in things which are ordained to the end; but it is ordained, of natural necessity, to the last end. This is evident from the fact that man is unable not to wish to be happy.

Reply Obj. 3. Happiness has a beginning owing to the condition of the participator: but it has no end by reason of the condition of the good, the participation of which makes man happy. Hence the beginning of happiness is from one cause, its endlessness is from another.

FIFTH ARTICLE

Whether Man Can Attain Happiness by His Natural Powers?

We proceed thus to the Fifth Article:—

Objection 1. It would seem that man can attain Happiness by his natural powers. For nature does not fail in necessary things. But nothing is so necessary to man as that by which he attains the last end. Therefore this is not lacking to human nature. Therefore man can attain Happiness by his natural powers.

Obj. 2. Further, since man is more noble than irrational creatures, it seems that he must be better equipped than they. But irrational creatures can attain their end by their natural powers. Much more therefore can man attain Happiness by his natural powers.

Obj. 3. Further, Happiness is a *perfect operation,* according to the Philosopher (*Ethic.*

vii. 13). Now the beginning of a thing belongs to the same principle as the perfecting thereof. Since, therefore, the imperfect operation, which is as the beginning in human operations, is subject to man's natural power, whereby he is master of his own actions; it seems that he can attain to perfect operation, *i.e.,* Happiness, by his natural powers.

On the contrary, Man is naturally the principle of his action, by his intellect and will. But final Happiness prepared for the saints, surpasses the intellect and will of man; for the Apostle says (1 Cor. ii. 9): *Eye hath not seen, nor ear heard, neither hath it entered into the heart of man, what things God hath prepared for them that love Him.* Therefore man cannot attain Happiness by his natural powers.

I answer that, Imperfect happiness that can be had in this life, can be acquired by man by his natural powers, in the same way as virtue, in whose operation it consists: on this point we shall speak further on (Q. 63). But man's perfect Happiness, as stated above (Q. 3, A. 8), consists in the vision of the Divine Essence. Now the vision of God's Essence surpasses the nature not only of man, but also of every creature, as was shown in the First Part (Q. 12, A. 4). For the natural knowledge of every creature is in keeping with the mode of his substance: thus it is said of the intelligence (*De Causis; Prop.* viii.) that *it knows things that are above it, and things that are below it, according to the mode of its substance.* But every knowledge that is according to the mode of created substance, falls short of the vision of the Divine Essence, which infinitely surpasses all created substance. Consequently neither man, nor any creature, can attain final Happiness by his natural powers.

Reply Obj. 1. Just as nature does not fail man in necessaries, although it has not provided him with weapons and clothing, as it provided other animals, because it gave him reason and hands, with which he is able to get these things for himself; so neither did it fail man in things necessary, although it gave him not the wherewithal to attain Happiness: since this it could not do. But it did give him freewill, with which he can turn to God, that He may make him happy. *For what we do by means of our friends, is done, in a sense, by ourselves* (*Ethic.* iii. 3).

Reply Obj. 2. The nature that can attain perfect good, although it needs help from without in order to attain it, is of more noble condition than a nature which cannot attain perfect good, but attains some imperfect good, although it need no help from without in order to attain it, as the Philosopher says (*De Cœlo* ii. 12). Thus he is better disposed to health who can attain perfect health, albeit by means of medicine, than he who can attain but imperfect health, without the help of medicine. And therefore the rational creature, which can attain the perfect good of happiness, but needs the Divine assistance for the purpose, is more perfect than the irrational creature, which is not capable of attaining this good, but attains some imperfect good by its natural powers.

Reply Obj. 3. When imperfect and perfect are of the same species, they can be caused by the same power. But this does not follow of necessity, if they be of different species: for not everything, that can cause the disposition of matter, can produce the final perfection. Now the imperfect operation, which is subject to man's natural power, is not of the same species as that perfect operation which is man's happiness: since operation takes its species from its object. Consequently the argument does not prove.

SIXTH ARTICLE

Whether Man Attains Happiness through the Action of Some Higher Creature?

We proceed thus to the Sixth Article:—

Objection 1. It would seem that man can be made happy through the action of some higher creature, viz., an angel. For since we observe a twofold order in things—one, of the parts of the universe to one another, the other, of the whole universe to a good which is outside the universe; the former order is ordained to the second as to its end (*Metaph.* xii. 10). Thus the mutual order of the parts of an army is dependent on the order of the whole army to the general. But the mutual order of the parts of the universe consists in the higher creatures acting on the lower, as stated in the First Part (Q. 109, A. 2): while happiness consists in the order of man to a good which is outside the universe, *i.e.*, God. Therefore man is made happy, through a higher creature, viz., an angel, acting on him.

Obj. 2. Further, that which is such in potentiality, can be reduced to act, by that which is such actually: thus what is potentially hot, is made actually hot, by something that is actually hot. But man is potentially happy. Therefore he can be made actually happy by an angel who is actually happy.

Obj. 3. Further, Happiness consists in an operation of the intellect, as stated above (Q. 3, A. 4). But an angel can enlighten man's intellect, as shown in the First Part (Q. 111, A. 1). Therefore an angel can make a man happy.

On the contrary, It is written (Ps. lxxxiii. 12): *The Lord will give grace and glory.*

I answer that, Since every creature is subject to the laws of nature, from the very fact that its power and action are limited: that which surpasses created nature, cannot be done by the power of any creature. Consequently if anything need to be done that is above nature, it is done by God immediately; such as raising the dead to life, restoring sight to the blind, and such like. Now it has been shown above (A. 5) that Happiness is a good surpassing created nature. Therefore it is impossible that it be bestowed through the action of any creature: but by God alone is man made happy,—if we speak of perfect Happiness. If, however, we speak of imperfect happiness, the same is to be said of it as of the virtue, in whose act it consists.

Rely Obj. 1. It often happens in the case of active powers ordained to one another, that it belongs to the highest power to reach the last end, while the lower powers contribute to the attainment of that last end, by causing a disposition thereto: thus to the art of sailing, which commands the art of ship-buiding, it belongs to use a ship for the end for which it was made. Thus, too, in the order of the universe, man is indeed helped by angels in the attainment of his last end, in respect of certain preliminary dispositions thereto: whereas he attains the last end itself through the First Agent, which is God.

Reply Obj. 2. When a form exists perfectly and naturally in something, it can be the principle of action on something else: for instance, a hot thing heats through heat. But if a form exist in something imperfectly and not naturally, it cannot be the principle whereby it is communicated to something else: thus the *intention* of color which is in the pupil, cannot make a thing white; nor indeed can everything enlightened or heated give heat or light to something else; for if they could, enlightening and heating would go on to infinity. But the light of glory, whereby God is seen, is in God perfectly and naturally; whereas in any creature, it is imperfectly and by likeness or participation. Consequently no creature can communicate its Happiness to another.

Reply Obj. 3. A happy angel enlightens the intellect of a man or of a lower angel, as to certain notions of the Divine works: but not as to the vision of the Divine Essence, as was stated in the First Part (Q. 106, A. 1): since in order to see this, all are immediately enlightened by God.

SEVENTH ARTICLE

Whether Any Good Works Are Necessary That Man May Receive Happiness from God?

We proceed thus to the Seventh Article:—

Objection 1. It would seem that no works

of man are necessary that he may obtain Happiness from God. For since God is an agent of infinite power, He requires before acting, neither matter, nor disposition of matter, but can forthwith produce the whole effect. But man's works, since they are not required for Happiness, as the efficient cause thereof, as stated above (A. 6), can be required only as dispositions thereto. Therefore God who does not require dispositions before acting, bestows Happiness without any previous works.

Obj. 2. Further, just as God is the immediate cause of Happiness, so is He the immediate cause of nature. But when God first established nature, He produced creatures without any previous disposition or action on the part of the creature, but made each one perfect forthwith in its species. Therefore it seems that He bestows Happiness on man without any previous works.

Obj. 3. Further, the Apostle says (Rom. iv. 6) that Happiness is of the man *to whom God reputeth justice without works.* Therefore no works of man are necessary for attaining Happiness.

On the contrary, It is written (Jo. xiii. 17): *If you know these things, you shall be blessed if you do them.* Therefore Happiness is obtained through works.

I answer that, Rectitude of the will, as stated above (Q. 4, A. 4), is necessary for Happiness; since it is nothing else than the right order of the will to the last end; and it is therefore necessary for obtaining the end, just as the right disposition of matter, in order to receive the form. But this does not prove that any work of man need precede his Happiness: for God could make a will having a right tendency to the end, and at the same time attaining the end; just as sometimes He disposes matter and at the same time introduces the form. But the order of Divine wisdom demands that it should not be thus; for as is stated in *De Cælo* ii. 12, *of those things that have a natural capacity for the perfect good, one has it without movement, some by one movement, some by several.* Now to possess the perfect good without movement, belongs to that which has it naturally: and to have Happiness naturally belongs to God alone. Therefore it belongs to God alone not to be moved towards Happiness by any previous operation. Now since Happiness surpasses every created nature, no pure creature can becomingly gain Happiness, without the movement of operation, whereby it tends thereto. But the angel, who is above man in the natural order, obtained it, according to the order of Divine wisdom, by one movement of a meritorious work, as was explained in the First Part (Q. 62, A. 5); whereas man obtains

it by many movements of works which are called merits. Wherefore also according to the Philosopher (*Ethic.* i. 9), happiness is the reward of works of virtue.

Reply Obj. 1. Works are necessary to man in order to gain Happiness; not on account of the insufficiency of the Divine power which bestows Happiness, but that the order in things be observed.

Reply Obj. 2. God produced the first creatures so that they were perfect forthwith, without any previous disposition or operation of the creature; because He instituted the first individuals of the various species, that through them nature might be propagated to their progeny. In like manner, because Happiness was to be bestowed on others through Christ, who is God and Man, *Who,* according to Heb. ii. 10, *had brought many children into glory;* therefore, from the very beginning of His conception, His soul was happy, without any previous meritorious operation. But this is peculiar to Him: for Christ's merit avails baptized children for the gaining of Happiness, though they have no merits of their own; because by Baptism they are made members of Christ.

Reply Obj. 3. The Apostle is speaking of the Happiness of Hope, which is bestowed on us by sanctifying grace, which is not given on account of previous works. For grace is not a term of movement, as Happiness is; rather is it the principle of the movement that tends towards Happiness.

EIGHTH ARTICLE

Whether Every Man Desires Happiness?

We proceed thus to the Eighth Article:—

Objection 1. It would seem that not all desire Happiness. For no man can desire what he knows not; since the apprehended good is the object of the appetite (*De Anima* iii. 10). But many know not what Happiness is. This is evident from the fact that, as Augustine says (*De Trin.* xiii. 4), *some thought that Happiness consists in pleasures of the body; some, in a virtue of the soul; some, in other things.* Therefore not all desire Happiness.

Obj. 2. Further, the essence of Happiness is the vision of the Divine Essence, as stated above (Q. 3, A. 8). But some consider it impossible for man to see the Divine Essence; wherefore they desire it not. Therefore all men do not desire Happiness.

Obj. 3. Further, Augustine says (*De Trin.* xiii. 5) that *happy is he who has all he desires, and desires nothing amiss.* But all do not desire this; for some desire certain things amiss, and yet they wish to desire such things Therefore all do not desire Happiness.

On the contrary, Augustine says (*De Trin.* xiii. 3): *If that actor had said: "You all wish to be happy; you do not wish to be unhappy," he would have said that which none would have failed to acknowledge in his will.* Therefore everyone desires to be happy.

I answer that, Happiness can be considered in two ways. First according to the general notion of happiness: and thus, of necessity, every man desires happiness. For the general notion of happiness consists in the perfect good, as stated above (AA. 3, 4). But since good is the object of the will, the perfect good of a man is that which entirely satisfies his will. Consequently to desire happiness is nothing else than to desire that one's will be satisfied. And this everyone desires. Secondly we may speak of Happiness according to its specific notion, as to that in which it consists. And thus all do not know Happiness; because they know not in what thing the general notion of happiness is found. And consequently, in this respect, not all desire it. Wherefore the reply to the first Objection is clear.

Reply Obj. 2. Since the will follows the apprehension of the intellect or reason; just as it happens that where there is no real distinction, there may be a distinction according to the consideration of reason; so does it happen that one and the same thing is desired in one way, and not desired in another. So that happiness may be considered as the final and perfect good, which is the general notion of happiness: and thus the will naturally and o. necessity tends thereto, as stated above. Again it can be considered under other special aspects, either on the part of the operation itself, or on the part of the operating power, or on the part of the object; and thus the will does not tend thereto of necessity.

Reply Obj. 3. This definition of Happiness given by some,—*Happy is the man that has all he desires,* or, *whose every wish is fulfilled,* is a good and adequate definition, if it be understood in a certain way; but an inadequate definition if understood in another. For if we understand it simply of all that man desires by his natural appetite, thus it is true that he who has all that he desires, is happy: since nothing satisfies man's natural desire, except the perfect good which is Happiness. But if we understand it of those things that man desires according to the apprehension of the reason, thus it does not belong to Happiness, to have certain things that man desires; rather does it belong to unhappiness, in so far as the possession of such things hinders man from having all that he desires naturally; thus it is that reason sometimes accepts as true things that are a hindrance to the knowledge of truth. And it was through taking this into consideration that Augustine added so as to include perfect Happiness,—that he *desires nothing amiss:* although the first part suffices if rightly understood, to wit, that *happy is he who has all he desires.*

QUESTION 6

Of the Voluntary and the Involuntary

(In Eight Articles)

SINCE therefore Happiness is to be gained by means of certain acts, we must in due sequence consider human acts, in order to know by what acts we may obtain Happiness, and by what acts we are prevented from obtaining it. But because operations and acts are concerned with things singular, consequently all practical knowledge is incomplete unless it take account of things in detail. The study of Morals, therefore, since it treats of human acts, should consider first the general principles; and secondly matters of detail.

In treating of the general principles, the points that offer themselves for our consideration are—(1) human acts themselves; (2) their principles. Now of human acts some are proper to man; others are common to man and animals. And since Happiness is man's proper good, those acts which are proper to man have a closer connection with Happiness than have those which are common to man and the other animals. First, then, we must consider those acts which are proper to man; secondly, those acts which are common to man and the other animals, and are called Passions. The first of these points offers a twofold consideration: (1) What makes a human act? (2) What distinguishes human acts?

And since those acts are properly called human, which are voluntary, because the will is the rational appetite, which is proper to man; we must consider acts in so far as they are voluntary.

First, then, we must consider the voluntary and involuntary in general; secondly, those acts which are voluntary, as being elicited by the will, and as issuing from the will immediately; thirdly, those acts which are voluntary, as being commanded by the will, which issue from the will through the medium of the other powers.

And because voluntary acts have certain circumstances, according to which we form our judgment concerning them, we must first consider the voluntary and the involuntary, and afterwards, the circumstances of those acts which are found to be voluntary or involuntary. Under the first head there are eight points of inquiry: (1) Whether there is anything voluntary in human acts? (2) Whether in irrational animals? (3) Whether there can be voluntariness without any action? (4) Whether violence can be done to the will? (5) Whether violence causes involuntariness? (6) Whether fear causes involuntariness? (7) Whether concupiscence causes involuntariness? (8) Whether ignorance causes involuntariness?

FIRST ARTICLE

Whether There Is Anything Voluntary in Human Acts?

We proceed thus to the First Article:—

Objection 1. It would seem that there is nothing voluntary in human acts. For that is voluntary *which has its principle within itself,* as Gregory of Nyssa,* Damascene (*De Fide Orthod.* ii. 24), and Aristotle (*Ethic.* iii. 1) declare. But the principle of human acts is not in man himself, but outside him: since man's appetite is moved to act, by the appetible object which is outside him, and is as a *mover unmoved* (*De Anima* iii. 10). Therefore there is nothing voluntary in human acts.

Obj. 2. Further, the Philosopher (*Phys.* viii. 2) proves that in animals no new movement arises that is not preceded by a motion from without. But all human acts are new, since none is eternal. Consequently, the principle of all human acts is from without: and therefore there is nothing voluntary in them.

Obj. 3. Further, he that acts voluntarily, can act of himself. But this is not true of man; for it is written (Jo. xv. 5): *Without Me you can do nothing.* Therefore there is nothing voluntary in human acts.

On the contrary, Damascene says (*De Fide Orthod.* ii) that *the voluntary is an act consisting in a rational operation.* Now such are human acts. Therefore there is something voluntary in human acts.

I answer that, There must needs be something voluntary in human acts. In order to make this clear, we must take note that the principle of some acts or movements is within the agent, or that which is moved; whereas the principle of some movements or acts is outside. For when a stone is moved upwards, the principle of this movement is outside the stone: whereas when it is moved downwards, the principle of this movement is in the stone. Now of those things that are moved by an in-

trinsic principle, some move themselves, some not. For since every agent or thing moved, acts or is moved for an end, as stated above (Q. 1, A. 2); those are perfectly moved by an intrinsic principle, whose intrinsic principle is one not only of movement but of movement for an end. Now in order for a thing to be done for an end, some knowledge of the end is necessary. Therefore, whatever so acts or is moved by an intrinsic principle, that it has some knowledge of the end, has within itself the principle of its act, so that it not only acts, but acts for an end. On the other hand, if a thing has no knowledge of the end, even though it have an intrinsic principle of action or movement, nevertheless the principle of acting or being moved for an end is not in that thing, but in something else, by which the principle of its action towards an end is imprinted on it. Wherefore such like things are not said to move themselves, but to be moved by others. But those things which have a knowledge of the end are said to move themselves because there is in them a principle by which they not only act but also act for an end. And consequently, since both are from an intrinsic principle, to wit, that they act and that they act for an end, the movements of such things are said to be voluntary: for the word *voluntary* implies that their movements and acts are from their own inclination. Hence it is that, according to the definitions of Aristotle, Gregory of Nyssa, and Damascene,† the voluntary is defined not only as having *a principle within* the agent, but also as implying *knowledge.* Therefore, since man especially knows the end of his work, and moves himself, in his acts especially is the voluntary to be found.

Reply Obj. 1. Not every principle is a first principle. Therefore, although it is essential to the voluntary act that its principle be within the agent, nevertheless it is not contrary to the nature of the voluntary act that this intrinsic principle be caused or moved by an extrinsic principle: because it is not essential to the voluntary act that its intrinsic principle be a first principle.—Yet again it must be observed that a principle of movement may happen to be first in a genus, but not first simply: thus in the genus of things subject to alteration, the first principle of alteration is a heavenly body, which nevertheless is not the first mover simply, but is moved locally by a higher mover. And so the intrinsic principle of the voluntary act, *i.e.,* the cognitive and appetitive power, is the first principle in the genus of appetitive movement, although it is moved by an extrinsic principle according to other species of movement.

---

* Nemesius, *De Natura Hom.* xxxii.　　† See objection 1.

Reply Obj. 2. New movements in animals are indeed preceded by a motion from without; and this in two respects. First, in so far as by means of an extrinsic motion an animal's senses are confronted with something sensible, which, on being apprehended, moves the appetite. Thus a lion, on seeing a stag in movement and coming towards him, begins to be moved towards the stag.—Secondly, in so far as some extrinsic motion produces a physical change in an animal's body, as in the case of cold or heat; and through the body being affected by the motion of an outward body, the sensitive appetite which is the power of a bodily organ, is also moved indirectly; thus it happens that through some alteration in the body the appetite is roused to the desire of something. But this is not contrary to the nature of voluntariness, as stated above (*ad* 1), for such movements caused by an extrinsic principle are of another genus of movement.

Reply Obj. 3. God moves man to act, not only by proposing the appetible to the senses, or by effecting a change in his body, but also by moving the will itself; because every movement either of the will or of nature, proceeds from God as the First Mover. And just as it is not incompatible with nature that the natural movement be from God as the First Mover, inasmuch as nature is an instrument of God moving it: so it is not contrary to the essence of a voluntary act, that it proceed from God, inasmuch as the will is moved by God. Nevertheless both natural and voluntary movements have this in common, that it is essential that they should proceed from a principle within the agent.

SECOND ARTICLE

Whether There Is Anything Voluntary in Irrational Animals?

We proceed thus to the Second Article:—

Objection 1. It would seem that there is nothing voluntary in irrational animals. For a thing is called *voluntary* from *voluntas* (*will*). Now since the will is in the reason (*De Anima* iii. 9), it cannot be in irrational animals. Therefore neither is there anything voluntary in them.

Obj. 2. Further, according as human acts are voluntary, man is said to be master of his actions. But irrational animals are not masters of their actions; for *they act not; rather are they acted upon*, as Damascene says (*De Fide Orthod.* ii. 27). Therefore there is no such thing as a voluntary act in irrational animals.

Obj. 3. Further, Damascene says (*ibid.*, 24)

* Nemesius, *De Nat. Hom.* xxxii.

that *voluntary acts lead to praise and blame.* But neither praise nor blame is due to the acts of irrational animals. Therefore such acts are not voluntary.

On the contrary, The Philosopher says (*Ethic.* iii. 2) that *both children and irrational animals participate in the voluntary.* The same is said by Damascene (*loc. cit.*) and Gregory of Nyssa.*

I answer that, As stated above (A. 1), it is essential to the voluntary act that its principle be within the agent, together with some knowledge of the end. Now knowledge of the end is twofold; perfect and imperfect. Perfect knowledge of the end consists in not only apprehending the thing which is the end, but also in knowing it under the aspect of end, and the relationship of the means to that end. And such knowledge belongs to none but the rational nature.—But imperfect knowledge of the end consists in mere apprehension of the end, without knowing it under the aspect of end, or the relationship of an act to the end. Such knowledge of the end is exercised by irrational animals, through their senses and their natural estimative power.

Consequently perfect knowledge of the end leads to the perfect voluntary; inasmuch as, having apprehended the end, a man can, from deliberating about the end and the means thereto, be moved, or not, to gain that end.— But imperfect knowledge of the end leads to the imperfect voluntary; inasmuch as the agent apprehends the end, but does not deliberate, and is moved to the end at once. Wherefore the voluntary in its perfection belongs to none but the rational nature: whereas the imperfect voluntary is within the competency of even irrational animals.

Reply Obj. 1. The will is the name of the rational appetite; and consequently it cannot be in things devoid of reason. But the word *voluntary* is derived from *voluntas* (*will*), and can be extended to those things in which there is some participation of will, by way of likeness thereto. It is thus that voluntary action is attributed to irrational animals, in so far as they are moved to an end, through some kind of knowledge.

Reply Obj. 2. The fact that man is master of his actions, is due to his being able to deliberate about them: for since the deliberating reason is indifferently disposed to opposite things, the will can be inclined to either. But it is not thus that voluntariness is in irrational animals, as stated above.

Reply Obj. 3. Praise and blame are the result of the voluntary act, wherein is the perfect voluntary; such as is not to be found in irrational animals.

THIRD ARTICLE

Whether There Can Be Voluntariness without Any Act?

We proceed thus to the Third Article:—

Objection 1. It would seem that voluntariness cannot be without any act. For that is voluntary which proceeds from the will. But nothing can proceed from the will, except through some act, at least an act of the will. Therefore there cannot be voluntariness without act.

Obj. 2. Further, just as one is said to wish by an act of the will, so when the act of the will ceases, one is said not to wish. But not to wish implies involuntariness, which is contrary to voluntariness. Therefore there can be nothing voluntary when the act of the will ceases.

Obj. 3. Further, knowledge is essential to the voluntary, as stated above (AA. 1, 2). But knowledge involves an act. Therefore voluntariness cannot be without some act.

On the contrary, The word *voluntary* is applied to that of which we are masters. Now we are masters in respect of to act and not to act, to will and not to will. Therefore just as to act and to will are voluntary, so also are not to act and not to will.

I answer. that, Voluntary is what proceeds from the will. Now one thing proceeds from another in two ways. First, directly; in which sense something proceeds from another inasmuch as this other acts; for instance, heating from heat. Secondly, indirectly; in which sense something proceeds from another through this other not acting; thus the sinking of a ship is set down to the helmsman, from his having ceased to steer.—But we must take note that the cause of what follows from want of action is not always the agent as not acting; but only then when the agent can and ought to act. For if the helmsman were unable to steer the ship or if the ship's helm be not entrusted to him, the sinking of the ship would not be set down to him, although it might be due to his absence from the helm.

Since, then, the will by willing and acting, is able, and sometimes ought, to hinder not-willing and not-acting; this not-willing and not-acting is imputed to, as though proceeding from, the will. And thus it is that we can have the voluntary without an act; sometimes without outward act, but with an interior act; for instance, when one wills not to act; and sometimes without even an interior act, as when one does not will to act.

Reply Obj. 1. We apply the word *voluntary* not only to that which proceeds from the will directly, as from its action; but also to that which proceeds from it indirectly as from its inaction.

Reply Obj. 2. *Not to wish* is said in two senses. First, as though it were one word, and the infinitive of *I-do-not-wish.* Consequently just as when I say *I do not wish to read,* the sense is, *I wish not to read;* so *not to wish to read* is the same as *to wish not to read,* and in this sense *not to wish* implies involuntariness. —Secondly it is taken as a sentence: and then no act of the will is affirmed. And in this sense *not to wish* does not imply involuntariness.

Reply Obj. 3. Voluntariness requires an act of knowledge in the same way as it requires an act of will; namely, in order that it be in one's power to consider, to wish and to act. And then, just as not to wish, and not to act, when it is time to wish and to act, is voluntary, so is it voluntary not to consider.

FOURTH ARTICLE

Whether Violence Can Be Done to the Will?

We proceed thus to the Fourth Article:—

Objection 1. It would seem that violence can be done to the will. For everything can be compelled by that which is more powerful. But there is something, namely, God, that is more powerful than the human will. Therefore it can be compelled, at least by Him.

Obj. 2. Further, every passive subject is compelled by its active principle, when it is changed by it. But the will is a passive force: for it is a *mover moved* (De Anima iii. 10). Therefore, since it is sometimes moved by its active principle, it seems that sometimes it is compelled.

Obj. 3. Further, violent movement is that which is contrary to nature. But the movement of the will is sometimes contrary to nature; as is clear of the will's movement to sin, which is contrary to nature, as Damascene says (De Fide Orthod. iv. 20). Therefore the movement of the will can be compelled.

On the contrary, Augustine says (De Civ. Dei v. 10) that what is done by the will is not done of necessity. Now, whatever is done under compulsion is done of necessity: consequently what is done by the will, cannot be compelled. Therefore the will cannot be compelled to act.

I answer that, The act of the will is twofold: one is its immediate act, as it were, elicited by it, namely, *to wish;* the other is an act of the will commanded by it, and put into execution by means of some other power, such as *to walk* and *to speak,* which are commanded by the will to be executed by means of the motive power.

As regards the commanded acts of the will, then, the will can suffer violence, in so far as violence can prevent the exterior members from executing the will's command. But as to the will's own proper act, violence cannot be done to the will.

The reason of this is that the act of the will is nothing else than an inclination proceeding from the interior principle of knowledge: just as the natural appetite is an inclination proceeding from an interior principle without knowledge. Now what is compelled or violent is from an exterior principle. Consequently it is contrary to the nature of the will's own act, that it should be subject to compulsion and violence: just as it is also contrary to the nature of a natural inclination or movement. For a stone may have an upward movement from violence, but that this violent movement be from its natural inclination is impossible. In like manner a man may be dragged by force: but it is contrary to the very notion of violence, that he be thus dragged of his own will.

Reply Obj. 1. God Who is more powerful than the human will, can move the will of man, according to Prov. xxi. 1: *The heart of the king is in the hand of the Lord; whithersoever He will He shall turn it.* But if this were by compulsion, it would no longer be by an act of the will, nor would the will itself be moved, but something else against the will.

Reply Obj. 2. It is not always a violent movement, when a passive subject is moved by its active principle; but only when this is done against the interior inclination of the passive subject. Otherwise every alteration and generation of simple bodies would be unnatural and violent: whereas they are natural by reason of the natural interior aptitude of the matter or subject to such a disposition. In like manner when the will is moved, according to its own inclination, by the appetible object, this movement is not violent but voluntary.

Reply Obj. 3. That to which the will tends by sinning, although in reality it is evil and contrary to the rational nature, nevertheless is apprehended as something good and suitable to nature, in so far as it is suitable to man by reason of some pleasurable sensation or some vicious habit.

FIFTH ARTICLE

Whether Violence Causes Involuntariness?

We proceed thus to the Fifth Article:—

Objection 1. It would seem that violence does not cause involuntariness. For we speak of voluntariness and involuntariness in respect of the will. But violence cannot be done to the will, as shown above (A. 4). Therefore violence cannot cause involuntariness.

Obj. 2. Further, that which is done involuntarily is done with grief, as Damascene (*De Fide Orthod.* ii. 24) and the Philosopher (*Ethic.* iii. 5) say. But sometimes a man suffers compulsion without being grieved thereby. Therefore violence does not cause involuntariness.

Obj. 3. Further, what is from the will cannot be involuntary. But some violent actions proceed from the will: for instance, when a man with a heavy body goes upwards; or when a man contorts his limbs in a way contrary to their natural flexibility. Therefore violence does not cause involuntariness.

On the contrary, The Philosopher (*Ethic.* iii. 1) and Damascene (*loc. cit.*) say that *things done under compulsion are involuntary.*

I answer that, Violence is directly opposed to the voluntary, as likewise to the natural. For the voluntary and the natural have this in common, that both are from an intrinsic principle; whereas violence is from an extrinsic principle. And for this reason, just as in things devoid of knowledge, violence effects something against nature: so in things endowed with knowledge, it effects something against the will. Now that which is against nature is said to be *unnatural;* and in like manner that which is against the will is said to be *involuntary.* Therefore violence causes involuntariness.

Reply Obj. 1. The involuntary is opposed to the voluntary. Now it has been said (A. 4) that not only the act, which proceeds immediately from the will, is called voluntary, but also the act commanded by the will. Consequently, as to the act which proceeds immediately from the will, violence cannot be done to the will, as stated above (*ibid.*): wherefore violence cannot make that act involuntary. But as to the commanded act, the will can suffer violence: and consequently in this respect violence causes involuntariness.

Reply Obj. 2. As that is said to be natural, which is according to the inclination of nature; so that is said to be voluntary, which is according to the inclination of the will. Now a thing is said to be natural in two ways. First, because it is from nature as from an active principle: thus it is natural for fire to produce heat. Secondly, according to a passive principle; because, to wit, there is in nature an inclination to receive an action from an extrinsic principle: thus the movement of the heavens is said to be natural, by reason of the natural aptitude in a heavenly body to receive such movement; although the cause of that movement is a voluntary agent. In like manner an act is said to be voluntary in two ways. First, in regard to action, for instance, when one wishes to be passive to another. Hence when action is brought to bear on something, by an extrinsic agent, as long as the will to suffer that action remains in the passive subject, there is not violence simply: for although the patient does nothing by way of action, he does something by being willing to suffer. Consequently this cannot be called involuntary.

Reply Obj. 3. As the Philosopher says (*Phys.* viii. 4) the movement of an animal, whereby at times an animal is moved against the natural inclination of the body, although it is not natural to the body, is nevertheless somewhat natural to the animal, to which it is natural to be moved according to its appetite. Accordingly this is violent, not simply but in a certain respect.—The same remark applies in the case of one who contorts his limbs in a way that is contrary to their natural disposition. For this is violent in a certain respect, *i.e.*, as to that particular limb; but not simply, *i.e.*, as to the man himself.

SIXTH ARTICLE

Whether Fear Causes Involuntariness Simply?

We proceed thus to the Sixth Article:—

Objection 1. It would seem that fear causes involuntariness simply. For just as violence regards that which is contrary to the will at the time, so fear regards a future evil which is repugnant to the will. But violence causes involuntariness simply. Therefore fear too causes involuntariness simply.

Obj. 2. Further, that which is such of itself, remains such, whatever be added to it: thus what is hot of itself, as long as it remains, is still hot, whatever be added to it. But that which is done through fear, is involuntary in itself. Therefore, even with the addition of fear, it is involuntary.

Obj. 3. Further, that which is such, subject to a condition, is such in a certain respect; whereas what is such, without any condition, is such simply: thus what is necessary, subject to a condition, is necessary in some respect: but what is necessary absolutely, is necessary simply. But that which is done through fear, is absolutely involuntary; and is not voluntary, save under a condition, namely, in order that the evil feared may be avoided. Therefore that which is done through fear, is involuntary simply.

On the contrary, Gregory of Nyssa* and the Philosopher (*Ethic.* iii. 1) say that such things are done through fear are *voluntary rather than involuntary.*

I answer that, As the Philosopher says (*Ethic.* iii) and likewise Gregory of Nyssa in his book on Man (Nemesius, *loc. cit.*), such things as are done through fear *are of a mixed character,* being partly voluntary and partly involuntary. For that which is done through fear, considered in itself, is not voluntary; but it becomes voluntary in this particular case, in order, namely, to avoid the evil feared.

But if the matter be considered aright, such things are voluntary rather than involuntary: for they are voluntary simply, but involuntary in a certain respect. For a thing is said to be simply, according as it is in act; but according as it is only in the apprehension, it is not simply, but in a certain respect. Now that which is done through fear, is in act in so far as it is done. For, since acts are concerned with singulars; and the singular, as such, is here and now; that which is done in act, in so far as it is here and now and under other individuating circumstances. And that which is done through fear, is voluntary, inasmuch as it is here and now, that is to say, in so far as, under the circumstances, it hinders a greater evil which was feared; thus the throwing of the cargo into the sea becomes voluntary during the storm, through fear of the danger: wherefore it is clear that it is voluntary simply. And hence it is that what is done out of fear is essentially voluntary, because its principle is within.—But if we consider what is done through fear, as outside this particular case, and inasmuch as it is repugnant to the will, this is merely a consideration of the mind. And consequently what is done through fear is involuntary, considered in that respect, that is to say, outside the actual circumstances of the case.

Reply Obj. 1. Things done through fear and compulsion, differ not only according to present and future time, but also in this, that the will does not consent, but is moved entirely counter to that which is done through compulsion: whereas what is done through fear, becomes voluntary, because the will is moved towards it, albeit not for its own sake, but on account of something else, that is, in order to avoid an evil which is feared. For the conditions of a voluntary act are satisfied, if it be done on account of something else voluntary: since the voluntary is not only what we wish, for its own sake, as an end, but also what we wish for the sake of something else, as an end. It is clear therefore that in what is done from compulsion, the will does nothing inwardly; whereas in what is done through fear, the will does something. Accordingly, as Gregory of Nyssa† says, in order to exclude things done through fear, a violent action is defined as not only one, *the principal whereof is from*

---

* Nemesius, *De Nat. Hom.* xxx. † Nemesius, *loc. cit.*

without, but with the addition, *in which he that suffers violence concurs not at all;* because the will of him that is in fear, does concur somewhat in that which he does through fear.

Reply Obj. 2. Things that are such absolutely, remain such, whatever be added to them; for instance, a cold thing, or a white thing: but things that are such relatively, vary according as they are compared with different things. For what is big in comparison with one thing, is small in comparison with another. Now a thing is said to be voluntary, not only for its own sake, as it were absolutely; but also for the sake of something else, as it were relatively. Accordingly, nothing prevents a thing which was not voluntary in comparison with one thing, from becoming voluntary when compared with another.

Reply Obj. 3. That which is done through fear, is voluntary without any condition, that is to say, according as it is actually done: but it is involuntary, under a certain condition, that is to say, if such a fear were not threatening. Consequently, this argument proves rather the opposite.

SEVENTH ARTICLE

Whether Concupiscence Causes Involuntariness?

We proceed thus to the Seventh Article:—

Objection 1. It would seem that concupiscence causes involuntariness. For just as fear is a passion, so is concupiscence. But fear causes involuntariness to a certain extent. Therefore concupiscence does so too.

Obj. 2. Further, just as the timid man through fear acts counter to that which he proposed, so does the incontinent, through concupiscence. But fear causes involuntariness to a certain extent. Therefore concupiscence does so also.

Obj. 3. Further, knowledge is necessary for voluntariness. But concupiscence impairs knowledge; for the Philosopher says (*Ethic.* vi. 5) that *delight,* or the lust of pleasure, *destroys the judgment of prudence.* Therefore concupiscence causes involuntariness.

On the contrary, Damascene says (*De Fide Orthod.* ii. 24): *The involuntary act deserves mercy or indulgence, and is done with regret.* But neither of these can be said of that which is done out of concupiscence. Therefore concupiscence does not cause involuntariness.

I answer that, Concupiscence does not cause involuntariness, but on the contrary makes something to be voluntary. For a thing is said to be voluntary, from the fact that the will is moved to it. Now concupiscence inclines the will to desire the object of concupiscence. Therefore the effect of concupiscence is to make something to be voluntary rather than involuntary.

Reply Obj. 1. Fear regards evil, but concupiscence regards good. Now evil of itself is counter to the will, whereas good harmonizes with the will. Therefore fear has a greater tendency than concupiscence to cause involuntariness.

Reply Obj. 2. He who acts from fear retains the repugnance of the will to that which he does, considered in itself. But he that acts from concupiscence, e.g., an incontinent man, does not retain his former will whereby he repudiated the object of his concupiscence; for his will is changed so that he desires that which previously he repudiated. Accordingly, that which is done out of fear is involuntary, to a certain extent, but that which is done from concupiscence is nowise involuntary. For the man who yields to concupiscence acts counter to that which he purposed at first, but not counter to that which he desires now; whereas the timid man acts counter to that which in itself he desires now.

Reply Obj. 3. If concupiscence were to destroy knowledge altogether, as happens with those whom concupiscence has rendered mad, it would follow that concupiscence would take away voluntariness. And yet properly speaking it would not result in the act being involuntary, because in things bereft of reason, there is neither voluntary nor involuntary. But sometimes in those actions which are done from concupiscence, knowledge is not completely destroyed, because the power of knowing is not taken away entirely, but only the actual consideration in some particular possible act. Nevertheless, this itself is voluntary, according as by voluntary we mean that which is in the power of the will, for example, *not to act* or *not to will,* and in like manner *not to consider;* for the will can resist the passion, as we shall state later on (Q. 10, A. 3; Q. 77, A. 7).

EIGHTH ARTICLE

Whether Ignorance Causes Involuntariness?

We proceed thus to the Eighth Article:—

Objection 1. It would seem that ignorance does not cause involuntariness. For *the involuntary act deserves pardon,* as Damascene says (*De Fide Orthod.* ii. 24). But sometimes that which is done through ignorance does not deserve pardon, according to 1 Cor. xiv. 38: *If any man know not, he shall not be known.* Therefore ignorance does not cause involuntariness.

Obj. 2. Further, every sin implies ignorance; according to Prov. xiv. 22: *They err, that work evil.* If, therefore, ignorance causes involuntariness, it would follow that every sin is involuntary: which is opposed to the saying of Augustine, that *every sin is voluntary* (*De Vera Relig.* xiv).

Obj. 3. Further, *involuntariness is not without sadness*, as Damascene says (*loc. cit*). But some things are done out of ignorance, but without sadness: for instance, a man may kill a foe, whom he wishes to kill, thinking at the time that he is killing a stag. Therefore ignorance does not cause involuntariness.

On the contrary, Damascene (*loc. cit.*) and the Philosopher (*Ethic.* iii. 1) say that *what is done through ignorance is involuntary.*

I answer that, If ignorance cause involuntariness, it is in so far as it deprives one of knowledge, which is a necessary condition of voluntariness, as was declared above (A. 1). But it is not every ignorance that deprives one of this knowledge. Accordingly, we must take note that ignorance has a threefold relationship to the act of the will: in one way, *concomitantly;* in another, *consequently;* in a third way, *antecedently.* — *Concomitantly,* when there is ignorance of what is done; but, so that even if it were known, it would be done. For then, ignorance does not induce one to wish this to be done, but it just happens that a thing is at the same time done and not known: thus in the example given (*Obj.* 3) a man did indeed wish to kill his foe, but killed him in ignorance, thinking to kill a stag. And ignorance of this kind, as the Philosopher states (*Ethic.* iii. 1), does not cause involuntariness, since it is not the cause of anything that is repugnant to the will: but it causes *non-voluntariness,* since that which is unknown cannot be actually willed. Ignorance is *consequent* to the act of the will, in so far as ignorance itself is voluntary: and this happens in two ways, in accordance with the two aforesaid modes of voluntary (A. 3). First, because the

act of the will is brought to bear on the ignorance: as when a man wishes not to know, that he may have an excuse for sin, or that he may not be withheld from sin; according to Job. xxi. 14: *We desire not the knowledge of Thy ways.* And this is called *affected ignorance.*—Secondly, ignorance is said to be voluntary, when it regards that which one can and ought to know: for in this sense *not to act* and *not to will* are said to be voluntary, as stated above (A. 3). And ignorance of this kind happens, either when one does not actually consider what one can and ought to consider;—this is called *ignorance of evil choice,* and arises from some passion or habit: or when one does not take the trouble to acquire the knowledge which one ought to have; in which sense, ignorance of the general principles of law, which one ought to know, is voluntary, as being due to negligence.—Accordingly, if in either of these ways, ignorance is voluntary, it cannot cause involuntariness simply. Nevertheless it causes involuntariness in a certain respect, inasmuch as it precedes the movement of the will towards the act, which movement would not be, if there were knowledge. Ignorance is *antecedent* to the act of the will, when it is not voluntary, and yet is the cause of man's willing what he would not will otherwise. Thus a man may be ignorant of some circumstance of his act, which he was not bound to know, the result being that he does that which he would not do, if he knew of that circumstance; for instance, a man, after taking proper precaution, may not know that someone is coming along the road, so that he shoots an arrow and slays a passer-by. Such ignorance causes involuntariness simply.

From this may be gathered the solution of the objections. For the first objection deals with ignorance of what a man is bound to know. The second, with ignorance of choice, which is voluntary to a certain extent, as stated above. The third, with that ignorance which is concomitant with the act of the will.

QUESTION 7

Of the Circumstances of Human Acts

(In Four Articles)

WE must now consider the circumstances of human acts: under which head there are four points of inquiry: (1) What is a circumstance? (2) Whether a theologian should take note of the circumstances of human acts? (3) How many circumstances are there? (4) Which are the most important of them?

FIRST ARTICLE

Whether a Circumstance Is an Accident of a Human Act?

We proceed thus to the First Article:—

Objection 1. It would seem that a circumstance is not an accident of a human act. For

Tully says (*De Invent. Rhetor.* i) that a circumstance is that from *which an orator adds authority and strength to his argument.* But oratorical arguments are derived principally from things pertaining to the essence of a thing, such as the definition, the genus, the species, and the like, from which also Tully declares that an orator should draw his arguments. Therefore a circumstance is not an accident of a human act.

Obj. 2. Further, *to be in* is proper to an accident. But that which surrounds (*circumstat*) is rather out than in. Therefore the circumstances are not accidents of human acts.

Obj. 3. Further, an accident has no accident. But human acts themselves are accidents. Therefore the circumstances are not accidents of acts.

On the contrary, The particular conditions of any singular thing are called its individuating accidents. But the Philosopher (*Ethic.* iii. 1) calls the circumstances particular things,* *i.e.,* the particular conditions of each act. Therefore the circumstances are individual accidents of human acts.

I answer that, Since, according to the Philosopher (*Peri Herm.* i), *words are the signs of what we understand,* it must needs be that in naming things we follow the process of intellectual knowledge. Now our intellectual knowledge proceeds from the better known to the less known. Accordingly with us, names of more obvious things are transferred so as to signify things less obvious: and hence it is that, as stated in *Metaph.* x. 4, *the notion of distance has been transferred from things that are apart locally, to all kinds of opposition:* and in like manner words that signify local movement are employed to designate all other movements, because bodies which are circumscribed by place, are best known to us. And hence it is that the word *circumstance* has passed from located things to human acts.

Now in things located, that is said to surround something, which is outside it, but touches it, or is placed near it. Accordingly, whatever conditions are outside the substance of an act, and yet in some way touch the human act, are called circumstances. Now what is outside a thing's substance, while it belongs to that thing, is called its accident. Wherefore the circumstances of human acts should be called their accidents.

Reply Obj. 1. The orator gives strength to his argument, in the first place, from the substance of the act; and, secondly, from the circumstances of the act. Thus a man becomes indictable, first, through being guilty of murder; secondly, through having done it fraudulently, or from motives of greed or at a holy

* τα καθ᾽ ἕκαστα.

time or place, and so forth. And so in the passage quoted, it is said pointedly that the orator *adds strength to his argument,* as though this were something secondary.

Reply Obj. 2. A thing is said to be an accident of something in two ways. First, from being in that thing: thus, whiteness is said to be an accident of Socrates. Secondly, because it is together with that thing in the same subject: thus, whiteness is an accident of the art of music, inasmuch as they meet in the same subject, so as to touch one another, as it were. And in this sense circumstances are said to be the accidents of human acts.

Reply Obj. 3. As stated above (*ad* 2), an accident is said to be the accident of an accident, from the fact that they meet in the same subject. But this happens in two ways. First, in so far as two accidents are both related to the same subject, without any relation to one another; as whiteness and the art of music in Socrates. Secondly, when such accidents are related to one another; as when the subject receives one accident by means of the other; for instance, a body receives color by means of its surface. And thus also is one accident said to be in another; for we speak of color as being in the surface.

Accordingly, circumstances are related to acts in both these ways. For some circumstances that have a relation to acts, belong to the agent otherwise than through the act; as place and condition of person; whereas others belong to the agent by reason of the act, as the manner in which the act is done.

SECOND ARTICLE

Whether Theologians Should Take Note of the Circumstances of Human Acts?

We proceed thus to the Second Article:—

Objection 1. It would seem that theologians should not take note of the circumstances of human acts. Because theologians do not consider human acts otherwise than according to their quality of good or evil. But it seems that circumstances cannot give quality to human acts; for a thing is never qualified, formally speaking, by that which is outside it; but by that which is in it. Therefore theologians should not take note of the circumstances of acts.

Obj. 2. Further, circumstances are the accidents of acts. But one thing may be subject to an infinity of accidents; hence the Philosopher says (*Metaph.* vi. 2) that *no art or science considers accidental being, except only the art of sophistry.* Therefore the theologian has not to consider circumstances.

Obj. 3. Further, the consideration of circumstances belongs to the orator. But oratory is not a part of theology. Therefore it is not a theologian's business to consider circumstances.

On the contrary, Ignorance of circumstances causes an act to be involuntary, according to Damascene (*De Fide Orthod.* ii 24) and Gregory of Nyssa.* But involuntariness excuses from sin, the consideration of which belongs to the theologian. Therefore circumstances also should be considered by the theologian.

I answer that, Circumstances come under the consideration of the theologian, for a threefold reason. First, because the theologian considers human acts, inasmuch as man is thereby directed to Happiness. Now, everything that is directed to an end should be proportionate to that end. But acts are made proportionate to an end by means of a certain commensurateness, which results from the due circumstances. Hence the theologian has to consider the circumstances.—Secondly, because the theologian considers human acts according as they are found to be good or evil, better or worse: and this diversity depends on circumstances, as we shall see further on (Q. 18, AA. 10, 11; Q. 73, A. 7).—Thirdly, because the theologian considers human acts under the aspect of merit and demerit, which is proper to human acts; and for this it is requisite that they be voluntary. Now a human act is deemed to be voluntary or involuntary, according to knowledge or ignorance of circumstances, as stated above (*cf.* Q. 6, A. 8). Therefore the theologian has to consider circumstances.

Reply Obj. 1. Good directed to the end is said to be useful; and this implies some kind of relation: wherefore the Philosopher says (*Ethic.* i 6) that *the good in the genus "relation" is the useful.* Now, in the genus *relation* a thing is denominated not only according to that which is inherent in the thing, but also according to that which is extrinsic to it: as may be seen in the expressions *right* and *left, equal* and *unequal,* and such like. Accordingly, since the goodness of acts consists in their utility to the end, nothing hinders their being called good or bad according to their proportion to extrinsic things that are adjacent to them.

Reply Obj. 2. Accidents which are altogether accidental are neglected by every art, by reason of their uncertainty and infinity. But such like accidents are not what we call circumstances; because circumstances, although, as stated above (A. 1), they are extrinsic to the act, nevertheless are in a kind of contact with it, by being related to it. Prop-

* Nemesius. *De Nat. Hom.* xxxi.

er accidents, however, come under the consideration of art.

Reply Obj. 3. The consideration of circumstances belongs to the moralist, the politician, and the orator. To the moralist, in so far as with respect to circumstances we find or lose the mean of virtue in human acts and passions. To the politician and to the orator, in so far as circumstances make acts to be worthy of praise or blame, of excuse or indictment. In different ways, however: because where the orator persuades, the politician judges. To the theologian this consideration belongs, in all the aforesaid ways: since to him all the other arts are subservient: for he has to consider virtuous and vicious acts, just as the moralist does; and with the orator and politician he considers acts according as they are deserving of reward or punishment.

THIRD ARTICLE

Whether the Circumstances Are Properly Set Forth in the Third Book of Ethics?

We proceed thus to the Third Article:—

Objection 1. It would seem that the circumstances are not properly set forth in *Ethic.* iii. 1. For a circumstance of an act is described as something outside the act. Now time and place answer to this description. Therefore there are only two circumstances, to wit, *when* and *where.*

Obj. 2. Further, we judge from the circumstances whether a thing is well or ill done. But this belongs to the mode of an act. Therefore all the circumstances are included under one, which is the *mode of acting.*

Obj. 3. Further, circumstances are not part of the substance of an act. But the causes of an act seem to belong to its substance. Therefore no circumstance should be taken from the cause of the act itself. Accordingly, neither *who,* nor *why,* nor *about what,* are circumstances: since *who* refers to the efficient cause, *why* to the final cause, and *about what* to the material cause.

On the contrary is the authority of the Philosopher in *Ethic.* iii. 1.

I answer that, Tully, in his Rhetoric (*De Invent. Rhetor.* i), gives seven circumstances, which are contained in this verse:

Quis, quid, ubi, quibus auxiliis, cur, quomodo, quando—
Who, what, where, by what aids, why, how, and when.

For in acts we must take note of *who* did it, *by what aids* or *instruments* he did it, *what* he did, *where* he did it, *why* he did it, *how* and *when* he did it. But Aristotle in *Ethic.* iii. 1 adds yet another, to wit, *about what,* which Tully includes in the circumstance *what.*

The reason of this enumeration may be set

down as follows. For a circumstance is described as something outside the substance of the act, and yet in a way touching it. Now this happens in three ways: first, inasmuch as it touches the act itself; secondly, inasmuch as it touches the cause of the act; thirdly, inasmuch as it touches the effect. It touches the act itself, either by way of measure, as *time* and *place;* or by qualifying the act as the *mode of acting.* It touches the effect, when we consider *what* is done. It touches the cause of the act, as to the final cause, by the circumstance *why;* as to the material cause, or object, in the circumstance *about what;* as to the principal efficient cause, in the circumstance *who;* and as to the instrumental efficient cause, in the circumstance *by what aids.*

Reply Obj. 1. Time and place surround (*circumstant*) the act by way of measure; but the others surround the act by touching it in any other way, while they are extrinsic to the substance of the act.

Reply Obj. 2. This mode *well* or *ill* is not a circumstance, but results from all the circumstances. But the mode which refers to a quality of the act is a special circumstance; for instance, that a man walk fast or slowly; that he strike hard or gently, and so forth.

Reply Obj. 3. A condition of the cause, on which the substance of the act depends, is not a circumstance; it must be an additional condition. Thus, in regard to the object, it is not a circumstance of theft that the object is another's property, for this belongs to the substance of the act; but that it be great or small. And the same applies to the other circumstances which are considered in reference to the other causes. For the end that specifies the act is not a circumstance, but some additional end. Thus, that a valiant man act *valiantly for the sake of* the good of the virtue or fortitude, is not a circumstance; but if he act valiantly for the sake of the delivery of the state, or of Christendom, or some such purpose. The same is to be said with regard to the circumstance *what;* for that a man by pouring water on someone should happen to wash him, is not a circumstance of the washing; but that in doing so he give him a chill, or scald him; heal him or harm him, these are circumstances.

FOURTH ARTICLE

Whether the Most Important Circumstances Are "Why" and "In What the Act Consists"?

We proceed thus to the Fourth Article:—
Objection 1. It would seem that these are

not the most important circumstances, namely, *why* and those *in which the act is,** as stated in *Ethic.* iii. 1. For those in which the act is seem to be place and time: and these do not seem to be the most important of the circumstances, since, of them all, they are the most extrinsic to the act. Therefore those things in which the act is are not the most important circumstances.

Obj. 2. Further, the end of a thing is extrinsic to it. Therefore it is not the most important circumstance.

Obj. 3. Further, that which holds the foremost place in regard to each thing, is its cause and its form. But the cause of an act is the person that does it; while the form of an act is the manner in which it is done. Therefore these two circumstances seem to be of the greatest importance.

On the contrary, Gregory of Nyssa† says that *the most important circumstances* are *why it is done* and *what is done.*

I answer that, As stated above (Q. 1, A. 1), acts are properly called human, inasmuch as they are voluntary. Now, the motive and object of the will is the end. Therefore that circumstance is the most important of all which touches the act on the part of the end, viz., the circumstance *why:* and the second in importance, is that which touches the very substance of the act, viz., the circumstance *what he did.* As to the other circumstances, they are more or less important, according as they more or less approach to these.

Reply Obj. 1. By those things *in which the act is* the Philosopher does not mean time and place, but those circumstances that are affixed to the act itself. Wherefore Gregory of Nyssa,† as though he were explaining the dictum of the Philosopher, instead of the latter's term,—*in which the act is,* said, *what is done.*

Reply Obj. 2. Although the end is not part of the substance of the act, yet it is the most important cause of the act, inasmuch as it moves the agent to act. Wherefore the moral act is specified chiefly by the end.

Reply Obj. 3. The person that does the act is the cause of that act, inasmuch as he is moved thereto by the end; and it is chiefly in this respect that he is directed to the act; while other conditions of the person have not such an important relation to the act.—As to the mode, it is not the substantial form of the act, for in an act the substantial form depends on the object and term or end; but it is, as it were, a certain accidental quality of the act.

* ἐν οἷς ἡ πρᾶξις.   † Nemesius, *De Nat. Hom.* xxxi.

QUESTION 8

Of the Will, in Regard to What It Wills

(In Three Articles)

WE must now consider the different acts of the will; and in the first place, those acts which belong to the will itself immediately, as being elicited by the will; secondly, those acts which are commanded by the will.

Now the will is moved to the end, and to the means to the end; we must therefore consider —(1) Those acts of the will whereby it is moved to the end; and (2) those whereby it is moved to the means. And since it seems that there are three acts of the will in reference to the end; viz., *volition, enjoyment,* and *intention;* we must consider—(1) Volition; (2) enjoyment; (3) intention.—Concerning the first, three things must be considered: (1) Of what things is the will? (2) By what is the will moved? (3) How is it moved?

Under the first head there are three points of inquiry: (1) Whether the will is of good only? (2) Whether it is of the end only, or also of the means? (3) If in any way it be of the means, whether it be moved to the end and to the means, by the same movement?

FIRST ARTICLE

Whether the Will Is of Good Only?

We proceed thus to the First Article:—

Objection 1. It would seem that the will is not of good only. For the same power regards opposites; for instance, sight regards white and black. But good and evil are opposites. Therefore the will is not only of good, but also of evil.

Obj. 2. Further, rational powers can be directed to opposite purposes, according to the Philosopher (*Metaph.* ix. 2). But the will is a rational power, since it is *in the reason,* as is stated in *De Anima* iii. 9. Therefore the will can be directed to opposites; and consequently its volition is not confined to good, but extends to evil.

Obj. 3. Further, good and being are convertible. But volition is directed not only to beings, but also to non-beings. For sometimes we wish *not to walk,* or *not to speak;* and again at times we wish for future things, which are not actual beings. Therefore the will is not of good only.

On the contrary, Dionysius says (*Div. Nom.* iv) that *evil is outside the scope of the will,* and that *all things desire good.*

I answer that, The will is a rational appetite. Now every appetite is only of something good. The reason of this is that the appetite is nothing else than an inclination of a person desirous of a thing towards that thing. Now every inclination is to something like and suitable to the thing inclined. Since, therefore, everything, inasmuch as it is being and substance, is a good, it must needs be that every inclination is to something good. And hence it is that the Philosopher says (*Ethic.* i. 1) that *the good is that which all desire.*

But it must be noted that, since every inclination results from a form, the natural appetite results from a form existing in the nature of things: while the sensitive appetite, as also the intellective or rational appetite, which we call the will, follows from an apprehended form. Therefore, just as the natural appetite tends to good existing in a thing; so the animal or voluntary appetite tends to a good which is apprehended. Consequently, in order that the will tend to anything, it is requisite, not that this be good in very truth, but that it be apprehended as good. Wherefore the Philosopher says (*Phys.* ii. 3) that *the end is a good, or an apparent good.*

Reply Obj. 1. The same power regards opposites, but it is not referred to them in the same way. Accordingly, the will is referred both to good and to evil: but to good by desiring it: to evil, by shunning it. Wherefore the actual desire of good is called *volition,** meaning thereby the act of the will; for it is in this sense that we are now speaking of the will. On the other hand, the shunning of evil is better described as *nolition:* wherefore, just as volition is of good, so nolition is of evil.

Reply Obj. 2. A rational power is not to be directed to all opposite purposes, but to those which are contained under its proper object; for no power seeks other than its proper object. Now, the object of the will is good. Wherefore the will can be directed to such opposite purposes as are contained under good, such as to be moved or to be at rest, to speak or to be silent, and such like: for the will can be directed to either under the aspect of good.

Reply Obj. 3. That which is not a being in nature, is considered as a being in the reason, wherefore negations and privations are said to be *beings of reason.* In this way, too, future

---

* In Latin,—*voluntas.* To avoid confusion with *voluntas* (the will) St. Thomas adds a word of explanation, which in the translation may appear superfluous.

things, in so far as they are apprehended, are beings. Accordingly, in so far as such like are beings, they are apprehended under the aspect of good; and it is thus that the will is directed to them. Wherefore the Philosopher says (*Ethic.* v. 1) that *to lack evil is considered as a good.*

SECOND ARTICLE

Whether Volition Is of the End Only, or Also of the Means?

We proceed thus to the Second Article:—

Objection 1. It would seem that volition is not of the means, but of the end only. For the Philosopher says (*Ethic.* iii. 2) that *volition is of the end, while choice is of the means.*

Obj. 2. Further, *For objects differing in genus there are corresponding different powers of the soul* (*Ethic.* vi. 1). Now, the end and the means are in different genera of good: because the end, which is a good either of rectitude or of pleasure, is in the genus *quality,* or *action,* or *passion;* whereas the good which is useful, and is directed to an end, is in the genus *relation* (*Ethic.* i. 6). Therefore, if volition is of the end, it is not of the means.

Obj. 3. Further, habits are proportionate to powers, since they are perfections thereof. But in those habits which are called practical arts, the end belongs to cne, and the means to another art; thus the use of a ship, which is its end, belongs to the (art of the) helmsman; whereas the building of the ship, which is directed to the end, belongs to the art of the shipwright. Therefore, since volition is of the end, it is not of the means.

On the contrary, In natural things, it is by the same power that a thing passes through the middle space, and arrives at the terminus. But the means are a kind of middle space, through which one arrives at the end or terminus. Therefore, if volition is of the end, it is also of the means.

I answer that, The word *voluntas* sometimes designates the power of the will, sometimes its act.* Accordingly, if we speak of the will as a power, thus it extends both to the end and to the means. For every power extends to those things in which may be considered the aspect of the object of that power in any way whatever: thus the sight extends to all things whatsoever that are in any way colored. Now the aspect of good, which is the object of the power of will, may be found not only in the end, but also in the means.

If, however, we speak of the will in regard to its act, then, properly speaking, volition is of the end only. Because every act denominated from a power, designates the simple act of that power: thus *to understand* designates

* See note on p. 626.

the simple act of the understanding. Now the simple act of a power is referred to that which is in itself the object of that power. But that which is good and willed in itself is the end. Wherefore volition, properly speaking, is of the end itself. On the other hand, the means are good and willed, not in themselves, but as referred to the end. Wherefore the will is directed to them, only in so far as it is directed to the end: so that what it wills in them, is the end. Thus, to understand, is properly directed to things that are known in themselves, *i.e.,* first principles: but we do not speak of understanding with regard to things known through first principles, except in so far as we see the principles in those things. For in morals the end is what principles are in speculative science (*cf. Ethic.* vii. 8).

Reply Obj. 1. The Philosopher is speaking of the will in reference to the simple act of the will; not in reference to the power of the will.

Reply Obj. 2. There are different powers for objects that differ in genus and are on an equality; for instance, sound and color are different genera of sensibles, to which are referred hearing and sight. But the useful and the righteous are not on an equality, but are as that which is of itself, and that which is in relation to another. Now such like objects are always referred to the same power; for instance, the power of sight perceives both color and light by which color is seen.

Reply Obj. 3. Not everything that diversifies habits, diversifies the powers: since habits are certain determinations of powers to certain special acts. Moreover, every practical art considers both the end and the means. For the art of the helmsman does indeed consider the end, as that which it effects; and the means, as that which it commands. On the other hand, the ship-building art considers the means as that which it effects; but it considers that which is the end, as that to which it refers what it effects. And again, in every practical art there is an end proper to it and means that belong properly to that art.

THIRD ARTICLE

Whether the Will Is Moved by the Same Act to the End and to the Means?

We proceed thus to the Third Article:—

Objection 1. It would seem that the will is moved by the same act, to the end and to the means. Because according to the Philosopher (*Topic* iii. 2) *where one thing is on account of another there is only one.* But the will does not will the means save on account of the end. Therefore it is moved to both by the same act.

Obj. 2. Further, the end is the reason for willing the means, just as light is the reason of seeing colors. But light and colors are seen by the same act. Therefore it is the same movement of the will, whereby it wills the end and the means.

Obj. 3. Further, it is one and the same natural movement which tends through the middle space to the terminus. But the means are in comparison to the end, as the middle space is to the terminus. Therefore it is the same movement of the will whereby it is directed to the end and to the means.

On the contrary, Acts are diversified according to their objects. But the end is a different species of good from the means, which are a useful good. Therefore the will is not moved to both by the same act.

I answer that, Since the end is willed in itself, whereas the means, as such, are only willed for the end, it is evident that the will can be moved to the end, without being moved to the means; whereas it cannot be moved to the means, as such, unless it is moved to the end. Accordingly the will is moved to the end in two ways: first, to the end absolutely and in itself; secondly, as the reason for willing the means. Hence it is evident that the will is moved by one and the same movement,—to the end, as the reason for willing the means; and to the means themselves. But it is another act whereby the will is moved to the end absolutely. And sometimes this act precedes the other in time; for example when a man first wills to have health, and afterwards deliberating by what means to be healed, wills to send for the doctor to heal him. The same happens in regard to the intellect: for at first a man understands the principles in themselves; but afterwards he understands them in the conclusions, inasmuch as he assents to the conclusions on account of the principles.

Reply Obj. 1. This argument holds in respect of the will being moved to the end as the reason for willing the means.

Reply Obj. 2. Whenever color is seen, by the same act the light is seen; but the light can be seen without the color being seen. In like manner whenever a man wills the means, by the same act he wills the end; but not conversely.

Reply Obj. 3. In the execution of a work, the means are as the middle space, and the end, as the terminus. Wherefore just as natural movement sometimes stops in the middle and does not reach the terminus; so sometimes one is busy with the means, without gaining the end. But in willing it is the reverse: for the will through (willing) the end comes to will the means; just as the intellect arrives at the conclusions through the principles which are called *means.* Hence it is that sometimes the intellect understands a mean, and does not proceed thence to the conclusion. And in like manner the will sometimes wills the end, and yet does not proceed to will the means.

The solution to the argument in the contrary sense is clear from what has been said above (A. 2 *ad* 2). For the useful and the righteous are not species of good in an equal degree, but are as that which is for its own sake and that which is for the sake of something else: wherefore the act of the will can be directed to one and not to the other; but not conversely.

QUESTION 9

Of That Which Moves the Will

(In Six Articles)

WE must now consider what moves the will: and under this head there are six points of inquiry: (1) Whether the will is moved by the intellect? (2) Whether it is moved by the sensitive appetite? (3) Whether the will moves itself? (4) Whether it is moved by an extrinsic principle? (5) Whether it is moved by a heavenly body? (6) Whether the will is moved by God alone as by an extrinsic principle?

FIRST ARTICLE

Whether the Will Is Moved by the Intellect?

We proceed thus to the First Article:—

Objection 1. It would seem that the will is not moved by the intellect. For Augustine says on Ps. cxviii. 20: *My soul hath coveted to long for Thy justifications:—The intellect flies ahead, the desire follows sluggishly or not at all: we know what is good, but deeds delight us not.* But it would not be so, if the will were moved by the intellect: because movement of the movable results from motion of the mover. Therefore the intellect does not move the will.

Obj. 2. Further, the intellect in presenting the appetible object to the will, stands in relation to the will, as the imagination in representing the appetible object to the sensitive appetite. But the imagination, in presenting the appetible object, does not move the sensitive appetite: indeed sometimes our imagination affects us no more than what is set before us in a picture, and moves us not at all

(*De Anima* ii. 3). Therefore neither does the intellect move the will.

Obj. 3. Further, the same is not mover and moved in respect of the same thing. But the will moves the intellect; for we exercise the intellect when we will. Therefore the intellect does not move the will.

On the contrary, The Philosopher says (De Anima iii. 10) that *the appetible object is a mover not moved, whereas the will is a mover moved.*

I answer that, A thing requires to be moved by something in so far as it is in potentiality to several things; for that which is in potentiality needs to be reduced to act by something actual; and to do this is to move. Now a power of the soul is seen to be in potentiality to different things in two ways: first, with regard to acting and not acting; secondly, with regard to this or that action. Thus the sight sometimes sees actually, and sometimes sees not: and sometimes it sees white, and sometimes black. It needs therefore a mover in two respects, viz., as to the exercise or use of the act, and as to the determination of the act. The first of these is on the part of the subject, which is sometimes acting, sometimes not acting: while the other is on the part of the object, by reason of which the act is specified.

The motion of the subject itself is due to some agent. And since every agent acts for an end, as was shown above (Q. 1, A. 2), the principle of this motion lies in the end. And hence it is that the art which is concerned with the end, by its command moves the art which is concerned with the means; just as the *art of sailing commands the art of shipbuilding* (*Phys.* ii. 2). Now good in general, which has the nature of an end, is the object of the will. Consequently, in this respect, the will moves the other powers of the soul to their acts, for we make use of the other powers when we will. For the end and perfection of every other power, is included under the object of the will as some particular good: and always the art or power to which the universal end belongs, moves to their acts the arts or powers to which belong the particular ends included in the universal end. Thus the leader of an army, who intends the common good—*i.e.*, the order of the whole army—by his command moves one of the captains, who intends the order of one company.

On the other hand, the object moves, by determining the act, after the manner of a formal principle, whereby in natural things actions are specified, as heating by heat. Now the first formal principle is universal *being* and *truth,* which is the object of the intellect. And therefore by this kind of motion the intellect moves the will, as presenting its object to it.

Reply Obj. 1. The passage quoted proves, not that the intellect does not move, but that it does not move of necessity.

Reply Obj. 2. Just as the imagination of a form without estimation of fitness or harmfulness, does not move the sensitive appetite; so neither does the apprehension of the true without the aspect of goodness and desirability. Hence it is not the speculative intellect that moves, but the practical intellect (*De Anima* iii. 9).

Reply Obj. 3. The will moves the intellect as to the exercise of its act; since even the true itself which is the perfection of the intellect, is included in the universal good, as a particular good. But as to the determination of the act, which the act derives from the object, the intellect moves the will; since the good itself is apprehended under a special aspect as contained in the universal true. It is therefore evident that the same is not mover and moved in the same respect.

SECOND ARTICLE

Whether the Will Is Moved by the Sensitive Appetite?

We proceed thus to the Second Article:—

Objection 1. It would seem that the will cannot be moved by the sensitive appetite. For *to move and to act is more excellent than to be passive,* as Augustine says (*Gen. ad lit.* xii. 16). But the sensitive appetite is less excellent than the will which is the intellectual appetite; just as sense is less excellent than intellect. Therefore the sensitive appetite does not move the will.

Obj. 2. Further, no particular power can produce a universal effect. But the sensitive appetite is a particular power, because it follows the particular apprehension of sense. Therefore it cannot cause the movement of the will, which movement is universal, as following the universal apprehension of the intellect.

Obj. 3. Further, as is proved in *Phys.* viii. 5, the mover is not moved by that which it moves, in such a way that there be reciprocal motion. But the will moves the sensitive appetite, inasmuch as the sensitive appetite obeys the reason. Therefore the sensitive appetite does not move the will.

On the contrary, It is written (James i. 14): *Every man is tempted by his own concupiscence, being drawn away and allured.* But man would not be drawn away by his concupiscence, unless his will were moved by the sensitive appetite, wherein concupiscence resides. Therefore the sensitive appetite moves the will.

I answer that, As stated above (A. 1), that which is apprehended as good and fitting, moves the will by way of object. Now, that a thing appear to be good and fitting, happens from two causes: namely, from the condition, either of the thing proposed, or of the one to whom it is proposed. For fitness is spoken of by way of relation; hence it depends on both extremes. And hence it is that taste, according as it is variously disposed, takes to a thing in various ways, as being fitting or unfitting. Wherefore as the Philosopher says (*Ethic.* iii. 5): *According as a man is, such does the end seem to him.*

Now it is evident that according to a passion of the sensitive appetite man is changed to a certain disposition. Wherefore according as man is affected by a passion, something seems to him fitting, which does not seem so when he is not so affected: thus that seems good to a man when angered, which does not seem good when he is calm. And in this way, the sensitive appetite moves the will, on the part of the object.

Reply Obj. 1. Nothing hinders that which is better simply and in itself, from being less excellent in a certain respect. Accordingly the will is simply more excellent than the sensitive appetite: but in respect of the man in whom a passion is predominant, in so far as he is subject to that passion, the sensitive appetite is more excellent.

Reply Obj. 2. Men's acts and choices are in reference to singulars. Wherefore from the very fact that the sensitive appetite is a particular power, it has great influence in disposing man so that something seems to him such or otherwise, in particular cases.

Reply Obj. 3. As the Philosopher says (*Polit.* i. 3), the reason, in which resides the will, moves, by its command, the irascible and concupiscible powers, not, indeed, *by a despotic sovereignty,* as a slave is moved by his master, but by a *royal and politic sovereignty,* as free men are ruled by their governor, and can nevertheless act counter to his commands. Hence both irascible and concupiscible can move counter to the will: and accordingly nothing hinders the will from being moved by them at times.

THIRD ARTICLE

Whether the Will Moves Itself?

We proceed thus to the Third Article:—

Objection 1. It would seem that the will does not move itself. For every mover, as such, is in act: whereas what is moved, is in potentiality; since *movement is the act of that which is in potentiality, as such.** Now the same is not in potentiality and in act, in respect of the same. Therefore nothing moves itself. Neither, therefore, can the will move itself.

* Aristotle, *Phys.* iii. 1.

Obj. 2. Further, the movable is moved on the mover being present. But the will is always present to itself. If, therefore, it moved itself, it would always be moving itself, which is clearly false.

Obj. 3. Further, the will is moved by the intellect, as stated above (A. 1). If, therefore, the will move itself, it would follow that the same thing is at once moved immediately by two movers; which seems unreasonable. Therefore the will does not move itself.

On the contrary, The will is mistress of its own act, and to it belongs to will and not to will. But this would not be so, had it not the power to move itself to will. Therefore it moves itself.

I answer that, As stated above (A. 1), it belongs to the will to move the other powers, by reason of the end which is the will's object. Now, as stated above (Q. 8, A. 2), the end is in things appetible, what the principle is in things intelligible. But it is evident that the intellect, through its knowledge of the principle, reduces itself from potentiality to act, as to its knowledge of the conclusions; and thus it moves itself. And, in like manner, the will, through its volition of the end, moves itself to will the means.

Reply Obj. 1. It is not in respect of the same that the will moves itself and is moved: wherefore neither is it in act and in potentiality in respect of the same. But forasmuch as it actually wills the end, it reduces itself from potentiality to act, in respect of the means, so as, in a word, to will them actually.

Reply Obj. 2. The power of the will is always actually present to itself; but the act of the will, whereby it wills an end, is not always in the will. But it is by this act that it moves itself. Accordingly it does not follow that it is always moving itself.

Reply Obj. 3. The will is moved by the intellect, otherwise than by itself. By the intellect it is moved on the part of the object: whereas it is moved by itself, as to the exercise of its act, in respect of the end.

FOURTH ARTICLE

Whether the Will Is Moved by an Exterior Principle?

We proceed thus to the Fourth Article:—

Objection 1. It would seem that the will is not moved by anything exterior. For the movement of the will is voluntary. But it is essential to the voluntary that it be from an intrinsic principle, just as it is essential to the natural act. Therefore the movement of the will is not from anything exterior.

Obj. 2. Further, the will cannot suffer violence, as was shown above (Q. 6, A. 4). But the violent act is one *the principle of which is* *outside the agent.** Therefore the will cannot be moved by anything exterior.

Obj. 3. Further, that which is sufficiently moved by one mover, needs not to be moved by another. But the will moves itself sufficiently. Therefore it is not moved by anything exterior.

On the contrary, The will is moved by the object, as stated above (A. 1). But the object of the will can be something exterior, offered to the sense. Therefore the will can be moved by something exterior.

I answer that, As far as the will is moved by the object, it is evident that it can be moved by something exterior. But in so far as it is moved in the exercise of its act, we must again hold it to be moved by some exterior principle.

For everything that is at one time an agent actually, and at another time an agent in potentiality, needs to be moved by a mover. Now it is evident that the will begins to will something, whereas previously it did not will it. Therefore it must, of necessity, be moved by something to will it. And, indeed, it moves itself, as stated above (A. 3), in so far as through willing the end it reduces itself to the act of willing the means. Now it cannot do this without the aid of counsel: for when a man wills to be healed, he begins to reflect how this can be attained, and through this reflection he comes to the conclusion that he can be healed by a physician: and this he wills. But since he did not always actually will to have health, he must, of necessity, have begun, through something moving him, to will to be healed. And if the will moved itself to will this, it must, of necessity, have done this with the aid of counsel following some previous volition. But this process could not go on to infinity. Wherefore we must, of necessity, suppose that the will advanced to its first movement in virtue of the instigation of some exterior mover, as Aristotle concludes in a chapter of the *Eudemian Ethics* (vii. 14).

Reply Obj. 1. It is essential to the voluntary act that its principle be within the agent: but it is not necessary that this inward principle be the first principle unmoved by another. Wherefore though the voluntary act has an inward proximate principle, nevertheless its first principle is from without. Thus, too, the first principle of the natural movement is from without, that, to wit, which moves nature.

Reply Obj. 2. For an act to be violent it is not enough that its principle be extrinsic, but we must add *without the concurrence of him that suffers violence.* This does not happen when the will is moved by an exterior principle: for it is the will that wills, though moved by another. But this movement would be vio-

* Aristotle, Ethic. iii. 1.

lent, if it were counter to the movement of the will: which in the present case is impossible; since then the will would will and not will the same thing.

Reply Obj. 3. The will moves itself sufficiently in one respect, and in its own order, that is to say as proximate agent; but it cannot move itself in every respect, as we have shown. Wherefore it needs to be moved by another as first mover.

FIFTH ARTICLE

Whether the Will Is Moved by a Heavenly Body?

We proceed thus to the Fifth Article:—

Objection 1. It would seem that the human will is moved by a heavenly body. For all various and multiform movements are reduced, as to their cause, to a uniform movement which is that of the heavens, as is proved in *Phys.* viii. 9. But human movements are various and multiform, since they begin to be, whereas previously they were not. Therefore they are reduced, as to their cause, to the movement of the heavens, which is uniform according to its nature.

Obj. 2. Further, according to Augustine (*De Trin.* iii. 4) *the lower bodies are moved by the higher.* But the movements of the human body, which are caused by the will, could not be reduced to the movement of the heavens, as to their cause, unless the will too were moved by the heavens. Therefore the heavens move the human will.

Obj. 3. Further, by observing the heavenly bodies astrologers foretell the truth about future human acts, which are caused by the will. But this would not be so, if the heavenly bodies could not move man's will. Therefore the human will is moved by a heavenly body.

On the contrary, Damascene says (*De Fide Orthod.* ii. 7) that *the heavenly bodies are not the causes of our acts.* But they would be, if the will, which is the principle of human acts, were moved by the heavenly bodies. Therefore the will is not moved by the heavenly bodies.

I answer that, It is evident that the will can be moved by the heavenly bodies in the same way as it is moved by its object; that is to say; in so far as exterior bodies, which move the will, through being offered to the senses, and also the organs themselves of the sensitive powers, are subject to the movements of the heavenly bodies.

But some have maintained that heavenly bodies have an influence on the human will, in the same way as some exterior agent moves the will, as to the exercise of its act.—But this is impossible. For the *will,* as stated in *De Anima* iii. 9, *is in the reason.* Now the reason is a power of the soul, not bound to a bodily organ: wherefore it follows that the will is a power absolutely incorporeal and immaterial. But it is evident that no body can act on what is incorporeal, but rather the reverse: because things incorporeal and immaterial have a power more formal and more universal than any corporeal things whatever. Therefore it is impossible for a heavenly body to act directly on the intellect or the will.—For this reason Aristotle (*De Anima* iii. 3) ascribed to those who held that intellect differs not from sense, the theory that *such is the will of men, as is the day which the father of men and of gods bring on** (referring to Jupiter, by whom they understand the entire heavens). For all the sensitive powers, since they are acts of bodily organs, can be moved accidentally, by the heavenly bodies—*i.e.*, through those bodies being moved, whose acts they are.

But since it has been stated (A. 2) that the intellectual appetite is moved, in a fashion, by the sensitive appetite, the movements of the heavenly bodies have an indirect bearing on the will; in so far as the will happens to be moved by the passions of the sensitive appetite.

Reply Obj. 1. The multiform movements of the human will are reduced to some uniform cause, which, however, is above the intellect and will. This can be said, not of any body, but of some superior immaterial substance. Therefore there is no need for the movement of the will to be referred to the movement of the heavens, as to its cause.

Reply Obj. 2. The movements of the human body are reduced, as to their cause, to the movement of a heavenly body, in so far as the disposition suitable to a particular movement, is somewhat due to the influence of heavenly bodies;—also, in so far as the sensitive appetite is stirred by the influence of heavenly bodies;—and again, in so far as exterior bodies are moved in accordance with the movement of heavenly bodies, at whose presence, the will begins to will or not to will something; for instance, when the body is chilled, we begin to wish to make the fire. But this movement of the will is on the part of the object offered from without: not on the part of an inward instigation.

Reply Obj. 3. As stated above (*cf.* P. I, Q. 84, AA. 6, 7) the sensitive appetite is the act of a bodily organ. Wherefore there is no reason why man should not be prone to anger or concupiscence, or some like passion, by reason of the influence of heavenly bodies, just as by reason of his natural complexion. But the majority of men are led by the passions, which the wise alone resist. Consequently, in

* *Odyssey* xviii. 135.

the majority of cases predictions about human acts, gathered from the observation of heavenly bodies, are fulfilled. Nevertheless, as Ptolemy says (*Centiloquium* v), *the wise man governs the stars:* which is as though to say that by resisting his passions, he opposes his will, which is free and nowise subject to the movement of the heavens, to such like effects of the heavenly bodies.

Or, as Augustine says (*Gen. ad lit.* ii. 17: *We must confess that when the truth is foretold by astrologers, this is due to some most hidden inspiration, to which the human mind is subject without knowing it. And since this is done in order to deceive man, it must be the work of the lying spirits.*

SIXTH ARTICLE

Whether the Will Is Moved by God Alone, As Exterior Principle?

We proceed thus to the Sixth Article:—

Objection 1. It would seem that the will is not moved by God alone as exterior principle. For it is natural that the inferior be moved by its superior: thus the lower bodies are moved by the heavenly bodies. But there is something which is higher than the will of man and below God, namely, the angel. Therefore man's will can be moved by an angel also, as exterior principle.

Obj. 2. Further, the act of the will follows the act of the intellect. But man's intellect is reduced to act, not by God alone, but also by the angel who enlightens it, as Dionysius says (*Cæl. Hier.* iv). For the same reason, therefore, the will also is moved by an angel.

Obj. 3. Further, God is not cause of other than good things, according to Gen. i. 31: *God saw all the things that He had made, and they were very good.* If, therefore man's will were moved by God alone, it would never be moved to evil: and yet it is the will whereby *we sin and whereby we do right,* as Augustine says (*Retract.* i. 9).

On the contrary, It is written (Phil. ii. 13): *It is God Who worketh in us* (Vulg.,—*you*) *both to will and to accomplish.*

I answer that, The movement of the will is from within, as also is the movement of nature. Now although it is possible for something to move a natural thing, without being the cause of the thing moved, yet that alone, which is in some way the cause of a thing's nature, can cause a natural movement in that thing. For a stone is moved upwards by a man, who is not the cause of the stone's nature, but this movement is not natural to the stone; but the natural movement of the stone is caused by no other than the cause of its nature. Wherefore it is said in *Phys.* viii. 4, that the generator moves locally heavy and light things. Accordingly man endowed with a will is sometimes moved by something that is not his cause; but that his voluntary movement be from an exterior principle that is not the cause of his will, is impossible.

Now the cause of the will can be none other than God. And this is evident for two reasons. First, because the will is a power of the rational soul, which is caused by God alone, by creation, as was stated in the First Part (Q. 90, A. 2).—Secondly, it is evident from the fact that the will is ordained to the universal good. Wherefore nothing else can be the cause of the will, except God Himself, Who is the universal good: while every other good is good by participation, and is some particular good, and a particular cause does not give a universal inclination. Hence neither can primary matter, which is potentiality to all forms, be created by some particular agent.

Reply Obj. 1. An angel is not above man in such a way as to be the cause of his will, as the heavenly bodies are the causes of natural forms, from which result the natural move, ments of natural bodies.

Reply Obj. 2. Man's intellect is moved by an angel, on the part of the object, which by the power of the angelic light is proposed to man's knowledge. And in this way the will also can be moved by a creature from without, as stated above (A. 4).

Reply Obj. 3. God moves man's will, as the Universal Mover, to the universal object of the will, which is good. And without this universal motion, man cannot will anything. But man determines himself by his reason to will this or that, which is true or apparent good.—Nevertheless, sometimes God moves some specially to the willing of something determinate, which is good; as in the case of those whom He moves by grace, as we shall state later on (Q. 109, A. 2).

QUESTION 10

Of the Manner in Which the Will Is Moved

(In Four Articles)

WE must now consider the manner in which the will is moved. Under this head there are four points of inquiry: (1) Whether the will is moved to anything naturally? (2) Whether it is moved of necessity by its object? (3) Whether it is moved of necessity by the lower appetite? (4) Whether it is moved of necessity by the exterior mover which is God?

FIRST ARTICLE

Whether the Will is Moved to Anything Naturally?

We proceed thus to the First Article:—

Objection 1. It would seem that the will is not moved to anything naturally. For the natural agent is condivided with the voluntary agent, as stated at the beginning of *Phys.* ii. 1. Therefore the will is not moved to anything naturally.

Obj. 2. Further, that which is natural is in a thing always: as *being hot* is in fire. But no movement is always in the will. Therefore no movement is natural to the will.

Obj. 3. Further, nature is determinate to one thing: whereas the will is referred to opposites. Therefore the will wills nothing naturally.

On the contrary, The movement of the will follows the movement of the intellect. But the intellect understands some things naturally. Therefore the will, too, wills some things naturally.

I answer that, As Boëthius says (*De Duabus Nat.*) and the Philosopher also (*Metaph.* v. 4) the word *nature* is used in a manifold sense. For sometimes it stands for the intrinsic principle in movable things. In this sense nature is either matter or the material form, as stated in *Phys.* ii. 1.—In another sense nature stands for any substance, or even for any being. And in this sense, that is said to be natural to a thing which befits it in respect of its substance. And this is that which of itself is in a thing. Now all things that do not of themselves belong to the thing in which they are, are reduced to something which belongs of itself to that thing, as to their principle. Wherefore, taking nature in this sense, it is necessary that the principle of whatever belongs to a thing, be a natural principle. This is evident in regard to the intellect: for the principles of intellectual knowledge are naturally known. In like manner the principle of voluntary movements must be something naturally willed.

Now this is good in general, to which the will tends naturally, as does each power to its object; and again it is the last end, which stands in the same relation to things appetible, as the first principles of demonstrations to things intelligible: and, speaking generally, it is all those things which belong to the willer according to his nature. For it is not only things pertaining to the will that the will desires, but also that which pertains to each power, and to the entire man. Wherefore man wills naturally not only the object of the will, but also other things that are appropriate to the other powers; such as the knowledge of truth, which befits the intellect; and to be and to live and other like things which regard the natural well-being; all of which are included in the object of the will, as so many particular goods.

Reply Obj. 1. The will is distinguished from nature as one kind of cause from another; for some things happen naturally and some are done voluntarily. There is, however, another manner of causing that is proper to the will, which is mistress of its act, besides the manner proper to nature, which is determinate to one thing. But since the will is founded on some nature, it is necessary that the movement proper to nature be shared by the will, to some extent: just as what belongs to a previous cause is shared by a subsequent cause. Because in every thing, being itself, which is from nature, precedes volition, which is from the will. And hence it is that the will wills something naturally.

Reply Obj. 2. In the case of natural things, that which is natural, as a result of the form only, is always in them actually, as heat is in fire. But that which is natural as a result of matter, is not always in them actually, but sometimes only in potentiality: because form is act, whereas matter is potentiality. Now movement is *the act of that which is in potentiality* (Aristotle, *Phys.* iii. 1). Wherefore that which belongs to, or results from, movement, in regard to natural things, is not always in them. Thus fire does not always move upwards, but only when it is outside its own place.* And in like manner it is not necessary that the will (which is reduced from potentiality to act, when it wills something), should always be in the act of volition; but only when it is in a certain determinate disposition. But God's will, which is pure act, is always in the act of volition.

Reply Obj. 3. To every nature there is one thing corresponding, proportionate, however, to that nature. For to nature considered as a genus, there corresponds something one generically; and to nature as species there corresponds something one specifically; and to the individualized nature there corresponds some one individual. Since, therefore, the will is an immaterial power like the intellect, some one general thing corresponds to it, naturally which is the good; just as to the intellect there corresponds some one general thing, which is the true, or being, or *what a thing is*. And under good in general are included many par-

ticular goods, to none of which is the will determined.

Whether the Will Is Moved, of Necessity, by Its Object?

We proceed thus to the Second Article:—

Objection 1. It seems that the will is moved, of necessity, by its object. For the object of the will is compared to the will as mover to movable, as stated in *De Anima* iii. 10. But a mover, if it be sufficient, moves the movable of necessity. Therefore the will can be moved of necessity by its object.

Obj. 2. Further, just as the will is an immaterial power, so is the intellect: and both powers are ordained to a universal object, as stated above (A. 1 *ad* 3). But the intellect is moved, of necessity, by its object: therefore the will also, by its object.

Obj. 3. Further, whatever one wills, is either the end, or something ordained to an end. But, seemingly, one wills an end necessarily: because it is like the principle in speculative matters, to which principle one assents of necessity. Now the end is the reason for willing the means; and so it seems that we will the means also necessarily. Therefore the will is moved of necessity by its object.

On the contrary, The rational powers, according to the Philosopher (*Metaph.* ix. 2) are directed to opposites. But the will is a rational power, since it is in the reason, as stated in *De Anima* iii. 9. Therefore the will is directed to opposites. Therefore it is not moved, of necessity, to either of the opposites.

I answer that, The will is moved in two ways: first, as to the exercise of its act; secondly, as to the specification of its act, derived from the object. As to the first way, no object moves the will necessarily, for no matter what the object be, it is in man's power not to think of it, and consequently not to will it actually. But as to the second manner of motion, the will is moved by one object necessarily, by another not. For in the movement of a power by its object, we must consider under what aspect the object moves the power. For the visible moves the sight, under the aspect of color actually visible. Wherefore if color be offered to the sight, it moves the sight necessarily: unless one turns one's eyes away; which belongs to the exercise of the act. But if the sight were confronted with something not in all respects colored actually, but only so in some respects, and in other respects not, the sight would not of necessity see such an object: for it might look at that part of the object which is not actually colored, and thus

* The Aristotelian theory was that fire's proper place is the fiery heaven, *i.e.*, the *Empyrean*.

it would not see it. Now just as the actually colored is the object of sight, so is good the object of the will. Wherefore if the will be offered an object which is good universally and from every point of view, the will tends to it of necessity, if it wills anything at all; since it cannot will the opposite. If, on the other hand, the will is offered an object that is not good from every point of view, it will not tend to it of necessity. And since lack of any good whatever, is a non-good, consequently, that good alone which is perfect and lacking in nothing, is such a good that the will cannot not-will it: and this is Happiness. Whereas any other particular goods, in so far as they are lacking in some good, can be regarded as non-goods: and from this point of view, they can be set aside or approved by the will, which can tend to one and the same thing from various points of view.

Reply Obj. 1. The sufficient mover of a power is none but that object that in every respect presents the aspect of the mover of that power. If, on the other hand, it is lacking in any respect, it will not move of necessity, as stated above.

Reply Obj. 2. The intellect is moved, of necessity, by an object, which is such as to be always and necessarily true: but not by that which may be either true or false—viz., by that which is contingent: as we have said of the good.

Reply Obj. 3. The last end moves the will necessarily, because it is the perfect good. In like manner whatever is ordained to that end, and without which the end cannot be attained, such as *to be* and *to live*, and the like. But other things without which the end can be gained, are not necessarily willed by one who wills the end: just as he who assents to the principle, does not necessarily assent to the conclusions, without which the principles can still be true.

THIRD ARTICLE

Whether the Will Is Moved, of Necessity, by the Lower Appetite?

We proceed thus to the Third Article:—

Objection 1. It would seem that the will is moved of necessity by a passion of the lower appetite. For the Apostle says (Rom. vii. 19): *The good which I will I do not; but the evil which I will not, that I do:* and this is said by reason of concupiscence, which is a passion. Therefore the will is moved of necessity by a passion.

Obj. 2. Further, as stated in *Ethic.* iii. 5, *according as a man is, such does the end seem to him.* But it is not in man's power to cast aside a passion at once. Therefore it is not in

man's power not to will that to which the passion inclines him.

Obj. 3. Further, a universal cause is not applied to a particular effect, except by means of a particular cause: wherefore the universal reason does not move save by means of a particular estimation, as stated in *De Anima* iii. 11. But as the universal reason is to the particular estimation, so is the will to the sensitive appetite. Therefore the will is not moved to will something particular, except through the sensitive appetite. Therefore, if the sensitive appetite happen to be disposed to some·thing, by reason of a passion, the will cannot be moved in a contrary sense.

On the contrary, It is written (Gen. iv. 7): *Thy lust* (Vulg.,—*The lust thereof*) *shall be under thee, and thou shalt have dominion over it.* Therefore man's will is not moved of necessity by the lower appetite.

I answer that, As stated above (Q. 9, A. 2), the passion of the sensitive appetite moves the will, in so far as the will is moved by its object: inasmuch as, to wit, man through being disposed in such and such a way by a passion, judges something to be fitting and good, which he would not judge thus were it not for the passion. Now this influence of a passion on man occurs in two ways. First, so that his reason is wholly bound, so that he has not the use of reason: as happens in those who through a violent access of anger or concupiscence become furious or insane, just as they may from some other bodily disorder; since such like passions do not take place without some change in the body. And of such the same is to be said as of irrational animals, which follow, of necessity, the impulse of their passions: for in them there is neither movement of reason, nor, consequently, of will.

Sometimes, however, the reason is not entirely engrossed by the passion, so that the judgment of reason retains, to a certain extent, its freedom: and thus the movement of the will remains in a certain degree. Accordingly in so far as the reason remains free, and not subject to the passion, the will's movement, which also remains, does not tend of necessity to that whereto the passion inclines it. Consequently, either there is no movement of the will in that man, and the passion alone holds its sway: or if there be a movement of the will, it does not necessarily follow the passion.

Reply Obj. 1. Although the will cannot prevent the movement of concupiscence from arising, of which the Apostle says: *The evil which I will not, that I do*—i.e., *I desire;* yet it is in the power of the will not to will to desire, or not to consent to concupiscence. And thus it does not necessarily follow the movement of concupiscence.

Reply Obj. 2. Since there is in man a two-fold nature, intellectual and sensitive; sometimes man is such and such uniformly in respect of his whole soul: either because the sensitive part is wholly subject to his reason, as in the virtuous; or because reason is entirely engrossed by passion, as in a madman. But sometimes, although reason is clouded by passion, yet something of the reason remains free. And in respect of this, man can either repel the passion entirely, or at least hold himself in check so as not to be led away by the passion. For when thus disposed, since man is variously disposed according to the various parts of the soul, a thing appears to him otherwise according to his reason, than it does according to a passion.

Reply Obj. 3. The will is moved not only by the universal good apprehended by the reason, but also by good apprehended by sense. Wherefore he can be moved to some particular good independently of a passion of the sensitive appetite. For we will and do many things without passion, and through choice alone; as is most evident in those cases wherein reason resists passion.

FOURTH ARTICLE

Whether the Will Is Moved of Necessity by the Exterior Mover Which Is God?

We proceed thus to the Fourth Article:—

Objection 1. It would seem that the will is moved of necessity by God. For every agent that cannot be resisted moves of necessity. But God cannot be resisted, because His power is infinite; wherefore it is written (Rom. ix. 19): *Who resisteth His will?* Therefore God moves the will of necessity.

Obj. 2. Further, the will is moved of necessity to whatever it wills naturally, as stated above (A. 2 *ad* 3). But *whatever God does in a thing is natural to it*, as Augustine says (*Contra Faust.* xxvi. 3). Therefore the will wills of necessity everything to which God moves it.

Obj. 3. Further, a thing is possible, if nothing impossible follows from its being supposed. But something impossible follows from the supposition that the will does not will that to which God moves it: because in that case God's operation would be ineffectual. Therefore it is not possible for the will not to will that to which God moves it. Therefore it wills it of necessity.

On the contrary, It is written (Ecclus. xv. 14): *God made man from the beginning, and left him in the hand of his own counsel.* Therefore He does not of necessity move man's will.

I answer that, As Dionysius says (*Div. Nom.* iv) *it belongs to Divine providence, not to destroy but to preserve the nature of things.* Wherefore it moves all things in accordance with their conditions; so that from necessary causes through the Divine motion, effects follow of necessity; but from contingent causes, effects follow contingently. Since, therefore, the will is an active principle, not determinate to one thing, but having an indifferent relation to many things, God so moves it, that He does not determine it of necessity to one thing, but its movement remains contingent and not necessary, except in those things to which it is moved naturally.

Reply Obj. 1. The Divine will extends not only to the doing of something by the thing which He moves, but also to its being done in a way which is fitting to the nature of that thing. And therefore it would be more repugnant to the Divine motion, for the will to be moved of necessity, which is not fitting to its nature; than for it to be moved freely, which is becoming to its nature.

Reply Obj. 2. That is natural to a thing, which God so works in it that it may be natural to it; for thus is something becoming to a thing, according as God wishes it to be becoming. Now He does not wish that whatever He works in things should be natural to them, for instance, that the dead should rise again. But this He does wish to be natural to each thing,—that it be subject to the Divine power.

Reply Obj. 3. If God moves the will to anything, it is incompatible with this supposition, that the will be not moved thereto. But it is not impossible simply. Consequently it does not follow that the will is moved by God necessarily.

QUESTION 11

Of Enjoyment,* Which Is an Act of the Will

(In Four Articles)

WE must now consider enjoyment: concerning which there are four points of inquiry: (1) Whether to enjoy is an act of the appetitive power? (2) Whether it belongs to the rational creature alone, or also to irrational animals? (3) Whether enjoyment is only of the last end? (4) Whether it is only of the end possessed?

* Or, Fruition.

FIRST ARTICLE

Whether to Enjoy Is an Act of the Appetitive Power?

We proceed thus to the First Article:—

Objection 1. It would seem that to enjoy belongs not only to the appetitive power. For to enjoy seems nothing else than to receive the fruit. But it is the intellect, in whose act Happiness consists, as shown above (Q. 3, A. 4), that receives the fruit of human life, which is Happiness. Therefore to enjoy is not an act of the appetitive power, but of the intellect.

Obj. 2. Further, each power has its proper end, which is its perfection: thus the end of sight is to know the visible; of the hearing, to perceive sounds; and so forth. But the end of a thing is its fruit. Therefore to enjoy belongs to each power, and not only to the appetite.

Obj. 3. Further, enjoyment implies a certain delight. But sensible delight belongs to sense, which delights in its object: and for the same reason, intellectual delight belongs to the intellect. Therefore enjoyment belongs to the apprehensive, and not to the appetitive power.

On the contrary, Augustine says (*De Doctr. Christ.,* i. 4 and *De Trin.* x. 10, 11): *To enjoy is to adhere lovingly to something for its own sake.* But love belongs to the appetitive power. Therefore also to enjoy is an act of the appetitive power.

I answer that, Fruitio (enjoyment) and *fructus* (fruit) seem to refer to the same, one being derived from the other; which from which, matters not for our purpose; though it seems probable that the one which is more clearly known, was first named. Now those things are most manifest to us which appeal most to the senses: wherefore it seems that the word "fruition" is derived from sensible fruits. But sensible fruit is that which we expect the tree to produce in the last place, and in which a certain sweetness is to be perceived. Hence fruition seems to have relation to love, or to the delight which one has in realizing the longed-for term, which is the end. Now the end and the good is the object of the appetitive power. Wherefore it is evident that fruition is the act of the appetitive power.

Reply Obj. 1. Nothing hinders one and the same thing from belonging, under different aspects, to different powers. Accordingly the vision of God, as vision, is an act of the intellect, but as a good and an end, is the object of the will. And as such is the fruition thereof: so that the intellect attains this end, as the executive power, but the will as the motive power, moving (the powers) towards the end and enjoying the end attained.

Reply Obj. 2. The perfection and end of every other power is contained in the object of the appetitive power, as the proper is contained in the common, as stated above (Q. 9, A. 1). Hence the perfection and end of each power, in so far as it is a good, belongs to the appetitive power. Wherefore the appetitive power moves the other powers to their ends; and itself realizes the end, when each of them reaches the end.

Reply Obj. 3. In delight there are two things: perception of what is becoming; and this belongs to the apprehensive power; and complacency in that which is offered as becoming: and this belongs to the appetitive power, in which power delight is formally completed.

SECOND ARTICLE

Whether to Enjoy Belongs to the Rational Creature Alone, or Also to Irrational Animals?

We proceed thus to the Second Article:—

Objection 1. It would seem that to enjoy belongs to men alone. For Augustine says (*De Doctr. Christ.* i. 22) that *it is given to us men to enjoy and to use.* Therefore other animals cannot enjoy.

Obj. 2. Further, to enjoy relates to the last end. But irrational animals cannot obtain the last end. Therefore it is not for them to enjoy.

Obj. 3. Further, just as the sensitive appetite is beneath the intellectual appetite, so is the natural appetite beneath the sensitive. If, therefore, to enjoy belongs to the sensitive appetite, it seems that for the same reason it can belong to the natural appetite. But this is evidently false, since the latter cannot delight in anything. Therefore the sensitive appetite cannot enjoy: and accordingly enjoyment is not possible for irrational animals.

On the contrary, Augustine says (QQ. 83, qu. 30): *It is not so absurd to suppose that even beasts enjoy their food and any bodily pleasure.*

I answer that, As was stated above (A. 1) to enjoy is not the act of the power that achieves the end as executor, but of the power that commands the achievement; for it has been said to belong to the appetitive power. Now things void of reason have indeed a power of achieving an end by way of execution, as that by which a heavy body has a downward tendency, whereas a light body has an upward tendency. Yet the power of command in respect of the end is not in them, but in some higher nature, which moves all nature by its command, just as in things endowed with knowledge, the appetite moves the other powers to their acts. Wherefore it is clear that things void of knowledge, although they attain an end, have no enjoyment of the end: this is only for those that are endowed with knowledge.

Now knowledge of the end is twofold: perfect and imperfect. Perfect knowledge of the end, is that whereby not only is that known which is the end and the good, but also the universal formality of the end and the good; and such knowledge belongs to the rational nature alone. On the other hand, imperfect knowledge is that by which the end and the good are known in the particular. Such knowledge is in irrational animals: whose appetitive powers do not command with freedom, but are moved according to a natural instinct to whatever they apprehend. Consequently, enjoyment belongs to the rational nature, in a perfect degree; to irrational animals, imperfectly; to other creatures, not at all.

Reply Obj. 1. Augustine is speaking there of perfect enjoyment.

Reply Obj. 2. Enjoyment need not be of the last end simply; but of that which each one chooses for his last end.

Reply Obj. 3. The sensitive appetite follows some knowledge; not so the natural appetite, especially in things void of knowledge.

Reply Obj. 4. Augustine is speaking there of imperfect enjoyment. This is clear from his way of speaking: for he says that *it is not so absurd to suppose that even beasts enjoy,* that is, as it would be, if one were to say that they *use.*

THIRD ARTICLE

Whether Enjoyment Is Only of the Last End?

We proceed thus to the Third Article:—

Objection 1. It would seem that enjoyment is not only of the last end. For the Apostle says (*Philem.* 20): *Yea, brother, may I enjoy thee in the Lord.* But it is evident that Paul had not placed his last end in a man. Therefore to enjoy is not only of the last end.

Obj. 2. Further, what we enjoy is the fruit. But the Apostle says (*Gal.* v. 22): *The fruit of the Spirit is charity, joy, peace,* and other like things, which are not in the nature of the last end. Therefore enjoyment is not only of the last end.

Obj. 3. Further, the acts of the will reflect on one another; for I will to will, and I love to love. But to enjoy is an act of the will: since *it is the will with which we enjoy,* as Augustine says (*De Trin.* x. 10). Therefore a man enjoys his enjoyment. But the last end of man is not enjoyment, but the uncreated good alone, which is God. Therefore enjoyment is not only of the last end.

On the contrary, Augustine says (*De Trin.* x. 11): *A man does not enjoy that which he desires for the sake of something else.* But the last end alone is that which man does not desire for the sake of something else. Therefore enjoyment is of the last end alone.

I answer that, As stated above (A. 1) the notion of fruit implies two things: first that it should come last; second, that it should calm the appetite with a certain sweetness and delight. Now a thing is last either simply or relatively; simply, if it be referred to nothing else; relatively, if it is the last in a particular series. Therefore that which is last simply, and in which one delights as in the last end, is properly called fruit; and this it is that one is properly said to enjoy.—But that which is delightful not in itself, but is desired, only as referred to something else, *e.g.,* a bitter potion for the sake of health, can nowise be called fruit.—And that which has something delightful about it, to which a number of preceding things are referred, may indeed be called fruit in a certain manner; but we cannot be said to enjoy it properly or as though it answered perfectly to the notion of fruit. Hence Augustine says (*De Trin.* x. 10) that *we enjoy what we know, when the delighted will is at rest therein.* But its rest is not absolute save in the possession of the last end: for as long as something is looked for, the movement of the will remains in suspense, although it has reached something. Thus in local movement, although any point between the two terms is a beginning and an end, yet it is not considered as an actual end, except when the movement stops there.

Reply Obj. 1. As Augustine says (*De Doctr. Christ.* i. 33), *if he had said, "May I enjoy thee," without adding "in the Lord," he would seem to have set the end of his love in him. But since he added that he set his end in the Lord, he implied his desire to enjoy Him:* as if we were to say that he expressed his enjoyment of his brother not as a term but as a means.

Reply Obj. 2. Fruit bears one relation to the tree that bore it, and another to man that enjoys it. To the tree indeed that bore it, it is compared as effect to cause; to the one enjoying it, as the final object of his longing and the consummation of his delight. Accordingly these fruits mentioned by the Apostle are so called because they are certain effects of the Holy Ghost in us, wherefore they are called *fruits of the Spirit:* but not as though we are to enjoy them as our last end. Or we may say with Ambrose that they are called fruits because *we should desire them for their own sake:* not indeed as though they were not ordained to the last end; but because they are such that we ought to find pleasure in them.

Reply Obj. 3. As stated above (Q. 1, A. 8; Q. 2, A. 7), we speak of an end in a twofold sense: first, as being the thing itself; secondly, as the attainment thereof. These are not, of course, two ends, but one end, considered in itself, and in its relation to something else. Accordingly God is the last end, as that which is ultimately sought for: while the enjoyment is as the attainment of this last end. And so, just as God is not one end, and the enjoyment of God, another: so it is the same enjoyment whereby we enjoy God, and whereby we enjoy our enjoyment of God. And the same applies to created happiness which consists in enjoyment.

FOURTH ARTICLE

Whether Enjoyment Is Only of the End Possessed?

We proceed thus to the Fourth Article:—

Objection 1. It would seem that enjoyment is only of the end possessed. For Augustine says (*De Trin.* x. 1) that *to enjoy is to use joyfully, with the joy, not of hope, but of possession.* But so long as a thing is not had, there is joy, not of possession but of hope. Therefore enjoyment is only of the end possessed.

Obj. 2. Further, as stated above (A. 3), enjoyment is not properly otherwise than of the last end: because this alone gives rest to the appetite. But the appetite has no rest save in the possession of the end. Therefore enjoyment, properly speaking, is only of the end possessed.

Obj. 3. Further, to enjoy is to lay hold of the fruit. But one does not lay hold of the fruit until one is in possession of the end. Therefore enjoyment is only of the end possessed.

On the contrary, to enjoy is to adhere lov-ingly to something for its own sake, as Augustine says (*De Doctr. Christ.* i. 4). But this is possible, even in regard to a thing which is not in our possession. Therefore it is possible to enjoy the end even though it be not possessed.

I answer that, To enjoy implies a certain relation of the will to the last end, according as the will has something by way of last end. Now an end is possessed in two ways; perfectly and imperfectly. Perfectly, when it is possessed not only in intention but also in reality; imperfectly, when it is possessed in intention only. Perfect enjoyment, therefore, is of the end already possessed: but imperfect enjoyment is also of the end possessed not really, but only in intention.

Reply Obj. 1. Augustine speaks there of perfect enjoyment.

Reply Obj. 2. The will is hindered in two ways from being at rest. First on the part of the object; by reason of its not being the last end, but ordained to something else: secondly on the part of the one who desires the end, by reason of his not being yet in possession of it. Now it is the object that specifies an act: but on the agent depends the manner of acting, so that the act be perfect or imperfect, as compared with the actual circumstances of the agent. Therefore enjoyment of anything but the last end is not enjoyment properly speaking, as falling short of the nature of enjoyment. But enjoyment of the last end, not yet possessed, is enjoyment properly speaking, but imperfect, on account of the imperfect way in which it is possessed.

Reply Obj. 3. One is said to lay hold of or to have an end, not only in reality, but also in intention, as stated above.

QUESTION 12

Of Intention

(In Five Articles)

WE must now consider Intention: concerning which there are five points of inquiry: (1) Whether intention is an act of the intellect or of the will? (2) Whether it is only of the last end? (3) Whether one can intend two things at the same time? (4) Whether intention of the end is the same act as volition of the means? (5) Whether intention is within the competency of irrational animals?

FIRST ARTICLE

Whether Intention Is an Act of the Intellect or of the Will?

We proceed thus to the First Article:—

Objection 1. It would seem that intention is an act of the intellect, and not of the will. For it is written (Matth. vi. 22): *If thy eye be single, thy whole body shall be lightsome:* where, according to Augustine (*De Serm. Dom. in Monte* ii. 13) the eye signifies intention. But since the eye is the organ of sight, it signifies the apprehensive power. Therefore intention is not an act of the appetitive but of the apprehensive power.

Obj. 2. Further, Augustine says (*ibid.*) that Our Lord spoke of intention as a light, when He said (Matth. vi. 23): *If the light that is in thee be darkness,* etc. But light pertains to knowledge. Therefore intention does too.

Obj. 3. Further, intention implies a kind of ordaining to an end. But to ordain is an act of reason. Therefore intention belongs not to the will but to the reason.

Obj. 4. Further, an act of the will is either of the end or of the means. But the act of the will in respect of the end is called volition, or enjoyment; with regard to the means, it is choice, from which intention is distinct. Therefore it is not an act of the will.

On the contrary, Augustine says (*De Trin.* xi. 4, 8, 9) that *the intention of the will unites the sight to the object seen; and the images retained in the memory, to the penetrating gaze of the soul's inner thought.* Therefore intention is an act of the will.

I answer that, Intention, as the very word denotes, signifies, *to tend to something.* Now both the action of the mover and the movement of the thing moved, tend to something. But that the movement of the thing moved tends to anything, is due to the action of the mover. Consequently intention belongs first and principally to that which moves to the end: hence we say that an architect or anyone who is in authority, by his command moves others to that which he intends. Now the will moves all the other powers of the soul to the end, as shown above (Q. 9, A. 1). Wherefore it is evident that intention, properly speaking, is an act of the will.

Reply Obj. 1. The eye designates intention figuratively, not because intention has reference to knowledge, but because it presupposes knowledge, which proposes to the will the end to which the latter moves; thus we foresee with the eye whither we should tend with our bodies.

Reply Obj. 2. Intention is called a light because it is manifest to him who intends. Wherefore works are called darkness, because a man knows what he intends, but knows not what the result may be, as Augustine expounds (*loc. cit.*).

Reply Obj. 3. The will does not ordain, but tends to something according to the order of reason. Consequently this word *intention* indicates an act of the will, presupposing the act whereby the reason orders something to the end.

Reply Obj. 4. Intention is an act of the will in regard to the end. Now the will stands in a threefold relation to the end. First, absolutely; and thus we have *volition,* whereby we will absolutely to have health and so forth. Secondly, it considers the end, as its place of rest; and thus *enjoyment* regards the end. Thirdly, it considers the end as the term towards which something is ordained; and thus *intention* regards the end. For when we speak of intending to have health, we mean not only that we will have it, but that we will have it by means of something else.

We proceed thus to the Second Article:—

Objection 1. It would seem that intention is only of the last end. For it is said in the book of Prosper's *Sentences* (*Sent.* 100): *The intention of the heart is a cry to God.* But God is the last end of the human heart. Therefore intention always regards the last end.

Obj. 2. Further, intention regards the end as the terminus, as stated above (A. 1 *ad* 4). But a terminus is something last. Therefore intention always regards the last end.

Obj. 3. Further, just as intention regards the end, so does enjoyment. But enjoyment is always of the last end. Therefore intention is too.

On the contrary, There is but one last end of human wills, viz., Happiness, as stated above (Q. 1, A. 7). If, therefore, intentions were only of the last end, men would not have different intentions: which is evidently false.

I answer that, As stated above (A. 1 *ad* 4), intention regards the end as a terminus of the movement of the will. Now a terminus of movement may be taken in two ways. First, the very last terminus, when the movement comes to a stop; this is the terminus of the whole movement. Secondly, some point midway, which is the beginning of one part of the movement, and the end or terminus of the other. Thus in the movement from A to C through B, C is the last terminus, while B is a terminus, but not the last. And intention can be both. Consequently though intention is always of the end, it need not be always of the last end.

Reply Obj. 1. The intention of the heart is called a cry to God, not that God is always the object of intention, but because He sees our intention.—Or because, when we pray, we direct our intention to God, which intention has the force of a cry.

Reply Obj. 2. A terminus is something last, not always in respect of the whole, but sometimes in respect of a part.

Reply Obj. 3. Enjoyment implies rest in the end; and this belongs to the last end alone. But intention implies movement towards an end, not rest. Wherefore the comparison proves nothing.

We proceed thus to the Third Article:—

Objection 1. It would seem that one cannot intend several things at the same time. For Augustine says (*De Serm. Dom. in Monte* ii

14, 16, 17) that man's intention cannot be directed at the same time to God and to bodily benefits. Therefore, for the same reason, neither to any other two things.

Obj. 2. Further, intention designates a movement of the will towards a terminus. Now there cannot be several termini in the same direction of one movement. Therefore the will cannot intend several things at the same time.

Obj. 3. Further, intention presupposes an act of reason or of the intellect. But *it is not possible to understand several things at the same time,* according to the Philosopher (*Topic.* ii. 10). Therefore neither is it possible to intend several things at the same time.

On the contrary, Art imitates nature. Now nature intends two purposes by means of one instrument: thus *the tongue* is *for the purpose of taste and speech* (*De Anima* ii. 8). Therefore, for the same reason, art or reason can at the same time direct one thing to two ends: so that one can intend several ends at the same time.

I answer that, The expression *two things* may be taken in two ways: they may be ordained to one another or not so ordained. And if they be ordained to one another, it is evident, from what has been said, that a man can intend several things at the same time. For intention is not only of the last end, as stated above (A. 2), but also of an intermediary end. Now a man intends at the same time, both the proximate and the last end; as the mixing of a medicine and the giving of health.

But if we take two things that are not ordained to one another, thus also a man can intend several things at the same time. This is evident from the fact that a man prefers one thing to another because it is the better of the two. Now one of the reasons for which one thing is better than another is that it is available for more purposes: wherefore one thing can be chosen in preference to another, because of the greater number of purposes for which it is available: so that evidently a man can intend several things at the same time.

Reply Obj. 1. Augustine means to say that man cannot at the same time direct his intention to God and to bodily benefits, as to two last ends: since, as stated above (Q. 1, A. 5), one man cannot have several last ends.

Reply Obj. 2. There can be several termini ordained to one another, of the same movement and in the same direction; but not unless they be ordained to one another. At the same time it must be observed that what is not one in reality may be taken as one by the reason. Now intention is a movement of the will to something already ordained by the reason, as stated above (A. 1 *ad* 3). Wherefore where we have many things in reality, we may take

them as one term of intention, in so far as the reason takes them as one: either because two things concur in the integrity of one whole, as a proper measure of heat and cold conduce to health; or because two things are included in one which may be intended. For instance, the acquiring of wine and clothing is included in wealth, as in something common to both; wherefore nothing hinders the man who intends to acquire wealth, from intending both the others.

Reply Obj. 3. As stated in the First Part (Q. 12, A. 10; Q. 58, A. 2; Q. 85, A. 4), it is possible to understand several things at the same time, in so far as, in some way, they are one.

FOURTH ARTICLE

Whether Intention of the End Is the Same Act As the Volition of the Means?

We proceed thus to the Fourth Article:—

Objection 1. It would seem that the intention of the end and the volition of the means are not one and the same movement. For Augustine says (*De Trin.* xi. 6) that *the will to see the window, has for its end the seeing of the window; and is another act from the will to see, through the window, the passersby.* But that I should will to see the passersby, through the window, belongs to intention; whereas that I will to see the window, belongs to the volition of the means. Therefore intention of end and the willing of the means are distinct movements of the will.

Obj. 2. Further, acts are distinct according to their objects. But the end and the means are distinct objects. Therefore the intention of the end and the willing of the means are distinct movements of the will.

Obj. 3. Further, the willing of the means is called choice. But choice and intention are not the same. Therefore intention of the end and the willing of the means are not the same movement of the will.

On the contrary, The means in relation to the end, are as the mid-space to the terminus. Now it is all the same movement that passes through the mid-space to the terminus, in natural things. Therefore in things pertaining to the will, the intention of the end is the same movement as the willing of the means.

I answer that, The movement of the will to the end and to the means can be considered in two ways. First, according as the will is moved to each of the aforesaid absolutely and in itself. And thus there are really two movements of the will to them. Secondly, it may be considered accordingly as the will is moved to the means for the sake of the end: and thus the movement of the will to the end and its movement to the means are one and the same thing. For when I say: *I wish to take medicine for the sake of health,* I signify no more than one movement of my will. And this is because the end is the reason for willing the means. Now the object, and that by reason of which it is an object, come under the same act; thus it is the same act of sight that perceives color and light, as stated above (Q. 8, A. 3 *ad* 2). And the same applies to the intellect; for if it consider principle and conclusion absolutely, it considers each by a distinct act; but when it assents to the conclusion on account of the principles, there is but one act of the intellect.

Reply Obj. 1. Augustine is speaking of seeing the window and of seeing, through the window, the passers-by, according as the will is moved to either absolutely.

Reply Obj. 2. The end, considered as a thing, and the means to that end, are distinct objects of the will. But in so far as the end is the formal object in willing the means, they are one and the same object.

Reply Obj. 3. A movement which is one as to the subject, may differ, according to our way of looking at it, as to its beginning and end, as in the case of ascent and descent (*Physic.* iii. 3). Accordingly, in so far as the movement of the will is to the means, as ordained to the end, it is called *choice:* but the movement of the will to the end as acquired by the means, is called *intention.* A sign of this is that we can have intention of the end without having determined the means which are the object of choice.

FIFTH ARTICLE

Whether Intention Is within the Competency of Irrational Animals?

We proceed thus to the Fifth Article:—

Objection 1. It would seem that irrational animals intend the end. For in things void of reason nature stands further apart from the rational nature, than does the sensitive nature in irrational animals. But nature intends the end even in things void of reason, as is proved

in *Phys.* ii. 8. Much more, therefore, do irrational animals intend the end.

Obj. 2. Further, just as intention is of the end, so is enjoyment. But enjoyment is in irrational animals, as stated above (Q. 11, A. 2). Therefore intention is too.

Obj. 3. Further, to intend an end belongs to one who acts for an end; since to intend is nothing else than to tend to something. But irrational animals act for an end; for an animal is moved either to seek food, or to do something of the kind. Therefore irrational animals intend an end.

On the contrary, Intention of an end implies ordaining something to an end: which belongs to reason. Since therefore irrational animals are void of reason, it seems that they do not intend an end.

I answer that, As stated above (A. 1), to intend is to tend to something; and this belongs to the mover and to the moved. According, therefore, as that which is moved to an end by another is said to intend the end, thus nature is said to intend an end, as being moved to its end by God, as the arrow is moved by the archer. And in this way, irrational animals intend an end, inasmuch as they are moved to something by natural instinct.—The other way of intending an end belongs to the mover; according as he ordains the movement of something, either his own or another's, to an end. This belongs to reason alone. Wherefore irrational animals do not intend an end in this way, which is to intend properly and principally, as stated above (A. 1).

Reply Obj. 1. This argument takes intention in the sense of being moved to an end.

Reply Obj. 2. Enjoyment does not imply the ordaining of one thing to another, as intention does, but absolute repose in the end.

Reply Obj. 3. Irrational animals are moved to an end, not as though they thought that they can gain the end by this movement; this belongs to one that intends; but through desiring the end by natural instinct, they are moved to an end, moved, as it were, by another, like other things that are moved naturally.

QUESTION 13

Of Choice, Which Is an Act of the Will with Regard to the Means

(In Six Articles)

WE must now consider the acts of the will with regard to the means. There are three of them: to choose, to consent, and to use. And choice is preceded by counsel. First of all, then, we must consider choice; secondly, counsel; thirdly, consent; fourthly, use.

Concerning choice there are six points of inquiry: (1) Of what power is it the act; of the will or of the reason? (2) Whether choice is to be found in irrational animals? (3) Whether choice is only the means, or sometimes also of the end? (4) Whether choice is only of things that we do ourselves? (5) Whether choice is only of possible things? (6) Whether man chooses of necessity or freely?

FIRST ARTICLE

Whether Choice Is an Act of Will or of Reason?

We proceed thus to the First Article:—

Objection 1. It would seem that choice is an act, not of will but of reason. For choice implies comparison, whereby one is given preference to another. But to compare is an act of reason. Therefore choice is an act of reason.

Obj. 2. Further, it is for the same faculty to form a syllogism, and to draw the conclusion. But, in practical matters, it is the reason that forms syllogisms. Since therefore choice is a kind of conclusion in practical matters, as stated in *Ethic.* vii. 3, it seems that it is an act of reason.

Obj. 3. Further, ignorance does not belong to the will but to the cognitive power. Now there is an *ignorance of choice,* as is stated in *Ethic.* iii. 1. Therefore it seems that choice does not belong to the will but to the reason.

On the contrary, The Philosopher says (*Ethic.* iii. 3) that choice is *the desire of things in our power.* But desire is an act of will. Therefore choice is too.

I answer that, The word choice implies something belonging to the reason or intellect, and something belonging to the will: for the Philosopher says (*Ethic.* vi. 2) that choice is either *intellect influenced by appetite or appetite influenced by intellect.* Now whenever two things concur to make one, one of them is formal in regard to the other. Hence Gregory of Nyssa* says that choice *is neither desire only, nor counsel only, but a combination of the two. For just as we say that an animal is composed of soul and body, and that it is neither a mere body, nor a mere soul, but both; so is it with choice.*

Now we must observe, as regards the acts of the soul, that an act belonging essentially to some power or habit, receives a form or species from a higher power or habit, according as an inferior is ordained by a superior: for if a man were to perform an act of fortitude for the love of God, that act is materially an act of fortitude, but formally, an act of charity. Now it is evident that, in a sense, reason precedes the will and ordains its act: in so far as the will tends to its object, according to the order of reason, since the apprehensive power presents the object to the appetite. Accordingly, that act whereby the will tends to something proposed to it as being good, through being ordained to the end by the reason, is materially an act of the will, but for-

* Nemesius, *De Nat. Hom.* xxxiii.

mally an act of the reason. Now in such like matters the substance of the act is as the matter in comparison to the order imposed by the higher power. Wherefore choice is substantially not an act of the reason but of the will: for choice is accomplished in a certain movement of the soul towards the good which is chosen. Consequently it is evidently an act of the appetitive power.

Reply Obj. 1. Choice implies a previous comparison; not that it consists in the comparison itself.

Reply Obj. 2. It is quite true that it is for the reason to draw the conclusion of a practical syllogism; and it is called *a decision* or *judgment,* to be followed by *choice.* And for this reason the conclusion seems to belong to the act of choice, as to that which results from it.

Reply Obj. 3. In speaking *of ignorance of choice,* we do not mean that choice is a sort of knowledge, but that there is ignorance of what ought to be chosen.

SECOND ARTICLE

Whether Choice Is to Be Found in Irrational Animals?

We proceed thus to the Second Article:

Objection 1. It would seem that irrational animals are able to choose. For choice *is the desire of certain things on account of an end,* as stated in *Ethic.* iii. 2, 3. But irrational animals desire something on account of an end: since they act for an end, and from desire. Therefore choice is in irrational animals.

Obj. 2. Further, the very word *electio* (choice) seems to signify the taking of something in preference to others. But irrational animals take something in preference to others: thus we can easily see for ourselves that a sheep will eat one grass and refuse another. Therefore choice is in irrational animals.

Obj. 3. Further, according to *Ethic.* vi. 12, *it is from prudence that a man makes a good choice of means.* But prudence is found in irrational animals: hence it is said in the beginning of *Metaph.* (i. 1) that *those animals which, like bees, cannot hear sounds, are prudent by instinct.* We see this plainly, in wonderful cases of sagacity manifested in the works of various animals, such as bees, spiders, and dogs. For a hound in following a stag, on coming to a crossroad, tries by scent whether the stag has passed by the first or the second road: and if he find that the stag has not passed there, being thus assured, takes to the third road without trying the scent; as though he were reasoning by way of exclusion, arguing that the stag must have passed by this way, since he did not pass by the others, and there is no other road. Therefore it seems that irrational animals are able to choose.

On the contrary, Gregory of Nyssa* says that *children and irrational animals act willingly but not from choice.* Therefore choice is not in irrational animals.

I answer that Since choice is the taking of one thing in preference to another it must of necessity be in respect of several things that can be chosen. Consequently in those things which are altogether determinate to one there is no place for choice. Now the difference between the sensitive appetite and the will is that, as stated above (Q. 1, A. 2 *ad* 3), the sensitive appetite is determinate to one particular thing, according to the order of nature; whereas the will, although determinate to one thing in general, viz., the good, according to the order of nature, is nevertheless indeterminate in respect of particular goods. Consequently choice belongs properly to the will, and not to the sensitive appetite which is all that irrational animals have. Wherefore irrational animals are not competent to choose.

Reply Obj. 1. Not every desire of one thing on account of an end is called choice: there must be a certain discrimination of one thing from another. And this cannot be except when the appetite can be moved to several things.

Reply Obj. 2. An irrational animal takes one thing in preference to another, because its appetite is naturally determinate to that thing. Wherefore as soon as an animal, whether by its sense or by its imagination, is offered something to which its appetite is naturally inclined, it is moved to that alone, without making any choice. Just as fire is moved upwards and not downwards, without its making any choice.

Reply Obj. 3. As stated in *Phys.* iii. 3 *movement is the act of the movable, caused by a mover.* Wherefore the power of the mover appears in the movement of that which it moves. Accordingly, in all things moved by reason, the order of reason which moves them is evident, although the things themselves are without reason: for an arrow through the motion of the archer goes straight towards the target, as though it were endowed with reason to direct its course. The same may be seen in the movements of clocks and all engines put together by the art of man. Now as artificial things are in comparison to human art, so are all natural things in comparison to the Divine art. And accordingly order is to be seen in things moved by nature, just as in things moved by reason, as is stated in *Phys.* ii. And thus it is that in the works of irrational animals we notice certain marks of sagacity, in so far as they have a natural inclination to set about their actions in a most orderly manner through being ordained by the Supreme art. For which reason, too, certain animals are called prudent or sagacious; and not because they reason or exercise any choice about things. This is clear from the fact that all that share in one nature, invariably act in the same way.

THIRD ARTICLE

Whether Choice Is Only of the Means, or Sometimes Also of the End?

We proceed thus to the Third Article:—

Objection 1. It would seem that choice is not only of the means. For the Philosopher says (*Ethic.* vi. 12) that *virtue makes us choose aright; but it is not the part of virtue, but of some other power to direct aright those things which are to be done for its sake.* But that for the sake of which something is done is the end. Therefore choice is of the end.

Obj. 2. Further, choice implies preference of one thing to another. But just as there can be preference of means, so can there be preference of ends. Therefore choice can be of ends, just as it can be of means.

On the contrary, The Philosopher says (*Ethic.* iii. 2) that *volition is of the end, but choice of the means.*

I answer that, As already stated (A. 1 *ad* 2), choice results from the decision or judgment which is, as it were, the conclusion of a practical syllogism. Hence that which is the conclusion of a practical syllogism, is the matter of choice. Now in practical things the end stands in the position of a principle, not of a conclusion, as the Philosopher says (*Phys.* ii. 9). Wherefore the end, as such, is not a matter of choice.

But just as in speculative knowledge nothing hinders the principle of one demonstration or of one science, from being the conclusion of another demonstration or science; while the first indemonstrable principle cannot be the conclusion of any demonstration or science; so too that which is the end in one operation, may be ordained to something as an end. And in this way it is a matter of choice. Thus in the work of a physician health is the end: wherefore it is not a matter of choice for a physician, but a matter of principle. Now the health of the body is ordained to the good of the soul, consequently with one who has charge of the soul's health, health or sickness may be a matter of choice; for the Apostle says (2 Cor. xii. 10): *For when I am weak, then am I powerful.* But the last end is nowise a matter of choice.

Reply Obj. 1. The proper ends of virtues

* Nemesius, *De Nat. Hom.* xxxiii.

are ordained to Happiness as to their last end. And thus it is that they can be a matter of choice.

Reply Obj. 2. As stated above (Q. 1, A. 5), there is but one last end. Accordingly wherever there are several ends, they can be the subject of choice, in so far as they are ordained to a further end.

FOURTH ARTICLE

Whether Choice Is of Those Things Only That Are Done by Us?

We proceed thus to the Fourth Article:—

Objection 1. It would seem that choice is not only in respect of human acts. For choice regards the means. Now, not only acts, but also the organs, are means (*Phys.* ii. 3). Therefore choice is not only concerned with human acts.

Obj. 2. Further, action is distinct from contemplation. But choice has a place even in contemplation; in so far as one opinion is preferred to another. Therefore choice is not concerned with human acts alone.

Obj. 3. Further, men are chosen for certain posts, whether secular or ecclesiastical, by those who exercise no action in their regard. Therefore choice is not concerned with human acts alone.

On the contrary, The Philosopher says (*Ethic.* iii. 2) that *no man chooses save what he can do himself.*

I answer that, Just as intention regards the end, so does choice regard the means. Now the end is either an action or a thing. And when the end is a thing, some human action must intervene; either in so far as man produces the thing which is the end, as the physician produces health (wherefore the production of health is said to be the end of the physician); or in so far as man, in some fashion, uses or enjoys the thing which is the end; thus for the miser, money or the possession of money is the end. The same is to be said of the means. For the means must needs be either an action; or a thing, with some action intervening whereby man either makes the thing which is the means, or puts it to some use. And thus it is that choice is always in regard to human acts.

Reply Obj. 1. The organs are ordained to the end, inasmuch as man makes use of them for the sake of the end.

Reply Obj. 2. In contemplation itself there is the act of the intellect assenting to this or that opinion. It is exterior action that is put in contradistinction to contemplation.

Reply Obj. 3. When a man chooses someone for a bishopric or some high position in the state, he chooses to name that man to that post. Else, if he had no right to act in the appointment of the bishop or official, he would have no right to choose. Likewise, whenever we speak of one thing being chosen in preference to another, it is in conjunction with some action of the chooser.

FIFTH ARTICLE

Whether Choice Is Only of Possible Things?

We proceed thus to the Fifth Article:—

Objection 1. It would seem that choice is not only of possible things. For choice is an act of the will, as stated above (A. 1). Now there is a willing of impossibilities (*Ethic.* iii. 2). Therefore there is also a choice of impossibilities.

Obj. 2. Further, choice is of things done by us, as stated above (A. 4). Therefore it matters not, as far as the act of choosing is concerned, whether one choose that which is impossible in itself, or that which is impossible to the chooser. Now it often happens that we are unable to accomplish what we choose: so that this proves to be impossible to us. Therefore choice is of the impossible.

Obj. 3. Further, to try to do a thing is to choose to do it. But the Blessed Benedict says (*Regula,* lxviii) that if the superior command what is impossible, it should be attempted. Therefore choice can be of the impossible.

On the contrary, The Philosopher says (*Ethic.* iii. *loc. cit.*) that *there is no choice of impossibilities.*

I answer that, As stated above (A. 4), our choice is always concerned with our actions. Now whatever is done by us, is possible to us. Therefore we must needs say that choice is only of possible things.

Moreover, the reason for choosing a thing is that it conduces to an end. But what is impossible cannot conduce to an end. A sign of this is that when men in taking counsel together come to something that is impossible to them, they depart, as being unable to proceed with the business.

Again, this is evident if we examine the previous process of the reason. For the means, which are the object of choice, are to the end, as the conclusion is to the principle. Now it is clear that an impossible conclusion does not follow from a possible principle. Wherefore an end cannot be possible, unless the means be possible. Now no one is moved to the impossible. Consequently no one would tend to the end, save for the fact that the means appear to be possible. Therefore the impossible is not the object of choice.

Reply Obj. 1. The will stands between the intellect and the external action: for the intellect proposes to the will its object, and the will causes the external action. Hence the principle of the movement in the will is to be found in the intellect, which apprehends something under the universal notion of good: but the term or perfection of the will's act is to be observed in its relation to the action whereby a man tends to the attainment of a thing; for the movement of the will is from the soul to the thing. Consequently the perfect act of the will is in respect of something that is good for one to do. Now this cannot be something impossible. Wherefore the complete act of the will is only in respect of what is possible and good for him that wills. But the incomplete act of the will is in respect of the impossible; and by some is called *velleity*, because, to wit, one would will (*vellet*) such a thing, were it possible. But choice is an act of the will, fixed on something to be done by the chooser. And therefore it is by no means of anything but what is possible.

Reply Obj. 2. Since the object of the will is the apprehended good, we must judge of the object of the will according as it is apprehended. And so, just as sometimes the will tends to something which is apprehended as good, and yet is not really good; so is choice sometimes made of something apprehended as possible to the chooser, and yet impossible to him.

Reply Obj. 3. The reason for this is that the subject should not rely on his own judgment to decide whether a certain thing is possible; but in each case should stand by his superior's judgment.

SIXTH ARTICLE

Whether Man Chooses of Necessity or Freely?

We proceed thus to the Sixth Article:—

Objection 1. It would seem that man chooses of necessity. For the end stands in relation to the object of choice, as the principle of that which follows from the principles, as declared in *Ethic.* vii. 8. But conclusions follow of necessity from their principles. Therefore man is moved of necessity from (willing) the end to the choice (of the means).

Obj. 2. Further, as stated above (A. 1 ad 2), choice follows the reason's judgment of what is to be done. But reason judges of necessity about some things: on account of the necessity of the premises. Therefore it seems that choice also follows of necessity.

Obj. 3. Further, if two things are absolutely equal, man is not moved to one more than to the other; thus if a hungry man, as Plato says (*cf. De Cœlo* ii. 13), be confronted on either side with two portions of food equally appetiz-

ing and at an equal distance, he is not moved towards one more than to the other; and he finds the reason of this in the immobility of the earth in the middle of the world. Now, if that which is equally (eligible) with something else cannot be chosen, much less can that be chosen which appears as less (eligible). Therefore if two or more things are available, of which one appears to be more (eligible), it is impossible to choose any of the others. Therefore that which appears to hold the first place is chosen of necessity. But every act of choosing is in regard to something that seems in some way better. Therefore every choice is made necessarily.

On the contrary, Choice is an act of a rational power; which according to the Philosopher (*Metaph.* ix. 2) stands in relation to opposites.

I answer that, Man does not choose of necessity. And this is because that which is possible not to be, is not of necessity. Now the reason why it is possible not to choose, or to choose, may be gathered from a twofold power in man. For man can will and not will, act and not act; again, he can will this or that, and do this or that. The reason of this is seated in the very power of the reason. For the will can tend to whatever the reason can apprehend as good. Now the reason can apprehend as good, not only this, viz., *to will* or *to act*, but also this, viz., *not to will* or *not to act*. Again, in all particular goods, the reason can consider an aspect of some good, and the lack of some good, which has the aspect of evil: and in this respect, it can apprehend any single one of such goods as to be chosen or to be avoided. The perfect good alone, which is Happiness, cannot be apprehended by the reason as an evil, or as lacking in any way. Consequently man wills Happiness of necessity, nor can he will not to be happy, or to be unhappy. Now since choice is not of the end, but of the means, as stated above (A. 3); it is not of the perfect good, which is Happiness, but of other particular goods. Therefore man chooses not of necessity, but freely.

Reply Obj. 1. The conclusion does not always of necessity follow from the principles, but only when the principles cannot be true if the conclusion is not true. In like manner, the end does not always necessitate in man the choosing of the means, because the means are not always such that the end cannot be gained without them; or, if they be such, they are not always considered in that light.

Reply Obj. 2. The reason's decision or judgment of what is to be done is about things that are contingent and possible to us. In such matters the conclusions do not follow of necessity from principles that are absolutely necessary but from such as are so conditionally; as, for instance, *If he runs, he is in motion.*

Reply Obj. 3. If two things be proposed as equal under one aspect, nothing hinders us from considering in one of them some particular point of superiority, so that the will has a bent towards that one rather than towards the other.

QUESTION 14

Of Counsel, Which Precedes Choice

(In Six Articles)

WE must now consider counsel; concerning which there are six points of inquiry: (1) Whether counsel is an inquiry? (2) Whether counsel is of the end or of the means? (3) Whether counsel is only of things that we do? (4) Whether counsel is of all things that we do? (5) Whether the process of counsel is one of analysis? (6) Whether the process of counsel is indefinite?

FIRST ARTICLE

Whether Counsel Is an Inquiry?

We proceed thus to the First Article:—

Objection 1. It would seem that counsel is not an inquiry. For Damascene says (*De Fide Orthod.* ii, 22) that counsel is *an act of the appetite.* But inquiry is not an act of the appetite. Therefore counsel is not an inquiry.

Obj. 2. Further, inquiry is a discursive act of the intellect: for which reason it is not found in God, Whose knowledge is not discursive, as we have shown in the First Part (Q. 14, A. 7). But counsel is ascribed to God: for it is written (Eph. i. 11) that *He worketh all things according to the counsel of His will.* Therefore counsel is not inquiry.

Obj. 3. Further, inquiry is of doubtful matters. But counsel is given in matters that are certainly good; thus the Apostle says (1 Cor. vii. 25): *Now concerning virgins I have no commandment of the Lord: but I give counsel.* Therefore, counsel is not an inquiry.

On the contrary, Gregory of Nyssa* says: *Every counsel is an inquiry; but not every inquiry is a counsel.*

I answer that, Choice, as stated above (Q. 13, A. 1 *ad* 2; A. 3), follows the judgment of the reason about what is to be done. Now there is much uncertainty in things that have to be done; because actions are concerned with contingent singulars, which by reason of their vicissitude, are uncertain. Now in things doubtful and uncertain the reason does not pronounce judgment, without previous inquiry: wherefore the reason must of necessity institute an inquiry before deciding on the objects of choice; and this inquiry is called

* Nemesius, *De Nat. Hom.* xxxiv.

counsel. Hence the Philosopher says (*Ethic.* iii. 2) that choice is the *desire of what has been already counselled.*

Reply Obj. 1. When the acts of two powers are ordained to one another, in each of them there is something belonging to the other power: consequently each act can be denominated from either power. Now it is evident that the act of the reason giving direction as to the means, and the act of the will tending to these means according to the reason's direction, are ordained to one another. Consequently there is to be found something of the reason, viz., order, in that act of the will, which is choice: and in counsel, which is an act of reason, something of the will,—both as matter (since counsel is of what man wills to do),—and as motive (because it is from willing the end, that man is moved to take counsel in regard to the means). And therefore, just as the Philosopher says (*Ethic.* vi. 2) that choice is *intellect influenced by appetite,* thus pointing out that both concur in the act of choosing; so Damascene says (*loc. cit.*) that counsel is *appetite based on inquiry,* so as to show that counsel belongs, in a way, both to the will, on whose behalf and by whose impulsion the inquiry is made, and to the reason that executes the inquiry.

Reply Obj. 2. The things that we say of God must be understood without any of the defects which are to be found in us: thus in us science is of conclusions derived by reasoning from causes to effects: but science when said of God, means sure knowledge of all effects in the First Cause, without any reasoning process. In like manner we ascribe counsel to God, as to the certainty of His knowledge or judgment, which certainty in us arises from the inquiry of counsel. But such inquiry has no place in God; wherefore in this respect it is not ascribed to God: in which sense Damascene says (*loc. cit.*): *God takes not counsel: those only take counsel who lack knowledge.*

Reply Obj. 3. It may happen that things which are most certainly good in the opinion of wise and spiritual men are not certainly good in the opinion of many, or at least of carnal-minded men. Consequently in such things counsel may be given.

SECOND ARTICLE

Whether Counsel Is of the End, or Only of the Means?

We proceed thus to the Second Article:—

Objection 1. It would seem that counsel is not only of the means but also of the end. For whatever is doubtful, can be the subject of inquiry. Now in things to be done by man there happens sometimes a doubt as to the end and not only as to the means. Since therefore inquiry as to what is to be done is counsel, it seems that counsel can be of the end.

Obj. 2. Further, the matter of counsel is human actions. But some human actions are ends, as stated in *Ethic.* i. 1. Therefore counsel can be of the end.

On the contrary, Gregory of Nyssa* says that *counsel is not of the end, but of the means.*

I answer that, The end is the principle in practical matters: because the reason of the means is to be found in the end. Now the principle cannot be called in question, but must be presupposed in every inquiry. Since therefore counsel is an inquiry, it is not of the end, but only of the means. Nevertheless it may happen that what is the end in regard to some things, is ordained to something else; just as also what is the principle of one demonstration, is the conclusion of another: and consequently that which is looked upon as the end in one inquiry, may be looked upon as the means in another; and thus it will become an object of counsel.

Reply Obj. 1. That which is looked upon as an end, is already fixed: consequently as long as there is any doubt about it, it is not looked upon as an end. Wherefore if counsel is taken about it, it will be counsel not about the end, but about the means.

Reply Obj. 2. Counsel is about operations, in so far as they are ordained to some end. Consequently if any human act be an end, it will not, as such, be the matter of counsel.

THIRD ARTICLE

Whether Counsel Is Only of Things That We Do?

We proceed thus to the Third Article:—

Objection 1. It would seem that counsel is not only of things that we do. For counsel implies some kind of conference. But it is possible for many to confer about things that are not subject to movement, and are not the result of our actions, such as the nature of various things. Therefore counsel is not only of things that we do.

Obj. 2. Further, men sometimes seek counsel about things that are laid down by law; hence we speak of counsel at law. And yet

those who seek counsel thus, have nothing to do in making the laws. Therefore counsel is not only of things that we do.

Obj. 3. Further, some are said to take consultation about future events; which, however, are not in our power. Therefore counsel is not only of things that we do.

Obj. 4. Further, if counsel were only of things that we do, no one would take counsel about what another does. But this is clearly untrue. Therefore counsel is not only of things that we do.

On the contrary, Gregory of Nyssa† says: *We take counsel of things that are within our competency and that we are able to do.*

I answer that, Counsel properly implies a conference held between several; the very word (*consilium*) denotes this, for it means a sitting together (*considium*), from the fact that many sit together in order to confer with one another. Now we must take note that in contingent particular cases, in order that anything be known for certain, it is necessary to take several conditions or circumstances into consideration, which it is not easy for one to consider, but are considered by several with greater certainty, since what one takes note of, escapes the notice of another; whereas in necessary and universal things, our view is brought to bear on matters much more absolute and simple, so that one man by himself may be sufficient to consider these things. Wherefore the inquiry of counsel is concerned, properly speaking, with contingent singulars. Now the knowledge of the truth in such matters does not rank so high as to be desirable of itself, as is the knowledge of things universal and necessary; but it is desired as being useful towards action, because actions bear on things singular and contingent. Consequently, properly speaking, counsel is about things done by us.

Reply Obj. 1. Counsel implies conference, not of any kind, but about what is to be done, for the reason given above.

Reply Obj. 2. Although that which is laid down by the law is not due to the action of him who seeks counsel, nevertheless it directs him in his action: since the mandate of the law is one reason for doing something.

Reply Obj. 3. Counsel is not only about what is done, but also about whatever has relation to what is done. And for this reason we speak of consulting about future events, in so far as man is induced to do or omit something, through the knowledge of future events.

Reply Obj. 4. We seek counsel about the actions of others, in so far as they are, in some way, one with us; either by union of affection —thus a man is solicitous about what concerns

---

* Nemesius, *De Nat. Hom.* xxxiv.   † Nemesius, *De Nat. Hom.* xxxiv.

his friend, as though it concerned himself; or after the manner of an instrument, for the principal agent and the instrument are, in a way, one cause, since one acts through the other; thus the master takes counsel about what he would do through his servant.

FOURTH ARTICLE

Whether Counsel Is about All Things That We Do?

We proceed thus to the Fourth Article:—

Objection 1. It would seem that counsel is about all things that we have to do. For choice is the *desire of what is counselled* as stated above (A. 1). But choice is about all things that we do. Therefore counsel is too.

Obj. 2. Further, counsel implies the reason's inquiry. But, whenever we do not act through the impulse of passion, we act in virtue of the reason's inquiry. Therefore there is counsel about everything that we do.

Obj. 3. Further, the Philosopher says (*Ethic.* iii. 3) that *if it appears that something can be done by more means than one, we take counsel by inquiring whereby it may be done most easily and best; but if it can be accomplished by one means, how it can be done by this.* But whatever is done, is done by one means or by several. Therefore counsel takes place in all things that we do.

On the contrary, Gregory of Nyssa* says that *counsel has no place in things that are done according to science or art.*

I answer that, Counsel is a kind of inquiry, as stated above (A. 1). But we are wont to inquire about things that admit of doubt; hence the process of inquiry, which is called an argument, *is a reason that attests something that admitted of doubt.*† Now, that something in relation to human acts admits of no doubt, arises from a twofold source. First, because certain determinate ends are gained by certain determinate means: as happens in the arts which are governed by certain fixed rules of action; thus a writer does not take counsel how to form his letters, for this is determined by art.—Secondly, from the fact that it little matters whether it is done this or that way; this occurs in minute matters, which help or hinder but little with regard to the end aimed at; and reason looks upon small things as mere nothings. Consequently there are two things of which we do not take counsel, although they conduce to the end, as the Philosopher says (*Ethic.* iii. 3): namely, minute things, and those which have a fixed way of being done, as in works produced by art, with the exception of those arts that admit of conjecture such as medicine, commerce, and the like, as Gregory of Nyssa‡ says.

Reply Obj. 1. Choice presupposes counsel by reason of its judgment or decision. Consequently when the judgment or decision is evident without inquiry, there is no need for the inquiry of counsel.

Reply Obj. 2. In matters that are evident, the reason makes no inquiry, but judges at once. Consequently there is no need of counsel in all that is done by reason.

Reply Obj. 3. When a thing can be accomplished by one means, but in different ways, doubt may arise, just as when it can be accomplished by several means: hence the need of counsel. But when not only the means, but also the way of using the means, is fixed, then there is no need of counsel.

FIFTH ARTICLE

Whether the Process of Counsel Is One of Analysis?

We proceed thus to the Fifth Article:—

Objection 1. It would seem that the process of counsel is not one of analysis. For counsel is about things that we do. But the process of our actions is not one of analysis, but rather one of synthesis, viz., from the simple to the composite. Therefore counsel does not always proceed by way of analysis.

Obj. 2. Further, counsel is an inquiry of the reason. But reason proceeds from things that precede to things that follow, according to the more appropriate order. Since then, the past precedes the present, and the present precedes the future, it seems that in taking counsel one should proceed from the past and present to the future: which is not an analytical process. Therefore the process of counsel is not one of analysis.

Obj. 3. Further, counsel is only of such things as are possible to us, according to *Ethic.* iii. 3. But the question as to whether a certain thing is possible to us, depends on what we are able or unable to do, in order to gain such and such an end. Therefore the inquiry of counsel should begin from things present.

On the contrary, The Philosopher says (*Ethic.* iii. 3) that *he who takes counsel seems to inquire and analyze.*

I answer that, In every inquiry one must begin from some principle. And if this principle precedes both in knowledge and in being, the process is not analytic, but synthetic: because to proceed from cause to effect is to proceed synthetically, since causes are more simple than effects. But if that which precedes in knowledge is later in the order of being, the process is one of analysis, as when our judgment deals with effects, which by analysis we trace to their simple causes. Now the principle in the inquiry of counsel is the end,

---

* Nemesius, *De Nat. Hom.* xxxiv.   † Cicero, *Topic. ad Trebat.*   ‡ Nemesius, *loc. cit.*

which precedes indeed in intention, but comes afterwards into execution. Hence the inquiry of counsel must needs be one of analysis, beginning that is to say, from that which is intended in the future, and continuing until it arrives at that which is to be done at once.

Reply Obj. 1. Counsel is indeed about action. But actions take their reason from the end; and consequently the order of reasoning about actions is contrary to the order of actions.

Reply Obj. 2. Reason begins with that which is first according to reason; but not always with that which is first in point of time.

Reply Obj. 3. We should not want to know whether something to be done for an end be possible, if it were not suitable for gaining that end. Hence we must first inquire whether it be conducive to the end, before considering whether it be possible.

SIXTH ARTICLE

Whether the Process of Counsel Is Indefinite?

We proceed thus to the Sixth Article:—

Objection 1. It would seem that the process of counsel is indefinite. For counsel is an inquiry about the particular things with which action is concerned. But singulars are infinite. Therefore the process of counsel is indefinite.

Obj. 2. Further, the inquiry of counsel has to consider not only what is to be done, but how to avoid obstacles. But every human action can be hindered, and an obstacle can be removed by some human reason. Therefore the inquiry about removing obstacles can go on indefinitely.

Obj. 3. Further, the inquiry of demonstrative science does not go on indefinitely, because one can come to principles that are self-evident, which are absolutely certain. But such like certainty is not to be had in contingent singulars, which are variable and uncertain. Therefore the inquiry of counsel goes on indefinitely.

On the contrary, No one is moved to that which he cannot possibly reach (*De Cœlo* i. 7). But it is impossible to pass through the infinite. If therefore the inquiry of counsel is infinite, no one would begin to take counsel. Which is clearly untrue.

I answer that, The inquiry of counsel is actually finite on both sides, on that of its principle and on that of its term. For a twofold principle is available in the inquiry of counsel. One is proper to it, and belongs to the very genus of things pertaining to operation: this is the end which is not the matter of counsel, but is taken for granted as its principle, as stated above (A. 2). The other principle is taken from another genus, so to speak; thus in demonstrative sciences one science postulates certain things from another, without inquirying into them. Now these principles which are taken for granted in the inquiry of counsel are any facts received through the senses—for instance, that this is bread or iron: and also any general statements known either through speculative or through practical science; for instance, that adultery is forbidden by God, or that man cannot live without suitable nourishment. Of such things counsel makes no inquiry.—But the term of inquiry is that which we are able to do at once. For just as the end is considered in the light of a principle, so the means are considered in the light of a conclusion. Wherefore that which presents itself as to be done first, holds the position of an ultimate conclusion whereat the inquiry comes to an end.—Nothing however prevents counsel from being infinite potentially, for as much as an infinite number of things may present themselves to be inquired into by means of counsel.

Reply Obj. 1. Singulars are infinite; not actually, but only potentially.

Reply Obj. 2. Although human action can be hindered, the hindrance is not always at hand. Consequently it is not always necessary to take counsel about removing the obstacle.

Reply Obj. 3. In contingent singulars, something may be taken for certain, not simply, indeed, but for the time being, and as far as it concerns the work to be done. Thus that Socrates is sitting is not a necessary statement; but that he is sitting, as long as he continues to sit, is necessary; and this can be taken for a certain fact.

QUESTION 15

Of Consent, Which Is an Act of the Will in Regard to the Means

(In Four Articles)

WE must now consider consent; concerning which there are four points of inquiry: (1) Whether consent is an act of the appetitive or of the apprehensive power? (2) Whether it is to be found in irrational animals? (3) Whether it is directed to the end or to the means? (4) Whether consent to an act belongs to the higher part of the soul only?

Whether Consent Is an Act of the Appetitive or of the Apprehensive Power?

We proceed thus to the First Article:—

Objection 1. It would seem that consent belongs only to the apprehensive part of the soul. For Augustine (*De Trin.* xii. 12) ascribes consent to the higher reason. But the reason is an apprehensive power. Therefore consent belongs to an apprehensive power.

Obj. 2. Further, consent is *co-sense.* But sense is an apprehensive power. Therefore consent is the act of an apprehensive power.

Obj. 3. Further, just as assent is an application of the intellect to something, so is consent. But assent belongs to the intellect, which is an apprehensive power. Therefore consent also belongs to an apprehensive power.

On the contrary, Damascene says (*De Fide Orthod.* ii. 22) that *if a man judge without affection for that of which he judges, there is no sentence, i.e.* consent. But affection belongs to the appetitive power. Therefore consent does also.

I answer that, Consent implies application of sense to something. Now it is proper to sense to take cognizance of things present; for the imagination apprehends the similitude of corporeal things, even in the absence of the things of which they bear the likeness; while the intellect apprehends universal ideas, which it can apprehend indifferently, whether the singulars be present or absent. And since the act of an appetitive power is a kind of inclination to the thing itself, the application of the appetitive power to the thing, in so far as it cleaves to it, gets by a kind of similitude, the name of sense, since, as it were, it acquires direct knowledge of the thing to which it cleaves, in so far as it takes complacency in it. Hence it is written (Wisd. i. 1): *Think of* (*Sentite*) *the Lord in goodness.* And on these grounds consent is an act of the appetitive power.

Reply Obj. 1. As stated in *De Anima* iii. 9, *the will is in the reason.* Hence, when Augustine ascribes consent to the reason, he takes reason as including the will.

Reply Obj. 2. Sense, properly speaking, belongs to the apprehensive faculty; but by way of similitude, in so far as it implies seeking acquaintance, it belongs to the appetive power, as stated above.

Reply Obj. 3. *Assentire* (*to assent*) is, to speak, *ad aliud sentire* (*to feel towards something*); and thus it implies a certain distance from that to which assent is given. But *consentire* (to consent) is *to feel with,* and this implies a certain union to the object of consent. Hence the will, to which it belongs to tend to

*In Latin rather than in English.

the thing itself, is more properly said to consent: whereas the intellect, whose act does not consist in a movement towards the thing, but rather the reverse, as we have stated in the First Part (Q.16, A. 1; Q. 27, A. 4; Q. 59, A. 2), is more properly said to assent: although one word is wont to be used for the other.* We may also say that the intellect assents, in so far as it is moved by the will.

Whether Consent Is to Be Found in Irrational Animals?

We proceed thus to the Second Article:—

Objection 1. It would seem that consent is to be found in irrational animals. For consent implies a determination of the appetite to one thing. But the appetite of irrational animals is determinate to one thing. Therefore consent is to be found in irrational animals.

Obj. 2. Further, if you remove what is first, you remove what follows. But consent precedes the accomplished act. If therefore there were no consent in irrational animals, there would be no act accomplished; which is clearly false.

Obj. 3. Further, men are sometimes said to consent to do something, through some passion; desire, for instance, or anger. But irrational animals act through passion. Therefore they consent.

On the contrary, Damascene says (*De Fide Orthod.* ii. 22) that *after judging, man approves and embraces the judgment of his counselling, and this is called the sentence, i.e.,* consent. But counsel is not in irrational animals. Therefore neither is consent.

I answer that, Consent, properly speaking, is not in irrational animals. The reason of this is that consent implies an application of the appetitive movement to something as to be done. Now to apply the appetitive movement to the doing of something, belongs to the subject in whose power it is to move the appetite: thus to touch a stone is an action suitable to a stick, but to apply the stick so that it touch the stone, belongs to one who has the power of moving the stick. But irrational animals have not the command of the appetitive movement; for this is in them through natural instinct. Hence in the irrational animal, there is indeed the movement of appetite, but it does not apply that movement to some particular thing. And hence it is that the irrational animal is not properly said to consent: this is proper to the rational nature, which has the command of the appetitive movement, and is able to apply or not to apply it to this or that thing.

Reply Obj. 1. In irrational animals the determination of the appetite to a particular thing is merely passive: whereas consent implies a determination of the appetite, which is active rather than merely passive.

Reply Obj. 2. If the first be removed, then what follows is removed, provided that, properly speaking, it follow from that only. But if something can follow from several things, it is not removed by the fact that one of them is removed; thus if hardening is the effect of heat and of cold (since bricks are hardened by fire, and frozen water is hardened by the cold), then by removing heat it does not follow that there is no hardening. Now the accomplishment of an act follows not only from consent, but also from the impulse of the appetite, such as is found in irrational animals.

Reply Obj. 3. The man who acts through passion is able not to follow the passion: whereas irrational animals have not that power. Hence the comparison fails.

THIRD ARTICLE

Whether Consent Is Directed to the End or to the Means?

We proceed thus to the Third Article:—

Objection 1. It would seem that consent is directed to the end. Because that on account of which a thing is such is still more such. But it is on account of the end that we consent to the means. Therefore, still more do we consent to the end.

Obj. 2. Further, the act of the intemperate man is his end, just as the act of the virtuous man is his end. But the intemperate man consents to his own act. Therefore consent can be directed to the end.

Obj. 3. Further, desire of the means is choice, as stated above (Q. 13, A. 1). If therefore consent were only directed to the means it would nowise differ from choice. And this is proved to be false by the authority of Damascene who says (*De Fide Orthod.* ii. 22) that *after the approval* which he calls *the sentence, comes the choice.* Therefore consent is not only directed to the means.

On the contrary, Damascene says (*ibid.*) that the *sentence, i.e.,* the consent, takes place *when man approves and embraces the judgment of his counsel.* But counsel is only about the means. Therefore the same applies to consent.

I answer that, Consent is the application of the appetitive movement to something that is already in the power of him who causes the application. Now the order of action is this: First there is the apprehension of the end; then the desire of the end; then the counsel about the means; then the desire of the means. Now the appetite tends to the last end natural-

ly: wherefore the application of the appetitive movement to the apprehended end has not the nature of consent, but of simple volition. But as to those things which come under consideration after the last end, in so far as they are directed to the end, they come under counsel: and so consent can be applied to them, in so far as the appetitive movement is applied to the judgment resulting from counsel. But the appetitive movement to the end is not applied to counsel: rather is counsel applied to it, because counsel presupposes the desire of the end. On the other hand, the desire of the means presupposes the decision of counsel. And therefore the application of the appetitive movement to counsel's decision is consent, properly speaking. Consequently, since counsel is only about the means, consent, properly speaking, is of nothing else but the means.

Reply Obj. 1. Just as the knowledge of conclusions through the principles is science, whereas the knowledge of the principles is not science, but something higher, namely, understanding; so do we consent to the means on account of the end, in respect of which our act is not consent but something greater, namely, volition.

Reply Obj. 2. Delight in his act, rather than the act itself, is the end of the intemperate man, and for sake of this delight he consents to that act.

Reply Obj. 3. Choice includes something that consent has not, namely, a certain relation to something to which something else is preferred: and therefore after consent there still remains a choice. For it may happen that by aid of counsel several means have been found conducive to the end, and through each of these meeting with approval, consent has been given to each: but after approving of many, we have given our preference to one by choosing it. But if only one meets with approval, then consent and choice do not differ in reality, but only in our way of looking at them; so that we call it consent, according as we approve of doing that thing; but choice according as we prefer it to those that do not meet with our approval.

FOURTH ARTICLE

Whether Consent to the Act Belongs Only to the Higher Part of the Soul?

We proceed thus to the Fourth Article:—

Objection 1. It would seem that consent to the act does not always belong to the higher reason. For *delight follows action, and perfects it, just as beauty perfects youth** (*Ethic.* x. 4). But consent to delight belongs to the

---

* οἶον τοῖς ἀκμαίοις ἡ ὥρα;—as youthful vigor perfects a man in his prime.

lower reason, as Augustine says (*De Trin.* xii. 12). Therefore consent to the act does not belong only to the higher reason.

Obj. 2. Further, an act to which we consent is said to be voluntary. But it belongs to many powers to produce voluntary acts. Therefore the higher reason is not alone in consenting to the act.

Obj. 3. Further, *the higher reason is that which is intent on the contemplation and consultation of things eternal,* as Augustine says (*De Trin.* xii. 7). But man often consents to an act not for eternal, but for temporal reasons, or even on account of some passion of the soul. Therefore consent to an act does not belong to the higher reason alone.

On the contrary, Augustine says (*De Trin.* xii. 12): *It is impossible for man to make up his mind to commit a sin, unless that mental faculty which has the sovereign power of urging his members to, or restraining them from, act, yield to the evil deed and become its slave.*

I answer that, The final decision belongs to him who holds the highest place, and to whom it belongs to judge of the others; for as long as judgment about some matter remains to be pronounced, the final decision has not been given. Now it is evident that it belongs to the higher reason to judge of all: since it is by the reason that we judge of sensible things; and of things pertaining to human principles we judge according to Divine principles, which is the function of the higher reason. Wherefore as long as a man is uncertain whether he resists or not, according to Divine principles, no judgment of the reason can be considered in the light of a final decision. Now the final decision of what is to be done is consent to the act. Therefore consent to the act belongs to the higher reason; but in that sense in which the reason includes the will, as stated above (A. 1 *ad* 1).

Reply Obj. 1. Consent to delight in the work done belongs to the higher reason, as also does consent to the work; but consent to delight in thought belongs to the lower reason, just as to the lower reason it belongs to think. Nevertheless the higher reason exercises judgment on the fact of thinking or not thinking, considered as an action; and in like manner on the delight that results. But in so far as the act of thinking is considered as ordained to a further act, it belongs to the lower reason. For that which is ordained to something else, belongs to a lower art or power than does the end to which it is ordained: hence the art which is concerned with the end is called the master or principal art.

Reply Obj. 2. Since actions are called voluntary from the fact that we consent to them, it does not follow that consent is an act of each power, but of the will which is in the reason, as stated above (A. 1 *ad* 1), and from which the voluntary act is named.

Reply Obj. 3. The higher reason is said to consent not only because it always moves to act, according to the eternal reasons; but also because it fails to dissent according to those same reasons.

QUESTION 16

Of Use, Which Is an Act of the Will in Regard to the Means

(In Four Articles)

WE must now consider use; concerning which there are four points of inquiry: (1) Whether use is an act of the will? (2) Whether it is to be found in irrational animals? (3) Whether it regards the means only, or the end also? (4) Of the relation of use to choice.

FIRST ARTICLE

Whether Use Is an Act of the Will?

We proceed thus to the First Article:—

Objection 1. It would seem that use is not an act of the will. For Augustine says (*De Doctr. Christ.* i. 4) that *to use is to refer that which is the object of use to the obtaining of something else.* But *to refer* something to another is an act of the reason to which it belongs to compare and to direct. Therefore use is an act of the reason and not of the will.

Obj. 2. Further, Damascene says (*De Fide Orthod.* ii. 22) that man *goes forward to the operation, and this is called impulse; then he makes use (of the powers) and this is called use.* But operation belongs to the executive power; and the act of the will does not follow the act of the executive power, on the contrary execution comes last. Therefore use is not an act of the will.

Obj. 3. Further, Augustine says (QQ. 83, qu. 30): *All things that were made were made for man's use, because reason with which man is endowed uses all things by its judgment of them.* But judgment of things created by God belongs to the speculative reason; which seems to be altogether distinct from the will, which is the principle of human acts. Therefore use is not an act of the will.

On the contrary, Augustine says (*De*

Trin. x. 11): *To use is to apply something to purpose of the will.*

I answer that, The use of a thing implies the application of that thing to an operation: hence the operation to which we apply a thing is called its use; thus the use of a horse is to ride, and the use of a stick is to strike. Now we apply to an operation not only the interior principles of action, viz., the powers of the soul or the members of the body; as the intellect, to understand; and the eye, to see; but also external things, as a stick, to strike. But it is evident that we do not apply external things to an operation save through the interior principles which are either the powers of the soul, or the habits of those powers, or the organs which are parts of the body. Now it has been shown above (Q. 9, A. 1) that it is the will which moves the soul's powers to their acts, and this is to apply them to operation. Hence it is evident that first and principally use belongs to the will as first mover; to the reason, as directing; and to the other powers as executing the operation, which powers are compared to the will which applies them to act, as the instruments are compared to the principal agent. Now action is properly ascribed, not to the instrument, but to the principal agent, as building is ascribed to the builder, but not to his tools. Hence it is evident that use is, properly speaking, an act of the will.

Reply Obj. 1. Reason does indeed refer one thing to another; but the will tends to that which is referred by the reason to something else. And in this sense to use is to refer one thing to another.

Reply Obj. 2. Damascene is speaking of use In so far as it belongs to the executive powers.

Reply Obj. 3. Even the speculative reason is applied by the will to the act of understanding or judging. Consequently the speculative reason is said to use, in so far as it is moved by the will, in the same way as the other powers.

SECOND ARTICLE

Whether Use Is to Be Found in Irrational Animals?

We proceed thus to the Second Article:—

Objection 1. It would seem that use is to be found in irrational animals. For it is better to enjoy than to use, because, as Augustine says (*De Trin.* x. 10): *We use things by referring them to something else which we are to enjoy.* But enjoyment is to be found in irrational animals, as stated above (Q. 11, A. 2). Much more, therefore, is it possible for them to use.

Obj. 2. Further, to apply the members to action is to use them. But irrational animals apply their members to action; for instance,

their feet, to walk; their horns, to strike. Therefore it is possible for irrational animals to use.

On the contrary, Augustine says (QQ. 83, qu. 30): *None but a rational animal can make use of a thing.*

I answer that, as stated above (A. 1), to use is to apply an active principle to action: thus to consent is to apply the appetitive movement to the desire of something, as stated above (Q. 15, AA. 1, 2, 3). Now he alone who has the disposal of a thing, can apply it to something else; and this belongs to him alone who knows how to refer it to something else, which is an act of the reason. And therefore none but a rational animal consents and uses.

Reply Obj. 1. To enjoy implies the absolute movement of the appetite to the appetible: whereas to use implies a movement of the appetite to something as directed to something else. If therefore we compare use and enjoyment in respect of their objects, enjoyment is better than use; because that which is appetible absolutely is better than that which is appetible only as directed to something else. But if we compare them in respect of the apprehensive power that precedes them, greater excellence is required on the part of use: because to direct one thing to another is an act of reason; whereas to apprehend something absolutely is within the competency even of sense.

Reply Obj. 2. Animals by means of their members do something from natural instinct; not through knowing the relation of their members to these operations. Wherefore, properly speaking, they do not apply their members to action, nor do they use them.

THIRD ARTICLE

Whether Use Regards Also the Last End?

We proceed thus to the Third Article:—

Objection 1. It would seem that use can regard also the last end. For Augustine says (*De Trin.* x. 11): *Whoever enjoys, uses.* But man enjoys the last end. Therefore he uses the last end.

Obj. 2. Further, *to use is to apply something to the purpose of the will* (ibid.). But the last end, more than anything else, is the object of the will's application. Therefore it can be the object of use.

Obj. 3. Further, Hilary says (*De Trin.* ii) that *Eternity is in the Father, Likeness in the Image, i.e.,* in the Son, *Use in the Gift, i.e.,* in the Holy Ghost. But the Holy Ghost, since He is God, is the last end. Therefore the last end can be the object of use.

On the contrary, Augustine says (QQ. 83, qu. 30): *No one rightly uses God, but one en-*

joys Him. But God alone is the last end. Therefore we cannot use the last end.

I answer that, Use, as stated above (A. 1), implies the application of one thing to another. Now that which is applied to another is regarded in the light of means to an end; and consequently use always regards the means. For this reason things that are adapted to a certain end are said to be *useful;* in fact their very usefulness is sometimes called use.

It must, however, be observed that the last end may be taken in two ways: first, simply; secondly, in respect of an individual. For since the end, as stated above (Q. 1, A. 8; Q. 2, A. 7), signifies sometimes the thing itself, and sometimes the attainment or possession of that thing (thus the miser's end is either money or the possession of it); it is evident that, simply speaking, the last end is the thing itself; for the possession of money is good only inasmuch as there is some good in money. But in regard to the individual, the obtaining of money is the last end; for the miser would not seek for money, save that he might have it. Therefore, simply and properly speaking, a man enjoys money, because he places his last end therein; but in so far as he seeks to possess it, he is said to use it.

Reply Obj. 1. Augustine is speaking of use in general, in so far as it implies the relation of an end to the enjoyment which a man seeks in that end.

Reply Obj. 2. The end is applied to the purpose of the will, that the will may find rest in it. Consequently this rest in the end, which is the enjoyment thereof, is in this sense called use of the end. But the means are applied to the will's purpose, not only in being used as means, but as ordained to something else in which the will finds rest.

Reply Obj. 3. The words of Hilary refer to use as applicable to rest in the last end; just as, speaking in a general sense, one may be said to use the end for the purpose of attaining it, as stated above. Hence Augustine says (*De Trin.* vi. 10) that *this love, delight, felicity, or happiness, is called use by him.*

FOURTH ARTICLE

Whether Use Precedes Choice?

We proceed thus to the Fourth Article:—

Objection 1. It would seem that use precedes choice. For nothing follows after choice, except execution. But use, since it belongs to the will, precedes execution. Therefore it precedes choice also.

Obj. 2. Further, the absolute precedes the relative. Therefore the less relative precedes the more relative. But choice implies two relations: one, of the thing chosen, in relation to the end; the other, of the thing chosen, in respect of that to which it is preferred; whereas use implies relation to the end only. Therefore use precedes choice.

Obj. 3. Further, the will uses the other powers in so far as it moves them. But the will moves itself too, as stated above (Q. 9, A. 3). Therefore it uses itself, by applying itself to act. But it does this when it consents. Therefore there is use in consent. But consent precedes choice as stated above (Q. 15, A. 3 *ad* 3). Therefore use does also.

On the contrary, Damascene says (*De Fide Orthod.* ii. 22) that *the will after choosing has an impulse to the operation, and afterwards it uses (the powers).* Therefore use follows choice.

I answer that, The will has a twofold relation to the thing willed. One, according as the thing willed is, in a way, in the willing subject, by a kind of proportion or order to the thing willed. Wherefore those things that are naturally proportionate to a certain end, are said to desire that end naturally.—Yet to have an end thus is to have it imperfectly. Now every imperfect thing tends to perfection. And therefore both the natural and the voluntary appetite tend to have the end in reality; and this is to have it perfectly. This is the second relation of the will to the thing willed.

Now the thing willed is not only the end, but also the means. And the last act that belongs to the first relation of the will to means, is choice; for there the will becomes fully proportionate, by willing the means fully. Use, on the other hand, belongs to the second relation of the will, in respect of which it tends to the realization of the thing willed. Wherefore it is evident that use follows choice; provided that by use we mean the will's use of the executive power in moving it. But since the will, in a way, moves the reason also, and uses it, we may take the use of the means, as consisting in the consideration of the reason, whereby it refers the means to the end. In this sense use precedes choice.

Reply Obj. 1. The motion of the will to the execution of the work, precedes execution, but follows choice. And so, since use belongs to that very motion of the will, it stands between choice and execution.

Reply Obj. 2. What is essentially relative is after the absolute; but the thing to which relation is referred need not come after. Indeed, the more a cause precedes, the more numerous the effects to which it has relation.

Reply Obj. 3. Choice precedes use, if they be referred to the same object. But nothing hinders the use of one thing preceding the choice of another. And since the acts of the will react on one another, in each act of the will we can find both consent and choice and use; so that we may say that the will consents to choose, and consents to consent, and uses itself in consenting and choosing. And such acts as are ordained to that which precedes, precede also.

QUESTION 17

Of the Acts Commanded by the Will

(In Nine Articles)

WE must now consider the acts commanded by the will; under which head there are nine points of inquiry: (1) Whether command is an act of the will or of the reason? (2) Whether command belongs to irrational animals? (3) Of the order between command and use; (4) Whether command and the commanded act are one act or distinct? (5) Whether the act of the will is commanded? (7) Whether the act of the sensitive appetite is commanded?(8) Whether the act of the vegetal soul is commanded? (9) Whether the acts of the external members are commanded?

FIRST ARTICLE

Whether Command Is an Act of the Reason or of the Will?

We proceed thus to the First Article:—

Objection 1. It would seem that command is not an act of the reason but of the will. For command is a kind of motion; because Avicenna says that there are four ways of moving, *by perfecting, by disposing, by commanding, and by counselling.* But it belongs to the will to move all the other powers of the soul, as stated above (Q. 9, A. 1). Therefore command is an act of the will.

Obj. 2. Further, just as to be commanded belongs to that which is subject, so, seemingly, to command belongs to that which is most free. But the root of liberty is especially in the will. Therefore to command belongs to the will.

Obj. 3. Further, command is followed at once by act. But the act of the reason is not followed at once by act: for he who judges that a thing should be done, does not do it at once. Therefore command is not an act of the reason, but of the will.

On the contrary, Gregory of Nyssa* and the Philosopher (*Ethic.* i. 13) say that *the appetite obeys reason.* Therefore command is an act of the reason.

I answer that, Command is an act of the reason, presupposing, however, an act of the will. In proof of this, we must take note that, since the acts of the reason and of the will can be brought to bear on one another, in so far

* Nemesius, *De Nat. Hom.* xvi.

as the reason reasons about willing, and the will wills to reason, the result is that the act of the reason precedes the act of the will, and conversely. And since the power of the preceding act continues in the act that follows, it happens sometimes that there is an act of the will in so far as it retains in itself something of an act of the reason, as we have stated in reference to use and choice; and conversely, that there is an act of the reason in so far as it retains in itself something of an act of the will.

Now, command is essentially indeed an act of the reason: for the commander orders the one commanded to do something, by way of intimation or declaration; and to order thus by intimating or declaring is an act of the reason. Now the reason can intimate or declare something in two ways. First, absolutely: and this intimation is expressed by a verb in the indicative mood, as when one person says to another: *This is what you should do.* Sometimes, however, the reason intimates something to a man by moving him thereto; and this intimation is expressed by a verb in the imperative mood; as when it is said to someone: *Do this.* Now the first mover, among the powers of the soul, to the doing of an act is the will, as stated above (Q. 9, A. 1). Since, therefore, the second mover does not move, save in virtue of the first mover, it follows that the very fact that the reason moves by commanding, is due to the power of the will. Consequently it follows that command is an act of the reason, presupposing an act of the will, in virtue of which the reason, by its command, moves (the power) to the execution of the act.

Reply Obj. 1. To command is to move, not anyhow, but by intimating and declaring to another; and this is an act of the reason.

Reply Obj. 2. The root of liberty is the will as the subject thereof; but it is the reason as its cause. For the will can tend freely towards various objects, precisely because the reason can have various perceptions of good. Hence philosophers define the free-will as being *a free judgment arising from reason,* implying that reason is the root of liberty.

Reply Obj. 3. This argument proves that command is an act of reason not absolutely, but with a kind of motion, as stated above.

SECOND ARTICLE

Whether Command Belongs to Irrational Animals?

We proceed thus to the Second Article:—

Objection 1. It would seem that command belongs to irrational animals. Because, according to Avicenna, *the power that commands movement is the appetite; and the power that executes movement is in the muscles and nerves.* But both powers are in irrational animals. Therefore command is to be found in irrational animals.

Obj. 2. Further, the condition of a slave is that of one who receives commands. But the body is compared to the soul as a slave to his master, as the Philosopher says (*Polit.* i. 2). Therefore the body is commanded by the soul, even in irrational animals, since they are composed of soul and body.

Obj. 3. Further, by commanding, man has an impulse towards an action. But impulse to action is to be found in irrational animals, as Damascene says (*De Fide Orthod.* ii. 22). Therefore command is to be found in irrational animals.

On the contrary, Command is an act of reason, as stated above (A. 1). But in irrational animals there is no reason. Neither, therefore, is there command.

I answer that, To command is nothing else than to direct someone to do something, by a certain motion of intimation. Now to direct is the proper act of reason. Wherefore it is impossible that irrational animals should command in any way, since they are devoid of reason.

Reply Obj. 1. The appetitive power is said to command movement, in so far as it moves the commanding reason. But this is only in man. In irrational animals the appetitive power is not, properly speaking, a commanding faculty, unless command be taken loosely for motion.

Reply Obj. 2. The body of the irrational animal is competent to obey; but its soul is not competent to command, because it is not competent to direct. Consequently there is no ratio there of commander and commanded; but only of mover and moved.

Reply Obj. 3. Impulse to action is in irrational animals otherwise than in man. For the impulse of man to action arises from the directing reason; wherefore his impulse is one of command. On the other hand, the impulse of the irrational animal arises from natural instinct; because as soon as they apprehend the fitting or the unfitting, their appetite is moved naturally to pursue or to avoid. Wherefore they are directed by another to act; and they themselves do not direct themselves to act.

Consequently in them is impulse but not command.

THIRD ARTICLE

Whether Use Precedes Command?

We proceed thus to the Third Article:—

Objection 1. It would seem that use precedes command. For command is an act of the reason presupposing an act of the will, as stated above (A. 1). But, as we have already shown (Q. 16, A. 1), use is an act of the will. Therefore use precedes command.

Obj. 2. Further, command is one of those things that are ordained to the end. But use is of those things that are ordained to the end. Therefore it seems that use precedes command.

Obj. 3. Further, every act of a power moved by the will is called use; because the will uses the other powers, as stated above (Q. 16, A. 1). But command is an act of the reason as moved by the will, as stated above (A. 1). Therefore command is a kind of use. Now the common precedes the proper. Therefore use precedes command.

On the contrary, Damascene says (*De Fide Orthod.* ii. 22) that impulse to action precedes use. But impulse to operation is given by command. Therefore command precedes use.

I answer that, use of that which is directed to the end, in so far as it is in the reason referring this to the end, precedes choice, as stated above (Q. 16, A. 4). Wherefore still more does it precede command.—On the other hand, use of that which is directed to the end, in so far as it is subject to the executive power, follows command; because use in the user is united to the act of the thing used; for one does not use a stick before doing something with the stick. But command is not simultaneous with the act of the thing to which the command is given: for it naturally precedes its fulfilment, sometimes, indeed, by priority of time. Consequently it is evident that command precedes use.

Reply Obj. 1. Not every act of the will precedes this act of the reason which is command; but an act of the will precedes, viz., choice; and an act of the will follows, viz., use. Because after counsel's decision, which is reason's judgment, the will chooses; and after choice, the reason commands that power which has to do what was chosen; and then, last of all, someone's will begins to use, by executing the command of reason; sometimes it is another's will, when one commands another; sometimes the will of the one that commands, when he commands himself to do something.

Reply Obj. 2. Just as act ranks before power, so does the object rank before the act. Now the object of use is that which is directed to the end. Consequently, from the fact that command precedes, rather than that it follows use.

Reply Obj. 3. Just as the act of the will in using the reason for the purpose of command, precedes the command; so also we may say that this act whereby the will uses the reason, is preceded by a command of reason; since the acts of these powers react on one another.

FOURTH ARTICLE

Whether Command and the Commanded Act Are One Act, or Distinct?

We proceed thus to the Fourth Article:—

Objection 1. It would seem that the commanded act is not one with the command itself. For the acts of different powers are themselves distinct. But the commanded act belongs to one power, and the command to another; since one is the power that commands, and the other is the power that receives the command. Therefore the commanded act is not one with the command.

Obj. 2. Further, whatever things can be separate from one another, are distinct: for nothing is severed from itself. But sometimes the commanded act is separate from the command: for sometimes the command is given, and the commanded act follows not. Therefore command is a distinct act from the act commanded.

Obj. 3. Further, whatever things are related to one another as precedent and consequent, are distinct. But command naturally precedes the commanded act. Therefore they are distinct.

On the contrary, The Philosopher says (*Topic.* iii. 2) that *where one thing is by reason of another, there is but one.* But there is no commanded act unless by reason of the command. Therefore they are one.

I answer that, Nothing prevents certain things being distinct in one respect, and one in another respect. Indeed, every multitude is one in some respect, as Dionysius says (*Div. Nom.* xiii). But a difference is to be observed in this, that some are simply many, and one in a particular respect: while with others it is the reverse. Now *one* is predicated in the same way as *being.* And substance is being simply, whereas accident or being *of reason* is a being only in a certain respect. Wherefore those things that are one in substance are one simply, though many in a certain respect. Thus, in the genus substance, the whole composed of its integral or essential parts, is one simply: because the whole is being and substance simply, and the parts are being and substances

in the whole. But those things which are distinct in substance, and one according to an accident, are distinct simply, and one in a certain respect: thus many men are one people, and many stones are one heap; which is unity of composition or order. In like manner also many individuals that are one in genus or species are many simply, and one in a certain respect: since to be one in genus or species is to be one according to the consideration of the reason.

Now just as in the genus of natural things, a whole is composed of matter and form (*e.g.,* man, who is one natural being, though he has many parts, is composed of soul and body); so, in human acts, the act of a lower power is in the position of matter in regard to the act of a higher power, in so far as the lower power acts in virtue of the higher power moving it: for thus also the act of the first mover is as the form in regard to the act of its instrument. Hence it is evident that command and the commanded act are one human act, just as a whole is one, yet in its parts, many.

Reply Obj. 1. If the distinct powers are not ordained to one another, their acts are diverse simply. But when one power is the mover of the other, then their acts are, in a way, one: since *the act of the mover and the act of the thing moved are one act* (*Phys.* iii. 3).

Reply Obj. 2. The fact that command and the commanded act can be separated from one another shows that they are different parts. Because the parts of a man can be separated from one another, and yet they form one whole.

Reply Obj. 3. In those things that are many in parts, but one as a whole, nothing hinders one part from preceding another. Thus the soul, in a way, precedes the body; and the heart, the other members.

FIFTH ARTICLE

Whether the Act of the Will Is Commanded?

We proceed thus to the Fifth Article:—

Objection 1. It would seem that the act of the will is not commanded. For Augustine says (*Conf.* viii. 9): *The mind commands the mind to will, and yet it does not.* But to will is the act of the will. Therefore the act of the will is not commanded.

Obj. 2. Further, to receive a command belongs to one who can understand the command. But the will cannot understand the command; for the will differs from the intellect, to which it belongs to understand. Therefore the act of the will is not commanded.

Obj. 3. Further, if one act of the will is commanded, for the same reason all are commanded. But if all the acts of the will are commanded, we must needs proceed to infinity; because the act of the will precedes the act of reason commanding, as stated above (A. 1); for if that act of the will be also commanded, this command will be preceded by another act of the reason, and so on to infinity. But to proceed to infinity is not possible. Therefore the act of the will is not commanded.

On the contrary, Whatever is in our power, is subject to our command. But the acts of the will, most of all, are in our power; since all our acts are said to be in our power, in so far as they are voluntary. Therefore the acts of the will are commanded by us.

I answer that, As stated above (A. 1), command is nothing else than the act of the reason directing, with a certain motion, something to act. Now it is evident that the reason can direct the act of the will: for just as it can judge it to be good to will something, so it can direct by commanding man to will. From this it is evident that an act of the will can be commanded.

Reply Obj. 1. As Augustine says (*ibid.*) when the mind commands itself perfectly to will, then already it wills: but that sometimes it commands and wills not, is due to the fact that it commands imperfectly. Now imperfect command arises from the fact that the reason is moved by opposite motives to command or not to command: wherefore it fluctuates between the two, and fails to command perfectly.

Reply Obj. 2. Just as each of the members of the body works not for itself alone but for the whole body; thus it is for the whole body that the eye sees; so is it with the powers of the soul. For the intellect understands, not for itself alone, but for all the powers; and the will wills not only for itself, but for all the powers too. Wherefore man, in so far as he is endowed with intellect and will, commands the act of the will for himself.

Reply Obj. 3. Since command is an act of reason, that act is commanded which is subject to reason. Now the first act of the will is not due to the direction of the reason but to the instigation of nature, or of a higher cause, as stated above (Q. 9, A. 4). Therefore there is no need to proceed to infinity.

SIXTH ARTICLE

Whether the Act of the Reason Is Commanded?

We proceed thus to the Sixth Article:—

Objection 1. It would seem that the act of the reason cannot be commanded. For it seems impossible for a thing to command itself. But it is the reason that commands, as stated above (A. 1). Therefore the act of the reason is not commanded.

Obj. 2. Further, that which is essential is different from that which is by participation. But the power whose act is commanded by reason, is rational by participation, as stated in *Ethic.* i. 13. Therefore the act of that power, which is essentially rational, is not commanded.

Obj. 3. Further, that act is commanded, which is in our power. But to know and judge the truth, which is the act of reason, is not always in our power. Therefore the act of the reason cannot be commanded.

On the contrary, That which we do of our free-will, can be done by our command. But the acts of the reason are accomplished through the free-will: for Damascene says (*De Fide Orthod.* ii. 22) that *by his free-will man inquires, considers, judges, approves.* Therefore the acts of the reason can be commanded.

I answer that, Since the reason re-acts on itself, just as it directs the acts of other powers, so can it direct its own act. Consequently its act can be commanded.

But we must take note that the act of the reason may be considered in two ways. First, as to the exercise of the act. And considered thus, the act of the reason can always be commanded: as when one is told to be attentive, and to use one's reason. Secondly, as to the object; in respect of which two acts of the reason have to be noticed. One is the act whereby it apprehends the truth about something. This act is not in our power: because it happens in virtue of a natural or supernatural light. Consequently in this respect, the act of the reason is not in our power, and cannot be commanded. The other act of the reason is that whereby it assents to what it apprehends. If, therefore, that which the reason apprehends is such that it naturally assents thereto, *e.g.,* the first principles, it is not in our power to assent or dissent to the like: assent follows naturally, and consequently, properly speaking, is not subject to our command. But some things which are apprehended do not convince the intellect to such an extent as not to leave it free to assent or dissent, or at least suspend its assent or dissent, on account of some cause or other; and in such things assent or dissent is in our power, and is subject to our command.

Reply Obj. 1. Reason commands itself, just as the will moves itself, as stated above (Q. 9, A. 3), that is to say, in so far as each power reacts on its own acts, and from one thing tends to another.

Reply Obj. 2. On account of the diversity of objects subject to the act of the reason, nothing prevents the reason from participating in itself: thus the knowledge of principles is participated in the knowledge of the conclusions.

The reply to the third objection is evident from what has been said.

We proceed thus to the Seventh Article:—

Objection 1. It would seem that the act of the sensitive appetite is not commanded. For the Apostle says (*Rom.* vii. 15): *For I do not that good which I will:* and a gloss explains this by saying that man lusts, although he wills not to lust. But to lust is an act of the sensitive appetite. Therefore the act of the sensitive appetite is not subject to our command.

Obj. 2. Further, corporeal matter obeys God alone, to the effect of formal transmutation, as was shown in the First Part (Q. 65, A. 4; Q. 91, A. 2; Q. 110, A. 2). But the act of the sensitive appetite is accompanied by a formal transmutation of the body, consisting in heat or cold. Therefore the act of the sensitive appetite is not subject to man's command.

Obj. 3. Further, the proper motive principle of the sensitive appetite is something apprehended by sense or imagination. But it is not always in our power to apprehend something by sense or imagination. Therefore the act of the sensitive appetite is not subject to our command.

On the contrary, Gregory of Nyssa* says: *That which obeys reason is twofold, the concupiscible and the irascible,* which belong to the sensitive appetite. Therefore the act of the sensitive appetite is subject to the command of reason.

I answer that, An act is subject to our command, in so far as it is in our power, as stated above (A. 5). Consequently in order to understand in what manner the act of the sensitive appetite is subject to the command of reason, we must consider in what manner it is in our power. Now it must be observed that the sensitive appetite differs from the intellective appetite, which is called the will, in the fact that the sensitive appetite is a power of a corporeal organ, whereas the will is not. Again, every act of a power that uses a corporeal organ, depends not only on a power of the soul, but also on the disposition of that corporeal organ: thus the act of vision depends on the power of sight, and on the condition of the eye, which condition is a help or a hindrance to that act. Consequently the act of the sensi-

Nemesius, De Nat. Hom. xvi,

tive appetite depends not only on the appetitive power, but also on the disposition of the body.

Now whatever part the power of the soul takes in the act, follows apprehension. And the apprehension of the imagination, being a particular apprehension, is regulated by the apprehension of reason, which is universal; just as a particular active power is regulated by a universal active power. Consequently in this respect the act of the sensitive appetite is subject to the command of reason.—On the other hand, condition or disposition of the body is not subject to the command of reason: and consequently in this respect, the movement of the sensitive appetite is hindered from being wholly subject to the command of reason.

Moreover it happens sometimes that the movement of the sensitive appetite is aroused suddenly in consequence of an apprehension of the imagination of sense. And then such movement occurs without the command of reason: although reason could have prevented it, had it foreseen. Hence the Philosopher says (*Polit.* i. 2) that the reason governs the irascible and concupiscible not by a *despotic supremacy,* which is that of a master over his slave; but by a *politic and royal supremacy,* whereby the free are governed, who are not wholly subject to command.

Reply Obj. 1. That man lusts, although he wills not to lust, is due to a disposition of the body, whereby the sensitive appetite is hindered from perfect compliance with the command of reason. Hence the Apostle adds (*ibid.*): *I see another law in my members, fighting against the law of my mind.*—This may also happen through a sudden movement of concupiscence, as stated above.

Reply Obj. 2. The condition of the body stands in a twofold relation to the act of the sensitive appetite. First, as preceding it: thus a man may be disposed in one way or another, in respect of his body, to this or that passion. Secondly, as consequent to it: thus a man becomes heated through anger. Now the condition that precedes, is not subject to the command of reason: since it is due either to nature, or to some previous movement, which cannot cease at once. But the condition that is consequent, follows the command of reason: since it results from the local movement of the heart, which has various movements according to the various acts of the sensitive appetite.

Reply Obj. 3. Since the external sensible is necessary for the apprehension of the senses, it is not in our power to apprehend anything by the senses, unless the sensible be present; which presence of the sensible is not always in our power. For it is then that man can use his senses if he will so to do; unless there be some obstacle on the part of the organ.—On the other hand, the apprehension of the imagination is subject to the ordering of reason, in proportion to the strength or weakness of the imaginative power. For that man is unable to imagine the things that reason considers, is either because they cannot be imagined, such as incorporeal things; or because of the weakness of the imaginative power, due to some organic indisposition.

EIGHTH ARTICLE

Whether the Act of the Vegetal Soul Is Commanded?

We proceed thus to the Eighth Article:—

Objection 1. It would seem that the acts of the vegetal soul are subject to the command of reason. For the sensitive powers are of higher rank than the vegetal powers. But the powers of the sensitive soul are subject to the command of reason. Much more, therefore, are the powers of the vegetal soul.

Obj. 2. Further, man is called a *little world*,* because the soul is in the body, as God is in the world. But God is in the world in such a way, that everything in the world obeys His command. Therefore all that is in man, even the powers of the vegetal soul, obey the command of reason.

Obj. 3. Further, praise and blame are awarded only to such acts as are subject to the command of reason. But in the acts of the nutritive and generative power, there is room for praise and blame, virtue and vice: as in the case of gluttony and lust, and their contrary virtues. Therefore the acts of these powers are subject to the command of reason.

On the contrary, Gregory of Nyssa† says that *the nutritive and generative power is one over which the reason has no control.*

I answer that, Some acts proceed from the natural appetite, others from the animal, or from the intellectual appetite: for every agent desires an end in some way. Now the natural appetite does not follow from some apprehension, as to the animal and the intellectual appetite. But the reason commands by way of apprehensive power. Wherefore those acts that proceed from the intellective or the animal appetite, can be commanded by reason: but not those acts that proceed from the natural appetite. And such are the acts of the vegetal soul; wherefore Gregory of Nyssa (Nemesius, —*loc. cit.*) says that *generation and nutrition belong to what are called natural powers.* Consequently the acts of the vegetal soul are not subject to the command of reason.

Reply Obj. 1. The more immaterial an act is, the more noble it is, and the more is it subject to the command of reason. Hence the very fact that the acts of the vegetal soul do not obey reason, shows that they rank lowest.

Reply Obj. 2. The comparison holds in a certain respect: because, to wit, as God moves the world, so the soul moves the body. But it does not hold in every respect: for the soul did not create the body out of nothing, as God created the world; for which reason the world is wholly subject to His command.

Reply Obj. 3. Virtue and vice, praise and blame do not affect the acts themselves of the nutritive and generative power, *i.e.*, digestion, and formation of the human body; but they affect the acts of the sensitive part, that are ordained to the acts of generation and nutrition; for example the desire for pleasure in the act of taking food or in the act of generation, and the right or wrong use thereof.

NINTH ARTICLE

Whether the Acts of the External Members Are Commanded?

We proceed thus to the Ninth Article:—

Objection 1. It would seem that the members of the body do not obey reason as to their acts. For it is evident that the members of the body are more distant from the reason, than the powers of the vegetal soul. But the powers of the vegetal soul do not obey reason, as stated above (A. 8). Therefore much less do the members of the body obey.

Obj. 2. Further, the heart is the principle of animal movement. But the movement of the heart is not subject to the command of reason: for Gregory of Nyssa‡ says that *the pulse is not controlled by reason.* Therefore the movement of the bodily members is not subject to the command of reason.

Obj. 3. Further, Augustine says (*De Civ. Dei* xiv. 16) that *the movement of the genital members is sometimes inopportune and not desired; sometimes when sought it fails, and whereas the heart is warm with desire, the body remains cold.* Therefore the movements of the members are not obedient to reason.

On the contrary, Augustine says (*Conf.* viii. 9): *The mind commands a movement of the hand, and so ready is the hand to obey, that scarcely can one discern obedience from command.*

I answer that, The members of the body are organs of the soul's powers. Consequently according as the powers of the soul stand in re-

---

* Aristotle, *Phys.* viii. 2.   † Nemesius, *De Nat. Hom.* xxii.   ‡ Nemesius, *De Nat. Hom.* xxii.

spect of obedience to reason, so do the members of the body stand in respect thereof. Since then the sensitive powers are subject to the command of reason, whereas the natural powers are not; therefore all movements of members, that are moved by the sensitive powers, are subject to the command of reason; whereas those movements of members, that arise from the natural powers, are not subject to the command of reason.

Reply Obj. 1. The members do not move themselves, but are moved through the powers of the soul; of which powers, some are in closer contact with the reason than are the powers of the vegetal soul.

Reply Obj. 2. In things pertaining to intellect and will, that which is according to nature stands first, whence all other things are derived: thus from the knowledge of principles that are naturally known, is derived knowledge of the conclusions; and from volition of the end naturally desired, is derived the choice of the means. So also in bodily movements the principle is according to nature. Now the principle of bodily movements begins with the movement of the heart. Consequently the movement of the heart is according to nature, and not according to the will: for like a proper accident, it results from life, which follows from the union of soul and body. Thus the movement of heavy and light things results from their substantial form: for which reason they are said to be moved by their generator, as the Philosopher states (*Phys.* viii. 4). Wherefore this movement is called *vital.* For which reason Gregory of Nyssa (Nemesius,—*loc. cit.*) says that, just as the movement of generation and nutrition does not obey reason, so neither does the pulse which is a vital movement. By the pulse he means the movement of the heart which is indicated by the pulse veins.

Reply Obj. 3. As Augustine says (*De Civ. Dei* xiv. 17, 20) it is in punishment of sin that the movement of these members does not obey reason: in this sense, that the soul is punished for its rebellion against God, by the insubmission of that member whereby original sin is transmitted to posterity.

But because, as we shall state later on, the effect of the sin of our first parent was that his nature was left to itself, through the withdrawal of the supernatural gift which God had bestowed on man, we must consider the natural cause of this particular member's insubmission to reason. This is stated by Aristotle (*De Causis Mot. Animal.*) who says that *the movements of the heart and of the organs of generation are involuntary,* and that the reason of this is as follows. These members are stirred at the occasion of some apprehension; in so far as the intellect and imagination represent such things as arouse the passions of the soul, of which passions these movements are a consequence. But they are not moved at the command of the reason or intellect, because these movements are conditioned by a certain natural change of heat and cold, which change is not subject to the command of reason. This is the case with these two organs in particular, because each is as it were a separate animal being, in so far as it is a principle of life; and the principle is virtually the whole. For the heart is the principle of the senses; and from the organ of generation proceeds the seminal virtue, which is virtually the entire animal. Consequently they have their proper movements naturally: because principles must needs be natural, as stated above (*Reply Obj.* 2).

QUESTION 18

Of the Good and Evil of Human Acts, in General

(In Eleven Articles)

WE must now consider the good and evil of human acts. First, how a human act is good or evil; secondly, what results from the good or evil of a human act, as merit or demerit, sin and guilt.

Under the first head there will be a threefold consideration: the first will be of the good and evil of human acts, in general; the second, of the good and evil of internal acts; the third, of the good and evil of external acts.

Concerning the first there are eleven points of inquiry: (1) Whether every human action is good, or are there evil actions? (2) Whether the good or evil of a human action is derived from its object? (3) Whether it is derived from a circumstance? (4) Whether it is derived from the end? (5) Whether a human action is good or evil in its species? (6) Whether an action has the species of good or evil from its end? (7) Whether the species derived from the end is contained under the species derived from the object, as under its genus, or conversely? (8) Whether any action is indifferent in its species? (9) Whether an individual action can be indifferent? (10 Whether a circumstance places a moral action in the species of good or evil? (11) Whether every circumstance that makes an action better or worse, places the moral action in the species of good or evil?

FIRST ARTICLE

Whether Every Human Action Is Good, or Are There Evil Actions?

We proceed thus to the First Article:—

Objection 1. It would seem that every human action is good, and that none is evil. For Dionysius says (*Div. Nom.* iv.) that evil acts not, save in virtue of the good. But no evil is done in virtue of the good. Therefore no action is evil.

Obj. 2. Further, nothing acts except in so far as it is in act. Now a thing is evil, not according as it is in act, but according as its potentiality is void of act; whereas in so far as its potentiality is perfected by act, it is good, as stated in *Metaph.* ix. 9. Therefore nothing acts in so far as it is evil, but only according as it is good. Therefore every action is good, and none is evil.

Obj. 3. Further, evil cannot be a cause, save accidentally, as Dionysius declares (*Div. Nom.* iv). But every action has some effect which is proper to it. Therefore no action is evil, but every action is good.

On the contrary, Our Lord said (Jo. iii. 20): *Every one that doth evil, hateth the light.* Therefore some actions of man are evil.

I answer that, We must speak of good and evil in actions as of good and evil in things: because such as everything is, such is the act that it produces. Now in things, each one has so much good as it has being: since good and being are convertible, as was stated in the First Part (Q. 5, AA. 1, 3). But God alone has the whole plenitude of His Being in a certain unity: whereas every other thing has its proper fulness of being in a certain multiplicity. Wherefore it happens with some things, that they have being in some respect, and yet they are lacking in the fulness of being due to them. Thus the fulness of human being requires a compound of soul and body, having all the powers and instruments of knowledge and movement: wherefore if any man be lacking in any of these, he is lacking in something due to the fulness of his being. So that as much as he has of being, so much has he of goodness: while so far as he is lacking in the fulness of his being, so far is he lacking in goodness, and is said to be evil: thus a blind man is possessed of goodness inasmuch as he lives; and of evil, inasmuch as he lacks sight. That, however, which has nothing of being or goodness, could not be said to be either evil or good. But since this same fulness of being is of the very essence of good, if a thing be lacking in its due fulness of being, it is not said to be good simply, but in a certain respect, inasmuch as it is a being; although it can be called a being simply, and a non-being in a certain respect, as was stated in the First Part (Q. 5, A. 1 *ad* 1). We must therefore say that every action has goodness, in so far as it has being: whereas it is lacking in goodness, in so far as it is lacking in something that is due to its fulness of being; and thus it is said to be evil: for instance if it lacks the quantity determined by reason, or its due place, or something of the kind.

Reply Obj. 1. Evil acts in virtue of deficient goodness. For if there were nothing of good there, there would be neither being nor possibility of action. On the other hand if good were not deficient, there would be no evil. Consequently the action done is a deficient good, which is good in a certain respect, but simply evil.

Reply Obj. 2. Nothing hinders a thing from being in act in a certain respect, so that it can act; and in a certain respect deficient in act, so as to cause a deficient act. Thus a blind man has in act the power of walking, whereby he is able to walk; but inasmuch as he is deprived of sight he suffers a defect in walking by stumbling when he walks.

Reply Obj. 3. An evil action can have a proper effect, according to the goodness and being that it has. Thus adultery is the cause of human generation, inasmuch as it implies union of male and female, but not inasmuch as it lacks the order of reason.

SECOND ARTICLE

Whether the Good or Evil of a Man's Action Is Derived from Its Object?

We proceed thus to the Second Article:—

Objection 1. It would seem that the good or evil of an action is not derived from its object. For the object of any action is a thing. But *evil is not in things, but in the sinner's use of them,* as Augustine says (*De Doctr. Christ.* iii. 12). Therefore the good or evil of a human action is not derived from its object.

Obj. 2. Further, the object is compared to the action as its matter. But the goodness of a thing is not from its matter, but rather from the form, which is an act. Therefore good and evil in actions is not derived from their object.

Obj. 3. Further, the object of an active power is compared to the action as effect to cause. But the goodness of a cause does not depend on its effect; rather is it the reverse. Therefore good or evil in actions is not derived from their object.

On the contrary, It is written (Osee ix. 10): *They became abominable as those things which they loved.* Now man becomes abominable to God on account of the malice of his action. Therefore the malice of his action is according to the evil objects that man loves. And the same applies to the goodness of his action.

I answer that, as stated above (A. 1) the good or evil of an action, as of other things, depends on its fulness of being or its lack of that fulness. Now the first thing that belongs to the fulness of being seems to be that which gives a thing its species. And just as a natural thing has its species from its form, so an action has its species from its object, as movement from its term. And therefore, just as the primary goodness of a natural thing is derived from its form, which gives it its species, so the primary goodness of a moral action is derived from its suitable object: hence some call such an action *good in its genus;* for instance, *to make use of what is one's own.* And just as, in natural things, the primary evil is when a generated thing does not realize its specific form (for instance, if instead of a man, something else be generated); so the primary evil in moral actions is that which is from the object, for instance, *to take what belongs to another.* And this action is said to be *evil in its genus,* genus here standing for species, just as we apply the term *mankind* to the whole human species.

Reply Obj. 1. Although external things are good in themselves, nevertheless they have not always a due proportion to this or that action. And so, inasmuch as they are considered as objects of such actions, they have not the quality of goodness.

Reply Obj. 2. The object is not the matter *of which* (a thing is made), but the matter *about which* (something is done); and stands in relation to the act as its form, as it were, through giving it its species.

Reply Obj. 3. The object of the human action is not always the object of an active power. For the appetitive power is, in a way, passive; in so far as it is moved by the appetible object; and yet it is a principle of human actions.—Nor again have the objects of the active powers always the nature of an effect, but only when they are already transformed: thus food when transformed is the effect of the nutritive power; whereas food before being transformed stands in relation to the nutritive power as the matter about which it exercises its operation. Now since the object is in some way the effect of the active power, it follows that it is the term of its action, and consequently that it gives it its form and species, since movement derives its species from its terms.—Moreover, although the goodness of an action is not caused by the goodness of its effect, yet an action is said to be good from the

fact that it can produce a good effect. Consequently the very proportion of an action to its effect is the measure of its goodness.

THIRD ARTICLE

Whether Man's Action Is Good or Evil from a Circumstance?

We proceed thus to the Third Article:—

Objection 1. It would seem that an action is not good or evil from a circumstance. For circumstances stand around (*circumstant*) an action, as being outside it, as stated above (Q. 7, A. 1). But *good and evil are in things themselves,* as is stated in *Metaph.* vi. 4. Therefore an action does not derive goodness or malice from a circumstance.

Obj. 2. Further, the goodness or malice of an action is considered principally in the doctrine of morals. But since circumstances are accidents of actions, it seems that they are outside the scope of art: because *no art takes notice of what is accidental* (*Metaph.* vi. 2). Therefore the goodness or malice of an action is not taken from a circumstance.

Obj. 3. Further, that which belongs to a thing, in respect of its substance, is not ascribed to it in respect of an accident. But good and evil belong to an action in respect of its substance; because an action can be good or evil in its genus as stated above (A. 2). Therefore an action is not good or bad from a circumstance.

On the contrary, the Philosopher says (*Ethic.* ii. 3) that a virtuous man acts as he should, and when he should, and so on in respect of the other circumstances. Therefore, on the other hand, the vicious man, in the matter of each vice, acts when he should not, or where he should not, and so on with the other circumstances. Therefore human actions are good or evil according to circumstances.

I answer that, In natural things, it is to be noted that the whole fulness of perfection due to a thing, is not from the mere substantial form, that gives it its species; since a thing derives much from supervening accidents, as man does from shape, color, and the like; and if any one of these accidents be out of due proportion, evil is the result. So it is with action. For the plenitude of its goodness does not consist wholly in its species, but also in certain additions which accrue to it by reason of certain accidents: and such are its due circumstances. Wherefore if something be wanting that is requisite as a due circumstance the action will be evil.

Reply Obj. 1. Circumstances are outside an action, inasmuch as they are not part of its essence; but they are in an action as accidents thereof. Thus, too, accidents in natural substances are outside the essence.

Reply Obj. 2. Every accident is not accidentally in its subject; for some are proper accidents; and of these every art takes notice. And thus it is that the circumstances of actions are considered in the doctrine of morals.

Reply Obj. 3. Since good and being are convertible; according as being is predicated of substance and of accident, so is good predicated of a thing both in respect of its essential being, and in respect of its accidental being; and this, both in natural things and in moral actions.

FOURTH ARTICLE

Whether a Human Action Is Good or Evil from Its End?

We proceed thus to the Fourth Article:—

Objection 1. It would seem that the good and evil in human actions are not from the end. For Dionysius says (*Div. Nom.* iv) that *nothing acts with a view to evil.* If therefore an action were good or evil from its end, no action would be evil. Which is clearly false.

Obj. 2. Further, the goodness of an action is something in the action. But the end is an extrinsic cause. Therefore an action is not said to be good or bad according to its end.

Obj. 3. Further, a good action may happen to be ordained to an evil end, as when a man gives an alms from vainglory; and conversely, an evil action may happen to be ordained to a good end, as a theft committed in order to give something to the poor. Therefore an action is not good or evil from its end.

On the contrary, Boëthius says (*De Differ. Topic.* ii) that *if the end is good, the thing is good, and if the end be evil, the thing also is evil.*

I answer that, The disposition of things as to goodness is the same as their disposition as to being. Now in some things the being does not depend on another, and in these it suffices to consider their being absolutely. But there are things the being of which depends on something else, and hence in their regard we must consider their being in its relation to the cause on which it depends. Now just as the being of a thing depends on the agent and the form, so the goodness of a thing depends on its end. Hence in the Divine Persons, Whose goodness does not depend on another, the measure of goodness is not taken from the end. Whereas human actions, and other things, the goodness of which depends on something else, have a measure of goodness from the end on which they depend, besides that goodness which is in them absolutely.

Accordingly a fourfold goodness may be considered in a human action. First, that which, as an action, it derives from its genus; because as much as it has of action and being so much has it of goodness, as stated above (A. 1). Secondly, it has goodness according to its species; which is derived from its suitable object. Thirdly, it has goodness from its circumstances, in respect, as it were, of its accidents. Fourthly, it has goodness from its end, to which it is compared as to the cause of its goodness.

Reply Obj. 1. The good in view of which one acts is not always a true good; but sometimes it is a true good, sometimes an apparent good. And in the latter event, an evil action results from the end in view.

Reply Obj. 2. Although the end is an extrinsic cause, nevertheless due proportion to the end, and relation to the end, are inherent to the action.

Reply Obj. 3. Nothing hinders an action that is good in one of the ways mentioned above, from lacking goodness in another way. And thus it may happen that an action which is good in its species or in its circumstances, is ordained to an evil end, or vice versa. However, an action is not good simply, unless it is good in all those ways: since *evil results from any single defect, but good from the complete cause,* as Dionysius says (*Div. Nom.* iv).

FIFTH ARTICLE

Whether a Human Action Is Good or Evil in Its Species?

We proceed thus to the Fifth Article:—

Objection 1. It would seem that good and evil in moral actions do not make a difference of species. For the existence of good and evil in actions is in conformity with their existence in things, as stated above (A. 1). But good and evil do not make a specific difference in things; for a good man is specifically the same as a bad man. Therefore neither do they make a specific difference in actions.

Obj. 2. Further, since evil is a privation, it is a non-being. But non-being cannot be a difference, according to the Philosopher (*Metaph.* iii. 3). Since therefore the difference constitutes the species, it seems that an action is not constituted in a species through being evil. Consequently good and evil do not diversify the species of human actions.

Obj. 3. Further, acts that differ in species produce different effects. But the same specific effect results from a good and from an evil action: thus a man is born of adulterous or of lawful wedlock. Therefore good and evil actions do not differ in species.

Obj. 4. Further, actions are sometimes said

to be good or bad from a circumstance, as stated above (A. 3). But since a circumstance is an accident, it does not give an action its species. Therefore human actions do not differ in species on account of their goodness or malice.

On the contrary, According to the Philosopher (*Ethic* ii. 1) *like habits produce like actions.* But a good and a bad habit differ in species, as liberality and prodigality. Therefore also good and bad actions differ in species.

I answer that, Every action derives its species from its object, as stated above (A. 2). Hence it follows that a difference of object causes a difference of species in actions. Now, it must be observed that a difference of objects causes a difference of species in actions, according as the latter are referred to one active principle, which does not cause a difference in actions, according as they are referred to another active principle. Because nothing accidental constitutes a species, but only that which is essential; and a difference of object may be essential in reference to one active principle, and accidental in reference to another. Thus to know color and to know sound, differ essentially in reference to sense, but not in reference to the intellect.

Now in human actions, good and evil are predicated in reference to the reason; because as Dionysius says (*Div. Nom.* iv), *the good of man is to be in accordance with reason,* and evil is *to be against reason.* For that is good for a thing which suits it in regard to its form; and evil, that which is against the order of its form. It is therefore evident that the difference of good and evil considered in reference to the object is an essential difference in relation to reason; that is to say, according as the object is suitable or unsuitable to reason. Now certain actions are called human or moral, inasmuch as they proceed from the reason. Consequently it is evident that good and evil diversify the species in human actions; since essential differences cause a difference of species.

Reply Obj. 1. Even in natural things, good and evil, inasmuch as something is according to nature, and something against nature, diversify the natural species; for a dead body and a living body are not of the same species. In like manner, good, inasmuch as it is in accord with reason, and evil, inasmuch as it is against reason, diversify the moral species.

Reply Obj. 2. Evil implies privation, not absolute, but affecting some potentiality. For an action is said to be evil in its species, not because it has no object at all; but because it has an object in disaccord with reason, for instance, to appropriate another's property.

Wherefore in so far as the object is something positive, it can constitute the species of an evil act.

Reply Obj. 3. The conjugal act and adultery, as compared to reason, differ specifically and have effects specifically different; because the one deserves praise and reward, the other, blame and punishment. But as compared to the generative power, they do not differ in species; and thus they have one specific effect.

Reply Obj. 4. A circumstance is sometimes taken as the essential difference of the object, as compared to reason; and then it can specify a moral act. And it must needs be so whenever a circumstance transforms an action from good to evil; for a circumstance would not make an action evil, except through being repugnant to reason.

SIXTH ARTICLE

Whether an Action Has the Species of Good or Evil from Its End?

We proceed thus to the Sixth Article:—

Objection 1. It would seem that the good and evil which are from the end do not diversify the species of actions. For actions derive their species from the object. But the end is altogether apart from the object. Therefore the good and evil which are from the end do not diversify the species of an action.

Obj. 2. Further, that which is accidental does not constitute the species, as stated above (A. 5). But it is accidental to an action to be ordained to some particular end; for instance, to give alms from vainglory. Therefore actions are not diversified as to species, according to the good and evil which are from the end.

Obj. 3. Further, acts that differ in species, can be ordained to the same end: thus to the end of vainglory, actions of various virtues and vices can be ordained. Therefore the good and evil which are taken from the end, do not diversify the species of action.

On the contrary, It has been shown above (Q. 1, A. 3) that human actions derive their species from the end. Therefore good and evil in respect of the end diversify the species of actions.

I answer that, Certain actions are called human, inasmuch as they are voluntary, as stated above (Q. 1, A. 1). Now, in a voluntary action, there is a twofold action, viz., the interior action of the will, and the external action: and each of these actions has its object. The end is properly the object of the interior act of the will: while the object of the external action, is that on which the action is brought to bear. Therefore just as the external action takes its species from the object on which it bears: so the interior act of the will takes its species from the end, as from its own proper object.

Now that which is on the part of the will is formal in regard to that which is on the part of the external action: because the will uses the limbs to act as instruments; nor have external actions any measure of morality, save in so far as they are voluntary. Consequently the species of a human act is considered formally with regard to the end, but materially with regard to the object of the external action. Hence the Philosopher says (*Ethic.* v. 2) that *he who steals that he may commit adultery, is, strictly speaking, more adulterer than thief.*

Reply Obj. 1. The end also has the character of an object, as stated above.

Reply Obj. 2. Although it is accidental to the external action to be ordained to some particular end, it is not accidental to the interior act of the will, which act is compared to the external act, as form to matter.

Reply Obj. 3. When many actions, differing in species, are ordained to the same end, there is indeed a diversity of species on the part of the external actions; but unity of species on the part of the internal action.

SEVENTH ARTICLE

Whether the Species Derived from the End Is Contained under the Species Derived from the Object, As under Its Genus, or Conversely?

We proceed thus to the Seventh Article:—

Objection 1. It would seem that the species of goodness derived from the end is contained under the species of goodness derived from the object, as a species is contained under its genus; for instance, when a man commits a theft in order to give an alms. For an action takes its species from its object, as stated above (AA. 2, 6). But it is impossible for a thing to be contained under another species, if this species be not contained under the proper species of that thing; because the same thing cannot be contained in different species that are not subordinate to one another. Therefore the species which is taken from the end, is contained under the species which is taken from the object.

Obj. 2. Further, the last difference always constitutes the most specific species. But the difference derived from the end seems to come after the difference derived from the object: because the end is something last. Therefore the species derived from the end, is contained under the species derived from the object, as its most specific species.

Obj. 3. Further, the more formal a difference is, the more specific it is: because difference is compared to genus, as form to matter. But the species derived from the end, is more formal than that which is derived from the object, as stated above (A. 6). Therefore the species derived from the end is contained under the species derived from the object, as the most specific species is contained under the subaltern genus.

On the contrary, Each genus has its determinate differences. But an action of one same species on the part of its object, can be ordained to an infinite number of ends: for instance, theft can be ordained to an infinite number of good and bad ends. Therefore the species derived from the end is not contained under the species derived from the object, as under its genus.

I answer that, The object of the external act can stand in a twofold relation to the end of the will: first, as being of itself ordained thereto; thus to fight well is of itself ordained to victory; secondly, as being ordained thereto accidentally; thus to take what belongs to another is ordained accidentally to the giving of alms. Now the differences that divide a genus, and constitute the species of that genus, must, as the Philosopher says (*Metaph.* vii. 12), divide that genus essentially: and if they divide it accidentally, the division is incorrect: as, if one were to say: *Animals are divided into rational and irrational; and the irrational into animals with wings, and animals without wings;* for *winged* and *wingless* are not essential determinations of the irrational being. But the following division would be correct: *Some animals have feet, some have no feet: and of those that have feet, some have two feet, some four, some many:* because the latter division is an essential determination of the former. Accordingly when the object is not of itself ordained to the end, the specific difference derived from the object is not an essential determination of the species derived from the end, nor is the reverse the case. Wherefore one of these species is not under the other; but then the moral action is contained under two species that are disparate, as it were. Consequently we say that he that commits theft for the sake of adultery, is guilty of a twofold malice in one action.—On the other hand, if the object be of itself ordained to the end, one of these differences is an essential determination of the other. Wherefore one of these species will be contained under the other.

It remains to be considered which of the two is contained under the other. In order to make this clear, we must first of all observe that the more particular the form is from which a difference is taken, the more specific is the difference. Secondly, that the more universal an agent is, the more universal a form does it cause. Thirdly, that the more remote an end is, the more universal the agent to which it corresponds; thus victory, which is the last end of the army, is the end intended by the commander in chief; while the right ordering of this or that regiment is the end intended by one of the lower officers. From all this it follows that the specific difference derived from the end, is more general; and that the difference derived from an object which of itself is ordained to that end, is a specific difference in relation to the former. For the will, the proper object of which is the end, is the universal mover in respect of all the powers of the soul, the proper objects of which are the objects of their particular acts.

Reply Obj. 1. One and the same thing, considered in its substance, cannot be in two species, one of which is not subordinate to the other. But in respect of those things which are superadded to the substance, one thing can be contained under different species. Thus one and the same fruit, as to its color, is contained under one species, *i.e.*, a white thing: and, as to its perfume, under the species of sweet-smelling things. In like manner an action which, as to its substance, is in one natural species, considered in respect to the moral conditions that are added to it, can belong to two species, as stated above (Q. 1, A. 3 *ad* 3).

Reply Obj. 2. The end is last in execution; but first in the intention of the reason, in regard to which moral actions receive their species.

Reply Obj. 3. Difference is compared to genus as form to matter, inasmuch as it actualizes the genus. On the other hand, the genus is considered as more formal than the species, inasmuch as it is something more absolute and less contracted. Wherefore also the parts of a definition are reduced to the genus of formal cause, as is stated in *Phys.* ii. 3. And in this sense the genus is the formal cause of the species; and so much the more formal, as it is more universal.

EIGHTH ARTICLE

Whether Any Action Is Indifferent in Its Species?

We proceed thus to the Eighth Article:—

Objection 1. It would seem that no action is indifferent in its species. For evil is the privation of good, according to Augustine (*Enchirid.* xi). But privation and habit are immediate contraries, according to the Philosopher (*Categor.* viii). Therefore there is no such thing as an action that is indifferent in its species, as though it were between good and evil.

Obj. 2. Further, human actions derive their species from their end or object, as stated above (A. 6; Q. 1, A. 3). But every end and every object is either good or bad. Therefore every human action is good or evil according to its species. None, therefore, is indifferent in its species.

Obj. 3. Further, as stated above (A. 1), an action is said to be good, when it has its due complement of goodness; and evil, when it lacks that complement. But every action must needs either have the entire plenitude of its goodness, or lack it in some respect. Therefore every action must needs be either good or bad in its species, and none is indifferent.

On the contrary, Augustine says (*De Serm. Dom. in Mont.* ii. 18), that *there are certain deeds of a middle kind, which can be done with a good or evil mind, of which it is rash to form a judgment.* Therefore some actions are indifferent according to their species.

I answer that, As stated above (AA. 2, 5), every action takes its species from its object; while human action, which is called moral, takes its species from the object, in relation to the principle of human actions, which is the reason. Wherefore if the object of an action includes something in accord with the order of reason, it will be a good action according to its species; for instance, to give alms to a person in want. On the other hand, if it includes something repugnant to the order of reason, it will be an evil act according to its species; for instance, to steal, which is to appropriate what belongs to another. But it may happen that the object of an action does not include something pertaining to the order of reason; for instance, to pick up a straw from the ground, to walk in the fields, and the like: and such actions are indifferent according to their species.

Reply Obj. 1. Privation is twofold. One is privation *as a result* (*privatum esse*), and this leaves nothing, but takes all away: thus blindness takes away sight altogether; darkness, light; and death, life. Between this privation and the contrary habit, there can be no medium in respect of the proper subject.—The other is privation *in process* (*privari*): thus sickness is privation of health; not that it takes health away altogether, but that it is a kind of road to the entire loss of health, occasioned by death. And since this sort of privation leaves something, it is not always the immediate contrary of the opposite habit. In this way evil is a privation of good, as Simplicius says in his commentary on the Categories: because it does not take away all good, but leaves some. Consequently there can be something between good and evil.

Reply Obj. 2. Every object or end has some goodness or malice, at least natural to it: but this does not imply moral goodness or malice, which is considered in relation to the reason, as stated above. And it is of this that we are here treating.

Reply Obj. 3. Not everything belonging to an action belongs also to its species. Wherefore although an action's specific nature may not contain all that belongs to the full complement of its goodness, it is not therefore an action specifically bad; nor is it specifically good. Thus a man in regard to his species is neither virtuous nor wicked.

NINTH ARTICLE

Whether an Individual Action Can Be Indifferent?

We proceed thus to the Ninth Article:—

Objection 1. It seems that an individual action can be indifferent. For there is no species that does not, or cannot, contain an individual. But an action can be indifferent in its species, as stated above (A. 8). Therefore an individual action can be indifferent.

Obj. 2. Further, individual actions cause like habits, as stated in *Ethic.* ii. 1. But a habit can be indifferent: for the Philosopher says (*Ethic.* iv. 1) that those who are of an even temper and prodigal disposition are not evil; and yet it is evident that they are not good, since they depart from virtue; and thus they are indifferent in respect of a habit. Therefore some individual actions are indifferent.

Obj. 3. Further, moral good belongs to virtue, while moral evil belongs to vice. But it happens sometimes that a man fails to ordain a specifically indifferent action to a vicious or virtuous end. Therefore an individual action may happen to be indifferent.

On the contrary, Gregory says in a homily (vi. *in Evang.*): *An idle word is one that lacks either the usefulness of rectitude or the motive of just necessity or pious utility,* while an idle word is an evil, because *men . . . shall render an account of it in the day of judgment* (Matth. xii. 36):—while if it does not lack the motive of just necessity or pious utility, it is good. Therefore every word is either good or bad. For the same reason every other action is either good or bad. Therefore no individual action is indifferent.

I answer that, It sometimes happens that an action is indifferent in its species, but considered in the individual it is good or evil. And the reason of this is because a moral action, as stated above (A. 3), derives its goodness not only from its object, whence it takes its species; but also from the circumstances, which are its accidents, as it were; just as something belongs to a man by reason of his individual accidents, which does not belong to him by reason of his species. And every individual action must needs have some circumstance that makes it good or bad, at least in respect of the intention of the end. For since it belongs to the reason to direct; if an action that proceeds from deliberate reason be not directed to the due end, it is, by that fact alone, repugnant to reason, and has the character of evil. But if it be directed to a due end, it is in accord with reason; wherefore it has the character of good. Now it must needs be either directed or not directed to a due end. Consequently every human action that proceeds from deliberate reason, if it be considered in the individual, must be good or bad.

If, however, it does not proceed from deliberate reason, but from some act of the imagination, as when a man strokes his beard, or moves his hand or foot; such an action, properly speaking, is not moral or human; since this depends on the reason. Hence it will be indifferent, as standing apart from the genus of moral actions.

Reply Obj. 1. For an action to be indifferent in its species can be understood in several ways. First in such a way that its species demands that it remain indifferent; and the objection proceeds on this line. But no action can be specifically indifferent thus: since no object of human action is such that it cannot be directed to good or evil, either through its end or through a circumstance.—Secondly, specific indifference of an action may be due to the fact that as far as its species is concerned, it is neither good nor bad. Wherefore it can be made good or bad by something else. Thus man, as far as his species is concerned, is neither white nor black; nor is it a condition of his species that he should not be black or white; but blackness or whiteness is superadded to man by other principles than those of his species.

Reply Obj. 3. The Philosopher states that a man is evil, properly speaking, if he be hurtful to others. And accordingly he says that the prodigal is not evil, because he hurts none save himself. And the same applies to all others who are not hurtful to other men. But we say here that evil, in general, is all that is repugnant to right reason. And in this sense every individual action is either good or bad, as stated above.

Reply Obj. 3. Whenever an end is intended by deliberate reason, it belongs either to the good of some virtue, or to the evil of some vice. Thus, if a man's action is directed to the support or repose of his body, it is also directed to the good of virtue, provided he direct his body itself to the good of virtue. The same clearly applies to other actions.

TENTH ARTICLE

Whether a Circumstance Places a Moral Action in the Species of Good or Evil?

We proceed thus to the Tenth Article:—

Objection 1. It would seem that a circumstance cannot place a moral action in the species of good or evil. For the species of an action is taken from its object. But circumstances differ from the object. Therefore circumstances do not give an action its species.

Obj. 2. Further, circumstances are as accidents in relation to the moral action, as stated above (Q. 7, A. 1). But an accident does not constitute the species. Therefore a circumstance does not constitute a species of good or evil.

Obj. 3. Further, one thing is not in several species. But one action has several circumstances. Therefore a circumstance does not place a moral action in a species of good or evil.

On the contrary, Place is a circumstance. But place makes a moral action to be in a certain species of evil; for theft of a thing from a holy place is a sacrilege. Therefore a circumstance makes a moral action to be specifically good or bad.

I answer that, Just as the species of natural things are constituted by their natural forms, so the species of moral actions are constituted by forms as conceived by the reason, as is evident from what was said above (A. 5). But since nature is determinate to one thing, nor can a process of nature go on to infinity, there must needs be some ultimate form, giving a specific difference, after which no further specific difference is possible. Hence it is that in natural things, that which is accidental to a thing, cannot be taken as a difference constituting the species. But the process of reason is not fixed to one particular term, for at any point it can still proceed further. And consequently that which, in one action, is taken as a circumstance added to the object that specifies the action, can again be taken by the directing reason, as the principal condition of the object that determines the action's species. Thus to appropriate another's property is specified by reason of the property being *another's*, and in this respect it is placed in the species of theft; and if we consider that action also in its bearing on place or time, then this will be an additional circumstance. But since the reason can direct as to place, time, and the like, it may happen that the condition as to place, in relation to the object, is considered as being in disaccord with reason: for instance, reason forbids damage to be done to a holy place. Consequently to steal from a

holy place has an additional repugnance to the order of reason. And thus place, which was first of all considered as a circumstance, is considered here as the principal condition of the object, and as itself repugnant to reason. And in this way, whenever a circumstance has a special relation to reason, either for or against, it must needs specify the moral action whether good or bad.

Reply Obj. 1. A circumstance, in so far as it specifies an action, is considered as a condition of the object, as stated above, and as being, as it were, a specific difference thereof.

Reply Obj. 2. A circumstance, so long as it is but a circumstance, does not specify an action, since thus it is a mere accident: but when it becomes a principal condition of the object, then it does specify the action.

Reply Obj. 3. It is not every circumstance that places the moral action in the species of good or evil; since not every circumstance implies accord or disaccord with reason. Consequently, although one action may have many circumstances, it does not follow that it is in many species. Nevertheless there is no reason why one action should not be in several, even disparate, moral species, as said above (A. 7 *ad* 1; Q. 1, A. 3 *ad* 3).

ELEVENTH ARTICLE

Whether Every Circumstance That Makes an Action Better or Worse, Places a Moral Action in a Species of Good or Evil?

We proceed thus to the Eleventh Article:—

Objection 1. It would seem that every circumstance relating to good or evil, specifies an action. For good and evil are specific differences of moral actions. Therefore that which causes a difference in the goodness or malice of a moral action, causes a specific difference, which is the same as to make it differ in species. Now that which makes an action better or worse, makes it differ in goodness and malice. Therefore it causes it to differ in species. Therefore every circumstance that makes an action better or worse, constitutes a species.

Obj. 2. Further, an additional circumstance either has in itself the character of goodness or malice, or it has not. If not, it cannot make the action better or worse; because what is not good, cannot make a greater good; and what is not evil, cannot make a greater evil. But if it has in itself the character of good or evil, for this very reason it has a certain species of good or evil. Therefore every circumstance that makes an action better or worse, constitutes a new species of good or evil.

Obj. 3. Further, according to Dionysius

(*Div. Nom.* iv), *evil is caused by each single defect.* Now every circumstance that increases malice, has a special defect. Therefore every such circumstance adds a new species of sin. And for the same reason, every circumstance that increases goodness, seems to add a new species of goodness: just as every unity added to a number makes a new species of number; since the good consists in *number, weight, and measure* (P. I, Q. 5, A. 5).

On the contrary, More and less do not change a species. But more and less is a circumstance of additional goodness or malice. Therefore not every circumstance that makes a moral action better or worse, places it in a species of good or evil.

I answer that, As stated above (A. 10), a circumstance gives the species of good or evil to a moral action, in so far as it regards a special order of reason. Now it happens sometimes that a circumstance does not regard a special order of reason in respect of good or evil, except on the supposition of another previous circumstance, from which the moral action takes its species of good or evil. Thus to take something in a large or small quantity, does not regard the order of reason in respect of good or evil, except a certain other condition be presupposed, from which the action takes its malice or goodness; for instance, if what is taken belongs to another, which makes the action to be discordant with reason.

Wherefore to take what belongs to another in a large or small quantity, does not change the species of the sin. Nevertheless it can aggravate or diminish the sin. The same applies to other evil or good actions. Consequently not every circumstance that makes a moral action better or worse, changes its species.

Reply Obj. 1. In things which can be more or less intense, the difference of more or less does not change the species: thus by differing in whiteness through being more or less white a thing is not changed in regard to its species of color. In like manner that which makes an action to be more or less good or evil, does not make the action differ in species.

Reply Obj. 2. A circumstance that aggravates a sin, or adds to the goodness of an action, sometimes has no goodness or malice in itself, but in regard to some other condition of the action, as stated above. Consequently it does not add a new species, but adds to the goodness or malice derived from this other condition of the action.

Reply Obj. 3. A circumstance does not always involve a distinct defect of its own; sometimes it causes a defect in reference to something else. In like manner a circumstance does not always add further perfection, except in reference to something else. And, for as much as it does, although it may add to the goodness or malice, it does not always change the species of good or evil.

QUESTION 19

Of the Goodness and Malice of the Interior Act of the Will

(In Ten Articles)

WE must now consider the goodness of the interior act of the will; under which head there are ten points of inquiry: (1) Whether the goodness of the will depends on the subject? (2) Whether it depends on the object alone? (3) Whether it depends on reason? (4) Whether it depends on the eternal law? (5) Whether erring reason binds? (6) Whether the will is evil if it follows the erring reason against the law of God? (7) Whether the goodness of the will in regard to the means, depends on the intention of the end? (8) Whether the degree of goodness or malice in the will depends on the degree of good or evil in the intention? (9) Whether the goodness of the will depends on its conformity to the Divine Will? (10) Whether it is necessary for the human will, in order to be good, to be conformed to the Divine Will, as regards the thing willed?

FIRST ARTICLE

Whether the Goodness of the Will Depends on the Object?

We proceed thus to the First Article:—

Objection 1. It would seem that the goodness of the will does not depend on the object. For the will cannot be directed otherwise than to what is good: since *evil is outside the scope of the will,* as Dionysius says (*Div. Nom.* iv). If therefore the goodness of the will depended on the object, it would follow that every act of the will is good, and none bad.

Obj. 2. Further, good is first of all in the end: wherefore the goodness of the end, as such, does not depend on any other, according to the Philosopher (*Ethic.* vi. 5), *goodness of action is the end, but goodness of making is never the end:* because the latter is always ordained to the thing made, as to its end. Therefore the goodness of the act of the will does not depend on any object.

Obj. 3. Further, such as a thing is, such does it make a thing to be. But the object of the will is good, by reason of the goodness of nature. Therefore it cannot give moral goodness to the will. Therefore the moral goodness of the will does not depend on the object.

On the contrary, the Philosopher says (*Ethic.* v. 1) that justice is that habit *from which men wish for just things*: and accordingly, virtue is a habit from which men wish for good things. But a good will is one which is in accordance with virtue. Therefore the goodness of the will is from the fact that a man wills that which is good.

I answer that, Good and evil are essential differences of the act of the will. Because good and evil of themselves regard the will; just as truth and falsehood regard reason; the act of which is divided essentially by the difference of truth and falsehood, for as much as an opinion is said to be true or false. Consequently good and evil will are acts differing in species. Now the specific difference in acts is according to objects, as stated above (Q. 18, A. 5). Therefore good and evil in the acts of the will is derived properly from the objects.

Reply Obj. 1. The will is not always directed to what is truly good, but sometimes to the apparent good; which has indeed some measure of good, but not of a good that is simply suitable to be desired. Hence it is that the act of the will is not always good, but sometimes evil.

Reply Obj. 2. Although an action can, in a certain way, be man's last end; nevertheless such action is not an act of the will, as stated above (Q. 1, A. 1 *ad 2*).

Reply Obj. 3. Good is presented to the will as its object by the reason: and in so far as it is in accord with reason, it enters the moral order, and causes moral goodness in the act of the will: because the reason is the principle of human and moral acts, as stated above (Q. 18, A. 5).

SECOND ARTICLE

Whether the Goodness of the Will Depends on the Object Alone?

We proceed thus to the Second Article:—

Objection 1. It would seem that the goodness of the will does not depend on the object alone. For the end has a closer relationship to the will than to any other power. But the acts of the other powers derive goodness not only from the object but also from the end, as we have shown above (Q. 18, A. 4). Therefore the act also of the will derives goodness not only from the object but also from the end.

Obj. 2. Further, the goodness of an action is derived not only from the object but also from the circumstances, as stated above (Q. 18, A. 3). But according to the diversity of circumstances there may be diversity of goodness and malice in the act of the will: for instance, if a man will, when he ought, where he ought, as much as he ought, and how he ought, or if he will as he ought not. Therefore the goodness of the will depends not only on the object, but also on the circumstances.

Obj. 3. Further, ignorance of circumstances excuses malice of the will, as stated above (Q. 6, A. 8). But it would not be so, unless the goodness or malice of the will depended on the circumstances. Therefore the goodness and malice of the will depend on the circumstances, and not only on the object.

On the contrary, An action does not take its species from the circumstances as such, as stated above (Q. 18, A. 10 *ad 2*). But good and evil are specific differences of the act of the will, as stated above (A. 1). Therefore the goodness and malice of the will depend, not on the circumstances, but on the object alone.

I answer that, In every genus, the more a thing is first, the more simple it is, and the fewer the principles of which it consists: thus primary bodies are simple. Hence it is to be observed that the first things in every genus, are, in some way, simple and consist of one principle. Now the principle of the goodness and malice of human actions is taken from the act of the will. Consequently the goodness and malice of the act of the will depend on some one thing; while the goodness and malice of other acts may depend on several things.

Now that one thing which is the principle in each genus, is not something accidental to that genus, but something essential thereto: because whatever is accidental is reduced to something essential, as to its principle. Therefore the goodness of the will's act depends on that one thing alone, which of itself causes goodness in the act; and that one thing is the object, and not the circumstances, which are accidents, as it were, of the act.

Reply Obj. 1. The end is the object of the will, but not of the other powers. Hence, in regard to the act of the will, the goodness derived from the object, does not differ from that which is derived from the end, as they differ in the acts of the other powers; except perhaps accidentally, in so far as one end depends on another, and one act of the will on another.

Reply Obj. 2. Given that the act of the will is fixed on some good, no circumstance can make that act bad. Consequently when it is said that a man wills a good when he ought not, or where he ought not, this can be understood in two ways. First, so that this circumstance is referred to the thing willed. And thus the act of the will is not fixed on something good: since to will to do something when it ought not to be done, is not to will something good. Secondly, so that the circumstance is referred to the act of willing. And thus, it is impossible to will something good when one ought not to, because one ought always to will what is good: except, perhaps, accidentally, in so far as a man by willing some particular good, is prevented from willing at the same time another good which he ought to will at that time. And then evil results, not from his willing that particular good, but from his not willing the other. The same applies to the other circumstances.

Reply Obj. 3. Ignorance of circumstances excuses malice of the will, in so far as the circumstance affects the thing willed: that is to say, in so far as a man ignores the circumstances of the act which he wills.

THIRD ARTICLE

Whether the Goodness of the Will Depends on Reason?

We proceed thus to the Third Article:—

Objection 1. It would seem that the goodness of the will does not depend on reason. For what comes first does not depend on what follows. But the good belongs to the will before it belongs to reason, as is clear from what has been said above (Q. 9, A. 1). Therefore the goodness of the will does not depend on reason.

Obj. 2. Further, the Philosopher says (*Ethic.* vi. 2) that the goodness of the practical intellect is *a truth that is in conformity with right desire*. But right desire is a good will. Therefore the goodness of the practical reason depends on the goodness of the will, rather than conversely.

Obj. 3. Further, the mover does not depend on that which is moved, but vice versa. But the will moves the reason and the other powers, as stated above (Q. 9, A. 1). Therefore the goodness of the will does not depend on reason.

On the contrary, Hilary says (*De Trin.* x): *It is an unruly will that persists in its desires in opposition to reason.* But the goodness of the will consists in not being unruly. Therefore the goodness of the will depends on its being subject to reason.

I answer that, As stated above (AA. 1, 2), the goodness of the will depends properly on the object. Now the will's object is proposed to it by reason. Because the good understood is the proportionate object of the will; while sensitive or imaginary good is proportionate not to the will but to the sensitive appetite: since the will can tend to the universal good, which reason apprehends; whereas the sensitive appetite tends only to the particular good, apprehended by the sensitive power. Therefore the goodness of the will depends on reason, in the same way as it depends on the object.

Reply Obj. 1. The good considered as such, *i.e.*, as appetible, pertains to the will before pertaining to the reason. But considered as true it pertains to the reason, before, under the aspect of goodness, pertaining to the will: because the will cannot desire a good that is not previously apprehended by reason.

Reply Obj. 2. The Philosopher speaks there of the practical intellect, in so far as it counsels and reasons about the means: for in this respect it is perfected by prudence. Now in regard to the means, the rectitude of the reason depends on its conformity with the desire of a due end: nevertheless the very desire of the due end presupposes on the part of reason a right apprehension of the end.

Reply Obj. 3. The will moves the reason in one way: the reason moves the will in another, viz., on the part of the object, as stated above (Q. 9, A. 1).

FOURTH ARTICLE

Whether the Goodness of the Will Depends on the Eternal Law?

We proceed thus to the Fourth Article:—

Objection 1. It would seem that the goodness of the human will does not depend on the eternal law. Because to one thing there is one rule and one measure. But the rule of the human will, on which its goodness depends, is right reason. Therefore the goodness of the will does not depend on the eternal law.

Obj. 2. Further, *a measure is homogeneous with the thing measured* (*Metaph.* x. 1). But the eternal law is not homogeneous with the human will. Therefore the eternal law cannot be the measure on which the goodness of the human will depends.

Obj. 3. Further, a measure should be most certain. But the eternal law is unknown to us. Therefore it cannot be the measure on which the goodness of our will depends.

On the contrary, Augustine says (*Contra Faust.* xxii. 27) that *sin is a deed, word or desire against the eternal law.* But malice of the will is the root of sin. Therefore, since malice is contrary to goodness, the goodness of the will depends on the eternal law.

I answer that, Wherever a number of causes are subordinate to one another, the effect depends more on the first than on the second cause: since the second cause acts only in virtue of the first. Now it is from the eternal law, which is the Divine Reason, that human reason is the rule of the human will, from which the human will derives its goodness. Hence it is written (Ps. iv. 6, 7): *Many say: Who showeth us good things? The light of Thy countenance, O Lord, is signed upon us:* as though to say: "The light of our reason is able to show us good things, and guide our will, in so far as it is the light of (*i.e.,* derived from) Thy countenance." It is therefore evident that the goodness of the human will depends on the eternal law much more than on human reason: and when human reason fails we must have recourse to the Eternal Reason.

Reply Obj. 1. To one thing there are not several proximate measures; but there can be several measures if one is subordinate to the other.

Reply Obj. 2. A proximate measure is homogeneous with the thing measured; a remote measure is not.

Reply Obj. 3. Although the eternal law is unknown to us according as it is in the Divine Mind: nevertheless, it becomes known to us somewhat, either by natural reason which is derived therefrom as its proper image; or by some sort of additional revelation.

FIFTH ARTICLE

Whether the Will Is Evil When It Is at Variance with Erring Reason?

We proceed thus to the Fifth Article:—

Objection 1. It would seem that the will is not evil when it is at variance with erring reason. Because the reason is the rule of the human will, in so far as it is derived from the eternal law, as stated above (A. 4). But erring reason is not derived from the eternal law. Therefore erring reason is not the rule of the human will. Therefore the will is not evil, if it be at variance with erring reason.

Obj. 2. Further, according to Augustine, the command of a lower authority does not bind if it be contrary to the command of a higher authority: for instance, if a provincial governor command something that is forbidden by the emperor. But erring reason sometimes proposes what is against the command of a higher power, namely, God Whose power is supreme. Therefore the decision of an erring reason does not bind. Consequently the will is not evil if it be at variance with erring reason.

Obj. 3. Further, every evil will is reducible to some species of malice. But the will that is at variance with erring reason is not reducible to some species of malice. For instance, if a man's reason err in telling him to commit fornication, his will in not willing to do so, can-

not be reduced to any species of malice. Therefore the will is not evil when it is at variance with erring reason.

On the contrary, As stated in the First Part (Q. 79, A. 13), conscience is nothing else than the application of knowledge to some action. Now knowledge is in the reason. Therefore when the will is at variance with erring reason, it is against conscience. But every such will is evil; for it is written (Rom. xiv. 23): *All that is not of faith—i.e.,* all that is against conscience—*is sin.* Therefore the will is evil when it is at variance with erring reason.

I answer that, Since conscience is a kind of dictate of the reason (for it is an application of knowledge to action, as was stated in the First Part, Q. 19, A. 13), to inquire whether the will is evil when it is at variance with erring reason, is the same as to inquire *whether an erring conscience binds.* On this matter, some distinguished three kinds of actions: for some are good generically; some are indifferent; some are evil generically. And they say that if reason or conscience tell us to do something which is good generically, there is no error: and in like manner if it tell us not to do something which is evil generically; since it is the same reason that prescribes what is good and forbids what is evil. On the other hand if a man's reason or conscience tells him that he is bound by precept to do what is evil in itself; or that what is good in itself, is forbidden, then his reason or conscience errs. In like manner if a man's reason or conscience tell him, that what is indifferent in itself, for instance to raise a straw from the ground, is forbidden or commanded, his reason or conscience errs. They say, therefore, that reason or conscience when erring in matters of indifference, either by commanding or by forbidding them, binds: so that the will which is at variance with that erring reason is evil and sinful. But they say that when reason or conscience errs in commanding what is evil in itself, or in forbidding what is good in itself and necessary for salvation, it does not bind; wherefore in such cases the will which is at variance with erring reason or conscience is not evil.

But this is unreasonable. For in matters of indifference, the will that is at variance with erring reason or conscience, is evil in some way on account of the object, on which the goodness or malice of the will depends; not indeed on account of the object according as it is in its own nature; but according as it is accidentally apprehended by reason as something evil to do or to avoid. And since the object of the will is that which is proposed by the reason, as stated above (A. 3), from the very fact that a thing is proposed by the reason as being evil, the will by tending thereto becomes evil. And this is the case not only in indifferent matters, but also in those that are good or evil in themselves. For not only indifferent matters can receive the character of goodness or malice accidentally; but also that which is good, can receive the character of evil, or that which is evil, can receive the character of goodness, on account of the reason apprehending it as such. For instance, to refrain from fornication is good: yet the will does not tend to this good except in so far as it is proposed by the reason. If, therefore, the erring reason propose it as an evil, the will tends to it as to something evil. Consequently the will is evil, because it wills evil, not indeed that which is evil in itself, but that which is evil accidentally, through being apprehended as such by the reason. In like manner, to believe in Christ is good in itself, and necessary for salvation: but the will does not tend thereto, except inasmuch as it is proposed by the reason. Consequently if it be proposed by the reason as something evil, the will tends to it as to something evil: not as if it were evil in itself, but because it is evil accidentally, through the apprehension of the reason. Hence the Philosopher says (*Ethic.* vii. 9) that *properly speaking the incontinent man is one who does not follow right reason; but accidentally, he is also one who does not follow false reason.* We must therefore conclude that, absolutely speaking, every will at variance with reason, whether right or erring, is always evil.

Reply Obj. 1. Although the judgment of an erring reason is not derived from God, yet the erring reason puts forward its judgment as being true, and consequently as being derived from God, from Whom is all truth.

Reply Obj. 2. The saying of Augustine holds good when it is known that the inferior authority prescribes something contrary to the command of the higher authority. But if a man were to believe the command of the proconsul to be the command of the emperor, in scorning the command of the proconsul he would scorn the command of the emperor. In like manner if a man were to know that human reason was dictating something contrary to God's commandment, he would not be bound to abide by reason: but then reason would not be entirely erroneous. But when erring reason proposes something as being commanded by God, then to scorn the dictate of reason is to scorn the commandment of God.

Reply Obj. 3. Whenever reason apprehends something as evil, it apprehends it under some species of evil; for instance, as being something contrary to a divine precept, or as giving scandal, or for some such like reason. And

then that evil is reduced to that species of malice.

Whether the Will Is Good When It Abides by Erring Reason?

We proceed thus to the Sixth Article:—

Objection 1. It would seem that the will is good when it abides by erring reason. For just as the will, when at variance with the reason, tends to that which reason judges to be evil; so, when in accord with the reason, it tends to what reason judges to be good. But the will is evil when it is at variance with reason, even when erring. Therefore even when it abides by erring reason, the will is good.

Obj. 2. Further, the will is always good, when it abides by the commandment of God and the eternal law. But the eternal law and God's commandment are proposed to us by the apprehension of the reason, even when it errs. Therefore the will is good, even when it abides by erring reason.

Obj. 3. Further, the will is evil when it is at variance with erring reason. If, therefore, the will is evil also when it abides by erring reason, it seems that the will is always evil when in conjunction with erring reason: so that in such a case a man would be in a dilemma, and, of necessity, would sin: which is unreasonable. Therefore the will is good when it abides by erring reason.

On the contrary, The will of those who slew the apostles was evil. And yet it was in accord with the erring reason, according to Jo. xvi. 2: *The hour cometh, that whosoever killeth you, will think that he doth a service to God.* Therefore the will can be evil, when it abides by erring reason.

I answer that, Whereas the previous question is the same as inquiring *whether an erring conscience binds;* so this question is the same as inquiring *whether an erring conscience excuses.* Now this question depends on what has been said above about ignorance. For it was said (Q. 6, A. 8) that ignorance sometimes causes an act to be involuntary, and sometimes not. And since moral good and evil consist in action in so far as it is voluntary, as was stated above (A. 2); it is evident that when ignorance causes an act to be involuntary, it takes away the character of moral good and evil; but not, when it does not cause the act to be involuntary. Again, it has been stated above (Q. 6, A. 8) that when ignorance is in any way willed, either directly or indirectly, it does not cause the act to be involuntary. And I call that ignorance *directly* voluntary, to which the act of the will tends: and that, *indirectly* voluntary, which is due to negligence, by reason of a man not wishing to know what he ought to know, as stated above (Q. 6, A. 8).

If then reason or conscience err with an error that is voluntary, either directly, or through negligence, so that one errs about what one ought to know; then such an error of reason or conscience does not excuse the will, that abides by that erring reason or conscience, from being evil. But if the error arise from ignorance of some circumstance, and without any negligence, so that it cause the act to be involuntary, then that error of reason or conscience excuses the will, that abides by that erring reason, from being evil. For instance, if erring reason tell a man that he should go to another man's wife, the will that abides by that erring reason is evil; since this error arises from ignorance of the Divine Law, which he is bound to know. But if a man's reason errs in mistaking another for his wife, and if he wish to give her her right when she asks for it, his will is excused from being evil: because this error arises from ignorance of a circumstance, which ignorance excuses, and causes the act to be involuntary.

Reply Obj. 1. As Dionysius says (*Div. Nom.* iv), *good results from the entire cause, evil from each particular defect.* Consequently in order that the thing to which the will tends be called evil, it suffices, either that it be evil in itself, or that it be apprehended as evil. But in order for it to be good, it must be good in both ways.

Reply Obj. 2. The eternal law cannot err, but human reason can. Consequently the will that abides by human reason, is not always right, nor is it always in accord with the eternal law.

Reply Obj. 3. Just as in syllogistic arguments, granted one absurdity, others must needs follow; so in moral matters, given one absurdity, others must follow too. Thus suppose a man to seek vainglory, he will sin, whether he does his duty for vainglory or whether he omit to do it. Nor is he in a dilemma about the matter: because he can put aside his evil intention. In like manner, suppose a man's reason or conscience to err through inexcusable ignorance, then evil must needs result in the will. Nor is this man in a dilemma: because he can lay aside his error, since his ignorance is vincible and voluntary.

SEVENTH ARTICLE

Whether the Goodness of the Will, As Regards the Means, Depends on the Intention of the End?

We proceed thus to the Seventh Article:—

Objection 1. It would seem that the goodness of the will does not depend on the in-

* Leonine ed.—*accompanying.*

tention of the end. For it has been stated above (A. 2) that the goodness of the will depends on the object alone. But as regards the means, the object of the will is one thing, and the end intended is another. Therefore in such matters the goodness of the will does not depend on the intention of the end.

Obj. 2. Further, to wish to keep God's commandment, belongs to a good will. But this can be referred to an evil end, for instance, to vainglory or covetousness, by willing to obey God for the sake of temporal gain. Therefore the goodness of the will does not depend on the intention of the end.

Obj. 3. Further, just as good and evil diversify the will, so do they diversify the end. But malice of the will does not depend on the malice of the end intended; since a man who wills to steal in order to give alms, has an evil will, although he intends a good end. Therefore neither does the goodness of the will depend on the goodness of the end intended.

On the contrary, Augustine says (*Confess.* ix. 3) that God rewards the intention. But God rewards a thing because it is good. Therefore the goodness of the will depends on the intention of the end.

I answer that, The intention may stand in a twofold relation to the act of the will; first, as preceding it, secondly as following* it. The intention precedes the act of the will causally, when we will something because we intend a certain end. And then the order to the end is considered as the reason of the goodness of the thing willed: for instance, when a man wills to fast for God's sake; because the act of fasting is specifically good from the very fact that it is done for God's sake. Wherefore, since the goodness of the will depends on the goodness of the thing willed, as stated above (AA. 1, 2), it must, of necessity, depend on the intention of the end.

On the other hand, intention follows the act of the will, when it is added to a preceding act of the will; for instance, a man may will to do something, and may afterwards refer it to God. And then the goodness of the previous act of the will does not depend on the subsequent intention, except in so far as that act is repeated with the subsequent intention.

Reply Obj. 1. When the intention is the cause of the act of willing, the order to the end is considered as the reason of the goodness of the object, as stated above.

Reply Obj. 2. The act of the will cannot be said to be good, if an evil intention is the cause of willing. For when a man wills to give an alms for the sake of vainglory, he wills that which is good in itself, under a species of evil; and therefore, as willed by him, it is evil. Wherefore his will is evil. If, however, the intention is subsequent to the act of the will, then the latter may be good: and the intention does not spoil that act of the will which preceded, but that which is repeated.

Reply Obj. 3. As we have already stated (A. 6 *ad* 1), *evil results from each particular defect, but good from the whole and entire cause.* Hence, whether the will tend to what is evil in itself, even under the species of good; or to the good under the species of evil, it will be evil in either case. But in order for the will to be good, it must tend to the good under the species of good; in other words, it must will the good for the sake of the good.

EIGHTH ARTICLE

Whether the Degree of Goodness or Malice in the Will Depends on the Degree of Good or Evil in the Intention?

We proceed thus to the Eighth Article:—

Objection 1. It would seem that the degree of goodness in the will depends on the degree of good in the intention. Because on Matth. xii. 35, *A good man out of the good treasure of his heart bringeth forth that which is good,* a gloss says: *A man does as much good as he intends.* But the intention gives goodness not only to the external action, but also to the act of the will, as stated above (A. 7). Therefore the goodness of a man's will is according to the goodness of his intention.

Obj. 2. Further, if you add to the cause, you add to the effect. But the goodness of the intention is the cause of the good will. Therefore a man's will is good, according as his intention is good.

Obj. 3. Further, in evil actions, a man sins in proportion to his intention: for if a man were to throw a stone with a murderous intention, he would be guilty of murder. Therefore, for the same reason, in good actions, the will is good in proportion to the good intended.

On the contrary, The intention can be good, while the will is evil. Therefore, for the same reason, the intention can be better, and the will less good.

I answer that, In regard to both the act, and the intention of the end, we may consider a twofold quantity: one, on the part of the object, by reason of a man willing or doing a good that is greater; the other, taken from the intensity of the act, according as a man wills or acts intensely; and this is more on the part of the agent.

If then we speak of these respective quantities from the point of view of the object, it is evident that the quantity in the act does not depend on the quantity in the intention. With regard to the external act this may happen in two ways. First, through the object that is ordained to the intended end not being proportionate to that end; for instance, if a man were to give ten pounds, he could not realize his intention, if he intended to buy a thing worth a hundred pounds. Secondly, on account of the obstacles that may supervene in regard to the exterior action, which obstacles we are unable to remove: for instance, a man intends to go to Rome, and encounters obstacles, which prevent him from going.—On the other hand, with regard to the interior act of the will, this happens in only one way: because the interior acts of the will are in our power, whereas the external actions are not. But the will can will an object that is not proportionate to the intended end: and thus the will that tends to that object considered absolutely, is not so good as the intention. Yet because the intention also belongs, in a way, to the act of the will,—inasmuch, to wit, as it is the reason thereof; it comes to pass that the quantity of goodness in the intention redounds upon the act of the will; that is to say, in so far as the will wills some great good for an end, although that by which it wills to gain so great a good, is not proportionate to that good.

But if we consider the quantity in the intention and in the act, according to their respective intensity, then the intensity of the intention redounds upon the interior act and the exterior act of the will: since the intention stands in relation to them as a kind of form, as is clear from what was said above (Q. 12, A. 4; Q. 18, A. 6). And yet considered materially, while the intention is intense, the interior or exterior act may be not so intense, materially speaking: for instance, when a man does not will with as much intensity to take medicine as he wills to regain health. Nevertheless the very fact of intending health intensely, redounds, as a formal principle, upon the intense volition of medicine.

We must observe, however, that the intensity of the interior or exterior act, may be referred to the intention as its object: as when a man intends to will intensely, or to do something intensely. And yet it does not follow that he wills or acts intensely; because the quantity of goodness in the interior or exterior act does not depend on the quantity of the good intended, as is shown above. And hence it is that a man does not merit as much as he intends to merit: because the quantity of merit is measured by the intensity of the act, as we shall show later on (Q. 20, A. 4; Q. 114, A. 4).

Reply Obj. 1. This gloss speaks of good as in the estimation of God, Who considers principally the intention of the end. Wherefore another gloss says on the same passage that *the treasure of the heart is the intention, according to which God judges our works.* For the goodness of the intention, as stated above, redounds, so to speak, upon the goodness of the will, which makes even the external act to be meritorious in God's sight.

Reply Obj. 2. The goodness of the intention is not the whole cause of a good will. Hence the argument does not prove.

Reply Obj. 3. The mere malice of the intention suffices to make the will evil: and therefore too, the will is as evil as the intention is evil. But the same reasoning does not apply to goodness, as stated above (*ad 2*).

NINTH ARTICLE

Whether the Goodness of the Will Depends on Its Conformity to the Divine Will?

We proceed thus to the Ninth Article:—

Objection 1. It would seem that the goodness of the human will does not depend on its conformity to the Divine will. Because it is impossible for man's will to be conformed to the Divine will; as appears from the word of Isaias (lv. 9): *As the heavens are exalted above the earth, so are My ways exalted above your ways, and My thoughts above your thoughts.* If therefore goodness of the will depended on its conformity to the divine will, it would follow that it is impossible for man's will to be good. Which is inadmissible.

Obj. 2. Further, just as our wills arise from the Divine will, so does our knowledge flow from the Divine knowledge. But our knowledge does not require to be conformed to God's knowledge; since God knows many things that we know not. Therefore there is no need for our will to be conformed to the Divine will.

Obj. 3. Further, the will is a principle of action. But our action cannot be conformed to God's. Therefore neither can our will be conformed to His.

On the contrary, It is written (Matth. xxvi. 39): *Not as I will, but as Thou wilt:* which words He said, because *He wishes man to be upright and to tend to God,* as Augustine expounds in the *Enchiridion.** But the rectitude of the will is its goodness. Therefore the goodness of the will depends on its conformity to the Divine will.

I answer that, As stated above (A. 7), the goodness of the will depends on the intention of the end. Now the last end of the human will is the Sovereign Good, namely, God, as stated above (Q. 1, A. 8; Q. 3, A. 1). Therefore the goodness of the human will requires it to be ordained to the Sovereign Good, that is, to God.

* *Enarr. in Ps.* xxxii., *serm.* i.

Now this Good is primarily and essentially compared to the Divine will, as its proper object. Again, that which is first in any genus is the measure and rule of all that belongs to that genus. Moreover, everything attains to rectitude and goodness, in so far as it is in accord with its proper measure. Therefore, in order that man's will be good it needs to be conformed to the Divine will.

Reply Obj. 1. The human will cannot be conformed to the will of God so as to equal it, but only so as to imitate it. In like manner human knowledge is conformed to the Divine knowledge, in so far as it knows truth: and human action is conformed to the Divine, in so far as it is becoming to the agent:—and this by way of imitation, not by way of equality.

From the above may be gathered the replies to the Second and Third Objections.

TENTH ARTICLE

Whether It is Necessary for the Human Will, in Order to Be Good, to Be Conformed to the Divine Will, as Regards the Thing Willed?

We proceed thus to the Tenth Article:—

Objection 1. It would seem that the human will need not always be conformed to the Divine will, as regards the thing willed. For we cannot will what we know not: since the apprehended good is the object of the will. But in many things we know not what God wills. Therefore the human will cannot be conformed to the Divine will as to the thing willed.

Obj. 2. Further, God wills to damn the man whom He foresees about to die in mortal sin. If therefore man were bound to conform his will to the Divine will, in the point of the thing willed, it would follow that a man is bound to will his own damnation. Which is inadmissible.

Obj. 3. Further, no one is bound to will what is against filial piety. But if man were to will what God wills, this would sometimes be contrary to filial piety: for instance, when God wills the death of a father: if his son were to will it also, it would be against filial piety. Therefore man is not bound to conform his will to the Divine will, as to the thing willed.

On the contrary, (1) On Ps. xxxii. 1, *Praise becometh the upright,* a gloss says: *That man has an upright heart, who wills what God wills.* But everyone is bound to have an upright heart. Therefore everyone is bound to will what God wills.

(2) Moreover, the will takes its form from the object, as does every act. If therefore man is bound to conform his will to the Divine will, it follows that he is bound to conform it, as to the thing willed.

(3) Moreover, opposition of wills arises from men willing different things. But whoever has a will in opposition to the Divine will, has an evil will. Therefore whoever does not conform his will to the Divine will, as to the thing willed, has an evil will.

I answer that, As is evident from what has been said above (AA. 3, 5), the will tends to its object, according as it is proposed by the reason. Now a thing may be considered in various ways by the reason, so as to appear good from one point of view, and not good from another point of view. And therefore if a man's will wills a thing to be, according as it appears to be good, his will is good: and the will of another man, who wills that thing not to be, according as it appears evil, is also good. Thus a judge has a good will, in willing a thief to be put to death, because this is just: while the will of another—*e.g.*, the thief's wife or son, who wishes him not to be put to death, inasmuch as killing is a natural evil, is also good.

Now since the will follows the apprehension of the reason or intellect; the more universal the aspect of the apprehended good, the more universal the good to which the will tends. This is evident in the example given above: because the judge has care of the common good, which is justice, and therefore he wishes the thief's death, which has the aspect of good in relation to the common estate; whereas the thief's wife has to consider the private good of the family, and from this point of view she wishes her husband, the thief, not to be put to death.—Now the good of the whole universe is that which is apprehended by God, Who is the Maker and Governor of all things: hence whatever He wills, He wills it under the aspect of the common good; this is His own Goodness, which is the good of the whole universe. On the other hand, the apprehension of a creature, according to its nature, is of some particular good, proportionate to that nature. Now a thing may happen to be good under a particular aspect, and yet not good under a universal aspect, or vice versa, as stated above. And therefore it comes to pass that a certain will is good from willing something considered under a particular aspect, which thing God wills not, under a universal aspect, and vice versa. And hence too it is, that various wills of various men can be good in respect of opposite things, for as much as, under various aspects, they wish a particular thing to be or not to be.

But a man's will is not right in willing a particular good, unless he refer it to the common good as an end: since even the natural appetite of each part is ordained to the common good of the whole. Now it is the end

that supplies the formal reason, as it were, of willing whatever is directed to the end. Consequently, in order that a man will some particular good with a right will, he must will that particular good materially, and the Divine and universal good, formally. Therefore the human will is bound to be conformed to the Divine will, as to that which is willed formally, for it is bound to will the Divine and universal good; but not as to that which is willed materially, for the reason given above.

At the same time in both these respects, the human will is conformed to the Divine, in a certain degree. Because inasmuch as it is conformed to the Divine will in the common aspect of the thing willed, it is conformed thereto in the point of the last end. While, inasmuch as it is not conformed to the Divine will in the thing willed materially, it is conformed to that will considered as efficient cause; since the proper inclination consequent to nature, or to the particular apprehension of some particular thing, comes to a thing from God as its efficient cause. Hence it is customary to say that a man's will, in this respect, is conformed to the Divine will, because it wills what God wishes him to will.

There is yet another kind of conformity in respect of the formal cause, consisting in man's willing something from charity, as God wills it. And this conformity is also reduced to the formal conformity, that is in respect of the last end, which is the proper object of charity.

Reply Obj. 1. We can know in a general way what God wills. For we know that whatever God wills, He wills it under the aspect of good. Consequently whoever wills a thing under any aspect of good, has a will conformed to the Divine will, as to the reason of the thing willed. But we know not what God wills in particular: and in this respect we are not bound to conform our will to the Divine will.

But in the state of glory, every one will see in each thing that he wills, the relation of that thing to what God wills in that particular matter. Consequently he will conform his will to God in all things not only formally, but also materially.

Reply Obj. 2. God does not will the damnation of a man, considered precisely as damnation, nor a man's death, considered precisely as death, because, *He wills all men to be saved* (1 Tim. ii. 4); but He wills such things under the aspect of justice. Wherefore in regard to such things it suffices for man to will the upholding of God's justice and of the natural order.

Wherefore the reply to the Third Objection is evident.

To the first argument advanced in a con-

trary sense, it should be said that a man who conforms his will to God's, in the aspect of reason of the thing willed, wills what God wills, more than the man, who conforms his will to God's, in the point of the very thing willed; because the will tends more to the end, than to that which is on account of the end.

To the second, it must be replied that the species and form of an act are taken from the object considered formally, rather than from the object considered materially.

To the third, it must be said that there is no opposition of wills when several people desire different things, but not under the same aspect: but there is opposition of wills, when under one and the same aspect one man wills a thing which another wills not. But there is no question of this here.

QUESTION 20

Of Goodness and Malice in External Human Actions

(In Six Articles)

WE must next consider goodness and malice as to external actions: under which head there are six points of inquiry: (1) Whether goodness and malice is first in the act of the will, or in the external action? (2) Whether the whole goodness or malice of the external action depends on the goodness of the will? (3) Whether the goodness and malice of the interior act are the same as those of the external action? (4) Whether the external action adds any goodness or malice to that of the interior act? (5) Whether the consequences of an external action increase its goodness or malice? (6) Whether one and the same external action can be both good and evil?

FIRST ARTICLE

Whether Goodness or Malice Is First in the Action of the Will, or in the External Action?

We proceed thus to the First Article:—

Objection 1. It would seem that good and evil are in the external action prior to being in the act of the will. For the will derives goodness from its object, as stated above (Q. 19, AA. 1, 2). But the external action is the object of the interior act of the will: for a man is said to will to commit a theft, or to will to give an alms. Therefore good and evil are in the external action, prior to being in the act of the will.

Obj. 2. Further, the aspect of good belongs first to the end: since what is directed to the end receives the aspect of good from its relation to the end. Now whereas the act of the will cannot be an end, as stated above (Q. 1, A. 1 *ad* 2), the act of another power can be an end. Therefore good is in the act of some other power prior to being in the act of the will.

Obj. 3. Further, the act of the will stands in a formal relation to the external action, as stated above (Q. 18, A. 6). But that which is formal is subsequent; since form is something added to matter. Therefore good and evil are in the external action, prior to being in the act of the will.

On the contrary, Augustine says (*Retract.* i. 9) that *it is by the will that we sin, and that we behave aright.* Therefore moral good and evil are first in the will.

I answer that, External actions may be said to be good or bad in two ways. First, in regard to their genus, and the circumstances connected with them: thus the giving of alms, if the required conditions be observed, is said to be good. Secondly, a thing is said to be good or evil, from its relation to the end: thus the giving of alms for vainglory is said to be evil. Now, since the end is the will's proper object, it is evident that this aspect of good or evil, which the external action derives from its relation to the end, is to be found first of all in the act of the will, whence it passes to the external action. On the other hand, the goodness or malice which the external action has of itself, on account of its being about due matter and its being attended by due circumstances, is not derived from the will, but rather from the reason. Consequently, if we consider the goodness of the external action, in so far as it comes from reason's ordination and apprehension, it is prior to the goodness of the act of the will: but if we consider it in so far as it is in the execution of the action done, it is subsequent to the goodness of the will, which is its principle.

Reply Obj. 1. The exterior action is the object of the will, inasmuch as it is proposed to the will by the reason, as a good apprehended and ordained by the reason: and thus it is prior to the good in the act of the will. But inasmuch as it is found in the execution of the action, it is an effect of the will, and is subsequent to the will.

Reply Obj. 2. The end precedes in the order of intention, but follows in the order of execution.

Reply Obj. 3. A form as received into matter, is subsequent to matter in the order of generation, although it precedes it in the order of nature: but inasmuch as it is in the active cause, it precedes in every way. Now the will is compared to the exterior action, as its efficient cause. Wherefore the goodness of the act of the will, as existing in the active cause, is the form of the exterior action.

SECOND ARTICLE

Whether the Whole Goodness and Malice of the External Action Depends on the Goodness of the Will?

We proceed thus to the Second Article:—

Objection 1. It would seem that the whole goodness and malice of the external action depend on the goodness of the will. For it is written (Matth. vii. 18): *A good tree cannot bring forth evil fruit, neither can an evil tree bring forth good fruit.* But, according to the gloss, the tree signifies the will, and fruit signifies works. Therefore, it is impossible for the interior act of the will to be good, and the external action evil, or vice versa.

Obj. 2. Further, Augustine says (*Retract.* i. 9) that there is no sin without the will. If therefore there is no sin in the will, there will be none in the external action. And so the whole goodness or malice of the external action depends on the will.

Obj. 3. Further, the good and evil of which we are speaking now are differences of the moral act. Now differences make an essential division in a genus, according to the Philosopher (*Metaph.* vii. 12). Since therefore an act is moral from being voluntary, it seems that goodness and malice in an act are derived from the will alone.

On the contrary, Augustine says (*Contra Mendac.* vii), that *there are some actions which neither a good end nor a good will can make good.*

I answer that, As stated above (A. 1), we may consider a twofold goodness or malice in the external action: one in respect of due matter and circumstances; the other in respect of the order to the end. And that which is in respect of the order to the end, depends entirely on the will: while that which is in respect of due matter or circumstances, depends on the reason: and on this goodness depends the goodness of the will, in so far as the will tends towards it.

Now it must be observed, as was noted above (Q. 19, A. 6 *ad* 1), that for a thing to be evil, one single defect suffices, whereas, for it to be good simply, it is not enough for it to be good in one point only, it must be good

in every respect. If therefore the will be good, both from its proper object and from its end, it follows that the external action is good. But if the will be good from its intention of the end, this is not enough to make the external action good: and if the will be evil either by reason of its intention of the end, or by reason of the act willed, it follows that the external action is evil.

Reply Obj. 1. If the good tree be taken to signify the good will, it must be in so far as the will derives goodness from the act willed and from the end intended.

Reply Obj. 2. A man sins by his will, not only when he wills an evil end; but also when he wills an evil act.

Reply Obj. 3. Voluntariness applies not only to the interior act of the will, but also to external actions, inasmuch as they proceed from the will and the reason. Consequently the difference of good and evil is applicable to both the interior and external act.

THIRD ARTICLE

Whether the Goodness and Malice of the External Action Are the Same As Those of the Interior Act?

We proceed thus to the Third Article:—

Objection 1. It would seem that the goodness and malice of the interior act of the will are not the same as those of the external action. For the principle of the interior act is the interior apprehensive or appetitive power of the soul; whereas the principle of the external action is the power that accomplishes the movement. Now where the principles of action are different, the actions themselves are different. Moreover, it is the action which is the subject of goodness or malice: and the same accident cannot be in different subjects. Therefore the goodness of the interior act cannot be the same as that of the external action.

Obj. 2. Further, *A virtue makes that, which has it, good, and renders its action good also* (*Ethic.* ii. 6). But the intellectual virtue in the commanding power is distinct from the moral virtue in the power commanded, as is declared in *Ethic.* i. 13. Therefore the goodness of the interior act, which belongs to the commanding power, is distinct from the goodness of the external action, which belongs to the power commanded.

Obj. 3. Further, the same thing cannot be cause and effect; since nothing is its own cause. But the goodness of the interior act is the cause of the goodness of the external action, or vice versa, as stated above (AA. 1, 2). Therefore it is not the same goodness in each.

On the contrary, It was shown above (Q. 18, A. 6) that the act of the will is the form, as it were, of the external action. Now that which results from the material and formal element is one thing. Therefore there is but one goodness of the internal and external act.

I answer that, As stated above (Q. 17, A. 4), the interior act of the will, and the external action, considered morally, are one act. Now it happens sometimes that one and the same individual act has several aspects of goodness or malice, and sometimes that it has but one. Hence we must say that sometimes the goodness or malice of the interior act is the same as that of the external action, and sometimes not. For as we have already said (AA. 1, 2), these two goodnesses or malices, of the internal and external acts, are ordained to one another. Now it may happen, in things that are subordinate to something else, that a thing is good merely from being subordinate; thus a bitter draught is good merely because it procures health. Wherefore there are not two goodnesses, one the goodness of health, and the other the goodness of the draught; but one and the same. On the other hand it happens sometimes that that which is subordinate to something else, has some aspect of goodness in itself, besides the fact of its being subordinate to some other good: thus a palatable medicine can be considered in the light of a pleasurable good, besides being conducive to health.

We must therefore say that when the external action derives goodness or malice from its relation to the end only, then there is but one and the same goodness of the act of the will which of itself regards the end, and of the external action, which regards the end through the medium of the act of the will. But when the external action has goodness or malice of itself, *i.e.*, in regard to its matter and circumstances, then the goodness of the external action is distinct from the goodness of the will in regarding the end; yet so that the goodness of the end passes into the external action, and the goodness of the matter and circumstances passes into the act of the will, as stated above (AA. 1, 2).

Reply Obj. 1. This argument proves that the internal and external actions are different in the physical order: yet distinct as they are in that respect, they combine to form one thing in the moral order, as stated above (Q. 17, A. 4).

Reply Obj. 2. As stated in *Ethic.* vi. 12, a moral virtue is ordained to the act of that virtue, which act is the end, as it were, of that virtue; whereas prudence, which is in the reason, is ordained to things directed to the end. For this reason various virtues are

necessary. But right reason in regard to the very end of a virtue has no other goodness than the goodness of that virtue, in so far as the goodness of the reason is participated in each virtue.

Reply Obj. 3. When a thing is derived by one thing from another, as from a univocal efficient cause, then it is not the same in both: thus when a hot thing heats, the heat of the heater is distinct from the heat of the thing heated, although it be the same specifically. But when a thing is derived by one thing from another, according to analogy or proportion, then it is one and the same in both: thus the healthiness which is in medicine or urine is derived from the healthiness of the animal's body; nor is health as applied to urine and medicine, distinct from health as applied to the body of an animal, of which health medicine is the cause, and urine the sign. It is in this way that the goodness of the external action is derived from the goodness of the will, and vice versa; viz., according to the order of one to the other.

FOURTH ARTICLE

Whether the External Action Adds Any Goodness or Malice to That of the Interior Act?

We proceed thus to the Fourth Article:—

Objection 1. It would seem that the external action does not add any goodness or malice to that of the interior action. For Chrysostom says (*Hom.* xix. *in Matth.*): *It is the will that is rewarded for doing good, or punished for doing evil.* Now works are the witnesses of tho will. Therefore God seeks for works not on His own account, in order to know how to judge; but for the sake of others, that all may understand how just He is. But good or evil is to be estimated according to God's judgment rather than according to the judgment of man. Therefore the external action adds no goodness or malice to that of the interior act.

Obj. 2. Further, the goodness and malice of the interior and external acts are one and the same, as stated above (A. 3). But increase is the addition of one thing to another. Therefore the external action does not add to the goodness or malice of the interior act.

Obj. 3. Further, the entire goodness of created things does not add to the Divine Goodness, because it is entirely derived therefrom. But sometimes the entire goodness of the external action is derived from the goodness of the interior act, and sometimes conversely, as stated above (AA. 1, 2). Therefore neither of them adds to the goodness or malice of the other.

On the contrary, Every agent intends to

attain good and avoid evil. If therefore by the external action no further goodness or malice be added, it is to no purpose that he who has a good or an evil will, does a good deed or refrains from an evil deed. Which is unreasonable.

I answer that, If we speak of the goodness which the external action derives from the will tending to the end, then the external action adds nothing to this goodness, unless it happens that the will in itself is made better in good things, or worse in evil things. This, seemingly, may happen in three ways. First in point of number; if, for instance, a man wishes to do something with a good or an evil end in view, and does not do it then, but afterwards wills and does it, the act of his will is doubled and a double good, or a double evil is the result.—Secondly, in point of extension: when, for instance, a man wishes to do something for a good or an evil end, and is hindered by some obstacle, whereas another man perseveres in the movement of the will until he accomplish it in deed; it is evident that the will of the latter is more lasting in good or evil, and in this respect, is better or worse.—Thirdly, in point of intensity: for there are certain external actions, which, in so far as they are pleasurable or painful, are such as naturally to make the will more intense or more remiss; and it is evident that the more intensely the will tends to good or evil, the better or worse it is.

On the other hand, if we speak of the goodness which the external action derives from its matter and due circumstances, thus it stands in relation to the will as its term and end. And in this way it adds to the goodness or malice of the will; because every inclination or movement is perfected by attaining its end or reaching its term. Wherefore the will is not perfect, unless it be such that, given the opportunity, it realizes the operation. But if this prove impossible, as long as the will is perfect, so as to realize the operation if it could; the lack of perfection derived from the external action, is simply involuntary. Now just as the involuntary deserves neither punishment nor reward in the accomplishment of good or evil deeds, so neither does it lessen reward or punishment, if a man through simple involuntariness fail to do good or evil.

Reply Obj. 1. Chrysostom is speaking of the case where a man's will is complete, and does not refrain from the deed save through the impossibility of achievement.

Reply Obj. 2. This argument applies to that goodness which the external action derives from the will as tending to the end. But the goodness which the external action takes from its matter and circumstances, is distinct from

that which it derives from the end; but it is not distinct from that which it has from the very act willed, to which it stands in the relation of measure and cause, as stated above (AA. 1, 2).

From this the reply to the Third Objection is evident.

FIFTH ARTICLE

Whether the Consequences of the External Action Increase Its Goodness or Malice?

We proceed thus to the Fifth Article:—

Objection 1. It would seem that the consequences of the external action increase its goodness or malice. For the effect pre-exists virtually in its cause. But the consequences result from the action as an effect from its cause. Therefore they pre-exist virtually in actions. Now a thing is judged to be good or bad according to its virtue, since a virtue *makes that which has it to be good (Ethic.* ii. 6). Therefore the consequences increase the goodness or malice of an action.

Obj. 2. Further, the good actions of his hearers are consequences resulting from the words of a preacher. But such goods as these redound to the merit of the preacher, as is evident from Phil. iv. 1: *My dearly beloved brethren, my joy and my crown.* Therefore the consequences of an action increase its goodness or malice.

Obj. 3. Further, punishment is not increased, unless the fault increases: wherefore it is written (Deut. xxv. 2): *According to the measure of the sin shall the measure also of the stripes be.* But the punishment is increased on account of the consequences; for it is written (Exod. xxi. 29): *But if the ox was wont to push with his horn yesterday and the day before, and they warned his master, and he did not shut him up, and he shall kill a man or a woman, then the ox shall be stoned, and his owner also shall be put to death.* But he would not have been put to death, if the ox, although he had not been shut up, had not killed a man. Therefore the consequences increase the goodness or malice of an action.

Obj. 4. Further, if a man do something which may cause death, by striking, or by sentencing, and if death does not ensue, he does not contract irregularity: but he would if death were to ensue. Therefore the consequences of an action increase its goodness or malice.

On the contrary, The consequences do not make an action that was evil, to be good; nor one that was good, to be evil. For instance, if a man give an alms to a poor man who makes bad use of the alms by committing a sin, this does not undo the good done by the giver; and, in like manner, if a man bear patiently a wrong done to him, the wrongdoer is not thereby excused. Therefore the consequences of an action do not increase its goodness or malice.

I answer that, The consequences of an action are either foreseen or not. If they are foreseen, it is evident that they increase the goodness or malice. For when a man foresees that many evils may follow from his action, and yet does not therefore desist therefrom, this shows his will to be all the more inordinate.

But if the consequences are not foreseen, we must make a distinction. Because if they follow from the nature of the action and in the majority of cases, in this respect, the consequences increase the goodness or malice of that action: for it is evident that an action is specifically better, if better results can follow from it; and specifically worse, if it is of a nature to produce worse results.—On the other hand, if the consequences follow by accident and seldom, then they do not increase the goodness or malice of the action: because we do not judge of a thing according to that which belongs to it by accident, but only according to that which belongs to it of itself.

Reply Obj. 1. The virtue of a cause is measured by the effect that flows from the nature of the cause, not by that which results by accident.

Reply Obj. 2. The good actions done by the hearers, result from the preacher's words, as an effect that flows from their very nature. Hence they redound to the merit of the preacher: especially when such is his intention.

Reply Obj. 3. The consequences for which that man is ordered to be punished, both follow from the nature of the cause, and are supposed to be foreseen. For this reason they are reckoned as punishable.

Reply Obj. 4. This argument would prove if irregularity were the result of the fault. But it is not the result of the fault, but of the fact, and of the obstacle to the reception of a sacrament.

SIXTH ARTICLE

Whether One and the Same External Action Can Be Both Good and Evil?

We proceed thus to the Sixth Article:—

Objection 1. It would seem that one and the same external action can be both good and evil. For *movement, if continuous, is one and the same (Phys.* v. 4). But one continuous movement can be both good and bad: for

instance, a man may go to church continuously, intending at first vainglory, and afterwards the service of God. Therefore one and the same action can be both good and evil.

Obj. 2. Further, according to the Philosopher *(Phys.* iii. 3), action and passion are one act. But the passion may be good, as Christ's was; and the action evil, as that of the Jews. Therefore one and the same act can be both good and evil.

Obj. 3. Further, since a servant is an instrument, as it were, of his master, the servant's action is his master's, just as the action of a tool is the workman's action. But it may happen that the servant's action result from his master's good will, and is therefore good: and from the evil will of the servant, and is therefore evil. Therefore the same action can be both good and evil.

On the contrary, The same thing cannot be the subject of contraries. But good and evil are contraries. Therefore the same action cannot be both good and evil.

I answer that, Nothing hinders a thing from being one, in so far as it is in one genus, and manifold, in so far as it is referred to another genus. Thus a continuous surface is one, considered as in the genus of quantity; and yet it is manifold, considered as to the genus of color, if it be partly white, and partly black. And accordingly, nothing hinders an action from being one, considered in the natural order; whereas it is not one, considered in the moral order; and vice versa, as we have stated above (A. 3 *ad* 1; Q. 18, A. 7 *ad* 1). For continuous walking is one action, considered in the natural order: but it may resolve itself into many actions, considered in the moral order, if a change take place in the walker's will, for the will is the principle of moral actions. If therefore we consider one action in the moral order, it is impossible for it to be morally both good and evil. Whereas if it be one as to natural and not moral unity, it can be both good and evil.

Reply Obj. 1. This continual movement which proceeds from various intentions, although it is one in the natural order, is not one in the point of moral unity.

Reply Obj. 2. Action and passion belong to the moral order, in so far as they are voluntary. And therefore in so far as they are voluntary in respect of wills that differ, they are two distinct things, and good can be in one of them while evil is in the other.

Reply Obj. 3. The action of the servant, in so far as it proceeds from the will of the servant, is not the master's action: but only in so far as it proceeds from the master's command. Wherefore the evil will of the servant does not make the action evil in this respect.

QUESTION 21

Of the Consequences of Human Actions by Reason of Their Goodness and Malice

(In Four Articles)

WE have now to consider the consequences of human actions by reason of their goodness and malice: and under this head there are four points of inquiry: (1) Whether a human action is right or sinful by reason of its being good or evil? (2) Whether it thereby deserves praise or blame? (3) Whether accordingly, it is meritorious or demeritorious? (4) Whether it is accordingly meritorious or demeritorious before God?

FIRST ARTICLE

Whether a Human Action Is Right or Sinful, in So Far As It is Good or Evil?

We proceed thus to the First Article:—

Objection 1. It seems that a human action is not right or sinful, in so far as it is good or evil. For *monsters are the sins of nature* (*Phys.* ii. 8). But monsters are not actions, but things engendered outside the order of nature. Now things that are produced according to art and reason imitate those that are produced according to nature (*ibid.*). Therefore an action is not sinful by reason of its being inordinate and evil.

Obj. 2. Further, sin, as stated in *Phys.* ii (*loc. cit.*), occurs in nature and art, when the end intended by nature or art is not attained. But the goodness or malice of a human action depends, before all, on the intention of the end, and on its achievement. Therefore it seems that the malice of an action does not make it sinful.

Obj. 3. Further, if the malice of an action makes it sinful, it follows that wherever there is evil, there is sin. But this is false: since punishment is not a sin, although it is an evil. Therefore an action is not sinful by reason of its being evil.

On the contrary, As shown above (Q. 19, A. 4), the goodness of a human action depends principally on the Eternal Law: and consequently its malice consists in its being in disaccord with the Eternal Law. But this is the very nature of sin; for Augustine says (*Contra Faust.* xxii. 27) that *sin is a word, deed, or desire, in opposition to the Eternal Law.* Therefore a human action is sinful by reason of its being evil.

I answer that, Evil is more comprehensive than sin, as also is good than right. For every privation of good, in whatever subject, is an evil: whereas sin consists properly in an action done for a certain end, and lacking due order to that end. Now the due order to an end is measured by some rule. In things that act according to nature, this rule is the natural force that inclines them to that end. When therefore an action proceeds from a natural force, in accord with the natural inclination to an end, then the action is said to be right: since the mean does not exceed its limits, viz., the action does not swerve from the order of its active principle to the end. But when an action strays from this rectitude, it comes under the notion of sin.

Now in those things that are done by the will, the proximate rule is the human reason, while the supreme rule is the Eternal Law. When, therefore, a human action tends to the end, according to the order of reason and of the Eternal Law, then that action is right: but when it turns aside from that rectitude, then it is said to be a sin. Now it is evident from what has been said (Q. 19, AA. 3, 4) that every voluntary action that turns aside from the order of reason and of the Eternal Law, is evil, and that every good action is in accord with reason and the Eternal Law. Hence it follows that a human action is right or sinful by reason of its being good or evil.

Reply Obj. 1. Monsters are called sins, inasmuch as they result from a sin in nature's action.

Reply Obj. 2. The end is twofold; the last end, and the proximate end. In the sin of nature, the action does indeed fail in respect of the last end, which is the perfection of the thing generated; but it does not fail in respect of any proximate end whatever; since when nature works it forms something. In like manner, the sin of the will always fails as regards the last end intended, because no voluntary evil action can be ordained to happiness, which is the last end: and yet it does not fail in respect of some proximate end: intended and achieved by the will. Wherefore also, since the very intention of this end is ordained to the last end, this same intention may be right or sinful.

Reply Obj. 3. Each thing is ordained to its end by its action: and therefore sin, which consists in straying from the order to the end, consists properly in an action. On the other hand, punishment regards the person of the sinner, as was stated in the First Part (Q. 48, A. 5, *ad* 4; A. 6, *ad* 3).

SECOND ARTICLE

Whether a Human Action Deserves Praise or Blame, by Reason of Its Being Good or Evil?

We proceed thus to the Second Article:—

Objection 1. It would seem that a human action does not deserve praise or blame by reason of its being good or evil. For *sin happens even in things done by nature* (*Phys.* ii. 8). And yet natural things are not deserving of praise or blame (*Ethic.* iii. 5). Therefore a human action does not deserve blame, by reason of its being evil or sinful; and, consequently, neither does it deserve praise, by reason of its being good.

Obj. 2. Further, just as sin occurs in moral actions, so does it happen in the productions of art: because as stated in *Phys.* ii. (*ibid.*), *it is a sin in a grammarian to write badly, and in a doctor to give the wrong medicine.* But the artist is not blamed for making something bad: because the artist's work is such, that he can produce a good or a bad thing, just as he lists. Therefore it seems that neither is there any reason for blaming a moral action, in the fact that it is evil.

Obj. 3. Further, Dionysius says (*Div. Nom.* iv) that evil is *weak and incapable.* But weakness or inability either takes away or diminishes guilt. Therefore a human action does not incur guilt from being evil.

On the contrary, The Philosopher says (*De Virt. et Vit.* i) that *virtuous deeds deserve praise, while deeds that are opposed to virtue deserve censure and blame.* But good actions are virtuous; because *virtue makes that which has it, good, and makes its action good* (*Ethic.* ii. 6): wherefore actions opposed to virtue are evil. Therefore a human action deserves praise or blame, through being good or evil.

I answer that, Just as evil is more comprehensive than sin, so is sin more comprehensive than blame. For an action is said to deserve praise or blame, from its being imputed to the agent: since to praise or to blame means nothing else than to impute to someone the malice or goodness of his action. Now an action is imputed to an agent, when it is in his power, so that he has dominion over it; and this is the case in all voluntary acts: because it is through his will that man has dominion over his actions, as was made clear above (Q. 1, AA. 1, 2). Hence it follows that good or evil, in voluntary actions alone, renders them worthy of praise or blame: and in such like actions, evil, sin and guilt are one and the same thing.

Reply Obj. 1. Natural actions are not in the power of the natural agent: since the action of nature is determinate. And, therefore, although there be sin in natural actions, there is no blame.

Reply Obj. 2. Reason stands in different relations to the productions of art, and to moral actions. In matters of art, reason is directed to a particular end, which is something devised by reason: whereas in moral matters, it is directed to the general end of all human life. Now a particular end is subordinate to the general end. Since therefore sin is a departure from the order to the end, as stated above (A. 1), sin may occur in two ways, in a production of art. First, by a departure from the particular end intended by the artist: and this sin will be proper to the art; for instance, if an artist produce a bad thing, while intending to produce something good; or produce something good, while intending to produce something bad. Secondly, by a departure from the general end of human life: and then he will be said to sin, if he intend to produce a bad work, and does so in effect, so that another is taken in thereby. But this sin is not proper to the artist as such, but as man. Consequently for the former sin the artist is blamed as an artist; while for the latter he is blamed as a man.—On the other hand, in moral matters, where we take into consideration the order of reason to the general end of human life, sin and evil are always due to a departure from the order of reason to the general end of human life. Wherefore man is blamed for such a sin, both as man and as a moral being. Hence the Philosopher says (*Ethic.* vi. 5) that *in art, he who sins voluntarily is preferable; but in prudence, as in the moral virtues,* which prudence directs, *he is the reverse.*

Reply Obj. 3. Weakness that occurs in voluntary evils, is subject to man's power: wherefore it neither takes away nor diminishes guilt.

THIRD ARTICLE

Whether a Human Action Is Meritorious or Demeritorious, in So Far As It Is Good or Evil?

We proceed thus to the Third Article:—

Objection 1. It would seem that a human action is not meritorious or demeritorious on account of its goodness or malice. For we speak of merit or demerit in relation to retribution, which has no place save in matters relating to another person. But good or evil actions are not all related to another person, for some are related to the person of the agent. Therefore not every good or evil human action is meritorious or demeritorious.

Obj. 2. Further, no one deserves punishment or reward for doing as he chooses with that of which he is master: thus if a man destroys what belongs to him, he is not punished, as if he had destroyed what belongs to another. But man is master of his own actions. Therefore a man does not merit punishment or reward, through putting his action to a good or evil purpose.

Obj. 3. Further, if a man acquire some good for himself, he does not on that account deserve to be benefited by another man: and the same applies to evil. Now a good action is itself a kind of good and perfection of the agent: while an inordinate action is his evil. Therefore a man does not merit or demerit, from the fact that he does a good or an evil deed.

On the contrary, It is written (Isa. iii. 10, 11): *Say to the just man that it is well; for he shall eat the fruit of his doings. Woe to the wicked unto evil; for the reward of his hands shall be given him.*

I answer that, We speak of merit and demerit, in relation to retribution, rendered according to justice. Now, retribution according to justice is rendered to a man, by reason of his having done something to another's advantage or hurt. It must, moreover, be observed that every individual member of a society is, in a fashion, a part and member of the whole society. Wherefore, any good or evil, done to the member of a society, redounds on the whole society: thus, who hurts the hand, hurts the man. When, therefore, anyone does good or evil to another individual, there is a twofold measure of merit or demerit in his action: first, in respect of the retribution owed to him by the individual to whom he has done good or harm; secondly, in respect of the retribution owed to him by the whole of society. —Now when a man ordains his action directly for the good or evil of the whole society, retribution is owed to him, before and above all, by the whole society; secondarily, by all the parts of society. Whereas when a man does that which conduces to his own benefit or disadvantage, then again is retribution owed to him, in so far as this too affects the community, forasmuch as he is a part of society: although retribution is not due to him, in so far as it conduces to the good or harm of an individual, who is identical with the agent: unless, perchance, he owe retribution to himself, by a sort of resemblance, in so far as man is said to be just to himself.

It is therefore evident that a good or evil action deserves praise or blame, in so far as it is in the power of the will: that it is right or sinful, according as it is ordained to the end; and that its merit or demerit depends on the recompense for justice or injustice towards another.

Reply Obj. 1. A man's good or evil actions, although not ordained to the good or evil of another individual, are nevertheless ordained to the good or evil of another, *i.e.*, the community.

Reply Obj. 2. Man is master of his actions; and yet, in so far as he belongs to another, *i.e.*, the community, of which he forms part, he merits or demerits, inasmuch as he disposes his actions well or ill: just as if he were to dispense well or ill other belongings of his, in respect of which he is bound to serve the community.

Reply Obj. 3. This very good or evil, which a man does to himself by his action, redounds to the community, as stated above.

FOURTH ARTICLE

Whether a Human Action Is Meritorious or Demeritorious before God, according As It Is Good or Evil?

We proceed thus to the Fourth Article:—

Objection 1. It would seem that man's actions, good or evil, are not meritorious or demeritorious in the sight of God. Because, as stated above (A. 3), merit and demerit imply relation to retribution for good or harm done to another. But a man's action, good or evil, does no good or harm to God; for it is written (Job xxxv. 6, 7): *If thou sin, what shalt thou hurt Him? . . . And if thou do justly, what shalt thou give Him?* Therefore a human action, good or evil, is not meritorious or demeritorious in the sight of God.

Obj. 2. Further, an instrument acquires no merit or demerit in the sight of him that uses it; because the entire action of the instrument belongs to the user. Now when man acts he is the instrument of the Divine power which is the principal cause of his action; hence it is written (Isa. x. 15): *Shall the axe boast itself against him that cutteth with it? Or shall the saw exalt itself against him by whom it is drawn?* where man while acting is evidently compared to an instrument. Therefore man merits or demerits nothing in God's sight, by good or evil deeds.

Obj. 3. Further, a human action acquires merit or demerit through being ordained to someone else. But not all human actions are ordained to God. Therefore not every good or evil action acquires merit or demerit in God's sight.

On the contrary, It is written (Eccles. xii. 14): *All things that are done, God will bring into judgment . . . whether it be good or evil.* Now judgment implies retribution, in respect of which we speak of merit and demerit. Therefore every human action, both good and evil, acquires merit or demerit in God's sight.

I answer that, A human action, as stated above (A. 3), acquires merit or demerit, through being ordained to someone else, either by reason of himself, or by reason of the community: and in each way, our actions, good and evil, acquire merit or demerit in the sight of God. On the part of God Himself, inasmuch as He is man's last end; and it is our duty to refer all our actions to the last end, as stated above (Q. 19, A. 10). Consequently, whoever does an evil deed, not referable to God, does not give God the honor due to Him as our last end.—On the part of the whole community of the universe, because in every community, he who governs the community, cares, first of all, for the common good; wherefore it is his business to award retribution for such things as are done well or ill in the community. Now God is the governor and ruler of the whole universe, as stated in the First Part (Q. 103, A. 5): and especially of rational creatures. Consequently it is evident that human actions acquire merit or demerit in reference to Him: else it would follow that human actions are no business of God's.

Reply Obj. 1. God in Himself neither gains nor loses anything by the action of man: but man, for his part, takes something from God, or offers something to Him, when he observes or does not observe the order instituted by God.

Reply Obj. 2. Man is so moved, as an instrument, by God, that, at the same time, he moves himself by his free-will, as was explained above (Q. 9, A. 6 *ad* 3). Consequently, by his action, he acquires merit or demerit in God's sight.

Reply Obj. 3. Man is not ordained to the body politic, according to all that he is and has; and so it does not follow that every action of his acquires merit or demerit in relation to the body politic. But all that man is, and can, and has, must be referred to God: and therefore every action of man, whether good or bad, acquires merit or demerit in the sight of God, as far as the action itself is concerned.

HUMAN ACTS (Cont'd)

Human Acts

Passions and Acts Common to Man and Animal

In General

1. Subject of the soul's passions.—Are passions in the soul?—Are they in the sensitive appetite or in the will?. — *22 / 3*
2. How they differ from one another.—Has a passion its contrary?—In the same power are there passions differing in species but not contrary?. — *23 / 4*
3. Their good and evil.—Are good and evil found in passions of the soul?—Is every passion morally evil?. — *24 / 4*
4. The relations of the irascible passions.—The four principal passions.—The relations existing among the passions. — *25 / 4*

In Particular

The Passions of the Concupiscible Appetite

1. Love
   1. Love Itself.—Is love a passion?—Is it the same as dilection?—How is it divided?. — *26 / 4*
   2. Its cause.—Is good the only cause of love?—Is knowledge?—Is any other passion of the soul its cause?. — *27 / 4*
   3. Its effects.—Is union an effect of love?—Is ecstasy?—Is zeal?—Is love the cause of all acts of love?. — *28 / 6*
2. Hatred.—Is evil the cause and object of hatred?—Is it stronger than love?—Can a man hate the truth?. — *29 / 6*
3. Concupiscence.—Is it of the sensitive appetite only?—Is it a special passion?—Is it natural?—Is it infinite?. — *30 / 4*
4. Delight
   1. In itself.—Is it a passion?—Does it differ from joy?—Is any delight not natural?. — *31 / 8*
   2. Its causes.—Whether operation, movement, sadness, doing good, cause pleasure. — *32 / 8*
   3. Its effects.—Spiritual expansion, a desire for further delight.—Does it impede the use of reason?. — *33 / 4*
   4. Its goodness and malice.—Is every pleasure evil?—Is pleasure the measure of moral good?. — *34 / 4*
5. Sorrow or Pain
   1. In itself.—Is pain a passion?—Is sorrow the same as pain?—The species of sorrow. — *35 / 8*
   2. Its causes.—Does loss, desire, or force cause sorrow?. — *36 / 4*
   3. Its effects.—Does pain burden the soul?—Weaken activity?. — *37 / 4*
   4. Its remedies.—Is pain assuaged by pleasure?—By the compassion of friends?—By sleep?. — *38 / 5*
   5. Its goodness and malice.—Is all sorrow evil?—Can it be virtuous?—Is pain the greatest evil?. — *39 / 4*

The Passions of the Irascible Appetite

1. Hope and Despair.—Is hope the same as desire?—Is hope in animals?—Is despair contrary to hope?. — *40 / 8*
2. Fear
   1. In itself.—Object of fear.—Its causes.—Effects.—Is there natural fear?. — *41 / 4*
   2. Its object.—Is good or evil the object of fear?—Are sudden things especially feared?. — *42 / 6*
   3. Its cause.—Is love the cause of fear?—Are defects?. — *43 / 2*
   4. Its effects.—Does it hinder action?—Does it cause contraction?. — *44 / 4*
3. Daring.—Is it contrary to fear?—Is it related to hope?. — *45 / 4*
4. Anger
   1. In itself.—Is its object good or evil?—Is it accompanied by an act of reason?. — *46 / 8*
   2. Its cause.—Is its motive always something done against the one who is angry?. — *47 / 4*
   3. Its effects.—Does it cause pleasure?—Does it hinder the use of reason?. — *48 / 4*

(Column headings at right: Question / Article)

QUESTION 22

Of the Subject of the Soul's Passions

(In Three Articles)

WE must now consider the passions of the soul: first, in general; secondly, in particular. Taking them in general, there are four things to be considered: (1) Their subject: (2) The difference between them: (3) Their mutual relationship: (4) Their malice and goodness.

Under the first head there are three points of inquiry: (1) Whether there is any passion in the soul? (2) Whether passion is in the appetitive rather than in the apprehensive part? (3) Whether passion is in the sensitive appetite rather than in the intellectual appetite, which is called the will?

FIRST ARTICLE

Whether Any Passion Is in the Soul?

We proceed thus to the First Article:—

Objection 1. It would seem that there is no passion in the soul. Because passivity belongs to matter. But the soul is not composed of matter and form, as stated in the First Part (Q. 75, A. 5). Therefore there is no passion in the soul.

Obj. 2. Further, passion is movement, as is stated in *Phys.* iii. 3. But the soul is not moved, as is proved in *De Anima* i. 3. Therefore passion is not in the soul.

Obj. 3. Further, passion is the road to corruption; since *every passion, when increased, alters the substance*, as is stated in *Topic.* vi. 6. But the soul is incorruptible. Therefore no passion is in the soul.

On the contrary, The Apostle says (Rom. vii. 5): *When we were in the flesh, the passions of sins which were by the law, did the work in our members.* Now sins are, properly speaking, in the soul. Therefore passions also, which are described as being *of sins*, are in the soul.

I answer that, The word *passive* is used in three ways. First, in a general way, according as whatever receives something is passive, although nothing is taken from it: thus we may say that the air is passive when it is lit up. But this is to be perfected rather than to be passive. Secondly, the word *passive* is employed in its proper sense, when something is received, while something else is taken away: and this happens in two ways. For sometimes that which is lost is unsuitable to the thing: thus when an animal's body is healed, it is said to be passive, because it receives health, and loses sickness.—At other times the contrary occurs: thus to ail is to be passive; because the ailment is received and health is lost. And here we have passion in its most proper ac-

ceptation. For a thing is said to be passive from its being drawn to the agent: and when a thing recedes from what is suitable to it, then especially does it appear to be drawn to something else. Moreover in *De Generat.* i. 3, it is stated that when a more excellent thing is generated from a less excellent, we have generation simply, and corruption in a particular respect: whereas the reverse is the case, when from a more excellent thing, a less excellent is generated. In these three ways it happens that passions are in the soul. For in the sense of mere reception, we speak of *feeling and understanding as being a kind of passion* (*De Anima* i. 5). But passion, accompanied by the loss of something, is only in respect of a bodily transmutation; wherefore passion properly so called cannot be in the soul, save accidentally, in so far, to wit, as the *composite* is passive. But here again we find a difference; because when this transmutation is for the worse, it has more of the nature of a passion, than when it is for the better: hence sorrow is more properly a passion than joy.

Reply Obj. 1. It belongs to matter to be passive in such a way as to lose something and to be transmuted: hence this happens only in those things that are composed of matter and form. But passivity, as implying mere reception, need not be in matter, but can be in anything that is in potentiality. Now, though the soul is not composed of matter and form, yet it has something of potentiality, in respect of which it is competent to receive or to be passive, according as the act of understanding is a kind of passion, as stated in *De Anima* iii. 4.

Reply Obj. 2. Although it does not belong to the soul in itself to be passive and to be moved, yet it belongs accidentally, as stated in *De Anima* i. 3.

Reply Obj. 3. This argument is true of passion accompanied by transmutation to something worse. And passion, in this sense, is not found in the soul, except accidentally: but the composite, which is corruptible, admits of it by reason of its own nature.

SECOND ARTICLE

Whether Passion Is in the Appetitive Rather Than in the Apprehensive Part?

We proceed thus to the Second Article:—

Objection 1. It would seem that passion is in the apprehensive part of the soul rather than in the appetitive. Because that which is first in any genus, seems to rank first among all things that are in that genus, and to be their cause, as is stated in *Metaph.* ii. 1. Now passion is found to be in the apprehensive, before being in the appetitive part: for the appetitive part is not affected unless there be a previous passion in the apprehensive part. Therefore passion is in the apprehensive part more than in the appetitive.

Obj. 2. Further, what is more active is less passive; for action is contrary to passion. Now the appetitive part is more active than the apprehensive. Therefore it seems that passion is more in the apprehensive part.

Obj. 3. Further, just as the sensitive appetite is the power of a corporeal organ, so is the power of sensitive apprehension. But passion in the soul occurs, properly speaking, in respect of a bodily transmutation. Therefore passion is not more in the sensitive appetitive than in the sensitive apprehensive part.

On the contrary, Augustine says (*De Civ. Dei* ix. 4) that *the movements of the soul, which the Greeks call πάθη, are styled by some of our writers, Cicero* for instance, disturbances; by some, affections or emotions; while others rendering the Greek more accurately, call them passions.* From this it is evident that the passions of the soul are the same as affections. But affections manifestly belong to the appetitive, and not to the apprehensive part. Therefore the passions are in the appetitive rather than in the apprehensive part.

I answer that, As we have already stated (A. 1) the word *passion* implies that the patient is drawn to that which belongs to the agent. Now the soul is drawn to a thing by the appetitive power rather than by the apprehensive power: because the soul has, through its appetitive power, an order to things as they are in themselves: hence the Philosopher says (*Metaph.* vi. 4) that *good and evil, i.e.,* the objects of the appetitive power, *are in things themselves.* On the other hand the apprehensive power is not drawn to a thing, as it is in itself; but knows it by reason of an *intention* of the thing, which *intention* it has in itself, or receives in its own way. Hence we find it stated (*ibid.*) that *the true and the false,* which pertain to knowledge, *are not in things, but in the mind.* Consequently it is evident that the nature of passion is consistent with the appetitive, rather than with the apprehensive part.

Reply Obj. 1. In things relating to perfection the case is the opposite, in comparison to things that pertain to defect. Because in things relating to perfection, intensity is in proportion to the approach to one first principle; to which the nearer a thing approaches, the more intense it is. Thus the intensity of a thing possessed of light depends on its approach to something endowed with light in a supreme degree, to which the nearer a thing approaches the more light it possesses. But in things that relate to defect, intensity depends, not on approach to something supreme, but in receding from that which is perfect; because therein consists the very notion of privation and defect. Wherefore the less a thing recedes from that which stands first, the less intense it is: and the result is that at first we always find some small defect, which afterwards increases as it goes on. Now passion pertains to defect, because it belongs to a thing according as it is in potentiality. Wherefore in those things that approach to the Supreme Perfection, *i.e.,* to God, there is but little potentiality and passion: while in other things, consequently, there is more. Hence also, in the supreme, *i.e.,* the apprehensive, power of the soul, passion is found less than in the other powers.

Reply Obj. 2. The appetitive power is said to be more active, because it is, more than the apprehensive power, the principle of the exterior action: and this for the same reason that it is more passive, namely, its being related to things as existing in themselves: since it is through the external action that we come into contact with things.

Reply Obj. 3. As stated in the First Part (Q. 78, A. 3), the organs of the soul can be changed in two ways. First, by a spiritual change, in respect of which the organ receives an *intention* of the object. And this is essential to the act of the sensitive apprehension: thus is the eye changed by the object visible, not by being colored, but by receiving an intention of color. But the organs are receptive of another and natural change, which affects their natural disposition; for instance, when they become hot or cold, or undergo some similar change. And whereas this kind of change is accidental to the act of the sensitive apprehension; for instance, if the eye be wearied through gazing intently at something, or be overcome by the intensity of the object: on the other hand, it is essential to the act of the sensitive appetite; wherefore the material element in the definitions of the movements of the appetitive part, is the natural change of the organ; for instance, *anger* is said to be a *kindling of the blood about the heart.* Hence it is evident that the notion of passion is more consistent with the act of the sensitive appetite, than with that of the sensitive apprehension, although both are actions of a corporeal organ.

---

* *Those things which the Greeks call πάθη, we prefer to call disturbances rather than diseases* (Tusc. iv. 5).

THIRD ARTICLE

Whether Passion Is in the Sensitive Appetite Rather Than in the Intellectual Appetite, Which Is Called the Will?

We proceed thus to the Third Article:—

Objection 1. It would seem that passion is not more in the sensitive than in the intellectual appetite. For Dionysius declares (*Div. Nom.* ii) Hierotheus *to be taught by a kind of yet more Godlike instruction; not only by learning Divine things, but also by suffering (patiens) them.* But the sensitive appetite cannot *suffer* Divine things, since its object is the sensible good. Therefore passion is in the intellectual appetite, just as it is also in the sensitive appetite.

Obj. 2. Further, the more powerful the active force, the more intense the passion. But the object of the intellectual appetite, which is the universal good, is a more powerful active force than the object of the sensitive appetite, which is a particular good. Therefore passion is more consistent with the intellectual than with the sensitive appetite.

Obj. 3. Further, joy and love are said to be passions. But these are to be found in the intellectual and not only in the sensitive appetite: else they would not be ascribed by the Scriptures to God and the angels. Therefore the passions are not more in the sensitive than in the intellectual appetite.

On the contrary, Damascene says (*De Fide Orthod.* ii. 22), while describing the animal passions: *Passion is a movement of the sensitive appetite when we imagine good or evil: in other words, passion is a movement of the irrational soul, when we think of good or evil.*

I answer that, As stated above (A. 1) passion is properly to be found where there is corporeal transmutation. This corporeal transmutation is found in the act of the sensitive appetite, and is not only spiritual, as in the sensitive apprehension, but also natural. Now there is no need for corporeal transmutation in the act of the intellectual appetite: because this appetite is not exercised by means of a corporeal organ. It is therefore evident that passion is more properly in the act of the sensitive appetite, than in that of the intellectual appetite; and this is again evident from the definitions of Damascene quoted above.

Reply Obj. 1. By *suffering* Divine things is meant being well affected towards them, and united to them by love: and this takes place without any alteration in the body.

Reply Obj. 2. Intensity of passion depends not only on the power of the agent, but also on the passibility of the patient: because things that are disposed to passion, suffer much even from petty agents. Therefore although the object of the intellectual appetite has greater activity than the object of the sensitive appetite, yet the sensitive appetite is more passive.

Reply Obj. 3. When love and joy and the like are ascribed to God or the angels, or to man in respect of his intellectual appetite, they signify simple acts of the will having like effects, but without passion. Hence Augustine says (*De Civ. Dei* ix. 5): *The holy angels feel no anger while they punish . . ., no fellow-feeling with misery while they relieve the unhappy: and yet ordinary human speech is wont to ascribe to them also these passions by name, because, although they have none of our weakness, their acts bear a certain resemblance to ours.*

QUESTION 23

How the Passions Differ from One Another

(In Four Articles)

WE must now consider how the passions differ from one another: and under this head there are four points of inquiry: (1) Whether the passions of the concupiscible part are different from those of the irascible part? (2) Whether the contrariety of passions in the irascible part is based on the contrariety of good and evil? (3) Whether there is any passion that has no contrary? (4) Whether, in the same power, there are any passions, differing in species, but not contrary to one another?

FIRST ARTICLE

Whether the Passions of the Concupiscible Part Are Different from Those of the Irascible Part?

We proceed thus to the First Article:—

Objection 1. It would seem that the same passions are in the irascible and concupiscible parts. For the Philosopher says (*Ethic.* ii. 5) that the passions of the soul are those emotions *which are followed by joy or sorrow.* But joy and sorrow are in the concupiscible part. Therefore all the passions are in the concupiscible part, and not some in the irascible, others in the concupiscible part.

Obj. 2. Further, on the words of Matth. xiii. 33, *The kingdom of heaven is like to leaven,* etc., Jerome's gloss says: *We should have prudence in the reason; hatred of vice, in the irascible faculty; desire of virtue, in the concupiscible part.* But hatred is in the concupiscible faculty, as also is love, of which it is the contrary, as is stated in *Topic*. ii. 7. Therefore the same passion is in the concupiscible and irascible faculties.

Obj. 3. Further, passions and actions differ specifically according to their objects. But the objects of the irascible and concupiscible passions are the same, viz., good and evil. Therefore the same passions are in the irascible and concupiscible faculties.

On the contrary, The acts of different powers differ in species; for instance, to see, and to hear. But the irascible and the concupiscible are two powers into which the sensitive appetite is divided, as stated in the First Part (Q. 81, A. 2). Therefore, since the passions are movements of the sensitive appetite, as stated above (Q. 22, A. 3), the passions of the irascible faculty are specifically distinct from those of the concupiscible part.

I answer that, The passions of the irascible part differ in species from those of the concupiscible faculty. For since different powers have different objects, as stated in the First Part (Q. 77, A. 3), the passions of different powers must of necessity be referred to different objects. Much more, therefore, do the passions of different faculties differ in species; since a greater difference in the object is required to diversify the species of the powers, than to diversify the species of passions or actions. For just as in the physical order, diversity of genus arises from diversity in the potentiality of matter, while diversity of species arises from diversity of form in the same matter; so in the acts of the soul, those that belong to different powers, differ not only in species but also in genus, while acts and passions regarding different specific objects, included under the one common object of a single power, differ as the species of that genus.

In order, therefore, to discern which passions are in the irascible, and which in the concupiscible, we must take the object of each of these powers. For we have stated in the First Part (Q. 81, A. 2) that the object of the concupiscible power is sensible good or evil, simply apprehended as such, which causes pleasure or pain. But, since the soul must, of necessity, experience difficulty or struggle at times, in acquiring some such good, or in avoiding some such evil, in so far as such good or evil is more than our animal nature can easily acquire or avoid; therefore this very good or evil, inasmuch as it is of an arduous or difficult nature, is the object of the irascible faculty. Therefore whatever passions regard good or evil absolutely, belong to the concupiscible power; for instance, joy, sorrow, love, hatred and such like: whereas those passions which regard good or bad as arduous, through being difficult to obtain or avoid, belong to the irascible faculty; such are daring, fear, hope and the like.

Reply Obj. 1. As stated in the First Part (*loc. cit.*), the irascible faculty is bestowed on animals, in order to remove the obstacles that hinder the concupiscible power from tending towards its object, either by making some good difficult to obtain, or by making some evil hard to avoid. The result is that all the irascible passions terminate in the concupiscible passions: and thus it is that even the passions which are in the irascible faculty are followed by joy and sadness which are in the concupiscible faculty.

Reply Obj. 2. Jerome ascribes hatred of vice to the irascible faculty, not by reason of hatred, which is properly a concupiscible passion; but on account of the struggle, which belongs to the irascible power.

Reply Obj. 3. Good, inasmuch as it is delightful, moves the concupiscible power. But if it prove difficult to obtain, from this very fact it has a certain contrariety to the concupiscible power: and hence the need of another power tending to that good. The same applies to evil. And this power is the irascible faculty. Consequently the concupiscible passions are specifically different from the irascible passions.

SECOND ARTICLE

Whether the Contrariety of the Irascible Passions Is Based on the Contrariety of Good and Evil?

We proceed thus to the Second Article:—

Objection 1. It would seem that the contrariety of the irascible passions is based on no other contrariety than that of good and evil. For the irascible passions are ordained to the concupiscible passions, as stated above (A. 1 *ad* 1). But the contrariety of the concupiscible passions is no other than that of good and evil; take, for instance, love and hatred, joy and sorrow. Therefore the same applies to the irascible passions.

Obj. 2. Further, passions differ according to their objects; just as movements differ according to their termini. But there is no other contrariety of movements, except that of the termini, as is stated in *Phys.* v. 3. Therefore there is no other contrariety of passions, save that of the objects. Now the object of the appetite is good or evil. Therefore in no appetitive power can there be contrariety of passions other than that of good and evil.

Obj. 3. Further, *every passion of the soul is by way of approach and withdrawal,* as Avicenna declares in his sixth book of *Physics*. Now approach results from the apprehension of good; withdrawal, from the apprehension of evil: since just as *good is what all desire*

(*Ethic.* i. 1), so evil is what all shun. Therefore, in the passions of the soul, there can be no other contrariety than that of good and evil.

On the contrary, Fear and daring are contrary to one another, as stated in *Ethic.* iii. 7. But fear and daring do not differ in respect of good and evil: because each regards some kind of evil. Therefore not every contrariety of the irascible passions is that of good and evil.

I answer that, Passion is a kind of movement, as stated in *Phys.* iii. 3. Therefore contrariety of passions is based on contrariety of movements or changes. Now there is a twofold contrariety in changes and movements, as stated in *Phys.* v. 5. One is according to approach and withdrawal in respect of the same term: and this contrariety belongs properly to changes, *i.e.,* to generation, which is a change *to being,* and to corruption, which is change *from being.* The other contrariety is according to opposition of termini, and belongs properly to movements: thus whitening, which is movement from black to white, is contrary to blackening, which is movement from white to black.

Accordingly there is a twofold contrariety in the passions of the soul: one, according to contrariety of objects, *i.e.,* of good and evil; the other, according to approach and withdrawal in respect of the same term. In the concupiscible passions the former contrariety alone is to be found; viz., that which is based on the objects: whereas in the irascible passions, we find both forms of contrariety. The reason of this is that the object of the concupiscible faculty, as stated above (A. 1), is sensible good or evil considered absolutely. Now good, as such, cannot be a term wherefrom, but only a term whereto, since nothing shuns good as such; on the contrary, all things desire it. In like manner, nothing desires evil, as such; but all things shun it: wherefore evil cannot have the aspect of a term whereto, but only of a term wherefrom. Accordingly every concupiscible passion in respect of good, tends to it, as love, desire and joy; while every concupiscible passion in respect of evil, tends from it, as hatred, avoidance or dislike, and sorrow. Wherefore, in the concupiscible passions, there can be no contrariety of approach and withdrawal in respect of the same object.

On the other hand, the object of the irascible faculty is sensible good or evil, considered not absolutely, but under the aspect of difficulty or arduousness. Now the good which is difficult or arduous, considered as good, is of such a nature as to produce in us a tendency to it, which tendency pertains to the passion of *hope;* whereas, considered as arduous or difficult, it makes us turn from it; and this pertains to the passion of *despair.* In like

manner the arduous evil, considered as an evil, has the aspect of something to be shunned; and this belongs to the passion of *fear:* but it also contains a reason for tending to it, as attempting something arduous, whereby to escape being subject to evil; and this tendency is called *daring.* Consequently, in the irascible passions we find contrariety in respect of good and evil (as between hope and fear): and also contrariety according to approach and withdrawal in respect of the same term (as between daring and fear).

From what has been said the replies to the objections are evident.

THIRD ARTICLE

Whether Any Passion of the Soul Has No Contrary?

We proceed thus to the Third Article:—

Objection 1. It would seem that every passion of the soul has a contrary. For every passion of the soul is either in the irascible or in the concupiscible faculty, as stated above (A. 1). But both kinds of passions have their respective modes of contrariety. Therefore every passion of the soul has its contrary.

Obj. 2. Further, every passion of the soul has either good or evil for its object; for these are the common objects of the appetitive part. But a passion having good for its object, is contrary to a passion having evil for its object. Therefore every passion has a contrary.

Obj. 3. Further, every passion of the soul is in respect of approach or withdrawal, as stated above (A. 2). But every approach has a corresponding contrary withdrawal, and vice versa. Therefore every passion of the soul has a contrary.

On the contrary, Anger is a passion of the soul. But no passion is set down as being contrary to anger, as stated in *Ethic.* iv. 5. Therefore not every passion has a contrary.

I answer that, The passion of anger is peculiar in this, that it cannot have a contrary, either according to approach and withdrawal, or according to the contrariety of good and evil. For anger is caused by a difficult evil already present: and when such an evil is present, the appetite must needs either succumb, so that it does not go beyond the limits of *sadness,* which is a concupiscible passion; or else it has a movement of attack on the hurtful evil, which movement is that of *anger.* But it cannot have a movement of withdrawal: because the evil is supposed to be already present or past. Thus no passion is contrary to anger according to contrariety of approach and withdrawal.

In like manner neither can there be according to contrariety of good and evil. Because the opposite of present evil is good obtained, which can no longer have the aspect of arduousness or difficulty. Nor, when once good is obtained, does there remain any other movement, except the appetite's repose in the good obtained; which repose belongs to joy, which is a passion of the concupiscible faculty.

Accordingly no movement of the soul can be contrary to the movement of anger, and nothing else than cessation from its movement is contrary thereto; thus the Philosopher says (*Rhetor.* ii. 3) that *calm is contrary to anger,* by opposition not of contrariety but of negation or privation.

From what has been said the replies to the objections are evident.

FOURTH ARTICLE

Whether in the Same Power, There Are Any Passions, Specifically Different, but Not Contrary to One Another?

We proceed thus to the Fourth Article:—

Objection 1. It would seem that there cannot be, in the same power, specifically different passions that are not contrary to one another. For the passions of the soul differ according to their objects. Now the objects of the soul's passions are good and evil; and on this distinction is based the contrariety of the passions. Therefore no passions of the same power, that are not contrary to one another, differ specifically.

Obj. 2. Further, difference of species implies a difference of form. But every difference of form is in respect of some contrariety, as stated in *Metaph.* ii. 8. Therefore passions of the same power, that are not contrary to one another, do not differ specifically.

Obj. 3. Further, since every passion of the soul consists in approach or withdrawal in respect of good or evil, it seems that every difference in the passions of the soul must needs arise from the difference of good and evil; or from the difference of approach and withdrawal; or from degrees in approach or withdrawal. Now the first two differences cause contrariety in the passions of the soul, as stated above (A. 2): whereas the third difference does not diversify the species; else the species of the soul's passions would be infinite. Therefore it is not possible for passions of the same power to differ in species, without being contrary to one another.

On the contrary, Love and joy differ in species, and are in the concupiscible power; and yet they are not contrary to one another; rather, in fact, one causes the other. Therefore in the same power there are passions that differ in species without being contrary to one another.

I answer that, Passions differ in accordance with their active causes, which, in the case of the passions of the soul, are their objects. Now the difference in active causes may be considered in two ways: first, from the point of view of their species or nature, as fire differs from water; secondly, from the point of view of the difference in their active power. In the passions of the soul we can treat the difference of their active or motive causes in respect of their motive power, as if they were natural agents. For every mover, in a fashion, either draws the patient to itself, or repels it from itself. Now in drawing it to itself, it does three things in the patient. Because, in the first place, it gives the patient an inclination or aptitude to tend to the mover: thus a light body, which is above, bestows lightness on the body generated, so that it has an inclination or aptitude to be above. Secondly, if the generated body be outside its proper place, the mover gives it movement towards that place. —Thirdly, it makes it to rest, when it shall have come to its proper place: since to the same cause are due, both rest in a place, and the movement to that place. The same applies to the cause of repulsion.

Now, in the movements of the appetitive faculty, good has, as it were, a force of attraction, while evil has a force of repulsion. In the first place, therefore, good causes, in the appetitive power, a certain inclination, aptitude or connaturalness in respect of good: and this belongs to the passion of *love:* the corresponding contrary of which is *hatred* in respect of evil.—Secondly, if the good be not yet possessed, it causes in the appetite a movement towards the attainment of the good beloved: and this belongs to the passion of *desire* or *concupiscence:* and contrary to it, in respect of evil, is the passion of *aversion* or *dislike.*— Thirdly, when the good is obtained, it causes the appetite to rest, as it were, in the good obtained: and this belongs to the passion of *delight* or *joy:* the contrary of which, in respect of evil, is *sorrow* or *sadness.*

On the other hand, in the irascible passions, the aptitude, or inclination to seek good, or to shun evil, is presupposed as arising from the concupiscible faculty, which regards good or evil absolutely. And in respect of good not yet obtained, we have *hope* and *despair.* In respect of evil not yet present we have *fear* and *daring.* But in respect of good obtained there is no irascible passion: because it is no longer considered in the light of something arduous, as stated above (A. 3). But evil already present gives rise to the passion of *anger.*

Accordingly it is clear that in the concupiscible faculty there are three couples of passions; viz., love and hatred, desire and aversion, joy and sadness. In like manner there are three groups in the irascible faculty; viz., hope and despair, fear and daring, and anger which has no contrary passion.

Consequently there are altogether eleven passions differing specifically; six in the concupiscible faculty, and five in the irascible; and under these all the passions of the soul are contained.

From this the replies to the objections are evident.

QUESTION 24

Of Good and Evil in the Passions of the Soul

(In Four Articles)

WE must now consider good and evil in the passions of the soul: and under this head there are four points of inquiry: (1) Whether moral good and evil can be found in the passions of the soul? (2) Whether every passion of the soul is morally evil? (3) Whether every passion increases or decreases the goodness or malice of an act? (4) Whether any passion is good or evil specifically?

FIRST ARTICLE

Whether Moral Good and Evil Can Be Found in the Passions of the Soul?

We proceed thus to the First Article:—

Objection 1. It would seem that no passion of the soul is morally good or evil. For moral good and evil are proper to man: since *morals are properly predicated of man*, as Ambrose says (*Super Luc., Prolog.*). But passions are not proper to man, for he has them in common with other animals. Therefore no passion of the soul is morally good or evil.

Obj. 2. Further, the good or evil of man consists in *being in accord, or in disaccord with reason*, as Dionysius says (*Div. Nom.* iv). Now the passions of the soul are not in the reason, but in the sensitive appetite, as stated above (Q. 22, A. 3). Therefore they have no connection with human, *i.e.*, moral, good or evil.

Obj. 3. Further, the Philosopher says (Ethic. ii. 5) that *we are neither praised nor blamed for our passions*. But we are praised and blamed for moral good and evil. Therefore the passions are not morally good or evil.

On the contrary, Augustine says (*De Civ. Dei* xiv. 7) while speaking of the passions of the soul: *They are evil if our love is evil; good if our love is good*.

I answer that, We may consider the passions of the soul in two ways: first, in themselves; secondly, as being subject to the command of the reason and will.—If then the passions be considered in themselves, to wit, as movements

* *Cf.* Q. 22, A. 2, footnote.

of the irrational appetite, thus there is no moral good or evil in them, since this depends on the reason, as stated above (Q. 18, A. 5). If, however, they be considered as subject to the command of the reason and will, then moral good and evil are in them. Because the sensitive appetite is nearer than the outward members to the reason and will; and yet the movements and actions of the outward members are morally good or evil, inasmuch as they are voluntary. Much more, therefore, may the passions, in so far as they are voluntary, be called morally good or evil. And they are said to be voluntary, either from being commanded by the will, or from not being checked by the will.

Reply Obj. 1. These passions, considered in themselves, are common to man and other animals: but, as commanded by the reason, they are proper to man.

Reply Obj. 2. Even the lower appetitive powers are called rational, in so far as *they partake of reason in some sort* (*Ethic.* i. 13).

Reply Obj. 3. The Philosopher says that we are neither praised nor blamed for our passions considered absolutely; but he does not exclude their becoming worthy of praise or blame, in so far as they are subordinate to reason. Hence he continues: *For the man who fears or is angry, is not praised . . . or blamed, but the man who is angry in a certain way, i.e., according to, or against reason.*

SECOND ARTICLE

Whether Every Passion of the Soul Is Evil Morally?

We proceed thus to the Second Article:—

Objection 1. It would seem that all the passions of the soul are morally evil. For Augustine says (*De Civ. Dei* ix. 4) that *some call the soul's passions diseases or disturbances of the soul*.* But every disease or disturbance of the soul is morally evil. Therefore every passion of the soul is evil morally.

Obj. 2. Further, Damascene says (*De Fide Orthod.* ii. 22) that *movement in accord with nature is an action, but movement contrary to nature is passion.* But in movements of the soul, what is against nature is sinful and morally evil: hence he says elsewhere (*ibid.* 4) that *the devil turned from that which is in accord with nature to that which is against nature.* Therefore these passions are morally evil.

Obj. 3. Further, whatever leads to sin, has an aspect of evil. But these passions lead to sin: wherefore they are called *the passions of sins* (Rom. vii. 5). Therefore it seems that they are morally evil.

On the contrary, Augustine says (*De Civ. Dei* xiv. 9) that *all these emotions are right in those whose love is rightly placed. . . . For they fear to sin, they desire to persevere; they grieve for sin, they rejoice in good works.*

I answer that, On this question the opinion of the Stoics differed from that of the Peripatetics: for the Stoics held that all passions are evil, while the Peripatetics maintained that moderate passions are good. This difference, although it appears great in words, is nevertheless, in reality, none at all, or but little, if we consider the intent of either school. For the Stoics did not discern between sense and intellect; and consequently neither between the intellectual and sensitive appetite. Hence they did not discriminate the passions of the soul from the movements of the will, in so far as the passions of the soul are in the sensitive appetite, while the simple movements of the will are in the intellectual appetite: but every rational movement of the appetitive part they call will, while they called passion, a movement that exceeds the limits of reason. Wherefore Cicero, following their opinion (*De Tusc. Quæst.* iii. 4) calls all passions *diseases of the soul:* whence he argues that *those who are diseased are unsound; and those who are unsound are wanting in sense.* Hence we speak of those who are wanting in sense as being *unsound.*

On the other hand, the Peripatetics give the name of *passions* to all the movements of the sensitive appetite. Wherefore they esteem them good, when they are controlled by reason; and evil when they are not controlled by reason. Hence it is evident that Cicero was wrong in disapproving (*ibid.*) of the Peripatetic theory of a mean in the passions, when he says that *every evil, though moderate, should be shunned; for, just as a body, though it be moderately ailing, is not sound; so, this mean in the diseases or passions of the soul, is not sound.* For passions are not called *diseases* or *disturbances* of the soul, save when they are not controlled by reason.

Hence the reply to the First Objection is evident.

Reply Obj. 2. In every passion there is an increase or decrease in the natural movement of the heart, according as the heart is moved more or less intensely by contraction and dilatation; and hence it derives the character of passion. But there is no need for passion to deviate always from the order of natural reason.

Reply Obj. 3. The passions of the soul, in so far as they are contrary to the order of reason, incline us to sin: but in so far as they are controlled by reason, they pertain to virtue.

THIRD ARTICLE

Whether Passion Increases or Decreases the Goodness or Malice of an Act?

We proceed thus to the Third Article:—

Objection 1. It would seem that every passion decreases the goodness of a moral action. For anything that hinders the judgment of reason, on which depends the goodness of a moral act, consequently decreases the goodness of the moral act. But every passion hinders the judgment of reason: for Sallust says (*Catilin.*): *All those that take counsel about matters of doubt, should be free from hatred, anger, friendship and pity.* Therefore passion decreases the goodness of a moral act.

Obj. 2. Further, the more a man's action is like to God, the better it is: hence the Apostle says (Eph. v. 1): *Be ye followers of God, as most dear children.* But *God and the holy angels feel no anger when they punish . . . no fellow-feeling with misery when they relieve the unhappy,* as Augustine says (*De Civ. Dei* ix. 5). Therefore it is better to do such like deeds without than with a passion of the soul.

Obj. 3. Further, just as moral evil depends on its relation to reason, so also does moral good. But moral evil is lessened by passion: for he sins less, who sins from passion, than he who sins deliberately. Therefore he does a better deed, who does well without passion, than he who does with passion.

On the contrary, Augustine says (*De Civ. Dei* ix. 5) that *the passion of pity is obedient to reason, when pity is bestowed without violating right, as when the poor are relieved, or the penitent forgiven.* But nothing that is obedient to reason lessens the moral good. Therefore a passion of the soul does not lessen moral good.

I answer that, As the Stoics held that every passion of the soul is evil, they consequently held that every passion of the soul lessens the goodness of an act; since the admixture of evil either destroys good altogether, or makes it to be less good. And this is true indeed, if by passions we understand none but the inordinate movements of the sensitive appetite, considered as disturbances or ailments. But if we give the name of passions to all the movements of the sensitive appetite, then it belongs to the perfection of man's good that his passions be moderated by reason. For since man's good is founded on reason as its root, that good will be all the more perfect, according as it extends to more things pertaining to man. Wherefore no one questions the fact that it belongs to the perfection of moral good, that the actions of the outward members be controlled by the law of reason. Hence, since the sensitive appetite can obey reason, as stated above (Q. 17, A. 7), it belongs to the perfection of moral or human good, that the passions themselves also should be controlled by reason.

Accordingly just as it is better that man should both will good and do it in his external act; so also does it belong to the perfection of moral good, that man should be moved unto good, not only in respect of his will, but also in respect of his sensitive appetite; according to Ps. lxxxiii. 3: *My heart and my flesh have rejoiced in the living God:* where by *heart* we are to understand the intellectual appetite, and by *flesh* the sensitive appetite.

Reply Obj. 1. The passions of the soul may stand in a twofold relation to the judgment of reason. First, antecedently: and thus, since they obscure the judgment of reason, on which the goodness of the moral act depends, they diminish the goodness of the act; for it is more praiseworthy to do a work of charity from the judgment of reason than from the mere passion of pity.—In the second place, consequently: and this in two ways. First, by way of redundance: because, to wit, when the higher part of the soul is intensely moved to anything, the lower part also follows that movement; and thus the passion that results in consequence, in the sensitive appetite, is a sign of the intensity of the will, and so indicates greater moral goodness.—Secondly, by way of choice; when, to wit, a man, by the judgment of his reason, chooses to be affected by a passion in order to work more promptly with the co-operation of the sensitive appetite. And thus a passion of the soul increases the goodness of an action.

Reply Obj. 2. In God and the angels there is no sensitive appetite, nor again bodily members: and so in them good does not depend on the right ordering of passions or of bodily actions, as it does in us.

Reply Obj. 3. A passion that tends to evil, and precedes the judgment of reason, diminishes sin; but if it be consequent in either of the ways mentioned above (*Reply Obj.* 1), it aggravates the sin, or else it is a sign of its being more grievous.

Whether Any Passion Is Good or Evil in Its Species?

We proceed thus to the Fourth Article:—

Objection 1. It would seem that no passion of the soul is good or evil morally according to its species. Because moral good and evil depend on reason. But the passions are in the sensitive appetite; so that accordance with reason is accidental to them. Since, therefore, nothing accidental belongs to a thing's species, it seems that no passion is good or evil according to its species.

Obj. 2. Further, acts and passions take their species from their object. If, therefore, any passion were good or evil, according to its species, it would follow that those passions the object of which is good, are specifically good, such as love, desire and joy: and that those passions, the object of which is evil, are specifically evil, as hatred, fear and sadness. But this is clearly false. Therefore no passion is good or evil according to its species.

Obj. 3. Further, there is no species of passion that is not to be found in other animals. But moral good is in man alone. Therefore no passion of the soul is good or evil according to its species.

On the contrary, Augustine says (*De Civ. Dei* ix. 5) that *pity is a kind of virtue.* Moreover, the Philosopher says (*Ethic.* ii. 7) that modesty is a praiseworthy passion. Therefore some passions are good or evil according to their species.

I answer that, We ought, seemingly, to apply to passions what has been said in regard to acts (Q. 18, AA. 5, 6; Q. 20, A. 1)—viz., that the species of a passion, as the species of an act, can be considered from two points of view. First, according to its natural genus; and thus moral good and evil have no connection with the species of an act or passion. Secondly, according to its moral genus, inasmuch as it is voluntary and controlled by reason. In this way moral good and evil can belong to the species of a passion, in so far as the object to which a passion tends, is, of itself, in harmony or in discord with reason: as is clear in the case of *shame* which is base fear; and of *envy* which is sorrow for another's good: for thus passions belong to the same species as the external act.

Reply Obj. 1. This argument considers the passions in their natural species, in so far as the sensitive appetite is considered in itself. But in so far as the sensitive appetite obeys reason, good and evil of reason are no longer accidentally in the passions of the appetite, but essentially.

Reply Obj. 2. Passions having a tendency to good, are themselves good, if they tend to that which is truly good, and in like manner, if they turn away from that which is truly evil. On the other hand, those passions which consist in aversion from good, and a tendency to evil, are themselves evil.

Reply Obj. 3. In irrational animals the sensitive appetite does not obey reason. Nevertheless, in so far as they are led by a kind of estimative power, which is subject to a higher, *i.e.,* the Divine, reason, there is a certain likeness of moral good in them, in regard to the soul's passions.

QUESTION 25

Of the Order of the Passions to One Another

(In Four Articles)

WE must now consider the order of the passions to one another: and under this head there are four points of inquiry: (1) The relation of the irascible passions to the concupiscible passions; (2) The relation of the concupiscible passions to one another; (3) The relation of the irascible passions to one another; (4) The four principal passions.

FIRST ARTICLE

Whether the Irascible Passions Precede the Concupiscible Passions, or Vice Versa?

We proceed thus to the First Article:—

Objection 1. It would seem that the irascible passions precede the concupiscible passions. For the order of the passions is that of their objects. But the object of the irascible faculty is the difficult good, which seems to be the highest good. Therefore the irascible passions seem to precede the concupiscible passions.

Obj. 2. Further, the mover precedes that which is moved. But the irascible faculty is compared to the concupiscible, as mover to that which is moved: since it is given to animals, for the purpose of removing the obstacles that hinder the concupiscible faculty from enjoying its object, as stated above (Q. 23, A. 1 *ad* 1; P. 1, Q. 81, A. 2). Now *that which removes an obstacle, is a kind of mover (Phys.* viii. 4). Therefore the irascible passions precede the concupiscible passions.

Obj. 3. Further, joy and sadness are concupiscible passions. But joy and sadness succeed to the irascible passions: for the Philosopher says (*Ethic* iv. 5) that *retaliation causes anger to cease, because it produces pleasure instead of the previous pain.* Therefore the concupiscible passions follow the irascible passions.

On the contrary, The concupiscible passions regard the absolute good, while the irascible passions regard a restricted, viz., the difficult, good. Since, therefore, the absolute good precedes the restricted good, it seems that the concupiscible passions precede the irascible.

I answer that, In the concupiscible passions there is more diversity than in the passions of the irascible faculty. For in the former we find something relating to movement—*e.g.,* desire; and something belonging to repose, *e.g.,* joy and sadness. But in the irascible passions there is nothing pertaining to repose, and only that which belongs to movement. The reason of this is that when we find rest in a thing, we no longer look upon it as something difficult or arduous; whereas such is the object of the irascible faculty.

Now since rest is the end of movement, it is first in the order of intention, but last in the order of execution. If, therefore, we compare the passions of the irascible faculty with those concupiscible passions that denote rest in good, it is evident that in the order of execution, the irascible passions take precedence of such like passions of the concupiscible faculty: thus hope precedes joy, and hence causes it, according to the Apostle (Rom. xii. 12): *Rejoicing in hope.* But the concupiscible passion which denotes rest in evil, viz., sadness, comes between two irascible passions: because it follows fear; since we become sad when we are confronted by the evil that we feared; while it precedes the movement of anger; since the movement of self-vindication, that results from sadness, is the movement of anger. And because it is looked upon as a good thing to pay back the evil done to us; when the angry man has achieved this he rejoices. Thus it is evident that every passion of the irascible faculty terminates in a concupiscible passion denoting rest, viz., either in joy or in sadness.

But if we compare the irascible passions to those concupiscible passions that denote movement, then it is clear that the latter take precedence: because the passions of the irascible faculty add something to those of the concupiscible faculty; just as the object of the irascible adds the aspect of arduousness or difficulty to the object of the concupiscible faculty. Thus hope adds to desire a certain effort, and a certain raising of the spirits to the realization of the arduous good. In like manner fear adds to aversion or detestation a certain lowness of spirits, on account of difficulty in shunning the evil.

Accordingly the passions of the irascible faculty stand between those concupiscible passions that denote movement towards good or evil, and those concupiscible passions that denote rest in good or evil. And it is therefore evident that the irascible passions both arise from and terminate in the passions of the concupiscible faculty.

Reply Obj. 1. This argument would prove, if the formal object of the concupiscible faculty were something contrary to the arduous, just as the formal object of the irascible faculty is that which is arduous. But because the object of the concupiscible faculty is good absolutely, it naturally precedes the object of the irascible, as the common precedes the proper.

Reply Obj. 2. The remover of an obstacle is not a direct but an accidental mover: and here we are speaking of passions as directly related to one another.—Moreover, the irascible passion removes the obstacle that hinders the concupiscible from resting in its object. Wherefore it only follows that the irascible passions precede those concupiscible passions that connote rest.—The third objection leads to the same conclusion.

SECOND ARTICLE

Whether Love Is the First of the Concupiscible Passions?

We proceed thus to the Second Article:—

Objection 1. It would seem that love is not the first of the concupiscible passions. For the concupiscible faculty is so called from concupiscence, which is the same passion as desire. But *things are named from their chief characteristic (De Anima* ii. 4). Therefore desire takes precedence of love.

Obj. 2. Further, love implies a certain union; since it is a *uniting and binding force,* as Dionysius states *(Div. Nom.* iv). But concupiscence or desire is a movement towards union with the thing coveted or desired. Therefore desire precedes love.

Obj. 3. Further, the cause precedes its effect. But pleasure is sometimes the cause of love: since some love on account of pleasure *(Ethic.* viii. 3, 4). Therefore pleasure precedes love; and consequently love is not the first of the concupiscible passions.

On the contrary, Augustine says *(De Civ. Dei* xiv. 7, 9) that all the passions are caused by love: since *love yearning for the beloved object, is desire; and, having and enjoying it, is joy.* Therefore love is the first of the concupiscible passions.

I answer that, Good and evil are the object of the concupiscible faculty. Now good naturally precedes evil; since evil is the privation of good. Wherefore all the passions, the object of which is good, are naturally before those, the object of which is evil,—that is to say, each precedes its contrary passion: because the quest of a good is the reason for shunning the opposite evil.

Now good has the aspect of an end, and the end is indeed first in the order of intention, but last in the order of execution. Consequently the order of the concupiscible passions can be considered either in the order of intention or in the order of execution. In the order of execution, the first place belongs to that which takes place first in the thing that tends to the end. Now it is evident that whatever tends to an end, has, in the first place, an aptitude or proportion to that end, for nothing tends to a disproportionate end; secondly, it is moved to that end; thirdly, it rests in the end, after having attained it. And this very aptitude or proportion of the appetite to good is love, which is complacency in good; while movement towards good is desire or concupiscence; and rest in good is joy or pleasure. Accordingly in this order, love precedes desire, and desire precedes pleasure.—But in the order of intention, it is the reverse: because the pleasure intended causes desire and love. For pleasure is the enjoyment of the good, which enjoyment is, in a way, the end, just as the good itself is, as stated above (Q. 11, A. 3 *ad* 3).

Reply Obj. 1. We name a thing as we understand it, for *words are signs of thoughts,* as the Philosopher states *(Peri Herm.* i. 1). Now in most cases we know a cause by its effect. But the effect of love, when the beloved object is possessed, is pleasure: when it is not possessed, it is desire or concupiscence: and, as Augustine says *(De Trin.* x. 12), *we are more sensible to love, when we lack that which we love.* Consequently of all the concupiscible passions, concupiscence is felt most; and for this reason the power is named after it.

Reply Obj. 2. The union of lover and beloved is twofold. There is real union, consisting in the conjunction of one with the other. This union belongs to joy or pleasure, which follows desire. There is also an affective union, consisting in an aptitude or proportion, in so far as one thing, from the very fact of its having an aptitude for and an inclination to another, partakes of it: and love betokens such a union. This union precedes the movement of desire.

Reply Obj. 3. Pleasure causes love, in so far as it precedes love in the order of intention.

THIRD ARTICLE

Whether Hope Is the First of the Irascible Passions?

We proceed thus to the Third Article:—

Objection 1. It would seem that hope is not the first of the irascible passions. Because the irascible faculty is denominated from anger. Since, therefore, *things are named from their chief characteristic* (*cf.* A. 2, *Obj.* 1), it seems that anger precedes and surpasses hope.

Obj. 2. Further, the object of the irascible faculty is something arduous. Now it seems more arduous to strive to overcome a contrary evil that threatens soon to overtake us, which pertains to daring; or an evil actually present, which pertains to anger; than to strive simply to obtain some good. Again, it seems more arduous to strive to overcome a present evil, than a future evil. Therefore anger seems to be a stronger passion than daring, and daring, than hope. And consequently it seems that hope does not precede them.

Obj. 3. Further, when a thing is moved towards an end, the movement of withdrawal precedes the movement of approach. But fear and despair imply withdrawal from something; while daring and hope imply approach towards something. Therefore fear and despair precede hope and daring.

On the contrary, The nearer a thing is to the first, the more it precedes others. But hope is nearer to love, which is the first of the passions. Therefore hope is the first of the passions in the irascible faculty.

I answer that, As stated above (A. 1) all the irascible passions imply movement towards something. Now this movement of the irascible faculty towards something may be due to two causes: one is the mere aptitude or proportion to the end; and this pertains to love or hatred, those whose object is good, or evil; and this belongs to sadness or joy. As a matter of fact, the presence of good produces no passion in the irascible, as stated above (Q. 23, AA. 3, 4); but the presence of evil gives rise to the passion of anger.

Since then in the order of generation or execution, proportion or aptitude to the end precedes the achievement of the end; it follows that, of all the irascible passions, anger is the last in the order of generation. And among the other passions of the irascible faculty, which imply a movement arising from love of good or hatred of evil, those whose object is good, viz., hope and despair, must naturally precede those whose object is evil, viz., daring and fear: yet so that hope precedes despair; since

hope is a movement towards good as such, which is essentially attractive, so that hope tends to good directly; whereas despair is a movement away from good, a movement which is consistent with good, not as such, but in respect of something else, wherefore its tendency from good is accidental, as it were. In like manner fear, through being a movement from evil, precedes daring.—And that hope and despair naturally precede fear and daring is evident from this,—that as the desire of good is the reason for avoiding evil, so hope and despair are the reason for fear and daring: because daring arises from the hope of victory, and fear arises from the despair of overcoming. Lastly, anger arises from daring: for no one is angry while seeking vengeance, unless he dare to avenge himself, as Avicenna observes in the sixth book of his *Physics*. Accordingly, it is evident that hope is the first of all the irascible passions.

And if we wish to know the order of all the passions in the way of generation, love and hatred are first; desire and aversion, second; hope and despair, third; fear and daring, fourth; anger, fifth; sixth and last, joy and sadness, which follow from all the passions, as stated in *Ethic.* ii. 5: yet so that love precedes hatred; desire precedes aversion; hope precedes despair; fear precedes daring; and joy precedes sadness, as may be gathered from what has been stated above.

Reply Obj. 1. Because anger arises from the other passions, as an effect from the causes that precede it, it is from anger, as being more manifest than the other passions, that the power takes its name.

Reply Obj. 2. It is not the arduousness but the good that is the reason for approach or desire. Consequently hope, which regards good more directly, takes precedence: although at times daring or even anger regards something more arduous.

Reply Obj. 3. The movement of the appetite is essentially and directly towards the good as towards its proper object; its movement from evil results from this. For the movement of the appetitive part is in proportion, not to natural movement, but to the intention of nature, which intends the end before intending the removal of a contrary, which removal is desired only for the sake of obtaining the end.

FOURTH ARTICLE

Whether These Are the Four Principal Passions,— Joy, Sadness, Hope, and Fear?

We proceed thus to the Fourth Article:—

Objection 1. It would seem that joy, sadness, hope and fear are not the four principal passions. For Augustine (*De Civ. Dei* xiv. 3, 7 *sqq.*) omits hope and puts desire in its place.

Obj. 2. Further, there is a twofold order in the passions of the soul: the order of intention, and the order of execution or generation. The principal passions should therefore be taken, either in the order of intention; and thus joy and sadness, which are the final passions, will be the principal passions; or in the order of execution or generation, and thus love will be the principal passion. Therefore joy and sadness, hope and fear should in no way be called the four principal passions.

Obj. 3. Further, just as daring is caused by hope, so fear is caused by despair. Either, therefore, hope and despair should be reckoned as principal passions, since they cause others: or hope and daring, from being akin to one another.

On the contrary, Boëthius (*De Consol.* i) in enumerating the four principal passions, says:

> Banish joys: banish fears:
> Away with hope: away with tears.

I answer that, These four are commonly called the principal passions. Two of them, viz., joy and sadness, are said to be principal because in them all the other passions have their completion and end; wherefore they arise from all the other passions, as is stated in *Ethic.* ii. 5.—Fear and hope are principal passions, not because they complete the others simply, but because they complete them as regards the movement of the appetite towards something: for in respect of good, movement begins in love, goes forward to desire, and ends in hope; while in respect of evil, it begins in hatred, goes on to aversion, and ends in fear.

—Hence it is customary to distinguish these four passions in relation to the present and the future: for movement regards the future, while rest is in something present: so that joy relates to present good, sadness relates to present evil; hope regards future good, and fear, future evil.

As to the other passions that regard good or evil, present or future, they all culminate in these four. For this reason some have said that these four are the principal passions, because they are general passions; and this is true, provided that by hope and fear we understand the appetite's common tendency to desire or shun something.

Reply Obj. 1. Augustine puts desire or covetousness in place of hope, in so far as they seem to regard the same object, viz., some future good.

Reply Obj. 2. These are called principal passions, in the order of intention and completion. And though fear and hope are not the last passions simply, yet they are the last of those passions that tend towards something as future. Nor can the argument be pressed any further except in the case of anger: yet neither can anger be reckoned a principal passion, because it is an effect of daring, which cannot be a principal passion, as we shall state further on (*Reply Obj.* 3).

Reply Obj. 3. Despair implies movement away from good; and this is, as it were, accidental: and daring implies movement towards evil; and this too is accidental. Consequently these cannot be principal passions; because that which is accidental cannot be said to be principal. And so neither can anger be called a principal passion, because it arises from daring.

QUESTION 26

Of the Passions of the Soul in Particular: and First, of Love

(In Four Articles)

WE have now to consider the soul's passions in particular, and (1) the passions of the concupiscible faculty; (2) the passions of the irascible faculty.

The first of these considerations will be threefold: since we shall consider (1) Love and hatred; (2) Desire and aversion; (3) Pleasure and sadness.

Concerning love, three points must be considered: (1) Love itself; (2) The cause of love; (3) The effects of love. Under the first head there are four points of inquiry: (1) Whether love is in the concupiscible power? (2) Whether love is a passion? (3) Whether love is the same as dilection?

(4) Whether love is properly divided into love of friendship, and love of concupiscence?

FIRST ARTICLE

Whether Love Is in the Concupiscible Power?

We proceed thus to the First Article:—

Objection 1. It would seem that love is not in the concupiscible power. For it is written (Wis. viii. 2): *Her,* namely, wisdom, *have I loved, and have sought her out from my youth.* But the concupiscible power, being a part of the sensitive appetite, cannot tend to wisdom, which is not apprehended by the senses. Therefore love is not in the concupiscible power.

Obj. 2. Further, love seems to be identified with every passion: for Augustine says (*De Civ. Dei* xiv. 7): *Love, yearning for the object beloved, is desire; having and enjoying it, is joy; fleeing what is contrary to it, is fear; and feeling what is contrary to it, is sadness.* But not every passion is in the concupiscible power; indeed, fear, which is mentioned in this passage, is in the irascible power. Therefore we must not say absolutely that love is in the concupiscible power.

Obj. 3. Further, Dionysius (*Div. Nom.* iv) mentions a *natural love.* But natural love seems to pertain rather to the natural powers, which belong to the vegetal soul. Therefore love is not simply in the concupiscible power.

On the contrary, The Philosopher says (*Topic.* ii. 7) that *love is in the concupiscible power.*

I answer that, Love is something pertaining to the appetite; since good is the object of both. Wherefore love differs according to the difference of appetites. For there is an appetite which arises from an apprehension existing, not in the subject of the appetite, but in some other: and this is called the *natural appetite.* Because natural things seek what is suitable to them according to their nature, by reason of an apprehension which is not in them, but in the Author of their nature, as stated in the First Part (Q. 6, A. 1 *ad* 2; Q. 103, A. 1 *ad* 1, 3).—And there is another appetite arising from an apprehension in the subject of the appetite, but from necessity and not from free-will. Such is, in irrational animals, the *sensitive appetite,* which, however, in man, has a certain share of liberty, in so far as it obeys reason.—Again, there is another appetite following freely from an apprehension in the subject of the appetite. And this is the rational or intellectual appetite, which is called the *will.*

Now in each of these appetites, the name *love* is given to the principle of movement towards the end loved. In the natural appetite the principle of this movement is the appetitive subject's connaturalness with the thing to which it tends, and may be called *natural love:* thus the connaturalness of a heavy body for the centre, is by reason of its weight and may be called *natural love.* In like manner the aptitude of the sensitive appetite or of the will to some good, that is to say, its very complacency in good, is called *sensitive love,* or *intellectual* or *rational love.* So that sensitive love is in the sensitive appetite, just as intellectual love is in the intellectual appetite. And it belongs to the concupiscible power, because it regards good absolutely, and not under the aspect of difficulty, which is the object of the irascible faculty.

Reply Obj. 1. The words quoted refer to intellectual or rational love.

Reply Obj. 2. Love is spoken of as being fear, joy, desire and sadness, not essentially but causally.

Reply Obj. 3. Natural love is not only in the powers of the vegetal soul, but in all the soul's powers, and also in all the parts of the body, and universally in all things: because, as Dionysius says (*Div. Nom.* iv), *Beauty and goodness are beloved by all things;* since each single thing has a connaturalness with that which is naturally suitable to it.

SECOND ARTICLE

Whether Love Is a Passion?

We proceed thus to the Second Article:—

Objection 1. It would seem that love is not a passion. For no power is a passion. But every love is a power, as Dionysius says (*Div. Nom.* iv). Therefore love is not a passion.

Obj. 2. Further, love is a kind of union or bond, as Augustine says (*De Trin.* viii. 10). But a union or bond is not a passion, but rather a relation. Therefore love is not a passion.

Obj. 3. Further, Damascene says (*De Fide Orthod.* ii. 22) that passion is a movement. But love does not imply the movement of the appetite; for this is desire, of which movement love is the principle. Therefore love is not a passion.

On the contrary, The Philosopher says (*Ethic.* viii. 5) that *love is a passion.*

I answer that, Passion is the effect of the agent on the patient. Now a natural agent produces a twofold effect on the patient: for in the first place it gives it the form; and secondly it gives it the movement that results from the form. Thus the generator gives the generated body both weight and the movement resulting from weight: so that weight, from being the principle of movement to the place, which is connatural to that body by reason of its weight, can, in a way, be called *natural love.* In the same way the appetible object gives the appetite, first, a certain adaptation to itself, which consists in complacency in that object; and from this follows movement towards the appetible object. For *the appetitive movement is circular,* as stated in *De Anima* iii. 10; because the appetible object moves the appetite, introducing itself, as it were, into its intention; while the appetite moves towards the realization of the appetible object, so that the movement ends where it began. Accordingly, the first change wrought in the appetite by the appetible object is called *love,* and is nothing else than complacency in that object; and from this complacency results a movement towards that same object, and this movement is *desire;* and lastly, there is rest which is *joy.* Since, therefore, love consists in a change wrought in the appetite by the appetible object, it is evident that love is a passion: properly so called, according as it is in the concupiscible faculty; in a wider and extended sense, according as it is in the will.

Reply Obj. 1. Since power denotes a principle of movement or action, Dionysius calls love a power, in so far as it is a principle of movement in the appetite.

Reply Obj. 2. Union belongs to love in so far as by reason of the complacency of the appetite, the lover stands in relation to that which he loves, as though it were himself or part of himself. Hence it is clear that love is not the very relation of union, but that union is a result of love. Hence, too, Dionysius says that *love is a unitive force (Div. Nom.* iv), and the Philosopher says (*Polit.* ii. 1) that union is the work of love.

Reply Obj. 3. Although love does not denote the movement of the appetite in tending towards the appetible object, yet it denotes that movement whereby the appetite is changed by the appetible object, so as to have complacency therein.

THIRD ARTICLE

Whether Love Is the Same As Dilection?

We proceed thus to the Third Article:—

Objection 1. It would seem that love is the same as dilection. For Dionysius says (*Div. Nom.* iv) that love is to dilection, *as four is to twice two, and as a rectilinear figure is to one composed of straight lines.* But these have the same meaning. Therefore love and dilection denote the same thing.

Obj. 2. Further, the movements of the appetite differ by reason of their objects. But the objects of dilection and love are the same. Therefore these are the same.

Obj. 3. Further, if dilection and love differ, it seems that it is chiefly in the fact that *dilection refers to good things, love to evil things, as some have maintained,* according to Augustine (*De Civ. Dei* xiv. 7). But they do not differ thus; because as Augustine says (*ibid.*) the holy Scripture uses both words in reference to either good or bad things. Therefore love and dilection do not differ: thus indeed Augustine concludes (*ibid.*) that *it is not one thing to speak of love, and another to speak of dilection.*

On the contrary, Dionysius says (*Div. Nom.* iv) that *some holy men have held that love means something more Godlike than dilection does.*

* Referring to the Latin *carus (dear).*

I answer that, We find four words referring in a way, to the same thing: viz., love, dilection, charity and friendship. They differ, however, in this, that *friendship,* according to the Philosopher (*Ethic.* viii. 5), *is like a habit,* whereas *love* and *dilection* are expressed by way of act or passion; and *charity* can be taken either way.

Moreover these three express act in different ways. For love has a wider signification than the others, since every dilection or charity is love, but not vice versa. Because dilection implies, in addition to love, a choice (*electionem*) made beforehand, as the very word denotes: and therefore dilection is not in the concupiscible power, but only in the will, and only in the rational nature.—Charity denotes, in addition to love, a certain perfection of love, in so far as that which is loved is held to be of great price, as the word itself implies.*

Reply Obj. 1. Dionysius is speaking of love and dilection, in so far as they are in the intellectual appetite; for thus love is the same as dilection.

Reply Obj. 2. The object of love is more general than the object of dilection: because love extends to more than dilection does, as stated above.

Reply Obj. 3. Love and dilection differ, not in respect of good and evil, but as stated. Yet in the intellectual faculty love is the same as dilection. And it is in this sense that Augustine speaks of love in the passage quoted: hence a little further on he adds that *a right will is well-directed love, and a wrong will is ill-directed love.* However, the fact that love, which is a concupiscible passion, inclines many to evil, is the reason why some assigned the difference spoken of.

Reply Obj. 4. The reason why some held that, even when applied to the will itself, the word *love* signifies something more Godlike than *dilection,* was because love denotes a passion, especially in so far as it is in the sensitive appetite; whereas dilection presupposes the judgment of reason. But it is possible for man to tend to God by love, being as it were passively drawn by Him, more than he can possibly be drawn thereto by his reason, which pertains to the nature of dilection, as stated above. And consequently love is more Godlike than dilection.

FOURTH ARTICLE

Whether Love Is Properly Divided into Love of Friendship and Love of Concupiscence?

We proceed thus to the Fourth Article:—

Objection 1. It would seem that love is not properly divided into love of friendship and love of concupiscence. For *love is a passion, while friendship is a habit,* according to the Philosopher (*Ethic.* viii. 5). But habit cannot be the member of a division of passions. Therefore love is not properly divided into love of concupiscence and love of friendship.

Obj. 2. Further, a thing cannot be divided by another member of the same division; for man is not a member of the same division as *animal.* But concupiscence is a member of the same division as love, as a passion distinct from love. Therefore concupiscence is not a division of love.

Obj. 3. Further, according to the Philosopher (*Ethic.* viii. 3) friendship is threefold, that which is founded on *usefulness,* that which is founded on *pleasure,* and that which is founded on *goodness.* But useful and pleasant friendship are not without concupiscence. Therefore concupiscence should not be contrasted with friendship.

On the contrary, We are said to love certain things, because we desire them: thus *a man is said to love wine, on account of its sweetness which he desires;* as stated in *Topic.* ii. 3. But we have no friendship for wine and suchlike things, as stated in *Ethic.* viii. 2. Therefore love of concupiscence is distinct from love of friendship.

I answer that, As the Philosopher says (*Rhet.* ii. 4), *to love is to wish good to someone.* Hence the movement of love has a twofold tendency: towards the good which a man wishes to someone,—to himself or to another, and towards that to which he wishes some good. Accordingly, man has love of concupi-scence towards the good that he wishes to another, and love of friendship, towards him to whom he wishes good.

Now the members of this division are related as primary and secondary: since that which is loved with the love of friendship is loved simply and for itself; whereas that which is loved with the love of concupiscence, is loved, not simply and for itself, but for something else. For just as that which has existence, is a being simply, while that which exists in another is a relative being; so, because good is convertible with being, the good, which itself has goodness, is good simply; but that which is another's good, is a relative good. Consequently the love with which a thing is loved, that it may have some good, is love simply; while the love, with which a thing is loved, that it may be another's good, is relative love.

Reply Obj. 1. Love is not divided into friendship and concupiscence, but into love of friendship, and love of concupiscence. For a friend is, properly speaking, one to whom we wish good: while we are said to desire, what we wish for ourselves.

Hence the Reply to the Second Objection is evident.

Reply Obj. 3. When friendship is based on usefulness or pleasure, a man does indeed wish his friend some good: and in this respect the character of friendship is preserved. But since he refers this good further to his own pleasure or use, the result is that friendship of the useful or pleasant, in so far as it is connected with love of concupiscence, loses the character of true friendship.

QUESTION 27

Of the Cause of Love

(*In Four Articles*)

WE must now consider the cause of love: and under this head there are four points of inquiry: (1) Whether good is the only cause of love? (2) Whether knowledge is a cause of love? (3) Whether likeness is a cause of love? (4) Whether any other passion of the soul is a cause of love?

FIRST ARTICLE

Whether Good Is the Only Cause of Love?

We proceed thus to the First Article:—

Objection 1. It would seem that good is not the only cause of love. For good does not cause love, except because it is loved. But it happens that evil also is loved, according to Ps. x. 6: *He that loveth iniquity, hateth his own soul:* else, every love would be good. Therefore good is not the only cause of love.

Obj. 2. Further, the Philosopher says (*Rhet.* ii. 4) that *we love those who acknowledge their evils.* Therefore it seems that evil is the cause of love.

Obj. 3. Further, Dionysius says (*Div. Nom.* iv) that not *the good* only but also *the beautiful is beloved by all.*

On the contrary, Augustine says (*De Trin.* viii. 3): *Assuredly, the good alone is beloved.* Therefore good alone is the cause of love.

I answer that, As stated above (Q. 26, A. 1), Love belongs to the appetitive power which is a passive faculty. Wherefore its object stands in relation to it as the cause of its movement or act. Therefore the cause of love must needs be love's object. Now the proper object of love is the good; because, as stated above (Q. 26, AA. 1, 2), love implies a certain connaturalness or complacency of the lover for the thing beloved, and to everything, that thing is a good, which is akin and proportionate to it. It follows, therefore, that good is the proper cause of love.

Reply Obj. 1. Evil is never loved except under the aspect of good, that is to say, in so far as it is good in some respect, and is considered as being good simply. And thus a certain love is evil, in so far as it tends to that which is not simply a true good. It is in this way that man *loves iniquity*, inasmuch as, by means of iniquity, some good is gained; pleasure, for instance, or money, or such like.

Reply Obj. 2. Those who acknowledge their evils, are beloved, not for their evils, but because they acknowledge them, for it is a good thing to acknowledge one's faults, in so far as it excludes insincerity or hypocrisy.

Reply Obj. 3. The beautiful is the same as the good, and they differ in aspect only. For since good is what all seek, the notion of good is that which calms the desire; while the notion of the beautiful is that which calms the desire, by being seen or known. Consequently those senses chiefly regard the beautiful, which are the most cognitive, viz., sight and hearing, as ministering to reason; for we speak of beautiful sights and beautiful sounds. But in reference to the other objects of the other senses, we do not use the expression *beautiful*, for we do not speak of beautiful tastes, and beautiful odors. Thus it is evident that beauty adds to goodness a relation to the cognitive faculty: so that *good* means that which simply pleases the appetite; while the *beautiful* is something pleasant to apprehend.

SECOND ARTICLE

Whether Knowledge Is a Cause of Love?

We proceed thus to the Second Article:—

Objection 1. It would seem that knowledge is not a cause of love. For it is due to love that a thing is sought. But some things are sought without being known, for instance, the sciences; for since *to have them is the same as to know them*, as Augustine says (QQ. 83, qu. 35), if we knew them we should have them, and should not seek them. Therefore knowledge is not the cause of love.

Obj. 2. Further, to love what we know not seems like loving something more than we know it. But some things are loved more than they are known: thus in this life God can be loved in Himself, but cannot be known in Himself. Therefore knowledge is not the cause of love.

Obj. 3. Further, if knowledge were the cause of love, there would be no love, where there is no knowledge. But in all things there is love, as Dionysius says (*Div. Nom.* iv); whereas there is not knowledge in all things. Therefore knowledge is not the cause of love.

On the contrary, Augustine proves (*De Trin.* x. 1, 2) that *none can love what he does not know.*

I answer that, As stated above (A. 1), good is the cause of love, as being its object. But good is not the object of the appetite, except as apprehended. And therefore love demands some apprehension of the good that is loved. For this reason the Philosopher (*Ethic.* ix. 5, 12) says that bodily sight is the beginning of sensitive love: and in like manner the contemplation of spiritual beauty or goodness is the beginning of spiritual love. Accordingly knowledge is the cause of love for the same reason as good is, which can be loved only if known.

Reply Obj. 1. He who seeks science, is not entirely without knowledge thereof: but knows something about it already in some respect, either in a general way, or in some one of its effects, or from having heard it commended, as Augustine says (*De Trin.* x. 1, 2). But to have it is not to know it thus, but to know it perfectly.

Reply Obj. 2. Something is required for the perfection of knowledge, that is not requisite for the perfection of love. For knowledge belongs to the reason, whose function it is to distinguish things which in reality are united, and to unite together, after a fashion, things that are distinct, by comparing one with another. Consequently the perfection of knowledge requires that man should know distinctly all that is in a thing, such as its parts, powers, and properties. On the other hand, love is in the appetitive power, which regards a thing as it is in itself: wherefore it suffices, for the perfection of love, that a thing be loved according as it is known in itself. Hence it is, therefore, that a thing is loved more than it is known; since it can be loved perfectly, even without being perfectly known. This is most evident in regard to the sciences, which some love through having a certain general knowledge of them: for instance, they know that rhetoric is a science that enables man to persuade others; and this is what they love in rhetoric. The same applies to the love of God.

Reply Obj. 3. Even natural love, which is in all things, is caused by a kind of knowledge, not indeed existing in natural things themselves, but in Him Who created their nature, as stated above (Q. 26, A. 1; *cf.* P. 1, Q. 6, A. 1 *ad* 2).

THIRD ARTICLE

Whether Likeness Is a Cause of Love?

We proceed thus to the Third Article:—

Objection 1. It would seem that likeness is not a cause of love. For the same thing is not the cause of contraries. But likeness is the cause of hatred; for it is written (Prov. xiii. 10) that *among the proud there are always contentions;* and the Philosopher says (*Ethic.* viii. 1) that *potters quarrel with one another.* Therefore likeness is not a cause of love.

Obj. 2. Further, Augustine says (*Confess.* iv. 14) that *a man loves in another that which he would not be himself: thus he loves an actor, but would not himself be an actor.* But it would not be so, if likeness were the proper cause of love; for in that case a man would love in another, that which he possesses himself, or would like to possess. Therefore likeness is not a cause of love.

Obj. 3. Further, everyone loves that which he needs, even if he have it not: thus a sick man loves health, and a poor man loves riches. But in so far as he needs them and lacks them, he is unlike them. Therefore not only likeness but also unlikeness is a cause of love.

Obj. 4. Further, the Philosopher says (*Rhet.* ii. 4) that *we love those who bestow money and health on us; and also those who retain their friendship for the dead.* But all are not such. Therefore likeness is not a cause of love.

On the contrary, It is written (Ecclus. xiii. 19): *Every beast loveth its like.*

I answer that, Likeness, properly speaking, is a cause of love. But it must be observed that likeness between things is twofold. One kind of likeness arises from each thing having the same quality actually: for example, two things possessing the quality of whiteness are said to be alike. Another kind of likeness arises from one thing having potentially and by way of inclination, a quality which the other has actually: thus we may say that a heavy body existing outside its proper place is like another heavy body that exists in its proper place: or again, according as potentiality bears a resemblance to its act; since act is contained, in a manner, in the potentiality itself.

Accordingly the first kind of likeness causes love of friendship or well-being. For the very fact that two men are alike, having, as it were, one form, makes them to be, in a manner, one in that form: thus two men are one thing in the species of humanity, and two white men are one thing in whiteness. Hence the affections of one tend to the other, as being one with him; and he wishes good to him as to himself. But the second kind of likeness causes love of concupiscence, or friendship founded on use-

fulness or pleasure: because whatever is in potentiality, as such, has the desire for its act; and it takes pleasure in its realization, if it be a sentient and cognitive being.

Now it has been stated above (Q. 26, A. 4), that in the love of concupiscence, the lover, properly speaking, loves himself, in willing the good that he desires. But a man loves himself more than another: because he is one with himself substantially, whereas with another he is one only in the likeness of some form. Consequently, if this other's likeness to him arising from the participation of a form, hinders him from gaining the good that he loves, he becomes hateful to him, not for being like him, but for hindering him from gaining his own good. This is why *potters quarrel among themselves,* because they hinder one another's gain: and why *there are contentions among the proud,* because they hinder one another in attaining the position they covet.

Hence the Reply to the First Objection is evident.

Reply Obj. 2. Even when a man loves in another what he loves not in himself, there is a certain likeness of proportion: because as the latter is to that which is loved in him, so is the former to that which he loves in himself: for instance, if a good singer love a good writer, we can see a likeness of proportion, inasmuch as each one has that which is becoming to him in respect of his art.

Reply Obj. 3. He that loves what he needs, bears a likeness to what he loves, as potentiality bears a likeness to its act, as stated above.

Reply Obj. 4. According to the same likeness of potentiality to its act, the illiberal man loves the man who is liberal, in so far as he expects from him something which he desires. The same applies to the man who is constant in his friendship as compared to one who is inconstant. For in either case friendship seems to be based on usefulness. We might also say that although not all men have these virtues in the complete habit, yet they have them according to certain seminal principles in the reason, in force of which principles the man who is not virtuous loves the virtuous man, as being in conformity with his own natural reason.

FOURTH ARTICLE

Whether Any Other Passion of the Soul Is a Cause of Love?

We proceed thus to the Fourth Article:—

Objection 1. It would seem that some other passion can be the cause of love. For the Philosopher (*Ethic.* viii. 3) says that some are loved for the sake of the pleasure they give.

But pleasure is a passion. Therefore another passion is a cause of love.

Obj. 2. Further, desire is a passion. But we love some because we desire to receive something from them: as happens in every friendship based on usefulness. Therefore another passion is a cause of love.

Obj. 3. Further, Augustine says (*De Trin.* x. 1: *When we have no hope of getting a thing, we love it but half-heartedly or not at all, even if we see how beautiful it is.* Therefore hope too is a cause of love.

On the contrary, All the other emotions of the soul are caused by love, as Augustine says (*De Civ. Dei* xiv. 7, 9).

I answer that, There is no other passion of the soul that does not presuppose love of some kind. The reason is that every other passion of the soul implies either movement towards something, or rest in something. Now every movement towards something, or rest in something, arises from some kinship or aptness to that thing; and in this does love consist.

Therefore it is not possible for any other passion of the soul to be universally the cause of every love. But it may happen that some other passion is the cause of some particular love: just as one good is the cause of another.

Reply Obj. 1. When a man loves a thing for the pleasure it affords, his love is indeed caused by pleasure; but that very pleasure is caused, in its turn, by another preceding love; for none takes pleasure save in that which is loved in some way.

Reply Obj. 2. Desire for a thing always presupposes love for that thing. But desire of one thing can be the cause of another thing's being loved; thus he that desires money, for this reason loves him from whom he receives it.

Reply Obj. 3. Hope causes or increases love; both by reason of pleasure, because it causes pleasure; and by reason of desire, because hope strengthens desire, since we do not desire so intensely that which we have no hope of receiving. Nevertheless hope itself is of a good that is loved.

QUESTION 28

Of the Effects of Love

(In Six Articles)

WE now have to consider the effects of love: under which head there are six points of inquiry: (1) Whether union is an effect of love? (2) Whether mutual indwelling is an effect of love? (3) Whether ecstasy is an effect of love? (4) Whether zeal is an effect of love? (5) Whether love is a passion that is hurtful to the lover? (6) Whether love is cause of all that the lover does?

FIRST ARTICLE

Whether Union Is an Effect of Love?

We proceed thus to the First Article:—

Objection 1. It would seem that union is not an effect of love. For absence is incompatible with union. But love is compatible with absence; for the Apostle says (Gal. iv. 18): *Be zealous for that which is good in a good thing always* (speaking of himself, according to a gloss), *and not only when I am present with you.* Therefore union is not an effect of love.

Obj. 2. Further, every union is either according to essence,—thus form is united to matter, accident to subject, and a part to the whole: or to another part in order to make up the whole: or according to likeness, in genus, species, or accident. But love does not cause union of essence; else love could not be between things essentially distinct. On the other

hand, love does not cause union of likeness, but rather is caused by it, as stated above (Q. 27, A. 3). Therefore union is not an effect of love.

Obj. 3. Further, the sense in act is the sensible in act, and the intellect in act is the thing actually understood. But the lover in act is not the beloved in act. Therefore union is the effect of knowledge rather than of love.

On the contrary, Dionysius says (*Div. Nom.* iv) that every love is a *unitive force.*

I answer that, The union of lover and beloved is twofold. The first is real union; for instance, when the beloved is present with the lover.—The second is union of affection: and this union must be considered in relation to the preceding apprehension; since movement of the appetite follows apprehension. Now love being twofold, viz., love of concupiscence, and love of friendship; each of these arises from a kind of apprehension of the oneness of the thing loved with the lover. For when we love a thing, by desiring it, we apprehend it as belonging to our well-being. In like manner when a man loves another with the love of friendship, he wills good to him, just as he wills good to himself: wherefore he apprehends him as his other self, in so far, to wit, as he wills good to him as to himself. Hence a friend is called a man's *other self* (*Ethic.* ix. 4), and

Augustine says (*Confess.* iv. 6), *Well did one say to his friend: Thou half of my soul.*

The first of these unions is caused *effectively* by love; because love moves man to desire and seek the presence of the beloved, as of something suitable and belonging to him. The second union is caused *formally* by love; because love itself is this union or bond. In this sense Augustine says (*De Trin.* viii. 10) that *love is a vital principle uniting, or seeking to unite two together, the lover, to wit, and the beloved.* For in describing it as *uniting* he refers to the union of affection, without which there is no love: and in saying that *it seeks to unite,* he refers to real union.

Reply Obj. 1. This argument is true of real union. That is necessary to pleasure as being its cause; desire implies the real absence of the beloved: but love remains whether the beloved be absent or present.

Reply Obj. 2. Union has a threefold relation to love. There is a union which causes love; and this is substantial union, as regards the love with which one loves oneself; while as regards the love wherewith one loves other things, it is the union of likeness, as stated above (Q. 27, A. 3). There is also a union which is essentially love itself. This union is according to a bond of affection, and is likened to substantial union, inasmuch as the lover stands to the object of his love, as to himself, if it be love of friendship; as to something belonging to himself, if it be love of concupiscence. Again there is a union, which is the effect of love. This is real union, which the lover seeks with the object of his love. Moreover this union is in keeping with the demands of love. for as the Philosopher relates (*Polit.* ii. 1), *Aristophanes stated that lovers would wish to be united both into one,* but since *this would result in either one or both being destroyed,* they seek a suitable and becoming union;—to live together, speak together, and be united together in other like things.

Reply Obj. 3. Knowledge is perfected by the thing known being united, through its likeness, to the knower. But the effect of love is that the thing itself which is loved, is, in a way, united to the lover, as stated above. Consequently the union caused by love is closer than that which is caused by knowledge.

SECOND ARTICLE

Whether Mutual Indwelling Is an Effect of Love?

We proceed thus to the Second Article:—

Objection 1. It would seem that love does not cause mutual indwelling, so that the lover be in the beloved and vice versa. For that which is in another is contained in it. But the same cannot be container and contents. Therefore love cannot cause mutual indwelling, so that the lover be in the beloved and vice versa.

Obj. 2. Further, nothing can penetrate within a whole, except by means of a division of the whole. But it is the function of the reason, not of the appetite where love resides, to divide things that are really united. Therefore mutual indwelling is not an effect of love.

Obj. 3. Further, if love involves the lover being in the beloved and vice versa, it follows that the beloved is united to the lover, in the same way as the lover is united to the beloved. But the union itself is love, as stated above (A. 1). Therefore it follows that the lover is always loved by the object of his love; which is evidently false. Therefore mutual indwelling is not an effect of love.

On the contrary, It is written (1 Jo. iv. 16): *He that abideth in charity abideth in God, and God in him.* Now charity is the love of God. Therefore, for the same reason, every love makes the beloved to be in the lover, and vice versa.

I answer that, This effect of mutual indwelling may be understood as referring both to the apprehensive and to the appetitive power. Because, as to the apprehensive power, the beloved is said to be in the lover, inasmuch as the beloved abides in the apprehension of the lover, according to Phil. i. 7, *For that I have you in my heart:* while the lover is said to be in the beloved, according to apprehension, inasmuch as the lover is not satisfied with a superficial apprehension of the beloved, but strives to gain an intimate knowledge of everything pertaining to the beloved, so as to penetrate into his very soul. Thus it is written concerning the Holy Ghost, Who Is God's Love, that He *searcheth all things, yea the deep things of God* (1 Cor. ii. 10).

As the appetitive power, the object loved is said to be in the lover, inasmuch as it is in his affections, by a kind of complacency: causing him either to take pleasure in it, or in its good, when present; or, in the absence of the object loved, by his longing, to tend towards it with the love of concupiscence, or towards the good that he wills to the beloved, with the love of friendship: not indeed from any extrinsic cause (as when we desire one thing on account of another, or wish good to another on account of something else), but because the complacency in the beloved is rooted in the lover's heart. For this reason we speak of love as being *intimate;* and of *the bowels of charity.* On the other hand, the lover is in the beloved, by the love of concupiscence and by the love of friendship, but not in the same way. For the love of concupiscence is not satisfied with any external or superficial possession or enjoyment of the beloved; but seeks to possess the beloved perfectly, by penetrating into his heart, as it were. Whereas, in the love of friendship, the lover is in the beloved, inasmuch as he reckons what is good or evil to his friend, as being so to himself; and his friend's will as his own, so that it seems as though he felt the good or suffered the evil in the person of his friend. Hence it is proper to friends *to desire the same things, and to grieve and rejoice at the same*, as the Philosopher says (*Ethic.* ix. 3 and *Rhet.* ii. 4). Consequently in so far as he reckons what affects his friend as affecting himself, the lover seems to be in the beloved, as though he were become one with him: but in so far as, on the other hand, he wills and acts for his friend's sake as for his own sake, looking on his friend as identified with himself, thus the beloved is in the lover.

In yet a third way, mutual indwelling in the love of friendship can be understood in regard to reciprocal love: inasmuch as friends return love for love, and both desire and do good things for one another.

Reply Obj. 1. The beloved is contained in the lover, by being impressed on his heart and thus becoming the object of his complacency. On the other hand, the lover is contained in the beloved, inasmuch as the lover penetrates, so to speak, into the beloved. For nothing hinders a thing from being both container and contents in different ways: just as a genus is contained in its species, and vice versa.

Reply Obj. 2. The apprehension of the reason precedes the movement of love. Consequently, just as the reason divides, so does the movement of love penetrate into the beloved, as was explained above.

Reply Obj. 3. This argument is true of the third kind of mutual indwelling, which is not to be found in every kind of love.

THIRD ARTICLE

Whether Ecstasy Is an Effect of Love?

We proceed thus to the Third Article:—

Objection 1. It would seem that ecstasy is not an effect of love. For ecstasy seems to imply loss of reason. But love does not always result in loss of reason: for lovers are masters of themselves at times. Therefore love does not cause ecstasy.

Obj. 2. Further, the lover desires the beloved to be united to him. Therefore he draws the beloved to himself, rather than betakes himself into the beloved, going forth out of himself as it were.

Obj. 3. Further, love unites the beloved to the lover, as stated above (A. 1). If, therefore, the lover goes out from himself, in order

to betake himself into the beloved, it follows that the lover always loves the beloved more than himself: which is evidently false. Therefore ecstasy is not an effect of love.

On the contrary, Dionysius says (*Div. Nom.* iv) that *the Divine love produces ecstasy,* and that *God Himself suffered ecstasy through love.* Since therefore according to the same author (*ibid.*), every love is a participated likeness of the Divine Love, it seems that every love causes ecstasy.

I answer that, To suffer ecstasy means to be placed outside oneself. This happens as to the apprehensive power and as to the appetitive power. As to the apprehensive power, a man is said to be placed outside himself, when he is placed outside the knowledge proper to him. This may be due to his being raised to a higher knowledge; thus, a man is said to suffer ecstasy, inasmuch as he is placed outside the connatural apprehension of his sense and reason, when he is raised up so as to comprehend things that surpass sense and reason: or it may be due to his being cast down into a state of debasement; thus a man may be said to suffer ecstasy, when he is overcome by violent passion or madness.—As to the appetitive power, a man is said to suffer ecstasy, when that power is borne towards something else, so that it goes forth out from itself, as it were.

The first of these ecstasies is caused by love dispositively, in so far, namely, as love makes the lover dwell on the beloved, as stated above (A. 2), and to dwell intently on one thing draws the mind from other things.—The second ecstasy is caused by love directly; by love of friendship, simply; by love of concupiscence, not simply but in a restricted sense. Because in love of concupiscence, the lover is carried out of himself, in a certain sense; in so far, namely, as not being satisfied with enjoying the good that he has, he seeks to enjoy something outside himself. But since he seeks to have this extrinsic good for himself, he does not go out from himself simply, and this movement remains finally within him. On the other hand, in the love of friendship, a man's affection goes out from itself simply; because he wishes and does good to his friend, by caring and providing for him, for his sake.

Reply Obj. 1. This argument is true of the first kind of ecstasy.

Reply Obj. 2. This argument applies to love of concupiscence, which, as stated above, does not cause ecstasy simply.

Reply Obj. 3. He who loves, goes out from himself, in so far as he wills the good of his friend and works for it. Yet he does not will the good of his friend more than his own good: and so it does not follow that he loves another more than himself.

FOURTH ARTICLE

Whether Zeal Is an Effect of Love?

We proceed thus to the Fourth Article:—

Objection 1. It would seem that zeal is not an effect of love. For zeal is a beginning of contention; wherefore it is written (1 Cor. iii. 3): *Whereas there is among you zeal* (Douay,—*envying*) *and contention,* etc. But contention is incompatible with love. Therefore zeal is not an effect of love.

Obj. 2. Further, the object of love is the good, which communicates itself to others. But zeal is opposed to communication; since it seems an effect of zeal, that a man refuses to share the object of his love with another: thus husbands are said to be jealous of (*zelare*) their wives, because they will not share them with others. Therefore zeal is not an effect of love.

Obj. 3. Further, there is no zeal without hatred, as neither is there without love: for it is written (Ps. lxxii. 3): *I had a zeal on occasion of the wicked.* Therefore it should not be set down as an effect of love any more than of hatred.

On the contrary, Dionysius says (*Div. Nom.* iv): *God is said to be a zealot, on account of his great love for all things.*

I answer that, Zeal, whatever way we take it, arises from the intensity of love. For it is evident that the more intensely a power tends to anything, the more vigorously it withstands opposition or resistance. Since therefore love is *a movement towards the object loved,* as *Augustine says* (QQ. 83, qu. 35), an intense love seeks to remove everything that opposes it.

But this happens in different ways according to love of concupiscence, and love of friendship. For in love of concupiscence he who desires something intensely, is moved against all that hinders his gaining or quietly enjoying the object of his love. It is thus that husbands are said to be jealous of their wives, lest association with others prove a hindrance to their exclusive individual rights. In like manner those who seek to excel, are moved against those who seem to excel, as though these were a hindrance to their excelling. And this is the zeal of envy, of which it is written (Ps. xxxvi. 1): *Be not emulous of evil doers, nor envy* (*zelaveris*) *them that work iniquity.*

On the other hand, love of friendship seeks the friend's good: wherefore, when it is intense, it causes a man to be moved against everything that opposes the friend's good. In this respect, a man is said to be zealous on behalf of his friend, when he makes a point of repelling whatever may be said or done against the friend's good. In this way, too, a man is said to be zealous on God's behalf, when he endeavors, to the best of his means, to repel whatever is contrary to the honor or will of God; according to 3 Kings xix. 14: *With zeal I have been zealous for the Lord of hosts.* Again on the words of Jo. ii. 17: *The zeal of Thy house hath eaten me up,* a gloss says that *a man is eaten up with a good zeal, who strives to remedy whatever evil he perceives; and if he cannot, bears with it and laments it.*

Reply Obj. 1. The Apostle is speaking in this passage of the zeal of envy; which is indeed the cause of contention, not against the object of love, but for it, and against that which is opposed to it.

Reply Obj. 2. Good is loved inasmuch as it can be communicated to the lover. Consequently whatever hinders the perfection of this communication, becomes hateful. Thus zeal arises from love of good.—But through defect of goodness, it happens that certain small goods cannot, in their entirety, be possessed by many at the same time: and from the love of such things arises the zeal of envy. But it does not arise, properly speaking, in the case of those things which, in their entirety, can be possessed by many: for no one envies another the knowledge of truth, which can be known entirely by many; except perhaps one may envy another his superiority in the knowledge of it.

Reply Obj. 3. The very fact that a man hates whatever is opposed to the object of his love, is the effect of love. Hence zeal is set down as an effect of love rather than of hatred.

FIFTH ARTICLE

Whether Love Is a Passion That Wounds the Lover?

We proceed thus to the Fifth Article:—

Objection 1. It would seem that love wounds the lover. For languor denotes a hurt in the one that languishes. But love causes languor: for it is written (Cant. ii. 5): *Stay me up with flowers, compass me about with apples; because I languish with love.* Therefore love is a wounding passion.

Obj. 2. Further, melting is a kind of dissolution. But love melts that in which it is: for it is written (Cant. v. 6): *My soul melted when my beloved spoke.* Therefore love is a dissolvent: therefore it is a corruptive and a wounding passion.

Obj. 3. Further, fervor denotes a certain excess of heat; which excess has a corruptive effect. But love causes fervor: for Dionysius (*Cæl. Hier.* vii) in reckoning the properties belonging to the Seraphim's love, includes *hot* and *piercing* and *most fervent.* Moreover it is said of love (Cant. viii. 6) that *its lamps are fire and flames.* Therefore love is a wounding and corruptive passion.

On the contrary, Dionysius says (*Div.* iv) that *everything loves itself with a love that holds it together, i.e.,* that preserves it. Therefore love is not a wounding passion, but rather one that preserves and perfects.

I answer that, As stated above (Q. 26, AA. 1, 2; Q. 27, A. 1), love denotes a certain adapting of the appetitive power to some good. Now nothing is hurt by being adapted to that which is suitable to it; rather, if possible, it is perfected and bettered. But if a thing be adapted to that which is not suitable to it, it is hurt and made worse thereby. Consequently love of a suitable good perfects and betters the lover; but love of a good which is unsuitable to the lover, wounds and worsens him. Wherefore man is perfected and bettered chiefly by the love of God: but is wounded and worsened by the love of sin, according to Osee ix. 10: *They became abominable, as those things which they loved.*

And let this be understood as applying to love in respect of its formal element, *i.e.,* in regard to the appetite. But in respect of the material element in the passion of love, *i.e.,* a certain bodily change, it happens that love is hurtful, by reason of this change being excessive: just as it happens in the senses, and in every act of a power of the soul that is exercised through the change of some bodily organ.

In reply to the objections, it is to be observed that four proximate effects may be ascribed to love: viz., melting, enjoyment, languor, and fervor. Of these the first is *melting,* which is opposed to freezing. For things that are frozen, are closely bound together, so as to be hard to pierce. But it belongs to love that the appetite is fitted to receive the good which is loved, inasmuch as the object loved is in the lover, as stated above (A. 2). Consequently the freezing or hardening of the heart is a disposition incompatible with love: while melting denotes a softening of the heart, whereby the heart shows itself to be ready for the entrance of the beloved.—If, then, the beloved is present and possessed, pleasure or enjoyment ensues. But if the beloved be absent, two passions arise; viz., sadness at its absence, which is denoted by *languor* (hence Cicero in *De Tuscul. Quæst.* iii. 11 applies the term *ailment* chiefly to sadness) ; and an intense desire to possess the beloved, which is signified by *fervor.*—And these are the effects of love considered formally, according to the relation of the appetitive power to its object. But in the passion of love, other effects ensue, proportionate to the above, in respect of a change in the organ.

SIXTH ARTICLE

Whether Love Is Cause of All That the Lover Does?

We proceed thus to the Sixth Article:—

Objection 1. It would seem that the lover does not do everything from love. For love is a passion, as stated above (Q. 26, A. 2). But man does not do everything from passion: for some things he does from choice, and some things from ignorance, as stated in *Ethic.* v. 8. Therefore not everything that a man does, is done from love.

Obj. 2. Further, the appetite is a principle of movement and action in all animals, as stated in *De Anima* iii. 10. If, therefore, whatever a man does is done from love, the other passions of the appetitive faculty are superfluous.

Obj. 3. Further, nothing is produced at one and the same time by contrary causes. But some things are done from hatred. Therefore all things are not done from love.

On the contrary, Dionysius says (*Div. Nom.* iv.) that *all things, whatever they do, they do for the love of good.*

I answer that, Every agent acts for an end, as stated above (Q. 1, A. 2). Now the end is the good desired and loved by each one. Wherefore it is evident that every agent, whatever it be, does every action from love of some kind.

Reply Obj. 1. This objection takes love as a passion existing in the sensitive appetite. But here we are speaking of love in a general sense, inasmuch as it includes intellectual, rational, animal, and natural love: for it is in this sense that Dionysius speaks of love in chap. iv. of *De Divinis Nominibus.*

Reply Obj. 2. As stated above (A. 5; Q. 27, A. 4) desire, sadness and pleasure, and consequently all the other passions of the soul, result from love. Wherefore very act that proceeds from any passion, proceeds also from love as from a first cause: and so the other passions, which are proximate causes, are not superfluous.

Reply Obj. 3. Hatred also is a result of love, as we shall state further on (Q. 29, A. 2).

QUESTION 29

Of Hatred

(In Six Articles)

WE must now consider hatred: concerning which there are six points of inquiry: (1) Whether evil is the cause and the object of hatred? (2) Whether love is the cause of hatred? (3) Whether hatred is stronger than love? (4) Whether a man can hate himself? (5) Whether a man can hate the truth? (6) Whether a thing can be the object of universal hatred?

FIRST ARTICLE

Whether Evil Is the Cause and Object of Hatred?

We proceed thus to the First Article:—

Objection 1. It would seem that evil is not the object and cause of hatred. For everything that exists, as such, is good. If therefore evil be the object of hatred, it follows that nothing but the lack of something can be the object of hatred: which is clearly untrue.

Obj. 2. Further, hatred of evil is praiseworthy; hence (2 Machab. iii. 1) some are praised for that *the laws were very well kept, because of the godliness of Onias the high-priest, and the hatred their souls* (Douay, *his soul) had of evil.* If, therefore, nothing but evil be the object of hatred, it would follow that all hatred is commendable: and this is clearly false.

Obj. 3. Further, the same thing is not at the same time both good and evil. But the same thing is lovable and hateful to different subjects. Therefore hatred is not only of evil, but also of good.

On the contrary, Hatred is the opposite of love. But the object of love is good, as stated above (Q. 26, A. 1; Q. 27, A. 1). Therefore the object of hatred is evil.

I answer that, Since the natural appetite is the result of apprehension (though this apprehension is not in the same subject as the natural appetite), it seems that what applies to the inclination of the natural appetite, applies also to the animal appetite, which does result from an apprehension in the same subject, as stated above (Q. 26, A. 1). Now, with regard to the natural appetite, it is evident, that just as each thing is naturally attuned and adapted to that which is suitable to it, wherein consists natural love; so has it a natural dissonance from that which opposes and destroys it; and this is natural hatred. So, therefore, in the animal appetite, or in the intellectual appetite, love is a certain harmony of the appetite with that which is apprehended as suitable; while hatred is dissonance of the appetite from that which is apprehended as repugnant and hurtful. Now, just as whatever is suitable, as such, bears the aspect of good; so whatever is repugnant, as such, bears the aspect of evil. And therefore, just as good is the object of love, so evil is the object of hatred.

Reply Obj. 1. Being, as such, has not the aspect of repugnance but only of fittingness; because being is common to all things. But being, inasmuch as it is this determinate being, has an aspect of repugnance to some determinate being. And in this way, one being is hateful to another, and is evil; though not in itself, but by comparison with something else.

Reply Obj. 2. Just as a thing may be apprehended as good, when it is not truly good; so a thing may be apprehended as evil, whereas it is not truly evil. Hence it happens sometimes that neither hatred of evil nor love of good is good.

Reply Obj. 3. To different things the same thing may be lovable or hateful: in respect of the natural appetite, owing to one and the same thing being naturally suitable to one thing, and naturally unsuitable to another: thus heat is becoming to fire and unbecoming to water: and in respect of the animal appetite, owing to one and the same thing being apprehended by one as good, by another as bad.

SECOND ARTICLE

Whether Love Is a Cause of Hatred?

We proceed thus to the Second Article:—

Objection 1. It would seem that love is not a cause of hatred. For *the opposite members of a division are naturally simultaneous* (*Prædic.* x). But love and hatred are opposite members of a division, since they are contrary to one another. Therefore they are naturally simultaneous. Therefore love is not the cause of hatred.

Obj. 2. Further, of two contraries, one is not the cause of the other. But love and hatred are contraries. Therefore love is not the cause of hatred.

Obj. 3. Further, that which follows is not the cause of that which precedes. But hatred precedes love, seemingly: since hatred implies a turning away from evil, whereas love implies a turning towards good. Therefore love is not the cause of hatred.

On the contrary, Augustine says (*De Civ. Dei* xiv. 7, 9) that all emotions are caused by love. Therefore hatred also, since it is an emotion of the soul, is caused by love.

I answer that, As stated above (A. 1), love consists in a certain agreement of the lover with the object loved, while hatred consists in a certain disagreement or dissonance. Now we should consider in each thing, what agrees with it, before that which disagrees: since a thing disagrees with another, through destroying or hindering that which agrees with it. Consequently love must needs precede hatred; and nothing is hated, save through being contrary to a suitable thing which is loved. And hence it is that every hatred is caused by love.

Reply Obj. 1. The opposite members of a division are sometimes naturally simultaneous, both really and logically; *e.g.,* two species of animal, or two species of color. Sometimes they are simultaneous logically, while, in reality, one precedes, and causes the other; *e.g.,* the species of numbers, figures and movements. Sometimes they are not simultaneous either really or logically; *e.g.,* substance and accident; for substance is in reality the cause of accident; and being is predicated of substance before it is predicated of accident, by a priority of reason, because it is not predicated of accident except inasmuch as the latter is in substance.—Now love and hatred are naturally simultaneous, logically but not really. Wherefore nothing hinders love from being the cause of hatred.

Reply Obj. 2. Love and hatred are contraries if considered in respect of the same thing. But if taken in respect of contraries, they are not themselves contrary, but consequent to one another: for it amounts to the same that one love a certain thing, or that one hate its contrary. Thus love of one thing is the cause of one's hating its contrary.

Reply Obj. 3. In the order of execution, the turning away from one term precedes the turning towards the other. But the reverse is the case in the order of intention: since approach to one term is the reason for turning away from the other. Now the appetitive movement belongs rather to the order of intention than to that of execution. Wherefore love precedes hatred: because each is an appetitive movement.

THIRD ARTICLE

Whether Hatred Is Stronger Than Love?

We proceed thus to the Third Article:—

Objection 1. It would seem that hatred is stronger than love. For Augustine says (QQ. 83, qu. 36): *There is no one who does not flee from pain, more than he desires pleas-*ure. But flight from pain pertains to hatred; while desire for pleasure belongs to love. Therefore hatred is stronger than love.

Obj. 2. Further, the weaker is overcome by the stronger. But love is overcome by hatred: when, that is to say, love is turned into hatred. Therefore hatred is stronger than love.

Obj. 3. Further, the emotions of the soul are shown by their effects. But man insists more on repelling what is hateful, than on seeking what is pleasant: thus also irrational animals refrain from pleasure for fear of the whip, as Augustine instances (*loc. cit.*). Therefore hatred is stronger than love.

On the contrary, Good is stronger than evil; because *evil does nothing except in virtue of good,* as Dionysius says (*Div. Nom.* iv). But hatred and love differ according to the difference of good and evil. Therefore love is stronger than hatred.

I answer that, It is impossible for an effect to be stronger than its cause. Now every hatred arises from some love as its cause, as above stated (A. 2). Therefore it is impossible for hatred to be stronger than love absolutely.

But furthermore, love must needs be, absolutely speaking, stronger than hatred. Because a thing is moved to the end more strongly than to the means. Now turning away from evil is directed as a means to the gaining of good. Wherefore, absolutely speaking, the soul's movement in respect of good is stronger than its movement in respect of evil.

Nevertheless hatred sometimes seems to be stronger than love, for two reasons. First, because hatred is more keenly felt than love. For, since the sensitive perception is accompanied by a certain impression; when once the impression has been received it is not felt so keenly as in the moment of receiving it. Hence the heat of a hectic fever, though greater, is nevertheless not felt so much as the heat of tertian fever; because the heat of the hectic fever is habitual and like a second nature. For this reason, love is felt more keenly in the absence of the object loved; thus Augustine says (*De Trin.* x. 12) that *love is felt more keenly when we lack what we love.* And for the same reason, the unbecomingness of that which is hated is felt more keenly than the becomingness of that which is loved.—Secondly, because comparison is made between a hatred and a love which are not mutually corresponding. Because, according to different degrees of good there are different degrees of love to which correspond different degrees of hatred. Wherefore a hatred that corresponds to a greater love, moves us more than a lesser love.

Hence it is clear how to reply to the First Objection. For the love of pleasure is less than the love of self-preservation, to which corresponds flight from pain. **Wherefore we flee from pain more than we love pleasure.**

Reply Obj. 2. Hatred would never overcome love, were it not for the greater love to which that hatred corresponds. Thus man loves himself, more than he loves his friend: and because he loves himself, his friend is hateful to him, if he oppose him.

Reply Obj. 3. The reason why we act with greater insistence in repelling what is hateful, is because we feel hatred more keenly.

FOURTH ARTICLE

Whether a Man Can Hate Himself?

We proceed thus to the Fourth Article:—

Objection 1. It would seem that a man can hate himself. For it is written (Ps. x. 6): *He that loveth iniquity, hateth his own soul.* But many love iniquity. Therefore many hate themselves.

Obj. 2. Further, him we hate, to whom we wish and work evil. But sometimes a man wishes and works evil to himself, *e.g.*, a man who kills himself. Therefore some men hate themselves.

Obj. 3. Further, Boëthius says (*De Consol.* ii) that *avarice makes a man hateful;* whence we may conclude that everyone hates a miser. But some men are misers. Therefore they hate themselves.

On the contrary, The Apostle says (Eph. v. 29) that *no man ever hated his own flesh.*

I answer that, Properly speaking, it is impossible for a man to hate himself. For everything naturally desires good, nor can anyone desire anything for himself, save under the aspect of good: for *evil is outside the scope of the will,* as Dionysius says (*Div. Nom.* iv). Now to love a man is to will good to him, as stated above (Q. 26, A. 4). Consequently, a man must, of necessity, love himself; and it is impossible for a man to hate himself, properly speaking.

But accidentally it happens that a man hates himself: and this in two ways. First, on the part of the good which a man wills to himself. For it happens sometimes that what is desired as good in some particular respect, is simply evil; and in this way, a man accidentally wills evil to himself; and thus hates himself.—Secondly, in regard to himself, to whom he wills good. For each thing is that which is predominant in it; wherefore the state is said to do what the king does, as if the king were the whole state. Now it is clear that man is principally the mind of man. And it happens that some men account themselves as being principally that which they are in

their material and sensitive nature. Wherefore they love themselves according to what they take themselves to be, while they hate that which they really are, by desiring what is contrary to reason.—And in both these ways, *he that loveth iniquity hateth* not only *his own soul,* but also himself.

Wherefore the reply to the First Objection is evident.

Reply Obj. 2. No man wills and works evil to himself, except he apprehend it under the aspect of good. For even they who kill themselves, apprehend death itself as a good, considered as putting an end to some unhappiness or pain.

Reply Obj. 3. The miser hates something accidental to himself, but not for that reason does he hate himself: thus a sick man hates his sickness for the very reason that he loves himself.—Or we may say that avarice makes man hateful to others, but not to himself. In fact, it is caused by inordinate self-love, in respect of which, man desires temporal goods for himself more than he should.

FIFTH ARTICLE

Whether a Man Can Hate the Truth?

We proceed thus to the Fifth Article:—

Objection 1. It would seem that a man cannot hate the truth. For good, true and being are convertible. But a man cannot hate good. Neither, therefore, can he hate the truth.

Obj. 2. Further, *All men have a natural desire for knowledge,* as stated in the beginning of the *Metaphysics* (i. 1). But knowledge is only of truth. Therefore truth is naturally desired and loved. But that which is in a thing naturally, is always in it. Therefore no man can hate the truth.

Obj. 3. Further, the Philosopher says (*Rhetor.* ii. 4) that *men love those who are straightforward.* But there can be no other motive for this save truth. Therefore man loves the truth naturally. Therefore he cannot hate it.

On the contrary, The Apostle says (Gal. iv. 16): *Am I become your enemy because I tell you the truth?* *

I answer that, Good, true and being are the same in reality, but differ as considered by reason. For good is considered in the light of something desirable, while being and true are not so considered: because good is *what all things seek.* Wherefore good, as such, cannot be the object of hatred, neither in general nor in particular.—Being and truth in general cannot be the object of hatred: because disagreement is the cause of hatred, and agreement is

---

* St. Thomas quotes the passage, probably from memory, as though it were an assertion: *I am become, etc.*

the cause of love; while being and truth are common to all things. But nothing hinders some particular being or some particular truth being an object of hatred, in so far as it is considered as hurtful and repugnant; since hurtfulness and repugnance are not incompatible with the notion of being and truth, as they are with the notion of good.

Now it may happen in three ways that some particular truth is repugnant or hurtful to the good we love. First, according as truth is in things as in its cause and origin. And thus man sometimes hates a particular truth, when he wishes that what is true were not true.— Secondly, according as truth is in man's knowledge, which hinders him from gaining the object loved: such is the case of those who wish not to know the truth of faith, that they may sin freely; in whose person it is said (Job xxi. 14): *We desire not the knowledge of Thy ways.*—Thirdly, a particular truth is hated, as being repugnant, inasmuch as it is in the intellect of another man: as, for instance, when a man wishes to remain hidden in his sin, he hates that anyone should know the truth about his sin. In this respect, Augustine says (*Confess.* x. 23) that men *love truth when it enlightens, they hate it when it reproves.* This suffices for the Reply to the First Objection.

Reply Obj. 2. The knowledge of truth is lovable in itself: hence Augustine says that men love it when it enlightens. But accidentally, the knowledge of truth may become hateful, in so far as it hinders one from accomplishing one's desire.

Reply Obj. 3. The reason why we love those who are straightforward is that they make known the truth, and the knowledge of the truth, considered in itself, is a desirable thing.

SIXTH ARTICLE

Whether Anything Can Be an Object of Universal Hatred?

We proceed thus to the Sixth Article:—

Objection 1. It would seem that a thing cannot be an object of universal hatred. Because hatred is a passion of the sensitive appetite, which is moved by an apprehension in the senses. But the senses cannot apprehend the universal. Therefore a thing cannot be an object of universal hatred.

Obj. 2. Further, hatred is caused by disagreement; and where there is disagreement, there is nothing in common. But the notion of universality implies something in common. Therefore nothing can be the object of universal hatred.

Obj. 3. Further, the object of hatred is evil.

But *evil is in things, and not in the mind* (*Metaph.* vi. 4). Since therefore the universal is in the mind only, which abstracts the universal from the particular, it would seem that hatred cannot have a universal object.

On the contrary, The Philosopher says (*Rhetor.* ii. 4) that *anger is directed to something singular, whereas hatred is also directed to a thing in general; for everybody hates the thief and the backbiter.*

I answer that, There are two ways of speaking of the universal: first, as considered under the aspect of universality; secondly, as considered in the nature to which it is ascribed: for it is one thing to consider the universal man, and another to consider a man as man. If, therefore, we take the universal, in the first way, no sensitive power, whether of apprehension or or appetite, can attain the universal: because the universal is obtained by abstraction from individual matter, on which every sensitive power is based.

Nevertheless the sensitive powers, both of apprehension and of appetite, can tend to something universally. Thus we say that the object of sight is color considered generically; not that the sight is cognizant of universal color, but because the fact that color is cognizable by the sight, is attributed to color, not as being this particular color, but simply because it is color. Accordingly hatred in the sensitive faculty can regard something universally: because this thing, by reason of its common nature, and not merely as an individual, is hostile to the animal—for instance, a wolf in regard to a sheep. Hence a sheep hates the wolf universally.—On the other hand, anger is always caused by something in particular: because it is caused by some action of the one that hurts us; and actions proceed from individuals. For this reason the Philosopher says (*ibid.*) that *anger is always directed to something singular, whereas hatred can be directed to a thing in general.*

But according as hatred is in the intellectual part, since it arises from the universal apprehension of the intellect, it can regard the universal in both ways.

Reply Obj. 1. The senses do not apprehend the universal, as such: but they apprehend something to which the character of universality is given by abstraction.

Reply Obj. 2. That which is common to all cannot be a reason of hatred. But nothing hinders a thing from being common to many, and at variance with others, so as to be hateful to them.

Reply Obj. 3. This argument considers the universal under the aspect of universality: and thus it does not come under the sensitive apprehension or appetite.

QUESTION 30

Of Concupiscence

(In Four Articles)

WE have now to consider concupiscence: under which head there are four points of inquiry: (1) Whether concupiscence is in the sensitive appetite only? (2) Whether concupiscence is a specific passion? (3) Whether some concupiscences are natural, and some not natural? (4) Whether concupiscence is infinite?

FIRST ARTICLE

Whether Concupiscence Is in the Sensitive Appetite Only?

We proceed thus to the First Article:—

Objection 1. It would seem that concupiscence is not only in the sensitive appetite. For there is a concupiscence of wisdom, according to Wis. vi. 21: *The concupiscence* (Douay, *desire*) *of wisdom bringeth to the everlasting kingdom.* But the sensitive appetite can have no tendency to wisdom. Therefore concupiscence is not only in the sensitive appetite.

Obj. 2. Further, the desire for the commandments of God is not in the sensitive appetite: in fact the Apostle says (Rom. vii. 18): *There dwelleth not in me, that is to say, in my flesh, that which is good.* But desire for God's commandments is an act of concupiscence, according to Ps. cxviii. 20: *My soul hath coveted* (*concupivit*) *to long for thy justifications.* Therefore concupiscence is not only in the sensitive appetite.

Obj. 3. Further, to each power, its proper good is a matter of concupiscence. Therefore concupiscence is in each power of the soul, and not only in the sensitive appetite.

On the contrary, Damascene says (*De Fide Orthod.* ii. 12) that *the irrational part which is subject and amenable to reason, is divided into the faculties of concupiscence and anger. This is the irrational part of the soul, passive and appetitive.* Therefore concupiscence is in the sensitive appetite.

I answer that, As the Philosopher says (*Rhetor.* i. 11), *concupiscence is a craving for that which is pleasant.* Now pleasure is twofold, as we shall state later on (Q. 31, AA. 3, 4): one is in the intelligible good, which is the good of reason; the other is in good perceptible to the senses. The former pleasure seems to belong to the soul alone: whereas the latter belongs to both soul and body: because the sense is a power seated in a bodily organ: wherefore sensible good is the good of the whole composite. Now concupiscence seems to be the craving for this latter pleasure, since it belongs to the united soul and body, as is implied by the Latin word *concupiscentia.* Therefore, properly speaking, concupiscence is in the sensitive appetite, and in the concupiscible faculty, which takes its name from it.

Reply Obj. 1. The craving for wisdom, or other spiritual goods, is sometimes called concupiscence; either by reason of a certain likeness; or on account of the craving in the higher part of the soul being so vehement that it overflows into the lower appetite, so that the latter also, in its own way, tends to the spiritual good, following the lead of the higher appetite, the result being that the body itself renders its service in spiritual matters, according to Ps. lxxxiii. 3: *My heart and my flesh have rejoiced in the living God.*

Reply Obj. 2. Properly speaking, desire may be not only in the lower, but also in the higher appetite. For it does not imply fellowship in craving, as concupiscence does; but simply movement towards the thing desired.

Reply Obj. 3. It belongs to each power of the soul to seek its proper good by the natural appetite, which does not arise from apprehension. But the craving for good, by the animal appetite, which arises from apprehension, belongs to the appetitive power alone. And to crave for a thing under the aspect of something delightful to the senses, wherein concupiscence properly consists, belongs to the concupiscible power.

SECOND ARTICLE

Whether Concupiscence Is a Specific Passion?

We proceed thus to the Second Article:—

Objection 1. It would seem that concupiscence is not a specific passion of the concupiscible power. For passions are distinguished by their objects. But the object of the concupiscible power is something delightful to the senses; and this is also the object of concupiscence, as the Philosopher declares (*Rhetor.* i. 11). Therefore concupiscence is not a specific passion of the concupiscible faculty.

Obj. 2. Further, Augustine says (QQ. 83, qu. 33) that *covetousness is the love of transitory things:* so that it is not distinct from love. But all specific passions are distinct from one another. Therefore concupiscence is not a specific passion in the concupiscible faculty.

Obj. 3. Further, to each passion of the concupiscible faculty there is a specific contrary passion in that faculty, as stated above (Q. 23, A. 4). But no specific passion of the concupiscible faculty is contrary to concupiscence. For Damascene says (*De Fide Orthod.* ii. 12) that *good when desired gives rise to concupiscence; when present, it gives joy: in like manner, the evil we apprehend makes us fear, the evil that is present makes us sad:* from which we gather that as sadness is contrary to joy, so is fear contrary to concupiscence. But fear is not in the concupiscible, but in the irascible part. Therefore concupiscence is not a specific passion of the concupiscible faculty.

On the contrary, Concupiscence is caused by love, and tends to pleasure, both of which are passions of the concupiscible faculty. Hence it is distinguished from the other concupiscible passions, as a specific passion.

I answer that, As stated above (A. 1; Q. 23, A. 1), the good which gives pleasure to the senses is the common object of the concupiscible faculty. Hence the various concupiscible passions are distinguished according to the differences of that good. Now the diversity of this object can arise from the very nature of the object, or from a diversity in its active power. The diversity, derived from the nature of the active object, causes a material difference of passions: while the difference in regard to its active power causes a formal diversity of passions, in respect of which the passions differ specifically.

Now the nature of the motive power of the end or of the good, differs according as it is really present, or absent: because, according as it is present, it causes the faculty to find rest in it; whereas, according as it is absent, it causes the faculty to be moved towards it. Wherefore the object of sensible pleasure causes love, inasmuch as, so to speak, it attunes and conforms the appetite to itself; it causes concupiscence, inasmuch as, when absent, it draws the faculty to itself; and it causes pleasure, inasmuch as, when present, it makes the faculty to find rest in itself. Accordingly, concupiscence is a passion differing *in species* from both love and pleasure.—But concupiscences of this or that pleasurable object differ *in number.*

Reply Obj. 1. Pleasurable good is the object of concupiscence, not absolutely, but considered as absent: just as the sensible, considered as past, is the object of memory. For these particular conditions diversify the species of passions, and even of the powers of the sensitive part, which regards particular things.

Reply Obj. 2. In the passage quoted we have causal, not essential, predication: for covetousness is not essentially love, but an effect of love.—We may also say that Augustine is taking covetousness in a wide sense, for any movement of the appetite in respect of good to come: so that it includes both love and hope.

Reply Obj. 3. The passion which is directly contrary to concupiscence has no name, and stands in relation to evil, as concupiscence in regard to good. But since, like fear, it regards the absent evil; sometimes it goes by the name of fear, just as hope is sometimes called covetousness. For a small good or evil is reckoned as though it were nothing: and consequently every movement of the appetite in future good or evil is called hope or fear, which regard good and evil as arduous.

THIRD ARTICLE

Whether Some Concupiscences Are Natural, and Some Not Natural?

We proceed thus to the Third Article:—

Objection 1. It would seem that concupiscences are not divided into those which are natural and those which are not. For concupiscence belongs to the animal appetite, as stated above (A. 1 *ad* 3). But the natural appetite is contrasted with the animal appetite. Therefore no concupiscence is natural.

Obj. 2. Further, material difference makes no difference of species, but only numerical difference;—a difference which is outside the purview of science. But if some concupiscences are natural, and some not, they differ only in respect of their objects; which amounts to a material difference, which is one of number only. Therefore concupiscences should not be divided into those that are natural and those that are not.

Obj. 3. Further, reason is contrasted with nature, as stated in *Phys.* ii. 5. If therefore in man there is a concupiscence which is not natural, it must needs be rational. But this is impossible: because, since concupiscence is a passion, it belongs to the sensitive appetite, and not to the will, which is the rational appetite. Therefore there are no concupiscences which are not natural.

On the contrary, The Philosopher (*Ethic.* iii. 11 and *Rhetor,* i. 11) distinguishes natural concupiscences from those that are not natural.

I answer that, As stated above (A. 1), concupiscence is the craving for pleasurable good. Now a thing is pleasurable in two ways. First, because it is suitable to the nature of the animal; for example, food, drink, and the like: and concupiscence of such pleasurable things is said to be natural.—Secondly, a thing is pleasurable because it is apprehended as suitable to the animal: as when one apprehends something as good and suitable, and consequently takes pleasure in it: and concupiscence of such pleasurable things is said to be not natural, and is more wont to be called *cupidity.*

Accordingly concupiscences of the first kind, or natural concupiscences, are common to men and other animals: because to both is there something suitable and pleasurable according to nature: and in these all men agree; wherefore the Philosopher (*Ethic.* iii. 11) calls them *common* and *necessary.*—But concupiscences of the second kind are proper to men, to whom it is proper to devise something as good and suitable, beyond that which nature requires. Hence the Philosopher says (*Rhetor.* i. 11) that the former concupiscences are *irrational,* but the latter, *rational.* And because different men reason differently, therefore the latter are also called (*Ethic.* iii. 11) *peculiar and acquired, i.e.,* in addition to those that are natural.

Reply Obj. 1. The same thing that is the object of the natural appetite, may be the object of the animal appetite, once it is apprehended. And in this way there may be an animal concupiscence for food, drink and the like, which are objects of the natural appetite.

Reply Obj. 2. The difference between those concupiscences that are natural and those that are not, is not merely a material difference; it is also, in a way, formal, in so far as it arises from a difference in the active object. Now the object of the appetite is the apprehended good. Hence diversity of the active object follows from diversity of apprehension: according as a thing is apprehended as suitable, either by absolute apprehension, whence arise natural concupiscences, which the Philosopher calls *irrational* (*Rhetor.* i. 11); or by apprehension together with deliberation, whence arise those concupiscences that are not natural, and which for this very reason the Philosopher calls *rational* (*ibid.*).

Reply Obj. 3. Man has not only universal reason, pertaining to the intellectual faculty; but also particular reason pertaining to the sensitive faculty, as stated in the First Part (Q. 78, A. 4; Q. 81, A. 3): so that even rational concupiscence may pertain to the sensitive appetite.—Moreover the sensitive appetite can be moved by the universal reason also, through the medium of the particular imagination.

FOURTH ARTICLE

Whether Concupiscence Is Infinite?

We proceed thus to the Fourth Article:—

Objection 1. It would seem that concupiscence is not infinite. For the object of concupiscence is good, which has the aspect of an end. But where there is infinity there is no end (*Metaph.* ii. 2). Therefore concupiscence cannot be infinite.

Obj. 2. Further, concupiscence is of the fitting good, since it proceeds from love. But the infinite is without proportion, and therefore unfitting. Therefore concupiscence cannot be infinite.

Obj. 3. Further, there is no passing through infinite things: and thus there is no reaching an ultimate term in them. But the subject of concupiscence is not delighted until he attain the ultimate term. Therefore, if concupiscence were infinite, no delight would ever ensue.

On the contrary, The Philosopher says (*Polit.* i. 3) that *since concupiscence is infinite, men desire an infinite number of things.*

I answer that, As stated above (A. 3), concupiscence is twofold; one is natural, the other is not natural. Natural concupiscence cannot be actually infinite: because it is of that which nature requires; and nature ever tends to something finite and fixed. Hence man never desires infinite meat, or infinite drink.—But just as in nature there is potential successive infinity, so can this kind of concupiscence be infinite successively; so that, for instance, after getting food, a man may desire food yet again; and so of anything else that nature requires: because these bodily goods, when obtained, do not last for ever, but fail. Hence Our Lord said to the woman of Samaria (Jo. iv. 13): *Whosoever drinketh of this water, shall thirst again.*

But non-natural concupiscence is altogether infinite. Because, as stated above (A. 3) it follows from the reason, and it belongs to the reason to proceed to infinity. Hence he that desires riches, may desire to be rich, not up to a certain limit, but to be simply as rich as possible.

Another reason may be assigned, according to the Philosopher (*Polit.* i. 3), why a certain concupiscence is finite, and another infinite. Because concupiscence of the end is always infinite: since the end is desired for its own sake, *e.g.,* health: and thus greater health is more desired, and so on to infinity; just as, if a white thing of itself dilates the sight, that which is more white dilates yet more. On the other hand, concupiscence of the means is not infinite, because the concupiscence of the means is in suitable proportion to the end. Consequently those who place their end in riches have an infinite concupiscence of riches; whereas those who desire riches, on account of the necessities of life, desire a finite measure of riches, sufficient for the necessities of life, as the Philosopher says (*ibid.*). The same applies to the concupiscence of any other things.

Reply Obj. 1. Every object of concupiscence

is taken as something finite: either because it is finite in reality, as being once actually desired; or because it is finite as apprehended. For it cannot be apprehended as infinite, since the infinite is that *from which, however much we may take, there always remains something to be taken* (*Phys.* iii. 6).

Reply Obj. 2. The reason is possessed of infinite power, in a certain sense, in so far as it can consider a thing infinitely, as appears in the addition of numbers and lines. Consequently, the infinite, taken in a certain way, is proportionate to reason. In fact the universal which the reason apprehends, is infinite in a sense, inasmuch as it contains potentially an infinite number of singulars.

Reply Obj. 3. In order that a man be delighted, there is no need for him to realize all that he desires: for he delights in the realization of each object of his concupiscence.

QUESTION 31

Of Delight * Considered in Itself

(In Eight Articles)

WE must now consider delight and sadness. Concerning delight four things must be considered: (1) Delight in itself; (2) The causes of delight; (3) Its effects; (4) Its goodness and malice.

Under the first head there are eight points of inquiry: (1) Whether delight is a passion? (2) Whether delight is subject to time? (3) Whether it differs from joy? (4) Whether it is in the intellectual appetite? (5) Of the delights of the higher appetite compared with the delight of the lower; (6) Of sensible delights compared with one another; (7) Whether any delight is non-natural? (8) Whether one delight can be contrary to another?

FIRST ARTICLE

Whether Delight Is a Passion?

We proceed thus to the First Article:—

Objection 1. It would seem that delight is not a passion. For Damascene (*De Fide Orthod.* ii. 22) distinguishes operation from passion, and says that *operation is a movement in accord with nature, while passion is a movement contrary to nature.* But delight is an operation, according to the Philosopher (*Ethic.* vii. 12, x. 5). Therefore delight is not a passion.

Obj. 2. Further, *To be passive is to be moved,* as stated in *Phys.* iii. 3. But delight does not consist in being moved, but in having been moved; for it arises from good already gained. Therefore delight is not a passion.

Obj. 3. Further, delight is a kind of a perfection of the one who is delighted; since it *perfects operation,* as stated in *Ethic.* x. 4, 5. But to be perfected does not consist in being passive or in being altered, as stated in *Phys.* vii. 3 and *De Anima* ii. 5. Therefore delight is not a passion.

On the contrary, Augustine (*De Civ. Dei* ix. 2, xiv. 5 sqq.) reckons delight, joy or gladness among the other passions of the soul.

* Or, Pleasure.   † *Phileb.* 32, 33.

I answer that, The movements of the sensitive appetite, are properly called passions, as stated above (Q. 22, A. 3). Now every emotion arising from a sensitive apprehension, is a movement of the sensitive appetite: and this must needs be said of delight, since, according to the Philosopher (*Rhetor.* i. 11) *delight is a certain movement of the soul and a sensible establishing thereof all at once, in keeping with the nature of the thing.*

In order to understand this, we must observe that just as in natural things some happen to attain to their natural perfections, so does this happen in animals. And though movement towards perfection does not occur all at once, yet the attainment of natural perfection does occur all at once. Now there is this difference between animals and other natural things, that when these latter are established in the state becoming their nature, they do not perceive it, whereas animals do. And from this perception there arises a certain movement of the soul in the sensitive appetite; which movement is called delight. Accordingly by saying that delight is *a movement of the soul,* we designate its genus. By saying that it is *an establishing in keeping with the thing's nature, i.e.,* with that which exists in the thing, we assign the cause of delight, viz., the presence of a becoming good. By saying that this establishing is *all at once,* we mean that this establishing is to be understood not as in the process of establishment, but as in the fact of complete establishment, in the term of the movement, as it were: for delight is not a *becoming* as Plato† maintained, but a *complete fact,* as stated in *Ethic.* vii. 12. Lastly, by saying that this establishing is *sensible,* we exclude the perfections of insensible things wherein there is no delight.—It is therefore evident that, since delight is a movement of the animal appetite arising from an apprehension of sense, it is a passion of the soul.

Reply Obj. 1. Connatural operation, which

is unhindered, is a second perfection, as stated in *De Anima* ii. 1: and therefore when a thing is established in its proper connatural and unhindered operation, delight follows, which consists in a state of completion, as observed above. Accordingly when we say that delight is an operation, we designate, not its essence, but its cause.

Reply Obj. 2. A twofold movement is to be observed in an animal: one, according to the intention of the end, and this belongs to the appetite; the other, according to the execution, and this belongs to the external operation. And so, although in him who has already gained the good in which he delights, the movement of execution ceases, by which he tends to the end; yet the movement of the appetitive faculty does not cease, since, just as before it desired that which it had not, so afterwards does it delight in that which it possesses. For though delight is a certain repose of the appetite, if we consider the presence of the pleasurable good that satisfies the appetite, nevertheless there remains the impression made on the appetite by its object, by reason of which delight is a kind of movement.

Reply Obj. 3. Although the name of passion is more appropriate to those passions which have a corruptive and evil tendency, such as bodily ailments, as also sadness and fear in the soul; yet some passions have a tendency to something good, as stated above (Q. 23, AA. 1, 4): and in this sense delight is called a passion.

SECOND ARTICLE

Whether Delight Is in Time?

We proceed thus to the Second Article:—

Objection 1. It would seem that delight is in time. For *delight is a kind of movement,* as the Philosopher says (*Rhetor.* i. 11). But all movement is in time. Therefore delight is in time.

Obj. 2. Further, a thing is said to last long and to be morose in respect of time. But some pleasures are called morose. Therefore pleasure is in time.

Obj. 3. Further, the passions of the soul are of one same genus. But some passions of the soul are in time. Therefore delight is too.

On the contrary, The Philosopher says (*Ethic.* x. 4) that *no one takes pleasure according to time.*

I answer that, A thing may be in time in two ways: first, by itself; secondly, by reason of something else, and accidentally as it were. For since time is the measure of successive things, those things are of themselves said to be in time, to which succession or something

pertaining to succession is essential: such are movement, repose, speech and such like. On the other hand, those things are said to be in time, by reason of something else and not of themselves, to which succession is not essential, but which are subject to something successive. Thus the fact of being a man is not essentially something successive; since it is not a movement, but the term of a movement or change, viz., of his being begotten: yet, because human being is subject to changeable causes, in this respect, to be a man is in time.

Accordingly, we must say that delight, of itself indeed, is not in time: for it regards good already gained, which is, as it were, the term of the movement. But if this good gained be subject to change, the delight therein will be in time accidentally: whereas if it be altogether unchangeable, the delight therein will not be in time, either by reason of itself or accidentally.

Reply Obj. 1. As stated in *De Anima* iii. 7, movement is twofold. One is *the act of something imperfect, i.e., of something existing in potentiality, as such:* this movement is successive and is in time. Another movement is *the act of something perfect, i.e., of something existing in act, e.g.,* to understand, to feel, and to will and such like, also to have delight. This movement is not successive, nor is it of itself in time.

Reply Obj. 2. Delight is said to be long lasting or morose, according as it is accidentally in time.

Reply Obj. 3. Other passions have not for their object a good obtained, as delight has. Wherefore there is more of the movement of the imperfect in them than in delight. And consequently it belongs more to delight not to be in time.

THIRD ARTICLE

Whether Delight Differs from Joy?

We proceed thus to the Third Article:—

Objection 1. It would seem that delight is altogether the same as joy. Because the passions of the soul differ according to their objects. But delight and joy have the same object, namely, a good obtained. Therefore joy is altogether the same as delight.

Obj. 2. Further, one movement does not end in two terms. But one and the same movement, that of desire, ends in joy and delight. Therefore delight and joy are altogether the same.

Obj. 3. Further, if joy differs from delight, it seems that there is equal reason for distinguishing gladness, exultation, and cheerfulness from delight, so that they would all be various passions of the soul. But this seems to be untrue. Therefore joy does not differ from delight.

On the contrary, We do not speak of joy in irrational animals; whereas we do speak of delight in them. Therefore joy is not the same as delight.

I answer that, Joy, as Avicenna states (*De Anima* iv), is a kind of delight. For we must observe that, just as some concupiscences are natural, and some not natural, but consequent to reason, as stated above (Q. 30, A. 3), so also some delights are natural, and some are not natural but rational. Or, as Damascene (*De Fide Orthod.* ii. 13) and Gregory of Nyssa* put it, *some delights are of the body, some are of the soul;* which amounts to the same. For we take delight both in those things which we desire naturally, when we get them, and in those things which we desire as a result of reason. But we do not speak of joy except when delight follows reason; and so we do not ascribe joy to irrational animals, but only delight.

Now whatever we desire naturally, can also be the object of reasoned desire and delight, but not vice versa. Consequently whatever can be the object of delight, can also be the object of joy in rational beings. And yet everything is not always the object of joy; since sometimes one feels a certain delight in the body, without rejoicing thereat according to reason. And accordingly delight extends to more things than does joy.

Reply Obj. 1. Since the object of the appetite of the soul is an apprehended good, diversity of apprehension pertains, in a way, to diversity of the object. And so delights of the soul, which are also called joys, are distinct from bodily delights, which are not called otherwise than delights: as we have observed above in regard to concupiscences (Q. 30, A. 3 *ad* 2).

Reply Obj. 2. A like difference is to be observed in concupiscences also: so that delight corresponds to concupiscence, while joy corresponds to desire, which seems to pertain more to concupiscence of the soul. Hence there is a difference of repose corresponding to the difference of movement.

Reply Obj. 3. These other names pertaining to delight are derived from the effects of delight; for *lætitia* (gladness) is derived from the *dilatation* of the heart, as if one were to say *latitia; exultation* is derived from the exterior signs of inward delight, which appear outwardly in so far as the inward joy breaks forth from its bounds; and *cheerfulness* is so called from certain special signs and effects of gladness. Yet all these names seem to belong to joy; for we do not employ them save in speaking of rational beings.

* Nemesius, *De Nat. Hom.* xviii.

Whether Delight Is in the Intellectual Appetite?

We proceed thus to the Fourth Article:—

Objection 1. It would seem that delight is not in the intellectual appetite. Because the Philosopher says (*Rhet.* i. 11) that *delight is a sensible movement.* But sensible movement is not in an intellectual power. Therefore delight is not in the intellectual appetite.

Obj. 2. Further, delight is a passion. But every passion is in the sensitive appetite. Therefore delight is only in the sensitive appetite.

Obj. 3. Further, delight is common to us and to the irrational animals. Therefore it is not elsewhere than in that power which we have in common with irrational animals.

On the contrary, It is written (Ps. xxxvi. 4): *Delight in the Lord.* But the sensitive appetite cannot reach to God; only the intellectual appetite can. Therefore delight can be in the intellectual appetite.

I answer that, As stated above (A. 3), a certain delight arises from the apprehension of the reason. Now on the reason apprehending something, not only the sensitive appetite is moved, as regards its application to some particular thing, but also the intellectual appetite, which is called the will. And accordingly, in the intellectual appetite or will there is that delight which is called joy, but not bodily delight.

However, there is this difference of delight in either power, that delight of the sensitive appetite is accompanied by a bodily transmutation, whereas delight of the intellectual appetite is nothing but the mere movement of the will. Hence Augustine says (*De Civ. Dei* xiv. 6) that *desire and joy are nothing else but a volition of consent to the things we wish.*

Reply Obj. 1. In this definition of the Philosopher, he uses the word *sensible* in its wide acceptation for any kind of perception. For he says (*Ethic.* x. 4) that *delight is attendant upon every sense, as it is also upon every act of the intellect and contemplation.*—Or we may say that he is defining delight of the sensitive appetite.

Reply Obj. 2. Delight has the character of passion, properly speaking, when accompanied by bodily transmutation. It is not thus in the intellectual appetite, but according to simple movement: for thus it is also in God and the angels. Hence the Philosopher says (*Ethic.* vii. 14) that *God rejoices by one simple act:* and Dionysius says at the end of *De Cœl. Hier.,* that *the angels are not susceptible to our passible delight, but rejoice together with God with the gladness of incorruption.*

Reply Obj. 3. In us there is delight, not only

in common with dumb animals, but also in common with angels. Wherefore Dionysius says (*ibid.*) that *holy men often take part in the angelic delights.* Accordingly we have delight, not only in the sensitive appetite, which we have in common with dumb animals, but also in the intellectual appetite, which we have in common with the angels.

FIFTH ARTICLE

Whether Bodily and Sensible Pleasures Are Greater Than Spiritual and Intellectual Pleasures?

We proceed thus to the Fifth Article:—

Objection 1. It would seem that bodily and sensible pleasures are greater than spiritual and intelligible pleasures. For all men seek some pleasure, according to the Philosopher (*Ethic.* x. 2, 4). But more seek sensible pleasures, than intelligible spiritual pleasures. Therefore bodily pleasures are greater.

Obj. 2. Further, the greatness of a cause is known by its effect. But bodily pleasures have greater effects; since *they alter the state of the body, and in some they cause madness* (*Ethic.* vii. 3). Therefore bodily pleasures are greater.

Obj. 3. Further, bodily pleasures need to be tempered and checked, by reason of their vehemence: whereas there is no need to check spiritual pleasures. Therefore bodily pleasures are greater.

On the contrary, It is written (Ps. cxviii. 103): *How sweet are Thy words to my palate; more than honey to my mouth!* And the Philosopher says (*Ethic.* x. 7) that *the greatest pleasure is derived from the operation of wisdom.*

I answer that, As stated above (A. 1), pleasure arises from union with a suitable object perceived or known. Now, in the operations of the soul, especially of the sensitive and intellectual soul, it must be noted that, since they do not pass into outward matter, they are acts or perfections of the agent, *e.g.,* to understand, to feel, to will, and the like: because actions which pass into outward matter, are actions and perfections rather of the matter transformed; for *movement is the act produced by the mover in the thing moved* (*Phys.* iii. 3). Accordingly the aforesaid actions of the sensitive and intellectual soul, are themselves a certain good of the agent, and are known by sense and intellect. Wherefore from them also does pleasure arise, and not only from their objects.

If therefore we compare intellectual pleasures with sensible pleasures, according as we delight in the very actions, for instance in sensitive and in intellectual knowledge; without doubt intellectual pleasures are much greater than sensible pleasures. For man takes much more delight in knowing something, by understanding it, than in knowing something by perceiving it with his sense. Because intellectual knowledge is more perfect; and because it is better known, since the intellect reflects on its own act more than sense does. Moreover intellectual knowledge is more beloved: for there is no one who would not forfeit his bodily sight rather than his intellectual vision, as beasts or fools are deprived thereof, as Augustine says in *De Civ. Dei* (*De Trin.* xiv. 14).

If, however, intellectual spiritual pleasures be compared with sensible bodily pleasures, then, in themselves and absolutely speaking, spiritual pleasures are greater. And this appears from the consideration of the three things needed for pleasure, viz., the good which is brought into conjunction, that to which it is conjoined, and the conjunction itself. For spiritual good is both greater and more beloved than bodily good: a sign whereof is that men abstain from even the greatest bodily pleasures, rather than suffer loss of honor which is an intellectual good.—Likewise the intellectual faculty is much more noble and more knowing than the sensitive faculty.—Also the conjunction is more intimate, more perfect and more firm. More intimate, because the senses stop at the outward accidents of a thing, whereas the intellect penetrates to the essence; for the object of the intellect is *what a thing is.* More perfect, because the conjunction of the sensible to the sense implies movement, which is an imperfect act: wherefore sensible pleasures are not perceived all at once, but some part of them is passing away, while some other part is looked forward to as yet to be realized, as is manifest in pleasures of the table and in sexual pleasures: whereas intelligible things are without movement: hence pleasures of this kind are realized all at once. More firm; because the objects of bodily pleasure are corruptible, and soon pass away; whereas spiritual goods are incorruptible.

On the other hand, in relation to us, bodily pleasures are more vehement, for three reasons. First, because sensible things are more known to us, than intelligible things.—Secondly, because sensible pleasures, through being passions of the sensitive appetite, are accompanied by some alteration in the body: whereas this does not occur in spiritual pleasures, save by reason of a certain reaction of the superior appetite on the lower. Thirdly, because bodily pleasures are sought as remedies for bodily defects or troubles, whence various griefs arise. Wherefore bodily pleasures, by reason of their succeeding griefs of this kind, are felt the more, and consequently are welcomed more than spiritual pleasures, which have no contrary griefs, as we shall state farther on (Q. 35, A. 5).

Reply Obj. 1. The reason why more seek bodily pleasures is because sensible goods are known better and more generally: and, again, because men need pleasures as remedies for many kinds of sorrow and sadness: and since the majority cannot attain spiritual pleasures, which are proper to the virtuous, hence it is that they turn aside to seek those of the body.

Reply Obj. 2. Bodily transmutation arises more from bodily pleasures, inasmuch as they are passions of the sensitive appetite.

Reply Obj. 3. Bodily pleasures are realized in the sensitive faculty which is governed by reason: wherefore they need to be tempered and checked by reason. But spiritual pleasures are in the mind, which is itself the rule: wherefore they are in themselves both sober and moderate.

SIXTH ARTICLE

Whether the Pleasures of Touch Are Greater Than the Pleasures Afforded by the Other Senses?

We proceed thus to the Sixth Article:—

Objection 1. It would seem that the pleasures of touch are not greater than the pleasures afforded by the other senses. Because the greatest pleasure seems to be that without which all joy is at an end. But such is the pleasure afforded by the sight, according to the words of Tobias v. 12: *What manner of joy shall be to me, who sit in darkness, and see not the light of heaven?* Therefore the pleasure afforded by the sight is the greatest of sensible pleasures.

Obj. 2. Further, *every one finds pleasure in what he loves*, as the Philosopher says (*Rhet.* i. 11). But *of all the senses the sight is loved most.** Therefore the greatest pleasure is that which is afforded by the sight.

Obj. 3. Further, the beginning of friendship which is for the sake of the pleasant is principally sight. But pleasure is the cause of such friendship. Therefore the greatest pleasure seems to be afforded by sight.

On the contrary, The Philosopher says (*Ethic.* iii. 10) that the greatest pleasures are those which are afforded by the touch.

I answer that, As stated above (Q. 25, A. 2 *ad* 1; Q. 27, A. 4 *ad* 1), everything gives pleasure according as it is loved. Now, as stated in *Metaph.* i. 1, the senses are loved for two reasons: for the purpose of knowledge, and on account of their usefulness. Wherefore the senses afford pleasure in both these ways. But because it is proper to man to apprehend knowledge itself as something good,

* *Metaph.* i. 1.

it follows that the former pleasures of the senses, *i.e.,* those which arise from knowledge, are proper to man: whereas pleasures of the senses, as loved for their usefulness, are common to all animals.

If therefore we speak of that sensible pleasure which is by reason of knowledge, it is evident that the sight affords greater pleasure than any other sense.—On the other hand, if we speak of that sensible pleasure which is by reason of usefulness, then the greatest pleasure is afforded by the touch. For the usefulness of sensible things is gauged by their relation to the preservation of the animal's nature. Now the sensible objects of touch bear the closest relation to this usefulness: for the touch takes cognizance of those things which are vital to an animal—namely, of things hot and cold and the like. Wherefore in this respect, the pleasures of touch are greater as being more closely related to the end. For this reason, too, other animals which do not experience sensible pleasure save by reason of usefulness, derive no pleasure from the other senses except as subordinated to the sensible objects of the touch: *for dogs do not take delight in the smell of hares, but in eating them;* . . . *nor does the lion feel pleasure in the lowing of an ox, but in devouring it* (*Ethic.* iii. 10).

Since then the pleasure afforded by touch is the greatest in respect of usefulness, and the pleasure afforded by sight the greatest in respect of knowledge; if anyone wish to compare these two, he will find that the pleasure of touch is, absolutely speaking, greater than the pleasure of sight, so far as the latter remains within the limits of sensible pleasure. Because it is evident that in everything, that which is natural is most powerful: and it is to these pleasures of the touch that the natural concupiscences, such as those of food, sexual union, and the like, are ordained.—If, however, we consider the pleasures of sight, inasmuch as sight is the handmaid of the mind, then the pleasures of sight are greater, forasmuch as intellectual pleasures are greater than sensible.

Reply Obj. 1. Joy, as stated above (A. 3), denotes pleasure of the soul; and this belongs principally to the sight. But natural pleasure belongs principally to the touch.

Reply Obj. 2. The sight is loved most, *on account of knowledge, because it helps us to distinguish many things* as is stated in the same passage (*Metaph.* i. 1).

Reply Obj. 3. Pleasure causes carnal love in one way; the sight, in another. For pleasure, especially that which is afforded by the touch, is the final cause of the friendship which is for the sake of the pleasant: whereas the sight is a cause like that from which a movement has its beginning, inasmuch as the beholder on seeing the lovable object receives an impression of its image, which entices him to love it and to seek its delight.

SEVENTH ARTICLE

Whether Any Pleasure Is Not Natural?

We proceed thus to the Seventh Article:—

Objection 1. It would seem that no pleasure is not natural. For pleasure is to the emotions of the soul what repose is to bodies. But the appetite of a natural body does not repose save in a connatural place. Neither, therefore, can the repose of the animal appetite, which is pleasure, be elsewhere than in something connatural. Therefore no pleasure is non-natural.

Obj. 2. Further, what is against nature is violent. But *whatever is violent causes grief* (*Metaph.* v. 5). Therefore nothing which is unnatural can give pleasure.

Obj. 3. Further, the fact of being established in one's own nature, if perceived, gives rise to pleasure, as is evident from the Philosopher's definition quoted above (A. 1). But it is natural to every thing to be established in its nature; because natural movement tends to a natural end. Therefore every pleasure is natural.

On the contrary, The Philosopher says (*Ethic.* vii. 5, 6) that some things are pleasant *not from nature but from disease.*

I answer that, We speak of that as being natural, which is in accord with nature, as stated in *Phys.* ii. 1. Now, in man, nature can be taken in two ways. First, inasmuch as intellect and reason is the principal part of man's nature, since in respect thereof he has his own specific nature. And in this sense, those pleasures may be called natural to man, which are derived from things pertaining to man in respect of his reason: for instance, it is natural to man to take pleasure in contemplating the truth and in doing works of virtue.—Secondly, nature in man may be taken as contrasted with reason, and as denoting that which is common to man and other animals, especially that part of man which does not obey reason. And in this sense, that which pertains to the preservation of the body, either as regards the individual, as food, drink, sleep, and the like, or as regards the species, as sexual intercourse, are said to afford man natural pleasure. Under each kind of pleasures, we find some that are *not natural* speaking absolutely, and yet *connatural* in some respect. For it happens in an individual that some one of the natural principles of the species is corrupted, so that something which is contrary to the specific nature, becomes accidentally natural to this individual: thus it is natural to this hot water to give heat. Consequently it happens that something which is not natural to man, either in regard to reason, or in regard to the preservation of the body, becomes connatural to this individual man, on account of there being some corruption of nature in him. And this corruption may be either on the part of the body,—from some ailment; thus to a man suffering from fever, sweet things seem bitter, and vice versa,—or from an evil temperament; thus some take pleasure in eating earth and coals and the like; or on the part of the soul; thus from custom some take pleasure in cannibalism or in the unnatural intercourse of man and beast, or other such like things, which are not in accord with human nature.

This suffices for the answers to the objections.

EIGHTH ARTICLE

Whether One Pleasure Can Be Contrary to Another?

We proceed thus to the Eighth Article:—

Objection 1. It would seem that one pleasure cannot be contrary to another. Because the passions of the soul derive their species and contrariety from their objects. Now the object of pleasure is the good. Since therefore good is not contrary to good, but *good is contrary to evil, and evil to good,* as stated in *Prædic.* viii; it seems that one pleasure is not contrary to another.

Obj. 2. Further, to one thing there is one contrary, as is proved in *Metaph.* x. 4. But sadness is contrary to pleasure. Therefore pleasure is not contrary to pleasure.

Obj. 3. Further, if one pleasure is contrary to another, this is only on account of the contrariety of the things which give pleasure. But this difference is material: whereas contrariety is a difference of form, as stated in *Metaph.* x. 4. Therefore there is no contrariety between one pleasure and another.

On the contrary, Things of the same genus that impede one another are contraries, as the Philosopher states (*Phys.* viii. 8). But some pleasures impede one another, as stated in *Ethic.* x. 5. Therefore some pleasures are contrary to one another.

I answer that, Pleasure, in the emotions of the soul, is likened to repose in natural bodies, as stated above (Q. 23, A. 4). Now one repose is said to be contrary to another when they are in contrary termini; thus *repose in a high place is contrary to repose in a low place* (*Phys.* v. 6). Wherefore it happens in the emotions of the soul that one pleasure is contrary to another.

Reply Obj. 1. This saying of the Philosopher is to be understood of good and evil as applied to virtues and vices: because one vice may be contrary to another vice, whereas no virtue can be contrary to another virtue. But in other things nothing prevents one good from being contrary to another, such as hot and cold, of which the former is good in relation to fire, the latter, in relation to water. And in this way one pleasure can be contrary to another.—That this is impossible with regard to the good of virtue, is due to the fact that virtue's good depends on fittingness in relation to some one thing—*i.e.*, the reason.

Reply Obj. 2. Pleasure, in the emotions of the soul, is likened to natural repose in bodies: because its object is something suitable and connatural, so to speak. But sadness is like a violent repose: because its object is disagreeable to the animal appetite, just as the place of violent repose is disagreeable to the natural appetite. Now natural repose is contrary both to violent repose of the same body, and to the natural repose of another, as stated in *Phys.* v. (*loc. cit.*). Wherefore pleasure is contrary both to another pleasure and to sadness.

Reply Obj. 3. The things in which we take pleasure, since they are the objects of pleasure, cause not only a material, but also a formal difference, if the formality of pleasurableness be different. Because difference in the formal object causes a specific difference in acts and passions, as stated above (Q. 23, AA. 1, 4; Q. 30, A. 2).

QUESTION 32

Of the Cause of Pleasure

(In Eight Articles)

WE must now consider the causes of pleasure: and under this head there are eight points of inquiry: (1) Whether operation is the proper cause of pleasure? (2) Whether movement is a cause of pleasure? (3) Whether hope and memory cause pleasure? (4) Whether sadness causes pleasure? (5) Whether the actions of others are a cause of pleasure to us? (6) Whether doing good to another is a cause of pleasure? (7) Whether likeness is a cause of pleasure? (8) Whether wonder is a cause of pleasure?

FIRST ARTICLE

Whether Operation Is the Proper Cause of Pleasure?

We proceed thus to the First Article:—

Objection 1. It would seem that operation is not the proper and first cause of pleasure. For, as the Philosopher says (*Rhet.* i. 11), *pleasure consists in a perception of the senses,* since knowledge is requisite for pleasure, as stated above (Q. 31, A. 1). But the objects of operations are knowable before the operations themselves. Therefore operation is not the proper cause of pleasure.

Obj. 2. Further, pleasure consists especially in an end gained: since it is this that is chiefly desired. But the end is not always an operation, but is sometimes the effect of the operation. Therefore operation is not the proper and direct cause of pleasure.

Obj. 3. Further, leisure and rest consist in cessation from work: and they are objects of pleasure (*Rhet.* i, *loc. cit.*). Therefore operation is not the proper cause of pleasure.

On the contrary, The Philosopher says (*Ethic.* vii. 12, 13; x. 4) that *pleasure is a connatural and uninterrupted operation.*

I answer that, As stated above (Q. 31, A. 1), two things are requisite for pleasure: namely, the attainment of the suitable good, and knowledge of this attainment. Now each of these consists in a kind of operation: because actual knowledge is an operation; and the attainment of the suitable good is by means of an operation. Moreover, the proper operation itself is a suitable good. Wherefore every pleasure must needs be the result of some operation.

Reply Obj. 1. The objects of operations are not pleasurable save inasmuch as they are united to us; either by knowledge alone, as when we take pleasure in thinking of or looking at certain things; or in some other way in addition to knowledge; as when a man takes pleasure in knowing that he has something good,—riches, honor, or the like; which would not be pleasurable unless they were apprehended as possessed. For as the Philosopher observes (*Polit.* ii. 2) *we take great pleasure in looking upon a thing as our own, by reason of the natural love we have for ourselves.* Now to have such like things is nothing else but to use them or to be able to use them: and this is through some operation. Wherefore it is evident that every pleasure is traced to some operation as its cause.

Reply Obj. 2. Even when it is not an operation, but the effect of an operation, that is the end, this effect is pleasant in so far as possessed or effected: and this implies use or operation.

Reply Obj. 3. Operations are pleasant, in

so far as they are proportionate and connatural to the agent. Now, since human power is finite, operation is proportionate thereto according to a certain measure. Wherefore if it exceed that measure, it will be no longer proportionate or pleasant, but, on the contrary, painful and irksome. And in this sense, leisure and play and other things pertaining to repose, are pleasant, inasmuch as they banish sadness which results from labor.

SECOND ARTICLE

Whether Movement Is a Cause of Pleasure?

We proceed thus to the Second Article:—

Objection 1. It would seem that movement is not a cause of pleasure. Because, as stated above (Q. 31, A. 1), the good which is obtained and is actually possessed, is the cause of pleasure: wherefore the Philosopher says (*Ethic.* vii. 12) that pleasure is not compared with generation, but with the operation of a thing already in existence. Now that which is being moved towards something has it not as yet; but, so to speak, is being generated in its regard, forasmuch as generation or corruption are united to every movement, as stated in *Phys.* viii. 3. Therefore movement is not a cause of pleasure.

Obj. 2. Further, movement is the chief cause of toil and fatigue in our works. But operations through being toilsome and fatiguing are not pleasant but disagreeable. Therefore movement is not a cause of pleasure.

Obj. 3. Further, movement implies a certain innovation, which is the opposite of custom. But things *which we are accustomed to, are pleasant*, as the Philosopher says(*Rhet.* i. 11). Therefore movement is not a cause of pleasure.

On the contrary, Augustine says (*Conf.* viii. 3): *What means this, O Lord my God, whereas Thou art everlasting joy to Thyself, and some things around Thee evermore rejoice in Thee? What means this, that this portion of things ebbs and flows alternately displeased and reconciled?* From these words we gather that man rejoices and takes pleasure in some kind of alternations: and therefore movement seems to cause pleasure.

I answer that, Three things are requisite for pleasure; two, *i.e.*, the one that is pleased and the pleasurable object conjoined to him; and a third, which is knowledge of this conjunction: and in respect of these three, movement is pleasant, as the Philosopher says (*Ethic.* vii. 14 and *Rhet.* i. 11). For as far as we who feel pleasure are concerned, change is pleasant to us because our nature is changeable; for which reason that which is suitable to us at one time

is not suitable at another,—thus to warm himself at a fire is suitable to man in winter and not in summer.—Again, on the part of the pleasing good which is united to us, change is pleasant. Because the continued action of an agent increases its effect: thus the longer a person remains near the fire, the more he is warmed and dried. Now the natural mode of being consists in a certain measure; and therefore when the continued presence of a pleasant object exceeds the measure of one's natural mode of being, the removal of that object becomes pleasant.—On the part of the knowledge itself (change becomes pleasant), because man desires to know something whole and perfect: when therefore a thing cannot be apprehended all at once as a whole, change in such a thing is pleasant, so that one part may pass and another succeed, and thus the whole be perceived. Hence Augustine says (*Conf.* iv. 11): *Thou wouldst not have the syllables stay, but fly away, that others may come, and thou hear the whole. And so whenever any one thing is made up of many, all of which do not exist together, all would please collectively more than they do severally, if all could be perceived collectively.*

If therefore there be any thing, whose nature is unchangeable; the natural mode of whose being cannot be exceeded by the continuation of any pleasing object; and which can behold the whole object of its delight at once,—to such a one change will afford no delight. And the more any pleasures approach to this, the more are they capable of being continual.

Reply Obj. 1. Although the subject of movement has not yet perfectly that to which it is moved, nevertheless it is beginning to have something thereof: and in this respect movement itself has something of pleasure. But it falls short of the perfection of pleasure; because the more perfect pleasures regard things that are unchangeable.—Moreover movement becomes the cause of pleasure, in so far as thereby something which previously was unsuitable, becomes suitable or ceases to be, as stated above.

Reply Obj. 2. Movement causes toil and fatigue, when it exceeds our natural aptitude. It is not thus that it causes pleasure, but by removing the obstacles to our natural aptitude.

Reply Obj. 3. What is customary becomes pleasant, in so far as it becomes natural: because custom is like a second nature. But the movement which gives pleasure is not that which departs from custom, but rather that which prevents the corruption of the natural mode of being, that might result from continued operation. And thus from the same cause of connaturalness, both custom and movement become pleasant.

THIRD ARTICLE

Whether Hope and Memory Cause Pleasure?

We proceed thus to the Third Article:—

Objection 1. It would seem that memory and hope do not cause pleasure. Because pleasure is caused by present good, as Damascene says (*De Fide Orthod.* ii. 12). But hope and memory regard what is absent: since memory is of the past, and hope of the future. Therefore memory and hope do not cause pleasure.

Obj. 2. Further, the same thing is not the cause of contraries. But hope causes affliction, according to Prov. xiii. 12: *Hope that is deferred afflicteth the soul.* Therefore hope does not cause pleasure.

Obj. 3. Further, just as hope agrees with pleasure in regarding good, so also do desire and love. Therefore hope should not be assigned as a cause of pleasure, any more than desire or love.

On the contrary, It is written (Rom. xii. 12): *Rejoicing in hope;* and (Ps. lxxvi. 4): *I remembered God, and was delighted.*

I answer that, Pleasure is caused by the presence of suitable good, in so far as it is felt, or perceived in any way. Now a thing is present to us in two ways. First, in knowledge—*i.e.,* according as the thing known is in the knower by its likeness; secondly, in reality—*i.e.,* according as one thing is in real conjunction of any kind with another, either actually or potentially. And since real conjunction is greater than conjunction by likeness, which is the conjunction of knowledge; and again, since actual is greater than potential conjunction: therefore the greatest pleasure is that which arises from sensation which requires the presence of the sensible object. The second place belongs to the pleasure of hope, wherein there is pleasurable conjunction, not only in respect of apprehension, but also in respect of the faculty or power of obtaining the pleasurable object. The third place belongs to the pleasure of memory, which has only the conjunction of apprehension.

Reply Obj. 1. Hope and memory are indeed of things which, absolutely speaking, are absent: and yet these are, after a fashion, present, *i.e.,* either according to apprehension only; or according to apprehension and possibility, at least supposed, of attainment.

Reply Obj. 2. Nothing prevents the same thing, in different ways, being the cause of contraries. And so hope, inasmuch as it implies a present appraising of a future good, causes pleasure; whereas, inasmuch as it implies absence of that good, it causes affliction.

Reply Obj. 3. Love and concupiscence also

* Gregory, *Moral.* iv.

cause pleasure. For everything that is loved becomes pleasing to the lover, since love is a kind of union or connaturalness of lover and beloved. In like manner every object of desire is pleasing to the one that desires, since desire is chiefly a craving for pleasure. However hope, as implying a certainty of the real presence of the pleasing good, that is not implied either by love or by concupiscence, is reckoned in preference to them as causing pleasure; and also in preference to memory, which is of that which has already passed away.

FOURTH ARTICLE

Whether Sadness Causes Pleasure?

We proceed thus to the Fourth Article:—

Objection 1. It would seem that sadness does not cause pleasure. For nothing causes its own contrary. But sadness is contrary to pleasure. Therefore it does not cause it.

Obj. 2. Further, contraries have contrary effects. But pleasures, when called to mind, cause pleasure. Therefore sad things, when remembered, cause sorrow and not pleasure.

Obj. 3. Further, as sadness is to pleasure, so is hatred to love. But hatred does not cause love, but rather the other way about, as stated above (Q. 29, A. 2). Therefore sadness does not cause pleasure.

On the contrary, It is written (Ps. xli. 4): *My tears have been my bread day and night:* where bread denotes the refreshment of pleasure. Therefore tears, which arise from sadness, can give pleasure.

I answer that, Sadness may be considered in two ways: as existing actually, and as existing in the memory: and in both ways sadness can cause pleasure. Because sadness, as actually existing, causes pleasure, inasmuch as it brings to mind that which is loved, the absence of which causes sadness; and yet the mere thought of it gives pleasure.—The recollection of sadness becomes a cause of pleasure, on account of the deliverance which ensued: because absence of evil is looked upon as something good; wherefore so far as a man thinks that he has been delivered from that which caused him sorrow and pain, so much reason has he to rejoice. Hence Augustine says in *De Civ. Dei* xxii. 31* that *oftentimes in joy we call to mind sad things . . . and in the season of health we recall past pains without feeling pain, . . . and in proportion are the more filled with joy and gladness:* and again (*Conf.* viii. 3) he says that *the more peril there was in the battle, so much the more joy will there be in the triumph.*

Reply Obj. 1. Sometimes accidentally a thing is the cause of its contrary: thus *that which is cold sometimes causes heat,* as stated in *Phys.* viii. 1. In like manner sadness is the accidental cause of pleasure, in so far as it gives rise to the apprehension of something pleasant.

Reply Obj. 2. Sad things, called to mind, cause pleasure, not in so far as they are sad and contrary to pleasant things; but in so far as man is delivered from them. In like manner the recollection of pleasant things, by reason of these being lost, may cause sadness.

Reply Obj. 3. Hatred also can be the accidental cause of love: *i.e.*, so far as some love one another, inasmuch as they agree in hating one and the same thing.

FIFTH ARTICLE

Whether the Actions of Others Are a Cause of Pleasure to Us?

We proceed thus to the Fifth Article:—

Objection 1. It would seem that the actions of others are not a cause of pleasure to us. Because the cause of pleasure is our own good when conjoined to us. But the actions of others are not conjoined to us. Therefore they are not a cause of pleasure to us.

Obj. 2. Further, action is the agent's own good. If, therefore, the actions of others are a cause of pleasure to us, for the same reason all goods belonging to others will be pleasing to us: which is evidently untrue.

Obj. 3. Further, action is pleasant through proceeding from an innate habit; hence it is stated in *Ethic.* ii. 3 that *we must reckon the pleasure which follows after action, as being the sign of a habit existing in us*. But the actions of others do not proceed from habits existing in us, but, sometimes, from habits existing in the agents. Therefore the actions of others are not pleasing to us, but to the agents themselves.

On the contrary, It is written in the second canonical epistle of John (*verse* 4): *I was exceeding glad that I found thy children walking in truth.*

I answer that, As stated above (A. 1; Q. 31, A. 1), two things are requisite for pleasure, namely, the attainment of one's proper good, and the knowledge of having obtained it. Wherefore the action of another may cause pleasure to us in three ways. First, from the fact that we obtain some good through the action of another. And in this way, the actions of those who do some good to us, are pleasing to us: since it is pleasant to be benefited by another.—Secondly, from the fact that another's action makes us to know or appreciate our own good: and for this reason men take pleasure in being praised or honored by others, because, to wit, they thus become aware of some good existing in themselves. And since

this appreciation receives greater weight from the testimony of good and wise men, hence men take greater pleasure in being praised and honored by them. And because a flatterer appears to praise, therefore flattery is pleasing to some. And as love is for something good, while admiration is for something great, so it is pleasant to be loved and admired by others, inasmuch as a man thus becomes aware of his own goodness or greatness, through their giving pleasure to others.—Thirdly, from the fact that another's actions, if they be good, are reckoned as one's own good, by reason of the power of love, which makes a man to regard his friend as one with himself. And on account of hatred, which makes one to reckon another's good as being in opposition to oneself, the evil action of an enemy becomes an object of pleasure: whence it is written (1 Cor. xiii. 6) that charity *rejoiceth not in iniquity, but rejoiceth with the truth.*

Reply Obj. 1. Another's action may be conjoined to me, either by its effect, as in the first way, or by knowledge, as in the second way; or by affection, as in the third way.

Reply Obj. 2. This argument avails for the third mode, but not for the first two.

Reply Obj. 3. Although the actions of another do not proceed from habits that are in me, yet they either produce in me something that gives pleasure; or they make me appreciate or know a habit of mine; or they proceed from the habit of one who is united to me by love.

SIXTH ARTICLE

Whether Doing Good to Another Is a Cause of Pleasure?

We proceed thus to the Sixth Article.—

Objection 1. It would seem that doing good to another is not a cause of pleasure. Because pleasure is caused by one's obtaining one's proper good, as stated above (AA. 1, 5; Q. 31, A. 1). But doing good pertains not to the obtaining but to the spending of one's proper good. Therefore it seems to be the cause of sadness rather than of pleasure.

Obj. 2. Further, the Philosopher says (*Ethic.* iv. 1) that *illiberality is more connatural to man than prodigality.* Now it is a mark of prodigality to do good to others; while it is a mark of illiberality to desist from doing good. Since therefore everyone takes pleasure in a connatural operation, as stated in *Ethic.* vii. 14 and x. 4, it seems that doing good to others is not a cause of pleasure.

Obj. 3. Further, contrary effects proceed from contrary causes. But man takes a natural pleasure in certain kinds of ill-doing, such as overcoming, contradicting or scolding others, or, if he be angry, in punishing them, as the Philosopher says (*Rhet.* i. 11). Therefore doing good to others is a cause of sadness rather than of pleasure.

On the contrary, The Philosopher says (*Polit.* ii. 2) that *it is most pleasant to give presents or assistance to friends and strangers.*

I answer that, Doing good to another may give pleasure in three ways. First, in consideration of the effect, which is the good conferred on another. In this respect, inasmuch as through being united to others by love, we look upon their good as being our own, we take pleasure in the good we do to others, especially to our friends, as in our own good.— Secondly, in consideration of the end; as when a man, from doing good to another, hopes to get some good for himself, either from God or from man: for hope is a cause of pleasure.— Thirdly, in consideration of the principle: and thus, doing good to another, can give pleasure in respect of a threefold principle. One is the faculty of doing good: and in this regard, doing good to another becomes pleasant, in so far as it arouses in man an imagination of abundant good existing in him, whereof he is able to give others a share. Wherefore men take pleasure in their children, and in their own works, as being things on which they bestow a share of their own good. Another principle is a man's habitual inclination to do good, by reason of which doing good becomes connatural to him: for which reason the liberal man takes pleasure in giving to others. The third principle is the motive: for instance when a man is moved by one whom he loves, to do good to someone: for whatever we do or suffer for a friend is pleasant, because love is the principal cause of pleasure.

Reply Obj. 1. Spending gives pleasure as showing forth one's good. But in so far as it empties us of our own good it may be a cause of sadness; for instance when it is excessive.

Reply Obj. 2. Prodigality is an excessive spending, which is unnatural: wherefore prodigality is said to be contrary to nature.

Reply Obj. 3. To overcome, to contradict and to punish, give pleasure, not as tending to another's ill, but as pertaining to one's own good, which man loves more than he hates another's ill. For it is naturally pleasant to overcome, inasmuch as it makes a man to appreciate his own superiority. Wherefore all those games in which there is a striving for the mastery, and a possibility of winning it, afford the greatest pleasure: and speaking generally all contests, in so far as they admit hope of victory.—To contradict and to scold can give pleasure in two ways. First, as making man imagine himself to be wise and excellent; since it belongs to wise men and elders to reprove and to scold. Secondly, in so far as by

scolding and reproving, one does good to another: for this gives one pleasure, as stated above.—It is pleasant to an angry man to punish, in so far as he thinks himself to be removing an apparent slight, which seems to be due to a previous hurt: for when a man is hurt by another, he seems to be slighted thereby; and therefore he wishes to be quit of this slight by paying back the hurt.—And thus it is clear that doing good to another may be of itself pleasant: whereas doing evil to another is not pleasant, except in so far as it seems to affect one's own good.

SEVENTH ARTICLE

Whether Likeness Is a Cause of Pleasure?

We proceed thus to the Seventh Article:—

Objection 1. It would seem that likeness is not a cause of pleasure. Because ruling and presiding seem to imply a certain unlikeness. But *it is natural to take pleasure in ruling and presiding,* as stated in *Rhet.* i. 11. Therefore unlikeness, rather than likeness, is a cause of pleasure.

Obj. 2. Further, nothing is more unlike pleasure than sorrow. But those who are burdened by sorrow are most inclined to seek pleasures, as the Philosopher says (*Ethic.* vii. 14). Therefore unlikeness, rather than likeness, is a cause of pleasure.

Obj. 3. Further, those who are satiated with certain delights, derive not pleasure but disgust from them; as when one is satiated with food. Therefore likeness is not a cause of pleasure.

On the contrary, Likeness is a cause of love, as above stated (Q. 27, A. 3): and love is the cause of pleasure. Therefore likeness is a cause of pleasure.

I answer that, Likeness is a kind of unity; hence that which is like us, as being one with us, causes pleasure; just as it causes love, as stated above (Q. 27, A. 3). And if that which is like us does not hurt our own good, but increase it, it is pleasurable simply; for instance one man in respect of another, one youth in relation to another.—But if it be hurtful to our own good, thus accidentally it causes disgust or sadness, not as being like and one with us, but as hurtful to that which is yet more one with us.

Now it happens in two ways that something like is hurtful to our own good. First, by destroying the measure of our own good, by a kind of excess; because good, especially bodily good, as health, is conditioned by a certain measure: wherefore superfluous food or any bodily pleasure, causes disgust.—Secondly, by being directly contrary to one's own good:

thus a potter dislikes other potters, not because they are potters, but because they deprive him of his own excellence or profits, which he seeks as his own good.

Reply Obj. 1. Since ruler and subject are in communion with one another, there is a certain likeness between them: but this likeness is conditioned by a certain superiority, since ruling and presiding pertain to the excellence of a man's own good: because they belong to men who are wise and better than others; the result being that they give man an idea of his own excellence.—Another reason is that by ruling and presiding, a man does good to others, which is pleasant.

Reply Obj. 2. That which gives pleasure to the sorrowful man, though it be unlike sorrow, bears some likeness to the man that is sorrowful: because sorrows are contrary to his own good. Wherefore the sorrowful man seeks pleasure as making for his own good, in so far as it is a remedy for its contrary. And this is why bodily pleasures, which are contrary to certain sorrows, are more sought than intellectual pleasures, which have no contrary sorrow, as we shall state later on (Q. 35, A. 5). And this explains why all animals naturally desire pleasure: because animals ever work through sense and movement. For this reason also young people are most inclined to seek pleasures; on account of the many changes to which they are subject, while yet growing. Moreover this is why the melancholic has a strong desire for pleasures, in order to drive away sorrow: because his *body is corroded by a base humor,* as stated in *Ethic.* vii. 14.

Reply Obj. 3. Bodily goods are conditioned by a certain fixed measure: wherefore surfeit of such things destroys the proper good, and consequently gives rise to disgust and sorrow, through being contrary to the proper good of man.

EIGHTH ARTICLE

Whether Wonder Is a Cause of Pleasure?

We proceed thus to the Eighth Article:—

Objection 1. It would seem that wonder is not a cause of pleasure. Because wonder is the act of one who is ignorant of the nature of something, as Damascene says. But knowledge, rather than ignorance, is a cause of pleasure. Therefore wonder is not a cause of pleasure.

Obj. 2. Further, wonder is the beginning of wisdom, being as it were, the road to the search of truth, as stated in the beginning of *Metaph.* (i. 2). But *it is more pleasant to think of what we know, than to seek for what we know not,* as the Philosopher says (*Ethic.*

x. 7): since in the latter case we encounter difficulties and hindrances, in the former not; while pleasure arises from an operation which is unhindered, as stated in *Ethic.* vii. 12, 13. Therefore wonder hinders rather than causes pleasure.

Obj. 3. Further, everyone takes pleasure in what he is accustomed to: wherefore the actions of habits acquired by custom, are pleasant. But *we wonder at what is unwonted,* as Augustine says (*Tract.* xxiv. *in Joan.*). Therefore wonder is contrary to the cause of pleasure.

On the contrary, The Philosopher says (*Rhet.* i. 11) that wonder is the cause of pleasure.

I answer that, It is pleasant to get what one desires, as stated above (Q. 23, A. 4): and therefore the greater the desire for the thing loved, the greater the pleasure when it is attained: indeed the very increase of desire brings with it an increase of pleasure, according as it gives rise to the hope of obtaining that which is loved, since it was stated above (A. 3 *ad* 3) that desire resulting from hope is a cause of pleasure.—Now wonder is a kind of desire for knowledge; a desire which comes to man when he sees an effect of which the cause either is unknown to him, or surpasses his knowledge or faculty of understanding. Consequently wonder is a cause of pleasure, in so far as it includes a hope of getting the knowledge which one desires to have. For this reason whatever is wonderful is pleasing, for instance things that are scarce. Also, representations of things, even of those which are not pleasant in themselves, give rise to pleasure; for the soul rejoices in comparing one thing with another, because comparison of one thing with another is the proper and connatural act of the reason, as the Philosopher says (*Poet.* iv). This again is why *it is more delightful to be delivered from great danger, because it is something wonderful,* as stated in *Rhet.* i. 11.

Reply Obj. 1. Wonder gives pleasure, not because it implies ignorance, but in so far as it includes the desire of learning the cause, and in so far as the wonderer learns something new, *i.e.,* that the cause is other than he had thought it to be.*

Reply Obj. 2. Pleasure includes two things; rest in the good, and perception of this rest. As to the former therefore, since it is more perfect to contemplate the known truth, than to seek for the unknown, the contemplation of what we know, is in itself more pleasing than the research of what we do not know. Nevertheless, as to the second, it happens that research is sometimes more pleasing accidentally,

* According to another reading:—that he is other than he thought himself to be.

in so far as it proceeds from a greater desire: for greater desire is awakened when we are conscious of our ignorance. This is why man takes the greatest pleasure in finding or learning things for the first time.

Reply Obj. 3. It is pleasant to do what we are wont to do, inasmuch as this is connatural to us, as it were. And yet things that are of rare occurrence can be pleasant, either as regards knowledge, from the fact that we desire to know something about them, in so far as they are wonderful; or as regards action, from the fact that *the mind is more inclined by desire to act intensely in things that are new*, as stated in *Ethic.* x. 4, since more perfect operation causes more perfect pleasure.

QUESTION 33

Of the Effects of Pleasure

(In Four Articles)

WE must now consider the effects of pleasure; and under this head there are four points of inquiry: (1) Whether expansion is an effect of pleasure? (2) Whether pleasure causes thirst or desire for itself? (3) Whether pleasure hinders the use of reason? (4) Whether pleasure perfects operation?

FIRST ARTICLE

Whether Expansion Is an Effect of Pleasure?

We proceed thus to the First Article:—

Objection 1. It would seem that expansion is not an effect of pleasure. For expansion seems to pertain more to love, according to the Apostle (2 Cor. vi. 11): *Our heart is enlarged.* Wherefore it is written (Ps. cxviii. 96) concerning the precept of charity: *Thy commandment is exceeding broad.* But pleasure is a distinct passion from love. Therefore expansion is not an effect of pleasure.

Obj. 2. Further, when a thing expands it is enabled to receive more. But receiving pertains to desire, which is for something not yet possessed. Therefore expansion seems to belong to desire rather than to pleasure.

Obj. 3. Further, contraction is contrary to expansion. But contraction seems to belong to pleasure, for the hand closes on that which we wish to grasp firmly: and such is the affection of appetite in regard to that which pleases it. Therefore expansion does not pertain to pleasure.

On the contrary, In order to express joy, it is written (Isa. lx. 5): *Thou shalt see and abound, thy heart shall wonder and be enlarged.* Moreover pleasure is called by the name of *laetitia*, as being derived from *dilatatio* (expansion), as stated above (Q. 31, A. 3, ad 3).

I answer that, Breadth (*latitudo*) is a dimension of bodily magnitude: hence it is not applied to the emotions of the soul, save metaphorically. Now expansion denotes a kind of movement towards breadth; and it belongs to pleasure in respect of the two things requisite for pleasure. One of these is on the part of the apprehensive power, which is cognizant of conjunction with some suitable good. As a result of this apprehension, man perceives that he has attained a certain perfection, which is a magnitude of the spiritual order: and in this respect man's mind is said to be magnified or expanded by pleasure.—The other requisite for pleasure is on the part of the appetitive power, which acquiesces in the pleasurable object, and rests therein, offering, as it were, to enfold it within itself. And thus man's affection is expanded by pleasure, as though it surrendered itself to hold within itself the object of its pleasure.

Reply Obj. 1. In metaphorical expressions nothing hinders one and the same thing from being attributed to different things according to different likenesses. And in this way expansion pertains to love by reason of a certain spreading out, in so far as the affection of the lover spreads out to others, so as to care, not only for his own interests, but also for what concerns others. On the other hand expansion pertains to pleasure, in so far as a thing becomes more ample in itself so as to become more capacious.

Reply Obj. 2. Desire includes a certain expansion arising from the imagination of the thing desired; but this expansion increases at the presence of the pleasurable object: because the mind surrenders itself more to that object when it is already taking pleasure in it, than when it desires it before possessing it; since pleasure is the end of desire.

Reply Obj. 3. He that takes pleasure in a thing holds it fast, by clinging to it with all his might: but he opens his heart to it that he may enjoy it perfectly.

SECOND ARTICLE

Whether Pleasure Causes Thirst or Desire for Itself?

We proceed thus to the Second Article:—

Objection 1. It would seem that pleasure does not cause desire for itself. Because all movement ceases when repose is reached. But pleasure is, as it were, a certain repose of the movement of desire, as stated above (Q. 23, A. 4; Q. 25, A. 2). Therefore the movement of desire ceases when pleasure is reached. Therefore pleasure does not cause desire.

Obj. 2. Further, a thing does not cause its contrary. But pleasure is, in a way, contrary to desire, on the part of the object: since desire regards a good which is not yet possessed, whereas pleasure regards the good that is possessed. Therefore pleasure does not cause desire for itself.

Obj. 3. Further, distaste is incompatible with desire. But pleasure often causes distaste. Therefore it does not cause desire.

On the contrary, Our Lord said (Jo. iv. 13): *Whosoever drinketh of this water, shall thirst again:* where, according to Augustine (*Tract.* xv. in *Joan.*), water denotes pleasures of the body.

I answer that, Pleasure can be considered in two ways; first, as existing in reality; secondly, as existing in the memory.—Again thirst, or desire, can be taken in two ways; first, properly, as denoting a craving for something not possessed; secondly, in general, as excluding distaste.

Considered as existing in reality, pleasure does not of itself cause thirst or desire for itself, but only accidentally; provided we take thirst or desire as denoting a craving for some thing not possessed: because pleasure is an emotion of the appetite in respect of something actually present.—But it may happen that what is actually present is not perfectly possessed: and this may be on the part of the thing possessed, or on the part of the possessor. On the part of the thing possessed, this happens through the thing possessed not being a simultaneous whole; wherefore one obtains possession of it successively, and while taking pleasure in what one has, one desires to possess the remainder: thus if a man is pleased with the first part of a verse, he desires to hear the second part, as Augustine says (*Conf.* iv. 11). In this way nearly all bodily pleasures cause thirst for themselves, until they are fully realized, because pleasures of this kind arise from some movement: as is evident in pleasures of the table.—On the part of the possessor, this happens when a man possesses a thing which is perfect in itself, yet does not possess it perfectly, but obtains possession of it little by little. Thus in this life, a faint perception of Divine knowledge affords us delight, and delight sets up a thirst or desire for perfect knowledge; in which sense we may understand the words of Ecclus. xxiv. 29: *They that drink me shall yet thirst.*

On the other hand, if by thirst or desire we understand the mere intensity of the emotion, that excludes distaste, thus more than all others spiritual pleasures cause thirst or desire for themselves. Because bodily pleasures become distasteful by reason of their causing an excess in the natural mode of being, when they are increased or even when they are protracted; as is evident in the case of pleasures of the table. This is why, when a man arrives at the point of perfection in bodily pleasures, he wearies of them, and sometimes desires another kind.—Spiritual pleasures, on the contrary, do not exceed the natural mode of being, but perfect nature. Hence when their point of perfection is reached, then do they afford the greatest delight: except, perchance, accidentally, in so far as the work of contemplation is accompanied by some operation of the bodily powers, which tire from protracted activity. And in this sense also we may understand those words of Ecclus. xxiv. 29: *They that drink me shall yet thirst:* for, even of the angels, who know God perfectly, and delight in Him, it is written (1 Pet. i. 12) that they *desire to look at* Him.

Lastly, if we consider pleasure, not as existing in reality, but as existing in the memory, thus it has of itself a natural tendency to cause thirst and desire for itself: when, to wit, man returns to that disposition, in which he was when he experienced the pleasure that is past. But if he be changed from that disposition, the memory of that pleasure does not give him pleasure, but distaste: for instance, the memory of food in respect of a man who has eaten to repletion.

Reply Obj. 1. When pleasure is perfect, then it includes complete rest; and the movement of desire, tending to what was not possessed, ceases. But when it is imperfect, then the desire, tending to what was not possessed, does not cease altogether.

Reply Obj. 2. That which is possessed imperfectly, is possessed in one respect, and in another respect is not possessed. Consequently it may be the object of desire and pleasure at the same time.

Reply Obj. 3. Pleasures cause distaste in one way, desire in another, as stated above.

THIRD ARTICLE

Whether Pleasure Hinders the Use of Reason?

We proceed thus to the Third Article:—

Objection 1. It would seem that pleasure does not hinder the use of reason. Because repose facilitates very much the due use of reason: wherefore the Philosopher says (*Phys.* vii. 3) that *while we sit and rest, the soul is inclined to knowledge and prudence;* and it is written (Wisd. viii. 16): *When I go into my house, I shall repose myself with her, i.e.,* wisdom. But pleasure is a kind of repose. Therefore it helps rather than hinders the use of reason.

Obj. 2. Further, things which are not in the same subject though they be contraries, do not hinder one another. But pleasure is in the appetitive faculty, while the use of reason is in the apprehensive power. Therefore pleasure does not hinder the use of reason.

Obj. 3. Further, that which is hindered by another, seems to be moved, as it were, thereby. But the use of an apprehensive power moves pleasure rather than is moved by it: because it is the cause of pleasure. Therefore pleasure does not hinder the use of reason.

On the contrary, The Philosopher says (*Ethic.* vi. 5), that *pleasure destroys the estimate of prudence.*

I answer that, As is stated in *Ethic.* x. 5, *appropriate pleasures increase activity . . . whereas pleasures arising from other sources are impediments to activity.* Accordingly there is a certain pleasure that is taken in the very act of reason, as when one takes pleasure in contemplating or in reasoning: and such pleasure does not hinder the act of reason, but helps it; because we are more attentive in doing that which gives us pleasure, and attention fosters activity.

On the other hand bodily pleasures hinder the use of reason in three ways. First, by distracting the reason. Because, as we have just observed, we attend much to that which pleases us. Now when the attention is firmly fixed on one thing, it is either weakened in respect of other things, or it is entirely withdrawn from them; and thus if the bodily pleasure be great, either it entirely hinders the use of reason, by concentrating the mind's attention on itself; or else it hinders it considerably.—Secondly, by being contrary to reason. Because some pleasures, especially those that are in excess, are contrary to the order of reason: and in this sense the Philosopher says that *bodily pleasures destroy the estimate of prudence, but not the speculative estimate,* to which they are not opposed, *for instance that the three angles of a triangle are together equal to two right angles.* In the first sense, however, they hinder both estimates.—Thirdly, by fettering the reason: in so far as bodily pleasure is followed by a certain alteration in the body, greater even than in the other passions, in proportion as the appetite is more vehemently affected towards a present than towards an absent thing. Now such bodily disturbances hinder the use of reason; as may be seen in the case of drunkards, in whom the use of reason is fettered or hindered.

Reply Obj. 1. Bodily pleasure implies indeed repose of the appetite in the object of pleasure; which repose is sometimes contrary to reason; but on the part of the body it always implies alteration. And in respect of both points, it hinders the use of reason.

Reply Obj. 2. The powers of appetite and of apprehension are indeed distinct parts, but belonging to the one soul. Consequently when the soul is very intent on the action of one part, it is hindered from attending to a contrary act of the other part.

Reply Obj. 3. The use of reason requires the due use of the imagination and of the other sensitive powers, which are exercised through a bodily organ. Consequently alteration in the body hinders the use of reason, because it hinders the acts of the imagination and of the other sensitive powers.

FOURTH ARTICLE

Whether Pleasure Perfects Operation?

We proceed thus to the Fourth Article:—

Objection 1. It would seem that pleasure does not perfect operation. For every human operation depends on the use of reason. But pleasure hinders the use of reason, as stated above (A. 3). Therefore pleasure does not perfect, but weakens human operation.

Obj. 2. Further, nothing perfects itself or its cause. But pleasure is an operation (*Ethic.* vii. 12, x. 4), *i.e.,* either in its essence or in its cause. Therefore pleasure does not perfect operation.

Obj. 3. Further, if pleasure perfects operation, it does so either as end, or as form, or as agent. But not as end; because operation is not sought for the sake of pleasure, but rather the reverse, as stated above (Q. 4, A. 2): nor as agent, because rather is it the operation that causes pleasure: nor again as form, because, according to the Philosopher (*Ethic.* x. 4), *pleasure does not perfect operation, as a habit does.* Therefore pleasure does not perfect operation.

On the contrary, The Philosopher says (*ibid.*) that *pleasure perfects operation.*

I answer that, Pleasure perfects operation in two ways. First, as an end: not indeed according as an end is that on *account of which a thing is;* but according as every good which is added to a thing and completes it, can be called its end. And in this sense the Philosopher says (*Ethic. x, loc. cit.*) that *pleasure perfects operation . . . as some end added to it:* that is to say, inasmuch as to this good, which is operation, is added another good, which is pleasure, denoting the repose of the appetite in a good that is presupposed.—Secondly, as agent; not indeed directly, for the Philosopher says (*ibid.*) that *pleasure per-*

fects operation, not as a physician makes a man healthy, but as health does: but it does so indirectly; inasmuch as the agent, through taking pleasure in his action, is more eagerly intent on it, and carries it out with greater care. And in this sense it is said in *Ethic.* x. 5, that *pleasures increase their appropriate activities, and hinder those that are not appropriate.*

Reply Obj. 1. It is not every pleasure that hinders the act of reason, but only bodily pleasure; for this arises, not from the act of reason, but from the act of the concupiscible faculty, which act is intensified by pleasure. On the contrary, pleasure that arises from the act of reason, strengthens the use of reason.

Reply Obj. 2. As stated in *Phys.* ii. 3, two things may be causes of one another, if one be the efficient, the other the final cause. And in this way, operation is the efficient cause of pleasure, while pleasure perfects operation by way of final cause, as stated above.

The Reply to the Third Objection is evident from what has been said.

QUESTION 34

Of the Goodness and Malice of Pleasures

(In Four Articles)

WE must now consider the goodness and malice of pleasures: under which head there are four points of inquiry: (1) Whether every pleasure is evil? (2) If not, whether every pleasure is good? (3) Whether any pleasure is the greatest good? (4) Whether pleasure is the measure or rule by which to judge of moral good and evil?

FIRST ARTICLE

Whether Every Pleasure Is Evil?

We proceed thus to the First Article:—

Objection 1. It would seem that every pleasure is evil. For that which destroys prudence and hinders the use of reason, seems to be evil in itself: since man's good is to be *in accord with reason,* as Dionysius says (*Div. Nom.* iv). But pleasure destroys prudence and hinders the use of reason; and so much the more, as the pleasure is greater: wherefore *in sexual pleasures,* which are the greatest of all, *it is impossible to understand anything,* as stated in *Ethic.* vii. 11. Moreover, Jerome says in his commentary on Matthew* that *at the time of conjugal intercourse, the presence of the Holy Ghost is not vouchsafed, even if it be a prophet that fulfils the conjugal duty.* Therefore pleasure is evil in itself; and consequently every pleasure is evil.

Obj. 2. Further, that which the virtuous man shuns, and the man lacking in virtue seeks, seems to be evil in itself, and should be avoided; because, as stated in *Ethic.* x. 5, *the virtuous man is a kind of measure and rule of human actions;* and the Apostle says (1 Cor. ii. 15): *The spiritual man judgeth all things.* But children and dumb animals, in whom there is no virtue, seek pleasure: whereas the man who is master of himself does not. Therefore pleasures are evil in themselves and should be avoided.

* Origen, *Hom.* vi. *in Num.*

Obj. 3. Further, *virtue and art are concerned about the difficult and the good* (*Ethic.* ii. 3). But no art is ordained to pleasure. Therefore pleasure is not something good.

On the contrary, It is written (Ps. xxxvi. 4): *Delight in the Lord.* Since, therefore, Divine authority leads to no evil, it seems that not every pleasure is evil.

I answer that, As stated in *Ethic.* x. 2, 3, some have maintained that all pleasure is evil. The reason seems to have been that they took account only of sensible and bodily pleasures which are more manifest; since, also in other respects, the ancient philosophers did not discriminate between the intelligible and the sensible, nor between intellect and sense (*cf. De Anima* iii. 3). And they held that all bodily pleasures should be reckoned as bad, and thus that man, being prone to immoderate pleasures, arrives at the mean of virtue by abstaining from pleasure.—But they were wrong in holding this opinion. Because, since none can live without some sensible and bodily pleasure, if they who teach that all pleasures are evil, are found in the act of taking pleasure; men will be more inclined to pleasure by following the example of their works instead of listening to the doctrine of their words: since, in human actions and passions, wherein experience is of great weight, example moves more than words.

We must therefore say that some pleasures are good, and that some are evil. For pleasure is a repose of the appetitive power in some loved good, and resulting from some operation; wherefore we may assign a twofold reason for this assertion. The first is in respect of the good in which a man reposes with pleasure. For good and evil in the moral order depend on agreement or disagreement with reason, as stated above (Q. 18, A. 5): just as in the order of nature, a thing is said to be natural, if it agrees with nature, and unnatural, if it disagrees. Accordingly, just as in the natural order there is a certain natural repose, whereby a thing rests in that which agrees with its nature, for instance, when a heavy body rests down below; and again an unnatural repose, whereby a thing rests in that which disagrees with its nature, as when a heavy body rests up aloft: so, in the moral order, there is a good pleasure, whereby the higher or lower appetite rests in that which is in accord with reason; and an evil pleasure, whereby the appetite rests in that which is discordant from reason and the law of God.

The second reason can be found by considering the actions, some of which are good, some evil. Now pleasures which are conjoined to actions are more akin to those actions, than desires, which precede them in point of time. Wherefore, since the desires of good actions are good, and of evil actions, evil; much more are the pleasures of good actions good, and those of evil actions evil.

Reply Obj. 1. As stated above (Q. 33, A. 3), it is not the pleasures which result from an act of reason, that hinder the reason or destroy prudence, but extraneous pleasures, such as the pleasures of the body. These indeed hinder the use of reason, as stated above (*ibid.*), either by contrariety of the appetite that rests in something repugnant to reason, which makes the pleasure morally bad; or by fettering the reason: thus in conjugal intercourse, though the pleasure be in accord with reason, yet it hinders the use of reason, on account of the accompanying bodily change. But in this case the pleasure is not morally evil; as neither is sleep, whereby the reason is fettered, morally evil, if it be taken according to reason: for reason itself demands that the use of reason be interrupted at times.—We must add, however, that although this fettering of the reason through the pleasure of conjugal intercourse has no moral malice, since it is neither a mortal nor a venial sin; yet it proceeds from a kind of moral malice, namely, from the sin of our first parent; because, as stated in the First Part (Q. 98, A. 2) the case was different in the state of innocence.

Reply Obj. 2. The temperate man does not shun all pleasures, but those that are immoderate, and contrary to reason. The fact that children and dumb animals seek pleasures, does not prove that all pleasures are evil: because they have from God their natural appetite, which is moved to that which is naturally suitable to them.

Reply Obj. 3. Art is not concerned with all kinds of good, but with the making of external things, as we shall state further on (Q. 57, A. 3). But actions and passions, which are

within us, are more the concern of prudence and virtue than of art. Nevertheless there is an art of making pleasure, namely, *the art of cookery and the art of making unguents,* as stated in *Ethic.* vii. 12.

SECOND ARTICLE

Whether Every Pleasure Is Good?

We proceed thus to the Second Article:—

Objection 1. It would seem that every pleasure is good. Because as stated in the First Part (Q. 5, A. 6), there are three kinds of good, the virtuous, the useful, and the pleasant. But everything virtuous is good; and in like manner everything useful is good. Therefore also every pleasure is good.

Obj. 2. Further, that which is not sought for the sake of something else, is good in itself, as stated in *Ethic.* i. 6, 7. But pleasure is not sought for the sake of something else; for it seems absurd to ask anyone why he seeks to be pleased. Therefore pleasure is good in itself. Now that which is predicated of a thing considered in itself, is predicated thereof universally. Therefore every pleasure is good.

Obj. 3. Further, that which is desired by all, seems to be good of itself: because good is *what all things seek,* as stated in *Ethic.* i. 1. But everyone seeks some kind of pleasure, even children and dumb animals. Therefore pleasure is good in itself: and consequently all pleasure is good.

On the contrary, It is written (Prov. ii. 14): *Who are glad when they have done evil, and rejoice in most wicked things.*

I answer that, While some of the Stoics maintained that all pleasures are evil, the Epicureans held that pleasure is good in itself, and that consequently all pleasures are good. They seem to have thus erred through not discriminating between that which is good simply, and that which is good in respect of a particular individual. That which is good simply, is good in itself. Now that which is not good in itself, may be good in respect of some individual in two ways. In one way, because it is suitable to him by reason of a disposition in which he is now, which disposition, however, is not natural: thus it is sometimes good for a leper to eat things that are poisonous, which are not suitable simply to the human temperament. In another way, through something unsuitable being esteemed suitable. And since pleasure is the repose of the appetite in some good, if the appetite reposes in that which is good simply, the pleasure will be pleasure simply, and good simply. But if a man's appetite repose in that which is good, not simply, but in respect of that particular man, then his pleasure will not be pleasure simply, but a pleasure to him; neither will it be good simply, but in a certain respect, or an apparent good.

Reply Obj. 1. The virtuous and the useful depend on accordance with reason, and consequently nothing is virtuous or useful, without being good. But the pleasant depends on agreement with the appetite, which tends sometimes to that which is discordant from reason. Consequently not every object of pleasure is good in the moral order which depends on the order of reason.

Reply Obj. 2. The reason why pleasure is not sought for the sake of something else is because it is repose in the end. Now the end may be either good or evil; although nothing can be an end except in so far as it is good in respect of such and such a man: and so too with regard to pleasure.

Reply Obj. 3. All things seek pleasure in the same way as they seek good: since pleasure is the repose of the appetite in good. But, just as it happens that not every good which is desired, is of itself and verily good; so not every pleasure is of itself and verily good.

THIRD ARTICLE

Whether Any Pleasure Is the Greatest Good?

We proceed thus to the Third Article:—

Objection 1. It would seem that no pleasure is the greatest good. Because nothing generated is the greatest good: since generation cannot be the last end. But pleasure is a consequence of generation: for the fact that a thing takes pleasure is due to its being established in its own nature, as stated above (Q. 31, A. 1). Therefore no pleasure is the greatest good.

Obj. 2. Further, that which is the greatest good cannot be made better by addition. But pleasure is made better by addition; since pleasure together with virtue is better than pleasure without virtue. Therefore pleasure is not the greatest good.

Obj. 3. Further, that which is the greatest good is universally good, as being good of itself: since that which is such of itself is prior to and greater than that which is such accidentally. But pleasure is not universally good, as stated above (A. 2). Therefore pleasure is not the greatest good.

On the contrary, Happiness is the greatest good: since it is the end of man's life. But Happiness is not without pleasure: for it is written (Ps. xv. 11): *Thou shalt fill me with joy with Thy countenance; at Thy right hand are delights even to the end.*

I answer that, Plato held neither with the Stoics, who asserted that all pleasures are evil, nor with the Epicureans, who maintained that all pleasures are good; but he said that some are good, and some evil; yet, so that no pleasure be the sovereign or greatest good. But, judging from his arguments, he fails in two points. First, because, from observing that sensible and bodily pleasure consists in a certain movement and *becoming,* as is evident in satiety from eating and the like; he concluded that all pleasure arises from some *becoming* and movement: and from this, since *becoming* and movement are the acts of something imperfect, it would follow that pleasure is not of the nature of ultimate perfection.—But this is seen to be evidently false as regards intellectual pleasures: because one takes pleasure, not only in the *becoming* of knowledge, for instance, when one learns or wonders, as stated above (Q. 32, A. 8 *ad* 2); but also in the act of contemplation, by making use of knowledge already acquired.

Secondly, because by greatest good he understood that which is the supreme good simply, *i.e.,* the good as existing apart from, and unparticipated by, all else, in which sense God is the Supreme Good; whereas we are speaking of the greatest good in human things. Now the greatest good of everything is its last end. And the end, as stated above (Q. 1, A. 8; Q. 2, A. 7) is twofold; namely, the thing itself, and the use of that thing; thus the miser's end is either money, or the possession of money. Accordingly, man's last end may be said to be either God Who is the Supreme Good simply; or the enjoyment of God, which implies a certain pleasure in the last end. And in this sense a certain pleasure of man may be said to be the greatest among human goods.

Reply Obj. 1. Not every pleasure arises from a *becoming;* for some pleasures result from perfect operations, as stated above. Accordingly nothing prevents some pleasure being the greatest good, although every pleasure is not such.

Reply Obj. 2. This argument is true of the greatest good simply, by participation of which all things are good; wherefore no addition can make it better: whereas in regard to other goods, it is universally true that any good becomes better by the addition of another good. —Moreover it might be said that pleasure is not something extraneous to the operation of virtue, but that it accompanies it, as stated in *Ethic.* i. 8.

Reply Obj. 3. That pleasure is the greatest good is due not to the mere fact that it is pleasure, but to the fact that it is perfect repose in the perfect good. Hence it does not follow that every pleasure is supremely good, or even good at all. Thus a certain science is supremely good, but not every science is.

FOURTH ARTICLE

Whether Pleasure Is the Measure or Rule by Which to Judge of Moral Good or Evil?

We proceed thus to the Fourth Article:—

Objection 1. It would seem that pleasure is not the measure or rule of moral good and evil. Because *that which is first in a genus is the measure of all the rest* (*Metaph.* x. 1). But pleasure is not the first thing in the moral genus, for it is preceded by love and desire. Therefore it is not the rule of goodness and malice in moral matters.

Obj. 2. Further, a measure or rule should be uniform; hence that movement which is the most uniform, is the measure and rule of all movements (*Metaph.* x. 1). But pleasures are various and multiform: since some of them are good, and some evil. Therefore pleasure is not the measure and rule of morals.

Obj. 3. Further, judgment of the effect from its cause is more certain than judgment of cause from effect. Now goodness or malice of operation is the cause of goodness or malice of pleasure: because *those pleasures are good which result from good operations, and those are evil which arise from evil operations,* as stated in *Ethic.* x. 5. Therefore pleasures are not the rule and measure of moral goodness and malice.

On the contrary, Augustine, commenting on Ps. vii. 10, *The searcher of hearts and reins is God,* says: *The end of care and thought is the pleasure which each one aims at achieving.* And the Philosopher says (*Ethic.* vii. 11) that *pleasure is the architect,* i.e., the principal, end,* in regard to which, we say absolutely that this is evil, and that, good.

I answer that, Moral goodness or malice depends chiefly on the will, as stated above (Q. 20, A. 1); and it is chiefly from the end that we discern whether the will is good or evil. Now the end is taken to be that in which the will reposes: and the repose of the will and of every appetite in the good is pleasure. And therefore man is reckoned to be good or bad chiefly according to the pleasure of the human will; since that man is good and virtuous, who takes pleasure in the works of virtue; and that man evil, who takes pleasure in evil works.

On the other hand, pleasures of the sensitive appetite are not the rule of moral goodness and malice; since food is universally pleasurable to the sensitive appetite both of good and of evil men. But the will of the good man takes pleasure in them in accordance with reason, to which the will of the evil man gives no heed.

Reply Obj. 1. Love and desire precede pleasure in the order of generation. But pleasure precedes them in the order of the end, which serves as a principle in actions; and it is by the principle, which is the rule and measure of such matters, that we form our judgment.

Reply Obj. 2. All pleasures are uniform in the point of their being the repose of the appetite in something good: and in this respect pleasure can be a rule or measure. Because that man is good, whose will rests in the true good: and that man evil, whose will rests in evil.

Reply Obj. 3. Since pleasure perfects operation as its end, as stated above (Q. 33, A. 4); an operation cannot be perfectly good, unless there be also pleasure in good: because the goodness of a thing depends on its end. And thus, in a way, the goodness of the pleasure is the cause of goodness in the operation.

QUESTION 35

Of Pain or Sorrow, in Itself

(In Eight Articles)

WE have now to consider pain and sorrow: concerning which we must consider: (1) Sorrow or pain in itself; (2) Its cause; (3) Its effects; (4) Its remedies; (5) Its goodness or malice.

Under the first head there are eight points of inquiry: (1) Whether pain is a passion of the soul? (2) Whether sorrow is the same as pain? (3) Whether sorrow or pain is contrary in pleasure? (4) Whether all sorrow is contrary to all pleasure? (5) Whether there is a sorrow contrary to the pleasure of contemplation? (6) Whether sorrow is to be shunned more than pleasure is to be sought? (7) Whether exterior pain is greater than interior? (8) Of the species of sorrow.

FIRST ARTICLE

Whether Pain Is a Passion of the Soul?

We proceed thus to the First Article:—

Objection 1. It would seem that pain is not a passion of the soul. Because no passion of the soul is in the body. But pain can be in the body, since Augustine says (*De Vera Relig.* xii), that *bodily pain is a sudden corruption*

---

* St. Thomas took *finis* as being the nominative, whereas it is the genitive —τοῦ τέλους; and the Greek reads *He* (i.e., the political philosopher), *is the architect of the end.*

of the well-being of that thing which the soul, by making evil use of it, made subject to corruption. Therefore pain is not a passion of the soul.

Obj. 2. Further, every passion of the soul belongs to the appetitive faculty. But pain does not belong to the appetitive, but rather to the apprehensive part: for Augustine says (*De Nat. Boni,* xx) that *bodily pain is caused by the sense resisting a more powerful body.* Therefore pain is not a passion of the soul.

Obj. 3. Further, every passion of the soul belongs to the animal appetite. But pain does not belong to the animal appetite, but rather to the natural appetite; for Augustine says (*Gen. ad lit.* viii. 14): *Had not some good remained in nature, we should feel no pain in being punished by the loss of good.* Therefore pain is not a passion of the soul.

On the contrary, Augustine (*De Civ. Dei* xiv. 8) reckons pain among the passions of the soul; quoting Virgil (*Æneid,* vi. 733):

> "Hence wild desires and grovelling fears
> And human laughter, human tears."
>
> (*Trl.* Conington.)

I answer that, Just as two things are requisite for pleasure; namely, conjunction with good and perception of this conjunction; so also two things are requisite for pain; namely, conjunction with some evil (which is in so far evil as it deprives one of some good), and perception of this conjunction. Now whatever is conjoined, if it have not the aspect of good or evil in regard to the being to which it is conjoined, cannot cause pleasure or pain. Whence it is evident that something under the aspect of good or evil is the object of pleasure or pain. But good and evil, as such, are objects of the appetite. Consequently it is clear that pleasure and pain belong to the appetite.

Now every appetitive movement or inclination consequent to apprehension, belongs to the intellective or sensitive appetite: since the inclination of the natural appetite is not consequent to an apprehension of the subject of that appetite, but to the apprehension of another, as stated in the First Part (Q. 103, AA. 1, 3). Since then pleasure and pain presuppose some sense or apprehension in the same subject, it is evident that pain, like pleasure, is in the intellective or sensitive appetite.

Again every movement of the sensitive appetite is called a passion, as stated above (Q. 22, AA. 1, 3): and especially those which tend to some defect. Consequently pain, according as it is in the sensitive appetite, is most properly called a passion of the soul: just as bodily ailments are properly called passions of the body. Hence Augustine (*De Civ. Dei*

* Quoting Cicero.

xiv. 7, 8*) reckons pain especially as being a kind of ailment.

Reply Obj. 1. We speak of pain of the body, because the cause of pain is in the body: as when we suffer something hurtful to the body. But the movement of pain is always in the soul; since *the body cannot feel pain unless the soul feel it,* as Augustine says (*Super Psalm.* lxxxvii. 4).

Reply Obj. 2. We speak of pain of the senses, not as though it were an act of the sensitive power; but because the senses are required for bodily pain, in the same way as for bodily pleasure.

Reply Obj. 3. Pain at the loss of good proves the goodness of the nature, not because pain is an act of the natural appetite, but because nature desires something as good, the removal of which being perceived, there results the passion of pain in the sensitive appetite.

SECOND ARTICLE

Whether Sorrow Is the Same As Pain?

We proceed thus to the Second Article:—

Objection 1. It would seem that sorrow is not pain. For Augustine says (*De Civ. Dei* xiv. 7) that *pain is used to express bodily suffering.* But sorrow is used more in reference to the soul. Therefore sorrow is not pain.

Obj. 2. Further, pain is only in respect of present evil. But sorrow can refer to both past and future evil: thus repentance is sorrow for the past, and anxiety is sorrow for the future. Therefore sorrow is quite different from pain.

Obj. 3. Further, pain seems not to follow save from the sense of touch. But sorrow can arise from all the senses. Therefore sorrow is not pain, and extends to more objects.

On the contrary, The Apostle says (Rom. ix. 2): *I have great sorrow* (Douay,—*sadness*) *and continual pain* (Douay,—*sorrow*) *in my heart,* thus denoting the same thing by sorrow and pain.

I answer that, Pleasure and pain can arise from a twofold apprehension, namely, from the apprehension of an exterior sense; and from the interior apprehension of the intellect or of the imagination. Now the interior apprehension extends to more objects than the exterior apprehension: because whatever things come under the exterior apprehension, come under the interior, but not conversely. Consequently that pleasure alone which is caused by an interior apprehension is called joy, as stated above (Q. 31, A. 3): and in like manner that pain alone which is caused by an interior apprehension, is called sorrow. And just as that pleasure which is caused by an exterior apprehension, is called pleasure but not joy; so too that pain which is caused by an exterior apprehension, is called pain indeed but not sorrow. Accordingly sorrow is a species of pain, as joy is a species of pleasure.

Reply Obj. 1. Augustine is speaking there of the use of the word: because *pain* is more generally used in reference to bodily pains, which are better known, than in reference to spiritual pains.

Reply Obj. 2. External sense perceives only what is present; but the interior cognitive power can perceive the present, past and future. Consequently sorrow can regard present, past and future: whereas bodily pain, which follows the apprehension of the external sense, can only regard something present.

Reply Obj. 3. The sensibles of touch are painful, not only in so far as they are disproportionate to the apprehensive power, but also in so far as they are contrary to nature: whereas the objects of the other senses can indeed be disproportionate to the apprehensive power, but they are not contrary to nature, save as they are subordinate to the sensibles of touch. Consequently man alone, who is a perfectly cognizant animal, takes pleasure in the objects of the other senses for their own sake; whereas other animals take no pleasure in them save as referable to the sensibles of touch, as stated in *Ethic.* iii. 10. Accordingly, in referring to the objects of the other senses, we do not speak of pain in so far as it is contrary to natural pleasure: but rather of sorrow, which is contrary to joy.—So then if pain be taken as denoting bodily pain, which is its more usual meaning, then it is contrasted with sorrow, according to the distinction of interior and exterior apprehension; although, on the part of the objects, pleasure extends further than does bodily pain. But if pain be taken in a wide sense, then it is the genus of sorrow, as stated above.

THIRD ARTICLE

Whether Sorrow or Pain Is Contrary to Pleasure?

We proceed thus to the Sixth Article:—

Objection 1. It would seem that sorrow is not contrary to pleasure. For one of two contraries is not the cause of the other. But sorrow can be the cause of pleasure; for it is written (*Matth.* v. 5): *Blessed are they that mourn, for they shall be comforted.* Therefore they are not contrary to one another.

Obj. 2. Further, one contrary does not denominate the other. But to some, pain or sorrow gives pleasure: thus Augustine says (*Conf.* iii. 2) that in stage-plays sorrow itself gives pleasure: and (*ibid.* iv. 5) that *weeping is a bitter thing, and yet it sometimes pleases us.* Therefore pain is not contrary to pleasure.

Obj. 3. Further, one contrary is not the

matter of the other; because contraries cannot co-exist together. But sorrow can be the matter of pleasure; for Augustine says (*De Pœnit.* xiii): *The penitent should ever sorrow, and rejoice in his sorrow.* The Philosopher too says (*Ethic.* ix. 4) that, on the other hand, *the evil man feels pain at having been pleased.* Therefore pleasure and pain are not contrary to one another.

On the contrary, Augustine says (*De Civ. Dei* xiv. 6) that *joy is the volition of consent to the things we wish: and that sorrow is the volition of dissent from the things we do not wish.* But consent and dissent are contraries. Therefore pleasure and sorrow are contrary to one another.

I answer that, As the Philosopher says (*Metaph.* x. 4), contrariety is a difference in respect of a form. Now the form or species of a passion or movement is taken from the object or term. Consequently, since the objects of pleasure and sorrow or pain, viz., present good and present evil, are contrary to one another, it follows that pain and pleasure are contrary to one another.

Reply Obj. 1. Nothing hinders one contrary causing the other accidentally: and thus sorrow can be the cause of pleasure. In one way, in so far as from sorrow at the absence of something, or at the presence of its contrary, one seeks the more eagerly for something pleasant: thus a thirsty man seeks more eagerly the pleasure of a drink, as a remedy for the pain he suffers. In another way, in so far as, from a strong desire for a certain pleasure, one does not shrink from undergoing pain, so as to obtain that pleasure. In each of these ways, the sorrows of the present life lead us to the comfort of the future life. Because by the mere fact that man mourns for his sins, or for the delay of glory, he merits the consolation of eternity. In like manner a man merits it when he shrinks not from hardships and straits in order to obtain it.

Reply Obj. 2. Pain itself can be pleasurable accidentally in so far as it is accompanied by wonder, as in stage-plays; or in so far as it recalls a beloved object to one's memory, and makes one feel one's love for the thing, whose absence gives us pain. Consequently, since love is pleasant, both pain and whatever else results from love, forasmuch as they remind us of our love, are pleasant. And, for this reason, we derive pleasure even from pains depicted on the stage: in so far as, in witnessing them, we perceive ourselves to conceive a certain love for those who are there represented.

Reply Obj. 3. The will and the reason reflect on their own acts, inasmuch as the acts themselves of the will and reason are considered under the aspect of good or evil. In this way sorrow can be the matter of pleasure, or vice versa, not essentially but accidentally: that is, in so far as either of them is considered under the aspect of good or evil.

FOURTH ARTICLE

Whether All Sorrow Is Contrary to All Pleasure?

We proceed thus to the Fourth Article:—

Objection 1. It would seem that all sorrow is contrary to all pleasure. Because, just as whiteness and blackness are contrary species of color, so pleasure and sorrow are contrary species of the soul's passions. But whiteness and blackness are universally contrary to one another. Therefore pleasure and sorrow are so too.

Obj. 2. Further, remedies are made of things contrary (to the evil). But every pleasure is a remedy for all manner of sorrow, as the Philosopher declares (*Ethic.* vii. 14). Therefore every pleasure is contrary to every sorrow.

Obj. 3. Further, contraries are hindrances to one another. But every sorrow hinders any kind of pleasure: as is evident from *Ethic.* x. 5. Therefore every sorrow is contrary to every pleasure.

On the contrary, The same thing is not the cause of contraries. But joy for one thing, and sorrow for the opposite thing, proceed from the same habit: thus from charity it happens that we *rejoice with them that rejoice,* and *weep with them that weep* (Rom. xii. 15). Therefore not every sorrow is contrary to every pleasure.

I answer that, As stated in *Metaph.* x. 4, contrariety is a difference in respect of a form. Now a form may be generic or specific. Consequently things may be contraries in respect of a generic form, as virtue and vice; or in respect of a specific form, as justice and injustice.

Now we must observe that some things are specified by absolute forms, *e.g.*, substances and qualities; whereas other things are specified in relation to something extrinsic, *e.g.*, passions and movements, which derive their species from their terms or objects. Accordingly in those things that are specified by absolute forms, it happens that species contained under contrary genera are not contrary as to their specific nature: but it does not happen for them to have any affinity or fittingness to one another. For intemperance and justice, which are in the contrary genera of virtue and vice, are not contrary to one another in respect of their specific nature; and yet they have no affinity or fittingness to one another.—On the other hand, in those things that are specified in relation to something extrinsic, it happens that

species belonging to contrary genera, are not only not contrary to one another, but also that they have a certain mutual affinity or fittingness. The reason of this is that where there is one same relation to two contraries, there is contrariety; *e.g.*, to approach to a white thing, and to approach to a black thing, are contraries; whereas contrary relations to contrary things, implies a certain likeness, *e.g.*, to recede from something white, and to approach to something black. This is most evident in the case of contradiction, which is the principle of opposition: because opposition consists in affirming and denying the same thing, *e.g.*, *white* and *not-white;* while there is fittingness and likeness in the affirmation of one contrary and the denial of the other, as, if I were to say *black* and *not white.*

Now sorrow and pleasure, being passions, are specified by their objects. According to their respective genera, they are contrary to one another: since one is a kind of *pursuit,* the other a kind of *avoidance,* which *are to the appetite, what affirmation and denial are to the intellect* (*Ethic.* vi. 2). Consequently sorrow and pleasure in respect of the same object, are specifically contrary to one another: whereas sorrow and pleasure in respect of objects that are not contrary but disparate, are not specifically contrary to one another, but are also disparate; for instance, sorrow at the death of a friend, and pleasure in contemplation. If, however, those diverse objects be contrary to one another, then pleasure and sorrow are not only not specifically contrary, but they also have a certain mutual fittingness and affinity: for instance to rejoice in good and to sorrow for evil

Reply Obj. 1. Whiteness and blackness do not take their species from their relationship to something extrinsic, as pleasure and sorrow do: wherefore the comparison does not hold.

Reply Obj. 2. Genus is taken from matter, as is stated in *Metaph.* viii. 2; and in accidents the subject takes the place of matter. Now it has been said above that pleasure and sorrow are generically contrary to one another. Consequently in every sorrow the subject has a disposition contrary to the disposition of the subject of pleasure: because in every pleasure the appetite is viewed as accepting what it possesses, and in every sorrow, as avoiding it. And therefore on the part of the subject every pleasure is a remedy for any kind of sorrow, and every sorrow is a hindrance of all manner of pleasure: but chiefly when pleasure is opposed to sorrow specifically.

Wherefore the Reply to the Third Objection is evident.—Or we may say that, although not every sorrow is specifically contrary to every pleasure, yet they are contrary to one another in regard to their effects: since one has the effect of strengthening the animal nature, while the other results in a kind of discomfort.

FIFTH ARTICLE

Whether There Is Any Sorrow Contrary to the Pleasure of Contemplation?

We proceed thus to the Fifth Article:—

Objection 1. It would seem that there is a sorrow that is contrary to the pleasure of contemplation. For the Apostle says (2 Cor. vii. 10): *The sorrow that is according to God, worketh penance steadfast unto salvation.* Now to look at God belongs to the higher reason, whose act is to give itself to contemplation, according to Augustine (*De Trin.* xii. 3, 4). Therefore there is a sorrow contrary to the pleasure of contemplation.

Obj. 2. Further, contrary things have contrary effects. If therefore the contemplation of one contrary gives pleasure, the other contrary will give sorrow: and so there will be a sorrow contrary to the pleasure of contemplation.

Obj. 3. Further, as the object of pleasure is good, so the object of sorrow is evil. But contemplation can be an evil: since the Philosopher says (*Metaph.* xii. 9) that *it is unfitting to think of certain things.* Therefore sorrow can be contrary to the pleasure of contemplation.

Obj. 4. Further, any work, so far as it is unhindered, can be a cause of pleasure, as stated in *Ethic.* vii. 12, 13, x. 4. But the work of contemplation can be hindered in many ways, either so as to destroy it altogether, or as to make it difficult. Therefore in contemplation there can be a sorrow contrary to the pleasure.

Obj. 5. Further, affliction of the flesh is a cause of sorrow. But, as it is written (Eccles. xii. 12) *much study is an affliction of the flesh.* Therefore contemplation admits of sorrow contrary to its pleasure.

On the contrary, It is written (Wis. viii. 16): *Her,* i.e., wisdom's, *conversation hath no bitterness nor her company any tediousness; but joy and gladness.* Now the conversation and company of wisdom are found in contemplation. Therefore there is no sorrow contrary to the pleasure of contemplation.

I answer that, The pleasure of contemplation can be understood in two ways. In one way, so that contemplation is the cause, but not the object of pleasure: and then pleasure is taken not in contemplating but in the thing contemplated. Now it is possible to contemplate something harmful and sorrowful,

* Nemesius,—*De Nat. Hom.* xviii.

just as to contemplate something suitable and pleasant. Consequently if the pleasure of contemplation be taken in this way, nothing hinders some sorrow being contrary to the pleasure of contemplation.

In another way, the pleasure of contemplation is understood, so that contemplation is its object and cause; as when one takes pleasure in the very act of contemplating. And thus, according to Gregory of Nyssa,* *no sorrow is contrary to that pleasure which is about contemplation:* and the Philosopher says the same (*Topic.* i. 13, *Ethic.* x. 3). This, however, is to be understood as being the case properly speaking. The reason is because sorrow is of itself contrary to pleasure in a contrary object: thus pleasure in heat is contrary to sorrow caused by cold. But there is no contrary to the object of contemplation: because contraries, as apprehended by the mind, are not contrary, but one is the means of knowing the other. Wherefore, properly speaking, there cannot be a sorrow contrary to the pleasure of contemplation.—Nor has it any sorrow annexed to it, as bodily pleasures have, which are like remedies against certain annoyances; thus a man takes pleasure in drinking through being troubled with thirst, but when the thirst is quite driven out, the pleasure of drinking ceases also. Because the pleasure of contemplation is not caused by one's being quit of an annoyance, but by the fact that contemplation is pleasant in itself: for pleasure is not a *becoming* but a perfect operation, as stated above (Q. 31, A. 1).

Accidentally, however, sorrow is mingled with the pleasure of apprehension; and this in two ways: first, on the part of an organ, secondly, through some impediment in the apprehension. On the part of an organ, sorrow or pain is mingled with apprehension, directly, as regards the apprehensive powers of the sensitive part, which have a bodily organ;—either from the sensible object disagreeing with the normal condition of the organ, as the taste of something bitter, and the smell of something foul;—or from the sensible object, though agreeable, being so continuous in its action on the sense, that it exceeds the normal condition of the organ, as stated above (Q. 33, A. 2), the result being that an apprehension which at first was pleasant becomes tedious.— But these two things cannot occur directly in the contemplation of the mind; because the mind has no corporeal organ: wherefore it was said in the authority quoted above that intellectual contemplation has neither *bitterness,* nor *tediousness.* Since, however, the human mind, in contemplation, makes use of the sensitive powers of apprehension, to whose acts weariness is incidental; therefore some affliction or pain is indirectly mingled with contemplation.

Nevertheless, in neither of these ways, is the pain thus accidentally mingled with contemplation, contrary to the pleasure thereof. Because pain caused by a hindrance to contemplation, is not contrary to the pleasure of contemplation, but rather is in affinity and in harmony with it, as is evident from what has been said above (A. 4): while pain or sorrow caused by bodily weariness, does not belong to the same genus, wherefore it is altogether disparate. Accordingly it is evident that no sorrow is contrary to pleasure taken in the very act of contemplation; nor is any sorrow connected with it save accidentally.

Reply Obj. 1. The *sorrow which is according to God*, is not caused by the very act of intellectual contemplation, but by something which the mind contemplates: viz., by sin, which the mind considers as contrary to the love of God.

Reply Obj. 2. Things which are contrary according to nature are not contrary according as they exist in the mind: for things that are contrary in reality are not contrary in the order of thought; indeed rather is one contrary the reason for knowing the other. Hence one and the same science considers contraries.

Reply Obj. 3. Contemplation, in itself, is never evil, since it is nothing else than the consideration of truth, which is the good of the intellect: it can, however, be evil accidentally, *i.e.*, in so far as the contemplation of a less noble object hinders the contemplation of a more noble object; or on the part of the object contemplated, to which the appetite is inordinately attached.

Reply Obj. 4. Sorrow caused by a hindrance to contemplation, is not contrary to the pleasure of contemplation, but is in harmony with it, as stated above.

Reply Obj. 5. Affliction of the flesh affects contemplation accidentally and indirectly, as stated above.

SIXTH ARTICLE

Whether Sorrow Is to Be Shunned More Than Pleasure Is to Be Sought?

We proceed thus to the Sixth Article:—

Objection 1. It would seem that sorrow is to be shunned more than pleasure is to be sought. For Augustine says (QQ. 83, qu. 63): *There is nobody that does not shun sorrow more than he seeks pleasure.* Now that which all agree in doing, seems to be natural. Therefore it is natural and right for sorrow to be shunned more than pleasure is sought.

Obj. 2. Further, the action of a contrary conduces to rapidity and intensity of movement: for *hot water freezes quicker and harder*, as the Philosopher says (*Meteor.* i. 12). But the shunning of sorrow is due to the contrariety of the cause of sorrow; whereas the desire for pleasure does not arise from any contrariety, but rather from the suitableness of the pleasant object. Therefore sorrow is shunned more eagerly than pleasure is sought.

Obj. 3. Further, the stronger the passion which a man resists according to reason, the more worthy is he of praise, and the more virtuous: since *virtue is concerned with the difficult and the good* (*Ethic.* ii. 3). But the brave man who resists the movement of shunning sorrow, is more virtuous than the temperate man, who resists the movement of desire for pleasure: since the Philosopher says (*Rhet.* ii. 4) that *the brave and the just are chiefly praised.* Therefore the movement of shunning sorrow is more eager than the movement of seeking pleasure.

On the contrary, Good is stronger than evil, as Dionysius declares (*Div. Nom.* iv). But pleasure is desirable for the sake of the good which is its object; whereas the shunning of sorrow is on account of evil. Therefore the desire for pleasure is more eager than the shunning of sorrow.

I answer that, The desire for pleasure is of itself more eager than the shunning of sorrow. The reason of this is that the cause of pleasure is a suitable good; while the cause of pain or sorrow is an unsuitable evil. Now it happens that a certain good is suitable without any repugnance at all: but it is not possible for any evil to be so unsuitable as not to be suitable in some way. Wherefore pleasure can be entire and perfect: whereas sorrow is always partial. Therefore desire for pleasure is naturally greater than the shunning of sorrow.—Another reason is because the good, which is the object of pleasure, is sought for its own sake: whereas the evil, which is the object of sorrow, is to be shunned as being a privation of good: and that which is by reason of itself is stronger than that which is by reason of something else.—Moreover we find a confirmation of this in natural movements. For every natural movement is more intense in the end, when a thing approaches the term that is suitable to its nature, than at the beginning, when it leaves the term that is unsuitable to its nature: as though nature were more eager in tending to what is suitable to it, than in shunning what is unsuitable. Therefore the inclination of the appetitive power is, of itself, more eager in tending to pleasure than in shunning sorrow.

But it happens accidentally that a man shuns sorrow more eagerly than he seeks pleasure: and this for three reasons. First, on the part of the apprehension. Because as Augustine says (*De Trin.* x. 12), *love is felt more keenly, when we lack that which we love.* Now from the lack of what we love, sorrow results, which is caused either by the loss of some loved good, or by the presence of some contrary evil. But pleasure suffers no lack of the good loved, for it rests in possession of it. Since then love is the cause of pleasure and sorrow, the latter is the more shunned, according as love is the more keenly felt on account of that which is contrary to it.—Secondly, on the part of the cause of sorrow or pain, which cause is repugnant to a good that is more loved than the good in which we take pleasure. For we love the natural well-being of the body more than the pleasure of eating: and consequently we would leave the pleasure of eating and the like, from fear of the pain occasioned by blows or other such causes, which are contrary to the well-being of the body.—Thirdly, on the part of the effect: namely, in so far as sorrow hinders not only one pleasure, but all.

Reply Obj. 1. The saying of Augustine that *sorrow is shunned more than pleasure is sought* is true accidentally but not simply. And this is clear from what he says after: *Since we see that the most savage animals are deterred from the greatest pleasures by fear of pain,* which pain is contrary to life which is loved above all.

Reply Obj. 2. It is not the same with movement from within and movement from without. For movement from within tends to what is suitable more than it recedes from that which is unsuitable; as we remarked above in regard to natural movement. But movement from without is intensified by the very opposition: because each thing strives in its own way to resist anything contrary to it, as aiming at its own preservation. Hence violent movement is intense at first, and slackens towards the end.—Now the movement of the appetitive faculty is from within: since it tends from the soul to the object. Consequently pleasure is, of itself, more to be sought than sorrow is to be shunned. But the movement of the sensitive faculty is from without, as it were from the object of the soul. Consequently the more contrary a thing is the more it is felt. And then too, accidentally, in so far as the senses are requisite for pleasure and pain, pain is shunned more than pleasure is sought.

Reply Obj. 3. A brave man is not praised because, in accordance with reason, he is not overcome by any kind of sorrow or pain whatever, but because he is not overcome by that which is concerned with the dangers of death. And this kind of sorrow is more shunned, than pleasures of the table or of sexual intercourse are sought, which latter pleasures are the object of temperance: thus life is loved more than food and sexual pleasure. But the temperate man is praised for refraining from pleasures of touch, more than for not shunning the pains which are contrary to them, as is stated in *Ethic.* iii. 11.

SEVENTH ARTICLE

Whether Outward Pain Is Greater Than Interior Sorrow?

We proceed thus to the Seventh Article:—

Objection 1. It would seem that outward pain is greater than interior sorrow of the heart. Because outward pain arises from a cause repugnant to the well-being of the body in which is life: whereas interior sorrow is caused by some evil in the imagination. Since, therefore, life is loved more than an imagined good, it seems that, according to what has been said above (A. 6), outward pain is greater than interior sorrow.

Obj. 2. Further, the reality moves more than its likeness does. But outward pain arises from the real conjunction of some contrary; whereas inward sorrow arises from the apprehended likeness of a contrary. Therefore outward pain is greater than inward sorrow.

Obj. 3. Further, a cause is known by its effect. But outward pain has more striking effects: since man dies sooner of outward pain than of interior sorrow. Therefore outward pain is greater and is shunned more than interior sorrow.

On the contrary, It is written (Ecclus. xxv. 17): *The sadness of the heart is every wound* (Douay,—*plague*), *and the wickedness of a woman is all evil.* Therefore, just as the wickedness of a woman surpasses all other wickedness, as the text implies; so sadness of the heart surpasses every outward wound.

I answer that, Interior and exterior pain agree in one point, and differ in two. They agree in this, that each is a movement of the appetitive power, as stated above (A. 1). But they differ in respect of those two things which are requisite for pain and pleasure; namely, in respect of the cause, which is a conjoined good or evil; and in respect of the apprehension. For the cause of outward pain is a conjoined evil repugnant to the body; while the cause of inward pain is a conjoined evil repugnant to the appetite. Again, outward pain arises from an apprehension of sense, chiefly of touch; while inward pain arises from an interior apprehension, of the imagination or of the reason.

If then we compare the cause of inward pain to the cause of outward pain, the former belongs, of itself, to the appetite to which both these pains belong: while the latter belongs to the appetite indirectly. Because inward pain arises from something being repugnant to the appetite itself, while outward pain arises from something being repugnant to the appetite, through being repugnant to the body. Now, that which is of itself is always prior to that which is by reason of another. Wherefore, from this point of view, inward pain surpasses outward pain.—In like manner also on the part of apprehension: because the apprehension of reason and imagination is of a higher order than the apprehension of the sense of touch.—Consequently inward pain is, simply and of itself, more keen than outward pain: a sign whereof is that one willingly undergoes outward pain in order to avoid inward pain: and in so far as outward pain is not repugnant to the interior appetite, it becomes in a manner pleasant and agreeable by way of inward joy. Sometimes, however, outward pain is accompanied by inward pain, and then the pain is increased. Because inward pain is not only greater than outward pain, it is also more universal: since whatever is repugnant to the body, can be repugnant to the interior appetite; and whatever is apprehended by sense may be apprehended by imagination and reason, but not conversely. Hence in the passage quoted above it is said expressively: *Sadness of the heart is every wound,* because even the pains of outward wounds are comprised in the interior sorrows of the heart.

Reply Obj. 1. Inward pain can also arise from things that are destructive of life. And then the comparison of inward to outward pain must not be taken in reference to the various evils that cause pain; but in regard to the various ways in which this cause of pain is compared to the appetite.

Reply Obj. 2. Inward pain is not caused by the apprehended likeness of a thing: for a man is not inwardly pained by the apprehended likeness itself, but by the thing which the likeness represents. And this thing is all the more perfectly apprehended by means of its likeness, as this likeness is more immaterial and abstract. Consequently inward pain is, of itself, greater, as being caused by a greater evil, forasmuch as evil is better known by an inward apprehension.

Reply Obj. 3. Bodily changes are more liable to be caused by outward pain, both from the fact that outward pain is caused by a corruptive conjoined corporally, which is a necessary condition of the sense of touch; and from the fact that the outward sense is more material than the inward sense, just as the sensitive appetite is more material than the intellective. For this reason, as stated above (Q. 22, A. 3; Q. 31, A. 5), the body undergoes a greater change from the movement of the

* Nemesius,—*De Nat. Hom.* xix.   † *Ibid.*

sensitive appetite: and, in like manner, from outward than from inward pain.

EIGHTH ARTICLE

Whether There Are Only Four Species of Sorrow?

We proceed thus to the Eighth Article:—

Objection 1. It would seem that Damascene's (*De Fide Orthod.* ii. 14) division of sorrow into four species is incorrect; viz., into *torpor, distress,* which Gregory of Nyssa* calls *anxiety,—pity,* and *envy.* For sorrow is contrary to pleasure. But there are not several species of pleasure. Therefore it is incorrect to assign different species of sorrow.

Obj. 2. Further, *Repentance* is a species of sorrow; and so are *indignation* and *jealousy,* as the Philosopher states (*Rhet.* ii. 9, 11). But these are not included in the above species. Therefore this division is insufficient.

Obj. 3. Further, the members of a division should be things that are opposed to one another. But these species are not opposed to one another. For according to Gregory† *torpor is sorrow depriving of speech: anxiety is the sorrow that weighs down; envy is sorrow for another's good; pity is sorrow for another's wrongs.* But it is possible for one to sorrow for another's wrongs, and for another's good, and at the same time to be weighed down inwardly, and outwardly to be speechless. Therefore this division is insufficient.

On the contrary stands the twofold authority of Gregory of Nyssa† and of Damascene.

I answer that, It belongs to the notion of a species that it is something added to the genus. But a thing can be added to a genus in two ways. First, as something belonging of itself to the genus, and virtually contained therein: thus *rational* is added to *animal.* Such an addition makes true species of a genus: as the Philosopher says (*Metaph.* vii. 12, viii. 2, 3). But, secondly, a thing may be added to a genus, that is, as it were, foreign to the notion conveyed by that genus: thus *white* or something of the kind may be added to *animal.* Such an addition does not make true species of the genus, according to the usual sense in which we speak of genera and species. But sometimes a thing is said to be a species of a certain genus, through having something foreign to that genus indeed, but to which the notion of that genus is applicable: thus a live coal or a flame is said to be a species of fire, because in each of them the nature of fire is applied to a foreign matter. In like manner we speak of astronomy and perspective as being species of mathematics, inasmuch as the principles of mathematics are applied to natural matter.

† Nemesius.

In accordance with this manner of speaking, the species of sorrow are reckoned by an application of the notion of sorrow to something foreign to it. This foreign matter may be taken on the part of the cause or the object, or of the effect. For the proper object of sorrow is *one's own evil*. Hence sorrow may be concerned for an object foreign to it either through one's being sorry for an evil that is not one's own; and thus we have *pity* which is sorrow for another's evil, considered, however, as one's own:—or through one's being sorry for something that is neither evil nor one's own, but another's good, considered, however, as one's own evil: and thus we have *envy*.—The proper effect of sorrow consists in a certain *flight of the appetite*. Wherefore the foreign element in the effect of sorrow, may be taken so as to affect the first part only, by excluding flight: and thus we have *anxiety* which weighs on the mind, so as to make escape seem impossible: hence it is also called *perplexity*. If, however, the mind be weighed down so much, that even the limbs become motionless, which belongs to *torpor*, then we have the foreign element affecting both, since there is neither flight, nor is the effect in the appetite. And the reason why torpor especially is said to deprive one of speech is because of all the external movements the voice is the best expression of the inward thought and desire, not only in men, but also in other animals, as is stated in *Polit.* i. 1.

Reply Obj. 1. Pleasure is caused by good, which has only one meaning: and so pleasure is not divided into several species as sorrow is; for the latter is caused by evil, which *happens in many ways*, as Dionysius says (*Div. Nom.* iv).

Reply Obj. 2. Repentance is for one's own evil, which is the proper object of sorrow: wherefore it does not belong to these species.—Jealousy and indignation are included in envy, as we shall explain later (II-II, Q. 36, A. 2).

Reply Obj. 3. This division is not according to opposite species; but according to the diversity of foreign matter to which the notion of sorrow is applied, as stated above.

QUESTION 36

Of the Causes of Sorrow or Pain

(In Four Articles)

WE must now consider the causes of sorrow: under which head there are four points of inquiry: (1) Whether sorrow is caused by the loss of a good or rather by the presence of an evil? (2) Whether desire is a cause of sorrow? (3) Whether the craving for unity is a cause of sorrow? (4) Whether an irresistible power is a cause of sorrow?

FIRST ARTICLE

Whether Sorrow Is Caused by the Loss of Good or by the Presence of Evil?

We proceed thus to the First Article:—

Objection 1. It would seem that sorrow is caused by the loss of a good rather than by the presence of an evil. For Augustine says (*De* viii. *Qq. Dulcit.*, qu. 1) that sorrow is caused by the loss of temporal goods. Therefore, in like manner, every sorrow is caused by the loss of some good.

Obj. 2. Further, it was said above (Q. 35, A. 4) that the sorrow which is contrary to a pleasure, has the same object as that pleasure. But the object of pleasure is good, as stated above (Q. 23, A. 4; Q. 31, A. 1; Q. 35, A. 3). Therefore sorrow is caused chiefly by the loss of good.

Obj. 3. Further, according to Augustine (*De Civ. Dei* xiv., 7, 9), love is the cause of sorrow, as of the other emotions of the soul. But the object of love is good. Therefore pain or sorrow is felt for the loss of good rather than for an evil that is present.

On the contrary, Damascene says (*De Fide Orthod.* ii. 12) that *the dreaded evil gives rise to fear, the present evil is the cause of sorrow.*

I answer that, If privations, as considered by the mind, were what they are in reality, this question would seem to be of no importance. For, as stated in the First Part (Q. 14, A. 10; Q. 48, A. 3), evil is the privation of good: and privation is in reality nothing else than the lack of the contrary habit; so that, in this respect, to sorrow for the loss of good, would be the same as to sorrow for the presence of evil. —But sorrow is a movement of the appetite in consequence of an apprehension: and even a privation, as apprehended, has the aspect of a being, wherefore it is called *a being of reason.* And in this way evil, being a privation, is regarded as a *contrary.* Accordingly, so far as the movement of the appetite is concerned, it makes a difference which of the two it regards chiefly, the present evil or the good which is lost.

Again, since the movement of the animal appetite holds the same place in the actions of the soul, as natural movement in natural things; the truth of the matter is to be found by considering natural movements. For if, in natural movements, we observe those of approach and withdrawal, approach is of itself directed to something suitable to nature; while withdrawal is of itself directed to something contrary to nature; thus a heavy body, of itself, withdraws from a higher place, and approaches naturally to a lower place. But if we consider the cause of both these movements, viz., gravity, then gravity itself inclines towards the lower place more than it withdraws from the higher place, since withdrawal from the latter is the reason for its downward tendency.

Accordingly, since, in the movements of the appetite, sorrow is a kind of flight or withdrawal, while pleasure is a kind of pursuit or approach; just as pleasure regards first the good possessed, as its proper object, so sorrow regards the evil that is present. On the other hand love, which is the cause of pleasure and sorrow, regards good rather than evil: and therefore, forasmuch as the object is the cause of a passion, the present evil is more properly the cause of sorrow or pain, than the good which is lost.

Reply Obj. 1. The loss itself of good is apprehended as an evil, just as the loss of evil is apprehended as a good: and in this sense Augustine says that pain results from the loss of temporal goods.

Reply Obj. 2. Pleasure and its contrary pain have the same object, but under contrary aspects: because if the presence of a particular thing be the object of pleasure, the absence of that same thing is the object of sorrow. Now one contrary includes the privation of the other, as stated in *Metaph.* x. 4: and consequently sorrow in respect of one contrary is, in a way, directed to the same thing under a contrary aspect.

Reply Obj. 3. When many movements arise from one cause, it does not follow that they all regard chiefly that which the cause regards chiefly, but only the first of them. And each of the others regards chiefly that which is suitable to it according to its own nature.

SECOND ARTICLE

Whether Desire Is a Cause of Sorrow?

We proceed thus to the Second Article:—

Objection 1. It would seem that desire is not a cause of pain or sorrow. Because sorrow of itself regards evil, as stated above (A. 1): whereas desire is a movement of the appetite towards good. Now movement towards one contrary is not a cause of the movement towards the other contrary. Therefore desire is not a cause of pain.

Obj. 2. Further, pain, according to Dama-

scene (*De Fide Orthod.* ii. 12), is caused by something present; whereas the object of desire is something future. Therefore desire is not a cause of pain.

Obj. 3. Further, that which is pleasant in itself is not a cause of pain. But desire is pleasant in itself, as the Philosopher says (*Rhet.* i. 11). Therefore desire is not a cause of pain or sorrow.

On the contrary, Augustine says (*Enchirid.* xxiv): *When ignorance of things necessary to be done, and desire of things hurtful, found their way in: error and pain stole an entrance in their company.* But ignorance is the cause of error. Therefore desire is a cause of sorrow.

I answer that, Sorrow is a movement of the animal appetite. Now, as stated above (A. 1) the appetitive movement is likened to the natural appetite; a likeness, that may be assigned to a twofold cause; one, on the part of the end, the other, on the part of the principle of movement. Thus, on the part of the end, the cause of a heavy body's downward movement is the lower place; while the principle of that movement is a natural inclination resulting from gravity.

Now the cause of the appetitive movement, on the part of the end, is the object of that movement. And thus, it has been said above (A. 1) that the cause of pain or sorrow is a present evil.—On the other hand, the cause, by way of principle, of that movement, is the inward inclination of the appetite; which inclination regards, first of all, the good, and in consequence, the rejection of a contrary evil. Hence the first principle of this appetitive movement is love, which is the first inclination of the appetite towards the possession of good: while the second principle is hatred, which is the first inclination of the appetite towards the avoidance of evil. But since concupiscence or desire is the first effect of love, which gives rise to the greatest pleasure, as stated above (Q. 32, A. 6); hence it is that Augustine often speaks of desire or concupiscence in the sense of love, as was also stated (Q. 30, A. 2 *ad* 2): and in this sense he says that desire is the universal cause of sorrow. Sometimes, however, desire taken in its proper sense, is the cause of sorrow. Because whatever hinders a movement from reaching its end is contrary to that movement. Now that which is contrary to the movement of the appetite, is a cause of sorrow. Consequently, desire becomes a cause of sorrow, in so far as we sorrow for the delay of a desired good, or for its entire removal. But it cannot be a universal cause of sorrow: since we sorrow more for the loss of present good, in which we have already taken pleasure, than for the withdrawal of future good which we desire to have.

Reply Obj. 1. The inclination of the appetite to the possession of good causes the inclination of the appetite to fly from evil, as stated above. And hence it is that the appetitive movements that regard good, are reckoned as causing the appetitive movements that regard evil.

Reply Obj. 2. That which is desired, though really future, is, nevertheless, in a way, present, inasmuch as it is hoped for.—Or we may say that although the desired good itself is future, yet the hindrance is reckoned as present, and so gives rise to sorrow.

Reply Obj. 3. Desire gives pleasure, so long as there is a hope of obtaining that which is desired. But, when hope is removed through the presence of an obstacle, desire causes sorrow.

THIRD ARTICLE

Whether the Craving for Unity Is a Cause of Sorrow?

We proceed thus to the Third Article:—

Objection 1. It would seem that the craving for unity is not a cause of sorrow. For the Philosopher says (*Ethic.* x. 3) that *this opinion,* which held repletion to be the cause of pleasure, and division* the cause of sorrow, *seems to have originated in pains and pleasures connected with food.* But not every pleasure or sorrow is of this kind. Therefore the craving for unity is not the universal cause of sorrow; since repletion pertains to unity, and division is the cause of multitude.

Obj. 2. Further, every separation is opposed to unity. If therefore sorrow were caused by a craving for unity, no separation would be pleasant: and this is clearly untrue as regards the separation of whatever is superfluous.

Obj. 3. Further, for the same reason we desire the conjunction of good and the removal of evil. But as conjunction regards unity, since it is a kind of union; so separation is contrary to unity. Therefore the craving for unity should not be reckoned, rather than the craving for separation, as causing sorrow.

On the contrary, Augustine says (*De Lib. Arb.* iii. 23), that *from the pain that dumb animals feel, it is quite evident how their souls desire unity, in ruling and quickening their bodies. For what else is pain but a feeling of impatience of division or corruption?*

I answer that, Forasmuch as the desire or craving for good is reckoned as a cause of sorrow, so must a craving for unity, and love, be accounted as causing sorrow. Because the good of each thing consists in a certain unity, inasmuch as each thing has, united in itself, the elements of which its perfection consists: wherefore the Platonists held that *one* is a principle, just as *good* is. Hence everything naturally desires unity, just as it desires goodness: and therefore, just as love or desire for good is a cause of sorrow, so also is the love or craving for unity.

Reply Obj. 1. Not every kind of union causes perfect goodness, but only that on which the perfect being of a thing depends. Hence neither does the desire of any kind of unity cause pain or sorrow, as some have maintained: whose opinion is refuted by the Philosopher from the fact that repletion is not always pleasant; for instance, when a man has eaten to repletion, he takes no further pleasure in eating; because repletion or union of this kind, is repugnant rather than conducive to perfect being. Consequently sorrow is caused by the craving, not for any kind of unity, but for that unity in which the perfection of nature consists.

Reply Obj. 2. Separation can be pleasant, either because it removes something contrary to a thing's perfection, or because it has some union connected with it, such as union of the sense to its object.

Reply Obj. 3. Separation from things hurtful and corruptive is desired, in so far as they destroy the unity which is due. Wherefore the desire for a such like separation is not the first cause of sorrow, whereas the craving for unity is.

FOURTH ARTICLE

Whether an Irresistible Power Is a Cause of Sorrow?

We proceed thus to the Fourth Article:—

Objection 1. It would seem that a greater power should not be reckoned a cause of sorrow. For that which is in the power of the agent is not present but future. But sorrow is for present evil. Therefore a greater power is not a cause of sorrow.

Obj. 2. Further, hurt inflicted is the cause of sorrow. But hurt can be inflicted even by a lesser power. Therefore a greater power should not be reckoned as a cause of sorrow.

Obj. 3. Further, the interior inclinations of the soul are the causes of the movements of appetite. But a greater power is something external. Therefore it should not be reckoned as a cause of sorrow.

On the contrary, Augustine says (*De Nat. Boni* xx): *Sorrow in the soul is caused by the will resisting a stronger power: while pain in the body is caused by sense resisting a stronger body.*

I answer that, As stated above (A. 1), a present evil, is cause of sorrow or pain, by way of object. Therefore that which is the cause of the evil being present, should be reckoned as

---

* Aristotle wrote ἔνδειαν, want; St. Thomas, in the Latin version read *incisionem;* should he have read *indigentiam?*

causing pain or sorrow. Now it is evident that it is contrary to the inclination of the appetite to be united with a present evil: and whatever is contrary to a thing's inclination does not happen to it save by the action of something stronger. Wherefore Augustine reckons a greater power as being the cause of sorrow.

But it must be noted that if the stronger power goes so far as to transform the contrary inclination into its own inclination, there will be no longer repugnance or violence: thus if a stronger agent, by its action on a heavy body, deprives it of its downward tendency, its consequent upward tendency is not violent but natural to it.

Accordingly if some greater power prevail so far as to take away from the will or the sensitive appetite, their respective inclinations, pain or sorrow will not result therefrom; such is the result only when the contrary inclination of the appetite remains. And hence Augustine says (*loc. cit.*) that sorrow is caused by the will *resisting a stronger power:* for were it not to resist, but to yield by consenting, the result would be not sorrow but pleasure.

Reply Obj. 1. A greater power causes sorrow, as acting not potentially but actually, *i.e.,* by causing the actual presence of the corruptive evil.

Reply Obj. 2. Nothing hinders a power which is not simply greater, from being greater in some respect: and accordingly it is able to inflict some harm. But if it be nowise stronger, it can do no harm at all: wherefore it cannot bring about that which causes sorrow.

Reply Obj. 3. External agents can be the causes of appetitive movements, in so far as they cause the presence of the object: and it is thus that a greater power is reckoned to be the cause of sorrow.

QUESTION 37

Of the Effects of Pain or Sorrow

(In Four Articles)

WE must now consider the effects of pain or or sorrow: under which head there are four points of inquiry: (1) Whether pain deprives one of the power to learn? (2) Whether the effect of sorrow or pain is to burden the soul? (3) Whether sorrow or pain weakens all activity? (4) Whether sorrow is more harmful to the body than all the other passions of the soul?

FIRST ARTICLE

Whether Pain Deprives One of the Power to Learn?

We proceed thus to the First Article:—

Objection 1. It would seem that pain does not deprive one of the power to learn. For it is written (Isa. xxvi. 9): *When Thou shalt do Thy judgments on the earth, the inhabitants of the world shall learn justice:* and further on (*verse* 16): *In the tribulation of murmuring Thy instruction was with them.* But the judgments of God and tribulation cause sorrow in men's hearts. Therefore pain or sorrow, far from destroying, increases the power of learning.

Obj. 2. Further, it is written (Isa. xxviii. 9): *Whom shall He teach knowledge? And whom shall He make to understand the hearing? Them that are weaned from the milk, that are drawn away from the breasts, i.e.,* from pleasures. But pain and sorrow are most destructive of pleasure; since sorrow hinders all pleasure, as stated in *Ethic.* vii. 14: and (Ecclus. xi. 29) it is stated that *the affliction of an hour maketh one forget great delights.* Therefore pain, instead of taking away, increases the faculty of learning.

Obj. 3. Further, inward sorrow surpasses outward pain, as stated above (Q. 35, A. 7). But man can learn while sorrowful. Much more, therefore, can he learn while in bodily pain.

On the contrary, Augustine says (*Soliloq.* i. 12): *Although during those days I was tormented with a violent tooth ache, I was not able to turn over in my mind other things than those I had already learnt; and as to learning anything, I was quite unequal to it, because it required undivided attention.*

I answer that, Since all the powers of the soul are rooted in the one essence of the soul, it must needs happen, when the intention of the soul is strongly drawn towards the action of one power, that it is withdrawn from the action of another power: because the soul, being one, can only have one intention. The result is that if one thing draws upon itself the entire intention of the soul, or a great portion thereof, anything else requiring considerable attention is incompatible therewith.

Now it is evident that sensible pain above all draws the soul's attention to itself; because it is natural for each thing to tend wholly to repel whatever is contrary to it, as may be observed even in natural things. It is likewise evident that in order to learn anything new, we require study and effort with a strong intention, as is clearly stated in Prov. ii. 4, 5: *If thou shalt seek* wisdom *as money, and shall* dig for her as for a treasure, then shalt thou understand learning (Vulg.,—the fear of the Lord). Consequently if the pain be acute, man is prevented at the time from learning anything: indeed it can be so acute, that, as long as it lasts, a man is unable to give his attention even to that which he knew already. —However a difference is to be observed according to the difference of love that a man has for learning or for considering: because the greater his love, the more will he retain the intention of his mind so as to prevent it from turning entirely to the pain.

Reply Obj. 1. Moderate sorrow, that does not cause the mind to wander, can conduce to the acquisition of learning especially in regard to those things by which a man hopes to be freed from sorrow. And thus, *in the tribulation of murmuring*, men are more apt to be taught of God.

Reply Obj. 2. Both pleasure and pain, in so far as they draw upon themselves the soul's intention, hinder the reason from the act of consideration, wherefore it is stated in *Ethic.* vii. 11 that *in the moment of sexual pleasure, a man cannot understand anything.* Nevertheless pain attracts the soul's intention more than pleasure does: thus we observe in natural things that the action of a natural body is more intense in regard to its contrary; for instance, hot water is more accessible to the action of cold, and in consequence freezes harder. If therefore pain or sorrow be moderate, it can conduce accidentally to the facility of learning, in so far as it takes away an excess of pleasure. But, of itself, it is a hindrance; and if it be intense, it prevents it altogether.

Reply Obj. 3. External pain arises from hurt done to the body, so that it involves bodily transmutation more than inward sorrow does: and yet the latter is greater in regard to the formal element of pain, which belongs to the soul. Consequently bodily pain is a greater hindrance to contemplation which requires complete repose, than inward sorrow is. Nevertheless if inward sorrow be very intense, it attracts the intention, so that man is unable to learn anything for the first time: wherefore on account of sorrow Gregory interrupted his commentary on Ezechiel (*Hom. .xxii in Ezechiel*).

SECOND ARTICLE

Whether the Effect of Sorrow or Pain Is to Burden the Soul?

We proceed thus to the Second Article:—

Objection 1. It would seem that it is not an effect of sorrow to burden the soul. For the Apostle says (2 Cor. vii. 11): *Behold this self-*

* Nemesius,—*De Nat. Hom.* xix.

same thing, that you were made sorrowful according to God, how great carefulness it worketh in you: yea defence, yea indignation, etc. Now carefulness and indignation imply that the soul is uplifted, which is contrary to being depressed. Therefore depression is not an effect of sorrow.

Obj. 2. Further, sorrow is contrary to pleasure. But the effect of pleasure is expansion: the opposite of which is not depression but contraction. Therefore depression should not be reckoned as an effect of sorrow.

Obj. 3. Further, sorrow consumes those who are afflicted therewith, as may be gathered from the words of the Apostle (2 Cor. ii. 7): *Lest perhaps such an one be swallowed up with overmuch sorrow.* But that which is depressed is not consumed; nay, it is weighed down by something heavy, whereas that which is consumed enters within the consumer. Therefore depression should not be reckoned an effect of sorrow.

On the contrary, Gregory of Nyssa* and Damascene (*De Fide Orthod.* ii. 14) speak of *depressing sorrow.*

I answer that, The effects of the soul's passions are sometimes named metaphorically, from a likeness to sensible bodies: for the reason that the movements of the animal appetite are like the inclinations of the natural appetite. And in this way fervor is ascribed to love, expansion to pleasure, and depression to sorrow. For a man is said to be depressed, through being hindered in his own movement by some weight. Now it is evident from what has been said above (Q. 23, A. 4; Q. 25, A. 4; Q. 36, A. 1) that sorrow is caused by a present evil: and this evil, from the very fact that it is repugnant to the movement of the will, depresses the soul, inasmuch as it hinders it from enjoying that which it wishes to enjoy. And if the evil which is the cause of sorrow be not so strong as to deprive one of the hope of avoiding it, although the soul be depressed in so far as, for the present, it fails to grasp that which it craves for; yet it retains the movement whereby to repulse that evil. If, on the other hand, the strength of the evil be such as to exclude the hope of evasion, then even the interior movement of the afflicted soul is absolutely hindered, so that it cannot turn aside either this way or that. Sometimes even the external movement of the body is paralyzed, so that a man becomes completely stupefied.

Reply Obj. 1. That uplifting of the soul ensues from the sorrow which is according to God, because it brings with it the hope of the forgiveness of sin.

Reply Obj. 2. As far as the movement of the appetite is concerned, contraction and depression amount to the same: because the soul, through being depressed so as to be unable to attend freely to outward things, withdraws to itself, closing itself up as it were.

Reply Obj. 3. Sorrow is said to consume man, when the force of the afflicting evil is such as to shut out all hope of evasion: and thus also it both depresses and consumes at the same time. For certain things, taken metaphorically, imply one another, which taken literally, appear to exclude one another.

THIRD ARTICLE

Whether Sorrow or Pain Weakens All Activity?

We proceed thus to the Third Article:—

Objection 1. It would seem that sorrow does not weaken all activity. Because carefulness is caused by sorrow, as is clear from the passage of the Apostle quoted above (A. 2, *Obj.* 1). But carefulness conduces to good work: wherefore the Apostle says (2 Tim. ii. 15): *Carefully study to present thyself . . . a workman that needeth not to be ashamed.* Therefore sorrow is not a hindrance to work, but helps one to work well.

Obj. 2. Further, sorrow causes desire in many cases, as stated in *Ethic.* vii. 14. But desire causes intensity of action. Therefore sorrow does too.

Obj. 3. Further, as some actions are proper to the joyful, so are others proper to the sorrowful; for instance, to mourn. Now a thing is improved by that which is suitable to it. Therefore certain actions are not hindered but improved by reason of sorrow.

On the contrary, The Philosopher says (*Ethic.* x. 4) that *pleasure perfects action,* whereas on the other hand, *sorrow hinders it* (*ibid.* 5).

I answer that, As stated above (A. 2), sorrow at times does not depress or consume the soul, so as to shut out all movement, internal or external; but certain movements are sometimes caused by sorrow itself. Accordingly action stands in a twofold relation to sorrow. First, as being the object of sorrow: and thus sorrow hinders any action: for we never do that which we do with sorrow, so well as that which we do with pleasure, or without sorrow. The reason for this is that the will is the cause of human actions: and consequently when we do something that gives pain, the action must of necessity be weakened in consequence.— Secondly, action stands in relation to sorrow, as to its principle and cause: and such action must needs be improved by sorrow: thus the more one sorrows on account of a certain thing, the more one strives to shake off sorrow, provided there is a hope of shaking it off: otherwise no movement or action would result from that sorrow.

From what has been said the replies to the objections are evident.

FOURTH ARTICLE

Whether Sorrow Is More Harmful to the Body Than the Other Passions of the Soul?

We proceed thus to the Fourth Article:—

Objection 1. It would seem that sorrow is not most harmful to the body. For sorrow has a spiritual existence in the soul. But those things which have only a spiritual existence do not cause a transmutation in the body: as is evident with regard to the images of colors, which images are in the air and do not give color to bodies. Therefore sorrow is not harmful to the body.

Obj. 2. Further if it be harmful to the body, this can only be due to its having a bodily transmutation in conjunction with it. But bodily transmutation takes place in all the passions of the soul, as stated above (Q. 22, AA. 1, 3). Therefore sorrow is not more harmful to the body than the other passions of the soul.

Obj. 3. Further, the Philosopher says (*Ethic.* vii. 3) that *anger and desire drive some to madness:* which seems to be a very great harm, since reason is the most excellent thing in man. Moreover, despair seems to be more harmful than sorrow; for it is the cause of sorrow. Therefore sorrow is not more harmful to the body than the other passions of the soul.

On the contrary, It is written (Prov. xvii. 22): *A joyful mind maketh age flourishing: a sorrowful spirit drieth up the bones:* and (*ibid.* xxv. 20). *As a moth doth by a garment, and a worm by the wood: so the sadness of a man consumeth the heart:* and (Ecclus. xxxviii. 19): *Of sadness cometh death.*

I answer that, Of all the soul's passions, sorrow is most harmful to the body. The reason of this is because sorrow is repugnant to man's life in respect of the species of its movement, and not merely in respect of its measure or quantity, as is the case with the other passions of the soul. For man's life consists in a certain movement, which flows from the heart to the other parts of the body: and this movement is befitting to human nature according to a certain fixed measure. Consequently if this movement goes beyond the right measure, it will be repugnant to man's life in respect of the measure of quantity; but not in respect of its specific character: whereas if this movement be hindered in its progress, it will be repugnant to life in respect of its species.

Now it must be noted that, in all the passions of the soul, the bodily transmutation which is their material element, is in conformity with and in proportion to the appetitive movement, which is the formal element: just as in everything matter is proportionate to form. Consequently those passions that imply a movement of the appetite in pursuit of something, are not repugnant to the vital movement as regards its species, but they may be repugnant thereto as regards its measure: such are love, joy, desire and the like; wherefore these passions conduce to the well-being of the body; though, if they be excessive, they may be harmful to it.—On the other hand, those passions which denote in the appetite a movement of flight or contraction, are repugnant to the vital movement, not only as regards its measure, but also as regards its species; wherefore they are simply harmful: such are fear and despair, and above all sorrow which depresses the soul by reason of a present evil, which makes a stronger impression than future evil.

Reply Obj. 1. Since the soul naturally moves the body, the spiritual movement of the soul is naturally the cause of bodily transmutation. Nor is there any parallel with spiritual images, because they are not naturally ordained to move such other bodies as are not naturally moved by the soul.

Reply Obj. 2. Other passions imply a bodily transmutation which is specifically in conformity with the vital movement: whereas sorrow implies a transmutation that is repugnant thereto, as stated above.

Reply Obj. 3. A lesser cause suffices to hinder the use of reason, than to destroy life: since we observe that many ailments deprive one of the use of reason, before depriving one of life. Nevertheless fear and anger cause very great harm to the body, by reason of the sorrow which they imply, and which arises from the absence of the thing desired. Moreover sorrow too sometimes deprives man of the use of reason: as may be seen in those who through sorrow become a prey to melancholy or madness.

QUESTION 38

Of the Remedies of Sorrow or Pain

(In Five Articles)

WE must now consider the remedies of pain or sorrow: under which head there are five points of inquiry: (1) Whether pain or sorrow is assuaged by every pleasure? (2) Whether it is assuaged by weeping? (3) Whether it is assuaged by the sympathy of friends? (4) Whether it is assuaged by contemplating the truth? (5) Whether it is assuaged by sleep and baths?

FIRST ARTICLE

Whether Pain or Sorrow Is Assuaged by Every Pleasure?

We proceed thus to the First Article:—

Objection 1. It would seem that not every pleasure assuages every pain or sorrow. For pleasure does not assuage sorrow, save in so far as it is contrary to it: for *remedies work by contraries* (*Ethic.* ii. 3). But not every pleasure is contrary to every sorrow; as stated above (Q. 35, A. 4). Therefore not every pleasure assuages every sorrow.

Obj. 2. Further, that which causes sorrow does not assuage it. But some pleasures cause sorrow; since, as stated in *Ethic.* ix. 4, *the wicked man feels pain at having been pleased.* Therefore not every pleasure assuages sorrow.

Obj. 3. Further, Augustine says (*Conf.* iv. 7) that he fled from his country, where he had been wont to associate with his friend, now dead: *for so should his eyes look for him less, where they were not wont to see him.* Hence we may gather that those things which united us to our dead or absent friends, become burdensome to us when we mourn their death or absence. But nothing united us more than the pleasures we enjoyed in common. Therefore these very pleasures become burdensome to us when we mourn. Therefore not every pleasure assuages every sorrow.

On the contrary, The Philosopher says (*Ethic.* vii. 14) that *sorrow is driven forth by pleasure, both by a contrary pleasure and by any other, provided it be intense.*

I answer that, As is evident from what has been said above (Q. 23, A. 4), pleasure is a kind of repose of the appetite in a suitable good; while sorrow arises from something unsuited to the appetite. Consequently in movements of the appetite pleasure is to sorrow, what, in bodies, repose is to weariness, which is due to a non-natural transmutation; for sorrow itself implies a certain weariness or ailing of the appetitive faculty. Therefore just as all repose of the body brings relief to any kind of weariness, ensuing from any non-natural cause; so every pleasure brings relief by assuaging any kind of sorrow, due to any cause whatever.

Reply Obj. 1. Although not every pleasure is specifically contrary to every sorrow, yet it is generically, as stated above (Q. 35, A. 4). And consequently, on the part of the disposition of the subject, any sorrow can be assuaged by any pleasure.

Reply Obj. 2. The pleasures of wicked men are not a cause of sorrow while they are enjoyed, but afterwards: that is to say, in so far as wicked men repent of those things in which they took pleasure. This sorrow is healed by contrary pleasures.

Reply Obj. 3. When there are two causes inclining to contrary movements, each hinders the other; yet the one which is stronger and more persistent, prevails in the end. Now when a man is made sorrowful by those things in which he took pleasure in common with a deceased or absent friend, there are two causes producing contrary movements. For the thought of the friend's death or absence, inclines him to sorrow: whereas the present good inclines him to pleasure. Consequently each is modified by the other. And yet, since the perception of the present moves more strongly than the memory of the past, and since love of self is more persistent than love of another; hence it is that, in the end, the pleasure drives out the sorrow. Wherefore a little further on (*loc. cit.*, 8) Augustine says that *his sorrow gave way to his former pleasures.*

SECOND ARTICLE

Whether Pain or Sorrow Is Assuaged by Tears?

We proceed thus to the Second Article:—

Objection 1. It would seem that tears do not assuage sorrow. Because no effect diminishes its cause. But tears or groans are an effect of sorrow, Therefore they do not diminish sorrow.

Obj. 2. Further, just as tears or groans are an effect of sorrow, so laughter is an effect of joy. But laughter does not lessen joy. Therefore tears do not lessen sorrow.

Obj. 3. Further, when we weep, the evil that saddens us is present to the imagination. But the image of that which saddens us increases sorrow, just as the image of a pleasant thing adds to joy. Therefore it seems that tears do not assuage sorrow.

On the contrary, Augustine says (*Conf.* iv. 7) that when he mourned the death of his friend, *in groans and in tears alone did he find some little refreshment.*

I answer that, Tears and groans naturally assuage sorrow: and this for two reasons. First, because a hurtful thing hurts yet more if we keep it shut up, because the soul is more intent on it: whereas if it be allowed to escape, the soul's intention is dispersed as it were on outward things, so that the inward sorrow is lessened. This is why when men, burdened with sorrow, make outward show of their sorrow, by tears or groans or even by words, their sorrow is assuaged.—Secondly, because an action, that befits a man according to his actual disposition, is always pleasant to him. Now tears and groans are actions befitting a man who is in sorrow or pain; and consequently they become pleasant to him. Since then, as stated above (A. 1), every pleasure assuages sorrow or pain somewhat, it follows that sorrow is assuaged by weeping and groans.

Reply Obj. 1. This relation of the cause to effect is opposed to the relation existing between the cause of sorrow and the sorrowing man. For every effect is suited to its cause, and consequently is pleasant to it; but the cause of sorrow is disagreeable to him that sorrows. Hence the effect of sorrow is not related to him that sorrows in the same way as the cause of sorrow is. For this reason sorrow is assuaged by its effect, on account of the aforesaid contrariety.

Reply Obj. 2. The relation of effect to cause is like the relation of the object of pleasure to him that takes pleasure in it: because in each case the one agrees with the other. Now every like thing increases its like. Therefore joy is increased by laughter and the other effects of joy: except they be excessive, in which case, accidentally, they lessen it.

Reply Obj. 3. The image of that which saddens us, considered in itself, has a natural tendency to increase sorrow: yet from the very fact that a man imagines himself to be doing that which is fitting according to his actual state, he feels a certain amount of pleasure. For the same reason if laughter escapes a man when he is so disposed that he thinks he ought to weep, he is sorry for it, as having done something unbecoming to him, as Cicero says (*De Tusc. Quæst.* iii. 27).

THIRD ARTICLE

Whether Pain and Sorrow Are Assuaged by the Sympathy of Friends?

We proceed thus to the Third Article:—

Objection 1. It would seem that the sorrow of sympathizing friends does not assuage our own sorrow. For contraries have contrary effects. Now as Augustine says (*Conf.* viii. 4), *when many rejoice together, each one has more exuberant joy, for they are kindled and inflamed one by the other.* Therefore, in like manner, when many are sorrowful, it seems that their sorrow is greater.

Obj. 2. Further, friendship demands mutual love, as Augustine declares (*Conf.* iv. 9). But a sympathizing friend is pained at the sorrow of his friend with whom he sympathizes. Consequently the pain of a sympathizing friend becomes, to the friend in sorrow, a further cause of sorrow: so that, his pain being doubled his sorrow seems to increase.

Obj. 3. Further, sorrow arises from every evil affecting a friend, as though it affected oneself: since *a friend is one's other self* (*Ethic.* ix. 4, 9). But sorrow is an evil. Therefore the sorrow of the sympathizing friend increases the sorrow of the friend with whom he sympathizes.

On the contrary, The Philosopher says (*Ethic.* ix. 11) that those who are in pain are consoled when their friends sympathize with them.

I answer that, When one is in pain, it is natural that the sympathy of a friend should afford consolation: whereof the Philosopher indicates a twofold reason (*Ethic.* ix. *ibid.*). The first is because, since sorrow has a depressing effect, it is like a weight whereof we strive to unburden ourselves: so that when a man sees others saddened by his own sorrow, it seems as though others were bearing the burden with him, striving, as it were, to lessen its weight; wherefore the load of sorrow becomes lighter for him: something like what occurs in the carrying of bodily burdens.—The second and better reason is because when a man's friends condole with him, he sees that he is loved by them, and this affords him pleasure, as stated above (Q. 32, A. 5). Consequently, since every pleasure assuages sorrow, as stated above (A. 1), it follows that sorrow is mitigated by a sympathizing friend.

Reply Obj. 1. In either case there is a proof of friendship, viz., when a man rejoices with the joyful, and when he sorrows with the sorrowful. Consequently each becomes an object of pleasure by reason of its cause.

Reply Obj. 2. The friend's sorrow itself would be a cause of sorrow: but consideration of its cause, viz., his love, gives rise rather to pleasure.

And this suffices for the reply to the Third Objection.

FOURTH ARTICLE

Whether Pain and Sorrow Are Assuaged by the Contemplation of Truth?

We proceed thus to the Fourth Article:—

Objection 1. It would seem that the contemplation of truth does not assuage sorrow. For it is written (Eccles. i. 18): *He that addeth knowledge addeth also sorrow* (Vulg.,—*labor*). But knowledge pertains to the contemplation of truth. Therefore the contemplation of truth does not assuage sorrow.

Obj. 2. Further, the contemplation of truth belongs to the speculative intellect. But *the*

speculative intellect is not a principle of movement; as stated in *De Anima* iii. 11. Therefore, since joy and sorrow are movements of the soul, it seems that the contemplation of truth does not help to assuage sorrow.

Obj. 3. Further, the remedy for an ailment should be applied to the part which ails. But contemplation of truth is in the intellect. Therefore it does not assuage bodily pain, which is in the senses.

On the contrary, Augustine says (*Soliloq.* i. 12): *It seemed to me that if the light of that truth were to dawn on our minds, either I should not feel that pain, or at least that pain would seem nothing to me.*

I answer that, As stated above (Q. 3, A. 5), the greatest of all pleasures consists in the contemplation of truth. Now every pleasure assuages pain as stated above (A. 1): hence the contemplation of truth assuages pain or sorrow, and the more so, the more perfectly one is a lover of wisdom. And therefore in the midst of tribulations men rejoice in the contemplation of Divine things and of future Happiness, according to James i. 2: *My brethren, count it all joy, when you shall fall into divers temptations:* and, what is more, even in the midst of bodily tortures this joy is found; as the *martyr Tiburtius, when he was walking barefoot on the burning coals, said: Methinks, I walk on roses, in the name of Jesus Christ.**

Reply Obj. 1. He that addeth knowledge, addeth sorrow, either on account of the difficulty and disappointment in the search of truth; or because knowledge makes man acquainted with many things that are contrary to his will. Accordingly, on the part of the things known, knowledge causes sorrow: but on the part of the contemplation of truth, it causes pleasure.

Reply Obj. 2. The speculative intellect does not move the mind on the part of the thing contemplated: but on the part of contemplation itself, which is man's good and naturally pleasant to him.

Reply Obj. 3. In the powers of the soul there is an overflow from the higher to the lower powers: and accordingly, the pleasure of contemplation, which is in the higher part, overflows so as to mitigate even that pain which is in the senses.

FIFTH ARTICLE

Whether Pain and Sorrow Are Assuaged by Sleep and Baths?

We proceed thus to the Fifth Article:—

Objection 1. It would seem that sleep and baths do not assuage sorrow. For sorrow is in

---

* *Cf.* Dominican Breviary, August 11th, commemoration of S. Tiburtius.

the soul: whereas sleep and baths regard the body. Therefore they do not conduce to the assuaging of sorrow.

Obj. 2. Further, the same effect does not seem to ensue from contrary causes. But these, being bodily things, are incompatible with the contemplation of truth which is a cause of the assuaging of sorrow, as stated above (A. 4). Therefore sorrow is not mitigated by the like.

Obj. 3. Further, sorrow and pain, in so far as they affect the body, denote a certain transmutation of the heart. But such remedies as these seem to pertain to the outward senses and limbs, rather than to the interior disposition of the heart. Therefore they do not assuage sorrow.

On the contrary, Augustine says (*Conf.* ix. 12): *I had heard that the bath had its name* ... *from the fact of its driving sadness from the mind.* And further on, he says: *I slept, and woke up again, and found my grief not a little assuaged:* and quotes the words from the hymn of Ambrose,† in which it is said that *Sleep restores the tired limbs to labor, refreshes the weary mind, and banishes sorrow.*

I answer that, As stated above (Q. 37, A. 4), sorrow, by reason of its specific nature, is repugnant to the vital movement of the body; and consequently whatever restores the bodily nature to its due state of vital movement, is opposed to sorrow and assuages it.—Moreover such remedies, from the very fact that they bring nature back to its normal state, are causes of pleasure; for this is precisely in what pleasure consists, as stated above (Q. 31, A. 1). Therefore, since every pleasure assuages sorrow, sorrow is assuaged by such like bodily remedies.

Reply Obj. 1. The normal disposition of the body, so far as it is felt, is itself a cause of pleasure, and consequently assuages sorrow.

Reply Obj. 2. As stated above (Q. 31, A. 8), one pleasure hinders another; and yet every pleasure assuages sorrow. Consequently it is not unreasonable that sorrow should be assuaged by causes which hinder one another.

Reply Obj. 3. Every good disposition of the body reacts somewhat on the heart, which is the beginning and end of bodily movements, as stated in *De Causa Mot. Animal.* xi.

QUESTION 39

Of the Goodness and Malice of Sorrow or Pain

(In Four Articles)

WE must now consider the goodness and malice of pain or sorrow: under which head there are four points of inquiry: (1) Whether all sorrow is evil? (2) Whether sorrow can be a virtuous good? (3) Whether it can be a useful good? (4) Whether bodily pain is the greatest evil?

FIRST ARTICLE

Whether All Sorrow Is Evil?

We proceed thus to the First Article:—

Objection 1. It would seem that all sorrow is evil. For Gregory of Nyssa‡ says: *All sorrow is evil, from its very nature.* Now what is naturally evil, is evil always and everywhere. Therefore all sorrow is evil.

Obj. 2. Further, that which all, even the virtuous, avoid, is evil. But all avoid sorrow, even the virtuous, since as stated in *Ethic.* vii. 11, *though the prudent man does not aim at pleasure, yet he aims at avoiding sorrow.* Therefore sorrow is evil.

Obj. 3. Further, just as bodily evil is the object and cause of bodily pain, so spiritual evil is the object and cause of sorrow in the

soul. But every bodily pain is a bodily evil. Therefore every spiritual sorrow is an evil of the soul.

On the contrary, Sorrow for evil is contrary to pleasure in evil. But pleasure in evil is evil: wherefore in condemnation of certain men, it is written (Prov. ii. 14), that *they are glad when they have done evil.* Therefore sorrow for evil is good.

I answer that, A thing may be good or evil in two ways: first considered simply and in itself; and thus all sorrow is an evil, because the mere fact of a man's appetite being uneasy about a present evil, is itself an evil, because it hinders the respose of the appetite in good.—Secondly, a thing is said to be good or evil, on the supposition of something else: thus shame is said to be good, on the supposition of a shameful deed done, as stated in *Ethic.* iv. 9. Accordingly, supposing the presence of something saddening or painful, it is a sign of goodness if a man is in sorrow or pain on account of this present evil. For if he were not to be in sorrow or pain, this could only be either because he feels it not, or because he does not reckon it as something unbecoming,

---

* *Balneum,* from the Greek βαλανεῖον.

† *Cf.* Sarum Breviary: First Sunday after the octave of the Epiphany, Hymn for first Vespers.

‡ Nemesius, *De Nat. Hom.* xix.

both of which are manifest evils. Consequently it is a condition of goodness, that, supposing an evil to be present, sorrow or pain should ensue. Wherefore Augustine says (*Gen. ad lit.* viii. 14): *It is also a good thing that he sorrows for the good he has lost: for had not some good remained in his nature, he could not be punished by the loss of good.*—Because, however, in the science of Morals, we consider things individually,—for actions are concerned about individuals,—that which is good on some supposition, should be considered as good: just as that which is voluntary on some supposition, is judged to be voluntary, as stated in *Ethic.* iii. 1, and likewise above (Q. 6, A. 6).

Reply Obj. 1. Gregory of Nyssa* is speaking of sorrow on the part of the evil that causes it, but not on the part of the subject that feels and rejects the evil.—And from this point of view all shun sorrow, inasmuch as they shun evil: but they do not shun the perception and rejection of evil.—The same also applies to bodily pain: because the perception and rejection of bodily evil is the proof of the goodness of nature.

This suffices for the Replies to the Second and Third Objections.

SECOND ARTICLE

Whether Sorrow Can Be a Virtuous Good?

We proceed thus to the Second Article:—

Objection 1. It would seem that sorrow is not a virtuous good. For that which leads to hell is not a virtuous good. But, as Augustine says (*Gen. ad lit.* xii. 33), *Jacob seems to have feared lest he should be troubled overmuch by sorrow, and so, instead of entering into the rest of the blessed, be consigned to the hell of sinners.* Therefore sorrow is not a virtuous good.

Obj. 2. Further, the virtuous good is praiseworthy and meritorious. But sorrow lessens praise or merit: for the Apostle says (*2 Cor.* ix. 7): *Everyone, as he hath determined in his heart, not with sadness, or of necessity.* Therefore sorrow is not a virtuous good.

Obj. 3. Further, as Augustine says (*De Civ. Dei* xiv. 15), *sorrow is concerned about those things which happen against our will.* But not to will those things which are actually taking place, is to have a will opposed to the decree of God, to Whose providence whatever is done is subject. Since, then, conformity of the human to the Divine will is a condition of the rectitude of the will, as stated above (Q. 19, A. 9), it seems that sorrow is incompatible with rectitude of the will, and that consequently it is not virtuous.

* Nemesius.

On the contrary, Whatever merits the reward of eternal life is virtuous. But such is sorrow; as is evident from Matth. v. 5: *Blessed are they that mourn, for they shall be comforted.* Therefore sorrow is a virtuous good.

I answer that, In so far as sorrow is good, it can be a virtuous good. For it has been said above (A. 1) that sorrow is a good inasmuch as it denotes perception and rejection of evil. These two things, as regards bodily pain, are a proof of the goodness of nature, to which it is due that the senses perceive, and that nature shuns, the harmful thing that causes pain. As regards interior sorrow, perception of the evil is sometimes due to a right judgment of reason; while the rejection of the evil is the act of the will, well disposed and detesting that evil. Now every virtuous good results from these two things, the rectitude of the reason and the will. Wherefore it is evident that sorrow may be a virtuous good.

Reply Obj. 1. All the passions of the soul should be regulated according to the rule of reason, which is the root of the virtuous good; but excessive sorrow, of which Augustine is speaking, oversteps this rule, and therefore it fails to be a virtuous good.

Reply Obj. 2. Just as sorrow for an evil arises from a right will and reason, which detest the evil, so sorrow for a good is due to a perverse reason and will, which detest the good. Consequently such sorrow is an obstacle to the praise and merit of the virtuous good; for instance, when a man gives an alms sorrowfully.

Reply Obj. 3. Some things do actually happen, not because God wills, but because He permits them to happen—such as sins. Consequently a will that is opposed to sin, whether in oneself or in another, is not discordant from the Divine will.—Penal evils happen actually, even by God's will. But it is not necessary for the rectitude of his will, that man should will them in themselves: but only that he should not revolt against the order of Divine justice, as stated above (Q. 19, A. 10).

THIRD ARTICLE

Whether Sorrow Can Be a Useful Good?

We proceed thus to the Third Article:—

Objection 1. It would seem that sorrow cannot be a useful good. For it is written (*Ecclus.* xxx. 25): *Sadness hath killed many, and there is no profit in it.*

Obj. 2. Further, choice is of that which is useful to an end. But sorrow is not an object of choice; in fact, *a thing without sorrow is to be chosen rather than the same thing with sorrow* (*Topic.* iii. 2). Therefore sorrow is not a useful good.

Obj. 3. Further, *Everything is for the sake of its own operation*, as stated in *De Cælo* ii. 3. But *sorrow hinders operation*, as stated in *Ethic.* x. 5. Therefore sorrow is not a useful good.

On the contrary, The wise man seeks only that which is useful. But according to Eccles. vii. 5, *the heart of the wise is where there is mourning, and the heart of fools where there is mirth*. Therefore sorrow is useful.

I answer that, A twofold movement of the appetite ensues from a present evil. One is that whereby the appetite is opposed to the present evil; and, in this respect, sorrow is of no use; because that which is present, cannot be not present.—The other movement arises in the appetite to the effect of avoiding or expelling the saddening evil: and, in this respect, sorrow is of use, if it be for something which ought to be avoided. Because there are two reasons for which it may be right to avoid a thing. First, because it should be avoided in itself, on account of its being contrary to good; for instance, sin. Wherefore sorrow for sin is useful as inducing man to avoid sin: hence the Apostle says (2 Cor. vii. 9): *I am glad: not because you were made sorrowful, but because you were made sorrowful unto penance.*—Secondly, a thing is to be avoided, not as though it were evil in itself, but because it is an occasion of evil; either through one's being attached to it, and loving it too much, or through one's being thrown headlong thereby into an evil, as is evident in the case of temporal goods. And, in this respect, sorrow for temporal goods may be useful; according to Eccles. vii. 3: *It is better to go to the house of mourning, than to the house of feasting: for in that we are put in mind of the end of all.*

Moreover, sorrow for that which ought to be avoided is always useful, since it adds another motive for avoiding it. Because the very evil is in itself a thing to be avoided: while everyone avoids sorrow for its own sake, just as everyone seeks the good, and pleasure in the good. Therefore just as pleasure in the good makes one seek the good more earnestly, so sorrow for evil makes one avoid evil more eagerly.

Reply Obj. 1. This passage is to be taken as referring to excessive sorrow, which consumes the soul: for such sorrow paralyzes the soul, and hinders it from shunning evil, as stated above (Q. 37, A. 2).

Reply Obj. 2. Just as any object of choice becomes less eligible by reason of sorrow, so that which ought to be shunned is still more to be shunned by reason of sorrow: and, in this respect, sorrow is useful.

Reply Obj. 3. Sorrow caused by an action

hinders that action: but sorrow for the cessation of an action, makes one do it more earnestly.

FOURTH ARTICLE

Whether Bodily Pain Is the Greatest Evil?

We proceed thus to the Fourth Article:—

Objection 1. It would seem that pain is the greatest evil. Because *the worst is contrary to the best* (*Ethic.* viii. 10). But a certain pleasure is the greatest good, viz., the pleasure of bliss. Therefore a certain pain is the greatest evil.

Obj. 2. Further, happiness is man's greatest good, because it is his last end. But man's Happiness consists in his *having whatever he will, and in willing naught amiss*, as stated above (Q. 3, A. 4, *Obj.* 5; Q. 5, A. 8, *Obj* 3). Therefore man's greatest good consists in the fulfilment of his will. Now pain consists in something happening contrary to the will, as Augustine declares (*De Civ. Dei* xiv. 6, 15). Therefore pain is man's greatest evil.

Obj. 3. Further, Augustine argues thus (*Soliloq.* i. 12): *We are composed of two parts, i.e., of a soul and a body, whereof the body is the inferior. Now the sovereign good is the greatest good of the better part: while the supreme evil is the greatest evil of the inferior part. But wisdom is the greatest good of the soul; while the worst thing in the body is pain. Therefore man's greatest good is to be wise: while his greatest evil is to suffer pain.*

On the contrary, Guilt is a greater evil than punishment, as was stated in the First Part (Q. 48, A. 6). But sorrow or pain belongs to the punishment of sin, just as the enjoyment of changeable things is an evil of guilt. For Augustine says (*De Vera Relig.* xii): *What is pain of the soul, except for the soul to be deprived of that which it was wont to enjoy, or had hoped to enjoy? And this is all that is called evil, i.e. sin, and the punishment of sin.* Therefore sorrow or pain is not man's greatest evil.

I answer that, It is impossible for any sorrow or pain to be man's greatest evil. For all sorrow or pain is either for something that is truly evil, or for something that is apparently evil, but good in reality. Now pain or sorrow for that which is truly evil cannot be the greatest evil: for there is something worse, namely, either not to reckon as evil that which is really evil, or not to reject it. Again, sorrow or pain, for that which is apparently evil, but really good, cannot be the greatest evil, for it would be worse to be altogether separated from that which is truly good. Hence it is impossible for any sorrow or pain to be man's greatest evil.

Reply Obj. 1. Pleasure and sorrow have two

good points in common: namely, a true judgment concerning good and evil; and the right order of the will in approving of good and rejecting evil. Thus it is clear that in pain or sorrow there is a good, by the removal of which they become worse: and yet there is not an evil in every pleasure, by the removal of which the pleasure is better. Consequently, a pleasure can be man's highest good, in the way above stated (Q. 34, A. 3): whereas sorrow cannot be man's greatest evil.

Reply Obj. 2. The very fact of the will being opposed to evil is a good. And for this reason, sorrow or pain cannot be the greatest evil; because it has an admixture of good.

Reply Obj. 3. That which harms the better thing is worse than that which harms the worse. Now a thing is called evil *because it harms,* as Augustine says (*Enchirid.* xii). Therefore that which is an evil to the soul is a greater evil than that which is an evil to the body. Therefore this argument does not prove: nor does Augustine give it as his own, but as taken from another.*

QUESTION 40

Of the Irascible Passions, and First, of Hope and Despair

(In Eight Articles)

WE must now consider the irascible passions: (1) Hope and despair; (2) Fear and daring; (3) Anger. Under first head there are eight points of inquiry: (1) Whether hope is the same as desire or cupidity? (2) Whether hope is in the apprehensive, or in the appetitive faculty? (3) Whether hope is in dumb animals? (4) Whether despair is contrary to hope? (5) Whether experience is a cause of hope? (6) Whether hope abounds in young men and drunkards? (7) Concerning the order of hope to love; (8) Whether hope conduces to action?

FIRST ARTICLE

Whether Hope Is the Same As Desii. or Cupidity?

We proceed thus to the First Article:—

Objection 1. It would seem that hope is the same as desire or cupidity. Because hope is reckoned as one of the four principal passions. But Augustine in setting down the four principal passions puts cupidity in the place of hope (*De Civ. Dei* xiv. 3, 7). Therefore hope is the same as cupidity or desire.

Obj. 2. Further, passions differ according to their objects. But the object of hope is the same as the object of cupidity or desire, viz., the future good. Therefore hope is the same as cupidity or desire.

Obj. 3. If it be said that hope, in addition to desire, denotes the possibility of obtaining the future good; on the contrary, whatever is accidental to the object does not make a different species of passion. But possibility of acquisition is accidental to a future good, which is the object of cupidity or desire, and of hope. Therefore hope does not differ specifically from desire or cupidity.

On the contrary, To different powers belong different species of passions. But hope

is in the irascible power; whereas desire or cupidity is in the concupiscible. Therefore hope differs specifically from desire or cupidity.

I answer that, The species of a passion is taken from the object. Now, in the object of hope, we may note four conditions. First, that it is something good; since, properly speaking, hope regards only the good; in this respect, hope differs from fear, which regards evil.— Secondly, that it is future; for hope does not regard that which is present and already possessed: in this respect, hope differs from joy which regards a present good.—Thirdly, that it must be something arduous and difficult to obtain, for we do not speak of any one hoping for trifles, which are in one's power to have at any time: in this respect, hope differs from desire or cupidity, which regards the future good absolutely: wherefore it belongs to the concupiscible, while hope belongs to the irascible faculty.—Fourthly, that this difficult thing is something possible to obtain: for one does not hope for that which one cannot get at all: and, in this respect, hope differs from despair. It is therefore evident that hope differs from desire, as the irascible passions differ from the concupiscible. For this reason, moreover, hope presupposes desire: just as all irascible passions presuppose the passions of the concupiscible faculty, as stated above (Q. 25, A. 1).

Rely Obj. 1. Augustine mentions desire instead of hope, because each regards future good; and because the good which is not arduous is reckoned as nothing: thus implying that desire seems to tend chiefly to the arduous good, to which hope tends likewise.

Reply Obj. 2. The object of hope is the future good considered, not absolutely, but as arduous and difficult of attainment, as stated above.

* Cornelius Celsus.

Reply Obj. 3. The object of hope adds not only possibility to the object of desire, but also difficulty: and this makes hope belong to another power, viz., the irascible, which regards something difficult, as stated in the First Part (Q. 81, A. 2). Moreover, possibility and impossibility are not altogether accidental to the object of the appetitive power: because the appetite is a principle of movement; and nothing is moved to anything except under the aspect of being possible; for no one is moved to that which he reckons impossible to get. Consequently hope differs from despair according to the difference of possible and impossible.

SECOND ARTICLE

Whether Hope Is in the Apprehensive or in the Appetitive Power?

We proceed thus to the Second Article:—

Objection 1. It would seem that hope belongs to the cognitive power. Because hope, seemingly, is a kind of awaiting; for the Apostle says (Rom. viii. 25): *If we hope for that which we see not; we wait for it with patience.* But awaiting seems to belong to the cognitive power, which we exercise by *looking out.* Therefore hope belongs to the cognitive power.

Obj. 2. Further, apparently hope is the same as confidence; hence when a man hopes he is said to be confident, as though to hope and to be confident were the same thing. But confidence, like faith, seems to belong to the cognitive power. Therefore hope does too.

Obj. 3. Further, certainty is a property of the cognitive power. But certainty is ascribed to hope. Therefore hope belongs to the cognitive power.

On the contrary, Hope regards good, as stated above (A. 1). Now good, as such, is not the object of the cognitive, but of the appetitive power. Therefore hope belongs, not to the cognitive, but to the appetitive power.

I answer that, Since hope denotes a certain stretching out of the appetite towards good, it evidently belongs to the appetitive power; since movement towards things belongs properly to the appetite: whereas the action of the cognitive power is accomplished not by the movement of the knower towards things, but rather according as the things known are in the knower. But since the cognitive power moves the appetite, by presenting its object to it; there arise in the appetite various movements according to various aspects of the apprehended object. For the apprehension of good gives rise to one kind of movement in the appetite, while the apprehension of evil gives rise to another: in like manner various movements arise from the apprehension of something present and of something future; of something considered absolutely, and of something considered as arduous; of something possible, and of something impossible. And accordingly hope is a movement of the appetitive power ensuing from the apprehension of a future good, difficult but possible to obtain; namely, a stretching forth of the appetite to such a good.

Reply Obj. 1. Since hope regards a possible good, there arises in man a twofold movement of hope; for a thing may be possible to him in two ways, viz., by his own power, or by another's. Accordingly when a man hopes to obtain something by his own power, he is not said to wait for it, but simply to hope for it. But, properly speaking, he is said to await that which he hopes to get by another's help as though to await (*exspectare*) implied keeping one's eyes on another (*ex alio spectare*), in so far as the apprehensive power, by going ahead, not only keeps its eye on the good which man intends to get, but also on the thing by whose power he hopes to get it; according to Ecclus. li. 10; *I looked for the succor of men.* Wherefore the movement of hope is sometimes called expectation, on account of the preceding inspection of the cognitive power.

Reply Obj. 2. When a man desires a thing and reckons that he can get it, he believes that he can get it, he believes that he will get it; and from this belief which precedes in the cognitive power, the ensuing movement in the appetite is called confidence. Because the movement of the appetite takes its name from the knowledge that precedes it, as an effect from a cause which is better known; for the apprehensive power knows its own act better than that of the appetite.

Reply Obj. 3. Certainty is ascribed to the movement, not only of the sensitive, but also of the natural appetite; thus we say that a stone is certain to tend downwards. This is owing to the inerrancy which the movement of the sensitive or even natural appetite derives from the certainty of the knowledge that precedes it.

THIRD ARTICLE

Whether Hope Is in Dumb Animals?

We proceed thus to the Third Article:—

Objection 1. It would seem that there is no hope in dumb animals. Because hope is for some future good, as Damascene says (*De Fide Orthod.* ii. 12). But knowledge of the future is not in the competency of dumb animals, whose knowledge is confined to the senses and does not extend to the future. Therefore there is no hope in dumb animals.

Obj. 2. Further, the object of hope is a future good, possible of attainment. But possi·

ble and impossible are differences of the true and the false, which are only in the mind, as the Philosopher states (*Metaph*. vi. 4). Therefore there is no hope in dumb animals, since they have no mind.

Obj. 3. Further, Augustine says (*Gen. ad lit.* ix. 14) that *animals are moved by the things that they see*. But hope is of things unseen: *for what a man seeth, why doth he hope for?* (Rom. viii. 24). Therefore there is no hope in dumb animals.

On the contrary, Hope is an irascible passion. But the irascible faculty is in dumb animals. Therefore hope is also.

I answer that, The internal passions of animals can be gathered from their outward movements: from which it is clear that hope is in dumb animals. For if a dog see a hare, or a hawk see a bird, too far off, it makes no movement towards it, as having no hope to catch it: whereas, if it be near, it makes a movement towards it, as being in hopes of catching it. Because, as stated above (Q. I, A. 2; Q. 26, A. 1; Q. 35, A. 1), the sensitive appetite of dumb animals, and likewise the natural appetite of insensible things, result from the apprehension of an intellect, just as the appetite of the intellectual nature, which is called the will. But there is a difference, in that the will is moved by an apprehension of the intellect in the same subject; whereas the movement of the natural appetite results from the apprehension of the separate Intellect, Who is the Author of nature; as does also the sensitive appetite of dumb animals, who act from a certain natural instinct. Consequently, in the actions of irrational animals and of other natural things, we observe a procedure which is similar to that which we observe in the actions of art: and in this way hope and despair are in dumb animals.

Reply Obj. 1. Although dumb animals do not know the future, yet an animal is moved by its natural instinct to something future, as though it foresaw the future. Because this instinct is planted in them by the Divine Intellect that foresees the future.

Reply Obj. 2. The object of hope is not the possible as differentiating the true, for thus the possible ensues from the relation of a predicate to a subject. The object of hope is the possible as compared to a power. For such is the division of the possible given in *Metaph*. v. 12, *i.e.*, into the two kinds we have just mentioned.

Reply Obj. 3. Although the thing which is future does not come under the object of sight; nevertheless through seeing something present, an animal's appetite is moved to seek or avoid something future.

Whether Despair Is Contrary to Hope?

We proceed thus to the Fourth Article:—

Objection 1. It would seem that despair is not contrary to hope. Because *to one thing there is one contrary* (*Metaph*. x. 5). But fear is contrary to hope. Therefore despair is not contrary to hope.

Obj. 2. Further, contraries seem to bear on the same thing. But hope and despair do not bear on the same thing: since hope regards the good, whereas despair arises from some evil that is in the way of obtaining good. Therefore hope is not contrary to despair.

Obj. 3. Further, movement is contrary to movement; while repose is in opposition to movement as a privation thereof. But despair seems to imply immobility rather than movement. Therefore it is not contrary to hope, which implies movement of stretching out towards the hoped-for good.

On the contrary, The very name of despair (*desperatio*) implies that it is contrary to hope (*spes*).

I answer that, As stated above (Q. 23, A. 2), there is a twofold contrariety of movements. One is in respect of approach to contrary terms: and this contrariety alone is to be found in the concupiscible passions, for instance between love and hatred. The other is according to approach and withdrawal with regard to the same term; and is to be found in the irascible passions, as stated above (*loc. cit*.). Now the object of hope, which is the arduous good, has the character of a principle of attraction, if it be considered in the light of something attainable; and thus hope tends thereto, for it denotes a kind of approach. But in so far as it is considered as unobtainable, it has the character of a principle of repulsion, because, as stated in *Ethic*. iii. 3, *when men come to an impossibility they disperse*. And this is how despair stands in regard to this object, wherefore it implies a movement of withdrawal: and consequently it is contrary to hope, as withdrawal is to approach.

Reply Obj. 1. Fear is contrary to hope, because their objects, *i.e.* good and evil, are contrary: for this contrariety is found in the irascible passions, according as they ensue from the passions of the concupiscible. But despair is contrary to hope, only by contrariety of approach and withdrawal.

Reply Obj. 2. Despair does not regard evil as such; sometimes, however, it regards evil accidentally, as making the difficult good impossible to obtain. But it can arise from the mere excess of good.

Reply Obj. 3. Despair implies not only privation of hope, but also a recoil from the thing desired, by reason of its being esteemed impossible to get. Hence despair, like hope, presupposes desire; because we neither hope for nor despair of that which we do not desire to have. For this reason, too, each of them regards the good, which is the object of desire.

FIFTH ARTICLE

Whether Experience Is a Cause of Hope?

We proceed thus to the Fifth Article:—

Objection 1. It would seem that experience is not a cause of hope. Because experience belongs to the cognitive power; wherefore the Philosopher says (*Ethic.* ii. 1) that *intellectual virtue needs experience and time.* But hope is not in the cognitive power, but in the appetite, as stated above (A. 2). Therefore experience is not a cause of hope.

Obj. 2. Further, the Philosopher says (*Rhet.* ii. 13) that *the old are slow to hope, on account of their experience;* whence it seems to follow that experience causes want of hope. But the same cause is not productive of opposites. Therefore experience is not a cause of hope.

Obj. 3. Further, the Philosopher says (*De Cælo* ii 5) that *to have something to say about everything, without leaving anything out, is sometimes a proof of folly.* But to attempt everything seems to point to great hopes; while folly arises from inexperience. Therefore inexperience, rather than experience, seems to be a cause of hope.

On the contrary, The Philosopher says (*Ethic.* iii 8) *some are hopeful, through having been victorious often and over many opponents:* which seems to pertain to experience. Therefore experience is a cause of hope.

I answer that, As stated above (A. 1), the object of hope is a future good, difficult but possible to obtain. Consequently a thing may be a cause of hope, either because it makes something possible to a man: or because it makes him think something possible. In the first way hope is caused by everything that increases a man's power; *e.g.* riches, strength, and, among others, experience: since by experience man acquires the faculty of doing something easily, and the result of this is hope. Wherefore Vegetius says (*De Re Milit.* i): *No one fears to do that which he is sure of having learned well.*

In the second way, hope is caused by everything that makes man think that he can obtain something: and thus both teaching and persuasion may be a cause of hope. And then again experience is a cause of hope, in so far as it makes him reckon something possible, which before his experience he looked upon as impossible.—However, in this way, experience can cause a lack of hope: because just as it makes a man think possible what he had previously thought impossible; so, conversely, experience makes a man consider as impossible that which hitherto he had thought possible. Accordingly experience causes hope in two ways, despair in one way: and for this reason we may say rather that it causes hope.

Reply Obj. 1. Experience in matters pertaining to action not only produces knowledge; it also causes a certain habit, by reason of custom, which renders the action easier. Moreover, the intellectual virtue itself adds to the power of acting with ease: because it shows something to be possible; and thus is a cause of hope.

Reply Obj. 2. The old are wanting in hope because of their experience, in so far as experience makes them think something impossible. Hence he adds (*ibid.*) that *many evils have befallen them.*

Reply Obj. 3. Folly and inexperience can be a cause of hope accidentally as it were, by removing the knowledge which would help one to judge truly a thing to be impossible. Wherefore inexperience is a cause of hope, for the same reason as experience causes lack of hope.

SIXTH ARTICLE

Whether Hope Abounds in Young Men and Drunkards?

We proceed thus to the Sixth Article:—

Objection 1. It would seem that youth and drunkenness are not causes of hope. Because hope implies certainty and steadiness; so much so that it is compared to an anchor (Heb. vi. 19). But young men and drunkards are wanting in steadiness; since their minds are easily changed. Therefore youth and drunkenness are not causes of hope.

Obj. 2. Further, as stated above (A. 5), the cause of hope is chiefly whatever increases one's power. But youth and drunkenness are united to weakness. Therefore they are not causes of hope.

Obj. 3. Further, experience is a cause of hope, as stated above (A. 5). But youth lacks experience. Therefore it is not a cause of hope.

On the contrary, The Philosopher says (*Ethic.* iii. 8) that *drunken men are hopeful:* and (*Rhet.* ii. 12) that *the young are full of hope.*

I answer that, Youth is a cause of hope for three reasons, as the Philosopher states in *Rhet.* ii. *ibid.:* and these three reasons may be gathered from the three conditions of the good which is the object of hope—namely, that it is future, arduous and possible, as stated above

(A. 1). For youth has much of the future before it, and little of the past: and therefore since memory is of the past, and hope of the future, it has little to remember and lives very much in hope.—Again, youths, on account of the heat of their nature, are full of spirit; so that their heart expands: and it is owing to the heart being expanded that one tends to that which is arduous; wherefore youths are spirited and hopeful.—Likewise they who have not suffered defeat, nor ¹ ad experience of obstacles to their efforts, are prone to count a thing possible to them. Wherefore youths, through inexperience of obstacles and of their own shortcomings, easily count a thing possible; and consequently are of good hope. Two of these causes are also in those who are in drink—viz., heat and high spirits, on account of wine, and heedlessness of dangers and shortcomings.—For the same reason all foolish and thoughtless persons attempt everything and are full of hope.

Reply Obj. 1. Although youths and men in drink lack steadiness in reality, yet they are steady in their own estimation, for they think that they will steadily obtain that which they hope for.

In like manner, in reply to the Second Objection, we must observe that young people and men in drink are indeed unsteady in reality: but, in their own estimation, they are capable, for they know not their shortcomings.

Reply Obj. 3. Not only experience, but also lack of experience, is, in some way, a cause of hope, as explained above, (A. 5 *ad* 3).

SEVENTH ARTICLE

Whether Hope Is a Cause of Love?

We proceed thus to the Seventh Article:—

Objection 1. It would seem that hope is not a cause of love. Because, according to Augustine (*De Civ. Dei* xiv. 7, 9), love is the first of the soul's emotions. But hope is an emotion of the soul. Therefore love precedes hope, and consequently hope does not cause love.

Obj. 2. Further, desire precedes hope. But desire is caused by love, as stated above (Q. 25, A. 2). Therefore hope, too, follows love, and consequently is not its cause.

Obj. 3. Further, hope causes pleasure, as stated above (Q. 32, A. 3). But pleasure is only of the good that is loved. Therefore love precedes hope.

On the contrary, The gloss commenting on Matth. i. 2, *Abraham begot Isaac, and Isaac begot Jacob,* says, *i.e., faith begets hope, and hope begets charity.* But charity is love. Therefore love is caused by hope.

I answer that, Hope can regard two things. For it regards as its object, the good which one hopes for. But since the good we hope for is something difficult but possible to obtain; and since it happens sometimes that what is difficult becomes possible to us, not through ourselves but through others; hence it is that hope regards also that by which something becomes possible to us.

In so far, then, as hope regards the good we hope to get, it is caused by love: since we do not hope save for that which we desire and love. — But in so far as hope regards one through whom something becomes possible to us, love is caused by hope, and not vice versa. Because by the very fact that we hope that good will accrue to us through someone, we are moved towards him as to our own good; and thus we begin to love him. Whereas from the fact that we love someone we do not hope in him, except accidentally, that is, in so far as we think that he returns our love. Wherefore the fact of being loved by another makes us hope in him; but our love for him is caused by the hope we have in him.

Wherefore the Replies to the Objections are evident.

EIGHTH ARTICLE

Whether Hope Is a Help or a Hindrance to Action?

We proceed thus to the Eighth Article:—

Objection 1. It would seem that hope is not a help but a hindrance to action. Because hope implies security. But security begets negligence which hinders action. Therefore hope is a hindrance to action.

Obj. 2. Further, sorrow hinders action, as stated above (Q. 37, A. 3). But hope sometimes causes sorrow: for it is written (Prov. xiii. 12): *Hope that is deferred afflicteth the soul.* Therefore hope hinders action.

Obj. 3. Further, despair is contrary to hope, as stated above (A. 4). But despair, especially in matters of war, conduces to action; for it is written (2 Kings ii. 26), that *it is dangerous to drive people to despair.* Therefore hope has a contrary effect, namely, by hindering action.

On the contrary, It is written (1 Cor. ix. 10) that *he that plougheth should plough in hope . . . to receive fruit:* and the same applies to all other actions.

I answer that, Hope of its very nature is a help to action by making it more intense: and this for two reasons. First, by reason of its object, which is a good, difficult but possible. For the thought of its being difficult arouses our attention; while the thought that it is possible is no drag on our effort. Hence it follows that by reason of hope man is intent on his action. Secondly, on account of its effect. Because hope, as stated above (Q. 32, A. 3), causes pleasure; which is a help to action, as stated above (Q. 33, A. 4). Therefore hope is conducive to action.

Reply Obj. 1. Hope regards a good to be obtained; security regards an evil to be avoided. Wherefore security seems to be contrary to fear rather than to belong to hope. Yet security does not beget negligence, save in so far as it lessens the idea of difficulty: whereby it also lessens the character of hope: for the things in which a man fears no hindrance, are no longer looked upon as difficult.

Reply Obj. 2. Hope of itself causes pleasure; it is by accident that it causes sorrow, as stated above (Q. 32, A. 3 *ad* 2).

Reply Obj. 3. Despair threatens danger in war, on account of a certain hope that attaches to it. For they who despair of flight, strive less to fly, but hope to avenge their death: and therefore in this hope they fight the more bravely, and consequently prove dangerous to the foe.

QUESTION 41

Of Fear, in Itself

(In Four Articles)

WE must now consider, in the first place, fear; and, secondly, daring. With regard to fear, four things must be considered: (1) Fear, in itself; (2) Its object; (3) Its cause; (4) Its effect. Under the first head there are four points of inquiry: (1) Whether fear is a passion of the soul? (2) Whether fear is a special passion? (3) Whether there is a natural fear? (4) Of the species of fear.

FIRST ARTICLE

Whether Fear Is a Passion of the Soul?

We proceed thus to the First Article:—

Objection 1. It would seem that fear is not a passion of the soul. For Damascene says (*De Fide Orthod.* iii. 23) that *fear is a power, by way of συϭτολή, — i.e., of contraction — desirous of vindicating nature.* But no virtue is a passion, as is proved in *Ethic.* ii. 5. Therefore fear is not a passion.

Obj. 2. Further, every passion is an effect due to the presence of an agent. But fear is not of something present, but of something future, as Damascene declares (*De Fide Orthod.* ii. 12). Therefore fear is not a passion.

Obj. 3. Further, every passion of the soul is a movement of the sensitive appetite, in consequence of an apprehension of the senses. But sense apprehends, not the future but the present. Since, then, fear is of future evil, it seems that it is not a passion of the soul.

On the contrary, Augustine (*De Civ. Dei* xiv. 5 *sqq.*) reckons fear among the other passions of the soul.

I answer that, Among the other passions of the soul, after sorrow, fear chiefly has the character of passion. For as we have stated above (Q. 22), the notion of passion implies first of all a movement of a passive power— *i.e.,* of a power whose object is compared to it as its active principle: since passion is the effect of an agent. In this way, both *to feel* and *to understand* are passions. Secondly, more properly speaking, passion is a movement of the appetitive power; and more properly still, it is a movement of an appetitive power that has a bodily organ, such movement being accompanied by a bodily transmutation. And, again, most properly those movements are called passions, which imply some deterioration. Now it is evident that fear, since it regards evil, belongs to the appetitive power, which of itself regards good and evil. Moreover, it belongs to the sensitive appetite: for it is accompanied by a certain transmutation—*i.e.,* contraction—as Damascene says (*cf. Obj.* 1). Again, it implies relation to evil as overcoming, so to speak, some particular good. Wherefore it has most properly the character of passion; less, however, than sorrow, which regards the present evil: because fear regards future evil, which is not so strong a motive as present evil.

Reply Obj. 1. Virtue denotes a principle of action: wherefore, in so far as the interior movements of the appetitive faculty are principles of external action, they are called virtues. But the Philosopher denies that passion is a virtue by way of habit.

Reply Obj. 2. Just as the passion of a natural body is due to the bodily presence of an agent, so is the passion of the soul due to the agent being present to the soul, although neither corporally nor really present: that is to say, in so far as the evil which is really future, is present in the apprehension of the soul.

Reply Obj. 3. The senses do not apprehend the future: but from apprehending the present, an animal is moved by natural instinct to hope for a future good, or to fear a future evil.

SECOND ARTICLE

Whether Fear Is a Special Passion?

We proceed thus to the Second Article:—

Objection 1. It would seem that fear is not a special passion. For Augustine says (QQ. 83, qu. 33) that *the man who is not distraught by fear, is neither harassed by desire, nor wounded by sickness*—i.e., sorrow—*nor tossed about in transports of empty joys*. Wherefore it seems that, if fear be set aside, all the other passions are removed. Therefore fear is not a special but a general passion.

Obj. 2. Further, the Philosopher says (*Ethic.* vi. 2) that *pursuit and avoidance in the appetite are what affirmation and denial are in the intellect*. But denial is nothing special in the intellect, as neither is affirmation, but something common to many. Therefore neither is avoidance anything special in the appetite. But fear is nothing but a kind of avoidance of evil. Therefore it is not a special passion.

Obj. 3. Further, if fear were a special passion, it would be chiefly in the irascible part. But fear is also in the concupiscible: since the Philosopher says (*Rhet.* ii. 5) that *fear is a kind of sorrow;* and Damascene says (*De Fide Orthod.* iii. 23) that fear is *a power of desire*: and both sorrow and desire are in the concupiscible faculty, as stated above (Q. 23, A. 4). Therefore fear is not a special passion, since it belongs to different powers.

On the contrary, Fear is condivided with the other passions of the soul, as is clear from Damascene (*De Fide Orthod.* ii. 12, 15).

I answer that, The passions of the soul derive their species from their objects: hence that is a special passion, which has a special object. Now fear has a special object, as hope has. For just as the object of hope is a future good, difficult but possible to obtain; so the object of fear is a future evil, difficult and irresistible. Consequently fear is a special passion of the soul.

Reply Obj. 1. All the passions of the soul arise from one source, viz., love, wherein they are connected with one another. By reason of this connection, when fear is put aside, the other passions of the soul are dispersed; not, however, as though it were a general passion.

Reply Obj. 2. Not every avoidance in the appetite is fear, but avoidance of a special object, as stated. Wherefore, though avoidance be something common, yet fear is a special passion.

Reply Obj. 3. Fear is nowise in the concupiscible: for it regards evil, not absolutely, but as difficult or arduous, so as to be almost unavoidable. But since the irascible passions arise from the passions of the concupiscible

faculty, and terminate therein, as stated above (Q. 25, A. 1); hence it is that what belongs to the concupiscible is ascribed to fear. For fear is called sorrow, in so far as the object of fear causes sorrow when present: wherefore the Philosopher says (*loc. cit.*) that fear arises *from the representation of a future evil which is either corruptive or painful.* In like manner desire is ascribed by Damascene to fear, because just as hope arises from the desire of good, so fear arises from avoidance of evil; while avoidance of evil arises from the desire of good, as is evident from what has been said above (Q. 25, A. 2; Q. 29, A. 2; Q. 36, A. 2).

THIRD ARTICLE

Whether There Is a Natural Fear?

We proceed thus to the Third Article:—

Objection 1. It would seem that there is a natural fear. For Damascene says (*De Fide Orthod.* iii. 23) that *there is a natural fear, through the soul refusing to be severed from the body.*

Obj. 2. Further, fear arises from love, as stated above (A. 2 *ad* 1). But there is a natural love, as Dionysius states (*Div. Nom.* iv). Therefore there is also a natural fear.

Obj. 3. Further, fear is opposed to hope, as stated above (Q. 40, A. 4 *ad* 1). But there is a hope of nature, as is evident from Rom. iv. 18, where it is said of Abraham that *against hope* of nature, *he believed in hope* of grace. Therefore there is also a fear of nature.

On the contrary, That which is natural is common to things animate and inanimate. But fear is not in things inanimate. Therefore there is no natural fear.

I answer that, A movement is said to be natural, because nature inclines thereto. Now this happens in two ways. First, so that it is entirely accomplished by nature, without any operation of the apprehensive faculty: thus to have an upward movement is natural to fire, and to grow is the natural movement of animals and plants.—Secondly, a movement is said to be natural, if nature inclines thereto, though it be accomplished by the apprehensive faculty alone: since, as stated above (Q. 10, A. 1), the movements of the cognitive and appetitive faculties are reducible to nature as to their first principle. In this way, even the acts of the apprehensive power, such as understanding, feeling, and remembering, as well as the movements of the animal appetite, are sometimes said to be natural.

And in this sense we may say that there is a natural fear; and it is distinguished from non-natural fear, by reason of the diversity of its object. For, as the Philosopher says

(*Rhet*. ii. 5), there is a fear of *corruptive evil*, which nature shrinks from on account of its natural desire to exist; and such fear is said to be natural. Again, there is a fear of *painful evil*, which is repugnant not to nature, but to the desire of the appetite; and such fear is not natural. In this sense we have stated above (Q. 26, A. 1 ; Q. 30, A. 3 ; Q. 31, A. 7) that love, desire, and pleasure are divisible into natural and non-natural.

But in the first sense of the word *natural*, we must observe that certain passions of the soul are sometimes said to be natural, as love, desire, and hope; whereas the others cannot be called natural. The reason of this is because love and hatred, desire and avoidance, imply a certain inclination to pursue what is good or to avoid what is evil; which inclination is to be found in the natural appetite also. Consequently there is a natural love; while we may also speak of desire and hope as being even in natural things devoid of knowledge.—On the other hand the other passions of the soul denote certain movements, whereto the natural inclination is nowise sufficient. This is due either to the fact that perception or knowledge is essential to these passions (thus we have said, Q. 31, AA. 1, 3 ; Q. 35, A. 1, that apprehension is a necessary condition of pleasure and sorrow), wherefore things devoid of knowledge cannot be said to take pleasure or to be sorrowful: or else it is because such like movements are contrary to the very nature of natural inclination: for instance, despair flies from good on account of some difficulty; and fear shrinks from repelling a contrary evil; both of which are contrary to the inclination of nature. Wherefore such like passions are in no way ascribed to inanimate beings.

Thus the Replies to the Objections are evident.

FOURTH ARTICLE

Whether the Species of Fear Are Suitably Assigned?

We proceed thus to the Fourth Article:—

Objection 1. It would seem that six species of fear are unsuitably assigned by Damascene (*De Fide Orthod.* ii. 15) ; namely, *laziness, shamefacedness, shame, amazement, stupor, and anxiety*. Because, as the Philosopher says (*Rhet.* ii. 5), *fear regards a saddening evil*. Therefore the species of fear should correspond to the species of sorrow. Now there are four species of sorrow, as stated above (Q. 35, A. 8). Therefore there should only be four species of fear corresponding to them.

Obj. 2. Further, that which consists in an action of our own is in our power. But fear regards an evil that surpasses our power, as

* Nemesius, *De Nat. Hom.* xx.   † Nemesius.

stated above (A. 2). Therefore laziness, shamefacedness, and shame, which regard our own actions, should not be reckoned as species of fear.

Obj. 3. Further, fear is of the future, as stated above (AA. 1, 2). But *shame regards a disgraceful deed already done*, as Gregory of Nyssa* says. Therefore shame is not a species of fear.

Obj. 4. Further, fear is only of evil. But amazement and stupor regard great and unwonted things, whether good or evil. Therefore amazement and stupor are not species of fear.

Obj. 5. Further, Philosophers have been led by amazement to seek the truth, as stated at the beginning of *Metaph*. But fear leads to flight rather than to search. Therefore amazement is not a species of fear.

On the contrary suffices the authority of Damascene and Gregory of Nyssa† (*cf. Obj.* 1, 3).

I answer that, As stated above (A. 2), fear regards a future evil which surpasses the power of him that fears, so that it is irresistible. Now man's evil, like his good, may be considered either in his action or in external things. In his action he has a twofold evil to fear. First, there is the toil that burdens his nature: and hence arises *laziness*, as when a man shrinks from work for fear of too much toil.—Secondly, there is the disgrace which damages him in the opinion of others. And thus, if disgrace is feared in a deed that is yet to be done, there is *shamefacedness*; if, however, it be in a deed already done, there is *shame*.

On the other hand, the evil that consists in external things may surpass man's faculty of resistance in three ways. First by reason of its magnitude; when, that is to say, a man considers some great evil the outcome of which he is unable to gauge: and then there is *amazement*.—Secondly, by reason of its being unwonted; because, to wit, some unwonted evil arises before us, and on that account is great in our estimation: and then there is *stupor*, which is caused by the representation of something unwonted.—Thirdly, by reason of its being unforeseen; because, to wit, it cannot be foreseen: thus future misfortunes are feared, and fear of this kind is called *anxiety*.

Reply Obj. 1. Those species of sorrow given above are not derived from the diversity of objects, but from the diversity of effects, and for certain special reasons. Consequently there is no need for those species of sorrow to correspond with these species of fear, which are derived from the proper division of the object of fear itself.

Reply Obj. 2. A deed considered as being

actually done, is in the power of the doer. But it is possible to take into consideration something connected with the deed, and surpassing the faculty of the doer, for which reason he shrinks from the deed. It is in this sense that laziness, shamefacedness, and shame are reckoned as species of fear.

Reply Obj. 3. The past deed may be the occasion of fear of future reproach or disgrace: and in this sense shame is a species of fear.

Reply Obj. 4. Not every amazement and stupor are species of fear, but that amazement which is caused by a great evil, and that stupor which arises from an unwonted evil.—Or else we may say that, just as laziness shrinks from the toil of external work, so amazement and stupor shrink from the difficulty of considering a great and unwonted thing, whether good or evil: so that amazement and stupor stand in relation to the act of the intellect, as laziness does to external work.

Reply Obj. 5. He who is amazed shrinks at present from forming a judgment of that which amazes him, fearing to fall short of the truth, but inquires afterwards: whereas he who is overcome by stupor fears both to judge at present, and to inquire afterwards. Wherefore amazement is a beginning of philosophical research: whereas stupor is a hindrance thereto.

QUESTION 42

Of the Object of Fear

(In Six Articles)

WE must now consider the object of fear: under which head there are six points of inquiry: (1) Whether good or evil is the object of fear? (2) Whether evil of nature is the object of fear? (3) Whether the evil of sin is an object of fear? (4) Whether fear itself can be feared? (5) Whether sudden things are especially feared? (6) Whether those things are more feared against which there is no remedy.

FIRST ARTICLE

Whether the Object of Fear Is Good or Evil?

We proceed thus to the First Article:—

Objection 1. It would seem that good is the object of fear. For Augustine says (QQ. 83, qu. 33) that *we fear nothing save to lose what we love and possess, or not to obtain that which we hope for.* But that which we love is good. Therefore fear regards good as its proper object.

Obj. 2. Further, the Philosopher says (*Rhet.* ii. 5) that *power and to be above another is a thing to be feared.* But this is a good thing. Therefore good is the object of fear.

Obj. 3. Further, there can be no evil in God. But we are commanded to fear God, according to Ps. xxxiii. 10: *Fear the Lord, all ye saints.* Therefore even the good is an object of fear.

On the contrary, Damascene says (*De Fide Orthod.* ii. 12) that fear is of future evil.

I answer that, Fear is a movement of the appetitive power. Now it belongs to the appetitive power to pursue and to avoid, as stated in *Ethic.* vi. 2: and pursuit is of good, while avoidance is of evil. Consequently whatever movement of the appetitive power implies pursuit, has some good for its object: and whatever movement implies avoidance, has an evil for its object. Wherefore, since fear implies an avoidance, in the first place and of its very nature it regards evil as its proper object.

It can, however, regard good also, in so far as referable to evil. This can be in two ways. In one way, inasmuch as an evil causes privation of good. Now a thing is evil from the very fact that it is a privation of some good. Wherefore, since evil is shunned because it is evil, it follows that it is shunned because it deprives one of the good that one pursues through love thereof. And in this sense Augustine says that there is no cause for fear, save loss of the good we love.

In another way, good stands related to evil as its cause: in so far as some good can by its power bring harm to the good we love: and so, just as hope, as stated above (Q. 40, A. 7), regards two things, namely, the good to which it tends, and the thing through which there is a hope of obtaining the desired good; so also does fear regard two things, namely, the evil from which it shrinks, and that good which, by its power, can inflict that evil. In this way God is feared by man, inasmuch as He can inflict punishment, spiritual or corporal. In this way, too, we fear the power of man; especially when it has been thwarted, or when it is unjust, because then it is more likely to do us a harm.

In like manner one fears *to be over another,* i.e., to lean on another, so that it is in his power to do us a harm: thus a man fears another, who knows him to be guilty of a crime, lest he reveal it to others.

This suffices for the Replies to the Objections.

SECOND ARTICLE

Whether Evil of Nature Is an Object of Fear?

We proceed thus to the Second Article:—

Objection 1. It would seem that evil of nature is not an object of fear. For the Philosopher says (*Rhet.* ii. 5) that *fear makes us take counsel.* But we do not take counsel about things which happen naturally, as stated in *Ethic.* iii. 3. Therefore evil of nature is not an object of fear.

Obj. 2. Further, natural defects such as death and the like are always threatening man. If therefore such like evils were an object of fear, man would needs be always in fear.

Obj. 3. Further, nature does not move to contraries. But evil of nature is an effect of nature. Therefore if a man shrinks from such like evils through fear thereof, this is not an effect of nature. Therefore natural fear is not of the evil of nature; and yet it seems that it should be.

On the contrary, The Philosopher says (*Ethic.* iii. 6) that *the most terrible of all things is death,* which is an evil of nature.

I answer that, As the Philosopher says (*Rhet.* ii. 5), fear is caused by the *imagination of a future evil which is either corruptive or painful.* Now just as a painful evil is that which is contrary to the will, so a corruptive evil is that which is contrary to nature: and this is the evil of nature. Consequently evil of nature can be the object of fear.

But it must be observed that evil of nature sometimes arises from a natural cause; and then it is called evil of nature, not merely from being a privation of the good of nature, but also from being an effect of nature; such are natural death and other like defects. But sometimes evil of nature arises from a nonnatural cause; such as violent death inflicted by an assailant. In either case evil of nature is feared to a certain extent, and to a certain extent not. For since fear arises *from the imagination of future evil,* as the Philosopher says (*loc. cit.*), whatever removes the imagination of the future evil, removes fear also. Now it may happen in two ways that an evil may not appear as about to be. First, through being remote and far off: for, on account of the distance, such a thing is considered as though it were not to be. Hence we either do not fear it, or fear it but little; for, as the Philosopher says (*Rhet.* ii. 5), *we do not fear things that are very far off; since all know that they shall die, but as death is not near, they heed it not.*—Secondly, a future evil is considered as though it were not to be, on account of its being inevitable, wherefore we look upon it as already present. Hence the Philosopher says (*Rhet.* ii. 5) that *those who are already on the scaffold, are not afraid,* seeing that they are on the very point of a death from which there is no escape; *but in order that a man be afraid, there must be some hope of escape for him.*

Consequently evil of nature is not feared if it be not apprehended as future: but if evil of nature, that is corruptive, be apprehended as near at hand, and yet with some hope of escape, then it will be feared.

Reply Obj. 1. The evil of nature sometimes is not an effect of nature, as stated above. But in so far as it is an effect of nature, although it may be impossible to avoid it entirely, yet it may be possible to delay it. And with this hope one may take counsel about avoiding it.

Reply Obj. 2. Although evil of nature ever threatens, yet it does not always threaten from near at hand: and consequently it is not always feared.

Reply Obj. 3. Death and other defects of nature are the effects of the common nature; and yet the individual nature rebels against them as far as it can. Accordingly, from the inclination of the individual nature arise pain and sorrow for such like evils, when present; fear when threatening in the future.

THIRD ARTICLE

Whether the Evil of Sin Is an Object of Fear?

We proceed thus to the Third Article:—

Objection 1. It would seem that the evil of sin can be an object of fear. For Augustine says on the canonical Epistle of John (*Tract.* ix), that *by chaste fear man fears to be severed from God.* Now nothing but sin severs us from God; according to Isa. lix. 2: *Your iniquities have divided between you and your God.* Therefore the evil of sin can be an object of fear.

Obj. 2. Further, Cicero says (*Quæst. Tusc.* iv. 4, 6) that *we fear when they are yet to come, those things which give us pain when they are present.* But it is possible for one to be pained or sorrowful on account of the evil of sin. Therefore one can also fear the evil of sin.

Obj. 3. Further, hope is contrary to fear. But the good of virtue can be the object of hope, as the Philosopher declares (*Ethic.* ix. 4): and the Apostle says (Gal. v. 10): *I have confidence in you in the Lord, that you will not be of another mind.* Therefore fear can regard evil of sin.

Obj. 4. Further, shame is a kind of fear, as stated above (Q. 41, A. 4). But shame regards a disgraceful deed, which is an evil of sin. Therefore fear does so likewise.

On the contrary, The Philosopher says (*Rhet.* ii. 5) that *not all evils are feared, for instance that someone be unjust or slow.*

I answer that, As stated above (Q. 40, A. 1; Q. 41, A. 2), as the object of hope is a future good difficult but possible to obtain, so the object of fear is a future evil, arduous and not to be easily avoided. From this we may gather that whatever is entirely subject to our power and will, is not an object of fear; and that nothing gives rise to fear save what is due to an external cause. Now human will is the proper cause of the evil of sin: and consequently evil of sin, properly speaking, is not an object of fear.

But since the human will may be inclined to sin by an extrinsic cause; if this cause have a strong power of inclination, in that respect a man may fear the evil of sin, in so far as it arises from that extrinsic cause: as when he fears to dwell in the company of wicked men, lest he be led by them to sin. But, properly speaking, a man thus disposed, fears the being led astray rather than the sin considered in its proper nature, *i.e.,* as a voluntary act; for considered in this light it is not an object of fear to him.

Reply Obj. 1. Separation from God is a punishment resulting from sin: and every punishment is, in some way, due to an extrinsic cause.

Reply Obj. 2. Sorrow and fear agree in one point, since each regards evil: they differ, however, in two points. First, because sorrow is about present evil, whereas fear is future evil. Secondly, because sorrow, being in the concupiscible faculty, regards evil absolutely; wherefore it can be about any evil, great or small; whereas fear, being in the irascible part, regards evil with the addition of a certain arduousness or difficulty; which difficulty ceases in so far as a thing is subject to the will. Consequently not all things that give us pain when they are present, make us fear when they are yet to come, but only some things, namely, those that are difficult.

Reply Obj. 3. Hope is of good that is obtainable. Now one may obtain a good either of oneself, or through another: and so, hope may be of an act of virtue, which lies within our own power. On the other hand, fear is of an evil that does not lie in our own power: and consequently the evil which is feared is always from an extrinsic cause; while the good that is hoped for may be both from an intrinsic and from an extrinsic cause.

Reply Obj. 4. As stated above (Q. 41, A. 4 *ad* 2, 3), shame is not fear of the very act of sin, but of the disgrace or ignominy which arises therefrom, and which is due to an extrinsic cause.

FOURTH ARTICLE

Whether Fear Itself Can Be Feared?

We proceed thus to the Fourth Article:—

Objection 1. It would seem that fear cannot be feared. For whatever is feared, is prevented from being lost, through fear thereof: thus a man who fears to lose his health, keeps it, through fearing its loss. If therefore a man be afraid of fear, he will keep himself from fear by being afraid: which seems absurd.

Obj. 2. Further, fear is a kind of flight. But nothing flies from itself. Therefore fear cannot be the object of fear.

Obj. 3. Further, fear is about the future. But fear is present to him that fears. Therefore it cannot be the object of his fear.

On the contrary, A man can love his own love, and can grieve at his own sorrow. Therefore, in like manner, he can fear his own fear.

I answer that, As stated above (A. 3), nothing can be an object of fear, save what is due to an extrinsic cause; but not that which ensues from our own will. Now fear partly arises from an extrinsic cause, and is partly subject to the will. It is due to an extrinsic cause, in so far as it is a passion resulting from the imagination of an imminent evil. In this sense it is possible for fear to be the object of fear, *i.e.,* a man may fear lest he should be threatened by the necessity of fearing, through being assailed by some great evil.—It is subject to the will, in so far as the lower appetite obeys reason; wherefore man is able to drive fear away. In this sense fear cannot be the object of fear, as Augustine says (QQ. 83, qu. 33). Lest, however, anyone make use of his arguments, in order to prove that fear cannot at all be the object of fear, we must add a solution to the same.

Reply Obj. 1. Not every fear is identically the same; there are various fears according to the various objects of fear. Nothing, then, prevents a man from keeping himself from fearing one thing, by fearing another, so that the fear which he has preserves him from the fear which he has not.

Reply Obj. 2. Since fear of an imminent evil is not identical with the fear of an imminent evil; it does not follow that a thing flies from itself, or that it is the same flight in both cases.

Reply Obj. 3. On account of the various kinds of fear already alluded to (*ad* 2) a man's present fear may have a future fear for its object.

FIFTH ARTICLE

Whether Sudden Things Are Especially Feared?

We proceed thus to the Fifth Article:—

Objection 1. It would seem that unwonted

and sudden things are not especially feared. Because, as hope is about good things, so fear is about evil things. But experience conduces to the increase of hope in good things. Therefore it also adds to fear in evil things.

Obj. 2. Further, the Philosopher says (*Rhet.* ii. 5) that *those are feared most, not who are quick-tempered, but who are gentle and cunning.* Now it is clear that those who are quick-tempered are more subject to sudden emotions. Therefore sudden things are less to be feared.

Obj. 3. Further, we think less about things that happen suddenly. But the more we think about a thing, the more we fear it; hence the Philosopher says (*Ethic.* iii. 8) that *some appear to be courageous through ignorance, but as soon as they discover that the case is different from what they expected, they run away.* Therefore sudden things are feared less.

On the contrary, Augustine says (*Conf.* ii. 6): *Fear is startled at things unwonted and sudden, which endanger things beloved, and takes forethought for their safety.*

I answer that, As stated above (A. 3 ; Q. 41, A. 2), the object of fear is an imminent evil, which can be repelled, but with difficulty. Now this is due to one of two causes: to the greatness of the evil, or to the weakness of him that fears; while unwontedness and suddenness conduce to both of these causes. First, it helps an imminent evil to seem greater. Because all material things, whether good or evil, the more we consider them, the smaller they seem. Consequently, just as sorrow for a present evil is mitigated in course of time, as Cicero states (*De Quæst. Tusc.* iii. 30) ; so, too, fear of a future evil is diminished by thinking about it beforehand.—Secondly, unwontedness and suddenness increase the weakness of him that fears, in so far as they deprive him of the remedies with which he might otherwise provide himself to forestall the coming evil, were it not for the evil taking him by surprise.

Reply Obj. 1. The object of hope is a good that it is possible to obtain. Consequently whatever increases a man's power, is of a nature to increase hope, and, for the same reason, to diminish fear, since fear is about an evil which cannot be easily repelled. Since, therefore, experience increases a man's power of action, therefore, as it increases hope, so does it diminish fear.

Reply Obj. 2. Those who are quick-tempered do not hide their anger; wherefore the harm they do others is not so sudden, as not to be foreseen. On the other hand, those who are gentle or cunning hide their anger; wherefore the harm which may be impending from them, cannot be foreseen, but takes one by surprise.

For this reason the Philosopher says that such men are feared more than others.

Reply Obj. 3. Bodily good or evil, considered in itself, seems greater at first. The reason for this is that a thing is more obvious when seen in juxtaposition with its contrary. Hence, when a man passes unexpectedly from penury to wealth, he thinks more of his wealth on account of his previous poverty: while, on the other hand, the rich man who suddenly becomes poor, finds poverty all the more disagreeable. For this reason sudden evil is feared more, because it seems more to be evil. —However, it may happen through some accident that the greatness of some evil is hidden; for instance if the foe hides himself in ambush: and then it is true that evil inspires greater fear through being much thought about.

SIXTH ARTICLE

Whether Those Things Are More Feared, for Which There Is No Remedy?

We proceed thus to the Sixth Article:—

Objection 1. It would seem that those things are not more to be feared, for which there is no remedy. Because it is a condition of fear, that there be some hope of safety, as stated above (A. 2). But an evil that cannot be remedied leaves no hope of escape. Therefore such things are not feared at all.

Obj. 2. Further, there is no remedy for the evil of death: since, in the natural course of things, there is no return from death to life. And yet death is not the most feared of all things, as the Philosopher says (*Rhet.* ii. 5). Therefore those things are not feared most, for which there is no remedy.

Obj. 3. Further, the Philosopher says (*Ethic.* i. 6) that *a thing which lasts long is no better than that which lasts but one day: nor is that which lasts for ever any better than that which is not everlasting:* and the same applies to evil. But things that cannot be remedied seem to differ from other things, merely in the point of their lasting long or for ever. Consequently they are not therefore any worse or more to be feared.

On the contrary, the Philosopher says (*Rhet.* ii. 5) that *those things are most to be feared which when done wrong cannot be put right, . . . or for which there is no help, or which are not easy.*

I answer that, The object of fear is evil: consequently whatever tends to increase evil, conduces to the increase of fear. Now evil is increased not only in its species of evil, but also in respect of circumstances, as stated above (Q. 18, A. 3). And of all the circumstances, longlastingness, or even everlastingness, seems to have the greatest bearing on the increase of evil. Because things that exist in time are measured, in a way, according to the duration of time: wherefore if it be an evil to suffer something for a certain length of time, we should reckon the evil doubled, if it be suffered for twice that length of time. And accordingly, to suffer the same thing for an infinite length of time, *i.e.*, for ever, implies, so to speak, an infinite increase. Now those evils which, after they have come, cannot be remedied at all, or at least not easily, are considered as lasting for ever or for a long time: for which reason they inspire the greatest fear.

Reply Obj. 1. Remedy for an evil is twofold. One, by which a future evil is warded off from coming. If such a remedy be removed, there is an end to hope and consequently to fear; wherefore we do not speak now of remedies of that kind. The other remedy is one by which an already present evil is removed: and of such a remedy we speak now.

Reply Obj. 2. Although death be an evil without remedy, yet, since it threatens not from near, it is not feared, as stated above (A. 2).

Reply Obj. 3. The Philosopher is speaking there of things that are good in themselves, *i.e.*, good specifically. And such like good is no better for lasting long or for ever: its goodness depends on its very nature.

QUESTION 43

Of the Cause of Fear

(In Two Articles)

WE must now consider the cause of fear: under which head there are two points of inquiry: (1) Whether love is the cause of fear? (2) Whether defect is the cause of fear?

FIRST ARTICLE

Whether Love Is the Cause of Fear?

We proceed thus to the First Article:—

Objection 1. It would seem that love is not the cause of fear. For that which leads to a thing is its cause. But *fear leads to the love of charity* as Augustine says on the canonical epistle of John (*Tract.* ix). Therefore fear is the cause of love, and not conversely.

Obj. 2. Further, the Philosopher says (*Rhet.* ii. 5) that *those are feared most from whom we dread the advent of some evil.* But the dread of evil being caused by someone, makes us hate rather than love him. Therefore fear is caused by hate rather than by love.

Obj. 3. Further, it has been stated above (Q. 42, A. 3) that those things which occur by our own doing are not fearful. But that which we do from love, is done from our inmost heart. Therefore fear is not caused by love.

On the contrary, Augustine says (QQ. 83, qu. 33): *There can be no doubt that there is no cause for fear save the loss of what we love, when we possess it, or the failure to obtain what we hope for.* Therefore all fear is caused by our loving something: and consequently love is the cause of fear.

I answer that, The objects of the soul's passions stand in relation thereto as the forms to things natural or artificial: because the passions of the soul take their species from their objects, as the aforesaid things do from their forms. Therefore, just as whatever is a cause of the form, is a cause of the thing constituted by that form, so whatever is a cause, in any way whatever, of the object, is a cause of the passion. Now a thing may be a cause of the object, either by way of efficient cause, or by way of material disposition. Thus the object of pleasure is good apprehended as suitable and conjoined: and its efficient cause is that which causes the conjunction, or the suitableness, or goodness, or apprehension of that good thing; while its cause by way of material disposition, is a habit or any sort of disposition by reason of which this conjoined good becomes suitable or is apprehended as such.

Accordingly, as to the matter in question, the object of fear is something reckoned as an evil to come, near at hand and difficult to avoid. Therefore that which can inflict such an evil, is the efficient cause of the object of fear, and, consequently, of fear itself. While that which renders a man so disposed that a thing is such an evil to him, is a cause of fear and of its object, by way of material disposition. And thus it is that love causes fear: since it is through his loving a certain good, that whatever deprives a man of that good is an evil to him, and that consequently he fears it as an evil.

Reply Obj. 1. As stated above (Q. 42, A. 1), fear, of itself and in the first place, regards the evil from which it recoils as being contrary to some loved good: and thus fear, of itself, is born of love.—But, in the second place, it regards the cause from which that evil ensues: so that sometimes, accidentally, fear gives rise to love; in so far as, for instance, through fear of God's punishments, man keeps His commandments, and thus begins to hope, while hope leads to love, as stated above (Q. 40, A. 7).

Reply Obj. 2. He, from whom evil is expected, is indeed hated at first; but afterwards, when once we begin to hope for good from him, we begin to love him. But the good, the contrary evil of which is feared, was loved from the beginning.

Reply Obj. 3. This argument is true of that which is the efficient cause of the evil to be feared: whereas love causes fear by way of material disposition, as stated above.

SECOND ARTICLE

Whether Defect Is the Cause of Fear?

We proceed thus to the Second Article:—

Objection 1. It would seem that defect is not a cause of fear. Because those who are in power are very much feared. But defect is contrary to power. Therefore defect is not a cause of fear.

Obj. 2. Further, the defect of those who are already being executed is extreme. But such like do not fear as stated in *Rhet.* ii. 5. Therefore defect is not a cause of fear.

Obj. 3. Further, contests arise from strength not from defect. But *those who contend fear those who contend with them (Rhet.* ii. 5). Therefore defect is not a cause of fear.

On the contrary, Contraries ensue from contrary causes. But *wealth, strength, a multitude of friends, and power drive fear away (Rhet.* ii. *ibid.).* Therefore fear is caused by lack of these.

I answer that, As stated above (A. 1), fear may be set down to a twofold cause: one is by way of a material disposition, on the part of him that fears; the other is by way of efficient cause, on the part of the person feared. As to the first then, some defect is, of itself, the cause of fear: for it is owing to some lack of power that one is unable easily to repulse a threatening evil. And yet, in order to cause fear, this defect must be according to a measure. For the defect which causes fear of a future evil, is less than the defect caused by evil present, which is the object of sorrow. And still greater would be the defect, if perception of the evil, or love of the good whose contrary is feared, were entirely absent.

But as to the second, power and strength are, of themselves, the cause of fear: because it is owing to the fact that the cause apprehended as harmful is powerful, that its effect cannot be repulsed. It may happen, however, in this respect, that some defect causes fear accidentally, in so far as owing to some defect someone wishes to hurt another; for instance, by reason of injustice, either because that other has already done him a harm, or because he fears to be harmed by him.

Reply Obj. 1. This argument is true of the cause of fear, on the part of the efficient cause.

Reply Obj. 2. Those who are already being executed, are actually suffering from a present evil; wherefore their defect exceeds the measure of fear.

Reply Obj. 3. Those who contend with one another are afraid, not on account of the power which enables them to contend: but on account of the lack of power, owing to which they are not confident of victory.

QUESTION 44

Of the Effects of Fear

(In Four Articles)

WE must now consider the effects of fear: under which head there are four points of inquiry: (1) Whether fear causes contraction? (2) Whether it makes men suitable for counsel? (3) Whether it makes one tremble? (4) Whether it hinders action?

FIRST ARTICLE

Whether Fear Causes Contraction?

We proceed thus to the First Article:—

Objection 1. It would seem that fear does not cause contraction. For when contraction takes place, the heat and vital spirits are withdrawn inwardly. But accumulation of heat and vital spirits in the interior parts of the body, dilates the heart unto endeavors of daring, as may be seen in those who are angered: while the contrary happens in those who are afraid. Therefore fear does not cause contraction.

Obj. 2. Further, when, as a result of contraction, the vital spirits and heat are accumulated in the interior parts, man cries out, as may be seen in those who are in pain. But those who fear utter nothing: on the contrary they lose their speech. Therefore fear does not cause contraction.

Obj. 3. Further, shame is a kind of fear, as stated above (Q. 41, A. 4). But *those who are ashamed blush,* as Cicero (*De Quæst. Tusc.* iv. 8), and the Philosopher (*Ethic.* iv. 9) observe. But blushing is an indication, not of contraction, but of the reverse. Therefore contraction is not an effect of fear.

On the contrary, Damascene says (*De Fide Orthod.* ii. 23) that *fear is a power according to* συστολή, i.e., contraction.

I answer that, As stated above (Q. 28, A. 5), in the passions of the soul, the formal element is the movement of the appetitive power, while the bodily transmutation is the material element. Both of these are mutually proportionate; and consequently the bodily transmutation assumes a resemblance to and the very nature of the appetitive movement. Now, as to the appetitive movement of the soul, fear implies a certain contraction: the reason of which is that fear arises from the imagination of some threatening evil which is difficult to repel, as stated above (Q. 41, A. 2). But that a thing be difficult to repel is due to lack of power, as stated above (Q. 43, A. 2): and the weaker a power is, the fewer the things to which it extends. Wherefore from the very imagination that causes fear there ensues a certain contraction in the appetite. Thus we observe in one who is dying that nature withdraws inwardly, on account of the lack of power: and again we see the inhabitants of a city, when seized with fear, leave the outskirts, and, as far as possible, make for the inner quarters. It is in resemblance to this contraction, which pertains to the appetite of the soul, that in fear a similar contraction of heat and vital spirits towards the inner parts takes place in regard to the body.

Reply Obj. 1. As the Philosopher says (*De Problem.* xxvii. 3), although in those who fear, the vital spirits recede from outer to the inner parts of the body, yet the movement of vital spirits is not the same in those who are angry and those who are afraid. For in those who are angry, by reason of the heat and subtlety of the vital spirits, which result from the craving for vengeance, the inward movement has an upward direction: wherefore the vital spirits and heat concentrate around the heart: the result being that an angry man is quick and brave in attacking.—But in those who are afraid, on account of the condensation caused by the cold, the vital spirits have a downward movement; the said cold being due to the imagined lack of power. Consequently the heat and vital spirits abandon the heart instead of concentrating around it: the result being that a man who is afraid is not quick to attack, but is more inclined to run away.

Reply Obj. 2. To everyone that is in pain, whether man or animal, it is natural to use all possible means of repelling the harmful thing that causes pain by its presence: thus we observe that animals, when in pain, attack with their jaws or with their horns. Now the greatest help for all purposes, in animals, is heat and vital spirits: wherefore when they are in pain, their nature stores up the heat and vital spirits within them, in order to make use thereof in repelling the harmful object. Hence the Philosopher says (*De Problem.* xxvii. 9) when the vital spirits and heat are concentrated together within, they require to find a vent in the voice: for which reason those who are in pain can scarcely refrain from crying aloud.—On the other hand, in those who are afraid, the internal heat and vital spirits move from the heart downwards, as stated above (*ad* 1): wherefore fear hinders speech which ensues from the emission of the vital spirits in an upward direction through the mouth: the result being that fear makes its subject speechless. For this reason, too, fear *makes its subject tremble,* as the Philosopher says (*De Problem.* xxvii. 1,6,7).

Reply Obj. 3. Mortal perils are contrary not only to the appetite of the soul, but also to nature. Consequently in such like fear, there is contraction not only in the appetite, but also in the corporeal nature: for when an animal is moved by the imagination of death, it experiences a contraction of heat towards the inner parts of the body, as though it were threatened by a natural death. Hence it is that *those who are in fear of death turn pale* (*Ethic.* iv. 9).—But the evil that shame fears, is contrary, not to nature, but only to the appetite of the soul. Consequently there results a contraction in this appetite, but not in fact, in the corporeal nature: in fact, the soul, as though contracted in itself, is free to set the vital spirits and heat in movement, so that they spread to the outward parts of the body: the result being that those who are ashamed blush.

SECOND ARTICLE

Whether Fear Makes One Suitable for Counsel?

We proceed thus to the Second Article:—

Objection 1. It would seem that fear does not make one suitable for counsel. For the same thing cannot be conducive to counsel, and a hindrance thereto. But fear hinders counsel: because every passion disturbs repose, which is requisite for the good use of reason. Therefore fear does not make a man suitable for counsel.

Obj. 2. Further, counsel is an act of reason, in thinking and deliberating about the future. But a certain fear *drives away all thought, and dislocates the mind,* as Cicero observes (*De Quæst. Tusc.* iv. 8). Therefore fear does not conduce to counsel, but hinders it.

Obj. 3. Further, just as we have recourse to counsel in order to avoid evil, so do we, in order to attain good things. But whereas fear is of evil to be avoided, so is hope of good things to be obtained. Therefore fear is not more conducive to counsel, than hope is.

On the contrary, The Philosopher says (*Rhet.* ii. 5) that *fear makes men of counsel.*

I answer that, A man of counsel may be taken in two ways. First from his being willing or anxious to take counsel. And thus fear makes men of counsel. Because, as the Philosopher says (*Ethic.* iii. 3), *we take counsel on great matters, because therein we distrust ourselves.* Now things which make us afraid, are not simply evil, but have a certain magnitude, both because they seem difficult to repel, and because they are apprehended as near to us, as stated above (Q. 42, A. 2). Wherefore men seek for counsel especially when they are afraid.

Secondly, a man of counsel means one who is apt for giving good counsel: and in this sense, neither fear nor any passion makes men of counsel. Because when a man is affected by a passion, things seem to him greater or smaller than they really are: thus to a lover, what he loves seems better; to him that fears, what he fears seems more dreadful. Consequently owing to the want of right judgment, every passion, considered in itself, hinders the faculty of giving good counsel.

This suffices for the Reply to the First Objection.

Reply Obj. 2. The stronger a passion is, the greater hindrance is it to the man who is swayed by it. Consequently, when fear is intense, man does indeed wish to take counsel, but his thoughts are so disturbed, that he can find no counsel. If, however, the fear be slight, so as to make a man wish to take counsel, without gravely disturbing the reason; it may even make it easier for him to take good counsel, by reason of his ensuing carefulness.

Reply Obj. 3. Hope also makes man a good counsellor: because, as the Philosopher says (*Rhet.* ii. 5), *no man takes counsel in matters he despairs of,* nor about impossible things, as he says in *Ethic.* iii. 3. But fear incites to counsel more than hope does. Because hope is of good things, as being possible of attainment; whereas fear is of evil things, as being difficult to repel, so that fear regards the aspect of difficulty more than hope does. And it is in matters of difficulty, especially when we distrust ourselves, that we take counsel, as stated above.

THIRD ARTICLE

Whether Fear Makes One Tremble?

We proceed thus to the Third Article:—

Objection 1. It would seem that trembling is not an effect of fear. Because trembling is occasioned by cold; thus we observe that a cold person trembles. Now fear does not seem to make one cold, but rather to cause a parching heat: a sign whereof is that those who fear are thirsty, especially if their fear be very great, as in the case of those who are being led to execution. Therefore fear does not cause trembling.

Obj. 2. Further, fæcal evacuation is occasioned by heat; hence laxative medicines are generally warm. But these evacuations are often caused by fear. Therefore fear apparently causes heat; and consequently does not cause trembling.

Obj. 3. Further, in fear, the heat is withdrawn from the outer to the inner parts of the body. If, therefore, man trembles in his outward parts, through the heat being withdrawn thus; it seems that fear should cause this trembling in all the external members. But such is not the case. Therefore trembling of the body is not caused by fear.

On the contrary, Cicero says (*De Quæst. Tusc.* iv. 8) that *fear is followed by trembling, pallor and chattering of the teeth.*

I answer that, As stated above (A. 1), in fear there takes place a certain contraction from the outward to the inner parts of the body, the result being that the outer parts become cold; and for this reason trembling is occasioned in these parts, being caused by a lack of power in controlling the members: which lack of power is due to the want of heat, which is the instrument whereby the soul moves those members, as stated in *De Anima* ii. 4.

Reply Obj. 1. When the heat withdraws from the outer to the inner parts, the inward heat increases, especially in the inferior or nutritive parts. Consequently the humid element being spent, thirst ensues; sometimes indeed the result is a loosening of the bowels, and urinary or even seminal evacuation.—Or else such like evacuations are due to contraction of the abdomen and testicles, as the Philosopher says (*De Problem.* xxii. 11).

This suffices for the Reply to the Second Objection.

Reply Obj. 3. In fear, heat abandons the heart, with a downward movement: hence in those who are afraid the heart especially trembles, as also those members which are connected with the breast where the heart resides. Hence those who fear tremble especially in their speech, on account of the tracheal artery being near the heart. The lower lip, too, and the lower jaw tremble, through their connection with the heart; which explains the chattering of the teeth. For the same reason the arms and hands tremble.—Or else because the aforesaid members are more mobile. For which reason the knees tremble in those who are afraid, according to Isa. xxxv. 3: *Strengthen ye the feeble hands, and confirm the trembling* (Vulg., *weak*) *knees.*

FOURTH ARTICLE

Whether Fear Hinders Action?

We proceed thus to the Fourth Article:—

Objection 1. It would seem that fear hinders action. For action is hindered chiefly by a disturbance in the reason, which directs action. But fear disturbs reason, as stated above (A. 2). Therefore fear hinders action.

Obj. 2. Further, those who fear while doing anything, are more apt to fail: thus a man who walks on a plank placed aloft, easily falls through fear; whereas, if he were to walk on the same plank down below, he would not fall, through not being afraid. Therefore fear hinders action.

Obj. 3. Further, laziness or sloth is a kind of fear. But laziness hinders action. Therefore fear does too.

On the contrary, The Apostle says (Phil. ii. 12): *With fear and trembling work out your salvation:* and he would not say this if fear were a hindrance to a good work. Therefore fear does not hinder a good action.

I answer that, Man's exterior actions are caused by the soul as first mover, but by the bodily members as instruments. Now action may be hindered both by defect of the instrument, and by defect of the principal mover. On the part of the bodily instruments, fear, considered in itself, is always apt to hinder exterior action, on account of the outward members being deprived, through fear, of their heat. But on the part of the soul, if the fear be moderate, without much disturbance of the reason, it conduces to working well, in so far as it causes a certain solicitude, and makes a man take counsel and work with greater attention.—If, however, fear increases so much as to disturb the reason, it hinders action even on the part of the soul. But of such a fear the Apostle does not speak.

This suffices for the Reply to the First Objection.

Reply Obj. 2. He that falls from a plank placed aloft, suffers a disturbance of his imagination, through fear of the fall that is pictured to his imagination.

Reply Obj. 3. Everyone in fear shuns that which he fears: and therefore, since laziness is a fear of work itself as being toilsome, it hinders work by withdrawing the will from it. But fear of other things conduces to action, in so far as it inclines the will to do that whereby a man escapes from what he fears.

QUESTION 45

Of Daring

(In Four Articles)

WE must now consider daring: under which head there are four points of inquiry: (1) Whether daring is contrary to fear? (2) How is daring related to hope? (3) Of the cause of daring; (4) Of its effect.

FIRST ARTICLE

Whether Daring Is Contrary to Fear?

We proceed thus to the First Article:—

Objection 1. It would seem that daring is not contrary to fear. For Augustine says (QQ. 83, qu. 31) that *daring is a vice.* Now vice is contrary to virtue. Since, therefore, fear is not a virtue but a passion, it seems that daring is not contrary to fear.

Obj. 2. Further, to one thing there is one contrary. But hope is contrary to fear. Therefore daring is not contrary to fear.

Obj. 3. Further, every passion excludes its opposite. But fear excludes safety; for Augustine says (*Conf.* ii. 6) that *fear takes forethought for safety.* Therefore safety is contrary to fear. Therefore daring is not contrary to fear.

On the contrary, The Philosopher says (*Rhet.* ii. 5) that *daring is contrary to fear.*

I answer that, It is of the essence of contraries to be *farthest removed from one another,* as stated in *Metaph.* x. 4. Now that which is farthest removed from fear, is daring: since fear turns away from the future hurt, on account of its victory over him that fears it; whereas daring turns on threatened danger, because of its own victory over that same danger. Consequently it is evident that daring is contrary to fear.

Reply Obj. 1. Anger, daring and all the names of the passions can be taken in two ways. First, as denoting absolutely movements of the sensitive appetite in respect of some object, good or bad: and thus they are names of passions.—Secondly, as denoting besides this movement, a straying from the order of reason: and thus they are names of vices. It is in this sense that Augustine speaks of daring: but we are speaking of it in the first sense.

Reply Obj. 2. To one thing, in the same respect, there are not several contraries; but in different respects nothing prevents one thing having several contraries. Accordingly it has been said above (Q. 23, A. 2; Q. 40, A. 4) that the irascible passions admit of a twofold contrariety: one, according to the opposition of good and evil, and thus fear is contrary to hope: the other, according to the opposition of approach and withdrawal, and thus daring is contrary to fear, and despair contrary to hope.

Reply Obj. 3. Safety does not denote something contrary to fear, but merely the exclusion of fear: for he is said to be safe, who fears not. Wherefore safety is opposed to fear, as a privation: while daring is opposed thereto as a contrary. And as contrariety implies privation, so daring implies safety.

SECOND ARTICLE

Whether Daring Ensues from Hope?

We proceed thus to the Second Article:—

Objection 1. It would seem that daring does not ensue from hope. Because daring regards evil and fearful things, as stated in *Ethic.* iii. 7. But hope regards good things, as stated above (Q. 40, A. 1). Therefore they have different objects and are not in the same order. Therefore daring does not ensue from hope.

Obj. 2. Further, just as daring is contrary to fear, so is despair contrary to hope. But fear does not ensue from despair: in fact despair excludes fear, as the Philosopher says (*Rhet.* ii. 5). Therefore daring does not result from hope.

Obj. 3. Further, daring is intent on something good, viz., victory. But it belongs to hope to tend to that which is good and difficult. Therefore daring is the same as hope; and consequently does not result from it.

On the contrary, The Philosopher says (*Ethic.* iii. 8) that *those who are hopeful are full of daring.* Therefore it seems that daring ensues from hope.

I answer that, As we have often stated (Q. 22, A. 2; Q. 35, A. 1; Q. 41, A. 1), all these passions belong to the appetitive power. Now every movement of the appetitive power is reducible to one either of pursuit or of avoidance. Again, pursuit or avoidance is of something either by reason of itself or by reason of something else. By reason of itself, good is the object of pursuit, and evil, the object of avoidance: but by reason of something else, evil can be the object of pursuit, through some good attaching to it; and good can be the object of avoidance, through some evil attaching to it. Now that which is by reason of something else, follows that which is by reason of itself. Consequently pursuit of evil follows pursuit of good; and avoidance of good follows avoidance of evil. Now these four things belong to four passions, since pursuit of good belongs to hope, avoidance of evil to fear, the pursuit

of the fearful evil belongs to daring, and the avoidance of good to despair. It follows, therefore, that daring results from hope; since it is in the hope of overcoming the threatening object of fear, that one attacks it boldly. But despair results from fear: since the reason why a man despairs is because he fears the difficulty attaching to the good he should hope for.

Reply Obj. 1. This argument would hold, if good and evil were not co-ordinate objects. But because evil has a certain relation to good, since it comes after good, as privation comes after habit; consequently daring which pursues evil, comes after hope which pursues good.

Reply Obj. 2. Although good, absolutely speaking, is prior to evil, yet avoidance of evil precedes avoidance of good; just as the pursuit of good precedes the pursuit of evil. Consequently just as hope precedes daring, so fear precedes despair. And just as fear does not always lead to despair, but only when it is intense; so hope does not always lead to daring, save only when it is strong.

Reply Obj. 3. Although the object of daring is an evil to which, in the estimation of the daring man, the good of victory is conjoined; yet daring regards the evil, and hope regards the conjoined good. In like manner despair regards directly the good which it turns away from, while fear regards the conjoined evil. Hence, properly speaking, daring is not a part of hope, but its effect: just as despair is an effect, not a part, of fear. For this reason, too, daring cannot be a principal passion.

THIRD ARTICLE

Whether Some Defect Is a Cause of Daring?

We proceed thus to the Third Article:—

Objection 1. It would seem that some defect is a cause of daring. For the Philosopher says (*De Problem.* xxvii. 4) that *lovers of wine are strong and daring.* But from wine ensues the effect of drunkenness. Therefore daring is caused by a defect.

Obj. 2. Further, the Philosopher says (*Rhet.* ii. 5) that *those who have no experience of danger are bold.* But want of experience is a defect. Therefore daring is caused by a defect.

Obj. 3. Further, those who have suffered wrongs are wont to be daring; *like the beasts when beaten,* as stated in *Ethic.* iii. 5. But the suffering of wrongs pertains to defect. Therefore daring is caused by a defect.

On the contrary, The Philosopher says (*Rhet.* ii. 5) that the cause of daring *is the presence in the imagination of the hope that the means of safety are nigh, and that the things to be feared are either non-existent or far off.* But anything pertaining to defect implies either the removal of the means of safety, or the proximity of something to be feared. Therefore nothing pertaining to defect is a cause of daring.

I answer that, As stated above (AA. 1, 2) daring results from hope and is contrary to fear: wherefore whatever is naturally apt to cause hope or banish fear, is a cause of daring. Since, however, fear and hope, and also daring, being passions, consist in a movement of the appetite, and in a certain bodily transmutation; a thing may be considered as the cause of daring in two ways, whether by raising hope, or by banishing of fear; in one way, on the part of the appetitive movement; in another way, on the part of the bodily transmutation.

On the part of the appetitive movement which follows apprehension, hope that leads to daring is roused by those things that make us reckon victory as possible. Such things regard either our own power, as bodily strength, experience of dangers, abundance of wealth, and the like; or they regard the powers of others, such as having a great number of friends or any other means of help, especially if a man trust in the Divine assistance: wherefore *those are more daring, with whom it is well in regard to godlike things,* as the Philosopher says (*Rhet.* ii. 5). Fear is banished, in this way, by the removal of threatening causes of fear; for instance, by the fact that a man has no enemies, through having harmed nobody, so that he is not aware of any imminent danger; since those especially appear to be threatened by danger, who have harmed others.

On the part of the bodily transmutation, daring is caused through the incitement of hope and the banishment of fear, by those things which raise the temperature about the heart. Wherefore the Philosopher says (*De Part. Animal.* iii. 4) that *those whose heart is small in size, are more daring; while animals whose heart is large are timid; because the natural heat is unable to give the same degree of temperature to a large as to a small heart; just as a fire does not heat a large house as well as it does a small house.* He says also (*De Problem.* xxvii. 4) that *those whose lungs contain much blood, are more daring, through the heat in the heart that results therefrom.* He says also in the same passage that *lovers of wine are more daring, on account of the heat of the wine:* hence it has been said above (Q. 40, A. 6) that drunkenness conduces to hope, since the heat in the heart banishes fear and raises hope, by reason of the dilatation and enlargement of the heart.

Reply Obj. 1. Drunkenness causes daring, not through being a defect, but through dilating the heart: and again through making a man think greatly of himself.

Reply Obj. 2. Those who have no experience of dangers are more daring, not on account of a defect, but accidentally, *i.e.,* in so far as through being inexperienced they do not know their own failings, nor the dangers that threaten. Hence it is that the removal of the cause of fear gives rise to daring.

Reply Obj. 3. As the Philosopher says (*Rhet.* ii. 5) *those who have been wronged are courageous, because they think that God comes to the assistance of those who suffer unjustly.*

Hence it is evident that no defect causes daring except accidentally, *i.e.,* in so far as some excellence attaches thereto, real or imaginary, either in oneself or in another.

FOURTH ARTICLE

Whether the Brave Are More Eager at First Than in the Midst of Danger?

We proceed thus to the Fourth Article:—

Objection 1. It would seem that the daring are not more eager at first than in the midst of danger. Because trembling is caused by fear, which is contrary to daring, as stated above (A. 1; Q. 44, A. 3). But the daring sometimes tremble at first, as the Philosopher says (*De Problem.* xxvii. 3). Therefore they are not more eager at first than in the midst of danger.

Obj. 2. Further, passion is intensified by an increase in its object: thus since a good is lovable, what is better is yet more lovable. But the object of daring is something difficult. Therefore the greater the difficulty, the greater the daring. But danger is more arduous and difficult when present. It is then therefore that daring is greatest.

Obj. 3. Further, anger is provoked by the infliction of wounds. But anger causes daring; for the Philosopher says (*Rhet.* ii. 5) that *anger makes man bold.* Therefore when man is in the midst of danger and when he is being beaten, then is he most daring.

On the contrary, It is said in *Ethic.* iii. 7 that *the daring are precipitate and full of eagerness before the danger, yet in the midst of dangers they stand aloof.*

I answer that, Daring, being a movement of the sensitive appetite, follows an apprehension of the sensitive faculty. But the sensitive faculty cannot make comparisons, nor can it inquire into circumstances; its judgment is instantaneous. Now it happens sometimes that it is impossible for a man to take note in an instant of all the difficulties of a certain situation: hence there arises the movement of daring to face the danger; so that when he comes to experience the danger, he feels the difficulty to be greater than he expected, and so gives way.

On the other hand, reason discusses all the difficulties of a situation. Consequently men of fortitude who face danger according to the judgment of reason, at first seem slack, because they face the danger not from passion but with due deliberation. Yet when they are in the midst of danger, they experience nothing unforeseen, but sometimes the difficulty turns out to be less than they anticipated; wherefore they are more persevering.—Moreover, it may be because they face the danger on account of the good of virtue which is the abiding object of their will, however great the danger may prove: whereas men of daring face the danger on account of a mere thought giving rise to hope and banishing fear, as stated above (A. 3).

Reply Obj. 1. Trembling does occur in men of daring, on account of the heat being withdrawn from the outer to the inner parts of the body, as occurs also in those who are afraid. But in men of daring the heat withdraws to the heart; whereas in those who are afraid, it withdraws to the inferior parts.

Reply Obj. 2. The object of love is good simply, wherefore if it be increased, love is increased simply. But the object of daring is a compound of good and evil; and the movement of daring towards evil presupposes the movement of hope towards good. If, therefore, so much difficulty be added to the danger that it overcomes hope, the movement of daring does not ensue, but fails.—But if the movement of daring does ensue, the greater the danger, the greater is the daring considered to be.

Reply Obj. 3. Hurt does not give rise to anger unless there be some kind of hope, as we shall see later on (Q. 46, A. 1). Consequently if the danger be so great as to banish all hope of victory, anger does not ensue.—It is true, however, that if anger does ensue, there will be greater daring.

QUESTION 46

Of Anger, in Itself

(In Eight Articles)

We must now consider anger: and (1) anger in itself; (2) the cause of anger and its remedy; (3) the effect of anger.

Under the first head there are eight points of inquiry: (1) Whether anger is a special passion? (2) Whether the object of anger is good or evil? (3) Whether anger is in the concupiscible faculty? (4) Whether anger is accompanied by an act of reason? (5) Whether anger is more natural than desire? (6) Whether anger is more grievous than hatred? (7) Whether anger is only towards those with whom we have a relation of justice? (8) Of the species of anger.

FIRST ARTICLE

Whether Anger Is a Special Passion?

We proceed thus to the First Article:—

Objection 1. It would seem that anger is not a special passion. For the irascible power takes its name from anger (*ira*). But there are several passions in this power, not only one. Therefore anger is not one special passion.

Obj. 2. Further, to every special passion there is a contrary passion; as is evident by going through them one by one. But no passion is contrary to anger, as stated above (Q. 23, A. 3). Therefore anger is not a special passion.

Obj. 3. Further, one special passion does not include another. But anger includes several passions: since it accompanies sorrow, pleasure, and hope, as the Philosopher states (*Rhet.* ii. 2). Therefore anger is not a special passion.

On the contrary, Damascene (*De Fide Orthod.* ii. 16) calls anger a special passion: and so does Cicero (*De Quœst. Tusc.* iv. 7).

I answer that, A thing is said to be general in two ways. First, by predication; thus *animal* is general in respect of all animals.—Secondly, by causality; thus the sun is the general cause of all things generated here below, according to Dionysius (*Div. Nom.* iv). Because just as a genus contains potentially many differences, according to a likeness of matter; so an efficient cause contains many effects according to its active power.—Now it happens that an effect is produced by the concurrence of various causes; and since every cause remains somewhat in its effect, we may say that, in yet a third way, an effect which is due to the concurrence of several causes, has a certain generality, inasmuch as several causes are, in a fashion, actually existing therein.

Accordingly in the first way, anger is not a general passion, but is condivided with the

other passions, as stated above (Q. 23, A. 4).—
In like manner, neither is it in the second
way: since it is not a cause of the other passions. But in this way love may be called a
general passion, as Augustine declares (*De
Civ. Dei* xiv. 7, 9), because love is the primary
root of all the other passions, as stated above
(Q. 27, A. 4). But, in a third way, anger may
be called a general passion, inasmuch as it is
caused by a concurrence of several passions.
Because the movement of anger does not arise
save on account of some pain inflicted, and
unless there be desire and hope of revenge:
for, as the Philosopher says (*Rhet.* ii. 2), *the
angry man hopes to punish; since he craves
for revenge as being possible.* Consequently
if the person, who inflicted the injury, excel
very much, anger does not ensue, but only
sorrow, as Avicenna states (*De Anima* iv. 6).

Reply Obj. 1. The irascible power takes its
name from *ira* (anger), not because every
movement of that power is one of anger; but
because all its movements terminate in anger;
and because, of all these movements, anger is
the most patent.

Reply Obj. 2. From the very fact that anger
is caused by contrary passions, *i.e.,* by hope,
which is of good, and by sorrow, which is of
evil, it includes in itself contrariety: and consequently it has no contrary outside itself.
Thus also in mixed colors there is no contrariety, except that of the simple colors from
which they are made.

Reply Obj. 3. Anger includes several passions, not indeed as a genus includes several
species; but rather according to the inclusion
of cause and effect.

SECOND ARTICLE

Whether the Object of Anger Is Good or Evil?

We proceed thus to the Second Article:—

Objection 1. It would seem that the object
of anger is evil. For Gregory of Nyssa* says
that anger is *the sword-bearer of desire*, inasmuch, to wit, as it assails whatever obstacle
stands in the way of desire. But an obstacle
has the character of evil. Therefore anger
regards evil as its object.

Obj. 2. Further, anger and hatred agree in
their effect, since each seeks to inflict harm
on another. But hatred regards evil as its
object, as stated above (Q. 29, A. 1). Therefore anger does also.

Obj. 3. Further, anger arises from sorrow;
wherefore the Philosopher says (*Ethic.* vii. 6)
that *anger acts with sorrow.* But evil is the
object of sorrow. Therefore it is also the object of anger.

On the contrary, Augustine says (*Conf.*

* Nemesius, *De Nat. Hom.* xxi.

ii. 6) that *anger craves for revenge.* But the
desire for revenge is a desire for something
good: since revenge belongs to justice. Therefore the object of anger is good.

Moreover, anger is always accompanied by
hope, wherefore it causes pleasure, as the
Philosopher says (*Rhet.* ii. 2). But the object
of hope and of pleasure is good. Therefore
good is also the object of anger.

I answer that, The movement of the appetitive power follows an act of the apprehensive
power. Now the apprehensive power apprehends a thing in two ways. First, by way of
an incomplex object, as when we understand
what a man is; secondly, by way of a complex
object, as when we understand that whiteness
is in a man. Consequently in each of these
ways the appetitive power can tend to both
good and evil:—by way of a simple and incomplex object, when the appetite simply follows and adheres to good, or recoils from evil:
and such movements are desire, hope, pleasure,
sorrow, and so forth:—by way of a complex
object, as when the appetite is concerned with
some good or evil being in, or being done to,
another, either seeking this or recoiling from
it. This is evident in the case of love and
hatred: for we love someone, in so far as we
wish some good to be in him; and we hate
someone, in so far as we wish some evil to be
in him. It is the same with anger; for when a
man is angry, he wishes to be avenged on
someone. Hence the movement of anger has
a twofold tendency: viz., to vengeance itself,
which it desires and hopes for as being a good,
wherefore it takes pleasure in it; and to the
person on whom it seeks vengeance, as to
something contrary and hurtful, which bears
the character of evil.

We must, however, observe a twofold difference in this respect, between anger on the
one side, and hatred and love on the other.
The first difference is that anger always regards two objects: whereas love and hatred
sometimes regard but one object, as when a
man is said to love wine or something of the
kind, or to hate it.—The second difference is,
that both the objects of love are good: since
the lover wishes good to someone, as to something agreeable to himself: while both the objects of hatred bear the character of evil: for the
man who hates, wishes evil to someone, as to
something disagreeable to him. Whereas anger regards one object under the aspect of
good, viz., vengeance, which it desires to have;
and the other object under the aspect of evil,
viz., the noxious person, on whom it seeks
to be avenged. Consequently it is a passion
somewhat made up of contrary passions.

This suffices for the Replies to the Objections.

THIRD ARTICLE

Whether Anger Is in the Concupiscible Faculty?

We proceed thus to the Third Article:—

Objection 1. It would seem that anger is in the concupiscible faculty. For Cicero says (*De Quæst. Tusc.* iv. 9) that anger is a kind of *desire*. But desire is in the concupiscible faculty. Therefore anger is too.

Obj. 2. Further, Augustine says in his Rule, that *anger grows into hatred:* and Cicero says (*loc. cit.*) that *hatred is inveterate anger.* But hatred, like love, is a concupiscible passion. Therefore anger is in the concupiscible faculty.

Obj. 3. Further, Damascene (*De Fide Orthod.* ii. 16) and Gregory of Nyssa* say that *anger is made up of sorrow and desire.* Both of these are in the concupiscible faculty. Therefore anger is a concupiscible passion.

On the contrary, The concupiscible is distinct from the irascible faculty. If, therefore, anger were in the concupiscible power, the irascible would not take its name from it.

I answer that, As stated above (Q. 23, A. 1), the passions of the irascible part differ from the passions of the concupiscible faculty, in that the objects of the concupiscible passions are good and evil absolutely considered, whereas the objects of the irascible passions are good and evil of a certain elevation or arduousness. Now it has been stated (A. 2) that anger regards two objects: viz., the vengeance that it seeks; and the person on whom it seeks vengeance; and in respect of both, anger requires a certain arduousness: for the movement of anger does not arise, unless there be some magnitude about both these objects; *since we make no ado about things that are naught or very minute,* as the Philosopher observes (*Rhet.* ii. 2). It is therefore evident that anger is not in the concupiscible, but in the irascible faculty.

Reply Obj. 1. Cicero gives the name of desire to any kind of craving for a future good, without discriminating between that which is arduous and that which is not. Accordingly he reckons anger as a kind of desire, inasmuch as it is a desire of vengeance. In this sense, however, desire is common to the irascible and concupiscible faculties.

Reply Obj. 2. Anger is said to grow into hatred, not as though the same passion which at first was anger, afterwards becomes hatred by becoming inveterate; but by a process of causality. For anger when it lasts a long time engenders hatred.

Reply Obj. 3. Anger is said to be composed of sorrow and desire, not as though they were its parts, but because they are its causes: and it has been said above (Q. 25, A. 2) that the

* Nemesius, *De Nat. Hom.* xxi.

concupiscible passions are the causes of the irascible passions.

FOURTH ARTICLE

Whether Anger Requires an Act of Reason?

We proceed thus to the Fourth Article:—

Objection 1. It would seem that anger does not require an act of reason. For, since anger is a passion, it is in the sensitive appetite. But the sensitive appetite follows an apprehension, not of reason, but of the sensitive faculty. Therefore anger does not require an act of reason.

Obj. 2. Further, dumb animals are devoid of reason: and yet they are seen to be angry. Therefore anger does not require an act of reason.

Obj. 3. Further, drunkenness fetters the reason; whereas it is conducive to anger. Therefore anger does not require an act of reason.

On the contrary, The Philosopher says (*Ethic.* vii. 6) that *anger listens to reason somewhat.*

I answer that, As stated above (A. 2), anger is a desire for vengeance. Now vengeance implies a comparison between the punishment to be inflicted and the hurt done; wherefore the Philosopher says (*Ethic.* vii. *loc. cit.*) that *anger, as if it had drawn the inference that it ought to quarrel with such a person, is therefore immediately exasperated.* Now to compare and to draw an inference is an act of reason. Therefore anger, in a fashion, requires an act of reason.

Reply Obj. 1. The movement of the appetitive power may follow an act of reason in two ways. In the first way, it follows the reason in so far as the reason commands: and thus the will follows reason, wherefore it is called the rational appetite. In another way, it follows reason in so far as the reason denounces, and thus anger follows reason. For the Philosopher says (*De Problem.* xxviii. 3) that *anger follows reason, not in obedience to reason's command, but as a result of reason's denouncing the injury.* Because the sensitive appetite is subject to the reason, not immediately but through the will.

Reply Obj. 2. Dumb animals have a natural instinct imparted to them by the Divine Reason, in virtue of which they are gifted with movements, both internal and external, like unto rational movements, as stated above (Q. 40, A. 3).

Reply Obj. 3. As stated in *Ethic.* vii. 6, *anger listens somewhat to reason* in so far as reason denounces the injury inflicted, *but listens not perfectly,* because it does not observe the rule of reason as to the measure of vengeance. Anger, therefore, requires an act of reason; and yet proves a hindrance to reason. Wherefore the Philosopher says (*De Problem.* iii. 2, 27) that those who are very drunk, so as to be incapable of the use of reason, do not get angry: but those who are slightly drunk, do get angry, through being still able, though hampered, to form a judgment of reason.

FIFTH ARTICLE

Whether Anger Is More Natural Than Desire?

We proceed thus to the Fifth Article:—

Objection 1. It would seem that anger is not more natural than desire. Because it is proper to man to be by nature a gentle animal. But *gentleness is contrary to anger,* as the Philosopher states (*Rhet.* ii. 3). Therefore anger is no more natural than desire, in fact it seems to be altogether unnatural to man.

Obj. 2. Further, reason is contrasted with nature: since those things that act according to reason, are not said to act according to nature. Now *anger requires an act of reason, but desire does not,* as stated in *Ethic.* vii. 6. Therefore desire is more natural than anger.

Obj. 3. Further, anger is a craving for vengeance: while desire is a craving for those things especially which are pleasant to the touch, viz., for pleasures of the table and for sexual pleasures. But these things are more natural to man than vengeance. Therefore desire is more natural than anger.

On the contrary, The Philosopher says (*Ethic.* vii. *loc. cit.*) that *anger is more natural than desire.*

I answer that, By *natural* we mean that which is caused by nature, as stated in *Phys.* ii. 1. Consequently the question as to whether a particular passion is more or less natural cannot be decided without reference to the cause of that passion. Now the cause of a passion, as stated above (Q. 36, A. 2), may be considered in two ways: first, on the part of the object; secondly, on the part of the subject. If then we consider the cause of anger and of desire, on the part of the object, thus desire, especially of pleasures of the table, and of sexual pleasures, is more natural than anger; in so far as these pleasures are more natural to man than vengeance.

If, however, we consider the cause of anger on the part of the subject, thus anger, in a manner, is more natural; and, in a manner, desire is more natural. Because the nature of an individual man may be considered either as to the generic, or as to the specific nature, or again as to the particular temperament of

the individual. If then we consider the generic nature, *i.e.,* the nature of this man considered as an animal; thus desire is more natural than anger; because it is from this very generic nature that man is inclined to desire those things which tend to preserve in him the life both of the species and of the individual.—If, however, we consider the specific nature, *i.e.,* the nature of this man as a rational being; then anger is more natural to man than desire, in so far as anger follows reason more than desire does. Wherefore the Philosopher says (*Ethic.* iv. 5) that *revenge* which pertains to anger *is more natural to man than meekness:* for it is natural to everything to rise up against things contrary and hurtful.—And if we consider the nature of the individual, in respect of his particular temperament, thus anger is more natural than desire; for the reason that anger is prone to ensue from the natural tendency to anger, more than desire, or any other passion, is to ensue from a natural tendency to desire, which tendencies result from a man's individual temperament. Because disposition to anger is due to a bilious temperament; and of all the humors, the bile moves quickest; for it is like fire. Consequently he that is temperamentally disposed to anger is sooner incensed with anger, than he that is temperamentally disposed to desire, is inflamed with desire: and for this reason the Philosopher says (*Ethic.* vii. 6) that a disposition to anger is more liable to be transmitted from parent to child, than a disposition to desire.

Reply Obj. 1. We may consider in man both the natural temperament on the part of the body, and the reason. On the part of the bodily temperament, a man, considered specifically, does not naturally excel others either in anger or in any other passion, on account of the moderation of his temperament. But other animals, for as much as their temperament recedes from this moderation and approaches to an extreme disposition, are naturally disposed to some excess of passion, such as the lion in daring, the hound in anger, the hare in fear, and so forth.—On the part of reason, however, it is natural to man, both to be angry and to be gentle: in so far as reason somewhat causes anger, by denouncing the injury which causes anger; and somewhat appeases anger, in so far as the angry man *does not listen perfectly to the command of reason,* as stated above (A. 4 *ad* 3).

Reply Obj. 2. Reason itself belongs to the nature of man: wherefore from the very fact that anger requires an act of reason, it follows that it is, in a manner, natural to man.

Reply Obj. 3. This argument regards anger and desire on the part of the object.

SIXTH ARTICLE

Whether Anger Is More Grievous than Hatred?

We proceed thus to the Sixth Article:—

Objection 1. It would seem that anger is more grievous than hatred. For it is written (Prov. xxvii. 4) that *anger hath no mercy, nor fury when it breaketh forth.* But hatred sometimes has mercy. Therefore anger is more grievous than hatred.

Obj. 2. Further, it is worse to suffer evil and to grieve for it, than merely to suffer it. But when a man hates, he is contented if the object of his hatred suffer evil: whereas the angry man is not satisfied unless the object of his anger know it and be aggrieved thereby, as the Philosopher says (*Rhet.* ii. 4). Therefore, anger is more grievous than hatred.

Obj. 3. Further, a thing seems to be so much the more firm according as more things concur to set it up: thus a habit is all the more settled through being caused by several acts. But anger is caused by the concurrence of several passions, as stated above (A. 1): whereas hatred is not. Therefore anger is more settled and more grievous than hatred.

On the contrary, Augustine, in his Rule, compares hatred to *a beam,* but anger to *a mote.*

I answer that, The species and nature of a passion are taken from its object. Now the object of anger is the same in substance as the object of hatred; since, just as the hater wishes evil to him whom he hates, so does the angry man wish evil to him with whom he is angry. But there is a difference of aspect: for the hater wishes evil to his enemy, as evil, whereas the angry man wishes evil to him with whom he is angry, not as evil but in so far as it has an aspect of good, that is, in so far as he reckons it as just, since it is a means of vengeance. Wherefore also it has been said above (A. 2) that hatred implies application of evil to evil, whereas anger denotes application of good to evil.—Now it is evident that to seek evil under the aspect of justice, is a lesser evil, than simply to seek evil to someone. Because to wish evil to someone under the aspect of justice, may be according to the virtue of justice, if it be in conformity with the order of reason; and anger fails only in this, that it does not obey the precept of reason in taking vengeance. Consequently it is evident that hatred is far worse and graver than anger.

Reply Obj. 1. In anger and hatred two points may be considered: namely, the thing desired, and the intensity of the desire. As to the thing desired, anger has more mercy than hatred has. For since hatred desires another's evil for evil's sake, it is satisfied with no particular measure of evil: because those things that are desired for their own sake, are desired without measure, as the Philosopher states (*Polit.* i. 3), instancing a miser with regard to riches. Hence it is written, (Ecclus. xii. 16): *An enemy . . . if he find an opportunity, will not be satisfied with blood.*—Anger, on the other hand, seeks evil only under the aspect of a just means of vengeance. Consequently when the evil inflicted goes beyond the measure of justice according to the estimate of the angry man, then he has mercy. Wherefore the Philosopher says (*Rhet.* ii. 4) that *the angry man is appeased if many evils befall, whereas the hater is never appeased.*

As to the intensity of the desire, anger excludes mercy more than hatred does; because the movement of anger is more impetuous, through the heating of the bile. Hence the passage quoted continues: *Who can bear the violence of one provoked?*

Reply Obj. 2. As stated above, an angry man wishes evil to someone, in so far as this evil is a means of just vengeance. Now vengeance is wrought by the infliction of a punishment: and the nature of punishment consists in being contrary to the will, painful, and inflicted for some fault. Consequently an angry man desires this, that the person whom he is hurting, may feel it and be in pain, and know that this has befallen him on account of the harm he has done the other. The hater, on the other hand, cares not for all this, since he desires another's evil as such.—It is not true, however, that an evil is worse through giving more pain: because *injustice and imprudence, although evil,* yet, being voluntary, *do not grieve those in whom they are,* as the Philosopher observes (*Rhet.* ii. 4).

Reply Obj. 3. That which proceeds from several causes, is more settled when these causes are of one kind: but it may be that one cause prevails over many others. Now hatred ensues from a more lasting cause than anger does. Because anger arises from an emotion of the soul due to the wrong inflicted; whereas hatred ensues from a disposition in a man, by reason of which he considers that which he hates to be contrary and hurtful to him. Consequently, as passion is more transitory than disposition or habit, so anger is less lasting than hatred; although hatred itself is a passion ensuing from this disposition. Hence the Philosopher says (*Rhet.* ii. 4) that *hatred is more incurable than anger.*

SEVENTH ARTICLE

Whether Anger Is Only towards Those to Whom One Has an Obligation of Justice?

We proceed thus to the Seventh Article:—

Objection 1. It would seem that anger is not only towards those to whom one has an obligation of justice. For there is no justice between man and irrational beings. And yet sometimes one is angry with irrational beings; thus, out of anger, a writer throws away his pen, or a rider strikes his horse. Therefore anger is not only towards those to whom one has an obligation of justice.

Obj. 2. Further, *there is no justice towards oneself . . . nor is there justice towards one's own* (*Ethic.* v. 6). But sometimes a man is angry with himself; for instance, a penitent, on account of his sin; hence it is written (Ps. iv. 5): *Be ye angry and sin not.* Therefore anger is not only towards those with whom one has a relation of justice.

Obj. 3. Further, justice and injustice can be of one man towards an entire class, or a whole community: for instance, when the state injures an individual. But anger is not towards a class but only towards an individual, as the Philosopher states (*Rhet.* ii. 4). Therefore properly speaking, anger is not towards those with whom one is in relation of justice or injustice.

The contrary, however, may be gathered from the Philosopher (*Rhet.* ii. 2, 3).

I answer that, As stated above (A. 6), anger desires evil as being a means of just vengeance. Consequently, anger is towards those to whom we are just or unjust: since vengeance is an act of justice, and wrong-doing is an act of injustice. Therefore both on the part of the cause, viz., the harm done by another, and on the part of the vengeance sought by the angry man, it is evident that anger concerns those to whom one is just or unjust.

Reply Obj. 1. As stated above (A. 4 *ad* 2), anger, though it follows an act of reason, can nevertheless be in dumb animals that are devoid of reason, in so far as through their natural instinct they are moved by their imagination to something like rational action. Since then in man there is both reason and imagination, the movement of anger can be aroused in man in two ways. First, when only his imagination denounces the injury: and, in this way, man is aroused to a movement of anger even against irrational and inanimate beings, which movement is like that which occurs in animals against anything that injures them.—Secondly, by the reason denouncing the injury: and thus, according to the Philosopher (*Rhet.* ii. 3), *it is impossible to be angry with insensible things, or with the dead:* both because they feel no pain, which is, above all, what the angry man seeks in those with whom he is angry: and because there is no question of

* *Cf.* Q. 29, 6.

vengeance on them, since they can do us no harm.

Reply Obj. 2. As the Philosopher says (*Ethic.* v. 11), *metaphorically speaking there is a certain justice and injustice between a man and himself,* in so far as the reason rules the irascible and concupiscible parts of the soul. And in this sense a man is said to be avenged on himself, and consequently, to be angry with himself. But properly, and in accordance with the nature of things, a man is never angry with himself.

Reply Obj. 3. The Philosopher (*Rhet.* ii. 4) assigns as one difference between hatred and anger, that *hatred may be felt towards a class, as we hate the entire class of thieves; whereas anger is directed only towards an individual.* The reason is that hatred arises from our considering a quality as disagreeing with our disposition; and this may refer to a thing in general or in particular. Anger, on the other hand, ensues from someone having injured us by his action. Now all actions are the deeds of individuals: and consequently anger is always pointed at an individual.—When the whole state hurts us, the whole state is reckoned as one individual.*

EIGHTH ARTICLE

Whether the Species of Anger Are Suitably Assigned?

We proceed thus to the Eighth Article:—

Objection 1. It would seem that Damascene (*De Fide Orthod.* ii. 16) unsuitably assigns three species of anger,—*wrath, ill-will* and *rancor.* For no genus derives its specific differences from accidents. But these three are diversified in respect of an accident: because *the beginning of the movement of anger is called wrath* (χόλος), *if anger continue it is called ill-will* (μῆνις); *while rancor* (κότος) *is anger waiting for an opportunity of vengeance.* Therefore these are not different species of anger.

Obj. 2. Further, Cicero says (*De Quæst. Tusc.* iv. 9) that *excandescentia* (*irascibility*) *is what the Greeks call* θύμωσις, *and is a kind of anger that arises and subsides intermittently;* while according to Damascene θύμωσις, is the same as κότος (*rancor*). Therefore κότος does not bide its time for taking vengeance, but in course of time spends itself.

Obj. 3. Further, Gregory (*Moral.* xxi. 4) gives three degrees of anger, namely, *anger without utterance, anger with utterance, and anger with perfection of speech,* corresponding to the three degrees mentioned by Our Lord (Matth. v. 22): *Whosoever is angry with his brother* (thus implying *anger without utterance*), and then, *whosoever shall say to his brother, "Raca"* (implying *anger with utter-*

ance yet without full expression), and lastly, *whosoever shall say "Thou fool"* (where we have *perfection of speech*). Therefore Damascene's division is imperfect, since it takes no account of utterance.

On the contrary, stands the authority of Damascene (*loc. cit.*) and Gregory of Nyssa.*

I answer that, The species of anger given by Damascene and Gregory of Nyssa are taken from those things which give increase to anger. This happens in three ways. First from facility of the movement itself, and he calls this kind of anger χόλος (*bile*) because it is quickly aroused. Secondly, on the part of the grief that causes anger, and which dwells some time in the memory; this belongs to μῆνις (*ill-will*) which is derived from μένειν (*to dwell*). Thirdly, on the part of that which the angry man seeks, viz., vengeance; and this pertains to κότος (*rancor*) which never rests until it is avenged.† Hence the Philosopher (*Ethic.* iv. 5) calls some angry persons ἀκρόχολοι

(*choleric*), because they are easily angered: some he calls πικροί (*bitter*), because they retain their anger for a long time; and some he calls χαλεποί (*ill-tempered*), because they never rest until they have retaliated.‡

Reply Obj. 1. All those things which give anger some kind of perfection are not altogether accidental to anger; and consequently nothing prevents them from causing a certain specific difference thereof.

Reply Obj. 2. Irascibility, which Cicero mentions, seems to pertain to the first species of anger, which consists in a certain quickness of temper, rather than to rancor (*furor*). And there is no reason why the Greek θύμωσις, which is denoted by the Latin *furor*, should not signify both quickness to anger, and firmness of purpose in being avenged.

Reply Obj. 3. These degrees are distinguished according to various effects of anger; and not according to degrees of perfection in the very movement of anger.

QUESTION 47

Of the Cause That Provokes Anger, and of the Remedies of Anger §

(In Four Articles)

WE must now consider the cause that provokes anger, and its remedies. Under this head there are four points of inquiry: (1) Whether the motive of anger is always something done against the one who is angry? (2) Whether slight or contempt is the sole motive of anger? (3) Of the cause of anger on the part of the angry person; (4) Of the cause of anger on the part of the person with whom one is angry.

FIRST ARTICLE

Whether the Motive of Anger Is Always Something Done against the One Who Is Angry?

We proceed thus to the First Article:—

Objection 1. It would seem that the motive of anger is not always something done against the one who is angry. Because man, by sinning, can do nothing against God; since it is written (Job xxxv. 6): *If thy iniquities be multiplied, what shalt thou do against Him?* And yet God is spoken of as being angry with man on account of sin, according to Ps. cv. 40: *The Lord was exceedingly angry with His people.* Therefore it is not always on account of something done against him, that a man is angry.

Obj. 2. Further, anger is a desire for vengeance. But one may desire vengeance for things done against others. Therefore we are not always angry on account of something done against us.

Obj. 3. Further, as the Philosopher says (*Rhet.* ii. 2) man is angry especially with those *who despise what he takes a great interest in; thus men who study philosophy are angry with those who despise philosophy,* and so forth. But contempt of philosophy does not harm the philosopher. Therefore it is not always a harm done to us that makes us angry.

Obj. 4. Further, he that holds his tongue when another insults him, provokes him to greater anger, as Chrysostom observes (*Hom.* xxii. *in Ep. ad Rom.*). But by holding his tongue he does the other no harm. Therefore a man is not always provoked to anger by something done against him.

On the contrary, The Philosopher says (*Rhet.* ii. 4) that *anger is always due to something done to oneself: whereas hatred may arise without anything being done to us, for we hate a man simply because we think him such.*

I answer that, As stated above (Q. 46, A. 6), anger is the desire to hurt another for the pur-

---

* Nemesius, *De Nat. Hom.* xxi.

† Eph. iv. 31. Let all bitterness and anger and indignation . . . be put away from you.

‡ *Cf.* II.-II. Q. 158, A. 5.

§ There is no further mention of these remedies in the text, except in Art. 4.

pose of just vengeance. Now unless some injury has been done, there is no question of vengeance: nor does any injury provoke one to vengeance, but only that which is done to the person who seeks vengeance: for just as everything naturally seeks its own good, so does it naturally repel its own evil. But injury done by anyone does not affect a man unless in some way it be something done against him. Consequently the motive of a man's anger is always something done against him.

Reply Obj. 1. We speak of anger in God, not as of a passion of the soul but as of judgment of justice, inasmuch as He wills to take vengeance on sin. Because the sinner, by sinning, cannot do God any actual harm: but so far as he himself is concerned, he acts against God in two ways. First, in so far as he despises God in His commandments. Secondly, in so far as he harms himself or another; which injury redounds to God, inasmuch as the person injured is an object of God's providence and protection.

Reply Obj. 2. If we are angry with those who harm others, and seek to be avenged on them, it is because those who are injured belong in some way to us: either by some kinship or by friendship, or at least because of the nature we have in common.

Reply Obj. 3. When we take a very great interest in a thing, we look upon it as our own good; so that if anyone despise it, it seems as though we ourselves were despised and injured.

Reply Obj. 4. Silence provokes the insulter to anger when he thinks it is due to contempt, as though his anger were slighted: and a slight is an action.

SECOND ARTICLE

Whether the Sole Motive of Anger Is Slight or Contempt?

We proceed thus to the Second Article:—

Objection 1. It would seem that slight or contempt is not the sole motive of anger. For Damascene says (*De Fide Orthod.* ii. 16) that we are angry *when we suffer, or think that we are suffering, an injury.* But one may suffer an injury without being despised or slighted. Therefore a slight is not the only motive of anger.

Obj. 2. Further, desire for honor and grief for a slight belong to the same subject. But dumb animals do not desire honor. Therefore they are not grieved by being slighted. And yet *they are roused to anger, when wounded,* as the Philosopher says (*Ethic.* iii. 8). Therefore a slight is not the sole motive of anger.

Obj. 3. Further, the Philosopher (*Rhet.* ii. 2) gives many other causes of anger, for instance, *being forgotten by others; that others should rejoice in our misfortunes; that they should make known our evils; being hindered from doing as we like.* Therefore being slighted is not the only motive for being angry.

On the contrary, The Philosopher says (*Rhet.* ii. *loc. cit.*) that anger is *a desire, with sorrow, for vengeance, on account of a seeming slight done unbecomingly.*

I answer that, All the causes of anger are reduced to slight. For slight is of three kinds, as stated in *Rhet.* ii., *ibid.,* viz., *contempt, despiteful treatment, i.e.,* hindering one from doing one's will, and *insolence:* and all motives of anger are reduced to these three. Two reasons may be assigned for this. First, because anger seeks another's hurt as being a means of just vengeance: wherefore it seeks vengeance in so far as it seems just. Now just vengeance is taken only for that which is done unjustly; hence that which provokes anger is always something considered in the light of an injustice. Wherefore the Philosopher says (*Rhet.* ii. 3) that *men are not angry, —if they think they have wronged some one and are suffering justly on that account; because there is no anger at what is just.* Now injury is done to another in three ways: namely, through ignorance, through passion, and through choice. Then, most of all, a man does an injustice, when he does an injury from choice, on purpose, or from deliberate malice, as stated in *Ethic.* v. 8. Wherefore we are most of all angry with those who, in our opinion, have hurt us on purpose. For if we think that some one has done us an injury through ignorance or through passion, either we are not angry with them at all, or very much less: since to do anything through ignorance or through passion takes away from the notion of injury, and to a certain extent calls for mercy and forgiveness. Those, on the other hand, who do an injury on purpose, seem to sin from contempt; wherefore we are angry with them most of all. Hence the Philosopher says (*Rhet.* ii. 3) that *we are either not angry at all, or not very angry with those who have acted through anger, because they do not seem to have acted slightingly.*

The second reason is because a slight is opposed to a man's excellence: because *men think little of things that are not worth much ado* (*Rhet.* ii. 2). Now we seek for some kind of excellence from all our goods. Consequently whatever injury is inflicted on us, in so far as it is derogatory to our excellence, seems to savor of a slight.

Reply Obj. 1. Any other cause, besides contempt, through which a man suffers an injury, takes away from the notion of injury: contempt or slight alone adds to the motive of anger, and consequently is of itself the cause of anger.

Reply Obj. 2. Although a dumb animal does not seek honor as such, yet it naturally seeks a certain superiority, and is angry with anything derogatory thereto.

Reply Obj. 3. Each of those causes amounts to some kind of slight. Thus forgetfulness is a clear sign of slight esteem, for the more we think of a thing the more is it fixed in our memory. Again if a man does not hesitate by his remarks to give pain to another, this seems to show that he thinks little of him: and those too who show signs of hilarity when another is in misfortune, seem to care little about his good or evil. Again he that hinders another from carrying out his will, without deriving thereby any profit to himself, seems not to care much for his friendship. Consequently all those things, in so far as they are signs of contempt, provoke anger.

THIRD ARTICLE

Whether a Man's Excellence Is the Cause of His Being Angry?

We proceed thus to the Third Article:—

Objection 1. It would seem that a man's excellence is not the cause of his being more easily angry. For the Philosopher says (*Rhet.* ii. 2) that *some are angry especially when they are grieved, for instance, the sick, the poor, and those who are disappointed.* But these things seem to pertain to defect. Therefore defect rather than excellence makes one prone to anger.

Obj. 2. Further, the Philosopher says (*ibid.*) that *some are very much inclined to be angry when they are despised for some failing or weakness of the existence of which there are grounds for suspicion; but if they think they excel in those points, they do not trouble.* But a suspicion of this kind is due to some defect. Therefore defect rather than excellence is a cause of a man being angry.

Obj. 3. Further, whatever savors of excellence makes a man agreeable and hopeful. But the Philosopher says (*Rhet.* ii. 3) that *men are not angry when they play, make jokes, or take part in a feast, nor when they are prosperous or successful, nor in moderate pleasures and well-founded hope.* Therefore excellence is not a cause of anger.

On the contrary, The Philosopher says (*ibid.* 9) that excellence makes men prone to anger.

I answer that, The cause of anger, in the man who is angry, may be taken in two ways.

First in respect of the motive of anger: and thus excellence is the cause of a man being easily angered. Because the motive of anger is an unjust slight, as stated above (A. 2). Now it is evident that the more excellent a man is, the more unjust is a slight offered him in the matter in which he excels. Consequently those who excel in any matter, are most of all angry, if they be slighted in that matter; for instance, a wealthy man in his riches, or an orator in his eloquence, and so forth.

Secondly, the cause of anger, in the man who is angry, may be considered on the part of the disposition produced in him by the motive aforesaid. Now it is evident that nothing moves a man to anger except a hurt that grieves him: while whatever savors of defect is above all a cause of grief; since men who suffer from some defect are more easily hurt. And this is why men who are weak, or subject to some other defect, are more easily angered, since they are more easily grieved.

This suffices for the Reply to the First Objection.

Reply Obj. 2. If a man be despised in a matter in which he evidently excels greatly, he does not consider himself the loser thereby, and therefore is not grieved: and in this respect he is less angered. But in another respect, in so far as he is more undeservedly despised, he has more reason for being angry: unless perhaps he thinks that he is envied or insulted not through contempt but through ignorance, or some other like cause.

Reply Obj. 3. All these things hinder anger in so far as they hinder sorrow. But in another respect they are naturally apt to provoke anger, because they make it more unseemly to insult anyone.

FOURTH ARTICLE

Whether a Person's Defect is a Reason for Being More Easily Angry with Him?

We proceed thus to the Fourth Article:—

Objection 1. It would seem that a person's defect is not a reason for being more easily angry with him. For the Philosopher says (*Rhet.* ii. 3) that *we are not angry with those who confess and repent and humble themselves; on the contrary, we are gentle with them. Wherefore dogs bite not those who sit down.* But these things savor of littleness and defect. Therefore littleness of a person is a reason for being less angry with him.

Obj. 2. Further, there is no greater defect than death. But anger ceases at the sight of death. Therefore defect of a person does not provoke anger against him.

Obj. 3. Further, no one thinks little of a man through his being friendly towards him. But we are more angry with friends, if they offend us or refuse to help us; hence it is written (Ps. liv. 13): *If my enemy had reviled me I would verily have borne with it.* Therefore a person's defect is not a reason for being more easily angry with him.

On the contrary, The Philosopher says (*Rhet.* ii. 2) that *the rich man is angry with the poor man, if the latter despise him; and in like manner the prince is angry with his subject.*

I answer that, As stated above (AA. 2, 3) unmerited contempt more than anything else is a provocative of anger. Consequently deficiency or littleness in the person with whom we are angry, tends to increase our anger, in so far as it adds to the unmeritedness of being despised. For just as the higher a man's position is, the more undeservedly he is despised; so the lower it is, the less reason he has for despising. Thus a nobleman is angry if he be insulted by a peasant; a wise man, if by a fool; a master, if by a servant.

If, however, the littleness or deficiency lessens the unmerited contempt, then it does not increase but lessens anger. In this way those who repent of their ill-deeds, and confess that they have done wrong, who humble themselves and ask pardon, mitigate anger, according to Prov. xv. 1: *A mild answer breaketh wrath:* because, to wit, they seem not to despise, but rather to think much of those before whom they humble themselves.

This suffices for the Reply to the First Objection.

Reply Obj. 2. There are two reasons why anger ceases at the sight of death. One is because the dead are incapable of sorrow and sensation; and this is chiefly what the angry seek in those with whom they are angered.—Another reason is because the dead seem to have attained to the limit of evils. Hence anger ceases in regard to all who are grievously hurt, in so far as this hurt surpasses the measure of just retaliation.

Reply Obj. 3. To be despised by one's friends seems also a greater indignity. Consequently if they despise us by hurting or by failing to help, we are angry with them for the same reason for which we are angry with those who are beneath us.

QUESTION 48

Of the Effects of Anger

(In Four Articles)

WE must now consider the effects of anger: under which head there are four points of inquiry: (1) Whether anger causes pleasure? (2) Whether above all it causes heat in the heart? (3) Whether above all it hinders the use of reason? (4) Whether it causes taciturnity?

FIRST ARTICLE

Whether Anger Causes Pleasure?

We proceed thus to the First Article:—

Objection 1. It would seem that anger does not cause pleasure. Because sorrow excludes pleasure. But anger is never without sorrow, since, as stated in *Ethic.* vii. 6, *everyone that acts from anger, acts with pain.* Therefore anger does not cause pleasure.

Obj. 2. Further, the Philosopher says (*Ethic.* iv. 5) that *vengeance makes anger to cease, because it substitutes pleasure for pain:* whence we may gather that the angry man derives pleasure from vengeance, and that vengeance quells his anger. Therefore on the advent of pleasure, anger departs: and consequently anger is not an effect united with pleasure.

Obj. 3. Further, no effect hinders its cause, since it is conformed to its cause. But pleasure hinders anger, as stated in *Rhet.* ii. 3. Therefore pleasure is not an effect of anger.

On the contrary, The Philosopher (*ibid.*) quotes the saying that anger is

"Sweet to the soul as honey to the taste."

—*Iliad,* xviii. 109, 110 (trl. POPE).

I answer that, As the Philosopher says (*Ethic.* vii. 14), pleasures, chiefly sensible and bodily pleasures, are remedies against sorrow: and therefore the greater the sorrow or anxiety, the more sensible are we to the pleasure which heals it, as is evident in the case of thirst which increases the pleasure of drink. Now it is clear from what has been said (Q. 47, AA. 1, 3), that the movement of anger arises from a wrong done that causes sorrow, for which sorrow vengeance is sought as a remedy. Consequently as soon as vengeance is present, pleasure ensues, and so much the greater according as the sorrow was greater.—Therefore if vengeance be really present, perfect pleasure ensues, entirely excluding sorrow, so that the movement of anger ceases. But before vengeance is really present, it becomes present to the angry man in two ways:—in one way, by hope; because none is angry except he hopes for vengeance, as stated above (Q. 46, A. 1);—in another way, by thinking of it continually, for to everyone that desires a thing it is pleasant to dwell on the thought of what he desires; wherefore the imaginings of dreams are pleasant. Accordingly an angry man takes pleasure in thinking much about vengeance. This pleasure, however, is not perfect, so as to banish sorrow and consequently anger.

Reply Obj. 1. The angry man does not grieve and rejoice at the same thing; he grieves for the wrong done, while he takes pleasure in the thought and hope of vengeance. Consequently sorrow is to anger as its beginning; while pleasure is the effect or terminus of anger.

Reply Obj. 2. This argument holds in regard to pleasure caused by the real presence of vengeance, which banishes anger altogether.

Reply Obj. 3. Pleasure that precedes hinders sorrow from ensuing, and consequently is a hindrance to anger. But pleasure felt in taking vengeance follows from anger.

SECOND ARTICLE

Whether Anger above All Causes Fervor in the Heart?

We proceed thus to the Second Article:—

Objection 1. It would seem that heat is not above all the effect of anger. For fervor, as stated above (Q. 28, A. 5; Q. 37, A. 2), belongs to love. But love, as above stated, is the beginning and cause of all the passions. Since then the cause is more powerful than its effect, it seems that anger is not the chief cause of fervor.

Obj. 2. Further, those things which, of themselves, arouse fervor, increase as time goes on; thus love grows stronger the longer it lasts. But in course of time anger grows weaker; for the Philosopher says (*Rhet.* ii. 3) that *time puts an end to anger.* Therefore fervor is not the proper effect of anger.

Obj. 3. Further, fervor added to fervor produces greater fervor. But *the addition of a greater anger banishes already existing anger,* as the Philosopher says (*ibid.*). Therefore anger does not cause fervor.

On the contrary, Damascene says (*De Fide Orth.* ii. 16) that *anger is fervor of the blood around the heart, resulting from an exhalation of the bile.*

I answer that, As stated above (Q. 44, A. 1), the bodily transmutation that occurs in the passions of the soul is proportionate to the movement of the appetite. Now it is evident that every appetite, even the natural appetite, tends with greater force to repel that which is contrary to it, if it be present: hence we see that hot water freezes harder, as though the cold acted with greater force on the hot object. Since then the appetitive movement of anger is caused by some injury inflicted, as by

a contrary that is present; it follows that the appetite tends with great force to repel the injury by the desire of vengeance; and hence ensues great vehemence and impetuosity in the movement of anger. And because the movement of anger is not one of recoil, which corresponds to the action of cold, but one of prosecution, which corresponds to the action of heat, the result is that the movement of anger produces fervor of the blood and vital spirits around the heart, which is the instrument of the soul's passions. And hence it is that, on account of the heart being so disturbed by anger, those chiefly who are angry betray signs thereof in their outer members. For, as Gregory says (*Moral.* v. 30) *the heart that is inflamed with the stings of its own anger beats quick, the body trembles, the tongue stammers, the countenance takes fire, the eyes grow fierce, they that are well known are not recognized. With the mouth indeed he shapes a sound, but the understanding knows not what it says.*

Reply Obj. 1. *Love itself is not felt so keenly as in the absence of the beloved,* as Augustine observes (*De Trin.* x. 12). Consequently when a man suffers from a hurt done to the excellence that he loves, he feels his love thereof the more: the result being that his heart is moved with greater heat to remove the hindrance to the object of his love; so that anger increases the fervor of love and makes it to be felt more.

Nevertheless, the fervor arising from heat differs according as it is to be referred to love or to anger. Because the fervor of love has a certain sweetness and gentleness; for it tends to the good that one loves: whence it is likened to the warmth of the air and of the blood. For this reason sanguine temperaments are more inclined to love; and hence the saying that *love springs from the liver,* because of the blood being formed there.—On the other hand, the fervor of anger has a certain bitterness with a tendency to destroy, for it seeks to be avenged on the contrary evil: whence it is likened to the heat of fire and of the bile, and for this reason Damascene says (*loc. cit.*) that it *results from an exhalation of the bile whence it takes its name* χολή.

Reply Obj. 2. Time, of necessity, weakens all those things, the causes of which are impaired by time. Now it is evident that memory is weakened by time; for things which happened long ago easily slip from our memory. But anger is caused by the memory of a wrong done. Consequently the cause of anger is impaired little by little as time goes on, until at length it vanishes altogether.—Moreover a wrong seems greater when it is first felt; and our estimate thereof is gradually lessened the further the sense of present wrong recedes into the past.—The same applies to love, so long as the cause of love is in the memory alone: wherefore the Philosopher says (*Ethic.* viii. 5) that *if a friend's absence lasts long, it seems to make men forget their friendship.* But in the presence of a friend, the cause of friendship is continually being multiplied by time: wherefore the friendship increases: and the same would apply to anger, were its cause continually multiplied.

Nevertheless the very fact that anger soon spends itself proves the strength of its fervor: for as a great fire is soon spent having burnt up all the fuel; so too anger, by reason of its vehemence, soon dies away.

Reply Obj. 3. Every power that is divided in itself is weakened. Consequently if a man being already angry with one, becomes angry with another, by this very fact his anger with the former is weakened. Especially is this so if his anger in the second case be greater: because the wrong done which aroused his former anger, will, in comparison with the second wrong, which is reckoned greater, seem to be of little or no account.

THIRD ARTICLE

Whether Anger above All Hinders the Use of Reason?

We proceed thus to the Third Article:—

Objection 1. It would seem that anger does not hinder the use of reason. Because that which presupposes an act of reason, does not seem to hinder the use of reason. But *anger listens to reason,* as stated in *Ethic.* vii. 6. Therefore anger does not hinder reason.

Obj. 2. Further, the more the reason is hindered, the less does man show his thoughts. But the Philosopher says (*Ethic.* vii. 6) that *an angry man is not cunning but is open.* Therefore anger does not seem to hinder the use of reason, as desire does; for desire is cunning, as he also states (*ibid.*).

Obj. 3. Further, the judgment of reason becomes more evident by juxtaposition of the contrary: because contraries stand out more clearly when placed beside one another. But this also increases anger: for the Philosopher says (*Rhet.* ii. 2) that *men are more angry if they receive unwonted treatment; for instance, honorable men, if they be dishonored:* and so forth. Therefore the same cause increases anger, and facilitates the judgment of reason. Therefore anger does not hinder the judgment of reason.

On the contrary, Gregory says (*Moral.* v. 30) that anger *withdraws the light of understanding, while by agitating it troubles the mind.*

I answer that, Although the mind or reason makes no use of a bodily organ in its proper act, yet, since it needs certain sensitive powers for the execution of its act, the acts of which powers are hindered when the body is disturbed, it follows of necessity that any disturbance in the body hinders even the judgment of reason; as is clear in the case of drunkenness or sleep. Now it has been stated (A. 2) that anger, above all, causes a bodily disturbance in the region of the heart, so much as to effect even the outward members. Consequently, of all the passions, anger is the most manifest obstacle to the judgment of reason, according to Ps. xxx. 10: *My eye is troubled with wrath.*

Reply Obj. 1. The beginning of anger is in the reason, as regards the appetitive movement, which is the formal element of anger. But the passion of anger forestalls the perfect judgment of reason, as though it listened but imperfectly to reason, on account of the commotion of the heat urging to instant action, which commotion is the material element of anger. In this respect it hinders the judgment of reason.

Reply Obj. 2. An angry man is said to be open, not because it is clear to him what he ought to do, but because he acts openly, without thought of hiding himself. This is due partly to the reason being hindered, so as not to discern what should be hidden and what done openly, nor to devise the means of hiding; and partly to the dilatation of the heart which pertains to magnanimity which is an effect of anger: wherefore the Philosopher says of the magnanimous man (*Ethic.* iv. 3) that *he is open in his hatreds and his friendships* . . . and *speaks and acts openly.*—Desire, on the other hand, is said to lie low and to be cunning, because, in many cases, the pleasurable things that are desired, savor of shame and voluptuousness, wherein man wishes not to be seen. But in those things that savor of manliness and excellence, such as matters of vengeance, man seeks to be in the open.

Reply Obj. 3. As stated above (*ad* 1), the movement of anger begins in the reason, wherefore the juxtaposition of one contrary with another facilitates the judgment of reason, on the same grounds as it increases anger. For when a man who is possessed of honor or wealth, suffers a loss therein, the loss seems all the greater, both on account of the contrast, and because it was unforeseen. Consequently it causes greater grief: just as a great good, through being received unexpectedly, causes greater delight. And in proportion to the increase of the grief that precedes, anger is increased also.

FOURTH ARTICLE

Whether Anger above All Causes Taciturnity?

We proceed thus to the Fourth Article:—

Objection 1. It would seem that anger does not cause taciturnity. Because taciturnity is opposed to speech. But increase of anger conduces to speech; as is evident from the degrees of anger laid down by Our Lord (Matth. v. 22): where He says: *Whosoever is angry with his brother;* and . . . *whosoever shall say to his brother, "Raca";* and . . . *whosoever shall say to his brother, "Thou fool."* Therefore anger does not cause taciturnity.

Obj. 2. Further, through failing to obey reason, man sometimes breaks out into unbecoming words: hence it is written (Prov. xxv. 28): *As a city that lieth open and is not compassed with walls, so is a man that cannot refrain his own spirit in speaking.* But anger, above all, hinders the judgment of reason, as stated above (A. 3). Consequently above all it makes one break out into unbecoming words. Therefore it does not cause taciturnity.

Obj. 3. Further, it is written (Matth. xii. 34): *Out of the abundance of the heart the mouth speaketh.* But anger, above all, causes a disturbance in the heart, as stated above (A. 2). Therefore above all it conduces to speech. Therefore it does not cause taciturnity.

On the contrary, Gregory says (*Moral.* v. 30) that *when anger does not vent itself outwardly by the lips, inwardly it burns the more fiercely.*

I answer that, As stated above (A. 3; Q. 46, A. 4), anger both follows an act of reason, and hinders the reason: and in both respects it may cause taciturnity. On the part of the reason, when the judgment of reason prevails so far, that although it does not curb the appetite in its inordinate desire for vengeance, yet it curbs the tongue from unbridled speech. Wherefore Gregory says (*Moral.* v. *loc. cit.*): *Sometimes when the mind is disturbed, anger, as if in judgment, commands silence.*—On the part of the impediment to reason because, as stated above (A. 2), the disturbance of anger reaches to those outward members, and chiefly to those members which reflect more distinctly the emotions of the heart, such as the eyes, face and tongue; wherefore, as observed above (A. 2), *the tongue stammers, the countenance takes fire, the eyes grow fierce.* Consequently anger may cause such a disturbance, that the tongue is altogether deprived of speech; and taciturnity is the result.

Reply Obj. 1. Anger sometimes goes so far as to hinder the reason from curbing the tongue: but sometimes it goes yet farther, so as to paralyze the tongue and other outward members.

And this suffices for the Reply to the Second Objection.

Reply Obj. 3. The disturbance of the heart may sometimes superabound to the extent that the movements of the outward members are hindered by the inordinate movement of the heart. Thence ensue taciturnity and immobility of the outward members; and sometimes even death.—If, however, the disturbance be not so great, then *out of the abundance of the heart* thus disturbed, the mouth proceeds to speak.

HABITS IN GENERAL

	Question	Article
Their Nature.—Is habit a quality?—Does it imply a relation to act?—Necessity of habit?	49	4
The Subject.—Is the soul subject of habit?—How?—Is habit in the intellect?	50	6
As to formation:—Is any habit from nature?—Is it caused by one act?	51	4
As to increase:—Do they increase by addition of repeated acts?	52	3
As to corruption:—Can a habit be diminished or corrupted?	53	3
Their Distinction.—Can many habits be in one power?—Can one habit be made up of many habits?	54	4

The Intrinsic Principles of Human Acts

1. Powers.—See Part I, Q. 77.

2. Habits
   1. In General..
      1. Their Nature.—Is habit a quality?—Does it imply a relation to act?—Necessity of habit?
      2. The Subject.—Is the soul subject of habit?—How?—Is habit in the intellect?
      3. Their Cause
         1. As to formation:—Is any habit from nature?—Is it caused by one act?
         2. As to increase:—Do they increase by addition of repeated acts?
         3. As to corruption:—Can a habit be diminished or corrupted?
      4. Their Distinction.—Can many habits be in one power?—Can one habit be made up of many habits?
   2. In Particular (See Part II-I, QQ. 55-89).

TREATISE ON HABITS

QUESTION 49

Of Habits in General, As to Their Substance

(In Four Articles)

AFTER treating of human acts and passions, we now pass on to the consideration of the principles of human acts, and firstly of intrinsic principles, secondly of extrinsic principles. The intrinsic principle is power and habit; but as we have treated of powers in the First Part (Q. 77. seqq.), it remains for us to consider them in general: in the second place we shall consider virtues and vices and other like habits, which are the principles of human acts.

Concerning habits in general there are four points to be considered: First, the substance of habits; second, their subject; third, the cause of their generation, increase, and corruption; fourth, how they are distinguished from one another.

Under the first head, there are four points of inquiry: (1) Whether habit is a quality? (2) Whether it is a distinct species of quality? (3) Whether habit implies an order to an act? (4) Of the necessity of habit.

FIRST ARTICLE

Whether Habit Is a Quality?

We proceed thus to the First Article:—

Objection 1. It would seem that habit is not a quality. For Augustine says (*Qq.* lxxxiii, qu. 73): *this word "habit" is derived from the verb "to have."* But *To have* belongs not only to quality, but also to the other categories: for we speak of ourselves as *having* quantity and money and other like things. Therefore habit is not a quality.

Obj. 2. Further, habit is reckoned as one of the predicaments; as may be clearly seen in the *Book on the Predicaments* (*Categor.* vi). But one predicament is not contained under another. Therefore habit is not a quality.

Obj. 2. Further, *every habit is a disposition*, as is stated in the *Book on the Predicaments* (*ibid.*). Now disposition is *the order of that which has parts*, as stated in *Metaph.* v, text. 24. But this belongs to the predicament *Position.* Therefore habit is not a quality.

On the contrary, The Philosopher says, in the *Book on the Predicaments* (*Categor.*

vi.) that *habit is a quality which it is difficult to change.*

I answer that, This word *habitus* (habit) is derived from *habere* (to have). Now habit is taken from this word in two ways; in one way, inasmuch as man, or any other thing, is said to *have* something; in another way, inasmuch as a particular thing has a relation (*se habet*) either in regard to itself, or in regard to something else.

Concerning the first, we must observe that *to have*, as said in regard to anything that is *had*, is common to the various predicaments. And so the Philosopher puts *to have* among the *post-predicaments*, so called because they result from the various predicaments; as, for instance, opposition, priority, posterity, and such like. Now among things which are had, there seems to be this distinction, that there are some in which there is no medium between the *haver* and that which is had: as, for instance, there is no medium between the subject and quality or quantity. Then there are some in which there is a medium, but only a relation: as, for instance, a man is said to have a companion or a friend. And, further, there are some in which there is a medium, not indeed an action or a passion, but something after the manner of action or passion: thus, for instance, something adorns or covers, and something else is adorned or covered: wherefore the Philosopher says (*Metaph.* v, text. 25) that *a habit is said to be, as it were, an action or a passion of the haver and that which is had;* as is the case in those things which we have about ourselves. And therefore these constitute a special genus of things, which comprised under the predicament of *habit*: of which the Philosopher says (*Metaph.* v., *ibid.*) that *there is a habit between clothing and the man who is clothed.*

But if *to have* be taken according as a thing has a relation in regard to itself or to something else; in that case habit is a quality; since this mode of having is in respect of some quality: and of this the Philosopher says (*Metaph.* v, *loc. cit.*) that *habit is a disposition whereby that which is disposed is disposed well or ill, and this, either in regard to itself* or in regard to another: thus health is a habit. And in this sense we speak of habit now. Wherefore we must say that habit is a quality.

Reply Obj. 1. This argument takes *to have* in the general sense: for thus it is common to many predicaments, as we have said.

Reply Obj. 2. This argument takes habit in the sense in which we understand it to be a medium between the haver, and that which is had: and in this sense it is a predicament, as we have said.

Reply Obj. 3. Disposition does always, indeed, imply an order of that which has parts: but this happens in three ways, as the Philosopher goes on at once to say (*ibid.*): namely, *either as to place, or as to power, or as to species.* In saying this, as Simplicius observes in his *Commentary on the Predicaments, he includes all dispositions:—bodily dispositions, when he says "as to place,"* and this belongs to the predicament *Position,* which is the order of parts in a place:—*when he says "as to power," he includes all those dispositions which are in course of formation and not yet arrived at perfect usefulness,* such as inchoate science and virtue:—*and when he says, "as to species," he includes perfect dispositions, which are called habits,* such as perfected science and virtue.

SECOND ARTICLE

Whether Habit Is a Distinct Species of Quality?

We thus proceed to the Second Article:—

It would seem that habit is not a distinct species of quality. Because, as we have said (A. 1), habit, in so far as it is a quality, is a disposition whereby that which is disposed is disposed well or ill. But this happens in regard to any quality: for a thing happens to be well or ill disposed in regard also to shape, and in like manner, in regard to heat and cold, and in regard to all such things. Therefore habit is not a distinct species of quality.

Obj. 2. Further, the Philosopher says in the *Book on the Predicaments (Categor.* vi), that heat and cold are dispositions or habits, just as sickness and health. Therefore habit or disposition is not distinct from the other species of quality.

Obj. 3. Further, *difficult to change* is not a difference belonging to the predicament of quality, but rather to movement or passion. Now, no genus should be contracted to a species by a difference of another genus; but *differences should be proper to a genus,* as the Philosopher says in *Metaph.* vii, text. 42. Therefore, since habit is *a quality difficult to change,* it seems not to be a distinct species of quality.

On the contrary, The Philosopher says in the *Book on the Predicaments (Categor.*vi) that *one species of quality is habit and disposition.*

I answer that, The Philosopher in the *Book of Predicaments (Categor.* vi) reckons disposition and habit as the first species of quality. Now Simplicius, in his *Commentary on the Predicaments,* explains the difference of these species as follows. He says *that some qualities are natural, and are in their subject in virtue of its nature, and are always there: but some are adventitious, being caused from without, and these can be lost. Now the latter,* i.e., those which are adventitious, *are habits and dispositions, differing in the point of being easily or difficultly lost. As to natural qualities, some regard a thing in the point of its being in a state of potentiality; and thus we have the second species of quality: while others regard a thing which is in act; and this either deeply rooted therein or only on its surface. If deeply rooted, we have the third species of quality: if on the surface, we have the fourth species of quality, as shape, and form which is the shape of an animated being.* But this distinction of the species of quality seems unsuitable. For there are many shapes, and passion-like qualities, which are not natural but adventitious: and there are also many dispositions which are not adventitious but natural, as health, beauty, and the like. Moreover, it does not suit the order of the species, since that which is the more natural is always first.

Therefore we must explain otherwise the distinction of dispositions and habits from other qualities. For quality, properly speaking, implies a certain mode of substance. Now mode, as Augustine says (*Gen. ad lit.* iv. 3), *is that which a measure determines:* wherefore it implies a certain determination according to a certain measure. Therefore, just as that in accordance with which the material potentiality (*potentia materiæ*) is determined to its substantial being, is called quality, which is a difference affecting substance, so that, in accordance with which the potentiality of the subject is determined to its accidental being, is called an accidental quality, which is also a kind of difference, as is clear from the Philosopher (*Metaph.* v, text. 19).

Now the mode of determination of the subject to accidental being may be taken in regard to the very nature of the subject, or in regard to action and passion resulting from its natural principles, which are matter and form; or again in regard to quantity. If we take the mode or determination of the subject in regard to quantity, we shall then have the fourth species of quality. And because quantity, considered in itself, is devoid of movement, and does not imply the notion of good or evil, so it does not concern the fourth species of quality whether a thing be well or ill disposed, nor quickly or slowly transitory.

But the mode of determination of the subject, in regard to action or passion, is considered in the second and third species of quality. And therefore in both, we take into account whether a thing be done with ease or difficulty; whether it be transitory or lasting. But in them, we do not consider anything pertaining to the notion of good or evil: because movements and passions have not the aspect of an end, whereas good and evil are said in respect of an end.

On the other hand, the mode or determination of the subject, in regard to the nature of the thing, belongs to the first species of quality, which is habit and disposition: for the Philosopher says (*Phys.* vii, text. 17), when speaking of habits of the soul and of the body, that they are *dispositions of the perfect to the best; and by perfect I mean that which is disposed in accordance with its nature.* And since the form itself and the nature of a thing is the end and the cause why a thing is made (*Phys.* ii., text. 23), therefore in the first species we consider both evil and good, and also changeableness, whether easy or difficult; inasmuch as a certain nature is the end of generation and movement. And so the Philosopher (*Metaph.* v, text. 25) defines habit, a *disposition whereby someone is disposed, well or ill;* and in *Ethic.* ii. 4, he says that by *habits we are directed well or ill in reference to the passions.* For when the mode is suitable to the thing's nature, it has the aspect of good: and when it is unsuitable, it has the aspect of evil. And since nature is the first object of consideration in anything, for this reason habit is reckoned as the first species of quality.

Reply Obj. 1. Disposition implies a certain order, as stated above (A. 1, *ad* 3). Wherefore a man is not said to be disposed by some quality except in relation to something else. And if we add *well or ill,* which belongs to the essential notion of habit, we must consider the quality's relation to the nature, which is the end. So in regard to shape, or heat, or cold, a man is not said to be well or ill disposed, except by reason of a relation to the nature of a thing, with regard to its suitability or unsuitability. Consequently even shapes and passion-like qualities, in so far as they are considered to be suitable or unsuitable to the nature of a thing, belong to habits or dispositions: for shape and color, according to their suitability to the nature of a thing, concern beauty: while heat and cold, according to their suitability to the nature of a thing, concern

health. And in this way heat and cold are put, by the Philosopher, in the first species of quality.

Wherefore it is clear how to answer the second objection: though some give another solution, as Simplicius says in his *Commentary on the Predicaments.*

Reply Obj. 3. This difference, *difficult to change,* does not distinguish habit from the other species of quality, but from disposition. Now disposition may be taken in two ways; in one way, as the genus of habit, for disposition is included in the definition of habit (*Metaph.* v, text. 25): in another way, according as it is divided against habit. Again, disposition, properly so called, can be divided against habit in two ways: first, as perfect and imperfect within the same species; and thus we call it a disposition, retaining the name of the genus, when it is had imperfectly, so as to be easily lost: whereas we call it a habit, when it is had perfectly, so as not to be lost easily. And thus a disposition becomes a habit, just as a boy becomes a man. Secondly, they may be distinguished as diverse species of the one subaltern genus: so that we call dispositions, those qualities of the first species, which by reason of their very nature are easily lost, because they have changeable causes; e.g., sickness and health: whereas we call habits those qualities which, by reason of their very nature, are not easily changed, in that they have unchangeable causes, e.g., sciences and virtues. And in this sense, disposition does not become habit. The latter explanation seems more in keeping with the intention of Aristotle: for in order to confirm this distinction he adduces the common mode of speaking, according to which, when a quality is, by reason of its nature, easily changeable, and, through some accident, becomes difficultly changeable, then it is called a habit: while the contrary happens in regard to qualities, by reason of their nature, difficultly changeable: for supposing a man to have a science imperfectly, so as to be liable to lose it easily, we say that he is disposed to that science, rather than that he has the science. From this it is clear that the word *habit* implies a certain lastingness: while the word *disposition* does not.

Nor does it matter that thus to be easy and difficult to change are specific differences (of a quality), although they belong to passion and movement, and not to the genus of quality. For these differences, though apparently accidental to quality, nevertheless designate differences which are proper and essential to quality. In the same way, in the genus of substance we often take accidental instead of substantial differences, in so far as by the former, essential principles are designated.

THIRD ARTICLE

Whether Habit Implies Order to an Act?

We proceed thus to the Third Article:—

Objection 1. It would seem that habit does not imply order to an act. For everything acts according as it is in act. But the Philosopher says (*De Anima* iii, text 8), that *when one is become knowing by habit, one is still in a state of potentiality, but otherwise than before learning.* Therefore habit does not imply the relation of a principle to an act.

Obj. 2. Further, that which is put in the definition of a thing, belongs to it essentially. But to be a principle of action, is put in the definition of power, as we read in *Metaph.* v., text. 17. Therefore to be the principle of an act belongs to power essentially. Now that which is essential is first in every genus. If therefore, habit also is a principle of act, it follows that it is posterior to power. And so habit and disposition will not be the first species of quality.

Obj. 3. Further, health is sometimes a habit, and so are leanness and beauty. But these do not indicate relation to an act. Therefore it is not essential to habit to be a principle of act.

On the contrary, Augustine says (*De Bono Conjug.* xxi) that *habit is that whereby something is done when necessary.* And the Commentator says (*De Anima* iii) that *habit is that whereby we act when we will.*

I answer that, To have relation to an act may belong to habit, both in regard to the nature of habit, and in regard to the subject in which the habit is. In regard to the nature of habit, it belongs to every habit to have relation to an act. For it is essential to habit to imply some relation to a thing's nature, in so far as it is suitable or unsuitable thereto. But a thing's nature, which is the end of generation, is further ordained to another end, which is either an operation, or the product of an operation, to which one attains by means of operation. Wherefore habit implies relation not only to the very nature of a thing, but also, consequently, to operation, inasmuch as this is the end of nature, or conducive to the end. Whence also it is stated (*Metaph.* v, text. 25) in the definition of habit, that it is a disposition whereby that which is disposed, is well or ill disposed either in regard to itself, that is to its nature, or in regard to something else, that is to the end.

But there are some habits, which even on the part of the subject in which they are, imply primarily and principally relation to an act. For, as we have said, habit primarily and of itself implies a relation to the thing's nature. If therefore the nature of the thing, in which

the habit is, consists in this very relation to an act, it follows that the habit principally implies relation to an act. Now it is clear that the nature and the notion of power is that it should be a principle of act. Wherefore every habit which is subjected in a power, implies principally relation to an act.

Reply Obj. 1. Habit is an act, in so far as it is a quality: and in this respect it can be a principle of operation. It is, however, in a state of potentiality in respect to operation. Wherefore habit is called first act, and operation, second act; as it is explained in *De Anima* ii., text. 5.

Reply Obj. 2. It is not of the essence of habit to be related to power, but to be related to nature. And as nature precedes action, to which power is related, therefore habit is put before power as a species of quality.

Reply Obj. 3. Health is said to be a habit, or a habitual disposition, in relation to nature, as stated above. But in so far as nature is a principle of act, it consequently implies a relation to act. Wherefore the Philosopher says (*De Hist. Animal.* x. 1), that man, or one of his members, is called healthy, *when he can perform the operation of a healthy man.* And the same applies to other habits.

FOURTH ARTICLE

Whether Habits Are Necessary?

We proceed thus to the Fourth Article:—

Objection 1. It would seem that habits are not necessary. For by habits we are well or ill disposed in respect of something, as stated above. But a thing is well or ill disposed by its form: for in respect of its form a thing is good, even as it is a being. Therefore there is no necessity for habits.

Obj. 2. Further, habit implies relation to an act. But power implies sufficiently a principle of act: for even the natural powers, without any habits, are principles of acts. Therefore there was no necessity for habits.

Obj. 3. Further, as power is related to good and evil, so also is habit: and as power does not always act, so neither does habit. Given, therefore, the powers, habits become superfluous.

On the contrary, Habits are perfections (*Phys.* vii, text. 17). But perfection is of the greatest necessity to a thing: since it is in the nature of an end. Therefore it was necessary that there should be habits.

I answer that, As we have said above (AA. 2, 3), habit implies a disposition in relation to a thing's nature, and to its operation or end, by reason of which disposition a thing is well or ill disposed thereto. Now for a thing to need to be disposed to something else, three conditions are necessary. The first condition is that which is disposed should be distinct from that to which it is disposed; and so, that it should be related to it as potentiality is to act. Whence, if there is a being whose nature is not composed of potentiality and act, and whose substance is its own operation, which itself is for itself, there we can find no room for habit and disposition, as is clearly the case in God.

The second condition is, that that which is in a state of potentiality in regard to something else, be capable of determination in several ways and to various things. Whence if something be in a state of potentiality in regard to something else, but in regard to that only, there we find no room for disposition and habit: for such a subject from its own nature has the due relation to such an act. Wherefore if a heavenly body be composed of matter and form, since that matter is not in a state of potentiality to another form, as we said in the First Part (Q. 56, A. 2), there is no need for disposition or habit in respect of the form, or even in respect of operation, since the nature of the heavenly body is not in a state of potentiality to more than one fixed movement.

The third condition is that in disposing the subject to one of those things to which it is in potentiality, several things should occur, capable of being adjusted in various ways: so as to dispose the subject well or ill to its form or to its operation. Wherefore the simple qualities of the elements which suit the natures of the elements in one single fixed way, are not called dispositions or habits, but *simple qualities*: but we call dispositions or habits, such things as health, beauty, and so forth, which imply the adjustment of several things which may vary in their relative adjustability. For this reason the Philosopher says (*Metaph.* v, text. 24, 25) that *habit is a disposition:* and disposition is *the order of that which has parts either as to place, or as to potentiality, or as to species,* as we have said above (A. 1 *ad* 3). Wherefore, since there are many things for whose natures and operations several things must concur which may vary in their relative adjustability, it follows that habit is necessary.

Reply Obj. 1. By the form the nature of a thing is perfected: yet the subject needs to be disposed in regard to the form by some disposition. But the form itself is further ordained to operation, which is either the end, or the means to the end. And if the form is limited to one fixed operation, no further disposition, besides the form itself, is needed for the operation. But if the form be such that it can operate in diverse ways, as the soul; it needs to be disposed to its operations by means of habits.

Reply Obj. 2. Power sometimes has a relation to many things: and then it needs to be determined by something else. But if a power has not a relation to many things, it does not need a habit to determine it, as we have said. For this reason the natural forces do not perform their operations by means of habits: because they are of themselves determined to one mode of operation.

Reply Obj. 3. The same habit has not a relation to good and evil, as will be made clear further on (Q. 34, A. 3): whereas the same power has a relation to good and evil. And, therefore, habits are necessary that the powers be determined to good.

QUESTION 50

Of the Subject of Habits

(In Six Articles)

WE consider next the subject of habits: and under this head there are six points of inquiry: (1) Whether there is a habit in the body? (2) Whether the soul is a subject of habit, in respect of its essence or in respect of its power? (3) Whether in the powers of the sensitive part there can be a habit? (4) Whether there is a habit in the intellect? (5) Whether there is a habit in the will? (6) Whether there is a habit in separate substances?

FIRST ARTICLE

Whether There Is a Habit in the Body?

We proceed thus to the First Article:—

Objection 1. It would seem that there is not a habit in the body. For, as the Commentator says (*De Anima* iii), *a habit is that whereby we act when we will.* But bodily actions are not subject to the will, since they are natural. Therefore there can be no habit in the body.

Obj. 2. Further, all bodily dispositions are easy to change. But habit is a quality, difficult to change. Therefore no bodily disposition can be a habit.

Obj. 3. Further, all bodily dispositions are subject to change. But change can only be in the third species of quality, which is divided against habit. Therefore there is no habit in the body.

On the contrary, The Philosopher says in the *Book of Predicaments* (*De Categor.* vi) that health of the body and incurable disease are called habits.

I answer that, As we have said above (Q. 49, AA. 2 seqq.), habit is a disposition of a subject which is in a state of potentiality either to form or to operation. Therefore in so far as habit implies disposition to operation, no habit is principally in the body as its subject. For every operation of the body proceeds either from a natural quality of the body or from the soul moving the body. Consequently, as to those operations which proceed from its nature, the body is not disposed by a habit: because the natural forces are determined to one mode of operation; and we have already said (Q. 49, A. 4) that it is when the subject is in potentiality to many things that a habitual disposition is required. As to the operations which proceed from the soul through the body, they belong principally to the soul, and secondarily to the body. Now habits are in proportion to their operations: whence *by like acts like habits are formed* (*Ethic.* ii. 1, 2). And therefore the dispositions to such operations are principally in the soul. But they can be secondarily in the body: to wit, in so far as the body is disposed and enabled with promptitude to help in the operations of the soul.

If, however, we speak of the disposition of the subject to form, thus a habitual disposition can be in the body, which is related to the soul as a subject is to its form. And in this way health and beauty and such like are called habitual dispositions. Yet they have not the nature of habit perfectly: because their causes, of their very nature, are easily changeable.

On the other hand, as Simplicius reports in his *Commentary on the Predicaments,* Alexander denied absolutely that habits or dispositions of the first species are in the body: and held that the first species of quality belonged to the soul alone. And he held that Aristotle mentions health and sickness in the *Book on the Predicaments* not as though they belonged to the first species of quality, but by way of example: so that he would mean that just as health and sickness may be easy or difficult to change, so also are all the qualities of the first species, which are called habits and dispositions. But this is clearly contrary to the intention of Aristotle: both because he speaks in the same way of health and sickness as examples, as of virtue and science; and because in *Physic.* vii, text. 17, he expressly mentions beauty and health among habits.

Reply Obj. 1. This objection runs in the sense of habit as a disposition to operation, and of those actions of the body which are from nature: but not in the sense of those

* ἴσως ἕξιν (*Categor.* viii).

actions which proceed from the soul, and the principle of which is the will.

Reply Obj. 2. Bodily dispositions are not simply difficult to change on account of the changeableness of their bodily causes. But they may be difficult to change by comparison to such a subject, because, to wit, as long as such a subject endures, they cannot be removed; or because they are difficult to change, by comparison to other dispositions. But qualities of the soul are simply difficult to change, on account of the unchangeableness of the subject. And therefore he does not say that health which is difficult to change is a habit simply: but that it is *as a habit,* as we read in the Greek.* On the other hand, the qualities of the soul are called habits simply.

Reply Obj. 3. Bodily dispositions which are in the first species of quality, as some maintained, differ from qualities of the third species, in this, that the qualities of the third species consist in some *becoming* and movement, as it were, wherefore they are called passions or passible qualities. But when they have attained to perfection (specific perfection, so to speak), they have then passed into the first species of quality. But Simplicius in his *Commentary* disapproves of this; for in this way heating would be in the third species, and heat in the first species of quality; whereas Aristotle puts heat in the third.

Wherefore Porphyrius, as Simplicius reports (*ibid.*), says that passion or passion-like quality, disposition and habit, differ in bodies by way of intensity and remissness. For when a thing receives heat in this only that it is being heated, and not so as to be able to give heat, then we have passion, if it is transitory; or passion-like quality if it is permanent. But when it has been brought to the point that it is able to heat something else, then it is a disposition; and if it goes so far as to be firmly fixed and to become difficult to change, then it will be a habit: so that disposition would be a certain intensity of passion or passion-like quality, and habit an intensity or disposition. But Simplicius disapproves of this, for such intensity and remissness do not imply diversity on the part of the form itself, but on the part of the diverse participation thereof by the subject; so that there would be no diversity among the species of quality. And therefore we must say otherwise that, as was explained above (Q. 49, A. 2 *ad* 1), the adjustment of the passion-like qualities themselves, according to their suitability to nature, implies the notion of disposition: and so, when a change takes place in these same passion-like qualities, which are heat and cold, moisture and dryness, there results a change as to sickness and health. But change does not occur in regard to like habits and dispositions, primarily and of themselves.

SECOND ARTICLE

Whether the Soul Is the Subject of Habit in Respect of Its Essence or in Respect of Its Power?

We proceed thus to the Second Article:—

Objection 1. It would seem that habit is in the soul in respect of its essence rather than in respect of its powers. For we speak of dispositions and habits in relation to nature, as stated above (Q. 49, A. 2). But nature regards the essence of the soul rather than the powers; because it is in respect of its essence that the soul is the nature of such a body and the form thereof. Therefore habits are in the soul in respect of its essence and not in respect of its powers.

Obj. 2. Further, accident is not the subject of accident. Now habit is an accident. But the powers of the soul are in the genus of accident, as we have said in the First Part (Q. 77, A. 1, *ad* 5). Therefore habit is not in the soul in respect of its powers.

Obj. 3. Further, the subject is prior to that which is in the subject. But since habit belongs to the first species of quality, it is prior to power, which belongs to the second species. Therefore habit is not in a power of the soul as its subject.

On the contrary, The Philosopher (*Ethic.* i. 13) puts various habits in the various powers of the soul.

I answer that, As we have said above (Q. 49, AA. 2, 3), habit implies a certain disposition in relation to nature or to operation. If therefore we take habit as having a relation to nature, it cannot be in the soul—that is, if we speak of human nature: for the soul itself is the form completing the human nature; so that, regarded in this way, habit or disposition is rather to be found in the body by reason of its relation to the soul, than in the soul by reason of its relation to the body.—But if we speak of a higher nature, of which man may become a partaker, according to 2 Peter i., *that we may be partakers of the Divine Nature:* thus nothing hinders some habit, namely, grace, from being in the soul in respect of its essence, as we shall state later on (Q. 110, A. 4).

On the other hand, if we take habit in its relation to operation, it is chiefly thus that habits are found in the soul: in so far as the soul is not determined to one operation, but is indifferent to many, which is a condition for a habit, as we have said above (Q. 49, A. 4). And since the soul is the principle of operation through its powers, therefore, re-

garded in this sense, habits are in the soul in respect of its powers.

Reply Obj. 1. The essence of the soul belongs to human nature, not as a subject requiring to be disposed to something further, but as a form and nature to which someone is disposed.

Reply Obj. 2. Accident is not of itself the subject of accident. But since among accidents themselves there is a certain order, the subject, according as it is under one accident, is conceived as the subject of a further accident. In this way we say that one accident is the subject of another; as superficies is the subject of color, in which sense power is the subject of habit.

Reply Obj. 3. Habit takes precedence of power, according as it implies a disposition to nature: whereas power always implies a relation to operation, which is posterior, since nature is the principle of operation. But the habit whose subject is a power, does not imply relation to nature, but to operation. Wherefore it is posterior to power. Or, we may say that habit takes precedence of power, as the complete takes precedence of the incomplete, and as act takes precedence of potentiality. For act is naturally prior to potentiality, though potentiality is prior in order of generation and time, as stated in *Metaph.* vii., text. 17; ix., text. 13.

THIRD ARTICLE

Whether There Can Be Any Habits in the Powers of the Sensitive Part?

We proceed thus to the Third Article:—

Objection 1. It would seem that there cannot be any habits in the powers of the sensitive part. For as the nutritive power is an irrational part, so is the sensitive power. But there can be no habits in the powers of the nutritive part. Therefore we ought not to put any habit in the powers of the sensitive part.

Obj. 2. Further, the sensitive parts are common to us and the brutes. But there are not any habits in brutes: for in them there is no will, which is put in the definition of habit, as we have said (Q. 49, A. 3). Therefore there are no habits in the sensitive powers.

Obj. 3. Further, the habits of the soul are sciences and virtues: and just as science is related to the apprehensive power, so is virtue related to the appetitive power. But in the sensitive powers there are no sciences: since science is of universals, which the sensitive powers cannot apprehend. Therefore, neither can there be habits of virtue in the sensitive part.

On the contrary, The Philosopher says (*Ethic.* iii. 10) that *some virtues,* **namely,** temperance and fortitude, *belong to the irrational part.*

I answer that, The sensitive powers can be considered in two ways: first, according as they act from natural instinct: secondly, according as they act at the command of reason. According as they act from natural instinct, they are ordained to one thing, even as nature is; but according as they act at the command of reason, they can be ordained to various things. And thus there can be habits in them, by which they are well or ill disposed in regard to something.

Reply Obj. 1. The powers of the nutritive part have not an inborn aptitude to obey the command of reason, and therefore there are no habits in them. But the sensitive powers have an inborn aptitude to obey the command of reason; and therefore habits can be in them: for in so far as they obey reason, in a certain sense they are said to be rational, as stated in *Ethic.* i. 13.

Reply Obj. 2. The sensitive powers of dumb animals do not act at the command of reason; but if they are left to themselves, such animals act from natural instinct: and so in them there are no habits ordained to operations. There are in them, however, certain dispositions in relation to nature, as health and beauty. But whereas by man's reason brutes are disposed by a sort of custom to do things in this or that way, so in this sense, to a certain extent, we can admit the existence of habits in dumb animals: wherefore Augustine says (QQ. lxxxiii., qu. 36): *We find the most untamed beasts, deterred by fear of pain, from that wherein they took the keenest pleasure; and whom this has become a custom in them, we say that they are tame and gentle.* But the habit is incomplete, as to the use of the will, for they have not that power of using or of refraining, which seems to belong to the notion of habit: and therefore, properly speaking, there can be no habits in them.

Reply Obj. 3. The sensitive appetite has an inborn aptitude to be moved by the rational appetite, as stated in *De Anima* iii., text 57: but the rational powers of apprehension have an inborn aptitude to receive from the sensitive powers. And therefore it is more suitable that habits should be in the powers of sensitive appetite than in the powers of sensitive apprehension, since in the powers of sensitive appetite habits do not exist except according as they act at the command of the reason. And yet even in the interior powers of sensitive apprehension, we may admit of certain habits whereby man has a facility of memory, thought or imagination: wherefore also the Philosopher says (*De Memor. et Remin.* ii)

* See First Part, Q. 79, A. 2, *ad* 2.

that *custom conduces much to a good memory:* the reason of which is that these powers also are moved to act at the command of the reason.

On the other hand the exterior apprehensive powers, as sight, hearing and the like, are not susceptive of habits, but are ordained to their fixed acts, according to the disposition of their nature, just as the members of the body, for there are no habits in them, but rather in the powers which command their movements.

Whether There Is Any Habit in the Intellect?

We proceed thus to the Fourth Article:—

Objection 1. It would seem that there are no habits in the intellect. For habits are in conformity with operations, as stated above (A. 1). But the operations of man are common to soul and body, as stated in *De Anima* i., text 64. Therefore also are habits. But the intellect is not an act of the body (*De Anima* iii., text. 6). Therefore the intellect is not the subject of a habit.

Obj. 2. Further, whatever is in a thing, is there according to the mode of that in which it is. But that which is form without matter, is act only: whereas what is composed of form and matter, has potentiality and act at the same time. Therefore nothing at the same time potential and actual can be in that which is form only, but only in that which is composed of matter and form. Now the intellect is form without matter. Therefore habit, which has potentiality at the same time as act, being a sort of medium between the two, cannot be in the intellect; but only in the *conjunctum,* which is composed of soul and body.

Obj. 3. Further, habit is a disposition whereby we are well or ill disposed in regard to something, as is said (*Metaph.* v., text. 25). But that anyone should be well or ill disposed to an act of the intellect is due to some disposition of the body: wherefore also it is stated (*De Anima* ii., text. 94) that *we observe men with soft flesh to be quick witted.* Therefore the habits of knowledge are not in the intellect, which is separate, but in some power which is the act of some part of the body.

On the contrary, The Philosopher (*Ethic.* vi. 2, 3, 10) puts science, wisdom and understanding, which is the habit of first principles, in the intellective part of the soul.

I answer that, concerning intellective habits there have been various opinions. Some, supposing that there was only one *possible** intellect for all men, were bound to hold that habits of knowledge are not in the intellect itself, but in the interior sensitive powers. For it is manifest that men differ in habits; and so it was impossible to put the habits of knowledge directly in that, which, being only one, would be common to all men. Wherefore if there were but one single *possible* intellect of all men, the habits of science, in which men differ from one another, could not be in the *possible* intellect as their subject, but would be in the interior sensitive powers, which differ in various men.

Now, in the first place, this supposition is contrary to the mind of Aristotle. For it is manifest that the sensitive powers are rational, not by their essence, but only by participation (*Ethic.* i. 13). Now the Philosopher puts the intellectual virtues, which are wisdom, science and understanding, in that which is rational by its essence. Wherefore they are not in the sensitive powers, but in the intellect itself. Moreover he says expressly (*De Anima* iii., text. 8, 18) that when the *possible* intellect is *thus identified with each thing*, that is, when it is reduced to act in respect of singulars by the intelligible species, *then it is said to be in act, as the knower is said to be in act; and this happens when the intellect can act of itself*, i.e., by considering: *and even then it is in potentiality in a sense; but not in the same way as before learning and discovering.* Therefore the *possible* intellect itself is the subject of the habit of science, by which the intellect, even though it be not actually considering, is able to consider. In the second place, this supposition is contrary to the truth. For as to whom belongs the operation, belongs also the power to operate, so to whom belongs the operation, belongs also the habit. But to understand and to consider is the proper act of the intellect. Therefore also the habit whereby one considers is properly in the intellect itself.

Reply Obj. 1. Some said, as Simplicius reports in his *Commentary on the Predicaments*, that, since every operation of man is to a certain extent an operation of the *conjunctum*, as the Philosopher says (*De Anima* i., text. 64); therefore no habit is in the soul only, but in the *conjunctum*. And from this it follows that no habit is in the intellect, for the intellect is separate, as ran the argument, given above. But the argument is not cogent. For habit is not a disposition of the object to the power, but rather a disposition of the power to the object: wherefore the habit needs to be in that power which is principle of the act, and not in that which is compared to the power as its object.

Now the act of understanding is not said to be common to soul and body, except in respect of the phantasm, as is stated in *De Anima.*, text. 66. But it is clear that the phantasm is compared as object to the passive intellect (*De Anima* iii., text. 3, 39). Whence it

follows that the intellective habit is chiefly on the part of the intellect itself; and not on the part of the phantasm, which is common to soul and body. And therefore we must say that the *possible* intellect is the subject of habit: for that is a competent subject of habit, which is in potentiality to many: and this belongs, above all, to the *possible* intellect. Wherefore the *possible* intellect is the subject of intellectual habits.

Reply Obj. 2. As potentiality to sensible being belongs to corporeal matter, so potentiality to intellectual being belongs to the *possible* intellect. Wherefore nothing forbids habit to be in the *possible* intellect, for it is midway between pure potentiality and perfect act.

Reply Obj. 3. Because the apprehensive powers inwardly prepare their proper objects for the *possible intellect*, therefore it is by the good disposition of these powers, to which the good disposition of the body co-operates, that man is rendered apt to understand. And so in a secondary way the intellective habit can be in these powers. But principally it is in the *possible* intellect.

FIFTH ARTICLE

Whether Any Habit Is in the Will?

We proceed thus to the Fifth Article:—

Objection 1. It would seem that there is not a habit in the will. For the habit which is in the intellect is the intelligible species, by means of which the intellect actually understands. But the will does not act by means of species. Therefore the will is not the subject of habit.

Obj. 2. Further, no habit is allotted to the active intellect, as there is to the *possible* intellect, because the former is an active power. But the will is above all an active power, because it moves all the powers to their acts, as stated above (Q. 9, A. 1). Therefore there is no habit in the will.

Obj. 3. Further, in the natural powers there is no habit, because, by reason of their nature, they are determinate to one thing. But the will, by reason of its nature, is ordained to tend to the good which reason directs. Therefore there is no habit in the will.

On the contrary, Justice is a habit. But justice is in the will; for it is *a habit whereby men will and do that which is just* (*Ethic.* v. 1). Therefore the will is the subject of a habit.

I answer that, Every power which may be variously directed to act, needs a habit whereby it is well disposed to its act. Now since the will is a rational power, it may be variously directed to act. And therefore in the will we must admit the presence of a habit whereby it is well disposed to its act. Moreover, from the very nature of habit, it is clear that it is principally related to the will; inasmuch as habit *is that which one uses when one wills*, as stated above (A. 1).

Reply Obj. 1. Even as in the intellect there is a species which is the likeness of the object; so in the will, and in every appetitive power, there must be something by which the power is inclined to its object; for the act of the appetitive power is nothing but a certain inclination, as we have said above (Q. 6, A. 4; Q. 22, A. 2). And therefore in respect of those things to which it is inclined sufficiently by the nature of the power itself, the power needs no quality to incline it. But since it is necessary, for the end of human life, that the appetitive power be inclined to something fixed, to which it is not inclined by the nature of the power, which has a relation to many and various things, therefore it is necessary that, in the will and in the other appetitive powers, there be certain qualities to incline them, and these are called habits.

Reply Obj. 2. The active intellect is active only, and in no way passive. But the will, and every appetitive power, is both mover and moved (*De Anima* iii., text. 54). And therefore the comparison between them does not hold; for to be susceptible of habit belongs to that which is somehow in potentiality.

Reply Obj. 3. The will from the very nature of the power is inclined to the good of the reason. But because this good is varied in many ways, the will needs to be inclined, by means of a habit, to some fixed good of the reason, in order that action may follow more promptly.

SIXTH ARTICLE

Whether There Are Habits in the Angels?

We proceed thus to the Sixth Article:—

Objection 1. It would seem that there are no habits in the angels. For Maximus, commentator of Dionysius (*Cœl. Hier.* vii), says: *It is not proper to suppose that there are intellectual* (i.e., spiritual) *powers in the divine intelligences* (i.e., in the angels) *after the manner of accidents, as in us: as though one were in the other as in a subject: for accident of any kind is foreign to them.* But every habit is an accident. Therefore there are no habits in the angels.

Obj. 2. Further, as Dionysius says (*Cœl. Hier.* iv): *The holy dispositions of the heavenly essences participate, above all other things, in God's goodness.* But that which is of itself (*per se*) is prior to and more powerful than that which is by another (*per aliud*).

Therefore the angelic essences are perfected of themselves unto conformity with God, and therefore not by means of habits. And this seems to have been the reasoning of Maximus, who in the same passage adds: *For if this were the case, surely their essence would not remain in itself, nor could it have been as far as possible deified of itself.*

Obj. 3. Further, habit is a disposition (*Metaph.* v, text. 25). But disposition, as is said in the same book, is *the order of that which has parts*. Since, therefore, angels are simple substances, it seems that there are no dispositions and habits in them.

On the contrary, Dionysius says (*Cœl. Hier.* vii) that the angels of the first hierarchy are called: *Fire-bearers and Thrones and Outpouring of Wisdom, by which is indicated the godlike nature of their habits.*

I answer that, Some have thought that there are no habits in the angels, and that whatever is said of them, is said essentially. Whence Maximus, after the words which we have quoted, says: *Their dispositions, and the powers which are in them, are essential, through the absence of matter in them.* And Simplicius says the same in his *Commentary on the Predicaments: Wisdom which is in the soul is its habit: but that which is in the intellect, is its substance. For everything divine is sufficient of itself, and exists in itself.*

Now this opinion contains some truth, and some error. For it is manifest from what we have said (Q. 49, A. 4) that only a being in potentiality is the subject of habit. So the above-mentioned commentators considered that angels are immaterial substances, and that there is no material potentiality in them, and on that account, excluded from them habit and any kind of accident. Yet since though there is no material potentiality in angels, there is still some potentiality in them (for to be pure act belongs to God alone), therefore, as far as potentiality is found to be in them, so far may habits be found in them. But because the potentiality of matter and the potentiality of intellectual substance are not of the same kind. Whence, Simplicius says in his *Commentary on the Predicaments* that: *The habits of the intellectual substance are not like the habits here below, but rather are they like simple and immaterial images which it contains in itself.*

However, the angelic intellect and the human intellect differ with regard to this habit. For the human intellect, being the lowest in the intellectual order, is in potentiality as regards all intelligible things, just as primal matter is in respect of all sensible forms; and therefore for the understanding of all things, it needs some habit. But the angelic intellect is not as a pure potentiality in the order of intelligible things, but as an act; not indeed as pure act (for this belongs to God alone), but with an admixture of some potentiality: and the higher it is, the less potentiality it has. And therefore, as we said in the First Part (Q. 55, A. 1), so far as it is in potentiality, so far is it in need of habitual perfection by means of intelligible species in regard to its proper operation: but so far as it is in act, through its own essence it can understand some things, at least itself, and other things according to the mode of its substance, as stated in *De Causis:* and the more perfect it is, the more perfectly will it understand.

But since no angel attains to the perfection of God, but all are infinitely distant therefrom; for this reason, in order to attain to God Himself, through intellect and will, the angels need some habits, being as it were in potentiality in regard to that Pure Act. Wherefore Dionysius says (*Cæl. Hier.* vii) that their habits are *godlike,* that is to say, that by them they are made like to God.

But those habits that are dispositions to the natural being are not in angels, since they are immaterial.

Reply Obj. 1. This saying of Maximus must be understood of material habits and accidents.

Reply Obj. 2. As to that which belongs to angels by their essence, they do not need a habit. But as they are not so far beings of themselves, as not to partake of Divine wisdom and goodness, therefore, so far as they need to partake of something from without, so far do they need to have habits.

Reply Obj. 3. In angels there are no essential parts: but there are potential parts, in so far as their intellect is perfected by several species, and in so far as their will has a relation to several things.

QUESTION 51

Of the Cause of Habits, As to Their Formation

(In Four Articles)

WE must next consider the cause of habits: and firstly, as to their formation; secondly, as to their increase; thirdly, as to their diminution and corruption. Under the first head there are four points of inquiry: (1) Whether any habit is from nature? (2) Whether any habit is caused by acts? (3) Whether a habit can be caused by one act? (4) Whether any habits are infused in man by God?

FIRST ARTICLE

Whether Any Habit Is from Nature?

We proceed thus to the First Article:—

Objection 1. It would seem that no habit is from nature. For the use of those things which are from nature does not depend on the will. But habit *is that which we use when we will,* as the Commentator says on *De Anima* iii. Therefore habit is not from nature.

Obj. 2. Further, nature does not employ two where one is sufficient. But the powers of the soul are from nature. If therefore the habits of the powers were from nature, habit and power would be one.

Obj. 3. Further, nature does not fail in necessaries. But habits are necessary in order to act well, as we have stated above (Q. 49, A. 4). If therefore any habits were from nature, it seems that nature would not fail to cause all necessary habits: but this is clearly false. Therefore habits are not from nature.

On the contrary, In *Ethic.* vi. 6, among other habits, place is given to understanding of first principles, which habit is from nature: wherefore also first principles are said to be known naturally.

I answer that, One thing can be natural to another in two ways. First in respect of the specific nature, as the faculty of laughing is natural to man, and it is natural to fire to have an upward tendency. Secondly, in respect of the individual nature, as it is natural to Socrates or Plato to be prone to sickness or inclined to health, in accordance with their respective temperaments.—Again, in respect of both natures, something may be called natural in two ways: first, because it entirely is from the nature; secondly, because it is partly from nature, and partly from an extrinsic principle. For instance, when a man is healed by himself, his health is entirely from nature; but when a man is healed by means of medicine, health is partly from nature, partly from an extrinsic principle.

Thus, then, if we speak of habit as a disposition of the subject in relation to form or nature, it may be natural in either of the foregoing ways. For there is a certain natural disposition demanded by the human species, so that no man can be without it. And this disposition is natural in respect of the specific nature. But since such a disposition has a certain latitude, it happens that different grades of this disposition are becoming to different men in respect of the individual nature. And this disposition may be either entirely from nature, or partly from nature, and partly from an extrinsic principle, as we have said of those who are healed by means of art.

But the habit which is a disposition to operation, and whose subject is a power of the soul, as stated above (Q. 50, A. 2), may be natural whether in respect of the specific nature or in respect of the individual nature:— in respect of the specific nature, on the part of the soul itself, which, since it is the form of the body, is the specific principle; but in respect of the individual nature, on the part of the body, which is the material principle. Yet in neither way does it happen that there are natural habits in man, so that they be entirely from nature. In the angels, indeed, this does happen, since they have intelligible species naturally impressed on them, which cannot be said of the human soul, as we said in the First Part (Q. 55, A. 2; Q. 84, A. 3).

There are, therefore, in man certain natural habits, owing their existence, partly to nature, and partly to some extrinsic principle: in one way, indeed, in the apprehensive powers; in another way, in the appetitive powers. For in the apprehensive powers there may be a natural habit by way of a beginning, both in respect of the specific nature, and in respect of the individual nature. This happens with regard to the specific nature, on the part of the soul itself: thus the understanding of first principles is called a natural habit. For it is owing to the very nature of the intellectual soul that man, having once grasped what is a whole and what is a part, should at once perceive that every whole is larger than its part: and in like manner with regard to other such principles. Yet what is a whole, and what is a part—this he cannot know except through the intelligible species which he has received from phantasms: and for this reason, the Philosopher at the end of the *Posterior Analytics* shows that knowledge of principles comes to us from the senses.

But in respect of the individual nature, a habit of knowledge is natural as to its beginning, in so far as one man, from the disposition of his organs of sense, is more apt than another to understand well, since we need the sensitive powers for the operation of the intellect.

In the appetitive powers, however, no habit is natural in its beginning, on the part of the soul itself, as to the substance of the habit; but only as to certain principles thereof, as, for instance, the principles of common law are called the *nurseries of virtue*. The reason of this is because the inclination to its proper objects, which seems to be the beginning of

a habit, does not belong to the habit, but rather to the very nature of the powers.

But on the part of the body, in respect of the individual nature, there are some appetitive habits by way of natural beginnings. For some are disposed from their own bodily temperament to chastity or meekness or such like.

Reply Obj. 1. This objection takes nature as divided against reason and will; whereas reason itself and will belong to the nature of man.

Reply Obj. 2. Something may be added even naturally to the nature of a power, while it cannot belong to the power itself. For instance, with regard to the angels, it cannot belong to the intellective power itself capable of knowing all things: for thus it would have to be the act of all things, which belongs to God alone. Because that by which something is known, must needs be the actual likeness of the thing known: whence it would follow, if the power of the angel knew all things by itself, that it was the likeness and act of all things. Wherefore there must needs be added to the angels' intellective power, some intelligible species, which are likenesses of things understood: for it is by participation of the Divine wisdom and not by their own essence, that their intellect can be actually those things which they understand. And so it is clear that not everything belonging to a natural habit can belong to the power.

Reply Obj. 3. Nature is not equally inclined to cause all the various kinds of habits: since some can be caused by nature, and some not, as we have said above. And so it does not follow that because some habits are natural, therefore all are natural.

SECOND ARTICLE

Whether Any Habit Is Caused by Acts?

We proceed thus to the Second Article:—

Objection 1. It would seem that no habit is caused by acts. For habit is a quality, as we have said above (Q. 49, A. 1). Now every quality is caused in a subject, according to the latter's receptivity. Since then the agent, inasmuch as it acts, does not receive but rather gives: it seems impossible for a habit to be caused in an agent by its own acts.

Obj. 2. Further, the thing wherein a quality is caused is moved to that quality, as may be clearly seen in that which is heated or cooled: whereas that which produces the act that causes the quality, moves, as may be seen in that which heats or cools. If therefore habits were caused in anything by its own act, it would follow that the same would be mover and moved, active and passive: which is impossible, as stated in *Physic.* iii. 8.

Obj. 3. Further, the effect cannot be more noble than its cause. But habit is more noble than the act which precedes the habit; as is clear from the fact that the latter produces more noble acts. Therefore habit cannot be caused by an act which precedes the habit.

On the contrary, The Philosopher (*Ethic.* ii, 1, 2) teaches that habits of virtue and vice are caused by acts.

I answer that, In the agent there is sometimes only the active principle of its act: for instance in fire there is only the active principle of heating. And in such an agent a habit cannot be caused by its own act: for which reason natural things cannot become accustomed or unaccustomed, as is stated in *Ethic.* ii. 1. But a certain agent is to be found, in which there is both the active and the passive principle of its act, as we see in human acts. For the acts of the appetitive power proceed from that same power according as it is moved by the apprehensive power presenting the object: and further, the intellective power, according as it reasons about conclusions, has, as it were, an active principle in a self-evident proposition. Wherefore by such acts habits can be caused in their agents; not indeed with regard to the first active principle, but with regard to that principle of the act, which principle is a mover moved. For everything that is passive and moved by another, is disposed by the action of the agent; wherefore if the acts be multiplied a certain quality is formed in the power which is passive and moved, which quality is called a habit: just as the habits of moral virtue are caused in the appetitive powers, according as they are moved by the reason, and as the habits of science are caused in the intellect, according as it is moved by first propositions.

Reply Obj. 1. The agent, as agent, does not receive anything. But in so far as it moves through being moved by another, it receives something from that which moves it: and thus is a habit caused.

Reply Obj. 2. The same thing, and in the same respect, cannot be mover and moved; but nothing prevents a thing from being moved by itself as to different respects, as is proved in *Phys.* viii., text. 28, 29.

Reply Obj. 3. The act which precedes the habit, in so far as it comes from an active principle, proceeds from a more excellent principle than is the habit caused thereby: just as the reason is a more excellent principle than the habit of moral virtue produced in the appetitive power by repeated acts, and as the understanding of first principles is a more excellent principle than the science of conclusions.

* See First Part, Q. 79, A. 2, *ad* 2.

THIRD ARTICLE

Whether a Habit Can Be Caused by One Act?

We proceed thus to the Third Article:—

Objection 1. It would seem that a habit can be caused by one act. For demonstration is an act of reason. But science, which is the habit of one conclusion, is caused by one demonstration. Therefore habit can be caused by one act.

Obj. 2. Further, as acts happen to increase by multiplication, so do they happen to increase by intensity. But a habit is caused by multiplication of acts. Therefore also if an act be very intense, it can be the generating cause of a habit.

Obj. 3. Further, health and sickness are habits. But it happens that a man is healed or becomes ill, by one act. Therefore one act can cause a habit.

On the contrary, The Philosopher (*Ethic.* i. 7): *As neither does one swallow nor one day make spring: so neither does one day nor a short time make a man blessed and happy.* But *happiness is an operation in respect of a habit of perfect virtue* (*Ethic.* i., ibid., 10, 13). Therefore a habit of virtue, and for the same reason, other habits, is not caused by one act.

I answer that, As we have said already (A. 2), habit is caused by act, because a passive power is moved by an active principle. But in order that some quality be caused in that which is passive, the active principle must entirely overcome the passive. Whence we see that because fire cannot at once overcome the combustible, it does not enkindle at once; but it gradually expels contrary dispositions, so that by overcoming it entirely, it may impress its likeness on it. Now it is clear that the active principle which is reason, cannot entirely overcome the appetitive power in one act: because the appetitive power is inclined variously, and to many things; while the reason judges in a single act, what should be willed in regard to various aspects and circumstances. Wherefore the appetitive power is not thereby entirely overcome, so as to be inclined like nature to the same thing, in the majority of cases; which inclination belongs to the habit of virtue. Therefore a habit of virtue cannot be caused by one act, but only by many.

But in the apprehensive powers, we must observe that there are two passive principles: one is the *possible** intellect itself; the other is the intellect which Aristotle (*De Anim.* iii., text 20) calls *passive,* and is the *particular reason,* that is the cogitative power, with memory and imagination. With regard then to the former passive principle, it is possible for a certain active principle to entirely overcome, by one act, the power of its passive principle:

thus one self-evident proposition convinces the intellect, so that it gives a firm assent to the conclusion, but a probable proposition cannot do this. Wherefore a habit of opinion needs to be caused by many acts of the reason, even on the part of the *possible* intellect: whereas a habit of science can be caused by a single act of the reason, so far as the *possible* intellect is concerned. But with regard to the lower apprehensive powers, the same acts need to be repeated many times for anything to be firmly impressed on the memory. And so the Philosopher says (*De Memor. et Remin.* 1) that *meditation strengthens memory.* Bodily habits, however, can be caused by one act, if the active principle is of great power: sometimes, for instance, a strong dose of medicine restores health at once.

Hence the solutions to the objections are clear.

FOURTH ARTICLE

Whether Any Habits Are Infused in Man by God?

We proceed thus to the Fourth Article:—

Objection 1. It would seem that no habit is infused in man by God. For God treats all equally. If therefore He infuses habits into some, He would infuse them into all: which is clearly untrue.

Obj. 2. Further, God works in all things according to the mode which is suitable to their nature: for *it belongs to Divine providence to preserve nature,* as Dionysius says (*Div. Nom.* iv). But habits are naturally caused in man by acts, as we have said above (A. 2). Therefore God does not cause habits to be in man except by acts.

Obj. 3. Further, If any habit be infused into man by God, man can by that habit perform many acts. But *from those acts a like habit is caused* (*Ethic.* ii. 1, 2). Consequently there will be two habits of the same species in the same man, one acquired, the other infused. Now this seems impossible: for two forms of the same species cannot be in the same subject. Therefore a habit is not infused into man by God.

On the contrary, it is written (Ecclus. xv.

5): *God filled him with the spirit of wisdom and understanding.* Now wisdom and understanding are habits. Therefore some habits are infused into man by God.

I answer that, Some habits are infused by God into man, for two reasons.

The first reason is because there are some habits by which man is disposed to an end which exceeds the proportion of human nature, namely, the ultimate and perfect happiness of man, as stated above (Q. 5, A. 5). And since habits need to be in proportion with that to which man is disposed by them, therefore is it necessary that those habits, which dispose to this end, exceed the proportion of human nature. Wherefore such habits can never be in man except by Divine infusion, as is the case with all gratuitous virtues.

The other reason is, because God can produce the effects of second causes, without these second causes, as we have said in the First Part (Q. 105, A. 6). Just as, therefore, sometimes, in order to show His power, He causes health, without its natural cause, but which nature could have caused, so also, at times, for the manifestation of His power, He infuses into man even those habits which can be caused by a natural power. Thus He gave to the apostles the science of the Scriptures and of all tongues, which men can acquire by study or by custom, but not so perfectly.

Reply Obj. 1. God, in respect of His Nature, is the same to all, but in respect of the order of His Wisdom, for some fixed motive, gives certain things to some, which He does not give to others.

Reply Obj. 2. That God works in all according to their mode, does not hinder God from doing what nature cannot do: but it follows from this that He does nothing contrary to that which is suitable to nature.

Reply Obj. 3. Acts produced by an infused habit, do not cause a habit, but strengthen the already existing habit; just as the remedies of medicine given to a man who is naturally healthy, do not cause a kind of health, but give new strength to the health he had before.

QUESTION 52

Of the Increase of Habits

(In Three Articles)

WE have now to consider the increase of habits; under which head there are three points of inquiry: (1) Whether habits increase? (2) Whether they increase by addition? (3) Whether each act increases the habit?

FIRST ARTICLE

Whether Habits Increase?

We proceed thus to the First Article:—

Objection 1. It would seem that habits cannot increase. For increase concerns quantity (*Phys.* v., text. 18). But habits are not in the genus quantity, but in that of quality. Therefore there can be no increase of habits.

Obj. 2. Further, habit is a perfection (*Phys.* vii., text. 17, 18). But since perfection conveys a notion of end and term, it seems that it cannot be more or less. Therefore a habit cannot increase.

Obj. 3. Further, those things which can be more or less are subject to alteration: for that which from being less hot becomes more hot, is said to be altered. But in habits there is no alteration, as is proved in *Phys.* vii., text. 15, 17. Therefore habits cannot increase.

On the contrary, Faith is a habit, and yet it increases: wherefore the disciples said to our Lord (Luke xvii. 5): *Lord, increase our faith.* Therefore habits increase.

I answer that, Increase, like other things pertaining to quantity, is transferred from bodily quantities to intelligible spiritual things, on account of the natural connection of the intellect with corporeal things, which come under the imagination. Now in corporeal quantities, a thing is said to be great, according as it reaches the perfection of quantity due to it; wherefore a certain quantity is reputed great in man, which is not reputed great in an elephant. And so also in forms, we say a thing is great because it is perfect. And since good has the nature of perfection, therefore *in things which are great, but not in quantity, to be greater is the same as to be better,* as Augustine says (*De Trin.* vi. 8).

Now the perfection of a form may be considered in two ways: first, in respect of the form itself: secondly, in respect of the participation of the form by its subject. In so far as we consider the perfections of a form in respect of the form itself, thus the form is said to be *little* or *great:* for instance great or little health or science. But in so far as we consider the perfection of a form in respect of the participation thereof by the subject, it is said to be *more* or *less:* for instance more or less white or healthy. Now this distinction is not to be understood as implying that the form has a being outside its matter or subject, but that it is one thing to consider the form according to its specific nature, and another to consider it in respect of its participation by a subject.

In this way, then, there were four opinions among philosophers concerning intensity and remission of habits and forms, as Simplicius relates in his *Commentary on the Predicaments.* For Plotinus and the other Platonists held that qualities and habits themselves were susceptible of more or less, for the reason that they were material, and so had a certain want

of definiteness, on account of the infinity of matter. Others, on the contrary, held that qualities and habits of themselves were not susceptible of more or less; but that the things affected by them (*qualia*) are said to be more or less, in respect of the participation of the subject: that, for instance, justice is not more or less, but the just thing. Aristotle alludes to this opinion in the *Predicaments* (*Categor.* vi). The third opinion was that of the Stoics, and lies between the two preceding opinions. For they held that some habits are of themselves susceptible of more and less, for instance, the arts; and that some are not, as the virtues. The fourth opinion was held by some who said that qualities and immaterial forms are not susceptible of more or less, but that material forms are.

In order that the truth in this matter be made clear, we must observe that, in respect of which a thing receives its species, must be something fixed and stationary, and as it were indivisible: for whatever attains to that thing, is contained under the species, and whatever recedes from it more or less, belongs to another species, more or less perfect. Wherefore, the Philosopher says (*Metaph.* viii., text. 10) that species of things are like numbers, in which addition or subtraction changes the species. If, therefore, a form, or anything at all, receives its specific nature in respect of itself, or in respect of something belonging to it, it is necessary that, considered in itself, it be something of a definite nature, which can be neither more nor less. Such are heat, whiteness and other like qualities which are not denominated from a relation to something else: and much more so, substance, which is *per se* being. But those things which receive their species from something to which they are related, can be diversified, in respect of themselves, according to more or less: and none the less they remain in the same species, on account of the one-ness of that to which they are related, and from which they receive their species. For example, movement is in itself more intense or more remiss: and yet it remains in the same species, on acount of the one-ness of the term by which it is specified. We may observe the same thing in health; for a body attains to the nature of health, according as it has a disposition suitable to an animal's nature, to which various dispositions may be suitable; which disposition is therefore variable as regards more or less, and withal the nature of health remains. Whence the Philosopher says (*Ethic.* x. 2, 3): *Health itself may be more or less: for the measure is not the same in all, nor is it always the same in one individual; but down to a certain point it may decrease and still remain health.*

Now these various dispositions and measures of health are by way of excess and defect: wherefore if the name of health were given to the most perfect measure, then we should not speak of health as greater or less.— Thus therefore it is clear how a quality or form may increase or decrease in itself, and how it cannot.

But if we consider a quality or form in respect of its participation by the subject, thus again we find that some qualities and forms are susceptive of more or less, and some not. Now Simplicius assigns the cause of this 'diversity to the fact that substance in itself cannot be susceptible of more or less, because it is *per se* being. And therefore every form which is participated substantially by its subject, cannot vary in intensity and remission: wherefore in the genus of substance nothing is said to be more or less. And because quantity is nigh to substance, and because shape follows on quantity, therefore is it that neither in these can there be such a thing as more or less. Whence the Philosopher says (*Phys.* vii., text. 15) that when a thing receives form and shape, it is not said to be altered, but to be made. But other qualities which are further removed from quantity, and are connected with passions and actions, are susceptible of more or less, in respect of their participation by the subject.

Now it is possible to explain yet further the reason of this diversity. For, as we have said, that from which a thing receives its species must remain indivisibly fixed and constant in something indivisible. Wherefore in two ways it may happen that a form cannot be participated more or less. First because the participator has its species in respect of that form. And for this reason no substantial form is participated more or less. Wherefore the Philosopher says (*Metaph.* viii., text. 10) that, *as a number cannot be more or less, so neither can that which is in the species of substance,* that is, in respect of its participation of the specific form: *but in so far as substance may be with matter, i.e.,* in respect of material dispositions, *more and less are found in substance.*

Secondly this may happen from the fact that the form is essentially indivisible: wherefore if anything participate that form, it must needs participate it in respect of its indivisibility. For this reason we do not speak of the species of number as varying in respect of more and less; because each species thereof is constituted by an indivisible unity. The same is to be said of the species of continuous quantity, which are denominated from numbers, as two-cubits-long, three-cubits-long, and of relations of quantity, as double and treble,

and of figures of quantity, as triangle and tetragon.

This same explanation is given by Aristotle in the *Predicaments* (*Categor.* vi), where in explaining why figures are not susceptible of more or less, he says: *Things which are given the nature of a triangle or a circle, are accordingly triangles and circles:* to wit, because indivisibility is essential to the motion of such, wherefore whatever participates their nature must participate it in its indivisibility.

It is clear, therefore, since we speak of habits and dispositions in respect of a relation to something (*Phys.* vii., text. 17), that in two ways intensity and remission may be observed in habits and dispositions. First, in respect of the habit itself: thus, for instance, we speak of greater or less health; greater or less science, which extends to more or fewer things. Secondly, in respect of participation by the subject: in so far as equal science or health is participated more in one than in another, according to a diverse aptitude arising either from nature, or from custom. For habit and disposition do not give species to the subject: nor again do they essentially imply indivisibility.

We shall say further on (Q. 66, A. 1) how it is with the virtues.

Reply Obj. 1. As the word *great* is taken from corporeal quantities and applied to the intelligible perfections of forms; so also is the word *growth,* the term of which is something great.

Reply Obj. 2. Habit is indeed a perfection, but not a perfection which is the term of its subject; for instance, a term giving the subject its specific being. Nor again does the nature of a habit include the notion of term, as do the species of numbers. Wherefore there is nothing to hinder it from being susceptive of more or less.

Reply Obj. 3 Alteration is primarily indeed in the qualities of the third species; but secondarily it may be in the qualities of the first species: for, supposing an alteration as to hot and cold, there follows in an animal an alteration as to health and sickness. In like manner, if an alteration take place in the passions of the sensitive appetite, or the sensitive powers of apprehension, an alteration follows as to science and virtue (*Phys.* viii., text. 20).

SECOND ARTICLE

Whether Habit Increases by Addition?

We proceed thus to the Second Article:—

Objection 1. It would seem that the increase of habits is by way of addition. For the word *increase,* as we have said, is transferred to forms, from corporeal quantities. But in corporeal quantities there is no increase without addition: wherefore (*De Gener.* i., text. 31) it is said that *increase is an addition to a magnitude already existing.* Therefore in habits also there is no increase without addition.

Obj. 2. Further, habit is not increased except by means of some agent. But every agent does something in the passive subject: for instance, that which heats, causes heat in that which is heated. Therefore there is no increase without addition.

Obj. 3. Further, as that which is not white, is in potentiality to be white: so that which is less white, is in potentiality to be more white. But that which is not white, is not made white except by the addition of whiteness. Therefore that which is less white, is not made more white, except by an added whiteness.

On the contrary, The Philosopher says (*Phys.* iv., text. 84): *That which is hot is made hotter, without making, in the matter, something hot, that was not hot, when the thing was less hot.* Therefore, in like manner, neither is any addition made in other forms when they increase.

I answer that, The solution of this question depends on what we have said above (A. 1). For we said that increase and decrease in forms which are capable of intensity and remissness, happen in one way not on the part of the very form considered in itself, through the diverse participation thereof by the subject. Wherefore such increase of habits and other forms, is not caused by an addition of form to form; but by the subject participating more or less perfectly, one and the same form. And just as, by an agent which is in act, something is made actually hot, beginning, as it were, to participate a form, not as though the form itself were made, as is proved in *Metaph.* vii., text. 32, so, by an intense action of the agent, something is made more hot, as it were participating the form more perfectly, not as though something were added to the form.

For if this increase in forms were understood to be by way of addition, this could only be either in the form itself or in the subject. If it be understood of the form itself, it has already been stated (A. 1) that such an addition or subtraction would change the species; even as the species of color is changed when a thing from being pale becomes white.—If, on the other hand, this addition be understood as applying to the subject, this could only be either because one part of the subject receives a form which it had not previously (thus we may say cold increases in a man who, after being cold in one part of his body, is cold in several parts), or because some other subject is added sharing in the same form (as when a

hot thing is added to another, or one white thing to another). But in either of these two ways we have not a more white or a more hot thing, but a greater white or hot thing.

Since, however, as stated above (A. 1), certain accidents are of themselves susceptible of more or less, in some of these we may find increase by addition. For movement increases by an addition either to the time it lasts, or to the course it follows: and yet the species remains the same on account of the one-ness of the term. Yet movement increases in intensity as to participation in its subject: i.e., in so far as the same movement can be executed more or less speedily or readily.—In like manner, science can increase in itself by addition; thus when anyone learns several conclusions of geometry, the same specific habit of science increases in that man. Yet a man's science increases, as to the subject's participation thereof, in intensity, in so far as one man is quicker and readier than another in considering the same conclusions.

As to bodily habits, it does not seem very probable that they receive increase by way of addition. For an animal is not said to be simply healthy or beautiful, unless it be such in all its parts. And if it be brought to a more perfect measure, this is the result of a change in the simple qualities, which are not susceptible of increase save in intensity on the part of the subject partaking of them.

How this question affects virtues we shall state further on (Q. 66, A. 1).

Reply Obj. 1. Even in bodily bulk increase is twofold. First, by addition of one subject to another; such is the increase of living things. Secondly, by mere intensity, without any addition at all; such is the case with things subject to rarefaction, as is stated in *Phys.* iv., text. 63.

Reply Obj. 2. The cause that increases a habit, always effects something in the subject, but not a new form. But it causes the subject to partake more perfectly of a pre-existing form, or it makes the form to extend further.

Reply Obj. 3. What is not already white, is potentially white, as not yet possessing the form of whiteness: hence the agent causes a new form in the subject. But that which is less hot or white, is not in potentiality to those forms, since it has them already actually: but it is in potentiality to a perfect mode of participation; and this it receives through the agent's action.

THIRD ARTICLE

Whether Every Act Increases Its Habit?

We proceed thus to the Third Article:—

Objection 1. It would seem that every act

increases its habit. For when the cause is increased the effect is increased. Now acts are causes of habits, as stated above (Q. 51, A. 2). Therefore a habit increases when its acts are multiplied.

Obj. 2. Further, of like things a like judgment should be formed. But all the acts proceeding from one and the same habit are alike (*Ethic.* ii. 1, 2). Therefore if some acts increase a habit, every act should increase it.

Obj. 3. Further, like is increased by like. But any act is like the habit whence it proceeds. Therefore every act increases its habit.

On the contrary, Opposite effects do not result from the same cause. But according to *Ethic.* ii. 2, some acts lessen the habit whence they proceed, for instance if they be done carelessly. Therefore it is not every act that increases a habit.

I answer that, Like acts cause like habits (*Ethic.* ii. 1, 2). Now things are like or unlike not only in respect of their qualities being the same or various, but also in respect of the same or a different mode of participation. For it is not only black that is unlike white, but also less white is unlike more white, since there is

movement from less white to more white, even as from one opposite to another, as is stated in *Physic.* v., text. 52.

But since use of habits depends on the will, as was shown above (Q. 50, A. 5); just as one who has a habit may fail to use it or may act contrary to it; so may he happen to use the habit by performing an act that is not in proportion to the intensity of the habit. Accordingly, if the intensity of the act correspond in proportion to the intensity of the habit, or even surpass it, every such act either increases the habit or disposes to an increase thereof, if we may speak of the increase of habits as we do of the increase of an animal. For not every morsel of food actually increases the animal's size, as neither does every drop of water hollow out the stone: but the multiplication of food results at last in an increase of the body. So, too, repeated acts cause a habit to grow. If, however, the act falls short of the intensity of the habit, such an act does not dispose to an increase of that habit, but rather to a lessening thereof.

From this it is clear how to solve the objections.

QUESTION 53

How Habits Are Corrupted or Diminished

(In Three Articles)

WE must now consider how habits are lost or weakened; and under this head there are three points of inquiry: (1) Whether a habit can be corrupted? (2) Whether it can be diminished? (3) How are habits corrupted or diminished?

FIRST ARTICLE

Whether a Habit Can Be Corrupted?

We proceed thus to the First Article:—

Objection 1. It would seem that a habit cannot be corrupted. For habit is within its subject like a second nature; wherefore it is pleasant to act from habit. Now so long as a thing is, its nature is not corrupted. Therefore neither can a habit be corrupted so long as its subject remains.

Obj. 2. Further, whenever a form is corrupted, this is due either to corruption of its subject, or to its contrary: thus sickness ceases through corruption of the animal, or through the advent of health. Now science, which is a habit, cannot be lost through corruption of its subject: since *the intellect,* which is its subject, *is a substance that is incorruptible* (*De Anima* i., text. 65). In like manner, neither can it be lost through the action of its con-

trary: since intelligible species are not contrary to one another (*Metaph.* vii., text. 52). Therefore the habit of science can nowise be lost.

Obj. 3. Further, all corruption results from some movement. But the habit of science, which is in the soul, cannot be corrupted by a direct movement of the soul itself, since the soul is not moved directly. It is, however, moved indirectly through the movement of the body: and yet no bodily change seems capable of corrupting the intelligible species residing in the intellect: since the intellect independently of the body is the proper abode of the species; for which reason it is held that that habits are not lost either through old age or through death. Therefore science cannot be corrupted. For the same reason neither can habits of virtue be corrupted, since they also are in the rational soul, and, as the Philosopher declares (*Ethic.* i, 10), *virtue is more lasting than learning.*

On the contrary, The Philosopher says (*De Long. et Brev. Vitæ* ii) that *forgetfulness and deception are the corruption of science.* Moreover, by sinning a man loses a habit of virtue: and again, virtues are engendered and corrupted by contrary acts (*Ethic.* ii. 2).

I answer that, A form is said to be corrupted directly by its contrary; indirectly, through its subject being corrupted. When therefore a habit has a corruptible subject, and a cause that has a contrary, it can be corrupted both ways. This is clearly the case with bodily habits—for instance, health and sickness.— But those habits that have an incorruptible subject, cannot be corrupted indirectly. There are, however, some habits which, while residing chiefly in an incorruptible subject, reside nevertheless secondarily in a corruptible subject; such is the habit of science which is chiefly indeed in the *possible* intellect, but secondarily in the sensitive powers of apprehenion, as stated above (Q. 50, A. 3 *ad* 3). Conequently the habit of science cannot be corupted indirectly, on the part of the *possible* intellect, but only on the part of the lower sensitive powers.

We must therefore inquire whether habits of this kind can be corrupted directly. If then there be a habit having a contrary, either on the part of itself or on the part of its cause, it can be corrupted directly: but if it has no contrary, it cannot be corrupted directly. Now it is evident that an intelligible species residing in the *possible* intellect, has no contrary; nor can the active intellect, which is the cause of that species, have a contrary. Wherefore if in the *possible* intellect there be a habit caused immediately by the active intellect, such a habit is incorruptible both directly and indirectly. Such are the habits of the first principles, both speculative and practical, which cannot be corrupted by any forgetfulness or deception whatever: even as the Philosopher says about prudence (*Ethic.* vi. 5) that *it cannot be lost by being forgotten.*— There is, however, in the *possible* intellect a habit caused by the reason, to wit, the habit of conclusions, which is called science, the cause of which something may be contrary in two ways. First, on the part of those very propositions which are the starting-point of the reason: for the assertion *Good is not good* is contrary to the assertion *Good is good (Peri Hermen.* ii). Secondly, on the part of the process of reasoning; forasmuch as a sophistical syllogism is contrary to a dialectic or demonstrative syllogism. Wherefore it is clear that a false reason car corrupt the habit of a true opinion or even of science. Hence the Philosopher, as stated above, says that *deception is the corruption of science.* As to virtues, some of them are intellectual, residing in reason itself, as stated in *Ethic.* vi. 1: and to these applies what we have said of science and opinion.—Some, however, viz., the moral virtues, are in the appetitive part of the soul; and the same may be said of the contrary vices. Now

the habits of the appetitive part are caused therein because it is natural to it to be moved by the reason. Therefore a habit either of virtue or of vice, may be corrupted by a judgment of reason, whenever its motion is contrary to such vice or virtue, whether through ignorance, passion or deliberate choice.

Reply Obj. 1. As stated in *Ethic.* vii. 10, a habit is like a second nature, and yet it falls short of it. And so it is that while the nature of a thing cannot in any way be taken away from a thing, a habit is removed, though with difficulty.

Reply Obj. 2. Although there is no contrary to intelligible species, yet there can be a contrary to assertions and to the process of reason, as stated above.

Reply Obj. 3. Science is not taken away by movement of the body, if we consider the root itself of the habit, but only as it may prove an obstacle to the act of science; in so far as the intellect, in its act, has need of the sensitive powers, which are impeded by corporal transmutation. But the intellectual movement of the reason can corrupt the habit of science, even as regards the very root of the habit. In like manner a habit of virtue can be corrupted. —Nevertheless when it is said that *virtue is more lasting than learning,* this must be understood in respect, not of the subject or cause, but of the act: because the use of virtue continues through the whole of life, whereas the use of learning does not.

SECOND ARTICLE

Whether a Habit Can Diminish?

We proceed thus to the Second Article:—

Objection 1. It would seem that a habit cannot diminish. Because a habit is a simple quality and form. Now a simple thing is possessed either wholly or not at all. Therefore although a habit can be lost it cannot diminish.

Obj. 2. Further, if a thing is befitting an accident, this is by reason either of the accident or of its subject. Now a habit does not become more or less intense by reason of itself; else it would follow that a species might be predicated of its individuals more or less. And if it can become less intense as to its participation by its subject, it would follow that something is accidental to a habit, proper thereto and not common to the habit and its subject. Now whenever a form has something proper to it besides its subject, that form can be separate, as stated in *De Anima* i., text. 13. Hence it follows that a habit is a separable form; which is impossible.

Obj. 3. Further, the very notion and nature

of a habit as of any accident, is inherence in a subject: wherefore any accident is defined with reference to its subject. Therefore if a habit does not become more or less intense in itself, neither can it in its inherence in its subject: and consequently it will be nowise less intense.

On the contrary, It is natural for contraries to be applicable to the same thing. Now increase and decrease are contraries. Since therefore a habit can increase, it seems that it can also diminish.

I answer that, Habits diminish, just as they increase, in two ways, as we have already explained (Q. 52, A. 1). And since they increase through the same cause as that which engenders them, so too they diminish by the same cause as that which corrupts them: since the diminishing of a habit is the road which leads to its corruption, even as, on the other hand, the engendering of a habit is a foundation of its increase.

Reply Obj. 1. A habit, considered in itself, is a simple form. It is not thus that it is subject to decrease; but according to the different ways in which its subject participates in it. This is due to the fact that the subject's potentiality is indeterminate, through its being able to participate a form in various ways, or to extend to a greater or a smaller number of things.

Reply Obj. 2. This argument would hold, if the essence itself of a habit were nowise subject to decrease. This we do not say; but that a certain decrease in the essence of a habit has its origin, not in the habit, but in its subject.

Reply Obj. 3. No matter how we take an accident, its very notion implies dependence on a subject, but in different ways. For if we take an accident in the abstract, it implies relation to a subject, which relation begins in the accident and terminates in the subject: for *whiteness* is *that whereby a thing is white.* Accordingly in defining an accident in the abstract, we do not put the subject as though it were the first part of the definition, viz., the genus; but we give it the second place, which is that of the difference; thus we say that *simitas* is *a curvature of the nose.* But if we take accidents in the concrete, the relation begins in the subject and terminates in the concrete, the relation begins in the subject and terminates at the accident: for *a white thing* is *something that has whiteness.* Accordingly in defining this kind of accident, we place the subject as the genus, which is the first part of a definition; for we say that a *simum* is a *snub-nose.*—Accordingly whatever is befitting an accident on the part of the subject, but is not of the very essence of the accident, is ascribed to that accident, not in the

abstract, but in the concrete. Such are increase and decrease in certain accidents: wherefore to be more or less white is not ascribed to whiteness but to a white thing. The same applies to habits and other qualities; save that certain habits increase or diminish by a kind of addition, as we have already clearly explained (Q. 52, A. 2).

THIRD ARTICLE

Whether a Habit Is Corrupted or Diminished through Mere Cessation from Act?

We proceed thus to the Third Article:—

Objection 1. It would seem that a habit is not corrupted or diminished through mere cessation from act. For habits are more lasting than passion-like qualities, as we have explained above (Q. 49, A. 2 *ad* 3; Q. 50, A. 1). But passion-like qualities are neither corrupted nor diminished by cessation from act: for whiteness is not lessened through not affecting the sight, nor heat through ceasing to make something hot. Therefore neither are habits diminished or corrupted through cessation from act.

Obj. 2. Further, corruption and diminution are changes. Now nothing is changed without a moving cause. Since therefore cessation from act does not imply a moving cause, it does not appear how a habit can be diminished or corrupted through cessation from act.

Obj. 3. Further, the habits of science and virtue are in the intellectual soul which is above time. Now those things that are above time are neither destroyed nor diminished by length of time. Neither, therefore, are such habits destroyed or diminished through length of time, if one fails for long to exercise them.

On the contrary, The Philosopher says (*De Long. et Brev. Vitæ* ii) that not only *deception,* but also *forgetfulness, is the corruption of science.* Moreover he says (*Ethic.* viii. 5) that *want of intercourse has dissolved many a friendship.* In like manner other habits of virtue are diminished or destroyed through cessation from act.

I answer that, As stated in *Phys.* vii., text. 27, a thing is a cause of movement in two ways. First, directly; and such a thing causes movement by reason of its proper form; thus fire causes heat. Secondly, indirectly; for instance, that which removes an obstacle. It is in this latter way that the destruction or diminution of a habit results through cessation from act, in so far, to wit, as we cease from exercising an act which overcame the causes that destroyed or weakened that habit. For it has been stated (A. 1) that habits are destroyed or diminished directly through some contrary agency. Consequently all habits that are gradually undermined by contrary agencies which need to be counteracted by acts proceeding from those habits, are diminished or even destroyed altogether by long cessation from act, as is clearly seen in the case both of science and of virtue. For it is evident that a habit of moral virtue makes a man ready to choose the mean in deeds and passions. And when a man fails to make use of his virtuous habit in order to moderate his own passions or deeds, the necessary result is that many passions and deeds fail to observe the mode of virtue, by reason of the inclination of the sensitive appetite and of other external agencies. Wherefore virtue is destroyed or lessened through cessation from act.—The same applies to the intellectual habits, which render man ready to judge aright of those things that are pictured by his imagination. Hence when man ceases to make use of his intellectual habits, strange fancies, sometimes in opposition to them, arise in his imagination; so that unless those fancies be, as it were, cut off or kept back by frequent use of his intellectual habits, man becomes less fit to judge aright, and sometimes is even wholly disposed to the contrary, and thus the intellectual habit is diminished or even wholly destroyed by cessation from act.

Reply Obj. 1. Even heat would be destroyed through ceasing to give heat, if, for this same reason, cold which is destructive of heat were to increase.

Reply Obj. 2. Cessation from act is a moving cause, conducive of corruption or diminution, by removing the obstacles thereto, as explained above.

Reply Obj. 3. The intellectual part of the soul, considered in itself, is above time, but the sensitive part is subject to time, and therefore in course of time it undergoes change as to the passions of the sensitive part, and also as to the powers of apprehension. Hence the Philosopher says (*Phys.* iv., text. 117) that time makes us forget.

QUESTION 54

Of the Distinction of Habits

(In Four Articles)

WE have now to consider the distinction of habits; and under this head there are four points of inquiry: (1) Whether many habits can be in one power? (2) Whether habits are distinguished by their objects? (3) Whether habits are divided into good and bad? (4) Whether one habit may be made up of many habits?

FIRST ARTICLE

Whether Many Habits Can Be in One Power?

We proceed thus to the First Article:—

Objection 1. It would seem that there cannot be many habits in one power. For when several things are distinguished in respect of the same thing, if one of them be multiplied, the others are too. Now habits and powers are distinguished in respect of the same thing, viz., their acts and objects. Therefore they are multiplied in like manner. Therefore there cannot be many habits in one power.

Obj. 2. Further, a power is a simple force. Now in one simple subject there cannot be diversity of accidents; for the subject is the cause of its accidents; and it does not appear how diverse effects can proceed from one simple cause. Therefore there cannot be many habits in one power.

Obj. 3. Further, just as the body is informed by its shape, so is a power informed by a habit. But one body cannot be informed at the same time by various shapes. Therefore neither can a power be informed at the same time by many habits. Therefore several habits cannot be at the same time in one power.

On the contrary, The intellect is one power; wherein, nevertheless, are the habits of various sciences.

I answer that, As stated above (Q. 49, A. 4), habits are dispositions of a thing that is in potentiality to something, either to nature, or to operation, which is the end of nature. As to those habits which are dispositions to nature, it is clear that several can be in one same subject: since in one subject we may take parts in various ways, according to the various dispositions of which parts there are various habits. Thus, if we take the humors as being parts of the human body, according to their disposition in respect of human nature, we have the habit or disposition of health: while, if we take like parts, such as nerves, bones, and flesh, the disposition of these in respect of nature is strength or weakness; whereas, if we take the limbs, i.e., the hands, feet, and so on, the disposition of these in proportion to nature, is beauty: and thus there are several habits or dispositions in the same subject.

If, however, we speak of those habits that are dispositions to operation, and belong properly to the powers; thus, again, there may be several habits in one power. The reason for this is that the subject of a habit is a passive power, as stated above (Q. 51, A. 2): for it is only an active power that cannot be the subject of a habit, as was clearly shown above (*ibid.*). Now a passive power is compared to the determinate act of any species, as matter to form: because, just as matter is determinate to one form by one agent, so, too, is a passive power determined by the nature of one active object to an act specifically one. Wherefore, just as several objects can move one passive power, so can one passive power be the subject of several acts or perfections specifically diverse. Now habits are qualities or forms adhering to a power, and inclining that power to acts of a determinate species. Consequently several habits, even as several specifically different acts, can belong to one power.

Reply Obj. 1. Even as in natural things, diversity of species is according to the form, and diversity of genus, according to matter, as stated in *Metaph.* v., text. 33 (since things that differ in matter belong to different genera): so, too, generic diversity of objects entails a difference of powers (wherefore the Philosopher says in *Ethic.* vi. 1, that *those objects that differ generically belong to different departments of the soul*); while specific difference of objects entails a specific difference of acts, and consequently of habits also. Now things that differ in genus differ in species, but not vice versa. Wherefore the acts and habits of different powers differ in species: but it does not follow that different habits are in different powers, for several can be in one power. And even as several genera may be included in one genus, and several species be contained in one species; so does it happen that there are several species of habits and powers.

Reply Obj. 2. Although a power is simple as to its essence, it is multiple virtually, inasmuch as it extends to many specifically different acts. Consequently there is nothing to prevent many superficially different habits from being in one power.

Reply Obj. 3. A body is informed by its shape as by its own terminal boundaries: whereas a habit is not the terminal boundary of a power, but the disposition of a power to an act as to its ultimate term. Consequently one same power cannot have several acts at the same time, except in so far as perchance one act is comprised in another; just as neither can a body have several shapes. save in so far

as one shape enters into another, as a three-sided in a four-sided figure. For the intellect cannot understand several things at the same time *actually;* and yet it can know several things at the same time *habitually.*

SECOND ARTICLE

Whether Habits Are Distinguished by Their Objects?

We proceed thus to the Second Article:—

Objection 1. It would seem that habits are not distinguished by their objects. For contraries differ in species. Now the same habit of science regards contraries: thus medicine regards the healthy and the unhealthy. Therefore habits are not distinguished by objects specifically distinct.

Obj. 2. Further, different sciences are different habits. But the same scientific truth belongs to different sciences: thus both the physicist and the astronomer prove the earth to be round, as stated in *Phys.* ii., text. 17. Therefore habits are not distinguished by their objects.

Obj. 3. Further, wherever the act is the same, the object is the same. But the same act can belong to different habits of virtue, if it be directed to different ends; thus to give money to anyone, if it be done for God's sake, is an act of charity; while, if it be done in order to pay a debt, it is an act of justice. Therefore the same object can also belong to different habits. Therefore diversity of habits does not follow diversity of objects.

On the contrary, Acts differ in species according to the diversity of their objects, as stated above (Q. 18, A. 5). But habits are dispositions to acts. Therefore habits also are distinguished according to the diversity of objects.

I answer that, A habit is both a form and a habit. Hence the specific distinction of habits may be taken in the ordinary way in which forms differ specifically; or according to that mode of distinction which is proper to habits. Accordingly forms are distinguished from one another in reference to the diversity of their active principles, since every agent produces its like in species.—Habits, however, imply order to something: and all things that imply order to something, are distinguished according to the distinction of the things to which they are ordained. Now a habit is a disposition implying a twofold order: viz., to nature, and to an operation consequent to nature.

Accordingly habits are specifically distinct in respect of three things. First, in respect of the active principles of such dispositions; secondly, in respect of nature; thirdly, in respect of specifically different objects, as will appear from what follows.

Reply Obj. 1. In distinguishing powers, or also habits, we must consider the object not in its material but in its formal aspect, which may differ in species or even in genus. And though the distinction between specific contraries is a real distinction, yet they are both known under one aspect, since one is known through the other. And consequently in so far as they concur in the one aspect of cognoscibility, they belong to one cognitive habit.

Reply Obj. 2. The physicist proves the earth to be round by one means, the astronomer by another: for the latter proves this by means of mathematics, e.g., by the shapes of eclipses, or something of the sort; while the former proves it by means of physics, e.g., by the movement of heavy bodies towards the center, and so forth. Now the whole force of a demonstration, which is *a syllogism producing science*, as stated in *Poster.* i, text. 5, depends on the mean. And consequently various means are as so many active principles, in respect of which the habits of science are distinguished.

Reply Obj. 3. As the Philosopher says (*Phys.* ii, text. 89; *Ethic.* vii. 8), the end is, in practical matters, what the principle is in speculative matters. Consequently diversity of ends demands a diversity of virtues, even as diversity of active principles does.—Moreover the ends are objects of the internal acts, with which, above all, the virtues are concerned, as is evident from what has been said (Q. 18, A. 6; Q. 19, A. 2 *ad* 1; Q. 34, A. 4).

THIRD ARTICLE

Whether Habits Are Divided into Good and Bad?

We proceed thus to the Third Article:—

Objection 1. It would seem that habits are not divided into good and bad. For good and bad are contraries. Now the same habit regards contraries, as was stated above (A. 2, *Obj.* 1). Therefore habits are not divided into good and bad.

Obj. 2. Further, good is convertible with being; so that, since it is common to all, it cannot be accounted a specific difference, as the Philosopher declares (*Topic.* iv). Again, evil, since it is a privation and a non-being, cannot differentiate any being. Therefore habits cannot be specifically divided into good and evil.

Obj. 3. Further, there can be different evil habits about one same object; for instance, intemperance and insensibility about matters of concupiscence: and in like manner there can be several good habits; for instance, human

virtue and heroic or godlike virtue, as the Philosopher clearly states (*Ethic.* vii. 1). Therefore, habits are not divided into good and bad.

On the contrary, A good habit is contrary to a bad habit, as virtue to vice. Now contraries are divided specifically into good and bad habits.

I answer that, As stated above (A. 2), habits are specifically distinct not only in respect of their objects and active principles, but also in their relation to nature. Now, this happens in two ways. First, by reason of their suitableness or unsuitableness to nature. In this way a good habit is specifically distinct from a bad habit: since a good habit is one which disposes to an act suitable to the agent's nature, while an evil habit is one which disposes to an act unsuitable to nature. Thus, acts of virtue are suitable to human nature, since they are according to reason, whereas acts of vice are discordant from human nature, since they are against reason. Hence it is clear that habits are distinguished specifically by the difference of good and bad.

Secondly, habits are distinguished in relation to nature, from the fact that one habit disposes to an act that is suitable to a lower nature, while another habit disposes to an act befitting a higher nature. And thus human virtue, which disposes to an act befitting human nature, is distinct from godlike or heroic virtue, which disposes to an act befitting some higher nature.

Reply Obj. 1. The same habit may be about contraries in so far as contraries agree in one common aspect. Never, however, does it happen that contrary habits are in one species: since contrariety of habits follows contrariety of aspect. Accordingly habits are divided into good and bad, namely, inasmuch as one habit is good, and another bad; but not by reason of one habit being something good, and another about something bad.

Reply Obj. 2. It is not the good which is common to every being, that is a difference constituting the species of a habit; but some determinate good by reason of suitability to some determinate, viz., the human, nature. In like manner the evil that constitutes a difference of habits is not a pure privation, but something determinate repugnant to a determinate nature.

Reply Obj. 3. Several good habits about one same specific thing are distinct in reference to their suitability to various natures, as stated above. But several bad habits in respect of one same action are distinct in reference to their diverse repugnance to that which is in keeping with nature: thus, various vices about one same matter are contrary to one virtue.

FOURTH ARTICLE

Whether One Habit Is Made Up of Many Habits?

We proceed thus to the Fourth Article:—

Objection 1. It would seem that one habit is made up of many habits. For whatever is engendered, not at once, but little by little, seems to be made up of several parts. But a habit is engendered, not at once, but little by little out of several acts, as stated above (Q. 51, A. 3). Therefore one habit is made up of several.

Obj. 2. Further, a whole is made up of its parts. Now many parts are assigned to one habit: thus Tully assigns many parts of fortitude, temperance, and other virtues. Therefore one habit is made up of many.

Obj. 3. Further, one conclusion suffices both for an act and for a habit of scientific knowledge. But many conclusions belong to but one science, to geometry, for instance, or to arithmetic. Therefore one habit is made up of many.

On the contrary, A habit, since it is a quality, is a simple form. But nothing simple is made up of many. Therefore one habit is not made up of many.

I answer that, A habit directed to operation, such as we are chiefly concerned with at present, is a perfection of a power. Now every perfection should be in proportion with that which it perfects. Hence, just as a power, while it is one, extends to many things, in so far as they have something in common, i.e., some general objective aspect, so also a habit extends to many things, in so far as they are related to one, for instance, to some specific objective aspect, or to one nature, or to one principle, as was clearly stated above (AA. 2, 3).

If then we consider a habit as to the extent of its object, we shall find a certain multiplicity therein. But since this multiplicity is directed to one thing, on which the habit is chiefly intent, hence it is that a habit is a simple quality, not composed of several habits, even though it extend to many things. For a habit does not extend to many things save in relation to one, whence it derives its unity.

Reply Obj. 1. That a habit is engendered little by little, is due, not to one part being engendered after another, but to the fact that the subject does not acquire all at once a firm and difficultly changeable disposition; and also to the fact that it begins by being imperfectly in the subject, and is gradually perfected. The same applies to other qualities.

Reply Obj. 2. The parts which are assigned to each cardinal virtue, are not integral parts that combine to form a whole; but subjective or potential parts, as we shall explain further on (Q. 57, A. 6 *ad* 4; II-II, Q. 48).

Reply Obj. 3. In any science, he who acquires, by demonstration, scientific knowledge of one conclusion, has the habit indeed, yet imperfectly. And when he obtains, by demonstration, the scientific knowledge of another conclusion, no additional habit is engendered in him: but the habit which was in him previously is perfected, forasmuch as it has increased in extent; because the conclusions and demonstrations of one science are co-ordinate, and one flows from another.

HABITS IN PARTICULAR
(Chart cont'd from p. 791)

(Chart cont'd from p. 791)

							Question	Article
The Intrinsic Principles of Human Acts (Cont'd)	2. Habits (Cont'd)	2. In Particular	1. Good Habits or Virtues	1. Virtues in Themselves	1. The Essence of virtue		55	4
					2. It Subject		56	6
						1. Intellectual virtues.—Wisdom, science, understanding of first principles	57	6
					2. Moral virtues of the appetitive faculty	1. The difference between moral and intellectual virtues	58	5
						2. Their distinction — 1. In relation to the passions	59	5
						2. From one another	60	5
						3. The difference between the chief or cardinal virtues and the others	61	5
					3. Its Division — 3. Theological Virtues:—Faith, Hope, Charity.—Are they specifically distinct from intellectual and moral virtues?		62	4
					4. Its Cause.—Whether virtue is in us by nature.—Whether moral virtues are in us by infusion		63	4
					5. Certain Properties of Virtues — 1. The mean of virtue		64	4
					2. The connections of virtues		65	5
					3. The equality among the virtues		66	6
					4. The duration of the virtues		67	6
				2. Matters Connected with Virtues	1. The gifts of the Holy Ghost.—Which and how many are they?—Do they differ from virtues?		68	8
					2. The beatitudes.—Do they differ from gifts and virtues?—Their number		69	4
					3. The fruits of the Holy Ghost.—Do they differ from beatitudes?—Their number		70	4
			2. Bad Habits: Sins and Vices—See Unit I, QQ. 71-89—Part II-I.					

QUESTION 55

Of the Virtues, As to Their Essence

(In Four Articles)

WE come now to the consideration of habits specifically. And since habits, as we have said (Q. 54, A. 3), are divided into good and bad, we must speak in the first place of good habits, which are virtues, and of other matters connected with them, namely the Gifts, Beatitudes and Fruits; in the second place, of bad habits, namely of vices and sins. Now five things must be considered about virtues: (1) the essence of virtue; (2) its subject; (3) the division of virtue; (4) the cause of virtue; (5) certain properties of virtue.

Under the first head, there are four points of inquiry: (1) Whether human virtue is a habit? (2) Whether it is an operative habit? (3) Whether it is a good habit? (4) Of the definition of virtue.

FIRST ARTICLE

Whether Human Virtue Is a Habit?

We proceed thus to the First Article:—

Objection 1. It would seem that human virtue is not a habit: For virtue is *the limit of power* (*De Cœlo* i., text. 116). But the limit of anything is reducible to the genus of that of which it is the limit; as a point is reducible to the genus of line. Therefore virtue is reducible to the genus of power, and not to the genus of habit.

Obj. 2. Further, Augustine says (*De Lib. Arb.* ii)* that *virtue is good use of free-will.* But use of free-will is an act. Therefore virtue is not a habit, but an act.

Obj. 3. Further, we do not merit by our habits, but by our actions: otherwise a man would merit continually, even while asleep. But we do merit by our virtues. Therefore virtues are not habits, but acts.

Obj. 4. Further, Augustine says (*De Moribus Eccl.* xv.) that *virtue is the order of love,* and (QQ. lxxxiii., qu. 30) that *the ordering which is called virtue consists in enjoying what we ought to enjoy, and using what we ought to use.* Now order, or ordering, denominates either an action or a relation. Therefore virtue is not a habit, but an action or a relation.

Obj. 5. Further, just as there are human virtues, so are there natural virtues. But natural virtues are not habits, but powers. Neither therefore are human virtues habits.

On the contrary, The Philosopher says (*Categ.* vi) that science and virtue are habits.

I answer that, Virtue denotes a certain perfection of a power. Now a thing's perfection is considered chiefly in regard to its end. But the end of power is act. Wherefore power is said to be perfect, according as it is determinate to its act.

Now there are some powers which of themselves are determinate to their acts; for instance, the active natural powers. And therefore these natural powers are in themselves called virtues. But the rational powers, which are proper to man, are not determinate to one particular action, but are inclined indifferently to many: and they are determinate to acts by means of habits, as is clear from what we have said above (Q. 49, A. 4). Therefore human virtues are habits.

Reply Obj. 1. Sometimes we give the name of a virtue to that to which the virtue is directed, namely, either to its object, or to its act: for instance, we give the name Faith, to that which we believe, or to the act of believing, as also to the habit by which we believe. When therefore we say that *virtue is the limit of power,* virtue is taken for the object of virtue. For the furthest point to which a power can reach, is said to be its virtue; for instance, if a man can carry a hundredweight and not more, his virtue† is put at a hundredweight, and not at sixty. But the objection takes virtue as being essentially the limit of power.

Reply Obj. 2. Good use of free-will is said to be a virtue, in the same sense as above (*ad* 1); that is to say, because it is that to which virtue is directed as to its proper act. For the act of virtue is nothing else than the good use of free-will.

Reply Obj. 3. We are said to merit by something in two ways. First, as by merit itself, just as we are said to run by running; and thus we merit by acts. Secondly, we are said to merit by something as by the principle whereby we merit, as we are said to run by the motive power; and thus are we said to merit by virtues and habits.

Reply Obj. 4. When we say that virtue is the order or ordering of love, we refer to the end to which virtue is ordered: because in us love is set in order by virtue.

---

* *Retract.* ix.; *cf. De Lib. Arb.* ii. 19.

† In English we should say *strength,* which is the original signification of the Latin *virtus*: thus we speak of an engine being so many horse-*power,* to indicate its *strength.*

Reply Obj. 5. Natural powers are of themselves determinate to one act: not so the rational powers. And so there is no comparison, as we have said.

SECOND ARTICLE

Whether Human Virtue Is an Operative Habit?

We proceed thus to the Second Article:—

Objection 1. It would seem that it is not essential to human virtue to be an operative habit. For Tully says (*Tuscul.* iv) that as health and beauty belong to the body, so virtue belongs to the soul. But health and beauty are not operative habits. Therefore neither is virtue.

Obj. 2. Further, in natural things we find virtue not only in reference to act, but also in reference to being: as is clear from the Philosopher (*De Cœlo* i), since some have a virtue to be always, while some have a virtue to be not always, but at some definite time. Now as natural virtue is in natural things, so is human virtue in rational beings. Therefore also human virtue is referred not only to act, but also to being.

Obj. 3. Further, the Philosopher says (*Phys.* vii., text. 17) that virtue *is the disposition of a perfect thing to that which is best.* Now the best thing to which man needs to be disposed by virtue is God Himself, as Augustine proves (*De Moribus Eccl.*, 3, 6, 14) to Whom the soul is disposed by being made like to Him. Therefore it seems that virtue is a quality of the soul in reference to God, likening it, as it were, to Him; and not in reference to operation. It is not, therefore, an operative habit.

On the contrary, The Philosopher (*Ethic.* ii. 6) says that *the virtue of a thing is that which makes its work good.*

I answer that, Virtue, from the very nature of the word, implies some perfection of power, as we have said above (A. 1). Wherefore, since power* is of two kinds, namely power in reference to being, and power in reference to act; the perfection of each of these is called virtue. But power in reference to being is on the part of matter, which is potential being, whereas power in reference to act, is on the part of the form, which is the principle of action, since everything acts in so far as it is in act.

Now man is so constituted that the body holds the place of matter, the soul that of form. The body, indeed, man has in common with other animals; and the same is to be said of the forces which are common to the soul and body: and only those forces which are proper to the soul, namely, the rational forces, belong to man alone. And therefore, human virtue, of which we are speaking now, cannot belong to

the body, but belongs only to that which is proper to the soul. Wherefore human virtue does not imply reference to being, but rather to act. Consequently it is essential to human virtue to be an operative habit.

Reply Obj. 1. Mode of action follows on the disposition of the agent: for such as a thing is, such is its act. And therefore, since virtue is the principle of some kind of operation, there must needs pre-exist in the operator in respect of virtue some corresponding disposition. Now virtue causes an ordered operation. Therefore virtue itself is an ordered disposition of the soul, in so far as, to wit, the powers of the soul are in some way ordered to one another, and to that which is outside. Hence virtue, inasmuch as it is a suitable disposition of the soul, is like health and beauty, which are suitable dispositions of the body. But this does not hinder virtue from being a principle of operation.

Reply Obj. 2. Virtue which is referred to being is not proper to man; but only that virtue which is referred to works of reason, which are proper to man.

Reply Obj. 3. As God's substance is His act, the highest likeness of man to God is in respect of some operation. Wherefore, as we have said above (Q. 3, A. 2), happiness or bliss by which man is made most perfectly conformed to God, and which is the end of human life, consists in an operation.

THIRD ARTICLE

Whether Human Virtue Is a Good Habit?

We proceed thus to the Third Article:—

Objection 1. It would seem that it is not essential to virtue that it should be a good habit. For sin is always taken in a bad sense. But there is a virtue even of sin; according to 1 Cor. xv. 56: *The virtue* (Douay,—*strength*) *of sin is the Law.* Therefore virtue is not always a good habit.

Obj. 2. Further, Virtue corresponds to power. But power is not only referred to good, but also to evil: according to Is. v.: *Woe to you that are mighty to drink wine, and stout men at drunkenness.* Therefore virtue also is referred to good and evil.

Obj. 3. Further, according to the Apostle (2 Cor. xii. 9): *Virtue* (Douay,—*Power*) *is made perfect in infirmity.* But infirmity is an evil. Therefore virtue is referred not only to good, but also to evil.

On the contrary, Augustine says (*De Moribus Eccl.* vi): *No one can doubt that virtue makes the soul exceeding good:* and the Philosopher says (*Ethic.* ii. 6): *Virtue is that*

* The one Latin word *potentia* is rendered *potentiality* in the first case, and *power* in the second.

which makes its possessor good, and his work good likewise.

I answer that, As we have said above (A. 1), virtue implies a perfection of power: wherefore the virtue of a thing is fixed by the limit of its power (*De Cælo* i). Now the limit of any power must needs be good: for all evil implies defect; wherefore Dionysius says (*Div. Nom.* ii) that every evil is a weakness. And for this reason the virtue of a thing must be regarded in reference to good. Therefore human virtue which is an operative habit, is a good habit, productive of good works.

Reply Obj. 1. Just as bad things are said metaphorically to be perfect, so are they said to be good: for we speak of a perfect thief or robber; and of a good thief or robber, as the Philosopher explains (*Metaph.* v., text. 21). In this way therefore virtue is applied to evil things: so that the *virtue* of sin is said to be law, in so far as occasionally sin is aggravated through the law, so as to attain to the limit of its possibility.

Reply Obj. 2. The evil of drunkenness and excessive drink, consists in a falling away from the order of reason. Now it happens that, together with this falling away from reason, some lower power is perfect in reference to that which belongs to its own kind, even in direct opposition to reason, or with some falling away therefrom. But the perfection of that power, since it is compatible with a falling away from reason, cannot be called a human virtue.

Reply Obj. 3. Reason is shown to be so much the more perfect, according as it is able to overcome or endure more easily the weakness of the body and of the lower powers. And therefore human virtue, which is attributed to reason, is said to be *made perfect in infirmity,* not of the reason indeed, but of the body and of the lower powers.

FOURTH ARTICLE

Whether Virtue Is Suitably Defined?

We proceed thus to the Fourth Article:—

Objection 1. It would seem that the definition, usually given, of virtue, is not suitable, to wit: *Virtue is a good quality of the mind, by which we live righteously, of which no one can make bad use, which God works in us, without us.* For virtue is man's goodness, since virtue it is that makes its subject good. But goodness does not seem to be good, as neither is whiteness white. It is therefore unsuitable to describe virtue as a *good quality.*

Obj. 2. Further, no difference is more common than its genus; since it is that which divides the genus. But *good* is more common than quality, since it is convertible with being.

* *Tract.* xxvii. *in Joan.: Serm.* xv. *de Verb. Ap.,* 11.

Therefore *good* should not be put in the definition of virtue, as a difference of quality.

Obj. 3. Further, as Augustine says (*De Trin.* xii. 3): *When we come across anything that is not common to us and the beasts of the field, it is something appertaining to the mind.* But there are virtues even of the irrational parts; as the Philosopher says (*Ethic.* iii. 10). Every virtue, therefore, is not a good quality *of the mind.*

Obj. 4. Further, righteousness seems to belong to justice; whence the righteous are called just. But justice is a species of virtue. It is therefore unsuitable to put *righteous* in the definition of virtue, when we say that virtue is that *by which we live righteously.*

Obj. 5. Further, whoever is proud of a thing, makes bad use of it. But many are proud of virtue, for Augustine says in his Rule, that *pride lies in wait for good works in order to slay them.* It is untrue, therefore, *that no one can make bad use of virtue.*

Obj. 6. Further, man is justified by virtue. But Augustine commenting on Jo. xv. 11: *He shall do greater things than these,* says:* *He who created thee without thee, will not justify thee without thee.* It is therefore unsuitable to say that *God works virtue in us, without us.*

On the contrary, We have the authority of Augustine from whose words this definition is gathered, and principally in *De Libero Arbitrio* ii. 19.

I answer that, This definition comprises perfectly the whole essential notion of virtue. For the perfect essential notion of anything is gathered from all its causes. Now the above definition comprises all the causes of virtue. For the formal cause of virtue, as of everything, is gathered from its genus and difference, when it is defined as *a good quality:* for *quality* is the genus of virtue, and the difference, *good.* But the definition would be more suitable if for *quality* we substitute *habit,* which is the proximate genus.

Now virtue has no matter *out of which* it is formed, as neither has any other accident; but it has matter *about which* it is concerned, and matter *in which* it exists, namely, the subject. The matter about which virtue is concerned is its object, and this could not be included in the above definition, because the object fixes the virtue to a certain species, and here we are giving the definition of virtue in general. And so for material cause we have the subject, which is mentioned when we say that virtue is a good quality *of the mind.*

The end of virtue, since it is an operative habit, is operation. But it must be observed, that some operative habits are always referred to evil, as vicious habits: others are sometimes referred to good, sometimes to evil; for in·

stance, opinion is referred both to the true and to the untrue: whereas virtue is a habit which is always referred to good: and so the distinction of virtue from those habits which are always referred to evil, is expressed in the words *by which we live righteously:* and its distinction from those habits which are sometimes directed unto good, sometimes unto evil, in the words, *of which no one makes bad use.*

Lastly, God is the efficient cause of infused virtue, to which this definition applies; and this is expressed in the words *which God works in us without us.* If we omit this phrase, the remainder of the definition will apply to all virtues in general, whether acquired or infused.

Reply Obj. 1. That which is first seized by the intellect is being: wherefore everything that we apprehend we consider as being, and consequently as one, and as good, which are convertible with being. Wherefore we say that essence is being and is one and is good; and that one-ness is being and one and good: and in like manner goodness. But this not the case with specific forms, as whiteness and health; for everything that we apprehend, is not apprehended with the notion of white and healthy. We must, however, observe that, as accidents and non-subsistent forms are called beings, not as if they themselves had being, but because things are by them; so also are they called good or one, not by some distinct goodness or one-ness, but because by them something is good or one. So also is virtue called good, because by it something is good.

Reply Obj. 2. Good, which is put in the definition of virtue, is not good in general which is convertible with being, and which extends further than quality, but the good as fixed by reason, with regard to which Dionysius says (*Div. Nom.* iv) *that the good of the soul is to be in accord with reason.*

Reply Obj. 3. Virtue cannot be in the irrational part of the soul, except in so far as this participates in the reason (*Ethic.* i. 13). And therefore reason, or the mind, is the proper subject of virtue.

Reply Obj. 4. Justice has a righteousness of its own by which it puts those outward things right which come into human use, and are the proper matter of justice, as we shall show further on (Q. 60, A. 2; II-II, Q. 58, A. 8). But the righteousness which denotes order to a due end and to the Divine law, which is the rule of the human will, as stated above (Q. 19, A. 4), is common to all virtues.

Reply Obj. 5. One can make bad use of a virtue objectively, for instance by having evil thoughts about a virtue, e.g., by hating it, or by being proud of it: but one cannot make bad use of virtue as principle of action, so that an act of virtue be evil.

Reply Obj. 6. Infused virtue is caused in us by God without any action on our part, but not without our consent. This is the sense of the words, *which God works in us without us.* As to those things which are done by us, God causes them in us, yet not without action on our part, for He works in every will and in every nature.

QUESTION 56

Of the Subject of Virtue

(In Six Articles)

WE now have to consider the subject of virtue, about which there are six points of inquiry: (1) Whether the subject of virtue is a power of the soul? (2) Whether one virtue can be in several powers? (3) Whether the intellect can be the subject of virtue? (4) Whether the irascible and concupiscible faculties can be the subject of virtue? (5) Whether the sensitive powers of apprehension can be the subject of virtue? (6) Whether the will can be the subject of virtue?

FIRST ARTICLE

Whether the Subject of Virtue Is a Power of the Soul?

We proceed thus to the First Article:—

Objection 1. It would seem that the subject of virtue is not a power of the soul. For Augustine says (*De Lib. Arb.* ii. 19) that *vir-* *tue is that by which we live righteously.* But we live by the essence of the soul, and not by a power of the soul. Therefore virtue is not in a power, but in the essence of the soul.

Obj. 2. Further, the Philosopher says (*Ethic.* ii. 6) that *virtue is that which makes its possessor good, and his work good likewise.* But as work is set up by power, so he that has a virtue is set up by the essence of the soul. Therefore virtue does not belong to the power, any more than to the essence of the soul.

Obj. 3. Further, power is in the second species of quality. But virtue is a quality, as we have said above (Q. 55, A. 4): and quality is not the subject of quality. Therefore a power of the soul is not the subject of virtue.

On the contrary, Virtue *is the limit of power* (*De Cælo* ii). But the limit is in that of which it is the limit. Therefore virtue is in a power of the soul.

I answer that, It can be proved in three ways that virtue belongs to a power of the soul. First, from the notion of the very essence of virtue, which implies perfection of a power; for perfection is in that which it perfects.— Secondly, from the fact that virtue is an operative habit, as we have said above (Q. 55, A. 2): for all operation proceeds from the soul through a power.—Thirdly, from the fact that virtue disposes to that which is best: for the best is the end, which is either a thing's operation, or something acquired by an operation proceeding from the thing's power. Therefore a power of the soul is the subject of virtue.

Reply Obj. 1. *To live* may be taken in two ways. Sometimes it is taken for the very existence of the living thing: in this way it belongs to the essence of the soul, which is the principle of existence in the living thing. But sometimes *to live* is taken for the operation of the living thing: in this sense, by virtue we live righteously, inasmuch as by virtue we perform righteous actions.

Reply Obj. 2. Good is either the end, or something referred to the end. And therefore, since the good of the worker consists in the work, this fact also, that virtue makes the worker good, is referred to the work, and consequently, to the power.

Reply Obj. 3. One accident is said to be the subject of another, not as though one accident could uphold another; but because one accident inheres to substance by means of another, as color to the body by means of the surface; so that surface is said to be the subject of color. In this way a power of the soul is said to be the subject of virtue.

SECOND ARTICLE

Whether One Virtue Can Be in Several Powers?

We proceed thus to the Second Article:—

Objection 1. It would seem that one virtue can be in several powers. For habits are known by their acts. But one act proceeds in various ways from several powers: thus walking proceeds from the reason as directing, from the will as moving, and from the motive power as executing. Therefore also one habit can be in several powers.

Obj. 2. Further, the Philosopher says (*Ethic.* ii. 4) that three things are required for virtue, namely: *to know, to will, and to work steadfastly.* But *to know* belongs to the intellect, and *to will* belongs to the will. Therefore virtue can be in several powers.

Obj. 3. Further, prudence is in the reason, since it is *the right reason of things to be done* (*Ethic.* vi. 5). And it is also in the will: for it cannot exist together with a perverse will (*ibid.,* 12). Therefore one virtue can be in two powers.

On the contrary, The subject of virtue is a power of the soul. But the same accident cannot be in several subjects. Therefore one virtue cannot be in several powers of the soul.

I answer that, It happens in two ways that one thing is subjected in two. First, so that it is in both on an equal footing. In this way it is impossible for one virtue to be in two powers: since diversity of powers follows the generic conditions of the objects, while diversity of habits follows the specific conditions thereof: and so wherever there is diversity of powers, there is diversity of habits; but not vice versa. In another way one thing can be subjected in two or more, not on an equal footing, but in a certain order. And thus one virtue can belong to several powers, so that it is in one chiefly, while it extends to others by a kind of diffusion, or by way of a disposition, in so far as one power is moved by another, and one power receives from another.

Reply Obj. 1. One act cannot belong to several powers equally, and in the same degree; but only from different points of view, and in various degrees.

Reply Obj. 2. *To know* is a condition required for moral virtue, inasmuch as moral virtue works according to right reason. But moral virtue is essentially in the appetite.

Reply Obj. 3. Prudence is really subjected in reason: but it presupposes as its principle the rectitude of the will, as we shall see further on (A. 3; Q. 57, A. 4).

THIRD ARTICLE

Whether the Intellect Can Be the Subject of Virtue?

We proceed thus to the Third Article:—

Objection 1. It would seem that the intellect is not the subject of virtue. For Augustine says (*De Moribus Eccl.* xv) that all virtue is love. But the subject of love is not the intellect, but the appetitive power alone. Therefore no virtue is in the intellect.

Obj. 2. Further, virtue is referred to good, as is clear from what has been said above (Q. 55, A. 3). Now good is not the object of the intellect, but of the appetitive power. Therefore the subject of virtue is not the intellect, but the appetitive power.

Obj. 3. Further, virtue is that *which makes its possessor good,* as the Philosopher says (*Ethic.* ii. 6). But the habit which perfects the intellect does not make its possessor good: since a man is not said to be a good man on account of his science or his art. Therefore the intellect is not the subject of virtue.

On the contrary, The mind is chiefly called

the intellect. But the subject of virtue is the mind, as is clear from the definition, above given, of virtue (Q. 55, A. 4). Therefore the intellect is the subject of virtue.

I answer that, As we have said above (Q. 55, A. 3), virtue is a habit by which we work well. Now a habit may be directed to a good act in two ways. First, in so far as by the habit a man acquires an aptness to a good act; for instance, by the habit of grammar man has the aptness to speak correctly. But grammar does not make a man always speak correctly: for a grammarian may be guilty of a barbarism or make a solecism: and the case is the same with other sciences and arts. Secondly, a habit may confer not only aptness to act, but also the right use of that aptness: for instance, justice not only gives man the prompt will to do just actions, but also makes him act justly.

And since good, and, in like manner, being, is said of a thing simply, in respect, not of what it is potentially, but of what it is actually: therefore from having habits of the latter sort, man is said simply to do good, and to be good; for instance, because he is just, or temperate; and in like manner as regards other such virtues. And since virtue is that *which makes its possessor good, and his work good likewise,* these latter habits are called virtuous simply; because they make the work to be actually good, and the subject good simply. But the first kind of habits are not called virtues simply: because they do not make the work good except in regard to a certain aptness, nor do they make their possessor good simply. For through being gifted in science or art, a man is said to be good, not simply, but relatively; for instance, a good grammarian, or a good smith. And for this reason science and art are often divided against virtue; while at other times they are called virtues (*Ethic.* vi. 2).

Hence the subject of a habit which is called a virtue in a relative sense, can be the intellect, and not only the practical intellect, but also the speculative, without any reference to the will: for thus the Philosopher (*Ethic.* vi. 3) holds that science, wisdom and understanding, and also art, are intellectual virtues. But the subject of a habit which is called a virtue simply, can only be the will, or some power in so far as it is moved by the will. And the reason of this is, that the will moves to their acts all those other powers that are in some way rational, as we have said above (Q. 9, A. 1; Q. 17, AA. 1, 5; P. I, Q. 82, A. 4): and therefore if man do well actually, this is because he has a good will. Therefore the virtue which makes a man to do well actually, and not

* Augustine: *Tract.* xxvi. *in Joan.*

merely to have the aptness to do well, must be either in the will itself; or in some power as moved by the will.

Now it happens that the intellect is moved by the will, just as are the other powers: for a man considers something actually, because he wills to do so. And therefore the intellect, in so far as it is subordinate to the will, can be the subject of virtue absolutely so called. And in this way the speculative intellect, or the reason, is the subject of Faith: for the intellect is moved by the command of the will to assent to what is of faith: for *no man believeth, unless he will.** But the practical intellect is the subject of prudence. For since prudence is the right reason of things to be done, it is a condition thereof that man be rightly disposed in regard to the principles of this reason of things to be done, that is in regard to their ends, to which man is rightly disposed by the rectitude of the will, just as to the principles of speculative truth he is rightly disposed by the natural light of the active intellect. And therefore as the subject of science, which is the right reason of speculative truths, is the speculative intellect in its relation to the active intellect, so the subject of prudence is the practical intellect in its relation to the right will.

Reply Obj. 1. The saying of Augustine is to be understood of virtue simply so called: not that every such virtue is love simply: but that it depends in some way on love, in so far as it depends on the will, whose first movement consists in love, as we have said above (Q. 25, AA. 1, 2, 3; Q. 27, A. 4; P. I., Q. 20, A. 1).

Reply Obj. 2. The good of each thing is its end: and therefore, as truth is the end of the intellect, so to know truth is the good act of the intellect. Whence the habit, which perfects the intellect in regard to the knowledge of truth, whether speculative or practical, is a virtue.

Reply Obj. 3. This objection considers virtue simply so called.

FOURTH ARTICLE

Whether the Irascible and Concupiscible Powers Are the Subject of Virtue?

We proceed thus to the Fourth Article:—

Objection 1. It would seem that the irascible and concupiscible powers cannot be the subject of virtue. For these powers are common to us and dumb animals. But we are now speaking of virtue as proper to man, since for this reason it is called human virtue. It is therefore impossible for human virtue to be in the irascible and concupiscible powers which are parts of the sensitive appetite, as we have said in the First Part (Q. 81, A. 2).

Obj. 2. Further, the sensitive appetite is a power which makes use of a corporeal organ. But the good of virtue cannot be in man's body: for the Apostle says (Rom. vii): *I know that good does not dwell in my flesh.* Therefore the sensitive appetite cannot be the subject of virtue.

Obj. 3. Further, Augustine proves (*De Moribus Eccl.* v) that virtue is not in the body but in the soul, for the reason that the body is ruled by the soul: wherefore it is entirely due to his soul that a man make good use of his body: *For instance, if my coachman, through obedience to my orders, guides well the horses which he is driving; this is all due to me.* But just as the soul rules the body, so also does the reason rule the sensitive appetite. Therefore that the irascible and concupiscible powers are rightly ruled, is entirely due to the rational powers. Now *virtue is that by which we live rightly,* as we have said above (Q. 55, A. 4). Therefore virtue is not in the irascible and concupiscible powers, but only in the rational powers.

Obj. 4. Further, *the principal act of moral virtue is choice* (*Ethic.* viii. 13). Now choice is not an act of the irascible and concupiscible powers, but of the rational power, as we have said above (Q. 13, A. 2). Therefore moral virtue is not in the irascible and concupiscible powers, but in the reason.

On the contrary, Fortitude is assigned to the irascible power, and temperance to the concupiscible power. Whence the Philosopher (*Ethic.* iii. 10) says that *these virtues belong to the irrational part of the soul.*

I answer that, The irascible and concupiscible powers can be considered in two ways. First, in themselves, in so far as they are parts of the sensitive appetite: and in this way they are not competent to be the subject of virtue. Secondly, they can be considered as participating in the reason, from the fact that they have a natural aptitude to obey reason. And thus the irascible or concupiscible power can be the subject of human virtue: for, in so far as it participates in the reason, it is the principle of a human act. And to these powers we must needs assign virtues.

For it is clear that there are some virtues in the irascible and concupiscible powers. Because an act, which proceeds from one power according as it is moved by another power, cannot be perfect, unless both powers be well disposed to the act: for instance, the act of a craftsman cannot be successful unless both the craftsman and his instrument be well disposed to act. Therefore in the matter of the operations of the irascible and concupiscible powers, according as they are moved by reason, there

must needs be some habit perfecting in respect of acting well, not only the reason, but also the irascible and concupiscible powers. And since the good disposition of the power which moves through being moved, depends on its conformity with the power that moves it: therefore the virtue which is in the irascible and concupiscible powers is nothing else but a certain habitual conformity of these powers to reason.

Reply Obj. 1. The irascible and concupiscible powers considered in themselves, as parts of the sensitive appetite, are common to us and dumb animals. But in so far as they are rational by participation, and are obedient to the reason, they are proper to man. And in this way they can be the subject of human virtue.

Reply Obj. 2. Just as human flesh has not of itself the good of virtue, but is made the instrument of a virtuous act, inasmuch as being moved by reason, we *yield our members to serve justice*; so also, the irascible and concupiscible powers, of themselves indeed, have not the good of virtue, but rather the infection of the "fomes": whereas, inasmuch as they are in conformity with reason, the good of reason is begotten in them.

Reply Obj. 3. The body is ruled by the soul, and the irascible and concupiscible powers by the reason, but in different ways. For the body obeys the soul blindly without any contradiction, in those things in which it has a natural aptitude to be moved by the soul: whence the Philosopher says (*Polit.* i. 3) that the *soul rules the body with a despotic command* as the master rules his slave: wherefore the entire movement of the body is referred to the soul. For this reason virtue is not in the body, but in the soul. But the irascible and concupiscible powers do not obey the reason blindly; on the contrary, they have their own proper movements, by which, at times, they go against reason, whence the Philosopher says (*ibid.*) that the *reason rules the irascible and concupiscible powers by a political command* such as that by which free men are ruled, who have in some respects a will of their own. And for this reason also must there be some virtues in the irascible and concupiscible powers, by which these powers are well disposed to act.

Reply Obj. 4. In choice there are two things, namely, the intention of the end, and this belongs to the moral virtue; and the preferential choice of that which is unto the end, and this belongs to prudence (*Ethic.* vi. 2, 5). But that the irascible and concupiscible powers have a right intention of the end in regard to the passions of the soul, is due to the good disposition of these powers. And therefore those moral virtues which are concerned with the passions are in the irascible and concupiscible powers, but prudence is in the reason.

FIFTH ARTICLE

Whether the Sensitive Powers of Apprehension Are the Subject of Virtue?

We proceed thus to the Fifth Article:—

Objection 1. It would seem that it is possible for virtue to be in the interior sensitive powers of apprehension. For the sensitive appetite can be the subject of virtue, in so far as it obeys reason. But the interior sensitive powers of apprehension obey reason: for the powers of imagination, of cogitation, and of memory* act at the command of reason. Therefore in these powers there can be virtue.

Obj. 2. Further, as the rational appetite, which is the will, can be hindered or helped in its act, by the sensitive appetite, so also can the intellect or reason be hindered or helped by the powers mentioned above. As, therefore, there can be virtue in the interior powers of appetite, so also can there be virtue in the interior powers of apprehension.

Obj. 3. Further, prudence is a virtue, of which Cicero (*De Invent. Rhetor.* ii) says that memory is a part. Therefore also in the power of memory there can be a virtue: and in like manner, in the other interior sensitive powers of apprehension.

On the contrary, All virtues are either intellectual or moral (*Ethic.* ii. 1). Now all the moral virtues are in the appetite; while the intellectual virtues are in the intellect or reason, as is clear from *Ethic.* vi. 1. Therefore there is no virtue in the interior sensitive powers of apprehension.

I answer that, In the interior sensitive powers of apprehension there are some habits. And this is made clear principally from what the Philosopher says (*De Memoria* ii), that *in remembering one thing after another, we become used to it; and use is a second nature.* Now a habit of use is nothing else than a habit acquired by use, which is like unto nature. Wherefore Tully says of virtue in his *Rhetoric* (*loc. cit.*) that *it is a habit like a second nature in accord with reason.* Yet, in man, that which he acquires by use, in his memory and other sensitive powers of apprehension, is not a habit properly so called, but something annexed to the habits of the intellective faculty, as we have said above (Q. 50, A. 4 *ad* 3).

Nevertheless even if there be habits in such powers, they cannot be called virtues. For virtue is a perfect habit, by which it never happens that anything but good is done: and so virtue must needs be in that power which

* *Cf.* P. I., Q. 78, A. 4.

consummates the good act. But the knowledge of truth is not consummated in the sensitive powers of apprehension: for such powers prepare the way to the intellective knowledge. And therefore in these powers there are none of the virtues, by which we know truth: these are rather in the intellect or reason.

Reply Obj. 1. The sensitive appetite is related to the will, which is the rational appetite, through being moved by it. And therefore the act of the appetitive power is consummated in the sensitive appetite: and for this reason the sensitive appetite is the subject of virtue. Whereas the sensitive powers of apprehension are related to the intellect rather through moving it; for the reason that the phantasms are related to the intellective soul, as colors to sight (*De Anima* iii., text. 18). And therefore the act of knowledge is terminated in the intellect; and for this reason the cognoscitive virtues are in the intellect itself, or the reason.

And thus is made clear the Reply to the Second Objection.

Reply Obj. 3. Memory is not a part of prudence, as species is of a genus, as though memory were a virtue properly so called: but one of the conditions required for prudence is a good memory; so that, in a fashion, it is after the manner of an integral part.

SIXTH ARTICLE

Whether the Will Can Be the Subject of Virtue?

We proceed thus to the Sixth Article:—

Objection 1. It would seem that the will is not the subject of virtue. Because no habit is required for that which belongs to a power by reason of its very nature. But since the will is in the reason, it is of the very essence of the will, according to the Philosopher (*De Anima* iii., text. 42), to tend to that which is good, according to reason. And to this good every virtue is ordered, since everything naturally desires its own proper good; for virtue, as Tully says in his *Rhetoric,* is a *habit like a second nature in accord with reason.* Therefore the will is not the subject of virtue.

Obj. 2. Further, every virtue is either intellectual or moral (*Ethic.* i., 13; ii. 1). But intellectual virtue is subjected in the intellect and reason, and not in the will: while moral virtue is subjected in the irascible and concupiscible powers which are rational by participation. Therefore no virtue is subjected in the will.

Obj. 3. Further, all human acts, to which virtues are ordained, are voluntary. If therefore there be a virtue in the will in respect of some human acts, in like manner there will be a virtue in the will in respect of all human acts. Either, therefore, there will be no virtue in any other power, or there will be two virtues ordained to the same act, which seems unreasonable. Therefore the will cannot be the subject of virtue.

On the contrary, Greater perfection is required in the mover than in the moved. But the will moves the irascible and concupiscible powers. Much more therefore should there be virtue in the will than in the irascible and concupiscible powers.

I answer that, Since the habit perfects the power in reference to act, then does the power need a habit perfecting it unto doing well, which habit is a virtue, when the power's own proper nature does not suffice for the purpose.

Now the proper nature of a power is seen in its relation to its object. Since, therefore, as we have said above (Q. 19, A. 3), the object of the will is the good of reason proportionate to the will, in respect of this the will does not need a virtue perfecting it. But if man's will is confronted with a good that exceeds its capacity, whether as regards the whole human species, such as Divine good, which transcends the limits of human nature, or as regards the individual, such as the good of one's neighbor, then does the will need virtue. And therefore such virtues as those which direct man's affections to God or to his neighbor are subjected in the will, as charity, justice, and such like.

Reply Obj. 1. This objection is true of those virtues which are ordained to the willer's own good; such as temperance and fortitude, which are concerned with the human passions, and the like, as is clear from what we have said (Q. 35, A. 6).

Reply Obj. 2. Not only the irascible and concupiscible powers are rational by participation but *the appetitive power altogether,* i.e., in its entirety (*Ethic.* 1. 13). Now the will is included in the appetitive power. And therefore whatever virtue is in the will must be a moral virtue, unless it be theological, as we shall see later on (Q. 62, A. 3).

Reply Obj. 3. Some virtues are directed to the good of moderated passion, which is the proper good of this or that man: and in these cases there is no need for virtue in the will, for the nature of the power suffices for the purpose, as we have said. This need exists only in the case of virtues which are directed to some extrinsic good.

QUESTION 57

Of the Intellectual Virtues

(In Six Articles)

WE now have to consider the various kinds of virtue: and (1) the intellectual virtues; (2) the moral virtues; (3) the theological virtues. Concerning the first there are six points of inquiry: (1) Whether habits of the speculative intellect are virtues? (2) Whether they are three, namely, wisdom, science and understanding? (3) Whether the intellectual habit, which is art, is a virtue? (4) Whether prudence is a virtue distinct from art? (5) Whether prudence is a virtue necessary to man? (6) Whether *eubulia, synesis* and *gnome* are virtues annexed to prudence?

FIRST ARTICLE

Whether the Habits of the Speculative Intellect Are Virtues?

We proceed thus to the First Article:—

Objection 1. It would seem that the habits of the speculative intellect are not virtues. For virtue is an operative habit, as we have said above (Q. 55, A. 2). But speculative habits are not operative: for speculative matter is distinct from practical, i.e., operative matter. Therefore the habits of the speculative intellect are not virtues.

Obj. 2. Further, virtue is about those things by which man is made happy or blessed: for *happiness is the reward of virtue* (*Ethic.* i. 9). Now intellectual habits do not consider human acts or other human goods, by which man acquires happiness, but rather things pertaining to nature or to God. Therefore such like habits cannot be called virtues.

Obj. 3. Further, science is a speculative habit. But science and virtue are distinct from one another as genera which are not subalternate, as the Philosopher proves in *Topic.* iv. Therefore speculative habits are not virtues.

On the contrary, The speculative habits alone consider necessary things which cannot be otherwise than they are. Now the Philosopher (*Ethic.* vi. 1) places certain intellectual virtues in that part of the soul which considers necessary things that cannot be otherwise than they are. Therefore the habits of the speculative intellect are virtues.

I answer that, Since every virtue is ordained to some good, as stated above (Q. 55, A. 3);

a habit, as we have already observed (Q. 56, A. 3), may be called a virtue for two reasons: first, because it confers aptness in doing good; secondly, because besides aptness, it confers the right use of it. The latter condition, as above stated (*ibid.*), belongs to those habits alone which affect the appetitive part of the soul: since it is the soul's appetitive power that puts all the powers and habits to their respective uses.

Since, then, the habits of the speculative intellect do not perfect the appetitive part, nor affect it in any way, but only the intellective part; they may indeed be called virtues in so far as they confer aptness for a good work, viz., the consideration of truth (since this is the good work of the intellect): yet they are not called virtues in the second way, as though they conferred the right use of a power or habit. For if a man possess a habit of speculative science, it does not follow that he is inclined to make use of it, but he is made able to consider the truth in those matters of which he has scientific knowledge:—that he make use of the knowledge which he has, is due to the motion of his will. Consequently a virtue which perfects the will, as charity or justice, confers the right use of these speculative habits. And in this way too there can be merit in the acts of these habits, if they be done out of charity: thus Gregory says (*Moral.* vi) that the *contemplative life has greater merit than the active life.*

Reply Obj. 1. Work is of two kinds, exterior and interior. Accordingly the practical or active faculty which is contrasted with the speculative faculty, is concerned with exterior work, to which the speculative habit is not ordained. Yet it is ordained to the interior act of the intellect which is to consider the truth. And in this way it is an operative habit.

Reply Obj. 2. Virtue is about certain things in two ways. In the first place a virtue is about its object. And thus these speculative virtues are not about those things whereby man is made happy; except perhaps, in so far as the word *whereby* indicates the efficient cause or object of complete happiness, i.e., God, Who is the supreme object of contemplation.—Secondly, a virtue is said to be about its acts: and in this sense the intellectual virtues are about those things whereby a man is made happy; both because the acts of these virtues can be meritorious, as stated above, and because they are a kind of beginning of perfect bliss, which consists in the contemplation of truth, as we have already stated (Q. 3, A. 7).

Reply Obj. 3. Science is contrasted with virtue taken in the second sense, wherein it belongs to the appetitive faculty.

Whether There Are Only Three Habits of the Speculative Intellect, Viz., Wisdom, Science and Understanding?

We proceed thus to the Second Article:—

Objection 1. It would seem unfitting to distinguish three virtues of the speculative intellect, viz., wisdom, science and understanding. Because a species is a kind of science, as stated in *Ethic.* vi. 7. Therefore wisdom should not be condivided with science among the intellectual virtues.

Obj. 2. Further, in differentiating powers, habits and acts in respect of their objects, we consider chiefly the formal aspect of these objects, as we have already explained (P. I., Q. 77, A. 3). Therefore diversity of habits is taken, not from their material objects, but from the formal aspect of those objects. Now the principle of a demonstration is the formal aspect under which the conclusion is known. Therefore the understanding of principles should not be set down as a habit or virtue distinct from the knowledge of conclusions.

Obj. 3. Further, an intellectual virtue is one which resides in the essentially rational faculty. Now even the speculative reason employs the dialectic syllogism for the sake of argument, just as it employs the demonstrative syllogism. Therefore as science, which is the result of a demonstrative syllogism, is set down as an intellectual virtue, so also should opinion be.

On the contrary, The Philosopher (*Ethic.* vi. 1) reckons these three alone as being intellectual virtues, viz., wisdom, science and understanding.

I answer that, As already stated (A. 1), the virtues of the speculative intellect are those which perfect the speculative intellect for the consideration of truth: for this is its good work. Now a truth is subject to a twofold consideration,—as known in itself, and as known through another. What is known in itself, is as a *principle*, and is at once understood by the intellect: wherefore the habit that perfects the intellect for the consideration of such truth is called *understanding*, which is the habit of principles.

On the other hand, a truth which is known through another, is understood by the intellect, not at once, but by means of the reason's inquiry, and is as a *term*. This may happen in two ways: first, so that it is the last in some particular genus; secondly, so that it is the ultimate term of all human knowledge. And, since *things that are knowable last from our standpoint, are knowable first and chiefly in their nature* (*Phys.* i., text. 2, 3); hence that which is last with respect to all human knowledge, is that which is knowable first and chiefly in its nature. And about these is *wisdom*, which considers the highest causes, as stated in *Metaph.* i. 1, 2. Wherefore it rightly judges all things and sets them in order, because there can be no perfect and universal judgment that is not based on the first causes.— But in regard to that which is last in this or that genus of knowable matter, it is *science* that perfects the intellect. Wherefore according to the different kinds of knowable matter, there are different habits of scientific knowledge; whereas there is but one wisdom.

Reply Obj. 1. Wisdom is a kind of science, in so far as it has that which is common to all the sciences; viz., to demonstrate conclusions from principles. But since it has something proper to itself above the other sciences, inasmuch as it judges of them all, not only as to their conclusions, but also as to their first principles, therefore it is a more perfect virtue than science.

Reply Obj. 2. When the formal aspect of the object is referred to a power or habit by one same act, there is no distinction of habit or power in respect of the formal aspect and of the material object: thus it belongs to the same power of sight to see both color, and light, which is the formal aspect under which color is seen, and is seen at the same time as the color. On the other hand, the principles of a demonstration can be considered apart, without the conclusion being considered at all. Again, they can be considered together with the conclusions, since the conclusions can be deduced from them. Accordingly, to consider the principles in this second way, belongs to science, which considers the conclusions also: while to consider the principles in themselves belongs to understanding.

Consequently, if we consider the point aright, these three virtues are distinct, not as being on a par with one another, but in a certain order. The same is to be observed in potential wholes, wherein one part is more perfect than another; for instance, the rational soul is more perfect than the sensitive soul; and the sensitive, than the vegetal. For it is thus that science depends on understanding as on a virtue of higher degree: and both of these depend on wisdom, as obtaining the highest place, and containing beneath itself both understanding and science, by judging both of the conclusions of science, and of the principles on which they are based.

Reply Obj. 3. As stated above (Q. 55, AA. 3, 4), a virtuous habit has a fixed relation to good, and is nowise referable to evil. Now the good of the intellect is truth, and falsehood is its evil. Wherefore those habits alone are called intellectual virtues, whereby we tell the truth and never tell a falsehood. But opinion and suspicion can be about both truth and falsehood: and so, as stated in *Ethic.* vi. 3, they are not intellectual virtues.

THIRD ARTICLE

Whether the Intellectual Habit, Art, Is a Virtue?

We proceed thus to the Third Article:—

Objection 1. It would seem that art is not an intellectual virtue. For Augustine says (*De Lib. Arb.* ii. 18, 19) that *no one makes bad use of virtue.* But one may make bad use of art: for a craftsman can work badly according to the knowledge of his art. Therefore art is not a virtue.

Obj. 2. Further, there is no virtue of a virtue. But *there is a virtue of art,* according to the Philosopher (*Ethic.* vi. 5). Therefore art is not a virtue.

Obj. 3. Further, the liberal arts excel the mechanical arts. But just as the mechanical arts are practical, so the liberal arts are speculative. Therefore, if art were an intellectual virtue, it would have to be reckoned among the speculative virtues.

On the contrary, The Philosopher (*Ethic.* vi. 3, 4) says that art is a virtue; and yet he does not reckon it among the speculative virtues, which, according to him, reside in the scientific part of the soul.

I answer that, Art is nothing else but *the right reason about certain works to be made.* And yet the good of these things depends, not on man's appetitive faculty being affected in this or that way, but on the goodness of the work done. For a craftsman, as such, is commendable, not for the will with which he does a work, but for the quality of the work. Art, therefore, properly speaking, is an operative habit. And yet it has something in common with the speculative habits: since the quality of the object considered by the latter is a matter of concern to them also, but not how the human appetite may be affected towards that object. For as long as the geometrician demonstrates the truth, it matters not how his appetitive faculty may be affected, whether he be joyful or angry: even as neither does this matter in a craftsman, as we have observed. And so art has the nature of a virtue in the same way as the speculative habits, in so far, to wit, as neither art nor speculative habit makes a good work as regards the use of the habit, which is the property of a virtue that perfects the appetite, but only as regards the aptness to work well.

Reply Obj. 1. When anyone endowed with an art produces bad workmanship, this is not the work of that art, in fact it is contrary to

the art: even as when a man lies, while knowing the truth, his words are not in accord with
his knowledge, but contrary thereto. Wherefore, just as science has always a relation to
good, as stated above (A. 2, *ad* 3), so it is with
art: and it is for this reason that it is called
a virtue. And yet it falls short of being a perfect virtue, because it does not make its possessor to use it well; for which purpose something further is requisite: although there cannot be a good use without the art.

Reply Obj. 2. In order that man may make
good use of the art he has, he needs a good will,
which is perfected by moral virtue; and for
this reason the Philosopher says that there is
a virtue of art; namely, a moral virtue, in so
far as the good use of art requires a moral virtue. For it is evident that a craftsman is inclined by justice, which rectifies his will, to
do his work faithfully.

Reply Obj. 3. Even in speculative matters
there is something by way of work: e.g., the
making of a syllogism or of a fitting speech,
or the work of counting or measuring. Hence
whatever habits are ordained to such like works
of the speculative reason, are, by a kind of
comparison, called arts indeed, but *liberal* arts,
in order to distinguish them from those arts
that are ordained to works done by the body,
which arts are, in a fashion, servile, inasmuch
as the body is in servile subjection to the soul,
and man, as regards his soul, is free (*liber*).
On the other hand, those sciences which are
not ordained to any such like work, are called
sciences simply, and not arts. Nor, if the liberal arts be more excellent, does it follow that
the notion of art is more applicable to them.

FOURTH ARTICLE

Whether Prudence Is a Distinct Virtue from Art?

We proceed thus to the Fourth Article:—

Objection 1. It would seem that prudence
is not a distinct virtue from art. For art
is the right reason about certain works. But
diversity of works does not make a habit cease
to be an art; since there are various arts about
works widely different. Since therefore prudence is also right reason about works, it seems
that it too should be reckoned a virtue.

Obj. 2. Further, prudence has more in common with art than the speculative habits have;
for they are both *about contingent matters that
may be otherwise than they are* (*Ethic.* vi.
4, 5). Now some speculative habits are called
arts. Much more, therefore, should prudence
be called an art.

Obj. 3. Further, it belongs to prudence, *to
be of good counsel* (*Ethic.* vi. 5). But counselling takes place in certain arts also, as stated

in *Ethic.* iii. 3, e.g., in the arts of warfare,
of seamanship, and of medicine. Therefore
prudence is not distinct from art.

On the contrary, The Philosopher distinguishes prudence from art (*Ethic.* vi. 5).

I answer that, Where the nature of virtue
differs, there is a different kind of virtue. Now
it has been stated above (A. 1; Q. 56, A. 3)
that some habits have the nature of virtue,
through merely conferring aptness for a good
work: while some habits are virtues, not only
through conferring aptness for a good work,
but also through conferring the use. But art
confers the mere aptness for good work; since
it does not regard the appetite; whereas prudence confers not only aptness for a good
work, but also the use: for it regards the appetite, since it presupposes the rectitude thereof.

The reason for this difference is that art is
the *right reason of things to be made;* whereas
prudence is the *right reason of things to be
done.* Now *making* and *doing* differ, as stated
in *Metaph.* ix., text. 16, in that *making* is an
action passing into outward matter, e.g., *to
build, to saw,* and so forth; whereas *doing* is
an action abiding in the agent, e.g., *to see, to
will,* and the like. Accordingly prudence stands
in the same relation to such like human actions,
consisting in the use of powers and habits, as
art does to outward makings: since each is the
perfect reason about the things with which it
is concerned. But perfection and rectitude of
reason in speculative matters, depend on the
principles from which reason argues; just as
we have said above (A. 2 *ad* 2) that science
depends on and presupposes understanding,
which is the habit of principles. Now in human acts the end is what the principles are in
speculative matters, as stated in *Ethic.* vii. 8.
Consequently, it is requisite for prudence,
which is right reason about things to be done,
that man be well disposed with regard to the
ends: and this depends on the rectitude of his
appetite. Wherefore, for prudence there is
need of a moral virtue, which rectifies the appetite. On the other hand the good of things
made by art is not the good of man's appetite,
but the good of those things themselves:
wherefore art does not presuppose rectitude
of the appetite. The consequence is that more
praise is given to a craftsman who is at fault
willingly, than to one who is unwillingly;
whereas it is more contrary to prudence to
sin willingly than unwillingly, since rectitude
of the will is essential to prudence, but not to
art.—Accordingly it is evident that prudence
is a virtue distinct from art.

Reply Obj. 1. The various kinds of things
made by art are all external to man: hence
they do not cause a different kind of virtue.
But prudence is right reason about human acts

themselves: hence it is a distinct kind of virtue, as stated above.

Reply Obj. 2. Prudence has more in common with art than a speculative habit has, if we consider their subject and matter: for they are both in the thinking part of the soul, and about things that may be otherwise than they are. But if we consider them as virtues, then art has more in common with the speculative habits, as is clear from what has been said.

Reply Obj. 3. Prudence is of good counsel about matters regarding man's entire life, and the end of human life. But in some arts there is counsel about matters concerning the ends proper to those arts. Hence some men, in so far as they are good counsellors in matters of warfare, or seamanship, are said to be prudent officers or pilots, but not simply prudent: only those are simply prudent who give good counsel about all the concerns of life.

FIFTH ARTICLE

Whether Prudence Is a Virtue Necessary to Man?

We proceed thus to the Fifth Article:—

Objection 1. It would seem that prudence is not a virtue necessary to lead a good life. For as art is to things that are made, of which it is the right reason, so is prudence to things that are done, in respect of which we judge of a man's life: for prudence is the right reason about these things, as stated in *Ethic.* vi. 5. Now art is not necessary in things that are made, save in order that they be made, but not after they have been made. Neither, therefore is prudence necessary to man in order to lead a good life, after he has become virtuous; but perhaps only in order that he may become virtuous.

Obj. 2. Further, *It is by prudence that we are of good counsel,* as stated in *Ethic.* vi. 5. But man can act not only from his own, but also from another's good counsel. Therefore man does not need prudence in order to lead a good life, but it is enough that he follow the counsels of prudent men.

Obj. 3. Further, an intellectual virtue is one by which one always tells the truth, and never a falsehood. But this does not seem to be the case with prudence: for it is not human never to err in taking counsel about what is to be done; since human actions are about things that may be otherwise than they are. Hence it is written (Wis. ix. 14): *The thoughts of mortal men are fearful, and our counsels uncertain.* Therefore it seems that prudence should not be reckoned an intellectual virtue.

On the contrary, It is reckoned with other virtues necessary for human life, when it is written (Wis. viii. 7) of Divine Wisdom: *She teacheth temperance and prudence and justice and fortitude, which are such things as men can have nothing more profitable in life.*

I answer that, Prudence is a virtue most necessary for human life. For a good life consists in good deeds. Now in order to do good deeds, it matters not only what a man does, but also how he does it; to wit, that he do it from right choice and not merely from impulse or passion. And, since choice is about things in reference to the end, rectitude of choice requires two things; namely, the due end, and something suitably ordained to that due end. Now man is suitably directed to his due end by a virtue which perfects the soul in the appetitive part, the object of which is the good and the end. And to that which is suitably ordained to the due end man needs to be rightly disposed by a habit in his reason, because counsel and choice, which are about things ordained to the end, are acts of the reason. Consequently an intellectual virtue is needed in the reason, to perfect the reason, and make it suitably affected towards things ordained to the end; and this virtue is prudence. Consequently prudence is a virtue necessary to lead a good life.

Reply Obj. 1. The good of an art is to be found, not in the craftsman, but in the product of the art, since art is right reason about things to be made: for since the making of a thing passes into external matter, it is a perfection not of the maker, but of the thing made, even as movement is the act of the thing moved: and art is concerned with the making of things. On the other hand, the good of prudence is in the active principle, whose activity is its perfection: for prudence is right reason about things to be done, as stated above (A. 4). Consequently art does not require of the craftsman that his act be a good act, but that his work be good. Rather would it be necessary for the thing made to act well (e.g., that a knife should carve well, or that a saw should cut well), if it were proper to such things to act, rather than to be acted on, because they have not dominion over their actions. Wherefore the craftsman needs art, not that he may live well, but that he may produce a good work of art, and have it in good keeping: whereas prudence is necessary to man, that he may lead a good life, and not merely that he may be a good man.

Reply Obj. 2. When a man does a good deed, not of his own counsel, but moved by that of another, his deed is not yet quite perfect, as regards his reason in directing him and his appetite in moving him. Wherefore, if he do a good deed, he does not do well simply; and yet this is required in order that he may lead a good life.

Reply Obj. 3. As stated in *Ethic.* vi. 2, truth is not the same for the practical as for the speculative intellect. Because the truth of the speculative intellect depends on conformity between the intellect and the thing. And since the intellect cannot be infallibly in conformity with things in contingent matters, but only in necessary matters, therefore no speculative habit about contingent things is an intellectual virtue, but only such as is is about necessary things.—On the other hand, the truth of the practical intellect depends on conformity with right appetite. This conformity has no place in necessary matters, which are not affected by the human will; but only in contingent matters which can be effected by us, whether they be matters of interior action, or the products of external work. Hence it is only about contingent matters that an intellectual virtue is assigned to the practical intellect, viz., art, as regards things to be made, and prudence, as regards things to be done.

SIXTH ARTICLE

Whether "Eubulia, Synesis and Gnome"* Are Virtues Annexed to Prudence?

We proceed thus to the Sixth Article:—

Objection 1. It would seem that εὐβουλία, σύνεσις. and γνώμη are unfittingly assigned as virtues annexed to prudence. For εὐβουλία is *a habit whereby we take good counsel* (*Ethic.* vi. 9). Now it *belongs to prudence to take good counsel,* as stated (*ibid.,* 5). Therefore εὐβουλία is not a virtue annexed to prudence, but rather is prudence itself.

Obj. 2. Further, it belongs to the higher to judge of the lower. The highest virtue would therefore seem to be the one whose act is judgment. Now σύνεσις enables us to judge well. Therefore σύνεσις is not a virtue annexed to prudence, but rather is a principal virtue.

Obj. 3. Further, just as there are various matters to pass judgment on, so are there different points on which one has to take counsel. But there is one virtue referring to all matters of counsel. Therefore, in order to judge well of what has to be done, there is no need, besides σύνεσις. of the virtue of γνώμη.

Obj. 4. Further, Cicero (*De Invent. Rhet.* iii) mentions three other parts of prudence; viz., *memory of the past, understanding of the present, and foresight of the future.* Moreover, Macrobius (*Super Somn. Scip.* 1) mentions yet others: viz., *caution, docility,* and the like. Therefore it seems that the above are not the only virtues annexed to prudence.

On the contrary stands the authority of the Philosopher (*Ethic.* vi 9, 10, 11), who as-

* εὐβουλία, σύνεσις, γνώμη.

signs these three virtues as being annexed to prudence.

I answer that, Wherever several powers are subordinate to one another, that power is the highest which is ordained to the highest act. Now there are three acts of reason in respect of anything done by man: the first of these is counsel; the second, judgment; the third, command. The first two correspond to those acts of the speculative intellect, which are inquiry and judgment, for counsel is a kind of inquiry: but the third is proper to the practical intellect, in so far as this is ordained to operation; for reason does not have to command in things that man cannot do. Now it is evident that in things done by man, the chief act is that of command, to which all the rest are subordinate. Consequently, that virtue which perfects the command, viz., prudence, as obtaining the highest place, has other secondary virtues annexed to it, viz., εὐστοχία, which perfects counsel; and σύνεσις and γνώμη, which are parts of prudence in relation to judgment, and of whose distinction we shall speak further on (*ad* 3).

Reply Obj. 1. Prudence makes us be of good counsel, not as though its immediate act consisted in being of good counsel, but because it perfects the latter act by means of a subordinate virtue, viz., εὐβουλία.

Reply Obj. 2. Judgment about what is to be done is directed to something further: for it may happen in some matter of action that a man's judgment is sound, while his execution is wrong. The matter does not attain to its final complement until the reason has commanded aright in the point of what has to be done.

Reply Obj. 3. Judgment of anything should be based on that thing's proper principles. But inquiry does not reach to the proper principles: because, if we were in possession of these, we should need no more to inquire, the truth would be already discovered. Hence only one virtue is directed to being of good counsel, whereas there are two virtues for good judgment: because difference is based not on common but on proper principles. Consequently, even in speculative matters, there is one science of dialectics, which inquires about all matters; whereas demonstrative sciences, which pronounce judgment, differ according to their different objects.—Σύνεσις and γνώμη differ in respect of the different rules on which judgment is based: for σύνεσις judges of actions according to the common law; while γνώμη bases its judgment on the natural law, in those cases where the common law fails to apply, as we shall explain further on (II-II, Q. 51, A. 4).

Reply Obj. 4. Memory, understanding, and

foresight, as also caution and docility and the like, are not virtues distinct from prudence: but are, as it were, integral parts thereof, in so far as they are all requisite for perfect prudence.—There are, moreover, subjective parts or species of prudence, e.g., domestic and political economy, and the like. But the three first named are, in a fashion, potential parts of prudence; because they are subordinate thereto, as secondary virtues to a principal virtue: and we shall speak of them later (II-II, Q. 48, *seqq.*).

QUESTION 58

Of the Difference between Moral and Intellectual Virtues

(In Five Articles)

WE must now consider moral virtues. We shall speak (1) of the difference between them and intellectual virtues; (2) of their distinction, one from another, in respect of their proper matter; (3) of the difference between the chief or cardinal virtues and the others.

Under the first head there are five points of inquiry: (1) Whether every virtue is a moral virtue? (2) Whether moral virtue differs from intellectual virtue? (3) Whether virtue is adequately divided into moral and intellectual virtue? (4) Whether there can be moral without intellectual virtue? (5) Whether, on the other hand, there can be intellectual without moral virtue?

FIRST ARTICLE

Whether Every Virtue Is a Moral Virtue?

We proceed thus to the First Article:—

Objection 1. It would seem that every virtue is a moral virtue. Because moral virtue is so called from the Latin *mos*, i.e., custom. Now, we can accustom ourselves to the acts of all the virtues. Therefore every virtue is a moral virtue.

Obj. 2. Further, the Philosopher says (*Ethic.* ii. 6) that moral virtue is *a habit of choosing the rational mean.* But every virtue is a habit of choosing: since the acts of any virtue can be done from choice. And, moreover, every virtue consists in following the rational mean in some way, as we shall explain further on (Q. 64, AA. 1, 2, 3). Therefore every virtue is a moral virtue.

Obj. 3. Further, Cicero says (*De Invent. Rhet.* ii) that *virtue is a habit like a second nature, in accord with reason.* But since every human virtue is directed to man's good, it must be in accord with reason: since man's good *consists in that which agrees with his reason,* as Dionysius states (*Div. Nom.* iv). Therefore every virtue is a moral virtue.

On the contrary, The Philosopher (*Ethic.* i. 13): *When we speak of a man's morals, we do not say that he is wise or intelligent, but that he is gentle or sober.* Accordingly, then,

wisdom and understanding are not moral virtues: and yet they are virtues, as stated above (Q. 57, A. 2). Therefore not every virtue is a moral virtue.

I answer that, In order to answer this question clearly, we must consider the meaning of the Latin word *mos;* for thus we shall be able to discover what a *moral* virtue is. Now *mos* has a twofold meaning. For sometimes it means custom, in which sense we read (Acts xv. 1): *Except you be circumcised after the manner (morem) of Moses, you cannot be saved.* Sometimes it means a natural or quasi-natural inclination to do some particular action, in which sense the word is applied to dumb animals. Thus we read (2 Macc. i. 2) that *rushing violently upon the enemy, like lions,* they slew them:* and the word is used in the same sense in Ps. lxvii. 7), where we read: *Who maketh men of one manner (moris) to dwell in a house.* For both these significations there is but one word in Latin; but in Greek there is a distinct word for each, for the word *ethos* is written sometimes with a long, and sometimes with a short *e.*

Now *moral* virtue is so called from *mos* in the sense of a natural or quasi-natural inclination to do some particular action. And the other meaning of *mos*, i.e., *custom,* is akin to this: because custom becomes a second nature, and produces an inclination similar to a natural one. But it is evident that inclination to an action belongs properly to the appetitive power, whose function it is to move all the powers to their acts, as explained above (Q. 9, A. 1). Therefore not every virtue is a moral virtue, but only those that are in the appetitive faculty.

Reply Obj. 1. This argument takes *mos* in the sense of *custom.*

Reply Obj. 2. Every act of virtue can be done from choice: but no virtue makes us choose aright, save that which is in the appetitive part of the soul: for it has been stated above that choice is an act of the appetitive faculty (Q. 13, A. 1). Wherefore a habit of choosing, i.e., a habit which is the principle

---

* *Leonum more,* i.e., as lions are in the habit of doing.

whereby we choose, is that habit alone which perfects the appetitive faculty: although the acts of other habits also may be a matter of choice.

Reply Obj. 3. Nature is the principle of movement (*Phys.* ii., text. 3). Now to move the faculties to act is the proper function of the appetitive power. Consequently to become as a second nature by consenting to the reason, is proper to those virtues which are in the appetitive faculty.

SECOND ARTICLE

Whether Moral Virtue Differs from Intellectual Virtue?

We proceed thus to the Second Article:—

Objection 1. It would seem that moral virtue does not differ from intellectual virtue. For Augustine says (*De Civ. Dei* iv. 21) *that virtue is the art of right conduct.* But art is an intellectual virtue. Therefore moral and intellectual virtue do not differ.

Obj. 2. Further, some authors put science in the definition of virtues: thus some define perseverance as a *science or habit regarding those things to which we should hold or not hold;* and holiness as a *science which makes man to be faithful and to do his duty to God.* Now science is an intellectual virtue. Therefore moral virtue should not be distinguished from intellectual virtue.

Obj. 3. Further, Augustine says (*Soliloq.* i. 6) that *virtue is the rectitude and perfection of reason.* But this belongs to the intellectual virtues, as stated in *Ethic.* vi. 13. Therefore moral virtue does not differ from intellectual.

Obj. 4. Further, a thing does not differ from that which is included in its definition. But intellectual virtue is included in the definition of moral virtue: for the Philosopher says (*Ethic.* ii. 6) that *moral virtue is a habit of choosing the mean appointed by reason as a prudent man would appoint it.* Now this right reason that fixes the mean of moral virtue, belongs to an intellectual virtue, as stated in *Ethic.* vi. 13. Therefore moral virtue does not differ from intellectual.

On the contrary, It is stated in *Ethic.* 1, 13 that *there are two kinds of virtue: some we call intellectual; some, moral.*

I answer that, Reason is the first principle of all human acts; and whatever other principles of human acts may be found, they obey reason somewhat, but in various ways. For some obey reason blindly and without any contradiction whatever: such are the limbs of the body, provided they be in a healthy condition, for as soon as reason commands, the hand or the foot proceeds to action. Hence the Philosopher says (*Polit.* i. 3) that *the soul rules the body like a despot,* i.e., as a master rules his slave, who has no right to rebel. Accordingly some held that all the active principles in man are subordinate to reason in this way. If this were true, for man to act well it would suffice that his reason be perfect. Consequently, since virtue is a habit perfecting man in view of his doing good actions, it would follow that it is only in the reason, so that there would be none but intellectual virtues. This was the opinion of Socrates, who said *every virtue is a kind of prudence,* as stated in *Ethic.* vi. 13. Hence he maintained that as long as a man is in possession of knowledge, he cannot sin; and that every one who sins, does so through ignorance.

Now this is based on a false supposition. Because the appetitive faculty obeys the reason, not blindly, but with a certain power of opposition; wherefore the Philosopher says (*Polit.* i. 3) that *reason commands the appetitive faculty by a politic power,* whereby a man rules over subjects that are free, having a certain right of opposition. Hence Augustine says on Ps. cxviii. (*serm.* 8) that *sometimes we understand* (what is right) *while desire is slow, or follows not at all,* in so far as the habits or passions of the appetitive faculty cause the use of reason to be impeded in some particular action. And in this way, there is some truth in the saying of Socrates that so long as a man is in possession of knowledge he does not sin: provided, however, that this knowledge is made to include the use of reason in this individual act of choice.

Accordingly for a man to do a good deed, it is requisite not only that his reason be well disposed by means of a habit of intellectual virtue; but also that his appetite be well disposed by means of a habit of moral virtue. And so moral differs from intellectual virtue, even as the appetite differs from the reason. Hence just as the appetite is the principle of human acts, in so far as it partakes of reason, so are moral habits to be considered virtues in so far as they are in conformity with reason.

Reply Obj. 1. Augustine usually applies the term *art* to any form of right reason; in which sense art includes prudence which is the right reason about things to be done, even as art is the right reason about things to be made. Accordingly, when he says that *virtue is the art of right conduct,* this applies to prudence essentially; but to other virtues, by participation, for as much as they are directed by prudence.

Reply Obj. 2. All such definitions, by whomsoever given, were based on the Socratic theory, and should be explained according to what we have said about art (*ad* 1).

The same applies to the Third Objection.

Reply Obj. 4. Right reason which is in accord with prudence is included in the definition of moral virtue, not as part of its essence, but as something belonging by way of participation to all the moral virtues, in so far as they are all under the direction of prudence.

THIRD ARTICLE

Whether Virtue Is Adequately Divided into Moral and Intellectual?

We proceed thus to the Third Article:—

Objection 1. It would seem that virtue is not adequately divided into moral and intellectual. For prudence seems to be a mean between moral and intellectual virtue, since it is reckoned among the intellectual virtues (*Ethic.* vi. 3, 5); and again is placed by all among the four cardinal virtues, which are moral virtues, as we shall show further on (Q. 61, A. 1). Therefore virtue is not adequately divided into intellectual and moral, as though there were no mean between them.

Obj. 2. Further, continency, perseverance, and patience are not reckoned to be intellectual virtues. Yet neither are they moral virtues; since they do not reduce the passions to a mean, and are consistent with an abundance of passion. Therefore virtue is not adequately divided into intellectual and moral.

Obj. 3. Further, faith, hope, and charity are virtues. Yet they are not intellectual virtues: for there are only five of these, viz., science, wisdom, understanding, prudence, and art, as stated above (Q. 57, AA. 2, 3, 5). Neither are they moral virtues: since they are not about the passions, which are the chief concern of moral virtue. Therefore virtue is not adequately divided into intellectual and moral.

On the contrary, The Philosopher says (*Ethic.* ii. 1) that *virtue is twofold, intellectual and moral.*

I answer that, Human virtue is a habit perfecting man in view of his doing good deeds. Now, in man there are but two principles of human actions, viz., the intellect or reason and the appetite: for these are the two principles of movement in man as stated in *De Anima,* iii, text, 48. Consequently every human virtue must needs be a perfection of one of these principles. Accordingly if it perfects man's speculative or practical intellect in order that his deed may be good, it will be an intellectual virtue: whereas if it perfects his appetite, it will be a moral virtue. It follows therefore that every human virtue is either intellectual or moral.

Reply Obj. 1. Prudence is essentially an intellectual virtue. But considered on the part of its matter, it has something in common with the moral virtues: for it is right reason about things to be done, as stated above (Q. 57,

A. 4). It is in this sense that it is reckoned with the moral virtues.

Reply Obj. 2. Continency and perseverance are not perfections of the sensitive appetite. This is clear from the fact that passions abound in the continent and persevering man, which would not be the case if his sensitive appetite were perfected by a habit making it conformable to reason. Continency and perseverance are, however, perfections of the rational faculty, and withstand the passions lest reason be led astray. But they fall short of being virtues: since intellectual virtue, which makes reason to hold itself well in respect of moral matters, presupposes a right appetite of the end, so that it may hold itself aright in respect of principles, i.e., the ends, on which it builds its argument: and this is wanting in the continent and persevering man. —Nor again can an action proceeding from two principles be perfect, unless each principle be perfected by the habit corresponding to that operation: thus, however perfect be the principal agent employing an instrument, it will produce an imperfect effect, if the instrument be not well disposed also. Hence if the sensitive appetite, which is moved by the rational faculty, is not perfect; however perfect the rational faculty may be, the resulting action will be imperfect: and consequently the principle of that action will not be a virtue.— And for this reason, continency, desisting from pleasures, and perseverance in the midst of pains, are not virtues, but something less than a virtue, as the Philosopher maintains (*Ethic.* vii. 1, 9).

Reply Obj. 3. Faith, hope, and charity are superhuman virtues: for they are virtues of man as sharing in the grace of God.

FOURTH ARTICLE

Whether There Can be Moral without Intellectual Virtue?

We proceed thus to the Fourth Article:—

Objection 1. It would seem that moral can be without intellectual virtue. Because moral virtue, as Cicero says (*De Invent. Rhet.* ii), is *a habit like a second nature in accord with reason.* Now though second nature may be in accord with some sovereign reason that moves it, there is no need for that reason to be united to nature in the same subject, as is evident of natural things devoid of knowledge. Therefore in a man there may be a moral virtue like a second nature, inclining him to consent to his reason, without his reason being perfected by an intellectual virtue.

Obj. 2. Further, by means of intellectual virtue man obtains perfect use of reason. But it happens at times that men are virtuous and acceptable to God, without being vigorous in the use of reason. Therefore it seems that moral virtue can be without intellectual.

Obj. 3. Further, moral virtue makes us inclined to do good works. But some, without depending on the judgment of reason, have a natural inclination to do good works. Therefore moral virtues can be without intellectual virtues.

On the contrary, Gregory says (*Moral.* xxii) that *the other virtues, unless we do prudently what we desire to do, cannot be real virtues.* But prudence is an intellectual virtue, as stated above (Q. 57, A. 5). Therefore moral virtues cannot be without intellectual virtues.

I answer that, Moral virtue can be without some of the intellectual virtues, viz., wisdom, science, and art; but not without understanding and prudence. Moral virtue cannot be without prudence, because it is a habit of choosing, i.e., making us choose well. Now in order that a choice be good, two things are required. First, that the intention be directed to a due end; and this is done by moral virtue, which inclines the appetitive faculty to the good that is in accord with reason, which is a due end. Secondly, that man take rightly those things which have reference to the end: and this he cannot do unless his reason counsel, judge and command aright, which is the function of prudence and the virtues annexed to it, as stated above (Q. 57, AA. 5, 6). Wherefore there can be no moral virtue without prudence: and consequently neither can there be without understanding. For it is by the virtue of understanding that we know self-evident principles both in speculative and in practical matters. Consequently just as right reason in speculative matters, in so far as it proceeds from naturally known principles, presupposes the understanding of those principles, so also does prudence, which is the right reason about things to be done.

Reply Obj. 1. The inclination of nature in things devoid of reason is without choice: wherefore such an inclination does not of necessity require reason. But the inclination of moral virtue is with choice: and consequently in order that it may be perfect it requires that reason be perfected by intellectual virtue.

Reply Obj. 2. A man may be virtuous without having full use of reason as to everything, provided he have it with regard to those things which have to be done virtuously. In this way all virtuous men have full use of reason. Hence those who seem to be simple, through lack of worldly cunning, may possibly be prudent, according to Matth. x. 16: *Be ye therefore prudent* (Douay,—*wise*) *as serpents, and simple as doves.*

* *Cf.* Plato, *Meno,* xli.

Reply Obj. 3. The natural inclination to a good of virtue is a kind of beginning of virtue, but is not perfect virtue. For the stronger this inclination is, the more perilous may it prove to be, unless it be accompanied by right reason, which rectifies the choice of fitting means towards the due end. Thus if a running horse be blind, the faster it runs the more heavily will it fall, and the more grievously will it be hurt. And consequently, although moral virtue be not right reason, as Socrates held, yet not only is it *according to right reason,* in so far as it inclines man to that which is, according to right reason, as the Platonists maintained;* but also it needs to be *joined with right reason,* as Aristotle declares (*Ethic.* vi. 13).

FIFTH ARTICLE

Whether There Can Be Intellectual without Moral Virtue?

We proceed thus to the Fifth Article:—

Objection 1. It would seem that there can be intellectual without moral virtue. Because perfection of what precedes does not depend on the perfection of what follows. Now reason precedes and moves the sensitive appetite. Therefore intellectual virtue, which is a perfection of the reason, does not depend on moral virtue, which is a perfection of the appetitive faculty; and can be without it.

Obj. 2. Further, morals are the matter of prudence, even as things makeable are the matter of art. Now art can be without its proper matter, as a smith without iron. Therefore prudence can be without the moral virtues, although of all the intellectual virtues, it seems most akin to the moral virtues.

Obj. 3. Further, prudence is *a virtue whereby we are of good counsel* (*Ethic.* vi. 9). Now many are of good counsel without having the moral virtues. Therefore prudence can be without a moral virtue.

On the contrary, To wish to do evil is directly opposed to moral virtue; and yet it is not opposed to anything that can be without moral virtue. Now it is contrary to prudence *to sin willingly* (*Ethic.* vi. 5). Therefore prudence cannot be without moral virtue.

I answer that, Other intellectual virtues can, but prudence cannot, be without moral virtue. The reason for this is that prudence is the right reason about things to be done (and this, not merely in general, but also in particular); about which things actions are. Now right reason demands principles from which reason proceeds to argue. And when reason argues about particular cases, it needs not only universal but also particular principles. As to universal principles of action, man is rightly disposed by the natural understanding of principles, whereby he understands that he should do no evil; or again by some practical science. But this is not enough in order that man may reason aright about particular cases. For it happens sometimes that the aforesaid universal principle, known by means of understanding or science, is destroyed in a particular case by a passion: thus to one who is swayed by concupiscence, when he is overcome thereby, the object of his desire seems good, although it is opposed to the universal judgment of his reason. Consequently, as by the habit of natural understanding or of science, man is made to be rightly disposed in regard to the universal principles of action; so, in order that he be rightly disposed with regard to the particular principles of action, viz., the ends, he needs to be perfected by certain habits, whereby it becomes connatural, as it were, to man to judge aright to the end. This is done by moral virtue: for the virtuous man judges aright of the end of virtue, because *such as a man is, such does the end seem to him* (*Ethic.* iii. 5).

Consequently the right reason about things to be done, viz., prudence, requires man to have moral virtue.

Reply Obj. 1. Reason, as apprehending the end, precedes the appetite for the end: but appetite for the end precedes the reason, as arguing about the choice of the means, which is the concern of prudence. Even so, in speculative matters the understanding of principles is the foundation on which the syllogism of the reason is based.

Reply Obj. 2. It does not depend on the disposition of our appetite whether we judge well or ill of the principles of art, as it does, when we judge of the end which is the principle in moral matters: in the former case our judgment depends on reason alone. Hence art does not require a virtue perfecting the appetite, as prudence does.

Reply Obj. 3. Prudence not only helps us to be of good counsel, but also to judge and command well. This is not possible unless impediment of the passions, destroying the judgment and command of prudence, be removed; and this is done by moral virtue.

QUESTION 59

Of Moral Virtue in Relation to the Passions

(In Five Articles)

WE must now consider the difference of one moral virtue from another. And since those moral virtues which are about the passions, differ accordingly to the difference of passions, we must consider (1) the relation of virtue to passion; (2) the different kinds of moral virtue in relation to the passions. Under the first head there are five points of inquiry: (1) Whether moral virtue is a passion? (2) Whether there can be moral virtue with passion? (3) Whether sorrow is compatible with moral virtue? (4) Whether every moral virtue is about a passion? (5) Whether there can be moral virtue without passion?

FIRST ARTICLE

Whether Moral Virtue Is a Passion?

We proceed thus to the First Article:—

Objection 1. It would seem that moral virtue is a passion. Because the mean is of the same genus as the extremes. But moral virtue is a mean between two passions. Therefore moral virtue is a passion.

Obj. 2. Further, virtue and vice, being contrary to one another, are in the same genus. But some passions are reckoned to be vices, such as envy and anger. Therefore some passions are virtues.

Obj. 3. Further, pity is a passion, since it is sorrow for another's ills, as stated above (Q. 35, A. 8). Now *Cicero the renowned orator did not hesitate to call pity a virtue,* as Augustine states in *De Civ. Dei* ix. 5. Therefore a passion may be a moral virtue.

On the contrary, It is stated in *Ethic.* ii. 5 that *passions are neither virtues nor vices.*

I answer that, Moral virtue cannot be a passion. This is clear for three reasons. First, because a passion is a movement of the sensitive appetite, as stated above (Q. 22, A. 3): whereas moral virtue is not a movement, but rather a principle of the movement of the appetite, being a kind of habit.—Secondly, because passions are not in themselves good or evil. For man's good or evil is something in reference to reason: wherefore the passions, considered in themselves, are referable both to good and to evil, for as much as they may accord or disaccord with reason. Now nothing of this sort can be a virtue: since virtue is referable to good alone, as stated above (Q. 55, A. 3).— Thirdly, because, granted that some passions are, in some way, referable to good only, or to evil only; even then the movement of passion, as passion, begins in the appetite, and ends in the reason, since the appetite tends to conformity with reason. On the other hand, the movement of virtue is the reverse, for it begins in the reason and ends in the appetite, inasmuch as the latter is moved by reason. Hence the definition of moral virtue (*Ethic.* ii. 6) states that it is *a habit of choosing the mean appointed by reason as a prudent man would appoint it.*

Reply Obj. 1. Virtue is a mean between passions, not by reason of its essence, but on account of its effect; because, to wit, it establishes the mean between passions.

Reply Obj. 2. If by vice we understand a habit of doing evil deeds, it is evident that no passion is a vice. But if vice is taken to mean sin which is a vicious act, nothing hinders a passion from being a vice, or, on the other hand, from concurring in an act of virtue; in so far as a passion is either opposed to reason or in accordance with reason.

Reply Obj. 3. Pity is said to be a virtue, i.e., an act of virtue, in so far as *that movement of the soul is obedient to reason; viz., when pity is bestowed without violating right, as when the poor are relieved, or the penitent forgiven,* as Augustine says (*ibid.*). But if by pity we understand a habit perfecting man so that he bestows pity reasonably, nothing hinders pity, in this sense, from being a virtue. The same applies to similar passions.

SECOND ARTICLE

Whether There Can Be Moral Virtue with Passion?

We proceed thus to the Second Article:—

Objection 1. It would seem that moral virtue cannot be with passion. For the Philosopher says (*Topic.* iv) that *a gentle man is one who is not passionate; but a patient man is one who is passionate but does not give way.* The same applies to all the moral virtues. Therefore all moral virtues are without passion.

Obj. 2. Further, virtue is a right affection of the soul, as health is of the body, as stated *Phys.* vii, text, 17: wherefore *virtue is a kind of health of the soul,* as Cicero says (*Quæst. Tuscul.* iv). But the soul's passions are *the soul's diseases,* as he says in the same book. Now health is incompatible with disease. Therefore neither is passion compatible with virtue.

Obj. 3. Further, moral virtue requires perfect use of reason even in particular matters. But the passions are an obstacle to this: for the Philosopher says (*Ethic.* vi. 5) that *pleasures destroy the judgment of prudence:* and Sallust says (*Catilin.*) that *when they,* i.e., the soul's passions, *interfere, it is not easy for the mind to grasp the truth.* Therefore passion is incompatible with moral virtue.

* *Noct. Attic.* xix. 1.

On the contrary, Augustine says (*De Civ. Dei* xiv. 6): *If the will is perverse, these movements,* viz., the passions, *are perverse also: but if it is upright, they are not only blameless, but even praiseworthy.* But nothing praiseworthy is incompatible with moral virtue. Therefore moral virtue does not exclude the passions, but is consistent with them.

I answer that, The Stoics and Peripatetics disagreed on this point, as Augustine relates (*De Civ. Dei* ix. 4). For the Stoics held that the soul's passions cannot be in a wise or virtuous man: whereas the Peripatetics, who were founded by Aristotle, as Augustine says (*ibid.*), maintained that the passions are compatible with moral virtue, if they be reduced to the mean.

This difference, as Augustine observes (*ibid.*), was one of words rather than of opinions. Because the Stoics, through not discriminating between the intellective appetite, i.e., the will, and the sensitive appetite, which is divided into irascible and concupiscible, did not, as the Peripatetics did, distinguish the passions from the other affections of the human soul, in the point of their being movements of the sensitive appetite, whereas the other emotions of the soul, which are not passions, are movements of the intellective appetite or will; but only in the point of the passions being, as they maintained, any emotions in disaccord with reason. These emotions could not be in a wise or virtuous man if they arose deliberately: while it would be possible for them to be in a wise man, if they arose suddenly: because, in the words of Aulus Gellius,* quoted by Augustine (*De Civ. Dei* ix., *loc. cit.*), *it is not in our power to call up the visions of the soul, known as its fancies; and when they arise from awesome things, they must needs disturb the mind of a wise man, so that he is slightly startled by fear, or depressed with sorrow,* in so far as *these passions forestall the use of reason without his approving of such things or consenting thereto.*

Accordingly, if the passions be taken for inordinate emotions, they cannot be in a virtuous man, so that he consent to them deliberately; as the Stoics maintained. But if the passions be taken for any movements of the sensitive appetite, they can be in a virtuous man, in so far as they are subordinate to reason. Hence Aristotle says (*Ethic.* ii. 3) that *some describe virtue as being a kind of freedom from passion and disturbance; this is incorrect, because the assertion should be qualified:* they should have said virtue is freedom from those passions *that are not as they should be as to manner and time.*

Reply Obj. 1. The Philosopher quotes this, as well as many other examples in his books on Logic, in order to illustrate, not his own mind, but that of others. It was the opinion of the Stoics that the passions of the soul were incompatible with virtue: and the Philosopher rejects this opinion (*Ethic.* ii, *loc. cit.*), when he says that virtue is not freedom from passion.—It may be said, however, that when he says that *a gentle man is not passionate,* we are to understand this of inordinate passion.

Reply Obj. 2. This and all similar arguments which Tully brings forward in *De Tuscul. Quæst.* iv take the passions in the tion of reason's command.

Reply Obj. 3. When a passion forestalls the judgment of reason, so as to prevail on the mind to give its consent, it hinders counsel and the judgment of reason. But when it follows that judgment, as through being commanded by reason, it helps towards the execution of reason's command.

THIRD ARTICLE

Whether Sorrow Is Compatible with Moral Virtue?

We proceed thus to the Third Article:—

Objection 1. It would seem that sorrow is incompatible with virtue. Because the virtues are effects of wisdom, according to Wis. viii. 7: *She.* i.e., Divine wisdom, *teacheth temperance, and prudence, and justice, and fortitude.* Now the *conversation* of wisdom *hath no bitterness,* as we read further on (*verse* 16). Therefore sorrow is incompatible with virtue also.

Obj. 2. Further, sorrow is a hindrance to work, as the Philosopher states (*Ethic.* vii. 13; x. 5). But a hindrance to good works is incompatible with virtue. Therefore sorrow is incompatible with virtue.

Obj. 3. Further, Tully calls sorrow a disease of the mind (*Tusc. Quæst.* iv). But disease of the mind is incompatible with virtue, which is a good condition of the mind. Therefore sorrow is opposed to virute and is incompatible with it.

On the contrary, Christ was perfect in virtue. But there was sorrow in Him, for He said (Matth. xxvi. 38): *My soul is sorrowful even unto death.* Therefore sorrow is compatible with virtue.

I answer that, As Augustine says (*De Civ. Dei* xiv. 8), the Stoics held that in the mind of the wise man there are three εὐπάθειαι, i.e., *three good passions,* in place of the three disturbances: viz., instead of covetousness, *desire;* instead of mirth, *joy;* instead of fear, *caution.* But they denied that anything corresponding to sorrow could be in the mind of a wise man, for two reasons.

First, because sorrow is for an evil that is already present. Now they held that no evil can happen to a wise man: for they thought that, just as man's only good is virtue, and

bodily goods are no good to man; so man's only evil is vice, which cannot be in a virtuous man. But this is unreasonable. For, since man is composed of soul and body, whatever conduces to preserve the life of the body, is some good to man; yet not his supreme good, because he can abuse it. Consequently the evil which is contrary to this good can be in a wise man, and can cause him moderate sorrow.—Again, although a virtuous man can be without grave sin, yet no man is to be found to live without committing slight sins, according to I Jo. i. 8: *If we say that we have no sin, we deceive ourselves.*—A third reason is because a virtuous man, though not actually in a state of sin, may have been so in the past. And he is to be commended if he sorrow for that sin, according to 2 Cor. vii. 10: *The sorrow that is according to God worketh penance steadfast unto salvation.*—Fourthly, because he may praiseworthily sorrow for another's sin. Therefore sorrow is compatible with moral virtue in the same way as the other passions are when moderated by reason.

Their second reason for holding this opinion was that sorrow is about evil present, whereas fear is for evil to come: even as pleasure is about a present good, while desire is for a future good. Now the enjoyment of a good possessed, or the desire to have good that one possesses not, may be consistent with virtue: but depression of the mind resulting from sorrow for a present evil, is altogether contrary to reason: wherefore it is incompatible with virtue. But this is unreasonable. For there is an evil which can be present to the virtuous man, as we have just stated; which evil is rejected by reason. Wherefore the sensitive appetite follows reason's rejection by sorrowing for that evil; yet moderately, according as reason dictates. Now it pertains to virtue that the sensitive appetite be conformed to reason, as stated above (A. 1, *ad* 2). Wherefore moderated sorrow for an object which ought to make us sorrowful, is a mark of virtue; as also the Philosopher says (*Ethic.* ii. 6, 7).—Moreover, this proves useful for avoiding evil: since, just as good is more readily sought for the sake of pleasure, so is evil more undauntedly shunned on account of sorrow.

Accordingly we must allow that sorrow for things pertaining to virtue is incompatible with virtue: since virtue rejoices in its own. On the other hand, virtue sorrows moderately for all that thwarts virtue, no matter how.

Reply Obj. 1. The passage quoted proves that the wise man is not made sorrowful by wisdom. Yet he sorrows for anything that hinders wisdom. Consequently there is no room for sorrow in the blessed, in whom there can be no hindrance to wisdom.

Reply Obj. 2. Sorrow hinders the work that makes us sorrowful: but it helps us to do more readily whatever banishes sorrow.

Reply Obj. 3. Immoderate sorrow is a disease of the mind: but moderate sorrow is the mark of a well-conditioned mind, according to the present state of life.

FOURTH ARTICLE

Whether All the Moral Virtues Are about the Passions?

We proceed thus to the Fourth Article:—

Objection 1. It would seem that all the moral virtues are about the passions. For the Philosopher says (*Ethic.* ii. 3) that *moral virtue is about objects of pleasure and sorrow.* But pleasure and sorrow are passions, as stated above (Q. 23, A. 4; Q. 31, A. 1; Q. 35, AA. 1, 2). Therefore all the moral virtues are about the passions.

Obj. 2. Further, the subject of the moral virtues is a faculty which is rational by participation, as the Philosopher states (*Ethic.* i. 13). But the passions are in this part of the soul, as stated above (Q. 22, A. 3). Therefore every moral virtue is about the passions.

Obj. 3. Further, some passion is to be found in every moral virtue: and so either all are about the passions, or none are. But some are about the passions, as fortitude and temperance, as stated in *Ethic.* iii. 6, 10. Therefore all the moral virtues are about the passions.

On the contrary, Justice, which is a moral virtue, is not about the passions; as stated in *Ethic.* v. 1, *seqq.*

I answer that, Moral virtue perfects the appetitive part of the soul by directing it to good as defined by reason. Now good as defined by reason is that which is moderated or directed by reason. Consequently there are moral virtues about all matters that are subject to reason's direction and moderation. Now reason directs, not only the passions of the sensitive appetite, but also the operations of the intellective appetite, i.e. the will, which is not the subject of a passion, as stated above (Q. 22, A. 3). Therefore not all the moral virtues are about passions, but some are about passions, some about operations.

Reply Obj. 1. The moral virtues are not all about pleasures and sorrows, as being their proper matter; but as being something resulting from their proper acts. For every virtuous man rejoices in acts of virtue, and sorrows for the contrary. Hence the Philosopher, after the words quoted, adds, *if virtues are about actions and passions; now every action and passion is followed by pleasure or sorrow, so that in this way virtue is about pleasures and sorrows,* viz., as about something that results from virtue.

Reply Obj. 2. Not only the sensitive appetite which is the subject of the passions, is rational by participation, but also the will, where there are no passions, as stated above.

Reply Obj. 3. Some virtues have passions as their proper matter, but some virtues not. Hence the comparison does not hold for all cases.

FIFTH ARTICLE

Whether There Can Be Moral Virtue without Passion?

We proceed thus to the Fifth Article:—

Objection 1. It would seem that moral virtue can be without passion. For the more perfect moral virtue is, the more does it overcome the passions. Therefore at its highest point of perfection it is altogether without passion.

Obj. 2. Further, then is a thing perfect, when it is removed from its contrary and from whatever inclines to its contrary. Now the passions incline us to sin which is contrary to virtue: hence (Rom. vii. 5) they are called *passions of sins.* Therefore perfect virtue is altogether without passion.

Obj. 3. Further, it is by virtue that we are conformed to God, as Augustine declares (*De Morib. Eccl.* vi. xi. xiii). But God does all things without passion at all. Therefore the most perfect virtue is without any passion.

On the contrary, No man is just who rejoices not in just deeds, as stated in *Ethic.* i. 8. But joy is a passion. Therefore justice cannot be without passion: and still less can the other virtues be.

I answer that, If we take the passions as being inordinate emotions, as the Stoics did, it is evident that in this sense perfect virtue is without the passions.—But if by passions we understand any movement of the sensitive appetite, it is plain that moral virtues, which are about the passions as about their proper matter, cannot be without passions. The reason for this is that otherwise it would follow that moral virtue makes the sensitive appetite altogether idle: whereas it is not the function of virtue to deprive the powers subordinate to reason of their proper activities, but to make them execute the commands of reason, by exercising their proper acts. Wherefore just as virtue directs the bodily limbs to their due external acts, so does it direct the sensitive appetite to its proper regulated movements.

Those moral virtues, however, which are not about the passions, but about operations, can be without passions. Such a virtue is justice: because it applies the will to its proper act, which is not a passion. Nevertheless, joy results from the act of justice; at least in the will, in which case it is not a passion. And if this joy be increased through the perfection of justice, it will overflow into the sensitive appetite; in so far as the lower powers follow the movement of the higher, as stated above (Q. 17, A. 7; Q. 24, A. 3). Wherefore by reason of this kind of overflow, the more perfect a virtue is, the more does it cause passion.

Reply Obj. 1. Virtue overcomes inordinate passion; it produces ordinate passion.

Reply Obj. 2. It is inordinate, not ordinate, passion that leads to sin.

Reply Obj. 3. The good of anything depends on the condition of its nature. Now there is no sensitive appetite in God and the angels, as there is in man. Consequently good operation in God and the angels is altogether without passion, as it is without a body: whereas the good operation of man is with passion, even as it is produced with the body's help.

QUESTION 60

How the Moral Virtues Differ from One Another

(In Five Articles)

WE must now consider how the moral virtues differ from one another : under which head there are five points of inquiry: (1) Whether there is only one moral virtue? (2) Whether those moral virtues which are about operations, are distinct from those which are about passions? (3) Whether there is but one moral virtue about operations? (4) Whether there are different moral virtues about different passions? (5) Whether the moral virtues differ in point of the various objects of the passions?

FIRST ARTICLE

Whether There Is Only One Moral Virtue?

We proceed thus to the First Article:—

Objection 1. It would seem that there is only one moral virtue. Because just as the direction of moral actions belongs to reason which is the subject of the intellectual virtues; so does their inclination belong to the appetite which is the subject of moral virtues. But there is only one intellectual virtue to direct all moral acts, viz., prudence. Therefore there is also but one moral virtue to give all moral acts their respective inclinations.

Obj. 2. Further, habits differ, not in respect of their material objects, but according to the formal aspect of their objects. Now the formal aspect of the good to which moral virtue is directed, is one thing, viz., the mean defined by reason. Therefore, seemingly, there is but one moral virtue.

Obj. 3. Further, things pertaining to morals are specified by their end, as stated above (Q. 1, A. 3). Now there is but one common end of all moral virtues, viz., happiness, while the proper and proximate ends are infinite in number. But the moral virtues themselves are not infinite in number. Therefore it seems that there is but one.

On the contrary, One habit cannot be in several powers, as stated above (Q. 56, A. 2).

But the subject of the moral virtues is the appetitive part of the soul, which is divided into several powers, as stated in the First Part (Q. 80, A. 2; Q. 81, A. 2). Therefore there cannot be only one moral virtue.

I answer that, As stated above (Q. 58, AA. 1, 2, 3), the moral virtues are habits of the appetitive faculty. Now habits differ specifically according to the specific differences of their objects, as stated above (Q. 54, A. 2). Again, the species of the object of appetite, as of any thing, depends on its specific form which it receives from the agent. But we must observe that the matter of the passive subject bears a twofold relation to the agent. For sometimes it receives the form of the agent, in the same kind specifically as the agent has that form, as happens with all univocal agents, so that if the agent be one specifically, the matter must of necessity receive a form specifically one: thus the univocal effect of fire is of necessity something in the species of fire.— Sometimes, however, the matter receives the form from the agent, but not in the same kind specifically as the agent, as is the case with non-univocal causes of generation: thus an animal is generated by the sun. In this case the forms received into matter are not of one species, but vary according to the adaptability of the matter to receive the influx of the agent: for instance, we see that owing to the one action of the sun, animals of various species are produced by putrefaction according to the various adaptability of matter.

Now it is evident that in moral matters the reason holds the place of commander and mover, while the appetitive power is commanded and moved. But the appetite does not receive the direction of reason univocally so to say; because it is rational, not essentially, but by participation (*Ethic.* i. 13). Consequently, objects made appetible by the direction of reason belong to various species, according to their various relations to reason:

so that it follows that moral virtues are of various species and are not one only.

Reply Obj. 1. The object of the reason is truth. Now in all moral matters, which are contingent matters of action, there is but one kind of truth. Consequently, there is but one virtue to direct all such matters, viz. prudence. —On the other hand, the object of the appetitive power is the appetible good, which varies in kind according to its various relations to reason, the directing power.

Reply Obj. 2. This formal element is one generically, on account of the unity of the agent: but it varies in species, on account of the various relations of the receiving matter, as explained above.

Reply Obj. 3. Moral matters do not receive their species from the last end, but from their proximate ends: and these, although they be infinite in number, are not infinite in species.

SECOND ARTICLE

Whether Moral Virtues about Operations Are Different from Those That Are About Passions?

We proceed thus to the Second Article:—

Objection 1. It would seem that moral virtues are not divided into those which are about operations and those which are about passions. For the Philosopher says (*Ethic.* ii. 3) that moral virtue is *an operative habit whereby we do what is best in matters of pleasure or sorrow.* Now pleasure and sorrow are passions, as stated above (Q. 31, A. 1; Q. 35, A. 1). Therefore the same virtue which is about passions is also about operations, since it is an operative habit.

Obj. 2. Further, the passions are principles of external action. If therefore some virtues regulate the passions, they must, as a consequence, regulate operations also. Therefore the same moral virtues are about both passions and operations.

Obj. 3. Further, the sensitive appetite is moved well or ill towards every external operation. Now movements of the sensitive appetite are passions. Therefore the same virtues that are about operations are also about passions.

On the contrary, The Philosopher reckons justice to be about operations; and temperance, fortitude, and gentleness, about passions (*Ethic.* ii. 3, 7; v. 1, *seqq.*).

I answer that, Operation and passion stand in a twofold relation to virtue. First, as its effects; and in this way every moral virtue has some good operations as its product; and a certain pleasure or sorrow, which are passions, as stated above (Q. 59, A. 4 *ad* 1).

Secondly, operation may be compared to moral virtue as the matter about which virtue is concerned: and in this sense those moral virtues which are about operations must needs differ from those which are about passions. The reason for this is that good and evil, in certain operations, are taken from the very nature of those operations, no matter how man may be affected towards them: viz. in so far as good and evil in them depend on their being commensurate with someone else. In operations of this kind there needs to be some power to regulate the operations in themselves: such are buying and selling, and all such operations in which there is an element of something due or undue to another. For this reason justice and its parts are properly about operations as their proper matter.—On the other hand, in some operations, good and evil depend only on commensuration with the agent. Consequently good and evil in these operations depend on the way in which man is affected to them. And for this reason in such like operations virtue must needs be chiefly about internal emotions which are called the passions of the soul, as is evidently the case with temperance, fortitude, and the like.

It happens, however, in operations which are directed to another, that the good of virtue is overlooked by reason of some inordinate passion of the soul. In such cases justice is destroyed in so far as the due measure of the external act is destroyed: while some other virtue is destroyed in so far as the internal passions exceed their due measure. Thus when through anger, one man strikes another, justice is destroyed in the undue blow; while gentleness is destroyed by the immoderate anger. The same may be clearly applied to other virtues.

This suffices for the Replies to the Objections. For the first considers operations as the effect of virtue, while the other two consider operation and passion as concurring in the same effect. But in some cases virtue is chiefly about operations, in others, about passions, for the reason given above.

THIRD ARTICLE

Whether There Is Only One Moral Virtue about Operations?

We proceed thus to the Third Article:—

Objection 1. It would seem that there is but one moral virtue about operations. Because the rectitude of all external operations seems to belong to justice. Now justice is but one virtue. Therefore there is but one virtue about operations.

Obj. 2. Further, those operations seem to differ most, which are directed on the one side to the good of the individual, and on the other to the good of the many. But this diversity does not cause diversity among the moral virtues: for the Philosopher says (*Ethic.* v. 1) that legal justice, which directs human acts to the common good, does not differ, save logically, from the virtue which directs a man's actions to one man only. Therefore diversity of operations does not cause a diversity of moral virtues.

Obj. 3. Further, if there are various moral virtues about various operations, diversity of moral virtues would needs follow diversity of operations. But this is clearly untrue: for it is the function of justice to establish rectitude in various kinds of commutations, and again in distributions, as is set down in *Ethic.* v. 2. Therefore there are not different virtues about different operations.

On the contrary, Religion is a moral virtue distinct from piety, both of which are about operations.

I answer that, All the moral virtues that are about operations agree in the one general notion of justice, which is in respect of something due to another: but they differ in respect of various special notions. The reason for this is that in external operations, the order of reason is established, as we have stated (A. 2), not according as how man is affected towards such operations, but according to the becomingness of the thing itself; from which becomingness we derive the notion of something due which is the formal aspect of justice: for, seemingly, it pertains to justice that a man give another his due. Wherefore all such virtues as are about operations, bear, in some way, the character of justice.—But the thing due is not of the same kind in all these virtues: for something is due to an equal in one way, to a superior, in another way, to an inferior, in yet another; and the nature of a debt differs according as it arises from a contract, a promise, or a favor already conferred. And corresponding to these various kinds of debt there are various virtues: e.g., *Religion* whereby we pay our debt to God; *Piety,* whereby we pay our debt to our parents or to our country; *Gratitude,* whereby we pay our debt to our benefactors, and so forth.

Reply Obj. 1. Justice properly so called is one special virtue, whose object is the perfect due, which can be paid in the equivalent. But the name of justice is extended also to all cases in which something due is rendered: in this sense it is not as a special virtue.

Reply Obj. 2. That justice which seeks the common good is another virtue from that which is directed to the private good of an individual: wherefore common right differs from private right; and Tully (*De Inv.* ii) reckons as a special virtue, piety which directs man to the good of his country.—But that justice

which directs man to the common good is a general virtue through its act of command: since it directs all the acts of the virtues to its own end, viz., the common good. And the virtues, in so far as they are commanded by that justice, receive the name of justice: so that virtue does not differ, save logically, from legal justice; just as there is only a logical difference between a virtue that is active of itself, and a virtue that is active through the command of another virtue.

Reply Obj. 3. There is the same kind of due in all the operations belonging to special justice. Consequently, there is the same virtue of justice, especially in regard to commutations. For it may be that distributive justice is of another species from commutative justice; but about this we shall inquire later on (II-II, Q. 61, A. 1).

FOURTH ARTICLE

Whether There Are Different Moral Virtues about Different Passions?

We proceed thus to the Fourth Article:—

Objection 1. It would seem that there are not different moral virtues about different passions. For there is but one habit about things that concur in their source and end: as is evident especially in the case of sciences. But the passions all concur in one source, viz., love; and they all terminate in the same end, viz., joy or sorrow, as we stated above (Q. 25, AA. 1, 2, 4; Q. 27, A. 4). Therefore there is but one moral virtue about all the passions.

Obj. 2. Further, if there were different moral virtues about different passions, it would follow that there are as many moral virtues as passions. But this clearly is not the case: since there is one moral virtue about contrary passions; namely, fortitude, about fear and daring; temperance, about pleasure and sorrow. Therefore there is no need for different moral virtues about different passions.

Obj. 3. Further, love, desire, and pleasure are passions of different species, as stated above (Q. 23, A. 4). Now there is but one virtue about all these three, viz., temperance. Therefore there are not different moral virtues about different passions.

On the contrary, Fortitude is about fear and daring; temperance about desire; meekness about anger; as stated in *Ethic.* iii. 6, 10; iv. 5.

I answer that, It cannot be said that there is only one moral virtue about all the passions: since some passions are not in the same power as other passions; for some belong to the irascible, others to the concupiscible faculty, as stated above (Q. 23, A. 1). On the other hand, neither does every diversity of passions necessarily suffice for a diversity of moral virtues. First, because some passions are in contrary opposition to one another, such as joy and sorrow, fear and daring, and so on. About such passions as are thus in opposition to one another there must needs be one same virtue. Because, since moral virtue consists in a kind of mean, the mean in contrary passions stands in the same ratio to both, even as in the natural order there is but one mean between contraries, e.g., between black and white.—Secondly, because there are different passions contradicting reason in the same manner, e.g. by impelling to that which is contrary to reason, or by withdrawing from that which is in accord with reason. Wherefore the different passions of the concupiscible faculty do not require different moral virtues, because their movements follow one another in a certain order, as being directed to the one same thing, viz., the attainment of some good or the avoidance of some evil: thus from love proceeds desire, and from desire we arrive at pleasure; and it is the same with the opposite passions, for hatred leads to avoidance or dislike, and this leads to sorrow.—On the other hand, the irascible passions are not all of one order, but are directed to different things: for daring and fear are about some great danger; hope and despair are about some difficult good; while anger seeks to overcome something contrary which has wrought harm. Consequently there are different virtues about such like passions: e.g., temperance, about the concupiscible passions; fortitude, about fear and daring; magnanimity, about hope and despair; meekness, about anger.

Reply Obj. 1. All the passions concur in one common principle and end; but not in one proper principle or end: and so this does not suffice for the unity of moral virtue.

Reply Obj. 2. Just as in the natural order the same principle causes movement from one extreme and movement towards the other; and as in the intellectual order contraries have one common ratio; so too between contrary passions there is but one moral virtue, which, like a second nature, consents to reason's dictates.

Reply Obj. 3. Those three passions are directed to the same object in a certain order, as stated above: and so they belong to the same virtue.

FIFTH ARTICLE

Whether the Moral Virtues Differ in Point of the Various Objects of the Passions?

We proceed thus to the Fifth Article:—

Objection 1. It would seem that the moral virtues do not differ according to the objects

* εὐτραπελία.

of the passions. For just as there are objects of passions, so are there objects of operations. Now those moral virtues that are about operations, do not differ according to the objects of those operations: for the buying and selling either of a house or of a horse belong to the one same virtue of justice. Therefore neither do those moral virtues that are about passions differ according to the objects of those passions.

Obj. 2. Further, the passions are acts or movements of the sensitive appetite. Now it needs a greater difference to differentiate habits than acts. Hence diverse objects which do not diversify the species of passions, do not diversify the species of moral virtue: so that there is but one moral virtue about all objects of pleasure, and the same applies to the other passions.

Obj. 3. Further, more or less do not change a species. Now various objects of pleasure differ only by reason of being more or less pleasurable. Therefore all objects of pleasure belong to one species of virtue: and for the same reason so do all fearful objects, and the same applies to others. Therefore moral virtue is not diversified according to the objects of the passions.

Obj. 4. Further, virtue hinders evil, even as it produces good. But there are various virtues about the desires for good things: thus temperance is about desires for the pleasure of touch, and *eutrapelia** about pleasures in games. Therefore there should be different virtues about fears of evils.

On the contrary, Chastity is about sexual pleasures, abstinence about pleasures of the table, and *eutrapelia* about pleasures in games.

I answer that, The perfection of a virtue depends on the reason; whereas the perfection of a passion depends on the sensitive appetite. Consequently virtues must needs be differentiated according to their relation to reason, but the passions according to their relation to the appetite. Hence the objects of the passions, according as they are variously related to the sensitive appetite, cause the different species of passions: while, according as they are related to reason, they cause the different species of virtues. Now the movement of reason is not the same as that of the sensitive appetite. Wherefore nothing hinders a difference of objects from causing diversity of passions, without causing diversity of virtues, as when one virtue is about several passions, as stated above (A. 4); and again, a difference of objects from causing different virtues, without causing a difference of passions, since several virtues are directed about one passion, e.g., pleasure.

And because diverse passions belonging to diverse powers, always belong to diverse virtues, as stated above (A. 4); therefore a difference of objects that corresponds to a difference of powers always causes a specific difference of virtues,—for instance the difference between that which is good absolutely speaking, and that which is good and difficult to obtain.—Moreover since the reason rules man's lower powers in a certain order, and even extends to outward things; hence, one single object of the passions, according as it is apprehended by sense, imagination, or reason, and again, according as it belongs to the soul, body, or external things, has various relations to reason, and consequently is of a nature to cause a difference of virtues. Consequently man's good which is the object of love, desire and pleasure, may be taken as referred either to a bodily sense, or to the inner apprehension of the mind: and this same good may be directed to man's good in himself, either in his body or in his soul, or to man's good in relation to other men. And every such difference, being differently related to reason, differentiates virtues.

Accordingly, if we take a good, and it be something discerned by the sense of touch, and something pertaining to the upkeep of human life either in the individual or in the species, such as the pleasures of the table or of sexual intercourse, it will belong to the virtue of *temperance*. As regards the pleasures of the other senses, they are not intense, and so do not present much difficulty to the reason: hence there is no virtue corresponding to them; for virtue, *like art, is about difficult things* (*Ethic.* ii. 3).

On the other hand, good discerned not by the senses, but by an inner power, and belonging to man in himself, is like money and honor; the former, by its very nature, being employable for the good of the body, while the latter is based on the apprehension of the mind. These goods again may be considered either absolutely, in which way they concern the concupiscible faculty, or as being difficult to obtain, in which way they belong to the irascible part: which distinction, however, has no place in pleasurable objects of touch; since such are of base condition, and are becoming to man in so far as he has something in common with irrational animals. Accordingly in reference to money considered as a good absolutely, as an object of desire, pleasure, or love, there is *liberality*: but if we consider this good as difficult to get, and as being the object of our hope, there is *magnificence*.* With regard to that good which we call honor, taken absolutely, as the object of love, we

have a virtue called *philotimia*,** i.e., *love of honor:* while if we consider it as hard to attain, and as an object of hope, then we have *magnanimity*. Wherefore liberality and *philotimia* seem to be in the concupiscible part, while magnificence and magnanimity are in the irascible.

As regards man's good in relation to other men, it does not seem hard to obtain, but is considered absolutely, as the object of the concupiscible passions. This good may be pleasurable to a man in his behavior towards another either in some serious matter, in actions, to wit, that are directed by reason to a due end, or in playful actions, viz., that are done for mere pleasure, and which do not stand in the same relation to reason as the former. Now one man behaves towards another in serious matters, in two ways. First, as being pleasant in his regard, by becoming speech and deeds: and this belongs to a virtue which Aristotle (*Ethic.* ii. 7) calls *friendship*,† and may be rendered *affability*. Secondly, one man behaves towards another by being frank with him, in words and deeds: this belongs to another virtue which (*Ethic.* iv. 7) he calls *truthfulness*.‡ For frankness is more akin to the reason than pleasure, and serious matters than play. Hence there is another virtue about the pleasures of games, which the Philosopher calls εὐτραπελία (*Ethic.* iv. 8).

It is therefore evident that, according to Aristotle, there are ten moral virtues about the passions, viz., fortitude, temperance, liberality, magnificence, magnanimity, *philotimia*, gentleness, friendship, truthfulness, and *eutrapelia*, all of which differ in respect of their diverse matter, passions, or objects: so that if we add *justice*, which is about operations, there will be eleven in all.

Reply Obj. 1. All objects of the same specific operation have the same relation to reason: not so all the objects of the same specific passion; because operations do not thwart reason as the passions do.

Reply Obj. 2. Passions are not differentiated by the same rule as virtues are, as stated above.

Reply Obj. 3. More and less do not cause a difference of species, unless they bear different relations to reason.

Reply Obj. 4. Good is a more potent mover than evil: because evil does not cause movement, save in virtue of good, as Dionysius states (*Div. Nom.* iv). Hence an evil does not prove an obstacle to reason, so as to require virtues unless that evil be great; there being, seemingly, one such evil corresponding to each kind of passion. Hence there is but one virtue, meekness, for every form of anger; and, again.

---

* μεγαλοπρέπεια. ** φιλοτιμία. † φιλία. ‡ ἀλήθεια.

but one virtue, fortitude, for all forms of daring.—On the other hand, good involves difficulty, which requires virtue, even if it be not a great good in that particular kind of passion. Consequently there are various moral virtues about desires, as stated above.

QUESTION 61

Of the Cardinal Virtues

(In Five Articles)

WE must now consider the cardinal virtues: under which head there are five points of inquiry: (1) Whether the moral virtues should be called cardinal or principal virtues? (2) Of their number; (3) Which are they? (4) Whether they differ from one another? (5) Whether they are fittingly divided into social, perfecting, perfect, and exemplar virtues?

FIRST ARTICLE

Whether the Moral Virtues Should Be Called Cardinal or Principal Virtues?

We proceed thus to the First Article:—

Objection 1. It would seem that moral virtues should not be called cardinal or principal virtues. For *the opposite members of a division are by nature simultaneous* (*Categor.* x), so that one is not principal rather than another. Now all the virtues are opposite members of the division of the genus *virtue*. Therefore none of them should be called principal.

Obj. 2. Further, the end is principal as compared to the means. But the theological virtues are about the end; while the moral virtues are about the means. Therefore the theological virtues, rather than the moral virtues, should be called principal or cardinal.

Obj. 3. Further, that which is essentially so is principal in comparison with that which is so by participation. But the intellectual virtues belong to that which is essentially rational: whereas the moral virtues belong to that which is rational by participation, as stated above (Q. 58, A. 3). Therefore the intellectual virtues are principal, rather than the moral virtues.

On the contrary, Ambrose in explaining the words, *Blessed are the poor in spirit* (Luke vi. 20) says: *We know that there are four cardinal virtues, viz., temperance, justice, prudence, and fortitude.* But these are moral virtues. Therefore the moral virtues are cardinal virtues.

I answer that, When we speak of virtue simply, we are understood to speak of human virtue. Now human virtue, as stated above (Q. 56, A. 3), is one that answers to the perfect idea of virtue, which requires rectitude of the appetite: for such like virtue not only confers the faculty of doing well, but also causes the good deed done. On the other hand, the name virtue is applied to one that answers imperfectly to the idea of virtue, and does not require rectitude of the appetite: because it merely confers the faculty of doing well without causing the good deed to be done. Now it is evident that the perfect is principal as compared to the imperfect: and so those virtues which imply rectitude of the appetite are called principal virtues. Such are the moral virtues, and prudence alone, of the intellectual virtues, for it is also something of a moral virtue, as was clearly shown above (Q. 57, A. 4). Consequently, those virtues which are called principal or cardinal are fittingly placed among the moral virtues.

Reply Obj. 1. When a univocal genus is divided into its species, the members of the division are on a par in the point of the generic idea; although considered in their nature as things, one species may surpass another in rank and perfection, as man in respect of other animals. But when we divide an analogous term, which is applied to several things, but to one before it is applied to another, nothing hinders one from ranking before another, even in the point of the generic idea; as the notion of being is applied to substance principally in relation to accident. Such is the division of virtue into the various kinds of virtue: since the good defined by reason is not found in the same way in all things.

Reply Obj. 2. The theological virtues are above man, as stated above (Q. 58, A. 3 *ad* 3). Hence they should properly be called not human, but *super-human* or godlike virtues.

Reply Obj. 3. Although the intellectual virtues, except in prudence, rank before the moral virtues, in the point of their subject, they do not rank before them as virtues; for a virtue, as such, regards good, which is the object of the appetite.

SECOND ARTICLE

Whether There Are Four Cardinal Virtues?

We proceed thus to the Second Article:—

Objection 1. It would seem that there are not four cardinal virtues. For prudence is the directing principle of the other moral virtues, as is clear from what has been said above (Q. 58, A. 4). But that which directs other things ranks before them. Therefore prudence alone is a principal virtue.

Obj. 2. Further, the principal virtues are, in a way, moral virtues. Now we are directed to moral works both by the practical reason, and by a right appetite, as stated in *Ethic.* vi. 2. Therefore there are only two cardinal virtues.

Obj. 3. Further, even among the other virtues one ranks higher than another. But in order that a virtue be principal, it needs not to rank above all the others, but above some. Therefore it seems that there are many more principal virtues.

On the contrary, Gregory says (*Moral.* ii): *The entire structure of good works is built on four virtues.*

I answer that, Things may be numbered either in respect of their formal principles, or according to the subjects in which they are: and either way we find that there are four cardinal virtues.

For the formal principle of the virtue of which we speak now is good as defined by reason; which good can be considered in two ways. First, as existing in the very act of reason: and thus we have one principal virtue, called *Prudence.*—Secondly, according as the reason puts its order into something else; either into operations, and then we have *Justice;* or into passions, and then we need two virtues. For the need of putting the order of reason into the passions is due to their thwarting reason: and this occurs in two ways. First, by the passions inciting to something against reason; and then the passions need a curb, which we call *Temperance.* Secondly, by the passions withdrawing us from following the dictate of reason, e.g., through fear of danger or toil: and then man needs to be strengthened for that which reason dictates, lest he turn back; and to this end there is *Fortitude.*

In like manner, we find the same number if we consider the subjects of virtue. For there are four subjects of the virtue we speak of now: viz., the power which is rational in its essence, and this is perfected by *Prudence;* and that which is rational by participation, and is threefold, the will, subject of *Justice,* the concupiscible faculty, subject of *Temperance,* and the irascible faculty, subject of *Fortitude.*

Reply Obj. 1. Prudence is the principal of all the virtues simply. The others are principal, each in its own genus.

Reply Obj. 2. That part of the soul which is rational by participation is threefold, as stated above.

Reply Obj. 3. All the other virtues among which one ranks before another, are reducible to the above four, both as to the subject and as to the formal principle.

THIRD ARTICLE

Whether Any Other Virtues Should Be Called Principal Rather Than These?

We proceed thus to the Third Article:—

Objection 1. It would seem that other virtues should be called principal rather than these. For, seemingly, the greatest is the principal in any genus. Now *magnanimity has a great influence on all the virtues* (*Ethic.* iv. 3). Therefore magnanimity should more than any be called a principal virtue.

Obj. 2. Further, that which strengthens the other virtues should above all be called a principal virtue. But such is humility: for Gregory says (*Hom.* iv. *in Ev.*) that *he who gathers the other virtues without humility is as one who carries straw against the wind.* Therefore humility seems above all to be a principal virtue.

Obj. 3. Further, that which is most perfect seems to be principal. But this applies to patience, according to James i. 4: *Patience hath a perfect work.* Therefore patience should be reckoned a principal virtue.

On the contrary, Cicero reduces all other virtues to these four (*De Invent. Rhet.* ii).

I answer that, As stated above (A. 2), these four are reckoned as cardinal virtues, in respect of the four formal principles of virtue as we understand it now. These principles are found chiefly in certain acts and passions. Thus the good which exists in the act of reason, is found chiefly in reason's command, but not in its counsel or its judgment, as stated above (Q. 57, A. 6). Again, good as defined by reason and put into our operations as something right and due, is found chiefly in commutations and distributions in respect of another person, and on a basis of equality. The good of curbing the passions is found chiefly in those passions which are most difficult to curb, viz., in the pleasures of touch. The good of being firm in holding to the good defined by reason, against the impulse of passion, is found chiefly in perils of death, which are most difficult to withstand.

Accordingly the above four virtues may be considered in two ways. First, in respect of their common formal principles. In this way they are called principal, being general, as it were, in comparison with all the virtues: so that, for instance, any virtue that causes good in reason's act of consideration, may be called prudence; every virtue that causes the good of right and due in operations, be called justice; every virtue that curbs and represses the passions, be called temperance; and every virtue that strengthens the mind against any passions whatever, be called fortitude. Many, both holy doctors, as also philosophers, speak about these virtues in this sense: and in this way the other virtues are contained under them.—Wherefore all the objections fail.

Secondly, they may be considered in point of their being denominated, each one from that which is foremost in its respective matter, and thus they are specific virtues, condivided with the others. Yet they are called principal in comparison with the other virtues, on account of the importance of their matter: so that prudence is the virtue which commands; justice, the virtue which is about due actions between equals; temperance, the virtue which suppresses desires for the pleasures of touch; and fortitude, the virtue which strengthens against dangers of death.—Thus again do the objections fail: because the other virtues may be principal in some other way, but these are called principal by reason of their matter, as stated above.

FOURTH ARTICLE

Whether the Four Cardinal Virtues Differ from One Another?

We proceed thus to the Fourth Article:—

Objection 1. It would seem that the above four virtues are not diverse and distinct from one another. For Gregory says (*Moral.* xxii. 1): *There is no true prudence, unless it be just, temperate and brave; no perfect temperance, that is not brave, just and prudent; no sound fortitude, that is not prudent, temperate and just; no real justice, without prudence, fortitude and temperance.* But this would not be so, if the above four virtues were distinct from one another: since the different species of one genus do not qualify one another. Therefore the aforesaid virtues are not distinct from one another.

Obj. 2. Further, among things distinct from one another the function of one is not attributed to another. But the function of temperance is attributed to fortitude: for Ambrose says (*De Offic.* xxxvi): *Rightly do we call it fortitude, when a man conquers himself, and is not weakened and bent by any enticement.* And of temperance he says (*ibid.*, xliii., xlv) that it *safeguards the manner and order in all things that we decide to do and say.* Therefore it seems that these virtues are not distinct from one another.

Obj. 3. Further, the Philosopher says (*Ethic.* ii. 4) that the necessary conditions of virtue are first of all *that a man should have knowledge; secondly, that he should exercise choice for a particular end; thirdly, that he should possess the habit and act with firmness and steadfastness.* But the first of these seems to belong to prudence which is rectitude of reason in things to be done; the second, i.e., choice, belongs to temperance, whereby a man, holding his passions on the curb, acts, not from passion but from choice; the third, that a man should act for the sake of a due end, implies a certain rectitude, which seemingly belongs to justice; while the last, viz., firmness and steadfastness, belongs to fortitude. Therefore each of these virtues is general in comparison to other virtues. Therefore they are not distinct from one another.

On the contrary, Augustine says (*De Moribus Eccl.* xi) that *there are four virtues, corresponding to the various emotions of love,* and he applies this to the four virtues mentioned above. Therefore the same four virtues are distinct from one another.

I answer that, As stated above (A. 3), these four virtues are understood differently by various writers. For some take them as signifying certain general conditions of the human mind, to be found in all the virtues: so that, to wit, prudence is merely a certain rectitude of discretion in any actions or matters whatever; justice, a certain rectitude of the mind, whereby man does what he ought in any matters; temperance, a disposition of the mind, moderating any passions or operations, so as to keep them within bounds; and fortitude, a disposition whereby the soul is strengthened for that which is in accord with reason, against any assaults of the passions, or the toil involved by any operations. To distinguish these four virtues in this way does not imply that justice, temperance and fortitude are distinct virtuous habits: because it is fitting that every moral virtue, from the fact that it is a *habit*, should be accompanied by a certain firmness so as not to be moved by its contrary: and this, we have said, belongs to fortitude. Moreover, inasmuch as it is a *virtue*, it is directed to good which involves the notion of right and due; and this, we have said, belongs to justice. Again, owing to the fact that it is a *moral virtue* partaking of reason, it observes the mode of reason in all things, and does not exceed its bounds, which has been stated to belong to temperance. It is only in the point of having discretion, which we ascribed to prudence, that there seems to be a distinction from the other three, inasmuch as discretion belongs essentially to reason; whereas the other three imply a certain share of reason by way of a kind of application (of reason) to passions or operations. According to the above explanation, then, prudence would be distinct from the other three virtues: but these would not be distinct from one another; for it is evident that one and the same virtue is both habit, and virtue, and moral virtue.

Others, however, with better reason, take these four virtues, according as they have their special determinate matter; each its own matter, in which special commendation is given to that general condition from which the virtue's name is taken as stated above (A. 3). In this way it is clear that the aforesaid virtues are distinct habits, differentiated in respect of their diverse objects.

Reply Obj. 1. Gregory is speaking of these four virtues in the first sense given above.—It may also be said that these four virtues qualify one another by a kind of overflow. For the qualities of prudence overflow on to the other virtues in so far as they are directed by prudence. And each of the others overflows on to the rest, for the reason that whoever can do what is harder, can do what is less difficult. Wherefore whoever can curb his desires for the pleasures of touch, so that they keep within bounds, which is a very hard thing to do, for this very reason is more able to check his daring in dangers of death, so as not to go too far, which is much easier; and in this sense fortitude is said to be temperate. Again, temperance is said to be brave, by reason of fortitude overflowing into temperance: in so far, to wit, as he whose mind is strengthened by fortitude against dangers of death, which is a matter of very great difficulty, is more able to remain firm against the onslaught of pleasures; for as Cicero says (*De Offic.* i), *it would be inconsistent for a man to be unbroken by fear, and yet vanquished by cupidity; or that he should be conquered by lust, after showing himself to be unconquered by toil.*

From this the Reply to the Second Objection is clear. For temperance observes the mean in all things, and fortitude keeps the mind unbent by the enticements of pleasures, —either in so far as these virtues are taken to denote certain general conditions of virtue, or in the sense that they overflow on to one another, as explained above.

Reply Obj. 3. These four general conditions of virtue set down by the Philosopher, are not proper to the aforesaid virtues. They may, however, be appropriated to them, in the way above stated.

FIFTH ARTICLE

Whether the Cardinal Virtues Are Fittingly Divided into Social Virtues, Perfecting, Perfect, and Exemplar Virtues?

We proceed thus to the Fifth Article:—

Objection 1. It would seem that these four virtues are unfittingly divided into exemplar virtues, perfecting virtues, perfect virtues, and social virtues. For as Macrobius says (*Super Somn. Scip.* 1), *the exemplar virtues are such as exist in the mind of God.* Now the Philosopher says (*Ethic.* x. 8) that *it is absurd to ascribe justice, fortitude, temperance, and prudence to God.* Therefore these virtues cannot be exemplar.

Obj. 2. Further, the *perfect* virtues are those which are without any passion: for Macrobius says (*ibid.*) that *in a soul that is cleansed, temperance has not to check worldly desires, for it has forgotten all about them: fortitude knows nothing about the passions; it does not have to conquer them.* Now it was stated above (Q. 59, A. 5) that the aforesaid virtues cannot be without passions. Therefore there is no such thing as *perfect* virtue.

Obj. 3. Further, he says (Macrobius,—*ibid.*) that the *perfecting* virtues are those of the man *who flies from human affairs and devotes himself exclusively to the things of God.* But it seems wrong to do this, for Cicero says (*De Offic.* i): *I reckon that it is not only unworthy of praise, but wicked for a man to say that he despises what most men admire, viz., power and office.* Therefore there are no *perfecting* virtues.

Obj. 4. Further, he says (Macrobius,—*ibid.*) that the *social* virtues are those *whereby good men work for the good of their country and for the safety of the city.* But it is only legal justice that is directed to the common weal, as the Philosopher states (*Ethic.* v. 1). Therefore other virtues should not be called *social.*

On the contrary, Macrobius says (*ibid.*): *Plotinus, together with Plato foremost among teachers of philosophy, says: "The four kinds of virtue are fourfold. In the first place there are social* virtues; secondly, there are perfecting† virtues; thirdly, there are perfect‡ virtues; and fourthly, there are exemplar virtues."*

I answer that, As Augustine says (*De Moribus Eccl.* vi), *the soul needs to follow something in order to give birth to virtue: this something is God: if we follow Him we shall*

---

* *Cf.* Chrysostom's fifteenth homily on St. Matthew, where he says: "The gentle, the modest, the merciful, the just man does not shut up his good deeds within himself. . . . He that is clean of heart and peaceful, and suffers persecution for the sake of the truth, lives for the common weal."

† *Virtutes purgatoriæ,* literally, *cleansing virtues.*

‡ *Virtutes purgati animi,* literally, *virtues of the clean soul.*

live aright. Consequently the exemplar of human virtue must needs pre-exist in God, just as in Him pre-exist the types of all things. Accordingly virtue may be considered as existing originally in God, and thus we speak of *exemplar* virtues: so that in God the Divine Mind itself may be called prudence; while temperance is the turning of God's gaze on Himself, even as in us it is that which conforms the appetite to reason. God's fortitude is His unchangeableness; His justice is the observance of the Eternal Law in His works, as Plotinus states (*cf.* Macrobius,—*ibid.*).

Again, since man by his nature is a social* animal, these virtues, in so far as they are in him according to the condition of his nature, are called *social* virtues; since it is by reason of them that man behaves himself well in the conduct of human affairs. It is in this sense that we have been speaking of these virtues until now.

But since it behooves man to do his utmost to strive onward even to Divine things, as even the Philosopher declares in *Ethic.* x. 7, and as Scripture often admonishes us,—for instance: *Be ye . . . perfect, as your heavenly Father is perfect* (*Matth.* v. 48), we must needs place some virtues between the social or human virtues, and the exemplar virtues which are Divine. Now these virtues differ by reason of a difference of movement and term: so that some are virtues of men who are on their way and tending towards the Divine similitude; and these are called *perfecting* virtues. Thus prudence, by contemplating the things of God, counts as nothing all things of the world, and directs all the thoughts of the soul to God alone;—temperance, so far as nature allows, neglects the needs of the body; fortitude prevents the soul from being afraid of neglecting the body and rising to heavenly things; and justice consists in the soul giving a wholehearted consent to follow the way thus proposed.—Besides these there are the virtues of those who have already attained to the Divine similitude: these are called the *perfect virtues.* —Thus prudence sees nought else but the things of God; temperance knows no earthly desires; fortitude has no knowledge of passion; and justice, by imitating the Divine Mind, is united thereto by an everlasting

* See note on page 849.

covenant. Such are the virtues attributed to the Blessed, or, in this life, to some who are at the summit of perfection.

Reply Obj. 1. The Philosopher is speaking of these virtues according as they relate to human affairs; for instance, justice, about buying and selling; fortitude, about fear; temperance, about desires; for in this sense it is absurd to attribute them to God.

Reply Obj. 2. Human virtues, that is to say, virtues of men living together in this world, are about the passions. But the virtues of those who have attained to perfect bliss are without passions. Hence Plotinus says (*cf.* Macrobius,—*loc. cit.*) that *the social virtues check the passions,* i.e., they bring them to the relative mean; *the second kind,* viz., the perfecting virtues, *uproot them; the third kind,* viz., the perfect virtues, *forget them; while it is impious to mention them in connection with virtues of the fourth kind,* viz., the exemplar virtues.—It may also be said that here he is speaking of passions as denoting inordinate emotions.

Reply Obj. 3. To neglect human affairs when necessity forbids is wicked; otherwise it is virtuous. Hence Cicero says a little earlier: *Perhaps one should make allowances for those who by reason of their exceptional talents have devoted themselves to learning; as also to those who have retired from public life on account of failing health, or for some other yet weightier motive; when such men yielded to others the power and renown of authority.* This agrees with what Augustine says (*De Civ. Dei* xix. 19): *The love of truth demands a hallowed leisure; charity necessitates good works. If no one lays this burden on us we may devote ourselves to the study and contemplation of truth; but if the burden is laid on us it is to be taken up under the pressure of charity.*

Reply Obj. 4. Legal justice alone regards the common weal directly: but by commanding the other virtues it draws them all into the service of the common weal, as the Philosopher declares (*Ethic.* v. 1). For we must take note that it concerns the human virtues, as we understand them here, to do well not only towards the community, but also towards the parts of the community, viz., towards the household, or even towards one individual.

QUESTION 62

Of the Theological Virtues

(In Four Articles)

WE must now consider the Theological Virtues: under which head there are four points of inquiry: (1) Whether there are any theological virtues? (2) Whether the theological virtues are distinct from the intellectual and moral virtues? (3) How many, and which are they? (4) Of their order.

FIRST ARTICLE

Whether There Are Any Theological Virtues?

We proceed thus to the First Article:—

Objection 1. It would seem that there are not any theological virtues. For according to *Phys.* vii., text. 17, *virtue is the disposition of a perfect thing to that which is best: and by perfect, I mean that which is disposed according to nature.* But that which is Divine is above man's nature. Therefore the theological virtues are not virtues of a man.

Obj. 2. Further, theological virtues are quasi-Divine virtues. But the Divine virtues are exemplars, as stated above (Q. 61, A. 5), which are not in us but in God. Therefore the theological virtues are not virtues of man.

Obj. 3. Further, the theological virtues are so called because they direct us to God, Who is the first beginning and last end of all things. But by the very nature of his reason and will, man is directed to his first beginning and end. Therefore there is no need for any habits of theological virtue, to direct the reason and will to God.

On the contrary, The precepts of the Law are about acts of virtue. Now the Divine Law contains precepts about the acts of faith, hope, and charity: for it is written (*Ecclus.* ii. 8, seqq.): *Ye that fear the Lord believe Him,* and again, *hope in Him,* and again, *love Him.* Therefore faith, hope, and charity are virtues directing us to God. Therefore they are theological virtues.

I answer that, Man is perfected by virtue, for those actions whereby he is directed to happiness, as was explained above (Q. 5, A. 7). Now man's happiness is twofold, as was also stated above (*ibid.,* A. 5). One is proportionate to human nature, a happiness, to wit, which man can obtain by means of his natural principles. The other is a happiness surpassing man's nature, and which man can obtain by the power of God alone, by a kind of participation of the Godhead, about which it is written (2 Pet. i. 4) that by Christ we are made *partakers of the Divine nature.* And because such happiness surpasses the capacity of human nature, man's natural principles which enable him to act well according to his capacity, do not suffice to direct man to this same happiness. Hence it is necessary for man to receive from God some additional principles, whereby he may be directed to supernatural happiness, even as he is directed to his connatural end, by means of his natural principles, albeit not without the Divine assistance. Such like principles are called *theological virtues:* first, because their object is God, inasmuch as they direct us aright to God: secondly, because they are infused in us by God alone: thirdly, because these virtues are not made known to us, save by Divine revelation, contained in Holy Writ.

Reply Obj. 1. A certain nature may be ascribed to a certain thing in two ways. First, essentially: and thus these theological virtues surpass the nature of man. Secondly, by participation, as kindled wood partakes of the nature of fire: and thus, after a fashion, man becomes a partaker of the Divine Nature, as stated above: so that these virtues are proportionate to man in respect of the Nature of which he is made a partaker.

Reply Obj. 2. These virtues are called Divine, not as though God were virtuous by reason of them, but because of them God makes us virtuous, and directs us to Himself. Hence they are not exemplar but exemplate virtues.

Reply Obj. 3. The reason and will are naturally directed to God, inasmuch as He is the beginning and end of nature, but in proportion to nature. But the reason and will, according to their nature, are not sufficiently directed to Him in so far as He is the object of supernatural happiness.

SECOND ARTICLE

Whether the Theological Virtues Are Distinct from the Intellectual and Moral Virtues?

We proceed thus to the Second Article:—

Objection 1. It would seem that the theological virtues are not distinct from the moral and intellectual virtues. For the theological virtues, if they be in a human soul, must needs perfect it, either as to the intellective, or as to the appetitive part. Now the virtues which perfect the intellective part are called intellectual; and the virtues which perfect the appetitive part, are called moral. Therefore, the theological virtues are not distinct from the moral and intellectual virtues.

Obj. 2. Further, the theological virtues are those which direct us to God.. Now, among the intellectual virtues there is one which directs us to God: this is wisdom, which is about Divine things, since it considers the highest cause. Therefore the theological virtues are not distinct from the intellectual virtues.

Obj. 3. Further, Augustine (*De Moribus Eccl.* xv) shows how the four cardinal virtues are the *order of love.* Now love is charity, which is a theological virtue. Therefore the moral virtues are not distinct from the theological.

On the contrary, That which is above man's nature is distinct from that which is according to his nature. But the theological virtues are above man's nature; while the intellectual and moral virtues are in proportion to his nature, as clearly shown above (Q. 58, A. 3). Therefore they are distinct from one another.

I answer that, As stated above (Q. 54, A. 2 *ad* 1), habits are specifically distinct from one another in respect of the formal difference of their objects. Now the object of the theological virtues is God Himself, Who is the last end of all, as surpassing the knowledge of our reason. On the other hand, the object of the intellectual and moral virtues is something comprehensible to human reason. Wherefore the theological virtues are specifically distinct from the moral and intellectual virtues.

Reply Obj. 1. The intellectual and moral virtues perfect man's intellect and appetite according to the capacity of human nature; the theological virtues, supernaturally.

Reply Obj. 2. The wisdom which the Philosopher (*Ethic.* vi. 3, 7) reckons as an intellectual virtue, considers Divine things so far as they are open to the research of human reason. Theological virtue, on the other hand, is about those same things so far as they surpass human reason.

Reply Obj. 3. Though charity is love, yet love is not always charity. When, then, it is stated that every virtue is the order of love, this can be understood either of love in the general sense, or of the love of charity. If it be understood of love, commonly so called, then each virtue is stated to be the order of love, in so far as each cardinal virtue requires ordinate emotions; and love is the root and cause of every emotion, as stated above (Q. 27, A. 4; Q. 28, A. 6 *ad* 2; Q. 41, A. 2 *ad* 1).—If, however, it be understood of the love of charity, it does not mean that every other virtue is charity essentially: but that all other vir-

tues depend on charity in some way, as we shall show further on (Q. 65, AA. 2, 4; II-II, Q. 23, A. 7).

THIRD ARTICLE

Whether Faith, Hope, and Charity Are Fittingly Reckoned as Theological Virtues?

We proceed thus to the Third Article:—

Objection 1. It would seem that faith, hope, and charity are not fittingly reckoned as three theological virtues. For the theological virtues are in relation to Divine happiness, what the natural inclination is in relation to the connatural end. Now among the virtues directed to the connatural end there is but one natural virtue, viz., the understanding of principles. Therefore there should be but one theological virtue.

Obj. 2. Further, the theological virtues are more perfect than the intellectual and moral virtues. Now faith is not reckoned among the intellectual virtues, but is something less than a virtue, since it is imperfect knowledge. Likewise hope is not reckoned among the moral virtues, but is something less than a virtue, since it is a passion. Much less therefore should they be reckoned as theological virtues.

Obj. 3. Further, the theological virtues direct man's soul to God. Now man's soul cannot be directed to God, save through the intellective part, wherein are the intellect and will. Therefore there should be only two theological virtues, one perfecting the intellect, the other, the will.

On the contrary, The Apostle says (1 Cor. xiii. 13): *Now there remain faith, hope, charity, these three.*

I answer that, As stated above (A. 1), the theological virtues direct man to supernatural happiness in the same way as by the natural inclination man is directed to his connatural end. Now the latter happens in respect of two things. First, in respect of the reason or intellect, in so far as it contains the first universal principles which are known to us by the natural light of the intellect, and which are reason's starting-point, both in speculative and in practical matters. Secondly, through the rectitude of the will which tends naturally to good as defined by reason.

But these two fall short of the order of supernatural happiness, according to 1 Cor. ii. 9: *The eye hath not seen, nor ear heard, neither hath it entered into the heart of man, what things God hath prepared for them that love Him.* Consequently in respect of both the above things man needed to receive in addition something supernatural to direct him to a supernatural end. First, as regards the intellect, man receives certain supernatural principles, which are held by means of a Divine light: these are the articles of faith, about which is faith.—Secondly, the will is directed to this end, both as to the movement of intention, which tends to that end as something attainable,—and this pertains to hope,—and as to a certain spiritual union, whereby the will is, so to speak, transformed into that end,— and this belongs to charity. For the appetite of a thing is moved and tends towards its connatural end naturally; and this movement is due to a certain conformity of the thing with its end.

Reply Obj. 1. The intellect requires intelligible species whereby to understand: consequently there is need of a natural habit in addition to the power. But the very nature of the will suffices for it to be directed naturally to the end, both as to the intention of the end and as to its conformity with the end. But the nature of the power is insufficient in either of these respects, for the will to be directed to things that are above its nature. Consequently there was need for an additional supernatural habit in both respects.

Reply Obj. 2. Faith and hope imply a certain imperfection: since faith is of things unseen, and hope, of things not possessed. Hence faith and hope, in things that are subject to human power, fall short of the notion of virtue. But faith and hope in things which are above the capacity of human nature surpass all virtue that is in proportion to man, according to 1 Cor. i. 25: *The weakness of God is stronger than men.*

Reply Obj. 3. Two things pertain to the appetite, viz., movement to the end, and conformity with the end by means of love. Hence there must needs be two theological virtues in the human appetite, namely, hope and charity.

FOURTH ARTICLE

Whether Faith Precedes Hope, and Hope Charity?

We proceed thus to the Fourth Article:—

Objection 1. It would seem that the order of the theological virtues is not that faith precedes hope, and hope charity. For the root precedes that which grows from it. Now charity is the root of all the virtues, according to Ephes. iii. 17: *Being rooted and founded in charity.* Therefore charity precedes the others.

Obj. 2. Further, Augustine says (*De Doctr. Christ.* i): *A man cannot love what he does not believe to exist. But if he believes and loves, by doing good works he ends in hoping.* Therefore it seems that faith precedes charity, and charity hope.

Obj. 3. Further, love is the principle of all our emotions, as stated above (A. 2 *ad* 3).

Now hope is a kind of emotion, since it is a passion, as stated above (Q. 25, A. 2). Therefore charity, which is love, precedes hope.

On the contrary, The Apostle enumerates them thus (1 Cor. xiii. 13): *Now there remain faith, hope, charity.*

I answer that, Order is twofold: order of generation, and order of perfection. By order of generation, in respect of which matter precedes form, and the imperfect precedes the perfect, in one same subject faith precedes hope, and hope charity, as to their acts: because habits are all infused together. For the movement of the appetite cannot tend to anything, either by hoping or loving, unless that thing be apprehended by the sense or by the intellect. Now it is by faith that the intellect apprehends the object of hope and love. Hence in the order of generation, faith precedes hope and charity.—In like manner a man loves a thing because he apprehends it as his good. Now from the very fact that a man hopes to be able to obtain some good through someone, he looks on the man in whom he hopes as a good of his own. Hence for the very reason that a man hopes in someone, he proceeds to love him: so that in the order of generation, hope precedes charity as regards their respective acts.

But in the order of perfection, charity precedes faith and hope: because both faith and hope are quickened by charity, and receive from charity their full complement as virtues. For thus charity is the mother and the root of all the virtues, inasmuch as it is the form of them all, as we shall state further on (II-II, Q. 23, A. 8).

This suffices for the Reply to the First Objection.

Reply Obj. 2. Augustine is speaking of that hope whereby a man hopes to obtain bliss through the merits which he has already: this belongs to hope quickened by and following charity. But it is possible for a man before having charity, to hope through merits not already possessed, but which he hopes to possess.

Reply Obj. 3. As stated above (Q. 40, A. 7), in treating of the passions, hope regards two things. One as its principal object, viz., the good hoped for. With regard to this, love always precedes hope: for good is never hoped for unless it be desired and loved.—Hope also regards the person from whom a man hopes to be able to obtain some good. With regard to this, hope precedes love at first; though afterwards hope is increased by love. Because from the fact that a man thinks that he can obtain a good through someone, he begins to love him: and from the fact that he loves him, he then hopes all the more in him.

QUESTION 63

Of the Cause of Virtues

(In Four Articles)

WE must now consider the cause of virtues; and under this head there are four points of inquiry: (1) Whether virtue is in us by nature? (2) Whether any virtue is caused in us by habituation? (3) Whether any moral virtues are in us by infusion? (4) Whether virtue acquired by habituation, is of the same species as infused virtue?

FIRST ARTICLE

Whether Virtue Is in Us by Nature?

We proceed thus to the First Article:—

Objection 1. It would seem that virtue is in us by nature. For Damascene says (*De Fide Orthod.* iii. 14): *Virtues are natural to us and are equally in all of us.* And Antony says in his sermon to the monks: *If the will contradicts nature it is perverse, if it follow nature, it is virtuous.* Moreover, a gloss on Matth. iv. 23, *Jesus went about,* etc., says: *He taught them natural virtues, i.e., chastity, justice, humility, which man possesses naturally.*

Obj. 2. Further, the virtuous good consists in accord with reason, as was clearly shown above (Q. 55, A. 4 *ad* 2). But that which accords with reason is natural to man; since reason is part of man's nature. Therefore virtue is in man by nature.

Obj. 3. Further, that which is in us from birth is said to be natural to us. Now virtues are in some from birth: for it is written (Job xxxi. 18): *From my infancy mercy grew up with me; and it came out with me from my mother's womb.* Therefore virtue is in man by nature.

On the contrary, Whatever is in man by nature is common to all men, and is not taken away by sin, since even in the demons natural gifts remain, as Dionysius states (*Div. Nom.* iv). But virtue is not in all men; and is cast out by sin. Therefore it is not in man by nature.

I answer that, With regard to corporeal forms, it has been maintained by some that they are wholly from within, by those, for instance, who upheld the theory of *latent forms.** Others held that forms are entirely from without, those, for instance, who thought that corporeal forms originated from some separate cause.—Others, however, esteemed that they are partly from within, in so far as they pre-exist potentially in matter; and part-

ly from without, in so far as they are brought into act by the agent.

In like manner with regard to sciences and virtues, some held that they are wholly from within, so that all virtues and sciences would pre-exist in the soul naturally, but that the hindrances to science and virtue, which are due to the soul being weighed down by the body, are removed by study and practice, even as iron is made bright by being polished. This was the opinion of the Platonists.—Others said that they are wholly from without, being due to the inflow of the active intellect, as Avicenna maintained.—Others said that sciences and virtues are in us by nature, so far as we are adapted to them, but not in their perfection: this is the teaching of the Philosopher (*Ethic.* ii. 1), and is nearer the truth.

To make this clear, it must be observed that there are two ways in which something is said to be natural to a man; one is according to his specific nature, the other according to his individual nature. And, since each thing derives its species from its form, and its individuation from matter, and, again, since man's form is his rational soul, while his matter is his body, whatever belongs to him in respect of his rational soul, is natural to him in respect of his specific nature; while whatever belongs to him in respect of the particular temperament of his body, is natural to him in respect of his individual nature. For whatever is natural to man in respect of his body, considered as part of his species, is to be referred, in a way, to the soul, in so far as this particular body is adapted to this particular soul.

In both these ways virtue is natural to man inchoatively. This is so in respect of the specific nature, in so far as in man's reason are to be found instilled by nature certain naturally known principles of both knowledge and action, which are the nurseries of intellectual and moral virtues, and in so far as there is in the will a natural appetite for good in accordance with reason. Again, this is so in respect of the individual nature, in so far as by reason of a disposition in the body, some are disposed either well or ill to certain virtues: because, to wit, certain sensitive powers are acts of certain parts of the body, according to the disposition of which these powers are helped or hindered in the exercise of their acts, and, in consequence, the rational powers also, which the aforesaid sensitive powers assist. In this way

---

* Anaxagoras; *cf.* P. I., Q. 45, A. 8; Q. 65, A.4.

one man has a natural aptitude for science, another for fortitude, another for temperance: and in these ways, both intellectual and moral virtues are in us by way of a natural aptitude, inchoatively,—but not perfectly, since nature is determined to one, while the perfection of these virtues does not depend on one particular mode of action, but on various modes, in respect of the various matters, which constitute the sphere of virtue's action, and according to various circumstances.

It is therefore evident that all virtues are in us by nature, according to aptitude and inchoation, but not according to perfection, except the theological virtues, which are entirely from without.

This suffices for the Replies to the Objections. For the first two argue about the nurseries of virtue which are in us by nature, inasmuch as we are rational beings.—The third objection must be taken in the sense that, owing to the natural disposition which the body has from birth, one has an aptitude for pity, another for living temperately, another for some other virtue.

SECOND ARTICLE

Whether Any Virtue Is Caused in Us by Habituation?

We proceed thus to the Second Article:—

Objection 1. It would seem that virtues cannot be caused in us by habituation. Because a gloss of Augustine,* commenting on Rom. xiv. 23, *All that is not of faith is sin,* says: *The whole life of an unbeliever is a sin: and there is no good without the Sovereign Good. Where knowledge of the truth is lacking, virtue is a mockery even in the best behaved people.* Now faith cannot be acquired by means of works, but is caused in us by God, according to Eph. ii. 8: *By grace you are saved through faith.* Therefore no acquired virtue can be in us by habituation.

Obj. 2. Further, sin and virtue are contraries, so that they are incompatible. Now man cannot avoid sin except by the grace of God, according to Wis. viii. 21: *I knew that I could not otherwise be continent, except God gave it.* Therefore neither can any virtues be caused in us by habituation, but only by the gift of God.

Obj. 3. Further, actions which lead toward virtue, lack the perfection of virtue. But an effect cannot be more perfect than its cause. Therefore a virtue cannot be caused by actions that precede it.

On the contrary, Dionysius says (*Div. Nom.* iv) that good is more efficacious than evil. But vicious habits are caused by evil

* *Cf. Lib. Sentent. Prosperi* cvi.

acts. Much more, therefore, can virtuous habits be caused by good acts.

I answer that, We have spoken above (Q. 51, AA. 2, 3) in a general way about the production of habits from acts; and speaking now in a special way of this matter in relation to virtue, we must take note that, as stated above (Q. 55, AA. 3, 4), man's virtue perfects him in relation to good. Now since the notion of good consists in *mode, species, and order,* as Augustine states (*De Nat. Boni.* iii), or in *number, weight, and measure,* as expressed in Wis. xi. 21, man's good must needs be appraised with respect to some rule. Now this rule is twofold, as stated above (Q. 19, AA. 3, 4), viz., human reason and Divine Law. And since Divine Law is the higher rule, it extends to more things, so that whatever is ruled by human reason, is ruled by the Divine Law too; but the converse does not hold.

It follows that human virtue directed to the good which is defined according to the rule of human reason can be caused by human acts: inasmuch as such acts proceed from reason, by whose power and rule the aforesaid good is established.—On the other hand, virtue which directs man to good as defined by the Divine Law, and not by human reason, cannot be caused by human acts, the principle of which is reason, but is produced in us by the Divine operation alone. Hence Augustine in giving the definition of the latter virtue inserts the words, *which God works in us without us* (*Super Ps.* cxviii, *Serm.* xxvi). It is also of these virtues that the First Objection holds good.

Reply Obj. 2. Mortal sin is incompatible with divinely infused virtue, especially if this be considered in its perfect state. But actual sin, even mortal, is compatible with humanly acquired virtue; because the use of a habit in us is subject to our will, as stated above (Q. 49, A. 3): and one sinful act does not destroy a habit of acquired virtue, since it is not an act but a habit, that is directly contrary to a habit. Wherefore, though man cannot avoid mortal sin without grace, so as never to sin mortally, yet he is not hindered from acquiring a habit of virtue, whereby he may abstain from evil in the majority of cases, and chiefly in matters most opposed to reason.— There are also certain mortal sins which man can nowise avoid without grace, those, namely, which are directly opposed to the theological virtues, which are in us through the gift of grace. This, however, will be more fully explained later (Q. 109, A. 4).

Reply Obj. 3. As stated above (A. 1; Q. 51, A. 1), certain seeds or principles of acquired virtue pre-exist in us by nature. These principles are more excellent than the virtues acquired through them: thus the understanding of speculative principles is more excellent than the science of conclusions, and the natural rectitude of the reason is more excellent than the rectification of the appetite which results through the appetite partaking of reason, which rectification belongs to moral virtue. Accordingly human acts, in so far as they proceed from higher principles, can cause acquired human virtues.

THIRD ARTICLE

Whether Any Moral Virtues Are in Us by Infusion?

We proceed thus to the Third Article:—

Objection 1. It would seem that no virtues besides the theological virtues are infused in us by God. Because God does not do by Himself, save perhaps sometimes miraculously, those things that can be done by second causes; for, as Dionysius says (*Cæl. Hier.* iv), *it is God's rule to bring about extremes through the mean.* Now intellectual and moral virtues can be caused in us by our acts, as stated above (A. 2). Therefore it is not reasonable that they should be caused in us by Infusion.

Obj. 2. Further, much less superfluity is found in God's works than in the works of nature. Now the theological virtues suffice to direct us to supernatural good. Therefore there are no other supernatural virtues needing to be caused in us by God.

Obj. 3. Further, nature does not employ two means where one suffices: much less does God. But God sowed the seeds of virtue in our souls, according to a gloss on Heb. i.* Therefore it is unfitting for him to cause in us other virtues by means of infusion.

On the contrary, It is written (Wis. viii. 7): *She teacheth temperance and prudence and justice and fortitude.*

I answer that, Effects must needs be proportionate to their causes and principles. Now all virtues, intellectual and moral, that are acquired by our actions, arise from certain natural principles pre-existing in us, as above stated (A. 1; Q. 51, A. 1): instead of which natural principles, God bestows on us the theological virtues, whereby we are directed to a supernatural end, as stated (Q. 62, A. 1). Wherefore we need to receive from God other habits corresponding, in due proportion, to the theological virtues, which habits are to the theological virtues, what the moral and intellectual virtues are to the natural principles of virtue.

Reply Obj. 1. Some moral and intellectual virtues can indeed be caused in us by our actions: but such are not proportionate to the

* *Cf.* Jerome on Gal. i. 15, 16.

theological virtues. Therefore it was necessary for us to receive, from God immediately, others that are proportionate to these virtues.

Reply Obj. 2. The theological virtues direct us sufficiently to our supernatural end, inchoatively: i.e., to God Himself immediately. But the soul needs further to be perfected by infused virtues in regard to other things, yet in relation to God.

Reply Obj. 3. The power of those naturally instilled principles does not extend beyond the capacity of nature. Consequently man needs in addition to be perfected by other principles in relation to his supernatural end.

FOURTH ARTICLE

Whether Virtue Acquired by Habituation Belongs to the Same Species As Infused Virtue?

We proceed thus to the Fourth Article:—

Objection 1. It would seem that infused virtue does not differ in species from acquired virtue. Because acquired and infused virtues, according to what has been said (A. 3), do not differ seemingly, save in relation to the last end. Now human habits and acts are specified, not by their last, but by their proximate end. Therefore the infused moral or intellectual virtue does not differ from the acquired virtue.

Obj. 2. Further, habits are known by their acts. But the act of infused and acquired temperance is the same, viz., to moderate desires of touch. Therefore they do not differ in species.

Obj. 3. Further, acquired and infused virtue differ as that which is wrought by God immediately, from that which is wrought by a creature. But the man whom God made, is of the same species as a man begotten naturally; and the eye which He gave to the man born blind, as one produced by the power of generation. Therefore it seems that acquired and infused virtue belong to the same species.

On the contrary, Any change introduced into the difference expressed in a definition involves a difference of species. But the definition of infused virtue contains the words, *which God works in us without us,* as stated above (Q. 55, A. 4). Therefore acquired virtue, to which these words cannot apply, is not of the same species as infused virtue.

I answer that, There is a twofold specific difference among habits. The first, as stated above (Q. 54, A. 2; Q. 56, A. 2; Q. 60, A. 1), is taken from the specific and formal aspects of their objects. Now the object of every virtue is a good considered as in that virtue's proper matter: thus the object of temperance is a good in respect of the pleasures connected with the concupiscence of touch. The formal aspect of this object is from reason which fixes the mean in these concupiscences: while the material element is something on the part of the concupiscences. Now it is evident that the mean that is appointed in such like concupiscences according to the rule of human reason, is seen under a different aspect from the mean which is fixed according to the Divine rule. For instance, in the consumption of food, the mean fixed by human reason, is that food should not harm the health of the body, nor hinder the use of reason: whereas, according to the Divine rule, it behooves man to *chastise his body, and bring it into subjection* (1 Cor. ix. 27), by abstinence in food, drink and the like. It is therefore evident that infused and acquired temperance differ in species; and the same applies to the other virtues.

The other specific difference among habits is taken from the things to which they are directed: for a man's health and a horse's are not of the same species, on account of the difference between the natures to which their respective healths are directed. In the same sense, the Philosopher says (*Polit.* iii. 3) that citizens have diverse virtues according as they are well directed to diverse forms of government. In the same way, too, those infused moral virtues, whereby men behave well in respect of their being *fellow-citizens with the saints, and of the household* (Douay,—*domestics) of God* (Eph. ii. 19), differ from the acquired virtues, whereby man behaves well in respect of human affairs.

Reply Obj. 1. Infused and acquired virtue differ not only in relation to the ultimate end, but also in relation to their proper objects, as stated.

Reply Obj. 2. Both acquired and infused temperance moderate desires for pleasures of touch, but for different reasons, as stated: wherefore their respective acts are not identical.

Reply Obj. 3. God gave the man born blind an eye for the same act as the act for which other eyes are formed naturally: consequently it was of the same species. It would be the same if God wished to give a man miraculously virtues, such as those that are acquired by acts. But the case is not so in the question before us, as stated.

QUESTION 64

Of the Mean of Virtue

(In Four Articles)

WE must now consider the properties of virtues: and (1) the mean of virtue, (2) the connection between virtues, (3) equality of virtues, (4) the duration of virtues. Under the first head there are four points of inquiry: (1) Whether moral virtue observes the mean? (2) Whether the mean of moral virtue is the real mean or the rational mean? (3) Whether the intellectual virtues observe the mean? (4) Whether the theological virtues do?

FIRST ARTICLE

Whether Moral Virtues Observe the Mean?

We proceed thus to the First Article:—

Objection 1. It would seem that moral virtue does not observe the mean. For the nature of a mean is incompatible with that which is extreme. Now the nature of virtue is to be something extreme; for it is stated in *De Cælo* i. that *virtue is the limit of power.* Therefore moral virtue does not observe the mean.

Obj. 2. Further, the maximum is not a mean. Now some moral virtues tend to a maximum: for instance magnanimity to very great honors, and magnificence to very large expenditure, as stated in *Ethic.* iv. 2, 3. Therefore not every moral virtue observes the mean.

Obj. 3. Further, if it is essential to a moral virtue to observe the mean, it follows that a moral virtue is not perfected, but on the contrary corrupted, through tending to something extreme. Now some moral virtues are perfected by tending to something extreme; thus virginity, which abstains from all sexual pleasure, observes the extreme, and is the most perfect chastity: and to give all to the poor is the most perfect mercy or liberality. Therefore it seems that it is not essential to moral virtue that it should observe the mean.

On the contrary, The Philosopher says (*Ethic.* ii. 6) that *moral virtue is a habit of choosing the mean.*

I answer that, As already explained (Q. 55, A. 3), the nature of virtue is that it should direct man to good. Now moral virtue is properly a perfection of the appetitive part of the soul in regard to some determinate matter: and the measure or rule of the appetitive movement in respect of appetible objects is the reason. But the good of that which is measured or ruled consists in its conformity with its rule: thus the good of things made by art is that they follow the rule of art. Consequently, in things of this sort, evil consists in discordance from their rule or measure. Now this may happen either by their exceeding the measure or by their falling short of it; as is clearly the case in all things ruled or measured. Hence it is evident that the good of moral virtue consists in conformity with the rule of reason.—Now it is clear that between excess and deficiency the mean is equality or conformity. Therefore it is evident that moral virtue observes the mean.

Reply Obj. 1. Moral virtue derives goodness from the rule of reason, while its matter consists in passions or operations. If therefore we compare moral virtue to reason, then, if we look at that which it has of reason, it holds the position of one extreme, viz. conformity; while excess and defect take the position of the other extreme, viz., deformity. But if we consider moral virtue in respect of its matter, then it holds the position of mean, in so far as it makes the passion conform to the rule of reason. Hence the Philosopher says (*Ethic.* ii. 6) that *virtue, as to its essence, is a mean state,* in so far as the rule of virtue is imposed on its proper matter: *but it is an extreme in reference to the "best" and "the excellent,"* viz., as to its conformity with reason.

Reply Obj. 2. In actions and passions the mean and the extremes depend on various circumstances: hence nothing hinders something from being extreme in a particular virtue as to one circumstance, while the same thing is a mean in respect of other circumstances, through being in conformity with reason. This is the case with magnanimity and magnificence. For if we look at the absolute quantity of the respective objects of these virtues, we shall call it an extreme and a maximum: but if we consider the quantity in relation to other circumstances, then it has the character of a mean: since these virtues tend to this maximum in accordance with the rule of reason, i.e., *where* it is right, *when* it is right, and for an *end* that is right. There will be excess, if one tends to this maximum *when* it is not right, or *where* it is not right, or for an undue *end;* and there will be deficiency if one fails to tend thereto *where* one ought, and *when* one ought. This agrees with the saying of the Philosopher (*Ethic.* iv. 3) that the *magnanimous man observes the extreme in quantity, but the mean in the right mode of his action.*

Reply Obj. 3. The same is to be said of virginity and poverty as of magnanimity. For virginity abstains from all sexual matters, and poverty from all wealth, for a right end, and in a right manner, i.e., according to God's word, and for the sake of eternal life. But if this be done in an undue manner, i.e., out of unlawful superstition, or again for vainglory, it will be in excess. And if it be not done when it ought to be done, or as it ought to be done,

it is a vice by deficiency: for instance, in those who break their vows of virginity or poverty

SECOND ARTICLE

Whether the Mean of Moral Virtue Is the Real Mean, or the Rational Mean?

We proceed thus to the Second Article:—

Objection 1. It would seem that the mean of moral virtue is not the rational mean, but the real mean. For the good of moral virtue consists in its observing the mean. Now, good, as stated in *Metaph.* ii, text, 8, is in things themselves. Therefore the mean of moral virtue is a real mean.

Obj. 2. Further, the reason is a power of apprehension. But moral virtue does not observe a mean between apprehensions, but rather a mean between operations or passions. Therefore the mean of moral virtue is not the rational, but the real mean.

Obj. 3. Further, a mean that is observed according to arithmetical or geometrical proportion is a real mean. Now such is the mean of justice, as stated in *Ethic.* v. 3. Therefore the mean of moral virtue is not the rational, but the real mean.

On the contrary, The Philosopher says (*Ethic.* ii. 6) that *moral virtue observes the mean fixed, in our regard, by reason.*

I answer that, The rational mean can be understood in two ways. First, according as the mean is observed in the act itself of reason, as though the very act of reason were made to observe the mean: in this sense, since moral virtue perfects not the act of reason, but the act of the appetitive power, the mean of moral virtue is not the rational mean.— Secondly, the mean of reason may be considered as that which the reason puts into some particular matter. In this sense every mean of moral virtue is a rational mean, since, as above stated (A. 1), moral virtue is said to observe the mean, through conformity with right reason.

But it happens sometimes that the rational mean is also the real mean: in which case the mean of moral virtue is the real mean, for instance, in justice. On the other hand, sometimes the rational mean is not the real mean, but is considered in relation to us: and such is the mean in all the other moral virtues. The reason for this is that justice is about operations, which deal with external things, wherein the right has to be established simply and absolutely, as stated above (Q. 60, A. 2): wherefore the rational mean in justice is the same as the real mean, in so far, to wit, as justice gives to each one his due, neither more nor less. But the other moral virtues deal with interior passions, wherein the right cannot be established in the same way, since men are variously situated in relation to their passions; hence the rectitude of reason has to be established in the passions, with due regard to us, who are moved in respect of the passions.

This suffices for the Replies to the Objections. For the first two arguments take the rational mean as being in the very act of reason, while the third argues from the mean of justice.

THIRD ARTICLE

Whether the Intellectual Virtues Observe the Mean?

We proceed thus to the Third Article:—

Objection 1. It would seem that the intellectual virtues do not observe the mean. Because moral virtue observes the mean by conforming to the rule of reason. But the intellectual virtues are in reason itself, so that they seem to have no higher rule. Therefore the intellectual virtues do not observe the mean.

Obj. 2. Further, the mean of moral virtue is fixed by an intellectual virtue: for it is stated in *Ethic.* ii. 6, that *virtue observes the mean appointed by reason, as a prudent man would appoint it.* If therefore intellectual virtues also observe the mean, this mean will have to be appointed for them by another virtue, so that there would be an indefinite series of virtues.

Obj. 3. Further, a mean is, properly speaking, between contraries, as the Philosopher explains (*Metaph.* x, text, 22, 23). But there seems to be no contrariety in the intellect; since contraries themselves, as they are in the intellect, are not in opposition to one another, but are understood together, as white and black, healthy and sick. Therefore there is no mean in the intellectual virtues.

On the contrary, Art is an intellectual virtue; and yet there is a mean in art (*Ethic.* ii 6). Therefore also intellectual virtue observes the mean.

I answer that, The good of anything consists in its observing the mean, by conforming with a rule or measure in respect of which it may happen to be excessive or deficient, as stated above (A. 1). Now intellectual virtue, like moral virtue, is directed to the good, as stated above (Q. 56, A. 3). Hence the good of an intellectual virtue consists in observing the mean, in so far as it is subject to a measure. Now the good of intellectual virtue is the true; in the case of contemplative virtue, it is the true taken absolutely (*Ethic.* vi. 2); in the case of practical virtue, it is the true in conformity with a right appetite.

Now truth apprehended by our intellect, if we consider it absolutely, is measured by things; since things are the measure of our intellect, as stated in *Metaph.* x, text, 5; because there is truth in what we think or say,

according as the thing is so or not. Accordingly the good of speculative intellectual virtue consists in a certain mean, by way of conformity with things themselves, in so far as the intellect expresses them as being what they are, or as not being what they are not: and it is in this that the nature of truth consists. There will be excess if something false is affirmed, as though something were, which in reality is not: and there will be deficiency if something is falsely denied, and declared not to be, whereas in reality it is.

The truth of practical intellectual virtue, if we consider it in relation to things, is by way of that which is measured; so that both in practical and in speculative intellectual virtues, the mean consists in conformity with things.—But if we consider it in relation to the appetite, it has the character of a rule and measure. Consequently the rectitude of reason is the mean of moral virtue, and also the mean of prudence,—of prudence as ruling and measuring, of moral virtue, as ruled and measured by that mean. In like manner the difference between excess and deficiency is to be applied in both cases.

Reply Obj. 1. Intellectual virtues also have their measure, as stated, and they observe the mean according as they conform to that measure.

Reply Obj. 2. There is no need for an indefinite series of virtues: because the measure and rule of intellectual virtue is not another kind of virtue, but things themselves.

Reply Obj. 3. The things themselves that are contrary have no contrariety in the mind, because one is the reason for knowing the other: nevertheless there is in the intellect contrariety of affirmation and negation, which are contraries, as stated at the end of *Peri Hermenias.* For though *to be* and *not to be* are not in contrary, but in contradictory opposition to one another, so long as we consider their signification in things themselves, for on the one hand we have *being* and on the other other we have simply *non-being;* yet if we refer them to the act of the mind, there is something positive in both cases. Hence *to be* and *not to be* are contradictory: but the opinion stating that *good is good* is contrary to the opinion stating that *good is not good:* and between two such contraries intellectual virtue observes the mean.

FOURTH ARTICLE

Whether the Theological Virtues Observe the Mean?

We proceed thus to the Fourth Article:—

Objection 1. It would seem that theological virtue observes the mean. For the good of other virtues consists in their observing the mean. Now the theological virtues surpass the others in goodness. Therefore much more does theological virtue observe the mean.

Obj. 2. Further, the mean of moral virtue depends on the appetite being ruled by reason; while the mean of intellectual virtue consists in the intellect being measured by things. Now theological virtue perfects both intellect and appetite, as stated above (Q. 62, A. 3). Therefore theological virtue also observes the mean.

Obj. 3. Further, hope, which is a theological virtue, is a mean between despair and presumption. Likewise faith holds a middle course between contrary heresies, as Boëthius states (*De Duab. Natur.* vii): thus, by confessing one Person and two natures in Christ, we observe the mean between the heresy of Nestorius, who maintained the existence of two persons and two natures, and the heresy of Eutyches, who held to one person and one nature. Therefore theological virtue observes the mean.

On the contrary, Wherever virtue observes the mean it is possible to sin by excess as well as by deficiency. But there is no sinning by excess against God, Who is the object of theological virtue: for it is written (*Ecclus.* xliii. 33): *Blessing the Lord, exalt Him as much as you can: for He is above all praise.* Therefore theological virtue does not observe the mean.

I answer that, As stated above (A. 1), the mean of virtue depends on conformity with virtue's rule or measure, in so far as one may exceed or fall short of that rule. Now the measure of theological virtue may be twofold. One is taken from the very nature of virtue, and thus the measure and rule of theological virtue is God Himself: because our faith is ruled according to Divine truth; charity, according to His goodness; hope, according to the immensity of His omnipotence and loving kindness. This measure surpasses all human power: so that never can we love God as much as He ought to be loved, nor believe and hope in Him as much as we should. Much less therefore can there be excess in such things. Accordingly the good of such virtues does not consist in a mean, but increases the more we approach to the summit.

The other rule or measure of theological virtue is by comparison with us: for although we cannot be borne towards God as much as we ought, yet we should approach to Him by believing, hoping and loving, according to the measure of our condition. Consequently it is possible to find a mean and extremes in theological virtue, accidentally and in reference to us.

Reply Obj. 1. The good of intellectual and moral virtues consists in a mean by reason of conformity with a measure that may be exceeded: whereas this is not so in the case of theological virtue, considered in itself, as stated above.

Reply Obj. 2. Moral and intellectual virtues perfect our intellect and appetite in relation to a created measure and rule; whereas the theological virtues perfect them in relation to an uncreated rule and measure. Wherefore the comparison fails.

Reply Obj. 3. Hope observes the mean between presumption and despair, in relation to us, in so far, to wit, as a man is said to be presumptuous, through hoping to receive from God a good in excess of his condition; or to despair through failing to hope for that which according to his condition he might hope for. But there can be no excess of hope in comparison with God, Whose goodness is infinite.—In like manner faith holds a middle course between contrary heresies, not by comparison with its object, which is God, in Whom we cannot believe too much; but in so far as human opinion itself takes a middle position between contrary opinions, as was explained above.

QUESTION 65

Of the Connection of Virtues

(In Five Articles)

WE must now consider the connection of virtues: under which head there are five points of inquiry: (1) Whether the moral virtues are connected with one another? (2) Whether the moral virtues can be without charity? (3) Whether charity can be without them? (4) Whether faith and hope can be without charity? (5) Whether charity can be without them?

FIRST ARTICLE

Whether the Moral Virtues Are Connected with One Another?

We proceed thus to the First Article:—

Objection 1. It would seem that the moral virtues are not connected with one another. Because moral virtues are sometimes caused by the exercise of acts, as is proved in

Ethic. ii. 1, 2. But man can exercise himself in the acts of one virtue, without exercising himself in the acts of some other virtue. Therefore it is possible to have one moral virtue without another.

Obj. 2. Further, Magnificence and magnanimity are moral virtues. Now a man may have other moral virtues without having magnificence or magnanimity: for the Philosopher says (*Ethic.* iv. 2, 3) that *a poor man cannot be magnificent,* and yet he may have other virtues; and (*ibid.*) that *he who is worthy of small things, and so accounts his worth, is modest, but not magnanimous.* Therefore the moral virtues are not connected with one another.

Obj. 3. Further, as the moral virtues perfect the appetitive part of the soul, so do the intellectual virtues perfect the intellective part. But the intellectual virtues are not mutually connected: since we may have one science, without having another. Neither, therefore, are the moral virtues connected with one another.

Obj. 4. Further, if the moral virtues are mutually connected, this can only be because they are united together in prudence. But this does not suffice to connect the moral virtues together. For, seemingly, one may be prudent about things to be done in relation to one virtue, without being prudent in those that concern another virtue: even as one may have the art of making certain things, without the art of making certain others. Now prudence is right reason about things to be done. Therefore the moral virtues are not necessarily connected with one another.

On the contrary, Ambrose says on Luke vi. 20: *The virtues are connected and linked together, so that whoever has one, is seen to have several:* and Augustine says (*De Trin.* vi. 4) that *the virtues that reside in the human mind are quite inseparable from one another:* and Gregory says (*Moral. xxii.* 1) that *one virtue without the other is either of no account whatever, or very imperfect:* and Cicero says (*Quæst. Tusc.* ii): *If you confess to not having one particular virtue, it must needs be that you have none at all.*

I answer that, Moral virtue may be considered either as perfect or as imperfect. An imperfect moral virtue, temperance for instance, or fortitude, is nothing but an inclination in us to do some kind of good deed, whether such inclination be in us by nature or by habituation. If we take the moral virtues in this way, they are not connected: since we find men who, by natural temperament or by being accustomed, are prompt in doing deeds of liberality, but are not prompt in doing deeds of chastity.

But the perfect moral virtue is a habit that inclines us to do a good deed well; and if we take moral virtues in this way, we must say that they are connected, as nearly all are agreed in saying. For this two reasons are given, corresponding to the different ways of assigning the distinction of the cardinal virtues. For, as we stated above (Q. 61, AA. 3, 4), some distinguish them according to certain general properties of the virtues: for instance, by saying that discretion belongs to prudence, rectitude to justice, moderation to temperance, and strength of mind to fortitude, in whatever matter we consider these properties to be. In this way the reason for the connection is evident: for strength of mind is not commended as virtuous, if it be without moderation or rectitude or discretion: and so forth. This, too, is the reason assigned for the connection by Gregory, who says (*Moral.* xxii. 1) that *a virtue cannot be perfect* as a virtue, *if isolated from the others:* for *there can be no true prudence without temperance, justice and fortitude:* and he continues to speak in like manner of the other virtues (*cf.* Q. 61, A. 4, Obj. 1). Augustine also gives the same reason (*De Trin.* vi. 4).

Others, however, differentiate these virtues in respect of their matters, and it is in this way that Aristotle assigns the reason for their connection (*Ethic.* vi. 13). Because, as stated above (Q. 58, A. 4), no moral virtue can be without prudence; since it is proper to moral virtue to make a right choice, for it is an elective habit. Now right choice requires not only the inclination to a due end, which inclination is the direct outcome of moral virtue, but also correct choice of things conducive to the end, which choice is made by prudence, that counsels, judges, and commands in those things that are directed to the end. In like manner one cannot have prudence unless one has the moral virtues: since prudence is *right reason about things to be done,* and the starting-point of reason is the end of the thing to be done, to which end man is rightly disposed by moral virtue. Hence, just as we cannot have speculative science unless we have the understanding of the principles, so neither can we have prudence without the moral virtues: and from this it follows clearly that the moral virtues are connected with one another.

Reply Obj. 1. Some moral virtues perfect man as regards his general state, in other words, with regard to those things which have to be done in every kind of human life. Hence man needs to exercise himself at the same time in the matters of all moral virtues. And if he exercise himself, by good deeds, in all such matters, he will acquire the habits of all the moral virtues. But if he exercise himself by good deeds in regard to one matter, but not in regard to another, for instance, by behaving well in matters of anger, but not in matters of concupiscence; he will indeed acquire a certain habit of restraining his anger; but this habit will lack the nature of virtue, through the absence of prudence, which is wanting in matters of concupiscence. In the same way, natural inclinations fail to have the complete character of virtue, if prudence be lacking.

But there are some moral virtues which perfect man with regard to some eminent state, such as magnificence and magnanimity; and since it does not happen to all in common to be exercised in the matter of such virtues, it is possible for a man to have the other moral virtues, without actually having the habits of these virtues,—provided we speak of acquired virtue. Nevertheless, when once a man has acquired those other virtues he possesses these in proximate potentiality. Because when, by practice, a man has acquired liberality in small gifts and expenditure, if he were to come in for a large sum of money, he would acquire the habit of magnificence with but little practice: even as a geometrician, by dint of little study, acquires scientific knowledge about some conclusion which had never been presented to his mind before. Now we speak of having a thing when we are on the point of having it, according to the saying of the Philosopher (*Phys.* ii, text, 56): *That which is scarcely lacking is not lacking at all.* This suffices for the Reply to the Second Objection.

Reply Obj. 3. The intellectual virtues are about divers matters having no relation to one another, as is clearly the case with the various sciences and arts. Hence we do not observe in them the connection that is to be found among the moral virtues, which are about passions and operations, that are clearly related to one another. For all the passions have their rise in certain initial passions, viz., love and hatred, and terminate in certain others, viz., pleasure and sorrow. In like manner all the operations that are the matter of moral virtue are related to one another, and to the passions. Hence the whole matter of moral virtues falls under the one rule of prudence.

Nevertheless, all intelligible things are related to first principles. And in this way, all the intellectual virtues depend on the understanding of principles; even as prudence depends on the moral virtues, as stated. On the other hand, the universal principles which are the object of the virtue of understanding of principles, do not depend on the conclusions, which are the objects of the other intellectual virtues, as do the moral virtues depend on pru-

dence, because the appetite, in a fashion, moves the reason, and the reason the appetite, as stated above (Q. 9, A. 1; Q. 58, A. 5 *ad* 1).

Reply Obj. 4. Those things to which the moral virtues incline, are as the principles of prudence: whereas the products of art are not the principles, but the matter of art. Now it is evident that, though reason may be right in one part of the matter, and not in another, yet in no way can it be called right reason, if it be deficient in any principle whatever. Thus, if a man be wrong about the principle, *A whole is greater than its part,* he cannot acquire the science of geometry, because he must necessarily wander from the truth in his conclusion.—Moreover, things *done* are related to one another, but not things *made,* as stated above (*ad* 3). Consequently the lack of prudence in one department of things to be done, would result in a deficiency affecting other things to be done: whereas this does not occur in things to be made.

SECOND ARTICLE

Whether Moral Virtues Can Be Without Charity?

We proceed thus to the Second Article:—

Objection 1. It would seem that moral virtue can be without charity. For it is stated in the *Liber Sentent. Prosperi* vii, that *every virtue save charity may be common to the good and bad.* But *charity can be in none except the good,* as stated in the same book. Therefore the other virtues can be had without charity.

Obj. 2. Further, moral virtues can be acquired by means of human acts, as stated in *Ethic.* ii. 1, 2, whereas charity cannot be had otherwise than by infusion, according to Rom. v. 5: *The charity of God is poured forth in our hearts by the Holy Ghost Who is given to us.* Therefore it is possible to have the other virtues without charity.

Obj. 3. Further, the moral virtues are connected together, through depending on prudence. But charity does not depend on prudence; indeed, it surpasses prudence, according to Eph. iii. 19: *The charity of Christ, which surpasseth all knowledge.* Therefore the moral virtues are not connected with charity, and can be without it.

On the contrary, It is written (1 Jo. iii. 14): *He that loveth not, abideth in death.* Now the spiritual life is perfected by the virtues, since it is *by them* that *we lead a good life,* as Augustine states (*De Lib. Arb.* ii. 17, 19). Therefore they cannot be without the love of charity.

I answer that, As stated above (Q. 63, A. 2), it is possible by means of human works to acquire moral virtues, in so far as they produce good works that are directed to an end not surpassing the natural power of man: and when they are acquired thus, they can be without charity, even as they were in many of the Gentiles.—But in so far as they produce good works in proportion to a supernatural last end, thus they have the character of virtue, truly and perfectly; and cannot be acquired by human acts, but are infused by God. Such like moral virtues cannot be without charity. For it has been stated above (A. 1; Q. 58, AA. 4, 5) that the other moral virtues cannot be without prudence; and that prudence cannot be without' the moral virtues, because these latter make man well disposed to certain ends, which are the starting-point of the procedure of prudence. Now for prudence to proceed aright, it is much more necessary that man be well disposed towards his ultimate end, which is the effect of charity, than that he be well disposed in respect of other ends, which is the effect of moral virtue: just as in speculative matters right reason has greatest need of the first indemonstrable principle, that *contradictories cannot both be true at the same time.* It is therefore evident that neither can infused prudence be without charity; nor, consequently, the other moral virtues, since they cannot be without prudence.

It is therefore clear from what has been said that only the infused virtues are perfect, and deserve to be called virtues simply: since they direct man well to the ultimate end. But the other virtues, those, namely, that are acquired, are virtues in a restricted sense, but not simply: for they direct man well in respect of the last end in some particular genus of action, but not in respect of the last end simply. Hence a gloss of Augustine* on the words, *All that is not of faith is sin* (Rom. xiv. 23), says: *He that fails to acknowledge the truth, has no true virtue, even if his conduct be good.*

Reply Obj. 1. Virtue, in the words quoted, denotes imperfect virtue. Else if we take moral virtue in its perfect state, *it makes its possessor good,* and consequently cannot be in the wicked.

Reply Obj. 2. This argument holds good of virtue in the sense of acquired virtue.

Reply Obj. 3. Though charity surpasses science and prudence, yet prudence depends on charity, as stated: and consequently so do all the infused moral virtues.

THIRD ARTICLE

Whether Charity Can Be without Moral Virtue?

We proceed thus to the Third Article:—

Objection 1. It would seem possible to have charity without the moral virtues. For when

* Cf. Lib. Sentent. Prosperi cvi.

one thing suffices for a certain purpose, it is superfluous to employ others. Now charity alone suffices for the fulfilment of all the works of virtue, as is clear from 1 Cor. xiii. 4, *seqq.*: *Charity is patient, is kind,* etc. Therefore it seems that if one has charity, other virtues are superfluous.

Obj. 2. Further, he that has a habit of virtue easily performs the works of that virtue, and those works are pleasing to him for their own sake: hence *pleasure taken in a work is a sign of habit (Ethic.* ii. 3). Now many have charity, being free from mortal sin, and yet they find it difficult to do works of virtue; nor are these works pleasing to them for their own sake, but only for the sake of charity. Therefore many have charity without the other virtues.

Obj. 3. Further, charity is to be found in every saint: and yet there are some saints who are without certain virtues. For Bede says (on Luke xvii. 10) that the saints are more humbled on account of their not having certain virtues, than rejoiced at the virtues they have. Therefore, if a man has charity, it does not follow of necessity that he has all the moral virtues.

On the contrary, The whole Law is fulfilled through charity, for it is written (Rom. xiii. 8): *He that loveth his neighbor, hath fulfilled the Law.* Now it is not possible to fulfil the whole Law, without having all the moral virtues: since the law contains precepts about all acts of virtue, as stated in *Ethic.* v. 1, 2. Therefore he that has charity, has all the moral virtues. Moreover, Augustine says in a letter (*Epist.* clxvii),† that charity contains all the cardinal virtues.

I answer that, All the moral virtues are infused together with charity. The reason for this is that God operates no less perfectly in works of grace than in works of nature. Now, in the works of nature, we find that whenever a thing contains a principle of certain works, it has also whatever is necessary for their execution: thus animals are provided with organs whereby to perform the actions that their souls empower them to do. Now it is evident that charity, inasmuch as it directs man to his last end, is the principle of all the good works that are referable to his last end. Wherefore all the moral virtues must needs be infused together with charity, since it is through them that man performs each different kind of good work.

It is therefore clear that the infused moral virtues are connected, not only through prudence, but also on account of charity: and, again, that whoever loses charity through

† Cf. Serm. xxxix. and xlvi. de Temp.

mortal sin, forfeits all the infused moral virtues.

Reply Obj. 1. In order that the act of a lower power be perfect, not only must there be perfection in the higher, but also in the lower power: for if the principal agent were well disposed, perfect action would not follow, if the instrument also were not well disposed. Consequently, in order that man work well in things referred to the end, he needs not only a virtue disposing him well to the end, but also those virtues which dispose him well to whatever is referred to the end: for the virtue which regards the end is the chief and moving principle in respect of those things that are referred to the end. Therefore it is necessary to have the moral virtues together with charity.

Reply Obj. 2. It happens sometimes that a man who has a habit, finds it difficult to act in accordance with the habit, and consequently feels no pleasure and complacency in the act, on account of some impediment supervening from without: thus a man who has a habit of science, finds it difficult to understand, through being sleepy or unwell. In like manner sometimes the habits of moral virtue experience difficulty in their works, by reason of certain contrary dispositions remaining from previous acts. This difficulty does not occur in respect of acquired moral virtue: because the repeated acts by which they are acquired, remove also the contrary dispositions.

Reply Obj. 3. Certain saints are said not to have certain virtues, in so far as they experience difficulty in the acts of those virtues, for the reason stated; although they have the habits of all the virtues.

FOURTH ARTICLE

Whether Faith and Hope Can Be without Charity?

We proceed thus to the Fourth Article:—

Objection 1. It would seem that faith and hope are never without charity. Because, since they are theological virtues, they seem to be more excellent than even the infused moral virtues. But the infused moral virtues cannot be without charity. Neither therefore can faith and hope be without charity.

Obj. 2. Further, *no man believes unwillingly* as Augustine says (*Tract.* xxvi. *in Joan.*). But charity is in the will as a perfection thereof, as stated above (Q. 62, A. 3). Therefore faith cannot be without charity.

Obj. 3. Further, Augustine says (*Enchiridion* viii) that *there can be no hope without love.* But love is charity: for it is of this love

that he speaks. Therefore hope cannot be without charity.

On the contrary, A gloss on Matth. i, 2 says that *faith begets hope, and hope, charity.* Now the begetter precedes the begotten, and can be without it. Therefore faith can be without hope; and hope, without charity.

I answer that, Faith and hope, like the moral virtues, can be considered in two ways; first in an inchoate state; secondly, as complete virtues. For since virtue is directed to the doing of good works, perfect virtue is that which gives the faculty of doing a perfectly good work, and this consists in not only doing what is good, but also in doing it well. Else, if what is done is good, but not well done, it will not be perfectly good; wherefore neither will the habit that is the principle of such an act, have the perfect character of virtue. For instance, if a man do what is just, what he does is good: but it will not be the work of a perfect virtue unless he do it well, i.e., by choosing rightly, which is the result of prudence; for which reason justice cannot be a perfect virtue without prudence.

Accordingly faith and hope can exist indeed in a fashion without charity: but they have not the perfect character of virtue without charity. For, since the act of faith is to believe in God; and since to believe is to assent to someone of one's own free will: to will not as one ought, will not be a perfect act of faith. To will as one ought is the outcome of charity which perfects the will: since every right movement of the will proceeds from a right love, as Augustine says (*De Civ. Dei* xiv. 9). Hence faith may be without charity, but not as a perfect virtue: just as temperance and fortitude can be without prudence. The same applies to hope. Because the act of hope consists in looking to God for future bliss. This act is perfect, if it is based on the merits which we have; and this cannot be without charity. But to expect future bliss through merits which one has not yet, but which one proposes to acquire at some future time, will be an imperfect act; and this is possible without charity. Consequently, faith and hope can be without charity; yet, without charity, they are not virtues properly so-called; because the nature of virtue requires that by it, we should not only do what is good, but also that we should do it well (*Ethic.* ii. 6).

Reply Obj. 1. Moral virtue depends on prudence: and not even infused prudence has the character of prudence without charity; for this involves the absence of due order to the first principle, viz., the ultimate end. On the other hand faith and hope, as such, do not depend either on prudence or charity; so that they can be without charity, although they are not virtues without charity, as stated.

Reply Obj. 2. This argument is true of faith considered as a perfect virtue.

Reply Obj. 3. Augustine is speaking here of that hope whereby we look to gain future bliss through merits which we have already; and this is not without charity.

FIFTH ARTICLE

Whether Charity Can Be without Faith and Hope?

We proceed thus to the Fifth Article:—

Objection 1. It would seem that charity can be without faith and hope. For charity is the love of God. But it is possible for us to love God naturally, without already having faith, or hope in future bliss. Therefore charity can be without faith and hope.

Obj. 2. Further, charity is the root of all the virtues, according to Ephes. iii. 17: *Rooted and founded in charity.* Now the root is sometimes without branches. Therefore charity can sometimes be without faith and hope, and the other virtues.

Obj. 3. Further, there was perfect charity in Christ. And yet He had neither faith nor hope: because He was a perfect comprehensor, as we shall explain further on (P. III, Q. 7, AA. 3, 4). Therefore charity can be without faith and hope.

On the contrary, The Apostle says (Heb. xi. 6): *Without faith it is impossible to please God;* and this evidently belongs most to charity, according to Prov. viii. 17: *I love them that love me.* Again, it is by hope that we are brought to charity, as stated above (Q. 62, A. 4). Therefore it is not possible to have charity without faith and hope.

I answer that, Charity signifies not only the love of God, but also a certain friendship with Him; which implies, besides love, a certain mutual return of love, together with mutual communion, as stated in *Ethic.* viii. 2. That this belongs to charity is evident from 1 Jo. iv. 16: *He that abideth in charity, abideth in God, and God in him,* and from 1 Cor. 1, 9, where it is written: *God is faithful, by Whom you are called unto the fellowship of His Son.* Now this fellowship of man with God, which consists in a certain familiar colloquy with Him, is begun here, in this life, by grace, but will be perfected in the future life, by glory; each of which things we hold by faith and hope. Wherefore just as friendship with a person would be impossible, if one disbelieved in, or despaired of, the possibility of their fellowship or familiar colloquy; so too, friendship with God, which is charity, is impossible without faith, so as to believe in this fellowship and colloquy with God, and to hope to attain to this fellowship. Therefore charity is quite impossible without faith and hope.

Reply Obj. 1. Charity is not any kind of love of God, but that love of God, by which He is loved as the object of bliss, to which object we are directed by faith and hope.

Reply Obj. 2. Charity is the root of faith and hope, in so far as it gives them the perfection of virtue. But faith and hope as such are the precursors of charity, as stated above (Q. 62, A. 4), and so charity is impossible without them.

Reply Obj. 3. In Christ there was neither faith nor hope, on account of their implying an imperfection. But instead of faith, He had manifest vision, and instead of hope, full comprehension*: so that in Him was perfect charity.

QUESTION 66

Of Equality among the Virtues

(In Six Articles)

WE must now consider equality among the virtues: under which head there are six points of inquiry: (1) Whether one virtue can be greater or less than another? (2) Whether all the virtues existing together in one subject are equal? (3) Of moral virtue in comparison with intellectual virtue; (4) Of the moral virtues as compared with one another; (5) Of the intellectual virtues in comparison with one another; (6) Of the theological virtues in comparison with one another.

* See above, Q. 4, A. 3.

FIRST ARTICLE

Whether One Virtue Can Be Greater or Less Than Another?

We proceed thus to the First Article:—

Objection 1. It would seem that one virtue cannot be greater or less than another. For it is written (Apoc. xxi. 16) that the sides of the city of Jerusalem are equal; and a gloss says that the sides denote the virtues. Therefore all virtues are equal; and consequently one cannot be greater than another.

Obj. 2. Further, a thing that, by its nature, consists in a maximum, cannot be more or less. Now the nature of virtue consists in a maximum, for virtue is *the limit of power,* as the Philosopher states (*De Cælo* i., text. 116); and Augustine says (*De Lib. Arb.* ii. 19) that *virtues are very great boons, and no one can use them to evil purpose.* Therefore it seems that one virtue cannot be greater or less than another.

Obj. 3. Further, the quantity of an effect is measured by the power of the agent. But perfect, viz. infused virtues, are from God Whose power is uniform and infinite. Therefore it seems that one virtue cannot be greater than another.

On the contrary, Wherever there can be increase and greater abundance, there can be inequality. Now virtues admit of greater abundance and increase: for it is written (Matth. v. 20): *Unless your justice abound more than that of the Scribes and Pharisees, you shall not enter into the kingdom of heaven:* and (Prov. xv. 5): *In abundant justice there is the greatest strength (virtus).* Therefore it seems that a virtue can be greater or less than another.

I answer that, When it is asked whether one virtue can be greater than another, the question can be taken in two senses. First, as applying to virtues of different species. In this sense it is clear that one virtue is greater than another; since a cause is always more excellent than its effect; and among effects, those nearest to the cause are the most excellent. Now it is clear from what has been said (Q. 18, A. 5; Q. 61, A. 2) that the cause and root of human good is the reason. Hence prudence which perfects the reason, surpasses in goodness the other moral virtues which perfect the appetitive power, in so far as it partakes of reason. And among these, one is better than another, according as it approaches nearer to the reason. Consequently justice, which is in the will, excels the remaining moral virtues; and fortitude, which is in the irascible part, stands before temperance, which is in the concupiscible, which has a smaller share of reason, as stated in *Ethic.* vii. 6.

The question can be taken in another way, as referring to virtues of the same species. In this way, according to what was said above (Q. 52, A. 1), when we were treating of the intensity of habits, virtue may be said to be greater or less in two ways: first, in itself; secondly with regard to the subject that partakes of it. If we consider it in itself, we shall call it great or little, according to the things to which it extends. Now whoever has a virtue, e.g., temperance, has it in respect of whatever temperance extends to. But this does not

apply to science and art: for every grammarian does not know everything relating to grammar. And in this sense the Stoics said rightly, as Simplicius states in his *Commentary on the Predicaments,* that virtue cannot be more or less, as science and art can; because the nature of virtue consists in a maximum.

If, however, we consider virtue on the part of the subject, it may then be greater or less, either in relation to different times, or in different men. Because one man is better disposed than another to attain to the mean of virtue which is defined by right reason; and this, on account of either greater habituation, or a better natural disposition, or a more discerning judgment of reason, or again a greater gift of grace, which is given to each one *according to the measure of the giving of Christ,* as stated in Ephes. iv. 9.—And here the Stoics erred, for they held that no man should be deemed virtuous, unless he were, in the highest degree, disposed to virtue. Because the nature of virtue does not require that man should reach the mean of right reason as though it were an indivisible point, as the Stoics thought; but it is enough that he should approach the mean, as stated in *Ethic.* ii. 6. Moreover, one same indivisible mark is reached more nearly and more readily by one than by another: as may be seen when several archers aim at a fixed target.

Reply Obj. 1. This equality is not one of absolute quantity, but of proportion: because all virtues grow in a man proportionately, as we shall see further on (A. 2).

Reply Obj. 2. This *limit* which belongs to virtue, can have the character of something *more or less* good, in the ways explained above: since, as stated, it is not an indivisible limit.

Reply Obj. 3. God does not work by necessity of nature, but according to the order of His wisdom, whereby He bestows on men various measures of virtue, according to Ephes. iv. 7: *To every one of you* (Vulg., *us*) *is given grace according to the measure of the giving of Christ.*

SECOND ARTICLE

Whether All the Virtues That Are Together in One Man, Are Equal?

We proceed thus to the Second Article:—

Objection 1. It would seem that the virtues in one same man are not all equally intense. For the Apostle says (1 Cor. vii. 7): *Everyone hath his proper gift from God; one after this manner, and another after that.* Now one gift would not be more proper than another to a man, if God infused all the virtues equally into each man. Therefore it seems that the virtues are not all equal in one and the same man.

Obj. 2. Further, if all the virtues were equally intense in one and the same man, it would follow that whoever surpasses another in one virtue, would surpass him in all the others. But this is clearly not the case: since various saints are specially praised for different virtues; e.g., Abraham for faith (Rom. iv.), Moses for his meekness (Num. vii. 3), Job for his patience (Tob. ii. 12). This is why of each Confessor the Church sings:*There was not found his like in keeping the law of the most High,** since each one was remarkable for some virtue or other. Therefore the virtues are not all equal in one and the same man.

Obj. 3. Further, the more intense a habit is, the greater one's pleasure and readiness in making use of it. Now experience shows that a man is more pleased and ready to make use of one virtue than of another. Therefore the virtues are not all equal in one and the same man.

On the contrary, Augustine says (*De Trin.* vi. 4) that *those who are equal in fortitude are equal in prudence and temperance,* and so on. Now it would not be so, unless all the virtues in one man were equal. Therefore all virtues are equal in one man.

I answer that, As explained above (A. 1), the comparative greatness of virtues can be understood in two ways. First, as referring to their specific nature: and in this way there is no doubt that in a man one virtue is greater than another, for example, charity, than faith and hope.—Secondly, it may be taken as referring to the degree of participation by the subject, according as a virtue becomes intense or remiss in its subject. In this sense all the virtues in one man are equal with an equality of proportion, in so far as their growth in man is equal: thus the fingers are unequal in size, but equal in proportion, since they grow in proportion to one another.

Now the nature of this equality is to be explained in the same way as the connection of virtues; for equality among virtues is their connection as to greatness. Now it has been stated above (Q. 65, A. 1) that a twofold connection of virtues may be assigned. The first is according to the opinion of those who understood these four virtues to be four general properties of virtues, each of which is found together with the other in any matter. In this way virtues cannot be said to be equal in any matter unless they have all these properties equal. Augustine alludes to this kind of equality (*De Trin.* vi. 4) when he says: *If you say these men are equal in fortitude, but that one is more prudent than the other; it follows*

that the fortitude of the latter is less prudent. Consequently they are not really equal in fortitude, since the former's fortitude is more prudent. You will find that this applies to the other virtues if you run over them all in the same way.

The other kind of connection among virtues followed the opinion of those who hold these virtues to have their own proper respective matters (Q. 65, AA. 1, 2). In this way the connection among moral virtues results from prudence, and, as to the infused virtues, from charity, and not from the inclination, which is on the part of the subject, as stated above (Q. 65, A. 1). Accordingly the nature of the equality among virtues can also be considered on the part of prudence, in regard to that which is formal in all the moral virtues: for in one and the same man, so long as his reason has the same degree of perfection, the mean will be proportionately defined according to right reason in each matter of virtue.

But in regard to that which is material in the moral virtues, viz. the inclination to the virtuous act, one may be readier to perform the act of one virtue, than the act of another virtue, and this either from nature, or from habituation, or again by the grace of God.

Reply Obj. 1. This saying of the Apostle may be taken to refer to the gifts of gratuitous grace, which are not common to all, nor are all of them equal in the one same subject. —We might also say that it refers to the measure of sanctifying grace, by reason of which one man has all the virtues in greater abundance than another man, on account of his greater abundance of prudence, or also of charity, in which all the infused virtues are connected.

Reply Obj. 2. One saint is praised chiefly for one virtue, another saint for another virtue, on account of his more admirable readiness for the act of one virtue than for the act of another virtue.

This suffices for the Reply to the Third Objection.

THIRD ARTICLE

Whether the Moral Virtues Are Better Than the Intellectual Virtues?

We proceed thus to the Third Article:—

Objection 1. It would seem that the moral virtues are better than the intellectual. Because that which is more necessary, and more lasting, is better. Now the moral virtues are *more lasting even than the sciences* (*Ethic.* i) which are intellectual virtues: and, moreover, they are more necessary for human life. Therefore they are preferable to the intellectual virtues.

* See *Lesson* in the Mass *Statuit* (Dominican Missal).

Obj. 2. Further, virtue is defined as *that which makes its possessor good.* Now man is said to be good in respect of moral virtue, and art in respect of intellectual virtue, except perhaps in respect of prudence alone. Therefore moral is better than intellectual virtue.

Obj. 3. Further, the end is more excellent than the means. But according to *Ethic.* vi. 12, *moral virtue gives right intention of the end; whereas prudence gives right choice of the means.* Therefore moral virtue is more excellent than prudence, which is the intellectual virtue that regards moral matters.

On the contrary, Moral virtue is in that part of the soul which is rational by participation; while intellectual virtue is in the essentially rational part, as stated in *Ethic.* i. 13. Now rational by essence is more excellent than rational by participation. Therefore intellectual virtue is better than moral virtue.

I answer that, A thing may be said to be greater or less in two ways: first, simply; secondly, relatively. For nothing hinders something from being better simply, e.g., *learning than riches,* and yet not better relatively, i.e.. *for one who is in want.** Now to consider a thing simply is to consider it in its proper specific nature. Accordingly, a virtue takes its species from its object, as explained above (Q. 54, A. 2; Q. 60, A. 1). Hence, speaking simply, that virtue is more excellent, which has the more excellent object. Now it is evident that the object of the reason is more excellent than the object of the appetite: since the reason apprehends things in the universal, while the appetite tends to things themselves, whose being is restricted to the particular. Consequently, speaking simply, the intellectual virtues, which perfect the reason, are more excellent than the moral virtues, which perfect the appetite.

But if we consider virtue in its relation to act, then moral virtue, which perfects the appetite, whose function it is to move the other powers to act, as stated above (Q. 9, A. 1), is more excellent.—And since virtue is so called from its being a principle of action, for it is the perfection of a power, it follows again that the nature of virtue agrees more with moral than with intellectual virtue, though the intellectual virtues are more excellent habits, simply speaking.

Reply Obj. 1. The moral virtues are more lasting than the intellectual virtues, because they are practised in matters pertaining to the life of the community. Yet it is evident that the objects of the sciences, which are necessary and invariable, are more lasting than the objects of moral virtue, which are certain particular matters of action.—That the moral virtues are more necessary for human life, proves that they are more excellent, not simply, but relatively. Indeed, the speculative intellectual virtues, from the very fact that they are not referred to something else, as a useful thing is referred to an end, are more excellent. The reason for this is that in them we have a kind of beginning of that happiness which consists in the knowledge of truth, as stated above (Q. 3, A. 6).

Reply Obj. 2. The reason why man is said to be good simply, in respect of moral virtue, but not in respect of intellectual virtue, is because the appetite moves the other powers to their acts, as stated above (Q. 56, A. 3). Wherefore this argument, too, proves merely that moral virtue is better relatively.

Reply Obj. 3. Prudence directs the moral virtues not only in the choice of the means, but also in appointing the end. Now the end of each moral virtue is to attain the mean in the matter proper to that virtue; which mean is appointed according to the right ruling of prudence, as stated in *Ethic.* ii. 6; vi. 13.

FOURTH ARTICLE

Whether Justice Is the Chief of the Moral Virtues?

We proceed thus to the Fourth Article:—

Objection 1. It would seem that justice is not the chief of the moral virtues. For it is better to give of one's own than to pay what is due. Now the former belongs to liberality, the latter to justice. Therefore liberality is apparently a greater virtue than justice.

Obj. 2. Further, the chief quality in a thing is, seemingly, that in which it is most perfect. Now, according to James i. 4, *Patience hath a perfect work* Therefore it would seem that patience is greater than justice.

Obj. 3. Further, *Magnanimity has a great influence on every virtue,* as stated in *Ethic.* iv. 3). Therefore it magnifies even justice. Therefore it is greater than justice.

On the contrary, The Philosopher says *Ethic.* v. 1) that *justice is the most excellent of the virtues.*

I answer that, A virtue considered in its species may be greater or less, either simply or relatively. A virtue is said to be greater simply, whereby a greater rational good shines forth, as stated above (A. 1). In this way justice is the most excellent of all the moral virtues, as being most akin to reason. This is made evident by considering its subject and its object: its subject, because this is the will, and the will is the rational appetite, as stated above (Q. 8, A. 1; Q. 26, A. 1): its object or matter, because it is about operations, whereby man is set in order not only in himself, but also in regard to another. Hence

---

** Aristotle, *Topic.* iii.

justice is the most excellent of virtues (Ethic. v., loc. cit.).—Among the other moral virtues, which are about the passions, the more excellent the matter in which the appetitive movement is subjected to reason, so much the more does the rational good shine forth in each. Now in things touching man, the chief of all is life, on which all other things depend. Consequently fortitude which subjects the appetitive movement to reason in matters of life and death, holds the first place among those moral virtues that are about the passions, but is subordinate to justice. Hence the Philosopher says (*Rhetor.* 1) that *those virtues must needs be greatest which receive the most praise: since virtue is a power of doing good. Hence the brave man and the just man are honored more than others; because the former,* i.e., fortitude, *is useful in war, and the latter,* i.e., justice, *both in war and in peace.*—After fortitude comes temperance, which subjects the appetite to reason in matters directly relating to life, in the one individual, or in the one species, viz., in matters of food and of sex.—And so these three virtues, together with prudence, are called principal virtues, in excellence also.

A virtue is said to be greater relatively, by reason of its helping or adorning a principal virtue: even as substance is more excellent simply than accident: and yet relatively some particular accident is more excellent than substance in so far as it perfects substance in some accidental mode of being.

Reply Obj. 1. The act of liberality needs to be founded on an act of justice, for *a man is not liberal in giving, unless he gives of his own (Polit.* ii. 3). Hence there could be no liberality apart from justice, which discerns between *meum* and *tuum:* whereas justice can be without liberality. Hence justice is simply greater than liberality, as being more universal, and as being its foundation: while liberality is greater relatively since it is an ornament and an addition to justice.

Reply Obj. 2. Patience is said to have *a perfect work,* by enduring evils, wherein it excludes not only unjust revenge, which is also excluded by justice; not only hatred, which is also suppressed by charity; nor only anger, which is calmed by gentleness; but also inordinate sorrow, which is the root of all the above. Wherefore it is more perfect and excellent through plucking up the root in this matter.—It is not, however, more perfect than all the other virtues simply. Because fortitude not only endures trouble without being disturbed, but also fights against it if necessary. Hence whoever is brave is patient; but the converse does not hold, for patience is a part of fortitude.

Reply Obj. 3. There can be no magnanimity without the other virtues, as stated in *Ethic.* iv. 3. Hence it is compared to them as their ornament, so that relatively it is greater than all the others, but not simply.

FIFTH ARTICLE

Whether Wisdom Is the Greatest of the Intellectual Virtues?

We proceed thus to the Fifth Article:—

Objection 1. It would seem that wisdom is not the greatest of the intellectual virtues. Because the commander is greater than the one commanded. Now prudence seems to command wisdom, for it is stated in *Ethic.* 1, 2 that political science, which belongs to prudence (*Ethic.* vi. 8), *orders that sciences should be cultivated in states, and to which of these each individual should devote himself, and to what extent.* Since, then, wisdom is one of the sciences, it seems that prudence is greater than wisdom.

Obj. 2. Further, it belongs to the nature of virtue to direct man to happiness: because virtue is *the disposition of a perfect thing to that which is best,* as stated in *Phys.* vii., text. 17. Now prudence is *right reason about things to be done,* whereby man is brought to happiness: whereas wisdom takes no notice of human acts, whereby man attains happiness. Therefore prudence is a greater virtue than wisdom.

Obj. 3. Further, the more perfect knowledge is, the greater it seems to be. Now we can have more perfect knowledge of human affairs, which are the subject of science, than of Divine things, which are the object of wisdom, which is the distinction given by Augustine (*De Trin.* xii. 14): because Divine things are incomprehensible, according to Job xxvi. 26: *Behold God is great, exceeding our knowledge.* Therefore science is a greater virtue than wisdom.

Obj. 4. Further, knowledge of principles is more excellent than knowledge of conclusions. But wisdom draws conclusions from indemonstrable principles which are the object of the virtue of understanding, even as other sciences do. Therefore understanding is a greater virtue than wisdom.

On the contrary, The Philosopher says (*Ethic.* vi. 7) that wisdom is *the head* among the intellectual virtues.

I answer that, As stated above (A. 3), the greatness of a virtue, as to its species, is taken from its object. Now the object of wisdom surpasses the objects of all the intellectual virtues: because wisdom considers the Supreme Cause, which is God, as stated at the beginning of the *Metaphysics.* And since it is by the cause that we judge of an effect, and by the higher cause that we judge of the lower effects; hence it is that wisdom exercises judgment over all the other intellectual virtues, directs them all, and is the architect of them all.

Reply Obj. 1. Since prudence is about human affairs, and wisdom about the Supreme Cause, it is impossible for prudence to be a greater virtue than wisdom, *unless*, as stated in *Ethic.* vi. 7, *man were the greatest thing in the world*. Wherefore we must say, as stated in the same book (*ibid.*), that prudence does not command wisdom, but vice versa: because *the spiritual man judgeth all things; and he himself is judged by no man* (1 Cor. ii. 15). For prudence has no business with supreme matters which are the object of wisdom: but its command covers things directed to wisdom, viz., how men are to obtain wisdom. Wherefore prudence, or political science, is, in this way, the servant of wisdom; for it leads to wisdom, preparing the way for her, as the doorkeeper for the king.

Reply Obj. 2. Prudence considers the means of acquiring happiness, but wisdom considers the very object of happiness, viz., the Supreme Intelligible. And if indeed the consideration of wisdom were perfect in respect of its object, there would be perfect happiness in the act of wisdom: but as, in this life, the act of wisdom is imperfect in respect of its principal object, which is God, it follows that the act of wisdom is a beginning or participation of future happiness, so that wisdom is nearer than prudence to happiness.

Reply Obj. 3. As the Philosopher says (*De Anima* i., text. 1), *one knowledge is preferable to another, either because it is about a higher object, or because it is more certain.* Hence if the objects be equally good and sublime, that virtue will be greater which possesses more certain knowledge. But a virtue which is less certain about a higher and better object, is preferable to that which is more certain about an object of inferior degree. Wherefore the Philosopher says (*De Cœlo* ii., text. 60) that *it is a great thing to be able to know something about celestial beings, though it be based on weak and probable reasoning;* and again (*De Part. Animal.* i. 5) that *it is better to know a little about sublime things, than much about mean things.*—Accordingly wisdom, to which knowledge about God pertains, is beyond the reach of man, especially in this life, so as to be his possession: for this *belongs to God alone* (*Metaph.* i. 2): and yet this little knowledge about God which we can have through wisdom is preferable to all other knowledge.

Reply Obj. 4. The truth and knowledge of indemonstrable principles depends on the meaning of the terms: for as soon as we know what is a whole, and what is a part, we know at once that every whole is greater than its part. Now to know the meaning of being and non-being, of whole and part, and of other things consequent to being, which are the terms whereof indemonstrable principles are constituted, is the function of wisdom: since universal being is the proper effect of the Supreme Cause, which is God. And so wisdom makes use of indemonstrable principles which are the object of understanding, not only by drawing conclusions from them, as other sciences do, but also by passing its judgment on them, and by vindicating them against those who deny them. Hence it follows that wisdom is a greater virtue than understanding.

SIXTH ARTICLE

Whether Charity Is the Greatest of the Theological Virtues?

We proceed thus to the Sixth Article:—

Objection 1. It would seem that charity is not the greatest of the theological virtues. Because, since faith is in the intellect, while hope and charity are in the appetitive power, it seems that faith is compared to hope and charity, as intellectual to moral virtue. Now intellectual virtue is greater than moral virtue, as was made evident above (Q. 62, A. 3). Therefore faith is greater than hope and charity.

Obj. 2. Further, when two things are added together, the result is greater than either one. Now hope results from something added to charity; for it presupposes love, as Augustine says (*Enchirid.* viii), and it adds a certain movement of stretching forward to the beloved. Therefore hope is greater than charity.

Obj. 3. Further, a cause is more noble than its effect. Now faith and hope are the cause of charity: for a gloss on Matth. 1. 3 says that *faith begets hope, and hope charity.* Therefore faith and hope are greater than charity.

On the contrary, The Apostle says (1 Cor. xiii. 13): *Now there remain faith, hope, charity, these three; but the greatest of these is charity.*

I answer that, As stated above (A. 3), the greatness of a virtue, as to its species, is taken from its object.—Now, since the three theological virtues look at God as their proper object, it cannot be said that any one of them is greater than another by reason of its having a greater object, but only from the fact that it approaches nearer than another to that object; and in this way charity is greater than the others. Because the others, in their very nature, imply a certain distance from the object: since faith is of what is not seen, and hope is of what is not possessed. But the love of charity is of that which is already possessed: since the beloved is, in a manner, in the lover, and, again, the lover is drawn by desire to union with the beloved; hence it is written (1 Jo. iv. 16): *He that abideth in charity, abideth in God, and God in him.*

Reply Obj. 1. Faith and hope are not related to charity in the same way as prudence to moral virtue; and for two reasons. First, because the theological virtues have an object surpassing the human soul: whereas prudence and the moral virtues are about things beneath man. Now in things that are above man, to love them is more excellent than to know them. Because knowledge is perfected by the known being in the knower: whereas love is perfected by the lover being drawn to the beloved. Now that which is above man is more excellent in itself than in man: since a thing is contained according to the mode of the container. But it is the other way about in things beneath man. Secondly, because

prudence moderates the appetitive movements pertaining to the moral virtues, whereas faith does not moderate the appetitive movement tending to God, which movement belongs to the theological virtues: it only shows the object. And this appetitive movement towards its object surpasses human knowledge, according to Ephes. iii. 19: *The charity of Christ which surpasseth all knowledge.*

Reply Obj. 2. Hope presupposes love of that which a man hopes to obtain; and such love is love of concupiscence, whereby he who desires good, loves himself rather than something else. On the other hand, charity implies love of friendship, to which we are led by hope, as stated above (Q. 62, A. 4).

Reply Obj. 3. An efficient cause is more noble than its effect: but not a disposing cause. For otherwise the heat of fire would be more noble than the soul, to which the heat disposes the matter. It is in this way that faith begets hope, and hope charity: in the sense, to wit, that one is a disposition to the other.

QUESTION 67

Of the Duration of Virtues after This Life

(In Six Articles)

WE must now consider the duration of virtues after this life, under which head there are six points of inquiry: (1) Whether the moral virtues remain after this life? (2) Whether the intellectual virtues remain? (3) Whether faith remains? (4) Whether hope remains? (5) Whether anything remains of faith or hope? (6) Whether charity remains?

FIRST ARTICLE

Whether the Moral Virtues Remain after This Life?

We proceed thus to the First Article:—

Objection 1. It would seem that the moral virtues do not remain after this life. For in the future state of glory men will be like angels, according to Matth. xxii. 30. But it is absurd to put moral virtues in the angels,* as stated in *Ethic.* x. 8. Therefore neither in man will there be moral virtues after this life.

Obj. 2. Further, moral virtues perfect man in the active life. But the active life does not remain after this life: for Gregory says (*Moral.* iv. 18): *The works of the active life pass away with the body.* Therefore moral virtues do not remain after this life.

Obj. 3. Further, temperance and fortitude, which are moral virtues, are in the irrational parts of the soul, as the Philosopher states (*Ethic.* iii. 10). Now the irrational parts of

the soul are corrupted, when the body is corrupted: since they are acts of bodily organs. Therefore it seems that the moral virtues do not remain after this life.

On the contrary, It is written (Wis. i. 15) that *justice is perpetual and immortal.*

I answer that, As Augustine says (*De Trin.* xiv. 9), Cicero held that the cardinal virtues do not remain after this life; and that, as Augustine says (*ibid.*), *in the other life men are made happy by the mere knowledge of that nature, than which nothing is better or more lovable, that Nature, to wit, which created all others.* Afterwards he concludes that these four virtues remain in the future life, but after a different manner.

In order to make this evident, we must note that in these virtues there is a formal element, and a quasi-material element. The material element in these virtues is a certain inclination of the appetitive part to the passions and operations according to a certain mode:—and since this mode is fixed by reason, the formal element is precisely this order of reason.

Accordingly we must say that these moral virtues do not remain in the future life, as regards their material element. For in the future life there will be no concupiscences and pleasures in matters of food and sex; nor fear and daring about dangers of death; nor distri-

---

* *Whatever relates to moral action is petty, and unworthy of the gods (Ethic. x. 8).*

butions and commutations of things employed in this present life. But, as regards the formal element, they will remain most perfect, after this life, in the Blessed, in as much as each one's reason will have most perfect rectitude in regard to things concerning him in respect of that state of life: and his appetitive power will be moved entirely according to the order of reason, in things pertaining to that same state. Hence Augustine says (*ibid.*) that *prudence will be there without any danger of error; fortitude, without the anxiety of bearing with evil; temperance, without the rebellion of the desires: so that prudence will neither prefer nor equal any good to God; fortitude will adhere to Him most steadfastly; and temperance will delight in Him Who knows no imperfection.* As to justice, it is yet more evident what will be its act in that life, viz. *to be subject to God:* because even in this life subjection to a superor is part of justice.

Reply Obj. 1. The Philosopher is speaking there of these moral virtues, as to their material element; thus he speaks of justice, as regards *commutations and distributions;* of fortitude, as to *matters of terror and danger;* of temperance, in respect of *lewd desires.*

The same applies to the Second Objection. For those things that concern the active life, belong to the material element of the virtues.

Reply Obj. 3. There is a twofold state after this life; one before the resurrection, during which the soul will be separate from the body; the other, after the resurrection, when the souls will be reunited to their bodies. In this state of resurrection, the irrational powers will be in the bodily organs, just as they now are. Hence it will be possible for fortitude to be in the irascible, and temperance in the concupiscible part, in so far as each power will be perfectly disposed to obey the reason. But in the state preceding the resurrection, the irrational parts will not be in the soul actually, but only radically in its essence, as stated in the First Part (Q. 77, A. 8). Wherefore neither will these virtues be actually, but only in their root, i.e. in the reason and will, wherein are certain nurseries of these virtues, as stated above (Q. 63, A. 1). Justice, however, will remain because it is in the will. Hence of justice it is specially said that it is *perpetual and immortal;* both by reason of its subject, since the will is incorruptible; and because its act will not change, as stated.

SECOND ARTICLE

Whether the Intellectual Virtues Remain after This Life?

We proceed thus to the Second Article:—
Objection 1. It would seem that the intel-

lectual virtues do not remain after this life. For the Apostle says (1 Cor. xiii. 8, 9) that *knowledge shall be destroyed,* and he states the reason to be because *we know in part.* Now just as the knowledge of science is in part, i.e., imperfect; so also is the knowledge of the other intellectual virtues, as long as this life lasts. Therefore all the intellectual virtues will cease after this life.

Obj. 2. Further, the Philosopher says (*Categor.* vi) that since science is a habit, it is a quality difficult to remove: for it is not easily lost, except by reason of some great change or sickness. But no bodily change is so great as that of death. Therefore science and the other intellectual virtues do not remain after death.

Obj. 3. Further, the intellectual virtues perfect the intellect so that it may perform its proper act well. Now there seems to be no act of the intellect after this life, since *the soul understands nothing without a phantasm* (*De Anima* iii., text. 30) ; and, after this life, the phantasms do not remain, since their only subject is an organ of the body. Therefore the intellectual virtues do not remain after this life.

On the contrary, The knowledge of what is universal and necessary is more constant than that of particular and contingent things. Now the knowledge of contingent particulars remains in man after this life; for instance, the knowledge of what one has done or suffered, according to Luke xvi. 25: *Son, remember that thou didst receive good things in thy life-time, and likewise Lazarus evil things.* Much more, therefore, does the knowledge of universal and necessary things remain, which belong to science and the other intellectual virtues.

I answer that, As stated in the First Part (Q. 79, A. 6), some have held that the intelligible species do not remain in the passive intellect except when it actually understands; and that so long as actual consideration ceases, the species are not preserved save in the sensitive powers which are acts of bodily organs, viz. in the powers of imagination and memory. Now these powers cease when the body is corrupted: and consequently, according to this opinion, neither science nor any other intellectual virtue will remain after this life when once the body is corrupted.

But this opinion is contrary to the mind of Aristotle, who states (*De Anima* iii., text 8) that *the possible intellect is in act when it is identified with each thing as knowing it; and yet, even then, it is in potentiality to consider it actually.*—It is also contrary to reason, because intelligible species are contained by the *possible* intellect immovably, according to the mode of their container: Hence the *possible* intellect is called *the abode of the species* (*De Anima* iii) because it preserves the intelligible species.

And yet the phantasms, by turning to which man understands in this life, by applying the intelligible species to them as stated in the First Part (Q. 84, A. 7; Q. 85, A. 1 *ad* 5), cease as soon as the body is corrupted. Hence, so far as the phantasms are concerned, which are the quasi-material element in the intellectual virtues, these latter cease when the body is destroyed: but as regards the intelligible species, which are in the *possible* intellect, the intellectual virtues remain. Now the species are the quasi-formal element of the intellectual virtues. Therefore these remain after this life, as regards their formal element, but not as regards their material element, just as we have stated concerning the moral virtues (A. 1).

Reply Obj. 1. The saying of the Apostle is to be understood as referring to the material element in science, and to the mode of understanding; because, to it, neither do the phantasms remain, when the body is destroyed; nor will science be applied by turning to the phantasms.

Reply Obj. 2. Sickness destroys the habit of science as to its material element, viz. the phantasms, but not as to the intelligible species, which are in the *possible* intellect.

Reply Obj. 3. As stated in the First Part (Q. 89, A. 1), the separated soul has a mode of understanding, other than by turning to the phantasms. Consequently science remains, yet not as to the same mode of operation; as we have stated concerning the moral virtues (A. 1).

THIRD ARTICLE

Whether Faith Remains after This Life?

We proceed thus to the Third Article:—

Objection 1. It would seem that faith remains after this life. Because faith is more excellent than science. Now science remains after this life, as stated above (A. 2). Therefore faith remains also.

Obj. 2. Further, it is written (1 Cor. iii. 11): *Other foundation no man can lay, but that which is laid; which is Christ Jesus,* i.e., faith in Jesus Christ. Now if the foundation is removed, that which is built upon it remains no more. Therefore, if faith remains not after this life, no other virtue remains.

Obj. 3. Further, the knowledge of faith and the knowledge of glory differ as perfect from imperfect. Now imperfect knowledge is compatible with perfect knowledge: thus in an angel there can be *evening* and *morning* knowledge;* and a man can have science through

*Cf. P. I., Q. 58, A. 6.

a demonstrative syllogism, together with opinion through a probable syllogism, about one same conclusion. Therefore after this life faith also is compatible with the knowledge of glory.

On the contrary, The Apostle says (2 Cor. v. 6, 7): *While we are in the body, we are absent from the Lord: for we walk by faith and not by sight.* But those who are in glory are not absent from the Lord, but present to Him. Therefore after this life faith does not remain in the life of glory.

I answer that, Opposition is of itself the proper cause of one thing being excluded from another, in so far, to wit, as wherever two things are opposite to one another, we find opposition of affirmation and negation. Now in some things we find opposition in respect of contrary forms; thus in colors we find white and black. In others we find opposition in respect of perfection and imperfection: wherefore in alterations, more and less are considered to be contraries, as when a thing from being less hot is made more hot (*Phys.* v, text. 19). And since perfect and imperfect are opposite to one another, it is impossible for perfection and imperfection to affect the same thing at the same time.

Now we must take note that sometimes imperfection belongs to a thing's very nature, and belongs to its species: even as lack of reason belongs to the very specific nature of a horse and an ox. And since a thing, so long as it remains the same identically, cannot pass from one species to another, it follows that if such an imperfection be removed, the species of that thing is changed: even as it would no longer be an ox or a horse, were it to be rational. Sometimes, however, the imperfection does not belong to the specific nature, but is accidental to the individual by reason of something else; even as sometimes lack of reason is accidental to a man, because he is asleep, or because he is drunk, or for some like reason; and it is evident, that if such an imperfection be removed, the thing remains substantially.

Now it is clear that imperfect knowledge belongs to the very nature of faith: for it is included in its definition; faith being defined as *the substance of things to be hoped for, the evidence of things that appear not* (Heb. xi. 1). Wherefore Augustine says (*Tract.* xl *in Joan.*): *What is faith? Believing without seeing.* But it is an imperfect knowledge that is of things unapparent or unseen. Consequently imperfect knowledge belongs to the very nature of faith: therefore it is clear that the knowledge of faith cannot be perfect and remain identically the same.

But we must also consider whether it is compatible with perfect knowledge: for there is nothing to prevent some kind of imperfect knowledge from being sometimes with perfect knowledge. Accordingly we must observe that knowledge can be imperfect in three ways: first, on the part of the knowable object; secondly, on the part of the medium; thirdly, on the part of the subject. The difference of perfect and imperfect knowledge on the part of the knowable object is seen in the *morning* and *evening* knowledge of the angels: for the "morning" knowledge is about things according to the being which they have in the Word, while the "evening" knowledge is about things according as they have being in their own natures, which being is imperfect in comparison with the First Being.—On the part of the medium, perfect and imperfect knowledge are exemplified in the knowledge of a conclusion through a demonstrative medium, and through a probable medium.—On the part of the subject the difference of perfect and imperfect knowledge applies to opinion, faith, and science. For it is essential to opinion that we assent to one of two opposite assertions with fear of the other, so that our adhesion is not firm: to science it is essential to have firm adhesion with intellectual vision, for science possesses certitude which results from the understanding of principles: while faith holds a middle place, for it surpasses opinion in so far as its adhesion is firm, but falls short of science in so far as it lacks vision.

Now it is evident that a thing cannot be perfect and imperfect in the same respect; yet the things which differ as perfect and imperfect can be together in the same respect in one and the same other thing. Accordingly, knowledge which is perfect on the part of the object is quite incompatible with imperfect knowledge about the same object; but they are compatible with one another in respect of the same medium or the same subject: for nothing hinders a man from having at one and the same time, through one and the same medium, perfect and imperfect knowledge about two things, one perfect, the other imperfect, e.g. about health and sickness, good and evil. —In like manner knowledge that is perfect on the part of the medium is incompatible with imperfect knowledge through one and the same medium: but nothing hinders them being about the same object or in the same subject: for one man can know the same conclusions through a probable and through a demonstrative medium.—Again, knowledge that is perfect on the part of the subject is incompatible with imperfect knowledge in the same subject. Now faith, of its very nature, contains an imperfection on the part of the subject, viz. that the believer sees not what he believes: whereas bliss, of its very nature, implies per-

fection on the part of the subject, viz. that the Blessed see that which makes them happy, as stated above (Q. 3, A. 8). Hence it is manifest that faith and bliss are incompatible in one and the same subject.

Reply Obj. 1. Faith is more excellent than science, on the part of the object, because its object is the First Truth. Yet science has a more perfect mode of knowing its object, which is not incompatible with vision which is the perfection of happiness, as the mode of faith is incompatible.

Reply Obj. 2. Faith is the foundation in as much as it is knowledge: consequently when this knowledge is perfected, the foundation will be perfected also.

The Reply to the Third Objection is clear from what has been said.

FOURTH ARTICLE

Whether Hope Remains after Death, in the State of Glory?

We proceed thus to the Fourth Article:—

Objection 1. It would seem that hope remains after death, in the state of glory. Because hope perfects the human appetite in a more excellent manner than the moral virtues. But the moral virtues remain after this life, as Augustine clearly states (*De Trin.* xiv. 9). Much more then does hope remain.

Obj. 2. Further, fear is opposed to hope. But fear remains after this life:—in the Blessed, filial fear, which abides for ever—in the lost, the fear of punishment. Therefore, in a like manner, hope can remain.

Obj. 3. Further, just as hope is of future good, so is desire. Now in the Blessed there is desire for future good; both for the glory of the body, which the souls of the Blessed desire, as Augustine declares (*Gen. ad. lit.* xii. 35); and for the glory of the soul, according to Ecclus. xxiv. 29: *They that eat me, shall yet hunger, and they that drink me, shall yet thirst,* and 1 Pet. i. 12: *On Whom the angels desire to look.* Therefore it seems that there can be hope in the Blessed after this life is past.

On the contrary, The Apostle says (Rom. viii. 24): *What a man seeth, why doth he hope for?* But the Blessed see that which is the object of hope, viz. God. Therefore they do not hope.

I answer that, As stated above (A. 3), that which, in its very nature, implies imperfection of its subject, is incompatible with the opposite perfection in that subject. Thus it is evident that movement of its very nature implies imperfection of its subject, since it is *the act of that which is in potentiality as such* (*Phys.* iii): so that as soon as this potentiality is brought into act, the movement ceases; for a thing does not continue to become white, when once it is made white. Now hope denotes a movement towards that which is not possessed, as is clear from what we have said above about the passion of hope (Q. 40, AA. 1, 2). Therefore when we possess that which we hope for, viz. the enjoyment of God, it will no longer be possible to have hope.

Reply Obj. 1. Hope surpasses the moral virtues as to its object, which is God. But the acts of the moral virtues are not incompatible with the perfection of happiness, as the act of hope is; except perhaps, as regards their matter, in respect of which they do not remain. For moral virtue perfects the appetite, not only in respect of what is not yet possessed, but also as regards something which is in our actual possession.

Reply Obj. 2. Fear is twofold, servile and filial, as we shall state further on (II-II, Q. 19, A. 2). Servile fear regards punishment, and will be impossible in the life of glory, since there will no longer be possibility of being punished.—Filial fear has two acts: one is an act of reverence to God, and with regard to this act, it remains: the other is an act of fear lest we be separated from God, and as regards this act, it does not remain. Because separation from God is in the nature of an evil: and no evil will be feared there, according to Prov. i. 33: *He . . . shall enjoy abundance without fear of evils.* Now fear is opposed to hope by opposition of good and evil, as stated above (Q. 23, A. 2; Q. 40, A. 1), and therefore the fear which will remain in glory is not opposed to hope. In the lost there can be fear of punishment, rather than hope of glory in the Blessed. Because in the lost there will be a succession of punishments, so that the notion of something future remains there, which is the object of fear: but the glory of the saints has no succession, by reason of its being a kind of participation of eternity, wherein there is neither past nor future, but only the present. —And yet, properly speaking, neither in the lost is there fear. For, as stated above (Q. 42, A. 2), fear is never without some hope of escape: and the lost will have no such hope. Consequently neither will there be fear in them; except speaking in a general way, in so far as any expectation of future evil is called fear.

Reply Obj. 3. As to the glory of the soul, there can be no desire in the Blessed, in so far as desire looks for something future, for the reason already given (*ad 2*). Yet hunger and thirst are said to be in them because they never weary, and for the same reason desire is said to be in the angels. With regard to the glory of the body, there can be desire in the souls

of the saints, but not hope, properly speaking; neither as a theological virtue, for thus its object is God, and not a created good; nor in its general signification. Because the object of hope is something difficult, as stated above (Q. 40, A. 1): while a good whose unerring cause we already possess, is not compared to us as something difficult. Hence he that has money is not, properly speaking, said to hope for what he can buy at once. In like manner those who have the glory of the soul are not, properly speaking, said to hope for the glory of the body, but only to desire it.

Whether Anything of Faith or Hope Remains in Glory?

We proceed thus to the Fifth Article:—

Objection 1. It would seem that something of faith and hope remains in glory. For when that which is proper to a thing is removed, there remains what is common; thus it is stated in *De Causis* that *if you take away rational, there remains living, and when you remove living, there remains being.* Now in faith there is something that it has in common with beatitude, viz. knowledge: and there is something proper to it, viz., darkness, for faith is knowledge in a dark manner. Therefore, the darkness of faith removed, the knowledge of faith still remains.

Obj. 2. Further, faith is a spiritual light of the soul, according to Ephes. i. 17, 18: *The eyes of your heart enlightened . . . in the knowledge of God;* yet this light is imperfect in comparison with the light of glory, of which it is written (Ps. xxxv. 10): *In Thy light we shall see light.* Now an imperfect light remains when a perfect light supervenes: for a candle is not extinguished when the sun's rays appear. Therefore it seems that the light of faith itself remains with the light of glory.

Obj. 3. Further, the substance of a habit does not cease through the withdrawal of its matter: for a man may retain the habit of liberality, though he have lost his money: yet he cannot exercise the act. Now the object of faith is the First Truth as unseen. Therefore when this ceases through being seen, the habit of faith can still remain.

On the contrary, Faith is a simple habit. Now a simple thing is either withdrawn entirely, or remains entirely. Since therefore faith does not remain entirely, but is taken away as stated above (A. 3), it seems that it is withdrawn entirely.

I answer that, Some have held that hope is taken away entirely: but that faith is taken away in part, viz. as to its obscurity, and remains in part, viz. as to the substance of its knowledge. And if this be understood to mean that it remains the same, not identically but generically, it is absolutely true; since faith is of the same genus, viz. knowledge, as the beatific vision. On the other hand, hope is not of the same genus as heavenly bliss: because it is compared to the enjoyment of bliss, as movement is to rest in the term of movement.

But if it be understood to mean that in heaven the knowledge of faith remains identically the same, this is absolutely impossible. Because when you remove a specific difference, the substance of the genus does not remain identically the same: thus if you remove the difference constituting whiteness, the substance of color does not remain identically the same, as though the identical color were at one time whiteness, and, at another, blackness. The reason is that genus is not related to difference as matter to form, so that the substance of the genus remains identically the same, when the difference is removed, as the substance of matter remains identically the same, when the form is changed: for genus and difference are not the parts of a species, else they would not be predicated of the species. But even as the species denotes the whole, i.e. the compound of matter and form in material things, so does the difference, and likewise the genus; the genus denotes the whole by signifying that which is material; the difference, by signifying that which is formal; the species, by signifying both. Thus, in man, the sensitive nature is as matter to the intellectual nature, and animal is predicated of that which has a sensitive nature, rational of that which has an intellectual nature, and man of that which has both. So that the one same whole is denoted by these three, but not under the same aspect.

It is therefore evident that, since the signification of the difference is confined to the genus if the difference be removed, the substance of the genus cannot remain the same: for the same animal nature does not remain, if another kind of soul constitute the animal. Hence it is impossible for the identical knowledge, which was previously obscure, to become clear vision. It is therefore evident that, in heaven, nothing remains of faith, either identically or specifically the same, but only generically, as stated.

Reply Obj. 1. If *rational* be withdrawn, the remaining *living* thing is the same, not identically, but generically, as stated.

Reply Obj. 2. The imperfection of candle-light is not opposed to the perfection of sunlight, since they do not regard the same subject: whereas the imperfection of faith and the perfection of glory are opposed to one another and regard the same subject. Consequently they are incompatible with one another, just as light and darkness in the air.

Reply Obj. 3. He that loses his money does not therefore lose the possibility of having money, and therefore it is reasonable for the habit of liberality to remain. But in the state of glory not only is the object of faith, which is the unseen, removed actually, but even its possibility, by reason of the unchangeableness of heavenly bliss: and so such a habit would remain to no purpose.

SIXTH ARTICLE

Whether Charity Remains after This Life, in Glory?

We proceed thus to the Sixth Article:—

Objection 1. It would seem that charity does not remain after this life, in glory. Because according to 1 Cor. xiii. 10, *when that which is perfect is come, that which is in part,* i.e. that which is imperfect, *shall be done away.* Now the charity of the wayfarer is imperfect. Therefore it will be done away when the perfection of glory is attained.

Obj. 2. Further, habits and acts are differentiated by their objects. But the object of love is good apprehended. Since therefore the apprehension of the present life differs from the apprehension of the life to come, it seems that charity is not the same in both cases.

Obj. 3. Further, things of the same kind can advance from imperfection to perfection by continuous increase. But the charity of the wayfarer can never attain to equality with the charity of heaven, however much it be increased. Therefore it seems that the charity of the wayfarer does not remain in heaven.

On the contrary, The Apostle says (1 Cor. xiii. 8): *Charity never falleth away.*

I answer that, As stated above (A. 3), when the imperfection of a thing does not belong to its specific nature, there is nothing to hinder the identical thing passing from imperfection to perfection, even as man is perfected by growth, and whiteness by intensity. Now charity is love, the nature of which does not include imperfection, since it may relate to an object either possessed or not possessed, either seen or not seen. Therefore charity is not done away by the perfection of glory, but remains identically the same.

Reply Obj. 1. The imperfection of charity is accidental to it; because imperfection is not included in the nature of love. Now although that which is accidental to a thing be withdrawn, the substance remains. Hence the imperfection of charity being done away, charity itself is not done away.

Reply Obj. 2. The object of charity is not knowledge itself; if it were, the charity of the wayfarer would not be the same as the charity of heaven: its object is the thing known, which remains the same, viz. God Himself.

Reply Obj. 3. The reason why the charity of the wayfarer cannot attain to the perfection of the charity of heaven, is a difference on the part of the cause: for vision is a cause of love, as stated in *Ethic.* ix. 5: and the more perfectly we know God, the more perfectly we love Him.

QUESTION 68

Of the Gifts

(In Eight Articles)

WE now come to consider the Gifts; under which head there are eight points of inquiry: (1) Whether the Gifts differ from the virtues? (2) Of the necessity of the Gifts? (3) Whether the Gifts are habits? (4) Which, and how many are they? (5) Whether the Gifts are connected? (6) Whether they remain in heaven? (7) Of their comparison with one another; (8) Of their comparison with the virtues.

FIRST ARTICLE

Whether the Gifts Differ from the Virtues?

We proceed thus to the First Article:—

Objection 1. It would seem that the gifts do not differ from the virtues. For Gregory commenting on Job. i. 2, *There were born to him seven sons,* says (*Moral.* i. 12): *Seven sons were born to us, when through the conception of heavenly thought, the seven virtues of the Holy Ghost take birth in us:* and he quotes the words of Isaias (xi. 2, 3): *And the Spirit . . . of understanding . . . shall rest upon him,* etc. where the seven gifts of the Holy Ghost are enumerated. Therefore the seven gifts of the Holy Ghost are virtues.

Obj. 2. Further, Augustine commenting on Matth. xii. 45, *Then he goeth and taketh with him seven other spirits,* etc., says (*De Quæst. Evang.* i. qu. 8): *The seven vices are opposed to the seven virtues of the Holy Ghost,* i.e. to the seven gifts. Now the seven vices are opposed to the seven virtues, commonly so called. Therefore the gifts do not differ from the virtues commonly so called.

Obj. 3. Further, things whose definitions are the same, are themselves the same. But the definition of virtue applies to the gifts; for each gift is *a good quality of the mind, whereby we lead a good life,* etc.* Likewise the definition of a gift can apply to the infused virtues: for a gift is *an unreturnable giving,* according to the Philosopher (*Topic.* iv. 4). Therefore the virtues and gifts do not differ from one another.

Obj. 4. Several of the things mentioned

* Cf. Q. 55, A. 4.

among the gifts, are virtues: for, as stated above (Q. 57, A. 2), wisdom, understanding, and knowledge are intellectual virtues, counsel pertains to prudence, piety is a kind of justice, and fortitude is a moral virtue. Therefore it seems that the gifts do not differ from the virtues.

On the contrary, Gregory (*Moral.* i. 12) distinguishes seven gifts, which he states to be denoted by the seven sons of Job, from the three theological virtues, which, he says, are signified by Job's three daughters. He also distinguishes (*Moral.* ii. 26) the same seven gifts from the four cardinal virtues, which he says were signified by the four corners of the house.

I answer that, If we speak of gift and virtue with regard to the notion conveyed by the words themselves, there is no opposition between them. Because the word *virtue* conveys the notion that it perfects man in relation to well-doing, while the word *gift* refers to the cause from which it proceeds. Now there is no reason why that which proceeds from one as a gift should not perfect another in well-doing: especially as we have already stated (Q. 63, A. 3) that some virtues are infused into us by God. Wherefore in this respect we cannot differentiate gifts from virtues. Consequently some have held that the gifts are not to be distinguished from the virtues.—But there remains no less a difficulty for them to solve; for they must explain why some virtues are called gifts and some not; and why among the gifts there are some, fear, for instance, that are not reckoned virtues.

Hence it is that others have said that the gifts should be held as being distinct from virtues; yet they have not assigned a suitable reason for this distinction, a reason, to wit, which would apply either to all the virtues, and to none of the gifts, or vice versa. For, seeing that of the seven gifts, four belong to the reason, viz. wisdom, knowledge, understanding and counsel, and three to the appetite, viz. fortitude, piety and fear; they held that the gifts perfect the free-will according as it is a faculty of the reason, while the virtues perfect it as a faculty of the will: since they observed only two virtues in the reason or intellect, viz. faith and prudence, the others being in the appetitive power or the affections. If this distinction were true, all the virtues would have to be in the appetite, and all the gifts in the reason.

Others observing that Gregory says (*Moral.* ii. 26) that *the gift of the Holy Ghost, by coming into the soul endows it with prudence, temperance, justice, and fortitude, and at the same time strengthens it against every kind of temptation by His sevenfold gift,* said that the virtues are given us that we may do good works, and the gifts, that we may resist temptation.—But neither is this distinction sufficient. Because the virtues also resist those temptations which lead to the sins that are contrary to the virtues; for everything naturally resists its contrary: which is especially clear with regard to charity, of which it is written (Cant. viii 7): *Many waters cannot quench charity.*

Others again, seeing that these gifts are set down in Holy Writ as having been in Christ, according to Isa. xi. 2, 3, said that the virtues are given simply that we may do good works, but the gifts, in order to conform us to Christ, chiefly with regard to His Passion, for it was then that these gifts shone with the greatest splendor.—Yet neither does this appear to be a satisfactory distinction. Because Our Lord Himself wished us to be conformed to Him, chiefly in humility and meekness, according to Matth. xi. 29: *Learn of Me, because I am meek and humble of heart,* and in charity, according to Jo. xv. 12: *Love one another, as I have loved you.* Moreover, these virtues were especially resplendent in Christ's Passion.

Accordingly, in order to differentiate the gifts from the virtues, we must be guided by the way in which Scripture expresses itself, for we find there that the term employed is *spirit* rather than *gift.* For thus it is written (Isa. xi. 2, 3): *The spirit . . . of wisdom and of understanding . . . shall rest upon him,* etc.: from which words we are clearly given to understand that these seven are there set down as being in us by Divine inspiration. Now inspiration denotes motion from without. For it must be noted that in man there is a twofold principle of movement, one within him, viz. the reason; the other extrinsic to him, viz. God, as stated above (Q. 9, AA. 4, 6): moreover the Philosopher says this in the chapter *On Good Fortune* (*Ethic. Eudem.* vii. 8).

Now it is evident that whatever is moved must be proportionate to its mover: and the perfection of the mobile as such, consists in a disposition whereby it is disposed to be well moved by its mover. Hence the more exalted

* ἀρετὴ ἡρωϊκὴ καὶ θεία.

the mover, the more perfect must be the disposition whereby the mobile is made proportionate to its mover: thus we see that a disciple needs a more perfect disposition in order to receive a higher teaching from his master. Now it is manifest that human virtues perfect man according as it is natural for him to be moved by his reason in his interior and exterior actions. Consequently man needs yet higher perfections, whereby to be disposed to be moved by God. These perfections are called gifts, not only because they are infused by God, but also because by them man is disposed to become amenable to the Divine inspiration, according to Isa. l. 5: *The Lord . . . hath opened my ear, and I do not resist; I have not gone back.* Even the Philosopher says in the chapter *On Good Fortune* (*Ethic. Eudem., loc. cit.*) that for those who are moved by Divine instinct, there is no need to take counsel according to human reason, but only to follow their inner promptings, since they are moved by a principle higher than human reason. This then is what some say, viz. that the gifts perfect man for acts which are higher than acts of virtue.

Reply Obj. 1. Sometimes these gifts are called virtues, in the broad sense of the word. Nevertheless, they have something over and above the virtues understood in this broad way, in so far as they are Divine virtues, perfecting man as moved by God. Hence the Philosopher (*Ethic.* vii. 1) above virtue commonly so called, places a kind of *heroic* or *divine virtue,** in respect of which some men are called *divine.*

Reply Obj. 2. The vices are opposed to the virtues, in so far as they are opposed to the good as appointed by reason; but they are opposed to the gifts, in as much as they are opposed to the Divine instinct. For the same thing is opposed both to God and to reason, whose light flows from God.

Reply Obj. 3. This definition applies to virtue taken in its general sense. Consequently, if we wish to restrict it to virtue as distinguished from the gifts, we must explain the words, *whereby we lead a good life* as referring to the rectitude of life which is measured by the rule of reason. Likewise the gifts, as distinct from infused virtue, may be defined as something given by God in relation to His motion; something, to wit, that makes man to follow well the promptings of God.

Reply Obj. 4. Wisdom is called an intellectual virtue, so far as it proceeds from the judgment of reason: but it is called a gift, according as its work proceeds from the Divine prompting. The same applies to the other virtues.

SECOND ARTICLE

Whether the Gifts Are Necessary to Man for Salvation?

We proceed thus to the Second Article:—

Objection 1. It would seem that the gifts are not necessary to man for salvation. Because the gifts are ordained to a perfection surpassing the ordinary perfection of virtue. Now it is not necessary for man's salvation that he should attain to a perfection surpassing the ordinary standard of virtue; because such perfection falls, not under the precept, but under a counsel. Therefore the gifts are not necessary to man for salvation.

Obj. 2. Further, it is enough, for man's salvation, that he behave well in matters concerning God and matters concerning man. Now man's behavior to God is sufficiently directed by the theological virtues; and his behavior towards men, by the moral virtues. Therefore the gifts are not necessary to man for salvation.

Obj. 3. Further, Gregory says (*Moral.* ii. 26) that *the Holy Ghost gives wisdom against folly, understanding against dullness, counsel against rashness, fortitude against fears, knowledge against ignorance, piety against hardness of our heart, and fear against pride.* But a sufficient remedy for all these things is to be found in the virtues. Therefore the gifts are not necessary to man for salvation.

On the contrary, Of all the gifts, wisdom seems to be the highest, and fear the lowest. Now each of these is necessary for salvation: since of wisdom it is written (*Wis.* vii. 28): *God loveth none but him that dwelleth with wisdom;* and of fear (Ecclus. i. 28): *He that is without fear cannot be justified.* Therefore the other gifts that are placed between these are also necessary for salvation.

I answer that, As stated above (A. 1), the gifts are perfections of man, whereby he is disposed so as to be amenable to the promptings of God. Wherefore in those matters where the prompting of reason is not sufficient, and there is need for the prompting of the Holy Ghost, there is, in consequence, need for a gift.

Now man's reason is perfected by God in two ways: first, with its natural perfection, to wit, the natural light of reason; secondly, with a supernatural perfection, to wit, the theological virtues, as stated above (Q. 62, A. 1). And, though this latter perfection is greater than the former, yet the former is possessed by man in a more perfect manner than the latter: because man has the former in his full possession, whereas he possesses the latter imperfectly, since we love and know God imperfectly. Now it is evident that anything that has a nature or a form or a virtue perfectly, can of itself work according to them: not, however, excluding the operation of God, Who works inwardly in every nature and in every will. On the other hand, that which has a nature, or form, or virtue imperfectly, cannot of itself work, unless it be moved by another. Thus the sun which possesses light perfectly, can shine by itself; whereas the moon which has the nature of light imperfectly, sheds only a borrowed light. Again, a physician, who knows the medical art perfectly, can work by himself; but his pupil, who is not yet fully instructed, cannot work by himself, but needs to receive instructions from him.

Accordingly, in matters subject to human reason, and directed to man's connatural end, man can work through the judgment of his reason. If, however, even in these things man receive help in the shape of special promptings from God, this will be out of God's superabundant goodness: hence, according to the philosophers, not every one that had the acquired moral virtues, had also the heroic or divine virtues. But in matters directed to the supernatural end, to which man's reason moves him, according as it is, in a manner, and imperfectly, informed by the theological virtues, the motion of reason does not suffice, unless it receive in addition the prompting or motion of the Holy Ghost, according to Rom. viii. 14, 17: *Whosoever are led by the Spirit of God, they are the sons of God . . . and if sons, heirs also:* and Ps. cxlii. 10: *Thy good Spirit shall lead me into the right land,* because, to wit, none can receive the inheritance of that land of the Blessed, except he be moved and led thither by the Holy Ghost. Therefore, in order to accomplish this end, it is necessary for man to have the gift of the Holy Ghost.

Reply Obj. 1. The gifts surpass the ordinary perfection of the virtues, not as regards the kind of works (as the counsels surpass the commandments), but as regards the manner of working, in respect of man being moved by a higher principle.

Reply Obj. 2. By the theological and moral virtues, man is not so perfected in respect of his last end, as not to stand in continual need of being moved by the yet higher promptings of the Holy Ghost, for the reason already given.

Reply Obj. 3. Whether we consider human reason as perfected in its natural perfection, or as perfected by the theological virtues, it does not know all things, nor all possible things. Consequently it is unable to avoid folly and other like things mentioned in the objection. God, however, to Whose knowledge and power all things are subject, by His motion safeguards us from all folly, ignorance, dullness of mind and hardness of heart, and the rest. Consequently the gifts of the Holy Ghost, which make us amenable to His promptings, are said to be given as remedies to these defects.

THIRD ARTICLE

Whether the Gifts of the Holy Ghost Are Habits?

We proceed thus to the Third Article:—

Objection 1. It would seem that the gifts of the Holy Ghost are not habits. Because a habit is a quality abiding in man, being defined as *a quality difficult to remove,* as stated in the *Predicaments (Categor.* vi.). Now it is proper to Christ that the gifts of the Holy Ghost rest in Him, as stated in Isa. xi. 2, 3. Moreover, it is written (Jo. i. 33): *He upon Whom thou shalt see the Spirit descending and remaining upon Him, He it is that baptizeth;* on which words Gregory comments as follows (*Moral.* ii. 27): *The Holy Ghost comes upon all the faithful; but, in a singular way, He dwells always in the Mediator.* Therefore the gifts of the Holy Ghost are not habits.

Obj. 2. Further, the gifts of the Holy Ghost perfect man according as he is moved by the Spirit of God, as stated above (AA. 1, 2). But in so far as man is moved by the Spirit of God, he is somewhat like an instrument in His regard. Now to be perfected by a habit is befitting, not an instrument, but a principal agent. Therefore the gifts of the Holy Ghost are not habits.

Obj. 3. Further, as the gifts of the Holy Ghost are due to Divine inspiration, so is the gift of prophecy. Now prophecy is not a habit: for *the spirit of prophecy does not always reside in the prophets,* as Gregory states (*Hom.* i. *in Ezechiel*). Neither, therefore, are the gifts of the Holy Ghost habits.

On the contrary, Our Lord in speaking of the Holy Ghost said to His disciples (Jo. xiv. 17): *He shall abide with you, and shall be in you.* Now the Holy Ghost is not in a man without His gifts. Therefore His gifts abide in man. Therefore they are not merely acts or passions but abiding habits.

I answer that, As stated above (A. 1), the gifts are perfections of man, whereby he becomes amenable to the promptings of the Holy Ghost. Now it is evident from what has been already said (Q. 56, A. 4; Q. 58, A. 2), that the moral virtues perfect the appetitive power according as it partakes somewhat of the reason, in so far, to wit, as it has a natural aptitude to be moved by the command of reason. Accordingly the gifts of the Holy Ghost, as compared with the Holy Ghost Himself, are related to man, even as the moral virtues, in comparison with the reason, are related to the appetitive power. Now the moral virtues are habits, whereby the powers of appetite are dis-

posed to obey reason promptly. Therefore the gifts of the Holy Ghost are habits whereby man is perfected to obey readily the Holy Ghost.

Reply Obj. 1. Gregory solves this objection (*ibid.*) by saying that *by those gifts without which one cannot obtain life, the Holy Ghost ever abides in all the elect, but not by His other gifts.* Now the seven gifts are necessary for salvation, as stated above (A. 2). Therefore, with regard to them, the Holy Ghost ever abides in holy men.

Reply Obj. 2. This argument holds, in the case of an instrument which has no faculty of action, but only of being acted upon. But man is not an instrument of that kind; for he is so acted upon by the Holy Ghost, that he also acts himself, in so far as he has a freewill. Therefore he needs a habit.

Reply Obj. 3. Prophecy is one of those gifts which are for the manifestation of the Spirit, not for the necessity of salvation: hence the comparison fails.

FOURTH ARTICLE

Whether the Seven Gifts of the Holy Ghost Are Suitably Enumerated?

We proceed thus to the Fourth Article:—

Objection 1. It would seem that seven gifts of the Holy Ghost are unsuitably enumerated. For in that enumeration four are set down corresponding to the intellectual virtues, viz., wisdom, understanding, knowledge, and counsel, which corresponds to prudence; whereas nothing is set down corresponding to art, which is the fifth intellectual virtue. Moreover, something is included corresponding to justice, viz., piety, and something corresponding to fortitude, viz., the gift of fortitude; while there is nothing to correspond to temperance. Therefore the gifts are enumerated insufficiently.

Obj. 2. Further, piety is a part of justice. But no part of fortitude is assigned to correspond thereto, but fortitude itself. Therefore justice itself, and not piety, ought to have been set down.

Obj. 3. Further, the theological virtues, more than any, direct us to God. Since, then, the gifts perfect man according as he is moved by God, it seems that some gifts, corresponding to the theological virtues, should have been included.

Obj. 4. Further, even as God is an object of fear, so is He of love, of hope, and of joy. Now love, hope, and joy are passions condivided with fear. Therefore, as fear is set down as a gift, so ought the other three.

Obj. 5. Further, wisdom is added in order to direct understanding; counsel, to direct fortitude; knowledge, to direct piety. Therefore, some gift should have been added for the purpose of directing fear. Therefore the seven gifts of the Holy Ghost are unsuitably enumerated.

On the contrary stands the authority of Holy Writ (Isa. xi. 2, 3).

I answer that, As stated above (A. 3), the gifts are habits perfecting man so that he is ready to follow the promptings of the Holy Ghost, even as the moral virtues perfect the appetitive powers so that they obey the reason. Now just as it is natural for the appetitive powers to be moved by the command of reason, so it is natural for all the forces in man to be moved by the instinct of God, as by a superior power. Therefore whatever powers in man can be the principles of human actions, can also be the subjects of gifts, even as they are virtues; and such powers are the reason and appetite.

Now the reason is speculative and practical: and in both we find the apprehension of truth (which pertains to the discovery of truth), and judgment concerning the truth. Accordingly, for the apprehension of truth, the speculative reason is perfected by *understanding;* the practical reason, by *counsel.* In order to judge aright, the speculative reason is perfected by *wisdom;* the practical reason by *knowledge.*—The appetitive power, in matters touching a man's relations to another, is perfected by *piety;* in matters touching himself, it is perfected by *fortitude* against the fear of dangers; and against inordinate lust for pleasures, by *fear,* according to Prov. xv. 27: *By the fear of the Lord every one declineth from evil,* and Ps. cxviii. 120: *Pierce Thou my flesh with Thy fear: for I am afraid of Thy judgments.*—Hence it is clear that these gifts extend to all those things to which the virtues, both intellectual and moral, extend.

Reply Obj. 1. The gifts of the Holy Ghost perfect man in matters concerning a good life: whereas art is not directed to such matters, but to external things that can be made, since art is the right reason, not about things to be done, but about things to be made (*Ethic.* vi. 4). However, we may say that, as regards the infusion of the gifts, the art is on the part of the Holy Ghost, Who is the principal mover, and not on the part of men, who are His organs when He moves them. The gift of fear corresponds, in a manner, to temperance: for just as it belongs to temperance, properly speaking, to restrain man from evil pleasures for the sake of the good appointed by reason, so does it belong to the gift of fear, to withdraw man from evil pleasures through fear of God.

Reply Obj. 2. Justice is so called from the rectitude of the reason, and so it is more suitably called a virtue than a gift. But the name of piety denotes the reverence which we give to our father and to our country. And since God is the Father of all, the worship of God is also called piety, as Augustine states (*De Civ. Dei* x. 1). Therefore the gift whereby a man, through reverence for God, works good to all, is fittingly called piety.

Reply Obj. 3. The mind of man is not moved by the Holy Ghost, unless in some way it be united to Him: even as the instrument is not moved by the craftsman, unless there be contact or some other kind of union between them. Now the primal union of man with God is by faith, hope and charity: and, consequently, these virtues are presupposed to the gifts, as being their roots. Therefore all the gifts correspond to these three virtues, as being derived therefrom.

Reply Obj. 4. Love, hope and joy have good for their object. Now God is the Sovereign Good: wherefore the names of these passions are transferred to the theological virtues which unite man to God. On the other hand, the object of fear is evil, which can nowise apply to God: hence fear does not denote union with God, but withdrawal from certain things through reverence for God. Hence it does not give its name to a theological virtue, but to a gift, which withdraws us from evil, for higher motives than moral virtue does.

Reply Obj. 5. Wisdom directs both the intellect and the affections of man. Hence two gifts are set down as corresponding to wisdom as their directing principle; on the part of the intellect, the gift of understanding; on the part of the affections, the gift of fear. Because the principal reason for fearing God is taken from a consideration of the Divine excellence, which wisdom considers.

FIFTH ARTICLE

Whether the Gifts of the Holy Ghost Are Connected?

We proceed thus to the Fifth Article:—

Objection 1. It would seem that the gifts are not connected, for the Apostle says (1 Cor. xii. 8): *To one . . . by the Spirit, is given the word of wisdom, and to another, the word of knowledge, according to the same Spirit.* Now wisdom and knowledge are reckoned among the gifts of the Holy Ghost. Therefore the gifts of the Holy Ghost are given to divers men, and are not connected together in the same man.

Obj. 2. Further, Augustine says (*De Trin.* xiv. 1) that *many of the faithful have not knowledge, though they have faith.* But some of the gifts, at least the gift of fear, accompany faith. Therefore it seems that the gifts are not necessarily connected together in one and the same man.

Obj. 3. Further, Gregory says (*Moral.* i) that wisdom *is of small account if it lack understanding, and understanding is wholly useless if it be not based upon wisdom.* . . . *Counsel is worthless, when the strength of fortitude is lacking thereto,* . . . *and fortitude is very weak if it be not supported by counsel.* . . . *Knowledge is nought if it hath not the use of piety,* . . . *and piety is very useless if it lack the discernment of knowledge,* . . . *and assuredly, unless it has these virtues with it, fear itself rises up to the doing of no good action:* from which it seems that it is possible to have one gift without another. Therefore the gifts of the Holy Ghost are not connected.

On the contrary, Gregory prefaces the passage above quoted, with the following remark: *It is worthy of note in this feast of Job's sons, that by turns they fed one another.* Now the sons of Job, of whom he is speaking, denote the gifts of the Holy Ghost. Therefore the gifts of the Holy Ghost are connected together by strengthening one another.

I answer that, The true answer to this question is easily gathered from what has been already set down. For it has been stated (A. 3) that as the powers of appetite are disposed by the moral virtues as regards the governance of reason, so all the powers of the soul are disposed by the gifts as regards the motion of Holy Ghost. Now the Holy Ghost dwells in us by charity, according to Rom. v. 5: *The charity of God is poured forth in our hearts by the Holy Ghost, Who is given to us,* even as our reason is perfected by prudence. Wherefore, just as the moral virtues are united together in prudence, so the gifts of the Holy Ghost are connected together in charity: so that whoever has charity has all the gifts of the Holy Ghost, none of which can one possess without charity.

Reply Obj. 1. Wisdom and knowledge can be considered in one way as gratuitous graces, in so far, to wit, as man so far abounds in the knowledge of things Divine and human, that he is able both to instruct the believer and confound the unbeliever. It is in this sense that the Apostle speaks, in this passage, about wisdom and knowledge: hence he mentions pointedly the *word* of wisdom and the *word* of knowledge. They may be taken in another way for the gifts of the Holy Ghost: and thus wisdom and knowledge are nothing else but perfections of the human mind, rendering it amenable to the promptings of the Holy Ghost in the knowledge of things Divine and human. Consequently it is clear that these gifts are in all who are possessed of charity.

Reply Obj. 2. Augustine is speaking there of knowledge, while expounding the passage of the Apostle quoted above (*Obj.* 1): hence

he is referring to knowledge, in the sense already explained, as a gratuitous grace. This is clear from the context which follows: *For it is one thing to know only what a man must believe in order to gain the blissful life, which is no other than eternal life; and another, to know how to impart this to godly souls, and to defend it against the ungodly, which latter the Apostle seems to have styled by the proper name of knowledge.*

Reply Obj. 3. Just as the connection of the cardinal virtues is proved in one way from the fact that one is, in a manner, perfected by another, as stated above (Q. 65, A. 1); so Gregory wishes to prove the connection of the gifts, in the same way, from the fact that one cannot be perfect without the other. Hence he had already observed that *each particular virtue is to the last degree destitute, unless one virtue lend its support to another.* We are therefore not to understand that one gift can be without another; but that if understanding were without wisdom, it would not be a gift; even as temperance, without justice, would not be a virtue.

SIXTH ARTICLE

Whether the Gifts of the Holy Ghost Remain in Heaven?

We proceed thus to the Sixth Article:—

Objection 1. It would seem that the gifts of the Holy Ghost do not remain in heaven. For Gregory says (*Moral.* ii. 26) that by means of His sevenfold gift the *Holy Ghost instructs the mind against all temptations.* Now there will be no temptations in heaven, according to Isa. xi. 9: *They shall not hurt, nor shall they kill in all My holy mountain.* Therefore there will be no gifts of the Holy Ghost in heaven.

Obj. 2. Further, the gifts of the Holy Ghost are habits, as stated above (A. 3). But habits are of no use, where their acts are impossible. Now the acts of some gifts are not possible in heaven; for Gregory says (*Moral.* i. 15) that *understanding* . . . *penetrates the truths heard,* . . . *counsel* . . . *stays us from acting rashly,* . . . *fortitude* . . . *has no fear of adversity,* . . . *piety satisfies the inmost heart with deeds of mercy,* all of which are incompatible with the heavenly state. Therefore these gifts will not remain in the state of glory.

Obj. 3. Further, some of the gifts perfect man in the contemplative life, e.g. wisdom and understanding: and some in the active life, e.g. piety and fortitude. Now the active life ends with this as Gregory states (*Moral.* vi). Therefore not all the gifts of the Holy Ghost will be in the state of glory.

On the contrary, Ambrose says (*De Spiritt*

Sancto i. 20): *The city of God, the heavenly Jerusalem is not washed with the waters of an earthly river: it is the Holy Ghost, of Whose outpouring we but taste, Who, proceeding from the Fount of life, seems to flow more abundantly in those celestial spirits, a seething torrent of sevenfold heavenly virtue.*

I answer that, We may speak of the gifts in two ways: first, as to their essence; and thus they will be most perfectly in heaven, as may be gathered from the passage of Ambrose, just quoted. The reason for this is that the gifts of the Holy Ghost render the human mind amenable to the motion of the Holy Ghost: which will be especially realized in heaven, where God will be *all in all* (1 Cor. xv. 28), and man entirely subject unto Him. Secondly, they may be considered as regards the matter about which their operations are: and thus, in the present life they have an operation about a matter, in respect of which they will have no operation in the state of glory. Considered in this way, they will not remain in the state of glory; just as we have stated to be the case with regard to the cardinal virtues (Q. 67, A. 1).

Reply Obj. 1. Gregory is speaking there of the gifts according as they are compatible with the present state: for it is thus that they afford us protection against evil temptations. But in the state of glory, where all evil will have ceased, we shall be perfected in good by the gifts of the Holy Ghost.

Reply Obj. 2. Gregory, in almost every gift, includes something that passes away with the present state, and something that remains in the future state. For he says that *wisdom strengthens the mind with the hope and certainty of eternal things;* of which two, hope passes, and certainty remains. Of understanding, he says *that it penetrates the truths heard, refreshing the heart and enlightening its darkness,* of which, hearing passes away, since *they shall teach no more every man . . . his brother* (Jerem. xxxi. 3, 4); but the enlightening of the mind remains. Of counsel he says that it *prevents us from being impetuous,* which is necessary in the present life; and also that *it makes the mind full of reason,* which is necessary even in the future state.—Of fortitude he says that it *fears not adversity,* which is necessary in the present life; and further, that it *sets before us the viands of confidence,* which remains also in the future life. With regard to knowledge he mentions only one thing, viz. that *she overcomes the void of ignorance,* which refers to the present state. When, however, he adds *in the womb of the mind,* this may refer figuratively to the fulness of knowledge, which belongs to the future state.—Of piety he says that *it satisfies the inmost heart*

with deeds of mercy. These words taken literally refer only to the present state: yet the inward regard for our neighbor, signified by *the inmost heart,* belongs also to the future state, when piety will achieve, not works of mercy, but fellowship of joy.—Of fear he says that *it oppresses the mind, lest it pride itself in present things,* which refers to the present state, and that *it strengthens it with the meat of hope for the future,* which also belongs to the present state, as regards hope, but may also refer to the future state, as regards being *strengthened* for things we hope for here, and obtain there.

Reply Obj. 3. This argument considers the gifts as to their matter. For the matter of the gifts will not be works of the active life; but all the gifts will have their respective acts about things pertaining to the contemplative life, which is the life of heavenly bliss.

SEVENTH ARTICLE

Whether the Gifts Are Set Down by Isaias in Their Order of Dignity?

We proceed thus to the Seventh Article:—

Objection 1. It would seem that the gifts are not set down by Isaias in their order of dignity. For the principal gift is, seemingly, that which, more than the others, God requires of man. Now God requires of man fear, more than the other gifts: for it is written (Deut. x. 12): *And now, Israel, what doth the Lord thy God require of thee, but that thou fear the Lord thy God?* and (Malach. i. 6): *If . . . I be a master, where is My fear?* Therefore it seems that fear, which is mentioned last, is not the lowest but the greatest of the gifts.

Obj. 2. Further, piety seems to be a kind of common good; since the Apostle says (1 Tim. iv. 8): *Piety (Douay,—Godliness) is profitable to all things.* Now a common good is preferable to particular goods. Therefore piety, which is given the last place but one, seems to be the most excellent gift.

Obj. 3. Further, knowledge perfects man's judgment, while counsel pertains to inquiry. But judgment is more excellent than inquiry. Therefore knowledge is a more excellent gift than counsel; and yet it is set down as being below it.

Obj. 4. Further, fortitude pertains to the appetitive power, while science belongs to reason. But reason is a more excellent power than the appetite. Therefore knowledge is a more excellent gift than fortitude; and yet the latter is given the precedence. Therefore the gifts are not set down in their order of dignity.

On the contrary, Augustine says (*De Serm. Dom. in Monte* i. 4): *It seems to me that the* sevenfold operation of the Holy Ghost, of which Isaias speaks, agrees in degrees and expression with these (of which we read in Matth. v. 3): but there is a difference of order, for there (viz. in Isaias) the enumeration begins with the more excellent gifts, here, with the lower gifts.

I answer that, The excellence of the gifts can be measured in two ways: first, simply, viz. by comparison to their proper acts as proceeding from their principles; secondly, relatively, viz. by comparison to their matter. If we consider the excellence of the gifts simply, they follow the same rule as the virtues, as to their comparison one with another; because the gifts perfect man for all the acts of the soul's powers, even as the virtues do, as stated above (A. 4). Hence, as the intellectual virtues have the precedence of the moral virtues, and among the intellectual virtues, the contemplative are preferable to the active, viz. wisdom, understanding and science to prudence and art (yet so that wisdom stands before understanding, and understanding before science, and prudence and synesis before eubulia): so also among the gifts, wisdom, understanding, knowledge, and counsel are more excellent than piety, fortitude, and fear; and among the latter, piety excels fortitude, and fortitude fear, even as justice surpasses fortitude, and fortitude temperance.—But in regard to their matter, fortitude and counsel precede knowledge and piety: because fortitude and counsel are concerned with difficult matters, whereas piety and knowledge regard ordinary matters. —Consequently the excellence of the gifts corresponds with the order in which they are enumerated; but so far as wisdom and understanding are given the preference to the others, their excellence is considered simply, while, so far as counsel and fortitude are preferred to knowledge and piety, it is considered with regard to their matter.

Reply Obj. 1. Fear is chiefly required as being the foundation, so to speak, of the perfection of the other gifts, for the fear of the Lord is the beginning of wisdom (Ps. cx. 10; Ecclus. i. 16), and not as though it were more excellent than the others. Because, in the order of generation, man departs from evil on account of fear (Prov. xvi. 16), before doing good works, and which result from the other gifts.

Reply Obj. 2. In the words quoted from the Apostle, piety is not compared with all God's gifts, but only with bodily exercise, of which he had said that it is profitable to little.

Reply Obj. 3. Although knowledge stands before counsel by reason of its judgment, yet counsel is more excellent by reason of its matter: for counsel is only concerned with matters

of difficulty (Ethic. iii. 3), whereas the judgment of knowledge embraces all matters.

Reply Obj. 4. The directive gifts which pertain to the reason are more excellent than the executive gifts, if we consider them in relation to their acts as proceeding from their powers, because reason transcends the appetite as a rule transcends the thing ruled. But on the part of the matter, counsel is united to fortitude as the directive power to the executive, and so is knowledge united to piety: because counsel and fortitude are concerned with matters of difficulty, while knowledge and piety are concerned with ordinary matters. Hence counsel together with fortitude, by reason of their matter, are given the preference to knowledge and piety.

EIGHTH ARTICLE

Whether the Virtues Are More Excellent Than the Gifts?

We proceed thus to the Eighth Article:—

Objection 1. It would seem that the virtues are more excellent than the gifts. For Augustine says (De Trin. xv. 18) while speaking of charity: No gift of God is more excellent than this. It is this alone which divides the children of the eternal kingdom from the children of eternal damnation. Other gifts are bestowed by the Holy Ghost, but, without charity, they avail nothing. But charity is a virtue. Therefore a virtue is more excellent than the gifts of the Holy Ghost.

Obj. 2. Further, that which is first naturally, seems to be more excellent. Now the virtues precede the gifts of the Holy Ghost; for Gregory says (Moral. ii. 26) that the gift of the Holy Ghost in the mind it works on, forms first of all justice, prudence, fortitude, temperance . . . and doth afterwards give it a temper in the seven virtues (viz. the gifts), so as against folly to bestow wisdom; against dullness, understanding; against rashness, counsel; against fear, fortitude; against ignorance, knowledge; against hardness of heart, piety; against piety, fear. Therefore the virtues are more excellent than the gifts.

Obj. 3. Further, Augustine says (De Lib. Arb. ii. 19) that the virtues cannot be used to evil purpose. But it is possible to make evil use of the gifts, for Gregory says (Moral. i. 18): We offer up the sacrifice of prayer . . . lest wisdom may uplift; or understanding, while it runs nimbly, deviate from the right path; or counsel, while it multiplies itself, grow into confusion; that fortitude, while it gives confidence, may not make us rash; lest knowledge, while it knows and yet loves not, may swell the mind; lest piety, while it swerves from the right line, may become dis-

torted; and lest fear, while it is unduly alarmed, may plunge us into the pit of despair. Therefore the virtues are more excellent than the gifts of the Holy Ghost.

On the contrary, The gifts are bestowed to assist the virtues and to remedy certain defects, as is shown in the passage quoted (*Obj.* 2), so that, seemingly, they accomplish what the virtues cannot. Therefore the gifts are more excellent than the virtues.

I answer that, As was shown above (Q. 58, A. 3; Q. 62, A. 1), there are three kinds of virtues: for some are theological, some intellectual, and some moral. The theological virtues are those whereby man's mind is united to God; the intellectual virtues are those whereby reason itself is perfected; and the moral virtues are those which perfect the powers of appetite in obedience to the reason. On the other hand the gifts of the Holy Ghost dispose all the powers of the soul to be amenable to the Divine motion.

Accordingly the gifts seem to be compared to the theological virtues, by which man is united to the Holy Ghost his Mover, in the same way as the moral virtues are compared to the intellectual virtues, which perfect the reason, the moving principle of the moral virtues. Wherefore as the intellectual virtues are more excellent than the moral virtues and control them, so the theological virtues are more excellent than the gifts of the Holy Ghost and regulate them. Hence Gregory says (*Moral.* i. 12) that *the seven sons,* i.e. the seven gifts, *never attain the perfection of the number ten, unless all that they do be done in faith, hope, and charity.*

But if we compare the gifts to the other virtues, intellectual and moral, then the gifts have the precedence of the virtues. Because the gifts perfect the soul's powers in relation to the Holy Ghost their Mover; whereas the virtues perfect, either the reason itself, or the other powers in relation to reason: and it is evident that the more exalted the mover, the more excellent the disposition whereby the thing moved requires to be disposed. Therefore the gifts are more perfect than the virtues.

Reply Obj. 1. Charity is a theological virtue; and such we grant to be more perfect than the gifts.

Reply Obj. 2. There are two ways in which one thing precedes another. One is in order of perfection and dignity, as love of God precedes love of our neighbor: and in this way the gifts precede the intellectual and moral virtues, but follow the theological virtues. The other is the order of generation or disposition: thus love of one's neighbor precedes love of God, as regards the act: and in this way moral and intellectual virtues precede the gifts, since man, through being well subordinate to his own reason, is disposed to be rightly subordinate to God.

Reply Obj. 3. Wisdom and understanding and the like are gifts of the Holy Ghost, according as they are quickened by charity, which *dealeth not perversely* (1 Cor. xiii. 4). Consequently wisdom and understanding and the like cannot be used to evil purpose, in so far as they are gifts of the Holy Ghost. But, lest they depart from the perfection of charity, they assist one another. This is what Gregory means to say.

QUESTION 69

Of the Beatitudes

(In Four Articles)

WE must now consider the beatitudes: under which head there are four points of inquiry: (1) Whether the beatitudes differ from the gifts and virtues? (2) Of the rewards of the beatitudes: whether they refer to this life? (3) Of the number of the beatitudes. (4) Of the fittingness of the rewards ascribed to beatitudes.

FIRST ARTICLE

Whether the Beatitudes Differ from the Virtues and Gifts?

We proceed thus to the First Article:—

Objection 1. It would seem that the beatitudes do not differ from the virtues and gifts. For Augustine (*De Serm. Dom. in Monte,* i. 4) assigns the beatitudes recited by Mat-

thew (v. 3, *seqq.*) to the gifts of the Holy Ghost; and Ambrose in his commentary on Luke vi. 20, *seqq.*, ascribes the beatitudes mentioned there, to the four cardinal virtues. Therefore the beatitudes do not differ from the virtues and gifts.

Obj. 2. Further, there are but two rules of the human will;—the reason and the eternal law, as stated above (Q. 19, A. 3; Q. 21, A. 1). Now the virtues perfect man in relation to reason; while the gifts perfect man in relation to the eternal law of the Holy Ghost, as is clear from what has been said (Q. 68, AA. 1, 3, *seqq.*). Therefore there cannot be anything else pertaining to the rectitude of the human will, besides the virtues and gifts. Therefore the beatitudes do not differ from them.

Obj. 3. Further, among the beatitudes are included meekness, justice, and mercy, which are said to be virtues. Therefore the beatitudes do not differ from the virtues and gifts.

On the contrary, Certain things are included among the beatitudes, that are neither virtues nor gifts, e.g. poverty, mourning, and peace. Therefore the beatitudes differ from the virtues and gifts.

I answer that, As stated above (Q. 2, A. 7; Q. 3, A. 1), happiness is the last end of human life. Now one is said to possess the end already, when one hopes to possess it; wherefore the Philosopher says (*Ethic. i.* 9) that *children are said to be happy because they are full of hope;* and the Apostle says (Rom. viii. 24): *We are saved by hope.* Again, we hope to obtain an end, because we are suitably moved towards that end, and approach thereto; and this implies some action. And a man is moved towards, and approaches the happy end by works of virtue, and above all by the works of the gifts, if we speak of eternal happiness, for which our reason is not sufficient, since we need to be moved by the Holy Ghost, and to be perfected with His gifts that we may obey and follow him. Consequently the beatitudes differ from the virtues and gifts, not as habit from habit, but as act from habit.

Reply Obj. 1. Augustine and Ambrose assign the beatitudes to the gifts and virtues, as acts are ascribed to habits. But the gifts are more excellent than the cardinal virtues, as stated above (Q. 68, A. 8). Wherefore Ambrose, in explaining the beatitudes propounded to the throng, assigns them to the cardinal virtues, whereas Augustine, who is explaining the beatitudes delivered to the disciples on the mountain, and so to those who were more perfect, ascribes them to the gifts of the Holy Ghost.

Reply Obj. 2. This argument proves that no other habits, besides the virtues and gifts, rectify human conduct.

Reply Obj. 3. Meekness is to be taken as denoting the act of meekness: and the same applies to justice and mercy. And though these might seem to be virtues, they are nevertheless ascribed to gifts, because the gifts perfect man in all matters wherein the virtues perfect him, as stated above (Q. 68, A. 2).

SECOND ARTICLE

Whether the Rewards Assigned to the Beatitudes Refer to This Life?

We proceed thus to the Second Article:—
Objection 1. It would seem that the rewards

* *Cf. De Serm. Dom. in Monte,* i. 1.

assigned to the beatitudes do not refer to this life. Because some are said to be happy because they hope for a reward, as stated above (A. 1). Now the object of hope is future happiness. Therefore these rewards refer to the life to come.

Obj. 2. Further, certain punishments are set down in opposition to the beatitudes, Luke vi. 25, where we read: *Woe to you that are filled; for you shall hunger. Woe to you that now laugh, for you shall mourn and weep.* Now these punishments do not refer to this life, because frequently men are not punished in this life, according to Job xxi. 13: *They spend their days in wealth.* Therefore neither do the rewards of the beatitudes refer to this life.

Obj. 3. Further, the kingdom of heaven which is set down as the reward of poverty is the happiness of heaven, as Augustine says (*De Civ. Dei* xix).* Again, abundant fullness is not to be had save in the life to come, according to Ps. xvi. 15: *I shall be filled* (Douay, —*satisfied*) *when Thy glory shall appear.*— Again, it is only in the future life that we shall see God, and that our Divine sonship will be made manifest, according to 1 Jo. iii. 2: *We are now the sons of God; and it hath not yet appeared what we shall be. We know that, when He shall appear, we shall be like to Him, because we shall see Him as He is.* Therefore these rewards refer to the future life.

On the contrary, Augustine says (*De Serm. Dom. in Monte* i. 4): *These promises can be fulfilled in this life, as we believe them to have been fulfilled in the apostles. For no words can express that complete change into the likeness even of an angel, which is promised to us after this life.*

I answer that, Expounders of Holy Writ are not agreed in speaking of these rewards. For some, with Ambrose (*Super Luc.* v.), hold that all these rewards refer to the life to come; while Augustine (*loc. cit.*) holds them to refer to the present life; and Chrysostom in his homilies (*In Matth.* xv) says that some refer to the future, and some to the present life.

In order to make the matter clear we must take note that hope of future happiness may be in us for two reasons. First, by reason of our having a preparation for, or a disposition to future happiness; and this is by way of merit; secondly, by a kind of imperfect inchoation of future happiness in holy men, even in this life. For it is one thing to hope that the tree will bear fruit, when the leaves begin to appear, and another, when we see the first signs of the fruit.

Accordingly, those things which are set down as merits in the beatitudes, are a kind of preparation for, or disposition to happiness, either perfect or inchoate: while those that are assigned as rewards, may be either perfect happiness, so as to refer to the future life, or some beginning of happiness, such as is found in those who have attained perfection, in which case they refer to the present life. Because when a man begins to make progress in the acts of the virtues and gifts, it is to be hoped that he will arrive at perfection, both as a wayfarer, and as a citizen of the heavenly kingdom.

Reply Obj. 1. Hope regards future happiness as the last end: yet it may also regard the assistance of grace as that which leads to that end, according to Ps. xxvii. 7: *In Him hath my heart hoped, and I have been helped.*

Reply Obj. 2. Although sometimes the wicked do not undergo temporal punishment in this life, yet they suffer spiritual punishment. Hence Augustine says (*Conf.* i): *Thou hast decreed, and it is so, Lord,—that the disordered mind should be its own punishment.* The Philosopher, too, says of the wicked (*Ethic.* ix. 4) that *their soul is divided against itself,* . . . *one part pulls this way, another that;* and afterwards he concludes, saying: *If wickedness makes a man so miserable, he should strain every nerve to avoid vice.*—In like manner, although, on the other hand, the good sometimes do not receive material rewards in this life, yet they never lack spiritual rewards, even in this life, according to Matth. xix. 29, and Mark x. 30: *Ye shall receive a hundred times as much even in this time.*

Reply Obj. 3. All these rewards will be fully consummated in the life to come: but meanwhile they are, in a manner, begun, even in this life. Because the *kingdom of heaven*, as Augustine says (*loc. cit.*), can denote the beginning of perfect wisdom, in so far as *the spirit* begins to reign in men.—The *possession* of the land denotes the well-ordered affections of the soul that rests, by its desire, on the solid foundation of the eternal inheritance, signified by *the land.*—They are *comforted* in this life, by receiving the Holy Ghost, Who is called the *Paraclete*, i.e., the Comforter.—They *have their fill*, even in this life, of that food of which Our Lord said (Jo. iv. 34): *My meat is to do the will of Him that sent Me.*—Again, in this life, men *obtain* God's *Mercy.*—Again, the eye being cleansed by the gift of understanding, we can, so to speak, *see God.*—Likewise, in this life, those who are the *peacemakers* of their own movements, approach to likeness to God, and are called *the children of God.* —Nevertheless these things will be more perfectly fulfilled in heaven.

* See Q. 3.

THIRD ARTICLE

Whether the Beatitudes Are Suitably Enumerated?

We proceed thus to the Third Article:—

Objection 1. It would seem that the beatitudes are unsuitably enumerated. For the beatitudes are assigned to the gifts, as stated above (A. 1, *ad* 1). Now some of the gifts, viz. wisdom and understanding, belong to the contemplative life: yet no beatitude is assigned to the act of contemplation, for all are assigned to matters connected with the active life. Therefore the beatitudes are insufficiently enumerated.

Obj. 2. Further, not only do the executive gifts belong to the active life, but also some of the directive gifts, e.g. knowledge and counsel: yet none of the beatitudes seems to be directly connected with the acts of knowledge or counsel. Therefore the beatitudes are insufficiently indicated.

Obj. 3. Further, among the executive gifts connected with the active life, fear is said to be connected with poverty, while piety seems to correspond to the beatitude of mercy: yet nothing is included directly connected with justice. Therefore the beatitudes are insufficiently enumerated.

Obj. 4. Further, many other beatitudes are mentioned in Holy Writ. Thus, it is written (Job v. 17): *Blessed is the man whom God correcteth;* and (Ps. i. 1): *Blessed is the man who hath not walked in the counsel of the ungodly;* and (Prov. iii. 13): *Blessed is the man that findeth wisdom.* Therefore the beatitudes are insufficiently enumerated.

Obj. 5. *On the other hand,* it seems that too many are mentioned. For there are seven gifts of the Holy Ghost: whereas eight beatitudes are indicated.

Obj. 6. Further, only four beatitudes are indicated in the sixth chapter of Luke. Therefore the seven or eight mentioned in Matth. v. are too many.

I answer that, These beatitudes are most suitably enumerated. To make this evident it must be observed that beatitude has been held to consist in one of three things: for some have ascribed it to a sensual life, some, to an active life, and some, to a contemplative life.* Now these three kinds of happiness stand in different relations to future beatitude, by hoping for which we are said to be happy. Because sensual happiness, being false and contrary to reason, is an obstacle to future beatitude; while happiness of the active life is a disposition of future beatitude; and contemplative happiness, if perfect, is the very essence of future beatitude, and, if imperfect, is a beginning thereof.

And so Our Lord, in the first place, indicated certain beatitudes as removing the obstacle of sensual happiness. For a life of pleasure consists of two things. First, in the affluence of external goods, whether riches or honors; from which man is withdrawn,—by a virtue so that he uses them in moderation,—and by a gift, in a more excellent way, so that he despises them altogether. Hence the first beatitude is: *Blessed are the poor in spirit*, which may refer either to the contempt of riches, or to the contempt of honors, which results from humility. Secondly, the sensual life consists in following the bent of one's passions, whether irascible or concupiscible. From following the irascible passions man is withdrawn,—by a virtue, so that they are kept within the bounds appointed by the ruling of reason,—and by a gift, in a more excellent manner, so that man, according to God's will, is altogether undisturbed by them: hence the second beatitude is: *Blessed are the meek*. From following the concupiscible passions, man is withdrawn,—by a virtue, so that man uses these passions in moderation,—and by a gift, so that, if necessary, he casts them aside altogether; nay more, so that, if need be, he makes a deliberate choice of sorrow;* hence the third beatitude is: *Blessed are they that mourn.*

Active life consists chiefly in man's relations with his neighbor, either by way of duty or by way of spontaneous gratuity. To the former we are disposed,—by a virtue, so that we do not refuse to do our duty to our neighbor, which pertains to justice;— and by a gift, so that we do the same much more heartily, by accomplishing works of justice with an ardent desire, even as a hungry and thirsty man eats and drinks with eager appetite. Hence the fourth beatitude is: *Blessed are they that hunger and thirst after justice.* With regard to spontaneous favors we are perfected,—by a virtue, so that we give where reason dictates we should give, e.g. to our friends or others united to us; which pertains to the virtue of liberality,— and by a gift, so that, through reverence for God, we consider only the needs of those on whom we bestow our gratuitous bounty: hence it is written (Luke xiv. 12, 13): *When thou makest a dinner or supper, call not thy friends, nor thy brethren*, etc. ... *but ... call the poor, the maimed*, etc.; which, properly, is to have mercy: hence the fifth beatitude is: *Blessed are the merciful.*

Those things which concern the contemplative life, are either final beatitude itself, or some beginning thereof: wherefore they are included in the beatitudes, not as merits, but as rewards. Yet the effects of the active life, which dispose man for the contemplative life,

*Cf. Q. 35, A. 3.

are included in the beatitudes. Now the effect of the active life, as regards those virtues and gifts whereby man is perfected in himself, is the cleansing of man's heart, so that it is not defiled by the passions: hence the sixth beatitude is: *Blessed are the clean of heart.* But as regards the virtues and gifts whereby man is perfected in relation to his neighbor, the effect of the active life is peace, according to Isaias xxxii. 17: *The work of justice shall be peace*: hence the seventh beatitude is *Blessed are the peacemakers.*

Reply Obj. 1. The acts of the gifts which belong to the active life are indicated in the merits: but the acts of gifts pertaining to the contemplative life are indicated in the rewards, for the reason given above. Because to *see God* corresponds to the gift of understanding; and to be like God by being adopted *children of God*, corresponds to the gift of wisdom.

Reply Obj. 2. In things pertaining to the active life, knowledge is not sought for its own sake, but for the sake of operation, as even the Philosopher states (*Ethic.* ii. 2). And therefore, since beatitude implies something ultimate, the beatitudes do not include the acts of those gifts which direct man in the active life, such acts, to wit, as are elicited by those gifts, as, e.g. to counsel is the act of counsel, and to judge, the act of knowledge: but, on the other hand, they include those operative acts of which the gifts have the direction, as, e.g. mourning in respect of knowledge, and mercy in respect of counsel.

Reply Obj. 3. In applying the beatitudes to the gifts we may consider two things. One is likeness of matter. In this way all the first five beatitudes may be assigned to knowledge and counsel as to their directing principles: whereas they must be distributed among the executive gifts: so that, to wit, hunger and thirst for justice, and mercy too, correspond to piety, which perfects man in his relations to others; meekness to fortitude, for Ambrose says on Luke vi. 22: *It is the business of fortitude to conquer anger, and to curb indignation*, fortitude being about the irascible passions: poverty and mourning to the gift of fear, whereby man withdraws from the lusts and pleasures of the world.

Secondly, we may consider the motives of the beatitudes: and, in this way, some of them will have to be assigned differently. Because the principal motive for meekness is reverence for God, which belongs to piety. The chief motive for mourning is knowledge, whereby man knows his failings and those of worldly things, according to Eccles. i. 18: *He that addeth knowledge, addeth also sorrow* (Vulg., *labor*). The principal motive for hungering after the works of justice, is fortitude of the soul: and the chief motive for being merciful is God's counsel, according to Dan. iv. 24: *Let my counsel be acceptable to the king* (Vulg., —*to thee, O king*): *and redeem thou thy sins with alms, and thy iniquities with works of mercy to the poor.*—It is thus that Augustine assigns them (*De Serm. Dom. in Monte* i. 4).

Reply Obj. 4. All the beatitudes mentioned in Holy Writ must be reduced to these, either as to the merits or as to the rewards: because they must all belong either to the active or to the contemplative life. Accordingly, when we read, *Blessed is the man whom the Lord correcteth*, we must refer this to the beatitude of mourning: when we read, *Blessed is the man that hath not walked in the counsel of the ungodly*, we must refer it to cleanness of heart: and when we read, *Blessed is the man that findeth wisdom*, this must be referred to the reward of the seventh beatitude. The same applies to all others that can be adduced.

Reply Obj. 5. The eighth beatitude is a confirmation and declaration of all those that precede. Because from the very fact that a man is confirmed in poverty of spirit, meekness, and the rest, it follows that no persecution will induce him to renounce them. Hence the eighth beatitude corresponds, in a way, to all the preceding seven.

Reply Obj. 6. Luke relates Our Lord's sermon as addressed to the multitude (vi. 17). Hence he sets down the beatitudes according to the capacity of the multitude, who know no other happiness than pleasure, temporal and earthly: wherefore by these four beatitudes Our Lord excludes four things which seem to belong to such happiness. The first of these is abundance of external goods, which he sets aside by saying: *Blessed are ye poor.*—The second is that man be well off as to his body, in food and drink and so forth; this he excludes by saying in the second place: *Blessed are ye that hunger.* The third is that it should be well with man as to joyfulness of heart, and this he puts aside by saying: *Blessed are ye that weep now.* The fourth is the outward favor of man; and this he excludes, saying, fourthly: *Blessed shall you be, when men shall hate you.* And as Ambrose says on Luke vi. 20, *poverty corresponds to temperance, which is unmoved by delights; hunger, to justice, since who hungers is compassionate and, through compassion gives; mourning, to prudence, which deplores perishable things; endurance of men's hatred belongs to fortitude.*

FOURTH ARTICLE

Whether the Rewards of the Beatitudes Are Suitably Enumerated?

We proceed thus to the Fourth Article:—

Objection 1. It would seem that the rewards of the beatitudes are unsuitably enumerated. Because the kingdom of heaven, which is eternal life, contains all good things. Therefore, once given the kingdom of heaven, no other rewards should be mentioned.

Obj. 2. Further, the kingdom of heaven is assigned as the reward, both of the first and of the eighth beatitude. Therefore, on the same ground, it should have been assigned to all.

Obj. 3. Further, the beatitudes are arranged in the ascending order, as Augustine remarks (*De Serm. Dom. in Monte* i. 4): whereas the rewards seem to be placed in the descending order, since to *possess the land* is less than to possess *the kingdom of heaven*. Therefore these rewards are unsuitably enumerated.

On the contrary stands the authority of Our Lord Who propounded these rewards.

I answer that, These rewards are most suitably assigned, considering the nature of the beatitudes in relation to the three kinds of happiness indicated above (A. 3). For the first three beatitudes concerned the withdrawal of man from those things in which sensual happiness consists: which happiness man desires by seeking the object of his natural desire, not where he should seek it, viz. in God, but in temporal and perishable things. Wherefore the rewards of the first three beatitudes correspond to these things which some men seek to find in earthly happiness. For men seek in external things, viz. riches and honors, a certain excellence and abundance, both of which are implied in the kingdom of heaven, whereby man attains to excellence and abundance of good things in God. Hence Our Lord promised the kingdom of heaven to the poor in spirit. Again, cruel and pitiless men seek by wrangling and fighting to destroy their enemies so as to gain security for themselves. Hence Our Lord promised the meek a secure and peaceful possession of the land of the living, whereby the solid reality of eternal goods is denoted. Again, men seek consolation for the toils of the present life, in the lusts and pleasures of the world. Hence Our Lord promises comfort to those that mourn.

Two other beatitudes belong to the works of active happiness, which are the works of virtues directing man in his relations to his neighbor: from which operations some men withdraw through inordinate love of their own good. Hence Our Lord assigns to these beatitudes rewards in correspondence with the motives for which men recede from them. For there are some who recede from acts of justice, and instead of rendering what is due, lay hands on what is not theirs, that they may abound in temporal goods. Wherefore Our

Lord promised those who hunger after justice, that they shall have their fill. Some, again, recede from works of mercy, lest they be busied with other people's misery. Hence Our Lord promised the merciful that they should obtain mercy, and be delivered from all misery.

The last two beatitudes belong to contemplative happiness or beatitude: hence the rewards are assigned in correspondence with the dispositions included in the merit. For cleanness of the eye disposes one to see clearly: hence the clean of heart are promised that they shall see God—Again, to make peace either in oneself or among others, shows a man to be a follower of God, Who is the God of unity and peace. Hence, as a reward, he is promised the glory of the Divine sonship, consisting in perfect union with God through consummate wisdom.

Reply Obj. 1. As Chrysostom says (*Hom.* xv. in *Matth.*), all these rewards are one in reality, viz. eternal happiness, which the human intellect cannot grasp. Hence it was necessary to describe it by means of various boons known to us, while observing due proportion to the merits to which those rewards are assigned.

Reply Obj. 2. Just as the eighth beatitude

is a confirmation of all the beatitudes, so it deserves all the rewards of the beatitudes. Hence it returns to the first, that we may understand all the other rewards to be attributed to it in consequence. Or else, according to Ambrose (*Super Luc.* v), the kingdom of heaven is promised to the poor in spirit, as regards the glory of the soul; but to those who suffer persecution in their bodies, it is promised as regards the glory of the body.

Reply Obj. 3. The rewards are also arranged in ascending order. For it is more to possess the land of the heavenly kingdom than simply to have it: since we have many things without possessing them firmly and peacefully. Again, it is more to be comforted in the kingdom than to have and possess it, for there are many things the possession of which is accompanied by sorrow. Again, it is more to have one's fill than simply to be comforted, because fulness implies abundance of comfort. And mercy surpasses satiety, for thereby man receives more than he merited or was able to desire. And yet more is it to see God, even as he is a greater man who not only dines at court, but also sees the king's countenance. Lastly, the highest place in the royal palace belongs to the king's son.

QUESTION 70

Of the Fruits of the Holy Ghost

(In Four Articles)

WE must now consider the Fruits of the Holy Ghost: under which head there are four points of inquiry: (1) Whether the fruits of the Holy Ghost are acts? (2) Whether they differ from the beatitudes? (3) Of their number? (4) Of their opposition to the works of the flesh.

FIRST ARTICLE

Whether the Fruits of the Holy Ghost Which the Apostle Enumerates (Gal. v.) Are Acts?

We proceed thus to the First Article:—

Objection 1. It would seem that the fruits of the Holy Ghost, enumerated by the Apostle (Gal. v. 22, 23), are not acts. For that which bears fruit, should not itself be called a fruit, else we should go on indefinitely. But our actions bear fruit: for it is written (Wis. iii. 15): *The fruit of good labor is glorious,* and (Jo. iv. 36): *He that reapeth receiveth wages, and gathereth fruit unto life everlasting.* Therefore our actions are not to be called fruits.

Obj. 2. Further, as Augustine says (*De Trin.* x. 10), *we enjoy* the things we know, when*

the will rests by rejoicing in them. But our will should not rest in our actions for their own sake. Therefore our actions should not be called fruits.

Obj. 3. Further, among the fruits of the Holy Ghost, the Apostle numbers certain virtues, viz. charity, meekness, faith, and chastity. Now virtues are not actions but habits, as stated above (Q. 55, A. 1). Therefore the fruits are not actions.

On the contrary, It is written (Matth. xii. 33): *By the fruit the tree is known;* that is to say, man is known by his works, as holy men explain the passage. Therefore human actions are called fruits.

I answer that, The word *fruit* has been transferred from the material to the spiritual world. Now fruit, among material things, is the product of a plant when it comes to perfection, and has a certain sweetness. This fruit has a twofold relation—to the tree that produces it, and to the man who gathers the fruit from the tree. Accordingly, in spiritual matters, we may take the word *fruit* in two ways:

**Fruimur,* from which verb we have the Latin *fructus* and the English *fruit.*

first, so that the fruit of man, who is likened to the tree, is that which he produces; secondly, so that man's fruit is what he gathers.

Yet not all that man gathers is fruit, but only that which is last and gives pleasure. For a man has both a field and a tree, and yet these are not called fruits; but that only which is last, to wit, that which man intends to derive from the field and from the tree. In this sense man's fruit is his last end which is intended for his enjoyment.

If, however, by man's fruit we understand a product of man, then human actions are called fruits: because operation is the second act of the operator, and gives pleasure if it is suitable to him. If then man's operation proceeds from man in virtue of his reason, it is said to be the fruit of his reason: but if it proceeds from him in respect of a higher power, which is the power of the Holy Ghost, then man's operation is said to be the fruit of the Holy Ghost, as of a Divine seed, for it is written (1 Jo. iii. 9): *Whosoever is born of God, committeth no sin, for His seed abideth in him.*

Reply Obj. 1. Since fruit is something last and final, nothing hinders one fruit bearing another fruit, even as one end is subordinate to another. And so our works, in so far as they are produced by the Holy Ghost working in us, are fruits: but, in so far as they are referred to the end which is eternal life, they should rather be called flowers: hence it is written (Ecclus. xxiv. 23): *My flowers are the fruits of honor and riches.*

Reply Obj. 2. When the will is said to delight in a thing for its own sake, this may be understood in two ways. First, so that the expression *for the sake of* be taken to designate the final cause; and in this way, man delights in nothing for its own sake, except the last end. Secondly, so that it express the formal cause; and in this way a man may delight in anything that is delightful by reason of its form. Thus it is clear that a sick man delights in health, for its own sake, as in an end; in a nice medicine, not as in an end, but as in something tasty; and in a nasty medicine, nowise for its own sake, but only for the sake of something else.—Accordingly we must say that man must delight in God for His own sake, as being his last end, and in virtuous deeds, not as being his end, but for the sake of their inherent goodness which is delightful to the virtuous. Hence Ambrose says (*De Parad.* xiii) that virtuous deeds are called fruits because *they refresh those that have them, with a holy and genuine delight.*

Reply Obj. 3. Sometimes the names of the virtues are applied to their actions: thus Augustine writes (*Tract.* xl. *in Joan.*): *Faith is*

to believe what thou seest not; and (*De Doctr.* Christ. iii. 10): *Charity is the movement of the soul in loving God and our neighbor.* It is thus that the names of the virtues are used in reckoning the fruits.

SECOND ARTICLE

Whether the Fruits Differ from the Beatitudes?

We proceed thus to the Second Article:—

Objection 1. It would seem that the fruits do not differ from the beatitudes. For the beatitudes are assigned to the gifts, as stated above (Q. 69, A. 1 *ad* i). But the gifts perfect man in so far as he is moved by the Holy Ghost. Therefore the beatitudes themselves are fruits of the Holy Ghost.

Obj. 2. Further, as the fruit of eternal life is to future beatitude which is that of actual possession, so are the fruits of the present life to the beatitudes of the present life, which are based on hope. Now the fruit of eternal life is identified with future beatitude. Therefore the fruits of the present life are the beatitudes.

Obj. 3. Further, fruit is essentially something ultimate and delightful. Now this is the very nature of beatitude, as stated above (Q. 3, A. 1; Q. 4, A. 1). Therefore fruit and beatitude have the same nature, and consequently should not be distinguished from one another.

On the contrary, Things divided into different species, differ from one another. But fruits and beatitudes are divided into different parts, as is clear from the way in which they are enumerated. Therefore the fruits differ from the beatitudes.

I answer that, More is required for a beatitude than for a fruit. Because it is sufficient for a fruit to be something ultimate and delightful; whereas for a beatitude, it must be something perfect and excellent. Hence all the beatitudes may be called fruits, but not vice versa. For the fruits are any virtuous deeds in which one delights: whereas the beatitudes are none but perfect works, and which, by reason of their perfection, are assigned to the gifts rather than to the virtues, as already stated (Q. 69, A. 1 *ad* 1).

Reply Obj. 1. This argument proves the beatitudes to be fruits, but not that all the fruits are beatitudes.

Reply Obj. 2. The fruit of eternal life is ultimate and perfect simply: hence it nowise differs from future beatitude. On the other hand the fruits of the present life are not simply ultimate and perfect; wherefore not all the fruits are beatitudes.

Reply Obj. 3. More is required for a beatitude than for a fruit, as stated.

THIRD ARTICLE

Whether the Fruits Are Suitably Enumerated by the Apostle?

We proceed thus to the Third Article:—

Objection 1. It would seem that the fruits are unsuitably enumerated by the Apostle (Gal. v. 22, 23). Because, elsewhere, he says that there is only one fruit of the present life; according to Rom. vi. 22: *You have your fruit unto sanctification.* Moreover it is written (Isa. xxvii. 9): *This is all the fruit . . . that the sin . . . be taken away.* Therefore we should not reckon twelve fruits.

Obj. 2. Further, fruit is the product of spiritual seed, as stated (A. 1). But Our Lord mentions (Matth. xiii. 23) a threefold fruit as growing from a spiritual seed in a good ground, viz. *hundredfold, sixtyfold* and *thirtyfold.* Therefore one should not reckon twelve fruits.

Obj. 3. Further, the very nature of fruit is to be something ultimate and delightful. But this does not apply to all the fruits mentioned by the Apostle: for patience and long-suffering seem to imply a painful object, while faith is not something ultimate, but rather something primary and fundamental. Therefore too many fruits are enumerated.

Obj. 4. *On the other hand,* It seems that they are enumerated insufficiently and incompletely. For it has been stated (A. 2) that all the beatitudes may be called fruits; yet not all are mentioned here. Nor is there anything corresponding to the acts of wisdom, and of many other virtues. Therefore it seems that the fruits are insufficiently enumerated.

I answer that, Tho number of the twelve fruits enumerated by the Apostle is suitable, and that there may be a reference to them in the twelve fruits of which it is written (Apoc. xxii. 2): *On both sides of the river was the tree of life bearing twelve fruits.* Since, however, a fruit is something that proceeds from a source as from a seed or root, the difference between these fruits must be gathered from the various ways in which the Holy Ghost proceeds in us: which process consists in this, that the mind of man is set in order, first of all, in regard to itself; secondly, in regard to things that are near it; thirdly, in regard to things that are below it.

Accordingly man's mind is well disposed in regard to itself when it has a good disposition towards good things and towards evil things. Now the first disposition of the human mind towards the good is effected by love, which is the first of our emotions and the root of them all, as stated above (Q. 27, A. 4). Wherefore among the fruits of the Holy Ghost, we reckon *charity,* wherein the Holy Ghost is given in a special manner, as in His own likeness, since He Himself is love. Hence it is written (Rom. v. 5): *The charity of God is poured forth in our hearts by the Holy Ghost, Who is given to us.*—The necessary result of the love of charity is joy: because every lover rejoices at being united to the beloved. Now charity has always actual presence of God Whom it loves, according to 1 Jo. iv. 16: *He that abideth in charity, abideth in God, and God in Him:* wherefore the sequel of charity is *joy.* Now the perfection of joy is peace in two respects. First, as regards freedom from outward disturbance; for it is impossible to rejoice perfectly in the beloved object, if one is disturbed in the enjoyment thereof; and again, if a man's heart is perfectly set at peace in one object, he cannot be disquieted by any other, since he accounts all others as nothing; hence it is written (Ps. cxviii. 165): *Much peace have they that love Thy Law, and to them there is no stumbling-block,* because, to wit, external things do not disturb them in their enjoyment of God. Secondly, as regards the calm of the restless desire: for he does not perfectly rejoice, who is not satisfied with the object of his joy. Now peace implies these two things, namely, that we be not disturbed by external things, and that our desires rest altogether in one object. Wherefore after charity and joy, *peace* is given the third place.—In evil things the mind has a good disposition, in respect of two things. First, by not being disturbed whenever evil threatens: which pertains to *patience;* secondly, by not being disturbed, whenever good things are delayed; which belongs to *long suffering,* since *to lack good is a kind of evil* (*Ethic.* v. 3).

Man's mind is well disposed as regards what is near him, viz. his neighbor, first, as to the will to do good; and to this belongs *goodness.* —Secondly, as to the execution of well-doing; and to this belongs *benignity,* for the benign are those in whom the salutary flame (*bonus ignis*) of love has enkindled the desire to be kind to their neighbor. Thirdly, as to his suffering with equanimity the evils his neighbor inflicts on him. To this belongs *meekness,* which curbs anger. Fourthly, in the point of our refraining from doing harm to our neighbor not only through anger, but also through fraud or deceit. To this pertains *faith,* if we take it as denoting fidelity. But if we take it for the faith whereby we believe in God, then man is directed thereby to that which is above him, so that he subject his intellect and, consequently, all that is his, to God.

Man is well disposed in respect of that which is below him, as regards external action, by *modesty,* whereby we observe the *mode* in all our words and deeds: as regards internal desires, by *continency* and *chastity:* whether these two differ because chastity withdraws man from unlawful desires, continency also from lawful desires: or because the continent man is subject to concupiscence, but is not led away; whereas the chaste man is neither subject to, nor led away from them.

Reply Obj. 1. Sanctification is effected by all the virtues, by which also sins are taken away. Consequently fruit is mentioned there in the singular, on account of its being generically one, though divided into many species which are spoken of as so many fruits.

Reply Obj. 2. The hundredfold, sixtyfold, and thirtyfold fruits do not differ as various species of virtuous acts, but as various degrees of perfection, even in the same virtue. Thus continency of the married state is said to be signified by the thirtyfold fruit; the continency of widowhood, by the sixtyfold; and virginal continency, by the hundredfold fruit. There are, moreover, other ways in which holy men distinguish three evangelical fruits according to the three degrees of virtue: and they speak of three degrees, because the perfection of anything is considered with respect to its beginning, its middle, and its end.

Reply Obj. 3. The fact of not being disturbed by painful things is something to delight in.—And as to faith, if we consider it as the foundation, it has the aspect of being ultimate and delightful, in as much as it contains certainty: hence a gloss expounds thus: *Faith, which is certainly about the unseen.*

Reply Obj. 4. As Augustine says on Gal. v. 22, 23, *the Apostle had no intention of teaching us how many* (either works of the flesh, or fruits of the Spirit) *there are; but to show how the former should be avoided, and the latter sought after.* Hence either more or fewer fruits might have been mentioned. Nevertheless, all the acts of the gifts and virtues can be reduced to these by a certain kind of fittingness, in so far as all the virtues and gifts must needs direct the mind in one of the above-mentioned ways. Wherefore the acts of wisdom and of any gifts directing to good, are reduced to charity, joy, and peace. The reason why he mentions these rather than others, is that these imply either enjoyment of good things, or relief from evils, which things seem to belong to the notion of fruit.

FOURTH ARTICLE

Whether the Fruits of the Holy Ghost Are Contrary to the Works of the Flesh?

We proceed thus to the Fourth Article:—

Objection 1. It would seem that the fruits of the Holy Ghost are not contrary to the works of the flesh, which the Apostle enumerates (Gal. v. 19, *seqq.*). Because contraries are in the same genus. But the works of the flesh are not called fruits. Therefore the fruits of the Spirit are not contrary to them.

Obj. 2. Further, one thing has one contrary. Now the Apostle mentions more works of the flesh than fruits of the Spirit. Therefore the fruits of the Spirit and the works of the flesh are not contrary to one another.

Obj. 3. Further, among the fruits of the Spirit, the first place is given to charity, joy, and peace: to which, fornication, uncleanness, and immodesty, which are the first of the works of flesh, are not opposed. Therefore the fruits of the Spirit are not contrary to the works of the flesh.

On the contrary, The Apostle says (*ibid.* 17) that *the flesh lusteth against the spirit, and the spirit against the flesh.*

I answer that, The works of the flesh and the fruits of the Spirit may be taken in two ways. First, in general: and in this way the fruits of the Holy Ghost considered in general are contrary to the works of the flesh. Because the Holy Ghost moves the human mind to that which is in accord with reason, or rather to that which surpasses reason: whereas the fleshly, viz. the sensitive, appetite draws man to sensible goods which are beneath him. Wherefore, since upward and downward are contrary movements in the physical order, so in human actions the works of the flesh are contrary to the fruits of the Spirit.

Secondly, both fruits and fleshly works as enumerated may be considered singly, each according to its specific nature. And in this they are not of necessity contrary each to each: because, as stated above (A. 3 *ad* 4), the Apostle did not intend to enumerate all the works, whether spiritual or carnal.—However, by a kind of adaptation, Augustine, commenting on Gal. v. 22, 23, contrasts the fruits with the carnal works, each to each. Thus *to fornication, which is the love of satisfying lust outside lawful wedlock, we may contrast charity, whereby the soul is wedded to God: wherein also is true chastity. By uncleanness we must understand whatever disturbances arise from fornication: and to these the joy of tranquillity is opposed. Idolatry, by reason of which war was waged against the Gospel of God, is opposed to peace. Against witchcrafts, enmities, contentions, emulations, wraths and quarrels, there is longsuffering, which helps us to bear the evils inflicted on us by those among whom we dwell; while kindness helps us to cure those evils; and goodness, to forgive them. In contrast to heresy there is faith; to envy, mildness; to drunkenness and revellings, continency.*

Reply Obj. 1. That which proceeds from a

tree against the tree's nature, is not called its fruit, but rather its corruption. And since works of virtue are connatural to reason, while works of vice are contrary to nature, therefore it is that works of virtue are called fruits, but not so works of vice.

Reply Obj. 2. Good happens in one way, *evil, in all manner of ways,* as Dionysius says (*Div. Nom.* iv.): so that to one virtue many vices are contrary. Consequently we must not be surprised if the works of the flesh are more numerous than the fruits of the spirit.

The Reply to the Third Objection is clear from what has been said.

SIN—ACTUAL—ORIGINAL

QUESTION 71

Of Vice and Sin Considered in Themselves

(In Six Articles)

WE have in the next place to consider vice and sin: about which six points have to be considered: (1) Vice and sin considered in themselves; (2) their distinction; (3) their comparison with one another; (4) the subject of sin; (5) the cause of sin; (6) the effect of sin.

Under the first head there are six points of inquiry: (1) Whether vice is contrary to virtue? (2) Whether vice is contrary to nature? (3) Which is worse, a vice or a vicious act? (4) Whether a vicious act is compatible with virtue? (5) Whether every sin includes action? (6) Of the definition of sin proposed by Augustine (*Contra Faust.* xxii): *Sin is a word, deed, or desire against the eternal law.*

FIRST ARTICLE

Whether Vice Is Contrary to Virtue?

We proceed thus to the First Article:—

Objection 1. It would seem that vice is not contrary to virtue. For one thing has one contrary, as proved in *Metaph.* x., text. 17. Now sin and malice are contrary to virtue. Therefore vice is not contrary to it: since vice applies also to undue disposition of bodily members or of any things whatever.

Obj. 2. Further, virtue denotes a certain perfection of power. But vice does not denote anything relative to power. Therefore vice is not contrary to virtue.

Obj. 3. Further, Cicero (*De Quœst. Tusc.* iv) says that *virtue is the soul's health.* Now sickness or disease, rather than vice, is opposed to health. Therefore vice is not contrary to virtue.

On the contrary, Augustine says (*De Perfect. Justit.* ii) that *vice is a quality in respect of which the soul is evil.* But *virtue is a quality which makes its subject good,* as was shown above (Q. 55, AA. 3, 4). Therefore vice is contrary to virtue.

I answer that, Two things may be considered in virtue,— the essence of virtue, and that to which virtue is ordained. In the essence of virtue we may consider something directly, and we may consider something consequently. Virtue implies *directly* a disposition whereby the subject is well disposed according to the mode of its nature: wherefore the Philosopher says (*Phys.* vii., text. 17) that *virtue is a disposition of a perfect thing to that which is best; and by perfect I mean that which is disposed according to its nature.* That which vir-

tue implies *consequently* is that it is a kind of goodness: because the goodness of a thing consists in its being well disposed according to the mode of its nature.—That to which virtue is directed is a good act, as was shown above (Q. 56, A. 3).

Accordingly three things are found to be contrary to virtue. One of these is *sin,* which is opposed to virtue in respect of that to which virtue is ordained: since, properly speaking, sin denotes an inordinate act; even as an act of virtue is an ordinate and due act:—in respect of that which virtue implies consequently, viz. that it is a kind of goodness, the contrary of virtue is *malice:*—while in respect of that which belongs to the essence of virtue directly, its contrary is *vice:* because the vice of a thing seems to consist in its not being disposed in a way befitting its nature: hence Augustine says (*De Lib. Arb.* iii): *Whatever is lacking for a thing's natural perfection may be called a vice.*

Reply Obj. 1. These three things are contrary to virtue, but not in the same respect: for sin is opposed to virtue, according as the latter is productive of a good work; malice, according as virtue is a kind of goodness; while vice is opposed to virtue properly as such.

Reply Obj. 2. Virtue implies not only perfection of power, the principle of action; but also the due disposition of its subject. The reason for this is because a thing operates according as it is in act: so that a thing needs to be well disposed if it has to produce a good work. It is in this respect that vice is contrary to virtue.

Reply Obj. 3. As Cicero says (*De Quœst. Tusc.* iv), *disease and sickness are vicious qualities,* for in speaking of the body *he calls it disease when the whole body is infected,* for instance, with fever or the like; he calls it sickness *when the disease is attended with weakness;* and vice *when the parts of the body are not well compacted together.* And although at times there may be disease in the body without sickness, for instance, when a man has a hidden complaint without being hindered outwardly from his wonted occupations; *yet, in the soul,* as he says, *these two things are indistinguishable, except in thought.* For whenever a man is ill-disposed inwardly, through some inordinate affection, he is rendered thereby unfit for fulfilling his duties: since *a tree is* known by its fruit, i.e. man by his works, according to Matth. xii. 33. But *vice of the soul*, as Cicero says (*ibid.*), *is a habit or affection of the soul discordant and inconsistent with itself through life*: and this is to be found even without disease and sickness, e.g. when a man sins from weakness or passion. Consequently vice is of wider extent than sickness or disease; even as virtue extends to more things than health; for health itself is reckoned a kind of virtue (*Phys.* vii., text. 17). Consequently vice is reckoned as contrary to virtue, more fittingly than sickness or disease.

SECOND ARTICLE

Whether Vice Is Contrary to Nature?

We proceed thus to the Second Article:—

Objection 1. It would seem that vice is not contrary to nature. Because vice is contrary to virtue, as stated above (A. 1). Now virtue is in us, not by nature but by infusion or habituation, as stated above (Q. 63, AA. 1, 2, 3). Therefore vice is not contrary to nature.

Obj. 2. Further, it is impossible to become habituated to that which is contrary to nature: thus *a stone never becomes habituated to upward movement* (*Ethic.* ii. 1). But some men become habituated to vice. Therefore vice is not contrary to nature.

Obj. 3. Further, anything contrary to a nature, is not found in the greater number of individuals possessed of that nature. Now vice is found in the greater number of men; for it is written (Matth. vii. 13): *Broad is the way that leadeth to destruction, and many there are who go in thereat.* Therefore vice is not contrary to nature.

Obj. 4. Further, sin is compared to vice, as act to habit, as stated above (A. 1). Now sin is defined as *a word, deed, or desire, contrary to the Law of God*, as Augustine shows (*Contra Faust.* xxii. 27). But the Law of God is above nature. Therefore we should say that vice is contrary to the Law, rather than to nature.

On the contrary, Augustine says (*De Lib. Arb.* iii. 13): *Every vice, simply because it is a vice, is contrary to nature.*

I answer that, As stated above (A. 1), vice is contrary to virtue. Now the virtue of a thing consists in its being well disposed in a manner befitting its nature, as stated above (A. 1). Hence the vice of any thing consists in its being disposed in a manner not befitting its nature, and for this reason is that thing *vituperated*, which word is derived from *vice* according to Augustine (*De Lib. Arb.* iii. 14).

But it must be observed that the nature of a thing is chiefly the form from which that thing derives its species. Now man derives his spe-

cies from his rational soul: and consequently whatever is contrary to the order of reason is, properly speaking, contrary to the nature of man, as man; while whatever is in accord with reason, is in accord with the nature of man, as man. Now *man's good is to be in accord with reason, and his evil is to be against reason*, as Dionysius states (*Div. Nom.* iv). Therefore human virtue, which makes a man good, and his work good, is in accord with man's nature, for as much as it accords with his reason: while vice is contrary to man's nature, in so far as it is contrary to the order of reason.

Reply Obj. 1. Although the virtues are not caused by nature as regards their perfection of being, yet they incline us to that which accords with reason, i.e. with the order of reason. For Cicero says (*De Inv. Rhet.* ii) that *virtue is a habit in accord with reason, like a second nature*: and it is in this sense that virtue is said to be in accord with nature, and on the other hand that vice is contrary to nature.

Reply Obj. 2. The Philosopher is speaking there of a thing being against nature, in so far as *being against nature* is contrary to *being from nature*: and not in so far as *being against nature* is contrary to *being in accord with nature*, in which latter sense virtues are said to be in accord with nature, in as much as they incline us to that which is suitable to nature.

Reply Obj. 3. There is a twofold nature in man, rational nature, and the sensitive nature. And since it is through the operation of his senses that man accomplishes acts of reason, hence there are more who follow the inclinations of the sensitive nature, than who follow the order of reason: because more reach the beginning of a business than achieve its completion. Now the presence of vices and sins in man is owing to the fact that he follows the inclination of his sensitive nature against the order of his reason.

Reply Obj. 4. Whatever is irregular in a work of art, is unnatural to the art which produced that work. Now the eternal law is compared to the order of human reason, as art to a work of art. Therefore it amounts to the same that vice and sin are against the order of human reason, and that they are contrary to the eternal law. Hence Augustine says (*De Lib. Arb.* iii. 6) that *every nature, as such, is from God; and is a vicious nature, in so far as it fails from the Divine art whereby it was made.*

THIRD ARTICLE

Whether Vice Is Worse Than a Vicious Act?

Objection 1. It would seem that vice, i.e. a bad habit, is worse than a sin, i.e. a bad act. For, as the more lasting a good is, the better it is, so the longer an evil lasts, the worse it is. Now a vicious habit is more lasting than vicious acts, that pass forthwith. Therefore a vicious habit is worse than a vicious act.

Obj. 2. Further, several evils are more to be shunned than one. But a bad habit is virtually the cause of many bad acts. Therefore a vicious habit is worse than a vicious act.

Obj. 3. Further, a cause is more potent than its effect. But a habit produces its actions both as to their goodness and as to their badness. Therefore a habit is more potent than its act, both in goodness and in badness.

On the contrary, A man is justly punished for a vicious act; but not for a vicious habit, so long as no act ensues. Therefore a vicious action is worse than a vicious habit.

I answer that, A habit stands midway between power and act. Now it is evident that both in good and in evil, act precedes power, as stated in *Metaph.* ix. 19. For it is better to do well than to be able to do well, and in like manner, it is more blameworthy to do evil, than to be able to do evil: whence it also follows that both in goodness and in badness, habit stands midway between power and act, so that, to wit, even as a good or evil habit stands above the corresponding power in goodness or in badness, so does it stand below the corresponding act. This is also made clear from the fact that a habit is not called good or bad, save in so far as it induces to a good or bad act: wherefore a habit is called good or bad by reason of the goodness or badness of its act: so that an act surpasses its habit in goodness or badness, since *the cause of a thing being such, is yet more so.*

Reply Obj. 1. Nothing hinders one thing from standing above another simply, and below it in some respect. Now a thing is deemed above another simply if it surpasses it in a point which is proper to both; while it is deemed above it in a certain respect, if it surpasses it in something which is accidental to both. Now it has been shown from the very nature of act and habit, that act surpasses habit both in goodness and in badness. Whereas the fact that habit is more lasting than act, is accidental to them, and is due to the fact that they are both found in a nature such that it cannot always be in action, and whose action consists in a transient movement. Consequently act simply excels in goodness and badness, but habit excels in a certain respect.

Reply Obj. 2. A habit is several acts, not simply, but in a certain respect, i.e., virtually. Wherefore this does not prove that habit precedes act simply, both in goodness and in badness.

Reply Obj. 3. Habit causes act by way of efficient causality: but act causes habit, by way of final causality, in respect of which we consider the nature of good and evil. Consequently act surpasses habit both in goodness and in badness.

FOURTH ARTICLE

Whether Sin Is Compatible with Virtue?

We proceed thus to the Fourth Article:—

Objection 1. It would seem that a vicious act, i.e. sin, is incompatible with virtue. For contraries cannot be together in the same subject. Now sin is, in some way, contrary to virtue, as stated above (A. 1). Therefore sin is incompatible with virtue.

Obj. 2. Further, sin is worse than vice, i.e. evil act than evil habit. But vice cannot be in the same subject with virtue: neither, therefore, can sin.

Obj. 3. Further, sin occurs in natural things, even as in voluntary matters (*Phys.* ii., text. 82). Now sin never happens in natural things, except through some corruption of the natural power; thus monsters are due to corruption of some elemental force in the seed, as stated in *Phys.* ii. Therefore no sin occurs in voluntary matters, except through the corruption of some virtue in the soul: so that sin and virtue cannot be together in the same subject.

On the contrary, The Philosopher says (*Ethic.* ii. 2, 3) that *virtue is engendered and corrupted by contrary causes.* Now one virtuous act does not cause a virtue, as stated above (Q. 51, A. 3): and, consequently, one sinful act does not corrupt virtue. Therefore they can be together in the same subject.

I answer that, Sin is compared to virtue, as evil act to good habit. Now the position of a habit in the soul is not the same as that of a form in a natural thing. For the form of a natural thing produces, of necessity, an operation befitting itself; wherefore a natural form is incompatible with the act of a contrary form: thus heat is incompatible with the act of cooling, and lightness with downward movement (except perhaps violence be used by some extrinsic mover): whereas the habit that resides in the soul, does not, of necessity, produce its operation, but is used by man when he wills. Consequently man, while possessing a habit, may either fail to use the habit, or produce a contrary act; and so a man having a virtue may produce an act of sin. And this sinful act, so long as there is but one, cannot corrupt virtue, if we compare the act to the virtue itself as a habit: since, just as habit is not engendered by one act, so neither is it destroyed by one act, as stated above (Q. 63, A. 2 *ad* 2). But if we compare the sinful act to the cause of the virtues, then it is possible for some virtues to be destroyed by one sinful act. For every mortal sin is contrary to charity, which is the root of all the infused virtues, as virtues; and consequently, charity being banished by one act of mortal sin, it follows that all the infused virtues are expelled *as virtues*. And I say on account of faith and hope, whose habits remain unquickened after mortal sin, so that they are no longer virtues. On the other hand, since venial sin is neither contrary to charity, nor banishes it, as a consequence, neither does it expel the other virtues. As to the acquired virtues, they are not destroyed by one act of any kind of sin.

Accordingly, mortal sin is incompatible with the infused virtues, but is consistent with acquired virtue: while venial sin is compatible with virtues, whether infused or acquired.

Reply Obj. 1. Sin is contrary to virtue, not by reason of itself, but by reason of its act. Hence sin is incompatible with the act, but not with the habit, of virtue.

Reply Obj. 2. Vice is directly contrary to virtue, even as sin to virtuous act: and so vice excludes virtue, just as sin excludes acts of virtue.

Reply Obj. 3. The natural powers act of necessity, and hence so long as the power is unimpaired, no sin can be found in the act. On the other hand, the virtues of the soul do not produce their acts of necessity; hence the comparison fails.

FIFTH ARTICLE

Whether Every Sin Includes an Action?

We proceed thus to the Fifth Article:—
Objection 1. It would seem that every sin includes an action. For as merit is compared with virtue, even so is sin compared with vice. Now there can be no merit without an action. Neither, therefore, can there be sin without action.

Obj. 2. Further, Augustine says (*De Lib. Arb.* iii. 18):* *So true is it that every sin is voluntary, that, unless it be voluntary, it is no sin at all.* Now nothing can be voluntary, save through an act of the will. Therefore every sin implies an act.

Obj. 3. Further, if sin could be without act, it would follow that a man sins as soon as he ceases doing what he ought. Now he who never does something that he ought to do, ceases continually doing what he ought. Therefore it would follow that he sins continually; and this is untrue. Therefore there is no sin without an act.

On the contrary, It is written (James iv. 17): *To him ... who knoweth to do good, and doth it not, to him it is a sin.* Now *not to do*

* *Cf. De Vera Relig.* xiv.

does not imply an act. Therefore sin can be without act.

I answer that, The reason for urging this question has reference to the sin of omission, about which there have been various opinions. For some say that in every sin of omission there is some act, either interior or exterior; —interior, as when a man wills *not to go to church,* when he is bound to go:—exterior, as when a man, at the very hour that he is bound to go to church (or even before), occupies himself in such a way that he is hindered from going. This seems, in a way, to amount to the same as the first, for whoever wills one thing that is incompatible with this other, wills, consequently, to go without this other: unless, perchance, it does not occur to him, that what he wishes to do, will hinder him from that which he is bound to do, in which case he might be deemed guilty of negligence. On the other hand, others say, that a sin of omission does not necessarily suppose an act: for the mere fact of not doing what one is bound to do is a sin.

Now each of these opinions has some truth in it. For if in the sin of omission we look merely at that in which the essence of the sin consists, the sin of omission will be sometimes with an interior act, as when a man wills *not to go to church:* while sometimes it will be without any act at all, whether interior or exterior, as when a man, at the time that he is bound to go to church, does not think of going or not going to church.

If, however, in the sin of omission, we consider also the causes, or occasions of the omission, then the sin of omission must of necessity include some act. For there is no sin of omission, unless we omit what we can do or not do: and that we turn aside so as not to do what we can do or not do, must needs be due to some cause or occasion, either united with the omission or preceding it. Now if this cause be not in man's power, the omission will not be sinful, as when anyone omits going to church on account of sickness: but if the cause or occasion be subject to the will, the omission is sinful; and such cause, in so far as it is voluntary, must needs always include some act, at least the interior act of the will: which act sometimes bears directly on the omission, as when a man wills *not to go to church,* because it is too much trouble; and in this case this act, of its very nature, belongs to the omission, because the volition of any sin whatever, pertains, of itself, to that sin, since voluntariness is essential to sin. Sometimes, however, the act of the will bears directly on something else, which hinders man from doing what he ought, whether this something else be united with the omission, as when a man wills to play at the time he ought to go to church,—or precede the omission, as when a man wills to sit up late at night, the result being that he does not go to church in the morning. In this case the act, interior or exterior, is accidental to the omission, since the omission follows outside the intention, and that which is outside the intention is said to be accidental (*Phys.* ii., text. 49, 50). Wherefore it is evident that then the sin of omission has indeed an act united with, or preceding the omission, but that this act is accidental to the sin of omission.

Now in judging about things, we must be guided by that which is proper to them, and not by that which is accidental: and consequently it is truer to say that a sin can be without any act; else the circumstantial acts and occasions would be essential to other actual sins.

Reply Obj. 1. More things are required for good than for evil, since *good results from a whole and entire cause, whereas evil results from each single defect, as* Dionysius states (*Div. Nom.* iv.): so that sin may arise from a man doing what he ought not, or by his not doing what he ought; while there can be no merit, unless a man do willingly what he ought to do: wherefore there can be no merit without act, whereas there can be sin without act.

Reply Obj. 2. The term *voluntary* is applied not only to that on which the act of the will is brought to bear, but also to that which we have the power to do or not to do, as stated in *Ethic.* iii. 5. Hence even not to will may be called voluntary, in so far as man has it in his power to will, and not to will.

Reply Obj. 3. The sin of omission is contrary to an affirmative precept which binds always, but not for always. Hence, by omitting to act, a man sins only for the time at which the affirmative precept binds him to act.

SIXTH ARTICLE

Whether Sin Is Fittingly Defined As a Word, Deed, or Desire Contrary to the Eternal Law?

We proceed thus to the Sixth Article:—

Objection 1. It would seem that sin is unfittingly defined by saying: *Sin is a word, deed, or desire, contrary to the eternal law.* Because *word, deed,* and *desire* imply an act; whereas not every sin implies an act, as stated above (A. 5). Therefore this definition does not include every sin.

Obj. 2. Further, Augustine says (*De duab. anim.* xii.): *Sin is the will to retain or obtain what justice forbids.* Now will is comprised under desire, in so far as desire denotes any act of the appetite. Therefore it was enough to say: *Sin is a desire contrary to the eternal law,* nor was there need to add *word* or *deed*.

Obj. 3. Further, sin apparently consists properly in aversion from the end: because good and evil are measured chiefly with regard to the end, as explained above (Q. 1, A. 3; Q. 18, AA. 4, 6; Q. 20, AA. 2, 3): wherefore, Augustine (*De Lib. Arb.* i) defines sin in reference to the end, by saying that *sin is nothing else than to neglect eternal things, and seek after temporal things:* and again he says (*Qq.* lxxxiii., qu. 30) *that all human wickedness consists in using what we should enjoy, and in enjoying what we should use.* Now the definition in question contains no mention of aversion from our due end: therefore it is an insufficient definition of sin.

Obj. 4. Further, a thing is said to be forbidden, because it is contrary to the law. Now not all sins are evil through being forbidden, but some are forbidden because they are evil. Therefore sin in general should not be defined as being against the law of God.

Obj. 5. Further, a sin denotes a bad human act, as was explained above (A. 1). Now man's evil is to be against reason, as Dionysius states (*Div. Nom.* iv). Therefore it would have been better to say that sin is against reason than to say that it is contrary to the eternal law.

On the contrary, the authority of Augustine suffices (*Contra Faust.* xxii. 27).

I answer that, As was shown above (A. 1), sin is nothing else than a bad human act. Now that an act is a human act is due to its being voluntary, as stated above (Q. 1, A. 1), whether it be voluntary, as being elicited by the will, e.g. to will or to choose, or as being commanded by the will, e.g. the exterior actions of speech or operation. Again, a human act is evil through lacking conformity with its due measure: and conformity of measure in a thing depends on a rule, from which if that thing depart, it is incommensurate. Now there are two rules of the human will: one is proximate and homogeneous, viz. the human reason; the other is the first rule, viz. the eternal law, which is God's reason, so to speak. Accordingly Augustine (*loc. cit.*) includes two things in the definition of sin; one, pertaining to the substance of a human act, and which is the matter, so to speak, of sin, when he says, *word, deed, or desire;* the other, pertaining to the nature of evil, and which is the form, as it were, of sin, when he says, *contrary to the eternal law.*

Reply Obj. 1. Affirmation and negation are reduced to one same genus: e.g. in Divine things, begotten and unbegotten are reduced to the genus *relation,* as Augustine states (*De Trin.* v. 6, 7): and so *word* and *deed* denote equally what is said and what is not said, what is done and what is not done.

Reply Obj. 2. The first cause of sin is in

the will, which commands all voluntary acts, in which alone is sin to be found: and hence it is that Augustine sometimes defines sin in reference to the will alone. But since external acts also pertain to the substance of sin, through being evil of themselves, as stated, it was necessary in defining sin to include something referring to external action.

Reply Obj. 3. The eternal law first and foremost directs man to his end, and in consequence, makes man to be well disposed in regard to things which are directed to the end: hence when he says, *contrary to the eternal law*, he includes aversion from the end and all other forms of inordinateness.

Reply Obj. 4. When it is said that not every sin is evil through being forbidden, this must be understood of prohibition by positive law. If, however, the prohibition be referred to the natural law, which is contained primarily in the eternal law, but secondarily in the natural code of the human reason, then every sin is evil through being prohibited: since it is contrary to natural law, precisely because it is inordinate.

Reply Obj. 5. The theologian considers sin chiefly as an offense against God; and the moral philosopher, as something contrary to reason. Hence Augustine defines sin with reference to its being *contrary to the eternal law*, more fittingly than with reference to its being contrary to reason; the more so, as the eternal law directs us in many things that surpass human reason, e.g. in matters of faith.

QUESTION 72

Of the Distinction of Sins

(In Nine Articles)

We must now consider the distinction of sins or vices: under which head there are nine points of inquiry: (1) Whether sins are distinguished specifically by their objects? (2) Of the distinction between spiritual and carnal sins; (3) Whether sins differ in reference to their causes? (4) Whether they differ with respect to those who are sinned against? (5) Whether sins differ in relation to the debt of punishment? (6) Whether they differ in regard to omission and commission? (7) Whether they differ according to their various stages? (8) Whether they differ in respect of excess and deficiency? (9) Whether they differ according to their various circumstances?

FIRST ARTICLE

Whether Sins Differ in Species according to Their Objects?

We proceed thus to the First Article:—

Objection 1. It would seem that sins do not differ in species, according to their objects. For acts are said to be good or evil, in relation, chiefly, to their end, as shown above (Q. 1, A. 3; Q. 18, AA. 4, 6). Since then sin is nothing else than a bad human act, as stated above (Q. 71, A. 1), it seems that sins should differ specifically according to their ends rather than according to their objects.

Obj. 2. Further, evil, being a privation, differs specifically according to the different species of opposites. Now sin is an evil in the genus of human acts. Therefore sins differ specifically according to their opposites rather than according to their objects.

Obj. 3. Further, if sins differed specifically according to their objects, it would be impossible to find the same specific sin with diverse objects: and yet such sins are to be found. For pride is about things spiritual and material as Gregory says (*Moral.* xxxiv. 18); and avarice is about different kinds of things. Therefore sins do not differ in species according to their objects.

On the contrary, Sin is a word, deed, or desire against God's law. Now words, deeds, and desires differ in species according to their various objects: since acts differ by their objects, as stated above (Q. 18, A. 2). Therefore sins also differ in species according to their objects.

I answer that, As stated above (Q. 71, A. 6), two things concur in the nature of sin, viz. the voluntary act, and its inordinateness, which consists in departing from God's law. Of these two, one is referred essentially to the sinner, who intends such and such an act in such and such matter; while the other, viz. the inordinateness of the act, is referred accidentally to the intention of the sinner, for *no one acts intending evil*, as Dionysius declares (*Div. Nom.* iv). Now it is evident that a thing derives its species from that which is essential and not from that which is accidental: because what is accidental is outside the specific nature. Consequently sins differ specifically on the part of the voluntary acts rather than of the inordinateness inherent to sin. Now voluntary acts differ in species according to their objects, as was proved above (Q. 18, A. 2). Therefore it follows that sins are properly distinguished in species by their objects.

Reply Obj. 1. The aspect of good is found chiefly in the end: and therefore the end stands in the relation of object to the act of the will which is at the root of every sin. Consequently it amounts to the same whether sins differ by their objects or by their ends.

Reply Obj. 2. Sin is not a pure privation but an act deprived of its due order: hence sins differ specifically according to the objects of their acts rather than according to their opposites, although, even if they were distinguished in reference to their opposite virtues, it would come to the same: since virtues differ specifically according to their objects, as stated above (Q. 60, A. 5).

Reply Obj. 3. In various things, differing in species or genus, nothing hinders our finding one formal aspect of the object, from which aspect sin receives its species. It is thus that pride seeks excellence in reference to various things; and avarice seeks abundance of things adapted to human use.

SECOND ARTICLE

Whether Spiritual Sins Are Fittingly Distinguished from Carnal Sins?

We proceed thus to the Second Article:—

Objection 1. It would seem that spiritual sins are unfittingly distinguished from carnal sins. For the Apostle says (Gal. v. 19): *The works of the flesh are manifest, which are fornication, uncleanness, immodesty, luxury, idolatry, witchcrafts,* etc., from which it seems that all kinds of sins are works of the flesh. Now carnal sins are called works of the flesh. Therefore carnal sins should not be distinguished from spiritual sins.

Obj. 2. Further, whosoever sins, walks according to the flesh, as stated in Rom. viii. 13: *If you live according to the flesh, you shall die. But if by the spirit you mortify the deeds of the flesh, you shall live.* Now to live or walk according to the flesh seems to pertain to the nature of carnal sin. Therefore carnal sins should not be distinguished from spiritual sins.

Obj. 3. Further, the higher part of the soul, which is the mind or reason, is called the spirit, according to Eph. iv. 23: *Be renewed in the spirit of your mind,* where spirit stands for reason, according to a gloss. Now every sin, which is committed in accordance with the flesh, flows from the reason by its consent; since consent in a sinful act belongs to the higher reason, as we shall state further on (Q. 74, A. 7). Therefore the same sins are both carnal and spiritual, and consequently they should not be distinguished from one another.

Obj. 4. Further, if some sins are carnal spe-

cifically, this, seemingly, should apply chiefly to those sins whereby man sins against his own body. But, according to the Apostle (1 Cor. vi. 18), *every sin that a man doth, is without the body: but he that committeth fornication, sinneth against his own body.* Therefore fornication would be the only carnal sin, whereas the Apostle (Eph. v. 3) reckons covetousness with the carnal sins.

On the contrary, Gregory (*Moral.* xxxi. 17) says that *of the seven capital sins five are spiritual, and two carnal.*

I answer that, As stated above (A. 1), sins take their species from their objects. Now every sin consists in the desire for some mutable good, for which man has an inordinate desire, and the possession of which gives him inordinate pleasure. Now, as explained above (Q. 31, A. 3), pleasure is twofold. One belongs to the soul, and is consummated in the mere apprehension of a thing possessed in accordance with desire; this can also be called spiritual pleasure, e.g. when one takes pleasure in human praise or the like. The other pleasure is bodily or natural, and is realized in bodily touch, and this can also be called carnal pleasure.

Accordingly, those sins which consist in spiritual pleasure, are called spiritual sins; while those which consist in carnal pleasure, are called carnal sins, e.g. gluttony, which consists in the pleasures of the table; and lust, which consists in sexual pleasures. Hence the Apostle says (2 Cor. vii. 1): *Let us cleanse ourselves from all defilement of the flesh and of the spirit.*

Reply Obj. 1. As a gloss says on the same passage, these vices are called works of the flesh, not as though they consisted in carnal pleasure; but flesh here denotes man, who is said to live according to the flesh, when he lives according to himself, as Augustine says (*De Civ. Dei* xiv. 2, 3). The reason of this is because every failing in the human reason is due in some way to the carnal sense. This suffices for the Reply to the Second Objection.

Reply Obj. 3. Even in the carnal sins there is a spiritual act, viz. the act of reason: but the end of these sins, from which they are named, is carnal pleasure.

Reply Obj. 4. As the gloss says (*ibid.*), *in the sin of fornication the soul is the body's slave in a special sense, because at the moment of sinning it can think of nothing else:* whereas the pleasure of gluttony, although carnal, does not so utterly absorb the reason.—It may also be said that in this sin, an injury is done to the body also, for it is defiled inordinately: wherefore by this sin alone is man said specially to sin against his body. While covetousness, which is reckoned among the carnal sins, stands here for adultery, which is the unjust appropriation of another's wife.—Again, it may be said that the thing in which the covetous man takes pleasure is something bodily, and in this respect covetousness is numbered with the carnal sins: but the pleasure itself does not belong to the body, but to the spirit, wherefore Gregory says (*loc. cit.*) that it is a spiritual sin.

THIRD ARTICLE

Whether Sins Differ Specifically in Reference to Their Causes?

We thus proceed to the Third Article:—

Objection 1. It would seem that sins differ specifically in reference to their causes. For a thing takes its species from that whence it derives its being. Now sins derive their being from their causes. Therefore they take their species from them also. Therefore they differ specifically in reference to their causes.

Obj. 2. Further, of all the causes the material cause seems to have least reference to the species. Now the object in a sin is like its material cause. Since, therefore, sins differ specifically according to their objects, it seems that much more do they differ in reference to their other causes.

Obj. 3. Further, Augustine, commenting on Ps. lxxix. 17, *Things set on fire and dug down,* says that *every sin is due either to fear inducing false humility, or to love enkindling us to undue ardor.* For it is written (1 Jo. ii. 16) that *all that is in the world, is the concupiscence of the flesh, or* (Vulg.,—*and*) *the concupiscence of the eyes, or* (Vulg.,—*and*) *the pride of life.* Now a thing is said to be in the world on account of sin, in as much as the world denotes lovers of the world, as Augustine observes (*Tract. ii. in Joan.*). Gregory, too (*Moral.* xxxi. 17), distinguishes all sins according to the seven capital vices. Now all these divisions refer to the causes of sins. Therefore, seemingly, sins differ specifically according to the diversity of their causes.

On the contrary, If this were the case all sins would belong to one species, since they are due to one cause. For it is written (Ecclus. x. 15) that *pride is the beginning of all sin,* and (1 Tim. vi. 10) that *the desire of money is the root of all evils.* Now it is evident that there are various species of sins. Therefore sins do not differ specifically according to their different causes.

I answer that, Since there are four kinds of causes, they are attributed to various things in various ways. Because the *formal* and *the material* cause regard properly the substance of a thing; and consequently substances differ in respect of their matter and form, both in species and in genus.—The *agent* and the *end* regard directly movement and operation: wherefore movements and operations differ specifically in respect of these causes; in different ways, however, because the natural active principles are always determined to the same acts; so that the different species of natural acts are taken not only from the objects, which are the ends or terms of those acts, but also from their active principles: thus heating and cooling are specifically distinct with reference to hot and cold. On the other hand, the active principles in voluntary acts, such as the acts of sins, are not determined, of necessity, to one act, and consequently from one active or motive principle, diverse species of sins can proceed: thus from fear engendering false humility man may proceed to theft, or murder, or to neglect the flock committed to his care; and these same things may proceed from love enkindling to undue ardor. Hence it is evident that sins do not differ specifically according to their various active or motive causes, but only in respect of diversity in the final cause, which is the end and object of the will. For it has been shown above (Q. 1, A. 3; Q. 18, AA. 4, 6) that human acts take their species from the end.

Reply Obj. 1. The active principles in voluntary acts, not being determined to one act, do not suffice for the production of human acts, unless the will be determined to one by the intention of the end, as the Philosopher proves (*Metaph.* ix., text. 15, 16), and consequently sin derives both its being and its species from the end.

Reply Obj. 2. Objects, in relation to external acts, have the character of matter *about which;* but, in relation to the interior act of the will, they have the character of end; and it is owing to this that they give the act its species. Nevertheless, even considered as the matter *about which,* they have the character of term, from which movement takes its species (*Phys.* v., text. 4; *Ethic.* x. 4); yet even terms of movement specify movements, in so far as term has the character of end.

Reply Obj. 3. These distinctions of sins are given, not as distinct species of sins, but to show their various causes.

FOURTH ARTICLE

Whether Sin Is Fittingly Divided into Sin against God, against Oneself, and against One's Neighbor?

We proceed thus to the Fourth Article:—

Objection 1. It would seem that sin is unfittingly divided into sin against God, against one's neighbor, and against oneself. For that which is common to all sins should not be reckoned as a part in the division of sin. But it is common to all sins to be against God: for it is stated in the definition of sin that it is *against God's law*, as stated above (Q. 66, A. 6). Therefore sin against God should not be reckoned a part of the division of sin.

Obj. 2. Further, every division should consist of things in opposition to one another. But these three kinds of sin are not opposed to one another: for whoever sins against his neighbor, sins against himself and against God. Therefore sin is not fittingly divided into these three.

Obj. 3. Further, specification is not taken from things external. But God and our neighbor are external to us. Therefore sins are not distinguished specifically with regard to them: and consequently sin is unfittingly divided according to these three.

On the contrary, Isidore (*De Summo Bono*), in giving the division of sins, says that *man is said to sin against himself, against God, and against his neighbor.*

I answer that, As stated above (Q. 71, AA. 1, 6), sin is an inordinate act. Now there should be a threefold order in man: one in relation to the rule of reason, in so far as all our actions and passions should be commensurate with the rule of reason:—another order is in relation to the rule of the Divine law, whereby man should be directed in all things: and if man were by nature a solitary animal, this twofold order would suffice.—But since man is naturally a civic and social animal, as is proved in *Polit.* i. 2, hence a third order is necessary, whereby man is directed in relation to other men among whom he has to dwell. Of these orders the second contains the first and surpasses it. For whatever things are comprised under the order of reason, are comprised under the order of God Himself. Yet some things are comprised under the order of God, which surpass the human reason, such as matters of faith, and things due to God alone. Hence he that sins in such matters, for instance, by heresy, sacrilege, or blasphemy, is said to sin against God. In like manner, the first order includes the third and surpasses it, because in all things wherein we are directed in reference to our neighbor, we need to be directed according to the order of reason. Yet in some things we are directed according to reason, in relation to ourselves only, and not in reference to our neighbor; and when man sins in these matters, he is said to sin against himself, as is seen in the glutton, the lustful, and the prodigal. But when man sins in matters concerning his neighbor, he is said to sin against his neighbor, as appears in the thief

* *Ex genere,* genus in this case denoting the species.

and the murderer. Now the things whereby man is directed to God, his neighbor, and himself are diverse. Wherefore this distinction of sins is in respect of their objects, according to which the species of sins are diversified: and consequently this distinction of sins is properly one of different species of sins: because the virtues also, to which sins are opposed, differ specifically in respect of these three. For it is evident from what has been said (Q. 62, AA. 1, 2, 3) that by the theological virtues man is directed to God; by temperance and fortitude, to himself; and by justice to his neighbor.

Reply Obj. 1. To sin against God is common to all sins, in so far as the order to God includes every human order; but in so far as order to God surpasses the other two orders, sin against God is a special kind of sin.

Reply Obj. 2. When several things, of which one includes another, are distinct from one another, this distinction is understood to refer, not to the part contained in another, but to that in which one goes beyond another. This may be seen in the division of numbers and figures: for a triangle is distinguished from a four-sided figure not in respect of its being contained thereby, but in respect of that in which it is surpassed thereby: and the same applies to the numbers three and four.

Reply Obj. 3. Although God and our neighbor are external to the sinner himself, they are not external to the act of sin, but are related to it as its object.

FIFTH ARTICLE
Whether the Division of Sins according to Their Debt of Punishment Diversifies Their Species?

We proceed thus to the Fifth Article:—

Objection 1. It would seem that the division of sins according to their debt of punishment diversifies their species; for instance, when sin is divided into *mortal* and *venial.* For things which are infinitely apart, cannot belong to the same species, nor even to the same genus. But venial and mortal sin are infinitely apart, since temporal punishment is due to venial sin, and eternal punishment to mortal sin; and the measure of the punishment corresponds to the gravity of the fault, according to Deut. xxv. 2: *According to the measure of the sin shall the measure also of the stripes be.* Therefore venial and mortal sins are not of the same genus, nor can they be said to belong to the same species.

Obj. 2. Further, some sins are mortal in virtue of their species,* as murder and adultery; and some are venial in virtue of their species,* as an idle word, and excessive laughter. Therefore venial and mortal sins differ specifically.

Obj. 3. Further, just as a virtuous act stands in relation to its reward, so does sin stand in relation to punishment. But the reward is the end of the virtuous act. Therefore punishment is the end of sin. Now sins differ specifically in relation to their ends, as stated above (A. 1 *ad* 1). Therefore they are also specifically distinct according to the debt of punishment.

On the contrary, Those things that constitute a species are prior to the species, e.g. specific differences. But punishment follows sin as the effect thereof. Therefore sins do not differ specifically according to the debt of punishment.

I answer that, In things that differ specifically we find a twofold difference:—the first causes the diversity of species, and is not to be found save in different species, e.g. *rational* and *irrational, animate* and *inanimate:*—the other difference is consequent to specific diversity; and though, in some cases, it may be consequent to specific diversity, yet, in others, it may be found within the same species; thus *white* and *black* are consequent to the specific diversity of crow and swan, and yet this difference is found within the one species of man.

We must therefore say that the difference between venial and mortal sin, or any other difference in respect of the debt of punishment, cannot be a difference constituting specific diversity. For what is accidental never constitutes a species; and what is outside the agent's intention is accidental (*Phys.* ii., text. 50). Now it is evident that punishment is outside the intention of the sinner, wherefore it is accidentally referred to sin on the part of the sinner. Nevertheless it is referred to sin by an extrinsic principle, viz. the justice of the judge, who imposes various punishments according to the various manners of sin. Therefore the difference derived from the debt of punishment, may be consequent to the specific diversity of sins, but cannot constitute it.

Now the difference between venial and mortal sin is consequent to the diversity of that inordinateness which constitutes the notion of sin. For inordinateness is twofold, one that destroys the principle of order, and another which, without destroying the principle of order, implies inordinateness in the things which follow the principle: thus, in an animal's body, the frame may be so out of order that the vital principle is destroyed; this is the inordinateness of death; while, on the other hand, saving the vital principle, there may be disorder in the bodily humors; and then there is sickness. Now the principle of the entire moral order is the last end, which

stands in the same relation to matters of action, as the indemonstrable principle does to matters of speculation (*Ethic.* vii. 8). Therefore when the soul is so disordered by sin as to turn away from its last end, viz. God, to Whom it is united by charity, there is mortal sin; but when it is disordered without turning away from God, there is venial sin. For even as in the body, the disorder of death which results from the destruction of the principle of life, is irreparable according to nature, while the disorder of sickness can be repaired by reason of the vital principle being preserved, so it is in matters concerning the soul. Because, in speculative matters, it is impossible to convince one who errs in the principles, whereas one who errs, but retains the principles, can be brought back to the truth by means of the principles. Likewise in practical matters, he who, by sinning, turns away from his last end, if we consider the nature of his sin, falls irreparably, and therefore is said to sin mortally and to deserve eternal punishment: whereas when a man sins without turning away from God, by the very nature of his sin, his disorder can be repaired, because the principle of the order is not destroyed; wherefore he is said to sin venially, because, to wit, he does not sin so as to deserve to be punished eternally.

Reply Obj. 1. Mortal and venial sins are infinitely apart as regards what they *turn away from,* not as regards what they *turn to,* viz. the object which specifies them. Hence nothing hinders the same species from including mortal and venial sins; for instance, in the species *adultery* the first movement is a venial sin; while an idle word, which is, generally speaking, venial, may even be a mortal sin.

Reply Obj. 2. From the fact that one sin is mortal by reason of its species, and another venial by reason of its species, it follows that this difference is consequent to the specific difference of sins, not that it is the cause thereof. And this difference may be found even in things of the same species, as stated above.

Reply Obj. 3. The reward is intended by him that merits or acts virtually; whereas the punishment is not intended by the sinner, but, on the contrary, is against his will. Hence the comparison fails.

SIXTH ARTICLE

Whether Sins of Commission and Omission Differ Specifically?

We proceed thus to the Sixth Article:—

Objection 1. It would seem that sins of commission and omission differ specifically. For *offense* and *sin* are condivided with one another (*Eph.* ii. 1), where it is written: *When you were dead in your offenses and sins,* which words a gloss explains, saying: *"Offenses," by omitting to do what was commanded, and "sins," by doing what was forbidden.* Whence it is evident that *offense* here denotes sins of omission; while *sin* denotes sins of commission. Therefore they differ specifically, since they are contrasted with one another as different species.

Obj. 2. Further, it is essential to sin to be against God's law, for this is part of its definition, as is clear from what has been said (Q. 71, A. 6). Now in God's law, the affirmative precepts, against which is the sin of omission, are different from the negative precepts, against which is the sin of commission. Therefore sins of omission and commission differ specifically.

Obj. 3. Further, omission and commission differ as affirmation and negation. Now affirmation and negation cannot be in the same species, since negation has no species; for *there is neither species nor difference of non-being,* as the Philosopher states (*Phys.* iv, text. 67). Therefore omission and commission cannot belong to the same species.

On the contrary, Omission and commission are found in the same species of sin. For the covetous man both takes what belongs to others, which is a sin of commission; and gives not of his own to whom he should give, which is a sin of omission. Therefore omission and commission do not differ specifically.

I answer that, There is a twofold difference in sins; a material difference and a formal difference: the material difference is to be observed in the natural species of the sinful act; while the formal difference is gathered from their relation to one proper end, which is also their proper object. Hence we find certain acts differing from one another in the material specific difference, which are nevertheless formally in the same species of sin, because they are directed to the one same end: thus strangling, stoning, and stabbing come under the one species of murder, although the actions themselves differ specifically according to the natural species.—Accordingly, if we refer to the material species in sins of omission and commission, they differ specifically, using species in a broad sense, in so far as negation and privation may have a species.—But if we refer to the formal species in sins of omission and commission, they do not differ specifically, because they are directed to the same end, and proceed from the same motive. For the covetous man, in order to hoard money, both robs, and omits to give what he ought, and in like manner, the glutton, to satiate his appetite, both eats too much and omits the prescribed fasts. The same applies to other sins: for in

things, negation is aways founded on affirmation, which, in a manner, is its cause. Hence in the physical order it comes under the same head, that fire gives forth heat, and that it does not give forth cold.

Reply Obj. 1. This division in respect of commission and omission, is not according to different formal species, but only according to material species, as stated.

Reply Obj. 2. In God's law, the necessity for various affirmative and negative precepts, was that men might be gradually led to virtue, first by abstaining from evil, being induced to this by the negative precepts, and afterwards by doing good, to which we are induced by the affirmative precepts. Wherefore the affirmative and negative precepts do not belong to different virtues, but to different degrees of virtue; and consequently they are not of necessity, opposed to sins of different species. Moreover sin is not specified by that from which it turns away, because in this respect it is a negation or privation, but by that to which it turns, in so far as sin is an act. Consequently sins do not differ specificaly according to the various precepts of the Law.

Reply Obj. 3. This objection considers the material diversity of sins. It must be observed, however, that although, properly speaking, negation is not in a species, yet it is allotted to a species by reduction to the affirmation on which it is based.

SEVENTH ARTICLE

Whether Sins Are Fittingly Divided into Sins of Thought, Word, and Deed?

We proceed thus to the Seventh Article:—

Objection 1. It would seem that sins are unfittingly divided into sins of thought, word, and deed. For Augustine (*De Trin.* xii. 12) describes three stages of sin, of which the first is *when the carnal sense offers a bait,* which is the sin of thought; the second stage is reached *when one is satisfied with the mere pleasure of thought;* and the third stage, *when consent is given to the deed.* Now these three belong to the sin of thought. Therefore it is unfitting to reckon sin of thought as one kind of sin.

Obj. 2. Further, Gregory (*Moral.* iv. 25) reckons four degrees of sin; the first of which is *a fault hidden in the heart;* the second, *when it is done openly;* the third, *when it is formed into a habit;* and the fourth, *when man goes so far as to presume on God's mercy or to give himself up to despair:* where no distinction is made between sins of deed and sins of word, and two other degrees of sin are added. Therefore the first division was unfitting.

Obj. 3. Further, there can be no sin of word

or deed unless there precede sin of thought. Therefore these sins do not differ specifically. Therefore they should not be condivided with one another.

On the contrary, Jerome in commenting on Ezech. xliii. 23, says: *The human race is subject to three kinds of sin, for when we sin, it is either by thought, or word, or deed.*

I answer that, Things differ specifically in two ways:—first, when each has the complete species; thus a horse and an ox differ specifically:—secondly, when the diversity of species is derived from diversity of degree in generation or movement: thus the building is the complete generation of a house, while the laying of the foundations, and the setting up of the walls are incomplete species, as the Philosopher declares (*Ethic.* x. 4); and the same can apply to the generation of animals.—Accordingly sins are divided into these three, viz., sins of thought, word, and deed, not as into various complete species: for the consummation of sin is in the deed, wherefore sins of deed have the complete species; but the first beginning of sin is its foundation, as it were, in the sin of thought; the second degree is the sin of word, in so far as man is ready to break out into a declaration of his thought; while the third degree consists in the consummation of the deed. Consequently these three differ in respect of the various degrees of sin. Nevertheless it is evident that these three belong to the one complete species of sin, since they proceed from the same motive. For the angry man, through desire of vengeance, is at first disturbed in thought, then he breaks out into words of abuse, and lastly he goes on to wrongful deeds; and the same applies to lust and to any other sin.

Reply Obj. 1. All sins of thought have the common note of secrecy, in respect of which they form one degree, which is, however, divided into three stages, viz. of cogitation, pleasure, and consent.

Reply Obj. 2. Sins of words and deed are both done openly, and for this reason Gregory (*loc. cit.*) reckons them under one head: whereas Jerome (*loc. cit.*) distinguishes between them, because in sins of word there is nothing but manifestation which is intended principally; while in sins of deed, it is the consummation of the inward thought which is principally intended, and the outward manifestation is by way of sequel. Habit and despair are stages following the complete species of sin, even as boyhood and youth follow the complete generation of a man.

Reply Obj. 3. Sin of thought and sin of word are not distinct from the sin of deed when they are united together with it, but

Isagog.; cf. Arist., *Metaph.* i.

when each is found by itself: even as one part of a movement is not distinct from the whole movement, when the movement is continuous, but only when there is a break in the movement.

EIGHTH ARTICLE

Whether Excess and Deficiency Diversify the Species of Sins

We proceed thus to the Eighth Article:—

Objection 1. It would seem that excess and deficiency do not diversify the species of sins. For excess and deficiency differ in respect of more and less. Now *more* and *less* do not diversify a species. Therefore excess and deficiency do not diversify the species of sins.

Obj. 2. Further, just as sin, in matters of action, is due to straying from the rectitude of reason, so falsehood, in speculative matters, is due to straying from the truth of the reality. Now the species of falsehood is not diversified by saying more or less than the reality. Therefore neither is the species of sin diversified by straying more or less from the rectitude of reason.

Obj. 3. Further, *one species cannot be made out of two,* as Porphyry declares.* Now excess and deficiency are united in one sin; for some are at once illiberal and wasteful—illiberality being a sin by deficiency, and prodigality, by excess. Therefore excess and deficiency do not diversify the species of sins.

On the contrary, Contraries differ specifically, for *contrariety is a difference of form,* as stated in *Metaph.* x., text. 13, 14. Now vices that differ according to excess and deficiency are contrary to one another, as illiberality to wastefulness. Therefore they differ specifically.

I answer that, While there are two things in sin, viz. the act itself and its inordinateness, in so far as sin is a departure from the order of reason and the Divine law, the species of sin is gathered, not from its inordinateness, which is outside the sinner's intention, as stated above (A. 1), but on the contrary, from the act itself as terminating in the object to which the sinner's intention is directed. Consequently wherever we find a different motive inclining the intention to sin, there will be a different species of sin. Now it is evident that the motive for sinning, in sins by excess, is not the same as the motive for sinning, in sins by deficiency; in fact, they are contrary to one another, just as the motive in the sin of intemperance is love for bodily pleasures, while the motive in the sin of insensibility is hatred of the same. Therefore these sins not only differ specifically, but are contrary to one another.

Reply Obj. 1. Although *more* and *less* do

not cause diversity of species, yet they are sometimes consequent to specific difference, in so far as they are the result of diversity of form; thus we may say that fire is lighter than air. Hence the Philosopher says (*Ethic.* viii. 1) that *those who held that there are no different species of friendship, by reason of its admitting of degree, were led by insufficient proof.* In this way to exceed reason or to fall short thereof belongs to sins specifically different, in so far as they result from different motives.

Reply Obj. 2. It is not the sinner's intention to depart from reason; and so sins of excess and deficiency do not become of one kind through departing from the one rectitude of reason. On the other hand, sometimes he who utters a falsehood, intends to hide the truth, wherefore in this respect, it matters not whether he tells more or less. If, however, departure from the truth be not outside the intention, it is evident that then one is moved by different causes to tell more or less; and in this respect there are different kinds of falsehood, as is evident of the *boaster*, who exceeds in telling untruths for the sake of fame, and the *cheat*, who tells less than the truth, in order to escape from paying his debts. This also explains how some false opinions are contrary to one another.

Reply Obj. 3. One may be prodigal and illiberal with regard to different objects: for instance one may be illiberal* in taking what one ought not, and prodigal in giving what one ought not: and nothing hinders contraries from being in the same subject, in different respects.

NINTH ARTICLE

Whether Sins Differ Specifically in Respect of Different Circumstances?

We proceed thus to the Ninth Article:—

Objection 1. It would seem that vices and sins differ specifically in respect of different circumstances. For, as Dionysius says (*Div. Nom.* iv), *evil results from each single defect.* Now individual defects are corruptions of individual circumstances. Therefore from the corruption of each circumstance there results a corresponding species of sin.

Obj. 2. Further, sins are human acts. But human acts sometimes take their species from circumstances, as stated above (Q. 18, A. 10). Therefore sins differ specifically according as different circumstances are corrupted.

* *Cf.* II-II. Q. 119, A. 1 *ad* 1.

Obj. 3. Further, diverse species are assigned to gluttony, according to the words contained in the following verse:

   Hastily, sumptuously, too much, greedily,
      daintily.

Now these pertain to various circumstances, for *hastily* means sooner than is right; *too much,* more than is right, and so on with the the others. Therefore the species of sin is diversified according to the various circumstances.

On the contrary, The Philosopher says (*Ethic.* iii. 7, iv. 1) that *every vice sins by doing more than one ought, and when one ought not;* and in like manner as to the other circumstances. Therefore the species of sins are not diversified in this respect.

I answer that, As stated above (A. 8), wherever there is a special motive for sinning, there is a different species of sin, because the motive for sinning is the end and object of sin. Now it happens sometimes that although different circumstances are corrupted, there is but one motive: thus the illiberal man, for the same motive, takes when he ought not, where he ought not, and more than he ought, and so on with the circumstances, since he does this through an inordinate desire of hoarding money: and in such cases the corruption of different circumstances does not diversify the species of sins, but belongs to one and the same species.

Sometimes, however, the corruption of different circumstances arises from different motives: for instance that a man eat hastily, may be due to the fact that he cannot brook the delay in taking food, on account of a rapid exhaustion of the digestive humors; and that he desire too much food, may be due to a naturally strong digestion; that he desire choice meats, is due to his desire for pleasure in taking food. Hence in such matters, the corruption of different circumstances entails different species of sins.

Reply Obj. 1. Evil, as such, is a privation, and so it has different species in respect of the things of which the subject is deprived, even as other privations. But sin does not take its species from the privation or aversion, as stated above (A. 1), but from turning to the object of the act.

Reply Obj. 2. A circumstance never transfers an act from one species to another, save when there is another motive.

Reply Obj. 3. In the various species of gluttony there are various motives, as stated.

QUESTION 73

Of the Comparison of One Sin with Another

(In Ten Articles)

WE must now consider the comparison of one sin with another; under which head there are ten points of inquiry: (1) Whether all sins and vices are connected with one another? (2) Whether all are equal? (3) Whether the gravity of sin depends on its object? (4) Whether it depends on the excellence of the virtue to which it is opposed? (5) Whether carnal sins are more grievous than spiritual sins? (6) Whether the gravity of sins depends on their causes? (7) Whether it depends on their circumstances? (8) Whether it depends on how much harm ensues? (9) Whether on the position of the person sinned against? (10) Whether sin is aggravated by reason of the excellence of the person sinning?

FIRST ARTICLE

Whether All Sins Are Connected with One Another?

We proceed thus to the First Article:—

Objection 1. It would seem that all sins are connected. For it is written (James ii. 10): *Whosoever shall keep the whole Law, but offend in one point, is become guilty of all.* Now to be guilty of transgressing all the precepts of Law, is the same as to commit all sins, because, as Ambrose says (*De Parad.* viii), *sin is a transgression of the Divine law, and disobedience of the heavenly commandments.* Therefore whoever commits one sin is guilty of all.

Obj. 2. Further, each sin banishes its opposite virtue. Now whoever lacks one virtue lacks them all, as was shown above (Q. 65, A. 1). Therefore whoever commits one sin, is deprived of all the virtues. But whoever lacks a virtue, has its opposite vice. Therefore whoever commits one sin, is guilty of all sins.

Obj. 3. Further, all virtues are connected, because they have a principle in common, as stated above (Q. 65, AA. 1, 2). Now as the virtues have a common principle, so have sins, because, as the love of God, which builds the city of God, is the beginning and root of all the virtues, so self-love, which builds the city of Babylon, is the root of all sins, as Augustine declares (*De Civ. Dei,* xiv. 28). Therefore all vices and sins are also connected so that whoever has one, has them all.

On the contrary, Some vices are contrary to one another, as the Philosopher states (*Ethic.* ii. 8). But contraries cannot be together in the same subject. Therefore it is impossible for all sins and vices to be connected with one another.

I answer that, The intention of the man who acts according to virtue in pursuance of his reason, is different from the intention of the sinner in straying from the path of reason. For the intention of every man acting according to virtue is to follow the rule of reason, wherefore the intention of all the virtues is directed to the same end, so that all the virtues are connected together in the right reason of things to be done, viz. prudence, as stated above (Q. 65, A. 1). But the intention of the sinner is not directed to the point of straying from the path of reason; rather is it directed to tend to some appetible good whence it derives its species. Now these goods, to which the sinner's intention is directed when departing from reason, are of various kinds, having no mutual connection; in fact they are sometimes contrary to one another. Since, therefore, vices and sins take their species from that to which they turn, it is evident that, in respect of that which completes a sin's species, sins are not connected with one another. For sin does not consist in passing from the many to the one, as is the case with virtues, which are connected, but rather in forsaking the one for the many.

Reply Obj. 1. James is speaking of sin, not as regards the thing to which it turns and which causes the distinction of sins, as stated above (Q. 72, A. 1), but as regards that from which sin turns away, in as much as man, by sinning, departs from a commandment of the law. Now all the commandments of the law are from one and the same, as he also says in the same passage, so that the same God is despised in every sin; and in this sense he says that whoever *offends in one point, is become guilty of all,* for as much as, by committing one sin, he incurs the debt of punishment through his contempt of God, which is the origin of all sins.

Reply Obj. 2. As stated above (Q. 71, A. 4), the opposite virtue is not banished by every act of sin; because venial sin does not destroy virtue; while mortal sin destroys infused virtue, by turning man away from God. Yet one act, even of mortal sin, does not destroy the habit of acquired virtue; though if such acts be repeated so as to engender a contrary habit, the habit of acquired virtue is destroyed, the destruction of which entails the loss of prudence, since when man acts against any virtue whatever, he acts against prudence, without which no moral virtue is possible, as stated above (Q. 58, A. 4; Q. 65, A. 1). Consequently all the moral virtues are destroyed as to the perfect and formal being of virtue, which they have in so far as they partake of prudence, yet there remain the inclinations to virtuous acts, which inclinations, however, are not virtues. Nevertheless it does not follow that for this reason man contracts all vices or sins— first, because several vices are opposed to one virtue, so that a virtue can be destroyed by one of them, without the others being present; secondly, because sin is directly opposed to virtue, as regards the virtue's inclination to act, as stated above (Q. 71, A. 1). Wherefore, as long as any virtuous inclinations remain, it cannot be said that man has the opposite vices or sins.

Reply Obj. 3. The love of God is unitive, in as much as it draws man's affections from the many to the one; so that the virtues, which flow from the love of God, are connected together. But self-love disunites man's affections among different things, in so far as man loves himself, by desiring for himself temporal goods, which are various and of many kinds: hence vices and sins, which arise from self-love, are not connected together.

SECOND ARTICLE

Whether All Sins Are Equal?

We proceed thus to the Second Article:—

Objection 1. It would seem that all sins are equal. Because sin is to do what is unlawful. Now to do what is unlawful is reproved in one and the same way in all things. Therefore sin is reproved in one and the same way. Therefore one sin is not graver than another.

Obj. 2. Further, every sin is a transgression of the rule of reason, which is to human acts what a linear rule is in corporeal things. Therefore to sin is the same as to pass over a line. But passing over a line occurs equally and in the same way, even if one go a long way from it or stay near it, since privations do not admit of more or less. Therefore all sins are equal.

Obj. 3. Further, sins are opposed to virtues. But all virtues are equal, as Cicero states (*Paradox.* iii). Therefore all sins are equal.

On the contrary, Our Lord said to Pilate (Jo. xix. 11): *He that hath delivered me to thee, hath the greater sin,* and yet it is evident that Pilate was guilty of some sin. Therefore one sin is greater than another.

I answer that, The opinion of the Stoics, which Cicero adopts in the book on *Paradoxes* (*loc. cit.*), was that all sins are equal: from which opinion arose the error of certain heretics, who not only hold all sins to be equal, but also maintain that all the pains of hell are equal. So far as can be gathered from the words of Cicero the Stoics arrived at their conclusion through looking at sin on the side of the privation only, in so far, to wit, as it is a departure from reason; wherefore considering simply that no privation admits of more or less, they held that all sins are equal. Yet, if we consider the matter carefully, we shall see that there are two kinds of privation. For there is a simple and pure privation, which consists, so to speak, in *being* corrupted; thus death is privation of life, and darkness is privation of light. Such like privations do not admit of more or less, because nothing remains of the opposite habit; hence a man is not less dead on the first day after his death, or on the third or fourth days, than after a year, when his corpse is already dissolved; and, in like manner, a house is no darker if the light be covered with several shades, than if it were covered by a single shade shutting out all the light.—There is, however, another privation which is not simple, but retains something of the opposite habit; it consists in *becoming* corrupted rather than in *being* corrupted, like sickness which is a privation of the due commensuration of the humors, yet so that something remains of that commensuration, else the animal would cease to live: and the same applies to deformity and the like. Such privations admit of more or less on the part of what remains or the contrary habit. For it matters much in sickness or deformity, whether one departs more or less from the due commensuration of humors or members. The same applies to vices and sins: because in them the privation of the due commensuration of reason is such as not to destroy the order of reason altogether; else evil, if total, destroys itself, as stated in *Ethic.* iv. 5. For the substance of the act, or the affection of the agent could not remain, unless something remained of the order of reason. Therefore it matters much to the gravity of a sin whether one departs more or less from the rectitude of reason: and accordingly we must say that sins are not all equal.

Reply Obj. 1. To commit sin is unlawful on account of some inordinateness therein: wherefore those which contain a greater inordinateness are more unlawful, and consequently graver sins.

Reply Obj. 2. This argument looks upon sin as though it were a pure privation.

Reply Obj. 3. Virtues are proportionately equal in one and the same subject: yet one virtue surpasses another in excellence according to its species; and again, one man is more virtuous than another, in the same species of virtue, as stated above (Q. 66, AA. 1, 2). Moreover, even if virtues were equal, it would not follow that vices are equal, since virtues are connected, and vices or sins are not.

THIRD ARTICLE

Whether the Gravity of Sins Varies according to Their Objects?

We proceed thus to the Third Article:—

Objection 1. It would seem that the gravity of sins does not vary according to their objects. Because the gravity of a sin pertains to its mode or quality: whereas the object is the matter of the sin. Therefore the gravity of sins does not vary according to their various objects.

Obj. 2. Further, the gravity of a sin is the intensity of its malice. Now sin does not derive its malice from its proper object to which it turns, and which is some appetible good, but rather from that which it turns away from. Therefore the gravity of sins does not vary according to their various objects.

Obj. 3. Further, sins that have different objects are of different kinds. But things of different kinds cannot be compared with one another, as is proved in *Phys.* vii., text. 30, *seqq.* Therefore one sin is not graver than another by reason of the difference of objects.

On the contrary, Sins take their species from their objects, as was shown above (Q. 72, A. 1). But some sins are graver than others in respect of their species, as murder is graver than theft. Therefore the gravity of sins varies according to their objects.

I answer that, As is clear from what has been said (Q. 71, A. 5), the gravity of sins varies in the same way as one sickness is graver than another: for just as the good of health consists in a certain commensuration of the humors, in keeping with an animal's nature, so the good of virtue consists in a certain commensuration of the human act in accord with the rule of reason. Now it is evident that the higher the principle the disorder of which causes the disorder in the humors, the graver is the sickness: thus a sickness which comes on the human body from the heart, which is the principle of life, or from some neighboring part, is more dangerous. Wherefore a sin must needs be so much the graver, as the disorder occurs in a principle which is higher in the order of reason. Now in matters of action the reason directs all things in view of the end: wherefore the higher the end which attaches to sins in human acts, the graver the sin. Now the object of an act

is its end, as stated above (Q.72, A. 3, *ad* 2); and consequently the difference of gravity in sins depends on their objects. Thus it is clear that external things are directed to man as their end, while man is further directed to God as his end. Wherefore a sin which is about the very substance of man, e.g. murder, is graver than a sin which is about external things, e.g. theft; and graver still is a sin committed directly against God, e.g. unbelief, blasphemy, and the like: and in each of these grades of sin, one sin will be graver than another according as it is about a higher or a lower principle. And forasmuch as sins take their species from their objects, the difference of gravity which is derived from the objects is first and foremost, as resulting from the species.

Reply Obj. 1. Although the object is the matter about which an act is concerned, yet it has the character of an end, in so far as the intention of the agent is fixed on it, as stated above (Q. 72, A. 3, *ad* 2). Now the form of a moral act depends on the end, as was shown above (Q. 72, A. 6; Q. 18, A. 6).

Reply Obj. 2. From the very fact that man turns unduly to some mutable good, it follows that he turns away from the immutable Good, which aversion completes the nature of evil. Hence the various degrees of malice in sins must needs follow the diversity of those things to which man turns.

Reply Obj. 3. All the objects of human acts are related to one another, wherefore all human acts are somewhat of one kind, in so far as they are directed to the last end. Therefore nothing prevents all sins from being compared with one another.

FOURTH ARTICLE

Whether the Gravity of Sins Depends on the Excellence of the Virtues to Which They Are Opposed?

We proceed thus to the Fourth Article:—

Objection 1. It would seem that the gravity of sins does not vary according to the excellence of the virtues to which they are opposed, so that, to wit, the graver sin is opposed to the greater virtue. For, according to Prov. xv. 5, *In abundant justice there is the greatest strength.* Now, as Our Lord says (Matth. v. 20, *seqq.*), abundant justice restrains anger, which is a less grievous sin than murder, which less abundant justice restrains. Therefore the least grievous sin is opposed to the greatest virtue.

Obj. 2. Further, it is stated in *Ethic.* ii 3 that *virtue is about the difficult and the good:* whence it seems to follow that the greater virtue is about what is more difficult. But it is a less grievous sin to fail in what is more difficult, than in what is less difficult. Therefore the less grievous sin is opposed to the greater virtue.

Obj. 3. Further, charity is a greater virtue than faith or hope (1 Cor. xiii. 13). Now hatred which is opposed to charity is a less grievous sin than unbelief or despair which are opposed to faith and hope. Therefore the less grievous sin is opposed to the greater virtue.

On the contrary, The Philosopher says (*Ethic.* viii. 10) that the *worst is opposed to the best.* Now in morals the best is the greatest virtue; and the worst is the most grievous sin. Therefore the most grievous sin is opposed to the greatest virtue.

I answer that, A sin is opposed to a virtue in two ways:—first, principally and directly; that is to wit, which is about the same object: because contraries are about the same thing. In this way, the more grievous sin must needs be opposed to the greater virtue: because, just as the degrees of gravity in a sin depend on the object, so also does the greatness of a virtue, since both sin and virtue take their species from the object, as shown above (Q. 60, A. 5; Q. 72, A. 1). Wherefore the greatest sin must needs be directly opposed to the greatest virtue, as being furthest removed from it in the same genus.—Secondly, the opposition of virtue to sin may be considered in respect of a certain extension of the virtue in checking sin. For the greater a virtue is, the further it removes man from the contrary sin, so that it withdraws man not only from that sin, but also from whatever leads to it. And thus it is evident that the greater a virtue is, the more it withdraws man also from less grievous sins: even as the more perfect health is, the more does it ward off even minor ailments. And in this way the less grievous sin is opposed to the greater virtue, on the part of the latter's effect.

Reply Obj. 1. This argument considers the opposition which consists in restraining from sin; for thus abundant justice checks even minor sins.

Reply Obj. 2. The greater virtue that is about a more difficult good is opposed directly to the sin which is about a more difficult evil. For in each case there is a certain superiority, in that the will is shown to be more intent on good or evil, through not being overcome by the difficulty.

Reply Obj. 3. Charity is not any kind of love, but the love of God: hence not any kind of hatred is opposed to it directly, but the hatred of God, which is the most grievous of all sins.

* The quotation is from *De Civ. Dei* ii. 4 and iv. 31.

Whether Carnal Sins Are of Less Guilt Than Spiritual Sins?

We proceed thus to the Fifth Article:—

Objection 1. It would seem that carnal sins are not of less guilt than spiritual sins. Because adultery is a more grievous sin than theft: for it is written (*Prov.* vi. 30, 32): *The fault is not so great when a man has stolen, . . . but he that is an adulterer, for the folly of his heart shall destroy his own soul.* Now theft belongs to covetousness, which is a spiritual sin; while adultery pertains to lust, which is a carnal sin. Therefore carnal sins are of greater guilt than spiritual sins.

Obj. 2. Further, Augustine says in his commentary on Leviticus* that *the devil rejoices chiefly in lust and idolatry.* But he rejoices more in the greater sin. Therefore, since lust is a carnal sin, it seems that the carnal sins are of most guilt.

Obj. 3. Further, the Philosopher proves (*Ethic.* vii. 6) that *it is more shameful to be incontinent in lust than in anger.* But anger is a spiritual sin, according to Gregory (*Moral.* xxxi. 17); while lust pertains to carnal sins. Therefore carnal sin is more grievous than spiritual sin.

On the contrary, Gregory says (*Moral.* xxxiii. 11) that carnal sins are of less guilt, but of more shame than spiritual sins.

I answer that, Spiritual sins are of greater guilt than carnal sins: yet this does not mean that each spiritual sin is of greater guilt than each carnal sin; but that, considering the sole difference between spiritual and carnal, spiritual sins are more grievous than carnal sins, other things being equal. Three reasons may be assigned for this. The first is on the part of the subject: because spiritual sins belong to the spirit, to which it is proper to turn to God, and to turn away from Him; whereas carnal sins are consummated in the carnal pleasure of the appetite, to which it chiefly belongs to turn to goods of the body; so that carnal sin, as such, denotes more a *turning to* something, and for that reason, implies a closer cleaving; whereas spiritual sin denotes more a *turning from* something, whence the notion of guilt arises; and for this reason it involves greater guilt.—A second reason may be taken on the part of the person against whom sin is committed: because carnal sin, as such, is against the sinner's own body, which he ought to love less, in the order of charity, than God and his neighbor, against whom he commits spiritual sins, and consequently spiritual sins, as such, are of greater guilt.—A third reason may be taken from the motive, since the stronger the impulse to sin, the less grievous the sin, as we shall state further on (A. 6). Now carnal sins have a stronger impulse, viz. our innate concupiscence of the flesh. Therefore spiritual sins, as such, are of greater guilt.

Reply Obj. 1. Adultery belongs not only to the sin of lust, but also to the sin of injustice, and in this respect may be brought under the head of covetousness, as a gloss observes on Eph. v. 5, *No fornicator, or unclean, or covetous person,* etc.; so that adultery is so much more grievous than theft, as a man loves his wife more than his chattels.

Reply Obj. 2. The devil is said to rejoice chiefly in the sin of lust, because it is of the greatest adhesion, and man can with difficulty be withdrawn from it. *For the desire of pleasure is insatiable,* as the Philosopher states (*Ethic.* iii. 12).

Reply Obj. 3. As the Philosopher himself says (*ibid.*), the reason why it is more shameful to be incontinent in lust than in anger, is that lust partakes less of reason; and in the same sense he says (*Ethic.* iii. 10) that *sins of intemperance are most worthy of reproach, because they are about those pleasures which are common to us and irrational animals:* hence, by these sins man is, so to speak, brutalized; for which same reason Gregory says (*loc. cit.*) that they are more shameful.

SIXTH ARTICLE

Whether the Gravity of a Sin Depends on Its Cause?

We proceed thus to the Sixth Article:—

Objection 1. It would seem that the gravity of a sin does not depend on its cause. Because the greater a sin's cause, the more forcibly it moves to sin, and so the more difficult is it to resist. But sin is lessened by the fact that it is difficult to resist; for it denotes weakness in the sinner, if he cannot easily resist sin; and a sin that is due to weakness is deemed less grievous. Therefore sin does not derive it gravity from its cause.

Obj. 2. Further, concupiscence is a general cause of sin; wherefore a gloss on Rom. vii. 7, *For I had not known concupiscence,* says: *The law is good, since by forbidding concupiscence, it forbids all evils.* Now the greater the concupiscence by which man is overcome, the less grievous his sin. Therefore the gravity of a sin is diminished by the greatness of its cause.

Obj. 3. Further, as rectitude of the reason is the cause of a virtuous act, so defect in the reason seems to be the cause of sin. Now the greater the defect in the reason, the less grievous the sin: so much so that he who lacks the use of reason, is altogether excused from sin, and he who sins through ignorance, sins less

grievously. Therefore the gravity of a sin is not increased by the greatness of its cause.

On the contrary, If the cause be increased, the effect is increased. Therefore the greater the cause of sin, the more grievous the sin.

I answer that, In the genus of sin, as in every other genus, two causes may be observed. The first is the direct and proper cause of sin, and is the will to sin: for it is compared to the sinful act, as a tree to its fruit, as a gloss observes on Matth. vii. 18, *A good tree cannot bring forth evil fruit:* and the greater this cause is, the more grievous will the sin be, since the greater the will to sin, the more grievously does man sin.

The other causes of sin are extrinsic and remote, as it were, being those whereby the will is inclined to sin. Among these causes we must make a distinction; for some of them induce the will to sin in accord with the very nature of the will: such is the end, which is the proper object of the will; and by a such like cause sin is made more grievous, because a man sins more grievously if his will is induced to sin by the intention of a more evil end.—Other causes incline the will to sin, against the nature and order of the will, whose natural inclination is to be moved freely of itself in accord with the judgment of reason. Wherefore those causes which weaken the judgment of reason (e.g. ignorance), or which weaken the free movement of the will (e.g. weakness, violence, fear, or the like), diminish the gravity of sin, even as they diminish its voluntariness; and so much so, that if the act be altogether involuntary, it is no longer sinful.

Reply Obj. 1. This argument considers the extrinsic moving cause, which diminishes voluntariness. The increase of such a cause diminishes the sin, as stated.

Reply Obj. 2. If concupiscence be understood to include the movement of the will, then, where there is greater concupiscence, there is a greater sin. But if by concupiscence we understand a passion, which is a movement of the concupiscible power, then a greater concupiscence, forestalling the judgment of reason and the movement of the will, diminishes the sin, because the man who sins, being stimulated by a greater concupiscence, falls through a more grievous temptation, wherefore he is less to be blamed. On the other hand, if concupiscence taken in this sense follows the judgment of reason, and the movement of the will, then the greater the concupiscence, the graver the sin: because sometimes the movement of concupiscence is redoubled by the will tending unrestrainedly to its object.

Reply Obj. 3. This argument considers the cause which renders the act involuntary, and such a cause diminishes the gravity of sin, as stated.

SEVENTH ARTICLE

Whether a Circumstance Aggravates a Sin?

We proceed thus to the Seventh Article:—

Objection 1. It would seem that a circumstance does not aggravate a sin. Because sin takes its gravity from its species. Now a circumstance does not specify a sin, for it is an accident thereof. Therefore the gravity of a sin is not taken from a circumstance.

Obj. 2. Further, a circumstance is either evil or not: if it is evil, it causes, of itself, a species of evil; and if it is not evil, it cannot make a thing worse. Therefore a circumstance nowise aggravates a sin.

Obj. 3. Further, the malice of a sin is derived from its turning away (from God). But circumstances affect sin on the part of the object to which it turns. Therefore they do not add to the sin's malice.

On the contrary, Ignorance of a circumstance diminishes sin: for he who sins through ignorance of a circumstance, deserves to be forgiven (*Ethic.* iii. 1). Now this would not be the case unless a circumstance aggravated a sin. Therefore a circumstance makes a sin more grievous.

I answer that, As the Philosopher says in speaking of habits of virtue (*Ethic.* ii. 1, 2), *it is natural for a thing to be increased by that which causes it.* Now it is evident that a sin is caused by a defect in some circumstance: because the fact that a man departs from the order of reason is due to his not observing the due circumstances in his action. Wherefore it is evident that it is natural for a sin to be aggravated by reason of its circumstances. This happens in three ways. First, in so far as a circumstance draws a sin from one kind to another: thus fornication is the intercourse of a man with one who is not his wife: but if to this be added the circumstance that the latter is the wife of another, the sin is drawn to another kind of sin, viz. injustice, in so far as he usurps another's property; and in this respect adultery is a more grievous sin than fornication.—Secondly, a circumstance aggravates a sin, not by drawing it into another genus, but only by multiplying the ratio of sin: thus if a wasteful man gives both when he ought not, and to whom he ought not to give, he commits the same kind of sin in more ways than if he were merely to give to whom he ought not, and for that very reason his sin is more grievous; even as that sickness is the graver which affects more parts of the body. Hence Cicero says (*Paradox.* iii) that *in taking his father's life a man commits many sins; for he outrages one who begot him, who fed*

him, who educated him, to whom he owes his lands, his house, his position in the republic. —Thirdly, a circumstance aggravates a sin by adding to the deformity which the sin derives from another circumstance: thus, taking another's property constitutes the sin of theft; but if to this be added the circumstance that much is taken of another's property, the sin will be more grievous; although in itself, to take more or less has not the character of a good or of an evil act.

Reply Obj. 1. Some circumstances do specify a moral act, as stated above (Q. 18, A. 10). Nevertheless a circumstance which does not give the species, may aggravate a sin; because, even as the goodness of a thing is weighed, not only in reference to its species, but also in reference to an accident, so the malice of an act is measured, not only according to the species of that act, but also according to a circumstance.

Reply Obj. 2 A circumstance may aggravate a sin either way. For if it is evil, it does not follow that it constitutes the sin's species; because it may multiply the ratio of evil within the same species, as stated above. And if it be not evil, it may aggravate a sin in relation to the malice of another circumstance.

Reply Obj. 3. Reason should direct the action not only as regards the object, but also as regards every circumstance. Therefore one may turn aside from the rule of reason through corruption of any single circumstance; for instance, by doing something when one ought not or where one ought not; and to depart thus from the rule of reason suffices to make the act evil. This turning aside from the rule of reason results from man's turning away from God, to Whom man ought to be united by right reason.

EIGHTH ARTICLE

Whether Sin Is Aggravated by Reason of Its Causing More Harm?

We proceed thus to the Eighth Article:—

Objection 1. It would seem that a sin is not aggravated by reason of its causing more harm. Because the harm done is an issue consequent to the sinful act. But the issue of an act does not add to its goodness or malice, as stated above (Q. 20, A. 5). Therefore a sin is not aggravated on account of its causing more harm.

Obj. 2. Further, harm is inflicted by sins against our neighbor. Because no one wishes to harm himself: and no one can harm God, according to Job xxxv. 6, 8: *If thy iniquities be multiplied, what shalt thou do against Him? . . . Thy wickedness may hurt a man that is like thee.* If, therefore, sins were aggravated through causing more harm, it would follow that sins against our neighbor are more grievous than sins against our God or oneself.

Obj. 3. Further, greater harm is inflicted on a man by depriving him of the life of grace, than by taking away his natural life; because the life of grace is better than the life of nature, so far that man ought to despise his natural life lest he lose the life of grace. Now, speaking absolutely, a man who leads a woman to commit fornication deprives her of the life of grace by leading her into mortal sin. If therefore a sin were more grievous on account of its causing a greater harm, it would follow that fornication, absolutely speaking, is a more grievous sin than murder, which is evidently untrue. Therefore a sin is not more grievous on account of its causing a greater harm.

On the contrary, Augustine says (*De Lib. Arb.* iii. 14): *Since vice is contrary to nature, a vice is the more grievous according as it diminishes the integrity of nature.* Now the diminution of the integrity of nature is a harm. Therefore a sin is graver according as it does more harm.

I answer that, Harm may bear a threefold relation to sin. Because sometimes the harm resulting from a sin is foreseen and intended, as when a man does something with a mind to harm another, e.g. a murderer or a thief. In this case the quantity of harm aggravates the sin directly, because then the harm is the direct object of the sin.—Sometimes the harm is foreseen, but not intended; for instance, when a man takes a short cut through a field, the result being that he knowingly injures the growing crops, although his intention is not to do this harm, but to commit fornication. In this case again the quantity of the harm done aggravates the sin; indirectly, however, in so far, to wit, as it is owing to his will being strongly inclined to sin, that a man does not forbear from doing, to himself or to another, a harm which he would not wish simply.—Sometimes, however, the harm is neither foreseen nor intended: and then if this harm is connected with the sinful act accidentally, it does not aggravate the sin directly; but, on account of his neglecting to consider the harm that might ensue, a man is deemed punishable for the evil results of his action if it be unlawful. If, on the other hand, the harm follow directly from the sinful act, although it be neither foreseen nor intended, it aggravates the sin directly, because whatever is directly consequent to a sin, belongs, in a manner, to the very species of that sin: for instance, if a man is a notorious fornicator, the result is that many are scandalized; and although such was not his intention, nor was it perhaps foreseen by him, yet it aggravates his sin directly.

But this does not seem to apply to penal harm, which the sinner himself incurs. Such like harm, if accidentally connected with the sinful act, and if neither foreseen nor intended, does not aggravate a sin, nor does it correspond with the gravity of the sin: for instance, if a man in running to slay, slips and hurts his foot. If, on the other hand, this harm is directly consequent to the sinful act, although perhaps it be neither foreseen nor intended, then greater harm does not make greater sin, but, on the contrary, a graver sin calls for the infliction of a greater harm. Thus, an unbeliever who has heard nothing about the pains of hell, would suffer greater pain in hell for a sin of murder than for a sin of theft: but his sin is not aggravated on account of his neither intending nor foreseeing this, as it would be in the case of a believer, who, seemingly, sins more grievously in the very fact that he despises a greater punishment, that he may satisfy his desire to sin; but the gravity of this harm is caused by the sole gravity of sin.

Reply Obj. 1. As we have already stated (Q. 20, A. 5), in treating of the goodness and malice of external actions, the result of an action if foreseen and intended adds to the goodness and malice of an act.

Reply Obj. 2. Although the harm done aggravates a sin, it does not follow that this alone renders a sin more grievous: in fact, it is inordinateness which of itself aggravates a sin. Wherefore the harm itself that ensues aggravates a sin, in so far only as it renders the act more inordinate. Hence it does not follow, supposing harm to be inflicted chiefly by sins against our neighbor, that such sins are the most grievous, since a much greater inordinateness is to be found in sins which man commits against God, and in some which he commits against himself.—Moreover we might say that although no man can do God any harm in His substance, yet he can endeavor to do so in things concerning Him, e.g. by destroying faith, by outraging holy things, which are most grievous sins.—Again, a man sometimes knowingly and freely inflicts harm on himself, as in the case of suicide, though this be referred finally to some apparent good, for example, delivery from some anxiety.

Reply Obj. 3. This argument does not prove, for two reasons: — first, because the murderer intends directly to do harm to his neighbors; whereas the fornicator who solicits the woman intends not harm but pleasure;—secondly, because murder is the direct and sufficient cause of bodily death; whereas no man can of himself be the sufficient cause of another's spiritual death, because no man dies spiritually except by sinning of his own will.

NINTH ARTICLE

Whether a Sin Is Aggravated by Reason of the Condition of the Person against Whom It Is Committed?

We proceed thus to the Ninth Article:—

Objection 1. It would seem that sin is not aggravated by reason of the condition of the person against whom it is committed. For if this were the case a sin would be aggravated chiefly by being committed against a just and holy man. But this does not aggravate a sin: because a virtuous man who bears a wrong with equanimity is less harmed by the wrong done him, than others, who, through being scandalized, are also hurt inwardly. Therefore the condition of the person against whom a sin is committed does not aggravate the sin.

Obj. 2. Further, if the condition of the person aggravated the sin, this would be still more the case if the person be near of kin, because, as Cicero says (*Paradox.* iii). *The man who kills his slave sins once: he that takes his father's life sins many times.* But the kinship of a person sinned against does not apparently aggravate a sin, because every man is most akin to himself; and yet it is less grievous to harm oneself than another, e.g. to kill one's own, than another's horse, as the Philosopher declares (*Ethic.* v. 11). Therefore kinship of the person sinned against does not aggravate the sin.

Obj. 3. Further, the condition of the person who sins aggravates a sin chiefly on account of his position or knowledge, according to Wis. vi. 7: *The mighty shall be mightily tormented,* and Luke xii. 47: *The servant who knew the will of his lord . . . and did it not . . . shall be beaten with many stripes.* Therefore, in like manner, on the part of the person sinned against, the sin is made more grievous by reason of his position and knowledge. But, apparently, it is not a more grievous sin to inflict an injury on a rich and powerful person than on a poor man, since *there is no respect of persons with God* (Col. iii. 25), according to Whose judgment the gravity of a sin is measured. Therefore the condition of the person sinned against does not aggravate the sin.

On the contrary, Holy Writ censures especially those sins that are committed against the servants of God. Thus it is written (3 Kings xix. 14): *They have destroyed Thy altars, they have slain Thy prophets with the sword.*—Moreover much blame is attached to the sin committed by a man against those who are akin to him, according to Mich. vii. 6: *the son dishonoreth the father, and the daughter riseth up against her mother.*—Fur-

thermore sins committed against persons of rank are expressly condemned: thus it is written (Job xxxiv. 18): *Who saith to the king: "Thou art an apostate"; who calleth rulers ungodly.* Therefore the condition of the person sinned against aggravates the sin.

I answer that, The person sinned against is, in a manner, the object of the sin. Now it has been stated above (A. 3) that the primary gravity of a sin is derived from its object; so that a sin is deemed to be so much the more grave, as its object is a more principal end. But the principal ends of human acts are God, man himself, and his neighbor: for whatever we do, it is on account of one of these that we do it; although one of them is subordinate to the other. Therefore the greater or lesser gravity of a sin, in respect of the person sinned against, may be considered on the part of these three.

First, on the part of God, to Whom man is the more closely united, as he is more virtuous or more sacred to God: so that an injury inflicted on such a person redounds on to God, according to Zach. ii. 8: *He that toucheth you, toucheth the apple of My eye.* Wherefore a sin is the more grievous, according as it is committed against a person more closely united to God by reason of personal sanctity, or official station.—On the part of man himself, it is evident that he sins all the more grievously, according as the person against whom he sins, is more united to him, either through natural affinity or kindness received or any other bond; because he seems to sin against himself rather than the other, and, for this very reason, sins all the more grievously, according to Ecclus. xiv. 5: *He that is evil to himself, to whom will he be good?*—On the part of his neighbor, a man sins the more grievously, according as his sin affects more persons: so that a sin committed against a public personage, e.g. a sovereign prince who stands in the place of the whole people, is more grievous than a sin committed against a private person; hence it is expressly prohibited (Exod. xxii. 28): *The prince of thy people thou shalt not curse.* In like manner it would seem that an injury done to a person of prominence, is all the more grave, on account of the scandal and the disturbance it would cause among many people.

Reply Obj. 1. He who inflicts an injury on a virtuous person, so far as he is concerned, disturbs him internally and externally; but that the latter is not disturbed internally is due to his goodness, which does not extenuate the sin of the injurer.

Reply Obj. 2. The injury which a man inflicts on himself in those things which are subject to the dominion of his will, for instance his possessions, is less sinful than if it were inflicted on another, because he does it of his own will; but in those things that are not subject to the dominion of his will, such as natural and spiritual goods, it is a graver sin to inflict an injury on oneself: for it is more grievous for a man to kill himself than another. Since, however, things belonging to our neighbor are not subject to the dominion of our will, the argument fails to prove, in respect of injuries done to such like things, that it is less grievous to sin in their regard, unless indeed our neighbor be willing, or give his approval.

Reply Obj. 3. There is no respect for persons if God punishes more severely those who sin against a person of higher rank; for this is done because such an injury redounds to the harm of many.

TENTH ARTICLE

Whether the Excellence of the Person Sinning Aggravates the Sin?

We proceed thus to the Tenth Article:—

Objection 1. It would seem that the excellence of the person sinning does not aggravate the sin. For man becomes great chiefly by cleaving to God, according to Ecclus. xxv. 13: *How great is he that findeth wisdom and knowledge! but there is none above him that feareth the Lord.* Now the more a man cleaves to God, the less is a sin imputed to him: for it is written (2 Paral. xxx. 18, 19): *The Lord Who is good will show mercy to all them, who with their whole heart seek the Lord the God of their fathers; and will not impute it to them that they are not sanctified.* Therefore a sin is not aggravated by the excellence of the person sinning.

Obj. 2. Further, *there is no respect of persons with God* (Rom. ii. 11). Therefore He does not punish one man more than another, for one and the same sin. Therefore a sin is not aggravated by the excellence of the person sinning.

Obj. 3. Further, no one should reap disadvantage from good. But he would, if his action were the more blameworthy on account of his goodness. Therefore a sin is not aggravated by reason of the excellence of the person sinning.

On the contrary, Isidore says (*De Summo Bono* ii. 18): *A sin is deemed so much the more grievous as the sinner is held to be a more excellent person.*

I answer that, Sin is twofold. There is a sin which takes us unawares on account of the weakness of human nature: and such like sins are less imputable to one who is more virtuous, because he is less negligent in checking those sins, which nevertheless human weakness does not allow us to escape altogether.—But there are other sins which proceed from deliberation: and these sins are all the more imputed to man according as he is more excellent. Four reasons may be assigned for this. First, because a more excellent person, e.g. one who excels in knowledge and virtue, can more easily resist sin; hence Our Lord said (Luke xii. 47) that the *servant who knew the will of his lord, . . . and did* it *not . . . shall be beaten with many stripes.*—Secondly, on account of ingratitude, because every good in which a man excels, is a gift of God, to Whom man is ungrateful when he sins: and in this respect any excellence, even in temporal goods, aggravates a sin, according to Wis. vi. 7: *The mighty shall be mightily tormented.*—Thirdly, on account of the sinful act being specially inconsistent with the excellence of the person sinning: for instance, if a prince were to violate justice, whereas he is set up as the guardian of justice, or if a priest were to be a fornicator, whereas he has taken the vow of chastity.—Fourthly, on account of the example or scandal; because, as Gregory says (*Pastor.* i. 2): *Sin becomes much more scandalous, when the sinner is honored for his position:* and the sins of the great are much more notorious and men are wont to bear them with more indignation.

Reply Obj. 1. The passage quoted alludes to those things which are done negligently when we are taken unawares through human weakness.

Reply Obj. 2. God does not respect persons in punishing the great more severely, because their excellence conduces to the gravity of their sin, as stated.

Reply Obj. 3. The man who excels in anything reaps disadvantage, not from the good which he has, but from his abuse thereof.

QUESTION 74

Of the Subject of Sin

(In Ten Articles)

WE must now consider the subject of vice or sin: under which head there are ten points of inquiry: (1) Whether the will can be the subject of sin? (2) Whether the will alone is the subject of sin? (3) Whether the sensuality can be the subject of sin? (4) Whether it can be the subject of mortal sin? (5) Whether the reason can be the subject of sin? (6) Whether morose delectation or non-morose delectation be subjected in the higher reason? (7) Whether the sin of consent in the act of sin is subjected in the higher reason? (8) Whether the lower reason can be the subject of mortal sin? (9) Whether the higher reason can be the subject of venial sin? (10) Whether there can be in the higher reason a venial sin directed to its proper object?

FIRST ARTICLE

Whether the Will Is a Subject of Sin?

We proceed thus to the First Article:—

Objection 1. It would seem that the will cannot be a subject of sin. For Dionysius says (*Div. Nom.* iv) that *evil is outside the will and the intention.* But sin has the character of evil. Therefore sin cannot be in the will.

Obj. 2. Further, the will is directed either to the good or to what seems good. Now from the fact that the will wishes the good, it does not sin: and that it wishes what seems good but is not truly good, points to a defect in the apprehensive power rather than in the will. Therefore sin is nowise in the will.

Obj. 3. Further, the same thing cannot be both subject and efficient cause of sin: because *the efficient and the material cause do not coincide* (*Phys.* 2, text. 70). Now the will is the efficient cause of sin: because the first cause of sinning is the will, as Augustine states (*De Duabus Anim.* x, 10, 11). Therefore it is not the subject of sin.

On the contrary, Augustine says (*Retract.* i. 9) that *it is by the will that we sin, and live righteously.*

I answer that, Sin is an act, as stated above (Q. 71, AA. 1, 6). Now some acts pass into external matter, e.g. *to cut* and *to burn*: and such like acts have for their matter and subject, the thing into which the action passes: thus the Philosopher states (*Phys.* iii, text. 18) that *movement is the act of the thing moved, caused by a mover.*—On the other hand, there

* Cf. *De Vera Relig.* xiv.

are acts which do not pass into external matter, but remain in the agent, e.g. *to desire* and *to know:* and such are all moral acts, whether virtuous or sinful. Consequently the proper subject of sin must needs be the power which is the principle of the act. Now since it is proper to moral acts that they are voluntary, as stated above (Q. 1, A. 1; Q. 18, A. 6), it follows that the will, which is the principle of voluntary acts, both of good acts, and of evil acts or sins, is the principle of sins. Therefore it follows that sin is in the will as its subject.

Reply Obj. 1. Evil is said to be outside the will, because the will does not tend to it under the aspect of evil. But since some evil is an apparent good, the will sometimes desires an evil, and in this sense sin is in the will.

Reply Obj. 2. If the defect in the apprehensive power were nowise subject to the will, there would be no sin, either in the will, or in the apprehensive power, as in the case of those whose ignorance is invincible. It remains therefore that when there is in the apprehensive power a defect that is subject to the will, this defect also is deemed a sin.

Reply Obj. 3. This argument applies to those efficient causes whose actions pass into external matter, and which do not move themselves, but move other things; the contrary of which is to be observed in the will; hence the argument does not prove.

SECOND ARTICLE

Whether the Will Alone Is the Subject of Sin?

We proceed thus to the Second Article:—

Objection 1. It would seem that the will alone is the subject of sin. For Augustine says (*De Duabus Anim.* x. 10) that *no one sins except by the will.* Now the subject of sin is the power by which we sin. Therefore the will alone is the subject of sin.

Obj. 2. Further, sin is an evil contrary to reason. Now good and evil pertaining to reason are the object of the will alone. Therefore the will alone is the subject of sin.

Obj. 3. Further, every sin is a voluntary act, because, as Augustine states (*De Lib. Arb.* iii. 18),* *so true is it that every sin is voluntary, that unless it be voluntary, it is no sin at all.* Now the acts of the other powers are not voluntary, except in so far as those powers are moved by the will; nor does this suffice for them to be the subject of sin, because then even the external members of the body, which are moved by the will, would be a subject of sin; which is clearly untrue. Therefore the will alone is the subject of sin.

On the contrary, Sin is contrary to virtue: and contraries are about one same thing. But the other powers of the soul, besides the will, are the subject of virtues, as stated above (Q. 56). Therefore the will is not the only subject of sin.

I answer that, As was shown above (A. 1), whatever is a principle of a voluntary act is a subject of sin. Now voluntary acts are not only those which are elicited by the will, but also those which are commanded by the will, as we stated above (Q. 6, A. 4) in treating of voluntariness. Therefore not only the will can be a subject of sin, but also all those powers which can be moved to their acts, or restrained from their acts, by the will; and these same powers are the subjects of good and evil moral habits, because act and habit belong to the same subject.

Reply Obj. 1. We do not sin except by the will as first mover; but we sin by the other powers as moved by the will.

Reply Obj. 2. Good and evil pertain to the will as its proper objects; but the other powers have certain determinate goods and evils, by reason of which they can be the subject of virtue, vice, and sin, in so far as they partake of will and reason.

Reply Obj. 3. The members of the body are not principles but merely organs of action: wherefore they are compared to the soul which moves them, as a slave who is moved but moves no other. On the other hand, the internal appetitive powers are compared to reason as free agents, because they both act and are acted upon, as is made clear in *Polit.* i. 3. Moreover, the acts of the external members are actions that pass into external matter, as may be seen in the blow that is inflicted in the sin of murder. Consequently there is no comparison.

THIRD ARTICLE

Whether There Can Be Sin in the Sensuality?

We proceed thus to the Third Article:—

Objection 1. It would seem that there cannot be sin in the sensuality. For sin is proper to man who is praised or blamed for his actions. Now the sensuality is common to us and irrational animals. Therefore sin cannot be in the sensuality.

Obj. 2. Further, *no man sins in what he cannot avoid,* as Augustine states (*De Lib. Arb.* iii. 18). But man cannot prevent the movement of the sensuality from being inordinate, since *the sensuality ever remains cor-*rupt, so long as we abide in this mortal life; wherefore it is signified by the serpent, as Augustine declares (*De Trin.* xii. 12, 13). Therefore the inordinate movement of the sensuality is not a sin.

Obj. 3. Further, that which man himself does not do is not imputed to him as a sin. Now *that alone do we seem to do ourselves, which we do with the deliberation of reason,* as the Philosopher says (*Ethic.* ix. 8). Therefore the movement of the sensuality, which is without the deliberation of reason, is not imputed to a man as a sin.

On the contrary, It is written (Rom. vii. 19): *The good which I will I do not; but the evil which I will not, that I do:* which words Augustine explains (*Contra Julian.* iii. 26; *De Verb. Apost.* xii. 2, 3), as referring to the evil of concupiscence, which is clearly a movement of the sensuality. Therefore there can be sin in the sensuality.

I answer that, As stated above (AA. 2, 3), sin may be found in any power whose act can be voluntary and inordinate, wherein consists the nature of sin. Now it is evident that the act of the sensuality can be voluntary, in so far as the sensuality, or sensitive appetite, is naturally inclined to be moved by the will. Wherefore it follows that sin can be in the sensuality.

Reply Obj. 1. Although some of the powers of the sensitive part are common to us and irrational animals, nevertheless, in us, they have a certain excellence through being united to the reason; thus we surpass other animals in the sensitive part for as much as we have the powers of cogitation and reminiscence, as stated in the First Part (Q. 78, A. 4). In the same way our sensitive appetite surpasses that of other animals by reason of a certain excellence consisting in its natural aptitude to obey the reason; and in this respect it can be the principle of a voluntary action, and, consequently, the subject of sin.

Reply Obj. 2. The continual corruption of the sensuality is to be understood as referring to the "fomes," which is never completely destroyed in this life, since, though the stain of original sin passes, its effect remains. However, this corruption of the "fomes" does not hinder man from using his rational will to check individual inordinate movements, if he be presentient of them, for instance by turning his thoughts to other things. Yet while he is turning his thoughts to something else, an inordinate movement may arise about this also: thus when a man, in order to avoid the movements of concupiscence, turns his thoughts away from carnal pleasures, to the considerations of science, sometimes an unpremeditated movement of vainglory will arise. Consequently a man cannot avoid all such movements, on account of the aforesaid corruption: but it is enough, for the conditions of a voluntary sin, that he be able to avoid each single one.

Reply Obj. 3. Man does not do perfectly himself what he does without the deliberation of reason, since the principal part of man does nothing therein: wherefore such is not perfectly a human act; and consequently it cannot be a perfect act of virtue or of sin, but is something imperfect of that kind. Therefore such movement of the sensuality as forestalls the reason, is a venial sin, which is something imperfect in the genus of sin.

FOURTH ARTICLE

Whether Mortal Sin Can Be in the Sensuality?

We proceed thus to the Fourth Article:—

Objection 1. It would seem that mortal sin can be in the sensuality. Because an act is discerned by its object. Now it is possible to commit a mortal sin about the objects of the sensuality, e.g. about carnal pleasures. Therefore the act of the sensuality can be a mortal sin, so that mortal sin can be found in the sensuality.

Obj. 2. Further, mortal sin is opposed to virtue. But virtue can be in the sensuality; for temperance and fortitude are virtues of the irrational parts, as the Philosopher states (*Ethic.* iii. 10). Therefore, since it is natural to contraries to be about the same subject, sensuality can be the subject of mortal sin.

Obj. 3. Further, venial sin is a disposition to mortal sin. Now disposition and habit are in the same subject. Since therefore venial sin may be in the sensuality, as stated above (A. 3 *ad* 3), mortal sin can be there also.

On the contrary, Augustine says (*Retract.* i. 23): *The inordinate movement of concupiscence, which is the sin of the sensuality, can even be in those who are in a state of grace,* in whom, however, mortal sin is not to be found. Therefore the inordinate movement of the sensuality is not a mortal sin.

I answer that, Just as a disorder which destroys the principle of the body's life causes the body's death, so too a disorder which destroys the principle of spiritual life, viz. the last end, causes spiritual death, which is mortal sin, as stated above (Q. 72, A. 5). Now it belongs to the reason alone, and not to the sensuality, to order anything to the end: and disorder in respect of the end can only belong to the power whose function it is to order others to the end. Wherefore mortal sin cannot be in the sensuality, but only in the reason.

Reply Obj. 1. The act of the sensuality can

concur towards a mortal sin: yet the fact of its being a mortal sin is due, not to its being an act of the sensuality, but to its being an act of reason, to whom the ordering to the end belongs. Consequently mortal sin is imputed, not to the sensuality, but to reason.

Reply Obj. 2. An act of virtue is perfected not only in that it is an act of the sensuality, but still more in the fact of its being an act of reason and will, whose function it is to choose: for the act of moral virtue is not without the exercise of choice: wherefore the act of moral virtue, which perfects the appetitive power, is always accompanied by an act of prudence, which perfects the rational power; and the same applies to mortal sin, as stated (*ad* 1).

Reply Obj. 3. A disposition may be related in three ways to that to which it disposes:—for sometimes it is the same thing and is in the same subject; thus inchoate science is a disposition to perfect science:—sometimes it is in the same subject, but is not the same thing; thus heat is a disposition to the form of fire:—sometimes it is neither the same thing, nor in the same subject, as in those things which are subordinate to one another in such a way that we can arrive at one through the other, e.g. goodness of the imagination is a disposition to science which is in the intellect. In this way the venial sin that is in the sensuality, may be a disposition to mortal sin, which is in the reason.

FIFTH ARTICLE

Whether Sin Can Be in the Reason?

We proceed thus to the Fifth Article:—

Objection 1. It would seem that sin cannot be in the reason. For the sin of any power is a defect thereof. But the fault of the reason is not a sin, on the contrary, it excuses sin: for a man is excused from sin on account of ignorance. Therefore sin cannot be in the reason.

Obj. 2. Further, the primary subject of sin is the will, as stated above (A. 1). Now reason precedes the will, since it directs it. Therefore sin cannot be in the reason.

Obj. 3. Further, there can be no sin except about things which are under our control. Now perfection and defect of reason are not among those things which are under our control: since by nature some are mentally deficient, and some shrewd-minded. Therefore no sin is in the reason.

On the contrary, Augustine says (*De Trin.* xii. 12) that sin is in the lower and in the higher reason.

I answer that, The sin of any power is an act of that power, as we have clearly shown (AA. 1, 2, 3). Now reason has a twofold act: one is its proper act in respect of its proper object, and this is the act of knowing the truth; the other is the act of the reason as directing the other powers. Now in both of these ways there may be sin in the reason. First, in so far as it errs in the knowledge of truth, which error is imputed to the reason as a sin, when it is in ignorance or error about what it is able and ought to know:—secondly, when it either commands the inordinate movements of the lower powers, or deliberately fails to check them.

Reply Obj. 1. This argument considers the defect in the proper act of the reason in respect of its proper object, and with regard to the case when it is a defect of knowledge about something which one is unable to know: for then this defect of reason is not a sin, and excuses from sin, as is evident with regard to the actions of madmen.—If, however, the defect of reason be about something which a man is able and ought to know, he is not altogether excused from sin, and the defect is imputed to him as a sin.—The defect which belongs only to the act of directing the other powers, is always imputed to reason as a sin, because it can always obviate this defect by means of its proper act.

Reply Obj. 2. As stated above (Q. 17, A. 1), when we were treating of the acts of the will and reason, the will moves and precedes the reason, in one way, and the reason moves and precedes the will in another: so that both the movement of the will can be called rational, and the act of the reason, voluntary. Accordingly sin is found in the reason, either through being a voluntary defect of the reason, or through the reason being the principle of the will's act.

The Reply to the Third Objection is evident from what has been said (*ad* 1).

SIXTH ARTICLE

Whether the Sin of Morose Delectation Is in the Reason?

We proceed thus to the Sixth Article:—

Objection 1. It would seem that the sin of morose delectation is not in the reason. For delectation denotes a movement of the appetitive power, as stated above (Q. 31, A. 1). But the appetitive power is distinct from the reason, which is an apprehensive power. Therefore morose delectation is not in the reason.

Obj. 2. Further, the object shows to which power an act belongs, since it is through the

*From the Latin mora,—delay.

act that the power is directed to its object. Now a morose delectation is sometimes about sensible goods, and not about the goods of the reason. Therefore the sin of morose delectation is not in the reason.

Obj. 3. Further, a thing is said to be morose* through taking a length of time. But length of time is no reason why an act should belong to a particular power. Therefore morose delectation does not belong to the reason.

On the contrary, Augustine says (*De Trin.* xii. 12) that *if the consent to a sensual delectation goes no further than the mere thought of the pleasure, I deem this to be like as though the woman alone had partaken of the forbidden fruit.* Now *the woman* denotes the lower reason, as he himself explains (*ibid.*). Therefore the sin of morose delectation is in the reason.

I answer that, As stated (A. 5), sin may be in the reason, not only in respect of reason's proper act, but sometimes in respect of its directing human actions. Now it is evident that reason directs not only external acts, but also internal passions. Consequently when the reason fails in directing the internal passions, sin is said to be in the reason, as also when it fails in directing external actions. Now it fails, in two ways, in directing internal passions: first, when it commands unlawful passions; for instance, when a man deliberately provokes himself to a movement of anger, or of lust:—secondly, when it fails to check the unlawful movement of a passion; for instance, when a man, having deliberately considered that a rising movement of passion is inordinate, continues, notwithstanding, to dwell (*immoratur*) upon it, and fails to drive it away. And in this sense the sin of morose delectation is said to be in the reason.

Reply Obj. 1. Delectation is indeed in the appetitive power as its proximate principle; but it is in the reason as its first mover, in accordance with what has been stated above (A. 1), viz. that actions which do not pass into external matter are subjected in their principles.

Reply Obj. 2. Reason has its proper elicited act about its proper object; but it exercises the direction of all the objects of those lower powers that can be directed by the reason: and accordingly delectation about sensible objects comes also under the direction of reason.

Reply Obj. 3. Delectation is said to be morose not from a delay of time, but because the reason in deliberating dwells (*immoratur*) thereon, and fails to drive it away, *deliberately holding and turning over what should have been cast aside as soon as it touched the mind,* as Augustine says (*De Trin.* xii. 12).

SEVENTH ARTICLE

Whether the Sin of Consent to the Act Is in the Higher Reason?

We proceed thus to the Seventh Article:—

Objection 1. It would seem that the sin of consent to the act is not in the higher reason. For consent is an act of the appetitive power, as stated above (Q. 15, A. 1): whereas the reason is an apprehensive power. Therefore the sin of consent to the act is not in the higher reason.

Obj. 2. Further, *the higher reason is intent on contemplating and consulting the eternal law,** as Augustine states (*De Trin.* xii. 7). But sometimes consent is given to an act, without consulting the eternal law: since man does not always think about Divine things, whenever he consents to an act. Therefore the sin of consent to the act is not always in the higher reason.

Obj. 3. Further, just as man can regulate his external actions according to the eternal law, so can he regulate his internal pleasures or other passions. But *consent to a pleasure without deciding to fulfil it by deed, belongs to the lower reason,* as Augustine states (*De Trin.* xii. 2). Therefore the consent to a sinful act should also be sometimes ascribed to the lower reason.

Obj. 4. Further, just as the higher reason excels the lower, so does the reason excel the imagination. Now sometimes man proceeds to act through the apprehension of the power of imagination, without any deliberation of his reason, as when, without premeditation, he moves his hand or foot. Therefore sometimes also the lower reason may consent to a sinful act, independently of the higher reason.

On the contrary, Augustine says (*De Trin.* xii. 12): *If the consent to the evil use of things that can be perceived by the bodily senses, so far approves of any sin, as to point, if possible, to its consummation by deed, we are to understand that the woman has offered the forbidden fruit to her husband.*

I answer that, Consent implies a judgment about the thing to which consent is given. For just as the speculative reason judges and delivers its sentence about intelligible matters, so the practical reason judges and pronounces sentence on matters of action. Now we must observe that in every case brought up for judgment, the final sentence belongs to the supreme court, even as we see that in speculative matters the final sentence touching any proposition is delivered by referring it to the first principles; since, so long as there remains

a yet higher principle, the question can yet be submitted to it: wherefore the judgment is still in suspense, the final sentence not being as yet pronounced. But it is evident that human acts can be regulated by the rule of human reason, which rule is derived from the created things that man knows naturally; and further still, from the rule of the Divine law, as stated above (Q. 19, A. 4). Consequently, since the rule of the Divine law is the higher rule, it follows that the ultimate sentence, whereby the judgment is finally pronounced, belongs to the higher reason which is intent on the eternal types. Now when judgment has to be pronounced on several points, the final judgment deals with that which comes last; and, in human acts, the action itself comes last, and the delectation which is the inducement to the action is a preamble thereto. Therefore the consent to an action belongs properly to the higher reason, while the consent to the delectation belongs to the lower reason, which delivers judgment in a lower court: although the higher reason can also judge of the delectation, since whatever is subject to the judgment of the lower court, is subject also to the judgment of the higher court, but not conversely.

Reply Obj. 1. Consent is an act of the appetitive power, not absolutely, but in consequence of an act of reason deliberating and judging, as stated above (Q. 15, A. 3). Because the fact that the consent is finally given to a thing is due to the fact that the will tends to that upon which the reason has already passed its judgment. Hence consent may be ascribed both to the will and to the reason.

Reply Obj. 2. The higher reason is said to consent, from the very fact that it fails to direct the human act according to the Divine law, whether or not it advert to the eternal law. For if it thinks of God's law, it holds it in actual contempt: and if not, it neglects it by a kind of omission. Therefore the consent to a sinful act always proceeds from the higher reason: because, as Augustine says (*De Trin.* xii. 12), *the mind cannot effectively decide on the commission of a sin, unless by its consent, whereby it wields its sovereign power of moving the members to action, or of restraining them from action, it become the servant or slave of the evil deed.*

Reply Obj. 3. The higher reason, by considering the eternal law, can direct or restrain the internal delectation, even as it can direct or restrain the external action: nevertheless, before the judgment of the higher reason is

---

* *Rationes æternæ,* cf. P. I, Q. 15, AA. 2, 3, where as in similar passages *ratio* has been rendered by the English *type,* because St. Thomas was speaking of the Divine *idea* as the archetype of the creature. Here the type or idea is a rule of conduct, and is identified with the eternal law (*cf.* A. 8, *Obj.* 1; A. 9).

pronounced the lower reason, while deliberating the matter in reference to temporal principles, sometimes approves of this delectation: and then the consent to the delectation belongs to the lower reason. If, however, after considering the eternal law, man persists in giving the same consent, such consent will then belong to the higher reason.

Reply Obj. 4. The apprehension of the power of imagination is sudden and indeliberate: wherefore it can cause an act before the higher or lower reason has time to deliberate. But the judgment of the lower reason is deliberate, and so requires time, during which the higher reason can also deliberate; consequently, if by its deliberation it does not check the sinful act, this will deservedly be imputed to it.

EIGHTH ARTICLE

Whether Consent to Delectation Is a Mortal Sin?

We proceed thus to the Eighth Article:—

Objection 1. It would seem that consent to delectation is not a mortal sin, for consent to delectation belongs to the lower reason, which does not consider the eternal types, i.e. the eternal law, and consequently does not turn away from them. Now every mortal sin consists in turning away from the Divine law, as is evident from Augustine's definition of mortal sin, which was quoted above (Q. 71, A. 6). Therefore consent to delectation is not a mortal sin.

Obj. 2. Further, consent to a thing is not evil, unless the thing to which consent is given be evil. Now *the cause of anything being such is yet more so, or at any rate not less.* Consequently the thing to which a man consents cannot be a lesser evil than his consent. But delectation without deed is not a mortal sin, but only a venial sin. Therefore neither is the consent to the delectation a mortal sin.

Obj. 3. Further, delectations differ in goodness and malice, according to the difference of the deeds, as the Philosopher states (*Ethic.* x. 3, 5). Now the inward thought is one thing, and the outward deed, e.g. fornication, is another. Therefore the delectation consequent to the act of inward thought, differs in goodness and malice from the pleasure of fornication, as much as the inward thought differs from the outward deed; and consequently there is a like difference of consent on either hand. But the inward thought is not a mortal sin, nor is the consent to that thought: and therefore neither is the consent to the delectation.

Obj. 4. Further, the external act of fornication or adultery is a mortal sin, not by reason of the delectation, since this is found also in the marriage act, but by reason of an inordinateness in the act itself. Now he that consents to the delectation does not, for this reason, consent to the inordinateness of the act. Therefore he seems not to sin mortally.

Obj. 5. Further, the sin of murder is more grievous than simple fornication. Now it is not a mortal sin to consent to the delectation resulting from the thought of murder. Much less therefore is it a mortal sin to consent to the delectation resulting from the thought of fornication.

Obj. 6. Further, the Lord's prayer is recited every day for the remission of venial sins, as Augustine asserts (*Enchirid.* lxxviii). Now Augustine teaches that consent to delectation may be driven away by means of the Lord's Prayer: for he says (*De Trin.* xii. 12) that *this sin is much less grievous than if it be decided to fulfil it by deed: wherefore we ought to ask pardon for such thoughts also, and we should strike our breasts and say: "Forgive us our trespasses."* Therefore consent to delectation is a venial sin.

On the contrary, Augustine adds after a few words: *Man will be altogether lost unless, through the grace of the Mediator, he be forgiven those things which are deemed mere sins of thought, since without the will to do them, he desires nevertheless to enjoy them.* But no man is lost except through mortal sin. Therefore consent to delectation is a mortal sin.

I answer that, There have been various opinions on this point, for some have held that consent to delectation is not a mortal sin, but only a venial sin, while others have held it to be a mortal sin, and this opinion is more common and more probable. For we must take note that since every delectation results from some action, as stated in *Ethic.* x 4, and again, that since every delectation has an object, it follows that every delectation may be compared to two things, viz. to the operation from which it results, and to the object in which a person takes delight. Now it happens that an action, just as a thing, is an object of delectation, because the action itself can be considered as a good and an end, in which the person who delights in it, rests. Sometimes the action itself, which results in delectation, is the object of delectation, in so far as the appetitive power, to which it belongs to take delight in anything, is brought to bear on the action itself as a good: for instance, when a man thinks and delights in his thought, in so far as his thought pleases him; while at other times the delight consequent to an action, e.g. a thought, has for its object another action, as being the object of his thought; and then his thought proceeds from the inclination of the appetite, not indeed to the thought, but to the action thought of. Accordingly a man who is thinking of fornication, may delight in either of two things: first, in the thought itself, secondly, in the fornication thought of. Now the delectation in the thought itself results from the inclination of the appetite to the thought; and the thought itself is not in itself a mortal sin; sometimes indeed it is only a venial sin, as when a man thinks of such a thing for no purpose; and sometimes it is no sin at all, as when a man has a purpose in thinking of it; for instance, he may wish to preach or dispute about it. Consequently such affection or delectation in respect of the thought of fornication is not a mortal sin in virtue of its genus, but is sometimes a venial sin and sometimes no sin at all: wherefore neither is it a mortal sin to consent to such a thought. In this sense the first opinion is true.

But that a man in thinking of fornication takes pleasure in the act thought of, is due to his desire being inclined to this act. Wherefore the fact that a man consents to such a delectation, amounts to nothing less than a consent to the inclination of his appetite to fornication: for no man takes pleasure except in that which is in conformity with his appetite. Now it is a mortal sin, if a man deliberately chooses that his appetite be conformed to what is in itself a mortal sin. Wherefore such a consent to delectation in a mortal sin, is itself a mortal sin, as the second opinion maintains.

Reply Obj. 1. Consent to delectation may be not only in the lower reason, but also in the higher reason, as stated above (A. 7). Nevertheless the lower reason may turn away from the eternal types, for, though it is not intent on them, as regulating according to them, which is proper to the higher reason, yet, it is intent on them, as being regulated according to them: and by turning from them in this sense, it may sin mortally; since even the acts of the lower powers and of the external members may be mortal sins, in so far as the direction of the higher reason fails in directing them according to the eternal types.

Reply Obj. 2. Consent to a sin that is venial in its genus, is itself a venial sin, and accordingly one may conclude that the consent to take pleasure in a useless thought about fornication, is a venial sin. But delectation in the act itself of fornication is, in its genus, a mortal sin: and that it be a venial sin before the consent is given, is accidental, viz. on account of the incompleteness of the act: which incompleteness ceases when the deliberate consent has been given, so that therefore it has its complete nature and is a mortal sin.

Reply Obj. 3. This argument considers the delectation which has the thought for its object.

Reply Obj. 4. The delectation which has an external act for its object, cannot be without complacency in the external act as such, even though there be no decision to fulfil it, on account of the prohibition of some higher authority: wherefore the act is inordinate, and consequently the delectation will be inordinate also.

Reply Obj. 5. The consent to delectation, resulting from complacency in an act of murder thought of, is a mortal sin also: but not the consent to delectation resulting from complacency in the thought of murder.

Reply Obj. 6. The Lord's Prayer is to be said in order that we may be preserved not only from venial sin, but also from mortal sin.

NINTH ARTICLE

Whether There Can Be Venial Sin in the Higher Reason As Directing the Lower Powers?

We proceed thus to the Ninth Article:—

Objection 1. It would seem that there cannot be venial sin in the higher reason as directing the lower powers, i.e., as consenting to a sinful act. For Augustine says (*De Trin.* xii. 7) that the *higher reason is intent on considering and consulting the eternal law.* But mortal sin consists in turning away from the eternal law. Therefore it seems that there can be no other than mortal sin in the higher reason.

Obj. 2. Further, the higher reason is the principle of the spiritual life, as the heart is of the body's life. But the diseases of the heart are deadly. Therefore the sins of the higher reason are mortal.

Obj. 3. Further, a venial sin becomes a mortal sin if it be done out of contempt. But it would seem impossible to commit even a venial sin, deliberately, without contempt. Since then the consent of the higher reason is always accompanied by deliberate consideration of the eternal law, it seems that it cannot be without mortal sin, on account of the contempt of the Divine law.

On the contrary, Consent to a sinful act belongs to the higher reason, as stated above (A. 7). But consent to an act of venial sin is itself a venial sin. Therefore a venial sin can be in the higher reason.

I answer that, As Augustine says (*De Trin.* xii. 7), the higher reason *is intent on contemplating or consulting the eternal law;* it contemplates it by considering its truth; it consults it by judging and directing other things according to it: and to this pertains the fact that by deliberating through the eternal types, it consents to an act or dissents from it. Now it may happen that the inordinateness of the act to which it consents, is not contrary to the eternal law, in the same way as mortal sin is, because it does not imply aversion from the last end, but is beside that law, as an act of venial sin is. Therefore when the higher reason consents to the act of a venial sin, it does not turn away from the eternal law: wherefore it sins, not mortally, but venially. This suffices for the Reply to the First Objection.

Reply Obj. 2. Disease of the heart is twofold:—one which is in the very substance of the heart, and affects its natural consistency, and such a disease is always mortal:—the other is a disease of the heart consisting in some disorder either of the movement or of the parts surrounding the heart, and such a disease is not always mortal. In like manner there is mortal sin in the higher reason whenever the order itself of the higher reason to its proper object which is the eternal law, is destroyed; but when the disorder leaves this untouched, the sin is not mortal but venial.

Reply Obj. 3. Deliberate consent to a sin does not always amount to contempt of the Divine law, but only when the sin is contrary to the Divine law.

TENTH ARTICLE

Whether Venial Sin Can Be in the Higher Reason As Such?

We proceed thus to the Tenth Article:—

Objection 1. It would seem that venial sin cannot be in the higher reason as such, i.e. as considering the eternal law. For the act of a power is not found to fail except that power be inordinately disposed with regard to its object. Now the object of the higher reason is the eternal law, in respect of which there can be no disorder without mortal sin. Therefore there can be no venial sin in the higher reason as such.

Obj. 2. Further, since the reason is a deliberative power, there can be no act of reason without deliberation. Now every inordinate movement in things concerning God, if it be deliberate, is a mortal sin. Therefore venial sin is never in the higher reason as such.

Obj. 3. Further, it happens sometimes that a sin which takes us unawares, is a venial sin. Now a deliberate sin is a mortal sin, through the reason, in deliberating, having recourse to some higher good, by acting against which, man sins more grievously; just as when the reason in deliberating about an inordinate pleasurable act, considers that it is contrary to the law of God, it sins more grievously in consenting, than if it only considered that it is contrary to moral virtue. But the higher reason cannot have recourse to any higher tribunal than its own object. Therefore if a movement that takes us unawares is not a mortal sin, neither will the subsequent deliberation make it a mortal sin; which is clearly false. Therefore there can be no venial sin in the higher reason as such.

On the contrary, A sudden movement of unbelief is a venial sin. But it belongs to the higher reason as such. Therefore there can be a venial sin in the higher reason as such.

I answer that, The higher reason regards its own object otherwise than the objects of the lower powers that are directed by the higher reason. For it does not regard the objects of the lower powers, except in so far as it consults the eternal law about them, and so it does not regard them save by way of deliberation. Now deliberate consent to what is a mortal sin in its genus, is itself a mortal sin; and consequently the higher reason always sins mortally, if the acts of the lower powers to which it consents are mortal sins.

With regard to its own object it has a twofold act, viz. simple *intuition,* and *deliberation,* in respect of which it again consults the eternal law about its own object. But in respect of simple intuition, it can have an inordinate movement about Divine things, as when a man suffers a sudden movement of unbelief. And although unbelief, in its genus, is a mortal sin, yet a sudden movement of unbelief is a venial sin, because there is no mortal sin unless it be contrary to the law of God. Now it is possible for one of the articles of faith to present itself to the reason suddenly under some other aspect, before the eternal law, i.e. the law of God, is consulted, or can be consulted, on the matter; as, for instance, when a man suddenly apprehends the resurrection of the dead as impossible naturally, and rejects it, as soon as he has thus apprehended it, before he has had time to deliberate and consider that this is proposed to our belief in accordance with the Divine law. If, however, the movement of unbelief remains after this deliberation, it is a mortal sin. Therefore, in sudden movements, the higher reason may sin venially in respect of its proper object, even if it be a mortal sin in its genus; or it may sin mortally by giving a deliberate consent; but in things pertaining to the lower powers, it always sins mortally, in things which are mortal sins in their genus, but not in those which are venial sins in their genus.

Reply Obj. 1. A sin which is against the eternal law, though it be mortal in its genus, may nevertheless be venial, on account of the incompleteness of a sudden action, as stated.

Reply Obj. 2. In matters of action, the simple intuition of the principles from which deliberation proceeds, belongs to the reason, as well as the act of deliberation: even as in speculative matters it belongs to the reason both to syllogize and to form propositions: consequently the reason also can have a sudden movement.

Reply Obj. 3. One and the same thing may be the subject of different considerations, of which one is higher than the other; thus the existence of God may be considered, either as possible to be known by the human reason, or as delivered to us by Divine revelation, which is a higher consideration. And therefore, although the object of the higher reason is, in its nature, something sublime, yet it is reducible to some yet higher consideration: and in this way, that which in the sudden movement was not a mortal sin, becomes a mortal sin in virtue of the deliberation which brought it into the light of a higher consideration, as was explained above.

QUESTION 75

Of the Causes of Sin, in General

(In Four Articles)

WE must now consider the causes of sin: (1) in general; (2) in particular. Under the first head there are four points of inquiry: (1) Whether sin has a cause? (2) Whether it has an internal cause? (3) Whether it has an external cause? (4) Whether one sin is the cause of another?

FIRST ARTICLE

Whether Sin Has a Cause?

We proceed thus to the First Article:—

Objection 1. It would seem that sin has no cause. For sin has the nature of evil, as stated above (Q. 71, A. 6). But evil has no cause, as Dionysius says (*Div. Nom.* iv). Therefore sin has no cause.

Obj. 2. Further, a cause is that from which something follows of necessity. Now that which is of necessity, seems to be no sin, for every sin is voluntary. Therefore sin has no cause.

Obj. 3. Further, if sin has a cause, this cause is either good or evil. It is not a good, because good produces nothing but good, for *a good tree cannot bring forth evil fruit* (Matth. vii. 18). Likewise neither can evil be the cause of sin, because the evil of punishment is a sequel to sin, and the evil of guilt is the same as sin. Therefore sin has no cause.

On the contrary, Whatever is done has a cause, for, according to Job v. 6, *nothing upon earth is done without a cause.* But sin is something done; since it is a *word, deed, or desire contrary to the law of God.* Therefore sin has a cause.

I answer that, A sin is an inordinate act. Accordingly, so far as it is an act, it can have a direct cause, even as any other act; but, so far as it is inordinate, it has a cause, in the same way as a negation or privation can have a cause. Now two causes may be assigned to a negation: in the first place, absence of the cause of affirmation; i.e. the negation of the cause itself, is the cause of the negation in itself; since the result of removing the cause is the removal of the effect: thus the absence of the sun is the cause of darkness. In the second place, the cause of an affirmation, of which a negation is a sequel, is the accidental cause of the resulting negation: thus fire by causing heat in virtue of its principal tendency, consequently causes a privation of cold. The first of these suffices to cause a simple negation. But, since the inordinateness of sin and of every evil is not a simple negation, but the privation of that which something ought naturally to have, such an inordinateness must needs have an accidental efficient cause. For that which naturally is and ought to be in a thing, is never lacking except on account of some impeding cause. And accordingly we are wont to say that evil, which consists in a certain privation, has a deficient cause, or an accidental efficient cause. Now every accidental cause is reducible to the direct cause. Since then sin, on the part of its inordinateness, has an accidental efficient cause, and on the part of the act, a direct efficient cause, it follows that the inordinateness of sin is a result of the cause of the act. Accordingly then, the will lacking the direction of the rule of reason and of the Divine law, and intent on some mutable good, causes the act of sin directly, and the inordinateness of the act, indirectly, and beside the intention: for the lack of order in the act results from the lack of direction in the will.

Reply Obj. 1. Sin signifies not only the privation of good, which privation is its inordinateness, but also the act which is the subject of that privation, which has the nature of evil: and how this evil has a cause, has been explained.

Reply Obj. 2. If this definition is to be verified in all cases, it must be understood as applying to a cause which is sufficient and not impeded. For it happens that a thing is the sufficient cause of something else, and that the effect does not follow of necessity, on account of some supervening impediment: else it would follow that all things happen of necessity, as is proved in *Metaph.* vi, text. 5. Accordingly, though sin has a cause, it does not follow that this is a necessary cause, since its effect can be impeded.

Reply Obj. 3. As stated above, the will in failing to apply the rule of reason or of the Divine law, is the cause of sin. Now the fact of not applying the rule of reason or of the Divine law, has not in itself the nature of evil, whether of punishment or of guilt, before it is applied to the act. Wherefore accordingly, evil is not the cause of the first sin, but some good lacking some other good.

SECOND ARTICLE

Whether Sin Has an Internal Cause?

We proceed thus to the Second Article:—

Objection 1. It would seem that sin has no internal cause. For that which is within a thing is always in it. If therefore sin had an internal cause, man would always be sinning, since given the cause, the effect follows.

Obj. 2. Further, a thing is not its own cause. But the internal movements of a man are sins. Therefore they are not the cause of sin.

Obj 3. Further, whatever is within man is either natural or voluntary. Now that which is natural cannot be the cause of sin, for sin is contrary to nature, as Damascene states (*De Fide Orthod.* ii. 3, iv. 21); while that which is voluntary, if it be inordinate, is already a sin. Therefore nothing intrinsic can be the cause of the first sin.

On the contrary, Augustine says (*De Duabus Anim.* x. 10, 11; *Retract.* i. 9) that *the will is the cause of sin.*

I answer that, As stated above (A. 1), the direct cause of sin must be considered on the part of the act. Now we may distinguish a twofold internal cause of human acts, one remote, the other proximate. The proximate internal cause of the human act is the reason and will, in respect of which man has a free-will; while the remote cause is the apprehension of the sensitive part, and also the sensitive appetite. For just as it is due to the judgment of reason, that the will is moved to something in accord with reason, so it is due to an apprehension of the senses that the sensitive appetite is inclined to something; which inclination sometimes influences the will and reason, as we shall explain further on (Q. 77, A. 1). Accordingly a double interior cause of sin may be assigned; one proximate, on the part of the reason and

will; the other remote, on the part of the imagination or sensitive appetite.

But since we have said above (A. 1 *ad 3*) that the cause of sin is some apparent good as motive, yet lacking the due motive, viz. the rule of reason or the Divine law, this motive which is an apparent good, appertains to the apprehension of the senses and to the appetite; while the lack of the due rule appertains to the reason, whose nature it is to consider this rule; and the completeness of the voluntary sinful act appertains to the will, so that the act of the will, given the conditions we have just mentioned, is already a sin.

Reply Obj. 1. That which is within a thing as its natural power, is always in it: but that which is within it, as the internal act of the appetitive or apprehensive power, is not always in it. Now the power of the will is the potential cause of sin, but is made actual by the preceding movements, both of the sensitive part, in the first place, and afterwards, of the reason. For it is because a thing is proposed as appetible to the senses, and because the appetite is inclined, that the reason sometimes fails to consider the due rule, so that the will produces the act of sin. Since therefore the movements that precede it are not always actual, neither is man always actually sinning.

Reply Obj. 2. It is not true that all the internal acts belong to the substance of sin, for this consists principally in the act of the will; but some precede and some follow the sin itself.

Reply Obj. 3. That which causes sin, as a power produces its act, is natural; and again, the movement of the sensitive part, from which sin follows, is natural sometimes, as, for instance, when anyone sins through appetite for food. Yet sin results in being unnatural from the very fact that the natural rule fails, which man, in accord with his nature, ought to observe.

THIRD ARTICLE

Whether Sin Has an External Cause?

We proceed thus to the Third Article:—

Objection 1. It would seem that sin has no external cause. For sin is a voluntary act. Now voluntary acts belong to principles that are within us, so that they have no external cause. Therefore sin has no external cause.

Obj. 2. Further, as nature is an internal principle, so is the will. Now in natural things sin can be due to no other than an internal cause; for instance, the birth of a monster is due to the corruption of some internal principle. Therefore in the moral order, sin can arise from no other than an internal cause. Therefore it has no external cause.

Obj. 3. Further, if the cause is multiplied, the effect is multiplied. Now the more numerous and weighty the external inducements to sin are, the less is a man's inordinate act imputed to him as a sin. Therefore nothing external is a cause of sin.

On the contrary, It is written (Num. xxi. 16): *Are not these they, that deceived the children of Israel by the counsel of Balaam, and made you transgress against the Lord by the sin of Phogor?* Therefore something external can be a cause of sin.

I answer that, As stated above (A. 2), the internal cause of sin is both the will, as completing the sinful act, and the reason, as lacking the due rule, and the appetite, as inclining to sin. Accordingly something external might be a cause of sin in three ways, either by moving the will itself immediately, or by moving the reason, or by moving the sensitive appetite. Now, as stated above (Q. 9, A. 6; Q. 10, A. 4), none can move the will inwardly save God alone, who cannot be a cause of sin, as we shall prove further on (Q. 79, A. 1). Hence it follows that nothing external can be a cause of sin, except by moving the reason, as a man or devil by enticing to sin; or by moving the sensitive appetite, as certain external sensibles move it. Yet neither does external enticement move the reason, of necessity, in matters of action, nor do things proposed externally, of necessity move the sensitive appetite, except perhaps it be disposed thereto in a certain way; and even the sensitive appetite does not, of necessity, move the reason and will. Therefore something external can be a cause moving to sin, but not so as to be a sufficient cause thereof: and the will alone is the sufficient completive cause of sin being accomplished.

Reply Obj. 1. From the very fact that the external motive causes of sin do not lead to sin sufficiently and necessarily, it follows that it remains in our power to sin or not to sin.

Reply Obj. 2. The fact that sin has an internal cause does not prevent its having an external cause; for nothing external is a cause of sin, except through the medium of the internal cause, as stated.

Reply Obj. 3. If the external causes inclining to sin be multiplied, the sinful acts are multiplied, because they incline to the sinful act in both greater numbers and greater frequency. Nevertheless the character of guilt is lessened, since this depends on the act being voluntary and in our power.

* Cf. *De Anima* ii.

FOURTH ARTICLE

Whether One Sin Is a Cause of Another?

We proceed thus to the Fourth Article:—

Objection 1. It would seem that one sin cannot be the cause of another. For there are four kinds of cause, none of which will fit in with one sin causing another. Because the end has the character of good; which is inconsistent with sin, which has the character of evil. In like manner neither can a sin be an efficient cause, since *evil is not an efficient cause, but is weak and powerless,* as Dionysius declares (*Div. Nom.* iv). The material and formal cause seems to have no place except in natural bodies, which are composed of matter and form. Therefore sin cannot have either a material or a formal cause.

Obj. 2. Further, *to produce its like belongs to a perfect thing,* as stated in *Meteor.* iv. 2.* But sin is essentially something imperfect. Therefore one sin cannot be a cause of another.

Obj. 3. Further, if one sin is the cause of a second sin, in the same way, yet another sin will be the cause of the first, and thus we go on indefinitely, which is absurd. Therefore one sin is not the cause of another.

On the contrary, Gregory says on Ezechiel (*Hom.* xi): *A sin that is not quickly blotted out by repentance, is both a sin and a cause of sin.*

I answer that, Forasmuch as a sin has a cause on the part of the act of sin, it is possible for one sin to be the cause of another, in the same way as one human act is the cause of another. Hence it happens that one sin may be the cause of another in respect of the four kinds of causes.—First, after the manner of an efficient or moving cause, both directly and indirectly. Indirectly, as that which removes an impediment is called an indirect cause of movement: for when man, by one sinful act, loses grace, or charity, or shame, or anything else that withdraws him from sin, he thereby falls into another sin, so that the first sin is the accidental cause of the second. Directly, as when, by one sinful act, man is disposed to commit more readily another like act: because acts cause dispositions and habits inclining to like acts.—Secondly, after the manner of a material cause, one sin is the cause of another, by preparing its matter: thus covetousness prepares the matter for strife, which is often about the wealth a man has amassed together.—Thirdly, after the manner of a final cause, one sin causes another, in so far as a man commits one sin for the sake of another which is his end;

as when a man is guilty or simony for the end of ambition, or form'ation for the purpose of theft.—And since the end gives the form to moral matters, as stated above (Q. 1, A. 3; Q. 18, AA. 4, 6), it follows that one sin is also the formal cause of another: because in the act of fornication committed for the purpose of theft, the former is material while the latter is formal.

Reply Obj. 1. Sin, in so far as it is inordinate, has the character of evil; but, in so far as it is an act, it has some good, at least apparent, for its end: so that, as an act, but not as being inordinate, it can be the cause, both final and efficient, of another sin.—A sin has matter, not *of which* but *about which* it is: and it has its form from its end. Consequently one sin can be the cause of another, in respect of the four kinds of cause, as stated above.

Reply Obj. 2. Sin is something imperfect on account of its moral imperfection on the part of its inordinateness. Nevertheless, as an act it can have natural perfection: and thus it can be the cause of another sin.

Reply Obj. 3. Not every cause of one sin is another sin; so there is no need to go on indefinitely: for one may come to one sin which is not caused by another sin.

QUESTION 76

Of the Causes of Sin, in Particular

(In Four Articles)

WE must now consider the causes of sin, in particular, and (1) The internal causes of sin; (2) its external causes; and (3) sins which are the causes of other sins. In view of what has been said above (A. 2), the first consideration will be threefold: so that in the first place we shall treat of ignorance, which is the cause of sin on the part of reason; secondly, of weakness or passion, which is the cause of sin on the part of the sensitive appetite; thirdly, of malice, which is the cause of sin on the part of the will.

Under the first head there are four points of inquiry: (1) Whether ignorance is a cause of sin? (2) Whether ignorance is a sin? (3) Whether it excuses from sin altogether? (4) Whether it diminishes sin?

FIRST ARTICLE

Whether Ignorance Can Be a Cause of Sin?

We proceed thus to the First Article:—

Objection 1. It would seem that ignorance cannot be a cause of sin: because a non-being is not the cause of anything. Now ignorance is a non-being, since it is a privation of knowledge. Therefore ignorance is not a cause of sin.

Obj. 2. Further, causes of sin should be reckoned in respect of sin being a *turning to* something, as was stated above (Q. 75, A. 1). Now ignorance seems to savor of *turning away* from something. Therefore it should not be reckoned a cause of sin.

Obj. 3. Further, every sin is seated in the will. Now the will does not turn to that which is not known, because its object is the good apprehended. Therefore ignorance cannot be a cause of sin.

On the contrary, Augustine says (*De Nat. et Grat.* lxvii) *that some sin through ignorance.*

I answer that, According to the Philosopher (*Phys.* viii. 27) a moving cause is twofold, direct and indirect. A direct cause is one that moves by its own power, as the generator is the moving cause of heavy and light things. An indirect cause, is either one that removes an impediment, or the removal itself of an impediment: and it is in this way that ignorance can be the cause of a sinful act; because it is a privation of knowledge perfecting the reason that forbids the act of sin, in so far as it directs human acts.

Now we must observe that the reason directs human acts in accordance with a twofold knowledge, universal and particular: because in conferring about what is to be done, it employs a syllogism, the conclusion of which is an act of judgment, or of choice, or an operation. Now actions are about singulars: wherefore the conclusion of a practical syllogism is a singular proposition. But a singular proposition does not follow from a universal proposition, except through the medium of a particular proposition: thus a man is restrained from an act of parricide, by the knowledge that it is wrong to kill one's father, and that this man is his father. Hence ignorance about either of these two propositions, viz. of the universal principle which is a rule of reason, or of the particular circumstance, could cause an act of parricide. Hence it is clear that not every kind of ignorance is the cause of a sin, but that alone which removes the knowledge which would prevent the sinful act. Consequently if a man's will be so disposed that he would not be restrained from the act of parricide, even though he recognized his father, his ignorance about his father is not the cause of his committing the sin, but is concomitant with the sin: wherefore such a man sins, not *through ignorance* but *in ignorance,* as the Philosopher states (*Ethic.* iii. 1).

Reply Obj. 1. Non-being cannot be the direct cause of anything: but it can be an accidental cause, as being the removal of an impediment.

Reply Obj. 2. As knowledge, which is removed by ignorance, regards sin as turning towards something, so too, ignorance of this respect of a sin is the cause of that sin, as removing its impediment.

Reply Obj. 3. The will cannot turn to that which is absolutely unknown: but if something be known in one respect, and unknown in another, the will can will it. It is thus that ignorance is the cause of sin: for instance, when a man knows that what he is killing is a man, but not that it is his own father; or when one knows that a certain act is pleasurable, but not that it is a sin.

SECOND ARTICLE

Whether Ignorance Is a Sin?

We proceed thus to the Second Article:—

Objection 1. It would seem that ignorance is not a sin. For sin is *a word, deed or desire contrary to God's law,* as stated above (Q. 71, A. 5). Now ignorance does not denote an act, either internal or external. Therefore ignorance is not a sin.

Obj. 2. Further, sin is more directly opposed to grace than to knowledge. Now privation of grace is not a sin, but a punishment resulting from sin. Therefore ignorance which is privation of knowledge is not a sin.

Obj. 3. Further, if ignorance is a sin, this can only be in so far as it is voluntary. But if ignorance is a sin, through being voluntary, it seems that the sin will consist in the act itself of the will, rather than in the ignorance. Therefore the ignorance will not be a sin, but rather a result of sin.

Obj. 4. Further, every sin is taken away by repentance, nor does any sin, except only original sin, pass as to guilt, yet remain in act. Now ignorance is not removed by repentance, but remains in act, all its guilt being removed by repentance. Therefore ignorance is not a sin, unless perchance it be original sin.

Obj. 5. Further, if ignorance be a sin, then a man will be sinning, as long as he remains in ignorance. But ignorance is continual in the one who is ignorant. Therefore a person in ignorance would be continually sinning, which is clearly false, else ignorance would be a most grievous sin. Therefore ignorance is not a sin.

On the contrary, Nothing but sin deserves punishment. But ignorance deserves punishment, according to 1 Cor. xiv. 38: *If any man*

know not, he shall not be known. Therefore ignorance is a sin.

I answer that, Ignorance differs from nescience, in that nescience denotes mere absence of knowledge; wherefore whoever lacks knowledge about anything, can be said to be nescient about it: in which sense Dionysius puts nescience in the angels (*Cœl. Hier.* vii). On the other hand, ignorance denotes privation of knowledge, i.e. lack of knowledge of those things that one has a natural aptitude to know. Some of these we are under an obligation to know, those, to wit, without the knowledge of which we are unable to accomplish a due act rightly. Wherefore all are bound in common to know the articles of faith, and the universal principles of right, and each individual is bound to know matters regarding his duty or state. Meanwhile there are other things which a man may have a natural aptitude to know, yet he is not bound to know them, such as the geometrical theorems, and contingent particulars, except in some individual case. Now it is evident that whoever neglects to have or do what he ought to have or do, commits a sin of omission. Wherefore through negligence, ignorance of what one is bound to know, is a sin; whereas it is not imputed as a sin to man, if he fails to know what he is unable to know. Consequently ignorance of such like things is called *invincible,* because it cannot be overcome by study. For this reason such like ignorance, not being voluntary, since it is not in our power to be rid of it, is not a sin: wherefore it is evident that no invincible ignorance is a sin. On the other hand, vincible ignorance is a sin, if it be about matters one is bound to know; but not, if it be about things one is not bound to know.

Reply Obj. 1. As stated above (Q. 71, A. 6, *ad* 1), when we say that sin is a *word, deed* or *desire,* we include the opposite negations, by reason of which omissions have the character of sin; so that negligence, in as much as ignorance is a sin, is comprised in the above definition of sin; in so far as one omits to say what one ought, or to do what one ought, or to desire what one ought, in order to acquire the knowledge which we ought to have.

Reply Obj. 2. Although privation of grace is not a sin in itself, yet by reason of negligence in preparing oneself for grace, it may have the character of sin, even as ignorance; nevertheless even here there is a difference, since man can acquire knowledge by his acts, whereas grace is not acquired by acts, but by God's favor.

Reply Obj. 3. Just as in a sin of transgression, the sin consists not only in the act of the will, but also in the act willed, which is commanded by the will; so in a sin of omission not only the act of the will is a sin, but also the omission, in so far as it is in some way voluntary; and accordingly, the neglect to know, or even lack of consideration is a sin.

Reply Obj. 4. Although when the guilt has passed away through repentance, the ignorance remains, according as it is a privation of knowledge, nevertheless the negligence does not remain, by reason of which the ignorance is said to be a sin.

Reply Obj. 5. Just as in other sins of omission, man sins actually only at the time at which the affirmative precept is binding, so is it with the sin of ignorance. For the ignorant man sins actually indeed, not continually, but only at the time for acquiring the knowledge that he ought to have.

THIRD ARTICLE

Whether Ignorance Excuses from Sin Altogether?

We proceed thus to the Third Article:—

Objection 1. It would seem that ignorance excuses from sin altogether. For as Augustine says (*Retract.* i. 9), every sin is voluntary. Now ignorance causes involuntariness, as stated above (Q. 6, A. 8). Therefore ignorance excuses from sin altogether

Obj. 2. Further, that which is done beside the intention, is done accidentally. Now the intention cannot be about what is unknown. Therefore what a man does through ignorance is accidental in human acts. But what is accidental does not give the species. Therefore nothing that is done through ignorance in human acts, should be deemed sinful or virtuous.

Obj. 3. Further, man is the subject of virtue and sin, inasmuch as he is partaker of reason. Now ignorance excludes knowledge which perfects the reason. Therefore Ignorance excuses from sin altogether.

On the contrary, Augustine says (*De Lib. Arb.* iii. 18) that *some things done through ignorance are rightly reproved.* Now those things alone are rightly reproved which are sins. Therefore some things done through ignorance are sins. Therefore ignorance does not altogether excuse from sin.

I answer that, Ignorance, by its very nature, renders the act which it causes involuntary. Now it has already been stated (AA. 1, 2) that ignorance is said to cause the act which the contrary knowledge would have prevented; so that this act, if knowledge were to hand, would be contrary to the will, which is the meaning of the word involuntary. If, however, the knowledge, which is removed by ignorance, would not have prevented the act, on account of the inclination of the will thereto, the lack of this knowledge does not make that man unwilling, but not willing, as stated in *Ethic.* iii. 1: and such like ignorance which is not the

cause of the sinful act, as already stated, since it does not make the act to be involuntary, does not excuse from sin. The same applies to any ignorance that does not cause, but follows or accompanies the sinful act.

On the other hand, ignorance which is the cause of the act, since it makes it to be involuntary, of its very nature excuses from sin, because voluntariness is essential to sin.—But it may fail to excuse altogether from sin, and this for two reasons. First, on the part of the thing itself which is not known. For ignorance excuses from sin, in so far as something is not known to be a sin. Now it may happen that a person ignores some circumstance of a sin, the knowledge of which circumstance would prevent him from sinning, whether it belong to the substance of the sin, or not; and nevertheless his knowledge is sufficient for him to be aware that the act is sinful;—for instance, if a man strike someone, knowing that it is a man (which suffices for it to be sinful) and yet be ignorant of the fact that it is his father, (which is a circumstance constituting another species of sin); or, suppose that he is unaware that this man will defend himself and strike him back, and that if he had known this, he would not have struck him (which does not affect the sinfulness of the act). Wherefore, though this man sins through ignorance, yet he is not altogether excused, because, notwithstanding, he has knowledge of the sin. Secondly, this may happen on the part of the ignorance itself, because, to wit, this ignorance is voluntary, either directly, as when a man wishes of set purpose to be ignorant of certain things that he may sin the more freely; or indirectly, as when a man, through stress of work or other occupations, neglects to acquire the knowledge which would restrain him from sin. For such like negligence renders the ignorance itself voluntary and sinful, provided it be about matters one is bound and able to know. Consequently this ignorance does not altogether excuse from sin. If, however, the ignorance be such as to be entirely involuntary, either through being invincible, or through being of matters one is not bound to know, then such like ignorance excuses from sin altogether.

Reply Obj. 1. Not every ignorance causes involuntariness, as stated above (Q. 6, A. 8). Hence not every ignorance excuses from sin altogether.

Reply Obj. 2. So far as voluntariness remains in the ignorant person, the intention of sin remains in him: so that, in this respect, his sin is not accidental.

Reply Obj. 3. If the ignorance be such as to exclude the use of reason entirely, it excuses from sin altogether, as is the case with madmen and imbeciles: but such is not always the ignorance that causes the sin; and so it does not always excuse from sin altogether.

FOURTH ARTICLE

Whether Ignorance Diminishes a Sin?

We proceed thus to the Fourth Article:—

Objection 1. It would seem that ignorance does not diminish a sin. For that which is common to all sins does not diminish sin. Now ignorance is common to all sins, for the Philosopher says (*Ethic.* iii. 1) that *every evil man is ignorant*. Therefore ignorance does not diminish sin.

Obj. 2. Further, one sin added to another makes a greater sin. But ignorance is itself a sin, as stated above (A. 2). Therefore it does not diminish a sin.

Obj. 3. Further, the same thing does not both aggravate and diminish sin. Now ignorance aggravates sin; for Ambrose commenting on Rom. ii. 4, *Knowest thou not that the benignity of God leadeth thee to penance?* says: *Thy sin is most grievous if thou knowest not.* Therefore ignorance does not diminish sin.

Obj. 4. Further, if any kind of ignorance diminishes a sin, this would seem to be chiefly the case as regards the ignorance which removes the use of reason altogether. Now this kind of ignorance does not diminish sin, but increases it: for the Philosopher says (*Ethic.* iii. 5) that the *punishment is doubled for a drunken man*. Therefore ignorance does not diminish sin.

On the contrary, Whatever is a reason for sin to be forgiven, diminishes sin. Now such is ignorance, as is clear from 1 Tim. i. 13: *I obtained . . . mercy . . . because I did it ignorantly.* Therefore ignorance diminishes or alleviates sin.

I answer that, Since every sin is voluntary, ignorance can diminish sin, in so far as it diminishes its voluntariness; and if it does not render it less voluntary, it nowise alleviates the sin. Now it is evident that the ignorance which excuses from sin altogether (through making it altogether involuntary) does not diminish a sin, but does away with it altogether. On the other hand, ignorance which is not the cause of the sin being committed, but is concomitant with it, neither diminishes nor increases the sin.

Therefore sin cannot be alleviated by any ignorance, but only by such as is a cause of the sin being committed, and yet does not excuse from the sin altogether. Now it happens sometimes that such like ignorance is directly and essentially voluntary, as when a man is purposely ignorant that he may sin more freely, and ignorance of this kind seems rather

to make the act more voluntary and more sinful, since it is through the will's intention to sin that he is willing to bear the hurt of ignorance, for the sake of freedom in sinning. Sometimes, however, the ignorance which is the cause of a sin being committed, is not directly voluntary, but indirectly or accidentally, as when a man is unwilling to work hard at his studies, the result being that he is ignorant, or as when a man willfully drinks too much wine, the result being that he becomes drunk and indiscreet, and this ignorance diminishes voluntariness and consequently alleviates the sin. For when a thing is not known to be a sin, the will cannot be said to consent to the sin directly, but only accidentally; wherefore, in that case there is less contempt, and therefore less sin.

Reply Obj. 1. The ignorance whereby *every evil man is ignorant,* is not the cause of sin being committed, but something resulting from that cause, viz. of the passion or habit inclining to sin.

Reply Obj. 2. One sin added to another makes more sins, but it does not always make a sin greater, since, perchance, the two sins do not coincide, but are separate. It may happen, if the first diminishes the second, that the two together have not the same gravity as one of them alone would have; thus murder is a more grievous sin if committed by a man when sober, than if committed by a man when drunk, although in the latter case there are two sins: because drunkenness diminishes the sinfulness of the resulting sin more than its own gravity implies.

Reply Obj. 3. The words of Ambrose may be understood as referring to simply affected ignorance; or they may have reference to a species of the sin of ingratitude, the highest degree of which is that man even ignores the benefits he has received; or again, they may be an allusion to the ignorance of unbelief, which undermines the foundation of the spiritual edifice.

Reply Obj. 4. The drunken man deserves a *double punishment* for the two sins which he commits, viz. drunkenness, and the sin which results from his drunkenness: and yet drunkenness, on account of the ignorance connected therewith, diminishes the resulting sin and more, perhaps, than the gravity of the drunkenness implies, as stated above (*ad* 2).—It might also be said that the words quoted refer to an ordinance of the legislator named Pittacus, who ordered drunkards to be more severely punished if they assaulted anyone; having an eye, not to the indulgence which the drunkard might claim, but to expediency, since more harm is done by the drunk than by the sober, as the Philosopher observes (*Polit.* ii).

QUESTION 77

Of the Cause o. Sin, on the Part of the Sensitive Appetite

(In Eight Articles)

WE must now consider the cause of sin, on the part of the sensitive appetite, as to whether a passion of the soul may be a cause of sin: and under this head there are eight points of inquiry: (1) Whether a passion of the sensitive appetite can move or incline the will? (2) Whether it can overcome the reason against the latter's knowledge? (3) Whether a sin resulting from a passion is a sin of weakness? (4) Whether the passion of self-love is the cause of every sin? (5) Of three causes mentioned in 1 Jo. ii. 16: *Concupiscence of the eyes, Concupiscence of the flesh,* and *Pride of life.* (6) Whether the passion which causes a sin diminishes it? (7) Whether passion excuses from sin altogether? (8) Whether a sin committed through passion can be mortal?

FIRST ARTICLE

Whether the Will Is Moved by a Passion of the Sensitive Appetite?

We proceed thus to the First Article:—

Objection 1. It would seem that the will is not moved by a passion of the sensitive appetite. For no passive power is moved except by its object. Now the will is a power both passive and active, inasmuch as it is mover and moved, as the Philosopher says of the appetitive power in general (*De Anima* iii, tent. 54) Since therefore the object of the will is not a passion of the sensitive appetite, but good defined by the reason, it seems that a passion of the sensitive appetite does not move the will.

Obj. 2. Further, the higher mover is not moved by the lower; thus the soul is not moved by the body. Now the will, which is the rational appetite, is compared to the sensitive appetite, as a higher mover to a lower: for the Philosopher says (*De Anima* iii, text. 57) that *the rational appetite moves the sensitive appetite, even as, in the heavenly bodies, one sphere moves another.* Therefore the will cannot be moved by a passion of the sensitive appetite.

Obj. 3. Further, nothing immaterial can be moved by that which is material. Now the will is an immaterial power, because it does not use a corporeal organ, since it is in the reason, as stated in *De Anima* iii, text. 42: whereas the sensitive appetite is a material force, since it is seated in an organ of the body. Therefore a passion of the sensitive

appetite cannot move the intellective appetite.

On the contrary, It is written (Dan. xiii. 56): *Lust hath perverted thy heart.*

I answer that, A passion of the sensitive appetite cannot draw or move the will directly; but it can do so indirectly, and this in two ways. First, by a kind of distraction: because, since all the soul's powers are rooted in the one essence of the soul, it follows of necessity that, when one power is intent in its act, another power becomes remiss, or is even altogether impeded, in its act, both because all energy is weakened through being divided, so that, on the contrary, through being centered on one thing, it is less able to be directed to several; and because, in the operations of the soul, a certain attention is requisite, and if this be closely fixed on one thing, less attention is given to another. In this way, by a kind of distraction, when the movement of the sensitive appetite is enforced in respect of any passion whatever, the proper movement of the rational appetite or will must, of necessity, become remiss or altogether impeded.

Secondly, this may happen on the part of the will's object, which is good apprehended by reason. Because the judgment and apprehension of reason is impeded on account of a vehement and inordinate apprehension of the imagination and judgment of the estimative power, as appears in those who are out of their mind. Now it is evident that the apprehension of the imagination and the judgment of the estimative power follow the passion of the sensitive appetite, even as the verdict of the taste follows the disposition of the tongue: for which reason we observe that those who are in some kind of passion, do not easily turn their imagination away from the object of their emotion, the result being that the judgment of the reason often follows the passion of the sensitive appetite, and consequently the will's movement follows it also, since it has a natural inclination always to follow the judgment of the reason.

Reply Obj. 1. Although the passion of the sensitive appetite is not the direct object of the will, yet it occasions a certain change in the judgment about the object of the will, as stated.

Reply Obj. 2. The higher mover is not directly moved by the lower; but, in a manner, it can be moved by it indirectly, as stated.

The Third Objection is solved in like manner.

SECOND ARTICLE

Whether the Reason Can Be Overcome by a Passion, against Its Knowledge?

We proceed thus to the Second Article:—

Objection 1. It would seem that the reason cannot be overcome by a passion, against its knowledge. For the stronger is not overcome by the weaker. Now knowledge, on account of its certitude, is the strongest thing in us. Therefore it cannot be overcome by a passion, which is weak and soon passes away.

Obj. 2. Further, the will is not directed save to the good or the apparent good. Now when a passion draws the will to that which is really good, it does not influence the reason against its knowledge; and when it draws it to that which is good apparently, but not really, it draws it to that which appears good to the reason. But what appears to the reason is in the knowledge of the reason. Therefore a passion never influences the reason against its knowledge.

Obj. 3. Further, if it be said that it draws the reason from its knowledge of something in general, to form a contrary judgment about a particular matter,—on the contrary, if a universal and a particular proposition be opposed, they are opposed by contradiction, e.g. *Every man*, and *Not every man*. Now if two opinions contradict one another, they are contrary to one another, as stated in *Peri Herm.* ii. If therefore anyone, while knowing something in general, were to pronounce an opposite judgment in a particular case, he would have two contrary opinions at the same time, which is impossible.

Obj. 4. Further, whoever knows the universal, knows also the particular which he knows to be contained in the universal: thus who knows that every mule is sterile, knows that this particular animal is sterile, provided he knows it to be a mule, as is clear from *Poster.* i., text. 2. Now he who knows something in general, e.g. that *no fornication is lawful*, knows this general proposition to contain, for example, the particular proposition, *This is an act of fornication*. Therefore it seems that his knowledge extends to the particular.

Obj. 5. Further, according to the Philosopher (*Peri Herm.* i.), *words express the thoughts of the mind*. Now it often happens that man, while in a state of passion, confesses that what he has chosen is an evil, even in that particular case. Therefore he has knowledge, even in particular.

Therefore it seems that the passions cannot draw the reason against its universal knowledge; because it is impossible for it to have universal knowledge together with an opposite particular judgment.

On the contrary, The Apostle says (Rom. vii. 23): *I see another law in my members, fighting against the law of my mind, and captivating me in the law of sin.* Now the law that is in the members is concupiscence, of which he had been speaking previously. Since then concupiscence is a passion, it seems that a passion draws the reason counter to its knowledge.

I answer that, As the Philosopher states (*Ethic.* vii. 2), the opinion of Socrates was that knowledge can never be overcome by passion; wherefore he held every virtue to be a kind of knowledge, and every sin a kind of ignorance. In this he was somewhat right, because, since the object of the will is a good or an apparent good, it is never moved to an evil, unless that which is not good appear good in some respect to the reason; so that the will would never tend to evil, unless there were ignorance or error in the reason. Hence it is written (Prov. xiv. 22): *They err that work evil.*

Experience, however, shows that many act contrary to the knowledge that they have, and this is confirmed by Divine authority, according to the words of Luke xii, 47: *The servant who knew the will of his lord . . . and did not . . . shall be beaten with many stripes,* and of James iv. 17: *To him . . . who knoweth to do good, and doth it not, to him it is a sin.* Consequently he was not altogether right, and it is necessary, with the Philosopher (*Ethic.* vii. 3) to make a distinction. Because, since man is directed to right action by a twofold knowledge, viz. universal and particular, a defect in either of them suffices to hinder the rectitude of the will and of the deed, as stated above (Q. 76, A. 1). It may happen, then, that a man has some knowledge in general, e.g. that no fornication is lawful, and yet he does not know in particular that this act, which is fornication, must not be done; and this suffices for the will not to follow the universal knowledge of the reason. Again, it must be observed that nothing prevents a thing which is known habitually from not being considered actually: so that it is possible for a man to have correct knowledge not only in general but also in particular, and yet not to consider his knowledge actually: and in such a case it does not seem difficult for a man to act counter to what he does not actually consider. Now, that a man sometimes fails to consider in particular what he knows habitually, may happen through mere lack of attention: for instance, a man who knows geometry, may not attend to the consideration of geometrical conclusions, which he is ready to consider at any moment. Sometimes man fails to consider actually what he knows habitually, on account of some hindrance supervening, e.g. some external occupation, or some bodily infirmity; and, in this way, a man who is in a state of passion, fails to consider in particular what he knows in general, in so far as the passions hinder him from considering it. Now it hinders him in three ways. First, by way of distraction, as explained above (A. 1). Secondly, by way of opposition, because a passion often inclines to something contrary to what man knows in general. Thirdly, by way of bodily transmutation, the result of which is that the reason is somehow fettered so as not to exercise its act freely; even as sleep or drunkenness, on account of some change wrought on the body, fetters the use of reason. That this takes place in the passions is evident from the fact that sometimes, when the passions are very intense, man loses the use of reason altogether: for many have gone out of their minds through excess of love or anger. It is in this way that passion draws the reason to judge in particular, against the knowledge which it has in general.

Reply Obj. 1. Universal knowledge, which is most certain, does not hold the foremost place in action, but rather particular knowledge, since actions are about singulars: wherefore it is not astonishing that, in matters of action, passion acts counter to universal knowledge, if the consideration of particular knowledge be lacking.

Reply Obj. 2. The fact that something appears good in particular to the reason, whereas it is not good, is due to a passion: and yet this particular judgment is contrary to the universal knowledge of the reason.

Reply Obj. 3. It is impossible for anyone to have an actual knowledge or true opinion about a universal affirmative proposition, and at the same time a false opinion about a particular negative proposition, or vice versa: but it may well happen that a man has true habitual knowledge about a universal affirmative proposition, and actually a false opinion about a particular negative: because an act is directly opposed, not to a habit, but to an act.

Reply Obj. 4. He that has knowledge in a universal, is hindered, on account of a passion, from reasoning about that universal, so as to draw the conclusion: but he reasons about another universal proposition suggested by the inclination of the passion, and draws his conclusion accordingly. Hence the Philosopher says (*Ethic.* vii. 3) that the syllogism of an incontinent man has four propositions, two particular and two universal, of which one is of the reason, e.g. No fornication is lawful, and the other, of passion, e.g. Pleasure is to be pursued. Hence passion fetters the reason, and hinders it from arguing and concluding

* Vulg.,—*The lust thereof shall be under thee.*

under the first proposition; so that while the passion lasts, the reason argues and concludes under the second.

Reply Obj. 5. Even as a drunken man sometimes gives utterance to words of deep signification, of which, however, he is incompetent to judge, his drunkenness hindering him; so a man who is in a state of passion, may indeed say in words that he ought not to do so and so, yet his inner thought is that he must do it, as stated in *Ethic.* vii. 3.

THIRD ARTICLE

Whether a Sin Committed through Passion, Should Be Called a Sin of Weakness?

We proceed thus to the Third Article:—

Objection 1. It would seem that a sin committed through passion should not be called a sin of weakness. For a passion is a vehement movement of the sensitive appetite, as stated above (A. 1). Now vehemence of movements is evidence of strength rather than of weakness. Therefore a sin committed through passion, should not be called a sin of weakness.

Obj. 2. Further, weakness in man regards that which is most fragile in him. Now this is the flesh; whence it is written (Ps. lxxvii. 39): *He remembered that they are flesh.* Therefore sins of weakness should be those which result from bodily defects, rather than those which are due to a passion.

Obj. 3. Further, man does not seem to be weak in respect of things which are subject to his will. Now it is subject to man's will, whether he do or do not the things to which his passions incline him, according to Gen. iv. 7: *Thy appetite shall be under thee,* and thou shalt have dominion over it.* Therefore sin committed through passion is not a sin of weakness.

On the contrary, Cicero (*De Quæst. Tusc.* iv) calls the passions diseases of the soul. Now weakness is another name for disease. Therefore a sin that arises from passion should be called a sin of weakness.

I answer that, The cause of sin is on the part of the soul, in which, chiefly, sin resides. Now weakness may be applied to the soul by way of likeness to weakness of the body. Accordingly, man's body is said to be weak, when it is disabled or hindered in the execution of its proper action, through some disorder of the body's parts, so that the humors and members of the human body cease to be subject to its governing and motive power. Hence a member is said to be weak, when it cannot do the work of a healthy member, the eye, for instance, when it cannot see clearly, as the Philosopher states (*De Hist. Animal.* x. 1). Therefore weakness of the soul is when the soul is hindered from fulfilling its proper action on account of a disorder in its parts. Now as the parts of the body are said to be out of order, when they fail to comply with the order of nature, so too the parts of the soul are said to be inordinate, when they are not subject to the order of reason, for the reason is the ruling power of the soul's parts. Accordingly, when the concupiscible or irascible power is affected by any passion contrary to the order of reason, the result being that an impediment arises in the aforesaid manner to the due action of man, it is said to be a sin of weakness. Hence the Philosopher (*Ethic.* vii. 8) compares the incontinent man to an epileptic, whose limbs move in a manner contrary to his intention.

Reply Obj. 1. Just as in the body the stronger the movement against the order of nature, the greater the weakness, so likewise, the stronger the movement of passion against the order of reason, the greater the weakness of the soul.

Reply Obj. 2. Sin consists chiefly in an act of the will, which is not hindered by weakness of the body: for he that is weak in body may have a will ready for action, and yet be hindered by a passion, as stated above (A. 1). Hence when we speak of sins of weakness, we refer to weakness of soul rather than of body. And yet even weakness of soul is called weakness of the flesh, in so far as it is owing to a condition of the flesh that the passions of the soul arise in us through the sensitive appetite being a power using a corporeal organ.

Reply Obj. 3. It is in the will's power to give or refuse its consent to what passion inclines us to do, and it is in this sense that our appetite is said to be under us; and yet this consent or dissent of the will is hindered in the way already explained (A. 1).

FOURTH ARTICLE

Whether Self-Love Is the Source of Every Sin?

We proceed thus to the Fourth Article:—

Objection 1. It would seem that self-love is not the source of every sin. For that which is good and right in itself is not the proper cause of sin. Now love of self is a good and right thing in itself: wherefore man is commanded to love his neighbor as himself (Levit. xix. 18). Therefore self-love cannot be the proper cause of sin.

Obj. 2. Further, the Apostle says (Rom. vii. 8): *Sin taking occasion by the commandment wrought in me all manner of concupiscence;* on which words a gloss says that *the law is good, since by forbidding concupiscence, it forbids all evils,* the reason for which is that concupiscence is the cause of every sin. Now

concupiscence is a distinct passion from love, as stated above (Q. 3, A. 2; Q. 23, A. 4). Therefore self-love is not the cause of every sin.

Obj. 3. Further, Augustine in commenting on Ps. lxxix. 17, *Things set on fire and dug down,* says that *every sin is due either to love arousing us to undue ardor or to fear inducing false humility.* Therefore self-love is not the only cause of sin.

Obj. 4. Further, as man sins at times through inordinate love of self, so does he sometimes through inordinate love of his neighbor. Therefore self-love is not the cause of every sin.

On the contrary, Augustine says (*De Civ. Dei* xiv. 28) that *self-love, amounting to contempt of God, builds up the city of Babylon.* Now every sin makes man a citizen of Babylon. Therefore self-love is the cause of every sin.

I answer that, As stated above (Q. 75, A. 1), the proper and direct cause of sin is to be considered on the part of the adherence to a mutable good; in which respect every sinful act proceeds from inordinate desire for some temporal good. Now the fact that anyone desires a temporal good inordinately, is due to the fact that he loves himself inordinately; for to wish anyone some good is to love him. Therefore it is evident that inordinate love of self is the cause of every sin.

Reply Obj. 1. Well ordered self-love, whereby man desires a fitting good for himself, is right and natural; but it is inordinate self-love, leading to the contempt of God, that Augustine (*loc. cit.*) reckons to be the cause of sin.

Reply Obj. 2. Concupiscence, whereby a man desires good for himself, is reduced to self-love as to its cause, as stated.

Reply Obj. 3. Man is said to love both the good he desires for himself, and himself to whom he desires it. Love, in so far as it is directed to the object of desire (e.g. a man is said to love wine or money) admits, as its cause, fear which pertains to avoidance of evil: for every sin arises either from inordinate desire for some good, or from inordinate avoidance of some evil. But each of these is reduced to self-love, since it is through loving himself that man either desires good things, or avoids evil things.

Reply Obj. 4. A friend is like another self (*Ethic.* ix): wherefore the sin which is committed through love for a friend, seems to be committed through self-love.

FIFTH ARTICLE

Whether Concupiscence of the Flesh, Concupiscence of the Eyes, and Pride of Life Are Fittingly Described As Causes of Sin?

We proceed thus to the Fifth Article:—

Objection 1. It would seem that *concupiscence of the flesh, concupiscence of the eyes, and pride of life* are unfittingly described as causes of sin. Because, according to the Apostle (1 Tim. vi. 10), *covetousness* is the root of all evils.* Now pride of life is not included in covetousness. Therefore it should not be reckoned among the causes of sin.

Obj. 2. Further, concupiscence of the flesh is aroused chiefly by what is seen by the eyes, according to Dan. xiii. 56: *Beauty hath deceived thee.* Therefore concupiscence of the eyes should not be condivided with concupiscence of the flesh.

Obj. 3. Further, concupiscence is desire for pleasure, as stated above (Q. 30, A. 2). Now objects of pleasure are perceived not only by the sight, but also by the other senses. Therefore *concupiscence of the hearing* and of the other senses should also have been mentioned.

Obj. 4. Further, just as man is induced to sin, through inordinate desire of good things, so is he also, through inordinate avoidance of evil things, as stated above (A. 4 *ad* 3). But nothing is mentioned here pertaining to avoidance of evil. Therefore the causes of sin are insufficiently described.

On the contrary, It is written (1 Jo. ii. 16): *All that is in the world is concupiscence of the flesh, or* (Vulg.,—*and*) *concupiscence of the eyes, or* (Vulg.,—*and*) *pride of life.* Now a thing is said to be *in the world* by reason of sin: wherefore it is written (*ibid* v. 19): *The whole world is seated in wickedness.* Therefore these three are causes of sin.

I answer that, As stated above (A. 4), inordinate self-love is the cause of every sin. Now self-love includes inordinate desire of good: for a man desires good for the one he loves. Hence it is evident that inordinate desire of good is the cause of every sin. Now good is, in two ways, the object of the sensitive appetite, wherein are the passions which are the cause of sin: first, absolutely, according as it is the object of the concupiscible part; secondly, under the aspect of difficulty, according as it is the object of the irascible part, as stated above (Q. 23, A. 1). Again, concupiscence is twofold, as stated above (Q. 30, A. 3). One is natural, and is directed to those things which sustain the nature of the body, whether as regards the preservation of the individual, such as food, drink, and the like, or as regards the preservation of the species, such as sexual matters: and the inordinate appetite of such things is called *concupiscence of the flesh.* The other is spiritual concupiscence, and is directed to those things which do not afford sustentation or pleasure in respect of the fleshly senses, but are delectable in respect of the apprehension or

* Douay,—*The desire of money.*

imagination, or some similar mode of perception; such are money, apparel, and the like; and this spiritual concupiscence is called *concupiscence of the eyes,* whether this be taken as referring to the sight itself, of which the eyes are the organ, so as to denote curiosity, according to Augustine's exposition (*Conf.* x); or to the concupiscence of things which are proposed outwardly to the eyes, so as to denote covetousness, according to the explanation of others.

The inordinate appetite of the arduous good pertains to the *pride of life;* for pride is the inordinate appetite of excellence, as we shall state further on (Q. 84, A. 2; (II-II, Q. 162, A. 1).

It is therefore evident that all passions that are a cause of sin can be reduced to these three: since all the passions of the concupiscible part can be reduced to the first two, and all the irascible passions to the third, which is not divided into two because all the irascible passions conform to spiritual concupiscence.

Reply Obj. 1. *Pride of life* is included in covetousness according as the latter denotes any kind of appetite for any kind of good. How covetousness, as a special vice, which goes by the name of *avarice,* is the root of all sins, shall be explained further on (Q. 84, A. 1).

Reply Obj. 2. Concupiscence of the eyes does not mean here the concupiscence for all things that can be seen by the eyes, but only for such things as afford, not carnal pleasure in respect of touch, but in respect of the eyes, i.e. of any apprehensive power.

Reply Obj. 3. The sense of sight is the most excellent of all the senses, and covers a larger ground, as stated in *Metaph.* i.: and so its name is transferred to all the other senses, and even to the inner apprehensions, as Augustine states (*De Verb. Dom.,* serm. xxxiii).

Reply Obj. 4. Avoidance of evil is caused by the appetite for good, as stated above (Q. 25, A. 2; Q. 39, A. 2); and so those passions alone are mentioned which incline to good, as being the causes of those which cause inordinately the avoidance of evil.

SIXTH ARTICLE

Whether Sin Is Alleviated on Account of a Passion?

We proceed thus to the Sixth Article:—

Objection 1. It would seem that sin is not alleviated on account of passion. For increase of cause adds to the effect: thus if a hot thing causes something to melt, a hotter will do so yet more. Now passion is a cause of sin, as stated (A. 5). Therefore the more intense the passion, the greater the sin. Therefore passion does not diminish sin, but increases it.

Obj. 2. Further, a good passion stands in the same relation to merit, as an evil passion does to sin. Now a good passion increases merit: for a man seems to merit the more, according as he is moved by a greater pity to help a poor man. Therefore an evil passion also increases rather than diminishes a sin.

Obj. 3. Further, a man seems to sin the more grievously, according as he sins with a more intense will. But the passion that impels the will makes it tend with greater intensity to the sinful act. Therefore passion aggravates a sin.

On the contrary, The passion of concupiscence is called a temptation of the flesh. But the greater the temptation that overcomes a man, the less grievous his sin, as Augustine states (*De Civ. Dei.* iv. 12).

I answer that, Sin consists essentially in an act of the free will, which is a faculty of the will and reason; while passion is a movement of the sensitive appetite. Now the sensitive appetite can be related to the free-will, antecedently and consequently: antecedently, according as a passion of the sensitive appetite draws or inclines the reason or will, as stated above (AA. 1, 2; Q. 10, A. 3); and consequently, in so far as the movements of the higher powers redound on to the lower, since it is not possible for the will to be moved to anything intensely, without a passion being aroused in the sensitive appetite.

Accordingly if we take passion as preceding the sinful act, it must needs diminish the sin: because the act is a sin in so far as it is voluntary, and under our control. Now a thing is said to be under our control, through the reason and will: and therefore the more the reason and will do anything of their own accord, and not through the impulse of a passion, the more is it voluntary and under our control. In this respect passion diminishes sin, in so far as it diminishes its voluntariness.

On the other hand, a consequent passion does not diminish a sin, but increases it; or rather it is a sign of its gravity, in so far, to wit, as it shows the intensity of the will towards the sinful act; and so it is true that the greater the pleasure or the concupiscence with which anyone sins, the greater the sin.

Reply Obj. 1. Passion is the cause of sin on the part of that to which the sinner turns. But the gravity of a sin is measured on the part of that from which he turns, which results accidentally from his turning to something else,—accidentally, i.e. beside his intention. Now an effect is increased by the increase, not of its accidental cause, but of its direct cause.

Reply Obj. 2. A good passion consequent to the judgment of reason increases merit; but if it precede, so that a man is moved to do well, rather by his passion than by the judgment of his reason, such a passion diminishes the goodness and praiseworthiness of his action.

Reply Obj. 3. Although the movement of the will incited by the passion is more intense, yet it is not so much the will's own movement, as if it were moved to sin by the reason alone.

Whether Passion Excuses from Sin Altogether?

We proceed thus to the Seventh Article:—

Objection 1. It would seem that passion excuses from sin altogether. For whatever causes an act to be involuntary, excuses from sin altogether. But concupiscence of the flesh, which is a passion, makes an act to be involuntary, according to Gal. v. 17: *The flesh lusteth against the spirit . . . so that you do not the things that you would.* Therefore passion excuses from sin altogether.

Obj. 2. Further, passion causes a certain ignorance of a particular matter, as stated above (A. 2; Q. 76, A. 3). But ignorance of a particular matter excuses from sin altogether, as stated above (Q. 6, A. 8). Therefore passion excuses from sin altogether.

Obj. 3. Further, disease of the soul is graver than disease of the body. But bodily disease excuses from sin altogether, as in the case of mad people. Much more, therefore, does passion, which is a disease of the soul.

On the contrary, The Apostle (Rom. vii. 5) speaks of the passions as *passions of sins,* for no other reason than that they cause sin: which would not be the case if they excused from sin altogether. Therefore passion does not excuse from sin altogether.

I answer that, An act which, in its genus, is evil, cannot be excused from sin altogether, unless it be rendered altogether involuntary. Consequently, if the passion be such that it renders the subsequent act wholly involuntary, it entirely excuses from sin; otherwise, it does not excuse entirely. In this matter two points apparently should be observed: first, that a thing may be voluntary either *in itself,* as when the will tends towards it directly; or *in its cause,* when the will tends towards that cause and not towards the effect; as is the case with one who wilfully gets drunk, for in that case he is considered to do voluntarily whatever he does through being drunk.—Secondly, we must observe that a thing is said to be voluntary *directly* or *indirectly;* directly, if the will tends towards it; indirectly, if the will could have prevented it, but did not.

Accordingly therefore we must make a distinction: because a passion is sometimes so strong as to take away the use of reason altogether, as in the case of those who are mad through love or anger; and then if such a passion were voluntary from the beginning, the act is reckoned a sin, because it is voluntary in its cause, as we have stated with regard to drunkenness. If, however, the cause be not voluntary but natural, for instance, if anyone through sickness or some such cause fall into such a passion as deprives him of the use of reason, his act is rendered wholly involuntary, and he is entirely excused from sin. Sometimes, however, the passion is not such as to take away the use of reason altogether; and then reason can drive the passion away, by turning to other thoughts, or it can prevent it from having its full effect; since the members are not put to work, except by the consent of reason, as stated above (Q. 17, A. 9): wherefore such a passion does not excuse from sin altogether.

Reply Obj. 1. The words, *So that you do not the things that you would* are not to be referred to outward deeds, but to the inner movement of concupiscence; for a man would wish never to desire evil, in which sense we are to understand the words of Rom. vii. 19: *The evil which I will not, that I do.*—Or again they may be referred to the will as preceding the passion, as is the case with the incontinent, who act counter to their resolution on account of their concupiscence.

Reply Obj. 2. The particular ignorance which excuses altogether, is ignorance of a circumstance, which a man is unable to know even after taking due precautions. But passion causes ignorance of law in a particular case, by preventing universal knowledge from being applied to a particular act, which passion the reason is able to drive away, as stated.

Reply Obj. 3. Bodily disease is involuntary: there would be a comparison, however, if it were voluntary, as we have stated about drunkenness, which is a kind of bodily disease.

EIGHTH ARTICLE

Whether a Sin Committed through Passion Can Be Mortal?

We proceed thus to the Eighth Article:—

Objection 1. It would seem that sin committed through passion cannot be mortal. Because venial sin is condivided with mortal sin. Now sin committed from weakness is venial, since it has in itself a motive for pardon (*venia*). Since therefore sin committed through passion is a sin of weakness, it seems that it cannot be mortal.

Obj. 2. Further, the cause is more powerful than its effect. But passion cannot be a mortal sin, for there is no mortal sin in the sensuality, as stated above (Q. 74, A. 4). Therefore a sin committed through passion cannot be mortal.

Obj. 3. Further, passion is a hindrance to reason, as explained above (AA. 1, 2). Now it belongs to the reason to turn to God, or to turn away from Him, which is the essence of a mortal sin. Therefore a sin committed through passion cannot be mortal.

On the contrary, The Apostle says (Rom. vii. 5) that *the passions of the sins . . . work* (Vulg.,—*did work*) *in our members to bring forth fruit unto death.* Now it is proper to mortal sin to bring forth fruit unto death. Therefore sin committed through passion may be mortal.

I answer that, Mortal sin, as stated above (Q. 72, A. 5), consists in turning away from our last end which is God, which aversion pertains to the deliberating reason, whose function it is also to direct towards the end. Therefore that which is contrary to the last end can happen not to be a mortal sin, only when the deliberating reason is unable to come to the rescue, which is the case in sudden movements. Now when anyone proceeds from passion to a sinful act, or to a deliberate consent, this does not happen suddenly: and so the deliberating reason can come to the rescue here, since it can drive the passion away, or at least prevent it from having its effect, as stated above: wherefore if it does not come to the rescue, there is a mortal sin; and it is thus, as we see, that many murders and adulteries are committed through passion.

Reply Obj. 1. A sin may be venial in three ways First, through its cause, i.e. through having cause to be forgiven, which cause lessens the sin; thus a sin that is committed through weakness or ignorance is said to be venial. Secondly, through its issue; thus every sin, through repentance, becomes venial, i.e. receives pardon (*veniam*). Thirdly, by its genus, e.g. an idle word. This is the only kind of venial sin that is opposed to mortal sin: whereas the objection regards the first kind.

Reply Obj. 2. Passion causes sin as regards the adherence to something. But that this be a mortal sin regards the aversion, which follows accidentally from the adherence, as stated above (A. 6, *ad* 1): hence the argument does not prove.

Reply Obj. 3. Passion does not always hinder the act of reason altogether: consequently the reason remains in possession of its free-will, so as to turn away from God, or turn to Him. If, however, the use of reason be taken away altogether, the sin is no longer either mortal or venial.

QUESTION 78

Of That Cause of Sin Which Is Malice

(In Four Articles)

WE must now consider the cause of sin on the part of the will, viz. malice: and under this head there are four points of inquiry: (1) Whether it is possible for anyone to sin through certain malice, i.e. purposely? (2) Whether everyone that sins through habit, sins through certain malice? (3) Whether every one that sins through certain malice, sins through habit? (4) Whether it is more grievous to sin through certain malice, than through passion?

FIRST ARTICLE

Whether Anyone Sins through Certain Malice?

We proceed thus to the First Article:—

Objection 1. It would seem that no one sins purposely, or through certain malice. Because ignorance is opposed to purpose or certain malice. Now *every evil man is ignorant*, according to the Philosopher (*Ethic.* iii. 1); and it is written (Prov. xiv. 22): *They err that work evil.* Therefore no one sins through certain malice.

Obj. 2. Further, Dionysius says (*Div. Nom.* iv) that *no one works intending evil.* Now to sin through malice seems to denote the intention of doing evil* in sinning, because an act is not denominated from that which is unintentional and accidental. Therefore no one sins through malice.

Obj. 3. Further, malice itself is a sin. If therefore malice is a cause of sin, it follows that sin goes on causing sin indefinitely, which is absurd. Therefore no one sins through malice.

On the contrary, It is written (Job xxxiv. 27): *(Who) as it were on purpose have revolted from God* (Vulg.,—*Him*), *and would not understand all His ways.* Now to revolt from God is to sin. Therefore some sin purposely or through certain malice.

I answer that, Man like any other being has naturally an appetite for the good; and so if his appetite incline away to evil, this is due to corruption or disorder in some one of the principles of man: for it is thus that sin occurs in the actions of natural things. Now the principles of human acts are the intellect, and the appetite, both rational (i.e. the will) and sensitive. Therefore even as sin occurs in

human acts, sometimes through a defect of the intellect, as when anyone sins through ignorance, and sometimes through a defect in the sensitive appetite, as when anyone sins through passion, so too does it occur through a defect consisting in a disorder of the will. Now the will is out of order when it loves more the lesser good. Again, the consequence of loving a thing less is that one chooses to suffer some hurt in its regard, in order to obtain a good that one loves more: as when a man, even knowingly, suffers the loss of a limb, that he may save his life which he loves more. Accordingly when an inordinate will loves some temporal good, e.g. riches or pleasure, more than the order of reason or Divine law, or Divine charity, or some such thing, it follows that it is willing to suffer the loss of some spiritual good, so that it may obtain possession of some temporal good. Now evil is merely the privation of some good; and so a man wishes knowingly a spiritual evil, which is evil simply, whereby he is deprived of a spiritual good, in order to possess a temporal good: wherefore he is said to sin through certain malice or on purpose, because he chooses evil knowingly.

Reply Obj. 1. Ignorance sometimes excludes the simple knowledge that a particular action is evil, and then man is said to sin through ignorance: sometimes it excludes the knowledge that a particular action is evil at this particular moment, as when he sins through passion: and sometimes it excludes the knowledge that a particular evil is not to be suffered for the sake of possessing a particular good, but not the simple knowledge that it is an evil: it is thus that a man is ignorant, when he sins through certain malice.

Reply Obj. 2. Evil cannot be intended by anyone for its own sake; but it can be intended for the sake of avoiding another evil, or obtaining another good, as stated above: and in this case anyone would choose to obtain a good intended for its own sake, without suffering loss of the other good; even as a lustful man would wish to enjoy a pleasure without offending God; but with the two set before him to choose from, he prefers sinning and thereby incurring God's anger, to being deprived of the pleasure.

Reply Obj. 3. The malice through which

---

* Alluding to the derivation of *Malitia* (malice) from *malum* (evil).

anyone sins, may be taken to denote habitual malice, in the sense in which the Philosopher (*Ethic.* v. 1) calls an evil habit by the name of malice, just as a good habit is called virtue: and in this way anyone is said to sin through malice when he sins through the inclination of a habit. It may also denote actual malice, whether by malice we mean the choice itself of evil (and thus anyone is said to sin through malice, in so far as he sins through making a choice of evil), or whether by malice we mean some previous fault that gives rise to a subsequent fault, as when anyone impugns the grace of his brother through envy. Nor does this imply that a thing is its own cause: for the interior act is the cause of the exterior act, and one sin is the cause of another; not indefinitely, however, since we can trace it back to some previous sin, which is not caused by any previous sin, as was explained above (Q. 75, A. 4 *ad* 3).

SECOND ARTICLE

Whether Everyone That Sins through Habit, Sins through Certain Malice?

We proceed thus to the Second Article:—

Objection 1. It would seem that not every one who sins through habit, sins through certain malice. Because sin committed through certain malice, seems to be most grievous. Now it happens sometimes that a man commits a slight sin through habit, as when he utters an idle word. Therefore sin committed from habit is not always committed through certain malice.

Obj. 2. Further, *Acts proceeding from habits are like the acts by which those habits were formed* (*Ethic.* ii. 1, 2). But the acts which precede a vicious habit are not committed through certain malice. Therefore the sins that arise from habit are not committed through certain malice.

Obj. 3. Further, when a man commits a sin through certain malice, he is glad after having done it, according to Prov. ii. 14: *Who are glad when they have done evil, and rejoice in most wicked things:* and this, because it is pleasant to obtain what we desire, and to do those actions which are connatural to us by reason of habit. But those who sin through habit, are sorrowful after committing a sin: because *bad men,* i.e. those who have a vicious habit, *are full of remorse* (*Ethic.* ix. 4). Therefore sins that arise from habit are not committed through certain malice.

On the contrary, A sin committed through certain malice is one that is done through choice of evil. Now we make choice of those things to which we are inclined by habit, as

stated in *Ethic.* vi. 2 with regard to virtuous habits. Therefore a sin that arises from habit is committed through certain malice.

I answer that, There is a difference between a sin committed by one who has the habit, and a sin committed through habit: for it is not necessary to use a habit, since it is subject to the will of the person who has that habit. Hence habit is defined as being *something we use when we will,* as stated above (Q. 50, A. 1). And thus, even as it may happen that one who has a vicious habit may break forth into a virtuous act, because a bad habit does not corrupt reason altogether, something of which remains unimpaired, the result being that a sinner does some works which are generically good; so too it may happen sometimes that one who has a vicious habit, acts, not from that habit, but through the uprising of a passion, or again through ignorance. But whenever he uses the vicious habit he must needs sin through certain malice: because to anyone that has a habit, whatever is befitting to him in respect of that habit, has the aspect of something lovable, since it thereby becomes, in a way, connatural to him, according as custom and habit are a second nature. Now the very thing which befits a man in respect of a vicious habit, is something that excludes a spiritual good: the result being that a man chooses a spiritual evil, that he may obtain possession of what befits him in respect of that habit: and this is to sin through certain malice. Wherefore it is evident that whoever sins through habit, sins through certain malice.

Reply Obj. 1. Venial sin does not exclude spiritual good, consisting in the grace of God or charity. Wherefore it is an evil, not simply, but in a relative sense: and for that reason the habit thereof is not a simple but a relative evil.

Reply Obj. 2. Acts proceeding from habits are of like species as the acts from which those habits were formed: but they differ from them as perfect from imperfect. Such is the difference between sin committed through certain malice and sin committed through passion.

Reply Obj. 3. He that sins through habit is always glad for what he does through habit, as long as he uses the habit. But since he is able not to use the habit, and to think of something else, by means of his reason, which is not altogether corrupted, it may happen that while not using the habit he is sorry for what he has done through the habit. And so it often happens that such a man is sorry for his sin not because sin in itself is displeasing to him, but on account of his reaping some disadvantage from the sin.

THIRD ARTICLE

Whether One Who Sins through Certain Malice, Sins through Habit?

We proceed thus to the Third Article:—

Objection 1. It would seem that whoever sins through certain malice, sins through habit. For the Philosopher says (*Ethic.* v. 9) that *an unjust action is not done as an unjust man does it,* i.e. through choice, *unless it be done through habit.* Now to sin through certain malice is to sin through making a choice of evil, as stated above (A. 1). Therefore no one sins through certain malice, unless he has the habit of sin.

Obj. 2. Further, Origen says (*Peri Archon* iii) that *a man is not suddenly ruined and lost, but must needs fall away little by little.* But the greatest fall seems to be that of the man who sins through certain malice. Therefore a man comes to sin through certain malice, not from the outset, but from inveterate custom, which may engender a habit.

Obj. 3. Further, whenever a man sins through certain malice, his will must needs be inclined of itself to the evil he chooses. But by the nature of that power man is inclined, not to evil but to good. Therefore if he chooses evil, this must be due to something supervening, which is passion or habit. Now when a man sins through passion, he sins not through certain malice, but through weakness, as stated (Q. 77, A. 3). Therefore whenever anyone sins through certain malice, he sins through habit.

On the contrary, The good habit stands in the same relation to the choice of something good, as the bad habit to the choice of something evil. But it happens sometimes that a man, without having the habit of a virtue, chooses that which is good according to that virtue. Therefore sometimes also a man, without having the habit of a vice, may choose evil, which is to sin through certain malice.

I answer that, The will is related differently to good and to evil. Because from the very nature of the power, it is inclined to the rational good, as its proper object; wherefore every sin is said to be contrary to nature. Hence, if a will be inclined, by its choice, to some evil, this must be occasioned by something else. Sometimes, in fact, this is occasioned through some defect in the reason, as when anyone sins through ignorance; and sometimes this arises through the impulse of the sensitive appetite, as when anyone sins through passion. Yet neither of these amounts to a sin through certain malice; for then alone does anyone sin through certain malice, when his will is moved to evil of its own accord. This may happen in two ways. First, through

his having a corrupt disposition inclining him to evil, so that, in respect of that disposition, some evil is, as it were, suitable and similar to him; and to this thing, by reason of its suitableness, the will tends, as to something good, because everything tends, of its own accord, to that which is suitable to it. Moreover this corrupt disposition is either a habit acquired by custom, or a sickly condition on the part of the body, as in the case of a man who is naturally inclined to certain sins, by reason of some natural corruption in himself.—Secondly, the will, of its own accord, may tend to an evil, through the removal of some obstacle: for instance, if a man be prevented from sinning, not through sin being in itself displeasing to him, but through hope of eternal life, or fear of hell, if hope give place to despair, or fear to presumption, he will end in sinning through certain malice, being freed from the bridle, as it were.

It is evident, therefore, that sin committed through certain malice, always presupposes some inordinateness in man, which, however, is not always a habit: so that it does not follow of necessity, if a man sins through certain malice, that he sins through habit.

Reply Obj. 1. To do an action as an unjust man does, may be not only to do unjust things through certain malice, but also to do them with pleasure, and without any notable resistance on the part of reason, and this occurs only in one who has a habit.

Reply Obj. 2. It is true that a man does not fall suddenly into sin from certain malice, and that something is presupposed; but this something is not always a habit, as stated above.

Reply Obj. 3. That which inclines the will to evil, is not always a habit or a passion, but at times is something else. Moreover, there is no comparison between choosing good and choosing evil: because evil is never without some good of nature, whereas good can be perfect without the evil of fault.

FOURTH ARTICLE

Whether It Is More Grievous to Sin through Certain Malice Than through Passion?

We proceed thus to the Fourth Article:—

Objection 1. It would seem that it is not more grievous to sin through certain malice than through passion. Because ignorance excuses from sin either altogether or in part. Now ignorance is greater in one who sins through certain malice, than in one who sins through passion; since he that sins through certain malice suffers from the worst form of ignorance, which according to the Philosopher (*Ethic.* vii. 8) is ignorance of principle, for he has a false estimation of the end, which is the principle in matters of action. Therefore there is more excuse for one who sins through certain malice, than for one who sins through passion.

Obj. 2. Further, the more a man is impelled to sin, the less grievous his sin, as is clear with regard to a man who is thrown headlong into sin by a more impetuous passion. Now he that sins through certain malice, is impelled by habit, the impulse of which is stronger than that of passion. Therefore to sin through habit is less grievous than to sin through passion.

Obj. 3. Further, to sin through certain malice is to sin through choosing evil. Now he that sins through passion, also chooses evil. Therefore he does not sin less than the man who sins through certain malice.

On the contrary, A sin that is committed on purpose, for this very reason deserves heavier punishment, according to Job xxxiv. 26: *He hath struck them as being wicked, in open sight, who, as it were, on purpose, have revolted from Him.* Now punishment is not increased except for a graver fault. Therefore a sin is aggravated through being done on purpose, i.e. through certain malice.

I answer that, A sin committed through malice is more grievous than a sin committed through passion, for three reasons. First, because, as sin consists chiefly in an act of the will, it follows that, other things being equal, a sin is all the more grievous, according as the movement of the sin belongs more to the will. Now when a sin is committed through malice, the movement of sin belongs more to the will, which is then moved to evil of its own accord, than when a sin is committed through passion, when the will is impelled to sin by something extrinsic, as it were. Wherefore a sin is aggravated by the very fact that it is committed through certain malice, and so much the more, as the malice is greater; whereas it is diminished by being committed through passion, and so much the more, as the passion is stronger.—Secondly, because the

passion which incites the will to sin, soon passes away, so that man repents of his sin, and soon returns to his good intentions; whereas the habit, through which a man sins, is a permanent quality, so that he who sins through malice, abides longer in his sin. For this reason the Philosopher (*Ethic.* vii. 8) compares the intemperate man, who sins through malice, to a sick man who suffers from a chronic disease, while he compares the incontinent man, who sins through passion, to one who suffers intermittently.—Thirdly, because he who sins through certain malice is ill-disposed in respect of the end itself, which is the principle in matters of action; and so the defect is more dangerous than in the case of the man who sins through passion, whose purpose tends to a good end, although this purpose is interrupted on account of the passion, for the time being. Now the worst of all defects is defect of principle. Therefore it is evident that a sin committed through malice is more grievous than one committed through passion.

Reply Obj. 1. Ignorance of choice, to which the objection refers, neither excuses nor diminishes a sin, as stated above (Q. 76, A. 4). Therefore neither does a greater ignorance of the kind make a sin to be less grave.

Reply Obj. 2. The impulse due to passion, is, as it were, due to a defect which is outside the will: whereas, by a habit, the will is inclined from within. Hence the comparison fails.

Reply Obj. 3. It is one thing to sin while choosing, and another to sin through choosing. For he that sins through passion, sins while choosing, but not through choosing, because his choosing is not for him the first principle of his sin; for he is induced through the passion, to choose what he would not choose, were it not for the passion. On the other hand, he that sins through certain malice, chooses evil of his own accord, in the way already explained (AA. 2, 3), so that his choosing, of which he has full control, is the principle of his sin: and for this reason he is said to sin *through* choosing.

QUESTION 79

Of the External Causes of Sin

(In Four Articles)

WE must now consider the external causes of sin, and (1) on the part of God; (2) on the part of the devil; (3) on the part of man.

Under the first head there are four points of inquiry: (1) Whether God is a cause of

sin? (2) Whether the act of sin is from God? (3) Whether God is the cause of spiritual blindness and hardness of heart? (4) Whether these things are directed to the salvation of those who are blinded or hardened?

FIRST ARTICLE

Whether God Is a Cause of Sin?

We proceed thus to the First Article:—

Objection 1. It would seem that God is a cause of sin. For the Apostle says of certain ones (Rom. i. 28): *God delivered them up to a reprobate sense, to do those things which are not right* (Douay,—*convenient*), and a gloss comments on this by saying that *God works in men's hearts, by inclining their wills to whatever He wills, whether to good or to evil.* Now sin consists in doing what is not right, and in having a will inclined to evil. Therefore God is to man a cause of sin.

Obj. 2. Further, it is written (Wis. xiv. 11): *The creatures of God are turned to an abomination; and a temptation to the souls of men.* But a temptation usually denotes a provocation to sin. Since therefore creatures were made by God alone, as was established in the First Part (Q. 44, A. 1), it seems that God is a cause of sin, by provoking man to sin.

Obj. 3. Further, the cause of the cause is the cause of the effect. Now God is the cause of the free-will, which itself is the cause of sin. Therefore God is the cause of sin.

Obj. 4. Further, every evil is opposed to good. But it is not contrary to God's goodness that He should cause the evil of punishment; since of this evil it is written (Isa. xlv. 7) that God creates evil, and (Amos iii. 6): *Shall there be evil in the city which God* (Vulg.,—*the Lord*) *hath not done?* Therefore it is not incompatible with God's goodness that He should cause the evil of fault.

On the contrary, It is written (Wis. xi. 25): *Thou . . . hatest none of the things which Thou hast made.* Now God hates sin, according to Wis. xiv. 9: *To God the wicked and his wickedness are hateful.* Therefore God is not a cause of sin.

I answer that, Man is, in two ways, a cause either of his own or of another's sin. First, directly, namely by inclining his or another's will to sin; secondly, indirectly, namely by not preventing someone from sinning. Hence (Ezech. iii. 18) it is said to the watchman: *If thou say not to the wicked: 'Thou shalt surely die'* * . . . *I will require his blood at thy hand.* —Now God cannot be directly the cause of sin, either in Himself or in another, since every sin is a departure from the order which is to God as the end: whereas God inclines and turns all things to Himself as to their last end, as Dionysius states (*Div. Nom.* i): so that it is impossible that He should be either

to Himself or to another the cause of departing from the order which is to Himself. Therefore He cannot be directly the cause of sin.— In like manner neither can He cause sin indirectly. For it happens that God does not give some the assistance, whereby they may avoid sin, which assistance were He to give, they would not sin. But He does all this according to the order of His wisdom and justice, since He Himself is Wisdom and Justice: so that if someone sin it is not imputable to Him as though He were the cause of that sin; even as a pilot is not said to cause the wrecking of the ship, through not steering the ship, unless he cease to steer while able and bound to steer: it is therefore evident that God is nowise a cause of sin.

Reply Obj. 1. As to the words of the Apostle, the solution is clear from the text. For if God delivered some up to a reprobate sense, it follows that they already had a reprobate sense, so as to do what was not right. Accordingly He is said to deliver them up to a reprobate sense, in so far as He does not hinder them from following that reprobate sense, even as we are said to expose a person to danger if we do not protect him.—The saying of Augustine (*De Grat. et Lib. Arb.* xxi, whence the gloss quoted is taken) to the effect that *God inclines men's wills to good and evil,* is to be understood as meaning that He inclines the will directly to good; and to evil, in so far as He does not hinder it, as stated above. And yet even this is due as being deserved through a previous sin.

Reply Obj. 2. When it is said the *creatures of God are turned 'to' an abomination, and a temptation to the souls of men,* the preposition *to* does not denote causality but sequel;† for God did not make the creatures that they might be an evil to man; this was the result of man's folly, wherefore the text goes on to say, *and a snare to the feet of the unwise,* who, to wit, in their folly, use creatures for a purpose other than that for which they were made.

Reply Obj. 3. The effect which proceeds from the middle cause, according as it is subordinate to the first cause, is reduced to that first cause; but if it proceed from the middle cause, according as it goes outside the order of the first cause, it is not reduced to that first cause: thus if a servant do anything contrary to his master's orders, it is not ascribed to the master as though he were the cause thereof. In like manner sin, which the free-will commits against the commandment of God, is not attributed to God as being its cause.

Reply Obj. 4. Punishment is opposed to the

---

* Vulg.,—*If, when I say to the wicked, "Thou shalt surely die," thou declare it not to him.*

† This is made clear by the Douay Version: the Latin *factæ sunt in abominationem* admits of the translation *were made to be an abomination,* which might imply causality.

good of the person punished, who is thereby deprived of some good or other: but fault is opposed to the good of subordination to God; and so it is directly opposed to the Divine goodness; consequently there is no comparison between fault and punishment.

SECOND ARTICLE

Whether the Act of Sin Is from God?

We proceed thus to the Second Article:—

Objection 1. It would seem that the act of sin is not from God. For Augustine says (*De Perfect. Justit.* ii) that *the act of sin is not a thing.* Now whatever is from God is a thing. Therefore the act of sin is not from God.

Obj. 2. Further, man is not said to be the cause of sin, except because he is the cause of the sinful act: for *no one works, intending evil,* as Dionysius states(*Div. Nom.* iv). Now God is not a cause of sin, as stated above (A. 1). Therefore God is not the cause of the act of sin.

Obj. 3. Further, some actions are evil and sinful in their species, as was shown above (Q. 18, AA. 2, 8). Now whatever is the cause of a thing, causes whatever belongs to it in respect of its species. If therefore God caused the act of sin, He would be the cause of sin, which is false, as was proved above (A. 1). Therefore God is not the cause of the act of sin.

On the contrary, The act of sin is a movement of the free-will. Now *the will of God is the cause of every movement,* as Augustine declares (*De Trin.* iii. 4, 9). Therefore God's will is the cause of the act of sin.

I answer that, The act of sin is both a being and an act; and in both respects it is from God. Because every being, whatever the mode of its being, must be derived from the First Being, as Dionysius declares (*Div. Nom.* 5), Again every action is caused by something existing in act, since nothing produces an action save in so far as it is in act; and every being in act is reduced to the First Act, viz. God, as to its cause, Who is act by His Essence. Therefore God is the cause of every action, in so far as it is an action.—But sin denotes a being and an action with a defect: and this defect is from a created cause, viz. the free-will, as falling away from the order of the First Agent, viz. God. Consequently this defect is not reduced to God as its cause, but to the free-will: even as the defect of limping is reduced to a crooked leg as its cause, but not to the motive power, which nevertheless causes whatever there is of movement in the limping. Accordingly God is the cause of the act of sin:

and yet He is not the cause of sin, because He does not cause the act to have a defect.

Reply Obj. 1. In this passage Augustine calls by the name of *thing,* that which is a thing simply, viz. substance; for in this sense the act of sin is not a thing.

Reply Obj. 2. Not only the act, but also the defect, is reduced to man as its cause, which defect consists in man not being subject to Whom he ought to be, although he does not intend this principally. Wherefore man is the cause of the sin: while God is cause of the act, in such a way, that nowise is He the cause of the defect accompanying the act, so that He is not the cause of the sin.

Reply Obj. 3. As stated above (Q. 72, A. 1), acts and habits do not take their species from the privation itself, wherein consists the nature of evil, but from some object, to which that privation is united: and so this defect which consists in not being from God, belongs to the species of the act consequently, and not as a specific difference.

THIRD ARTICLE

Whether God Is the Cause of Spiritual Blindness and Hardness of Heart?

We proceed thus to the Third Article:—

Objection 1. It would seem that God is not the cause of spiritual blindness and hardness of heart. For Augustine says (*Qq.* lxxxiii, qu. 3) that God is not the cause of that which makes man worse. Now man is made worse by spiritual blindness and hardness of heart. Therefore God is not the cause of spiritual blindness and hardness of heart.

Obj. 2. Further, Fulgentius says (*De Dupl. Prædest.* i. 19): *God does not punish what He causes.* Now God punishes the hardened heart, according to Ecclus. iii. 27: *A hard heart shall fear evil at the last.* Therefore God is not the cause of hardness of heart.

Obj. 3. Further, the same effect is not put down to contrary causes. But the cause of spiritual blindness is said to be the malice of man, according to Wis. ii. 21: *For their own malice blinded them,* and again, according to 2 Cor. iv. 4: *The god of this world hath blinded the minds of unbelievers:* which causes seem to be opposed to God. Therefore God is not the cause of spiritual blindness and hardness of heart.

On the contrary, It is written (Isa. vi. 10): *Blind the heart of this people, and make their ears heavy,* and Rom. ix. 18: *He hath mercy on whom He will, and whom He will He hardeneth.*

I answer that, Spiritual blindness and hardness of heart imply two things. One is the movement of the human mind in cleaving to evil, and turning away from the Divine light; and as regards this, God is not the cause of spiritual blindness and hardness of heart, just as He is not the cause of sin. The other thing is the withdrawal of grace, the result of which is that the mind is not enlightened by God to see aright, and man's heart is not softened to live aright; and as regards this God is the cause of spiritual blindness and hardness of heart.

Now we must consider that God is the universal cause of the enlightening of souls, according to Jo. i. 9: *That was the true light which enlighteneth every man that cometh into this world,* even as the sun is the universal cause of the enlightening of bodies, though not in the same way; for the sun enlightens by necessity of nature, whereas God works freely, through the order of His wisdom. Now although the sun, so far as it is concerned, enlightens all bodies, yet if it be encountered by an obstacle in a body, it leaves it in darkness, as happens to a house whose window-shutters are closed, although the sun is in no way the cause of the house being darkened, since it does not act of its own accord in failing to light up the interior of the house; and the cause of this is the person who closed the shutters. On the other hand, God, of His own accord, withholds His grace from those in whom He finds an obstacle: so that the cause of grace being withheld is not only the man who raises an obstacle to grace; but God, Who, of His own accord, withholds His grace. In this way, God is the cause of spiritual blindness, deafness of ear, and hardness of heart.

These differ from one another in respect of the effects of grace, which both perfects the intellect by the gift of wisdom, and softens the affections by the fire of charity. And since two of the senses excel in rendering service to the intellect, viz. sight and hearing, of which the former assists *discovery,* and the latter, *teaching,* hence it is that spiritual *blindness* corresponds to sight, *heaviness of the ears* to hearing, and *hardness of heart* to the affections.

Reply Obj. 1. Blindness and hardheartedness, as regards the withholding of grace, are punishments, and therefore, in this respect, they make man no worse. It is because he is already worsened by sin that he incurs them, even as other punishments.

Reply Obj. 2. This argument considers hardheartedness in so far as it is a sin.

Reply Obj. 3. Malice is the demeritorious cause of blindness, just as sin is the cause of punishment: and in this way too, the devil is said to blind, in so far as he induces man to sin.

FOURTH ARTICLE

Whether Blindness and Hardness of Heart Are Directed to the Salvation of Those Who Are Blinded and Hardened?

We proceed thus to the Fourth Article:—

Objection 1. It would seem that blindness and hardness of heart are always directed to the salvation of those who are blinded and hardened. For Augustine says (*Enchir.* xi) that *as God is supremely good, He would nowise allow evil to be done, unless He could draw some good from every evil.* Much more, therefore, does He direct to some good, the evil of which He Himself is the cause. Now God is the cause of blindness and hardness of heart, as stated above (A. 3). Therefore they are directed to the salvation of those who are blinded and hardened.

Obj. 2. Further, it is written (Wis. i. 13) that *God hath no pleasure in the destruction of the ungodly.** Now He would seem to take pleasure in their destruction, if He did not turn their blindness to their profit: just as a physician would seem to take pleasure in torturing the invalid, if he did not intend to heal the invalid when he prescribes a bitter medicine for him. Therefore God turns blindness to the profit of those who are blinded.

Obj. 3. Further, *God is not a respecter of persons* (Acts x. 34). Now He directs the blinding of some, to their salvation, as in the case of some of the Jews, who were blinded so as not to believe in Christ, and, through not believing, to slay Him, and afterwards were seized with compunction, and converted, as related by Augustine (*De Quæst. Evang.* iii). Therefore God turns all blindness to the spiritual welfare of those who are blinded.

Obj. 4. On the other hand, According to Rom. iii. 8, evil should not be done, that good may ensue. Now blindness is an evil. Therefore God does not blind some for the sake of their welfare.

I answer that, Blindness is a kind of preamble to sin. Now sin has a twofold relation, —to one thing directly, viz. to the sinner's damnation;—to another, by reason of God's mercy or providence, viz. that the sinner may be healed, in so far as God permits some to fall into sin, that by acknowledging their sin, they may be humbled and converted, as Augustine states (*De Nat. et Grat.* xxii). Therefore blindness, of its very nature, is directed to the damnation of those who are blinded; for which reason it is accounted an effect of reprobation. But, through God's mercy, temporary blindness is directed medicinally to the spiritual welfare of those who are blinded.

* Vulg.,—*God made not death, neither hath He pleasure in the destruction of the living.*

This mercy, however, is not vouchsafed to all those who are blinded, but only to the predestinated, to whom *all things work together unto good* (Rom. viii. 28). Therefore as regards some, blindness is directed to their healing; but as regards others, to their damnation; as Augustine says (*De Quæst. Evang., loc. cit.*).

Reply Obj. 1. Every evil that God does, or permits to be done, is directed to some good; yet not always to the good of those in whom the evil is, but sometimes to the good of others, or of the whole universe: thus He directs the sin of tyrants to the good of the martyrs, and the punishment of the lost to the glory of His justice.

Reply Obj. 2. God does not take pleasure in the loss of man, as regards the loss itself, but by reason of His justice, or of the good that ensues from the loss.

Reply Obj. 3. That God directs the blindness of some to their spiritual welfare, is due to His mercy; but that the blindness of others is directed to their loss is due to His justice: and that He vouchsafes His mercy to some, and not to all, does not make God a respecter of persons, as explained in the First Part (Q. 23, A. 5, *ad* 3).

Reply Obj. 4. Evil of fault must not be done, that good may ensue; but evil of punishment must be inflicted for the sake of good.

QUESTION 80

Of the Cause of Sin, As Regards the Devil

(In Four Articles)

WE must now consider the cause of sin, as regards the devil; and under this head there are four points of inquiry: (1) Whether the devil is directly the cause of sin? (2) Whether the devil induces us to sin, by persuading us inwardly? (3) Whether he can make us sin of necessity? (4) Whether all sins are due to the devil's suggestion?

FIRST ARTICLE

Whether the Devil Is Directly the Cause of Man's Sinning?

We proceed thus to the First Article:—

Objection 1. It would seem that the devil is directly the cause of man's sinning. For sin consists directly in an act of the appetite. Now Augustine says (*De Trin.* iv. 12) that *the devil inspires his friends with evil desires;* and Bede, commenting on Acts v. 3, says that the devil *draws the mind to evil desires;* and Isidore says (*De Summo Bono* ii. 41, iii. 5) that the devil *fills men's hearts with secret lusts.* Therefore the devil is directly the cause of sin.

Obj. 2. Further, Jerome says (*Contra Jovin.* ii. 2) that *as God is the perfecter of good, so is the devil the perfecter of evil.* But God is directly the cause of our good. Therefore the devil is directly the cause of our sins.

Obj. 3. Further, the Philosopher says in a chapter of the *Eudemein Ethics* (vii. 18): *There must needs be some extrinsic principle of human counsel.* Now human counsel is not only about good things but also about evil things. Therefore, as God moves man to take good counsel, and so is the cause of good, so the devil moves him to take evil counsel, and consequently is directly the cause of sin,

On the contrary, Augustine proves (*De Lib. Arb.* i. 11) that *nothing else than his own will makes man's mind the slave of his desire.* Now man does not become a slave to his desire, except through sin. Therefore the cause of sin cannot be the devil, but man's own will alone.

I answer that, Sin is an action: so that a thing can be directly the cause of sin, in the same way as anyone is directly the cause of an action; and this can only happen by moving that action's proper principle to act. Now the proper principle of a sinful action is the will, since every sin is voluntary. Consequently nothing can be directly the cause of sin, except that which can move the will to act.

Now the will, as stated above (Q. 9, AA. 3, 4, 6), can be moved by two things:—first by its object, inasmuch as the apprehended appetible is said to move the appetite:—secondly by that agent which moves the will inwardly to will, and this is no other than the will itself, or God, as was shown above (*loc. cit.*). Now God cannot be the cause of sin, as stated above (Q. 79, A. 1). Therefore it follows that in this respect, a man's will alone is directly the cause of his sin.

As regards the object, a thing may be understood as moving the will in three ways.—First, the object itself which is proposed to the will: thus we say that food arouses man's desire to eat.—Secondly, he that proposes or offers this object.—Thirdly, he that persuades the will that the object proposed has an aspect of good, because he also, in a fashion, offers the will its proper object, which is a real or apparent good of reason.—Accordingly, in the first way the sensible things, which approach from without, move a man's will to sin.—In the second and third ways, either the devil or a man may incite to sin, either by offering an object of appetite to the senses, or by persuading the reason. But in none of these three ways can anything be the direct cause of sin, because the will is not, of necessity, moved by any object except the last end, as stated above (Q. 10, AA. 1, 2). Consequently neither the thing offered from without, nor he that proposes it, nor he that persuades, is the sufficient cause of sin. Therefore it follows that the devil is a cause of sin, neither directly nor sufficiently, but only by persuasion, or by proposing the object of appetite.

Reply Obj. 1. All these, and other like authorities, if we meet with them, are to be understood as denoting that the devil induces man to affection for a sin, either by suggesting to him, or by offering him objects of appetite.

Reply Obj. 2. This comparison is true in so far as the devil is somewhat the cause of our sins, even as God is in a certain way the cause of our good actions, but does not extend to the mode of causation: for God causes good things in us by moving the will inwardly, whereas the devil cannot move us in this way.

Reply Obj. 3. God is the universal principle of all inward movements of man; but that the human will be determined to an evil counsel, is directly due to the human will, and to the devil as persuading or offering the object of appetite.

SECOND ARTICLE

Whether the Devil Can Induce Man to Sin, by Internal Instigations?

We proceed thus to the Second Article:—

Objection 1. It would seem that the devil cannot induce man to sin, by internal instigations. Because the internal movements of the soul are vital functions. Now no vital functions can be exercised except by an intrinsic principle, not even those of the vegetal soul, which are the lowest of vital functions. Therefore the devil cannot instigate man to evil through his internal movements.

Obj. 2. Further, all the internal movements arise from the external senses according to the order of nature. Now it belongs to God alone to do anything beside the order of nature, as was stated in the First Part (Q. 110, A. 4). Therefore the devil cannot effect anything in man's internal movements, except in respect of things which are perceived by the external senses.

Obj. 3. Further, the internal acts of the soul are to understand and to imagine. Now the devil can do nothing in connection with either of these, because, as stated in the First Part

* *De Insomn.* iii, iv.

(Q. 111, AA. 2, 3, *ad* 2), the devil cannot impress species on the human intellect, nor does it seem possible for him to produce imaginary species, since imaginary forms, being more spiritual, are more excellent than those which are in sensible matter, which, nevertheless, the devil is unable to produce, as is clear from what we have said in the First Part (Q. 110, A. 2; Q. 111, AA. 2, 3 *ad* 2). Therefore the devil cannot through man's internal movements induce him to sin.

On the contrary, In that case, the devil would never tempt man, unless he appeared visibly; which is evidently false.

I answer that, The interior part of the soul is intellective and sensitive; and the intellective part contains the intellect and the will. As regards the will, we have already stated (A. 1; P. I., Q. 111, A. 1) what is the devil's relation thereto. Now the intellect, of its very nature, is moved by that which enlightens it in the knowledge of truth, which the devil has no intention of doing in man's regard; rather does he darken man's reason so that it may consent to sin, which darkness is due to the imagination and sensitive appetite. Consequently the operation of the devil seems to be confined to the imagination and sensitive appetite, by moving either of which he can induce man to sin. For his operation may result in presenting certain forms to the imagination; and he is able to incite the sensitive appetite to some passion or other.

The reason of this is, that as stated in the First Part (Q. 110, A. 3), the corporeal nature has a natural aptitude to be moved locally by the spiritual nature: so that the devil can produce all those effects which can result from the local movement of bodies here below, except he be restrained by the Divine power. Now the representation of forms to the imagination is due, sometimes, to local movement: for the Philosopher says (*De Somno et Vigil.*)* that *when an animal sleeps, the blood descends in abundance to the sensitive principle, and the movements descend with it, viz. the impressions left by the action of sensible objects, which impressions are preserved by means of sensible species, and continue to move the apprehensive principle, so that they appear just as though the sensitive principles were being affected by them at the time.* Hence such a local movement of the vital spirits or humors can be procured by the demons, whether man sleep or wake: and so it happens that man's imagination is brought into play.

In like manner, the sensitive appetite is incited to certain passions according to certain fixed movements of the heart and the vital spirits: wherefore the devil can co-operate in this also. And through certain passions being aroused in the sensitive appetite, the result is that man more easily perceives the movement or sensible image which is brought in the manner explained, before the apprehensive principle, since, as the Philosopher observes (*ibid.*), *lovers are moved, by even a slight likeness, to an apprehension of the beloved.* It also happens, through the rousing of a passion, that what is put before the imagination, is judged, as being something to be pursued, because, to him who is held by a passion, whatever the passion inclines him to, seems good. In this way the devil induces man inwardly to sin.

Reply Obj. 1. Although vital functions are always from an intrinsic principle, yet an extrinsic agent can co-operate with them, even as external heat co-operates with the functions of the vegetal soul, that food may be more easily digested.

Reply Obj. 2. This apparition of imaginary forms is not altogether outside the order of nature, nor is it due to a command alone, but according to local movement, as explained above.

Consequently the Reply to the Third Objection is clear, because these forms are received originally from the senses.

THIRD ARTICLE

Whether the Devil Can Induce Man to Sin of Necessity?

We proceed thus to the Third Article:—

Objection 1. It would seem that the devil can induce man to sin of necessity. Because the greater can compel the lesser. Now it is said of the devil (Job xli. 24) that *there is no power on earth that can compare with him.* Therefore he can compel man to sin, while he dwells on the earth.

Obj. 2. Further, man's reason cannot be moved except in respect of things that are offered outwardly to the senses, or are represented to the imagination: because *all our knowledge arises from the senses, and we cannot understand without a phantasm* (*De Anima* iii, text. 30, 39). Now the devil can move man's imagination, as stated above (A. 2); and also the external senses, for Augustine says (*Qq.* lxxxiii, qu. 12) that *this evil,* of which, to wit, the devil is the cause, *extends gradually through all the approaches to the senses, it adapts itself to shapes, blends with colors, mingles with sounds, seasons every flavor.* Therefore it can incline man's reason to sin of necessity.

Obj. 3. Further, Augustine says (*De Civ. Dei* xix. 4) that *there is some sin when the flesh lusteth against the spirit.* Now the devil can cause concupiscence of the flesh, even as

other passions, in the way explained above (A. 2). Therefore he can induce man to sin of necessity.

On the contrary, It is written (1 Pet. v. 8): *Your adversary the devil, as a roaring lion, goeth about seeking whom he may devour.* Now it would be useless to admonish thus, if it were true that man were under the necessity of succumbing to the devil. Therefore he cannot induce man to sin of necessity.

Further, It is likewise written (James iv. 7): *Be subject ... to God, but resist the devil, and he will fly from you,* which would be said neither rightly nor truly, if the devil were able to compel us, in any way whatever, to sin; for then neither would it be possible to resist him, nor would he fly from those who do. Therefore he does not compel to sin.

I answer that, The devil, by his own power, unless he be restrained by God, can compel anyone to do an act which, in its genus, is a sin; but he cannot bring about the necessity of sinning. This is evident from the fact that man does not resist that which moves him to sin, except by his reason; the use of which the devil is able to impede altogether, by moving the imagination and the sensitive appetite; as is the case with one who is possessed. But then, the reason being thus fettered, whatever man may do, it is not imputed to him as a sin. If, however, the reason is not altogether fettered, then, in so far as it is free, it can resist sin, as stated above (Q. 77, A. 7.). It is consequently evident that the devil can nowise compel man to sin.

Reply Obj. 1. Not every power that is greater than man, can move man's will; God alone can do this, as stated above (Q. 9, A. 6).

Reply Obj. 2. That which is apprehended by the senses or the imagination does not move the will, of necessity, so long as man has the use of reason; nor does such an apprehension always fetter the reason.

Reply Obj. 3. The lusting of the flesh against the spirit, when the reason actually resists it, is not a sin, but is matter for the exercise of virtue. That reason does not resist, is not in the devil's power; wherefore he cannot bring about the necessity of sinning.

FOURTH ARTICLE

Whether All the Sins of Men Are Due to the Devil's Suggestion?

We proceed thus to the Fourth Article:—

Objection 1. It would seem that all the sins of men are due to the devil's suggestion. For Dionysius says (*Div. Nom.* iv) that the *crowd of demons are the cause of all evils, both to themselves and to others.*

Obj. 2. Further, whoever sins mortally, becomes the slave of the devil, according to Jo. viii. 34: *Whosoever committeth sin is the slave* (Douay,—*servant*) *of sin.* Now *by whom a man is overcome, of the same also he is the slave* (2 Pet. ii. 19). Therefore whoever commits a sin, has been overcome by the devil.

Obj. 3. Further, Gregory says (*Moral.* iv. 10) the sin of the devil is irreparable, because he sinned at no other's suggestion. Therefore, if any men were to sin of their own free-will and without suggestion from any other, their sin would be irremediable: which is clearly false. Therefore all the sins of men are due to the devil's suggestion.

On the contrary, It is written (*De Eccl. Dogm.* lxxxii): *Not all our evil thoughts are incited by the devil; sometimes they are due to a movement of the free-will.*

I answer that, the devil is the occasional and indirect cause of all our sins, in so far as he induced the first man to sin, by reason of whose sin human nature is so infected, that we are all prone to sin: even as the burning of wood might be imputed to the man who dried the wood so as to make it easily inflammable.—He is not, however, the direct cause of all the sins of men, as though each were the result of his suggestion. Origen proves this (*Peri Archon iii.* 2) from the fact that even if the devil were no more, men would still have the desire for food, sexual pleasures and the like; which desire might be inordinate, unless it were subordinate to reason, a matter that is subject to the free-will.

Reply Obj. 1. The crowd of demons are the cause of all our evils, as regards their original cause, as stated.

Reply Obj. 2. A man becomes another's slave not only by being overcome by him, but also by subjecting himself to him spontaneously: it is thus that one who sins of his own accord, becomes the slave of the devil.

Reply Obj. 3. The devil's sin was irremediable, not only because he sinned without another's suggestion; but also because he was not already prone to sin, on account of any previous sin; which can be said of no sin of man.

QUESTION 81

Of the Cause of Sin, on the Part of Man

(In Five Articles)

WE must now consider the cause of sin, on the part of man. Now, while man, like the devil, is the cause of another's sin, by outward suggestion, he has a certain special manner of causing sin, by way of origin. Wherefore we must speak about original sin, the consideration of which will be three-fold: (1) Of its transmission; (2) of its essence; (3) of its subject.

Under the first head there are five points of inquiry: (1) Whether man's first sin is transmitted, by way of origin to his descendants? (2) Whether all the other sins of our first parent, or of any other parents, are transmitted to their descendants, by way of origin? (3) Whether original sin is contracted by all those who are begotten of Adam by way of seminal generation? (4) Whether it would be contracted by anyone formed miraculously from some part of the human body? (5) Whether original sin would have been contracted if the woman, and not the man, had sinned?

FIRST ARTICLE

Whether the First Sin of Our First Parent Is Contracted by His Descendants, by Way of Origin?

We proceed thus to the First Article:—

Objection 1. It would seem that the first sin of our first parent is not contracted by others, by way of origin. For it is written (Ezech. xviii. 20): *The son shall not bear the iniquity of the father.* But he would bear the iniquity if he contracted it from him. Therefore no one contracts any sin from one of his parents by way of origin.

Obj. 2. Further, an accident is not transmitted by way of origin, unless its subject be also transmitted, since accidents do not pass from one subject to another. Now the rational soul which is the subject of sin, is not transmitted by way of origin, as was shown in the First Part (Q. 118, A. 2). Therefore neither can any sin be transmitted by way of origin.

Obj. 3. Further, whatever is transmitted by way of human origin, is caused by the semen. But the semen cannot cause sin, because it lacks the rational part of the soul, which alone can be a cause of sin. Therefore no sin can be contracted by way of origin.

Obj. 4. Further, that which is more perfect in nature, is more powerful in action. Now perfect flesh cannot infect the soul united to it, else the soul could not be cleansed of original sin, so long as it is united to the body. Much less, therefore, can the semen infect the soul.

Obj. 5. Further, the Philosopher says (*Ethic.*

iii. 5); *No one finds fault with those who are ugly by nature, but only those who are so through want of exercise and through carelessness.* Now those are said to be *naturally ugly,* who are so from their origin. Therefore nothing which comes by way of origin is blameworthy or sinful.

On the contrary, The Apostle says (Rom. v. 12): *By one man sin entered into this world, and by sin death.* Nor can this be understood as denoting imitation or suggestion, since it is written (Wis. ii. 24): *By the envy of the devil, death came into the world.* It follows therefore that through origin from the first man sin entered into the world.

I answer that, According to the Catholic Faith we are bound to hold that the first sin of the first man is transmitted to his descendants, by way of origin. For this reason children are taken to be baptized soon after their birth, to show that they have to be washed from some uncleanness. The contrary is part of the Pelagian heresy, as is clear from Augustine in many of his books.*

In endeavoring to explain how the sin of our first parent could be transmitted by way of origin to his descendants, various writers have gone about it in various ways. For some, considering that the subject of sin is the rational soul, maintained that the rational soul is transmitted with the semen, so that thus an infected soul would seem to produce other infected souls. Others, rejecting this as erroneous, endeavored to show how the guilt of the parent's soul can be transmitted to the children, even though the soul be not transmitted, from the fact that defects of the body are transmitted from parent to child, thus a leper may beget a leper, or a gouty man may be the father of a gouty son, on account of some seminal corruption, although this corruption is not leprosy or gout. Now since the body is proportioned to the soul, and since the soul's defects redound into the body, and vice versa, in like manner, say they, a culpable defect of the soul is passed on to the child, through the transmission of the semen, albeit the semen itself is not the subject of guilt.

But all these explanations are insufficient. Because, granted that some bodily defects are transmitted by the way of origin from parent to child, and granted that even some defects of the soul are transmitted in consequence, on account of a defect in the bodily habit, as in the case of idiots begetting idiots; nevertheless the fact of having a defect by the way of origin seems to exclude the notion of guilt, which is essentially something voluntary. Wherefore granted that the rational soul were

transmitted, from the very fact that the stain on the child's soul is not in its will, it would cease to be a guilty stain binding its subject to punishment; for, as the Philosopher says (*Ethic.* iii. 5), *no one reproaches a man born blind; one rather takes pity on him.*

Therefore we must explain the matter otherwise by saying that all men born of Adam may be considered as one man, inasmuch as they have one common nature, which they receive from their first parents; even as in civil matters, all who are members of one community are reputed as one body, and the whole community as one man. Indeed Poryphyry says (*Prædic., De Specie*) that *by sharing the same species, many men are one man.* Accordingly the multitude of men born of Adam, are as so many members of one body. Now the action of one member of the body, of the hand for instance, is voluntary not by the will of that hand, but by the will of the soul, the first mover of the members. Wherefore a murder which the hand commits would not be imputed as a sin to the hand, considered by itself as apart from the body, but is imputed to it as something belonging to man and moved by man's first moving principle. In this way, then, the disorder which is in this man born of Adam, is voluntary, not by his will, but by the will of his first parent, who, by the movement of generation, moves all who originate from him, even as the soul's will moves all the members to their actions. Hence the sin which is thus transmitted by the first parent to his descendants is called *original,* just as the sin which flows from the soul into the bodily members is called *actual.* And just as the actual sin that is committed by a member of the body, is not the sin of that member, except inasmuch as that member is a part of the man, for which reason it is called a *human sin;* so original sin is not the sin of this person, except inasmuch as this person receives his nature from his first parent, for which reason it is called the *sin of nature,* according to Eph. ii. 3: *We . . . were by nature children of wrath.*

Reply Obj. 1. The son is said not to bear the iniquity of his father, because he is not punished for his father's sin, unless he share in his guilt. It is thus in the case before us: because guilt is transmitted by the way of origin from father to son, even as actual sin is transmitted through being imitated.

Reply Obj. 2. Although the soul is not transmitted, because the power in the semen is not able to cause the rational soul, nevertheless the motion of the semen is a disposition to the transmission of the rational soul:

---

* For instance *Retract.* i. 9; *De Pecc. Merit. et Remiss.* ix.; *Contra Julian.* i. 3, iii. 1; *De Dono Persev.* xi., xii.

so that the semen by its own power transmits the human nature from parent to child, and with that nature, the stain which infects it: for he that is born is associated with his first parent in his guilt, through the fact that he inherits his nature from him by a kind of movement which is that of generation.

Reply Obj. 3. Although the guilt is not actually in the semen, yet human nature is there virtually, accompanied by that guilt.

Reply Obj. 4. The semen is the principle of generation, which is an act proper to nature, by helping it to propagate itself. Hence the soul is more infected by the semen, than by the flesh which is already perfect, and already affixed to a certain person.

Reply Obj. 5. A man is not blamed for that which he has from his origin, if we consider the man born, in himself. But if we consider him as referred to a principle, then he may be reproached for it: thus a man may from his birth be under a family disgrace, on account of a crime committed by one of his forbears.

SECOND ARTICLE

Whether Also Other Sins of the First Parent or of Nearer Ancestors Are Transmitted to Their Descendants?

We proceed thus to the Second Article:—

Objection 1. It would seem that also other sins, whether of the first parent or of nearer ancestors, are transmitted to their descendants. For punishment is never due unless for fault. Now some are punished by the judgment of God for the sin of their immediate parents, according to Exod. xx. 5: *I am . . . God, . . . jealous, visiting the iniquity of the fathers upon the children, unto the third and fourth generation.* Furthermore, according to human law, the children of those who are guilty of high treason are disinherited. Therefore the guilt of nearer ancestors is also transmitted to their descendants.

Obj. 2. Further, a man can better transmit to another, that which he has of himself, than that which he has received from another: thus fire heats better than hot water does. Now a man transmits to his children, by the way, of origin, the sin which he has from Adam. Much more therefore should he transmit the sin which he has contracted of himself.

Obj. 3. Further, the reason why we contract original sin from our first parent is because we were in him as in the principle of our nature, which he corrupted. But we were likewise in our nearer ancestors, as in principles of our nature, which however it be corrupt, can be corrupted yet more by sin, according

* *Ep. ad Auxilium,* ccl.

to Apoc. xxii. 11: *He that is filthy, let him be filthier still.* Therefore children contract, by the way of origin, the sins of their nearer ancestors, even as they contract the sin of their first parent.

On the contrary, Good is more self-diffusive than evil. But the merits of the nearer ancestors are not transmitted to their descendants. Much less therefore are their sins.

I answer that, Augustine puts this question in the *Enchiridion,* xlvi, xlvii, and leaves it unsolved. Yet if we look into the matter carefully we shall see that it is impossible for the sins of the nearer ancestors, or even any other but the first sin of our first parent to be transmitted by the way of origin. The reason is that a man begets his like in species but not in individual. Consequently those things that pertain directly to the individual, such as personal actions and matters affecting them, are not transmitted by parents to their children: for a grammarian does not transmit to his son the knowledge of grammar that he has acquired by his own studies. On the other hand, those things that concern the nature of the species, are transmitted by parents to their children, unless there be a defect of nature: thus a man with eyes begets a son having eyes, unless nature fails. And if nature be strong, even certain accidents of the individual pertaining to natural disposition, are transmitted to the children, e.g. fleetness of body, acuteness of intellect, and so forth; but nowise those that are purely personal, as stated above.

Now just as something may belong to the person as such, and also something through the gift of grace, so may something belong to the nature as such, viz. whatever is caused by the principles of nature, and something too through the gift of grace. In this way original justice, as stated in the First Part (Q. 100, A. 1), was a gift of grace, conferred by God on all human nature in our first parent. This gift the first man lost by his first sin. Wherefore as that original justice together with the nature was to have been transmitted to his posterity, so also was its disorder. — Other actual sins, however, whether of the first parent or of others, do not corrupt the nature as nature, but only as the nature of that person, i.e. in respect of the proneness to sin: and consequently other sins are not transmitted.

Reply Obj. 1. According to Augustine in his letter to Avitus,* children are never inflicted with spiritual punishment on account of their parents, unless they share in their guilt, either in their origin, or by imitation, because every soul is God's immediate property, as stated in Ezech. xviii. 4. Sometimes, however, by Divine or human judgment, children receive bodily punishment on their parents' account, inasmuch as the child, as to its body, is part of its father.

Reply Obj. 2. A man can more easily transmit that which he has of himself, provided it be transmissible. But the actual sins of our nearer ancestors are not transmissible, because they are purely personal, as stated above.

Reply Obj. 3. The first sin infects nature with a human corruption pertaining to nature; whereas other sins infect it with a corruption pertaining only to the person.

THIRD ARTICLE

Whether the Sin of the First Parent Is Transmitted, by the Way of Origin, to All Men?

We proceed thus to the Third Article:—

Objection 1. It would seem that the sin of the first parent is not transmitted, by the way of origin, to all men. Because death is a punishment consequent upon original sin. But not all those, who are born of the seed of Adam, will die: since those who will be still living at the coming of our Lord, will never die, as, seemingly, may be gathered from 1 Thessal. iv. 14: *We who are alive . . . unto the coming of the Lord, shall not prevent them who have have slept.* Therefore they do not contract original sin.

Obj. 2. Further, no one gives another what he has not himself. Now a man who has been baptized has not original sin. Therefore he does not transmit it to his children.

Obj. 3. Further, the gift of Christ is greater than the sin of Adam, as the Apostle declares (Rom. v. 15, *seqq.*). But the gift of Christ is not transmitted to all men: neither, therefore, is the sin of Adam.

On the contrary, The Apostle says (Rom. v. 12): *Death passed upon all men in whom all have sinned.*

I answer that, According to the Catholic Faith we must firmly believe that, Christ alone excepted, all men descended from Adam contract original sin from him; else all would not need redemption* which is through Christ; and this is erroneous. The reason for this may be gathered from what has been stated (A. 1), viz. that original sin, in virtue of the sin of our first parent, is transmitted to his posterity, just as, from the soul's will, actual sin is transmitted to the members of the body, through their being moved by the will. Now it is evident that actual sin can be transmitted to all such members as have an inborn aptitude to be moved by the will. Therefore original sin is transmitted to all those who are moved by Adam by the movement of generation.

Reply Obj. 1. It is held with greater proba-

Cf. Translator's note inserted before P. III, Q. 27.

bility and more commonly that all those that are alive at the coming of our Lord, will die, and rise again shortly, as we shall state more fully in the Third Part (Suppl., Q. 78, A. 1, *Obj.* 1).—If, however, it be true, as others hold, that they will never die, (an opinion which Jerome mentions among others in a letter to Minerius, on the Resurrection of the Body—*Ep.* cxix), then we must say in reply to the objection, that although they are not to die, the debt of death is none the less in them, and that the punishment of death will be remitted by God, since He can also forgive the punishment due for actual sins.

Reply Obj. 2. Original sin is taken away by Baptism as to the guilt, in so far as the soul recovers grace as regards the mind. Nevertheless original sin remains in its effect as regards the "fomes," which is the disorder of the lower parts of the soul and of the body itself, in respect of which, and not of the mind, man exercises his power of generation. Consequently those who are baptized transmit original sin: since they do not beget as being renewed in Baptism, but as still retaining something of the oldness of the first sin.

Reply Obj. 3. Just as Adam's sin is transmitted to all who are born of Adam corporally, so is the grace of Christ transmitted to all that are begotten of Him spiritually, by faith and Baptism: and this, not only unto the removal of the sin of their first parent, but also unto the removal of actual sins, and the obtaining of glory.

FOURTH ARTICLE

Whether Original Sin Would Be Contracted by a Person Formed Miraculously from Human Flesh?

We proceed thus to the Fourth Article:—

Objection 1. It would seem that original sin would be contracted by a person formed miraculously from human flesh. For a gloss on Gen. iv. 1 says that *Adam's entire posterity was corrupted in his loins, because they were not severed from him in the place of life, before he sinned, but in the place of exile after he had sinned.* But if a man were to be formed in the aforesaid manner, his flesh would be severed in the place of exile. Therefore it would contract original sin.

Obj. 2. Further, original sin is caused in us by the soul being infected through the flesh. But man's flesh is entirely corrupted. Therefore a man's soul would contract the infection of original sin, from whatever part of the flesh it was formed.

Obj. 3. Further, original sin comes upon all from our first parent, in so far as we were all in him when he sinned. But those who might be formed out of human flesh would have been in Adam. Therefore they would contract original sin.

On the contrary, They would not have been in Adam *according to seminal virtue,* which alone is the cause of the transmission of original sin, as Augustine states (*Gen. ad lit.* x. 18, *seqq.*).

I answer that, As stated above (AA. 1, 3), original sin is transmitted from the first parent to his posterity, inasmuch as they are moved by him through generation, even as the members are moved by the soul to actual sin. Now there is no movement to generation except by the active power of generation: so that those alone contract original sin, who are descended from Adam through the active power of generation originally derived from Adam, i.e. who are descended from him through seminal power; for the seminal power is nothing else than the active power of generation. But if anyone were to be formed by God out of human flesh, it is evident that the active power would not be derived from Adam. Consequently he would not contract original sin: even as a hand would have no part in a human sin, if it were moved, not by the man's will, but by some external mover.

Reply Obj. 1. Adam was not in the place of exile until after his sin. Consequently it is not on account of the place of exile, but on account of the sin, that original sin is transmitted to those to whom his active generation extends.

Reply Obj. 2. The flesh does not corrupt the soul, except in so far as it is the active principle in generation, as we have stated.

Reply Obj. 3. If a man were to be formed from human flesh, he would have been in Adam, *by way of bodily substance,** but not according to seminal virtue, as stated above. Therefore he would not contract original sin.

FIFTH ARTICLE

Whether If Eve, and Not Adam, Had Sinned, Their Children Would Have Contracted Original Sin?

We proceed thus to the Fifth Article:—

Objection 1. It would seem that if Eve, and not Adam, had sinned, their children would have contracted original sin. Because we contract original sin from our parents, in so far as we were once in them, according to the word of the Apostle (Rom. v. 12): *In whom all have sinned.* Now a man pre-exists in his mother as well as in his father. Therefore a man would have contracted original sin from his mother's sin as well as from his father's.

Obj. 2. Further, if Eve, and not Adam, had sinned, their children would have been born liable to suffering and death, since it is *the mother* that *provides the matter in generation* as the Philosopher states (*De Gener. Animal.* ii. 1, 4), while death and liability to suffering are the necessary results of matter. Now liability to suffering and the necessity of dying are punishments of original sin. Therefore if Eve, and not Adam, had sinned, their children would contract original sin.

Obj. 3. Further, Damascene says (*De Fide Orthod.* iii. 3) that *the Holy Ghost came upon the Virgin,* (of whom Christ was to be born without original sin) *purifying her.* But this purification would not have been necessary, if the infection of original sin were not contracted from the mother. Therefore the infection of original sin is contracted from the mother: so that if Eve had sinned, her children would have contracted original sin, even if Adam had not sinned.

On the contrary, The Apostle says (Rom. v. 12): *By one man sin entered into this world.* Now if the woman would have transmitted original sin to her children, he should have said that it entered by two, since both of them sinned, or rather that it entered by a woman, since she sinned first. Therefore original sin is transmitted to the children, not by the mother, but by the father.

I answer that, The solution of this question is made clear by what has been said. For it has been stated (A. 1) that original sin is transmitted by the first parent in so far as he is the mover in the begetting of his children: wherefore it has been said (A. 4) that if anyone were begotten materially only, of human flesh, they would not contract original sin. Now it is evident that in the opinion of philosophers, the active principle of generation is from the father, while the mother provides the matter. Therefore original sin is contracted, not from the mother, but from the father: so that, accordingly, if Eve, and not Adam, had sinned, their children would not contract original sin: whereas, if Adam, and not Eve, had sinned, they would contract it.

Reply Obj. 1. The child pre-exists in its father as in its active principle, and in its mother, as in its material and passive principle. Consequently the comparison fails.

Reply Obj. 2. Some hold that if Eve, and not Adam, had sinned, their children would be immune from the sin, but would have been subject to the necessity of dying and to other forms of suffering that are a necessary result of the matter which is provided by the mother, not as punishments, but as actual defects.— This, however, seems unreasonable. Because,

---

* The expression is S. Augustine's (*Gen. ad lit.* x). *Cf. Summa Theologica,* P. III, Q. 31., A. 6, Reply to First Objection.

as stated in the First Part (Q. 97, AA. 1, 2 ad 4), immortality and impassibility, in the original state, were a result, not of the condition of matter, but of original justice, whereby the body was subjected to the soul, so long as the soul remained subject to God. Now privation of original justice is original sin. If, therefore, supposing Adam had not sinned, original sin would not have been transmitted to posterity on account of Eve's sin; it is evident that the children would not have been deprived of original justice: and consequently they would not have been liable to suffer and subject to the necessity of dying.

Reply Obj. 3. This prevenient purification in the Blessed Virgin was not needed to hinder the transmission of original sin, but because it behooved the Mother of God *to shine with the greatest purity.** For nothing is worthy to receive God unless it be pure, according to Ps. xcii. 5: *Holiness becometh Thy House, O Lord.*

QUESTION 82

Of Original Sin, As to Its Essence

(In Four Articles)

WE must now consider original sin as to its essence, and under this head there are four points of inquiry: (1) Whether original sin is a habit? (2) Whether there is but one original sin in each man? (3) Whether original sin is concupiscence? (4) Whether original sin is equally in all?

FIRST ARTICLE

Whether Original Sin Is a Habit?

We proceed thus to the First Article:—

Objection 1. It would seem that original sin is not a habit. For original sin is the absence of original justice, as Anselm states (*De Concep. Virg.* ii, iii, xxvi), so that original sin is a privation. But privation is opposed to habit. Therefore original sin is not a habit.

Obj. 2. Further, actual sin has the nature of fault more than original sin, in so far as it is more voluntary. Now the habit of actual sin has not the nature of a fault, else it would follow that a man while asleep, would be guilty of sin. Therefore no original habit has the nature of a fault.

Obj. 3. Further, in wickedness act always precedes habit, because evil habits are not infused, but acquired. Now original sin is not preceded by an act. Therefore original sin is not a habit.

On the contrary, Augustine says in his book on the Baptism of infants (*De Pecc. Merit. et Remiss.* i. 39) that on account of original sin little children have the aptitude of concupiscence though they have not the act. Now aptitude denotes some kind of habit. Therefore original sin is a habit.

I answer that, As stated above (Q. 49, A. 4; Q. 50, A. 1), habit is twofold. The first is a habit whereby power is inclined to an act: thus science and virtue are called habits. In this way original sin is not a habit.—The second kind of habit is the disposition of a complex nature, whereby that nature is well or ill disposed to something, chiefly when such a disposition has become like a second nature, as in the case of sickness or health. In this sense original sin is a habit. For it is an inordinate disposition, arising from the destruction of the harmony which was essential to original justice, even as bodily sickness is an inordinate disposition of the body, by reason of the destruction of that equilibrium which is essential to health. Hence it is that original sin is called the *languor of nature.*†

Reply Obj. 1. As bodily sickness is partly a privation, in so far as it denotes the destruction of the equilibrium of health, and partly something positive, viz. the very humors that are inordinately disposed, so too original sin denotes the privation of original justice, and besides this, the inordinate disposition of the parts of the soul. Consequently it is not a pure privation, but a corrupt habit.

Reply Obj. 2. Actual sin is an inordinateness of an act: whereas original sin, being the sin of nature, is an inordinate disposition of nature, and has the character of fault through being transmitted from our first parent, as stated above (Q. 81, A. 1). Now this inordinate disposition of nature is a kind of habit, whereas the inordinate disposition of an act is not: and for this reason original sin can be a habit, whereas actual sin cannot.

Reply. Obj. 3. This objection considers the habit which inclines a power to an act: but original sin is not this kind of habit. Nevertheless a certain inclination to an inordinate act does follow from original sin, not directly, but indirectly, viz. by the removal of the obstacle, i.e. original justice, which hindered inordinate movements: just as an inclination to inordinate bodily movements results indirectly from bodily sickness. Nor is it necessary to

---

* *Cf.* Anselm,—*De Concep. Virg.* xviii.   † *Cf.* Augustine,—*In Ps.* cxviii, *serm.* iii.

say that original sin is a habit *infused*, or a habit *acquired* (except by the act of our first parent, but not by our own act): but it is a habit *inborn* due to our corrupt origin.

SECOND ARTICLE

Whether There Are Several Original Sins in One Man?

We proceed thus to the Second Article:—

Objection 1. It would seem that there are many original sins in one man. For it is written (Ps. l. 7): *Behold I was conceived in iniquities, and in sins did my mother conceive me.* But the sin in which a man is conceived is original sin. Therefore there are several original sins in man.

Obj. 2. Further, one and the same habit does not incline its subject to contraries: since the inclination of habit is like that of nature which tends to one thing. Now original sin, even in one man, inclines to various and contrary sins. Therefore original sin is not one habit; but several.

Obj. 3. Further, original sin infects every part of the soul. Now the different parts of the soul are different subjects of sin, as shown above (Q. 74). Since then one sin cannot be in different subjects, it seems that original sin is not one but several.

On the contrary, It is written (Jo. i. 29): *Behold the Lamb of God, behold Him Who taketh away the sin of the world:* and the reason for the employment of the singular is that the *sin of the world* is original sin, as a gloss expounds this passage.

I answer that, In one man there is one original sin. Two reasons may be assigned for this. The first is on the part of the cause of original sin. For it has been stated (Q. 81, A. 2) that the first sin alone of our first parent was transmitted to his posterity. Wherefore in one man original sin is one in number; and in all men, it is one in proportion, i.e. in relation to its first principle.—The second reason may be taken from the very essence of original sin. Because in every inordinate disposition, unity of species depends on the cause, while the unity of number is derived from the subject. For example, take bodily sickness: various species of sickness proceed from different causes, e.g. from excessive heat or cold, or from a lesion in the lung or liver; while one specific sickness in one man will be one in number.—Now the cause of this corrupt disposition that is called original sin, is one only, viz. the privation of original justice, removing the subjection of man's mind to God. Consequently original sin is specifically one, and, in one man, can be only one in number; while, in different men, it is one in species and in proportion, but is numerically many.

Reply Obj. 1. The employment of the pural, —*in sins*, may be explained by the custom of the Divine Scriptures in the frequent use of the plural for the singular, e.g. *They are dead that sought the life of the child;*—or by the fact that all actual sins virtually pre-exist in original sin, as in a principle so that it is virtually many;—or by the fact of there being many deformities in the sin of our first parent, viz. pride, disobedience, gluttony, and so forth;—or by several parts of the soul being infected by original sin.

Reply Obj. 2. Of itself and directly, i.e. by its own form, one habit cannot incline its subject to contraries. But there is no reason why it should not do so, indirectly and accidentally, i.e., by the removal of an obstacle: thus, when the harmony of a mixed body is destroyed, the elements have contrary local tendencies. In like manner, when the harmony of original justice is destroyed, the various powers of the soul have various opposite tendencies.

Reply Obj. 3. Original sin infects the different parts of the soul, in so far as they are the parts of one whole; even as original justice held all the soul's parts together in one. Consequently there is but one original sin: just as there is but one fever in one man, although the various parts of the body are affected.

THIRD ARTICLE

Whether Original Sin Is Concupiscence?

We proceed thus to the Third Article:—

Objection 1. It would seem that original sin is not concupiscence. For every sin is contrary to nature, according to Damascene (*De Fide Orthod.* ii. 4, 30). But concupiscence is in accordance with nature, since it is the proper act of the concupiscible faculty which is a natural power. Therefore concupiscence is not original sin.

Obj. 2. Further, through original sin *the passions of sins* are in us, according to the Apostle (Rom. vii. 5). Now there are several other passions besides concupiscence, as stated above (Q. 23, A. 4). Therefore original sin is not concupiscence any more than another passion.

Obj. 3. Further, by original sin, all the parts of the soul are disordered, as stated above (A. 2, *Obj.* 3). But the intellect is the highest of the soul's parts, as the Philosopher states (*Ethic.* x. 7). Therefore original sin is ignorance rather than concupiscence.

On the contrary, Augustine says (*Retract.* i. 15): *Concupiscence is the guilt of original sin.*

I answer that, Everything takes its species from its form: and it has been stated (A. 2) that the species of original sin is taken from its cause. Consequently the formal element of original sin must be considered in respect of the cause of original sin. But contraries have contrary causes. Therefore the cause of original sin must be considered with respect to the cause of original justice, which is opposed to it. Now the whole order of original justice consists in man's will being subject to God: which subjection, first and chiefly, was in the will, whose function it is to move all the other parts to the end, as stated above (Q. 9, A. 1), so that the will being turned away from God, all the other powers of the soul become inordinate. Accordingly the privation of original justice, whereby the will was made subject to God, is the formal element in original sin; while every other disorder of the soul's powers, is a kind of material element in respect of original sin. Now the inordinateness of the other powers of the soul consists chiefly in their turning inordinately to mutable good; which inordinateness may be called by the general name of concupiscence. Hence original sin is concupiscence, materially, but privation of original justice, formally.

Reply Obj. 1. Since, in man, the concupiscible power is naturally governed by reason, the act of concupiscence is so far natural to man, as it is in accord with the order of reason; while, in so far as it trespasses beyond the bounds of reason, it is, for a man, contrary to reason. Such is the concupiscence of original sin.

Reply Obj. 2. As stated above (Q. 25, A. 1), all the irascible passions are reducible to concupiscible passions, as holding the principle place: and of these, concupiscence is the most impetuous in moving, and is felt most, as stated above (*ibid.*, A. 2, *ad* 1). Therefore original sin is ascribed to concupiscence, as being the chief passion, and as including all the others, in a fashion.

Reply Obj. 3. As, in good things, the intellect and reason stand first, so conversely in evil things, the lower part of the soul is found to take precedence, for it clouds and draws the reason, as stated above (Q. 77, AA. 1, 2; Q. 80, A. 2). Hence original sin is called concupiscence rather than ignorance, although ignorance is comprised among the material defects of original sin.

FOURTH ARTICLE

Whether Original Sin Is Equally in All?

We proceed thus to the Fourth Article:—

Objection 1. It would seem that original sin is not equally in all. Because original sin is inordinate concupiscence, as stated above (A. 3). Now all are not equally prone to acts of concupiscence. Therefore original sin is not equally in all.

Obj. 2. Further, original sin is an inordinate disposition of the soul, just as sickness is an inordinate disposition of the body. But sickness is subject to degrees. Therefore original sin is subject to degrees.

Obj. 3. Further, Augustine says (*De Nup. et Concup.* i. 23) that *lust transmits original sin to the child.* But the act of generation may be more lustful in one than in another. Therefore original sin may be greater in one than in another.

On the contrary, Original sin is the sin of nature, as stated above (Q. 81, A. 1). But nature is equally in all. Therefore original sin is too.

I answer that, There are two things in original sin: one is the privation of original justice; the other is the relation of this privation to the sin of our first parent, from whom it is transmitted to man through his corrupt origin. As to the first, original sin has no degrees, since the gift of original justice is taken away entirely; and privations that remove something entirely, such as death and darkness, cannot be more or less, as stated above (Q. 73, A. 2). In like manner, neither is this possible, as to the second: since all are related equally to the first principle of our corrupt origin, from which principle original sin takes the nature of guilt; for relations cannot be more or less. Consequently it is evident that original sin cannot be more in one than in another.

Reply Obj. 1. Through the bond of original justice being broken, which held together all the powers of the soul in a certain order, each power of the soul tends to its own proper movement, and the more impetuously, as it is stronger. Now it happens that some of the soul's powers are stronger in one man than in another, on account of the different bodily temperaments. Consequently if one man is more prone than another to acts of concupiscence, this is not due to original sin, because the bond of original justice is equally broken in all, and the lower parts of the soul are, in all, left to themselves equally; but it is due to the various dispositions of the powers, as stated.

Reply Obj. 2. Sickness of the body, even sickness of the same species, has not an equal cause in all; for instance if a fever be caused by corruption of the bile, the corruption may be greater or less, and nearer to, or further from a vital principle. But the cause of original sin is equal in all, so that there is no comparison.

Reply Obj. 3. It is not the actual lust that transmits original sin: for, supposing God were to grant to a man to feel no inordinate lust in the act of generation, he would still transmit original sin; we must understand this to be habitual lust, whereby the sensitive appetite is not kept subject to reason by the bonds of original justice. This lust is equally in all.

QUESTION 83

Of the Subject of Original Sin

(In Four Articles)

WE must now consider the subject of original sin, under which head there are four points of inquiry: (1) Whether the subject of original sin is the flesh rather than the soul? (2) If it be the soul, whether this be through its essence, or through its powers? (3) Whether the will prior to the other powers is the subject of original sin? (4) Whether certain powers of the soul are specially infected, viz. the generative power, the concupiscible part, and the sense of touch?

FIRST ARTICLE

Whether Original Sin Is More in the Flesh Than in the Soul?

We proceed thus to the First Article:—

Objection 1. It would seem that original sin is more in the flesh than in the soul. Because the rebellion of the flesh against the mind arises from the corruption of original sin. Now the root of this rebellion is seated in the flesh: for the Apostle says *(Rom.* vii. 23): *I see another law in my members fighting against the law of my mind.* Therefore original sin is seated chiefly in the flesh.

Obj. 2. Further, a thing is more in its cause than in its effect: thus heat is in the heating fire more than in the hot water. Now the soul is infected with the corruption of original sin by the carnal semen. Therefore original sin is in the flesh rather than in the soul.

Obj. 3. Further, we contract original sin from our first parent, in so far as we were in him by reason of seminal virtue. Now our souls were not in him thus, but only our flesh. Therefore original sin is not in the soul, but in the flesh.

Obj. 4. Further, the rational soul created by God is infused into the body. If therefore the soul were infected with original sin, it would follow that it is corrupted in its creation or infusion: and thus God would be the cause of sin, since He is the author of the soul's creation and infusion.

Obj. 5. Further, no wise man pours a precious liquid into a vessel, knowing that the vessel will corrupt the liquid. But the rational soul is more precious than any liquid. If therefore the soul, by being united with the body, could be corrupted with the infection of original sin, God, Who is wisdom itself, would never infuse the soul into such a body. And yet He does; wherefore it is not corrupted by the flesh. Therefore original sin is not in the soul but in the flesh.

On the contrary, The same is the subject of a virtue and of the vice or sin contrary to that virtue. But the flesh cannot be the subject of virtue: for the Apostle says (Rom. vii. 18): *I know that there dwelleth not in me, that is to say, in my flesh, that which is good.* Therefore the flesh cannot be the subject of original sin, but only the soul.

I answer that, One thing can be in another in two ways. First, as in its cause, either principal, or instrumental; secondly, as in its subject. Accordingly the original sin of all men was in Adam indeed, as in its principal cause, according to the words of the Apostle (Rom. v. 12): *In whom all have sinned:* whereas it is in the bodily semen, as in its instrumental cause, since it is by the active power of the semen that original sin together with human nature is transmitted to the child. But original sin can nowise be in the flesh as its subject, but only in the soul.

The reason for this is that, as stated above (Q. 81, A. 1), original sin is transmitted from the will of our first parent to his posterity by a certain movement of generation, in the same way as actual sin is transmitted from any man's will to his other parts. Now in this transmission it is to be observed, that whatever accrues from the motion of the will consenting to sin, to any part of man that can in any way share in that guilt, either as its subject or as its instrument, has the character of sin. Thus from the will consenting to gluttony, concupiscence of food accrues to the concupiscible faculty, and partaking of food accrues to the hand and the mouth, which, in so far as they are moved by the will to sin, are the instruments of sin. But that further action is evoked in the nutritive power and the internal members, which have no natural aptitude for being moved by the will, does not bear the character of guilt.

Accordingly, since the soul can be the subject of guilt, while the flesh, of itself, cannot be the subject of guilt; whatever accrues to the soul from the corruption of the first sin, has the character of guilt, while whatever accrues to the flesh, has the character, not of guilt but of punishment: so that, therefore, the soul is the subject of original sin, and not the flesh.

Reply Obj. 1. As Augustine says (*Retract.* i. 27),* the Apostle is speaking, in that passage, of man already redeemed, who is delivered from guilt, but is still liable to punishment, by reason of which sin is stated to dwell *in the flesh.* Consequently it follows that the flesh is the subject, not of guilt, but of punishment.

Reply Obj. 2. Original sin is caused by the semen as instrumental cause. Now there is no need for anything to be more in the instrumental cause than in the effect; but only in the principal cause: and, in this way, original sin was in Adam more fully, since iu him it had the nature of actual sin.

Reply Obj. 3. The soul of any individual man was in Adam, in respect of his seminal power, not indeed as in its effective principle, but as in a dispositive principle: because the bodily semen, which is transmitted from Adam, does not of its own power produce the rational soul, but disposes the matter for it.

Reply Obj. 4. The corruption of original sin is nowise caused by God, but by the sin alone of our first parent through carnal generation. And so, since creation implies a relation in the soul to God alone, it cannot be said that the soul is tainted through being created.—On the other hand, infusion implies relation both to God infusing and to the flesh into which the soul is infused. And so, with regard to God infusing, it cannot be said that the soul is stained through being infused; but only with regard to the body into which it is infused.

Reply Obj. 5. The common good takes precedence of private good. Wherefore God, according to His wisdom, does not overlook the general order of things (which is that such a soul be infused into such a body), lest this soul contract a singular corruption: all the more that the nature of the soul demands that it should not exist prior to its infusion into the body, as stated in the First Part (Q. 90, A. 4; Q. 118, A. 3). And it is better for the soul to be thus, according to its nature, than not to be at all, especially since it can avoid damnation, by means of grace.

SECOND ARTICLE

Whether Original Sin Is in the Essence of the Soul Rather Than in the Powers?

We proceed thus to the Second Article:—

Objection 1. It would seem that original sin is not in the essence of the soul rather than in

* *Cf.* QQ. lxxxiii., qu. 66.

the powers. For the soul is naturally apt to be the subject of sin, in respect of those parts which can be moved by the will. Now the soul is moved by the will, not as to its essence but only as to the powers. Therefore original sin is in the soul, not according to its essence, but only according to the powers.

Obj. 2. Further, original sin is opposed to original justice. Now original justice was in a power of the soul, because power is the subject of virtue. Therefore original sin also is in a power of the soul, rather than in its essence.

Obj. 3. Further, just as original sin is derived by the soul from the flesh, so is it derived by the powers from the essence. But original sin is more in the soul than in the flesh. Therefore it is more in the powers than in the essence of the soul.

Obj. 4. Further, original sin is said to be concupiscence, as stated (Q. 82, A. 3). But concupiscence is in the powers of the soul. Therefore original sin is also.

On the contrary, Original sin is called the sin of nature, as stated above (Q. 81, A. 1). Now the soul is the form and nature of the body, in respect of its essence and not in respect of its powers, as stated in the First Part (Q. 76, A. 6). Therefore the soul is the subject of original sin chiefly in respect of its essence.

I answer that, The subject of a sin is chiefly that part of the soul to which the motive cause of that sin primarily pertains: thus if the motive cause of a sin is sensual pleasure, which regards the concupiscible power through being its proper object, it follows that the concupiscible power is the proper subject of that sin. Now it is evident that original sin is caused through our origin. Consequently that part of the soul which is first reached by man's origin, is the primary subject of original sin. Now the origin reaches the soul as the term of generation, according as it is the form of the body: and this belongs to the soul in respect of its essence, as was proved in the First Part (Q. 76, A. 6). Therefore the soul, in respect of its essence, is the primary subject of original sin.

Reply Obj. 1. As the motion of the will of an individual reaches to the soul's powers and not to its essence, so the motion of the will of the first generator, through the channel of generation, reaches first of all to the essence of the soul, as stated.

Reply Obj. 2. Even original justice pertained radically to the essence of the soul, because it was God's gift to human nature, to which the essence of the soul is related before the powers. For the powers seem to regard the person, in as much as they are the principles of personal acts. Hence they are the proper subjects of actual sins, which are the sins of the person.

Reply Obj. 3. The body is related to the soul as matter to form, which though it comes second in order of generation, nevertheless comes first in the order of perfection and nature. But the essence of the soul is related to the powers, as a subject to its proper accidents, which follow their subject both in the order of generation and in that of perfection. Consequently the comparison fails.

Reply Obj. 4. Concupiscence, in relation to original sin, holds the position of matter and effect, as stated above (Q. 82, A. 3).

THIRD ARTICLE

Whether Original Sin Infects the Will before the Other Powers?

We proceed thus to the Third Article:—

Objection 1. It would seem that original sin does not infect the will before the other powers. For every sin belongs chiefly to that power by whose act it was caused. Now original sin is caused by an act of the generative power. Therefore it seems to belong to the generative power more than to the others.

Obj. 2. Further, original sin is transmitted through the carnal semen. But the other powers of the soul are more akin to the flesh than the will is, as is evident with regard to all the sensitive powers, which use a bodily organ. Therefore original sin is in them more than in the will.

Obj. 3. Further, the intellect precedes the will, for the object of the will is only the good understood. If therefore original sin infects all the powers of the soul, it seems that it must first of all infect the intellect, as preceding the others.

On the contrary, Original justice has a prior relation to the will, because it is *rectitude of the will*, as Anselm states (*De Concep. Virg.* iii). Therefore original sin, which is opposed to it, also has a prior relation to the will.

I answer that, Two things must be considered in the infection of original sin. First, its inherence to its subject; and in this respect it regards first the essence of the soul, as stated above (A. 2). In the second place we must consider its inclination to act; and in this way it regards the powers of the soul. It must therefore regard first of all that power in which is seated the first inclination to commit a sin, and this is the will, as stated above (Q. 74, AA. 1, 2). Therefore original sin regards first of all the will.

Reply Obj. 1. Original sin, in man, is not caused by the generative power of the child, but by the act of the parental generative power. Consequently, it does not follow that the child's generative power is the subject of original sin.

Reply Obj. 2. Original sin spreads in two ways; from the flesh to the soul, and from the essence of the soul to the powers. The former follows the order of generation, the latter follows the order of perfection. Therefore, although the other, viz. the sensitive powers, are more akin to the flesh, yet, since the will, being the higher power, is more akin to the essence of the soul, the infection of original sin reaches it first.

Reply Obj. 3. The intellect precedes the will, in one way, by proposing its object to it. In another way, the will precedes the intellect, in the order of motion to act, which motion pertains to sin.

FOURTH ARTICLE

Whether the Aforesaid Powers Are More Infected Than the Others?

We proceed thus to the Fourth Article:—

Objection 1. It would seem that the aforesaid powers are not more infected than the others. For the infection of original sin seems to pertain more to that part of the soul which can be first the subject of sin. Now this is the rational part, and chiefly the will. Therefore that power is most infected by original sin.

Obj. 2. Further, no power of the soul is infected by guilt, except in so far as it can obey reason. Now the generative power cannot obey reason, as stated in *Ethic.* i. 13. Therefore the generative power is not the most infected by original sin.

Obj. 3. Further, of all the senses the sight is the most spiritual and the nearest to reason, in so far as *it shows us how a number of things differ* (*Met.* i). But the infection of guilt is first of all in the reason. Therefore the sight is more infected than touch.

On the contrary, Augustine says (*De Civ. Dei* xiv. 16, *seqq.,* 24) that the infection of original sin is most apparent in the movements of the members of generation, which are not subject to reason. Now those members serve the generative power in the mingling of sexes, wherein there is the delectation of touch, which is the most powerful incentive to concupiscence. Therefore the infection of original sin regards these three chiefly, viz. the generative power, the concupiscible faculty and the sense of touch.

I answer that, Those corruptions especially are said to be infectious, which are of such a nature as to be transmitted from one subject to another; hence contagious diseases, such as leprosy and murrain and the like, are said to be infectious. Now the corruption of original sin is transmitted by the act of generation, as stated above (Q. 81, A. 1). Therefore the powers which concur in this act, are chiefly said to be infected. Now this act serves the generative power, in as much as it is directed to generation; and it includes delectation of the touch, which is the most powerful object of the concupiscible faculty. Consequently, while all the parts of the soul are said to be corrupted by original sin, these three are said specially to be corrupted and infected.

Reply Obj. 1. Original sin, in so far as it inclines to actual sins, belongs chiefly to the will, as stated above (A. 3). But in so far as it is transmitted to the offspring, it belongs to the aforesaid powers proximately, and to the will, remotely.

Reply Obj. 2. The infection of actual sin belongs only to the powers which are moved by the will of the sinner. But the infection of original sin is not derived from the will of the contractor, but through his natural origin, which is effected by the generative power. Hence it is this power that is infected by original sin.

Reply Obj. 3. Sight is not related to the act of generation except in respect of remote disposition, in so far as the concupiscible species is seen through the sight. But the delectation is completed in the touch. Wherefore the aforesaid infection is ascribed to the touch rather than to the sight.

QUESTION 84

Of the Cause of Sin, in Respect of One Sin Being the Cause of Another

(In Four Articles)

WE must now consider the cause of sin, in so far as one sin can be the cause of another. Under this head there are four points of inquiry: (1) Whether covetousness is the root of all sins? (2) Whether pride is the beginning of every sin? (3) Whether other special sins should be called capital vices, besides pride and covetousness? (4) How many capital vices there are, and which are they?

FIRST ARTICLE

Whether Covetousness Is the Root of All Sins?

We proceed thus to the First Article.—

Objection 1. It would seem that covetousness is not the root of all sins. For covetousness, which is immoderate desire for riches, is opposed to the virtue of liberality. But liberality is not the root of all virtues. Therefore covetousness is not the root of all sins.

Obj. 2. Further, the desire for the means proceeds from desire for the end. Now riches, the desire for which is called covetousness, are not desired except as being useful for some end, as stated in *Ethic.* i. 5. Therefore covetousness is not the root of all sins, but proceeds from some deeper root.

Obj. 3. Further, it often happens that avarice, which is another name for covetousness, arises from other sins; as when a man desires money through ambition, or in order to sate his gluttony. Therefore it is not the root of all sins.

On the contrary, The Apostle says (1 Tim. vi. 10): *The desire of money is the root of all evil.*

I answer that, According to some, covetous-

ness may be understood in different ways.—First, as denoting inordinate desire for riches: and thus it is a special sin.—Secondly, as denoting inordinate desire for any temporal good: and thus it is a genus comprising all sins, because every sin includes an inordinate turning to a mutable good, as stated above (Q. 72, A. 2).—Thirdly, as denoting an inclination of a corrupt nature to desire corruptible goods inordinately: and they say that in this sense covetousness is the root of all sins, comparing it to the root of a tree, which draws its sustenance from earth, just as every sin grows out of the love of temporal things.

Now, though all this is true, it does not seem to explain the mind of the Apostle when he states that covetousness is the root of all sins. For in that passage he clearly speaks against those who, because they *will become rich, fall into temptation, and into the snare of the devil . . . for covetousness is the root of all evils.* Hence it is evident that he is speaking of covetousness as denoting the inordinate desire for riches. Accordingly, we must say that covetousness, as denoting a special sin, is called the root of all sins, in likeness to the root of a tree, in furnishing sustenance to the whole tree. For we see that by riches man acquires the means of committing any sin whatever, and of sating his desire for any sin whatever, since money helps man to obtain all manner of temporal goods, according to Eccles. x. 19: *All things obey money:* so that in this sense desire for riches is the root of all sins.

Reply Obj. 1. Virtue and sin do not arise from the same source. For sin arises from the desire of mutable good; and consequently the desire of that good which helps one to obtain all temporal goods, is called the root of all sins. But virtue arises from the desire for the immutable Good; and consequently charity, which is the love of God, is called the root of the virtues, according to Eph. iii. 17: *Rooted and founded in charity.*

Reply Obj. 2. The desire of money is said to be the root of sins, not as though riches were sought for their own sake, as being the last end; but because they are much sought after as useful for any temporal end. And since a universal good is more desirable than a particular good, they move the appetite more than any individual goods, which along with many others can be procured by means of money.

Reply Obj. 3. Just as in natural things we do not ask what always happens, but what happens most frequently, for the reason that the nature of corruptible things can be hindered, so as not always to act in the same way; so also in moral matters, we consider what happens in the majority of cases, not what happens invariably, for the reason that the will does not act of necessity. So when we say that covetousness is the root of all evils, we do not assert that no other evil can be its root, but that other evils more frequently arise therefrom, for the reason given.

SECOND ARTICLE

Whether Pride Is the Beginning of Every Sin?

We proceed thus to the Second Article:—

Objection 1. It would seem that pride is not the beginning of every sin. For the root is a beginning of a tree, so that the beginning of a sin seems to be the same as the root of sin. Now covetousness is the root of every sin, as stated above (A. 1). Therefore it is also the beginning of every sin, and not pride.

Obj. 2. Further, it is written (Ecclus. x. 14): *The beginning of the pride of man is apostasy* (Douay,—*to fall off*) *from God.* But apostasy from God is a sin. Therefore another sin is the beginning of pride, so that the latter is not the beginning of every sin.

Obj. 3. Further, the beginning of every sin would seem to be that which causes all sins. Now this is inordinate self-love, which, according to Augustine (*De Civ. Dei* xiv), *builds up the city of Babylon.* Therefore self-love and not pride, is the beginning of every sin.

On the contrary, It is written (Ecclus. x. 15): *Pride is the beginning of all sin.*

I answer that, Some say pride is to be taken in three ways. First, as denoting inordinate desire to excel; and thus it is a special sin.— Secondly, as denoting actual contempt of God, to the effect of not being subject to His commandment; and thus, they say, it is a generic sin.—Thirdly, as denoting an inclination to this contempt, owing to the corruption of nature; and in this sense they say that it is the beginning of every sin, and that it differs from covetousness, because covetousness regards sin as turning towards the mutable good by which sin is, as it were, nourished and fostered, for which reason covetousness is called the *root;* whereas pride regards sin as turning away from God, to Whose commandment man refuses to be subject, for which reason it is called the *beginning,* because the beginning of evil consists in turning away from God.

Now though all this is true, nevertheless it does not explain the mind of the wise man who said (*loc. cit.*): *Pride is the beginning of all sin.* For it is evident that he is speaking of pride as denoting inordinate desire to excel, as is clear from what follows (*verse* 17): *God hath overturned the thrones of proud princes;* indeed this is the point of nearly the whole chapter. We must therefore say that pride, even as denoting a special sin, is the beginning of every sin. For we must take note that, in voluntary actions, such as sins, there is a twofold order, of intention, and of execution. In the former order, the principle is the end, as we have stated many times before (Q. 1, A. 1 *ad* 1; Q. 18, A. 7 *ad* 2; Q. 15, A. 1 *ad* 2; Q. 25, A. 2). Now man's end in acquiring all temporal goods is that, through their means, he may have some perfection and excellence. Therefore, from this point of view, pride, which is the desire to excel, is said to be the *beginning* of every sin.—On the other hand, in the order of execution, the first place belongs to that which by furnishing the opportunity of fulfilling all desires of sin, has the character of a root, and such are riches; so that, from this point of view, covetousness is said to be the *root* of all evils, as stated above (A. 1).

This suffices for the Reply to the First Objection.

Reply Obj. 2. Apostasy from God is stated to be the beginning of pride, in so far as it denotes a turning away from God, because from the fact that man wishes not to be subject to God, it follows that he desires inordinately his own excellence in temporal things. Wherefore, in the passage quoted, apostasy from God does not denote the special sin, but rather that general condition of every sin, consisting in its turning away from God.—It may also be said that apostasy from God is said to be the beginning of pride, because it is the first species of pride. For it is characteristic of pride to be unwilling to be subject to any superior, and especially to God; the result being that a man is unduly lifted up, in respect of the other species of pride.

Reply Obj. 3. In desiring to excel, man loves himself, for to love oneself is the same as to desire some good for oneself. Consequently it amounts to the same whether we reckon pride or self-love as the beginning of every evil.

THIRD ARTICLE

Whether Any Other Special Sins, Besides Pride and Avarice, Should Be Called Capital?

We proceed thus to the Third Article:—

Objection 1. It would seem that no other special sins, besides pride and avarice, should be called capital. Because *the head seems to be to an animal, what the root is to a plant,* as stated in *De Anima* ii, text. 38: for the roots are like a mouth. If therefore covetousness is called the *root of all evils,* it seems that it alone, and no other sin, should be called a capital vice.

Obj. 2. Further, the head bears a certain relation of order to the other members, in so far as sensation and movement follow from the head. But sin implies privation of order. Therefore sin has not the character of head: so that no sins should be called capital.

Obj. 3. Further, capital crimes are those which receive capital punishment. But every kind of sin comprises some that are punished thus. Therefore the capital sins are not certain specific sins.

On the contrary, Gregory (*Moral.* xxxi. 17) enumerates certain special vices under the name of capital.

I answer that, The word capital is derived from *caput* (*a head*). Now the head, properly speaking, is that part of an animal's body, which is the principle and director of the whole animal. Hence, metaphorically speaking, every principle is called a head, and even men who direct and govern others are called heads. Accordingly a capital vice is so called, in the first place, from *head* taken in the proper sense, and thus the name *capital* is given to a sin for which capital punishment is inflicted. It is not in this sense that we are now speaking of capital sins, but in another sense, in which the term *capital* is derived from head, taken metaphorically for a principle or director of others. In this way a capital vice is one from which other vices arise, chiefly by being their final cause, which origin is formal, as stated above (Q. 72, A. 6). Wherefore a capital vice is not only the principle of others, but is also their director and, in a way, their leader: because the art or habit, to which the end belongs, is always the principle and the commander in matters concerning the means. Hence Gregory (*Moral.* xxxi. 17) compares these capital vices to the *leaders of an army.*

Reply Obj. 1. The term *capital* is taken from *caput* and applied to something connected with, or partaking of the head, as having some property thereof, but not as being the head taken literally. And therefore the capital vices are not only those which have the character of primary origin, as covetousness which is called the *root,* and pride which is called the beginning, but also those which have the character of proximate origin in respect of several sins.

Reply Obj. 2. Sin lacks order in so far as it turns away from God, for in this respect it is an evil, and evil, according to Augustine (*De Natura Boni* iv.), is *the privation of mode, species and order.* But in so far as sin implies a turning to something, it regards some good: wherefore, in this respect, there can be order in sin.

Reply Obj. 3. This objection considers capital sin as so called from the punishment it deserves, in which sense we are not taking it here.

FOURTH ARTICLE

Whether the Seven Capital Vices Are Suitably Reckoned?

We proceed thus to the Fourth Article:—

Objection 1. It would seem that we ought not to reckon seven capital vices, viz. vainglory, envy, anger, sloth, covetousness, gluttony, lust. For sins are opposed to virtues. But there are four principal virtues, as stated above (Q. 61, A. 2). Therefore there are only four principal or capital vices.

Obj. 2. Further, the passions of the soul are causes of sin, as stated above (Q. 77). But there are four principal passions of the soul; two of which, viz. hope and fear, are not mentioned among the above sins, whereas certain vices are mentioned to which pleasure and sadness belong, since pleasure belongs to gluttony and lust, and sadness to sloth and envy. Therefore the principal sins are unfittingly enumerated.

Obj. 3. Further, anger is not a principal passion. Therefore it should not be placed among the principal vices.

Obj. 4. Further, just as covetousness or avarice is the root of sin, so is pride the beginning of sin, as stated above (A. 2). But avarice is reckoned to be one of the capital vices. Therefore pride also should be placed among the capital vices.

Obj. 5. Further, some sins are committed which cannot be caused through any of these: as, for instance, when one sins through ignorance, or when one commits a sin with a good intention, e.g. steals in order to give an alms.

Therefore the capital vices are insufficiently enumerated.

On the contrary, stands the authority of Gregory who enumerates them in this way (*Moral.* xxxi. 17).

I answer that, As stated above (A. 3), the capital vices are those which give rise to others, especially by way of final cause. Now this kind of origin may take place in two ways. First, on account of the condition of the sinner, who is disposed so as to have a strong inclination for one particular end, the result being that he frequently goes forward to other sins. But this kind of origin does not come under the consideration of art, because man's particular dispositions are infinite in number.—Secondly, on account of a natural relationship of the ends to one another: and it is in this way that most frequently one vice arises from another, so that this kind of origin can come under the consideration of art.

Accordingly therefore, those vices are called capital, whose ends have certain fundamental reasons for moving the appetite; and it is in respect of these fundamental reasons that the capital vices are differentiated. Now a thing moves the appetite in two ways. First, directly and of its very nature: thus good moves the appetite to seek it, while evil, for the same reason, moves the appetite to avoid it. Secondly, indirectly and on account of something else, as it were: thus one seeks an evil on account of some attendant good, or avoids a good on account of some attendant evil.

Again, man's good is threefold. For, in the first place, there is a certain good of the soul, which derives its aspect of appetibility, merely through being apprehended, viz. the excellence of honor and praise, and this good is sought inordinately by *vainglory.*—Secondly, there is the good of the body, and this regards either the preservation of the individual, e.g. meat and drink, which good is pursued inordinately by *gluttony,*—or the preservation of the species, e.g. sexual intercourse, which good is sought inordinately by *lust.*—Thirdly, there is external good, viz. riches, to which *covetousness* is referred. These same four vices avoid inordinately the contrary evils.

Or again,—good moves the appetite chiefly through possessing some property of happiness, which all men seek naturally. Now in the first place happiness implies perfection, since happiness is a perfect good, to which belongs excellence or renown, which is desired by *pride* or *vainglory.* Secondly, it implies satiety, which *covetousness* seeks in riches that give promise thereof. Thirdly, it implies pleasure, without which happiness is impossible, as stated in *Ethic.* i. 7, x. 6, 7, 8, and this *gluttony* and *lust* pursue.

On the other hand, avoidance of good on account of an attendant evil occurs in two ways. For this happens either in respect of one's own good, and thus we have *sloth,* which is sadness about one's spiritual good, on account of the attendant bodily labor:—or else it happens in respect of another's good, and this, if it be without recrimination, belongs to *envy,* which is sadness about another's good as being a hindrance to one's own excellence, while if it be with recrimination with a view to vengeance, it is *anger.* Again, these same vices seek the contrary evils.

Reply Obj. 1. Virtue and vice do not origi-nate in the same way: since virtue is caused by the subordination of the appetite to reason, or to the immutable good, which is God, whereas vice arises from the appetite for mutable good. Wherefore there is no need for the principal vices to be contrary to the principal virtues.

Reply Obj. 2. Fear and hope are irascible passions. Now all the passions of the irascible part arise from passions of the concupiscible part; and these are all, in a way, directed to pleasure or sorrow. Hence pleasure and sorrow have a prominent place among the capital sins, as being the most important of the passions, as stated above (Q. 25, A. 4).

Reply Obj. 3. Although anger is not a principal passion, yet it has a distinct place among the capital vices, because it implies a special kind of movement in the appetite, in so far as recrimination against another's good has the aspect of a virtuous good, i.e. of the right to vengeance.

Reply Obj. 4. Pride is said to be the beginning of every sin, in the order of the end, as stated above (A. 2): and it is in the same order that we are to consider the capital sin as being principal. Wherefore pride, like a universal vice, is not counted along with the others, but is reckoned as the *queen of them all,* as Gregory states (*Moral.* xxxi. 27). But covetousness is said to be the root from another point of view, as stated above (AA. 1, 2).

Reply Obj. 5. These vices are called capital because others, most frequently, arise from them: so that nothing prevents some sins from arising out of other causes.—Nevertheless we might say that all the sins which are due to ignorance, can be reduced to sloth, to which pertains the negligence of a man who declines to acquire spiritual goods on account of the attendant labor; for the ignorance that can cause sin, is due to negligence, as stated above (Q. 76, A. 2). That a man commit a sin with a good intention, seems to point to ignorance, in so far as he knows not that evil should not be done that good may come of it.

QUESTION 85

Of the Effects of Sin, and, First, of the Corruption of the Good of Nature

(In Six Articles)

WE must now consider the effects of sin; and (1) the corruption of the good of nature; (2) the stain on the soul; (3) the debt of punishment.

Under the first head there are six points of inquiry: (1) Whether the good of nature is diminished by sin? (2) Whether it can be taken away altogether? (3) Of the four wounds, mentioned by Bede, with which human nature is stricken in consequence of sin. (4) Whether privation of mode, species and order is an effect of sin? (5) Whether death and other bodily defects are the result of sin? (6) Whether they are, in any way, natural to man?

FIRST ARTICLE

Whether Sin Diminishes the Good of Nature?

We proceed thus to the First Article:—

Objection 1. It would seem that sin does not diminish the good of nature. For man's sin is no worse than the devil's. But natural good remains unimpaired in devils after sin, as Dionysius states (*Div. Nom.* iv). Therefore neither does sin diminish the good of human nature.

Obj. 2. Further, when that which follows is changed, that which precedes remains unchanged, since substance remains the same when its accidents are changed. But nature exists before the voluntary action. Therefore, when sin has caused a disorder in a voluntary act, nature is not changed on that account, so that the good of nature be diminished.

Obj. 3. Further, sin is an action, while diminution is a passion. Now no agent is passive by the very reason of its acting, although it is possible for it to act on one thing, and to be passive as regards another. Therefore he who sins, does not, by his sin, diminish the good of his nature.

Obj. 4. Further, no accident acts on its subject; because that which is patient is a potential being, while that which is subjected to an accident, is already an actual being as regards that accident. But sin is in the good of nature as an accident in a subject. Therefore sin does not diminish the good of nature, since to diminish is to act.

On the contrary, A certain man going down from Jerusalem to Jericho (Luke x. 30), i.e. *to the corruption of sin, was stripped of his gifts, and wounded in his nature,* as Bede* expounds the passage. Therefore sin diminishes the good of nature.

I answer that, The good of human nature is threefold. First, there are the principles of which nature is constituted, and the properties that flow from them, such as the powers of the soul, and so forth. Secondly, since man has from nature an inclination to virtue, as stated above (Q. 60, A. 1; Q. 63, A. 1), this inclination to virtue is a good of nature. Thirdly, the gift of original justice, conferred on the whole human nature in the person of the first man, may be called a good of nature.

Accordingly, the first-mentioned good of nature is neither destroyed nor diminished by sin. The third good of nature was entirely destroyed through the sin of our first parent. But the second good of nature, viz. the natural inclination to virtue, is diminished by sin. Because human acts produce an inclination to like acts, as stated above (Q. 50, A.1). Now from the very fact that a thing becomes inclined to one of two contraries, its inclination to the other contrary must needs be diminished. Wherefore as sin is opposed to virtue, from the very fact that a man sins, there results a diminution of that good of nature, which is the inclination to virtue.

Reply Obj. 1. Dionysius is speaking of the first-mentioned good of nature, which consists in *being, living and understanding,* as anyone may see who reads the context.

Reply Obj. 2. Although nature precedes the voluntary action, it has an inclination to a certain voluntary action. Wherefore nature is not changed in itself, through a change in the voluntary action: it is the inclination that is changed in so far as it is directed to its term.

Reply Obj. 3. A voluntary action proceeds from various powers, active and passive. The result is that through voluntary actions something is caused or taken away in the man who acts, as we stated when treating of the production of habits (Q. 51, A. 2).

Reply Obj. 4. An accident does not act effectively on its subject, but it acts on it formally, in the same sense as when we say that whiteness makes a thing white. In this way there is nothing to hinder sin from diminishing the good of nature; but only in so far as sin is itself a diminution of the good of nature, through being an inordinateness of action. But as regards the inordinateness of the agent, we

* The quotation is from the *Glossa Ordinaria* of Strabo.

must say that such like inordinateness is caused by the fact that in the acts of the soul, there is an active, and a passive element: thus the sensible object moves the sensitive appetite, and the sensitive appetite inclines the reason and will, as stated above (Q. 77, AA. 1, 2). The result of this is the inordinateness, not as though an accident acted on its own subject, but in so far as the object acts on the power, and one power acts on another and puts it out of order.

SECOND ARTICLE

Whether the Entire Good of Human Nature Can Be Destroyed by Sin?

We proceed thus to the Second Article:—

Objection 1. It would seem that the entire good of human nature can be destroyed by sin. For the good of human nature is finite, since human nature itself is finite. Now any finite thing is entirely taken away, if the subtraction be continuous. Since therefore the good of nature can be continually diminished by sin, it seems that in the end it can be entirely taken away.

Obj. 2. Further, in a thing of one nature, the whole and the parts are uniform, as is evidently the case with air, water, flesh and all bodies with similar parts. But the good of nature is wholly uniform. Since therefore a part thereof can be taken away by sin, it seems that the whole can also be taken away by sin.

Obj. 3. Further, the good of nature, that is weakened by sin, is aptitude for virtue. Now this aptitude is destroyed entirely in some on account of sin: thus the lost cannot be restored to virtue any more than the blind can to sight. Therefore sin can take away the good of nature entirely.

On the contrary, Augustine says (*Enchirid.* xiv) that *evil does not exist except in some good.* But the evil of sin cannot be in the good of virtue or of grace, because they are contrary to it. Therefore it must be in the good of nature, and consequently it does not destroy it entirely.

I answer that, As stated above (A. 1), the good of nature, that is diminished by sin, is the natural inclination to virtue, which is befitting to man from the very fact that he is a rational being; for it is due to this that he performs actions in accord with reason, which is to act virtuously. Now sin cannot entirely take away from man the fact that he is a rational being, for then he would no longer be capable of sin. Wherefore it is not possible for this good of nature to be destroyed entirely.

Since, however, this same good of nature may be continually diminished by sin, some,

in order to illustrate this, have made use of the example of a finite thing being diminished indefinitely, without being entirely destroyed. For the Philosopher says (*Phys.* i, text. 37) that if from a finite magnitude a continual subtraction be made in the same quantity, it will at last be entirely destroyed, for instance if from any finite length I continue to subtract the length of a span. If, however, the subtraction be made each time in the same proportion, and not in the same quantity, it may go on indefinitely, as, for instance, if a quantity be halved, and one half be diminished by half, it will be possible to go on thus indefinitely, provided that what is subtracted in each case be less than what was subtracted before.—But this does not apply to the question at issue, since a subsequent sin does not diminish the good of nature less than a previous sin, but perhaps more, if it be a more grievous sin.

We must, therefore, explain the matter otherwise by saying that the aforesaid inclination is to be considered as a middle term between two others: for it is based on the rational nature as on its root, and tends to the good of virtue, as to its term and end. Consequently its diminution may be understood in two ways: first, on the part of its root, secondly, on the part of its term. In the first way, it is not diminished by sin, because sin does not diminish nature, as stated above (A. 1). But it is diminished in the second way, in so far as an obstacle is placed against its attaining its term. Now if it were diminished in the first way, it would needs be entirely destroyed at last by the rational nature being entirely destroyed. Since, however, it is diminished on the part of the obstacle which is placed against its attaining its term, it is evident that it can be diminished indefinitely, because obstacles can be placed indefinitely, inasmuch as man can go on indefinitely adding sin to sin: and yet it cannot be destroyed entirely, because the root of this inclination always remains. An example of this may be seen in a transparent body, which has an inclination to receive light, from the very fact that it is transparent; yet this inclination or aptitude is diminished on the part of supervening clouds, although it always remains rooted in the nature of the body.

Reply Obj. 1. This objection avails when diminution is made by subtraction. But here the diminution is made by raising obstacles, and this neither diminishes nor destroys the root of the inclination, as stated above.

Reply Obj. 2. The natural inclination is indeed wholly uniform: nevertheless it stands in relation both to its principle and to its term, in respect of which diversity of relation, it is diminished on the one hand, and not on the other.

Reply. Obj. 3. Even in the lost the natural inclination to virtue remains, else they would have no remorse of conscience. That it is not reduced to act is owing to their being deprived of grace by Divine justice. Thus even in a blind man the aptitude to see remains in the very root of his nature, inasmuch as he is an animal naturally endowed with sight: yet this aptitude is not reduced to act, for the lack of a cause capable of reducing it, by forming the organ requisite for sight.

THIRD ARTICLE

Whether Weakness, Ignorance, Malice and Concupiscence Are Suitably Reckoned As the Wounds of Nature Consequent upon Sin?

We proceed thus to the Third Article:—

Objection 1. It would seem that weakness, ignorance, malice and concupiscence are not suitably reckoned as the wounds of nature consequent upon sin. For one same thing is not both effect and cause of the same thing. But these are reckoned to be causes of sin, as appears from what has been said above (Q. 76, A. 1; Q. 77, AA. 3, 5; Q. 78, A. 1). Therefore they should not be reckoned as effects of sin.

Obj. 2. Further, malice is the name of a sin. Therefore it should have no place among the effects of sin.

Obj. 3. Further, concupiscence is something natural, since it is the act of the concupiscible power. But that which is natural should not be reckoned a wound of nature. Therefore concupiscence should not be reckoned a wound of nature.

Obj. 4. Further, it has been stated (Q. 77, A. 3) that to sin from weakness is the same as to sin from passion. But concupiscence is a passion. Therefore it should not be condivided with weakness.

Obj. 5. Further, Augustine (*De Nat. et Grat.* lxvii. 67) reckons *two things to be punishments inflicted on the soul of the sinner,* viz. *ignorance and difficulty,* from which arise *error and vexation,* which four do not coincide with the four in question. Therefore it seems that one or the other reckoning is incomplete.

On the contrary, The authority of Bede suffices.*

I answer that, As a result of original justice, the reason had perfect hold over the lower parts of the soul, while reason itself was perfected by God and was subject to Him. Now this same original justice was forfeited through the sin of our first parent, as already stated (Q. 81, A. 2); so that all the powers of the

soul are left, as it were, destitute of their proper order, whereby they are naturally directed to virtue; which destitution is called a wounding of nature.

Again, there are four of the soul's powers that can be the subject of virtue, as stated above (Q. 61, A. 2), viz. the reason, where prudence resides, the will, where justice is, the irascible, the subject of fortitude, and the concupiscible, the subject of temperance. Therefore in so far as the reason is deprived of its order to the true, there is the wound of ignorance; in so far as the will is deprived of its order to the good, there is the wound of malice; in so far as the irascible is deprived of its order to the arduous, there is the wound of weakness; and in so far as the concupiscible is deprived of its order to the delectable, moderated by reason, there is the wound of concupiscence.

Accordingly these are the four wounds inflicted on the whole of human nature as a result of our first parent's sin. But since the inclination to the good of virtue is diminished in each individual on account of actual sin, as was explained above (AA. 1, 2), these four wounds are also the result of other sins, in so far as, through sin, the reason is obscured, especially in practical matters, the will hardened to evil, good actions become more difficult, and concupiscence more impetuous.

Reply Obj. 1. There is no reason why the effect of one sin should not be the cause of another: because the soul, through sinning once, is more easily inclined to sin again.

Reply Obj. 2. Malice is not to be taken here as a sin, but as a certain proneness of the will to evil, according to the words of Gen. viii. 21: *Man's senses are prone to evil from his youth.*†

Reply Obj. 3. As stated above (Q. 82, A. 3, *ad* 1), concupiscence is natural to man, in so far as it is subject to reason: whereas, in so far as it goes beyond the bounds of reason, it is unnatural to man.

Reply Obj. 4. Speaking in a general way, every passion can be called a weakness, in so far as it weakens the soul's strength and clogs the reason. Bede, however, took weakness in the strict sense, as contrary to fortitude which pertains to the irascible.

Reply Obj. 5. The *difficulty* which is mentioned in this book of Augustine, includes the three wounds affecting the appetitive powers, viz. *malice, weakness* and *concupiscence,* for it is owing to these three that a man finds it difficult to tend to the good. *Error* and *vexation* are consequent wounds, since a man is vexed through being weakened in respect of the objects of his concupiscence.

* Reference not known.

† Vulg., *The imagination and thought of man's heart are prone to evil from his youth.*

FOURTH ARTICLE

Whether Privation of Mode, Species and Order Is the Effect of Sin?

We proceed thus to the Fourth Article:—

Objection 1. It would seem that privation of mode, species and order is not the effect of sin. For Augustine says (*De Natura Boni* iii) that *where these three abound, the good is great; where they are less, there is less good; where they are not, there is no good at all.* But sin does not destroy the good of nature. Therefore it does not destroy mode, species and order.

Obj. 2. Further, nothing is its own cause. But sin itself is the *privation of mode, species and order,* as Augustine states (*De Natura Boni* iv). Therefore privation of mode, species and order is not the effect of sin.

Obj. 3. Further, different effects result from different sins. Now since mode, species and order are diverse, their corresponding privations must be diverse also, and, consequently, must be the result of different sins. Therefore privation of mode, species and order is not the effect of each sin.

On the contrary, Sin is to the soul what weakness is to the body, according to Ps. vi. 3, *Have mercy on me, O Lord, for I am weak.* Now weakness deprives the body of mode, species and order. Therefore sin deprives the soul of mode, species and order.

I answer that, As stated in the First Part (Q. 5, A. 5), mode, species and order are consequent upon every created good, as such, and also upon every being. Because every being and every good as such depends on its form from which it derives its *species.* Again, any kind of form, whether substantial or accidental, of anything whatever, is according to some measure, wherefore it is stated in *Metaph.* viii. that *the forms of things are like numbers,* so that a form has a certain *mode* corresponding to its measure. Lastly, owing to its form, each thing has a relation of *order* to something else.

Accordingly there are different grades of mode, species and order, corresponding to the different degrees of good. For there is a good belonging to the very substance of nature, which good has its mode, species and order, and is neither destroyed nor diminished by sin. There is again the good of the natural inclination, which also has its mode, species and order; and this is diminished by sin, as stated above (AA. 1, 2), but is not entirely destroyed. Again, there is the good of virtue and grace: this too has its mode, species and order, and is entirely taken away by sin. Lastly, there is a good consisting in the ordinate act itself, which also has its mode, species

and order, the privation of which is essentially sin. Hence it is clear both how sin is privation of mode, species and order, and how it destroys or diminishes mode, species and order.

This suffices for the Replies to the first two Objections.

Reply Obj. 3. Mode, species and order follow one from the other, as explained above: and so they are destroyed or diminished together.

FIFTH ARTICLE

Whether Death and Other Bodily Defects Are the Result of Sin?

We proceed thus to the Fifth Article:—

Objection 1. It would seem that death and other bodily defects are not the result of sin. Because equal causes have equal effects. Now these defects are not equal in all, but abound in some more than in others, whereas original sin, from which especially these defects seem to result, is equal in all, as stated above (Q. 82, A. 4). Therefore death and suchlike defects are not the result of sin.

Obj. 2. Further, if the cause is removed, the effect is removed. But these defects are not removed, when all sin is removed by Baptism or Penance. Therefore they are not the effect of sin.

Obj. 3. Further, actual sin has more of the character of guilt than original sin has. But actual sin does not change the nature of the body by subjecting it to some defect. Much less, therefore, does original sin. Therefore death and other bodily defects are not the result of sin.

On the contrary, The Apostle says (Rom. v. 12). *By one man sin entered into this world, and by sin death.*

I answer that, One thing causes another in two ways: first, by reason of itself; secondly, accidentally. By reason of itself, one thing is the cause of another, if it produces its effect by reason of the power of its nature or form, the result being that the effect is directly intended by the cause. Consequently, as death and such like defects are beside the intention of the sinner, it is evident that sin is not, of itself, the cause of these defects. Accidentally, one thing is the cause of another if it causes it by removing an obstacle: thus it is stated in *Phys.* viii, text. 32, that *by displacing a pillar a man moves accidentally the stone resting thereon.* In this way the sin of our first parent is the cause of death and all such like defects in human nature, in so far as by the sin of our first parent original justice was taken away, whereby not only were the lower powers of the soul held together under the control of reason, without any disorder whatever, but also the whole body was held together in subjection to the soul, without any defect, as stated in the First Part (Q. 97, A. 1). Wherefore, original justice being forfeited through the sin of our first parent; just as human nature was stricken in the soul by the disorder among the powers, as stated above (A. 3; Q. 82, A. 3), so also it became subject to corruption, by reason of disorder in the body.

Now the withdrawal of original justice has the character of punishment, even as the withdrawal of grace has. Consequently, death and all consequent bodily defects are punishments of original sin. And although the defects are not intended by the sinner, nevertheless they are ordered according to the justice of God Who inflicts them as punishments.

Reply Obj. 1. Causes that produce their effects of themselves, if equal, produce equal effects: for if such causes be increased or diminished, the effect is increased or diminished. But equal causes of an obstacle being removed, do not point to equal effects. For supposing a man employs equal force in displacing two columns, it does not follow that the movements of the stones resting on them will be equal; but that one will move with the greater velocity, which has the greater weight according to the property of its nature, to which it is left when the obstacle to its falling is removed. Accordingly, when original justice is removed, the nature of the human body is left to itself, so that according to diverse natural temperaments, some men's bodies are subject to more defects, some to fewer, although original sin is equal in all.

Reply Obj. 2. Both original and actual sin are removed by the same cause that removes these defects, according to the Apostle (Rom. viii. 11): *He ... shall quicken ... your mortal bodies, because of His Spirit that dwelleth in you:* but each is done according to the order of Divine wisdom, at a fitting time. Because it is right that we should first of all be conformed to Christ's sufferings, before attaining to the immortality and impassibility of glory, which was begun in Him, and by Him acquired for us. Hence it behooves that our bodies should remain, for a time, subject to suffering, in order that we may merit the impassibility of glory, in conformity with Christ.

Reply Obj. 3. Two things may be considered in actual sin, the substance of the act, and the aspect of fault. As regards the substance of the act, actual sin can cause a bodily defect: thus some sicken and die through eating too much. But as regards the fault, it deprives us of grace which is given to us that we may regulate the acts of the soul, but not that we may ward off defects of the body, as

original justice did. Wherefore actual sin does not cause those defects, as original sin does.

SIXTH ARTICLE

Whether Death and Other Defects Are Natural to Man?

We proceed thus to the Sixth Article:—

Objection 1. It would seem that death and such like defects are natural to man. For *the corruptible and the incorruptible differ generically* (*Metaph.* x, text. 26). But man is of the same genus as other animals which are naturally corruptible. Therefore man is naturally corruptible.

Obj. 2. Further, whatever is composed of contraries is naturally corruptible, as having within itself the cause of its corruption. But such is the human body. Therefore it is naturally corruptible.

Obj. 3. Further, a hot thing naturally consumes moisture. Now human life is preserved by hot and moist elements. Since therefore the vital functions are fulfilled by the action of natural heat, as stated in *De Anima* ii, text. 50, it seems that death and such like defects are natural to man.

On the contrary, 1. God made in man whatever is natural to him. Now *God made not death* (Wis. i. 13). Therefore death is not natural to man.

2. Further, that which is natural cannot be called either a punishment or an evil: since what is natural to a thing is suitable to it. But death and such like defects are the punishment of original sin, as stated above (A. 5). Therefore they are not natural to man.

3. Further, matter is proportionate to form, and everything to its end. Now man's end is everlasting happiness, as stated above (Q. 2, A. 7; Q. 5, AA. 3, 4): and the form of the human body is the rational soul, as was proved in the First Part (Q. 75, A. 6). Therefore the human body is naturally incorruptible.

I answer that, We may speak of any corruptible thing in two ways; first, in respect of its universal nature, secondly, as regards its particular nature. A thing's particular nature is its own power of action and self-preservation. And in respect of this nature, every corruption and defect is contrary to nature, as stated in *De Cœlo* ii, text. 37, since this power tends to the being and preservation of the thing to which it belongs.

On the other hand, the universal nature is an active force in some universal principle of nature, for instance in some heavenly body; or again belonging to some superior substance, in which sense God is said by some to be *the Nature Who makes nature.* This force intends the good and the preservation of the universe, for which alternate generation and corruption in things are requisite: and in this respect corruption and defect in things are natural, not indeed as regards the inclination of the form which is the principle of being and perfection, but as regards the inclination of matter which is allotted proportionately to its particular form according to the discretion of the universal agent. And although every form intends perpetual being as far as it can, yet no form of a corruptible being can achieve its own perpetuity, except the rational soul; for the reason that the latter is not entirely subject to matter, as other forms are; indeed it has an immaterial operation of its own, as stated in the First Part (Q. 75, A. 2). Consequently as regards his form, incorruption is more natural to man than to other corruptible things. But since that very form has a matter composed of contraries, from the inclination of that matter there results corruptibility in the whole. In this respect man is naturally corruptible as regards the nature of his matter left to itself, but not as regards the nature of his form.

The first three objections argue on the side of the matter; while the other three argue on the side of the form. Wherefore in order to solve them, we must observe that the form of man which is the rational soul, in respect of its incorruptibility is adapted to its end, which is everlasting happiness: whereas the human body, which is corruptible, considered in respect of its nature, is, in a way, adapted to its form, and, in another way, it is not. For we may note a twofold condition in any matter, one which the agent chooses, and another which is not chosen by the agent, and is a natural condition of matter. Thus, a smith in order to make a knife, chooses a matter both hard and flexible, which can be sharpened so as to be useful for cutting, and in respect of this condition iron is a matter adapted for a knife: but that iron be breakable and inclined to rust, results from the natural disposition of iron, nor does the workman choose this in the iron, indeed he would do without it if he could: wherefore this disposition of matter is not adapted to the workman's intention, nor to the purpose of his art. In like manner the human body is the matter chosen by nature in respect of its being of a mixed temperament, in order that it may be most suitable as an organ of touch and of the other sensitive and motive powers. Whereas the fact that it is corruptible is due to a condition of matter, and is not chosen by nature: indeed nature would choose an incorruptible matter if it could. But God, to Whom every nature is subject, in forming man supplied the defect of nature, and by the gift of original justice, gave the body a certain incorruptibility, as was stated in the First Part (Q. 97, A. 1). It is in this sense that it is said that *God made not death*, and that death is the punishment of sin.

This suffices for the Replies to the Objections.

QUESTION 86

Of the Stain of Sin

(In Two Articles)

WE must now consider the stain of sin; under which head there are two points of inquiry: (1) Whether an effect of sin is a stain on the soul? (2) Whether it remains in the soul after the act of sin?

FIRST ARTICLE

Whether Sin Causes a Stain on the Soul?

We proceed thus to the First Article:—

Objection 1. It would seem that sin causes no stain on the soul. For a higher nature cannot be defiled by contact with a lower nature: hence the sun's ray is not defiled by contact with tainted bodies, as Augustine says (*Contra Quinque Hæreses* v). Now the human soul is of a much higher nature than mutable things, to which it turns by sinning. Therefore it does not contract a stain from them by sinning.

Obj. 2. Further, sin is chiefly in the will, as stated above (Q. 74, AA. 1, 2). Now the will is in the reason, as stated in *De Anima* iii, text. 42. But the reason or intellect is not stained by considering anything whatever; rather indeed is it perfected thereby. Therefore neither is the will stained by sin.

Obj. 3. Further, if sin causes a stain, this stain is either something positive, or a pure privation. If it be something positive, it can only be either a disposition or a habit: for it seems that nothing else can be caused by an act. But it is neither disposition nor habit: for it happens that a stain remains even after the removal of a disposition or habit; for instance, in a man who after committing a mortal sin of prodigality, is so changed as to fall into a sin of the opposite vice. Therefore the stain does not denote anything positive in the soul.—Again, neither is it a pure privation. Because all sins agree on the part of aversion and privation of grace: and so it would follow that there is but one stain caused by all sins. Therefore the stain is not the effect of sin.

On the contrary, It was said to Solomon (Ecclus. xlvii. 22): *Thou hast stained thy glory:* and it is written (Ephes. v. 27): *That He might present it to Himself a glorious church not having spot or wrinkle:* and in each case it is question of the stain of sin. Therefore a stain is the effect of sin.

I answer that, A stain is properly ascribed to corporeal things, when a comely body loses its comeliness through contact with another body, e.g. a garment, gold or silver, or the like. Accordingly a stain is ascribed to spiritual things in like manner. Now man's soul has a twofold comeliness; one from the refulgence of the natural light of reason, whereby he is directed in his actions; the other, from the refulgence of the Divine light, viz. of wisdom and grace, whereby man is also perfected for the purpose of doing good and fitting actions. Now, when the soul cleaves to things by love, there is a kind of contact in the soul: and when man sins, he cleaves to certain things, against the light of reason and of the Divine law, as shown above (Q. 71, A. 6). Wherefore the loss of comeliness occasioned by this contact, is metaphorically called a stain on the soul.

Reply Obj. 1. The soul is not defiled by inferior things, by their own power, as though they acted on the soul: on the contrary, the soul, by its own action, defiles itself, through cleaving to them inordinately, against the light of reason and of the Divine law.

Reply Obj. 2. The action of the intellect is accomplished by the intelligible thing being in the intellect, according to the mode of the intellect, so that the intellect is not defiled, but perfected, by them. On the other hand, the act of the will consists in a movement towards things themselves, so that love attaches the soul to the thing loved. Thus it is that the soul is stained, when it cleaves inordinately, according to Osee ix. 10: *They . . . became abominable as those things were which they loved.*

Reply Obj. 3. The stain is neither something positive in the soul, nor does it denote a pure privation: it denotes a privation of the soul's brightness in relation to its cause, which is sin; wherefore diverse sins occasion diverse stains. It is like a shadow, which is the privation of light through the interposition of a body, and which varies according to the diversity of the interposed bodies.

SECOND ARTICLE

Whether the Stain Remains in the Soul after the Act of Sin?

We proceed thus to the Second Article:—

Objection 1. It would seem that the stain does not remain in the soul after the act of sin. For after an action, nothing remains in the soul except habit or disposition. But the stain is not a habit or disposition, as stated above (A. 1, *Obj.* 3). Therefore the stain does not remain in the soul after the act of sin.

Obj. 2. Further, the stain is to the sin what the shadow is to the body, as stated above (A. 1, *ad* 3). But the shadow does not remain when the body has passed by. Therefore the stain does not remain in the soul when the act of sin is past.

Obj. 3. Further, every effect depends on its cause. Now the cause of the stain is the act of sin. Therefore when the act of sin is no longer there, neither is the stain in the soul.

On the contrary, It is written (Jos. xxii. 17): *Is it a small thing to you that you sinned with Beelphegor, and the stain of that crime remaineth in you* (Vulg.,—*us*) *to this day?*

I answer that, The stain of sin remains in the soul even when the act of sin is past. The reason for this is that the stain, as stated above (A. 1), denotes a blemish in the brightness of the soul, on account of its withdrawing from the light of reason or of the Divine law. And therefore so long as man remains out of this light, the stain of sin remains in him: but as soon as, moved by grace, he returns to the Divine light and to the light o. reason, the stain is removed. For although the act of sin ceases, whereby man withdrew from the light of reason and of the Divine law, man does not at once return to the state in which he was before, and it is necessary that his will should have a movement contrary to the previous movement. Thus if one man be parted from another on account of some kind of movement, he is not reunited to him as soon as the movement ceases, but he needs to draw nigh to him and to return by a contrary movement.

Reply Obj. 1. Nothing positive remains in the soul after the act of sin, except the disposition or habit; but there does remain something privative, viz. the privation of union with the Divine light.

Reply Obj. 2. After the interposed body has passed by, the transparent body remains in the same position and relation as regards the illuminating body, and so the shadow passes at once. But when the sin is past, the soul does not remain in the same relation to God: and so there is no comparison.

Reply Obj. 3. The act of sin parts man from God, which parting causes the defect of brightness, just as local movement causes local parting. Wherefore, just as when movement ceases, local distance is not removed, so neither, when the act of sin ceases, is the stain removed.

QUESTION 87

Of the Debt of Punishment

(In Eight Articles)

WE must now consider the debt of punishment. We shall consider (1) the debt itself; (2) mortal and venial sin, which differ in respect of the punishment due to them.

Under the first head there are eight points of inquiry: (1) Whether the debt of punishment is an effect of sin? (2) Whether one sin can be the punishment of another? (3) Whether any sin incurs a debt of eternal punishment? (4) Whether sin incurs a debt of punishment that is infinite in quantity? (5) Whether every sin incurs a debt of eternal and infinite punishment? (6) Whether the debt of punishment can remain after sin? (7) Whether every punishment is inflicted for a sin? (8) Whether one person can incur punishment for another's sin?

FIRST ARTICLE

Whether the Debt of Punishment Is an Effect of Sin?

We proceed thus to the First Article:—

Objection 1. It would seem that the debt of punishment is not an effect of sin. For that which is accidentally related to a thing, does not seem to be its proper effect. Now the debt of punishment is accidentally related to sin, for it is beside the intention of the sinner. Therefore the debt of punishment is not an effect of sin.

Obj. 2. Further, evil is not the cause of good. But punishment is good, since it is just, and is from God. Therefore it is not an effect of sin, which is evil.

Obj. 3. Further, Augustine says (*Conf.* i) that *every inordinate affection is its own punishment.* But punishment does not incur a further debt of punishment, because then it would go on indefinitely. Therefore sin does not incur the debt of punishment.

On the contrary, It is written (Rom. ii. 9): *Tribulation and anguish upon every soul of man that worketh evil.* But to work evil is to sin. Therefore sin incurs a punishment which is signified by the words *tribulation and anguish.*

I answer that, It has passed from natural things to human affairs that whenever one thing rises up against another, it suffers some detriment therefrom. For we observe in natural things that when one contrary supervenes, the other acts with greater energy, for which reason *hot water freezes more rapidly,* as stated in *Meteor.* i. 12. Wherefore we find that the natural inclination of man is to repress those who rise up against him. Now it is evident that all things contained in an order, are, in a manner, one, in relation to the principle of that order. Consequently, whatever rises up against an order, is put down by that order or by the principle thereof. And because sin is an inordinate act, it is evident that whoever sins, commits an offense against an order: wherefore he is put down, in consequence, by that same order, which repression is punishment.

Accordingly, man can be punished with a threefold punishment corresponding to the three orders to which the human will is subject. In the first place a man's nature is subjected to the order of his own reason; secondly, it is subjected to the order of another man who governs him either in spiritual or in temporal matters, as a member either of the state or of the household; thirdly, it is subjected to the universal order of the Divine government. Now each of these orders is disturbed by sin, for the sinner acts against his reason, and against human and Divine law. Wherefore he incurs a threefold punishment; one, inflicted by himself, viz. remorse of conscience; another, inflicted by man; and a third, inflicted by God.

Reply Obj. 1. Punishment follows sin, inasmuch as this is an evil by reason of its being inordinate. Wherefore just as evil is accidental to the sinner's act, being beside his intention, so also is the debt of punishment.

Reply Obj. 2. Further, a just punishment may be inflicted either by God or by man: wherefore the punishment itself is the effect of sin, not directly but dispositively. Sin, however, makes man deserving of punishment, and that is an evil: for Dionysius says (*Div. Nom.* iv) that *punishment is not an evil, but to deserve punishment, is.* Consequently the debt of punishment is considered to be directly the effect of sin.

Reply Obj. 3. This punishment of the *inordinate affection* is due to sin as overturning the order of reason. Nevertheless sin incurs a further punishment, through disturbing the order of the Divine or human law.

SECOND ARTICLE

Whether Sin Can Be the Punishment of Sin?

We proceed thus to the Second Article:—

Objection 1. It would seem that sin cannot be the punishment of sin. For the purpose of punishment is to bring man back to the good of virtue, as the Philosopher declares (*Ethic.* x. 9). Now sin does not bring man back to the good of virtue, but leads him in the opposite direction. Therefore sin is not the punishment of sin.

Obj. 2. Further, just punishments are from God, as Augustine says (*Qq.* lxxxiii, qu. 82). But sin is not from God, and is an injustice. Therefore sin cannot be the punishment of sin.

Obj. 3. Further, the nature of punishment is to be something against the will. But sin is something from the will, as shown above (Q. 74, AA. 1, 2). Therefore sin cannot be the punishment of sin.

On the contrary, Gregory says (*Hom.* xi. *in Ezech.*) that some sins are punishments of others.

I answer that, We may speak of sin in two ways: first, in its essence, as such; secondly, as to that which is accidental thereto. Sin as such can nowise be the punishment of another. Because sin considered in its essence is something proceeding from the will, for it is from this that it derives the character of guilt. Whereas punishment is essentially something against the will, as stated in the First Part (Q. 48, A. 5). Consequently it is evident that sin regarded in its essence can nowise be the punishment of sin.

On the other hand, sin can be the punishment of sin accidentally in three ways. First, when one sin is the cause of another, by removing an impediment thereto. For passions, temptations of the devil, and the like are causes of sin, but are impeded by the help of Divine grace which is withdrawn on account of sin. Wherefore since the withdrawal of grace is a punishment, and is from God, as stated above (Q. 79, A. 3), the result is that the sin which ensues from this is also a punishment accidentally. It is in this sense that the Apostle speaks (Rom. i. 24) when he says: *Wherefore God gave them up to the desires of their heart,* i.e. to their passions; because, to wit, when men are deprived of the help of Divine grace, they are overcome by their passions. In this way sin is always said to be the punishment of a preceding sin.—Secondly, by reason of the substance of the act, which is such as to cause pain, whether it be an interior act, as is clearly the case with anger or envy, or an exterior act, as is the case with one who endures considerable trouble and loss in order to achieve a sinful act, according to

Wis. v. 7: *We wearied ourselves in the way of iniquity.*—Thirdly, on the part of the effect, so that one sin is said to be a punishment by reason of its effect. In the last two ways, a sin is a punishment not only in respect of a preceding sin, but also with regard to itself.

Reply Obj. 1. Even when God punishes men by permitting them to fall into sin, this is directed to the good of virtue. Sometimes indeed it is for the good of those who are punished, when, to wit, men arise from sin, more humble and more cautious. But it is always for the amendment of others, who seeing some men fall from sin to sin, are the more fearful of sinning.—With regard to the other two ways, it is evident that the punishment is intended for the sinner's amendment, since the very fact that man endures toil and loss in sinning, is of a nature to withdraw man from sin.

Reply Obj. 2. This objection considers sin essentially as such: and the same answer applies to the Third Objection.

THIRD ARTICLE

Whether Any Sin Incurs a Debt of Eternal Punishment?

We proceed thus to the Third Article:—

Objection 1. It would seem that no sin incurs a debt of eternal punishment. For a just punishment is equal to the fault, since justice is equality: wherefore it is written (Isa. xxvii. 8): *In measure against measure, when it shall be cast off, thou shalt judge it.* Now sin is temporal. Therefore it does not incur a debt of eternal punishment.

Obj. 2. Further, *punishments are a kind of medicine* (*Ethic.* ii. 3). But no medicine should be infinite, because it is directed to an end, and *what is directed to an end, is not infinite,* as the Philosopher states (*Polit.* i. 6). Therefore no punishment should be infinite.

Obj. 3. Further, no one does a thing always unless he delights in it for its own sake. But *God hath not pleasure in the destruction of men* (Vulg.,—*of the living*). Therefore He will not inflict eternal punishment on man.

Obj. 4. Further, nothing accidental is infinite. But punishment is accidental, for it is not natural to the one who is punished. Therefore it cannot be of infinite duration.

On the contrary, It is written (Matth. xxv. 46): *These shall go into everlasting punishment;* and (Mark iii. 29): *He that shall blaspheme against the Holy Ghost, shall never have forgiveness, but shall be guilty of an everlasting sin.*

I answer that, As stated above (A. 1), sin incurs a debt of punishment through disturbing an order. But the effect remains so long as the cause remains. Wherefore so long as the disturbance of the order remains the debt of punishment must needs remain also. Now disturbance of an order is sometimes reparable, sometimes irreparable: because a defect which destroys the principle is irreparable, whereas if the principle be saved, defects can be repaired by virtue of that principle. For instance, if the principle of sight be destroyed, sight cannot be restored except by Divine power; whereas, if the principle of sight be preserved, while there arise certain impediments to the use of sight, these can be remedied by nature or by art. Now in every order there is a principle whereby one takes part in that order. Consequently if a sin destroys the principle of the order whereby man's will is subject to God, the disorder will be such as to be considered in itself, irreparable, although it is possible to repair it by the power of God. Now the principle of this order is the last end, to which man adheres by charity. Therefore whatever sins turn man away from God, so as to destroy charity, considered in themselves, incur a debt of eternal punishment.

Reply Obj. 1. Punishment is proportionate to sin in point of severity, both in Divine and in human judgments. In no judgment, however, as Augustine says (*De Civ. Dei* xxi. 11) is it requisite for punishment to equal fault in point of duration. For the fact that adultery or murder is committed in a moment does not call for a momentary punishment: in fact they are punished sometimes by imprisonment or banishment for life,—sometimes even by death; wherein account is not taken of the time occupied in killing, but rather of the expediency of removing the murderer from the fellowship of the living, so that this punishment, in its own way, represents the eternity of punishment inflicted by God. Now according to Gregory (*Dial.* iv. 44) it is just that he who has sinned against God in his own eternity should be punished in God's eternity. A man is said to have sinned in his own eternity, not only as regards continual sinning throughout his whole life, but also because, from the very fact that he fixes his end in sin, he has the will to sin everlastingly. Wherefore Gregory says (*ibid.*) that the *wicked would wish to live without end, that they might abide in their sins for ever.*

Reply Obj 2. Even the punishment that is inflicted according to human laws, is not always intended as a medicine for the one who is punished, but sometimes only for others: thus when a thief is hanged, this is not for his own amendment, but for the sake of others, that at least they may be deterred from crime through fear of the punishment, according to Prov. xix. 25: *The wicked man being scourged,*

the fool shall be wiser. Accordingly the eternal punishments inflicted by God on the reprobate, are medicinal punishments for those who refrain from sin through the thought of those punishments, according to Ps. lix. 6: *Thou hast given a warning to them that fear Thee, that they may flee from before the bow, that Thy beloved may be delivered.*

Reply Obj. 3. God does not delight in punishments for their own sake; but He does delight in the order of His justice, which requires them.

Reply Obj. 4. Although punishment is related indirectly to nature, nevertheless it is essentially related to the disturbance of the order, and to God's justice. Wherefore, so long as the disturbance lasts, the punishment endures.

FOURTH ARTICLE

Whether Sin Incurs a Debt of Punishment Infinite in Quantity?

We proceed thus to the Fourth Article:—

Objection 1. It would seem that sin incurs a debt of punishment infinite in quantity. For it is written (Jerem. x. 24): *Correct me, O Lord, but yet with judgment: and not in Thy fury, lest Thou bring me to nothing.* Now God's anger or fury signifies metaphorically the vengeance of Divine justice: and to be brought to nothing is an infinite punishment, even as to make a thing out of nothing denotes infinite power. Therefore according to God's vengeance, sin is awarded a punishment infinite in quantity.

Obj. 2. Further, quantity of punishment corresponds to quantity of fault, according to Deut. xxv. 2: *According to the measure of the sin shall the measure also of the stripes be.* Now a sin which is committed against God, is infinite: because the gravity of a sin increases according to the greatness of the person sinned against (thus it is a more grievous sin to strike the sovereign than a private individual), and God's greatness is infinite. Therefore an infinite punishment is due for a sin committed against God.

Obj. 3. Further, a thing may be infinite in two ways, in duration, and in quantity. Now the punishment is infinite in duration. Therefore it is infinite in quantity also.

On the contrary, If this were the case, the punishments of all mortal sins would be equal; because one infinite is not greater than another.

I answer that, Punishment is proportionate to sin. Now sin comprises two things. First, there is the turning away from the immutable good, which is infinite, wherefore, in this respect, sin is infinite. Secondly, there is the inordinate turning to mutable good. In this respect sin is finite, both because the mutable good itself is finite, and because the movement of turning towards it is finite, since the acts of a creature cannot be infinite. Accordingly, in so far as sin consists in turning away from something, its corresponding punishment is the *pain of loss,* which also is infinite, because it is the loss of the infinite good, i.e. God. But in so far as sin turns inordinately to something, its corresponding punishment is the *pain of sense,* which also is finite.

Reply Obj. 1. It would be inconsistent with Divine justice for the sinner to be brought to nothing absolutely, because this would be incompatible with the perpetuity of punishment that Divine justice requires, as stated above (A. 3). The expression *to be brought to nothing* is applied to one who is deprived of spiritual goods, according to 1 Cor. xiii. 2: *If I . . . have not charity, I am nothing.*

Reply Obj. 2. This argument considers sin as turning away from something, for it is thus that man sins against God.

Reply Obj. 3. Duration of punishment corresponds to duration of fault, not indeed as regards the act, but on the part of the stain, for as long as this remains, the debt of punishment remains. But punishment corresponds to fault in the point of severity. And a fault which is irreparable, is such that, of itself, it lasts for ever; wherefore it incurs an everlasting punishment. But it is not infinite as regards the thing it turns to; wherefore, in this respect, it does not incur punishment of infinite quantity.

FIFTH ARTICLE

Whether Every Sin Incurs a Debt of Eternal Punishment?

We proceed thus to the Fifth Article:—

Objection 1. It would seem that every sin incurs a debt of eternal punishment. Because punishment, as stated above (A. 4), is proportionate to the fault. Now eternal punishment differs infinitely from temporal punishment: whereas no sin, apparently, differs infinitely from another, since every sin is a human act, which cannot be infinite. Since therefore some sins incur a debt of everlasting punishment, as stated above (A. 4), it seems that no sin incurs a debt of mere temporal punishment.

Obj. 2. Further, original sin is the least of all sins, wherefore Augustine says (*Enchir.* xciii) that *the lightest punishment is incurred by those who are punished for original sin alone.* But original sin incurs everlasting punishment, since children who have died in original sin through not being baptized, will never see the kingdom of God, as is shown by our Lord's words (Jo. iii. 3): *Unless a man*

be born again, he cannot see the kingdom of God. Much more, therefore, will the punishments of all other sins be everlasting.

Obj. 3. Further, a sin does not deserve greater punishment through being united to another sin; for Divine justice has allotted its punishment to each sin. Now a venial sin deserves eternal punishment if it be united to a mortal sin in a lost soul, because in hell there is no remission of sins. Therefore venial sin by itself deserves eternal punishment. Therefore temporal punishment is not due for any sin.

On the contrary, Gregory says (*Dial.* iv. 39), that certain slighter sins are remitted after this life. Therefore all sins are not punished eternally.

I answer that, As stated above (A. 3), a sin incurs a debt of eternal punishment, in so far as it causes an irreparable disorder in the order of Divine justice, through being contrary to the very principle of that order, viz. the last end. Now it is evident that in some sins there is disorder indeed, but such as not to involve contrariety in respect of the last end, but only in respect of things referable to the end, in so far as one is too much or too little intent on them without prejudicing the order to the last end: as, for instance, when a man is too fond of some temporal thing, yet would not offend God for its sake, by breaking one of His commandments. Consequently such sins do not incur everlasting, but only temporal punishment.

Reply Obj. 1. Sins do not differ infinitely from one another in respect of their turning towards mutable good, which constitutes the substance of the sinful act; but they do differ infinitely in respect of their turning away from something. Because some sins consist in turning away from the last end, and some in a disorder affecting things referable to the end: and the last end differs infinitely from the things that are referred to it.

Reply Obj. 2. Original sin incurs everlasting punishment, not on account of its gravity, but by reason of the condition of the subject, viz. a human being deprived of grace, without which there is no remission of sin.

The same answer applies to the Third Objection about venial sin. Because eternity of punishment does not correspond to the quantity of the sin, but to its irremissibility, as stated above (A. 3).

SIXTH ARTICLE

Whether the Debt of Punishment Remains after Sin?

We proceed thus to the Sixth Article:—

Objection 1. It would seem that there remains no debt of punishment after sin. For if the cause be removed the effect is removed. But sin is the cause of the debt of punishment. Therefore, when the sin is removed, the debt of punishment ceases also.

Obj. 2. Further, sin is removed by man returning to virtue. Now a virtuous man deserves, not punishment, but reward. Therefore, when sin is removed, the debt of punishment no longer remains.

Obj. 3. Further, *Punishments are a kind of medicine (Ethic.* ii. 3). But a man is not given medicine after being cured of his disease. Therefore, when sin is removed the debt of punishment does not remain.

On the contrary, It is written (2 Kings xii. 13, 14): *David said to Nathan: I have sinned against the Lord. And Nathan said to David: The Lord also hath taken away thy sin; thou shalt not die. Nevertheless because thou hast given occasion to the enemies of the Lord to blaspheme . . . the child that is born to thee shall die.* Therefore a man is punished by God even after his sin is forgiven: and so the debt of punishment remains, when the sin has been removed.

I answer that, Two things may be considered in sin: the guilty act, and the consequent stain. Now it is evident that in all actual sins, when the act of sin has ceased, the guilt remains; because the act of sin makes man deserving of punishment, in so far as he transgresses the order of Divine justice, to which he cannot return except he pay some sort of penal compensation, which restores him to the equality of justice; so that, according to the order of Divine justice, he who has been too indulgent to his will, by transgressing God's commandments, suffers, either willingly or unwillingly, something contrary to what he would wish. This restoration of the equality of justice by penal compensation is also to be observed in injuries done to one's fellow men. Consequently it is evident that when the sinful or injurious act has ceased there still remains the debt of punishment.

But if we speak of the removal of sin as to the stain, it is evident that the stain of sin cannot be removed from the soul, without the soul being united to God, since it was through being separated from Him that it suffered the loss of its brightness, in which the stain consists, as stated above (Q. 86, A. 1). Now man is united to God by his will. Wherefore the stain of sin cannot be removed from man, unless his will accept the order of Divine justice, that is to say, unless either of his own accord he take upon himself the punishment of his past sin, or bear patiently the punishment which God inflicts on him; and in both ways punishment avails for satisfaction. Now when punishment is satisfactory, it loses somewhat

of the nature of punishment: for the nature of punishment is to be against the will; and although satisfactory punishment, absolutely speaking, is against the will, nevertheless in this particular case and for this particular purpose, it is voluntary. Consequently it is voluntary simply, but involuntary in a certain respect, as we have explained when speaking of the voluntary and the involuntary (Q. 6, A. 6). We must, therefore, say that, when the stain of sin has been removed, there may remain a debt of punishment, not indeed of punishment simply, but of satisfactory punishment.

Reply Obj. 1. Just as after the act of sin has ceased, the stain remains, as stated above (Q. 86, A. 2), so the debt of punishment also can remain. But when the stain has been removed, the debt of punishment does not remain in the same way, as stated.

Reply Obj. 2. The virtuous man does not deserve punishment simply, but he may deserve it as satisfactory: because his very virtue demands that he should do satisfaction for his offenses against God or man.

Reply Obj. 3. When the stain is removed, the wound of sin is healed as regards the will. But punishment is still requisite in order that the other powers of the soul be healed, since they were disordered by the sin committed, so that, to wit, the disorder may be remedied by the contrary of that which caused it. Moreover punishment is requisite in order to restore the equality of justice, and to remove the scandal given to others, so that those who were scandalized at the sin may be edified by the punishment, as may be seen in the example of David quoted above.

SEVENTH ARTICLE

Whether Every Punishment Is Inflicted for a Sin?

We proceed thus to the Seventh Article:—

Objection 1. It would seem that not every punishment is inflicted for a sin. For it is written (Jo. ix. 3, 2) about the man born blind: *Neither hath this man sinned, nor his parents . . . that he should be born blind.* In like manner we see that many children, those also who have been baptized, suffer grievous punishments, fevers, for instance, diabolical possession, and so forth, and yet there is no sin in them after they have been baptized. Moreover before they are baptized, there is no more sin in them than in the other children who do not suffer such things. Therefore not every punishment is inflicted for a sin.

Obj. 2. Further, that sinners should thrive and that the innocent should be punished seem to come under the same head. Now each of these is frequently observed in human affairs, for it is written about the wicked (Ps. lxxii. 5): *They are not in the labor of men: neither shall they be scourged like other men;* and (Job. xxi. 7): (*Why then do*) *the wicked live, are* (*they*) *advanced, and strengthened with riches* (*?*)*; and (Habac. i. 13): *Why lookest Thou upon the contemptuous* (Vulg.,—*them that do unjust things*), *and holdest Thy peace, when the wicked man oppresseth* (Vulg.,—*devoureth*), *the man that is more just than himself?* Therefore not every punishment is inflicted for a sin.

Obj. 3. Further, it is written of Christ (1 Pet. ii. 22) that *He did no sin, nor was guile found in His mouth.* And yet it is said (*ibid.*, 21) that He *suffered for us.* Therefore punishment is not always inflicted by God for sin.

On the contrary, It is written (Job iv. 7, seqq.): *Who ever perished innocent? Or when were the just destroyed? On the contrary, I have seen those who work iniquity . . . perishing by the blast of God;* and Augustine writes (*Retract.* i) that *all punishment is just, and is inflicted for a sin.*

I answer that, As already stated (A. 6), punishment can be considered in two ways,— simply, and as being satisfactory. A satisfactory punishment is, in a way, voluntary. And since those who differ as to the debt of punishment, may be one in will by the union of love, it happens that one who has not sinned, bears willingly the punishment for another: thus even in human affairs we see men take the debts of another upon themselves.—If, however, we speak of punishment simply, in respect of its being something penal, it has always a relation to a sin in the one punished. Sometimes this is a relation to actual sin, as when a man is punished by God or man for a sin committed by him. Sometimes it is a relation to original sin: and this, either principally or consequently,—principally, the punishment of original sin is that human nature is left to itself, and deprived of original justice: and consequently, all the penalties which result from this defect in human nature.

Nevertheless we must observe that sometimes a thing seems penal, and yet is not so simply. Because punishment is a species of evil, as stated in the First Part. (Q. 48, A. 5). Now evil is privation of good. And since man's good is manifold, viz. good of the soul, good of the body, and external goods, it happens sometimes that man suffers the loss of a lesser good, that he may profit in a greater good, as when he suffers loss of money for the sake of bodily health, or loss of both of these, for the sake of his soul's health and the glory of God. In such cases the loss is an evil to man, not simply but relatively; wherefore it does not

answer to the name of punishment simply, but of medicinal punishment, because a medical man prescribes bitter potions to his patients, that he may restore them to health. And since such like are not punishments properly speaking, they are not referred to sin as their cause, except in a restricted sense: because the very fact that human nature needs a treatment of penal medicines, is due to the corruption of nature which is itself the punishment of original sin. For there was no need, in the state of innocence, for penal exercises in order to make progress in virtue; so that whatever is penal in the exercise of virtue, is reduced to original sin as its cause.

Reply Obj. 1. Such like defects of those who are born with them, or which children suffer from, are the effects and the punishments of original sin, as stated above (Q. 85, A. 5); and they remain even after baptism, for the cause stated above (*ibid.*, ad 2): and that they are not equally in all, is due to the diversity of nature, which is left to itself, as stated above (*ibid.*, ad 1). Nevertheless, they are directed by Divine providence, to the salvation of men, either of those who suffer, or of others who are admonished by their means—and also to the glory of God.

Reply Obj. 2. Temporal and bodily goods are indeed goods of man, but they are of small account: whereas spiritual goods are man's chief goods. Consequently it belongs to Divine justice to give spiritual goods to the virtuous, and to award them as much temporal goods or evils, as suffices for virtue: for, as Dionysius says (*Div. Nom.* viii), *Divine justice does not enfeeble the fortitude of the virtuous man, by material gifts.* The very fact that others receive temporal goods, is detrimental to their spiritual good; wherefore the psalm quoted concludes (*verse 6*): *Therefore pride hath held them fast.*

Reply Obj. 3. Christ bore a satisfactory punishment, not for His, but for our sins.

EIGHTH ARTICLE

Whether Anyone Is Punished for Another's Sin?

We proceed thus to the Eighth Article:—

Objection 1. It would seem that one may be punished for another's sin. For it is written (*Exod.* xx. 5): *I am . . . God . . . jealous, visiting the iniquity of the fathers upon the children, unto the third and fourth generation of them that hate Me;* and (Matth. xxiii. 35): *That upon you may come all the just blood that hath been shed upon the earth.*

Obj. 2. Further, human justice springs from Divine justice. Now, according to human justice, children are sometimes punished for their

* The words in brackets show the readings of the Vulgate.

parents, as in the case of high treason. Therefore also according to Divine justice, one is punished for another's sin.

Obj. 3. Further, if it be replied that the son is punished, not for the father's sin, but for his own, inasmuch as he imitates his father's wickedness; this would not be said of the children rather than of outsiders, who are punished in like manner as those whose crimes they imitate. It seems, therefore, that children are punished, not for their own sins, but for those of their parents.

On the contrary, It is written (Ezech. xviii. 20): *The son shall not bear the iniquity of the father.*

I answer that, If we speak of that satisfactory punishment, which one takes upon oneself voluntarily, one may bear another's punishment, in so far as they are, in some way, one, as stated above (A. 7).—If, however, we speak of punishment inflicted on account of sin, inasmuch as it is penal, then each one is punished for his own sin only, because the sinful act is something personal.—But if we speak of a punishment that is medicinal, in this way it does happen that one is punished for another's sin. For it has been stated (A. 7) that ills sustained in bodily goods or even in the body itself, are medicinal punishments intended for the health of the soul. Wherefore there is no reason why one should not have such like punishments inflicted on one for another's sin, either by God or by man; e.g. on children for their parents, or on servants for their masters, inasmuch as they are their property so to speak; in such a way, however, that, if the children or the servants take part in the sin, this penal ill has the character of punishment in regard to both the one punished and the one he is punished for. But if they do not take part in the sin, it has the character of punishment in regard to the one for whom the punishment is borne, while, in regard to the one who is punished, it is merely medicinal (except accidentally, if he consent to the other's sin), since it is intended for the good of his soul, if he bears it patiently.

With regard to spiritual punishments, these are not merely medicinal, because the good of the soul is not directed to a yet higher good. Consequently no one suffers loss in the goods of the soul without some fault of his own.

* *Ep. ad Auxilium,* ccl.

Wherefore, as Augustine says (*Ep. ad Avit.*),* such like punishments are not inflicted on one for another's sin, because, as regards the soul, the son is not the father's property. Hence the Lord assigns the reason for this by saying (Ezech. xviii. 4): *All souls are Mine.*

Reply Obj. 1. Both the passages quoted should, seemingly, be referred to temporal or bodily punishments, in so far as children are the property of their parents, and posterity, of their forefathers.—Else, if they be referred to spiritual punishments, they must be understood in reference to the imitation of sin, wherefore in Exodus these words are added, *Of them that hate Me,* and in the chapter quoted from Matthew (*verse 32*) we read: *Fill ye up then the measure of your fathers.* —The sins of the fathers are said to be punished in their children, because the latter are the more prone to sin through being brought up amid their parents' crimes, both by becoming accustomed to them, and by imitating their parents' example, conforming to their authority as it were. Moreover they deserve heavier punishment if, seeing the punishment of their parents, they fail to mend their ways. —The text adds, *to the third and fourth generation,* because men are wont to live long enough to see the third and fourth generation, so that both the children can witness their parents' sins so as to imitate them, and the parents can see their children's punishments so as to grieve for them.

Reply Obj. 2. The punishments which human justice inflicts on one for another's sin are bodily and temporal. They are also remedies or medicines against future sins, in order that either they who are punished, or others may be restrained from similar faults.

Reply Obj. 3. Those who are near of kin are said to be punished, rather than outsiders, for the sins of others, both because the punishment of kindred redounds somewhat upon those who sinned, as stated above, in so far as the child is the father's property, and because the examples and the punishments that occur in one's own household are more moving. Consequently when a man is brought up amid the sins of his parents, he is more eager to imitate them, and if he is not deterred by their punishments, he would seem to be the more obstinate, and, therefore, to deserve more severe punishment.

QUESTION 88

Of Venial and Mortal Sin

(In Six Articles)

In the next place, since venial and mortal sins differ in respect of the debt of punishment, we must consider them. First, we shall consider venial sin as compared with mortal sin; secondly, we shall consider venial sin in itself.

Under the first head there are six points of inquiry: (1) Whether venial sin is fittingly condivided with mortal sin? (2) Whether they differ generically? (3) Whether venial sin is a disposition to mortal sin? (4) Whether a venial sin can become mortal? (5) Whether a venial sin can become mortal by reason of an aggravating circumstance? (6) Whether a mortal sin can become venial?

FIRST ARTICLE

Whether Venial Sin Is Fittingly Condivided with Mortal Sin?

We proceed thus to the First Article:—

Objection 1. It would seem that venial sin is unfittingly condivided with mortal sin. For Augustine says (*Contra Faust.* xxii. 27): *Sin is a word, deed or desire contrary to the eternal law.* But the fact of being against the eternal law makes a sin to be mortal. Consequently every sin is mortal. Therefore venial sin is not condivided with mortal sin.

Obj. 2. Further, the Apostle says (1 Cor. x. 31): *Whether you eat or drink, or whatsoever else you do; do all to the glory of God.* Now whoever sins breaks this commandment, because sin is not done for God's glory. Consequently, since to break a commandment is to commit a mortal sin, it seems that whoever sins, sins mortally.

Obj. 3. Further, whoever cleaves to a thing by love, cleaves either as enjoying it, or as using it, as Augustine states (*De Doctr. Christ.* i. 3, 4). But no person, in sinning, cleaves to a mutable good as using it: because he does not refer it to that good which gives us happiness, which, properly speaking, is to use, according to Augustine (*ibid.*). Therefore whoever sins enjoys a mutable good. Now *to enjoy what we should use is human perverseness,* as Augustine again says (*Qq.* lxxxiii, qu. 30). Therefore, since *perverseness** denotes a mortal sin, it seems that whoever sins, sins mortally.

Obj. 4. Further, whoever approaches one term, from that very fact turns away from the opposite. Now whoever sins, approaches a mutable good, and, consequently turns away from the immutable good, so that he sins mortally. Therefore venial sin is unfittingly condivided with mortal sin.

On the contrary, Augustine says (*Tract.* xli *in Joan.*), that *a crime is one that merits damnation, and a venial sin, one that does not.* But a crime denotes a mortal sin. Therefore venial sin is fittingly condivided with mortal sin.

I answer that, Certain terms do not appear to be mutually opposed, if taken in their proper sense, whereas they are opposed if taken metaphorically: thus *to smile* is not opposed to *being dry;* but if we speak of the smiling meadows when they are decked with flowers and fresh with green hues this is opposed to drought. In like manner if mortal be taken literally as referring to the death of the body, it does not imply opposition to venial, nor belong to the same genus. But if mortal be taken metaphorically, as applied to sin, it is opposed to that which is venial.

For sin, being a sickness of the soul, as stated above (Q. 71, A. 1 *ad* 3; Q. 72, A. 5; Q. 74, A. 9 *ad* 2), is said to be mortal by comparison with a disease, which is said to be mortal, through causing an irreparable defect consisting in the corruption of a principle, as stated above (Q. 72, A. 5). Now the principle of the spiritual life, which is a life in accord with virtue, is the order to the last end, as stated above (*ibid.;* Q. 87, A. 3): and if this order be corrupted, it cannot be repaired by any intrinsic principle, but by the power of God alone, as stated above (Q. 87, A. 3), because disorders in things referred to the end, are repaired through the end, even as an error about conclusions can be repaired through the truth of the principles. Hence the defect of order to the last end cannot be repaired through something else as a higher principle, as neither can an error about principles. Wherefore such sins are called mortal, as being irreparable. On the other hand, sins which imply a disorder in things referred to the end, the order to the end itself being preserved, are called venial: because a sin receives its acquittal (*veniam*) when the debt of punishment is taken away, and this ceases when the sin ceases, as explained above (Q. 87, A. 6).

Accordingly, mortal and venial are mutually opposed as reparable and irreparable: and I

* The Latin *pervertere* means to overthrow, to destroy, hence *perversion* of God's law is a mortal sin.

say this with reference to the intrinsic principle, but not to the Divine power, which can repair all diseases, whether of the body or of the soul. Therefore venial sin is fittingly condivided with mortal sin.

Reply Obj. 1. The division of sin into venial and mortal is not a division of a genus into its species which have an equal share of the generic nature: but it is the division of an analogous term into its parts, of which it is predicated, of the one first, and of the other afterwards. Consequently the perfect notion of sin, which Augustine gives, applies to mortal sin. On the other hand, venial sin is called a sin, in reference to an imperfect notion of sin, and in relation to mortal sin: even as an accident is called a being, in relation to substance, in reference to the imperfect notion of being. For it is not *against* the law, since he who sins venially neither does what the law forbids, nor nor omits what the law prescribes to be done; but he acts *beside* the law, through not observing the mode of reason, which the law intends.

Reply Obj. 2. This precept of the Apostle is affirmative, and so it does not bind for all times. Consequently everyone who does not actually refer all his actions to the glory of God, does not therefore act against this precept. In order, therefore, to avoid mortal sin each time that one fails actually to refer an action to God's glory, it is enough to refer oneself and all that one has to God habitually. Now venial sin excludes only actual reference of the human act to God's glory, and not habitual reference: because it does not exclude charity, which refers man to God habitually. Therefore it does not follow that he who sins venially, sins mortally.

Reply Obj. 3. He that sins venially, cleaves to temporal good, not as enjoying it, because he does not fix his end in it, but as using it, by referring it to God, not actually but habitually.

Reply Obj. 4. Mutable good is not considered to be a term in contraposition to the immutable good, unless one's end is fixed therein: because what is referred to the end has not the character of finality.

SECOND ARTICLE

Whether Mortal and Venial Sin Differ Generically?

We proceed thus to the Second Article:—

Objection 1. It would seem that venial and mortal sin do not differ generically, so that some sins be generically mortal, and some generically venial. Because human acts are considered to be generically good or evil according to their matter or object, as stated above (Q. 18, A. 2). Now either mortal or venial sin may be committed in regard to any object or matter: since man can love any mu-

table good, either less than God, which may be a venial sin, or more than God, which is a mortal sin. Therefore venial and mortal sin do not differ generically.

Obj. 2. Further, as stated above (A. 1; Q. 72, A. 5; Q. 87, A. 3), a sin is called mortal when it is irreparable, venial when it can be repaired. Now irreparability belongs to sin committed out of malice, which, according to some, is irremissible: whereas reparability belongs to sins committed through weakness or ignorance, which are remissible. Therefore mortal and venial sin differ as sin committed through malice differs from sin committed through weakness or ignorance. But, in this respect, sins differ, not in genus but in cause, as stated above (Q. 77, A. 8, *ad* 1). Therefore venial and mortal sin do not differ generically.

Obj. 3. Further, it was stated above (Q. 74, A. 3, *ad* 3; A. 10) that sudden movements both of the sensuality and of the reason are venial sins. But sudden movements occur in every kind of sin. Therefore no sins are generically venial.

On the contrary, Augustine, in a sermon on Purgatory (*De Sanctis*, serm. xli), enumerates certain generic venial sins, and certain generic mortal sins.

I answer that, Venial sin is so called from *venia* (*pardon*). Consequently a sin may be called venial, first of all, because it has been pardoned: thus Ambrose says that *penance makes every sin venial:* and this is called venial *from the result.*—Secondly, a sin is called venial because it does not contain anything either partially or totally, to prevent its being pardoned:—partially, as when a sin contains something diminishing its guilt, e.g. a sin committed through weakness or ignorance: and this is called venial *from the cause:*—totally, through not destroying the order to the last end, wherefore it deserves temporal, but not everlasting punishment. It is of this venial sin that we wish to speak now.

For as regards the first two, it is evident that they have no determinate genus: whereas venial sin, taken in the third sense, can have a determinate genus, so that one sin may be venial generically, and another generically mortal, according as the genus or species of an act is determined by its object. For, when the will is directed to a thing that is in itself contrary to charity, whereby man is directed to his last end, the sin is mortal by reason of its object. Consequently it is a mortal sin generically, whether it be contrary to the love of God, e.g. blasphemy, perjury, and the like, or against the love of one's neighbor, e.g. murder, adultery, and such like: wherefore such sins are mortal by reason of their genus.—Sometimes, however, the sinner's will is directed to a thing containing a certain inordinateness, but which is not contrary to the love of God and one's neighbor, e.g. an idle word, excessive laughter, and so forth: and such sins are venial by reason of their genus.

Nevertheless, since moral acts derive their character of goodness and malice, not only from their objects, but also from some disposition of the agent, as stated above (Q. 18, AA. 4, 6), it happens sometimes that a sin which is venial generically by reason of its object, becomes mortal on the part of the agent, either because he fixes his last end therein, or because he directs it to something that is a mortal sin in its own genus; for example, if a man direct an idle word to the commission of adultery. In like manner it may happen, on the part of the agent, that a sin generically mortal becomes venial, by reason of the act being imperfect, i.e. not deliberated by reason, which is the proper principle of an evil act, as we have said above in reference to sudden movements of unbelief.

Reply Obj. 1. The very fact that anyone chooses something that is contrary to divine charity, proves that he prefers it to the love of God, and consequently, that he loves it more than he loves God. Hence it belongs to the genus of some sins, which are of themselves contrary to charity, that something is loved more than God; so that they are mortal by reason of their genus.

Reply Obj. 2. This argument considers those sins which are venial from their cause.

Reply Obj. 3. This argument considers those sins which are venial by reason of the imperfection of the act.

THIRD ARTICLE

Whether Venial Sin is a Disposition to Mortal Sin?

We proceed thus to the Third Article:—

Objection 1. It would seem that venial sin is not a disposition to mortal sin. For one contrary does not dispose to another. But venial and mortal sin are condivided as contrary to one another, as stated above (A. 1). Therefore venial sin is not a disposition to mortal sin.

Obj. 2. Further, an act disposes to something of like species, wherefore it is stated in *Ethic.* ii. 1, 2, that *from like acts like dispositions and habits are engendered.* But mortal and venial sin differ in genus or species, as stated above (A. 2). Therefore venial sin does not dispose to mortal sin.

Obj. 3. Further, if a sin is called venial because it disposes to mortal sin, it follows that whatever disposes to mortal sin is a venial sin. Now every good work disposes to mortal sin; wherefore Augustine says in his Rule

(*Ep.* ccxi) that *pride lies in wait for good works that it may destroy them.* Therefore even good works would be venial sins, which is absurd.

On the contrary, It is written (Ecclus. xix. 1): *He that contemneth small things shall fall by little and little.* Now he that sins venially seems to contemn small things. Therefore by little and little he is disposed to fall away altogether into mortal sin.

I answer that, A disposition is a kind of cause; wherefore as there is a twofold manner of cause, so is there a twofold manner of disposition. For there is a cause which moves directly to the production of the effect, as a hot thing heats: and there is a cause which moves indirectly, by removing an obstacle, as he who displaces a pillar is said to displace the stone that rests on it. Accordingly an act of sin disposes to something in two ways. First, directly, and thus it disposes to an act of like species. In this way, a sin generically venial does not, primarily and of its nature, dispose to a sin generically mortal, for they differ in species. Nevertheless, in this same way, a venial sin can dispose, by way of consequence, to a sin which is mortal on the part of the agent: because the disposition or habit may be so far strengthened by acts of venial sin, that the lust of sinning increases, and the sinner fixes his end in that venial sin: since the end for one who has a habit, as such, is to work according to that habit; and the consequence will be that, by sinning often venially, he becomes disposed to a mortal sin. Secondly, a human act disposes to something by removing an obstacle thereto. In this way a sin generically venial can dispose to a sin generically mortal. Because he that commits a sin generically venial, turns aside from some particular order; and through accustoming his will not to be subject to the due order in lesser matters, is disposed not to subject his will even to the order of the last end, by choosing something that is a mortal sin in its genus.

Reply Obj. 1. Venial and mortal sin are not condivided in contrariety to one another, as though they were species of one genus, as stated above (A. 1, *ad* 1), but as an accident is condivided with substance. Wherefore as an accident can be a disposition to a substantial form, so can a venial sin dispose to mortal.

Reply Obj. 2. Venial sin is not like mortal sin in species; but it is in genus, inasmuch as they both imply a defect of due order, albeit in different ways, as stated (AA. 1, 2).

Reply Obj. 3. A good work is not, of itself, a disposition to mortal sin; but it can be the matter or occasion of mortal sin accidentally; whereas a venial sin, of its very nature, disposes to mortal sin, as stated.

FOURTH ARTICLE

Whether a Venial Sin Can Become Mortal?

We proceed thus to the Fourth Article:—

Objection 1. It would seem that a venial sin can become a mortal sin. For Augustine in explaining the words of Jo. iii. 36, *He that believeth not the Son, shall not see life,* says (*Tract.* xii *in Joan.*): *The slightest, i.e.* venial, *sins kill if we make little of them.* Now a sin is called mortal through causing the spiritual death of the soul. Therefore a venial sin can become mortal.

Obj. 2. Further, a movement in the sensuality before the consent of reason, is a venial sin, but after consent, is a mortal sin, as stated above (Q. 74, A. 8, *ad* 2). Therefore a venial sin can become mortal.

Obj. 3. Further, venial and mortal sin differ as curable and incurable disease, as stated above (A. 1). But a curable disease may become incurable. Therefore a venial sin may become mortal.

Obj. 4. Further, a disposition may become a habit. Now venial sin is a disposition to mortal, as stated (A. 3). Therefore a venial sin can become mortal.

On the contrary, Things that differ infinitely are not changed into one another. Now venial and mortal sin differ infinitely, as is evident from what has been said above (Q. 72, A. 5, *ad* 1; Q. 87, A. 5, *ad* 1). Therefore a venial sin cannot become mortal.

I answer that, The fact of a venial sin becoming a mortal sin may be understood in three ways. First, so that the same identical act be at first a venial, and then a mortal sin. This is impossible: because a sin, like any moral act, consists chiefly in an act of the will: so that an act is not one morally, if the will be changed, although the act be continuous physically. If, however, the will be not changed, it is not possible for a venial sin to become mortal.

Secondly, this may be taken to mean that a sin generically venial, becomes mortal. This is possible, in so far as one may fix one's end in that venial sin, or direct it to some mortal sin as end, as stated above (A. 2).

Thirdly, this may be understood in the sense of many venial sins constituting one mortal sin. If this be taken as meaning that many venial sins added together make one mortal sin, it is false, because all the venial sins in the world cannot incur a debt of punishment equal to that of one mortal sin. This is evident as regards the duration of the punishment, since mortal sin incurs a debt of eternal punishment, while venial sin incurs a debt of temporal punishment, as stated above (Q. 87,

* See Q. 74, A. 6.

AA. 3, 5).—It is also evident as regards the pain of loss, because mortal sins deserve to be punished by the privation of seeing God, to which no other punishment is comparable, as Chrysostom states (*Hom.* xxiv *in Matth.*). —It is also evident as regards the pain of sense, as to the remorse of conscience; although as to the pain of fire, the punishments may perhaps not be improportionate to one another.

If, however, this be taken as meaning that many venial sins make one mortal sin dispositively, it is true, as was shown above (A. 3) with regard to the two different manners of disposition, whereby venial sin disposes to mortal sin.

Reply Obj. 1. Augustine is referring to the fact of many venial sins making one mortal sin dispositively.

Reply Obj. 2. The very same movement of the sensuality which preceded the consent of reason can never become a mortal sin; but the movement of the reason in consenting is a mortal sin.

Reply Obj. 3. Disease of the body is not an act, but an abiding disposition; wherefore, while remaining the same disease, it may undergo change. On the other hand, venial sin is a transient act, which cannot be taken up again: so that in this respect the comparison fails.

Reply Obj. 4. A disposition that becomes a habit, is like an imperfect thing in the same species; thus imperfect science, by being perfected, becomes a habit. On the other hand, venial sin is a disposition to something differing generically, even as an accident which disposes to a substantial form, into which it is never changed.

FIFTH ARTICLE

Whether a Circumstance Can Make a Venial Sin to Be Mortal?

We proceed thus to the Fifth Article:—

Objection 1. It would seem that a circumstance can make a venial sin mortal. For Augustine says in a sermon on Purgatory (*De Sanctis,* serm. xli) that *if anger continue for a long time, or if drunkenness be frequent, they become mortal sins.* But anger and drunkenness are not mortal but venial sins generically, else they would always be mortal sins. Therefore a circumstance makes a venial sin to be mortal.

Obj. 2. Further, the Master says (*2 Sentent.,* D. xxiv) that delectation, if morose,* is a mortal sin, but that if it be not morose, it is a venial sin. Now moroseness is a circumstance. Therefore a circumstance makes a venial sin to be mortal.

Obj. 3. Further, evil and good differ more than venial and mortal sin, both of which are generically evil. But a circumstance makes a good act to be evil, as when a man gives an alms for vainglory. Much more, therefore, can it make a venial sin to be mortal.

On the contrary, Since a circumstance is an accident, its quantity cannot exceed that of the act itself, derived from the act's genus, because the subject always excels its accident. If, therefore, an act be venial by reason of its genus, it cannot become mortal by reason of an accident: since, in a way, mortal sin infinitely surpasses the quantity of venial sin, as is evident from what has been said (Q. 72, A. 5, *ad* 1; Q. 87, A. 5, *ad* 1).

I answer that, As stated above (Q. 7, A. 1; Q. 18, A. 5, *ad* 4; AA. 10, 11), when we were treating of circumstances, a circumstance, as such, is an accident of the moral act: and yet a circumstance may happen to be taken as the specific difference of a moral act, and then it loses its nature of circumstance, and constitutes the species of the moral act. This happens in sins when a circumstance adds the deformity of another genus; thus when a man has knowledge of another woman than his wife, the deformity of his act is opposed to chastity; but if this other be another man's wife, there is an additional deformity opposed to justice which forbids one to take what belongs to another; and accordingly this circumstance constitutes a new species of sin known as adultery.

It is, however, impossible for a circumstance to make a venial sin become mortal, unless it adds the deformity of another species. For it has been stated above (A 1) that the deformity of a venial sin consists in a disorder affecting things that are referred to the end, whereas the deformity of a mortal sin consists in a disorder about the last end. Consequently it is evident that a circumstance cannot make a venial sin to be mortal, so long as it remains a circumstance, but only when it transfers the sin to another species, and becomes, as it were, the specific difference of the moral act.

Reply Obj. 1 Length of time is not a circumstance that draws a sin to another species, nor is frequency or custom, except perhaps by something accidental supervening. For an action does not acquire a new species through being repeated or prolonged, unless by chance something supervene in the repeated or prolonged act to change its species, e.g. disobedience, contempt, or the like.

We must therefore reply to the objection by saying that since anger is a movement of the soul tending to the hurt of one's neighbor, if the angry movement tend to a hurt which is a mortal sin generically, such as murder or robbery, that anger will be a mortal sin generically: and if it be a venial sin, this will be due to the imperfection of the act, in so far as it is a sudden movement of the sensuality: whereas, if it last a long time, it returns to its generic nature, through the consent of reason.—If, on the other hand, the hurt to which the angry movement tends, is a sin generically venial, for instance, if a man be angry with someone, so as to wish to say some trifling word in jest that would hurt him a little, the anger will not be a mortal sin, however long it last, unless perhaps accidentally; for instance, if it were to give rise to great scandal or something of the kind.

With regard to drunkenness we reply that it is a mortal sin by reason of its genus; for, that a man, without necessity, and through the mere lust of wine, make himself unable to use his reason, whereby he is directed to God and avoids committing many sins, is expressly contrary to virtue. That it be a venial sin, is due to some sort of ignorance or weakness, as when a man is ignorant of the strength of the wine, or of his own unfitness, so that he has no thought of getting drunk, for in that case the drunkenness is not imputed to him as a sin, but only the excessive drink. If, however, he gets drunk frequently, this ignorance no longer avails as an excuse, for his will seems to choose to give way to drunkenness rather than to refrain from excess of wine: wherefore the sin returns to its specific nature.

Reply Obj. 2. Morose delectation is not a mortal sin except in those matters which are mortal sins generically. In such matters, if the delectation be not morose, there is a venial sin through imperfection of the act, as we have said with regard to anger (*ad* 1): because anger is said to be lasting, and delectation to be morose, on account of the approval of the deliberating reason.

Reply Obj. 3. A circumstance does not make a good act to be evil, unless it constitute the species of a sin, as we have stated above (Q. 18, A. 5, *ad* 4).

SIXTH ARTICLE

Whether a Mortal Sin Can Become Venial?

We proceed thus to the Sixth Article:—

Objection 1. It would seem that a mortal sin can become venial. Because venial sin is equally distant from mortal, as mortal sin is from venial. But a venial sin can become mortal, as stated above (A. 5). Therefore also a mortal sin can become venial.

Obj. 2. Further, venial and mortal sin are said to differ in this, that he who sins mortally loves a creature more than God, while he who sins venially loves the creature less than God. Now it may happen that a person in committing a sin generically mortal, loves a creature less than God; for instance, if anyone being ignorant that simple fornication is a mortal sin, and contrary to the love of God, commits the sin of fornication, yet so as to be ready, for the love of God, to refrain from that sin if he knew that by committing it he was acting counter to the love of God. Therefore his will be a venial sin; and accordingly a mortal sin can become venial.

Obj. 3. Further, as stated above (A. 5, *Obj.* 3), good is more distant from evil, than venial from mortal sin. But an act which is evil in itself, can become good; thus to kill a man may be an act of justice, as when a judge condemns a thief to death. Much more therefore can a mortal sin become venial.

On the contrary, An eternal thing can never become temporal. But mortal sin deserves eternal punishment, whereas venial sin deserves temporal punishment. Therefore a mortal sin can never become venial.

I answer that, Venial and mortal differ as perfect and imperfect in the genus of sin, as stated above (A. 1, *ad* 1). Now the imperfect can become perfect, by some sort of addition: and, consequently, a venial sin can become mortal, by the addition of some deformity pertaining to the genus of mortal sin, as when a man utters an idle word for the purpose of fornication. On the other hand, the perfect cannot become imperfect, by addition; and so a mortal sin cannot become venial, by the addition of a deformity pertaining to the genus of venial sin, for the sin is not diminished if a man commit fornication in order to utter an idle word; rather is it aggravated by the additional deformity.

Nevertheless a sin which is generically mortal, can become venial by reason of the imperfection of the act, because then it does not completely fulfil the conditions of a moral act, since it is not a deliberate, but a sudden act, as is evident from what we have said above (A. 2). This happens by a kind of subtraction, namely, of deliberate reason. And since a moral act takes its species from deliberate reason, the result is that by such a subtraction the species of the act is destroyed.

Reply Obj. 1. Venial differs from mortal as imperfect from perfect, even as a boy differs from a man. But the boy becomes a man and not vice versa. Hence the argument does not prove.

Reply Obj. 2. If the ignorance be such as to excuse sin altogether, as the ignorance of a madman or an imbecile, then he that commits fornication in a state of such like ignorance, commits no sin either mortal or venial. But if the ignorance be not invincible, then the ignorance itself is a sin, and contains within itself the lack of the love of God, in so far as a man neglects to learn those things whereby he can safeguard himself in the love of God.

Reply Obj. 3. As Augustine says (*Contra Mendacium* vii), *those things which are evil in themselves, cannot be well done for any good end.* Now murder is the slaying of the innocent, and this can nowise be well done. But, as Augustine states (*De Lib. Arb.* i. 4, 5), the judge who sentences a thief to death, or the soldier who slays the enemy of the common weal, are not murderers.

QUESTION 89

Of Venial Sin in Itself

(In Six Articles)

We must now consider venial sin in itself, and under this head there are six points of inquiry: (1) Whether venial sin causes a stain in the soul? (2) Of the different kinds of venial sin, as denoted by *wood, hay, stubble* (1 Cor. iii. 12); (3) Whether man could sin venially in the state of innocence? (4) Whether a good or a wicked angel can sin venially? (5) Whether the movements of unbelievers are venial sins? (6) Whether venial sin can be in a man with original sin alone?

FIRST ARTICLE

Whether Venial Sin Causes a Stain in the Soul?

We proceed thus to the First Article:—

Objection 1. It would seem that venial sin causes a stain in the soul. For Augustine says (*De Pœnit.*),* that if venial sins be multiplied, they destroy the beauty of our souls so as to deprive us of the embraces of our heavenly spouse. But the stain of sin is nothing else but the loss of the soul's beauty. Therefore venial sins cause a stain in the soul.

Obj. 2. Further, mortal sin causes a stain in the soul, on account of the inordinateness of the act and of the sinner's affections. But, in venial sin, there is an inordinateness of the act and of the affections. Therefore venial sin causes a stain in the soul.

Obj. 3. Further, the stain on the soul is caused by contact with a temporal thing,

* *Hom.* 50 *inter L., 2.*

through love thereof, as stated above (Q. 86, A. 1). But, in venial sin, the soul is in contact with a temporal thing through inordinate love. Therefore venial sin brings a stain on the soul.

On the contrary, It is written (*Eph.* v. 27): *That He might present it to Himself a glorious church, not having spot or wrinkle,* on which the gloss says: *i.e. some grievous sin.* Therefore it seems proper to mortal sin to cause a stain in the soul.

I answer that, As stated above (Q. 86, A. 1), a stain denotes a loss of comeliness due to contact with something, as may be seen in corporeal matters, from which the term has been transferred to the soul, by way of similitude. Now just as in the body there is a twofold comeliness, one resulting from the inward disposition of the members and colors, the other resulting from outward refulgence supervening, so too, in the soul, there is a twofold comeliness one habitual, and, so to speak, intrinsic, the other, actual, like an outward flash of light. Now venial sin is a hindrance to actual comeliness, but not to habitual comeliness, because it neither destroys nor diminishes the habit of charity and of the other virtues, as we shall show further on (II-II, Q. 24, A. 10; Q. 133, A. 1 *ad* 2), but only hinders their acts. On the other hand, a stain denotes something permanent in the thing stained, wherefore it seems in the nature of a loss of habitual rather than of actual comeliness. Therefore, properly speaking, venial sin does not cause a stain in the soul. If, however, we find it stated anywhere that it does induce a stain, this is in a restricted sense, in so far as it hinders the comeliness that results from acts of virtue.

Reply Obj. 1. Augustine is speaking of the case in which many venial sins lead to mortal sin dispositively: because otherwise they would not sever the soul from the embrace of its heavenly spouse.

Reply Obj. 2. In mortal sin, the inordinateness of the act destroys the habit of virtue, but not in venial sin.

Reply Obj. 3. In mortal sin the soul comes into contact with a temporal thing as its end, so that the shedding of the light of grace, which accrues to those who, by charity, cleave to God as their last end, is entirely cut off. On the contrary, in venial sin, man does not cleave to a creature as his last end: hence there is no comparison.

SECOND ARTICLE

Whether Venial Sins Are Suitably Designated As "Wood, Hay, and Stubble"?

We proceed thus to the Second Article:—
Objection 1. It would seem that venial sins

are unsuitably designated as *wood, hay,* and *stubble* (1 Cor. iii. 12). Because wood, hay, and stubble are said (*ibid.*) to be built on a spiritual foundation. Now venial sins are something outside a spiritual foundation, even as false opinions are outside the pale of science. Therefore venial sins are not suitably designated as wood, hay, and stubble.

Obj. 2. Further, he who builds wood, hay, and stubble, *shall be saved yet so as by fire* (*verse* 15). But sometimes the man who commits a venial sin, will not be saved, even by fire, e.g. when a man dies in mortal sin to which venial sins are attached. Therefore venial sins are unsuitably designated by wood, hay, and stubble.

Obj. 3. Further, according to the Apostle (*verse* 12) those who build *gold, silver, precious stones,* i.e., love of God and our neighbor, and good works, are others from those who build wood, hay, stubble. But those even who love God and their neighbor, and do good works, commit venial sins: for it is written (1 Jo. i. 8): *If we say that we have no sin, we deceive ourselves.* Therefore venial sins are not suitably designated by these three.

Obj. 4. Further, there are many more than three differences and degrees of venial sins. Therefore they are unsuitably comprised under these three.

On the contrary, The Apostle says (1 Cor. iii. 15) that the man who builds up wood, hay, stubble, *shall be saved yet so as by fire,* so that he will suffer punishment, but not everlasting. Now the debt of temporal punishment belongs properly to venial sin, as stated above (Q. 87, A. 5). Therefore these three signify venial sins.

I answer that, Some have understood the *foundation* to be dead faith, upon which some build good works, signified by gold, silver, and precious stones, while others build mortal sins, which according to them are designated by wood, hay, and stubble. But Augustine disapproves of this explanation (*De Fide et Oper.* xv), because, as the Apostle says (Gal. v 21), he who does the works of the flesh, *shall not obtain the kingdom of God,* which signifies to be saved; whereas the Apostle says that he who builds wood, hay, and stubble *shall be saved yet so as by fire.* Consequently wood, hay, stubble cannot be understood to denote mortal sins.

Others say that wood, hay, stubble designate good works, which are indeed built upon the spiritual edifice, but are mixed with venial sins: as, when a man is charged with the care of a family, which is a good thing, excessive love of his wife, or of his children or of his possessions insinuates itself into his life, under

God however, so that, to wit, for the sake of these things he would be unwilling to do anything in opposition to God.—But neither does this seem to be reasonable. For it is evident that all good works are referred to the love of God, and one's neighbor, wherefore they are designated by *gold, silver,* and *precious stones,* and consequently not by *wood, hay,* and *stubble.*

We must therefore say that the very venial sins that insinuate themselves into those who have a care for earthly things, are designated by wood, hay, and stubble. For just as these are stored in a house, without belonging to the substance of the house, and can be burnt, while the house is saved, so also venial sins are multiplied in a man, while the spiritual edifice remains, and for them, man suffers fire, either of temporal trials in this life, or of purgatory after this life, and yet he is saved for ever.

Reply Obj. 1. Venial sins are not said to be built upon the spiritual foundation, as though they were laid directly upon it, but because they are laid beside it; in the same sense as it is written (Ps. cxxxvi. 1): *Upon the waters of Babylon,* i.e. *beside the waters:* because venial sins do not destroy the spiritual edifice.

Reply Obj. 2. It is not said that everyone who builds wood, hay, and stubble, shall be saved as by fire, but only those who build *upon the foundation.* And this foundation is not dead faith, as some have esteemed, but faith quickened by charity, according to Eph. iii. 17: *Rooted and founded in charity.* Accordingly, he that dies in mortal sin with venial sins, has indeed wood, hay, and stubble, but not built upon the spiritual edifice; and consequently he will not be saved so as by fire.

Reply Obj. 3. Although those who are withdrawn from the care of temporal things, sin venially sometimes, yet they commit but slight venial sins, and in most cases they are cleansed by the fervor of charity: wherefore they do not build up venial sins, because these do not remain long in them. But the venial sins of those who are busy about earthly things remain longer, because they are unable to have such frequent recourse to the fervor of charity in order to remove them.

Reply Obj. 4. As the Philosopher says (*De Cœlo* i, text. 2), *all things are comprised under three, the beginning, the middle, and the end.* Accordingly all degrees of venial sins are reduced to three, viz. to *wood,* which remains longer in the fire; *stubble,* which is burnt up at once; and *hay,* which is between these two: because venial sins are removed by fire, quickly or slowly, according as man is more or less attached to them.

Whether Man Could Commit a Venial Sin in the State of Innocence?

We proceed thus to the Third Article:—

Objection 1. It would seem that man could commit a venial sin in the state of innocence. Because on 1 Tim. ii. 14, *Adam was not seduced,* a gloss says: *Having no experience of God's severity, it was possible for him to be so mistaken as to think that what he had done was a venial sin.* But he would not have thought this unless he could have committed a venial sin. Therefore he could commit a venial sin without sinning mortally.

Obj. 2. Further, Augustine says (*Gen. ad lit.* xi. 5): *We must not suppose that the tempter would have overcome man, unless first of all there had arisen in man's soul a movement of vainglory which should have been checked.* Now the vainglory which preceded man's defeat, which was accomplished through his falling into mortal sin, could be nothing more than a venial sin.—In like manner, Augustine says (*ibid.*) that *man was allured by a certain desire of making the experiment, when he saw that the woman did not die when she had taken the forbidden fruit.*—Again there seems to have been a certain movement of unbelief in Eve, since she doubted what the Lord had said, as appears from her saying (Gen. iii. 3): *Lest perhaps we die.* Now these apparently were venial sins. Therefore man could commit a venial sin before he committed a mortal sin.

Obj. 3. Further, mortal sin is more opposed to the integrity of the original state, than venial sin is. Now man could sin mortally notwithstanding the integrity of the original state. Therefore he could also sin venially.

On the contrary, Every sin deserves some punishment. But nothing penal was possible in the state of innocence, as Augustine declares (*De Civ. Dei* xiv. 10). Therefore he could not commit a sin that would not deprive him of that state of integrity. But venial sin does not change man's state. Therefore he could not sin venially.

I answer that, It is generally admitted that man could not commit a venial sin in the state of innocence. This, however, is not to be understood as though on account of the perfection of his state, the sin which is venial for us would have been mortal for him, if he had committed it. Because the dignity of a person is a circumstance that aggravates a sin, but it does not transfer it to another species, unless there be an additional deformity by reason of disobedience, or vow or the like, which does not apply to the question in point. Consequently what is venial in itself could not be changed into mortal by reason of the excellence of the original state. We must therefore understand this to mean that he could not sin venially, because it was impossible for him to commit a sin which was venial in itself, before losing the integrity of the original state by sinning mortally.

The reason for this is because venial sin occurs in us, either through the imperfection of the act, as in the case of sudden movements, in a genus of mortal sin or through some inordinateness in respect of things referred to the end, the due order to the end being safeguarded. Now each of these happens on account of some defect of order, by reason of the lower powers not being checked by the higher. Because the sudden rising of a movement of the sensuality in us is due to the sensuality not being perfectly subject to reason: and the sudden rising of a movement in the reason itself is due, in us, to the fact that the execution of the act of reason is not subject to the act of deliberation which proceeds from a higher good, as stated above (Q. 74, A. 10); and that the human mind be out of order as regards things directed to the end, the due order to the end being safeguarded, is due to the fact that the things referred to the end are not infallibly directed under the end, which holds the highest place, being the beginning, as it were, in matters concerning the appetite, as stated above (Q. 10, AA. 1, 2, *ad 3*; Q. 72, A. 5). Now, in the state of innocence, as stated in the First Part (Q. 95, A. 1), there was an unerring stability of order, so that the lower powers were always subjected to the higher, so long as man remained subject to God, as Augustine says (*De Civ. Dei* xiv. 13). Hence there could be no inordinateness in man, unless first of all the highest part of man were not subject to God, which constitutes a mortal sin. From this it is evident that, in the state of innocence, man could not commit a venial sin, before committing a mortal sin.

Reply Obj. 1. In the passage quoted, venial is not taken in the same sense as we take it now; but by venial sin we mean that which is easily forgiven.

Reply Obj. 2. This vainglory which preceded man's downfall, was his first mortal sin, for it is stated to have preceded his downfall into the outward act of sin. This vainglory was followed, in the man, by the desire to make an experiment, and, in the woman, by doubt, for she gave way to vainglory, merely through hearing the serpent mention the precept, as though she refused to be held in check by the precept.

Reply Obj. 3. Mortal sin is opposed to the integrity of the original state in the fact of its destroying that state: this a venial sin cannot do. And because the integrity of the primitive state is incompatible with any inordinateness whatever, the result is that the first man could not sin venially, before committing a mortal sin.

FOURTH ARTICLE

Whether a Good or a Wicked Angel Can Sin Venially?

We proceed thus to the Fourth Article:—

Objection 1. It would seem that a good or a wicked angel can sin venially. Because man agrees with the angels, in the higher part of his soul which is called the mind, according to Gregory, who says (*Hom.* xxix *in Ev.*) that *man understands in common with the angels.* But man can commit a venial sin in the higher part of his soul. Therefore an angel can commit a venial sin also.

Obj. 2. Further, He that can do more, can do less. But an angel could love a created good more than God, and he did, by sinning mortally. Therefore he could also love a creature less than God inordinately, by sinning venially.

Obj. 3. Further, wicked angels seem to do certain things which are venial sins generically, by provoking man to laughter, and other like frivolities. Now the circumstance of the person does not make a mortal sin to be venial, as stated above (A. 3), unless there be a special prohibition, which is not the case in point. Therefore an angel can sin venially.

On the contrary, The perfection of an angel is greater than that of man in the primitive state. But man could not sin venially in the primitive state, and much less, therefore, can an angel.

I answer that, An angel's intellect, as stated in the First Part (Q. 58, A. 3; Q. 79, A. 8), is not discursive, i.e. it does not proceed from principles to conclusions, so as to understand both separately, as we do. Consequently, whenever the angelic intellect considers a conclusion, it must, of necessity, consider it in its principles. Now in matters of appetite, as we have often stated (Q. 8, A. 2; Q. 10, A. 1; Q. 72, A. 5), ends are like principles, while the means are like conclusions. Wherefore an angel's mind is not directed to the means, except as they stand under the order to the end. Consequently, from their very nature, they can have no inordinateness in respect of the means, unless at the same time they have an inordinateness in respect of the end, and this is a mortal sin. Now good angels are not moved to the means, except in subordination to the due end which is God: wherefore all their actions are acts of charity, so that no venial sin can be in them. On the other hand, wicked angels are moved to nothing except in subordination to the end which is their sin of pride. Therefore they sin mortally in everything that they do of their own will.—This does not apply to the appetite for the natural good, which appetite we have stated to be in them P. I, Q. 63, A. 4; Q. 64, A. 2 *ad* 5).

Reply Obj. 1. Man does indeed agree with the angels in the mind or intellect, but he differs in his mode of understanding, as stated above.

Reply Obj. 2. An angel could not love a creature less than God, without, at the same time, either referring it to God, as the last end, or to some inordinate end, for the reason given above.

Reply Obj. 3. The demons incite man to all such things which seem to be venial, that he may become used to them, so as to lead him on to mortal sin. Consequently in all such things they sin mortally, on account of the end they have in view.

FIFTH ARTICLE

Whether the First Movements of the Sensuality in Unbelievers Are Mortal Sins?

We proceed thus to the Fifth Article:—

Objection 1. It would seem that the first movements of the sensuality in unbelievers are mortal sins. For the Apostle says (Rom. viii. 1) that *there is . . . no condemnation to them that are in Christ Jesus, who walk not according to the flesh:* and he is speaking there of the concupiscence of the sensuality, as appears from the context (ch. vii). Therefore the reason why concupiscence is not a matter of condemnation to those who walk not according to the flesh, i.e. by consenting to concupiscence, is because they are in Christ Jesus. But unbelievers are not in Christ Jesus. Therefore in unbelievers this is a matter of condemnation. Therefore the first movements of unbelievers are mortal sins.

Obj. 2. Further, Anselm says (*De Gratia et Lib. Arb.* vii): *Those who are not in Christ, when they feel the sting of the flesh, follow the road of damnation, even if they walk not according to the flesh.* But damnation is not due save to mortal sin. Therefore, since man feels the sting of the flesh in the first movements of concupiscence, it seems that the first movements of concupiscence in unbelievers are mortal sins.

Obj. 3. Further, Anselm says (*ibid.*): *Man was so made that he was not liable to feel concupiscence.* Now this liability seems to be remitted to man by the grace of Baptism, which the unbeliever has not. Therefore every act of concupiscence in an unbeliever, even

without his consent, is a mortal sin, because he acts against his duty.

On the contrary, It is stated in Acts x. 34 that *God is not a respecter of persons.* Therefore He does not impute to one unto condemnation, what He does not impute to another. But He does not impute first movements to believers, unto condemnation. Neither therefore does He impute them to unbelievers.

I answer that, It is unreasonable to say that the first movements of unbelievers are mortal sins, when they do not consent to them. This is evident for two reasons. First, because the sensuality itself cannot be the subject of mortal sin, as stated above (Q. 79, A. 4). Now the sensuality has the same nature in unbelievers as in believers. Therefore it is not possible for the mere movements of the sensuality in unbelievers, to be mortal sins.

Secondly, from the state of the sinner. Because excellence of the person never diminishes sin, but, on the contrary, increases it, as stated above (Q. 73, A. 10). Therefore a sin is not less grievous in a believer than in an unbeliever, but much more so. For the sins of an unbeliever are more deserving of forgiveness, on account of their ignorance, according to 1 Tim. i. 13: *I obtained the mercy of God, because I did it ignorantly in* my *unbelief:* whereas the sins of believers are more grievous on account of the sacraments of grace, according to Heb. x. 29: *How much more, do you think, he deserveth worse punishments . . . who hath esteemed the blood of the testament unclean, by which he was sanctified?*

Reply Obj. 1. The Apostle is speaking of the condemnation due to original sin, which condemnation is remitted by the grace of Jesus Christ, although the *fomes* of concupiscence remain. Wherefore the fact that believers are subject to concupiscence is not in them a sign of the condemnation due to original sin, as it is in unbelievers.

In this way also is to be understood the saying of Anselm, wherefore the Reply to the Second Objection is evident.

Reply Obj. 3. This freedom from liability to concupiscence was a result of original justice. Wherefore that which is opposed to such liability pertains, not to actual but to original sin.

SIXTH ARTICLE

Whether Venial Sin Can Be in Anyone with Original Sin Alone?

We proceed thus to the Sixth Article:—

Objection 1. It would seem that venial sin can be in a man with original sin alone. For disposition precedes habit. Now venial sin is a disposition to mortal sin, as stated above

(Q. 88, A. 3). Therefore in an unbeliever, in whom original sin is not remitted, venial sin exists before mortal sin: and so sometimes unbelievers have venial together with original sin, and without mortal sins.

Obj. 2. Further, venial sin has less in common, and less connection with mortal sin, than one mortal sin has with another. But an unbeliever in the state of original sin, can commit one mortal sin without committing another. Therefore he can also commit a venial sin without committing a mortal sin.

Obj. 3. Further, it is possible to fix the time at which a child is first able to commit an actual sin: and when the child comes to that time, it can stay a short time at least, without committing a mortal sin, because this happens in the worst criminals. Now it is possible for the child to sin venially during that space of time, however short it may be. Therefore venial sin can be in anyone with original sin alone and without mortal sin.

On the contrary, Man is punished for original sin in the children's limbo, where there is no pain of sense, as we shall state further on (Suppl., Q. 69, A. 6): whereas men are punished in hell for no other than mortal sin. Therefore there will be no place where a man can be punished for venial sin with no other than original sin.

I answer that, It is impossible for venial sin to be in anyone with original sin alone, and without mortal sin. The reason for this is because before a man comes to the age of discretion, the lack of years hinders the use of reason and excuses him from mortal sin, wherefore, much more does it excuse him from venial sin, if he does anything which is such

generically. But when he begins to have the use of reason, he is not entirely excused from the guilt of venial or mortal sin. Now the first thing that occurs to a man to think about then, is to deliberate about himself. And if he then direct himself to the due end, he will, by means of grace, receive the remission of original sin: whereas if he does not then direct himself to the due end, as far as he is capable of discretion at that particular age, he will sin mortally, through not doing that which is in his power to do. Accordingly thenceforward there cannot be venial sin in him without mortal, until afterwards all sin shall have been remitted to him through grace.

Reply Obj. 1. Venial sin precedes mortal sin not as a necessary, but as a contingent disposition, just as work sometimes disposes to fever, but not as heat disposes to the form of fire.

Reply Obj. 2. Venial sin is prevented from being with original sin alone, not on account of its want of connection or likeness, but on account of the lack of use of reason, as stated above.

Reply Obj. 3. The child that is beginning to have the use of reason can refrain from other mortal sins for a time, but it is not free from the aforesaid sin of omission, unless it turn to God as soon as possible. For the first thing that occurs to a man who has discretion, is to think of himself, and to direct other things to himself as to their end, since the end is the first thing in the intention. Therefore this is the time when man is bound by God's affirmative precept, which the Lord expressed by saying (Zach. i. 3): *Turn ye to Me ... and I will turn to you.*

ON LAW—THE EXTRINSIC PRINCIPLES OF HUMAN ACTS

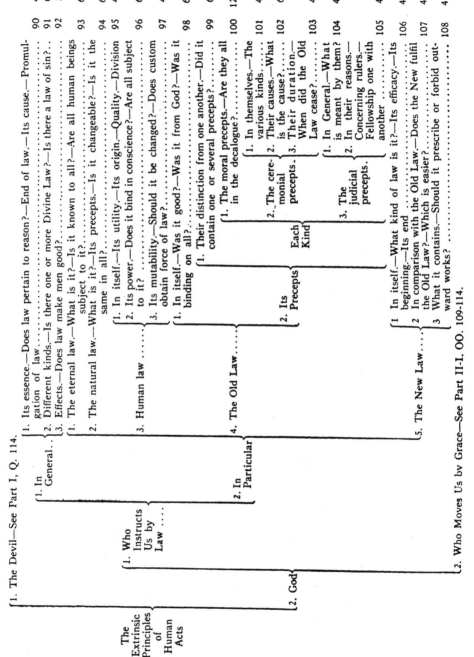

TREATISE ON LAW

QUESTION 90

Of the Essence of Law

(In Four Articles)

WE have now to consider the extrinsic principles of acts. Now the extrinsic principle inclining to evil is the devil, of whose temptations we have spoken in the First Part (Q. 114). But the extrinsic principle moving to good is God, Who both instructs us by means of His Law, and assists us by His Grace: wherefore in the first place we must speak of law; in the second place, of grace.

Concerning law, we must consider—(1) Law itself in general; (2) its parts. Concerning law in general three points offer themselves for our consideration: (1) Its essence; (2) The different kinds of law; (3) The effects of law.

Under the first head there are four points of inquiry: (1) Whether law is something pertaining to reason? (2) Concerning the end of law; (3) Its cause; (4) The promulgation of law.

FIRST ARTICLE

Whether Law Is Something Pertaining to Reason?

We proceed thus to the First Article:—

Objection 1. It would seem that law is not something pertaining to reason. For the Apostle says (Rom. vii. 23): *I see another law in my members,* etc. But nothing pertaining to reason is in the members; since the reason does not make use of a bodily organ. Therefore law is not something pertaining to reason.

Obj. 2. Further, in the reason there is nothing else but power, habit, and act. But law is not the power itself of reason. In like manner, neither is it a habit of reason: because the habits of reason are the intellectual virtues of which we have spoken above (Q. 57). Nor again is it an act of reason: because then law would cease, when the act of reason ceases, for instance, while we are asleep. Therefore law is nothing pertaining to reason.

Obj. 3. Further, the law moves those who are subject to it to act aright. But it belongs properly to the will to move to act, as is evident from what has been said above (Q. 9, A. 1). Therefore law pertains, not to the reason, but to the will; according to the words of the Jurist (*Lib.* i. *ff.*, *De Const. Prin.* leg. i): *Whatsoever pleaseth the sovereign, has force of law.*

On the contrary, It belongs to the law to command and to forbid. But it belongs to reason to command, as stated above (Q. 17, A. 1). Therefore law is something pertaining to reason.

I answer that, Law is a rule and measure of acts, whereby man is induced to act or is restrained from acting: for *lex* (law) is derived from *ligare* (to bind), because it binds one to act. Now the rule and measure of human acts is the reason, which is the first principle of human acts, as is evident from what has been stated above (Q. 1, A. 1 *ad* 3); since it belongs to the reason to direct to the end, which is the first principle in all matters of action, according to the Philosopher (*Phys.* ii). Now that which is the principle in any genus, is the rule and measure of that genus: for instance, unity in the genus of numbers, and the first movement in the genus of movements. Consequently it follows that law is something pertaining to reason.

Reply Obj. 1. Since law is a kind of rule and measure, it may be in something in two ways. First, as in that which measures and rules: and since this is proper to reason, it follows that, in this way, law is in the reason alone.—Secondly, as in that which is measured and ruled. In this way, law is in all those things that are inclined to something by reason of some law: so that any inclination arising from a law, may be called a law, not essentially but by participation as it were. And thus the inclination of the members to concupiscence is called *the law of the members.*

Reply Obj. 2. Just as, in external action, we may consider the work and the work done, for instance the work of building and the house built; so in the acts of reason, we may consider the act itself of reason, i.e., to understand and to reason, and something produced by this act. With regard to the speculative reason, this is first of all the definition; secondly, the proposition; thirdly, the syllogism or argument. And since also the practical reason makes use of a syllogism in respect of the work to be done, as stated above (Q. 13, A. 3; Q. 76, A. 1) and as the Philosopher teaches (*Ethic.* vii. 3); hence we find in the practical reason something that holds the same position in regard to operations, as, in the speculative intellect, the proposition holds in regard to conclusions. Such like universal propositions of the practical intellect that are directed to actions have the nature of law. And these propositions are sometimes under our actual consideration, while sometimes they are retained in the reason by means of a habit.

Reply Obj. 3. Reason has its power of moving from the will, as stated above (Q. 17, A. 1): for it is due to the fact that one wills the end, that the reason issues its commands as regards things ordained to the end. But in order that the volition of what is commanded may have the nature of law, it needs to be in accord with some rule of reason. And in this sense is to be understood the saying that the will of the sovereign has the force of law; otherwise the sovereign's will would savor of lawlessness rather than of law.

SECOND ARTICLE

Whether the Law Is Always Something Directed to the Common Good?

We proceed thus to the Second Article:—

Objection 1. It would seem that the law is not always directed to the common good as to its end. For it belongs to law to command and to forbid. But commands are directed to certain individual goods. Therefore the end of the law is not always the common good.

Obj. 2. Further, the law directs man in his actions. But human actions are concerned with particular matters. Therefore the law is directed to some particular good.

Obj. 3. Further, Isidore says (*Etym.* v. 3): *If the law is based on reason, whatever is based on reason will be a law.* But reason is the foundation not only of what is ordained to the common good, but also of that which is directed to private good. Therefore the law Is not only directed to the good of all, but also to the private good of an individual.

On the contrary, Isidore says (*Etym.* v. 21) that *laws are enacted for no private profit, but for the common benefit of the citizens.*

I answer that, As stated above (A. 1), the law belongs to that which is a principle of human acts, because it is their rule and measure. Now as reason is a principle of human acts, so in reason itself there is something which is the principle in respect of all the rest: wherefore to this principle chiefly and mainly law must needs be referred.—Now the first principle in practical matters, which are the object of the practical reason, is the last end: and the last end of human life is bliss or happiness, as stated above (Q. 2, A. 7; Q. 3, A. 1). Consequently the law must needs regard principally the relationship to happiness. Moreover, since every part is ordained to the whole, as imperfect to perfect; and since one man is a part of the perfect community, the law must needs regard properly the relationship to universal happiness. Wherefore the

Philosopher, in the above definition of legal matters mentions both happiness and the body politic: for he says (*Ethic.* v. 1) that we call those legal matters *just, which are adapted to produce and preserve happiness and its parts for the body politic:* since the state is a perfect community, as he says in *Polit.* i. 1.

Now in every genus, that which belongs to it chiefly is the principle of the others, and the others belong to that genus in subordination to that thing: thus fire, which is chief among hot things, is the cause of heat in mixed bodies, and these are said to be hot in so far as they have a share of fire. Consequently, since the law is chiefly ordained to the common good, any other precept in regard to some individual work, must needs be devoid of the nature of a law, save in so far as it regards the common good. Therefore every law is ordained to the common good.

Reply Obj. 1. A command denotes an application of a law to matters regulated by the law. Now the order to the common good, at which the law aims, is applicable to particular ends. And in this way commands are given even concerning particular matters.

Reply Obj 2. Actions are indeed concerned with particular matters: but those particular matters are referable to the common good, not as to a common genus or species, but as to a common final cause, according as the common good is said to be the common end.

Reply Obj. 3. Just as nothing stands firm with regard to the speculative reason except that which is traced back to the first indemonstrable principles, so nothing stands firm with regard to the practical reason, unless it be directed to the last end which is the common good: and whatever stands to reason in this sense, has the nature of a law.

THIRD ARTICLE

Whether the Reason of Any Man Is Competent to Make Laws?

We proceed thus to the Third Article:—

Objection 1. It would seem that the reason of any man is competent to make laws. For the Apostle says (Rom. ii. 14) that *when the Gentiles, who have not the law, do by nature those things that are of the law, . . . they are a law to themselves.* Now he says this of all in general. Therefore anyone can make a law for himself.

Obj. 2. Further, as the Philosopher says (*Ethic.* ii. 1), *the intention of the lawgiver is to lead men to virtue.* But every man can lead another to virtue. Therefore the reason of any man is competent to make laws.

Obj. 3. Further, just as the sovereign of a state governs the state, so every father of a family governs his household. But the sovereign of a state can make laws for the state. Therefore every father of a family can make laws for his household.

On the contrary, Isidore says (*Etym.* v. 10): *A law is an ordinance of the people, whereby something is sanctioned by the Elders together with the Commonalty.*

I answer that, A law, properly speaking, regards first and foremost the order to the common good. Now to order anything to the common good, belongs either to the whole people, or to someone who is the viceregent of the whole people. And therefore the making of a law belongs either to the whole people or to a public personage who has care of the whole people: since in all other matters the directing of anything to the end concerns him to whom the end belongs.

Reply Obj. 1. As stated above (A. 1 *ad* 1), a law is in a person not only as in one that rules, but also by participation as in one that is ruled. In the latter way each one is a law to himself, in so far as he shares the direction that he receives from one who rules him. Hence the same text goes on: *Who show the work of the law written in their hearts.*

Reply Obj. 2. A private person cannot lead another to virtue efficaciously: for he can only advise, and if his advice be not taken, it has no coercive power, such as the law should have, in order to prove an efficacious inducement to virtue, as the Philosopher says (*Ethic.* x. 9). But this coercive power is vested in the whole people or in some public personage, to whom it belongs to inflict penalties, as we shall state further on (Q. 92, A. 2 *ad* 3; II-II, Q. 64, A. 3). Wherefore the framing of laws belongs to him alone.

Reply Obj. 3. As one man is a part of the household, so a household is a part of the state: and the state is a perfect community, according to *Polit.* i. 1. And therefore, as the good of one man is not the last end, but is ordained to the common good; so too the good of one household is ordained to the good of a single state, which is a perfect community. Consequently he that governs a family, can indeed make certain commands or ordinances, but not such as to have properly the force of law.

FOURTH ARTICLE

Whether Promulgation Is Essential to a Law?

We proceed thus to the Fourth Article:—

Objection 1. It would seem that promulgation is not essential to a law. For the natural law above all has the character of law. But the natural law needs no promulgation. Therefore it is not essential to a law that it be promulgated.

Obj. 2. Further, it belongs properly to a law to bind one to do or not to do something. But the obligation of fulfilling a law touches not only those in whose presence it is promulgated, but also others. Therefore promulgation is not essential to a law.

Obj. 3. Further, the binding force of a law extends even to the future, since *laws are binding in matters of the future,* as the jurists say (*Cod.* 1., tit. *De lege et constit.* leg. vii). But promulgation concerns those who are present. Therefore it is not essential to a law.

On the contrary, It is laid down in the *Decretals,* dist. 4, that *laws are established when they are promulgated.*

I answer that, As stated above (A. 1), a law is imposed on others by way of a rule and measure. Now a rule or measure is imposed by being applied to those who are to be ruled and measured by it. Wherefore, in order that a law obtain the binding force which is proper to a law, it must needs be applied to the men who have to be ruled by it. Such application is made by its being notified to them by promulgation. Wherefore promulgation is necessary for the law to obtain its force.

Thus from the four preceding articles, the definition of law may be gathered; and it is nothing else than an ordinance of reason for the common good, made by him who has care of the community, and promulgated.

Reply Obj. 1. The natural law is promulgated by the very fact that God instilled it into man's mind so as to be known by him naturally.

Reply Obj. 2. Those who are not present when a law is promulgated, are bound to observe the law, in so far as it is notified or can be notified to them by others, after it has been promulgated.

Reply Obj. 3. The promulgation that takes place now, extends to future time by reason of the durability of written characters, by which means it is continually promulgated. Hence Isidore says (*Etym.* v. 3; ii. 10) that *lex* (law) *is derived from legere* (to read) *because it is written.*

QUESTION 91

Of the Various Kinds of Law

(In Six Articles)

WE must now consider the various kinds of law: under which head there are six points of inquiry: (1) Whether there is an eternal law? (2) Whether there is a natural law? (3) Whether there is a human law? (4) Whether there is a Divine law? (5) Whether there is one Divine law, or several? (6) Whether there is a law of sin?

FIRST ARTICLE

Whether There Is an Eternal Law?

We proceed thus to the First Article:—

Objection 1. It would seem that there is no eternal law. Because every law is imposed on someone. But there was not someone from eternity on whom a law could be imposed: since God alone was from eternity. Therefore no law is eternal.

Obj. 2. Further, promulgation is essential to law. But promulgation could not be from eternity: because there was no one to whom it could be promulgated from eternity. Therefore no law can be eternal.

Obj. 3. Further, a law implies order to an end. But nothing ordained to an end is eternal: for the last end alone is eternal. Therefore no law is eternal.

On the contrary, Augustine says (*De Lib. Arb.* i. 6): *That Law which is the Supreme Reason cannot be understood to be otherwise than unchangeable and eternal.*

I answer that, As stated above (Q. 90, A. 1 *ad* 2; AA. 3, 4), a law is nothing else but a dictate of practical reason emanating from the ruler who governs a perfect community. Now it is evident, granted that the world is ruled by Divine Providence, as was stated in the First Part (Q. 22, AA. 1, 2), that the whole community of the universe is governed by Divine Reason. Wherefore the very Idea of the government of things in God the Ruler of the universe, has the nature of a law. And since the Divine Reason's conception of things is not subject to time but is eternal, according to Prov. viii. 23, therefore it is that this kind of law must be called eternal.

Reply Obj. 1. Those things that are not in themselves, exist with God, inasmuch as they are foreknown and preordained by Him, according to Rom. iv. 17: *Who calls those things that are not, as those that are.* Accordingly the eternal concept of the Divine law bears the character of an eternal law, in so far as it is ordained by God to the government of things foreknown by Him.

Reply Obj. 2. Promulgation is made by word of mouth or in writing; and in both ways the eternal law is promulgated: because both the Divine Word and the writing of the Book of Life are eternal. But the promulgation cannot be from eternity on the part of the creature that hears or reads.

Reply Obj. 3. The law implies order to the end actively, in so far as it directs certain things to the end; but not passively,—that is to say, the law itself is not ordained to the end,—except accidentally, in a governor whose end is extrinsic to him, and to which end his law must needs be ordained. But the end of the Divine government is God Himself, and His law is not distinct from Himself. Wherefore the eternal law is not ordained to another end.

SECOND ARTICLE

Whether There Is in Us a Natural Law?

We proceed thus to the Second Article:—

Objection 1. It would seem that there is no natural law in us. Because man is governed sufficiently by the eternal law: for Augustine says (*De Lib. Arb.* i) that *the eternal law is that by which it is right that all things should be most orderly.* But nature does not abound in superfluities as neither does she fail in necessaries. Therefore no law is natural to man.

Obj. 2. Further, by the law man is directed, in his acts, to the end, as stated above (Q. 90, A. 2). But the directing of human acts to their end is not a function of nature, as is the case in irrational creatures, which act for an end solely by their natural appetite; whereas man acts for an end by his reason and will. Therefore no law is natural to man.

Obj. 3. Further, the more a man is free, the less is he under the law. But man is freer than all the animals, on account of his free-will, with which he is endowed above all other animals. Since therefore other animals are not subject to a natural law, neither is man subject to a natural law.

On the contrary, A gloss on Rom. ii. 14: *When the Gentiles, who have not the law, do by nature those things that are of the law,* comments as follows: *Although they have no written law, yet they have the natural law, whereby each one knows, and is conscious of, what is good and what is evil.*

I answer that, As stated above (Q. 90, A. 1 *ad* 1), law, being a rule and measure, can be in a person in two ways: in one way, as in him that rules and measures; in another way, as in that which is ruled and measured, since a thing is ruled and measured, in so far as it partakes of the rule or measure. Wherefore, since all things subject to Divine providence are ruled and measured by the eternal law, as was stated above (A. 1); it is evident that all things partake somewhat of the eternal law, in so far as, namely, from its being imprinted on them, they derive their respective inclinations to their proper acts and ends. Now among all others, the rational creature is subject to Divine providence in the most excellent way, in so far as it partakes of a share of providence, by being provident both for itself and for others. Wherefore it has a share of the Eternal Reason, whereby it has a natural inclination to its proper act and end: and this participation of the eternal law in the rational creature is called the natural law. Hence the Psalmist after saying (Ps. iv. 6): *Offer up the sacrifice of justice,* as though someone asked what the works of justice are, adds: *Many say, Who showeth us good things?* in answer to which question he says: *The light of Thy countenance, O Lord, is signed upon us:* thus implying that the light of natural reason, whereby we discern what is good and what is evil, which is the function of the natural law, is nothing else than an imprint on us of the Divine light. It is therefore evident that the natural law is nothing else than the rational creature's participation of the eternal law.

Reply Obj. 1. This argument would hold, if the natural law were something different from the eternal law: whereas it is nothing but a participation thereof, as stated above.

Reply Obj. 2. Every act of reason and will in us is based on that which is according to nature, as stated above (Q. 10, A. 1): for every act of reasoning is based on principles that are known naturally, and every act of appetite in respect of the means is derived from the natural appetite in respect of the last end. Accordingly the first direction of our acts to their end must needs be in virtue of the natural law.

Reply Obj. 3. Even irrational animals partake in their own way of the Eternal Reason, just as the rational creature does. But because the rational creature partakes thereof in an intellectual and rational manner, therefore the participation of the eternal law in the rational creature is properly called a law, since a law is something pertaining to reason, as stated above (Q. 90, A. 1). Irrational creatures, however, do not partake thereof in a rational manner, wherefore there is no participation of the eternal law in them, except by way of similitude.

THIRD ARTICLE

Whether There Is a Human Law?

We proceed thus to the Third Article:—

Objection 1. It would seem that there is not a human law. For the natural law is a participation of the eternal law, as stated above (A. 2). Now through the eternal law *all things are most orderly,* as Augustine states (*De Lib. Arb.* i. 6). Therefore the natural law suffices for the ordering of all human affairs. Consequently there is no need for a human law.

Obj. 2. Further, a law bears the character of a measure, as stated above (Q. 90, A. 1). But human reason is not a measure of things, but vice versa, as stated in *Metaph.* x, text. 5. Therefore no law can emanate from human reason.

Obj. 3. Further, a measure should be most certain, as stated in *Metaph.* x, text. 3. But the dictates of human reason in matters of conduct are uncertain, according to Wis. ix. 14: *The thoughts of mortal men are fearful, and our counsels uncertain.* Therefore no law can emanate from human reason.

On the contrary, Augustine (*De Lib. Arb.* i. 6) distinguishes two kinds of law, the one eternal, the other temporal, which he calls human.

I answer that, As stated above (Q. 90, A. 1, *ad* 2), a law is a dictate of the practical reason. Now it is to be observed that the same procedure takes place in the practical and in the speculative reason: for each proceeds from principles to conclusions, as stated above (*ibid.*). Accordingly we conclude that just as, in the speculative reason, from naturally known indemonstrable principles, we draw the conclusions of the various sciences, the knowledge of which is not imparted to us by nature, but acquired by the efforts of reason, so too it is from the precepts of the natural law, as from general and indemonstrable principles, that the human reason needs to proceed to the more particular determination of certain matters. These particular determinations, devised by human reason, are called human laws, provided the other essential conditions of law be observed, as stated above (Q. 90, AA. 2, 3, 4). Wherefore Tully says in his *Rhetoric* (*De Invent. Rhet.* ii) that *justice has its source in nature; thence certain things came into custom by reason of their utility; afterwards these things which emanated from nature and were approved by custom, were sanctioned by fear and reverence for the law.*

Reply Obj. 1. The human reason cannot have a full participation of the dictate of the Divine Reason, but according to its own mode, and imperfectly. Consequently, as on the part of the speculative reason, by a natural participation of Divine Wisdom, there is in us the knowledge of certain general principles, but not proper knowledge of each single truth, such as that contained in the Divine Wisdom; so too, on the part of the practical reason, man has a natural participation of the eternal law, according to certain general principles, but not as regards the particular determinations of individual cases, which are, however, contained in the eternal law. Hence the need for human reason to proceed further to sanction them by law.

Reply Obj. 2. Human reason is not, of itself, the rule of things: but the principles impressed on it by nature, are general rules and measures of all things relating to human conduct, whereof the natural reason is the rule and measure, although it is not the measure of things that are from nature.

Reply Obj. 3. The practical reason is concerned with practical matters, which are singular and contingent: but not with necessary things, with which the speculative reason is concerned. Wherefore human laws cannot have that inerrancy that belongs to the demonstrated conclusions of sciences. Nor is it necessary for every measure to be altogether unerring and certain, but according as it is possible in its own particular genus.

FOURTH ARTICLE

Whether There Was Any Need for a Divine Law?

We proceed thus to the Fourth Article:—

Objection 1. It would seem that there was no need for a Divine law. Because, as stated above (A. 2), the natural law is a participation in us of the eternal law. But the eternal law is a Divine law, as stated above (A. 1). Therefore there is no need for a Divine law in addition to the natural law, and human laws derived therefrom.

Obj. 2. Further, it is written (Ecclus. xv. 14) that *God left man in the hand of his own counsel.* Now counsel is an act of reason, as stated above (Q. 14, A. 1). Therefore man was left to the direction of his reason. But a dictate of human reason is a human law as stated above (A. 3). Therefore there is no need for man to be governed also by a Divine law.

Obj. 3. Further, human nature is more self-sufficing than irrational creatures. But irrational creatures have no Divine law besides the natural inclination impressed on them. Much less, therefore, should the rational creature have a Divine law in addition to the natural law.

On the contrary, David prayed God to set His law before him, saying (Ps. cxviii. 33): *Set before me for a law the way of Thy justifications, O Lord.*

I answer that, Besides the natural and the human law it was necessary for the directing of human conduct to have a Divine law. And this for four reasons. First, because it is by law that man is directed how to perform his proper acts in view of his last end. And indeed if man were ordained to no other end than that which is proportionate to his natural faculty, there would be no need for man to have any further direction on the part of his reason, besides the natural law and human law which is derived from it. But since man is ordained to an end of eternal happiness which is inproportionate to man's natural faculty, as stated above (Q. 5, A. 5), therefore it was necessary that, besides the natural and the human law, man should be directed to his end by a law given by God.

Secondly, because, on account of the uncertainty of human judgment, especially on contingent and particular matters, different people form different judgments on human acts; whence also different and contrary laws result. In order, therefore, that man may know without any doubt what he ought to do and what he ought to avoid, it was necessary for man to be directed in his proper acts by a law given by God, for it is certain that such a law cannot err.

Thirdly, because man can make laws in those matters of which he is competent to judge. But man is not competent to judge of interior movements, that are hidden, but only of exterior acts which appear: and yet for the perfection of virtue it is necessary for man to conduct himself aright in both kinds of acts. Consequently human law could not sufficiently curb and direct interior acts; and it was necessary for this purpose that a Divine law should supervene.

Fourthly, because, as Augustine says (*De Lib. Arb.* i. 5, 6), human law cannot punish or forbid all evil deeds: since while aiming at doing away with all evils, it would do away with many good things, and would hinder the advance of the common good, which is necessary for human intercourse. In order, therefore, that no evil might remain unforbidden and unpunished, it was necessary for the Divine law to supervene, whereby all sins are forbidden.

And these four causes are touched upon in Ps. cxviii. 8, where it is said: *The law of the Lord is unspotted, i.e.,* allowing no foulness of sin; *converting souls,* because it directs not only exterior, but also interior acts; *the testimony of the Lord is faithful,* because of the certainty of what is true and right; *giving wisdom to little ones,* by directing man to an end supernatural and Divine.

Reply Obj. 1. By the natural law the eternal law is participated proportionately to the capacity of human nature. But to his supernatural end man needs to be directed in a yet higher way. Hence the additional law given by God, whereby man shares more perfectly in the eternal law.

Reply Obj. 2. Counsel is a kind of inquiry: hence it must proceed from some principles. Nor is it enough for it to proceed from principles imparted by nature, which are the precepts of the natural law, for the reasons given above: but there is need for certain additional principles, namely, the precepts of the Divine law.

Reply Obj. 3. Irrational creatures are not ordained to an end higher than that which is proportionate to their natural powers: consequently the comparison fails.

FIFTH ARTICLE

Whether There Is But One Divine Law?

We proceed thus to the Fifth Article:—

Objection 1. It would seem that there is but one Divine law. Because, where there is one king in one kingdom there is but one law. Now the whole of mankind is compared to God as to one king, according to Ps. xlvi. 8: *God is the King of all the earth.* Therefore there is but one Divine law.

Obj. 2. Further, every law is directed to the end which the lawgiver intends for those for whom he makes the law. But God intends one and the same thing for all men; since according to 1 Tim. ii. 4: *He will have all men to be saved, and to come to the knowledge of the truth.* Therefore there is but one Divine law.

Obj. 3. Further, the Divine law seems to be more akin to the eternal law, which is one, than the natural law, according as the revelation of grace is of a higher order than natural knowledge. Therefore much more is the Divine law but one.

On the contrary, The Apostle says (Heb. vii. 12): *The priesthood being translated, it is necessary that a translation also be made of the law.* But the priesthood is twofold, as stated in the same passage, viz., the levitical priesthood, and the priesthood of Christ. Therefore the Divine law is twofold, namely the Old Law and the New Law.

I answer that, As stated in the First Part (Q. 30, A. 3), distinction is the cause of number. Now things may be distinguished in two ways. First, as those things that are altogether specifically different, e.g., a horse and an ox. Secondly, as perfect and imperfect in the same species, e.g., a boy and a man: and in this way the Divine law is divided into Old and New. Hence the Apostle (Gal. iii. 24, 25) compares the state of man under the Old Law to that of a child *under a pedagogue;* but the state under the New Law, to that of a full grown man, who is *no longer under a pedagogue.*

Now the perfection and imperfection of these two laws is to be taken in connection with the three conditions pertaining to law, as stated above. For, in the first place, it belongs to law to be directed to the common good as to its end, as stated above (Q. 90, A. 2). This good may be twofold. It may be a sensible and earthly good; and to this, man was directly ordained by the Old Law: wherefore, at the very outset of the law, the people were invited to the earthly kingdom of the Chananæans (Exod. iii. 8, 17). Again it may be an intelligible and heavenly good: and to this, man is ordained by the New Law. Wherefore, at the very beginning of His preaching, Christ invited men to the kingdom of heaven, saying (Matth. iv. 17): *Do penance, for the kingdom of heaven is at hand.* Hence Augustine says (*Contra Faust.* iv) that *promises of temporal goods are contained in the Old Testament, for which reason it is called old; but the promise of eternal life belongs to the New Testament.*

Secondly, it belongs to the law to direct human acts according to the order of righteousness (A. 4): wherein also the New Law surpasses the Old Law, since it directs our internal acts, according to Matth. v. 20: *Unless your justice abound more than that of the Scribes and Pharisees, you shall not enter into the kingdom of heaven.* Hence the saying that *the Old Law restrains the hand, but the New Law controls the mind* (3 Sentent., D. xl).

Thirdly, it belongs to the law to induce men to observe its commandments. This the Old Law did by the fear of punishment: but the New Law, by love, which is poured into our hearts by the grace of Christ, bestowed in the New Law, but foreshadowed in the Old. Hence Augustine says (*Contra Adimant. Manich. discip.* xvii) that *there is little difference* between the Law and the Gospel—fear and love.*

Reply Obj. 1. As the father of a family issues different commands to the children and to the adults, so also the one King, God, in His one kingdom, gave one law to men, while they were yet imperfect, and another more

---

* The *little difference* refers to the Latin words *timor* and *amor,—fear* and *love.*

perfect law, when, by the preceding law, they had been led to a greater capacity for Divine things.

Reply Obj. 2. The salvation of man could not be achieved otherwise than through Christ, according to Acts iv. 12: *There is no other name . . . given to men, whereby we must be saved.* Consequently the law that brings all to salvation could not be given until after the coming of Christ. But before His coming it was necessary to give to the people, of whom Christ was to be born, a law containing certain rudiments of righteousness unto salvation, in order to prepare them to receive Him.

Reply Obj. 3. The natural law directs man by way of certain general precepts, common to both the perfect and the imperfect: wherefore it is one and the same for all. But the Divine law directs man also in certain particular matters, to which the perfect and imperfect do not stand in the same relation. Hence the necessity for the Divine law to be twofold, as already explained.

SIXTH ARTICLE

Whether There Is a Law in the Fomes of Sin?

We proceed thus to the Sixth Article:—

Objection 1. It would seem that there is no law of the "fomes" of sin. For Isidore says (*Etym.* v) that the *law is based on reason.* But the "fomes" of sin is not based on reason, but deviates from it. Therefore the "fomes" has not the nature of a law.

Obj. 2. Further, every law is binding, so that those who do not obey it are called transgressors. But man is not called a transgressor, from not following the instigations of the "fomes"; but rather from his following them. Therefore the "fomes" has not the nature of a law.

Obj. 3. Further, the law is ordained to the common good, as stated above (Q. 90, A. 2). But the "fomes" inclines us, not to the common, but to our own private good. Therefore the "fomes" has not the nature of sin.

On the contrary, The Apostle says (Rom. vii. 23): *I see another law in my members, fighting against the law of my mind.*

I answer that, As stated above (A. 2; Q. 90, A. 1 *ad* 1), the law, as to its essence, resides in him that rules and measures; but, by way of participation, in that which is ruled and measured; so that every inclination or ordination which may be found in things subject to the law, is called a law by participation, as stated above (*ibid.*). Now those who are subject to a law may receive a twofold inclination from the lawgiver. First, in so far as he directly inclines his subjects to something; sometimes

indeed different subjects to different acts; in this way we may say that there is a military law and a mercantile law. Secondly, indirectly; thus by the very fact that a lawgiver deprives a subject of some dignity, the latter passes into another order, so as to be under another law, as it were: thus if a soldier be turned out of the army, he becomes a subject of rural or of mercantile legislation.

Accordingly under the Divine Lawgiver various creatures have various natural inclinations, so that what is, as it were, a law for one, is against the law for another: thus I might say that fierceness is, in a way, the law of a dog, but against the law of a sheep or another meek animal. And so the law of man, which, by the Divine ordinance, is allotted to him, according to his proper natural condition, is that he should act in accordance with reason: and this law was so effective in the primitive state, that nothing either beside or against reason could take man unawares. But when man turned his back on God, he fell under the influence of his sensual impulses: in fact this happens to each one individually, the more he deviates from the path of reason, so that, after a fashion, he is likened to the beasts that are led by the impulse of sensuality, according to Ps. xlviii. 21: *Man, when he was in honor, did not understand: he hath been compared to senseless beasts, and made like to them.*

So, then, this very inclination of sensuality which is called the "fomes," in other animals has simply the nature of a law (yet only in so far as a law may be said to be in such things), by reason of a direct inclination. But in man, it has not the nature of law in this way, rather is it a deviation from the law of reason. But since, by the just sentence of God, man is destitute of original justice, and his reason bereft of its vigor, this impulse of sensuality, whereby he is led, in so far as it is a penalty following from the Divine law depriving man of his proper dignity, has the nature of a law.

Reply Obj. 1. This argument considers the "fomes" in itself, as an incentive to evil. It is not thus that it has the nature of a law, as stated above, but according as it results from the justice of the Divine law: it is as though we were to say that the law allows a nobleman to be condemned to hard labor for some misdeed.

Reply Obj. 2. This argument considers law in the light of a rule or measure: for it is in this sense that those who deviate from the law become transgressors. But the "fomes" is not a law in this respect, but by a kind of participation, as stated above.

Reply Obj. 3. This argument considers the "fomes" as to its proper inclination, and not as to its origin. And yet if the inclination of sensuality be considered as it is in other animals, thus it is ordained to the common good, namely, to the preservation of nature in the species or in the individual. And this is in man also, in so far as sensuality is subject to reason. But it is called the "fomes" in so far as it strays from the order of reason.

QUESTION 92

Of the Effects of Law

(In Two Articles)

WE must now consider the effects of law; under which head there are two points of inquiry: (1) Whether an effect of law is to make men good? (2) Whether the effects of law are to command, to forbid, to permit, and to punish, as the Jurist states?

FIRST ARTICLE

Whether an Effect of Law Is to Make Men Good?

We proceed thus to the First Article:—

Objection 1. It seems that it is not an effect of law to make men good. For men are good through virtue, since virtue, as stated in *Ethic.* ii. 6 is *that which makes its subject good.* But virtue is in man from God alone, because He it is Who *works it in us without us,* as we stated above (Q. 55, A. 4) in giving the definition of virtue. Therefore the law does not make men good.

Obj. 2. Further, Law does not profit a man unless he obeys it. But the very fact that a man obeys a law is due to his being good. Therefore in man goodness is presupposed to the law. Therefore the law does not make men good.

Obj. 3. Further, Law is ordained to the common good, as stated above (Q. 90, A. 2). But some behave well in things regarding the community, who behave ill in things regarding themselves. Therefore it is not the business of the law to make men good.

Obj. 4. Further, some laws are tyrannical, as the Philosopher says (*Polit.* iii. 6). But a tyrant does not intend the good of his subjects, but considers only his own profit. Therefore law does not make men good.

On the contrary, The Philosopher says (*Ethic.* ii. 1) that the *intention of every lawgiver is to make good citizens.*

I answer that, as stated above (Q. 90, A. 1 ad 2; AA. 3, 4), a law is nothing else than a dictate of reason in the ruler by whom his subjects are governed. Now the virtue of any subordinate thing consists in its being well subordinated to that by which it is regulated: thus we see that the virtue of the irascible and concupiscible faculties consists in their being obedient to reason; and accordingly *the virtue of every subject consists in his being*

well subjected to his ruler, as the Philosopher says (*Polit.* i). But every law aims at being obeyed by those who are subject to it. Consequently it is evident that the proper effect of law is to lead its subjects to their proper virtue: and since virtue is *that which makes its subject good,* it follows that the proper effect of law is to make those to whom it is given, good, either simply or in some particular respect. For if the intention of the lawgiver is fixed on true good, which is the common good regulated according to Divine justice, it follows that the effect of the law is to make men good simply. If, however, the intention of the lawgiver is fixed on that which is not simply good, but useful or pleasurable to himself, or in opposition to Divine justice; then the law does not make men good simply, but in respect to that particular government. In this way good is found even in things that are bad of themselves: thus a man is called a good robber, because he works in a way that is adapted to his end.

Reply Obj. 1. Virtue is twofold, as explained above (Q. 63, A. 2), viz., acquired and infused. Now the fact of being accustomed to an action contributes to both, but in different ways; for it causes the acquired virtue; while it disposes to infused virtue, and preserves and fosters it when it already exists. And since law is given for the purpose of directing human acts; as far as human acts conduce to virtue, so far does law make men good. Wherefore the Philosopher says in the second book of the *Politics* (*Ethic.* ii) that *lawgivers make men good by habituating them to good works.*

Reply Obj. 2. It is not always through perfect goodness of virtue that one obeys the law, but sometimes it is through fear of punishment, and sometimes from the mere dictates of reason, which is a beginning of virtue, as stated above (Q. 63, A. 1).

Reply Obj. 3. The goodness of any part is considered in comparison with the whole; hence Augustine says (*Conf.* iii) that *unseemly is the part that harmonizes not with the whole.* Since then every man is a part of the state, it is impossible that a man be good, unless he be well proportionate to the common good: nor can the whole be well consistent unless its parts be proportionate to it. Consequently the common good of the state cannot flourish, unless the citizens be virtuous, at least those whose business it is to govern. But it is enough for the good of the community, that the other citizens be so far virtuous that they obey the commands of their rulers. Hence the Philosopher says (*Polit.* iii. 2) that *the virtue of a sovereign is the same as that of a good man, but the virtue of any common citizen is not the same as that of a good man.*

Reply Obj. 4. A tyrannical law, through not being according to reason, is not a law, absolutely speaking, but rather a perversion of law; and yet in so far as it is something in the nature of a law, it aims at the citizens' being good. For all it has in the nature of a law consists in its being an ordinance made by a superior to his subjects, and aims at being obeyed by them, which is to make them good, not simply, but with respect to that particular government.

SECOND ARTICLE

Whether the Acts of Law Are Suitably Assigned?

We proceed thus to the Second Article:—

Objection 1. It would seem that the acts of law are not suitably assigned as consisting in *command, prohibition, permission* and *punishment.* For *every law is a general precept,* as the jurist states (*ibid.*). But command and precept are the same. Therefore the other three are superfluous.

Obj. 2. Further, the effect of a law is to induce its subjects to be good, as stated above (A. 1). But counsel aims at a higher good than a command does. Therefore it belongs to law to counsel rather than to command.

Obj. 3. Further, just as punishment stirs a man to good deeds, so does reward. Therefore if to punish is reckoned an effect of law, so also is to reward.

Obj. 4. Further, the intention of a lawgiver is to make men good, as stated above (A. 1). But he that obeys the law, merely through fear of being punished, is not good: because *although a good deed may be done through servile fear,* i.e., *fear of punishment, it is not done well,* as Augustine says (*Contra duas Epist. Pelag.* ii). Therefore punishment is not a proper effect of law.

On the contrary, Isidore says (*Etym.* v. 19): *Every law either permits something, as:* "*A brave man may demand his reward*": or forbids something, as: "*No man may ask a consecrated virgin in marriage*": or punishes, as: "*Let him that commits a murder be put to death.*"

I answer that, Just as an assertion is a dictate of reason asserting something, so is a law a dictate of reason, commanding something. Now it is proper to reason to lead from one thing to another. Wherefore just as, in demonstrative sciences, the reason leads us from certain principles to assent to the conclusion, so it induces us by some means to assent to the precept of the law.

Now the precepts of law are concerned with human acts, in which the law directs, as stated above (Q. 90, AA. 1, 2; Q. 91, A. 4). Again, there are three kinds of human acts: for, as stated above (Q. 18, A. 8), some acts are good generically, viz., acts of virtue; and in respect of these the act of the law is a precept or command, for *the law commands all acts of virtue* (*Ethic.* v. 1). Some acts are evil generically, viz., acts of vice, and in respect of these the law forbids. Some acts are generically indifferent, and in respect of these the law permits; and all acts that are either not distinctly good or not distinctly bad may be called indifferent.—And it is the fear of punishment that law makes use of in order to ensure obedience: in which respect punishment is an effect of law.

Reply Obj. 1. Just as to cease from evil is a kind of good, so a prohibition is a kind of precept: and accordingly, taking precept in a wide sense, every law is a kind of precept.

Reply Obj. 2. To advise is not a proper act of law, but may be within the competency even of a private person, who cannot make a law. Wherefore too the Apostle, after giving a certain counsel (1 Cor. vii. 12) says: *I speak, not the Lord.* Consequently it is not reckoned as an effect of law.

Reply Obj. 3. To reward may also pertain to anyone: but to punish pertains to none but the framer of the law, by whose authority the pain is inflicted. Wherefore to reward is not reckoned an effect of law, but only to punish.

Reply Obj. 4. From becoming accustomed to avoid evil and fulfil what is good, through fear of punishment, one is sometimes led on to do so likewise, with delight and of one's own accord. Accordingly, law, even by punishing, leads men on to being good.

QUESTION 93

Of the Eternal Law

(In Six Articles)

WE must now consider each law by itself; and (1) The eternal law; (2) The natural law; (3) The human law; (4) The old law; (5) The new law, which is the law of the Gospel. Of the sixth law which is the law of the "fomes," suffice what we have said when treating of original sin.

Concerning the first there are six points of inquiry: (1) What is the eternal law? (2) Whether it is known to all? (3) Whether every law is derived from it? (4) Whether necessary things are subject to the eternal law? (5) Whether natural contingencies are subject to the eternal law? (6) Whether all human things are subject to it?

FIRST ARTICLE

Whether the Eternal Law Is a Sovereign Type* Existing in God?

We proceed thus to the First Article:—

Objection 1. It would seem that the eternal law is not a sovereign type existing in God. For there is only one eternal law. But there are many types of things in the Divine mind; for Augustine says (*Qq.* lxxxiii, qu. 46) that God *made each thing according to its type.* Therefore the eternal law does not seem to be a type existing in the Divine mind.

Obj. 2. Further, it is essential to a law that it be promulgated by word, as stated above (Q. 90, A. 4). But Word is a Personal name in God, as stated in the First Part (Q. 34, A. 1): whereas type refers to the Essence. Therefore the eternal law is not the same as a Divine type.

Obj. 3. Further, Augustine says (*De Vera Relig.* xxx): *We see a law above our minds, which is called truth.* But the law which is above our minds is the eternal law. Therefore truth is the eternal law. But the idea of truth is not the same as the idea of a type. Therefore the eternal law is not the same as the sovereign type.

On the contrary, Augustine says (*De Lib. Arb.* i. 6) that *the eternal law is the sovereign type, to which we must always conform.*

I answer that, Just as in every artificer there pre-exists a type of the things that are made by his art, so too in every governor there must pre-exist the type of the order of those things that are to be done by those who are

* *Ratio.*

subject to his government. And just as the type of the things yet to be made by an art is called the art or exemplar of the products of that art, so too the type in him who governs the acts of his subjects, bears the character of a law, provided the other conditions be present which we have mentioned above (Q. 90). Now God, by His wisdom, is the Creator of all things in relation to which He stands as the artificer to the products of his art, as stated in the First Part (Q. 14, A. 8). Moreover He governs all the acts and movements that are to be found in each single creature, as was also stated in the First Part (Q. 103, A. 5). Wherefore as the type of the Divine Wisdom, inasmuch as by It all things are created, has the character of art, exemplar or idea; so the type of Divine Wisdom, as moving all things to their due end, bears the character of law. Accordingly the eternal law is nothing else than the type of Divine Wisdom, as directing all actions and movements.

Reply Obj. 1. Augustine is speaking in that passage of the ideal types which regard the proper nature of each single thing; and consequently in them there is a certain distinction and plurality, according to their different relations to things, as stated in the First Part (Q. 15, A. 2). But law is said to direct human acts by ordaining them to the common good, as stated above (Q. 90, A. 2). And things, which are in themselves different, may be considered as one, according as they are ordained to one common thing. Wherefore the eternal law is one since it is the type of this order.

Reply Obj. 2. With regard to any sort of word, two points may be considered: viz., the word itself, and that which is expressed by the word. For the spoken word is something uttered by the mouth of man, and expresses that which is signified by the human word. The same applies to the human mental word, which is nothing else than something conceived by the mind, by which man expresses his thoughts mentally. So then in God the Word conceived by the intellect of the Father is the name of a Person: but all things that are in the Father's knowledge, whether they refer to the Essence or to the Persons, or to the works of God, are expressed by this Word, as Augustine declares (*De Trin.* xv. 14). And among other things expressed by this Word, the eternal law itself is expressed thereby. Nor does it follow that the eternal law is a Personal name in God: yet it is appropriated to the Son, on account of the kinship between type and word.

Reply Obj. 3. The types of the Divine intellect do not stand in the same relation to things, as the types of the human intellect. For the human intellect is measured by things, so that a human concept is not true by reason of itself, but by reason of its being consonant with things, since *an opinion is true or false according as it answers to the reality.* But the Divine intellect is the measure of things: since each thing has so far truth in it, as it represents the Divine intellect, as was stated in the First Part (Q. 16, A. 1). Consequently the Divine intellect is true in itself; and its type is truth itself.

SECOND ARTICLE

Whether the Eternal Law Is Known to All?

We proceed thus to the Second Article:—

Objection 1. It would seem that the eternal law is not known to all. Because, as the Apostle says (1 Cor. ii. 11), *the things that are of God no man knoweth, but the Spirit of God.* But the eternal law is a type existing in the Divine mind. Therefore it is unknown to all save God alone.

Obj. 2. Further, as Augustine says (*De Lib. Arb.* i. 6) *the eternal law is that by which it is right that all things should be most orderly.* But all do not know how all things are most orderly. Therefore all do not know the eternal law.

Obj. 3. Further, Augustine says (*De Vera Relig.* xxxi) that *the eternal law is not subject to the judgment of man.* But according to *Ethic.* i. *any man can judge well of what he knows.* Therefore the eternal law is not known to us.

On the contrary, Augustine says (*De Lib. Arb.* i. 6) that *knowledge of the eternal law is imprinted on us.*

I answer that, A thing may be known in two ways: first, in itself; secondly, in its effect, wherein some likeness of that thing is found: thus someone not seeing the sun in its substance, may know it by its rays. So then no one can know the eternal law, as it is in itself, except the blessed who see God in His Essence. But every rational creature knows it in its reflection, greater or less. For every knowledge of truth is a kind of reflection and participation of the eternal law, which is the unchangeable truth, as Augustine says (*De Vera Relig.* xxxi). Now all men know the truth to a certain extent, at least as to the common principles of the natural law: and as to the others, they partake of the knowledge of truth, some more, some less; and in this

respect are more or less cognizant of the eternal law.

Reply Obj. 1. We cannot know the things that are of God, as they are in themselves; but they are made known to us in their effects, according to Rom. i. 20: *The invisible things of God . . . are clearly seen, being understood by the things that are made.*

Reply Obj. 2. Although each one knows the eternal law according to his own capacity, in the way explained above, yet none can comprehend it: for it cannot be made perfectly known by its effects. Therefore it does not follow that anyone who knows the eternal law in the way aforesaid, knows also the whole order of things, whereby they are most orderly.

Reply Obj. 3. To judge of a thing may be understood in two ways. First, as when a cognitive power judges of its proper object, according to Job. xii. 11: *Doth not the ear discern words, and the palate of him that eateth, the taste?* It is to this kind of judgment that the Philosopher alludes when he says that *anyone can judge well of what he knows,* by judging, namely, whether what is put forward is true. In another way we speak of a superior judging of a subordinate by a kind of practical judgment, as to whether he should be such and such or not. And thus none can judge of the eternal law.

THIRD ARTICLE

Whether Every Law Is Derived from the Eternal Law?

We proceed thus to the Third Article:—

Objection 1. It would seem that not every law is derived from the eternal law. For there is a law of the "fomes," as stated above (Q. 91, A. 6), which is not derived from that Divine law which is the eternal law, since thereunto pertains the *prudence of the flesh,* of which the Apostle says (Rom. viii. 7), that *it cannot be subject to the law of God.* Therefore not every law is derived from the eternal law.

Obj. 2. Further, nothing unjust can be derived from the eternal law, because, as stated above (A. 2, *Obj.* 2), *the eternal law is that, according to which it is right that all things should be most orderly.* But some laws are unjust, according to Isa. x. 1: *Woe to them that make wicked laws.* Therefore not every law is derived from the eternal law.

Obj. 3. Further, Augustine says (*De Lib. Arb.* i. 5) that *the law which is framed for ruling the people, rightly permits many things which are punished by Divine providence.* But the type of Divine providence is the eternal law, as stated above (A. 1). Therefore not even every good law is derived from the eternal law.

On the contrary, Divine Wisdom says

(Prov. viii. 15): *By Me kings reign, and lawgivers decree just things.* But the type of Divine Wisdom is the eternal law, as stated above (A. 1). Therefore all laws proceed from the eternal law.

I answer that, As stated above (Q. 90, AA. 1, 2), the law denotes a kind of plan directing acts towards an end. Now wherever there are movers ordained to one another, the power of the second mover must needs be derived from the power of the first mover; since the second mover does not move except in so far as it is moved by the first. Wherefore we observe the same in all those who govern, so that the plan of government is derived by secondary governors from the governor in chief; thus the plan of what is to be done in a state flows from the king's command to his inferior administrators: and again in things of art the plan of whatever is to be done by art flows from the chief craftsman to the under-craftsmen, who work with their hands. Since then the eternal law is the plan of government in the Chief Governor, all the plans of government in the inferior governors must be derived from the eternal law. But these plans of inferior governors are all other laws besides the eternal law. Therefore all laws, in so far as they partake of right reason, are derived from the eternal law. Hence Augustine says (*De Lib. Arb.* i. 6) that *in temporal law there is nothing just and lawful, but what man has drawn from the eternal law.*

Reply Obj. 1. The "fomes" has the nature of law in man, in so far as it is a punishment resulting from Divine justice; and in this respect it is evident that it is derived from the eternal law. But in so far as it denotes a proneness to sin, it is contrary to the Divine law, and has not the nature of law, as stated above (Q. 91, A. 6).

Reply Obj. 2. Human law has the nature of law in so far as it partakes of right reason; and it is clear that, in this respect, it is derived from the eternal law. But in so far as it deviates from reason, it is called an unjust law, and has the nature, not of law but of violence. Nevertheless even an unjust law, in so far as it retains some appearance of law, though being framed by one who is in power, is derived from the eternal law; since all power is from the Lord God, according to Rom. xiii. 1.

Reply Obj. 3. Human law is said to permit certain things, not as approving of them, but as being unable to direct them. And many things are directed by the Divine law, which human law is unable to direct, because more things are subject to a higher than to a lower cause. Hence the very fact that human law does not meddle with matters it cannot direct,

comes under the ordination of the eternal law. It would be different, were human law to sanction what the eternal law condemns. Consequently it does not follow that human law is not derived from the eternal law, but that it is not on a perfect equality with it.

FOURTH ARTICLE

Whether Necessary and Eternal Things Are Subject to the Eternal Law?

We proceed thus to the Fourth Article:—

Objection 1. It would seem that necessary and eternal things are subject to the eternal law. For whatever is reasonable is subject to reason. But the Divine will is reasonable, for it is just. Therefore it is subject to (the Divine) reason. But the eternal law is the Divine reason. Therefore God's will is subject to the eternal law. But God's will is eternal. Therefore eternal and necessary things are subject to the eternal law.

Obj. 2. Further, whatever is subject to the King, is subject to the King's law. Now the Son, according to 1 Cor. xv. 28, 24, *shall be subject . . . to God and the Father, . . . when He shall have delivered up the Kingdom to Him.* Therefore the Son, Who is eternal, is subject to the eternal law.

Obj. 3. Further, the eternal law is Divine providence as a type. But many necessary things are subject to Divine providence: for instance, the stability of incorporeal substances and of the heavenly bodies. Therefore even necessary things are subject to eternal law.

On the contrary, Things that are necessary cannot be otherwise, and consequently need no restraining. But laws are imposed on men, in order to restrain them from evil, as explained above (Q. 92, A. 2). Therefore necessary things are not subject to the eternal law.

I answer that, As stated above (A. 1), the eternal law is the type of the Divine government. Consequently whatever is subject to the Divine government, is subject to the eternal law: while if anything is not subject to the Divine government, neither is it subject to the eternal law. The application of this distinction may be gathered by looking around us. For those things are subject to human government, which can be done by man; but what pertains to the nature of man is not subject to human government; for instance, that he should have a soul, hands, or feet. Accordingly all that is in things created by God, whether it be contingent or necessary, is subject to the eternal law: while things pertaining to the Divine Nature or Essence are not subject to the eternal law, but are the eternal law itself.

Reply Obj. 1. We may speak of God's will

in two ways. First, as to the will itself: and thus, since God's will is His very Essence, it is subject neither to the Divine government, nor to the eternal law, but is the same thing as the eternal law. Secondly, we may speak of God's will, as to the things themselves that God wills about creatures; which things are subject to the eternal law, in so far as they are planned by Divine Wisdom. In reference to these things God's will is said to be reasonable (*rationalis*): though regarded in itself it should rather be called their type (*ratio*).

Reply Obj. 2. God the Son was not made by God, but was naturally born of God. Consequently He is not subject to Divine providence or to the eternal law: but rather is Himself the eternal law by a kind of appropriation, as Augustine explains (*De Vera Relig.* xxxi). But He is said to be subject to the Father by reason of His human nature, in respect of which also the Father is said to be greater than He.

The third objection we grant, because it deals with those necessary things that are created.

Reply Obj. 4. As the Philosopher says (*Metaph.* v., text. 6), some necessary things have a cause of their necessity: and thus they derive from something else the fact that they cannot be otherwise. And this is in itself a most effective restraint; for whatever is restrained, is said to be restrained in so far as it cannot do otherwise than it is allowed to.

FIFTH ARTICLE

Whether Natural Contingents Are Subject to the Eternal Law?

We proceed thus to the Fifth Article:—

Objection 1. It would seem that natural contingents are not subject to the eternal law. Because promulgation is essential to law, as stated above (Q. 90, A. 4). But a law cannot be promulgated except to rational creatures, to whom it is possible to make an announcement. Therefore none but rational creatures are subject to the eternal law; and consequently natural contingents are not.

Obj. 2. Further, *Whatever obeys reason partakes somewhat of reason*, as stated in *Ethic.* i. But the eternal law is the supreme type, as stated above (A. 1). Since then natural contingents do not partake of reason in any way, but are altogether void of reason, it seems that they are not subject to the eternal law.

Obj. 3. Further, the eternal law is most efficient. But in natural contingents defects occur. Therefore they are not subject to the eternal law.

On the contrary, It is written (Prov. viii. 29): *When He compassed the sea with its bounds, and set a law to the waters, that they should not pass their limits.*

I answer that, We must speak otherwise of the law of man, than of the eternal law which is the law of God. For the law of man extends only to rational creatures subject to man. The reason of this is because law directs the actions of those that are subject to the government of someone: wherefore, properly speaking, none imposes a law on his own actions. Now whatever is done regarding the use of irrational things subject to man, is done by the act of man himself moving those things, for these irrational creatures do not move themselves, but are moved by others, as stated above (Q. 1, A. 2). Consequently man cannot impose laws on irrational beings, however much they may be subject to him. But he can impose laws on rational beings subject to him, in so far as by his command or pronouncement of any kind, he imprints on their minds a rule which is a principle of action.

Now just as man, by such pronouncement, impresses a kind of inward principle of action on the man that is subject to him, so God imprints on the whole of nature the principles of its proper actions. And so, in this way, God is said to command the whole of nature, according to Ps. cxlviii. 6: *He hath made a decree, and it shall not pass away.* And thus all actions and movements of the whole of nature are subject to the eternal law. Consequently irrational creatures are subject to the eternal law, through being moved by Divine providence; but not, as rational creatures are, through understanding the Divine commandment.

Reply Obj. 1. The impression of an inward active principle is to natural things, what the promulgation of law is to men: because law, by being promulgated, imprints on man a directive principle of human actions, as stated above.

Reply Obj. 2. Irrational creatures neither partake of nor are obedient to human reason: whereas they do partake of the Divine Reason by obeying it; because the power of Divine Reason extends over more things than human reason does. And as the members of the human body are moved at the command of reason, and yet do not partake of reason, since they have no apprehension subordinate to reason; so too irrational creatures are moved by God, without, on that account, being rational.

Reply Obj. 3. Although the defects which occur in natural things are outside the order of particular causes, they are not outside the order of universal causes, especially of the First

Cause, *i.e.*, God, from Whose providence nothing can escape, as stated in the First Part (Q. 22, A. 2). And since the eternal law is the type of Divine providence, as stated above (A. 1), hence the defects of natural things are subject to the eternal law.

SIXTH ARTICLE

Whether All Human Affairs Are Subject to the Eternal Law?

We proceed thus to the Sixth Article:—

Objection 1. It would seem that not all human affairs are subject to the eternal law. For the Apostle says (Gal. v. 18): *If you are led by the spirit you are not under the law.* But the righteous who are the sons of God by adoption, are led by the spirit of God, according to Rom. viii. 14: *Whosoever are led by the spirit of God, they are the sons of God.* Therefore not all men are under the eternal law.

Obj. 2. Further, the Apostle says (Rom. viii. 7): *The prudence* (Vulg., *wisdom*) *of the flesh is an enemy to God: for it is not subject to the law of God.* But many are those in whom the prudence of the flesh dominates. Therefore all men are not subject to the eternal law which is the law of God.

Obj. 3. Further, Augustine says (*De Lib. Arb.* i. 6) that *the eternal law is that by which the wicked deserve misery, the good, a life of blessedness.* But those who are already blessed, and those who are already lost, are not in the state of merit. Therefore they are not under the eternal law.

On the contrary, Augustine says (*De Civ. Dei,* xix. 12): *Nothing evades the laws of the most high Creator and Governor, for by Him the peace of the universe is administered.*

I answer that, There are two ways in which a thing is subject to the eternal law, as explained above (A. 5): first, by partaking of the eternal law by way of knowledge; secondly, by way of action and passion, i.e., by partaking of the eternal law by way of an inward motive principle: and in this second way, irrational creatures are subject to the eternal law, as stated above (*ibid.*). But since the rational nature, together with that which it has in common with all creatures, has something proper to itself inasmuch as it is rational, consequently it is subject to the eternal law in both ways; because while each rational creature has some knowledge of the eternal law, as stated above (A. 2), it also has a natural inclination to that which is in harmony with the eternal law; for *we are naturally adapted to be the recipients of virtue* (*Ethic.* ii. 1).

Both ways, however, are imperfect, and to a certain extent destroyed, in the wicked; because in them the natural inclination to virtue is corrupted by vicious habits, and, moreover, the natural knowledge of good is darkened by passions and habits of sin. But in the good both ways are found more perfect: because in them, besides the natural knowledge of good, there is the added knowledge of faith and wisdom; and again, besides the natural inclination to good, there is the added motive of grace and virtue.

Accordingly, the good are perfectly subject to the eternal law, as always acting according to it: whereas the wicked are subject to the eternal law, imperfectly as to their actions, indeed, since both their knowledge of good, and their inclination thereto, are imperfect; but this imperfection on the part of action is supplied on the part of passion, in so far as they suffer what the eternal law decrees concerning them, according as they fail to act in harmony with that law. Hence Augustine says (*De Lib. Arb.* i. 15): *I esteem that the righteous act according to the eternal law;* and (*De Catech. Rud.* xviii): *Out of the just misery of the souls which deserted Him, God knew how to furnish the inferior parts of His creation with most suitable laws.*

Reply Obj. 1. This saying of the Apostle may be understood in two ways. First, so that a man is said to be under the law, through being pinned down thereby, against his will, as by a load. Hence, on the same passage a gloss says that *he is under the law, who refrains from evil deeds, through fear of the punishment threatened by the law, and not from love of virtue.* In this way the spiritual man is not under the law, because he fulfils the law willingly, through charity which is poured into his heart by the Holy Ghost. Secondly, it can be understood as meaning that the works of a man, who is led by the Holy Ghost, are the works of the Holy Ghost rather than his own. Therefore, since the Holy Ghost is not under the law, as neither is the Son, as stated above (A. 4 *ad* 2); it follows that such works, in so far as they are of the Holy Ghost, are not under the law. The Apostle witnesses to this when he says (2 Cor. iii. 17): *Where the Spirit of the Lord is, there is liberty.*

Reply Obj. 2. The prudence of the flesh cannot be subject to the law of God as regards action; since it inclines to actions contrary to the Divine law: yet it is subject to the law of God, as regards passion; since it deserves to suffer punishment according to the law of Divine justice. Nevertheless in no man does the prudence of the flesh dominate so far as to destroy the whole good of his nature: and consequently there remains in man the inclination to act in accordance with the eternal law.

For we have seen above (Q. 85, A. 2) that sin does not destroy entirely the good of nature.

Reply Obj. 3. A thing is maintained in the end and moved towards the end by one and the same cause: thus gravity which makes a heavy body rest in the lower place is also the cause of its being moved thither. We therefore reply that as it is according to the eternal law that some deserve happiness, others unhappiness, so is it by the eternal law that some are maintained in a happy state, others in an unhappy state. Accordingly both the blessed and the damned are under the eternal law.

QUESTION 94

Of the Natural Law

(In Six Articles)

WE must now consider the natural law; concerning which there are six points of inquiry: (1) What is the natural law? (2) What are the precepts of the natural law? (3) Whether all acts of virtue are prescribed by the natural law? (4) Whether the natural law is the same in all? (5) Whether it is changeable? (6) Whether it can be abolished from the heart of man?

FIRST ARTICLE

Whether the Natural Law Is a Habit?

We proceed thus to the First Article:—

Objection 1. It would seem that the natural law is a habit. Because, as the Philosopher says (*Ethic.* ii. 5), *there are three things in the soul, power, habit, and passion.* But the natural law is not one of the soul's powers: nor is it one of the passions; as we may see by going through them one by one. Therefore the natural law is a habit.

Obj. 2. Further, Basil* says that the conscience or *synderesis is the law of our mind;* which can only apply to the natural law. But the *synderesis* is a habit, as was shown in the First Part (Q. 79, A. 12). Therefore the natural law is a habit.

Obj. 3. Further, the natural law abides in man always, as will be shown further on (A. 6). But man's reason, which the law regards, does not always think about the natural law. Therefore the natural law is not an act, but a habit.

On the contrary, Augustine says (*De Bono Conjug.* xxi) that *a habit is that whereby something is done when necessary.* But such is not the natural law: since it is in infants and in the damned who cannot act by it. Therefore the natural law is not a habit.

I answer that, A thing may be called a habit in two ways. First, properly and essentially: and thus the natural law is not a habit. For it has been stated above (Q. 90, A. 1 *ad* 2) that the natural law is something appointed

* Damascene, *De Fide Orthod.* iv. 22.

by reason, just as a proposition is a work of reason. Now that which a man does is not the same as that whereby he does it: for he makes a becoming speech by the habit of grammar. Since then a habit is that by which we act, a law cannot be a habit properly and essentially.

Secondly, the term habit may be applied to that which we hold by a habit: thus faith may mean that which we hold by faith. And accordingly, since the precepts of the natural law are sometimes considered by reason actually, while sometimes they are in the reason only habitually, in this way the natural law may be called a habit. Thus, in speculative matters, the indemonstrable principles are not the habit itself whereby we hold those principles, but are the principles the habit of which we possess.

Reply Obj. 1. The Philosopher proposes there to discover the genus of virtue; and since it is evident that virtue is a principle of action, he mentions only those things which are principles of human acts, viz., powers, habits and passions. But there are other things in the soul besides these three: there are acts; thus *to will* is in the one that wills; again, things known are in the knower; moreover its own natural properties are in the soul, such as immortality and the like.

Reply Obj. 2. Synderesis is said to be the law of our mind, because it is a habit containing the precepts of the natural law, which are the first principles of human actions.

Reply Obj. 3. This argument proves that the natural law is held habitually; and this is granted.

To the argument advanced in the contrary sense we reply that sometimes a man is unable to make use of that which is in him habitually, on account of some impediment: thus, on account of sleep, a man is unable to use the habit of science. In like manner, through the deficiency of his age, a child cannot use the habit of understanding of principles, or the natural law, which is in him habitually.

SECOND ARTICLE

Whether the Natural Law Contains Several Precepts, or One Only?

We proceed thus to the Second Article:—

Objection 1. It would seem that the natural law contains, not several precepts, but one only. For law is a kind of precept, as stated above (Q. 92, A. 2). If therefore there were many precepts of the natural law, it would follow that there are also many natural laws.

Obj. 2. Further, the natural law is consequent to human nature. But human nature, as a whole, is one; though, as to its parts, it is manifold. Therefore, either there is but one precept of the law of nature, on account of the unity of nature as a whole; or there are many, by reason of the number of parts of human nature. The result would be that even things relating to the inclination of the concupiscible faculty belong to the natural law.

Obj. 3. Further, law is something pertaining to reason, as stated above (Q. 90, A. 1). Now reason is but one in man. Therefore there is only one precept of the natural law.

On the contrary, The precepts of the natural law in man stand in relation to practical matters, as the first principles to matters of demonstration. But there are several first indemonstrable principles. Therefore there are also several precepts of the natural law.

I answer that, As stated above (Q. 91, A. 3), the precepts of the natural law are to the practical reason, what the first principles of demonstrations are to the speculative reason; because both are self-evident principles. Now a thing is said to be self-evident in two ways: first, in itself; secondly, in relation to us. Any proposition is said to be self-evident in itself, if its predicate is contained in the notion of the subject: although, to one who knows not the definition of the subject, it happens that such a proposition is not self-evident. For instance, this proposition, *Man is a rational being,* is, in its very nature, self-evident, since who says *man,* says *a rational being:* and yet to one who knows not what a man is, this proposition is not self-evident. Hence it is that, as Boethius says (*De Hebdom.*), certain axioms or propositions are universally self-evident to all; and such are those propositions whose terms are known to all, as, *Every whole is greater than its part,* and, *Things equal to one and the same are equal to one another.* But some propositions are self-evident only to the wise, who understand the meaning of the terms of such propositions: thus to one who understands that an angel is not a body, it is self-evident that an angel is not circumscriptively in a place: but this is not evident

* *Pandect. Just.* I., tit. i.

to the unlearned, for they cannot grasp it.

Now a certain order is to be found in those things that are apprehended universally. For that which, before aught else, falls under apprehension, is *being,* the notion of which is included in all things whatsoever a man apprehends. Wherefore the first indemonstrable principle is that *the same thing cannot be affirmed and denied at the same time,* which is based on the notion of *being* and *not-being:* and on this principle all others are based, as is stated in *Metaph.* iv, text. 9. Now as *being* is the first thing that falls under the apprehension simply, so *good* is the first thing that falls under the apprehension of the practical reason, which is directed to action: since every agent acts for an end under the aspect of good. Consequently the first principle in the practical reason is one founded on the notion of good, viz., that *good is that which all things seek after.* Hence this is the first precept of law, that *good is to be done and pursued, and evil is to be avoided.* All other precepts of the natural law are based upon this: so that whatever the practical reason naturally apprehends as man's good (or evil) belongs to the precepts of the natural law as something to be done or avoided.

Since, however, good has the nature of an end, and evil, the nature of a contrary, hence it is that all those things to which man has a natural inclination, are naturally apprehended by reason as being good, and consequently as objects of pursuit, and their contraries as evil, and objects of avoidance. Wherefore according to the order of natural inclinations, is the order of the precepts of the natural law. Because in man there is first of all an inclination to good in accordance with the nature which he has in common with all substances: inasmuch as every substance seeks the preservation of its own being, according to its nature: and by reason of this inclination, whatever is a means of preserving human life, and of warding off its obstacles, belongs to the natural law. Secondly, there is in man an inclination to things that pertain to him more specially, according to that nature which he has in common with other animals: and in virtue of this inclination, those things are said to belong to the natural law, *which nature has taught to all animals,** such as sexual intercourse, education of offspring and so forth. Thirdly, there is in man an inclination to good, according to the nature of his reason, which nature is proper to him: thus man has a natural inclination to know the truth about God, and to live in society: and in this respect, whatever pertains to this inclination belongs to the natural law; for instance, to shun ignorance, to avoid offending those among whom one has to live, and other such things regarding the above inclination.

Reply Obj. 1. All these precepts of the law of nature have the character of one natural law, inasmuch as they flow from one first precept.

Reply Obj. 2. All the inclinations of any parts whatsoever of human nature, *e.g.*, of the concupiscible and irascible parts, in so far as they are ruled by reason, belong to the natural law, and are reduced to one first precept, as stated above: so that the precepts of the natural law are many in themselves, but are based on one common foundation.

Reply Obj. 3. Although reason is one in itself, yet it directs all things regarding man; so that whatever can be ruled by reason, is contained under the law of reason.

THIRD ARTICLE

Whether All Acts of Virtue Are Prescribed by the Natural Law?

We proceed thus to the Third Article:—

Objection 1. It would seem that not all acts of virtue are prescribed by the natural law. Because, as stated above (Q. 90, A. 2) it is essential to a law that it be ordained to the common good. But some acts of virtue are ordained to the private good of the individual, as is evident especially in regards to acts of temperance. Therefore not all acts of virtue are the subject of natural law.

Obj. 2. Further, every sin is opposed to some virtuous act. If therefore all acts of virtue are prescribed by the natural law, it seems to follow that all sins are against nature: whereas this applies to certain special sins.

Obj. 3. Further, those things which are according to nature are common to all. But acts of virtue are not common to all: since a thing is virtuous in one, and vicious in another. Therefore not all acts of virtue are prescribed by the natural law.

On the contrary, Damascene says (*De Fide Orthod.* iii. 4) that *virtues are natural.* Therefore virtuous acts also are a subject of the natural law.

I answer that, We may speak of virtuous acts in two ways: first, under the aspect of virtuous; secondly, as such and such acts considered in their proper species. If then we speak of acts of virtue, considered as virtuous, thus all virtuous acts belong to the natural law. For it has been stated (A. 2) that to the natural law belongs everything to which a man is inclined according to his nature. Now each thing is inclined naturally to an operation that is suitable to it according to its form: thus fire is inclined to give heat. Wherefore, since the rational soul is the proper form of man, there

is in every man a natural inclination to act according to reason: and this is to act according to virtue. Consequently, considered thus, all acts of virtue are prescribed by the natural law: since each one's reason naturally dictates to him to act virtuously. But if we speak of virtuous acts, considered in themselves, i.e., in their proper species, thus not all virtuous acts are prescribed by the natural law: for many things are done virtuously, to which nature does not incline at first; but which, through the inquiry of reason, have been found by men to be conducive to well-living.

Reply Obj. 1. Temperance is about the natural concupiscences of food, drink and sexual matters, which are indeed ordained to the natural common good, just as other matters of law are ordained to the moral common good.

Reply Obj. 2. By human nature we may mean either that which is proper to man—and in this sense all sins, as being against reason, are also against nature, as Damascene states (*De Fide Orthod.* ii. 30) : or we may mean that nature which is common to man and other animals; and in this sense, certain special sins are said to be against nature; thus contrary to sexual intercourse, which is natural to all animals, is unisexual lust, which has received the special name of the unnatural crime.

Reply Obj. 3. This argument considers acts in themselves. For it is owing to the various conditions of men, that certain acts are virtuous for some, as being proportionate and becoming to them, while they are vicious for others, as being out of proportion to them.

FOURTH ARTICLE

Whether the Natural Law Is the Same in All Men?

We proceed thus to the Fourth Article:—

Objection 1. It would seem that the natural law is not the same in all. For it is stated in the Decretals (*Dist.* i) that *the natural law is that which is contained in the Law and the Gospel.* But this is not common to all men; because, as it is written (Rom. x. 16), *all do not obey the gospel.* Therefore the natural law is not the same in all men.

Obj. 2. Further, *Things which are according to the law are said to be just,* as stated in *Ethic.* v. But it is stated in the same book that nothing is so universally just as not to be subject to change in regard to some men. Therefore even the natural law is not the same in all men.

Obj. 3. Further, as stated above (AA. 2, 3), to the natural law belongs everything to which a man is inclined according to his nature. Now different men are naturally inclined to different things; some to the desire of pleasures, others to the desire of honors, and other men to other things. Therefore there is not one natural law for all.

On the contrary, Isidore says (*Etym.* v. 4): *The natural law is common to all nations.*

I answer that, As stated above (AA. 2, 3), to the natural law belongs those things to which a man is inclined naturally: and among these it is proper to man to be inclined to act according to reason. Now the process of reason is from the common to the proper, as stated in *Phys.* i. The speculative reason, however, is differently situated in this matter, from the practical reason. For, since the speculative reason is busied chiefly with necessary things, which cannot be otherwise than they are, its proper conclusions, like the universal principles, contain the truth without fail. The practical reason, on the other hand, is busied with contingent matters, about which human actions are concerned: and consequently, although there is necessity in the general principles, the more we descend to matters of detail, the more frequently we encounter defects. Accordingly then in speculative matters truth is the same in all men, both as to principles and as to conclusions: although the truth is not known to all as regards the conclusions, but only as regards the principles which are called common notions. But in matters of action, truth or practical rectitude is not the same for all, as to matters of detail, but only as to the general principles: and where there is the same rectitude in matters of detail, it is not equally known to all.

It is therefore evident that, as regards the general principles whether of speculative or of practical reason, truth or rectitude is the same for all, and is equally known by all. As to the proper conclusions of the speculative reason, the truth is the same for all, but is not equally known to all: thus it is true for all that the three angles of a triangle are together equal to two right angles, although it is not known to all. But as to the proper conclusions of the practical reason, neither is the truth or rectitude the same for all, nor, where it is the same, is it equally known by all. Thus it is right and true for all to act according to reason: and from this principle it follows as a proper conclusion, that goods entrusted to another should be restored to their owner. Now this is true for the majority of cases: but it may happen in a particular case that it would be injurious, and therefore unreasonable, to restore goods held in trust; for instance if they are claimed for the purpose of fighting against one's country. And this principle will be found to fail the more, according as we descend further into detail, *e.g.,* if one were to say that goods held in trust should be restored with such and such a guarantee, or in

such and such a way; because the greater the number of conditions added, the greater the number of ways in which the principle may fail, so that it be not right to restore or not to restore.

Consequently we must say that the natural law, as to general principles, is the same for all, both as to rectitude and as to knowledge. But as to certain matters of detail, which are conclusions, as it were, of those general principles, it is the same for all in the majority of cases, both as to rectitude and as to knowledge; and yet in some few cases it may fail, both as to rectitude, by reason of certain obstacles (just as natures subject to generation and corruption fail in some few cases on account of some obstacle), and as to knowledge, since in some the reason is perverted by passion, or evil habit, or an evil disposition of nature; thus formerly, theft, although it is expressly contrary to the natural law, was not considered wrong among the Germans, as Julius Cæsar relates (*De Bello Gall.* vi).

Reply Obj. 1. The meaning of the sentence quoted is not that whatever is contained in the Law and the Gospel belongs to the natural law, since they contain many things that are above nature; but that whatever belongs to the natural law is fully contained in them. Wherefore Gratian, after saying that *the natural law is what is contained in the Law and the Gospel,* adds at once, by way of example, *by which everyone is commanded to do to others as he would be done by.*

Reply Obj. 2. The saying of the Philosopher is to be understood of things that are naturally just, not as general principles, but as conclusions drawn from them, having rectitude in the majority of cases, but failing in a few.

Reply Obj. 3. As, in man, reason rules and commands the other powers, so all the natural inclinations belonging to the other powers must needs be directed according to reason. Wherefore it is universally right for all men, that all their inclinations should be directed according to reason.

FIFTH ARTICLE

Whether the Natural Law Can Be Changed?

We proceed thus to the Fifth Article:—

Objection 1. It would seem that the natural law can be changed. Because on Ecclus. xvii. 9, *He gave them instructions, and the law of life,* the gloss says: *He wished the law of the letter to be written, in order to correct the law of nature.* But that which is corrected is changed. Therefore the natural law can be changed.

Obj. 2. Further, the slaying of the innocent,

adultery, and theft are against the natural law. But we find these things changed by God: as when God commanded Abraham to slay his innocent son (Gen. xxii. 2); and when he ordered the Jews to borrow and purloin the vessels of the Egyptians (Exod. xii. 35); and when He commanded Osee to take to himself *a wife of fornications* (Osee i. 2). Therefore the natural law can be changed.

Obj. 3. Further, Isidore says (*Etym.* v. 4) that *the possession of all things in common, and universal freedom, are matters of natural law.* But these things are seen to be changed by human laws. Therefore it seems that the natural law is subject to change.

On the contrary, It is said in the Decretals (*Dist.* v): *The natural law dates from the creation of the rational creature. It does not vary according to time, but remains unchangeable.*

I answer that, A change in the natural law may be understood in two ways. First, by way of addition. In this sense nothing hinders the natural law from being changed: since many things for the benefit of human life have been added over and above the natural law, both by the Divine law and by human laws.

Secondly, a change in the natural law may be understood by way of subtraction, so that what previously was according to the natural law, ceases to be so. In this sense, the natural law is altogether unchangeable in its first principles: but in its secondary principles, which, as we have said (A. 4), are certain detailed proximate conclusions drawn from the first principles, the natural law is not changed so that what it prescribes be not right in most cases. But it may be changed in some particular cases of rare occurrence, through some special causes hindering the observance of such precepts, as stated above (A. 4).

Reply Obj. 1. The written law is said to be given for the correction of the natural law, either because it supplies what was wanting to the natural law; or because the natural law was perverted in the hearts of some men, as to certain matters, so that they esteemed those things good which are naturally evil; which perversion stood in need of correction.

Reply Obj. 2. All men alike, both guilty and innocent, die the death of nature: which death of nature is inflicted by the power of God on account of original sin, according to 1 Kings ii. 6: *The Lord killeth and maketh alive.* Consequently, by the command of God, death can be inflicted on any man, guilty or innocent, without any injustice whatever.— In like manner adultery is intercourse with another's wife; who is allotted to him by the law emanating from God. Consequently inter-

course with any woman, by the command of God, is neither adultery nor fornication.—The same applies to theft, which is the taking of another's property. For whatever is taken by the command of God, to Whom all things belong, is not taken against the will of its owner, whereas it is in this that theft consists.—Nor is it only in human things, that whatever is commanded by God is right; but also in natural things, whatever is done by God, is, in some way, natural, as stated in the First Part (Q. 105, A. 6 *ad* 1).

Reply Obj. 3. A thing is said to belong to the natural law in two ways. First, because nature inclines thereto: *e.g.,* that one should not do harm to another. Secondly, because nature did not bring in the contrary: thus we might say that for man to be naked is of the natural law, because nature did not give him clothes, but art invented them. In this sense, *the possession of all things in common and universal freedom* are said to be of the natural law, because, to wit, the distinction of possessions and slavery were not brought in by nature, but devised by human reason for the benefit of human life. Accordingly the law of nature was not changed in this respect, except by addition.

SIXTH ARTICLE

Whether the Law of Nature Can Be Abolished from the Heart of Man?

We proceed thus to the Sixth Article:—

Objection 1. It would seem that the natural law can be abolished from the heart of man. Because on Rom. ii. 14, *When the Gentiles who have not the law,* etc., a gloss says that *the law of righteousness, which sin had blotted out, is graven on the heart of man when he is restored by grace.* But the law of righteousness is the law of nature. Therefore the law of nature can be blotted out.

Obj. 2. Further, the law of grace is more efficacious than the law of nature. But the law of grace is blotted out by sin. Much more therefore can the law of nature be blotted out.

Obj. 3. Further, that which is established by law is made just. But many things are enacted by men, which are contrary to the law of nature. Therefore the law of nature can be abolished from the heart of man.

On the contrary, Augustine says (*Conf.* ii): *Thy law is written in the hearts of men, which iniquity itself effaces not.* But the law which is written in men's hearts is the natural law. Therefore the natural law cannot be blotted out.

I answer that, As stated above (AA. 4, 5), there belong to the natural law, first, certain most general precepts, that are known to all; and secondly, certain secondary and more detailed precepts, which are, as it were, conclusions following closely from first principles. As to those general principles, the natural law, in the abstract, can nowise be blotted out from men's hearts. But it is blotted out in the case of a particular action, in so far as reason is hindered from applying the general principle to a particular point of practice, on account of concupiscence or some other passion, as stated above (Q. 77, A. 2).—But as to the other, *i.e.*, the secondary precepts, the natural law can be blotted out from the human heart, either by evil persuasions, just as in speculative matters errors occur in respect of necessary conclusions; or by vicious customs and corrupt habits, as among some men, theft, and even unnatural vices, as the Apostle states (Rom. i), were not esteemed sinful.

Reply Obj. 1. Sin blots out the law of nature in particular cases, not universally, except perchance in regard to the secondary precepts of the natural law, in the way stated above.

Reply Obj. 2. Although grace is more efficacious than nature, yet nature is more essential to man, and therefore more enduring.

Reply Obj. 3. This argument is true of the secondary precepts of the natural law, against which some legislators have framed certain enactments which are unjust.

QUESTION 95

Of Human Law

(In Four Articles)

WE must now consider human law; and (1) this law considered in itself; (2) its power; (3) its mutability. Under the first head there are four points of inquiry: (1) Its utility. (2) Its origin. (3) Its quality. (4) Its division.

FIRST ARTICLE

Whether It Was Useful for Laws to Be Framed by Men?

We proceed thus to the First Article:—

Objection 1. It would seem that it was not useful for laws to be framed by men. Because the purpose of every law is that man be made good thereby, as stated above (Q. 92, A. 1). But men are more to be induced to be good willingly by means of admonitions, than against their will, by means of laws. Therefore there was no need to frame laws.

Obj. 2. Further, As the Philosopher says (*Ethic.* v. 4), *men have recourse to a judge as to animate justice.* But animate justice is better than inanimate justice, which is contained in laws. Therefore it would have been better for the execution of justice to be entrusted to the decision of judges, than to frame laws in addition.

Obj. 3. Further, every law is framed for the direction of human actions, as is evident from what has been stated above (Q. 90, AA. 1, 2). But since human actions are about singulars, which are infinite in number, matters pertaining to the direction of human actions cannot be taken into sufficient consideration except by a wise man, who looks into each one of them. Therefore it would have been better for human acts to be directed by the judgment of wise men, than by the fram-

ing of laws. Therefore there was no need of human laws.

On the contrary, Isidore says (*Etym.* v. 20): *Laws were made that in fear thereof human audacity might be held in check, that innocence might be safeguarded in the midst of wickedness, and that the dread of punishment might prevent the wicked from doing harm.* But these things are most necessary to mankind. Therefore it was necessary that human laws should be made.

I answer that, As stated above (Q. 63, A. 1; Q. 94, A. 3), man has a natural aptitude for virtue; but the perfection of virtue must be acquired by man by means of some kind of training. Thus we observe that man is helped by industry in his necessities, for instance, in food and clothing. Certain beginnings of these he has from nature, viz., his reason and his hands; but he has not the full complement, as other animals have, to whom nature has given sufficiency of clothing and food. Now it is difficult to see how man could suffice for himself in the matter of this training: since the perfection of virtue consists chiefly in withdrawing man from undue pleasures, to which above all man is inclined, and especially the young, who are more capable of being trained. Consequently a man needs to receive this training from another, whereby to arrive at the perfection of virtue. And as to those young people who are inclined to acts of virtue, by their good natural disposition, or by custom, or rather by the gift of God, paternal training suffices, which is by admonitions. But since some are found to be depraved, and prone to vice, and not easily amenable to words, it was necessary for such to be restrained from evil by force and fear, in order that, at least, the might desist from evil-doing, and leave others in peace, and that they themselves, by being habituated in this way, might be brought to do willingly what hitherto they did from fear, and thus become virtuous. Now this kind of training, which compels through fear of punishment, is the discipline of laws. Therefore, in order that man might have peace and virtue, it was necessary for laws to be framed: for, as the Philosopher says (*Polit.* i. 2), *as man is the most noble of animals if he be perfect in virtue, so is he the lowest of all, if he be severed from law and righteousness;* because man can use his reason to devise means of satisfying his lusts and evil passions, which other animals are unable to do.

Reply Obj. 1. Men who are well disposed are led willingly to virtue by being admonished better than by coercion: but men who are evilly disposed are not led to virtue unless they are compelled.

Reply Obj. 2. As the Philosopher says (*Rhet.* i. 1), *it is better that all things be regulated by law, than left to be decided by judges:* and this for three reasons. First, because it is easier to find a few wise men competent to frame right laws, than to find the many who would be necessary to judge aright of each single case.—Secondly, because those who make laws consider long beforehand what laws to make; whereas judgment on each single case has to be pronounced as soon as it arises: and it is easier for man to see what is right, by taking many instances into consideration, than by considering one solitary fact.—Thirdly, because lawgivers judge in the abstract and of future events; whereas those who sit in judgment judge of things present, towards which they are affected by love, hatred, or some kind of cupidity; wherefore their judgment is perverted.

Since then the animated justice of the judge is not found in every man, and since it can be deflected, therefore it was necessary, whenever possible, for the law to determine how to judge, and for very few matters to be left to the decision of men.

Reply Obj. 3. Certain individual facts which cannot be covered by the law *have necessarily to be committed to judges,* as the Philosopher says in the same passage: for instance, *concerning something that has happened or not happened,* and the like.

SECOND ARTICLE

Whether Every Human Law Is Derived from the Natural Law?

We proceed thus to the Second Article:—
Objection 1. It would seem that not every

human law is derived from the natural law. For the Philosopher says (*Ethic.* v. 7) that *the legal just is that which originally was a matter of indifference.* But those things which arise from the natural law are not matters of indifference. Therefore the enactments of human laws are not all derived from the natural law.

Obj. 2. Further, positive law is contrasted with natural law, as stated by Isidore (*Etym.* v. 4) and the Philosopher (*Ethic.* v, *loc. cit.*). But those things which flow as conclusions from the general principles of the natural law belong to the natural law, as stated above (Q. 94, A. 4). Therefore that which is established by human law does not belong to the natural law.

Obj. 3. Further, the law of nature is the same for all; since the Philosopher says (*Ethic* v. 7) that *the natural just is that which is equally valid everywhere.* If therefore human laws were derived from the natural law, it would follow that they too are the same for all: which is clearly false.

Obj. 4. Further, it is possible to give a reason for things which are derived from the natural law. But *it is not possible to give the reason for all the legal enactments of the lawgivers,* as the jurist says.* Therefore not all human laws are derived from the natural law.

On the contrary, Tully says (*Rhetor.* ii): *Things which emanated from nature and were approved by custom, were sanctioned by fear and reverence for the laws.*

I answer that, As Augustine says (*De Lib. Arb.* i. 5), *that which is not just seems to be no law at all:* wherefore the force of a law depends on the extent of its justice. Now in human affairs a thing is said to be just, from being right, according to the rule of reason. But the first rule of reason is the law of nature, as is clear from what has been stated above (Q. 91, A. 2 *ad* 2). Consequently every human law has just so much of the nature of law, as it is derived from the law of nature. But if in any point it deflects from the law of nature, it is no longer a law but a perversion of law.

But it must be noted that something may be derived from the natural law in two ways: first, as a conclusion from premises, secondly, by way of determination of certain generalities. The first way is like to that by which, in sciences, demonstrated conclusions are drawn from the principles: while the second mode is likened to that whereby, in the arts, general forms are particularized as to details: thus the craftsman needs to determine the general form of a house to some particular shape. Some things are therefore derived from the general

* *Pandect. Justin.* lib. i. ff., tit. iii., v., *De Leg. et Senat.*

principles of the natural law, by way of conclusions; *e.g.*, that *one must not kill* may be derived as a conclusion from the principle that *one should do harm to no man:* while some are derived therefrom by way of determination; *e.g.*, the law of nature has it that the evil-doer should be punished; but that he be punished in this or that way, is a determination of the law of nature.

Accordingly both modes of derivation are found in the human law. But those things which are derived in the first way, are contained in human law not as emanating therefrom exclusively, but have some force from the natural law also. But those things which are derived in the second way, have no other force than that of human law.

Reply Obj. 1. The Philosopher is speaking of those enactments which are by way of determination or specification of the precepts of the natural law.

Reply Obj. 2. This argument avails for those things that are derived from the natural law, by way of conclusions.

Reply Obj. 3. The general principles of the natural law cannot be applied to all men in the same way on account of the great variety of human affairs: and hence arises the diversity of positive laws among various people.

Reply Obj. 4. These words of the Jurist are to be understood as referring to decisions of rulers in determining particular points of the natural law: on which determinations the judgment of expert and prudent men is based as on its principles; in so far, to wit, as they see at once what is the best thing to decide. Hence the Philosopher says (*Ethic.* vi. 11) that in such matters, *we ought to pay as much attention to the undemonstrated sayings and opinions of persons who surpass us in experience, age and prudence, as to their demonstrations.*

THIRD ARTICLE

Whether Isidore's Description of the Quality of Positive Law Is Appropriate?

We proceed thus to the Third Article:—

Objection 1. It would seem that Isidore's description of the quality of positive law is not appropriate, when he says (*Etym.* v. 21): *Law shall be virtuous, just, possible to nature, according to the custom of the country, suitable to place and time, necessary, useful; clearly expressed, lest by its obscurity it lead to misunderstanding; framed for no private benefit, but for the common good.* Because he had previously expressed the quality of law in three conditions, saying that *law is anything*

* *Pandect. Just. lib. xxv. ff., tit. iii., De Leg. et Senat.*

founded on reason, provided that it foster religion, be helpful to discipline, and further the common weal. Therefore it was needless to add any further conditions to these.

Obj. 2. Further, Justice is included in honesty, as Tully says (*De Offic.* vii). Therefore after saying *honest* it was superfluous to add *just.*

Obj. 3. Further, written law is condivided with custom, according to Isidore (*Etym.* ii. 10). Therefore it should not be stated in the definition of law that it is *according to the custom of the country.*

Obj. 4. Further, a thing may be necessary in two ways. It may be necessary simply, because it cannot be otherwise: and that which is necessary in this way, is not subject to human judgment, wherefore human law is not concerned with necessity of this kind. Again a thing may be necessary for an end: and this necessity is the same as usefulness. Therefore it is superfluous to say both *necessary* and *useful.*

On the contrary stands the authority of Isidore.

I answer that, Whenever a thing is for an end, its form must be determined proportionately to that end; as the form of a saw is such as to be suitable for cutting (*Phys.* ii, text. 88). Again, everything that is ruled and measured must have a form proportionate to its rule and measure. Now both these conditions are verified of human law: since it is both something ordained to an end; and is a rule or measure ruled or measured by a higher measure. And this higher measure is twofold, viz., the Divine law and the natural law, as explained above (A. 2; Q. 93, A. 3). Now the end of human law is to be useful to man, as the jurist states.* Wherefore Isidore in determining the nature of law, lays down, at first, three conditions; viz., that it *foster religion,* inasmuch as it is proportionate to the Divine law; that it be *helpful to discipline,* inasmuch as it is proportionate to the natural law; and that it *further the common weal,* inasmuch as it is proportionate to the utility of mankind.

All the other conditions mentioned by him are reduced to these three. For it is called virtuous because it fosters religion. And when he goes on to say that it should be *just, possible to nature, according to the customs of the country, adapted to place and time,* he implies that it should be helpful to discipline. For human discipline depends first on the order of reason, to which he refers by saying *just:* —secondly, it depends on the ability of the agent; because discipline should be adapted to each one according to his ability, taking also into account the ability of nature (for the same burdens should be not laid on children as on adults); and should be according to human customs; since man cannot live alone in society, paying no heed to others:—thirdly, it depends on certain circumstances, in respect of which he says, *adapted to place and time.*—The remaining words, *necessary, useful,* etc., mean that law should further the common weal: so that *necessity* refers to the removal of evils; *usefulness* to the attainment of good; *clearness of expression,* to the need of preventing any harm ensuing from the law itself.—And since, as stated above (Q. 90, A. 2), law is ordained to the common good, this is expressed in the last part of the description.

This suffices for the Replies to the Objections.

FOURTH ARTICLE

Whether Isidore's Division of Human Laws Is Appropriate?

We proceed thus to the Fourth Article:—

Objection 1. It would seem that Isidore wrongly divided human statutes or human law (*Etym.* v. 4 *seqq.*). For under this law he includes the *law of nations,* so called, because, as he says, *nearly all nations use it.* But as he says, *natural law is that which is common to all nations.* Therefore the law of nations is not contained under positive human law, but rather under natural law.

Obj. 2. Further, those laws which have the same force, seem to differ not formally but only materially. But *statutes, decrees of the commonalty, senatorial decrees,* and the like which he mentions (*ibid.,* 9), all have the same force. Therefore they do not differ, except materially. But art takes no notice of such a distinction: since it may go on to infinity. Therefore this division of human laws is not appropriate.

Obj. 3. Further, just as, in the state, there are princes, priests and soldiers, so are there other human offices. Therefore it seems that, as this division includes *military law,* and *public law,* referring to priests and magistrates; so also it should include other laws pertaining to the other offices of the state.

Obj. 4. Further, those things that are accidental should be passed over. But it is accidental to law that it be framed by this or that man. Therefore it is unreasonable to divide laws according to the names of lawgivers, so that one be called the *Cornelian* law, another the *Falcidian* law, etc.

On the contrary, The authority of Isidore (Obj. 1) suffices.

I answer that, A thing can of itself be divided in respect of something contained in the notion of that thing. Thus a soul either rational or irrational is contained in the notion of animal: and therefore animal is divided properly and of itself in respect of its being rational or irrational; but not in the point of its being white or black, which are entirely beside the notion of animal. Now, in the notion of human law, many things are contained, in respect of any of which human law can be divided properly and of itself. For in the first place it belongs to the notion of human law, to be derived from the law of nature, as explained above (A. 2). In this respect positive law is divided into the *law of nations* and *civil law,* according to the two ways in which something may be derived from the law of nature, as stated above (A. 2). Because, to the law of nations belong those things which are derived from the law of nature, as conclusions from premises, *e.g.,* just buyings and sellings, and the like, without which men cannot live together, which is a point of the law of nature, since man is by nature a social animal, as is proved in *Polit.* i. 2. But those things which are derived from the law of nature by way of particular determination, belong to the civil law, according as each state decides on what is best for itself.

Secondly, it belongs to the notion of human law, to be ordained to the common good of the state. In this respect human law may be divided according to the different kinds of men who work in a special way for the common good: *e.g.,* priests, by praying to God for the people; princes, by governing the people; soldiers, by fighting for the safety of the people. Wherefore certain special kinds of law are adapted to these men.

Thirdly, it belongs to the notion of human law, to be framed by that one who governs the community of the state, as shown above (Q. 90, A. 3). In this respect, there are various human laws according to the various forms of government. Of these, according to the Philosopher (*Polit.* iii. 10) one is *monarchy,* i.e., when the state is governed by one; and then we have *Royal Ordinances.* Another form is *aristocracy,* i.e., government by the best men or men of highest rank; and then we have the *Authoritative legal opinions* (*Responsa Prudentum*) and *Decrees of the Senate* (*Senatus consulta*). Another form is *oligarchy,* i.e., government by a few rich and powerful men; and then we have *Prætorian,* also called *Honorary,* law. Another form of government is that of the people, which is called *democracy,* and there we have *Decrees of the commonalty* (*Plebiscita*). There is also tyrannical government, which is altogether corrupt, which, therefore, has no corresponding law.

Finally, there is a form of government made up of all these, and which is the best: and in this respect we have law sanctioned by the *Lords and Commons,* as stated by Isidore (*loc. cit.*).

Fourthly, it belongs to the notion of human law to direct human actions. In this respect, according to the various matters of which the law treats, there are various kinds of laws, which are sometimes named after their authors: thus we have the *Lex Julia* about adultery, the *Lex Cornelia* concerning assassins, and so on, differentiated in this way, not on account of the authors, but on account of the matters to which they refer.

Reply Obj. 1. The law of nations is indeed, in some way, natural to man, in so far as he is a reasonable being, because it is derived from the natural law by way of a conclusion that is not very remote from its premises. Wherefore men easily agreed thereto. Nevertheless it is distinct from the natural law, especially from that natural law which is common to all animals.

The Replies to the other Objections are evident from what has been said.

QUESTION 96

Of the Power of Human Law

(In Six Articles)

WE must now consider the power of human law. Under this head there are six points of inquiry: (1) Whether human law should be framed for the community? (2) Whether human law should repress all vices? (3) Whether human law is competent to direct all acts of virtue? (4) Whether it binds man in conscience? (5) Whether all men are subject to human law? (6) Whether those who are under the law may act beside the letter of the law?

FIRST ARTICLE

Whether Human Law Should Be Framed for the Community Rather Than for the Individual?

We proceed thus to the First Article:—

Objection 1. It would seem that human law should be framed not for the community, but rather for the individual. For the Philosopher says (*Ethic.* v. 7) that *the legal just . . . includes all particular acts of legislation . . . and all those matters which are the subject of decrees,* which are also individual matters, since decrees are framed about individual actions. Therefore law is framed not only for the community, but also for the individual.

Obj. 2. Further, law is the director of human acts, as stated above (Q. 90, AA. 1, 2). But human acts are about individual matters. Therefore human laws should be framed, not for the community, but rather for the individual.

Obj. 3. Further, law is a rule and measure of human acts, as stated above (Q. 90, AA. 1, 2). But a measure should be most certain, as stated in *Metaph.* x. Since therefore in human acts no general proposition can be so certain as not to fail in some individual cases, it seems that laws should be framed not in general but for individual cases.

On the contrary, The jurist says (*Pandect. Justin.* lib. i, tit. iii, art. ii, *De legibus,* etc.) that *laws should be made to suit the majority of instances; and they are not framed according to what may possibly happen in an individual case.*

I answer that, Whatever is for an end should be proportionate to that end. Now the end of law is the common good; because, as Isidore says (*Etym.* v. 21) that *law should be framed, not for any private benefit, but for the common good of all the citizens.* Hence human laws should be proportionate to the common good. Now the common good comprises many things. Wherefore law should take account of many things, as to persons, as to matters, and as to times. Because the community of the state is composed of many persons; and its good is procured by many actions; nor is it established to endure for only a short time, but to last for all time by the citizens succeeding one another, as Augustine says (*De Civ. Dei* ii. 21; xxii. 6).

Reply Obj. 1. The Philosopher (*Ethic.* v. 7) divides the legal just, i.e., positive law, into three parts. For some things are laid down simply in a general way: and these are the general laws. Of these he says that *the legal is that which originally was a matter of indifference, but which, when enacted, is so no longer:* as the fixing of the ransom of a captive.—Some things affect the community in one respect, and individuals in another. These are called *privileges,* i.e., *private laws,* as it were, because they regard private persons, although their power extends to many matters; and in regard to these, he adds, *and further, all particular acts of legislation.*—Other matters are legal, not through being laws, but through being applications of general laws to particular cases: such are decrees which have the force of law; and in regard to these, he adds *all matters subject to decrees*.

Reply Obj. 2. A principle of direction should be applicable to many; wherefore (*Metaph.* x, text. 4) the Philosopher says that all things belonging to one genus, are measured by one, which is the principle in that genus. For if there were as many rules or measures as there are things measured or ruled, they would cease to be of use, since their use consists in being applicable to many things. Hence law would be of no use, if it did not extend further than to one single act. Because the decrees of prudent men are made for the purpose of directing individual actions; whereas law is a general precept, as stated above (Q. 92, A. 2, Obj. 2).

Reply Obj. 3. *We must not seek the same degree of certainty in all things* (*Ethic.* i. 3). Consequently in contingent matters, such as natural and human things, it is enough for a thing to be certain, as being true in the greater number of instances, though at times and less frequently it fail.

SECOND ARTICLE

Whether It Belongs to the Human Law to Repress All Vices?

We proceed thus to the Second Article:—

Objection 1. It would seem that it belongs to human law to repress all vices. For Isidore says (*Etym.* v. 20) that *laws were made in order that, in fear thereof, man's audacity might be held in check*. But it would not be held in check sufficiently, unless all evils were repressed by law. Therefore human law should repress all evils.

Obj. 2. Further, the intention of the lawgiver is to make the citizens virtuous. But a man cannot be virtuous unless he forbear from all kinds of vice. Therefore it belongs to human law to repress all vices.

Obj. 3. Further, human law is derived from the natural law, as stated above (Q. 95, A. 2). But all vices are contrary to the law of nature. Therefore human law should repress all vices.

On the contrary, We read in *De Lib. Arb.* i. 5: *It seems to me that the law which is written for the governing of the people rightly permits these things, and that Divine providence punishes them*. But Divine providence punishes nothing but vices. Therefore human law rightly allows some vices, by not repressing them.

I answer that, As stated above (Q. 90, AA. 1, 2), law is framed as a rule or measure of human acts. Now a measure should be homogeneous with that which it measures, as stated in *Metaph.* x, text. 3, 4, since different things are measured by different measures. Where-

fore laws imposed on men should also be in keeping with their condition, for, as Isidore says (*Etym.* v. 21), law should be *possible both according to nature, and according to the customs of the country*. Now possibility or faculty of action is due to an interior habit or disposition: since the same thing is not possible to one who has not a virtuous habit, as is possible to one who has. Thus the same is not possible to a child as to a full-grown man: for which reason the law for children is not the same as for adults, since many things are permitted to children, which in an adult are punished by law or at any rate are open to blame. In like manner many things are permissible to men not perfect in virtue, which would be intolerable in a virtuous man.

Now human law is framed for a number of human beings, the majority of whom are not perfect in virtue. Wherefore human laws do not forbid all vices, from which the virtuous abstain, but only the more grievous vices, from which it is possible for the majority to abstain; and chiefly those that are to the hurt of others, without the prohibition of which human society could not be maintained: thus human law prohibits murder, theft and suchlike.

Reply Obj. 1. Audacity seems to refer to the assailing of others. Consequently it belongs to those sins chiefly whereby one's neighbor is injured: and these sins are forbidden by human law, as stated.

Reply Obj. 2. The purpose of human law is to lead men to virtue, not suddenly, but gradually. Wherefore it does not lay upon the multitude of imperfect men the burdens of those who are already virtuous, viz., that they should abstain from all evil. Otherwise these imperfect ones, being unable to bear such precepts, would break out into yet greater evils: thus it is written (Prov. xxx. 33): *He that violently bloweth his nose, bringeth out blood;* and (Matth. ix. 17) that if *new wine*, i.e., precepts of a perfect life, is *put into old bottles*, i.e., into imperfect men, *the bottles break, and the wine runneth out*, i.e., the precepts are despised, and those men, from contempt, break out into evils worse still.

Reply Obj. 3. The natural law is a participation in us of the eternal law: while human law falls short of the eternal law. Now Augustine says (*De Lib. Arb.* i. 5): *The law which is framed for the government of states, allows and leaves unpunished many things that are punished by Divine providence. Nor, if this law does not attempt to do everything, is this a reason why it should be blamed for what it does*. Wherefore, too, human law does not prohibit everything that is forbidden by the natural law.

THIRD ARTICLE

Whether Human Law Prescribes Acts of All the Virtues?

We proceed thus to the Third Article:—

Objection 1. It would seem that human law does not prescribe acts of all the virtues. For vicious acts are contrary to acts of virtue. But human law does not prohibit all vices, as stated above (A. 2). Therefore neither does it prescribe all acts of virtue.

Obj. 2. Further, a virtuous act proceeds from a virtue. But virtue is the end of law; so that whatever is from a virtue, cannot come under a precept of law. Therefore human law does not prescribe all acts of virtue.

Obj. 3. Further, law is ordained to the common good, as stated above (Q. 90, A. 2). But some acts of virtue are ordained, not to the common good, but to private good. Therefore the law does not prescribe all acts of virtue.

On the contrary, The Philosopher says (*Ethic.* v. 1) that the law *prescribes the performance of the acts of a brave man,* . . . *and the acts of the temperate man,* . . . *and the acts of the meek man: and in like manner as regards the other virtues and vices, prescribing the former, forbidding the latter.*

I answer that, The species of virtues are distinguished by their objects, as explained above (Q. 54, A. 2; Q. 60, A. 1; Q. 62, A. 2). Now all the objects of virtues can be referred either to the private good of an individual, or to the common good of the multitude: thus matters of fortitude may be achieved either for the safety of the state, or for upholding the rights of a friend, and in like manner with the other virtues. But law, as stated above (Q. 90, A. 2) is ordained to the common good. Wherefore there is no virtue whose acts cannot be prescribed by the law. Nevertheless human law does not prescribe concerning all the acts of every virtue: but only in regard to those that are ordainable to the common good,—either immediately, as when certain things are done directly for the common good,—or mediately, as when a lawgiver prescribes certain things pertaining to good order, whereby the citizens are directed in the upholding of the common good of justice and peace.

Reply Obj. 1. Human law does not forbid all vicious acts, by the obligation of a precept, as neither does it prescribe all acts of virtue. But it forbids certain acts of each vice, just as it prescribes some acts of each virtue.

Reply Obj. 2. An act is said to be an act of virtue in two ways. First, from the fact that a man does something virtuous; thus the act of justice is to do what is right, and an act of fortitude is to do brave things: and in this way law prescribes certain acts of virtue.— Secondly an act of virtue is when a man does a virtuous thing in a way in which a virtuous man does it. Such an act always proceeds from virtue: and it does not come under a precept of law, but is the end at which every lawgiver aims.

Reply Obj. 3. There is no virtue whose act is not ordainable to the common good, as stated above, either mediately or immediately.

FOURTH ARTICLE

Whether Human Law Binds a Man in Conscience?

We proceed thus to the Fourth Article:—

Objection 1. It would seem that human law does not bind a man in conscience. For an inferior power has no jurisdiction in a court of higher power. But the power of man, which frames human law, is beneath the Divine power. Therefore human law cannot impose its precept in a Divine court, such as is the court of conscience.

Obj. 2. Further, the judgment of conscience depends chiefly on the commandments of God. But sometimes God's commandments are made void by human laws, according to Matth. xv. 6: *You have made void the commandment of God for your tradition.* Therefore human law does not bind a man in conscience.

Obj. 3. Further, human laws often bring loss of character and injury on man, according to Isa. x. 1 *et seq.: Woe to them that make wicked laws, and when they write, write injustice; to oppress the poor in judgment, and do violence to the cause of the humble of My people.* But it is lawful for anyone to avoid oppression and violence. Therefore human laws do not bind man in conscience.

On the contrary, It is written (1 Pet. ii. 19): *This is thankworthy, if for conscience* . . . *a man endure sorrows, suffering wrongfully.*

I answer that, Laws framed by man are either just or unjust. If they be just, they have the power of binding in conscience, from the eternal law whence they are derived, according to Prov. viii. 15: *By Me kings reign, and lawgivers decree just things.* Now laws are said to be just, both from the end, when, to wit, they are ordained to the common good,—and from their author, that is to say, when the law that is made does not exceed the power of the lawgiver,—and from their form, when, to wit, burdens are laid on the subjects, according to an equality of proportion and with a view to the common good. For, since one man is a part of the community, each man in all that he is and has, belongs to the community; just as a part, in all that it is, belongs to the whole; wherefore nature inflicts a loss on the part, in order to save the whole: so that on this account, such laws as these, which impose proportionate burdens, are just and binding in conscience, and are legal laws.

On the other hand laws may be unjust in two ways: first, by being contrary to human good, through being opposed to the things mentioned above:—either in respect of the end, as when an authority imposes on his subjects burdensome laws, conducive, not to the common good, but rather to his own cupidity or vainglory;—or in respect of the author, as when a man makes a law that goes beyond the power committed to him;—or in respect of the form, as when burdens are imposed unequally on the community, although with a view to the common good. The like are acts of violence rather than laws; because, as Augustine says (*De Lib. Arb.* i. 5), *a law that is not just, seems to be no law at all.* Wherefore such laws do not bind in conscience, except perhaps in order to avoid scandal or disturbance, for which cause a man should even yield his right, according to Matth. v. 40, 41: *If a man . . . take away thy coat, let go thy cloak also unto him; and whosoever will force thee one mile, go with him other two.*

Secondly, laws may be unjust through being opposed to the Divine good: such are the laws of tyrants inducing to idolatry, or to anything else contrary to the Divine law: and laws of this kind must nowise be observed, because, as stated in Acts v. 29, *we ought to obey God rather than men.*

Reply Obj. 1. As the Apostle says (Rom. viii, 1, 2), all human power is from God . . . *therefore he that resisteth the power,* in matters that are within its scope, *resisteth the ordinance of God;* so that he becomes guilty according to his conscience.

Reply Obj. 2. This argument is true of laws that are contrary to the commandments of God, which is beyond the scope of (human) power. Wherefore in such matters human law should not be obeyed.

Reply Obj. 3. This argument is true of a law that inflicts unjust hurt on its subjects. The power that man holds from God does not extend to this: wherefore neither in such matters is man bound to obey the law, provided he avoid giving scandal or inflicting a more grievous hurt.

FIFTH ARTICLE

Whether All Are Subject to the Law?

We proceed thus to the Fifth Article:—

Objection 1. It would seem that not all are

subject to the law. For those alone are subject to a law for whom a law is made. But the Apostle says (1 Tim. i. 9): *The law is not made for the just man.* Therefore the just are not subject to the law.

Obj. 2. Further, Pope Urban says*: *He that is guided by a private law need not for any reason be bound by the public law.* Now all spiritual men are led by the private law of the Holy Ghost, for they are the sons of God, of whom it is said (Rom. viii. 14): *Whosoever are led by the Spirit of God, they are the sons of God.* Therefore not all men are subject to human law.

Obj. 3. Further, the jurist says† that *the sovereign is exempt from the laws.* But he that is exempt from the law is not bound thereby. Therefore not all are subject to the law.

On the contrary, The Apostle says (Rom. xiii. 1): *Let every soul be subject to the higher powers.* But subjection to a power seems to imply subjection to the laws framed by that power. Therefore all men should be subject to human law.

I answer that, As stated above (Q. 90, AA. 1, 2; A. 3 ad 2), the notion of law contains two things; first, that it is a rule of human acts; secondly, that it has coercive power. Wherefore a man may be subject to law in two ways. First, as the regulated is subject to the regulator: and, in this way, whoever is subject to a power, is subject to the law framed by that power. But it may happen in two ways that one is not subject to a power. In one way, by being altogether free from its authority: hence the subjects of one city or kingdom are not bound by the laws of the sovereign of another city or kingdom, since they are not subject to his authority. In another way, by being under a yet higher law; thus the subject of a proconsul should be ruled by his command, but not in those matters in which the subject receives his orders from the emperor: for in these matters, he is not bound by the mandate of the lower authority, since he is directed by that of a higher. In this way, one who is simply subject to a law, may not be subject thereto in certain matters, in respect of which he is ruled by a higher law.

Secondly, a man is said to be subject to a law as the coerced is subject to the coercer. In this way the virtuous and righteous are not subject to the law, but only the wicked. Because coercion and violence are contrary to the will: but the will of the good is in harmony with the law, whereas the will of the wicked is discordant from it. Wherefore in this sense the good are not subject to the law, but only the wicked.

Reply Obj. 1. This argument is true of subjection by way of coercion: for, in this way, *the law is not made for the just men:* because *they are a law to themselves,* since they *shew the work of the law written in their hearts,* as the Apostle says (Rom. ii. 14, 15). Consequently the law does not enforce itself upon them as it does on the wicked.

Reply Obj. 2. The law of the Holy Ghost is above all law framed by man: and therefore spiritual men, in so far as they are led by the law of the Holy Ghost, are not subject to the law in those matters that are inconsistent with the guidance of the Holy Ghost. Nevertheless the very fact that spiritual men are subject to law, is due to the leading of the Holy Ghost, according to 1 Pet. ii. 13: *Be ye subject . . . to every human creature for God's sake.*

Reply Obj. 3. The sovereign is said to be *exempt from the law,* as to its coercive power; since, properly speaking, no man is coerced by himself, and law has no coercive power save from the authority of the sovereign. Thus then is the sovereign said to be exempt from the law, because none is competent to pass sentence on him, if he acts against the law. Wherefore on Ps. L. 6: *To Thee only have I sinned,* a gloss says that *there is no man who can judge the deeds of a king.*—But as to the directive force of law, the sovereign is subject to the law by his own will, according to the statement (*Extra, De Constit.* cap. *Cum omnes*) that *whatever law a man makes for another, he should keep himself. And a wise authority* says: "Obey the law that thou makest thyself."* Moreover the Lord reproaches those who *say and do not;* and who *bind heavy burdens and lay them on men's shoulders, but with a finger of their own they will not move them* (Matth. xxiii. 3, 4). Hence, in the judgment of God, the sovereign is not exempt from the law, as to its directive force; but he should fulfil it of his own freewill and not of constraint.—Again the sovereign is above the law, in so far as, when it is expedient, he can change the law, and dispense in it according to time and place.

SIXTH ARTICLE

Whether He Who Is Under a Law May Act Beside the Letter of the Law?

We proceed thus to the Sixth Article:—

Objection 1. It seems that he who is subject to a law may not act beside the letter of the law. For Augustine says (*De Vera Relig.* xxxi): *Although men judge about temporal laws when they make them, yet when once they are made they must pass judgment not* on them, but according to them. But if anyone disregard the letter of the law, saying that he observes the intention of the lawgiver, he seems to pass judgment on the law. Therefore it is not right for one who is under a law to disregard the letter of the law, in order to observe the intention of the lawgiver.

Obj. 3. Further, he alone is competent to interpret the law who can make the law. But those who are subject to the law cannot make the law. Therefore they have no right to interpret the intention of the lawgiver, but should always act according to the letter of the law.

Obj. 3. Further, every wise man knows how to explain his intention by words. But those who framed the laws should be reckoned wise: for Wisdom says (Prov. viii. 15): *By Me kings reign, and lawgivers decree just things.* Therefore we should not judge of the intention of the lawgiver otherwise than by the words of the law.

On the contrary, Hilary says (*De Trin.* iv): *The meaning of what is said is according to the motive for saying it: because things are not subject to speech, but speech to things.* Therefore we should take account of the motive of the lawgiver, rather than of his very words.

I answer that, As stated above (A. 4), every law is directed to the common weal of men, and derives the force and nature of law accordingly. Hence the jurist says*: *By no reason of law, or favor of equity, is it allowable for us to interpret harshly, and render burdensome, those useful measures which have been enacted for the welfare of man.* Now it happens often that the observance of some point of law conduces to the common weal in the majority of instances, and yet, in some cases, is very hurtful. Since then the lawgiver cannot have in view every single case, he shapes the law according to what happens most frequently, by directing his attention to the common good. Wherefore if a case arise wherein the observance of that law would be hurtful to the general welfare, it should not be observed. For instance, suppose that in a besieged city it be an established law that the gates of the city are to be kept closed, this is good for public welfare as a general rule: but, if it were to happen that the enemy are in pursuit of certain citizens, who are defenders of the city, it would be a great loss to the city, if the gates were not opened to them: and so in that case the gates ought to be opened, contrary to the letter of the law, in order to maintain the common weal, which the lawgiver had in view.

Nevertheless it must be noted, that if the

---

* Dionysius Cato, *Dist. de Moribus.*   * *Pandect. Justin.* lib. i. ff., tit. 3, *De Leg. et Senat.*

observance of the law according to the letter does not involve any sudden risk needing instant remedy, it is not competent for everyone to expound what is useful and what is not useful to the state: those alone can do this who are in authority, and who, on account of such like cases, have the power to dispense from the laws. If, however, the peril be so sudden as not to allow of the delay involved by referring the matter to authority, the mere necessity brings with it a dispensation, since necessity knows no law.

Reply Obj. 1. He who in a case of necessity acts beside the letter of the law, does not judge of the law; but of a particular case in which he sees that the letter of the law is not to be observed.

Reply Obj. 2. He who follows the intention of the lawgiver, does not interpret the law simply; but in a case in which it is evident, by reason of the manifest harm, that the lawgiver intended otherwise. For if it be a matter of doubt, he must either act according to the letter of the law, or consult those in power.

Reply Obj. 3. No man is so wise as to be able to take account of every single case; wherefore he is not able sufficiently to express in words all those things that are suitable for the end he has in view. And even if a lawgiver were able to take all the cases into consideration, he ought not to mention them all, in order to avoid confusion: but should frame the law according to that which is of most common occurrence.

QUESTION 97

Of Change in Laws

(In Four Articles)

WE must now consider change in laws: under which head there are four points of inquiry: (1) Whether human law is changeable? (2) Whether it should be always changed, whenever anything better occurs? (3) Whether it is abolished by custom, and whether custom obtains the force of law? (4) Whether the application of human law should be changed by dispensation of those in authority?

FIRST ARTICLE

Whether Human Law Should Be Changed in Any Way?

We proceed thus to the First Article:—

Objection 1. It would seem that human law should not be changed in any way at all. Because human law is derived from the natural law, as stated above (Q. 95, A. 2). But the natural law endures unchangeably. Therefore human law should also remain without any change.

Obj. 2. Further, as the Philosopher says (*Ethic.* v. 5), a measure should be absolutely stable. But human law is the measure of human acts, as stated above (Q. 90, AA 1, 2). Therefore it should remain without change.

Obj. 3. Further, it is of the essence of law to be just and right, as stated above (Q. 95, A. 2). But that which is right once is right always. Therefore that which is law once, should be always law.

On the contrary, Augustine says (*De Lib. Arb.* i. 6): *A temporal law, however just, may be justly changed in course of time.*

I answer that, As stated above (Q. 91, A. 3), human law is a dictate of reason, whereby human acts are directed. Thus there may be two causes for the just change of human law: one on the part of reason; the other on the part of man whose acts are regulated by law. The cause on the part of reason is that it seems natural to human reason to advance gradually from the imperfect to the perfect. Hence, in speculative sciences, we see that the teaching of the early philosophers was imperfect, and that it was afterwards perfected by those who succeeded them. So also in practical matters: for those who first endeavored to discover something useful for the human community, not being able by themselves to take everything into consideration, set up certain institutions which were deficient in many ways; and these were changed by subsequent lawgivers who made institutions that might prove less frequently deficient in respect of the common weal.

On the part of man, whose acts are regulated by law, the law can be rightly changed on account of the changed condition of man, to whom different things are expedient according to the difference of his condition. An example is proposed by Augustine (*De Lib. Arb.* i. 6): *If the people have a sense of moderation and responsibility, and are most careful guardians of the common weal, it is right to enact a law allowing such a people to choose their own magistrates for the government of the commonwealth. But if, as time goes on, the same people become so corrupt as to sell their votes, and entrust the government to scoundrels and criminals; then the right of appointing their public officials is rightly forfeit to such a people, and the choice devolves to a few good men*

Reply. Obj. 1. The natural law is a participation of the eternal law, as stated above (Q. 91, A. 2), and therefore endures without change, owing to the unchangeableness and perfection of the Divine Reason, the Author of nature. But the reason of man is changeable and imperfect: wherefore his law is subject to change.—Moreover the natural law contains certain universal precepts, which are everlasting: whereas human law contains certain particular precepts, according to various emergencies.

Reply Obj. 2. A measure should be as enduring as possible. But nothing can be absolutely unchangeable in things that are subject to change. And therefore human law cannot be altogether unchangeable.

Reply Obj. 3. In corporal things, right is predicated absolutely: and therefore, as far as itself is concerned, always remains right. But right is predicated of law with reference to the common weal, to which one and the same thing is not always adapted, as stated above: wherefore rectitude of this kind is subject to change.

SECOND ARTICLE

Whether Human Law Should Always Be Changed, Whenever Something Better Occurs?

We proceed thus to the Second Article:—

Objection 1. It would seem that human law should be changed, whenever something better occurs. Because human laws are devised by human reason, like other arts. But in the other arts, the tenets of former times give place to others, if something better occurs. Therefore the same should apply to human laws.

Obj. 2. Further, by taking note of the past we can provide for the future. Now unless human laws had been changed when it was found possible to improve them, considerable inconvenience would have ensued; because the laws of old were crude in many points. Therefore it seems that laws should be changed, whenever anything better occurs to be enacted.

Obj. 3. Further, human laws are enacted about single acts of man. But we cannot acquire perfect knowledge in singular matters, except by experience, which *requires time,* as stated in *Ethic.* ii. Therefore it seems that as time goes on it is possible for something better to occur for legislation.

On the contrary, It is stated in the Decretals (*Dist.* xii. 5): *It is absurd, and a detestable shame, that we should suffer those traditions to be changed which we have received from the fathers of old.*

I answer that, As stated above (A. 1), human law is rightly changed, in so far as such change is conducive to the common weal. But, to a certain extent, the mere change of law is of itself prejudicial to the common good: because custom avails much for the observance of laws, seeing that what is done contrary to general custom, even in slight matters, is looked upon as grave. Consequently, when a law is changed, the binding power of the law is diminished, in so far as custom is abolished. Wherefore human law should never be changed, unless, in some way or other, the common weal be compensated according to the extent of the harm done in this respect. Such compensation may arise either from some very great and very evident benefit conferred by the new enactment; or from the extreme urgency of the case, due to the fact that either the existing law is clearly unjust, or its observance extremely harmful. Wherefore the jurist says* that *in establishing new laws, there should be evidence of the benefit to be derived, before departing from a law which has long been considered just.*

Reply Obj. 1. Rules of art derive their force from reason alone: and therefore whenever something better occurs, the rule followed hitherto should be changed. But *laws derive very great force from custom,* as the Philosopher states (*Polit.* ii. 5): consequently they should not be quickly changed.

Reply Obj. 2. This argument proves that laws ought to be changed: not in view of any improvement, but for the sake of a great benefit or in a case of great urgency, as stated above. This answer applies also to the Third Objection.

THIRD ARTICLE

Whether Custom Can Obtain Force of Law?

We proceed thus to the Third Article:—

Objection 1. It would seem that custom cannot obtain force of law, nor abolish a law. Because human law is derived from the natural law and from the Divine law, as stated above (Q. 93, A. 3; Q. 95, A. 2). But human custom cannot change either the law of nature or the Divine law. Therefore neither can it change human law.

Obj. 2. Further, many evils cannot make one good. But he who first acted against the law, did evil. Therefore by multiplying such acts, nothing good is the result. Now a law is something good; since it is a rule of human acts. Therefore law is not abolished by custom, so that the mere custom should obtain force of law.

Obj. 3. Further, the framing of laws belongs to those public men whose business it is to govern the community; wherefore private

* *Pandect. Justin.* lib. i. ff., tit. 4, *De Constit. Princip.*

individuals cannot make laws. But custom grows by the acts of private individuals. Therefore custom cannot obtain force of law, so as to abolish the law.

On the contrary, Augustine says (*Ep. ad Casulan.* xxxvi): *The customs of God's people and the institutions of our ancestors are to be considered as laws. And those who throw contempt on the customs of the Church ought to be punished as those who disobey the law of God.*

I answer that, All law proceeds from the reason and will of the lawgiver; the Divine and natural laws from the reasonable will of God; the human law from the will of man, regulated by reason. Now just as human reason and will, in practical matters, may be made manifest by speech, so may they be made known by deeds: since seemingly a man chooses as good that which he carries into execution. But it is evident that by human speech, law can be both changed and expounded, in so far as it manifests the interior movement and thought of human reason. Wherefore by actions also, especialy if they be repeated, so as to make a custom, law can be changed and expounded; and also something can be established which obtains force of law, in so far as by repeated external actions, the inward movement of the will, and concepts of reason are most effectually declared; for when a thing is done again and again, it seems to proceed from a deliberate judgment of reason. Accordingly, custom has the force of a law, abolishes law, and is the interpreter of law.

Reply Obj. 1. The natural and Divine laws proceed from the Divine will, as stated above. Wherefore they cannot be changed by a custom proceeding from the will of man, but only by Divine authority. Hence it is that no custom can prevail over the Divine or natural laws: for Isidore says (*Synon.* ii. 16): *Let custom yield to authority: evil customs should be eradicated by law and reason.*

Reply Obj. 2. As stated above (Q. 96, A. 6), human laws fail in some cases: wherefore it is possible sometimes to act beside the law; namely, in a case where the law fails; yet the act will not be evil. And when such cases are multiplied, by reason of some change in man, then custom shows that the law is no longer useful: just as it might be declared by the verbal promulgation of a law to the contrary. If, however, the same reason remains, for which the law was useful hitherto, then it is not the custom that prevails against the law, but the law that overcomes the custom: unless perhaps the sole reason for the law seeming useless, be that it is not *possible according*

Cf. Q. 95, A. 3.

*to the custom of the country,** which has been stated to be one of the conditions of law. For it is not easy to set aside the custom of a whole people.

Reply Obj. 3. The people among whom a custom is introduced may be of two conditions. For if they are free, and able to make their own laws, the consent of the whole people expressed by a custom counts far more in favor of a particular observance, than does the authority of the sovereign, who has not the power to frame laws, except as representing the people. Wherefore although each individual cannot make laws, yet the whole people can. If however the people have not the free power to make their own laws, or to abolish a law made by a higher authority; nevertheless with such a people a prevailing custom obtains force of law, in so far as it is tolerated by those to whom it belongs to make laws for that people: because by the very fact that they tolerate it they seem to approve of that which is introduced by custom.

FOURTH ARTICLE

Whether the Rulers of the People Can Dispense from Human Laws?

We proceed thus to the Fourth Article:—

Objection 1. It would seem that the rulers of the people cannot dispense from human laws. For the law is established for the *common weal,* as Isidore says (*Etym.* v. 21). But the common good should not be set aside for the private convenience of an individual: because, as the Philosopher says (*Ethic.* i. 2), *the good of the nation is more godlike than the good of one man.* Therefore it seems that a man should not be dispensed from acting in compliance with the general law.

Obj. 2. Further, those who are placed over others are commanded as follows (Deut. i. 17): *You shall hear the little as well as the great; neither shall you respect any man's person, because it is the judgment of God.* But to allow one man to do that which is equally forbidden to all, seems to be respect of persons. Therefore the rulers of a community cannot grant such dispensations, since this is against a precept of the Divine law.

Obj. 3. Further, human law, in order to be just, should accord with the natural and Divine laws: else it would not *foster religion,* nor be *helpful to discipline,* which is requisite to the nature of law, as laid down by Isidore (*Etym.* v. 3). But no man can dispense from the Divine and natural laws. Neither, therefore, can he dispense from the human law.

On the contrary, The Apostle says (1 Cor. ix. 17): *A dispensation is committed to me.*

I answer that, Dispensation, properly speaking, denotes a measuring out to individuals of some common goods: thus the head of a household is called a dispenser, because to each member of the household he distributes work and necessaries of life in due weight and measure. Accordingly in every community a man is said to dispense, from the very fact that he directs how some general precept is to be fulfilled by each individual. Now it happens at times that a precept, which is conducive to the common weal as a general rule, is not good for a particular individual, or in some particular case, either because it would hinder some greater good, or because it would be the occasion of some evil, as explained above (Q. 96, A. 6). But it would be dangerous to leave this to the discretion of each individual, except perhaps by reason of an evident and sudden emergency, as stated above (*ibid.*). Consequently he who is placed over a community is empowered to dispense in a human law that rests upon his authority, so that, when the law fails in its application to persons or circumstances, he may allow the precept of the law not to be observed. If however he grant this permission without any such reason, and of his mere will, he will be an unfaithful or an imprudent dispenser: unfaithful, if he has not the common good in view; imprudent, if he ignores the reasons for granting dispensations. Hence Our Lord says (Luke

xii. 42): *Who, thinkest thou, is the faithful and wise dispenser* (Douay,—*steward*), *whom his lord setteth over his family?*

Reply Obj. 1. When a person is dispensed from observing the general law, this should not be done to the prejudice of, but with the intention of benefiting, the common good.

Reply Obj. 2. It is not respect of persons if unequal measures are served out to those who are themselves unequal. Wherefore when the condition of any person requires that he should reasonably receive special treatment, it is not respect of persons if he be the object of special favor.

Reply Obj. 3. Natural law, so far as it contains general precepts, which never fail, does not allow of dispensation. In the other precepts, however, which are as conclusions of the general precepts, man sometimes grants a dispensation: for instance, that a loan should not be paid back to the betrayer of his country, or something similar. But to the Divine law each man stands as a private person to the public law to which he is subject. Wherefore just as none can dispense from public human law, except the man from whom the law derives its authority, or his delegate; so, in the precepts of the Divine law, which are from God, none can dispense but God, or the man to whom He may give special power for that purpose.

QUESTION 98

Of the Old Law

(In Six Articles)

IN due sequence we must now consider the Old Law; and (1) The Law itself; (2) Its precepts. Under the first head there are six points of inquiry: (1) Whether the Old Law was good? (2) Whether it was from God? (3) Whether it came from Him through the angels? (4) Whether it was given to all? (5) Whether it was binding on all? (6) Whether it was given at a suitable time?

FIRST ARTICLE

Whether the Old Law Was Good?

We proceed thus to the First Article:—

Objection 1. It would seem that the Old Law was not good. For it is written (Ezech. xx. 25): *I gave them statutes that were not good, and judgments in which they shall not live.* But a law is not said to be good except on account of the goodness of the precepts that it contains. Therefore the Old Law was not good.

Obj. 2. Further, it belongs to the goodness

of a law that it conduce to the common welfare, as Isidore says (*Etym.* v. 3). But the Old Law was not salutary; rather was it deadly and hurtful. For the Apostle says (Rom. vii. 8, *seq.*): *Without the law sin was dead. And I lived some time without the law. But when the commandment came sin revived; and I died.* Again he says (Rom. v. 20): *Law entered in that sin might abound.* Therefore the Old Law was not good.

Obj. 3. Further, it belongs to the goodness of the law that it should be possible to obey it, both according to nature, and according to human custom. But such the Old Law was not: since Peter said (Acts xv. 10): *Why tempt you (God) to put a yoke on the necks of the disciples, which neither our fathers nor we have been able to bear?* Therefore it seems that the Old Law was not good.

On the contrary, The Apostle says (Rom. vii. 12): *Wherefore the law indeed is holy, and the commandment holy, and just, and good.*

I answer that, Without any doubt, the Old

Law was good. For just as a doctrine is shown to be good by the fact that it accords with right reason, so is a law proved to be good if it accords with reason. Now the Old Law was in accordance with reason. Because it repressed concupiscence which is in conflict with reason, as evidenced by the commandment, *Thou shalt not covet thy neighbor's goods* (Exod. xx. 17). Moreover the same law forbade all kinds of sin; and these too are contrary to reason. Consequently it is evident that it was a good law. The Apostle argues in the same way (Rom. vii): *I am delighted,* says he *(verse 22), with the law of God, according to the inward man:* and again *(verse 16):* I *consent to the law, that is good.*

But it must be noted that the good has various degrees, as Dionysius states (*Div. Nom.* iv): for there is a perfect good, and an imperfect good. In things ordained to an end, there is perfect goodness when a thing is such that it is sufficient in itself to conduce to the end: while there is imperfect goodness when a thing is of some assistance in attaining the end, but is not sufficient for the realization thereof. Thus a medicine is perfectly good, if it gives health to a man; but it is imperfect, if it helps to cure him, without being able to bring him back to health. Again it must be observed that the end of human law is different from the end of Divine law. For the end of human law is the temporal tranquillity of the state, which end law effects by directing external actions, as regards those evils which might disturb the peaceful condition of the state. On the other hand, the end of the Divine law is to bring man to that end which is everlasting happiness; which end is hindered by any sin, not only of external, but also of internal action. Consequently that which suffices for the perfection of human law, viz., the prohibition and punishment of sin, does not suffice for the perfection of the Divine law: but it is requisite that it should make man altogether fit to partake of everlasting happiness. Now this cannot be done save by the grace of the Holy Ghost, whereby *charity,* which fulfilleth the law, . . . *is spread abroad in our hearts* (Rom. v. 5): since *the grace of God is life everlasting (ibid.* vi. 23). But the Old Law could not confer this grace, for this was reserved to Christ; because, as it is written (Jo. i. 17), the law was given *by Moses, grace and truth came by Jesus Christ.* Consequently the Old Law was good indeed, but imperfect, according to Heb. vii. 19: *The law brought nothing to perfection.*

Reply Obj. 1. The Lord refers there to the ceremonial precepts; which are said not to be good, because they did not confer grace unto the remission of sins, although by fulfilling these precepts man confessed himself a sinner. Hence it is said pointedly, *and judgments in which they shall not live;* i.e., whereby they are unable to obtain life; and so the text goes on: *And I polluted them,* i.e., showed them to be polluted, *in their own gifts, when they offered all that opened the womb, for their offenses.*

Reply Obj. 2. The law is said to have been deadly, as being not the cause, but the occasion of death, on account of its imperfection: in so far as it did not confer grace enabling man to fulfil what it prescribed, and to avoid what it forbade. Hence this occasion was not given to men, but taken by them. Wherefore the Apostle says *(ibid.* 11): *Sin, taking occasion by the commandment, seduced me, and by it killed me.* In the same sense when it is said that *the law entered in that sin might abound,* the conjunction *that* must be taken as consecutive and not final: in so far as men, taking occasion from the law, sinned all the more, both because a sin became more grievous after law had forbidden it, and because concupiscence increased, since we desire a thing the more from its being forbidden.

Reply Obj. 3. The yoke of the law could not be borne without the help of grace, which the law did not confer: for it is written (Rom. ix. 16): *It is not of him that willeth, nor of him that runneth,* viz., that he wills and runs in the commandments of God, *but of God that showeth mercy.* Wherefore it is written (Ps. cxviii. 32): *I have run the way of Thy commandments, when Thou didst enlarge my heart,* i.e., by giving me grace and charity.

SECOND ARTICLE

Whether the Old Law Was from God?

We proceed thus to the Second Article:—

Objection 1. It would seem that the Old Law was not from God. For it is written (Deut. xxxii. 4): *The works of God are perfect.* But the Law was imperfect, as stated above (A. 1). Therefore the Old Law was not from God.

Obj. 2. Further, it is written (Eccles. iii. 14): *I have learned that all the works which God hath made continue for ever.* But the Old Law does not continue for ever: since the Apostle says (Heb. vii. 18): *There is indeed a setting aside of the former commandment, because of the weakness and unprofitableness thereof.* Therefore the Old Law was not from God.

Obj. 3. Further, a wise lawgiver should remove, not only evil, but also the occasions of evil. But the Old Law was an occasion of sin, as stated above (A. 1 *ad* 2). Therefore the giving of such a law does not appertain to

God, to Whom *none is like among the lawgivers* (Job. xxxvi. 22).

Obj. 4. Further, it is written (1 Tim. ii. 4) that God *will have all men to be saved.* But the Old Law did not suffice to save man, as stated above (A. 1). Therefore the giving of such a law did not appertain to God. Therefore the Old Law was not from God.

On the contrary, Our Lord said (Matth. xv. 6) while speaking to the Jews, to whom the Law was given: *You have made void the commandment of God for your tradition.* And shortly before (*verse* 4) He had said: *Honor thy father and mother,* which is contained expressly in the Old Law (Exod. xx. 12; Deut. v. 16). Therefore the Old Law was from God.

I answer that, The Old Law was given by the good God, Who is the Father of Our Lord Jesus Christ. For the Old Law ordained men to Christ in two ways. First by bearing witness to Christ; wherefore He Himself says (Luke xxiv. 44): *All things must needs be fulfilled, which are written in the law . . ., and in the prophets, and in the psalms, concerning Me:* and (Jo. v. 46): *If you did believe Moses, you would perhaps believe Me also; for he wrote of Me.*—Secondly, as a kind of disposition, since by withdrawing men from idolatrous worship, it enclosed (*concludebat*) them in the worship of one God, by Whom the human race was to be saved through Christ. Wherefore the Apostle says (Gal. iii. 23): *Before the faith came, we were kept under the law shut up* (*conclusi*), *unto that faith which was to be revealed.* Now it is evident that the same thing it is, which gives a disposition to the end, and which brings to the end; and when I say *the same,* I mean that it does so either by itself or through its subjects. For the devil would not make a law whereby men would be led to Christ, Who was to cast him out, according to Matth. xii. 26: *If Satan cast out Satan, his kingdom is divided* (Vulg.,—*he is divided against himself*). Therefore the Old Law was given by the same God, from Whom came salvation to man, through the grace of Christ.

Reply Obj. 1. Nothing prevents a thing being not perfect simply, and yet perfect in respect of time: thus a boy is said to be perfect, not simply, but with regard to the condition of time. So, too, precepts that are given to children are perfect in comparison with the condition of those to whom they are given, although they are not perfect simply. Hence the Apostle says (Gal. iii. 24): *The law was our pedagogue in Christ.*

Reply Obj. 2. Those works of God endure for ever which God so made that they would endure for ever; and these are His perfect works. But the Old Law was set aside when

there came the perfection of grace; not as though it were evil, but as being weak and useless for this time; because, as the Apostle goes on to say, *the law brought nothing to perfection:* hence he says (Gal. iii. 25): *After the faith is come, we are no longer under a pedagogue.*

Reply Obj. 3. As stated above (Q. 79, A. 4), God sometimes permits certain ones to fall into sin, that they may thereby be humbled. So also did He wish to give such a law as men by their own forces could not fulfill, so that, while presuming on their own powers, they might find themselves to be sinners, and being humbled might have recourse to the help of grace.

Reply Obj. 4. Although the Old Law did not suffice to save man, yet another help from God besides the Law was available for man, viz., faith in the Mediator, by which the fathers of old were justified even as we are. Accordingly God did not fail man by giving him insufficient aids to salvation.

THIRD ARTICLE

Whether the Old Law Was Given through the Angels?

We proceed thus to the Third Article:—

Objection 1. It seems that the Old Law was not given through the angels, but immediately by God. For an angel means a *messenger;* so that the word *angel* denotes ministry, not lordship, according to Ps. cii. 20, 21: *Bless the Lord, all ye His Angels . . . you ministers of His.* But the Old Law is related to have been given by the Lord: for it is written (Exod. xx. 1): *And the Lord spoke . . . these words,* and further on: *I am the Lord Thy God.* Moreover the same expression is often repeated in Exodus, and in the later books of the Law. Therefore the Law was given by God immediately.

Obj. 2. Further, according to Jo. i. 17, *the Law was given by Moses.* But Moses received it from God immediately: for it is written (Exod. xxxiii. 11): *The Lord spoke to Moses face to face, as a man is wont to speak to his friend.* Therefore the Old Law was given by God immediately.

Obj. 3. Further, it belongs to the sovereign alone to make a law, as stated above (Q. 90, A. 3). But God alone is Sovereign as regards the salvation of souls: while the angels are the *ministering spirits,* as stated in Heb. i. 14. Therefore it was not meet for the Law to be given through the angels, since it is ordained to the salvation of souls.

On the contrary, The Apostle said (Gal. iii. 19) that the Law was *given* (Vulg.,—*ordained*) *by angels in the hand of a Mediator.* And Stephen said (Acts vii. 53): (*Who*) *have received the Law by the disposition of angels.*

I answer that, The Law was given by God through the angels. And besides the general reason given by Dionysius (*Cœl. Hier.* iv), viz., that *the gifts of God should be brought to men by means of the angels,* there is a special reason why the Old Law should have been given through them. For it has been stated (AA. 1, 2) that the Old Law was imperfect, and yet disposed man to that perfect salvation of the human race, which was to come through Christ. Now it is to be observed that wherever there is an order of powers or arts, he that holds the highest place, himself exercises the principal and perfect acts; while those things which dispose to the ultimate perfection are effected by him through his subordinates: thus the ship-builder himself rivets the planks together, but prepares the material by means of the workmen who assist him under his direction. Consequently it was fitting that the perfect law of the New Testament should be given by the incarnate God immediately; but that the Old Law should be given to men by the ministers of God, i.e., by the angels. It is thus that the Apostle at the beginning of his epistle to the Hebrews (i. 2) proves the excellence of the New Law over the Old; because in the New Testament *God . . . hath spoken to us by His Son,* whereas in the Old Testament *the word was spoken by angels* (ii. 2).

Reply Obj. 1. As Gregory says at the beginning of his *Morals (Præf., chap.* i), *the angel who is described to have appeared to Moses, is sometimes mentioned as an angel, sometimes as the Lord: an angel, in truth, in respect of that which was subservient to the external delivery; and the Lord, because He was the Director within, Who supported the effectual power of speaking.* Hence also it is that the angel spoke as personating the Lord.

Reply. Obj. 2. As Augustine says (*Gen. ad lit.* xii. 27), it is stated in Exodus that *the Lord spoke to Moses face to face;* and shortly afterwards we read: *"Show me Thy glory."* Therefore he perceived what he saw and he desired what he saw not. Hence he did not see the very Essence of God; and consequently he was not taught by Him immediately. Accordingly when Scripture states that *He spoke to him face to face,* this is to be understood as expressing the opinion of the people, who thought that Moses was speaking with God mouth to mouth, when God spoke and appeared to him, by means of a subordinate creature, i.e., an angel and a cloud.— Again we may say that this vision *face to face* means some kind of sublime and familiar contemplation, inferior to the vision of the Divine Essence.

Reply Obj. 3. It is for the sovereign alone to make a law by his own authority; but sometimes after making a law, he promulgates it through others. Thus God made the Law by His own authority, but He promulgated it through the angels.

FOURTH ARTICLE

Whether the Old Law Should Have Been Given to the Jews Alone?

We proceed thus to the Fourth Article:—

Objection 1. It would seem that the Old Law should not have been given to the Jews alone. For the Old Law disposed men for the salvation which was to come through Christ, as stated above (AA. 2, 3). But that salvation was to come not to the Jews alone but to all nations, according to Isa. xlix. 6: *It is a small thing that thou shouldst be my servant to raise up the tribes of Jacob, and to convert the dregs of Israel. Behold I have given thee to be the light of the Gentiles, that thou mayest be My salvation, even to the farthest part of the earth.* Therefore the Old Law should have been given to all nations, and not to one people only.

Obj. 2. Further, according to Acts x. 34, 35, *God is not a respecter of persons: but in every nation, he that feareth Him, and worketh justice, is acceptable to Him.* Therefore the way of salvation should not have been opened to one people more than to another.

Obj. 3. Further, the law was given through the angels, as stated above (A. 3). But God always vouchsafed the ministrations of the angels not to the Jews alone, but to all nations: for it is written (Ecclus. xvii. 14): *Over every nation He set a ruler.* Also on all nations He bestows temporal goods, which are of less account with God than spiritual goods. Therefore He should have given the Law also to all peoples.

On the contrary, It is written (Rom. iii. 1, 2): *What advantage then hath the Jew? . . . Much every way. First indeed, because the words of God were committed to them:* and (Ps. cxlvii. 9): *He hath not done in like manner to every nation: and His judgments He hath not made manifest unto them.*

I answer that, It might be assigned as a reason for the Law being given to the Jews rather than to other peoples, that the Jewish people alone remained faithful to the worship of one God, while the others turned away to idolatry; wherefore the latter were unworthy to receive the Law, lest a holy thing should be given to dogs.

But this reason does not seem fitting: because that people turned to idolatry, even after the Law had been made, which was more grievous, as is clear from Exod. xxxii. and from Amos v. 25, 26: *Did you offer victims and sacrifices to Me in the desert for forty years, O house of Israel? But you carried a tabernacle for your Moloch, and the image of your idols, the star of your god, which you made to yourselves.* Moreover it is stated expressly (Deut. ix. 6): *Know therefore that the Lord thy God giveth thee not this excellent land in possession for thy justices, for thou art a very stiff-necked people:* but the real reason is given in the preceding verse: *That the Lord might accomplish His word, which He promised by oath to thy fathers Abraham, Isaac, and Jacob.*

What this promise was is shown by the Apostle, who says (Gal. iii. 16) that *to Abraham were the promises made and to his seed. He saith not, "And to his seeds," as of many: but as of one, "And to thy seed, which is Christ."* And so God vouchsafed both the Law and other special boons to that people, on account of the promise made to their fathers that Christ should be born of them. For it was fitting that the people, of whom Christ was to be born, should be signalized by a special sanctification, according to the words of Levit. xix. 2: *Be ye holy, because I . . . am holy.*—Nor again was it on account of the merit of Abraham himself that this promise was made to him, viz., that Christ should be born of his seed: but of gratuitous election and vocation. Hence it is written (Isa. xli. 2): *Who hath raised up the just one from the east, hath called him to follow him?*

It is therefore evident that it was merely from gratuitous election that the patriarchs received the promise, and that the people sprung from them received the law; according to Deut. iv. 36, 37: *Ye did* (Vulg.,—*Thou didst*) *hear His words out of the midst of the fire, because He loved thy fathers, and chose their seed after them.*—And if again it be asked why He chose this people, and not another, that Christ might be born thereof; a fitting answer is given by Augustine (*Tract. super Joan.* xxvi.): *Why He draweth one and draweth not another, seek not thou to judge, if thou wish not to err.*

Reply Obj. 1 Although the salvation, which was to come through Christ, was prepared for all nations, yet it was necessary that Christ should be born of one people, which, for this reason, was privileged above other peoples; according to Rom. ix. 4: *To whom,* namely the Jews, *belongeth the adoption as of children (of God), . . . and the testament, and the giving of the Law; . . . whose are the fathers, and of whom is Christ according to the flesh.*

Reply Obj. 2. Respect of persons takes place in those things which are given according to

due; but it has no place in those things which are bestowed gratuitously. Because he who, out of generosity, gives of his own to one and not to another, is not a respecter of persons: but if he were a dispenser of goods held in common, and were not to distribute them according to personal merits, he would be a respecter of persons. Now God bestows the benefits of salvation on the human race gratuitously: wherefore He is not a respecter of persons, if He gives them to some rather than to others. Hence Augustine says (*De Prædest. Sanct.* viii): *All whom God teaches, he teaches out of pity; but whom He teaches not, out of justice He teaches not:* for this is due to the condemnation of the human race for the sin of the first parent.

Reply Obj. 3. The benefits of grace are forfeited by man on account of sin: but not the benefits of nature. Among the latter are the ministries of the angels, which the very order of various natures demands, viz., that the lowest beings be governed through the intermediate beings: and also bodily aids, which God vouchsafes not only to men, but also to beasts, according to Ps. xxxv. 7: *Men and beasts Thou wilt preserve, O Lord.*

FIFTH ARTICLE

Whether All Men Were Bound to Observe the Old Law

We proceed thus to the Fifth Article:—

Objection 1. It would seem that all men were bound to observe the Old Law. Because whoever is subject to the king, must needs be subject to his law. But the Old Law was given by God, Who is *King of all the earth* (Ps. xlvi. 8). Therefore all the inhabitants of the earth were bound to observe the Law.

Obj. 2. Further, the Jews could not be saved without observing the Old Law: for it is written (Deut. xxvii. 26): *Cursed be he that abideth not in the words of this law, and fulfilleth them not in work.* If therefore other men could be saved without the observance of the Old Law, the Jews would be in a worse plight than other men.

Obj. 3. Further, the Gentiles were admitted to the Jewish ritual and to the observances of the Law: for it is written (Exod. xii. 48): *If any stranger be willing to dwell among you, and to keep the Phase of the Lord, all his males shall first be circumcised, and then shall he celebrate it according to the manner; and he shall be as he that is born in the land.* But it would have been useless to admit strangers to the legal observances according to the Divine ordinance, if they could have been saved without the observance of the Law. Therefore none could be saved without observing the Law.

On the contrary, Dionysius says (*Cœl. Hier.* ix) that many of the Gentiles were brought back to God by the angels. But it is clear that the Gentiles did not observe the Law. Therefore some could be saved without observing the Law.

I answer that, The Old Law showed forth the precepts of the natural law, and added certain precepts of its own. Accordingly, as to those precepts of the natural law contained in the Old Law, all were bound to observe the Old Law; not because they belonged to the Old Law, but because they belonged to the natural law. But as to those precepts which were added by the Old Law, they were not binding on any save the Jewish people alone. The reason of this is because the Old Law, as stated above (A. 4), was given to the Jewish people, that it might receive a prerogative of holiness, in reverence for Christ Who was to be born of that people. Now whatever laws are enacted for the special sanctification of certain ones, are binding on them alone: thus clerics who are set aside for the service of God are bound to certain obligations to which the laity are not bound; likewise religious are bound by their profession to certain works of perfection, to which people living in the world are not bound. In like manner this people was bound to certain special observances, to which other peoples were not bound. Wherefore it is written (Deut. xviii. 13): *Thou shalt be perfect and without spot before the Lord thy God:* and for this reason they used a kind of form of profession, as appears from Deut. xxvi. 3: *I profess this day before the Lord thy God,* etc.

Reply Obj. 1. Whoever are subject to a king, are bound to observe his law which he makes for all in general. But if he orders certain things to be observed by the servants of his household, others are not bound thereto.

Reply Obj. 2. The more a man is united to God, the better his state becomes: wherefore the more the Jewish people were bound to the worship of God, the greater their excellence over other peoples. Hence it is written (Deut. iv. 8): *What other nation is there so renowned that hath ceremonies and just judgments, and all the law?* In like manner, from this point of view, the state of clerics is better than that of the laity, and the state of religious than that of folk living in the world.

Reply Obj. 3. The Gentiles obtained salvation more perfectly and more securely under the observances of the Law than under the mere natural law: and for this reason they were admitted to them. So too the laity are now admitted to the ranks of the clergy, and secular persons to those of the religious, although they can be saved without this.

Whether the Old Law Was Suitably Given at the Time of Moses?

We proceed thus to the Sixth Article:—

Objection 1. It would seem that the Old Law was not suitably given at the time of Moses. Because the Old Law disposed man for the salvation which was to come through Christ, as stated above (AA. 2, 3). But man needed this salutary remedy immediately after he had sinned. Therefore the Law should have been given immediately after sin.

Obj. 2. Further, the Old Law was given for the sanctification of those from whom Christ was to be born. Now the promise concerning the *seed, which is Christ* (Gal. iii. 16) was first made to Abraham, as related in Gen. xii. 7. Therefore the Law should have been given at once at the time of Abraham.

Obj. 3. Further, as Christ was born of those alone who descended from Noe through Abraham, to whom the promise was made; so was He born of no other of the descendants of Abraham but David, to whom the promise was renewed, according to 2 Kings xxiii. 1: *The man to whom it was appointed concerning the Christ of the God of Jacob . . . said.* Therefore the Old Law should have been given after David, just as it was given after Abraham.

On the contrary, The Apostle says (Gal. iii. 19) that the Law *was set because of transgressions, until the seed should come, to whom He made the promise, being ordained by angels in the hand of a Mediator:*—ordained, i.e., *given in orderly fashion,* as the gloss explains. Therefore it was fitting that the Old Law should be given in this order of time.

I answer that, It was most fitting for the Law to be given at the time of Moses. The reason for this may be taken from two things in respect of which every law is imposed on two kinds of men. Because it is imposed on some men who are hard-hearted and proud, whom the law restrains and tames: and it is imposed on good men, who, through being instructed by the law, are helped to fulfil what they desire to do. Hence it was fitting that the Law should be given at such a time as would be appropriate for the overcoming of man's pride. For man was proud of two things, viz., of knowledge and of power. He was proud of his knowledge, as though his natural reason could suffice him for salvation: and accordingly, in order that his pride might be overcome in this matter, man was left to the guidance of his reason without the help of a written law: and man was able to learn from experience that his reason was deficient, since about the time of Abraham man had fallen headlong into idolatry and the most shameful vices. Wherefore, after those times, it was necessary for a written law to be given as a remedy for human ignorance: because *by the Law is the knowledge of sin* (Rom. iii. 20).— But, after man had been instructed by the Law, his pride was convinced of his weakness, through his being unable to fulfil what he knew. Hence, as the Apostle concludes (Rom. viii. 3, 4), *what the Law could not do in that it was weak through the flesh, God sent* (Vulg.,—*sending*) *His own Son, . . . that the justification of the Law might be fulfilled in us.* With regard to good men, the Law was given to them as a help; which was most needed by the people, at the time when the natural law began to be obscured on account of the exuberance of sin: for it was fitting that this help should be bestowed on men in an orderly manner, so that they might be led from imperfection to perfection; wherefore it was becoming that the Old Law should be given between the law of nature and the law of grace.

Reply Obj. 1. It was not fitting for the Old Law to be given at once after the sin of the first man: both because man was so confident in his own reason, that he did not acknowledge his need of the Old Law; and because as yet the dictate of the natural law was not darkened by habitual sinning.

Reply Obj. 2. A law should not be given save to the people, since it is a general precept, as stated above (Q. 90, AA. 2, 3); wherefore at the time of Abraham God gave men certain familiar, and, as it were, household precepts: but when Abraham's descendants had multiplied, so as to form a people, and when they had been freed from slavery, it was fitting that they should be given a law; for *slaves are not that part of the people or state to which it is fitting for the law to be directed,* as the Philosopher says (*Polit.* iii. 2, 4, 5).

Reply Obj. 3. Since the Law had to be given to the people, not only those, of whom Christ was born, received the Law, but the whole people, who were marked with the seal of circumcision, which was the sign of the promise made to Abraham, and in which he believed, according to Rom. iv. 11: hence even before David, the Law had to be given to that people as soon as they were collected together.

QUESTION 99

Of the Precepts of the Old Law

(In Six Articles)

WE must now consider the precepts of the Old Law; and (1) how they are distinguished from one another; (2) each kind of precept. Under the first head there are six points of inquiry: (1) Whether the Old Law contains several precepts or only one? (2) Whether the Old Law contains any moral precepts? (3) Whether it contains ceremonial precepts in addition to the moral precepts? (4) Whether besides these it contains judicial precepts? (5) Whether it contains any others besides these? (6) How the Old Law induced men to keep its precepts.

FIRST ARTICLE

Whether the Old Law Contains Only One Precept?

We proceed thus to the First Article:—

Objection 1. It would seem that the Old Law contains but one precept. Because a law is nothing else than a precept, as stated above (Q. 90, AA. 2, 3). Now there is but one Old Law. Therefore it contains but one precept.

Obj. 2. Further, the Apostle says (Rom. xiii. 9): *If there be any other commandment, it is comprised in this word: Thou shalt love thy neighbor as thyself.* But this is only one commandment. Therefore the Old Law contained but one commandment.

Obj. 3. Further, it is written (Matth. vii. 12): *All things . . . whatsoever you would that men should do to you, do you also to them. For this is the Law and the prophets.* But the whole of the Old Law is comprised in the Law and the prophets. Therefore the whole of the Old Law contains but one commandment.

On the contrary, The Apostle says (Ephes. ii. 15): *Making void the Law of commandments contained in decrees:* where he is referring to the Old Law, as the gloss comments on the passage. Therefore the Old Law comprises many commandments.

I answer that, Since a precept of law is binding, it is about something which must be done: and, that a thing must be done, arises from the necessity of some end. Hence it is evident that a precept implies, in its very idea, relation to an end, in so far as a thing is commanded as being necessary or expedient to an end. Now many things may happen to be necessary or expedient to an end; and, accordingly, precepts may be given about various things as being ordained to one end. Consequently we must say that all the precepts of the Old Law are one in respect of their relation to one end: and yet they are many in respect of the diversity of those things that are ordained to that end.

Reply Obj. 1. The Old Law is said to be one as being ordained to one end: yet it comprises various precepts, according to the diversity of the things which it directs to the end. Thus also the art of building is one according to the unity of its end, because it aims at the building of a house: and yet it contains various rules, according to the variety of acts ordained thereto.

Reply Obj. 2. As the Apostle says (1 Tim. i. 5), *the end of the commandment is charity;* since every law aims at establishing friendship, either between man and man, or between man and God. Wherefore the whole Law is comprised in this one commandment, *Thou shalt love thy neighbor as thyself,* as expressing the end of all commandments: because love of one's neighbor includes love of God, when we love our neighbor for God's sake. Hence the Apostle put this commandment in place of the two which are about the love of God and of one's neighbor, and of which Our Lord said (Matth. xxii. 40): *On these two commandments dependeth the whole Law and the prophets.*

Reply Obj. 3. As stated in *Ethic.* ix. 8, *friendship towards another arises from friendship towards oneself,* in so far as man looks on another as on himself. Hence when it is said, *All things whatsoever you would that men should do to you, do you also to them,* this is an explanation of the rule of neighborly love contained implicitly in the words, *Thou shalt love thy neighbor as thyself:* so that it is an explanation of this commandment.

SECOND ARTICLE

Whether the Old Law Contains Moral Precepts?

We proceed thus to the Second Article:—

Objection 1. It would seem that the Old Law contains no moral precepts. For the Old Law is distinct from the law of nature, as stated above (Q. 91, AA. 4, 5; Q. 98, A. 5). But the moral precepts belong to the law of nature. Therefore they do not belong to the Old Law.

Obj. 2. Further, the Divine Law should have come to man's assistance where human reason fails him: as is evident in regard to things that are of faith, which are above reason. But man's reason seems to suffice for the moral precepts. Therefore the moral precepts do not belong to the Old Law, which is a Divine law.

Obj. 3. Further, the Old Law is said to be *the letter* that *killeth* (2 Cor. iii. 6). But the moral precepts do not kill, but quicken, according to Ps. cxviii. 93: *Thy justifications I will never forget, for by them Thou hast given me life.* Therefore the moral precepts do not belong to the Old Law.

On the contrary, It is written (Ecclus. xvii. 9): *Moreover, He gave them discipline* (Douay,—*instructions*) *and the law of life for an inheritance.* Now discipline belongs to morals; for the gloss on Heb. xii. 11: *Now all chastisement* (*disciplina*), etc., says: *Discipline is an exercise in morals by means of difficulties.* Therefore the Law which was given by God comprised moral precepts.

I answer that, The Old Law contained some moral precepts; as is evident from Exod. xx. 13, 15: *Thou shalt not kill, Thou shalt not steal.* This was reasonable: because, just as the principal intention of human law is to create friendship between man and man; so the chief intention of the Divine law is to establish man in friendship with God. Now since likeness is the reason of love, according to Ecclus. xiii. 19: *Every beast loveth its like;* there cannot possibly be any friendship of man to God, Who is supremely good, unless man become good: wherefore it is written (Levit. xix. 2; *cf.* xi. 45): *You shall be holy, for I am holy.* But the goodness of man is virtue, which *makes its possessor good* (*Ethic.* ii. 6). Therefore it was necessary for the Old Law to include precepts about acts of virtue: and these are the moral precepts of the Law.

Reply Obj. 1. The Old Law is distinct from the natural law, not as being altogether different from it, but as something added thereto. For just as grace presupposes nature, so must the Divine law presuppose the natural law.

Reply Obj. 2. It was fitting that the Divine law should come to man's assistance not only in those things for which reason is insufficient, but also in those things in which human reason may happen to be impeded. Now human reason could not go astray in the abstract, as to the universal principles of the natural law; but through being habituated to sin, it became obscured in the point of things to be done in detail. But with regard to the other moral precepts, which are like conclusions drawn from the universal principles of the natural law, the reason of many men went astray, to the extent of judging to be lawful, things that are evil in themselves. Hence there was need for the authority of the Divine law to rescue man from both these defects. Thus among the articles of faith not only are those things set forth to which reason cannot reach, such as the Trinity of the Godhead; but also those to which right reason can attain, such as the Unity of the Godhead; in order to remove the manifold errors to which reason is liable.

Reply Obj. 3. As Augustine proves (*De Spiritu et Litera* xiv), even the letter of the law is said to be the occasion of death, as to the moral precepts; in so far as, to wit, it prescribes what is good, without furnishing the aid of grace for its fulfilment.

THIRD ARTICLE

Whether the Old Law Comprises Ceremonial, Besides Moral, Precepts?

We proceed thus to the Third Article:—

Objection 1. It would seem that the Old Law does not comprise ceremonial, besides moral, precepts. For every law that is given to man is for the purpose of directing human actions. Now human actions are called moral, as stated above (Q. 1, A. 3). Therefore it seems that the Old Law given to men should not comprise other than moral precepts.

Obj. 2. Further, those precepts that are styled ceremonial seem to refer to the Divine worship. But Divine worship is the act of a virtue, viz., religion, which, as Tully says (*De Invent.* ii) *offers worship and ceremony to the Godhead.* Since, then, the moral precepts are about acts of virtue, as stated above (A. 2), it seems that the ceremonial precepts should not be distinct from the moral.

Obj. 3. Further, the ceremonial precepts seem to be those which signify something figuratively. But, as Augustine observes (*De Doctr. Christ.* ii. 3, 4), *of all signs employed by men words hold the first place.* Therefore there was no need for the Law to contain ceremonial precepts about certain figurative actions.

On the contrary, It is written (Deut. iv. 13, 14): *Ten words ... He wrote in two tables of stone; and He commanded me at that time that I should teach you the ceremonies and judgments which you shall do.* But the ten commandments of the Law are moral precepts. Therefore besides the moral precepts there are others which are ceremonial.

I answer that, As stated above (A. 2), the Divine law is instituted chiefly in order to direct men to God; while human law is instituted chiefly in order to direct men in relation to one another. Hence human laws have not concerned themselves with the institution of anything relating to Divine worship except as affecting the common good of mankind: and for this reason they have devised many institutions relating to Divine matters, ac-

* *Fact. et Dict. Memor.* i. 1.

cording as it seemed expedient for the formation of human morals; as may be seen in the rites of the Gentiles. On the other hand the Divine law directed men to one another according to the demands of that order whereby man is directed to God, which order was the chief aim of that law. Now man is directed to God not only by the interior acts of the mind, which are faith, hope, and love, but also by certain external works, whereby man makes profession of his subjection to God: and it is these works that are said to belong to the Divine worship. This worship is called *ceremony,*—the *munia,* i.e., gifts, of *Ceres* (who was the goddess of fruits), as some say: because, at first, offerings were made to God from the fruits:—or because, as Valerius Maximus states,* the word *ceremony* was introduced among the Latins, to signify the Divine worship, being derived from a town near Rome called *Caere:* since, when Rome was taken by the Gauls, the sacred chattels of the Romans were taken thither and most carefully preserved. Accordingly those precepts of the Law which refer to the Divine worship are specially called ceremonial.

Reply Obj. 1. Human acts extend also to the Divine worship: and therefore the Old Law given to man contains precepts about these matters also.

Reply Obj. 2. As stated above (Q. 91, A. 3), the precepts of the natural law are general, and require to be determined: and they are determined both by human law and by Divine law. And just as these very determinations which are made by human law are said to be, not of natural, but of positive law; so the determinations of the precepts of the natural law, effected by the Divine law, are distinct from the moral precepts which belong to the natural law. Wherefore to worship God, since it is an act of virtue, belongs to a moral precept; but the determination of this precept, namely that He is to be worshipped by such and such sacrifices, and such and such offerings, belongs to the ceremonial precepts. Consequently the ceremonial precepts are distinct from the moral precepts.

Reply Obj. 3. As Dionysius says (*Cœl. Hier.* i), the things of God cannot be manifested to men except by means of sensible similitudes. Now these similitudes move the soul more when they are not only expressed in words, but also offered to the senses. Wherefore the things of God are set forth in the Scriptures not only by similitudes expressed in words, as in the case of metaphorical expressions; but also by similitudes of things set before the eyes, which pertains to the ceremonial precepts.

FOURTH ARTICLE

Whether, Besides the Moral and Ceremonial Precepts, There Are Also Judicial Precepts?

We proceed thus to the Fourth Article:—

Objection 1. It would seem that there are no judicial precepts in addition to the moral and ceremonial precepts in the Old Law. For Augustine says (*Contra Faust.* vi. 2) that in the Old Law there are *precepts concerning the life we have to lead, and precepts regarding the life that is foreshadowed*. Now the precepts of the life we have to lead are moral precepts; and the precepts of the life that is foreshadowed are ceremonial. Therefore besides these two kinds of precepts we should not put any judicial precepts in the Law.

Obj. 2. Further, a gloss on Ps. cxviii. 102, *I have not declined from Thy judgments,* says, —i.e., *from the rule of life Thou hast set for me.* But a rule of life belongs to the moral precepts. Therefore the judicial precepts should not be considered as distinct from the moral precepts.

Obj. 3. Further, judgment seems to be an act of justice, according to Ps. xciii. 15: *Until justice be turned into judgment.* But acts of justice, like the acts of other virtues, belong to the moral precepts. Therefore the moral precepts include the judicial precepts, and consequently should not be held as distinct from them.

On the contrary, It is written (Deut. vi. 1): *These are the precepts, and ceremonies, and judgments:* where *precepts* stands for *moral precepts* antonomastically. Therefore there are judicial precepts besides moral and ceremonial precepts.

I answer that, As stated above (AA. 2, 3), it belongs to the Divine law to direct men to one another and to God. Now each of these belongs in the abstract to the dictates of the natural law, to which dictates the moral precepts are to be referred: yet each of them has to be determined by Divine or human law, because naturally known principles are universal, both in speculative and in practical matters. Accordingly just as the determination of the universal principle about Divine worship is effected by the ceremonial precepts, so the determination of the general precepts of that justice which is to be observed among men is effected by the judicial precepts.

We must therefore distinguish three kinds of precept in the Old Law; viz., *moral* precepts, which are dictated by the natural law; *ceremonial* precepts, which are determinations of the Divine worship; and *judicial* precepts, which are determinations of the justice to be maintained among men. Wherefore the Apostle (Rom. vii. 12) after saying that the *Law is holy,* adds that *the commandment is just, and holy, and good: just,* in respect of the judicial precepts; *holy,* with regard to the ceremonial precepts (since the word *sanctus—holy—*is applied to that which is consecrated to God); and *good,* i.e., conducive to virtue, as to the moral precepts.

Reply Obj. 1. Both the moral and the judicial precepts aim at the ordering of human life: and consequently they are both comprised under one of the heads mentioned by Augustine, viz., under the precepts of the life we have to lead.

Reply Obj. 2. Judgment denotes execution of justice, by an application of the reason to individual cases in a determinate way. Hence the judicial precepts have something in common with the moral precepts, in that they are derived from reason; and something in common with the ceremonial precepts, in that they are determinations of general precepts. This explains why sometimes *judgments* comprise both judicial and moral precepts, as in Deut. v. 1: *Hear, O Israel, the ceremonies and judgments;* and sometimes judicial and ceremonial precepts, as in Levit. xviii. 4: *You shall do My judgments, and shall observe My precepts,* where *precepts* denotes moral precepts, while *judgments* refers to judicial and ceremonial precepts.

Reply Obj. 3. The act of justice, in general, belongs to the moral precepts; but its determination to some special kind of act belongs to the judicial precepts

FIFTH ARTICLE

Whether the Old Law Contains Any Others Besides the Moral, Judicial, and Ceremonial Precepts?

We proceed thus to the Fifth Article:—

Objection 1. It would seem that the Old Law contains others besides the moral, judicial, and ceremonial precepts. Because the judicial precepts belong to the act of justice, which is between man and man; while the ceremonial precepts belong to the act of religion, whereby God is worshipped. Now besides these there are many other virtues, viz., temperance, fortitude, liberality, and several others, as stated above (Q. 60, A. 5). Therefore besides the aforesaid precepts, the Old Law should comprise others.

Obj. 2. Further, it is written (Deut. xi. 1): *Love the Lord thy God, and observe His precepts and ceremonies, His judgments and commandments.* Now precepts concern moral matters, as stated above (A. 4). Therefore besides the moral, judicial, and ceremonial precepts, the Law contains others which are called *commandments.**

Obj. 3. Further, it is written (Deut. vi. 17): *Keep the precepts of the Lord thy God, and the testimonies and ceremonies which I have* (Vulg.,—*He hath*) *commanded thee.* Therefore in addition to the above, the Law comprises *testimonies.*

Obj. 4. Further, it is written (Ps. cxviii. 93): *Thy justifications* (i.e., *Thy Law,* according to a gloss) *I will never forget.* Therefore in the Old Law there are not only moral, ceremonial, and judicial precepts, but also others, called *justifications.*

On the contrary, It is written (Deut. vi. 1): *These are the precepts and ceremonies and judgments which the Lord your God commanded . . . you.* And these words are placed at the beginning of the Law. Therefore all the precepts of the Law are included under them.

I answer that, Some things are included in the Law by way of precept; other things, as being ordained to the fulfilment of the precepts. Now the precepts refer to things which have to be done: and to their fulfilment man is induced by two considerations, viz., the authority of the lawgiver, and the benefit derived from the fulfilment, which benefit consists in the attainment of some good, useful, pleasurable or virtuous, or in the avoidance of some contrary evil. Hence it was necessary that in the Old Law certain things should be set forth to indicate the authority of God the lawgiver: e.g., Deut. vi. 4: *Hear, O Israel, the Lord our God is one Lord;* and Gen. i. 1: *In the beginning God created heaven and earth:* and these are called *testimonies.*— Again it was necessary that in the Law certain rewards should be appointed for those who observe the Law, and punishments for those who transgress; as it may be seen in Deut. xxviii: *If thou wilt hear the voice of the Lord Thy God . . . He will make thee higher than all the nations,* etc.: and these are called *justifications,* according as God punishes or rewards certain ones justly.

The things that have to be done do not come under the precept except in so far as they have the character of a duty. Now a duty is twofold: one according to the rule of reason; the other according to the rule of a law which prescribes that duty: thus the Philosopher distinguishes a twofold just,—moral and legal (*Ethic.* v. 7).

Moral duty is twofold: because reason dictates that something must be done, either as being so necessary that without it the order of virtue would be destroyed; or as being useful for the better maintaining of the order of virtue. And in this sense some of the moral precepts are expressed by way of absolute command or prohibition, as *Thou shalt not kill, Thou shalt not steal:* and these are properly called *precepts.* Other things are prescribed or forbidden, not as an absolute duty, but as something better to be done. These may be called *commandments;* because they are expressed by way of inducement and persuasion: an example whereof is seen in Exod. xxii. 26: *If thou take of thy neighbor a garment in pledge, thou shalt give it him again before sunset;* and in other like cases. Wherefore Jerome (*Præfat. in Comment. super Marc.*) says that *justice is in the precepts, charity in the commandments.*—Duty as fixed by the Law, belongs to the *judicial* precepts, as regards human affairs; to the *ceremonial* precepts, as regards Divine matters.

Nevertheless those ordinances also which refer to punishments and rewards may be called *testimonies,* in so far as they testify to the Divine justice.—Again all the precepts of the Law may be styled *justifications,* as being executions of legal justice.—Furthermore the commandments may be distinguished from the precepts, so that those things be called *precepts* which God Himself prescribed; and those things *commandments* which He enjoined (*mandavit*) through others, as the very word seems to denote.

From this it is clear that all the precepts of the Law are either moral, ceremonial, or judicial; and that other ordinances have not the character of a precept, but are directed to the observance of the precepts, as stated above.

Reply Obj. 1. Justice alone, of all the virtues, implies the notion of duty. Consequently moral matters are determinable by law in so far as they belong to justice: of which virtue religion is a part, as Tully says (*De Invent.* ii). Wherefore the legal just cannot be anything foreign to the ceremonial and judicial precepts.

The Replies to the other Objections are clear from what has been said.

SIXTH ARTICLE

Whether the Old Law Should Have Induced Men to the Observance of Its Precepts, by Means of Temporal Promises and Threats?

We proceed thus to the Sixth Article:—

Objection 1. It would seem that the Old Law should not have induced men to the observance of its precepts, by means of temporal promises and threats. For the purpose of the Divine law is to subject man to God by fear

* The *commandments* (*mandata*) spoken of here and in the body of this article are not to be confused with the Commandments (*præcepta*) in the ordinary acceptance of the word.

and love: hence it is written (Deut. x. 12): *And now, Israel, what doth the Lord thy God require of thee, but that thou fear the Lord thy God, and walk in His ways, and love Him?* But the desire for temporal goods leads man away from God: for Augustine says (*Qq.* lxxxiii, qu. 36), that *covetousness is the bane of charity.* Therefore temporal promises and threats seem to be contrary to the intention of a lawgiver: and this makes a law worthy of·rejection, as the Philosopher declares (*Polit.* ii. 6).

Obj. 2. Further, the Divine law is more excellent than human law. Now, in sciences, we notice that the loftier the science, the higher the means of persuasion that it employs. Therefore, since human law employs temporal threats and promises, as means of persuading man, the Divine law should have used, not these, but more lofty means.

Obj. 3. Further, the reward of righteousness and the punishment of guilt cannot be that which befalls equally the good and the wicked. But as stated in Eccles. ix. 2, *all temporal things equally happen to the just and to the wicked, to the good and to the evil, to the clean and to the unclean, to him that offereth victims, and to him that despiseth sacrifices.* Therefore temporal goods or evils are not suitably set forth as punishments or rewards of the commandments of the Divine law.

On the contrary, It is written (Isa. i. 19, 20): *If you be willing, and will hearken to Me, you shall eat the good things of the land. But if you will not, and will provoke Me to wrath: the sword shall devour you.*

I answer that, As in speculative sciences men are persuaded to assent to the conclusions by means of syllogistic arguments, so too in every law, men are persuaded to observe its precepts by means of punishments and rewards. Now it is to be observed that, in speculative sciences, the means of persuasion are adapted to the conditions of the pupil: wherefore the process of argument in sciences should be ordered becomingly, so that the instruction is based on principles more generally known. And thus also he who would persuade a man to the observance of any precepts, needs to move him at first by things for which he has an affection; just as children are induced to do something, by means of little childish gifts. Now it has

been said above (Q. 98, AA. 1, 2, 3) that the Old Law disposed men 'ɔ (the coming of) Christ, as the imperfect disposes to the perfect, wherefore it was given to a people as yet imperfect in comparison to the perfection which was to result from Christ's coming: and for this reason, that people is compared to a child that is still under a pedagogue (Gal. iii. 24). But the perfection of man consists in his despising temporal things and cleaving to things spiritual, as is clear from the words of the Apostle (Phil. iii. 13, 15): *Forgetting the things that are behind, I stretch* (Vulg.,—*and stretching*) *forth myself to those that are before. . . . Let us therefore, as many as are perfect, be thus minded.* Those who are yet imperfect desire temporal goods, albeit in subordination to God: whereas the perverse place their end in temporalities. It was therefore fitting that the Old Law should conduct men to God by means of temporal goods for which the imperfect have an affection.

Reply Obj. 1. Covetousness whereby man places his end in temporalities, is the bane of charity. But the attainment of temporal goods which man desires in subordination to God is a road leading the imperfect to the love of God, according to Ps. xlviii. 19: *He will praise Thee, when Thou shalt do well to him.*

Reply Obj. 2. Human law persuades men by means of temporal rewards or by punishments to be inflicted by men: whereas the Divine law persuades men by means of rewards or punishments to be received from God. In this respect it employs higher means.

Reply Obj. 3. As anyone can see, who reads carefully the story of the Old Testament, the common weal of the people prospered under the Law as long as they obeyed it; and as soon as they departed from the precepts of the Law they were overtaken by many calamities. But certain individuals, although they observed the justice of the Law, met with misfortunes, —either because they had already become spiritual (so that misfortune might withdraw them all the more from attachment to temporal things, and that their virtue might be tried);—or because, while outwardly fulfilling the works of the Law, their heart was altogether fixed on temporal goods, and far removed from God, according to Isa. xxix. 13 (Matth. xv. 8): *This people honoreth Me with their lips; but their heart is far from Me.*

QUESTION 100

Of the Moral Precepts of the Old Law

(In Twelve Articles)

WE must now consider each kind of precept of the Old Law: and (1) the moral precepts, (2) the ceremonial precepts, (3) the judicial precepts. Under the first head there are twelve points of inquiry: (1) Whether all the moral precepts of the Old Law belong to the law of nature? (2) Whether the moral precepts of the Old Law are about the acts of all the virtues? (3) Whether all the moral precepts of the Old Law are reducible to the ten precepts of the decalogue? (4) How the precepts of the decalogue are distinguished from one another: (5) Their number; (6) Their order; (7) The manner in which they were given; (8) Whether they are dispensable? (9) Whether the mode of observing a virtue comes under the precept of the Law? (10) Whether the mode of charity comes under the precept? (11) The distinction of other moral precepts. (12) Whether the moral precepts of the Old Law justified man?

FIRST ARTICLE

Whether All the Moral Precepts of the Old Law Belong to the Law of Nature?

We proceed thus to the First Article:—

Objection 1. It would seem that not all the moral precepts belong to the law of nature. For it is written (Ecclus. xvii 9): *Moreover He gave them instructions, and the law of life for an inheritance.* But instruction is in contradistinction to the law of nature; since the law of nature is not learnt, but instilled by natural instinct. Therefore not all the moral precepts belong to the natural law.

Obj. 2. Further, the Divine law is more perfect than human law. But human law adds certain things concerning good morals, to those that belong to the law of nature: as is evidenced by the fact that the natural law is the same in all men, while these moral institutions are various for various people. Much more reason therefore was there why the Divine law should add to the law of nature, ordinances pertaining to good morals.

Obj. 3. Further, just as natural reason leads to good morals in certain matters, so does faith: hence it is written (Gal. v. 6) that faith *worketh by charity.* But faith is not included in the law of nature; since that which is of faith is above nature. Therefore not all the moral precepts of the Divine law belong to the law of nature.

On the contrary, The Apostle says (Rom. ii. 14) that *the Gentiles, who have not the Law, do by nature those things that are of the Law:* which must be understood of things pertaining to good morals. Therefore all the moral precepts of the Law belong to the law of nature.

I answer that, The moral precepts, distinct from the ceremonial and judicial precepts, are about things pertaining of their very nature to good morals. Now since human morals depend on their relation to reason, which is the proper principle of human acts, those morals are called good which accord with reason, and those are called bad which are discordant from reason. And as every judgment of speculative reason proceeds from the natural knowledge of first principles, so every judgment of practical reason proceeds from principles known naturally, as stated above (Q. 94, AA. 2, 4): from which principles one may proceed in various ways to judge of various matters. For some matters connected with human actions are so evident, that after very little consideration one is able at once to approve or disapprove of them by means of these general first principles: while some matters cannot be the subject of judgment without much consideration of the various circumstances, which all are not competent to do carefully, but only those who are wise: just as it is not possible for all to consider the particular conclusions of sciences, but only for those who are versed in philosophy: and lastly there are some matters of which man cannot judge unless he be helped by Divine instruction; such as the articles of faith.

It is therefore evident that since the moral precepts are about matters which concern good morals; and since good morals are those which are in accord with reason; and since also every judgment of human reason must needs be derived in some way from natural reason; it follows, of necessity, that all the moral precepts belong to the law of nature; but not all in the same way. For there are certain things which the natural reason of every man, of its own accord and at once, judges to be done or not to be done: *e.g., Honor thy father and thy mother,* and, *Thou shalt not kill, Thou shalt not steal:* and these belong to the law of nature absolutely.—And there are certain things which, after a more careful consideration, wise men deem obligatory. Such belong to the law of nature, yet so that they need to be inculcated, the wiser teaching the less wise: e.g., *Rise up before the hoary head, and honor the person of the aged man,* and the like.—And there are some things, to judge of which, human reason needs Divine instruction, whereby we are taught about the things of God: e.g., *Thou shalt not make to thyself a graven thing, nor the likeness of anything; Thou shalt not take the name of the Lord thy God in vain.*

This suffices for the Replies to the Objections.

SECOND ARTICLE

Whether the Moral Precepts of the Law Are about All the Acts of Virtue?

We proceed thus to the Second Article:—

Objection 1. It would seem that the moral precepts of the Law are not about all the acts of virtue. For observance of the precepts of the Old Law is called justification, according to Ps. cxviii. 8: *I will keep Thy justifications.* But justification is the execution of justice. Therefore the moral precepts are only about acts of justice.

Obj. 2. Further, that which comes under a precept has the character of a duty. But the character of duty belongs to justice alone and to none of the other virtues, for the proper act of justice consists in rendering to each one his due. Therefore the precepts of the moral law are not about the acts of the other virtues, but only about the acts of justice.

Obj. 3. Further, every law is made for the common good, as Isidore says (*Etym.* v. 21). But of all the virtues justice alone regards the common good, as the Philosopher says (*Ethic.* v. 1). Therefore the moral precepts are only about the acts of justice.

On the contrary, Ambrose says (*De Paradiso* viii) that *a sin is a transgression of the Divine law, and a disobedience to the commandments of heaven.* But there are sins contrary to all the acts of virtue. Therefore it belongs to the Divine law to direct all the acts of virtue.

I answer that, Since the precepts of the Law are ordained to the common good, as stated above (Q. 90, A. 2), the precepts of the Law must needs be diversified according to the various kinds of community: hence the Philosopher (*Polit.* iv. 1) teaches that the laws which are made in a state which is ruled by a king must be different from the laws of a state which is ruled by the people, or by a few powerful men in the state. Now human law is ordained for one kind of community, and the Divine law for another kind. Because human law is ordained for the civil community, implying mutual duties of man and his fellows: and men are ordained to one another

by outward acts, whereby men live in communion with one another. This life in common of man with man pertains to justice, whose proper function consists in directing the human community. Wherefore human law makes precepts only about acts of justice; and if it commands acts of other virtues, this is only in so far as they assume the nature of justice, as the Philosopher explains (*Ethic.* v. 1).

But the community for which the Divine law is ordained, is that of men in relation to God, either in this life or in the life to come. And therefore the Divine law proposes precepts about all those matters whereby men are well ordered in their relations to God. Now man is united to God by his reason or mind, in which is God's image. Wherefore the Divine law proposes precepts about all those matters whereby human reason is well ordered. But this is effected by the acts of all the virtues: since the intellectual virtues set in good order the acts of the reason in themselves: while the moral virtues set in good order the acts of the reason in reference to the interior passions and exterior actions. It is therefore evident that the Divine law fittingly proposes precepts about the acts of all the virtues: yet so that certain matters, without which the order of virtue, which is the order of reason, cannot even exist, come under an obligation of precept; while other matters, which pertain to the well-being of perfect virtue, come under an admonition of counsel.

Reply Obj. 1. The fulfilment of the commandments of the Law, even of those which are about the acts of the other virtues, has the character of justification, inasmuch as it is just that man should obey God: or again, inasmuch as it is just that all that belongs to man should be subject to reason.

Reply Obj. 2. Justice properly so called regards the duty of one man to another: but all the other virtues regard the duty of the lower powers to reason. It is in relation to this latter duty that the Philosopher speaks (*Ethic.* v. 11) of a kind of metaphorical justice.

The Reply to the Third Objection is clear from what has been said about the different kinds of community.

THIRD ARTICLE

Whether All the Moral Precepts of the Old Law Are Reducible to the Ten Precepts of the Decalogue?

We proceed thus to the Third Article:—

Objection 1. It would seem that not all the moral precepts of the Old Law are reducible to the ten precepts of the decalogue. For the first and principal precepts of the Law are, *Thou shalt love the Lord thy God,* and, *Thou shalt love thy neighbor,* as stated in Matth. xxii. 37, 39. But these two are not contained in the precepts of the decalogue. Therefore not all the moral precepts are contained in the precepts of the decalogue.

Obj. 2. Further, the moral precepts are not reducible to the ceremonial precepts, but rather vice versa. But among the precepts of the decalogue, one is ceremonial, viz., *Remember that thou keep holy the Sabbath-day.* Therefore the moral precepts are not reducible to all the precepts of the decalogue.

Obj. 3. Further, the moral precepts are about all the acts of virtue. But among the precepts of the decalogue are only such as regard acts of justice; as may be seen by going through them all. Therefore the precepts of the decalogue do not include all the moral precepts.

On the contrary, The gloss on Matth. v. 11: *Blessed are ye when they shall revile you,* etc., says that *Moses, after propounding the ten precepts, set them out in detail.* Therefore all the precepts of the Law are so many parts of the precepts of the decalogue.

I answer that, The precepts of the decalogue differ from the other precepts of the Law, in the fact that God Himself is said to have given the precepts of the decalogue; whereas He gave the other precepts to the people through Moses. Wherefore the decalogue includes those precepts the knowledge of which man has immediately from God. Such are those which with but slight reflection can be gathered at once from the first general principles: and those also which become known to man immediately through divinely infused faith. Consequently two kinds of precepts are not reckoned among the precepts of the decalogue: viz., first general principles, for they need no further promulgation after being once imprinted on the natural reason to which they are self-evident; as, for instance, that one should do evil to no man, and other similar principles:—and again those which the careful reflection of wise men shows to be in accord with reason; since the people receive these principles from God, through being taught by wise men. Nevertheless both kinds of precepts are contained in the precepts of the decalogue; yet in different ways. For the first general principles are contained in them, as principles in their proximate conclusions; while those which are known through wise men are contained, conversely, as conclusions in their principles.

Reply Obj. 1. Those two principles are the first general principles of the natural law, and are self-evident to human reason, either through nature or through faith. Wherefore all the precepts of the decalogue are referred to these, as conclusions to general principles.

Reply Obj. 2. The precept of the Sabbath observance is moral in one respect, in so far as it commands man to give some time to the things of God, according to Ps. xlv. 11: *Be still and see that I am God.* In this respect it is placed among the precepts of the decalogue: but not as to the fixing of the time, in which respect it is a ceremonial precept.

Reply Obj. 3. The notion of duty is not so patent in the other virtues as it is in justice. Hence the precepts about the acts of the other virtues are not so well known to the people as are the precepts about acts of justice. Wherefore the acts of justice especially come under the precepts of the decalogue, which are the primary elements of the Law.

FOURTH ARTICLE

Whether the Precepts of the Decalogue Are Suitably Distinguished from One Another?

We proceed thus to the Fourth Article:—

Objection 1. It would seem that the precepts of the decalogue are unsuitably distinguished from one another. For worship is a virtue distinct from faith. Now the precepts are about acts of virtue. But that which is said at the beginning of the decalogue, *Thou shalt not have strange gods before Me,* belongs to faith: and that which is added, *Thou shalt not make . . . any graven thing,* etc., belongs to worship. Therefore these are not one precept, as Augustine asserts (Qq. *in Exod.,* qu. lxxi), but two.

Obj. 2. Further, the affirmative precepts in the Law are distinct from the negative precepts; *e.g., Honor thy father and thy mother,* and, *Thou shalt not kill.* But this, *I am the Lord thy God,* is affirmative: and that which follows, *Thou shalt not have strange gods before Me,* is negative. Therefore these are two precepts, and do not, as Augustine says (*loc. cit.*), make one.

Obj. 3. Further, the Apostle says (Rom. vii. 7): *I had not known concupiscence, if the Law did not say: "Thou shalt not covet."* Hence it seems that this precept, *Thou shalt not covet,* is one precept; and, therefore, should not be divided into two.

On the contrary stands the authority of Augustine who, in commenting on Exodus (*loc. cit.*) distinguishes three precepts as referring to God, and seven as referring to our neighbor.

I answer that, The precepts of the decalogue are differently divided by different authorities. For Hesychius commenting on Levit. xxvi. 26, *Ten women shall bake your bread in one oven,* says that the precept of the Sabbath-day observance is not one of the ten precepts, because its observance, in the letter, is not binding for all time. But he distinguishes four precepts pertaining to God, the first being, *I am the Lord thy God;* the second, *Thou shalt not have strange gods before Me,* (thus also Jerome distinguishes these two precepts, in his commentary on Osee x. 10, *On thy*—Vulg., *their*—*two iniquities*); the third precept according to him is, *Thou shalt not make to thyself any graven thing;* and the fourth, *Thou shalt not take the name of the Lord thy God in vain.* He states that there are six precepts pertaining to our neighbor; the first, *Honor thy father and thy mother;* the second, *Thou shalt not kill;* the third, *Thou shalt not commit adultery;* the fourth, *Thou shalt not steal;* the fifth, *Thou shalt not bear false witness;* the sixth, *Thou shalt not covet.*

But, in the first place, it seems unbecoming for the precept of the Sabbath-day observance to be put among the precepts of the decalogue, if it nowise belonged to the decalogue. Secondly, because, since it is written (Matth. vi. 24), *No man can serve two masters,* the two statements, *I am the Lord thy God,* and, *Thou shalt not have strange gods before Me* seem to be of the same nature and to form one precept. Hence Origen (*Hom.* viii *in Exod.*), who also distinguishes four precepts as referring to God, unites these two under one precept; and reckons in the second place, *Thou shalt not make . . . any graven thing;* as third, *Thou shalt not take the name of the Lord thy God in vain;* and as fourth, *Remember that thou keep holy the Sabbath-day.* The other six he reckons in the same way as Hesychius.

Since, however, the making of graven things or the likeness of anything is not forbidden except as to the point of their being worshipped as gods—for God commanded an image of the Seraphim (Vulg.,—Cherubim) to be made and placed in the tabernacle, as related in Exod. xxv. 18—Augustine more fittingly unites these two, *Thou shalt not have strange gods before Me,* and, *Thou shalt not make . . . any graven thing,* into one precept. Likewise to covet another's wife, for the purpose of carnal knowledge, belongs to the concupiscence of the flesh; whereas, to covet other things, which are desired for the purpose of possession, belongs to the concupiscence of the eyes; wherefore Augustine reckons as distinct precepts, that which forbids the coveting of another's goods, and that which prohibits the coveting of another's wife. Thus he distinguishes three precepts as referring to God, and seven as referring to our neighbor. And this is better.

Reply Obj. 1. Worship is merely a declaration of faith: wherefore the precepts about worship should not be reckoned as distinct from those about faith. Nevertheless precepts should be given about worship rather than about faith, because the precept about faith is presupposed to the precepts of the decalogue, as is also the precept of charity. For just as the first general principles of the natural law are self-evident to a subject having natural reason, and need no promulgation; so also to believe in God is a first and self-evident principle to a subject possessed of faith: *for he that cometh to God, must believe that He is* (Heb. xi. 6). Hence it needs no other promulgation than the infusion of faith.

Reply Obj. 2. The affirmative precepts are distinct from the negative, when one is not comprised in the other: thus that man should honor his parents does not include that he should not kill another man; nor does the latter include the former. But when an affirmative precept is included in a negative, or vice versa, we do not find that two distinct precepts are given: thus there is not one precept saying that *Thou shalt not steal,* and another binding one to keep another's property intact, or to give it back to its owner. In the same way there are not different precepts about believing in God, and about not believing in strange gods.

Reply Obj. 3. All covetousness has one common ratio: and therefore the Apostle speaks of the commandment about covetousness as though it were one. But because there are various special kinds of covetousness, therefore Augustine distinguishes different prohibitions against coveting: for covetousness differs specifically in respect of the diversity of actions or things coveted, as the Philosopher says (*Ethic.* x. 5).

FIFTH ARTICLE

Whether the Precepts of the Decalogue Are Suitably Set Forth?

We proceed thus to the Fifth Article:—

Objection 1. It would seem that the precepts of the decalogue are unsuitably set forth. Because sin, as stated by Ambrose (*De Paradiso* viii), is *a transgression of the Divine law and a disobedience to the commandments of heaven.* But sins are distinguished according as man sins against God, or his neighbor, or himself. Since, then, the decalogue does not include any precepts directing man in his relations to himself, but only such as direct him in his relations to God and himself, it seems that the precepts of the decalogue are insufficiently enumerated.

Obj. 2. Further, just as the Sabbath-day observance pertained to the worship of God, so also did the observance of other solemnities, and the offering of sacrifices. But the decalogue contains a precept about the Sabbathday observance. Therefore it should contain others also, pertaining to the other solemnities, and to the sacrificial rite.

Obj. 3. Further, as sins against God include the sin of perjury, so also do they include blasphemy, or other ways of lying against the teaching of God. But there is a precept forbidding perjury, *Thou shalt not take the name of the Lord thy God in vain.* Therefore there should be also a precept of the decalogue forbidding blasphemy and false doctrine.

Obj. 4. Further, just as man has a natural affection for his parents, so has he also for his children. Moreover the commandment of charity extends to all our neighbors. Now the precepts of the decalogue are ordained unto charity, according to 1 Tim. i. 5: *The end of the commandment is charity.* Therefore as there is a precept referring to parents, so should there have been some precepts referring to children and other neighbors.

Obj. 5. Further, in every kind of sin, it is possible to sin in thought or in deed. But in some kinds of sin, namely in theft and adultery, the prohibition of sins of deed, when it is said, *Thou shalt not commit adultery, Thou shalt not steal,* is distinct from the prohibition of the sin of thought, when it is said, *Thou shalt not covet thy neighbor's goods,* and, *Thou shalt not covet thy neighbor's wife.* Therefore the same should have been done in regard to the sins of homicide and false witness.

Obj. 6. Further, just as sin happens through disorder of the concupiscible faculty, so does it arise through disorder of the irascible part. But some precepts forbid inordinate concupiscence, when it is said, *Thou shalt not covet.* Therefore the decalogue should have included some precepts forbidding the disorders of the irascible faculty. Therefore it seems that the ten precepts of the decalogue are unfittingly enumerated.

On the contrary, It is written (Deut. iv. 13): *He shewed you His covenant, which He commanded you to do, and the ten words that He wrote in two tables of stone.*

I answer that, As stated above (A. 2), just as the precepts of human law direct man in his relations to the human community, so the precepts of the Divine law direct man in his relations to a community or commonwealth of men under God. Now in order that any man may dwell aright in a community, two things are required: the first is that he behave well to the head of the community; the other is that he behave well to those who are his fellows and partners in the community. It is therefore necessary that the Divine law should contain in the first place precepts ordering

man in his relations to God; and in the second place, other precepts ordering man in his relations to other men who are his neighbors and live with him under God.

Now man owes three things to the head of the community: first, fidelity; secondly, reverence; thirdly, service. Fidelity to his master consists in his not giving sovereign honor to another: and this is the sense of the first commandment, in the words *Thou shalt not have strange gods.*—Reverence to his master requires that he should do nothing injurious to him: and this is conveyed by the second commandment, *Thou shalt not take the name of the Lord thy God in vain.*—Service is due to the master in return for the benefits which his subjects receive from him: and to this belongs the third commandment of the sanctification of the Sabbath in memory of the creation of all things.

To his neighbors a man behaves himself well both in particular and in general. In particular, as to those to whom he is indebted, by paying his debts: and in this sense is to be taken the commandment about honoring one's parents.—In general, as to all men, by doing harm to none, either by deed, or by word, or by thought. By deed, harm is done to one's neighbor,—sometimes in his person, i.e., as to his personal existence; and this is forbidden by the words, *Thou shalt not kill:*—sometimes in a person united to him, as to the propagation of offspring; and this is prohibited by the words, *Thou shalt not commit adultery:*—sometimes in his possessions, which are directed to both the aforesaid; and with regard to this it is said, *Thou shalt not steal.* —Harm done by word is forbidden when it is said, *Thou shalt not bear false witness against thy neighbor:*—harm done by thought is forbidden in the words, *Thou shalt not covet.*

The three precepts that direct man in his behavior towards God may also be differentiated in this same way. For the first refers to deeds; wherefore it is said, *Thou shalt not make . . . a graven thing:* the second, to words; wherefore it is said, *Thou shalt not take the name of the Lord thy God in vain:* the third, to thoughts; because the sanctification of the Sabbath, as the subject of a moral precept, requires repose of the heart in God.— Or, according to Augustine (*In Ps.* xxxii: *Conc.* 1), by the first commandment we reverence the unity of the First Principle; by the second, the Divine truth; by the third, His goodness whereby we are sanctified, and wherein we rest as in our last end.

Reply Obj. 1. This objection may be answered in two ways. First, because the precepts of the decalogue can be reduced to the precepts of charity. Now there was need for man to receive a precept about loving God and his neighbor, because in this respect the natural law had become obscured on account of sin: but not about the duty of loving oneself, because in this respect the natural law retained its vigor: or again, because love of oneself is contained in the love of God and of one's neighbor: since true self-love consists in directing oneself to God. And for this reason the decalogue includes those precepts only which refer to our neighbor and to God.

Secondly, it may be answered that the precepts of the decalogue are those which the people received from God immediately; wherefore it is written (Deut. x. 4): *He wrote in the tables, according as He had written before, the ten words, which the Lord spoke to you.* Hence the precepts of the decalogue need to be such as the people can understand at once. Now a precept implies the notion of duty. But it is easy for a man, especially for a believer, to understand that, of necessity, he owes certain duties to God and to his neighbor. But that, in matters which regard himself and not another, man has, of necessity, certain duties to himself, is not so evident: for, at the first glance, it seems that everyone is free in matters that concern himself. And therefore the precepts which prohibit disorders of a man with regard to himself, reach the people through the instruction of men who are versed in such matters; and, consequently, they are not contained in the decalogue.

Reply Obj. 2. All the solemnities of the Old Law were instituted in celebration of some Divine favor, either in memory of past favors, or in sign of some favor to come: in like manner all the sacrifices were offered up with the same purpose. Now of all the Divine favors to be commemorated the chief was that of the Creation, which was called to mind by the sanctification of the Sabbath; wherefore the reason for this precept is given in Exod. xx. 11: *In six days the Lord made heaven and earth,* etc. And of all future blessings, the chief and final was the repose of the mind in God, either, in the present life, by grace, or, in the future life, by glory; which repose was also foreshadowed in the Sabbath-day observance: wherefore it is written (Isa. lviii. 13): *If thou turn away thy foot from the Sabbath, from doing thy own will in My holy day, and call the Sabbath delightful, and the holy of the Lord glorious.* Because these favors first and chiefly are borne in mind by men, especially by the faithful.—But other solemnities were celebrated on account of certain particular favors temporal and transitory, such as the celebration of the Passover in memory of the past favor of the delivery from Egypt, and as a sign of the future Passion of Christ, which though temporal and transitory, brought us to the repose of the spiritual Sabbath. Consequently, the Sabbath alone, and none of the other solemnities and sacrifices, is mentioned in the precepts of the decalogue.

Reply Obj. 3. As the Apostle says (Heb. vi. 16), *men swear by one greater than themselves; and an oath for confirmation is the end of all their controversy.* Hence, since oaths are common to all, inordinate swearing is the matter of a special prohibition by a precept of the decalogue. According to one interpretation, however, the words, *Thou shalt not take the name of the Lord thy God in vain,* are a prohibition of false doctrine, for one gloss expounds them thus: *Thou shalt not say that Christ is a creature.*

Reply Obj. 4. That a man should not do harm to anyone is an immediate dictate of his natural reason: and therefore the precepts that forbid the doing of harm are binding on all men. But it is not an immediate dictate of natural reason that a man should do one thing in return for another, unless he happen to be indebted to someone. Now a son's debt to his father is so evident that one cannot get away from it by denying it: since the father is the principle of generation and being, and also of upbringing and teaching. Wherefore the decalogue does not prescribe deeds of kindness or service to be done to anyone except to one's parents. On the other hand parents do not seem to be indebted to their children for any favors received, but rather the reverse is the case.—Again, a child is a part of his father; and *parents love their children as being a part of themselves,* as the Philosopher states (*Ethic.* viii. 12). Hence, just as the decalogue contains no ordinance as to man's behavior towards himself, so, for the same reason, it includes no precept about loving one's children.

Reply Obj. 5. The pleasure of adultery and the usefulness of wealth, in so far as they have the character of pleasurable or useful good, are of themselves, objects of appetite: and for this reason they needed to be forbidden not only in the deed but also in the desire. But murder and falsehood are, of themselves, objects of repulsion (since it is natural for man to love his neighbor and the truth): and are desired only for the sake of something else. Consequently with regard to sins of murder and false witness, it was necessary to proscribe, not sins of thought, but only sins of deed.

Reply Obj. 6. As stated above (Q. 25, A. 1), all the passions of the irascible faculty arise from the passions of the concupiscible part. Hence, as the precepts of the decalogue are, as it were, the first elements of the Law, there was no need for mention of the irascible passions, but only of the concupiscible passions.

SIXTH ARTICLE

Whether the Ten Precepts of the Decalogue Are Set in Proper Order?

We proceed thus to the Sixth Article:—

Objection 1. It would seem that the ten precepts of the decalogue are not set in proper order. Because love of one's neighbor is seemingly previous to love of God, since our neighbor is better known to us than God is; according to 1 Jo. iv. 20: *He that loveth not his brother, whom he seeth, how can he love God, Whom he seeth not?* But the first three precepts belong to the love of God, while the other seven pertain to the love of our neighbor. Therefore the precepts of the decalogue are not set in proper order.

Obj. 2. Further, acts of virtue are prescribed by the affirmative precepts, and acts of vice are forbidden by the negative precepts. But according to Boëthius in his commentary on the *Categories*,* vices should be uprooted before virtues are sown. Therefore among the precepts concerning our neighbor, the negative precepts should have preceded the affirmative.

Obj. 3. Further, the precepts of the Law are about men's actions. But actions of thought precede actions of word or outward deed. Therefore the precepts about not coveting, which regard our thoughts, are unsuitably placed last in order.

On the contrary, The Apostle says (Rom. xiii. 1): *The things that are of God, are well ordered* (Vulg.,—*Those that are, are ordained of God*). But the precepts of the decalogue were given immediately by God, as stated above (A. 3). Therefore they are arranged in becoming order.

I answer that, As stated above (AA. 3, 5 *ad* 1), the precepts of the decalogue are such as the mind of man is ready to grasp at once. Now it is evident that a thing is so much the more easily grasped by the reason, as its contrary is more grievous and repugnant to reason. Moreover, it is clear, since the order of reason begins with the end, that, for a man to be inordinately disposed towards his end, is supremely contrary to reason. Now the end of human life and society is God. Consequently it was necessary for the precepts of the decalogue, first of all, to direct man to God; since the contrary to this is most grievous. Thus also, in an army, which is ordained to the commander as to its end, it is requisite first that the soldier should be subject to the commander, and the opposite of

* Lib. iv., cap. *De Oppos.*

this is most grievous; and secondly it is requisite that he should be in co-ordination with the other soldiers.

Now among those things whereby we are ordained to God, the first is that man should be subjected to Him faithfully, by having nothing in common with His enemies. The second is that he should show Him reverence: the third that he should offer Him service. Thus, in an army, it is a greater sin for a soldier to act treacherously and make a compact with the foe, than to be insolent to his commander: and this last is more grievous than if he be found wanting in some point of service to him.

As to the precepts that direct man in his behavior towards his neighbor, it is evident that it is more repugnant to reason, and a more grievous sin, if man does not observe the due order as to those persons to whom he is most indebted. Consequently, among those precepts that direct man in his relations to his neighbor, the first place is given to that one which regards his parents. Among the other precepts we again find the order to be according to the gravity of sin. For it is more grave and more repugnant to reason, to sin by deed than by word; and by word than by thought. And among sins of deed, murder which destroys life in one already living is more grievous than adultery, which imperils the life of the unborn child; and adultery is more grave than theft, which regards external goods.

Reply Obj. 1. Although our neighbor is better known than God by the way of the senses, nevertheless the love of God is the reason for the love of our neighbor, as shall be declared later on (II-II, Q. 25, A. 1; Q. 26, A. 2). Hence the precepts ordaining man to God demanded precedence of the others.

Reply Obj. 2. Just as God is the universal principle of being in respect of all things, so is a father a principle of being in respect of his son. Therefore the precept regarding parents was fittingly placed after the precepts regarding God. This argument holds in respect of affirmative and negative precepts about the same kind of deed: although even then it is not altogether cogent. For although in the order of execution, vices should be uprooted before virtues are sown, according to Ps. xxxiii. 15: *Turn away from evil, and do good,* and Isa. i. 16, 17: *Cease to do perversely; learn to do well;* yet, in the order of knowledge, virtue precedes vice, because *the crooked line is known by the straight* (*De Anima* i): and *by the law is the knowledge of sin* (Rom. iii. 20). Wherefore the affirmative precept demanded the first place. However, this is not the reason for the order, but that which is given above. Because in the precepts regarding God, which belong to the first table, an affirmative precept is placed last, since its transgression implies a less grievous sin.

Reply Obj. 3. Although sin of thought stands first in the order of execution, yet its prohibition holds a later position in the order of reason.

SEVENTH ARTICLE

Whether the Precepts of the Decalogue Are Suitably Formulated?

We proceed thus to the Seventh Article:—

Objection 1. It would seem that the precepts of the decalogue are unsuitably formulated. Because the affirmative precepts direct man to acts of virtue, while the negative precepts withdraw him from acts of vice. But in every matter there are virtues and vices opposed to one another. Therefore in whatever matter there is an ordinance of a precept of the decalogue, there should have been an affirmative and a negative precept. Therefore it was unfitting that affirmative precepts should be framed in some matters, and negative precepts in others.

Obj. 2. Further, Isidore says (*Etym.* ii. 10) that every law is based on reason. But all the precepts of the decalogue belong to the Divine law. Therefore the reason should have been pointed out in each precept, and not only in the first and third.

Obj. 3. Further, by observing the precepts man deserves to be rewarded by God. But the Divine promises concern the rewards of the precepts. Therefore the promise should have been included in each precept, and not only in the second and fourth.

Obj. 4. Further, the Old Law is called *the law of fear,* in so far as it induced men to observe the precepts, by means of the threat of punishments. But all the precepts of the decalogue belong to the Old Law. Therefore a threat of punishment should have been included in each, and not only in the first and second.

Obj. 5. Further, all the commandments of God should be retained in the memory: for it is written (Prov. iii. 3): *Write them in the tables of thy heart.* Therefore it was not fitting that mention of the memory should be made in the third commandment only. Consequently it seems that the precepts of the decalogue are unsuitably formulated.

On the contrary, It is written (Wis. xi. 21) that *God made all things, in measure, number and weight.* Much more therefore did He observe a suitable manner in formulating His Law.

I answer that, The highest wisdom is contained in the precepts of the Divine law: wherefore it is written (Deut. iv. 6): *This is your wisdom and understanding in the sight of nations.* Now it belongs to wisdom to arrange all things in due manner and order. Therefore it must be evident that the precepts of the Law are suitably set forth.

Reply Obj. 1. Affirmation of one thing always leads to the denial of its opposite: but the denial of one opposite does not always lead to the affirmation of the other. For it follows that if a thing is white, it is not black: but it does not follow that if it is not black, it is white: because negation extends further than affirmation. And hence too, that one ought not to do harm to another, which pertains to the negative precepts, extends to more persons, as a primary dictate of reason, than that one ought to do someone a service or kindness. Nevertheless it is a primary dictate of reason that man is a debtor in the point of rendering a service or kindness to those from whom he has received kindness, if he has not yet repaid the debt. Now there are two whose favors no man can sufficiently repay, viz., God and man's father, as stated in *Ethic.* viii. 14. Therefore it is that there are only two affirmative precepts; one about the honor due to parents, the other about the celebration of the Sabbath in memory of the Divine favor.

Reply Obj. 2. The reasons for the purely moral precepts are manifest; hence there was no need to add the reason. But some of the precepts include ceremonial matter, or a determination of a general moral precept; thus the first precept includes the determination, *Thou shalt not make a graven thing;* and in the third precept the Sabbath-day is fixed. Consequently there was need to state the reason in each case.

Reply Obj. 3. Generally speaking, men direct their actions to some point of utility. Consequently in those precepts in which it seemed that there would be no useful result, or that some utility might be hindered, it was necessary to add a promise of reward. And since parents are already on the way to depart from us, no benefit is expected from them: wherefore a promise of reward is added to the precept about honoring one's parents. The same applies to the precept forbidding idolatry: since thereby it seemed that men were hindered from receiving the apparent benefit which they think they can get by entering into a compact with the demons.

Reply Obj. 4. Punishments are necessary against those who are prone to evil, as stated in *Ethic.* x. 9. Wherefore a threat of punishment is only affixed to those precepts of the law which forbade evils to which men were prone. Now men were prone to idolatry by reason of the general custom of the nations. Likewise men are prone to perjury on account of the frequent use of oaths. Hence it is that a threat is affixed to the first two precepts.

Reply Obj. 5. The commandment about the Sabbath was made in memory of a past blessing. Wherefore special mention of the memory is made therein.—Or again, the commandment about the Sabbath has a determination affixed to it that does not belong to the natural law, wherefore this precept needed a special admonition.

EIGHTH ARTICLE

Whether the Precepts of the Decalogue Are Dispensable?

We proceed thus to the Eighth Article:—

Objection 1. It would seem that the precepts of the decalogue are dispensable. For the precepts of the decalogue belong to the natural law. But the natural law fails in some cases and is changeable, like human nature, as the Philosopher says (*Ethic.* v. 7). Now the failure of law to apply in certain particular cases is a reason for dispensation, as stated above (Q. 96, A. 6; Q. 97, A. 4). Therefore a dispensation can be granted in the precepts of the decalogue.

Obj. 2. Further, man stands in the same relation to human law as God does to Divine law. But man can dispense with the precepts of a law made by man. Therefore, since the precepts of the decalogue are ordained by God, it seems that God can dispense with them. Now our superiors are God's vicegerents on earth; for the Apostle says (2 Cor. ii. 10): *For what I have pardoned, if I have pardoned anything, for your sakes have I done it in the person of Christ.* Therefore superiors can dispense with the precepts of the decalogue.

Obj. 3. Further, among the precepts of the decalogue is one forbidding murder. But it seems that a dispensation is given by men in this precept: for instance, when according to the prescription of human law, such as evildoers or enemies are lawfully slain. Therefore the precepts of the decalogue are dispensable.

Obj. 4. Further, the observance of the Sabbath is ordained by a precept of the decalogue. But a dispensation was granted in this precept; for it is written (1 Machab. ii. 4): *And they determined in that day, saying: Whosoever shall come up to fight against us on the Sabbath-day, we will fight against him.* Therefore the precepts of the decalogue are dispensable.

On the contrary are the words of Isa.

xxiv. 5, where some are reproved for that *they have changed the ordinance, they have broken the everlasting covenant;* which, seemingly, apply principally to the precepts of the decalogue. Therefore the precepts of the decalogue cannot be changed by dispensation.

I answer that, As stated above (*loc. cit. cf. Obj.* 1), precepts admit of dispensation, when there occurs a particular case in which, if the letter of the law be observed, the intention of the lawgiver is frustrated. Now the intention of every lawgiver is directed first and chiefly to the common good; secondly, to the order of justice and virtue, whereby the common good is preserved and attained. If therefore there be any precepts which contain the very preservation of the common good, or the very order of justice and virtue, such precepts contain the intention of the lawgiver, and therefore are indispensable. For instance, if in some community a law were enacted, such as this,—that no man should work for the destruction of the commonwealth, or betray the state to its enemies, or that no man should do anything unjust or evil, such precepts would not admit of dispensation. But if other precepts were enacted, subordinate to the above, and determining certain special modes of procedure, these latter precepts would admit of dispensation, in so far as the omission of these precepts in certain cases would not be prejudicial to the former precepts which contain the intention of the lawgiver. For instance if, for the safeguarding of the commonwealth, it were enacted in some city that from each ward some men should keep watch as sentries in case of siege, some might be dispensed from this on account of some greater utility.

Now the precepts of the decalogue contain the very intention of the lawgiver, who is God. For the precepts of the first table, which direct us to God, contain the very order to the common and final good, which is God; while the precepts of the second table contain the order of justice to be observed among men, that nothing undue be done to anyone, and that each one be given his due; for it is in this sense that we are to take the precepts of the decalogue. Consequently the precepts of the decalogue admit of no dispensation whatever.

Reply Obj. 1. The Philosopher is not speaking of the natural law which contains the very order of justice: for it is a never-failing principle that *justice should be preserved.* But he is speaking in reference to certain fixed modes of observing justice, which fail to apply in certain cases.

Reply Obj. 2. As the Apostle says (2 Tim. ii. 13), God *continueth faithful, He cannot deny Himself.* But He would deny Himself if He were to do away with the very order of His own justice, since He is justice itself. Wherefore God cannot dispense a man so that it be lawful for him not to direct himself to God, or not to be subject to His justice, even in those matters in which men are directed to one another.

Reply Obj. 3. The slaying of a man is forbidden in the decalogue, in so far as it bears the character of something undue: for in this sense the precept contains the very essence of justice. Human law cannot make it lawful for a man to be slain unduly. But it is not undue for evil-doers or foes of the common weal to be slain: hence this is not contrary to the precept of the decalogue; and such a killing is no murder as forbidden by that precept, as Augustine observes (*De Lib. Arb.* i. 4).— In like manner when a man's property is taken from him, if it be due that he should lose it, this is not theft or robbery as forbidden by the decalogue.

Consequently when the children of Israel, by God's command, took away the spoils of the Egyptians, this was not theft; since it was due to them by the sentence of God.— Likewise when Abraham consented to slay his son, he did not consent to murder, because his son was due to be slain by the command of God, Who is Lord of life and death: for He it is Who inflicts the punishment of death on all men, both godly and ungodly, on account of the sin of our first parent, and if a man be the executor of that sentence by Divine authority, he will be no murderer any more than God would be.—Again Osee, by taking unto himself a wife of fornications, or an adulterous woman, was not guilty either of adultery or of fornication. because he took unto himself one who was his by command of God, Who is the Author of the institution of marriage.

Accordingly, therefore, the precepts of the decalogue, as to the essence of justice which they contain, are unchangeable: but as to any determination by application to individual actions,—for instance that this or that be murder, theft, or adultery, or not—in this point they admit of change; sometimes by Divine authority alone, namely, in such matters as are exclusively of Divine institution, as marriage and the like; sometimes also by human authority, namely in such matters as are subject to human jurisdiction: for in this respect men stand in the place of God: and yet not in all respects.

Reply Obj. 4. This determination was an interpretation rather than a dispensation. For a man is not taken to break the Sabbath, if he does something necessary for human welfare; as Our Lord proves (Matth. xii. 3 *seq.*).

NINTH ARTICLE

Whether the Mode of Virtue Falls under the Precept of the Law?

We proceed thus to the Ninth Article:—

Objection 1. It would seem that the mode of virtue falls under the precept of the law. For the mode of virtue is that deeds of justice should be done justly, that deeds of fortitude should be done bravely, and in like manner as to the other virtues. But it is commanded (Deut. xvi. 20) that *thou shalt follow justly after that which is just.* Therefore the mode of virtue falls under the precept.

Obj. 2. Further, that which belongs to the intention of the lawgiver comes chiefly under the precept. But the intention of the lawgiver is directed chiefly to make men virtuous, as stated in *Ethic.* ii: and it belongs to a virtuous man to act virtuously. Therefore the mode of virtue falls under the precept.

Obj. 3. Further, the mode of virtue seems to consist properly in working willingly and with pleasure. But this falls under a precept of the Divine law, for it is written (Ps. xcix. 2): *Serve ye the Lord with gladness;* and (2 Cor. ix. 7): *Not with sadness or necessity: for God loveth a cheerful giver;* whereupon the gloss says: *Whatever ye do, do gladly; and then you will do it well; whereas if you do it sorrowfully, it is done in thee, not by thee.* Therefore the mode of virtue falls under the precept of the law.

On the contrary, No man can act as a virtuous man acts unless he has the habit of virtue, as the Philosopher explains (*Ethic.* ii. 4, v. 8). Now whoever transgresses a precept of the law, deserves to be punished. Hence it would follow that a man who has not the habit of virtue, would deserve to be punished, whatever he does. But this is contrary to the intention of the law, which aims at leading man to virtue, by habituating him to good works. Therefore the mode of virtue does not fall under the precept.

I answer that, As stated above (Q. 90, A. 3 *ad* 2), a precept of law has compulsory power. Hence that on which the compulsion of the law is brought to bear, falls directly under the precept of the law. Now the law compels through fear of punishment, as stated in *Ethic.* x. 9, because that properly falls under the precept of the law, for which the penalty of the law is inflicted. But Divine law and human law are differently situated as to the appointment of penalties; since the penalty of the law is inflicted only for those things which come under the judgment of the lawgiver: for the law punishes in accordance with the verdict given. Now man, the framer of human law, is competent to judge only of outward acts; because *man seeth those things that appear*, according to 1 Kings xvi. 7: while God alone, the framer of the Divine law, is competent to judge of the inward movements of wills, according to Ps. vii. 10: *The searcher of hearts and reins is God.*

Accordingly, therefore, we must say that the mode of virtue is in some sort regarded both by human and by Divine law; in some respect it is regarded by the Divine, but not by the human law; and in another way, it is regarded neither by the human nor by the Divine law. Now the mode of virtue consists in three things, as the Philosopher states in *Ethic.* ii. The first is that man should act *knowingly:* and this is subject to the judgment of both Divine and human law; because what a man does in ignorance, he does accidentally. Hence according to both human and Divine law, certain things are judged in respect of ignorance to be punishable or pardonable.

The second point is that a man should act *deliberately*, i.e., *from choice, choosing that particular action for its own sake;* wherein a twofold internal movement is implied, of volition and of intention, about which we have spoken above (QQ. 8, 12): and concerning these two, Divine law alone, and not human law, is competent to judge. For human law does not punish the man who wishes to slay, but slays not: whereas the Divine law does, according to Matth. v. 22: *Whosoever is angry with his brother, shall be in danger of the judgment.*

The third point is that he should *act from a firm and immovable principle:* which firmness belongs properly to a habit, and implies that the action proceeds from a rooted habit. In this respect, the mode of virtue does not fall under the precept either of Divine or of human law, since neither by man nor by God is he punished as breaking the law, who gives due honor to his parents and yet has not the habit of filial piety.

Reply Obj. 1. The mode of doing acts of justice, which falls under the precept, is that they be done in accordance with right; but not that they be done from the habit of justice.

Reply Obj. 2. The intention of the lawgiver is twofold. His aim, in the first place, is to lead men to something by the precepts of the law: and this is virtue. Secondly, his intention is brought to bear on the matter itself of the precept: and this is something leading or disposing to virtue, viz., an act of virtue. For the end of the precept and the matter of the precept are not the same: just as neither in other things is the end the same as that which conduces to the end.

Reply Obj. 3. That works of virtue should be done without sadness, falls under the precept of the Divine law; for whoever works with sadness works unwillingly. But to work with pleasure, i.e., joyfully or cheerfully, in one respect falls under the precept, viz., in so far as pleasure ensues from the love of God and one's neighbor (which love falls under the precept), and love causes pleasure: and in another respect does not fall under the precept, in so far as pleasure ensues from a habit; for *pleasure taken in a work proves the existence of a habit*, as stated in *Ethic.* ii. 3. For an act may give pleasure either on account of its end, or through its proceeding from a becoming habit.

TENTH ARTICLE

Whether the Mode of Charity Falls under the Precept of the Divine Law?

We proceed thus to the Tenth Article:—

Objection 1. It would seem that the mode of charity falls under the precept of the Divine law. For it is written (Matth. xix. 17): *If thou wilt enter into life, keep the commandments:* whence it seems to follow that the observance of the commandments suffices for entrance into life. But good works do not suffice for entrance into life, except they be done from charity: for it is written (1 Cor. xiii. 3): *If I should distribute all my goods to feed the poor, and if I should deliver my body to be burned, and have not charity, it profiteth me nothing.* Therefore the mode of charity is included in the commandment.

Obj. 2. Further, the mode of charity consists properly speaking in doing all things for God. But this falls under the precept; for the Apostle says (1 Cor. x. 31): *Do all to the glory of God.* Therefore the mode of charity falls under the precept.

Obj. 3. Further, if the mode of charity does not fall under the precept, it follows that one can fulfil the precepts of the law without having charity. Now what can be done without charity can be done without grace, which is always united with charity. Therefore one can fulfil the precepts of the law without grace. But this is the error of Pelagius, as Augustine declares (*De Hæres.* lxxxviii). Therefore the mode of charity is included in the commandment.

On the contrary, Whoever breaks a commandment sins mortally. If therefore the mode of charity falls under the precept, it follows that whoever acts otherwise than from charity sins mortally. But whoever has not charity, acts otherwise than from charity. Therefore it follows that whoever has not charity, sins mortally in whatever he does, however good this may be in itself: which is absurd.

I answer that, Opinions have been contrary on this question. For some have said absolutely that the mode of charity comes under the precept; and yet that it is possible for one not having charity to fulfil this precept: because he can dispose himself to receive charity from God. Nor (say they) does it follow that a man not having charity sins mortally whenever he does something good of its kind: because it is an affirmative precept that binds one to act from charity, and is binding not for all time, but only for such time as one is in a state of charity.—On the other hand, some have said that the mode of charity is altogether outside the precept.

Both these opinions are true up to a certain point. Because the act of charity can be considered in two ways. First, as an act by itself: and thus it falls under the precept of the law which specially prescribes it, viz., *Thou shalt love the Lord thy God,* and *Thou shalt love thy neighbor.* In this sense, the first opinion is true. Because it is not impossible to observe this precept which regards the act of charity; since man can dispose himself to possess charity, and when he possesses it, he can use it. Secondly, the act of charity can be considered as being the mode of the acts of the other virtues, i.e., inasmuch as the acts of the other virtues are ordained to charity, which is *the end of the commandment,* as stated in 1 Tim. i. 5: for it has been said above (Q. 12, A. 4) that the intention of the end is a formal mode of the act ordained to that end. In this sense the second opinion is true in saying that the mode of charity does not fall under the precept, that is to say that this commandment, *Honor thy father,* does not mean that a man must honor his father from charity, but merely that he must honor him. Wherefore he that honors his father, yet has not charity, does not break this precept: although he does break the precept concerning the act of charity, for which reason he deserves to be punished.

Reply Obj. 1. Our Lord did not say, *If thou wilt enter into life, keep one commandment;* but *keep* all *the commandments:* among which is included the commandment concerning the love of God and our neighbor.

Reply Obj. 2. The precept of charity contains the injunction that God should be loved from our whole heart, which means that all things would be referred to God. Consequently man cannot fulfil the precept of charity, unless he also refer all things to God. Wherefore he that honors his father and mother, is bound to honor them from charity, not in virtue of the precept, *Honor thy father and mother,* but in virtue of the precept, *Thou shalt love the*

Lord thy God with thy whole heart. And since these are two affirmative precepts, not binding for all times, they can be binding, each one at a different time: so that it may happen that a man fulfils the precept of honoring his father and mother, without at the same time breaking the precept concerning the omission of the mode of charity.

Reply Obj. 3. Man cannot fulfil all the precepts of the law, unless he fulfil the precept of charity, which is impossible without charity. Consequently it is not possible, as Pelagius maintained, for man to fulfil the law without grace.

ELEVENTH ARTICLE

Whether It Is Right to Distinguish Other Moral Precepts of the Law Besides the Decalogue?

We proceed thus to the Eleventh Article:—

Objection 1. It would seem that it is wrong to distinguish other moral precepts of the law besides the decalogue. Because, as Our Lord declared (Matth. xxii. 40), *on these two commandments* of charity *dependeth the whole law and the prophets.* But these two commandments are explained by the ten commandments of the decalogue. Therefore there is no need for other moral precepts.

Obj. 2. Further, the moral precepts are distinct from the judicial and ceremonial precepts, as stated above (Q. 99, AA. 3, 4). But the determinations of the general moral precepts belong to the judicial and ceremonial precepts: and the general moral precepts are contained in the decalogue, or are even presupposed to the decalogue, as stated above (A. 3). Therefore it was unsuitable to lay down other moral precepts besides the decalogue.

Obj. 3. Further, the moral precepts are about the acts of all the virtues, as stated above (A. 2). Therefore, as the Law contains, besides the decalogue, moral precepts pertaining to religion, liberality, mercy, and chastity; so there should have been added some precepts pertaining to the other virtues, for instance, fortitude, sobriety, and so forth. And yet such is not the case. It is therefore unbecoming to distinguish other moral precepts in the Law besides those of the decalogue.

On the contrary, It is written (Ps. xviii. 8): *The law of the Lord is unspotted, converting souls.* But man is preserved from the stain of sin, and his soul is converted to God by other moral precepts besides those of the decalogue. Therefore it was right for the Law to include other moral precepts.

I answer that, As is evident from what has been stated (Q. 99, AA. 3, 4), the judicial and ceremonial precepts derive their force from their institution alone: since before they were instituted, it seemed of no consequence whether things were done in this or that way. But the moral precepts derive their efficacy from the very dictate of natural reason, even if they were never included in the Law. Now of these there are three grades: for some are most certain, and so evident as to need no promulgation; such as the commandments of the love of God and our neighbor, and others like these, as stated above (A. 3), which are, as it were, the ends of the commandments; wherefore no man can have an erroneous judgment about them. Some precepts are more detailed, the reason of which even an uneducated man can easily grasp; and yet they need to be promulgated, because human judgment, in a few instances, happens to be led astray concerning them: these are the precepts of the decalogue. Again, there are some precepts the reason of which is not so evident to everyone, but only to the wise; these are moral precepts added to the decalogue, and given to the people by God through Moses and Aaron.

But since the things that are evident are the principles whereby we know those that are not evident, these other moral precepts added to the decalogue are reducible to the precepts of the decalogue, as so many corollaries. Thus the first commandment of the decalogue forbids the worship of strange gods: and to this are added other precepts forbidding things relating to the worship of idols: thus it is written (Deut. xviii. 10, 11): *Neither let there be found among you anyone that shall expiate his son or daughter, making them to pass through the fire: . . . neither let there be any wizard nor charmer, nor anyone that consulteth pythonic spirits, or fortune-tellers, or that seeketh the truth from the dead.*—The second commandment forbids perjury. To this is added the prohibition of blasphemy (Levit. xxiv. 15 *seq.*) and the prohibition of false doctrine (Deut. xiii).—To the third commandment are added all the ceremonial precepts.—To the fourth commandment prescribing the honor due to parents, is added the precept about honoring the aged, according to Levit. xix. 32: *Rise up before the hoary head, and honor the person of the aged man;* and likewise all precepts prescribing the reverence to be observed towards our betters, or kindliness towards our equals or inferiors.—To the fifth commandment, which forbids murder, is added the prohibition of hatred and of any kind of violence inflicted on our neighbor, according to Levit. xix. 16: *Thou shalt not stand against the blood of thy neighbor:* likewise the prohibition against hating one's brother (*ibid.* 17): *Thou shalt not hate thy brother in thy*

heart.—To the sixth commandment which forbids adultery, is added the prohibition about whoredom, according to Deut. xxiii. 17: *There shall be no whore among the daughters of Israel, nor whoremonger among the sons of Israel;* and the prohibition against unnatural sins, according to Levit. xviii. 22, 23: *Thou shalt not lie with mankind . . . thou shalt not copulate with any beast.*—To the seventh commandment which prohibits theft, is added the precept forbidding usury, according to Deut. xxiii. 19: *Thou shalt not lend to thy brother money to usury;* and the prohibition against fraud, according to Deut. xxv. 13: *Thou shalt not have divers weights in thy bag;* and universally all prohibitions relating to peculations and larceny.—To the eighth commandment, forbidding false testimony, is added the prohibition against false judgment, according to Exod. xxiii. 2: *Neither shalt thou yield in judgment, to the opinion of the most part, to stray from the truth;* and the prohibition against lying (*ibid.* 7): *Thou shalt fly lying;* and the prohibition against detraction, according to Levit. xix. 16: *Thou shalt not be a detractor, nor a whisperer among the people.*—To the other two commandments no further precepts are added, because thereby are forbidden all kinds of evil desires.

Reply Obj. 1. The precepts of the decalogue are ordained to the love of God and our neighbor as pertaining evidently to our duty towards them; but the other precepts are so ordained as pertaining thereto less evidently.

Reply Obj. 2. It is in virtue of their institution that the ceremonial and judicial precepts *are determinations of the precepts of the decalogue*, not by reason of a natural instinct, as in the case of the superadded moral precepts.

Reply Obj. 3. The precepts of a law are ordained for the common good, as stated above (Q. 90, A. 2). And since those virtues which direct our conduct towards others pertain directly to the common good, as also does the virtue of chastity, in so far as the generative act conduces to the common good of the species; hence precepts bearing directly on these virtues are given, both in the decalogue and in addition thereto. As to the act of fortitude there are the order to be given by the commanders in the war, which is undertaken for the common good: as is clear from Deut. xx. 3, where the priest is commanded (to speak thus): *Be not afraid, do not give back.* In like manner the prohibition of acts of gluttony is left to paternal admonition, since it is contrary to the good of the household; hence it is said (Deut. xxi. 20) in the person of parents: *He slighteth hearing our admonitions, he giveth himself to revelling, and to debauchery and banquetings.*

TWELFTH ARTICLE

Whether the Moral Precepts of the Old Law Justified Man?

We proceed thus to the Twelfth Article:—

Objection 1. It would seem that the moral precepts of the Old Law justified man. Because the Apostle says (Rom. ii. 13): *For not the hearers of the Law are justified before God, but the doers of the Law shall be justified.* But the doers of the Law are those who fulfil the precepts of the Law. Therefore the fulfilling of the precepts of the Law was a cause of justification.

Obj. 2. Further, it is written (Levit. xviii. 5): *Keep My laws and My judgments, which if a man do, he shall live in them.* But the spiritual life of man is through justice. Therefore the fulfilling of the precepts of the Law was a cause of justificat'on.

Obj. 3. Further, the Divine law is more efficacious than human law. But human law justifies man; since there is a kind of justice consisting in fulfilling the precepts of law. Therefore the precepts of the Law justified man.

On the contrary, The Apostle says (2 Cor. iii. 6): *The letter killeth:* which, according to Augustine (*De Spir. et Lit.* xiv), refers even to the moral precepts. Therefore the moral precepts did not cause justice.

I answer that, Just as *healthy* is said properly and first of that which is possessed of health, and secondarily of that which is a sign or a safeguard of health; so justification means first and properly the causing of justice; while secondarily and improperly, as it were, it may denote a sign of justice or a disposition thereto. If justice be taken in the last two ways, it is evident that it was conferred by the precepts of the Law; in so far, to wit, as they disposed men to the justifying grace of Christ, which they also signified, because as Augustine says (*Contra Faust.* xxii. 24), *even the life of that people foretold and foreshadowed Christ.*

But if we speak of justification properly so called, then we must notice that it can be considered as in the habit or as in the act: so that accordingly justification may be taken in two ways. First, according as man is made just, by becoming possessed of the habit of justice: secondly, according as he does works of justice, so that in this sense justification is nothing else than the execution of justice. Now justice, like the other virtues, may denote either the acquired or the infused virtue, as is clear from what has been stated (Q. 63, A. 4). The acquired virtue is caused by works; but the infused virtue is caused by God Himself through His grace. The latter is true justice, of which we are speaking now, and in this respect of which a man is said to be just before God, according to Rom. iv. 2: *If Abraham were justified by works, he hath whereof to glory, but not before God.* Hence this justice could not be caused by the moral precepts, which are about human actions: wherefore the moral precepts could not justify man by causing justice.

If, on the other hand, by justification we understand the execution of justice, thus all the precepts of the Law justified man, but in various ways. Because the ceremonial precepts taken as a whole contained something just in itself, in so far as they aimed at offering worship to God; whereas taken individually they contained that which is just, not in itself, but by being a determination of the Divine law. Hence it is said of these precepts that they did not justify man save through the devotion and obedience of those who complied with them.—On the other hand the moral and judicial precepts, either in general or also in particular, contained that which is just in itself: but the moral precepts contained that which is just in itself according to that *general justice* which is *every virtue* according to *Ethic.* v, 1; whereas the judicial precepts belonged to *special justice,* which is about contracts connected with the human mode of life, between one man and another.

Reply Obj. 1. The Apostle takes justification for the execution of justice.

Reply Obj. 2. The man who fulfilled the precepts of the Law is said to live in them, because he did not incur the penalty of death, which the Law inflicted on its transgressors: in this sense the Apostle quotes this passage (Gal. iii. 12).

Reply Obj. 3. The precepts of human law justify man by acquired justice: it is not about this that we are inquiring now, but only about that justice which is before God.

QUESTION 101

Of the Ceremonial Precepts in Themselves

(In Four Articles)

WE must now consider the ceremonial precepts: and first we must consider them in themselves; secondly, their cause; thirdly, their duration. Under the first head there are four points of inquiry: (1) The nature of the ceremonial precepts: (2) Whether they are figurative? (3) Whether there should have been many of them? (4) Of their various kinds.

FIRST ARTICLE

Whether the Nature of the Ceremonial Precepts Consists in Their Pertaining to the Worship of God?

We proceed thus to the First Article:—

Objection 1. It would seem that the nature of the ceremonial precepts does not consist in their pertaining to the worship of God. Because, in the Old Law, the Jews were given certain precepts about abstinence from food (Levit. xi); and about refraining from certain kinds of clothes, *e.g.* (Levit. xix. 19): *Thou shalt not wear a garment that is woven of two sorts;* and again (Num. xv. 38): *To make to themselves fringes in the corners of their garments.* But these are not moral precepts; since they do not remain in the New Law. Nor are they judicial precepts; since they do not pertain to the pronouncing of judgment between man and man. Therefore they are ceremonial precepts. Yet they seem in no way to pertain to the worship of God. Therefore the nature of the ceremonial precepts does not consist in their pertaining to Divine Worship.

Obj. 2. Further, some state that the ceremonial precepts are those which pertain to solemnities; as though they were so called from the *cerei* (candles) which are lit up on those occasions. But many other things besides solemnities pertain to the worship of God. Therefore it does not seem that the ceremonial precepts are so called from their pertaining to the Divine worship.

Obj. 3. Further, some say that the ceremonial precepts are patterns, i.e., rules, of salvation: because the Greek χαῖρε is the same as the Latin *salve.* But all the precepts of the Law are rules of salvation, and not only those that pertain to the worship of God. Therefore not only those precepts which pertain to the Divine worship are called ceremonial.

Obj. 4. Further, Rabbi Moses says (*Doct. Perplex.* iii) that the ceremonial precepts are those for which there is no evident reason. But there is evident reason for many things pertaining to the worship of God; such as the observance of the Sabbath, the feasts of the Passover and of the Tabernacles, and many other things, the reason for which is set down in the Law. Therefore the ceremonial precepts are not those which pertain to the worship of God.

On the contrary, It is written (Exod. xviii. 19, 20): *Be thou to the people in those things that pertain to God . . . and . . . shew the people the ceremonies and the manner of worshipping.*

I answer that, As stated above (Q. 99, A. 4), the ceremonial precepts are determinations of the moral precepts whereby man is directed to God, just as the judicial precepts are determinations of the moral precepts whereby he is directed to his neighbor. Now man is directed to God by the worship due to Him. Wherefore those precepts are properly called ceremonial, which pertain to the Divine worship. —The reason for their being so called was given above (*ibid.,* A. 3), when we established the distinction between the ceremonial and other precepts.

Reply Obj. 1. The Divine worship includes not only sacrifices and the like, which seem to be directed to God immediately, but also those things whereby His worshippers are duly prepared to worship Him: thus too in other matters, whatever is preparatory to the end comes under the science whose object is the end. Accordingly those precepts of the Law which regard the clothing and food of God's worshippers, and other such matters, pertain to a certain preparation of the ministers, with the view of fitting them for the Divine worship: just as those who administer to a king make use of certain special observances. Consequently such are contained under the ceremonial precepts.

Reply Obj. 2. The alleged explanation of the name does not seem very probable: especially as the Law does not contain many instances of the lighting of candles in solemnities; since, even the lamps of the Candlestick were furnished with *oil of olives,* as stated in Levit. xxiv. 2. Nevertheless we may say that all things pertaining to the Divine worship were more carefully observed on solemn festivals: so that all ceremonial precepts may be included under the observance of solemnities.

Reply Obj. 3. Neither does this explanation of the name appear to be very much to the point, since the word *ceremony* is not Greek but Latin. We may say, however, that, since man's salvation is from God, those precepts above all seem to be rules of salvation, which direct man to God: and accordingly those which refer to Divine worship are called ceremonial precepts.

Reply Obj. 4. This explanation of the ceremonial precepts has a certain amount of probability: not that they are called ceremonial precisely because there is no evident reason for them; this is a kind of consequence. For, since the precepts referring to the Divine worship must needs be figurative, as we shall state further on (A. 2), the consequence is that the reason for them is not so very evident.

SECOND ARTICLE

Whether the Ceremonial Precepts Are Figurative?

We proceed thus to the Second Article:—

Objection 1. It would seem that the ceremonial precepts are not figurative. For it is the duty of every teacher to express himself in such a way as to be easily understood, as Augustine states (*De Doctr. Christ.* iv. 4, 10) and this seems very necessary in the framing of a law: because precepts of law are proposed to the populace; for which reason a law should be manifest, as Isidore declares (*Etym.* v. 21). If therefore the precepts of the Law were given as figures of something, it seems unbecoming that Moses should have delivered these precepts without explaining what they signified.

Obj. 2. Further, whatever is done for the worship of God, should be entirely free from unfittingness. But the performance of actions in representation of others, seems to savor of the theatre or of the drama: because formerly the actions performed in theatres were done to represent the actions of others. Therefore it seems that such things should not be done for the worship of God. But the ceremonial precepts are ordained to the Divine worship, as stated above (A. 1). Therefore they should not be figurative.

Obj. 3. Further, Augustine says (*Enchirid.* iii., iv) that *God is worshipped chiefly by faith, hope, and charity.* But the precepts of faith, hope, and charity are not figurative. Therefore the ceremonial precepts should not be figurative.

Obj. 4. Further, Our Lord said (Jo. iv. 24): *God is a spirit, and they that adore Him, must adore Him in spirit and in truth.* But a figure is not the very truth: in fact one is condivided with the other. Therefore the ceremonial precepts, which refer to the Divine worship, should not be figurative.

On the contrary, The Apostle says (Coloss. ii. 16, 17): *Let no man . . . judge you in meat or in drink, or in respect of a festival day, or of the new moon, or of the sabbaths, which are a shadow of things to come.*

I answer that, As stated above (A. 1; Q. 99, AA. 3, 4), the ceremonial precepts are those which refer to the worship of God. Now the Divine worship is twofold: internal, and external. For since man is composed of soul and body, each of these should be applied to the worship of God; the soul by an interior worship; the body by an outward worship: hence it is written (Ps. lxxxiii. 3): *My heart and my flesh have rejoiced in the living God.* And as the body is ordained to God through the soul, so the outward worship is ordained to the internal worship. Now interior worship consists in the soul being united to God by the intellect and affections. Wherefore according to the various ways in which the intellect and affections of the man who worships God are rightly united to God, his external actions are applied in various ways to the Divine worship.

For in the state of future bliss, the human intellect will gaze on the Divine Truth in Itself. Wherefore the external worship will not consist in anything figurative, but solely in the praise of God, proceeding from the inward knowledge and affection, according to Isa. li. 3: *Joy and gladness shall be found therein, thanksgiving and the voice of praise.*

But in the present state of life, we are unable to gaze upon the Divine Truth in Itself, and we need the ray of Divine light to shine upon us under the form of certain sensible figures, as Dionysius states (*Cœl. Hier.* i); in various ways, however, according to the various states of human knowledge. For under the Old Law, neither was the Divine Truth manifest in Itself, nor was the way leading to that manifestation as yet opened out, as the Apostle declares (Heb. ix. 8). Hence the external worship of the Old Law needed to be figurative not only of the future truth to be manifested in our heavenly country, but also of Christ, Who is the way leading to that heavenly manifestation. But under the New Law this way is already revealed: and therefore it needs no longer to be foreshadowed as something future, but to be brought to our minds as something past or present: and the truth of the glory to come, which is not yet revealed, alone needs to be foreshadowed. This is what the Apostle says (Heb. xi. 1): *The Law has* (Vulg.,—*having*) *a shadow of the good things to come, not the very image of the things:* for a shadow is less than an image; so that the image belongs to the New Law, but the shadow to the Old.

Reply Obj. 1. The things of God are not to be revealed to man except in proportion to his capacity: else he would be in danger of downfall, were he to despise what he cannot grasp. Hence it was more beneficial that the Divine mysteries should be revealed to uncultured people under a veil of figures, that thus they might know them at least implicitly by using those figures to the honor of God.

Reply Obj. 2. Just as human reason fails to grasp poetical expressions on account of their being lacking in truth, so does it fail to grasp Divine things perfectly, on account of the sublimity of the truth they contain: and therefore in both cases there is need of signs by means of sensible figures.

Reply Obj. 3. Augustine is speaking there of internal worship; to which, however, external worship should be ordained, as stated above.

The same answer applies to the Fourth Objection: because men were taught by Him to practice more perfectly the spiritual worship of God.

THIRD ARTICLE

Whether There Should Have Been Many Ceremonial Precepts?

We proceed thus to the Third Article:—

Objection 1. It would seem that there should not have been many ceremonial precepts. For those things which conduce to an end should be proportionate to that end. But the ceremonial precepts, as stated above (AA. 1, 2), are ordained to the worship of God, and to the foreshadowing of Christ. Now *there is but one God, of Whom are all things, . . . and one Lord Jesus Christ, by Whom are all things* (1 Cor. viii. 6). Therefore there should not have been many ceremonial precepts.

Obj. 2. Further, the great number of the ceremonial precepts was an occasion of transgression, according to the words of Peter (Acts xv. 10): *Why tempt you God, to put a yoke upon the necks of the disciples, which neither our fathers nor we have been able to bear?* Now the transgression of the Divine precepts is an obstacle to man's salvation. Since, therefore, every law should conduce to man's salvation, as Isidore says (*Etym.* v. 3), it seems that the ceremonial precepts should not have been given in great number.

Obj. 3. Further, the ceremonial precepts referred to the outward and bodily worship of God, as stated above (A. 2). But the Law should have lessened this bodily worship: since it directed men to Christ, Who taught them to worship God *in spirit and in truth*, as stated in John iv. 23. Therefore there should not have been many ceremonial precepts.

On the contrary, It is written (Osee viii. 12): *I shall write to them* (Vulg.,—*him*) *My manifold laws;* and (Job. xi. 6): *That He might show thee the secrets of His wisdom, and that His Law is manifold.*

I answer that, As stated above (Q. 96, A. 1), every law is given to a people. Now a people contains two kinds of men: some, prone to evil, who have to be coerced by the precepts of the law, as stated above (Q. 95, A. 1); some, inclined to good, either from nature or from custom, or rather from grace; and the like have to be taught and improved by means of the precepts of the law. Accordingly, with regard to both kinds of men it was expedient that the Old Law should contain many ceremonial precepts. For in that people there were many prone to idolatry; wherefore it was necessary to recall them by means of ceremonial precepts from the worship of idols to the worship of God. And since men served idols in many ways, it was necessary on the other hand to devise many means of repressing every single one: and again, to lay many obligations on such like men, in order that being burdened, as it were, by their duties to the Divine worship, they might have no time for the service of idols. As to those who were inclined to good, it was again necessary that there should be many ceremonial precepts; both because thus their mind was turned to God in many ways, and more continually; and because the mystery of Christ, which was foreshadowed by these ceremonial precepts, brought many boons to the world, and afforded men many considerations, which needed to be signified by various ceremonies.

Reply Obj. 1. When that which conduces to an end is sufficient to conduce thereto, then one such thing suffices for one end: thus one remedy, if it be efficacious, suffices sometimes to restore man to health, and then the remedy needs not to be repeated. But when that which conduces to an end is weak and imperfect, it needs to be multiplied: thus many remedies are given to a sick man, when one is not enough to heal him. Now the ceremonies of the Old Law were weak and imperfect, both for representing the mystery of Christ, on account of its surpassing excellence; and for subjugating men's minds to God. Hence the Apostle says (Heb. vii. 18, 19): *There is a setting aside of the former commandment because of the weakness and unprofitableness thereof, for the law brought nothing to perfection.* Consequently these ceremonies needed to be in great number.

Reply Obj. 2. A wise lawgiver should suffer lesser transgressions, that the greater may be avoided. And therefore, in order to avoid the sin of idolatry, and the pride which would arise in the hearts of the Jews, were they to fulfil all the precepts of the Law, the fact that they would in consequence find many occasions of disobedience did not prevent God from giving them many ceremonial precepts.

Reply Obj. 3. The Old Law lessened bodily worship in many ways. Thus it forbade sacrifices to be offered in every place and by any person. Many such like things did it enact for the lessening of bodily worship; as Rabbi Moses the Egyptian testifies (*Doct. Perplex.* iii). Nevertheless it behooved not to attenuate the bodily worship of God so much as to allow men to fall away into the worship of idols.

FOURTH ARTICLE

Whether the Ceremonies of the Old Law Are Suitably Divided into Sacrifices, Sacred Things, Sacraments, and Observances?

We proceed thus to the Fourth Article:—

Objection 1. It would seem that the ceremonies of the Old Law are unsuitably divided into *sacrifices, sacred things, sacraments and observances.* For the ceremonies of the Old Law foreshadowed Christ. But this was done only by the sacrifices, which foreshadowed the sacrifice in which Christ *delivered Himself an oblation and a sacrifice to God* (Eph. v. 2). Therefore none but the sacrifices were ceremonies.

Obj. 2. Further, the Old Law was ordained to the New. But in the New Law the sacrifice is the Sacrament of the Altar. Therefore in the Old Law there should be no distinction between *sacrifices* and *sacraments.*

Obj. 3. Further, a *sacred thing* is something dedicated to God: in which sense the tabernacle and its vessels were said to be consecrated. But all the ceremonial precepts were ordained to the worship of God, as stated above (A. 1). Therefore all ceremonies were sacred things. Therefore *sacred things* should not be taken as a part of the ceremonies.

Obj. 4. Further, *observances* are so called from having to be observed. But all the precepts of the Law had to be observed: for it is written (Deut. viii. 11): *Observe* (Douay,—*Take heed*) *and beware lest at any time thou forget the Lord thy God, and neglect His commandments and judgments and ceremonies.* Therefore the *observances* should not be considered as a part of the ceremonies.

Obj. 5. Further, the solemn festivals are reckoned as part of the ceremonial: since they were a shadow of things to come (Coloss. ii. 16, 17): and the same may be said of the obla-

tions and gifts, as appears from the words of the Apostle (Heb. ix. 9): and yet these do not seem to be included in any of those mentioned above. Therefore the above division of ceremonies is unsuitable.

On the contrary, In the Old Law each of the above is called a ceremony. For the sacrifices are called ceremonies (Num. xv. 24): *They shall offer a calf . . . and the sacrifices and libations thereof, as the ceremonies require.* Of the sacrament of Order it is written (Levit. vii. 35): *This is the anointing of Aaron and his sons in the ceremonies.* Of sacred things also it is written (Exod. xxxviii. 21): *These are the instruments of the tabernacle of the testimony . . . in the ceremonies of the Levites.* And again in the observances it is written (3 Kings ix. 6): *If you . . . shall turn away from following Me, and will not observe* (Douay,—*keep*) *My . . . ceremonies which I have set before you.*

I answer that, As stated above (AA. 1, 2), the ceremonial precepts are ordained to the Divine worship. Now in this worship we may consider the worship itself, the worshippers, and the instruments of worship. The worship consists specially in *sacrifices,* which are offered up in honor of God.—The instruments of worship refer to the *sacred things,* such as the tabernacle, the vessels and so forth.—With regard to the worshippers two points may be considered. The first point is their preparation for Divine worship, which is effected by a sort of consecration either of the people or of the ministers; and to this the *sacraments* refer. The second point is their particular mode of life, whereby they are distinguished from those who do not worship God: and to this pertain the *observances,* for instance, in matters of food, clothing, and so forth.

Reply Obj. 1. It was necessary for the sacrifices to be offered both in some certain place and by some certain men: and all this pertained to the worship of God. Wherefore just as their sacrifices signified Christ the victim, so too their sacraments and sacred things foreshadowed the sacraments and sacred things of the New Law; while their observances foreshadowed the mode of life of the people under the New Law: all of which things pertain to Christ.

Reply Obj. 2. The sacrifice of the New Law, viz., the Eucharist, contains Christ Himself, the Author of our Sanctification: for *He* sanctified *the people by His own blood* (Heb. xiii. 12). Hence this Sacrifice is also a sacrament. But the sacrifices of the Old Law did not contain Christ, but foreshadowed Him; hence they are not called sacraments. In order to signify this there were certain sacraments apart from the sacrifices of the Old Law, which sacraments were figures of the sanctification to come. Nevertheless to certain consecrations certain sacrifices were united.

Reply Obj. 3. The sacrifices and sacraments were of course sacred things. But certain things were sacred, through being dedicated to the Divine worship, and yet were not sacrifices or sacraments: wherefore they retained the common designation of sacred things.

Reply Obj. 4. Those things which pertained to the mode of life of the people who worshipped God, retained the common designation of observances, in so far as they fell short of the above. For they were not called sacred things, because they had no immediate connection with the worship of God, such as the tabernacle and its vessels had. But by a sort of consequence they were matters of ceremony, in so far as they affected the fitness of the people who worshipped God.

Reply Obj. 5. Just as the sacrifices were offered in a fixed place, so were they offered at fixed times: for which reason the solemn festivals seem to be reckoned among the sacred things.—The oblations and gifts are counted together with the sacrifices; hence the Apostle says (Heb. v. 1): *Every high-priest taken from among men, is ordained for men in things that appertain to God, that he may offer up gifts and sacrifices.*

QUESTION 102

Of the Causes of the Ceremonial Precepts

(In Six Articles)

WE must now consider the causes of the ceremonial precepts: under which head there are six points of inquiry: (1) Whether there was any cause for the ceremonial precepts? (2) Whether the cause of the ceremonial precepts was literal or figurative? (3) The causes of the sacrifices; (4) The causes of the sacraments; (5) The causes of the sacred things; (6) The causes of the observances.

FIRST ARTICLE

Whether There Was Any Cause for the Ceremonial Precepts?

We proceed thus to the First Article:—

Objection 1. It would seem that there was was no cause for the ceremonial precepts. Because on Ephes. ii. 15, *Making void the law of the commandments,* the gloss says, i.e., *making void the Old Law as to the carnal observances, by substituting decrees,* i.e., *evangelical precepts, which are based on reason.* But if the observances of the Old Law were based on reason, it would have been useless to void them by the reasonable decrees of the New Law. Therefore there was no reason for the ceremonial observances of the Old Law.

Obj. 2. Further, the Old Law succeeded the law of nature. But in the law of nature there was a precept for which there was no reason save that man's obedience might be tested; as Augustine says *(Gen. ad lit.* viii. 6, 13), concerning the prohibition about the tree of life. Therefore in the Old Law there should have been some precepts for the purpose of testing man's obedience, having no reason in themselves.

Obj. 3. Further, man's works are called moral according as they proceed from reason. If therefore there is any reason for the ceremonial precepts, they would not differ from the moral precepts. It seems therefore that there was no cause for the ceremonial precepts: for the reason of a precept is taken from some cause.

On the contrary, It is written (Ps. xviii. 9): *The commandment of the Lord is lightsome, enlightening the eyes.* But the ceremonial precepts are commandments of God. Therefore they are lightsome: and yet they would not be so, if they had no reasonable cause. Therefore the ceremonial precepts have a reasonable cause.

I answer that, Since, according to the Philosopher *(Metaph.* i. 2), it is the function of a *wise man to do everything in order,* those things which proceed from the Divine wisdom must needs be well ordered, as the Apostle states (Rom. xiii. 1). Now there are two conditions required for things to be well ordered. First, that they be ordained to their due end, which is the principle of the whole order in matters of action: since those things that happen by chance outside the intention of the end, or which are not done seriously but for fun, are said to be inordinate. Secondly, that which is done in view of the end should be proportionate to the end. From this it follows that the reason for whatever conduces to the end is taken from the end: thus the reason for the disposition of a saw is taken from cutting, which is its end, as stated in *Phys.* ii. 9. Now it is evident that the ceremonial precepts, like all the other precepts of the Law, were institutions of Divine wisdom: hence it is written (Deut. iv. 6): *This is your wisdom and understanding in the sight of nations.* Consequently we must needs say that the ceremonial precepts were ordained to a certain end, wherefrom their reasonable causes can be gathered.

Reply Obj. 1. It may be said that there was no reason for the observances of the Old Law, in the sense that there was no reason in the very nature of the thing done: for instance that a garment should not be made of wool and linen. But there could be a reason' for them in relation to something else: namely, in so far as something was signified or excluded thereby. On the other hand, the decrees of the New Law, which refer chiefly to faith and the love of God, are reasonable from the very nature of the act.

Reply Obj. 2. The reason for the prohibition concerning the tree of knowledge of good and evil was not that this tree was naturally evil: and yet this prohibition was reasonable in its relation to something else, in as much as it signified something. And so also the ceremonial precepts of the Old Law were reasonable on account of their relation to something else.

Reply Obj. 3. The moral precepts in their very nature have reasonable causes: as for instance, *Thou shalt not kill, Thou shalt not steal.* But the ceremonial precepts have a reasonable cause in their relation to something else, as stated above.

SECOND ARTICLE

Whether the Ceremonial Precepts Have a Literal Cause or Merely a Figurative Cause?

We proceed thus to the Second Article:—

Objection 1. It would seem that the ceremonial precepts have not a literal, but merely a figurative, cause. For among the ceremonial precepts, the chief was circumcision and the sacrifice of the paschal lamb. But neither of these had any but a figurative cause: because each was given as a sign. For it is written (Gen. xvii. 11): *You shall circumcise the flesh of your foreskin, that it may be for a sign of the covenant between Me and you:* and of the celebration of the Passover it is written (Exod. xiii. 9): *It shall be as a sign in thy hand, and as a memorial before thy eyes.* Therefore much more did the other ceremonial precepts have none but a figurative reason.

Obj. 2. Further, an effect is proportionate to its cause. But all the ceremonial precepts are figurative, as stated above (Q. 101, A. 2). Therefore they have no other than a figurative cause.

Obj. 3. Further, if it be a matter of indifference whether a certain thing, considered in itself, be done in a particular way or not, it seems that it has not a literal cause. Now there are certain points in the ceremonial pre-

cepts, which appear to be a matter of indifference, as to whether they be done in one way or in another: for instance, the number of animals to be offered, and other such particular circumstances. Therefore there is no literal cause for the precepts of the Old Law.

On the contrary, Just as the ceremonial precepts foreshadowed Christ, so did the stories of the Old Testament: for it is written (1 Cor. x. 11) that *all (these things) happened to them in figure.* Now in the stories of the Old Testament, besides the mystical or figurative, there is the literal sense. Therefore the ceremonial precepts had also literal, besides their figurative causes.

I answer that, As stated above (A. 1), the reason for whatever conduces to an end must be taken from that end. Now the end of the ceremonial precepts was twofold: for they were ordained to the Divine worship, for that particular time, and to the foreshadowing of Christ; just as the words of the prophets regarded the time being in such a way as to be utterances figurative of the time to come, as Jerome says on Osee i. 3. Accordingly the reasons for the ceremonial precepts of the Old Law can be taken in two ways. First, in respect of the Divine worship which was to be observed for that particular time: and these reasons are literal: whether they refer to the shunning of idolatry; or recall certain Divine benefits; or remind men of the Divine excellence; or point out the disposition of mind which was then required in those who worshipped God.—Secondly, their reasons can be gathered from the point of view of their being ordained to foreshadow Christ: and thus their reasons are figurative and mystical: whether they be taken from Christ Himself and the Church, which pertains to the allegorical sense; or to the morals of the Christian people, which pertains to the moral sense; or to the state of future glory, in as much as we are brought thereto by Christ, which refers to the anagogical sense.

Reply Obj. 1. Just as the use of metaphorical expressions in Scripture belongs to the literal sense, because the words are employed in order to convey that particular meaning; so also the meaning of those legal ceremonies which commemorated certain Divine benefits, on account of which they were instituted, and of others similar which belonged to that time, does not go beyond the order of literal causes. Consequently when we assert that the cause of the celebration of the Passover was its signification of the delivery from Egypt, or that circumcision was a sign of God's covenant with Abraham, we assign the literal cause.

Reply Obj. 2. This argument would avail, if the ceremonial precepts had been given merely as figures of things to come, and not for the purpose of worshipping God then and there.

Reply Obj. 3. As we stated when speaking of human laws (Q. 96, AA. 1, 6), there is a reason for them in the abstract, but not in regard to particular conditions, which depend on the judgment of those who frame them; so also many particular determinations in the ceremonies of the Old Law have no literal cause, but only a figurative cause; whereas in the abstract they have a literal cause.

THIRD ARTICLE

Whether a Suitable Cause Can Be Assigned for the Ceremonies Which Pertained to Sacrifices?

We proceed thus to the Third Article:—

Objection 1. It would seem that no suitable cause can be assigned for the ceremonies pertaining to sacrifices. For those things which were offered in sacrifice, are those which are necessary for sustaining human life: such as certain animals and certain loaves. But God needs no such sustenance; according to Ps. xlix. 13: *Shall I eat the flesh of bullocks? Or shall I drink the blood of goats?* Therefore such sacrifices were unfittingly offered to God.

Obj. 2. Further, only three kinds of quadrupeds were offered in sacrifice to God, viz., oxen, sheep and goats; of birds, generally the turtledove and the dove; but specially, in the cleansing of a leper, an offering was made of sparrows. Now many other animals are more noble than these. Since therefore whatever is best should be offered to God, it seems that not only of these three should sacrifices have been offered to Him.

Obj. 3. Further, just as man has received from God the dominion over birds and beasts, so also has he received dominion over fishes. Consequently it was unfitting for fishes to be excluded from the divine sacrifices.

Obj. 4. Further, turtledoves and doves indifferently are commanded to be offered up. Since then the young of the dove are commanded to be offered, so also should the young of the turtledove.

Obj. 5. Further, God is the Author of life, not only of men, but also of animals, as is clear from Gen. i. 20, *seq.* Now death is opposed to life. Therefore it was fitting that living animals rather than slain animals should be offered to God, especially as the Apostle admonishes us (Rom. xii. 1), to present our bodies *a living sacrifice, holy, pleasing unto God.*

Obj. 6. Further, if none but slain animals were offered in sacrifice to God, it seems that it mattered not how they were slain. Therefore it was unfitting that the manner of im-

molation should be determined, especially as regards birds (Levit. i. 15, *seq.*).

Obj. 7. Further, every defect in an animal is a step towards corruption and death. If therefore slain animals were offered to God, it was unreasonable to forbid the offering of an imperfect animal, *e.g.*, a lame, or a blind, or otherwise defective animal.

Obj. 8. Further, those who offer victims to God should partake thereof, according to the words of the Apostle (1 Cor. x. 18): *Are not they that eat of the sacrifices partakers of the altar?* It was therefore unbecoming for the offerers to be denied certain parts of the victims, namely, the blood, the fat, the breastbone and the right shoulder.

Obj. 9. Further, just as holocausts were offered up in honor of God, so also were the peace-offerings and sin-offerings. But no female animal was offered up to God as a holocaust, although holocausts were offered of both quadrupeds and birds. Therefore it was inconsistent that female animals should be offered up in peace-offerings and sin-offerings, and that nevertheless birds should not be offered up in peace-offerings.

Obj. 10. Further, all the peace-offerings seem to be of one kind. Therefore it was unfitting to make a distinction among them, so that it was forbidden to eat the flesh of certain peace-offerings on the following day, while it was allowed to eat the flesh of other peace-offerings, as laid down in Levit. vii. 15, *seq.*

Obj. 11. Further, all sins agree in turning us from God. Therefore, in order to reconcile us to God, one kind of sacrifice should have been offered up for all sins.

Obj. 12. Further, all animals that were offered up in sacrifice, were offered in one way, viz., slain. Therefore it does not seem to be suitable that products of the soil should be offered up in various ways; for sometimes an offering was made of ears of corn, sometimes of flour, sometimes of bread, this being baked sometimes in an oven, sometimes in a pan, sometimes on a gridiron.

Obj. 13. Further, whatever things are serviceable to us should be recognized as coming from God. It was therefore unbecoming that besides animals, nothing but bread, wine, oil, incense, and salt should be offered to God.

Obj. 14. Further, bodily sacrifices denote the inward sacrifice of the heart, whereby man offers his soul to God. But in the inward sacrifice, the sweetness, which is denoted by honey, surpasses the pungency which salt represents; for it is written (Ecclus. xxiv. 27): *My spirit is sweet above honey.* Therefore it was unbecoming that the use of honey, and of leaven which makes bread savory, should be forbidden in a sacrifice; while the use was prescribed, of salt which is pungent, and of incense which has a bitter taste. Consequently it seems that things pertaining to the ceremonies of the sacrifices have no reasonable cause.

On the contrary, It is written (Levit. i. 13): *The priest shall offer it all and burn it all upon the altar, for a holocaust, and most sweet savor to the Lord.* Now according to Wis. vii. 28, *God loveth none but him that dwelleth with wisdom:* whence it seems to follow that whatever is acceptable to God is wisely done. Therefore these ceremonies of the sacrifices were wisely done, as having reasonable causes.

I answer that, As stated above (A. 2), the ceremonies of the Old Law had a twofold cause, viz., a literal cause, according as they were intended for Divine worship; and a figurative or mystical cause, according as they were intended to foreshadow Christ: and on either hand the ceremonies pertaining to the sacrifices can be assigned to a fitting cause.

For, according as the ceremonies of the sacrifices were intended for the divine worship, the causes of the sacrifices can be taken in two ways. First, in so far as the sacrifice represented the directing of the mind to God, to which the offerer of the sacrifice was stimulated. Now in order to direct his mind to God aright, man must recognize that whatever he has is from God as from its first principle, and direct it to God as its last end. This was denoted in the offerings and sacrifices, by the fact that man offered some of his own belongings in honor of God, as though in recognition of his having received them from God, according to the saying of David (1 Paral. xxix. 14): *All things are Thine: and we have given Thee what we received of Thy hand.* Wherefore in offering up sacrifices man made protestation that God is the first principle of the creation of all things, and their last end, to which all things must be directed.—And since, for the human mind to be directed to God aright, it must recognize no first author of things other than God, nor place its end in any other; for this reason it was forbidden in the Law to offer sacrifice to any other but God, according to Exod. xxii. 20: *He that sacrificeth to gods, shall be put to death, save only to the Lord.* Wherefore another reasonable cause may be assigned to the ceremonies of the sacrifices, from the fact that thereby men were withdrawn from offering sacrifices to idols. Hence too it is that the precepts about the sacrifices were not given to the Jewish people until after they had fallen into idolatry, by worshipping the molten calf: as though those sacrifices were instituted, that the people, being ready to offer sacrifices, might offer those sacrifices to God rather than to idols. Thus it is written (Jer. vii. 22): *I spake not to your fathers and I commanded them not, in the day that I brought them out of the land of Egypt, concerning the matter of burnt-offerings and sacrifices.*

Now of all the gifts which God vouchsafed to mankind after they had fallen away by sin, the chief is that He gave His Son; wherefore it is written (Jo. iii. 16): *God so loved the world, as to give His only-begotten Son; that whosoever believeth in Him, may not perish, but may have life everlasting.* Consequently the chief sacrifice is that whereby Christ Himself *delivered Himself . . . to God for an odor of sweetness* (Eph. v. 2). And for this reason all the other sacrifices of the Old Law were offered up in order to foreshadow this one individual and paramount sacrifice,—the imperfect forecasting the perfect. Hence the Apostle says (Heb. x. 11) that the priest of the Old Law *often* offered *the same sacrifices, which can never take away sins: but* Christ offered *one sacrifice for sins, for ever.* And since the reason of the figure is taken from that which the figure represents, therefore the reasons of the figurative sacrifices of the Old Law should be taken from the true sacrifice of Christ.

Reply Obj. 1. God did not wish these sacrifices to be offered to Him on account of the things themselves that were offered, as though He stood in need of them: wherefore it is written (Isa. i. 11): *I desire not holocausts of rams, and fat of fatlings, and blood of calves and lambs and buckgoats.* But, as stated above, He wished them to be offered to Him, in order to prevent idolatry;—in order to signify the right ordering of man's mind to God; —and in order to represent the mystery of the Redemption of man by Christ.

Reply Obj. 2. In all the respects mentioned above (*ad* 1), there was a suitable reason for these animals, rather than others, being offered up in sacrifice to God. First, in order to prevent idolatry. Because idolaters offered all other animals to their gods, or made use of them in their sorceries: while the Egyptians (among whom the people had been dwelling) considered it abominable to slay these animals, wherefore they used not to offer them in sacrifice to their gods. Hence it is written (Exod. viii. 26): *We shall sacrifice the abominations of the Egyptians to the Lord our God.* For they worshipped the sheep; they reverenced the ram (because demons appeared under the form thereof); while they employed oxen for agriculture, which was reckoned by them as something sacred.

Secondly, this was suitable for the aforesaid right ordering of man's mind to God: and in two ways.—First, because it is chiefly by means of these animals that human life is sustained: and moreover they are most clean, and partake of a most clean food: whereas other animals are either wild, and not deputed to ordinary use among men: or, if they be tame, they have unclean food, as pigs and geese: and nothing but what is clean should be offered to God.—These birds especially were offered in sacrifice, because there were plenty of them in the land of promise.—Secondly, because the sacrificing of these animals represented purity of heart. Because as the gloss says on Levit. i, *We offer a calf, when we overcome the pride of the flesh; a lamb, when we restrain our unreasonable motions; a goat, when we conquer wantonness; a turtledove, when we keep chaste; unleavened bread, when we feast on the unleavened bread of sincerity.* And it is evident that the dove denotes charity and simplicity of heart.

Thirdly, it was fitting that these animals should be offered, that they might foreshadow Christ. Because, as the gloss observes, *Christ is offered in the calf, to denote the strength of the cross; in the lamb, to signify His innocence; in the ram, to foreshadow His headship; and in the goat, to signify the likeness of "sinful flesh."** The turtledove and dove denoted the union of the two natures; or else the turtledove signified chastity; while the dove was a figure of charity. *The wheat-flour foreshadowed the sprinkling of believers with the water of Baptism.*

Reply Obj. 3. Fish through living in water are further removed from man than other animals, which, like man, live in the air. Again, fish die as soon as they are taken out of water; hence they could not be offered in the temple like other animals.

Reply Obj. 4. Among turtledoves the older ones are better than the young; while with doves the case is the reverse. Wherefore, as Rabbi Moses observes (*Doct. Perplex.,* iii), turtledoves and young doves are commanded to be offered, because nothing should be offered to God but what is best.

Reply Obj. 5. The animals which were offered in sacrifice were slain, because it is by being killed that they become useful to man, forasmuch as God gave them to man for food. Wherefore also they were burnt with fire: because it is by being cooked that they are made fit for human consumption.—Moreover the slaying of the animals signified the destruction of sins: and also that man deserved death on account of his sins; as though those animals were slain in man's stead, in order to betoken the expiation of sins.—Again the slaying of these animals signified the slaying of Christ.

Reply Obj. 6. The Law fixed the special manner of slaying the sacrificial animals in order to exclude other ways of killing, whereby idolaters sacrificed animals to idols.—Or again, as Rabbi Moses says (*loc. cit.*), the

* An allusion to Col. ii. 11 (*Textus Receptus*).

Law chose that manner of slaying which was least painful to the slain animal. This excluded cruelty on the part of the offerers, and any mangling of the animals slain.

Reply Obj. 7. It is because unclean animals are wont to be held in contempt among men, that it was forbidden to offer them in sacrifice to God: and for this reason too they were forbidden (Deut. xxiii. 18) to offer *the hire of a strumpet or the price of a dog in the house of . . . God.* For the same reason they did not offer animals before the seventh day, because such were abortive as it were, the flesh being not yet firm on account of its exceeding softness.

Reply Obj. 8. There were three kinds of sacrifices. There was one in which the victim was entirely consumed by fire: this was called a *holocaust*, i.e., *all burnt.* For this kind of sacrifice was offered to God specially to show reverence to ᵁis majesty, and love of His goodness: and typified the state of perfection as regards the fulfilment of the counsels. Wherefore the whole was burnt up: so that as the whole animal by being dissolved into vapor soared aloft, so it might denote that the whole man, and whatever belongs to him, are subject to the authority of God, and should be offered to Him.

Another sacrifice was the *sin-offering*, which was offered to God on account of man's need for the forgiveness of sin: and this typifies the state of penitents in satisfying for sins. It was divided into two parts: for one part was burnt; while the other was granted to the use of the priests to signify that remission of sins is granted by God through the ministry of His priests. When, however, this sacrifice was offered for the sins of the whole people, or specially for the sin of the priest, the whole victim was burnt up. For it was not fitting that the priests should have the use of that which was offered for their own sins, to signify that nothing sinful should remain in them. Moreover, this would not be satisfaction for sin: for if the offering were granted to the use of those for whose sins it was offered, it would seem to be the same as if it had not been offered.

The third kind of sacrifice was called the *peace-offering*, which was offered to God, either in thanksgiving, or for the welfare and prosperity of the offerers, in acknowledgment of benefits already received or yet to be received: and this typifies the state of those who are proficient in the observance of the commandments. These sacrifices were divided into three parts: for one part was burnt in honor of God; another part was allotted to the use of the priests; and the third part to the use of the offerers; in order to signify that man's salvation is from God, by the direction of God's ministers, and through the co-operation of those who are saved.

But it was the universal rule that the blood and fat were not allotted to the use either of the priests or of the offerers: the blood being poured out at the foot of the altar, in honor of God, while the fat was burnt upon the altar (Levit. ix. 9, 10). The reason for this was, first, in order to prevent idolatry: because idolaters used to drink the blood and eat the fat of the victims, according to Deut. xxxii. 38: *Of whose victims they eat the fat, and drank the wine of their drink-offerings.*—Secondly, in order to form them to a right way of living. For they were forbidden the use of the blood that they might abhor the shedding of human blood; wherefore it is written (Gen. ix. 4, 5): *Flesh with blood you shall not eat: for I will require the blood of your lives:*—and they were forbidden to eat the fat, in order to withdraw them from lasciviousness; hence it is written (Ezech. xxxiv. 3): *You have killed that which was fat.*—Thirdly, on account of the reverence due to God: because blood is most necessary for life, for which reason *life* is said to be *in the blood* (Levit. xvii. 11, 14): while fat is a sign of abundant nourishment. Wherefore, in order to show that to God we owe both life and a sufficiency of all good things, the blood was poured out, and the fat burnt up in His honor.—Fourthly, in order to foreshadow the shedding of Christ's blood, and the abundance of His charity, whereby He offered Himself to God for us.

In the peace-offerings, the breast-bone and the right shoulder were allotted to the use of the priest, in order to prevent a certain kind uf divination which is known as *spatulamantia,* so called because it was customary in divining to use the shoulder-blade (*spatula*), and the breast-bone of the animals offered in sacrifice; wherefore these things were taken away from the offerers.—This also denoted the priest's need of wisdom in the heart, to instruct the people,—this was signified by the breast-bone, which covers the heart; and his need of fortitude, in order to bear with human frailty—and this was signified by the right shoulder.

Reply Obj. 9. Because the holocaust was the most perfect kind of sacrifice, therefore none but a male was offered for a holocaust: because the female is an imperfect animal.— The offering of turtledoves and doves was on account of the poverty of the offerers, who were unable to offer bigger animals. And since peace-victims were offered freely, and no one was bound to offer them against his will, hence these birds were offered not among the peace-victims, but among the holocausts

and victims for sin, which man was obliged to offer at times. Moreover these birds, on account of their lofty flight, were befitting the perfection of the holocausts: and were suitable for sin-offerings, because their song is doleful.

Reply Obj. 10. The holocaust was the chief of all the sacrifices: because all was burnt in honor of God, and nothing of it was eaten. The second place in holiness, belongs to the sacrifice for sins, which was eaten in the court only, and on the very day of the sacrifice (Lev. vii. 6, 15). The third place must be given to the peace-offerings of thanksgiving, which were eaten on the same day, but anywhere in Jerusalem. Fourth in order were the *ex-voto* peace-offerings, the flesh of which could be eaten even on the morrow. The reason for this order is that man is bound to God, chiefly on account of His majesty; secondly, on account of the sins he has committed; thirdly, because of the benefits he has already received from Him; fourthly, by reason of the benefits he hopes to receive from Him.

Reply Obj. 11. Sins are more grievous by reason of the state of the sinner, as stated above (Q. 73, A. 10): wherefore different victims are commanded to be offered for the sin of a priest, or of a prince, or of some other private individual. *But,* as Rabbi Moses says (*loc. cit.*), *we must take note that the more grievous the sin, the lower the species of animal offered for it. Wherefore the goat, which is a very base animal, was offered for idolatry; while a calf was offered for a priest's ignorance, and a ram for the negligence of a prince.*

Reply Obj. 12. In the matter of sacrifices the Law had in view the poverty of the offerers; so that those who could not have a four-footed animal at their disposal, might at least offer a bird; and that he who could not have a bird might at least offer bread; and that if a man had not even bread he might offer flour or ears of corn.

The figurative cause is that the bread signifies Christ Who is the *living bread* (Jo. vi. 41, 51). He was indeed an ear of corn, as it were, during the state of the law of nature, in the faith of the patriarchs; He was like flour in the doctrine of the Law of the prophets; and He was like perfect bread after He had taken human nature; baked in the fire, i.e., formed by the Holy Ghost in the oven of the virginal womb; baked again in a pan by the toils which He suffered in the world; and consumed by fire on the cross as on a gridiron.

Reply Obj. 13. The products of the soil are useful to man, either as food, and of these bread was offered; or as drink, and of these wine was offered; or as seasoning, and of these oil and salt were offered; or as healing, and of these they offered incense, which both smells sweetly and binds easily together.

Now the bread foreshadowed the flesh of Christ; and the wine, His blood, whereby we were redeemed; oil betokens the grace of Christ; salt, His knowledge; incense, His prayer.

Reply Obj. 14. Honey was not offered in the sacrifices to God, both because it was wont to be offered in the sacrifices to idols; and in order to denote the absence of all carnal sweetness and pleasure from those who intend to sacrifice to God.—Leaven was not offered, to denote the exclusion of corruption. Perhaps too, it was wont to be offered in the sacrifices to idols.

Salt, however, was offered, because it wards off the corruption of putrefaction: for sacrifices offered to God should be incorrupt. Moreover, salt signifies the discretion of wisdom, or again, mortification of the flesh.

Incense was offered to denote devotion of the heart, which is necessary in the offerer; and again, to signify the odor of a good name: for incense is composed of matter, both rich and fragrant. And since the sacrifice *of jealousy* did not proceed from devotion, but rather from suspicion, therefore incense was not offered therein (Num. v. 15).

FOURTH ARTICLE

Whether Sufficient Reason Can Be Assigned for the Ceremonies Pertaining to Holy Things?

We proceed thus to the Fourth Article:—

Objection 1. It would seem that no sufficient reason can be assigned for the ceremonies of the Old Law that pertain to holy things. For Paul said (Acts xvii. 24): *God Who made the world and all things therein; He being Lord of heaven and earth, dwelleth not in temples made by hands.* It was therefore unfitting that in the Old Law a tabernacle or temple should be set up for the worship of God.

Obj. 2. Further, the state of the Old Law was not changed except by Christ. But the tabernacle denoted the state of the Old Law. Therefore it should not have been changed by the building of a temple.

Obj. 3. Further, the Divine law, more than any other indeed, should lead man to the worship of God. But an increase of divine worship requires multiplication of altars and temples; as is evident in regard to the New Law. Therefore it seems that also under the Old Law there should have been not only one tabernacle or temple, but many.

Obj. 4. Further, the tabernacle or temple was ordained to the worship of God. But in God we should worship above all His unity and simplicity. Therefore it seems unbecoming for the tabernacle or temple to be divided by means of veils.

Obj. 5. Further, the power of the First Mover, i.e., God, appears first of all in the east, for it is in that quarter that the first movement begins. But the tabernacle was set up for the worship of God. Therefore it should have been built so as to point to the east rather than the west.

Obj. 6. Further, the Lord commanded (Exod. xx. 4) that they should *not make . . . a graven thing, nor the likeness of anything.* It was therefore unfitting for graven images of the cherubin to be set up in the tabernacle or temple. In like manner, the ark, the propitiatory, the candlestick, the table, the two altars, seem to have been placed there without reasonable cause.

Obj. 7. Further, the Lord commanded (Exod. xx. 24): *You shall make an altar of earth unto Me:* and again (*ibid.,* 26): *Thou shalt not go up by steps unto My altar.* It was therefore unfitting that subsequently they should be commanded to make an altar of wood laid over with gold or brass; and of such a height that it was impossible to go up to it except by steps. For it is written (Exod. xxvii. 1, 2): *Thou shalt make also an altar of setim wood, which shall be five cubits long, and as many broad, . . . and three cubits high . . . and thou shalt cover it with brass:* and (Exod. xxx. 1, 3): *Thou shalt make . . . an altar to burn incense, of setim wood . . . and thou shalt overlay it with the purest gold.*

Obj. 8. Further, in God's works nothing should be superfluous; for not even in the works of nature is anything superfluous to be found. But one cover suffices for one tabernacle or house. Therefore it was unbecoming to furnish the tabernacle with many coverings, viz., curtains, curtains of goats' hair, rams' skins dyed red, and violet-colored skins (Exod. xxvi).

Obj. 9. Further, exterior consecration signifies interior holiness, the subject of which is the soul. It was therefore unsuitable for the tabernacle and its vessels to be consecrated, since they were inanimate things.

Obj. 10. Further, it is written (Ps. xxxiii. 2): *I will bless the Lord at all times, His praise shall always be in my mouth.* But the solemn festivals were instituted for the praise of God. Therefore it was not fitting that certain days should be fixed for keeping solemn festivals; so that it seems that there was no suitable cause for the ceremonies relating to holy things.

On the contrary, The Apostle says (Heb.

viii. 4) that those who *offer gifts according to the law, . . . serve unto the example and shadow of heavenly things. As it was answered to Moses, when he was to finish the tabernacle: See, says He, that thou make all things according to the pattern which was shown thee on the mount.* But that is most reasonable, which presents a likeness to heavenly things. Therefore the ceremonies relating to holy things had a reasonable cause.

I answer that, The chief purpose of the whole external worship is that man may give worship to God. Now man's tendency is to reverence less those things which are common, and indistinct from other things; whereas he admires and reveres those things which are distinct from others in some point of excellence. Hence too it is customary among men for kings and princes, who ought to be reverenced by their subjects, to be clothed in more precious garments, and to possess vaster and more beautiful abodes. And for this reason it behooved special times, a special abode, special vessels, and special ministers to be appointed for the divine worship, so that thereby the soul of man might be brought to greater reverence for God.

In like manner the state of the Old Law, as observed above (A. 2; Q. 100, A. 12; Q. 101, A. 2), was instituted that it might foreshadow the mystery of Christ. Now that which foreshadows something should be determinate, so that it may present some likeness thereto. Consequently, certain special points had to be observed in matters pertaining to the worship of God.

Reply Obj. 1. The divine worship regards two things: namely, God Who is worshipped, and men, who worship Him. Accordingly God, Who is worshipped, is confined to no bodily place: wherefore there was no need, on His part, for a tabernacle or temple to be set up. But men, who worship Him, are corporeal beings: and for their sake there was need for a special tabernacle or temple to be set up for the worship of God, for two reasons. First, that through coming together with the thought that the place was set aside for the worship of God, they might approach thither with greater reverence. Secondly, that certain things relating to the excellence of Christ's Divine or human nature might be signified by the arrangement of various details in such temple or tabernacle.

To this Solomon refers (3 Kings viii. 27) when he says: *If heaven and the heavens of heavens cannot contain Thee, how much less this house which I have built* for Thee? And further on (*ibid.* 29, 30) he adds: *That Thy eyes may be open upon this house . . . of which Thou hast said: My name shall be there; . . .* *that Thou mayest hearken to the supplication of Thy servant and of Thy people Israel.* From this it is evident that the house of the sanctuary was set up, not in order to contain God, as abiding therein locally, but that God's name might dwell there, i.e., that God might be made known there by means of things done and said there; and that those who prayed there might, through reverence for the place, pray more devoutly, so as to be heard more readily.

Reply Obj. 2. Before the coming of Christ, the state of the Old Law was not changed as regards the fulfilment of the Law, which was effected in Christ alone: but it was changed as regards the condition of the people that were under the Law. Because, at first, the people were in the desert, having no fixed abode: afterwards they were engaged in various wars with the neighboring nations; and lastly, at the time of David and Solomon, the state of that people was one of great peace. And then for the first time the temple was built in the place which Abraham, instructed by God, had chosen for the purpose of sacrifice. For it is written (Gen. xxii. 2) that the Lord commanded Abraham to *offer* his son *for a holocaust upon one of the mountains which I will show thee:* and it is related further on (*ibid.* 14) that *he called the name of that place, The Lord seeth,* as though, according to the Divine prevision, that place were chosen for the worship of God. Hence it is written (Deut. xii. 5, 6): *You shall come to the place which the Lord your God shall choose . . . and you shall offer . . . your holocausts and victims.*

Now it was not meet for that place to be pointed out by the building of the temple before the aforesaid time; for three reasons assigned by Rabbi Moses. First, lest the Gentiles might seize hold of that place. Secondly, lest the Gentiles might destroy it. The third reason is lest each tribe might wish that place to fall to their lot, and strifes and quarrels be the result. Hence the temple was not built until they had a king who would be able to quell such quarrels. Until that time a portable tabernacle was employed for divine worship, no place being as yet fixed for the worship of God. This is the literal reason for the distinction between the tabernacle and the temple.

The figurative reason may be assigned to the fact that they signify a twofold state. For the tabernacle, which was changeable, signifies the state of the present changeable life: whereas the temple, which was fixed and stable, signifies the state of future life which is altogether unchangeable. For this reason it is said that in the building of the temple no sound was heard of hammer or saw, to signify that all movements of disturbance will be far removed from the future state.—Or else the tabernacle signifies the state of the Old Law; while the temple built by Solomon betokens the state of the New Law. Hence the Jews alone worked at the building of the tabernacle; whereas the temple was built with the co-operation of the Gentiles, viz., the Tyrians and Sidonians.

Reply Obj. 3. The reason for the unity of the temple or tabernacle may be either literal or figurative. The literal reason was the exclusion of idolatry. For the Gentiles put up various temples to various gods: and so, to strengthen in the minds of men their belief in the unity of the Godhead, God wished sacrifices to be offered to Him in one place only. —Another reason was in order to show that bodily worship is not acceptable of itself: and so they were restrained from offering sacrifices anywhere and everywhere. But the worship of the New Law, in the sacrifice whereof spiritual grace is contained, is of itself acceptable to God; and consequently the multiplication of altars and temples is permitted in the New Law.

As to those matters that regarded the spiritual worship of God, consisting in the teaching of the Law and the Prophets, there were, even under the Old Law, various places, called synagogues, appointed for the people to gather together for the praise of God; just as now there are places called churches in which the Christian people gather together for the divine worship. Thus our church takes the place of both temple and synagogue: since the very sacrifice of the Church is spiritual; wherefore with us the place of sacrifice is not distinct from the place of teaching. The figurative reason may be that hereby is signied the unity of the Church, whether militant or triumphant.

Reply Obj. 4. Just as the unity of the temple or tabernacle betokened the unity of God, or the unity of the Church, so also the division of the tabernacle or temple signified the distinction of those things that are subject to God, and from which we arise to the worship of God. Now the tabernacle was divided into two parts: one was called the *Holy of Holies,* and was placed to the west; the other was called the *Holy Place,** which was situated to the east. Moreover there was a court facing the tabernacle. Accordingly there are two reasons for this distinction. One is in respect of the tabernacle being ordained to the worship of God. Because the different parts of the world are thus betokened by the division of the tabernacle. For that part which was called the Holy of Holies signified the higher world,

which is that of spiritual substances: while that part which is called the Holy Place signified the corporeal world.—Hence the Holy Place was separated from the Holy of Holies by a veil, which was of four different colors (denoting the four elements), viz., of linen, signifying earth, because linen, i.e., flax, grows out of the earth; purple, signifying water, because the purple tint was made from certain shells found in the sea; violet, signifying air, because it has the color of the air; and scarlet twice dyed, signifying fire:—and this because matter composed of the four elements is a veil between us and incorporeal substances. Hence the high-priest alone, and that once a year, entered into the inner tabernacle, i.e., the Holy of Holies: whereby we are taught that man's final perfection consists in his entering into that (higher) world: whereas into the outward tabernacle, i.e., the Holy Place, priests entered every day: whereas the people were only admitted to the court; because the people are able to perceive material things, the inner nature of which only wise men by dint of study are able to discover.

But with regard to the figurative reason, the outward tabernacle, which was called the Holy Place, betokened the state of the Old Law, as the Apostle says (Heb. ix. 6, *seq.*): because into that tabernacle *the priests always entered accomplishing the offices of sacrifices.* But the inner tabernacle, which was called the Holy of Holies, signified either the glory of heaven or the spiritual state of the New Law, which is a kind of beginning of the glory to come. To the latter state Christ brought us; and this was signified by the high-priest entering alone, once a year, into the Holy of Holies.—The veil betokened the concealing of the spiritual sacrifices under the sacrifices of old. This veil was adorned with four colors: viz., that of linen, to designate purity of the flesh; purple, to denote the sufferings which the saints underwent for God; scarlet twice dyed, signifying the twofold love of God and our neighbor; and violet, in token of heavenly contemplation.—With regard to the state of the Old Law the people and the priests were situated differently from one another. For the people saw the mere corporeal sacrifices which were offered in the court: whereas the priests were intent on the inner meaning of the sacrifices, because their faith in the mysteries of Christ was more explicit. Hence they entered into the outer tabernacle. This outer tabernacle was divided from the court by a veil; because some matters relating to the mystery of Christ were hidden from the people, while they were known to the priests: though they were not fully revealed to them, as they were

---

* Or *Sanctuary.* The Douay version uses both expressions.

subsequently in the New Testament (*cf.* Ephes. iii. 5).

Reply Obj. 5. Worship towards the west was introduced in the Law to the exclusion of idolatry: because all the Gentiles, in reverence to the sun, worshipped towards the east; hence it is written (Ezech. viii. 16) that certain men *had their backs towards the temple of the Lord, and their faces to the east, and they adored towards the rising of the sun.* Accordingly, in order to prevent this, the tabernacle had the Holy of Holies to westward, that they might adore toward the west. A figurative reason may also be found in the fact that the whole state of the first tabernacle was ordained to foreshadow the death of Christ, which is signified by the west, according to Ps. lxvii. 5: *Who ascendeth unto the west; the Lord is His name.*

Reply Obj. 6. Both literal and figurative reasons may be assigned for the things contained in the tabernacle. The literal reason is in connection with the divine worship. And because, as already observed (*ad* 4), the inner tabernacle, called the Holy of Holies, signified the higher world of spiritual substances, hence that tabernacle contained three things, viz., *the ark of the testament in which was a golden pot that had manna, and the rod of Aaron that had blossomed, and the tables* (Heb. ix. 4) on which were written the ten commandments of the Law. Now the ark stood between two *cherubim* that looked one towards the other: and over the ark was a table, called the *propitiatory*, raised above the wings of the cherubim, as though it were held up by them; and appearing, to the imagination, to be the very seat of God. For this reason it was called the *propitiatory*, as though the people received propitiation thence at the prayers of the high-priest. And so it was held up, so to speak, by the cherubim, in obedience, as it were, to God: while the ark of the testament was like the foot-stool to Him that sat on the propitiatory.—These three things denote three things in that higher world: namely, God Who is above all, and incomprehensible to any creature. Hence no likeness of Him was set up; to denote His invisibility. But there was something to represent his seat; since, to wit, the creature, which is beneath God, as the seat is under the sitter, is comprehensible.—Again in that higher world there are spiritual substances called angels. These are signified by the two cherubim, looking one towards the other, to show that they are at peace with one another, according to Job xxv. 2: *Who maketh peace in . . . high places.* For this reason, too, there was more than one cherub, to betoken the multitude of heavenly spirits, and to prevent their receiving worship

from those who had been commanded to worship but one God.—Moreover there are, enclosed as it were in that spiritual world, the intelligible types of whatsoever takes place in this world, just as in every cause are enclosed the types of its effects, and in the craftsman the types of the works of his craft. This was betokened by the ark, which represented, by means of the three things it contained, the three things of greatest import in human affairs. These are wisdom, signified by the tables of the testament; the power of governing, betokened by the rod of Aaron; and life, denoted by the manna which was the means of sustenance.—Or else these three signified the three Divine attributes, viz., wisdom, in the tables; power, in the rod; goodness, in the manna,—both by reason of its sweetness, and because it was through the goodness of God that it was granted to man, wherefore it was preserved as a memorial of the Divine mercy.—Again, these three things were represented in Isaias' vision. For he *saw the Lord sitting upon a throne high and elevated;* and the seraphim standing by; and that the house was filled with the glory of the Lord; wherefore the seraphim cried out: *All the earth is full of His glory* (Isa. vi. 1, 3).—And so the images of the seraphim were set up, not to be worshipped, for this was forbidden by the first commandment; but as a sign of their function, as stated above.

The outer tabernacle, which denotes this present world, also contained three things, viz., the *altar of incense,* which was directly opposite the ark; the *table of proposition,* with the twelve loaves of proposition on it, which stood on the northern side; and the *candlestick,* which was placed towards the south. These three things seem to correspond to the three which were enclosed in the ark; and they represented the same things as the latter, but more clearly: because, in order that wise men, denoted by the priests entering the temple, might grasp the meaning of these types, it was necessary to express them more manifestly than they are in the Divine or angelic mind. —Accordingly the candlestick betokened, as a sensible sign thereof, the wisdom which was expressed on the tables (of the Law) in intelligible words.—The altar of incense signified the office of the priest, whose duty it was to bring the people to God: and this was signified also by the rod: because on that altar the sweet-smelling incense was burnt, signifying the holiness of the people acceptable to God: for it is written (Apoc. viii. 3) that the smoke of the sweet-smelling spices signifies the *justifications of the saints* (*cf. ibid.* xix. 8). Moreover it was fitting that the dignity of the priesthood should be denoted, in the ark, by the rod, and, in the outer tabernacle, by the altar of incense: because the priest is the mediator between God and the people, governing the people by Divine power, denoted by the rod; and offering to God the fruit of His government, i.e., the holiness of the people, on the altar of incense, so to speak.—The table signified the sustenance of life, just as the manna did: but the former, a more general and a coarser kind of nourishment; the latter, a sweeter and more delicate.—Again, the candlestick was fittingly placed on the southern side, while the table was placed to the north: because the south is the right-hand side of the world, while the north is the left-hand side, as stated in *De Cælo et Mundo* ii; and wisdom, like other spiritual goods, belongs to the right hand, while temporal nourishment belongs to the left, according to Prov. iii. 16: *In her left hand (are) riches and glory.* And the priestly power is midway between temporal goods and spiritual wisdom; because thereby both spiritual wisdom and temporal goods are dispensed.

Another literal signification may be assigned. For the ark contained the tables of the Law, in order to prevent forgetfulness of the Law, wherefore it is written (Exod. xxiv. 12): *I will give thee two tables of stone, and the Law, and the commandments which I have written: that thou mayest teach them* to the children of Israel.—The rod of Aaron was placed there to restrain the people from insubordination to the priesthood of Aaron; wherefore it is written (Num. xvii. 10): *Carry back the rod of Aaron into the tabernacle of the testimony, that it may be kept there for a token of the rebellious children of Israel.*— The manna was kept in the ark to remind them of the benefit conferred by God on the children of Israel in the desert; wherefore it is written (Exod. xvi. 32): *Fill a gomor of it, and let it be kept unto generations to come hereafter, that they may know the bread wherewith I fed you in the wilderness.*—The candlestick was set up to enhance the beauty of the temple, for the magnificence of a house depends on its being well lighted. Now the candlestick had seven branches, as Josephus observes (*Antiquit.* iii. 7, 8), to signify the seven planets, wherewith the whole world is illuminated. Hence the candlestick was placed towards the south; because for us the course of the planets is from that quarter.—The altar of incense was instituted that there might always be in the tabernacle a sweet-smelling smoke; both through respect for the tabernacle, and as a remedy for the stenches arising from the shedding of blood and the slaying of animals. For men despise evil-smelling things as being vile, whereas sweet-smelling

things are much appreciated.—The table was placed there to signify that the priests who served the temple should take their food in the temple: wherefore, as stated in Matth. xii. 4, it was lawful for none but the priests to eat the twelve loaves which were put on the table in memory of the twelve tribes. And the table was not placed in the middle directly in front of the propitiatory, in order to exclude an idolatrous rite: for the Gentiles, on the feasts of the moon, set up at a table in front of the idol of the moon, wherefore it is written (Jerem. vii. 18): *The women knead the dough, to make cakes to the queen of heaven.*

In the court outside the tabernacle was the altar of holocausts, on which sacrifices of those things which the people possessed were offered to God: and consequently the people who offered these sacrifices to God by the hands of the priest could be present in the court. But the priests alone, whose function it was to offer the people to God, could approach the inner altar, whereon the very devotion and holiness of the people was offered to God. And this altar was put up outside the tabernacle and in the court, to the exclusion of idolatrous worship: for the Gentiles placed altars inside the temples to offer up sacrifices thereon to idols.

The figurative reason for all these things may be taken from the relation of the tabernacle to Christ, who was foreshadowed therein. Now it must be observed that to show the imperfection of the figures of the Law, various figures were instituted in the temple to betoken Christ. For He was foreshadowed by the *propitiatory*, since He is *a propitiation for our sins* (1 Jo. ii. 2).—This propitiatory was fittingly carried by cherubim, since of Him it is written (Heb. i. 6): *Let all the angels of God adore Him.*—He is also signified by the ark: because just as the ark was made of setim-wood, so was Christ's body composed of most pure members. Moreover it was gilded: for Christ was full of wisdom and charity, which are betokened by gold. And in the ark was a golden pot, i.e., His holy soul, having manna, i.e., *all the fulness of the Godhead* (Coloss. ii. 9). Also there was a rod in the ark, i.e., His priestly power: for *He was made a . . . priest for ever* (Heb. vi. 20). And therein were the tables of the Testament, to denote that Christ Himself is a lawgiver.—Again, Christ was signified by the candlestick, for He said Himself (Jo. viii. 12): *I am the Light of the world;* while the seven lamps denoted the seven gifts of the Holy Ghost. He is also betokened in the table, because He is our spiritual food, according to Jo. vi. 41, 51: *I am the living bread:* and the twelve loaves signified the twelve apostles, or their teaching. —Or again, the candlestick and table may signify the Church's teaching, and faith, which also enlightens and refreshes.—Again, Christ is signified by the two altars of holocausts and incense. Because all works of virtue must be offered by us to God through Him; both those whereby we afflict the body, which are offered, as it were, on the altar of holocausts; and those which, with greater perfection of mind, are offered to God in Christ, by the spiritual desires of the perfect, on the altar of incense, as it were, according to Heb. xiii. 15: *By Him therefore let us offer the sacrifice of praise always to God.*

Reply Obj. 7. The Lord commanded an altar to be made for the offering of sacrifices and gifts, in honor of God, and for the upkeep of the ministers who served the tabernacle. Now concerning the construction of the altar the Lord issued a twofold precept. One was at the beginning of the Law (Exod. xx. 24, seq.) when the Lord commanded them to make *an altar of earth,* or at least *not of hewn stones;* and again, not to make the altar high, so as to make it necessary to *go up* to it *by steps.* This was in detestation of idolatrous worship: for the Gentiles made their altars ornate and high, thinking that there was something holy and divine in such things. For this reason, too, the Lord commanded (Deut. xvi. 21): *Thou shalt plant no grove, nor any tree near the altar of the Lord thy God:* since idolaters were wont to offer sacrifices beneath trees, on account of the pleasantness and shade afforded by them.—There was also a figurative reason for these precepts. Because we must confess that in Christ, Who is our altar, there is the true nature of flesh, as regards His humanity—and this is to make an altar of earth; and again, in regard to His God-head, we must confess His equality with the Father,—and this is *not to go up* to the altar by steps. Moreover we should not couple the doctrine of Christ to that of the Gentiles, which provokes men to lewdness.

But when once the tabernacle had been constructed to the honor of God, there was no longer reason to fear these occasions of idolatry. Wherefore the Lord commanded the altar of holocausts to be made of brass, and to be conspicuous to all the people; and the altar of incense, which was visible to none but the priests. Nor was brass so precious as to give the people an occasion for idolatry.

Since, however, the reason for the precept, *Thou shalt not go up by steps unto My altar* (Exod. xx. 26) is stated to have been *lest thy nakedness be discovered,* it should be observed that this too was instituted with the purpose of preventing idolatry, for in the feasts of Priapus the Gentiles uncovered their nakedness before the people. But later on the priests were prescribed the use of loin-cloths for the sake of decency: so that without any danger the altar could be placed so high that the priests when offering sacrifices would go up by steps of wood, not fixed but movable.

Reply Obj. 8. The body of the tabernacle consisted of boards placed on end, and covered on the inside with curtains of four different colors, viz., twisted linen, violet, purple, and scarlet twice dyed. These curtains, however, covered the sides only of the tabernacle; and the roof of the tabernacle was covered with violet-colored skins; and over this there was another covering of rams' skins dyed red; and over this there was a third curtain made of goats' hair, which covered not only the roof of the tabernacle, but also reached to the ground and covered the boards of the tabernacle on the outside. The literal reason of these coverings taken altogether was the adornment and protection of the tabernacle, that it might be an object of respect. Taken singly, according to some, the curtains denoted the starry heaven, which is adorned with various stars; the curtain (of goats' skin) signified the waters which are above the firmament; the skins dyed red denoted the empyrean heaven, where the angels are; the violet skins, the heaven of the Blessed Trinity.

The figurative meaning of these things is that the boards of which the tabernacle was constructed signify the faithful of Christ, who compose the Church. The boards were covered on the inner side by curtains of four colors: because the faithful are inwardly adorned with the four virtues: for *the twisted linen,* as the gloss observes, *signifies the flesh refulgent with purity; violet signifies the mind desirous of heavenly things; purple denotes the flesh subject to passions; the twice dyed scarlet betokens the mind in the midst of the passions enlightened by the love of God and our neighbor.* The coverings of the building designate prelates and doctors, who ought to be conspicuous for their heavenly manner of life, signified by the violet colored skins: and who should also be ready to suffer martyrdom, denoted by the skins dyed red; and austere of life and patient in adversity, betokened by the curtains of goats' hair, which were exposed to wind and rain, as the gloss observes.

Reply Obj. 9. The literal reason for the sanctification of the tabernacle and vessels was that they might be treated with greater reverence, being deputed, as it were, to the divine worship by this consecration.—The figurative reason is that this sanctification signified the sanctification of the living tabernacle, i.e., the faithful of whom the Church of Christ is composed.

Reply Obj. 10. Under the Old Law there were seven temporal solemnities, and one continual solemnity, as may be gathered from Num. xxviii, xxix. There was a continual teast, since the lamb was sacrificed every day, morning and evening: and this continual feast of an abiding sacrifice signified the perpetuity of Divine bliss. Of the temporal feasts the first was that which was repeated every week. This was the solemnity of the *Sabbath*, celebrated in memory of the work of the creation of the universe.—Another solemnity, viz., *the New Moon*, was repeated every month, and was observed in memory of the work of the Divine government. For the things of this lower world owe their variety chiefly to the movement of the moon; wherefore this feast was kept at the new moon: and not at the full moon, to avoid the worship of idolaters who used to offer sacrifices to the moon at that particular time.—And these two blessings are bestowed in common on the whole human race; and hence they were repeated more frequently.

The other five feasts were celebrated once a year: and they commemorated the benefits which had been conferred especially on that people. For there was the feast of the *Passover* in the first month to commemorate the blessing of being delivered out of Egypt.— The feast of *Pentecost* was celebrated fifty days later, to recall the blessing of the giving of the Law.—The other three feasts were kept in the seventh month, nearly the whole of which was solemnized by them, just as tne seventh day. For on the first of the seventh month was the feast of *Trumpets,* in memory of the delivery of Isaac, when Abraham found the ram caught by its horns, which they represented by the horns which they blew.—The feast of Trumpets was a kind of invitation whereby they prepared themselves to keep the following feast which was kept on the tenth day. This was the feast of *Expiation,* in memory of the blessing whereby, at the prayer of Moses, God forgave the people's sin of worshipping the calf. After this was the feast of *Scenopegia* or of *Tents,* which was kept for seven days, to commemorate the blessing of being protected and led by God through the desert, where they lived in tents. Hence during this feast they had to take *the fruits of the fairest tree,* i.e., the citron, *and trees of dense foliage,** i.e., the myrtle, which is fragrant, *and branches of palm-trees, and willows of the brook,* which retain their greenness a long time; and these are to be found in the Land of promise; to signify that God had

* Douay and A. V. and R. V. read: *Boughs of thick trees.*

brought them through the arid land of the wilderness to a land of delights.—On the eighth day another feast was observed, of *Assembly and Congregation,* on which the people collected the expenses necessary for the divine worship: and it signified the uniting of the people and the peace granted to them in the Land of promise.

The figurative reason for these feasts was that the continual sacrifice of the lamb foreshadowed the perpetuity of Christ, Who is the *Lamb of God,* according to Heb. xiii. 8: *Jesus Christ yesterday and to-day, and the same for ever.*—The Sabbath signified the spiritual rest bestowed by Christ, as stated in Heb. iv. The Neomenia, which is the beginning of the new moon, signified the enlightening of the primitive Church by Christ's preaching and miracles.—The feast of Pentecost signified the Descent of the Holy Ghost on the apostles.— The feast of Trumpets signified the preaching of the apostles.—The feast of Expiation signified the cleansing of the Christian people from sins: and the feast of Tabernacles signified their pilgrimage in this world, wherein they walk by advancing in virtue.—The feast of Assembly or Congregation foreshadowed the assembly of the faithful in the kingdom of heaven: wherefore this feast is described as *most holy* (Levit. xxiii. 36). These three feasts followed immediately on one another, because those who expiate their vices should advance in virtue, until they come to see God, as stated in Ps. lxxxiii. 8.

FIFTH ARTICLE

Whether There Can Be Any Suitable Cause for the Sacraments of the Old Law?

We proceed thus to the Fifth Article:—

Objection 1. It would seem that there can be no suitable cause for the sacraments of the Old Law. Because those things that are done for the purpose of divine worship should not be like the observances of idolaters: since it is written (Deut. xii. 31): *Thou shalt not do in like manner to the Lord thy God: for they have done to their gods all the abominations which the Lord abhorreth.* Now worshippers of idols used to knive themselves to the shedding of blood: for it is related (3 Kings xviii. 28) that they *cut themselves after their manner with knives and lancets, till they were all covered with blood.* For this reason the Lord commanded (Deut. xiv. 1): *You shall not cut yourselves nor make any baldness for the dead.* Therefore it was unfitting for circumcision to be prescribed by the Law (Levit. xii. 3).

Obj. 2. Further, those things which are

done for the worship of God should be marked with decorum and gravity; according to Ps. xxxiv. 18: *I will praise Thee in a grave* (Douay,—*strong) people*. But it seems to savor of levity for a man to eat with haste. Therefore it was unfittingly commanded (Exod. xii. 11) that they should eat the Paschal lamb *in haste*. Other things too relative to the eating of the lamb were prescribed, which seem altogether unreasonable.

Obj. 3. Further, the sacraments of the Old Law were figures of the sacraments of the New Law. Now the Paschal lamb signified the sacrament of the Eucharist, according to 1 Cor. v. 7: *Christ our Pasch is sacrificed.* Therefore there should also have been some sacraments in the Old Law to foreshadow the other sacraments of the New Law, such as Confirmation, Extreme Unction, and Matrimony, and so forth.

Obj. 4. Further, purification can scarcely be done except by removing something impure. But as far as God is concerned, no bodily thing is reputed impure, because all bodies are God's creatures; and *every creature of God is good, and nothing to be rejected that is received with thanksgiving* (1 Tim. iv. 4). It was therefore unfitting for them to be purified after contact with a corpse, or any similar corporeal infection.

Obj. 5. Further, it is written (Ecclus. xxxiv. 4): *What can be made clean by the unclean?* But the ashes of the red heifer* which was burnt, were unclean, since they made a man unclean: for it is stated (Num. xix. 7 *seq.*) that the priest who immolated her was rendered unclean *until the evening;* likewise he that burnt her; and he that gathered up her ashes. Therefore it was unfittingly prescribed there that the unclean should be purified by being sprinkled with those cinders.

Obj. 6. Further, sins are not something corporeal that can be carried from one place to another: nor can man be cleansed from sin by means of something unclean. It was therefore unfitting for the purpose of expiating the sins of the people that the priest should confess the sins of the children of Israel on one of the buck-goats, that it might carry them away into the wilderness: while they were rendered unclean by the other, which they used for the purpose of purification, by burning it together with the calf outside the camp; so that they had to wash their clothes and their bodies with water (Levit. xvi).

Obj. 7. Further, what is already cleansed should not be cleansed again. It was therefore unfitting to apply a second purification to a man cleansed from leprosy, or to a house; as laid down in Levit. xiv.

Obj. 8. Further, spiritual uncleanness cannot be cleansed by material water or by shaving the hair. Therefore it seems unreasonable that the Lord ordered (Exod. xxx. 18 *seq.*) the making of a brazen laver with its foot, that the priests might wash their hands and feet before entering the temple; and that He commanded (Num. viii. 7) the Levites to be sprinkled with the water of purification, and to shave all the hairs of their flesh.

Obj. 9. Further, that which is greater cannot be cleansed by that which is less. Therefore it was unfitting that, in the Law, the higher and lower priests, as stated in Levit. viii,† and the Levites, according to Num. viii. should be consecrated with any bodily anointing, bodily sacrifices, and bodily oblations.

Obj. 10. Further, as stated in 1 Kings xvi. 7, *Man seeth those things that appear, but the Lord beholdeth the heart.* But those things that appear outwardly in man are the disposition of his body and his clothes. Therefore it was unfitting for certain special garments to be appointed to the higher and lower priests, as related in Exod. xxviii.‡ It seems, moreover, unreasonable that anyone should be debarred from the priesthood on account of defects in the body, as stated in Levit. xxi. 17, seq.: *Whosoever of thy seed throughout their families, hath a blemish, he shall not offer bread to his God . . . if he be blind, if he be lame*, etc. It seems, therefore, that the sacraments of the Old Law were unreasonable.

On the contrary, It is written (Levit. xx. 8): *I am the Lord that sanctify you.* But nothing unreasonable is done by God, for it is written (Ps. ciii. 24): *Thou hast made all things in wisdom.* Therefore there was nothing without a reasonable cause in the sacraments of the Old Law, which were ordained to the sanctification of man.

I answer that, As stated above (Q. 101, A. 4), the sacraments are, properly speaking, things applied to the worshippers of God for their consecration so as, in some way, to depute them to the worship of God. Now the worship of God belonged in a general way to the whole people; but in a special way, it belonged to the priests and Levites, who were the ministers of divine worship. Consequently, in these sacraments of the Old Law, certain things concerned the whole people in general; while others belonged to the ministers.

In regard to both, three things were necessary. The first was to be established in the state of worshipping God: and this institution was brought about,—for all in general, by circumcision, without which no one was admitted to any of the legal observances,—and for the priests, by their consecration. The

---

* *Cf.* Heb. ix. 13.   † *Cf.* Exod. xxix.   ‡ *Cf.* Levit viii. 7, *seq.*

second thing required was the use of those things that pertain to divine worship. And thus, as to the people, there was the partaking of the paschal banquet, to which no uncircumcised man was admitted, as is clear from Exod. xii. 43 *seq.*: and, as to the priests, the offering of the victims, and the eating of the loaves of proposition and of other things that were allotted to the use of the priests.—The third thing required was the removal of all impediments to divine worship, viz., of uncleannesses. And then, as to the people, certain purifications were instituted for the removal of certain external uncleannesses; and also expiations from sins; while, as to the priests and Levites, the washing of hands and feet and the shaving of the hair was instituted.

And all these things had reasonable causes, both literal, in so far as they were ordained to the worship of God for the time being, and figurative, in so far as they were ordained to foreshadow Christ: as we shall see by taking them one by one.

Reply Obj. 1. The chief literal reason for circumcision was in order that man might profess his belief in one God. And because Abraham was the first to sever himself from the infidels, by going out from his house and kindred, for this reason he was the first to receive circumcision. This reason is set forth by the Apostle (Rom. iv. 9, *seq.*) thus: *He received the sign of circumcision, a seal of the justice of the faith which he had, being uncircumcised;* because, to wit, we are told that *unto Abraham faith was reputed to justice,* for the reason that *against hope he believed in hope,* i.e., against the hope that is of nature he believed in the hope that is of grace, *that he might be made the father of many nations,* when he was an old man, and his wife an old and barren woman. And in order that this declaration, and imitation of Abraham's faith, might be fixed firmly in the hearts of the Jews, they received in their flesh such a sign as they could not forget, wherefore it is written (Gen. xvii. 13): *My covenant shall be in your flesh for a perpetual covenant.* This was done on the eighth day, because until then a child is very tender, and so might be seriously injured; and is considered as something not yet consolidated: wherefore neither are animals offered before the eighth day. And it was not delayed after that time, lest some might refuse the sign of circumcision on account of the pain: and also lest the parents, whose love for their children increases as they become used to their presence and as they grow older, should withdraw their children from circumcision.—A second reason may have been the weakening of concupiscence in that member.—A third motive may have been

to revile the worship of Venus and Priapus, which gave honor to that part of the body.— The Lord's prohibition extended only to the cutting of oneself in honor of idols: and such was not the circumcision of which we have been speaking.

The figurative reason for circumcision was that it foreshadowed the removal of corruption, which was to be brought about by Christ, and will be perfectly fulfilled in the eighth age, which is the age of those who rise from the dead. And since all corruption of guilt and punishment comes to us through our carnal origin, from the sin of our first parent, therefore circumcision was applied to the generative member. Hence the Apostle says (Coloss. ii. 11): *You are circumcised* in Christ *with circumcision not made by hand in despoiling of the body of the flesh, but in the circumcision of* Our Lord Jesus *Christ.*

Reply Obj. 2. The literal reason of the paschal banquet was to commemorate the blessing of being led by God out of Egypt. Hence by celebrating this banquet they declared that they belonged to that people which God had taken to Himself out of Egypt. For when they were delivered from Egypt, they were commanded to sprinkle the lamb's blood on the transoms of their house doors, as though declaring that they were averse to the rites of the Egyptians who worshipped the ram. Wherefore they were delivered by the sprinkling or rubbing of the blood of the lamb on the door-posts, from the danger of extermination which threatened the Egyptians.

Now two things are to be observed in their departure from Egypt: namely, their haste in going, for the Egyptians pressed them to go forth speedily, as related in Exod. xii. 33; and there was the danger that anyone who did not hasten to go with the crowd might be slain by the Egyptians. Their haste was shown in two ways. First by what they ate. For they were commanded to eat unleavened bread, as a sign *that it could not be leavened, the Egyptians pressing them to depart;* and to eat roast meat, for this took less time to prepare; and that they should not break a bone thereof, because in their haste there was no time to break bones. Secondly, as to the manner of eating. For it is written: *You shall gird your reins, and you shall have shoes on your feet, holding staves in your hands, and you shall eat in haste:* which clearly designates men at the point of starting on a journey. To this also is to be referred the command: *In one house shall it be eaten, neither shall you carry forth of the flesh thereof out of the house:* because, to wit, on account of their haste, they could not send any gifts of it.

The stress they suffered while in Egypt was denoted by the wild lettuces. The figurative reason is evident, because the sacrifice of the paschal lamb signified the sacrifice of Christ according to 1 Cor. v. 7: *Christ our pasch is sacrificed*. The blood of the lamb, which ensured deliverance from the destroyer, by being sprinkled on the transoms, signified faith in Christ's Passion, in the hearts and on the lips of the faithful, by which same Passion we are delivered from sin and death, according to 1 Pet. i. 18: *You were . . . redeemed . . . with the precious blood . . . of a lamb unspotted*. The partaking of its flesh signified the eating of Christ's body in the Sacrament; and the flesh was roasted at the fire to signify Christ's Passion or charity. And it was eaten with unleavened bread to signify the blameless life of the faithful who partake of Christ's body, according to 1 Cor. v. 8: *Let us feast . . . with the unleavened bread of sincerity and truth*. The wild lettuces were added to denote repentance for sins, which is required of those who receive the body of Christ. Their loins were girt in sign of chastity: and the shoes of their feet are the examples of our dead ancestors. The staves they were to hold in their hands denoted pastoral authority: and it was commanded that the paschal lamb should be eaten in one house, i.e., in a catholic church, and not in the conventicles of heretics.

Reply Obj. 3. Some of the sacraments of the New Law had corresponding figurative sacraments in the Old Law. For Baptism, which is the sacrament of Faith, corresponds to circumcision. Hence it is written (Col. ii. 11, 12): *You are circumcised . . . in the circumcision of* Our Lord Jesus Christ; *buried with Him in Baptism*. In the New Law the sacrament of the Eucharist corresponds to the banquet of the paschal lamb. The sacrament of Penance in the New Law corresponds to all the purifications of the Old Law. The sacrament of Orders corresponds to the consecration of the pontiff and of the priests. To the sacrament of Confirmation, which is the sacrament of the fulness of grace, there would be no corresponding sacrament of the Old Law, because the time of fulness had not yet come, since *the Law brought no man* (Vulg.,—*nothing*) *to perfection* (Heb. vii. 19). The same applies to the sacrament of Extreme Unction, which is an immediate preparation for entrance into glory, to which the way was not yet opened out in the Old Law, since the price had not yet been paid. Matrimony did indeed exist under the Old Law, as a function of nature, but not as the sacrament of the union of Christ with the Church, for that union was not as yet brought about. Hence under the Old Law it was allowable to give a

bill of divorce, which is contrary to the nature of a sacrament.

Reply Obj. 4. As already stated, the purifications of the Old Law were ordained for the removal of impediments to the divine worship: which worship is twofold; viz., spiritual, consisting in devotion of the mind to God; and corporal, consisting in sacrifices, oblations, and so forth. Now men are hindered in the spiritual worship by sins, whereby men were said to be polluted, for instance, by idolatry, murder, adultery, or incest. From such pollutions men were purified by certain sacrifices, offered either for the whole community in general, or also for the sins of individuals; not that those carnal sacrifices had of themselves the power of expiating sin; but that they signified that expiation of sins which was to be effected by Christ, and of which those of old became partakers by protesting their faith in the Redeemer, while taking part in the figurative sacrifices.

The impediments to external worship consisted in certain bodily uncleannesses; which were considered in the first place as existing in man, and consequently in other animals also, and in man's clothes, dwelling-place, and vessels. In man himself uncleanness was considered as arising partly from himself and partly from contact with unclean things. Anything proceeding from man was reputed unclean that was already subject to corruption, or exposed thereto: and consequently since death is a kind of corruption, the human corpse was considered unclean. In like manner, since leprosy arises from corruption of the humors, which break out externally and infect other persons, therefore were lepers also considered unclean; and, again, women suffering from a flow of blood, whether from weakness, or from nature (either at the monthly course or at the time of conception); and, for the same reason, men were reputed unclean if they suffered from a flow of seed, whether due to weakness, to nocturnal pollution, or to sexual intercourse. Because every humor issuing from man in the aforesaid ways involves some unclean infection. Again, man contracted uncleanness by touching any unclean thing whatever.

Now there was both a literal and a figurative reason for these uncleannesses. The literal reason was taken from the reverence due to those things that belong to the divine worship: both because men are not wont, when unclean, to touch precious things: and in order that by rarely approaching sacred things they might have greater respect for them. For since man could seldom avoid all the aforesaid uncleannesses, the result was that men could seldom approach to touch things belonging to the worship of God, so that when they did approach, they did so with greater reverence and humility. Moreover, in some of these the literal reason was that men should not be kept away from worshipping God through fear of coming in contact with lepers and others similarly afflicted with loathsome and contagious diseases. In others, again, the reason was to avoid idolatrous worship; because in their sacrificial rites the Gentiles sometimes employed human blood and seed. All these bodily uncleannesses were purified either by the mere sprinkling of water, or, in the case of those which were more grievous, by some sacrifice of expiation for the sin which was the occasion of the uncleanness in question.

The figurative reason for these uncleannesses was that they were figures of various sins. For the uncleanness of any corpse signifies the uncleanness of sin, which is the death of the soul. The uncleanness of leprosy betokened the uncleanness of heretical doctrine: both because heretical doctrine is contagious just as leprosy is, and because no doctrine is so false as not to have some truth mingled with error, just as on the surface of a leprous body one may distinguish the healthy parts from those that are infected. The uncleanness of a woman suffering from a flow of blood denotes the uncleanness of idolatry, on account of the blood which is offered up. The uncleanness of the man who has suffered seminal loss signifies the uncleanness of empty words, for *the seed is the word of God*. The uncleanness of sexual intercourse and of the woman in child-birth signifies the uncleanness of original sin. The uncleanness of the woman in her periods signifies the uncleanness of a mind that is sensualized by pleasure. Speaking generally, the uncleanness contracted by touching an unclean thing denotes the uncleanness arising from consent in another's sin, according to 2 Cor. vi. 17: *Go out from among them, and be ye separate . . . and touch not the unclean thing.*

Moreover, this uncleanness arising from the touch was contracted even by inanimate objects; for whatever was touched in any way by an unclean man, became itself unclean. Wherein the Law attenuated the superstition of the Gentiles, who held that uncleanness was contracted not only by touch, but also by speech or looks, as Rabbi Moses states (*Doct. Perplex.* iii) of a woman in her periods. The mystical sense of this was that *to God the wicked and his wickedness are hateful alike* (Wis. xiv. 9).

There was also an uncleanness of inanimate things considered in themselves, such as the uncleanness of leprosy in a house or in clothes. For just as leprosy occurs in men through a corrupt humor causing putrefaction and corruption in the flesh; so, too, through some corruption and excess of humidity or dryness, there arises sometimes a kind of corruption in the stones with which a house is built, or in clothes. Hence the Law called this corruption by the name of leprosy, whereby a house or a garment was deemed to be unclean: both because all corruption savored of uncleanness, as stated above, and because the Gentiles worshipped their household gods as a preservative against this corruption. Hence the Law prescribed such houses, where this kind of corruption was of a lasting nature, to be destroyed; and such garments to be burnt, in order to avoid all occasion of idolatry. There was also an uncleanness of vessels, of which it is written (Num. xix. 15): *The vessel that hath no cover, and binding over it, shall be unclean.* The cause of this uncleanness was that anything unclean might easily drop into such vessels, so as to render them unclean. Moreover, this command aimed at the prevention of idolatry. For idolaters believed that if mice, lizards, or the like, which they used to sacrifice to the idols, fell into the vessels or into the water, these became more pleasing to the gods. Even now some women let down uncovered vessels in honor of the nocturnal deities which they call *Janæ*.

The figurative reason of these uncleannesses is that the leprosy of a house signified the uncleanness of the assembly of heretics; the leprosy of a linen garment signified an evil life arising from bitterness of mind; the leprosy of a woolen garment denoted the wickedness of flatterers; leprosy in the warp signified the vices of the soul; leprosy on the woof denoted sins of the flesh, for as the warp is in the woof, so is the soul in the body. The vessel that has neither cover nor binding, betokens a man who lacks the veil of taciturnity, and who is unrestrained by any severity of discipline.

Reply Obj. 5. As stated above (*ad* 4), there was a twofold uncleanness in the Law; one by way of corruption in the mind or in the body; and this was the graver uncleanness; the other was by mere contact with an unclean thing, and this was less grave, and was more easily expiated. Because the former uncleanness was expiated by sacrifices for sins, since all corruption is due to sin, and signifies sin: whereas the latter uncleanness was expiated by the mere sprinkling of a certain water, of which water we read in Num. xix. For there God commanded them to take a red cow in memory of the sin they had committed in worshipping a calf. And a cow is mentioned rather than a calf, because it was thus that the Lord was wont to designate the synagogue, according to Osee iv. 16: *Israel hath gone astray like a wanton heifer:* and this was, perhaps, because they worshipped heifers after the custom of Egypt, according to Osee x. 5: *(They) have worshipped the kine of Bethaven.* And in detestation of the sin of idolatry it was sacrificed outside the camp; in fact, whenever sacrifice was offered up in expiation of the multitude of sins, it was all burnt outside the camp. Moreover, in order to show that this sacrifice cleansed the people from all their sins, *the priest* dipped *his finger in her blood,* and sprinkled *it over against the door of the tabernacle seven times;* for the number seven signifies universality. Further, the very sprinkling of blood pertained to the detestation of idolatry, in which the blood that was offered up was not poured out, but was collected together, and men gathered round it to eat in honor of the idols. Likewise it was burnt by fire, either because God appeared to Moses in a fire, and the Law was given from the midst of fire; or to denote that idolatry, together with all that was connected therewith, was to be extirpated altogether; just as the cow was burnt *with her skin and her flesh, her blood and dung being delivered to the flames.* To this burning were added *cedar-wood, and hyssop, and scarlet twice dyed,* to signify that just as cedar-wood is not liable to putrefaction, and scarlet twice dyed does not easily lose its color, and hyssop retains its odor after it has been dried; so also was this sacrifice for the preservation of the whole people, and for their good behavior and devotion. Hence it is said of the ashes of the cow: *That they may be reserved for the multitude of the children of Israel.* Or, according to Josephus (*Antiq. iii, 8, 9, 10*), the four elements are indicated here: for *cedar-wood* was added to the fire, to signify the earth, on account of its earthiness; *hyssop,* to signify the air, on account of its smell; *scarlet twice dyed,* to signify water, for the same reason as purple, on account of the dyes which are taken out of the water:—thus denoting the fact that this sacrifice was offered to the Creator of the four elements. And since this sacrifice was offered for the sin of idolatry, both *he that burned her,* and *he that gathered up the ashes,* and *he that sprinkled the water* in which the ashes were placed, were deemed unclean in detestation of that sin, in order to show that whatever was in any way connected with idolatry should be cast aside as being unclean. From this uncleanness they were purified by the mere washing of their clothes; nor did they need to be sprinkled with the water on account of this kind of uncleanness, because otherwise the process would have been unending, since he that sprinkled the water became unclean, so that if he were

to sprinkle himself he would remain unclean; and if another were to sprinkle him, that one would have become unclean, and in like manner, whoever might sprinkle him, and so on indefinitely.

The figurative reason of this sacrifice was that the red cow signified Christ in respect of his assumed weakness, denoted by the female sex; while the color of the cow designated the blood of His Passion. And the *red cow was of full age,* because all Christ's works are perfect, *in which there* was *no blemish; and* which had *not carried the yoke,* because Christ was innocent, nor did He carry the yoke of sin. It was commanded to be taken to Moses, because they blamed Him for transgressing the law of Moses by breaking the Sabbath. And it was commanded to be delivered *to Eleazar the priest,* because Christ was delivered into the hands of the priests to be slain. It was immolated *without the camp,* because Christ *suffered outside the gate* (Heb. xiii. 12). And the priest dipped *his finger in her blood,* because the mystery of Christ's Passion should be considered and imitated.

It was sprinkled *over against . . . the tabernacle,* which denotes the synagogue, to signify either the condemnation of the unbelieving Jews, or the purification of believers; and this *seven times,* in token either of the seven gifts of the Holy Ghost, or of the seven days wherein all time is comprised. Again, all things that pertain to the Incarnation of Christ should be burnt with fire, i.e., they should be understood spiritually; for the *skin* and *flesh* signified Christ's outward works; the *blood* denoted the subtle inward force which quickened His external deeds; the *dung* betokened His weariness, His thirst, and all such like things pertaining to His weakness. Three things were added, viz., *cedar-wood,* which denotes the height of hope or contemplation; *hyssop,* in token of humility or faith; *scarlet twice dyed,* which denotes twofold charity; for it is by these three that we should cling to Christ suffering. The ashes of this burning were gathered by *a man that is clean,* because the relics of the Passion came into the possession of the Gentiles, who were not guilty of Christ's death. The ashes were put into water for the purpose of expiation, because Baptism receives from Christ's Passion the power of washing away sins. The priest who immolated and burned the cow, and he who burned, and he who gathered together the ashes, were unclean, as also he that sprinkled the water: either because the Jews became unclean through putting Christ to death, whereby our sins are expiated; and this, until the evening, i.e., until the end of the world, when the remnants of Israel will be converted; or else because they who handle sacred things with a view to the cleansing of others contract certain uncleannesses, as Gregory says (*Pastor.* ii. 5); and this until the evening, i.e., until the end of this life.

Reply Obj. 6. As stated above (*ad* 5), an uncleanness which was caused by corruption either of mind or of body was expiated by sin-offerings. Now special sacrifices were wont to be offered for the sins of individuals: but since some were neglectful about expiating such sins and uncleannesses; or, through ignorance, failed to offer this expiation; it was laid down that once a year, on the tenth day of the seventh month, a sacrifice of expiation should be offered for the whole people. And because, as the Apostle says (Heb. vii. 28), *the Law maketh men priests, who have infirmity,* it behooved the priest first of all to offer a calf for his own sins, in memory of Aaron's sin in fashioning the molten calf; and, besides, to offer a ram for a holocaust, which signified that the priestly sovereignty denoted by the ram, who is the head of the flock, was to be ordained to the glory of God.—Then he offered two he-goats for the people: one of which was offered in expiation of the sins of the multitude. For the he-goat is an evil-smelling animal; and from its skin clothes are made having a pungent odor; to signify the stench, uncleanness and the sting of sin. After this he-goat had been immolated, its blood was taken, together with the blood of the calf, into the Holy of Holies, and the entire sanctuary was sprinkled with it; to signify that the tabernacle was cleansed from the uncleannesses of the children of Israel. But the corpses of the he-goat and calf which had been offered up for sin had to be burnt, to denote the destruction of sins. They were not, however, burnt on the altar: since none but holocausts were burnt thereon; but it was prescribed that they should be burnt without the camp, in detestation of sin: for this was done whenever sacrifice was offered for a grievous sin, or for the multitude of sins. The other goat was let loose into the wilderness: not indeed to offer it to the demons, whom the Gentiles worshipped in desert places, because it was unlawful to offer aught to them; but in order to point out the effect of the sacrifice which had been offered up. Hence the priest put his hand on its head, while confessing the sins of the children of Israel: as though that goat were to carry them away into the wilderness, where it would be devoured by wild beasts, because it bore the punishment of the people's sins. And it was said to bear the sins of the people, either because the forgiveness of the people's sins was signified by its

being let loose, or because on its head written lists of sins were fastened.

The figurative reason of these things was that Christ was foreshadowed both by the calf, on account of His power; and by the ram, because He is the Head of the faithful; and by the he-goat, on account of *the likeness of sinful flesh* (Rom. viii. 3). Moreover, Christ was sacrificed for the sins of both priests and people: since both those of high and those of low degree are cleansed from sin by His Passion. The blood of the calf and of the goat was brought into the Holies by the priest, because the entrance to the kingdom of heaven was opened to us by the blood of Christ's Passion. Their bodies were burnt without the camp, because *Christ suffered without the gate*, as the Apostle declares (Heb. xiii. 12). The scape-goat may denote either Christ's Godhead Which went away into solitude when the Man Christ suffered, not by going to another place, but by restraining His power: or it may signify the base concupiscence which we ought to cast away from ourselves, while we offer up to Our Lord acts of virtue.

With regard to the uncleanness contracted by those who burnt these sacrifices, the reason is the same as that which we assigned (*ad* 5) to the sacrifice of the red heifer.

Reply Obj. 7. The legal rite did not cleanse the leper of his deformity, but declared him to be cleansed. This is shown by the words of Lev. xiv. 3, *seq.*, where it is said that the priest, *when he shall find that the leprosy is cleansed*, shall command *him that is to be purified*: consequently, the leper was already healed: but he was said to be purified in so far as the verdict of the priest restored him to the society of men and to the worship of God. It happened sometimes, however, that bodily leprosy was miraculously cured by the legal rite, when the priest erred in his judgment.

Now this purification of a leper was twofold: for, in the first place, he was declared to be clean; and, secondly, he was restored, as clean, to the society of men and to the worship of God, to wit, after seven days. At the first purification the leper who sought to be cleansed offered for himself *two living sparrows, . . . cedar-wood, and scarlet, and hyssop*, in such wise that a sparrow and the hyssop should be tied to the cedar-wood with a scarlet thread, so that the cedar-wood was like the handle of an aspersory: while the hyssop and sparrow were that part of the aspersory which was dipped into the blood of the other sparrow which was *immolated . . . over living waters*. These things he offered as an antidote to the four defects of leprosy: for cedar-wood, which is not subject to putrefaction, was offered against the putrefaction; hyssop, which is a sweet-smelling herb, was offered up against the stench; a living sparrow was offered up against numbness; and scarlet, which has a vivid color, was offered up against the repulsive color of leprosy. The living sparrow was let loose to fly away into the plain, because the leper was restored to his former liberty.

On the eighth day he was admitted to divine worship, and was restored to the society of men; but only after having shaved all the hair of his body, and washed his clothes, because leprosy rots the hair, infects the clothes, and gives them an evil smell. Afterwards a sacrifice was offered for his sin, since leprosy was frequently a result of sin: and some of the blood of the sacrifice was put on the tip of the ear of the man that was to be cleansed, *and on the thumb of his right hand, and the great toe of his right foot;* because it is in these parts that leprosy is first diagnosed and felt. In this rite, moreover, three liquids were employed: viz., blood, against the corruption of the blood; oil, to denote the healing of the disease; and living waters, to wash away the filth.

The figurative reason was that the Divine and human natures in Christ were denoted by the two sparrows, one of which, in likeness of His human nature, was offered up in an earthen vessel over living waters, because the waters of Baptism are sanctified by Christ's Passion. The other sparrow, in token of His impassible Godhead, remained living, because the Godhead cannot die: hence it flew away, for the Godhead could not be encompassed by the Passion. Now this living sparrow, together with the cedar-wood and scarlet and cochineal, and hyssop, i.e., faith, hope, and charity, as stated above (*ad* 5), was put into the water for the purpose of sprinkling, because we are baptized in the faith of the God-Man. By the waters of Baptism or of his tears man washes his clothes, i.e., his works, and all his hair, i.e., his thoughts. The tip of the right ear of the man to be cleansed is moistened with some of the blood and oil, in order to strengthen his hearing against harmful words; and the thumb and toe of his right hand and foot are moistened that his deeds may be holy. Other matters pertaining to this purification, or to that also of any other uncleannesses, call for no special remark, beyond what applies to other sacrifices, whether for sins or for trespasses.

Reply Objs. 8 *and* 9. Just as the people were initiated by circumcision to the divine worship, so were the ministers by some special purification or consecration: wherefore

they are commanded to be separated from other men, as being specially deputed, rather than others, to the ministry of the divine worship. And all that was done touching them in their consecration or institution, was with a view to show that they were in possession of a prerogative of purity, power, and dignity. Hence three things were done in the institution of ministers: for first, they were purified; secondly, they were adorned* and consecrated; thirdly, they were employed in the ministry. All in general used to be purified by washing in water, and by certain sacrifices; but the Levites in particular shaved all the hair of their bodies, as stated in Lev. viii. (*cf.* Num. viii).

With regard to the high-priests and priests the consecration was performed as follows. First, when they had been washed, they were clothed with certain special garments in designation of their dignity. In particular, the high-priest was anointed on the head with the oil of unction: to denote that the power of consecration was poured forth by him on to others, just as oil flows from the head on to the lower parts of the body; according to Ps. cxxxii. 2: *Like the precious ointment on the head that ran down upon the beard, the beard of Aaron.* But the Levites received no other consecration besides being offered to the Lord by the children of Israel through the hands of the high-priest, who prayed for them. The lesser priests were consecrated on the hands only, which were to be employed in the sacrifices. The tip of their right ear and the thumb of their right hand, and the great toe of their right foot were tinged with the blood of the sacrificial animal, to denote that they should be obedient to God's law in offering the sacrifices (this is denoted by touching their right ear); and that they should be careful and ready in performing the sacrifices (this is signified by the moistening of the right foot and hand). They themselves and their garments were sprinkled with the blood of the animal that had been sacrificed, in memory of the blood of the lamb by which they had been delivered in Egypt. At their consecration the following sacrifices were offered: a calf, for sin, in memory of Aaron's sin in fashioning the molten calf; a ram, for a holocaust, in memory of the sacrifice of Abraham, whose obedience it behooved the high-priest to imitate; again, a ram of consecration, which was as a peace-offering, in memory of the delivery from Egypt through the blood of the lamb; and a basket of bread, in memory of the manna vouchsafed to the people.

In reference to their being destined to the

* *Ornabantur.* Some editions have *ordinabantur,—were ordained:* the former reading is a reference to Lev. viii. 7-9.

ministry, the fat of the ram, one roll of bread, and the right shoulder were placed on their hands, to show that they received the power of offering these things to the Lord: while the Levites were initiated to the ministry by being brought into the tabernacle of the covenant, as being destined to the ministry touching the vessels of the sanctuary.

The figurative reason of these things was that those who are to be consecrated to the spiritual ministry of Christ, should be first of all purified by the waters of Baptism, and by the waters of tears, in their faith in Christ's Passion, which is a sacrifice both of expiation and of purification. They have also to shave all the hair of their body, i.e., all evil thoughts. They should, moreover, be decked with virtues, and be consecrated with the oil of the Holy Ghost, and with the sprinkling of Christ's blood. And thus they should be intent on the fulfilment of their spiritual ministry.

Reply Obj. 10. As already stated (A. 4), the purpose of the Law was to induce men to have reverence for the divine worship: and this in two ways;—first, by excluding from the worship of God whatever might be an object of contempt; secondly, by introducing into the divine worship all that seemed to savor of reverence. And, indeed, if this was observed in regard to the tabernacle and its vessels, and in the animals to be sacrificed, much more was it to be observed in the very ministers. Wherefore, in order to obviate contempt for the ministers, it was prescribed that they should have no bodily stain or defect: since men so deformed are wont to be despised by others. For the same reason it was also commanded that the choice of those who were to be destined to the service of God was not to be made in a broadcast manner from any family, but according to their descent from one particular stock, thus giving them distinction and nobility.

In order that they might be revered, special ornate vestments were appointed for their use, and a special form of consecration. This indeed is the general reason of ornate garments. But the high-priest in particular had eight vestments. First, he had a linen tunic.—Secondly, he had a purple tunic; round the bottom of which were placed *little bells* and *pomegranates of violet, and purple, and scarlet twice dyed.*—Thirdly, he had the ephod, which covered his shoulders and his breast down to the girdle; and it was made of gold, and violet and purple, and scarlet twice dyed and twisted linen: and on his shoulders he bore two onyx stones, on which were graven the names of the children of Israel.—Fourthly, he

had the rational, made of the same material; it was square in shape, and was worn on the breast, and was fastened to the ephod. On this rational there were twelve precious stones set in four rows, on which also were graven the names of the children of Israel, in token that the priest bore the burden of the whole people, since he bore their names on his shoulders; and that it was his duty ever to think of their welfare, since he wore them on his breast, bearing them in his heart, so to speak. And the Lord commanded the *Doctrine and Truth* to be put in the rational: for certain matters regarding moral and dogmatic truth were written on it. The Jews indeed pretend that on the rational was placed a stone which changed color according to the various things which were about to happen to the children of Israel: and this they call the *Truth and Doctrine.*—Fifthly, he wore a belt or girdle made of the four colors mentioned above.—Sixthly, there was the tiara or mitre which was made of linen.—Seventhly, there was the golden plate which hung over his forehead; on it was inscribed the Lord's name.—Eighthly, there were *the linen breeches to cover the flesh of their nakedness,* when they went up to the sanctuary or altar.—Of these eight vestments the lesser priests had four, viz., the linen tunic and breeches, the belt and the tiara.

According to some, the literal reason for these vestments was that they denoted the disposition of the terrestrial globe; as though the high-priest confessed himself to be the minister of the Creator of the world, wherefore it is written (Wis. xviii. 24): *In the robe of Aaron was the whole world* described. For the linen breeches signified the earth out of which the flax grows. The surrounding belt signified the ocean which surrounds the earth. The violet tunic denoted the air by its color: its little bells betoken the thunder; the pomegranates, the lightning. The ephod, by its many colors, signified the starry heaven; the two onyx stones denoted the two hemispheres, or the sun and moon. The twelve precious stones on the breast are the twelve signs of the zodiac: and they are said to have been placed on the rational, because in heaven are the types (*rationes*) of earthly things, according to Job xxxviii. 33: *Dost thou know the order of heaven, and canst thou set down the reason (rationem) thereof on the earth?* The turban or tiara signified the empyrean: the golden plate was a token of God, the governor of the universe.

The figurative reason is evident. Because bodily stains or defects wherefrom the priests had to be immune, signify the various vices and sins from which they should be free. Thus it is forbidden that he should be blind, i.e. he ought not to be ignorant: he must not be lame, i.e., vacillating and uncertain of purpose: that he must not have *a little, or a great, or a crooked nose*, i.e., that he should not, from lack of discretion, exceed in one direction or in another, or even exercise some base occupation: for the nose signifies discretion, because it discerns odors. It is forbidden that he should have *a broken foot* or *hand*, i.e., he should not lose the power of doing good works or of advancing in virtue. He is rejected, too, if he have a swelling either in front or behind (Vulg.,—*if he be crook-backed*): by which is signified too much love of earthly things:—if he be blear-eyed, i.e., if his mind is darkened by carnal affections: for running of the eyes is caused by a flow of matter. He is also rejected if he have *a pearl in his eye*, i.e., if he presumes in his own estimation that he is clothed in the white robe of righteousness. Again, he is rejected *if he have a continued scab*, i.e., lustfulness of the flesh: also, if he have *a dry scurf*, which covers the body without giving pain, and is a blemish on the comeliness of the members; which denotes avarice. Lastly, he is rejected *if he have a rupture* or hernia; through baseness rending his heart, though it appear not in his deeds.

The vestments denote the virtues of God's ministers. Now there are four things that are necessary to all His ministers, viz., chastity denoted by the breeches; a pure life, signified by the linen tunic; the moderation of discretion, betokened by the girdle; and rectitude of purpose, denoted by the mitre covering the head.—But the high-priests needed four other things in addition to these. First, a continual recollection of God in their thoughts; and this was signified by the golden plate worn over the forehead, with the name of God engraved thereon. Secondly, they had to bear with the shortcomings of the people: this was denoted by the ephod which they bore on their shoulders. Thirdly, they had to carry the people in their mind and heart by the solicitude of charity, in token of which they wore the rational. Fourthly, they had to lead a godly life by performing works of perfection; and this was signified by the violet tunic. Hence little golden bells were fixed to the bottom of the violet tunic, which bells signified the teaching of divine things united in the high-priest to his godly mode of life. In addition to these were the pomegranates, signifying unity of faith and concord in good morals: because his doctrine should hold together in such a way that it should not rend asunder the unity of faith and peace.

* *Cf.* Deut. xiv.

SIXTH ARTICLE

Whether There Was Any Reasonable Cause for the Ceremonial Observances?

We proceed thus to the Sixth Article:—

Objection 1. It would seem that there was no reasonable cause for the ceremonial observances. Because, as the Apostle says (1 Tim. iv. 4), *every creature of God is good, and nothing to be rejected that is received with thanksgiving.* It was therefore unfitting that they should be forbidden to eat certain foods, as being unclean according to Lev. xi.*

Obj. 2. Further, just as animals are given to man for food, so also are herbs: wherefore it is written (Gen. ix. 3): *As the green herbs have I delivered all* flesh *to you.* But the Law did not distinguish any herbs from the rest as being unclean, although some are most harmful, for instance, those that are poisonous. Therefore it seems that neither should any animals have been prohibited as being unclean.

Obj. 3. Further, if the matter from which a thing is generated be unclean, it seems that likewise the thing generated therefrom is unclean. But flesh is generated from blood. Since therefore all flesh was not prohibited as unclean, it seems that in like manner neither should blood have been forbidden as unclean; nor the fat which is engendered from blood.

Obj. 4. Further, Our Lord said (Matth. x. 28; *cf.* Luke xii. 4), that those should not be feared *that kill the body*, since after death they *have no more that they can do:* which would not be true if after death harm might come to man through anything done with his body. Much less therefore does it matter to an animal already dead how its flesh be cooked. Consequently there seems to be no reason in what is said, Exod. xxiii. 19: *Thou shalt not boil a kid in the milk of its dam.*

Obj. 5. Further, all that is first brought forth of man and beast, as being most perfect, is commanded to be offered to the Lord (Exod. xiii). Therefore it is an unfitting command that is set forth in Lev. xix. 23: *when you shall be come into the land, and shall have planted in it fruit trees, you shall take away the uncircumcision†* *of them,* i.e., the first crops, and they *shall be unclean to you, neither shall you eat of them.*

Obj. 6. Further, clothing is something extraneous to man's body. Therefore certain kinds of garments should not have been forbidden to the Jews: for instance (Lev. xix. 19): *Thou shalt not wear a garment that is woven of two sorts:* and (Deut. xxii. 5): *A woman shall not be clothed with man's apparel, neither shall a man use woman's apparel:* and further on (verse 11): *Thou shalt not wear a*

† *Præputia,* which Douay version renders *first fruits.*

garment that is woven of woolen and linen together.

Obj. 7. Further, to be mindful of God's commandments concerns not the body but the heart. Therefore it is unsuitably prescribed (Deut. vi. 8, *seq.*) that they should *bind* the commandments of God *as a sign* on their hands; and that they should *write them in the entry;* and (Num. xv. 38, *seq.*) that they should *make to themselves fringes in the corners of their garments, putting in them ribands of blue, . . . they may remember . . . the commandments of the Lord.*

Obj. 8. Further, the Apostle says (1 Cor. ix. 9) that God does not *take care for oxen,* and, therefore, neither of other irrational animals. Therefore without reason is it commanded (Deut. xxii. 6): *If thou find, as thou walkest by the way, a bird's nest in a tree . . . thou shalt not take the dam with her young;* and (Deut. xxv. 4): *Thou shalt not muzzle the ox that treadeth out thy corn;* and (Lev. xix. 19): *Thou shalt not make thy cattle to gender with beasts of any other kind.*

Obj. 9. Further, no distinction was made between clean and unclean plants. Much less therefore should any distinction have been made about the cultivation of plants. Therefore it was unfittingly prescribed (Lev. xix. 19): *Thou shalt not sow thy field with different seeds;* and (Deut. xxii. 9, *seq.*): *Thou shalt sow thy vineyard with divers seeds;* and: *Thou shalt not plough with an ox and an ass together.*

Obj. 10. Further, it is apparent that inanimate things are most of all subject to the power of man. Therefore it was unfitting to debar man from taking the silver and gold of which idols were made, or anything they found in the houses of idols, as expressed in the commandment of the Law (Deut. vii. 25, *seq.*). It also seems an absurd commandment set forth in Deut. xxiii. 13, that they should *dig round about and . . . cover with earth that which they were eased of.*

Obj. 11. Further, piety is required especially in priests. But it seems to be an act of piety to assist at the burial of one's friends: wherefore Tobias is commended for so doing (Tob. i. 20, *seqq.*). In like manner it is sometimes an act of piety to marry a loose woman, because she is thereby delivered from sin and infamy. Therefore it seems inconsistent for these things to be forbidden to priests (Lev. xxi).

On the contrary, It is written (Deut. xviii. 14): *But thou art otherwise instructed by the Lord thy God:* from which words we may gather that these observances were instituted by God to be a special prerogative of that people. Therefore they are not without reason or cause.

I answer that, The Jewish people, as stated above (A. 5), were specially chosen for the worship of God, and among them the priests themselves were specially set apart for that purpose. And just as other things that are applied to the divine worship, need to be marked in some particular way so that they be worthy of the worship of God; so too in that people's, and specially the priests', mode of life, there needed to be certain special things befitting the divine worship, whether spiritual or corporal. Now the worship prescribed by the Law foreshadowed the mystery of Christ: so that whatever they did was a figure of things pertaining to Christ, according to 1 Cor. x. 11: *All these things happened to them in figures.* Consequently the reasons for these observances may be taken in two ways, first according to their fittingness to the worship of God; secondly, according as they foreshadow something touching the Christian mode of life.

Reply Obj. 1. As stated above (A. 5 ad 4, 5), the Law distinguished a twofold pollution or uncleanness; one, that of sin, whereby the soul was defiled; and another consisting in some kind of corruption, whereby the body was in some way infected. Speaking then of the first-mentioned uncleanness, no kind of food is unclean, or can defile a man, by reason of its nature; wherefore we read (Matth. xv. 11): *Not that which goeth into the mouth defileth a man; but what cometh out of the mouth, this defileth a man:* which words are explained (verse 17) as referring to sins. Yet certain foods can defile the soul accidentally; in so far as man partakes of them against obedience or a vow, or from excessive concupiscence; or through their being an incentive to lust, for which reason some refrain from wine and flesh-meat.

If, however, we speak of bodily uncleanness, consisting in some kind of corruption, the flesh of certain animals is unclean, either because like the pig they feed on unclean things; or because their life is among unclean surroundings: thus certain animals, like moles and mice and such like, live underground, whence they contract a certain unpleasant smell; or because their flesh, through being too moist or too dry, engenders corrupt humors in the human body. Hence they were forbidden to eat the flesh of flat-footed animals, i.e., animals having an uncloven hoof, on account of their earthiness; and in like manner they were forbidden to eat the flesh of animals that have many clefts in their feet, because such are very fierce and their flesh is very dry, such as the flesh of lions and the like. For the same reason they were forbidden to eat certain birds of prey the flesh of which is very dry, and certain water-fowl on account of their exceeding humidity. In like manner certain fish lacking fins and scales were prohibited on account of their excessive moisture; such as eels and the like. They were, however, allowed to eat ruminants and animals with a divided hoof, because in such animals the humors are well absorbed, and their nature well balanced: for neither are they too moist, as is indicated by the hoof; nor are they too earthy, which is shown by their having not a flat but a cloven hoof. Of fishes they were allowed to partake of the drier kinds, of which the fins and scales are an indication, because thereby the moist nature of the fish is tempered. Of birds they were allowed to eat the tamer kinds, such as hens, partridges, and the like.—Another reason was detestation of idolatry: because the Gentiles, and especially the Egyptians, among whom they had grown up, offered up these forbidden animals to their idols, or employed them for the purpose of sorcery: whereas they did not eat those animals which the Jews were allowed to eat, but worshipped them as gods, or abstained, for some other motive, from eating them, as stated above (A. 3 ad 2). The third reason was to prevent excessive care about food: wherefore they were allowed to eat those animals which could be procured easily and promptly.

With regard to blood and fat, they were forbidden to partake of those of any animal whatever without exception. Blood was forbidden, both in order to avoid cruelty, that they might abhor the shedding of human blood, as stated above (A. 3 ad 8); and in order to shun the idolatrous rite whereby it was customary for men to collect the blood and to gather together around it for a banquet in honor of the idols, to whom they held the blood to be most acceptable. Hence the Lord commanded the blood to be poured out and to be covered with earth (Lev. xvii. 13).—For the same reason they were forbidden to eat animals that had been suffocated or strangled: because the blood of these animals would not be separated from the body: or because this form of death is very painful to the victim; and the Lord wished to withdraw them from cruelty even in regard to irrational animals, so as to be less inclined to be cruel to other men, through being used to be kind to beasts. They were forbidden to eat the fat: both because idolaters ate it in honor of their gods; and because it used to be burnt in honor of God; and, again, because blood and fat are not nutritious, which is the cause assigned by Rabbi Moses (Doct. Perplex. iii).—The reason why they were forbidden to eat the sinews

is given in Gen. xxxii. 32, where it is stated that the children of Israel . . . eat not the sinew . . . because he touched the sinew of Jacob's thigh and it shrank.

The figurative reason for these things is that all these animals signified certain sins, in token of which those animals were prohibited. Hence Augustine says (Contra Faustum vi. 7): If the swine and lamb be called in question, both are clean by nature, because all God's creatures are good: yet the lamb is clean, and the pig is unclean in a certain signication. Thus if you speak of a foolish, and of a wise man, each of these expressions is clean considered in the nature of the sound, letters and syllables of which it is composed: but in signification, the one is clean, the other unclean. The animal that chews the cud and has a divided hoof, is clean in signification. Because division of the hoof is a figure of the two Testaments: or of the Father and Son: or of the two natures in Christ: of the distinction of good and evil. While chewing the cud signifies meditation on the Scriptures and a sound understanding thereof; and whoever lacks either of these is spiritually unclean.—In like manner those fish that have scales and fins are clean in signification. Because fins signify the heavenly or contemplative life; while scales signify a life of trials, each of which is required for spiritual cleanness.—Of birds certain kinds were forbidden. In the eagle which flies at a great height, pride is forbidden: in the griffon which is hostile to horses and men, cruelty of powerful men is prohibited. The osprey, which feeds on very small birds, signifies those who oppress the poor. The kite, which is full of cunning, denotes those who are fraudulent in their dealings. The vulture, which follows an army, expecting to feed on the carcases of the slain, signifies those who like others to die or to fight among themselves that they may gain thereby. Birds of the raven kind signify those who are blackened by their lusts; or those who lack kindly feelings, for the raven did not return when once it had been let loose from the ark. The ostrich which, though a bird, cannot fly, and is always on the ground, signifies those who fight for God's cause, and at the same time are taken up with worldly business. The owl which sees clearly at night, but cannot see in the daytime, denotes those who are clever in temporal affairs, but dull in spiritual matters. The gull, which both flies in the air and swims in the water, signifies those who are partial both to Circumcision and to Baptism: or else it denotes those who would fly by contemplation, yet dwell in the waters of sensual delights. The hawk, which helps men to seize the prey, is a figure of those who assist the strong to prey on the poor. The screech-owl, which seeks its food by night but hides by day, signifies the lustful man who seeks to lie hidden in his deeds of darkness. The cormorant, so constituted that it can stay a long time under water, denotes the glutton who plunges into the waters of pleasure. The ibis is an African bird with a long beak, and feeds on snakes; and perhaps it is the same as the stork: it signifies the envious man, who refreshes himself with the ills of others, as with snakes. The swan is bright in color, and by the aid of its long neck extracts its food from deep places on land or water: it may denote those who seek earthly profit through an external brightness of virtue. The bittern is a bird of the East: it has a long beak, and its jaws are furnished with follicules, wherein it stores its food at first, after a time proceeding to digest it: it is a figure of the miser, who is excessively careful in hoarding up the necessities of life. The coot* has this peculiarity apart from other birds, that it has a webbed foot for swimming, and a cloven foot for walking: for it swims like a duck in the water, and walks like a partridge on land: it drinks only when it bites, since it dips all its food in water: it is a figure of a man who will not take advice, and does nothing but what is soaked in the water of his own will. The heron,† commonly called a falcon, signifies those whose *feet are swift to shed blood* (Ps. xiii. 3). The plover,‡ which is a garrulous bird, signifies the gossip. The hoopoe, which builds its nest on dung, feeds on fœtid ordure, and whose song is like a groan, denotes worldly grief which works death in those who are unclean. The bat, which flies near the ground, signifies those who being gifted with worldly knowledge, seek none but earthly things.—Of fowls and quadrupeds those alone were permitted which have the hind-legs longer than the forelegs, so that they can leap: whereas those were forbidden which cling rather to the earth: because those who abuse the doctrine of the four Evangelists, so that they are not lifted up thereby, are reputed unclean.—By the prohibition of blood, fat and nerves, we are to understand the forbidding of cruelty, lust, and bravery in committing sin.

Reply Obj. 2. Men were wont to eat plants and other products of the soil even before the deluge: but the eating of flesh seems to have been introduced after the deluge; for it is written (Gen. ix. 3): *Even as the green herbs have I delivered . . . all* flesh *to you.* The rea-

son for this was that the eating of the products of the soil savors rather of a simple life; whereas the eating of flesh savors of delicate and over-careful living. For the soil gives birth to the herb of its own accord; and such like products of the earth may be had in great quantities with very little effort: whereas no small trouble is necessary either to rear or to catch an animal. Consequently God being wishful to bring His people back to a more simple way of living, forbade them to eat many kinds of animals, but not those things that are produced by the soil.—Another reason may be that animals were offered to idols, while the products of the soil were not.

The Reply to the Third Objection is clear from what has been said (*ad* 1).

Reply Obj. 4. Although the kid that is slain has no perception of the manner in which its flesh is cooked, yet it would seem to savor of heartlessness if the dam's milk, which was intended for the nourishment of her offspring, were served up on the same dish.—It might also be said that the Gentiles in celebrating the feasts of their idols prepared the flesh of kids in this manner, for the purpose of sacrifice or banquet: hence (Exod. xxiii) after the solemnities to be celebrated under the Law had been foretold, it is added: *Thou shalt not boil a kid in the milk of its dam.* The figurative reason for this prohibition is this:—the kid, signifying Christ, on account of *the likeness of sinful flesh* (Rom. viii. 3), was not to be seethed, i.e., slain, by the Jews, *in the milk of its dam,* i.e., during His infancy.—Or else it signifies that the kid, i.e., the sinner, should not be boiled in the milk of its dam, i.e., should not be cajoled by flattery.

Reply Obj. 5. The Gentiles offered their gods the first-fruits, which they held to bring them good luck: or they burnt them for the purpose of sorcery. Consequently (the Israelites) were commanded to look upon the fruits of the first three years as unclean: for in that country nearly all trees bear fruit in three years' time; those trees, to wit, that are cultivated either from seed, or from a graft, or from a cutting: but it seldom happens that the fruit-stones or seeds encased in a pod are sown: since it would take a longer time for these to bear fruit: and the Law considered what happened most frequently. The fruits, however, of the fourth year, as being the firstlings of clean fruits, were offered to God: and from the fifth year onward they were eaten.

The figurative reason was that this fore-

---

* Douay,—*porphyrion.* St. Thomas's description tallies with the coot or moorhen: though of course he is mistaken about the feet differing from one another.

† Vulg.—*herodionem.*

‡ Here, again, the Douay translators transcribed from the Vulgate,—*charadrion; charadrius* is the generic name for all plovers.

shadowed the fact that after the three states of the Law (the first lasting from Abraham to David, the second, until they were carried away to Babylon, the third until the time of Christ), the Fruit of the Law, i.e., Christ, was to be offered to God.—Or again, that we should mistrust our first efforts, on account of their imperfection.

Reply Obj. 6. It is said of a man in Ecclus. xix. 27, that *the attire of the body . . . shows what he is.* Hence the Lord wished His people to be distinguished from other nations, not only by the sign of circumcision, which was in the flesh, but also by a certain difference of attire. Wherefore they were forbidden to wear garments woven of woolen and linen together, and for a woman to be clothed with man's apparel, or *vice versa,* for two reasons. First, to avoid idolatrous worship. Because the Gentiles, in their religious rites, used garments of this sort, made of various materials. Moreover in the worship of Mars, women put on men's armor; while, conversely, in the worship of Venus men donned women's attire.— The second reason was to preserve them from lust: because the employment of various materials in the making of garments signified inordinate union of sexes, while the use of male attire by a woman, or *vice versa,* has an incentive to evil desires, and offers an occasion of lust. The figurative reason is that the prohibition of wearing a garment woven of woolen and linen signified that it was forbidden to unite the simplicity of innocence, denoted by wool, with the duplicity of malice, betokened by linen.—It also signifies that woman is forbidden to presume to teach, or perform other duties of men: or that man should not adopt the effeminate manners of a woman.

Reply Obj. 7. As Jerome says on Matth. xxiii. 6, *the Lord commanded them to make violet-colored fringes in the four corners of their garments, so that the Israelites might be distinguished from other nations.* Hence, in this way, they professed to be Jews: and consequently the very sight of this sign reminded them of their law.

When we read: *Thou shalt bind them on thy hand, and they shall be ever before thy eyes* (Vulg.,—*they shall be and shall move between thy eyes*),—*the Pharisees gave a false interpretation to these words, and wrote the decalogue of Moses on a parchment, and tied it on their foreheads like a wreath, so that it moved in front of their eyes:* whereas the intention of the Lord in giving this commandment was that they should be bound in their hands, i.e., in their works; and that they should be before their eyes, i.e., in their thoughts. The violet-colored fillets which were inserted in

their cloaks signify the godly intention which should accompany our every deed.—It may, however, be said that, because they were a carnal-minded and stiff-necked people, it was necessary for them to be stirred by these sensible things to the observance of the Law.

Reply Obj. 8. Affection in man is twofold: It may be an affection of reason, or it may be an affection of passion. If a man's affection be one of reason, it matters not how man behaves to animals, because God has subjected all things to man's power, according to Ps. viii. 8: *Thou hast subjected all things under his feet:* and it is in this sense that the Apostle says that *God has no care for oxen;* because God does not ask of man what he does with oxen or other animals.

But if man's affection be one of passion, then it is moved also in regard to other animals: for since the passion of pity is caused by the afflictions of others; and since it happens that even irrational animals are sensible to pain, it is possible for the affection of pity to arise in a man with regard to the sufferings of animals. Now it is evident that if a man practice a pitiful affection for animals, he is all the more disposed to take pity on his fellow-men: wherefore it is written (Prov. xii. 10): *The just regardeth the lives of his beasts: but the bowels of the wicked are cruel.* Consequently the Lord, in order to inculcate pity to the Jewish people, who were prone to cruelty, wished them to practice pity even with regard to dumb animals, and forbade them to do certain things savoring of cruelty to animals. Hence He prohibited them to *boil a kid in the milk of its dam,* and to *muzzle the ox that treadeth out the corn;* and to slay *the dam with her young.* It may, nevertheless, be also said that these prohibitions were made in hatred of idolatry. For the Egyptians held it to be wicked to allow the ox to eat of the grain while threshing the corn. Moreover certain sorcerers were wont to ensnare the mother bird with her young during incubation, and to employ them for the purpose of securing fruitfulness and good luck in bringing up children:—also because it was held to be a good omen to find the mother sitting on her young.

As to the mingling of animals of divers species, the literal reason may have been threefold. The first was to show detestation for the idolatry of the Egyptians, who employed various mixtures in worshipping the planets, which produce various effects, and on various kinds of things according to their various conjunctions.—The second reason was in condemnation of unnatural sins.—The third reason was the entire removal of all occasions of concupiscence. Because animals of different species do not easily breed, unless this be brought about by man; and movements of lust are aroused by seeing such things. Wherefore in the Jewish traditions we find it prescribed, as stated by Rabbi Moses, that men shall turn away their eyes from such sights.

The figurative reason for these things is that the necessities of life should not be withdrawn from the ox that treadeth the corn, i.e., from the preacher bearing the sheaves of doctrine, as the Apostle states (1 Cor. ix. 4, *seqq.*).—Again, we should not take the dam with her young: because in certain things we have to keep the spiritual senses, i.e., the offspring, and set aside the observance of the letter, i.e., the mother, for instance, in all the ceremonies of the Law. It is also forbidden that beasts of burden, i.e., any of the common people, should be allowed to engender, i.e., to have any connection, with animals of another kind, i.e., with Gentiles or Jews.

Reply Obj. 9. All these minglings were forbidden in agriculture; literally, in detestation of idolatry. For the Egyptians in worshipping the stars employed various combinations of seeds, animals and garments, in order to represent the various conjunctions of the stars.—Or else all these minglings were forbidden in detestation of the unnatural vice.

They have, however, a figurative reason. For the prohibition: *Thou shalt not sow thy field with different seeds*, is to be understood, in the spiritual sense, of the prohibition to sow strange doctrine in the Church, which is a spiritual vineyard.—Likewise *the field*, i.e., the Church, must not be sown *with different seeds*, i.e., with Catholic and heretical doctrines.—Neither is it allowed to plough *with an ox and an ass together;* thus a fool should not accompany a wise man in preaching, for one would hinder the other.

Reply Obj. 10.* Silver and gold were reasonably forbidden (Deut. vii) not as though they were not subject to the power of man, but because, like the idols themselves, all materials out of which idols were made, were anathematized as hateful in God's sight. This is clear from the same chapter, where we read further on (verse 26): *Neither shalt thou bring anything of the idol into thy house, lest thou become an anathema, like it.* Another reason was lest, by taking silver and gold, they should be led by avarice into idolatry to which the Jews were inclined. The other precept (Deut. xxiii) about covering up excretions, was just and becoming, both for the sake of bodily cleanliness; and in order to keep the air wholesome; and by reason of the respect due to the tabernacle of the covenant which stood in the midst of the camp, wherein the Lord was said to dwell; as is clearly set forth in the same passage, where after

expressing the command, the reason thereof is at once added, to wit: *For the Lord thy God walketh in the midst of thy camp, to deliver thee, and to give up thy enemies to thee, and let thy camp be holy (i.e.,* clean), *and let no uncleanness appear therein.* The figurative reason for this precept, according to Gregory (*Moral.* xxxi), is that sins which are the fetid excretions of the mind should be covered over by repentance, that we may become acceptable to God, according to Ps. xxxi. 1: *Blessed are they whose iniquities are forgiven and whose sins are covered.* Or else according to a gloss, that we should recognize the unhappy condition of human nature, and humbly cover and purify the stains of a puffed-up and proud spirit in the deep furrow of self-examination.

Reply Obj. 11. Sorcerers and idolatrous priests made use, in their rites, of the bones and flesh of dead men. Wherefore, in order to extirpate the customs of idolatrous worship, the Lord commanded that the priests of inferior degree, who at fixed times served in the temple, should not *incur an uncleanness at the death* of anyone except of those who were closely related to them, viz., their father or mother, and others thus near of kin to them. But the high-priest had always to be ready for the service of the sanctuary; wherefore he was absolutely forbidden to approach the dead, however nearly related to him.—They were also forbidden to marry *a harlot* or *one that has been put away,* or any other than a virgin: both on account of the reverence due to the priesthood, the honor of which would seem to be tarnished by such a marriage: and for the sake of the children who would be disgraced by the mother's shame: which was most of all to be avoided when the priestly dignity was passed on from father to son.—Again, they were commanded to shave neither head nor beard, and not to make incisions in their flesh, in order to exclude the rites of idolatry. For the priests of the Gentiles shaved both head and beard, wherefore it is written (Baruch vi. 30): *Priests sit in their temples having their garments rent, and their heads and beards shaven.* Moreover, in worshipping their idols *they cut themselves with knives and lancets* (3 Kings xviii. 28). For this reason the priests of the Old Law were commanded to do the contrary.

The spiritual reason for these things is that priests should be entirely free from dead works, i.e., sins. And they should not shave their heads, i.e., set wisdom aside; nor should they shave their beards, i.e., set aside the perfection of wisdom; nor rend their garments or cut their flesh, i.e., they should not incur the sin of schism.

* The Reply to the Tenth Objection is lacking in the codices. The solution given here is found in some editions, and was supplied by Nicolai.

QUESTION 103

Of the Duration of the Ceremonial Precepts

(In Four Articles)

WE must now consider the duration of the ceremonial precepts: under which head there are four points of inquiry: (1) Whether the ceremonial precepts were in existence before the Law? (2) Whether at the time of the Law the ceremonies of the Old Law had any power of justification? (3) Whether they ceased at the coming of Christ? (4) Whether it is a mortal sin to observe them after the coming of Christ?

FIRST ARTICLE

Whether the Ceremonies of the Law Were in Existence before the Law?

We proceed thus to the First Article:—

Objection 1. It would seem that the ceremonies of the Law were in existence before the Law. For sacrifices and holocausts were ceremonies of the Old Law, as stated above (Q. 101, A. 4). But sacrifices and holocausts preceded the Law: for it is written (Gen. iv. 3, 4) that *Cain offered, of the fruits of the earth, gifts to the Lord,* and that *Abel offered of the firstlings of his flock, and of their fat.* Noe also *offered holocausts* to the Lord (Gen. xviii. 20), and Abraham did in like manner (Gen. xxii. 13). Therefore the ceremonies of the Old Law preceded the Law.

Obj. 2. Further, the erecting and consecrating of the altar were part of the ceremonies relating to holy things. But these preceded the Law. For we read (Gen. xiii. 18) that *Abraham . . . built . . . an altar to the Lord;* and (Gen. xxviii. 18) that *Jacob . . . took the stone . . . and set it up for a title, pouring oil upon the top of it.* Therefore the legal ceremonies preceded the Law.

Obj. 3. Further, the first of the legal sacraments seems to have been circumcision. But circumcision preceded the Law, as appears from Gen. xvii. In like manner the priesthood preceded the Law; for it is written (Gen. xiv. 18) that *Melchisedech . . . was the priest of the most high God.* Therefore the sacramental ceremonies preceded the Law.

Obj. 4. Further the distinction of clean from unclean animals belongs to the ceremonies of observances, as stated above (Q. 100, 2, A. 6 *ad* 1). But this distinction preceded the Law; for it is written (Gen. vii. 2, 3): *Of all clean beasts take seven and seven . . . but of the beasts that are unclean, two and two.*

Therefore the legal ceremonies preceded the Law.

On the contrary, It is written (Deut. vi. 1): *These are the precepts, and ceremonies . . . which the Lord your God commanded that I should teach you.* But they would not have needed to be taught about these things, if the aforesaid ceremonies had been already in existence. Therefore the legal ceremonies did not precede the Law.

I answer that, As is clear from what has been said (Q. 101, A. 2; Q. 102, A. 2), the legal ceremonies were ordained for a double purpose; the worship of God, and the foreshadowing of Christ. Now whoever worships God must needs worship Him by means of certain fixed things pertaining to external worship. But the fixing of the divine worship belongs to the ceremonies; just as the determining of our relations with our neighbor is a matter determined by the judicial precepts, as stated above (Q. 99, A. 4). Consequently, as among men in general there were certain judicial precepts, not indeed established by Divine authority, but ordained by human reason; so also there were some ceremonies fixed, not by the authority of any law, but according to the will and devotion of those that worship God. Since, however, even before the Law some of the leading men were gifted with the spirit of prophecy, it is to be believed that a heavenly instinct, like a private law, prompted them to worship God in a certain definite way, which would be both in keeping with the interior worship, and a suitable token of Christ's mysteries, which were foreshadowed also by other things that they did, according to 1 Cor. x. 11: *All . . . things happened to them in figure.* Therefore there were some ceremonies before the Law, but they were not legal ceremonies, because they were not as yet established by legislation.

Reply Obj. 1. The patriarchs offered up these oblations, sacrifices and holocausts previously to the Law, out of a certain devotion of their own will, according as it seemed proper to them to offer up in honor of God those things which they had received from Him, and thus to testify that they worshipped God Who is the beginning and end of all.

Reply Obj. 2. They also established certain sacred things, because they thought that the honor due to God demanded that certain places should be set apart from others for the purpose of divine worship.

Reply Obj. 3. The sacrament of circumcision was established by command of God before the Law. Hence it cannot be called a sacrament of the Law as though it were an institution of the Law, but only as an observance included in the Law. Hence Our Lord said (Jo. vii. 22) that circumcision was *not of Moses, but of his fathers.*—Again, among those who worshipped God, the priesthood was in existence before the Law by human appointment, for the Law allotted the priestly dignity to the firstborn.

Reply Obj. 4. The distinction of clean from unclean animals was in vogue before the Law, not with regard to eating them, since it is written (Gen. ix. 3): *Everything that moveth and liveth shall be meat for you:* but only as to the offering of sacrifices, because they used only certain animals for that purpose. If, however, they did make any distinction in regard to eating; it was not that it was considered illegal to eat such animals, since this was not forbidden by any law, but from dislike or custom: thus even now we see that certain foods are looked upon with disgust in some countries, while people partake of them in others.

SECOND ARTICLE

Whether, at the Time of the Law, the Ceremonies of the Old Law Had Any Power of Justification?

We proceed thus to the Second Article:—

Objection 1. It would seem that the ceremonies of the Old Law had the power of justification at the time of the Law. Because expiation from sin and consecration pertains to justification. But it is written (Exod. xxix. 21) that the priests and their apparel were consecrated by the sprinkling of blood and the anointing of oil; and (Levit. xvi. 16) that, by sprinkling the blood of the calf, the priest expiated *the sanctuary from the uncleanness of the children of Israel, and from their transgressions and . . . their sins.* Therefore the ceremonies of the Old Law had the power of justification.

Obj. 2. Further, that by which man pleases God pertains to justification, according to Ps. x. 8: *The Lord is just and hath loved justice.* But some pleased God by means of ceremonies, according to Levit. x. 19: *How could I . . . please the Lord in the ceremonies, having a sorrowful heart?* Therefore the ceremonies of the Old Law had the power of justification.

Obj. 3. Further, things relating to the divine worship regard the soul rather than the body, according to Ps. xviii. 8: *The Law of the Lord is unspotted, converting souls.* But the leper was cleansed by means of the ceremonies of the Old Law, as stated in Lev. xiv. Much more therefore could the ceremonies of the Old Law cleanse the soul by justifying it.

On the contrary, The Apostle says (Gal. ii)*: If there had been a law given which could justify* (Vulg.,—*give life*), *Christ died in vain,* i.e., without cause. But this is inadmissible. Therefore the ceremonies of the Old Law did not confer justice.

I answer that, As stated above (Q. 102, A. 5 ad 4), a two-fold uncleanness was distinguished in the Old Law. One was spiritual and is the uncleanness of sin. The other was corporal, which rendered a man unfit for divine worship; thus a leper, or anyone that touched carrion, was said to be unclean: and thus uncleanness was nothing but a kind of irregularity. From this uncleanness, then, the ceremonies of the Old Law had the power to cleanse: because they were ordered by the Law to be employed as remedies for the removal of the aforesaid uncleannesses which were contracted in consequence of the prescription of the Law. Hence the Apostle says (Heb. ix. 13) that *the blood of goats and of oxen, and the ashes of a heifer, being sprinkled, sanctify such as are defiled, to the cleansing of the flesh.* And just as this uncleanness which was washed away by such like ceremonies, affected the flesh rather than the soul, so also the ceremonies themselves are called by the Apostle shortly before (verse 10) justices of the flesh: *justices of the flesh,* says he, *being laid on them until the time of correction.*

On the other hand, they had no power of cleansing from uncleanness of the soul, i.e., from the uncleanness of sin. The reason of this was that at no time could there be expiation from sin, except through Christ, *Who taketh away the sins* (Vulg.,—*sin*) *of the world* (Jo. i. 29). And since the mystery of Christ's Incarnation and Passion had not yet really taken place, those ceremonies of the Old Law could not really contain in themselves a power flowing from Christ already incarnate and crucified, such as the sacraments of the New Law contain. Consequently they could not cleanse from sin: thus the Apostle says (Heb. x. 4) that *it is impossible that with the blood of oxen and goats sin should be taken away;* and for this reason he calls them (Gal. iv. 9) *weak and needy elements:* weak indeed, because they cannot take away sin; but this weakness results from their being needy, i.e., from the fact that they do not contain grace within themselves.

---

* The first words of the quotation are from iii. 21: St. Thomas probably quoting from memory, substituted them for ii. 21, which runs thus: *If justice be by the Law, then Christ died in vain.*

However, it was possible at the time of the Law, for the minds of the faithful, to be united by faith to Christ incarnate and crucified; so that they were justified by faith in Christ: of which faith the observance of these ceremonies was a sort of profession, inasmuch as they foreshadowed Christ. Hence in the Old Law certain sacrifices were offered up for sins, not as though the sacrifices themselves washed sins away, but because they were professions of faith which cleansed from sin. In fact, the Law itself implies this in the terms employed: for it is written (Lev. iv. 26, v. 16) that in offering the sacrifice for sin *the priest shall pray for him . . . and it shall be forgiven him,* as though the sin were forgiven, not in virtue of the sacrifices, but through the faith and devotion of those who offered them.—It must be observed, however, that the very fact that the ceremonies of the Old Law washed away uncleanness of the body, was a figure of that expiation from sins which was effected by Christ.

It is therefore evident that under the state of the Old Law the ceremonies had no power of justification.

Reply Obj. 1. That sanctification of priests and their sons, and of their apparel or of anything else belonging to them, by sprinkling them with blood, had no other effect but to appoint them to the divine worship, and to remove impediments from them, *to the cleansing of the flesh,* as the Apostle states (Heb. ix. 13), in token of that sanctification whereby *Jesus* sanctified *the people by His own blood (ibid.* xiii. 12).—Moreover, the expiation must be understood as referring to the removal of these bodily uncleannesses, not to the forgiveness of sin. Hence even the sanctuary which could not be the subject of sin is stated to be expiated.

Reply Obj. 2. The priests pleased God in the ceremonies by their obedience and devotion, and by their faith in the reality foreshadowed; not by reason of the things considered in themselves.

Reply Obj. 3. Those ceremonies which were prescribed in the cleansing of a leper, were not ordained for the purpose of taking away the defilement of leprosy. This is clear from the fact that these ceremonies were not applied to a man until he was already healed: hence it is written (Lev. xiv, 3, 4) that the priest, *going out of the camp, when he shall find that the leprosy is cleansed, shall command him that is to be purified to offer,* etc.; whence it is evident that the priest was appointed the judge of leprosy, not before, but after cleansing. But these ceremonies were employed for the purpose of taking away the uncleanness of irregularity.—They do say, however, that if a priest were to err in his judgment, the leper would be cleansed miraculously by the power of God, but not in virtue of the sacrifice. Thus also it was by miracle that the thigh of the adulterous woman rotted, when she had drunk the water *on which* the priest had *heaped curses,* as stated in Num. v. 19-27.

THIRD ARTICLE

Whether the Ceremonies of the Old Law Ceased at the Coming of Christ?

We proceed thus to the Third Article:—

Objection 1. It would seem that the ceremonies of the Old Law did not cease at the coming of Christ. For it is written (Baruch iv. 1): *This is the book of the commandments of God, and the law that is for ever.* But the legal ceremonies were part of the Law. Therefore the legal ceremonies were to last for ever.

Obj. 2. Further, the offering made by a leper after being cleansed was a ceremony of the Law. But the Gospel commands the leper, who has been cleansed, to make this offering (Matth. viii. 4). Therefore the ceremonies of the Old Law did not cease at Christ's coming.

Obj. 3. Further, as long as the cause remains, the effect remains. But the ceremonies of the Old Law had certain reasonable causes, inasmuch as they were ordained to the worship of God, besides the fact that they were intended to be figures of Christ. Therefore the ceremonies of the Old Law should not have ceased.

Obj. 4. Further, circumcision was instituted as a sign of Abraham's faith: the observance of the sabbath, to recall the blessing of creation: and other solemnities, in memory of other Divine favors, as stated above (Q. 102, A. 4 *ad* 10; A. 5 *ad* 1). But Abraham's faith is ever to be imitated even by us: and the blessing of creation and other Divine favors should never be forgotten. Therefore at least circumcision and the other legal solemnities should not have ceased.

On the contrary, The Apostle says (Coloss. ii. 16, 17): *Let no man . . . judge you in meat or in drink, or in respect of a festival day, or of the new moon, or of the sabbaths, which are a shadow of things to come:* and (Heb. viii. 13): *In saying a new (testament), he hath made the former old: and that which decayeth and groweth old, is near its end.*

I answer that, All the ceremonial precepts of the Old Law were ordained to the worship of God, as stated above (Q. 101, AA. 1, 2). Now external worship should be in proportion to the internal worship, which consists in faith, hope, and charity. Consequently exterior worship had to be subject to variations according to the variations in the internal worship, in which a threefold state may be distinguished. One state was in respect of faith and hope, both in heavenly goods, and in the means of obtaining them,—in both of these considered as things to come. Such was the state of faith and hope in the Old Law.—Another state of the interior worship is that in which we have faith and hope in heavenly goods as things to come; but in the means of obtaining heavenly goods, as in things present or past. Such is the state of the New Law.—The third state is that in which both are possessed as present; wherein nothing is believed in as lacking, nothing hoped for as being yet to come. Such is the state of the Blessed.

In this state of the Blessed, then, nothing in regard to the worship of God will be figurative; there will be naught but *thanksgiving and voice of praise* (Isa. li. 3). Hence it is written concerning the city of the Blessed (Apoc. xxi. 22): *I saw no temple therein: for the Lord God Almighty is the temple thereof, and the Lamb.* Proportionately, therefore, the ceremonies of the first-mentioned state which fore-shadowed the second and third states, had need to cease at the advent of the second state; and other ceremonies had to be introduced which would be in keeping with the state of divine worship for that particular time, wherein heavenly goods are a thing of the future, but the Divine favors whereby we obtain the heavenly boons are a thing of the present.

Reply Obj. 1. The Old Law is said to be *for ever* simply and absolutely, as regards its moral precepts; but as regards the ceremonial precepts it lasts for ever in respect of the reality which those ceremonies foreshadowed.

Reply Obj. 2. The mystery of the redemption of the human race was fulfilled in Christ's Passion: hence Our Lord said then: *It is consummated* (Jo. xix. 30). Consequently the prescriptions of the Law must have ceased then altogether through their reality being fulfilled. As a sign of this, we read that at the Passion of Christ *the veil of the temple was rent* (Matth. xxvii. 51). Hence, before Christ's Passion, while Christ was preaching and working miracles, the Law and the Gospel were concurrent, since the mystery of Christ had already begun, but was not as yet consummated. And for this reason Our Lord, before His Passion, commanded the leper to observe the legal ceremonies.

Reply Obj. 3. The literal reasons already given (Q. 102) for the ceremonies refer to the divine worship, which was founded on faith in that which was to come. Hence, at the advent of Him Who was to come, both that worship ceased, and all the reasons referring thereto.

Reply Obj. 4. The faith of Abraham was commended in that he believed in God's promise concerning his seed to come, in which all nations were to be blessed. Wherefore, as long as this seed was yet to come, it was necessary to make profession of Abraham's faith by means of circumcision. But now that it is consummated, the same thing needs to be declared by means of another sign, viz., Baptism, which, in this respect, took the place of circumcision, according to the saying of the Apostle (Coloss. ii. 11, 12): *You are circumcised with circumcision not made by hand, in despoiling of the body of the flesh, but in the circumcision of Christ, buried with Him in Baptism.*

As to the sabbath, which was a sign recalling the first creation, its place is taken by the *Lord's Day*, which recalls the beginning of the new creature in the Resurrection of Christ.—In like manner other solemnities of the Old Law are supplanted by new solemnities: because the blessings vouchsafed to that people, foreshadowed the favors granted us by Christ. Hence the feast of the Passover gave place to the feast of Christ's Passion and Resurrection: the feast of Pentecost when the Old Law was given, to the feast of Pentecost on which was given the Law of the living spirit: the feast of the New Moon, to Lady Day, when appeared the first rays of the sun, i.e., Christ, by the fulness of grace: the feast of Trumpets, to the feasts of the Apostles: the feast of Expiation, to the feasts of Martyrs and Confessors: the feast of Tabernacles, to the feast of the Church Dedication: the feast of the Assembly and Collection, to feast of the Angels, or else to the feast of All Hallows.

FOURTH ARTICLE

Whether Since Christ's Passion the Legal Ceremonies Can Be Observed without Committing Mortal Sin?

We proceed thus to the Fourth Article:—

Objection 1. It would seem that since Christ's Passion the legal ceremonies can be observed without committing mortal sin. For we must not believe that the apostles committed mortal sin after receiving the Holy Ghost: since by His fulness they were *endued with power from on high* (Luke xxiv. 49). But the apostles observed the legal ceremonies after the coming of the Holy Ghost: for it is stated (Acts xvi. 3) that Paul circumcised Timothy: and (Acts xxi. 26) that Paul, at the advice of James, *took the men, and . . . being purified with them, entered into the temple, giving notice of the accomplishment of the days of purification, until an oblation should be offered for every one of them.* Therefore the legal ceremonies can be observed since the

Passion of Christ without committing mortal sin.

Obj. 2. Further, one of the legal ceremonies consisted in shunning the fellowship of Gentiles. But the first Pastor of the Church complied with this observance; for it is stated (Gal. ii. 12) that, *when* certain men *had come* to Antioch, Peter *withdrew and separated himself* from the Gentiles. Therefore the legal ceremonies can be observed since Christ's Passion without committing mortal sin.

Obj. 3. Further, the commands of the apostles did not lead men into sin. But it was commanded by apostolic decree that the Gentiles should observe certain ceremonies of the Law: for it is written (Acts xv. 28, 29): *It hath seemed good to the Holy Ghost and to us, to lay no further burden upon you than these necessary things: that you abstain from things sacrificed to idols, and from blood, and from things strangled, and from fornication.* Therefore the legal ceremonies can be observed since Christ's Passion without committing mortal sin.

On the contrary, The Apostle says (Gal. v. 2): *If you be circumcised, Christ shall profit you nothing.* But nothing save mortal sin hinders us from receiving Christ's fruit. Therefore since Christ's Passion it is a mortal sin to be circumcised, or to observe the other legal ceremonies.

I answer that, All ceremonies are professions of faith, in which the interior worship of God consists. Now man can make profession of his inward faith, by deeds as well as by words: and in either profession, if he make a false declaration, he sins mortally. Now, though our faith in Christ is the same as that of the fathers of old; yet, since they came before Christ, whereas we come after Him, the same faith is expressed in different words, by us and by them. For by them was it said: *Behold a virgin shall conceive and bear a son,* where the verbs are in the future tense: whereas we express the same by means of verbs in the past tense, and say that she *conceived and bore.* In like manner the ceremonies of the Old Law betokened Christ as having yet to be born and to suffer: whereas our sacraments signify Him as already born and having suffered. Consequently, just as it would be a mortal sin now for anyone, in making a profession of faith, to say that Christ is yet to be born, which the fathers of old said devoutly and truthfully; so too it would be a mortal sin now to observe those ceremonies which the fathers of old fulfilled with devotion and fidelity. Such is the teaching Augustine (*Contra Faust.* xix. 16), who says: *It is no longer promised that He shall be born, shall suffer and rise again, truths of which their sacra-*

ments were a kind of image: but it is declared that He is already born, has suffered and risen again; of which our sacraments, in which Christians share, are the actual representation.

Reply Obj. 1. On this point there seems to have been a difference of opinion between Jerome and Augustine. For Jerome (*Super Galat.* ii. 11, seq.) distinguished two periods of time. One was the time previous to Christ's Passion, during which the legal ceremonies were neither dead, since they were obligatory, and did expiate in their own fashion; nor deadly, because it was not sinful to observe them. But immediately after Christ's Passion they began to be not only dead, so as no longer to be either effectual or binding; but also deadly, so that whoever observed them was guilty of mortal sin. Hence he maintained that after the Passion the apostles never observed the legal ceremonies in real earnest; but only by a kind of pious pretense, lest, to wit, they should scandalize the Jews and hinder their conversion. This pretense, however, is to be understood, not as though they did not in reality perform those actions, but in the sense that they performed them without the mind to observe the ceremonies of the Law: thus a man might cut away his foreskin for health's sake, not with the intention of observing legal circumcision.

But since it seems unbecoming that the apostles, in order to avoid scandal, should have hidden things pertaining to the truth of life and doctrine, and that they should have made use of pretense, in things pertaining to the salvation of the faithful; therefore Augustine (*Epist.* lxxxii) more fittingly distinguished three periods of time. One was the time that preceded the Passion of Christ, during which the legal ceremonies were neither deadly nor dead: another period was after the publication of the Gospel, during which the legal ceremonies are both dead and deadly. The third is a middle period, viz., from the Passion of Christ until the publication of the Gospel, during which the legal ceremonies were dead indeed, because they had neither effect nor binding force; but were not deadly, because it was lawful for the Jewish converts to Christianity to observe them, provided they did not put their trust in them so as to hold them to be necessary unto salvation, as though faith in Christ could not justify without the legal observances. On the other hand, there was no reason why those who were converted from heathendom to Christianity should observe them. Hence Paul circumcised Timothy, who was born of a Jewish mother; but was unwilling to circumcise Titus, who was of heathen nationality.

The reason why the Holy Ghost did not

wish the converted Jews to be debarred at once from observing the legal ceremonies, while converted heathens were forbidden to observe the rites of heathendom, was in order to show that there is a difference between these rites. For heathenish ceremonial was rejected as absolutely unlawful, and as prohibited by God for all time; whereas the legal ceremonial ceased as being fulfilled through Christ's Passion, being instituted by God as a figure of Christ.

Reply Obj. 2. According to Jerome, Peter withdrew himself from the Gentiles by pretense, in order to avoid giving scandal to the Jews, of whom he was the Apostle. Hence he did not sin at all in acting thus. On the other hand, Paul in like manner made a pretense of blaming him, in order to avoid scandalizing the Gentiles, whose Apostle he was.—But Augustine disapproves of this solution: because in the canonical Scripture (viz., Gal. ii. 11), wherein we must not hold anything to be false, Paul says that Peter *was to be blamed.* Consequently it is true that Peter was at fault: and Paul blamed him in very truth and not with pretense. Peter, however, did not sin, by observing the legal ceremonial for the time being; because this was lawful for him who was a converted Jew. But he did sin by excessive minuteness in the observance of the legal rites lest he should scandalize the Jews, the result being that he gave scandal to the Gentiles.

Reply Obj. 3. Some have held that this prohibition of the apostles is not to be taken literally, but spiritually: namely, that the prohibition of blood signifies the prohibition of murder; the prohibition of things strangled, that of violence and rapine; the prohibition of things offered to idols, that of idolatry; while fornication is forbidden as being evil in itself:

which opinion they gathered from certain glosses, which expound these prohibitions in a mystical sense.—Since, however, murder and rapine were held to be unlawful even by the Gentiles, there would have been no need to give this special commandment to those who were converted to Christ from heathendom. Hence others maintain that those foods were forbidden literally, not to prevent the observance of legal ceremonies, but in order to prevent gluttony. Thus Jerome says on Ezech. xliv. 31 (*The priest shall not eat of anything that is dead*): He condemns those priests who from gluttony did not keep these precepts.

But since certain foods are more delicate than these and more conducive to gluttony, there seems no reason why these should have been forbidden more than the others.

We must therefore follow the third opinion, and hold that these foods were forbidden literally, not with the purpose of enforcing compliance with the legal ceremonies, but in order to further the union of Gentiles and Jews living side by side. Because blood and things strangled were loathsome to the Jews by ancient custom; while the Jews might have suspected the Gentiles of relapse into idolatry if the latter had partaken of things offered to idols. Hence these things were prohibited for the time being, during which the Gentiles and Jews were to become united together. But as time went on, with the lapse of the cause, the effect lapsed also, when the truth of the Gospel teaching was divulged, wherein Our Lord taught that *not that which entereth into the mouth defileth a man* (Matth. xv. 11); and that *nothing is to be rejected that is received with thanksgiving* (1 Tim. iv. 4).—With regard to fornication a special prohibition was made, because the Gentiles did not hold it to be sinful.

QUESTION 104

Of the Judicial Precepts

(In Four Articles)

WE must now consider the judicial precepts: and first of all we shall consider them in general; in the second place we shall consider their reasons. Under the first head there are four points of inquiry: (1) What is meant by the judicial precepts? (2) Whether they are figurative? (3) Their duration. (4) Their division.

FIRST ARTICLE

Whether the Judicial Precepts Were Those Which Directed Man in Relation to His Neighbor?

We proceed thus to the First Article:—

Objection 1. It would seem that the judicial precepts were not those which directed man in his relations to his neighbor. For judicial precepts take their name from *judgment.* But there are many things that direct man as to his neighbor, which are not subordinate to judgment. Therefore the judicial precepts were not those which directed man in his relations to his neighbor.

Obj. 2. Further, the judicial precepts are distinct from the moral precepts, as stated above (Q. 99, A. 4). But there are many moral precepts which direct man as to his neighbor: as is evidently the case with the seven precepts of the second table. Therefore the judicial precepts are not so called from directing man as to his neighbor.

Obj. 3. Further, as the ceremonial precepts relate to God, so do the judicial precepts relate to one's neighbor, as stated above (Q. 99, A. 4; Q. 101, A. 1). But among the ceremonial precepts there are some which concern man himself, such as observances in matter of food and apparel, of which we have already spoken (Q. 102, A. 6 *ad* 1, 6). Therefore the judicial precepts are not so called from directing man as to his neighbor.

On the contrary, It is reckoned (Ezech. xviii. 8) among other works of a good and just man, that *he hath executed true judgment between man and man.* But judicial precepts are so called from *judgment.* Therefore it seems that the judicial precepts were those which directed the relations between man and man.

I answer that, As is evident from what we have stated above (Q. 95, A. 2; Q. 99, A. 4), in every law, some precepts derive their binding force from the dictate of reason itself, because natural reason dictates that something ought to be done or to be avoided. These are called *moral* precepts: since human morals are based on reason.—At the same time there are other precepts which derive their binding force, not from the very dictate of reason (because, considered in themselves, they do not imply an obligation of something due or undue); but from some institution, Divine or human: and such are certain determinations of the moral precepts. When therefore the moral precepts are fixed by Divine institution in matters relating to man's subordination to God, they are called *ceremonial* precepts: but when they refer to man's relations to other men, they are called *judicial* precepts. Hence there are two conditions attached to the judicial precepts: viz., first, that they refer to man's relations to other men; secondly, that they derive their binding force not from reason alone, but in virtue of their institution.

Reply Obj. 1. Judgments emanate through the official pronouncement of certain men who are at the head of affairs, and in whom the judicial power is vested. Now it belongs to those who are at the head of affairs to regulate not only litigious matters, but also voluntary contracts which are concluded between man and man, and whatever matters concern the community at large and the government thereof. Consequently the judicial precepts are not only those which concern actions at law; but also all those that are directed to the ordering of one man in relation to another, which ordering is subject to the direction of the sovereign as supreme judge.

Reply Obj. 2. This argument holds in respect of those precepts which direct man in his relations to his neighbor, and derive their binding force from the mere dictate of reason.

Reply Obj. 3. Even in those precepts which direct us to God, some are moral precepts, which the reason itself dictates when it is quickened by faith; such as that God is to be loved and worshipped. There are also ceremonial precepts, which have no binding force except in virtue of their Divine institution. Now God is concerned not only with the sacrifices that are offered to Him, but also with whatever relates to the fitness of those who offer sacrifices to Him and worship Him. Because men are ordained to God as to their end; wherefore it concerns God and, consequently, is a matter of ceremonial precept, that man should show some fitness for the divine worship. On the other hand, man is not ordained to his neighbor as to his end, so as to need to be disposed in himself with regard to his neighbor, for such is the relationship of a slave to his master, since a slave *is his master's in all that he is,* as the Philosopher says (*Polit.* i. 2). Hence there are no judicial precepts ordaining man in himself; all such precepts are moral: because the reason, which is the principal in moral matters, holds the same position, in man, with regard to things that concern him, as a prince or judge holds in the state.—Nevertheless we must take note that, since the relations of man to his neighbor are more subject to reason than the relations of man to God, there are more precepts whereby man is directed in his relations to his neighbor, than whereby he is directed to God. For the same reason there had to be more ceremonial than judicial precepts in the Law.

SECOND ARTICLE

Whether the Judicial Precepts Were Figurative?

We proceed thus to the Second Article:—

Objection 1. It would seem that the judicial precepts were not figurative. Because it seems proper to the ceremonial precepts to be instituted as figures of something else. Therefore, if the judicial precepts are figurative, there will be no difference between the judicial and ceremonial precepts.

Obj. 2. Further, just as certain judicial precepts were given to the Jewish people, so also were some given to other heathen peoples. But the judicial precepts given to other peoples were not figurative, but stated what had to be done. Therefore it seems that neither were the judicial precepts of the Old Law figures of anything.

Obj. 3. Further, those things which relate to the divine worship had to be taught under certain figures, because the things of God are above our reason, as stated above (Q. 101, A. 2, *ad* 2). But things concerning our neighbor are not above our reason. Therefore the judicial precepts which direct us in relation to our neighbor should not have been figurative.

On the contrary, The judicial precepts are expounded both in the allegorical and in the moral sense (Exod. xxi).

I answer that, A precept may be figurative in two ways. First, primarily and in itself: because, to wit, it is instituted principally that it may be the figure of something. In this way the ceremonial precepts are figurative; since they were instituted for the very purpose that they might foreshadow something relating to the worship of God and the mystery of Christ. —But some precepts are figurative, not primarily and in themselves, but consequently. In this way the judicial precepts of the Old Law are figurative. For they were not instituted for the purpose of being figurative, but in order that they might regulate the state of that people according to justice and equity. Nevertheless they did foreshadow something consequently: since, to wit, the entire state of that people, who were directed by these precepts, was figurative, according to 1 Cor. x. 11: *All . . . things happened to them in figure.*

Reply Obj. 1. The ceremonial precepts are not figurative in the same way as the judicial precepts, as explained above.

Reply Obj. 2. The Jewish people were chosen by God that Christ might be born of them. Consequently the entire state of that people had to be prophetic and figurative, as Augustine states (*Contra Faust.* xxii. 24). For this reason even the judicial precepts that were given to this people were more figurative than those which were given to other nations. Thus, too, the wars and deeds of this people are expounded in the mystical sense: but not the wars and deeds of the Assyrians or Romans, although the latter are more famous in the eyes of men.

Reply Obj. 3. In this people the direction of man in regard to his neighbor, considered in itself, was subject to reason. But in so far as it was referred to the worship of God, it was above reason: and in this respect it was figurative.

THIRD ARTICLE

Whether the Judicial Precepts of the Old Law Bind for Ever?

We proceed thus to the Third Article:—

Objection 1. It would seem that the judicial precepts of the Old Law bind for ever. Be-

cause the judicial precepts relate to the virtue of justice: since a judgment is an execution of the virtue of justice. Now *justice is perpetual and immortal* (Wis. i. 15). Therefore the judicial precepts bind for ever.

Obj. 2. Further, Divine institutions are more enduring than human institutions. But the judicial precepts of human laws bind for ever. Therefore much more do the judicial precepts of the Divine Law.

Obj. 3. Further, the Apostle says (Heb. vii. 18) that *there is a setting aside of the former commandment, because of the weakness and unprofitableness thereof.* Now this is true of the ceremonial precept, which *could* (Vulg.,—*can*) *not, as to the conscience, make him perfect that serveth only in meats and in drinks, and divers washings and justices of the flesh,* as the Apostle declares (Heb. ix. 9, 10). On the other hand, the judicial precepts were useful and efficacious in respect of the purpose for which they were instituted, viz., to establish justice and equity among men. Therefore the judicial precepts of the Old Law are not set aside, but still retain their efficacy.

On the contrary, The Apostle says (Heb. vii. 12) that *the priesthood being translated it is necessary that a translation also be made of the Law.* But the priesthood was transferred from Aaron to Christ. Therefore the entire Law was also transferred. Therefore the judicial precepts are no longer in force.

I answer that, The judicial precepts did not bind for ever, but were annulled by the coming of Christ: yet not in the same way as the ceremonial precepts. For the ceremonial precepts were annulled so far as to be not only *dead,* but also deadly to those who observe them since the coming of Christ, especially since the promulgation of the Gospel. On the other hand, the judicial precepts are dead indeed, because they have no binding force: but they are not deadly. For if a sovereign were to order these judicial precepts to be observed in his kingdom, he would not sin: unless perchance they were observed, or ordered to be observed, as though they derived their binding force through being institutions of the Old Law: for it would be a deadly sin to intend to observe them thus.

The reason for this difference may be gathered from what has been said above (A. 2). For it has been stated that the ceremonial precepts are figurative primarily and in themselves, as being instituted chiefly for the purpose of foreshadowing the mysteries of Christ to come.—On the other hand, the judicial precepts were not instituted that they might be figures, but that they might shape the state of that people who were directed to Christ

Consequently, when the state of that people changed with the coming of Christ, the judicial precepts lost their binding force: for the Law was a pedagogue, leading men to Christ, as stated in Gal. iii. 24. Since, however, these judicial precepts are instituted, not for the purpose of being figures, but for the performance of certain deeds, the observance thereof is not prejudicial to the truth of faith. But the intention of observing them, as though one were bound by the Law, is prejudicial to the truth of faith: because it would follow that the former state of the people still lasts, and that Christ has not yet come.

Reply Obj. 1. The obligation of observing justice is indeed perpetual. But the determination of those things that are just, according to human or Divine institution, must needs be different, according to the different states of mankind.

Reply Obj. 2. The judicial precepts established by men retain their binding force for ever, so long as the state of government remains the same. But if the state or nation pass to another form of government, the laws must needs be changed. For democracy, which is government by the people, demands different laws from those of oligarchy, which is government by the rich, as the Philosopher shows (*Polit.* iv. 1). Consequently when the state of that people changed, the judicial precepts had to be changed also.

Reply Obj. 3. Those judicial precepts directed the people to justice and equity, in keeping with the demands of that state. But after the coming of Christ, there had to be a change in the state of that people, so that in Christ there was no distinction between Gentile and Jew, as there had been before. For this reason the judicial precepts needed to be changed also.

FOURTH ARTICLE

Whether It Is Possible to Assign a Distinct Division of the Judicial Precepts?

We proceed thus to the Fourth Article:—

Objection 1. It would seem that it is impossible to assign a distinct division of the judicial precepts. Because the judicial precepts direct men in their relations to one another. But those things which need to be directed, as pertaining to the relationship between man and man, and which are made use of by men, are not subject to division, since they are infinite in number. Therefore it is not possible to assign a distinct division of the judicial precepts.

Obj. 2. Further, the judicial precepts are decisions on moral matters. But moral precepts do not seem to be capable of division,

except in so far as they are reducible to the precepts of the decalogue. Therefore there is no distinct division of the judicial precepts.

Obj. 3. Further, because there is a distinct division of the ceremonial precepts, the Law alludes to this division, by describing some as *sacrifices*, others as *observances*. But the Law contains no allusion to a division of the judicial precepts. Therefore it seems that they have no distinct division.

On the contrary, Wherever there is order there must needs be division. But the notion of order is chiefly applicable to the judicial precepts, since thereby that people was ordained. Therefore it is most necessary that they should have a distinct division.

I answer that, Since law is the art, as it were, of directing or ordering the life of man, as in every art there is a distinct division in the rules of art, so, in every law, there must be a distinct division of precepts: else the law would be rendered useless by confusion. We must therefore say that the judicial precepts of the Old Law, whereby men were directed in their relations to one another, are subject to division according to the divers ways in which man is directed.

Now in every people a fourfold order is to be found: one, of the people's sovereign to his subjects; a second, of the subjects among themselves; a third, of the citizens to foreigners; a fourth, of members of the same household, such as the order of the father to his son; of the wife to her husband; of the master to his servant: and according to these four orders we may distinguish different kinds of judicial precepts in the Old Law. For certain precepts are laid down concerning the institution of the sovereign and relating to his office, and about the respect due to him: this is one part of the judicial precepts.—Again, certain precepts are given in respect of a man to his fellow citizens: for instance, about buying and selling, judgments and penalties: this is the second part of the judicial precepts.—Again, certain precepts are enjoined with regard to foreigners: for instance, about wars waged against their foes, and about the way to receive travelers and strangers: this is the third part of the judicial precepts.—Lastly, certain precepts are given relating to home life: for instance, about servants, wives and children: this is the fourth part of the judicial precepts.

Reply Obj. 1. Things pertaining to the ordering of relations between one man and another are indeed infinite in number: yet they are reducible to certain distinct heads, according to the different relations in which one man stands to another, as stated above.

Reply Obj. 2. The precepts of the decalogue held the first place in the moral order, as stated above (Q. 100, A. 3): and consequently it is fitting that other moral precepts should be distinguished in relation to them. But the judicial and ceremonial precepts have a different binding force, derived, not from natural reason, but from their institution alone. Hence there is a distinct reason for distinguishing them.

Reply Obj. 3. The Law alludes to the division of the judicial precepts in the very things themselves which are prescribed by the judicial precepts of the Law.

QUESTION 105

Of the Reason for the Judicial Precepts

(In Four Articles)

WE must now consider the reason for the judicial precepts: under which head there are four points of inquiry: (1) Concerning the reason for the judicial precepts relating to the rulers; (2) Concerning the fellowship of one man with another; (3) Concerning matters relating to foreigners; (4) Concerning things relating to domestic matters.

FIRST ARTICLE

Whether the Old Law Enjoined Fitting Precepts Concerning Rulers?

We proceed thus to the First Article:—

Objection 1. It would seem that the Old Law made unfitting precepts concerning rulers. Because, as the Philosopher says (*Polit.* iii. 4), *the ordering of the people depends mostly on the chief ruler.* But the Law contains no precept relating to the institution of the chief ruler; and yet we find therein prescriptions concerning the inferior rulers: firstly (Exod. xviii. 21): *Provide out of all the people wise* (Vulg.,—*able*) *men,* etc.; again (Num. xi. 16): *Gather unto Me seventy men of the ancients of Israel;* and again (Deut. i. 13): *Let Me have from among you wise and understanding men,* etc. Therefore the Law provided insufficiently in regard to the rulers of the people.

Obj. 2. Further, *The best gives of the best,* as Plato states (*Tim.* ii). Now the best ordering of a state or of any nation is to be ruled by a king: because this kind of government approaches nearest in resemblance to the Divine government, whereby God rules the world from the beginning. Therefore the Law should have set a king over the people, and they should not have been allowed a choice in the matter, as indeed they were allowed (Deut. xvii. 14, 15): *When thou . . . shalt say: I will set a king over me . . . thou shalt set him,* etc.

Obj. 3. Further, according to Matth. xii. 25: *Every kingdom divided against itself shall be made desolate:* a saying which was verified in the Jewish people, whose destruction was brought about by the division of the kingdom. But the Law should aim chiefly at things pertaining to the general well-being of the people. Therefore it should have forbidden the kingdom to be divided under two kings: nor should this have been introduced even by Divine authority; as we read of its being introduced by the authority of the prophet Ahias the Silonite (3 Kings xi. 29 *seq.*).

Obj. 4. Further, just as priests are instituted for the benefit of the people in things concerning God, as stated in Heb. v. 1; so are rulers set up for the benefit of the people in human affairs. But certain things were allotted as a means of livelihood for the priests and Levites of the Law: such as the tithes and first-fruits, and many like things. Therefore in like manner certain things should have been determined for the livelihood of the rulers of the people: the more that they were forbidden to accept presents, as is clearly stated in Exod. xxiii. 8: *You shall not* (Vulg.,—*Neither shalt thou*) *take bribes, which even blind the wise, and pervert the words of the just.*

Obj. 5. Further, as a kingdom is the best form of government, so is tyranny the most corrupt. But when the Lord appointed the king, He established a tyrannical law; for it is written (1 Kings viii. 11): *This will be the right of the king, that shall reign over you: He will take your sons,* etc. Therefore the Law made unfitting provision with regard to the institution of rulers.

On the contrary, The people of Israel is commended for the beauty of its order (Num. xxiv. 5): *How beautiful are thy tabernacles, O Jacob, and thy tents, O Israel.* But the beautiful ordering of a people depends on the right establishment of its rulers. Therefore the Law made right provision for the people with regard to its rulers.

I answer that, Two points are to be observed concerning the right ordering of rulers in a state or nation. One is that all should take some share in the government: for this form of constitution ensures peace among the people, commends itself to all, and is most enduring, as stated in *Polit.* ii. 6. The other point is to be observed in respect of the kinds of government, or the different ways in which the constitutions are established. For whereas these differ in kind, as the Philosopher states (*Polit.* iii. 5), nevertheless the first place is held by the *kingdom,* where the power of government is vested in one; and *aristocracy,* which signifies government by the best, where the power of government is vested in a few. Accordingly, the best form of government is in a state or kingdom, wherein one is given the power to preside over all; while under him are others having governing powers: and yet a government of this kind is shared by all, both because all are eligible to govern, and because the rulers are chosen by all. For this is the best form of polity, being partly kingdom, since there is one at the head of all; partly aristocracy, in so far as a number of persons are set in authority; partly democracy, i.e., government by the people, in so far as the rulers can be chosen from the people, and the people have the right to choose their rulers.

Such was the form of government established by the Divine Law. For Moses and his successors governed the people in such a way that each of them was ruler over all; so that there was a kind of kingdom. Moreover, seventy-two men were chosen, who were elders in virtue: for it is written (Deut. i. 15): *I took out of your tribes men wise and honorable, and appointed them rulers:* so that there was an element of aristocracy. But it was a democratical government in so far as the rulers were chosen from all the people; for it is written (Exod. xviii. 21): *Provide out of all the people wise* (Vulg.,—*able*) *men,* etc.; and, again, in so far as they were chosen by the people; wherefore it is written (Deut. i. 13): *Let me have from among you wise* (Vulg.,—*able*) *men,* etc. Consequently it is evident that the ordering of the rulers was well provided for by the Law.

Reply Obj. 1. This people was governed under the special care of God: wherefore it is written (Deut. vii. 6): *The Lord thy God hath chosen thee to be His peculiar people:* and this is why the Lord reserved to Himself the institution of the chief ruler. For this too did Moses pray (Num. xxvii. 16): *May the Lord the God of the spirits of all the flesh provide a man, that may be over this multitude.* Thus by God's orders Josue was set at the head in place of Moses: and we read about each of the judges who succeeded Josue that God raised ... up a saviour for the people, and that the spirit of the Lord was in them (Judges iii. 9, 10, 15). Hence the Lord did not leave the choice of a king to the people; but reserved this to Himself, as appears from Deut. xvii. 15: *Thou shalt set him whom the Lord thy God shall choose.*

Reply Obj. 2. A kingdom is the best form of government of the people, so long as it is not corrupt. But since the power granted to a king is so great, it easily degenerates into tyranny, unless he to whom this power is given be a very virtuous man: for it is only the virtuous man that conducts himself well in the midst of prosperity, as the Philosopher observes (*Ethic.* iv. 3). Now perfect virtue is to be found in few: and especially were the Jews inclined to cruelty and avarice, which vices above all turn men into tyrants. Hence from the very first the Lord did not set up the kingly authority with full power, but gave them judges and governors to rule them. But afterwards when the people asked Him to do so, being indignant with them, so to speak, He granted them a king, as is clear from His words to Samuel (1 Kings viii. 7): *They have not rejected thee, but Me, that I should not reign over them.*

Nevertheless, as regards the appointment of a king, He did establish the manner of election from the very beginning (Deut. xvii. 14, seqq.): and then He determined two points: first, that in choosing a king they should wait for the Lord's decision; and that they should not make a man of another nation king, because such kings are wont to take little interest in the people they are set over, and consequently to have no care for their welfare:—secondly, He prescribed how the king after his appointment should behave, in regard to himself; namely, that he should not accumulate chariots and horses, nor wives, nor immense wealth: because through craving for such things princes become tyrants and forsake justice.—He also appointed the manner in which they were to conduct themselves towards God: namely, that they should continually read and ponder on God's Law, and should ever fear and obey God.—Moreover, He decided how they should behave towards their subjects: namely, that they should not proudly despise them, or ill-treat them, and that they should not depart from the paths of justice.

Reply Obj. 3. The division of the kingdom, and a number of kings, was rather a punishment inflicted on that people for their many dissensions, specially against the just rule of David, than a benefit conferred on them for their profit. Hence it is written (Osee xiii. 11): *I will give thee a king in My wrath;* and (*ibid.* viii. 4): *They have reigned, but not by Me: they have been princes, and I knew not.*

Reply Obj. 4. The priestly office was bequeathed by succession from father to son: and this, in order that it might be held in greater respect, if not any man from the people could become a priest: since honor was given to them out of reverence for the divine worship. Hence it was necessary to put aside certain things for them both as to tithes and as to first-fruits, and, again, as to oblations and sacrifices, that they might be afforded a means of livelihood. On the other hand, the rulers, as stated above, were chosen from the whole people; wherefore they had their own possessions, from which to derive a living: and so much the more, since the Lord forbade even a king to have superabundant wealth to make too much show of magnificence: both because he could scarcely avoid the excesses of pride and tyranny, arising from such things, and because, if the rulers were not very rich, and if their office involved much work and anxiety, it would not tempt the ambition of the common people; and would not become an occasion of sedition.

Reply Obj. 5. That right was not given to the king by Divine institution: rather was it foretold that kings would usurp that right, by framing unjust laws, and by degenerating into tyrants who preyed on their subjects. This is clear from the context that follows: *And you shall be his slaves* (Douay, *servants*): which is significative of tyranny, since a tyrant rules his subjects as though they were his slaves. Hence Samuel spoke these words to deter them from asking for a king; since the narrative continues: *But the people would not hear the voice of Samuel.*—It may happen, however, that even a good king, without being a tyrant, may take away the sons, and make them tribunes and centurions; and may take many things from his subjects in order to secure the common weal.

SECOND ARTICLE

Whether the Judicial Precepts Were Suitably Framed As to the Relations of One Man with Another?

We proceed thus to the Second Article:—

Objection 1. It would seem that the judicial precepts were not suitably framed as regards the relations of one man with another. Because men cannot live together in peace, if one man takes what belongs to another. But this seems to have been approved by the Law: since it is written (Deut. xxiii. 24): *Going into thy neighbor's vineyard, thou mayst eat as many grapes as thou pleasest.* Therefore the Old Law did not make suitable provisions for man's peace.

Obj. 2. Further, one of the chief causes of the downfall of states has been the holding of property by women, as the Philosopher says (*Polit.* ii. 6). But this was introduced by the Old Law; for it is written (Num. xxvii. 8): *When a man dieth without a son,*

his inheritance shall pass to his daughter. Therefore the Law made unsuitable provision for the welfare of the people.

Obj. 3. Further, it is most conducive to the preservation of human society that men may provide themselves with necessaries by buying and selling, as stated in *Polit.* i. But the Old Law took away the force of sales; since it prescribes that in the 50th year of the jubilee all that is sold shall return to the vendor (Levit. xxv. 28). Therefore in this matter the Law gave the people an unfitting command.

Obj. 4. Further, man's needs require that men should be ready to lend: which readiness ceases if the creditors do not return the pledges: hence it is written (Ecclus. xxix. 10): *Many have refused to lend, not out of wickedness, but they were afraid to be defrauded without cause.* And yet this was encouraged by the Law. First, because it prescribed (Deut. xv. 2): *He to whom any thing is owing from his friend or neighbor or brother, cannot demand it again, because it is the year of remission of the Lord;* and (Exod. xxii. 15) it is stated that if a borrowed animal should die while the owner is present, the borrower is not bound to make restitution. Secondly, because the security acquired through the pledge is lost: for it is written (Deut. xxiv. 10): *When thou shalt demand of thy neighbor any thing that he oweth thee, thou shalt not go into his house to take away a pledge;* and again (verses 12, 13): *The pledge shall not lodge with thee that night, but thou shalt restore it to him presently.* Therefore the Law made insufficient provision in the matter of loans.

Obj. 5. Further, considerable risk attaches to goods deposited with a fraudulent depositary: wherefore great caution should be observed in such matters: hence it is stated in 2 Mach. iii. 15 that *the priests . . . called upon Him from heaven, Who made the law concerning things given to be kept, that He would preserve them safe, for them that had deposited them.* But the precepts of the Old Law observed little caution in regard to deposits: since it is prescribed (Exod. xxii. 10, 11) that when goods deposited are lost, the owner is to stand by the oath of the depositary. Therefore the Law made unsuitable provision in this matter.

Obj. 6. Further, just as a workman offers his work for hire, so do men let houses and so forth. But there is no need for the tenant to pay his rent as soon as he takes a house. Therefore it seems an unnecessarily hard prescription (Lev. xix. 13) that *the wages of him that hath been hired by thee shall not abide with thee until the morning.*

Obj. 7. Further, since there is often pressing need for a judge, it should be easy to gain access to one. It was therefore unfitting that the Law (Deut. xvii. 8, 9) should command them to go to a fixed place to ask for judgment on doubtful matters.

Obj. 8. Further, it is possible that not only two, but three or more, should agree to tell a lie. Therefore it is unreasonably stated (Deut. xix. 15) that *in the mouth of two or three witnesses every word shall stand.*

Obj. 9. Further, punishment should be fixed according to the gravity of the fault: for which reason also it is written (Deut. xxv. 2): *According to the measure of the sin, shall the measure also of the stripes be.* Yet the Law fixed unequal punishments for certain faults: for it is written (Exod. xxii. 1) that the thief *shall restore five oxen for one ox, and four sheep for one sheep.* Moreover, certain slight offenses are severely punished: thus (Num. xv. 32, *seqq.*) a man is stoned for gathering sticks on the sabbath day: and (Deut. xxi. 18, *seqq*) the unruly son is commanded to be stoned on account of certain small transgressions, viz., because *he gave himself to revelling . . . and banquetings.* Therefore the Law prescribed punishments in an unreasonable manner.

Obj. 10. Further, as Augustine says (*De Civ. Dei* xxi. 11), *Tully writes that the laws recognize eight forms of punishment, indemnity, prison, stripes, retaliation, public disgrace, exile, death, slavery.* Now some of these were prescribed by the Law. *Indemnity,* as when a thief was condemned to make restitution fivefold or fourfold. *Prison,* as when (Num. xv. 34) a certain man is ordered to be imprisoned. *Stripes,* thus (Deut. xxv. 2), *if they see that the offender be worthy of stripes; they shall lay him down, and shall cause him to be beaten before them. Public disgrace* was brought on to him who refused to take to himself the wife of his deceased brother, for she took off *his shoe from his foot,* and did *spit in his face* (*ibid.* 9). It prescribed the *death* penalty, as is clear from Lev. xx. 9: *He that curseth his father, or mother, dying let him die.* The Law also recognized the *lex talionis,* by prescribing (Exod. xxi. 24): *Eye for eye, tooth for tooth.* Therefore it seems unreasonable that the Law should not have inflicted the two other punishments, viz., *exile* and *slavery.*

Obj. 11. Further, no punishment is due except for a fault. But dumb animals cannot commit a fault. Therefore the Law is unreasonable in punishing them (Exod. xxi. 29): *If the ox . . . shall kill a man or a woman, it shall be stoned:* and (Lev. xx. 16):

The woman that shall lie under any beast, shall be killed together with the same. Therefore it seems that matters pertaining to the relations of one man with another were unsuitably regulated by the Law.

Obj. 12. Further, the Lord commanded (Exod. xxi. 12) a murderer to be punished with death. But the death of a dumb animal is reckoned of much less account than the slaying of a man. Hence murder cannot be sufficiently punished by the slaying of a dumb animal. Therefore it is unfittingly prescribed (Deut. xxi. 1, 4) that *when there shall be found . . . the corpse of a man slain, and it is not known who is guilty of the murder . . . the ancients* of the nearest city *shall take a heifer of the herd, that hath not drawn in the yoke, nor ploughed the ground, and they shall bring her into a rough and stony valley, that never was ploughed, nor sown; and there they shall strike off the head of the heifer.*

On the contrary, It is recalled as a special blessing (Ps. cxlvii. 20) that *He hath not done in like manner to every nation; and His judgments He hath not made manifest to them.*

I answer that, As Augustine says (*De Civ. Dei* ii. 21), quoting Tully, *a nation is a body of men united together by consent to the law and by community of welfare.* Consequently it is of the essence of a nation that the mutual relations of the citizens be ordered by just laws. Now the relations of one man with another are twofold: some are effected under the guidance of those in authority: others are effected by the will of private individuals. And since whatever is subject to the power of an individual can be disposed of according to his will, hence it is that the decision of matters between one man and another, and the punishment of evildoers, depend on the direction of those in authority, to whom men are subject. On the other hand, the power of private persons is exercised over the things they possess: and consequently their dealings with one another, as regards such things, depend on their own will, for instance in buying, selling, giving, and so forth. Now the Law provided sufficiently in respect of each of these relations between one man and another. For it established judges, as is clearly indicated in Deut. xvi. 18: *Thou shalt appoint judges and magistrates in all its* (Vulg.,—*thy*) *gates, . . . that they may judge the people with just judgment.* It also directed the manner of pronouncing just judgments, according to Deut. i. 16, 17: *Judge that which is just, whether he be one of your own country or a stranger: there shall be no difference of persons.* It also removed an occasion of pronouncing unjust judgment, by forbidding judges to accept bribes (Exod. xxiii. 8; Deut. xvi. 19). It prescribed the number of witnesses, viz., two or three: and it appointed certain punishments to certain crimes, as we shall state farther on (ad 10).

But with regard to possessions, it is a very good thing, says the Philosopher (*Polit.* ii. 2) that the things possessed should be distinct, and that the use thereof should be partly common, and partly granted to others by the will of the possessors. These three points were provided for by the Law. Because, in the first place, the possessions themselves were divided among individuals: for it is written (Num. xxxiii. 53, 54): *I have given you* the land *for a possession: and you shall divide it among you by lot.* And since many states have been ruined through want of regulations in the matter of possessions, as the Philosopher observes (*Polit.* ii. 6); therefore the Law provided a threefold remedy against the irregularity of possessions. The first was that they should be divided equally, wherefore it is written (Num. xxxiii. 54): *To the more you shall give a larger part, and to the fewer, a lesser.* A second remedy was that possessions could not be alienated for ever, but after a certain lapse of time should return to their former owner, so as to avoid confusion of possessions (*cf. ad* 3). The third remedy aimed at the removal of this confusion, and provided that the dead should be succeeded by their next of kin: in the first place, the son; secondly, the daughter; thirdly, the brother; fourthly, the father's brother; fifthly, any other next of kin. Furthermore, in order to preserve the distinction of property, the Law enacted that heiresses should marry within their own tribe, as recorded in Num. xxxvi. 6.

Secondly, the Law commanded that, in some respects, the use of things should belong to all in common. Firstly, as regards the care of them; for it was prescribed (Deut. xxii. 1-4). *Thou shalt not pass by, if thou seest thy brother's ox or his sheep go astray; but thou shalt bring them back to thy brother,* and in like manner as to other things.—Secondly, as regards fruits. For all alike were allowed on entering a friend's vineyard to eat of the fruit, but not to take any away. And, specially, with respect to the poor, it was prescribed that the forgotten sheaves, and the bunches of grapes and fruit, should be left behind for them (Lev. xix. 9; Deut. xxiv. 19). Moreover, whatever grew in the seventh year was common property, as stated in Exod. xxiii. 11 and Lev. xxv. 4.

Thirdly, the law recognized the transference of goods by the owner. There was a purely gratuitous transfer: thus it is written (Deut. xiv. 28, 29): *The third day thou shalt separate another tithe . . . and the Levite . . . and the stranger, and the fatherless, and the widow . . . shall come and shall eat and be filled.* And there was a transfer for a consideration, for instance, by selling and buying, by letting out and hiring, by loan and also by deposit, concerning all of which we find that the Law made ample provision. Consequently it is clear that the Old Law provided sufficiently concerning the mutual relations of one man with another.

Reply Obj. 1. As the Apostle says (Rom. xiii. 8), *he that loveth his neighbor hath fulfilled the Law:* because, to wit, all the precepts of the Law, chiefly those concerning our neighbor, seem to aim at the end that men should love one another. Now it is an effect of love that men give their own goods to others: because, as stated in 1 John iii. 17: *He that . . . shall see his brother in need, and shall shut up his bowels from him: how doth the charity of God abide in him?* Hence the purpose of the Law was to accustom men to give of their own to others readily: thus the Apostle (1 Tim. vi. 18) commands the rich *to give easily and to communicate to others.* Now a man does not give easily to others if he will not suffer another man to take some little thing from him without any great injury to him. And so the Law laid down that it should be lawful for a man, on entering his neighbor's vineyard, to eat of the fruit there: but not to carry any away, lest this should lead to the infliction of a grievous harm, and cause a disturbance of the peace: for among well-behaved people, the taking of a little does not disturb the peace; in fact, it rather strengthens friendship and accustoms men to give things to one another.

Reply Obj. 2. The Law did not prescribe that women should succeed to their father's estate except in default of male issue: failing which it was necessary that succession should be granted to the female line in order to comfort the father, who would have been sad to think that his estate would pass to strangers. Nevertheless the Law observed due caution in the matter, by providing that those women who succeeded to their father's estate, should marry within their own tribe, in order to avoid confusion of tribal possessions, as stated in Num. xxxvi. 7, 8.

Reply Obj. 3. As the Philosopher says (*Polit.* ii. 4), the regulation of possessions conduces much to the preservation of a state or nation. Consequently, as he himself observes, it was forbidden by the law in some of the heathen states, *that anyone should sell his possessions, except to avoid a manifest loss.* For if possessions were to be sold indiscriminately, they might happen to come into the hands of a few: so that it might become necessary for a state or country to become void of inhabitants. Hence the Old Law, in order to remove this danger, ordered things in such a way that while provision was made for men's needs, by allowing the sale of possessions to avail for a certain period, at the same time the said danger was removed, by prescribing the return of those possessions after that period had elapsed. The reason for this law was to prevent confusion of possessions, and to ensure the continuance of a definite distinction among the tribes.

But as the town houses were not allotted to distinct estates, therefore the Law allowed them to be sold in perpetuity, like movable goods. Because the number of houses in a town was not fixed, whereas there was a fixed limit to the amount of estates, which could not be exceeded, while the number of houses in a town could be increased. On the other hand, houses situated not in a town, but *in a village that hath no walls,* could not be sold in perpetuity: because such houses are built merely with a view to the cultivation and care of possessions; wherefore the Law rightly made the same prescription in regard to both (Lev. xxv).

Reply Obj. 4. As stated above (*ad* 1), the purpose of the Law was to accustom men to its precepts, so as to be ready to come to one another's assistance: because this is a very great incentive to friendship. The Law granted these facilities for helping others in the matter not only of gratuitous and absolute donations, but also of mutual transfers: because the latter kind of succor is more frequent and benefits the greater number: and it granted facilities for this purpose in many ways. First of all by prescribing that men should be ready to lend, and that they should not be less inclined to do so as the year of remission drew nigh, as stated in Deut. xv. 7, *seqq.*—Secondly, by forbidding them to burden a man to whom they might grant a loan, either by exacting usury, or by accepting necessities of life in security; and by prescribing that when this had been done they should be restored at once. For it is written (Deut. xxiii. 19): *Thou shalt not lend to thy brother money to usury:* and (xxiv. 6): *Thou shalt not take the nether nor the upper millstone to pledge; for he hath pledged his life to thee:* and (Exod. xxii. 26): *If thou take of thy neighbor a garment in pledge, thou shalt give it him again before sunset.*—Thirdly, by forbidding them to be importunate in exacting payment. Hence it is written (Exod. xxii. 25): *If thou lend money to any of my people that is poor that dwelleth with thee, thou shalt not be hard upon them as an extortioner.* For this reason, too, it is enacted (Deut. xxiv. 10, 11): *When thou shalt demand of thy neighbor anything that he oweth thee, thou shalt not go into his house to take away a pledge, but thou shalt stand without, and he shall bring out to thee what he hath:* both because a man's house is his surest refuge, wherefore it is offensive to a man to be set upon in his own house; and because the Law does not allow the creditor to take away whatever he likes in security, but rather permits the debtor to give what he needs least.—Fourthly, the Law prescribed that debts should cease altogether after the lapse of seven years. For it was probable that those who could conveniently pay their debts, would do so before the seventh year, and would not defraud the lender without cause. But if they were altogether insolvent, there was the same reason for remitting the debt from love for them, as there was for renewing the loan on account of their need.

As regards animals granted in loan, the Law enacted that if, through the neglect of the person to whom they were lent, they perished or deteriorated in his absence, he was bound to make restitution. But if they perished or deteriorated while he was present and taking proper care of them, he was not bound to make restitution, especially if they were hired for a consideration: because they might have died or deteriorated in the same way if they had remained in possession of the lender, so that if the animal had been saved through being lent, the lender would have gained something by the loan which would no longer have been gratuitous. And especially was this to be observed when animals were hired for a consideration: because then the owner received a certain price for the use of the animals; wherefore he had no right to any profit, by receiving indemnity for the animal, unless the person who had charge of it were negligent. In the case, however, of animals not hired for a consideration, equity demanded that he should receive something by way of restitution at least to the value of the hire of the animal that had perished or deteriorated.

Reply Obj. 5. The difference between a loan and a deposit is that a loan is in respect of goods transferred for the use of the person to whom they are transferred, whereas a deposit is for the benefit of the depositor. Hence in certain cases there was a stricter obligation of returning a loan than of restoring goods held in deposit. Because the latter might be lost in two ways. First, unavoidably: i.e., either through a natural cause, for instance if an animal held in deposit were to die or depreciate in value; or through an extrinsic cause, for instance, if it were taken by an enemy, or devoured by a beast (in which case, however, a man was bound to restore to the owner whatever was left of the animal thus slain): whereas in the other cases mentioned above, he was not bound to make restitution; but only to take an oath in order to clear himself of suspicion. Secondly, the goods deposited might be lost through an avoidable cause, for instance by theft: and then the depositary was bound to restitution on account of his neglect. But, as stated above (*ad* 4), he who held an animal on loan, was bound to restitution, even if he were absent when it depreciated or died: because he was held responsible for less negligence than a depositary, who was only held responsible in case of theft.

Reply Obj. 6. Workmen who offer their labor for hire, are poor men who toil for their daily bread: and therefore the Law commanded wisely that they should be paid at once, lest they should lack food. But they who offer other commodities for hire, are wont to be rich: nor are they in such need of their price in order to gain a livelihood: and consequently the comparison does not hold.

Reply Obj. 7. The purpose for which judges are appointed among men, is that they may decide doubtful points in matters of justice. Now a matter may be doubtful in two ways. First, among simple-minded people: and in order to remove doubts of this kind, it was prescribed (Deut. xvi. 18) that *judges and magistrates* should be appointed in each tribe, *to judge the people with just judgment.*—Secondly, a matter may be doubtful even among experts: and therefore, in order to remove doubts of this kind, the Law prescribed that all should foregather in some chief place chosen by God, where there would be both the high-priest, who would decide doubtful matters relating to the ceremonies of divine worship; and the chief judge of the people, who would decide matters relating to the judgments of men: just as even now cases are taken from a lower to a higher court either by appeal or by consultation. Hence it is written (Deut. xvii. 8, 9): *If thou perceive that there be among you a hard and doubtful matter in judgment, . . . and thou see that the words of the judges within thy gates do vary; arise and go up to the place, which the Lord thy God shall choose; and thou shalt come to the priests of the Levitical race, and to the judge that shall be at that time.* But such like doubtful matters did not often occur for judgment: wherefore the people were not burdened on this account.

Reply Obj. 8. In the business affairs of men, there is no such thing as demonstrative and infallible proof, and we must be content with a certain conjectural probability, such as that which an orator employs to persuade. Consequently, although it is quite possible for two

or three witnesses to agree to a falsehood, yet it is neither easy nor probable that they succeed in so doing: wherefore their testimony is taken as being true, especially if they do not waver in giving it, or are not otherwise suspect. Moreover, in order that witnesses might not easily depart from the truth, the Law commanded that they should be most carefully examined, and that those who were found untruthful should be severely punished, as stated in Deut. xix. 16, *seqq.*

There was, however, a reason for fixing on this particular number, in token of the unerring truth of the Divine Persons, Who are sometimes mentioned as two, because the Holy Ghost is the bond of the other two Persons; and sometimes as three: as Augustine observes on Jo. viii. 17: *In your law it is written that the testimony of two men is true.*

Reply Obj. 9. A severe punishment is inflicted not only on account of the gravity of a fault, but also for other reasons. First, on account of the greatness of the sin, because a greater sin, other things being equal, deserves a greater punishment. Secondly, on account of a habitual sin, since men are not easily cured of habitual sin except by severe punishments. Thirdly, on account of a great desire for or a great pleasure in the sin: for men are not easily deterred from such sins unless they be severely punished. Fourthly, on account of the facility of committing a sin and of concealing it: for such like sins, when discovered, should be more severely punished in order to deter others from committing them.

Again, with regard to the greatness of a sin, four degrees may be observed, even in respect of one single deed. The first is when a sin is committed unwillingly; because then, if the sin be altogether involuntary, man is altogether excused from punishment; for it is written (Deut. xxii. 25, *seqq.*) that a damsel who suffers violence in a field is not guilty of death, because *she cried, and there was no man to help her.* But if a man sinned in any way voluntarily, and yet through weakness, as for instance when a man sins from passion, the sin is diminished: and the punishment, according to true judgment, should be diminished also; unless perchance the common weal requires that the sin be severely punished in order to deter others from committing such sins, as stated above.—The second degree is when a man sins through ignorance: and then he was held to be guilty to a certain extent, on account of his negligence in acquiring knowledge: yet he was not punished by the judges but expiated his sin by sacrifices. Hence it is written (Lex. iv. 2): *The soul that sinneth through ignorance, etc.* This is, however, to be taken as applying to ignorance of fact; and not to ignorance of the Divine precept, which all were bound to know.—The third degree was when a man sinned from pride, i.e., through deliberate choice or malice: and then he was punished according to the greatness of the sin.*—The fourth degree was when a man sinned from stubbornness or obstinacy: and then he was to be utterly cut off as a rebel and a destroyer of the commandment of the Law.†

Accordingly we must say that, in appointing the punishment for theft, the Law considered what would be likely to happen most frequently (Exod. xxii. 1-9): wherefore, as regards theft of other things which can easily be safeguarded from a thief, the thief restored only twice their value. But sheep cannot be easily safeguarded from a thief, because they graze in the fields: wherefore it happened more frequently that sheep were stolen in the fields. Consequently the Law inflicted a heavier penalty, by ordering four sheep to be restored for the theft of one. As to cattle, they were yet more difficult to safeguard, because they are kept in the fields, and do not graze in flocks as sheep do; wherefore a yet more heavy penalty was inflicted in their regard, so that five oxen were to be restored for one ox. And this I say, unless perchance the animal itself were discovered in the thief's possession: because in that case he had to restore only twice the number, as in the case of other thefts: for there was reason to presume that he intended to restore the animal, since he kept it alive.—Again, we might say, according to a gloss, that *a cow is useful in five ways: it may be used for sacrifice, for ploughing, for food, for milk, and its hide is employed for various purposes:* and therefore for one cow five had to be restored. But the sheep was useful in four ways: *for sacrifice, for meat, for milk, and for its wool.*—The unruly son was slain, not because he ate and drank: but on account of his stubbornness and rebellion, which was always punished by death, as stated above.— As to the man who gathered sticks on the sabbath, he was stoned as a breaker of the Law, which commanded the sabbath to be observed, to testify the belief in the newness of the world, as stated above (Q. 100, A. 5): wherefore he was slain as an unbeliever.

Reply Obj. 10. The Old Law inflicted the death penalty for the more grievous crimes, viz., for those which are committed against God, and for murder, for stealing a man, irreverence towards one's parents, adultery and incest. In the case of theft of other things it inflicted punishment by indemnification: while in the case of blows and mutilation it authorized punishment by retaliation; and

likewise for the sin of bearing false witness. In other faults of less degree it prescribed the punishment of stripes or of public disgrace.

The punishment of slavery was prescribed by the Law in two cases. First, in the case of a slave who was unwilling to avail himself of the privilege granted by the Law, whereby he was free to depart in the seventh year of remission: wherefore he was punished by remaining a slave for ever.—Secondly, in the case of a thief, who had not wherewith to make restitution, as stated in Exod. xxii. 3.

The punishment of absolute exile was not prescribed by the Law: because God was worshipped by that people alone, whereas all other nations were given to idolatry: wherefore if any man were exiled from that people absolutely, he would be in danger of falling into idolatry. For this reason it is related (1 Kings xxvi. 19) that David said to Saul: *They are cursed in the sight of the Lord, who have cast me out this day, that I should not dwell in the inheritance of the Lord, saying: Go, serve strange gods.* There was, however, a restricted sort of exile: for it is written in Deut. xix. 4‡ that *he that striketh* (Vulg.,— *killeth) his neighbor ignorantly, and is proved to have had no hatred against him, shall flee to one of the cities* of refuge and *abide there until the death of the high-priest.* For then it became lawful for him to return home, because when the whole people thus suffered a loss they forgot their private quarrels, so that the next of kin of the slain were not so eager to kill the slayer.

Reply Obj. 11. Dumb animals were ordered to be slain, not on account of any fault of theirs; but as a punishment to their owners, who had not safeguarded their beasts from these offenses. Hence the owner was more severely punished if his ox had butted anyone *yesterday or the day before* (in which case steps might have been taken to avoid the danger), than if it had taken to butting suddenly.—Or again, the animal was slain in detestation of the sin; and lest men should be horrified at the sight thereof.

Reply Obj. 12. The literal reason for this commandment, as Rabbi Moses declares (*Doct. Perplex.* iii), was because the slayer was frequently from the nearest city: wherefore the slaying of the calf was a means of investigating the hidden murder. This was brought about in three ways. In the first place the elders of the city swore that they had taken every measure for safeguarding the roads. Secondly, the owner of the heifer was indemnified for the slaying of his beast, and if the murder was previously discovered, the beast was not slain. Thirdly, the place, where

*Cf. Deut. xxv. 2.   † Cf. Num. xv. 30, 31.   ‡ Cf. Num. xxxv. 25.

the heifer was slain, remained uncultivated. Wherefore, in order to avoid this twofold loss, the men of that city would readily make known the murderer, if they knew who he was: and it would seldom happen but that some word or sign would escape about the matter.—Or again, this was done in order to frighten people, in detestation of murder. Because the slaying of a heifer, which is a useful animal and full of strength, especially before it has been put under the yoke, signified that whoever committed murder, however useful and strong he might be, was to forfeit his life; and that, by a cruel death, which was implied by the striking off of its head; and that the murderer, as vile and abject, was to be cut off from the fellowship of men, which was betokened by the fact that the heifer after being slain was left to rot in a rough and uncultivated place.

Mystically, the heifer taken from the herd signifies the flesh of Christ; which had not drawn a yoke, since it had done no sin; nor did it plough the ground, i.e., it never knew the stain of revolt. The fact of the heifer being killed in an uncultivated valley signified the despised death of Christ, whereby all sins are washed away, and the devil is shown to be the arch-murderer.

THIRD ARTICLE

Whether the Judicial Precepts Regarding Foreigners Were Framed in a Suitable Manner?

We proceed thus to the Third Article:—

Objection 1. It would seem that the judicial precepts regarding foreigners were not suitably framed. For Peter said (Acts x. 34, 35): *In very deed I perceive that God is not a respecter of persons, but in every nation, he that feareth Him and worketh justice is acceptable to Him.* But those who are acceptable to God should not be excluded from the Church of God. Therefore it is unsuitably commanded (Deut. xxiii. 3) that *the Ammonite and the Moabite, even after the tenth generation, shall not enter into the church of the Lord for ever:* whereas, on the other hand, it is prescribed (*ibid* 7) to be observed with regard to certain other nations: *Thou shalt not abhor the Edomite, because he is thy brother; nor the Egyptian because thou wast a stranger in his land.*

Obj. 2. Further, we do not deserve to be punished for those things which are not in our power. But it is not in a man's power to be an eunuch, or born of a prostitute. Therefore it is unsuitably commanded (Deut. xxiii. 1, 2) that *an eunuch and one born of a prostitute shall not enter into the church of the Lord.*

Obj. 3. Further, the Old Law mercifully

forbade strangers to be molested: for it is written (Exod. xxii. 21): *Thou shalt not molest a stranger, nor afflict him; for yourselves also were strangers in the land of Egypt:* and (xxiii. 9): *Thou shalt not molest a stranger, for you know the hearts of strangers, for you also were strangers in the land of Egypt.* But it is an affliction to be burdened with usury. Therefore the Law unsuitably permitted them (Deut. xxiii. 19, 20) to lend money to the stranger for usury.

Obj. 4. Further, men are much more akin to us than trees. But we should show greater care and love for these things that are nearest to us, according to Ecclus. xiii. 19: *Every beast loveth its like: so also every man him that is nearest to himself.* Therefore the Lord unsuitably commanded (Deut. xx. 13-19) that all the inhabitants of a captured hostile city were to be slain, but that the fruit-trees should not be cut down.

Obj. 5. Further, every one should prefer the common good of virtue to the good of the individual. But the common good is sought in a war which men fight against their enemies. Therefore it is unsuitably commanded (Deut. xx. 5-7) that certain men should be sent home, for instance a man that had built a new house, or who had planted a vineyard, or who had married a wife.

Obj. 6. Further, no man should profit by his own fault. But it is a man's fault if he be timid or faint-hearted: since this is contrary to the virtue of fortitude. Therefore the timid and faint-hearted are unfittingly excused from the toil of battle (Deut. xx. 8).

On the contrary, Divine Wisdom declares (Prov viii. 8): *All my words are just, there is nothing wicked nor perverse in them.*

I answer that, Man's relations with foreigners are two-fold: peaceful, and hostile: and in directing both kinds of relation the Law contained suitable precepts. For the Jews were offered three opportunities of peaceful relations with foreigners. First, when foreigners passed through their land as travelers.—Secondly, when they came to dwell in their land as new-comers. And in both these respects the Law made kind provision in its precepts: for it is written (Exod. xxii 21): *Thou shalt not molest a stranger (advenam);* and again (*ibid.* xxiii. 9): *Thou shalt not molest a stranger (peregrino).*—Thirdly, when any foreigners wished to be admitted entirely to their fellowship and mode of worship. With regard to these a certain order was observed. For they were not at once admitted to citizenship: just as it was the law with some nations that no one was deemed a citizen except after two or three generations, as the Philosopher says (*Polit.* iii. 1). The reason for this was that if foreigners were allowed to meddle with the affairs of a nation as soon as they settled down in its midst, many dangers might occur, since the foreigners not yet having the common good firmly at heart might attempt something hurtful to the people. Hence it was that the Law prescribed in respect of certain nations that had close relations with the Jews (viz., the Egyptians among whom they were born and educated, and the Idumeans, the children of Esau, Jacob's brother), that they should be admitted to the fellowship of the people after the third generation; whereas others (with whom their relations had been hostile, such as the Ammonites and Moabites) were never to be admitted to citizenship; while the Amalekites, who were yet more hostile to them, and had no fellowship of kindred with them, were to be held as foes in perpetuity: for it is written (Exod. xvii. 16): *The war of the Lord shall be against Amalec from generation to generation.*

In like manner with regard to hostile relations with foreigners, the Law contained suitable precepts. For, in the first place, it commanded that war should be declared for a just cause: thus it is commanded (Deut. xx. 10) that when they advanced to besiege a city, they should at first make an offer of peace.—Secondly, it enjoined that when once they had entered on a war they should undauntedly persevere in it, putting their trust in God. And in order that they might be the more heedful of this command, it ordered that on the approach of battle the priest should hearten them by promising them God's aid.—Thirdly, it prescribed the removal of whatever might prove an obstacle to the fight, and that certain men, who might be in the way, should be sent home.—Fourthly, it enjoined that they should use moderation in pursuing the advantage of victory, by sparing women and children, and by not cutting down the fruit-trees of that country.

Reply Obj. 1. The Law excluded the men of no nation from the worship of God and from things pertaining to the welfare of the soul: for it is written (Exod. xii. 48): *If any stranger be willing to dwell among you, and to keep the Phase of the Lord; all his males shall first be circumcised, and then shall he celebrate it according to the manner, and he shall be as that which is born in the land.* But in temporal matters concerning the public life of the people, admission was not granted to everyone at once, for the reason given above: but to some, i.e., the Egyptians and Idumeans, in the third generation; while others were excluded in perpetuity, in detestation of their past offense, i.e., the peoples of Moab, Ammon, and Amalec. For just as one man is

punished for a sin committed by him, in order that others seeing this may be deterred and refrain from sinning; so too may one nation or city be punished for a crime, that others may refrain from similar crimes.

Nevertheless it was possible by dispensation for a man to be admitted to citizenship on account of some act of virtue: thus it is related (Judith xiv. 6) that Achior, the captain of the children of Ammon, *was joined to the people of Israel, with all the succession of his kindred.*—The same applies to Ruth the Moabite, who was *a virtuous woman* (Ruth iii. 11): although it may be said that this prohibition regarded men and not women, who are not competent to be citizens absolutely speaking.

Reply Obj. 2. As the Philosopher says (*Polit.* iii. 3), a man is said to be a citizen in two ways: first, simply; secondly, in a restricted sense. A man is a citizen simply if he has all the rights of citizenship, for instance, the right of debating or voting in the popular assembly. On the other hand, any man may be called citizen, only in a restricted sense, if he dwells within the state, even common people or children or old men, who are not fit to enjoy power in matters pertaining to the common weal. For this reason bastards, by reason of their base origin, were excluded from the *ecclesia,* i.e., from the popular assembly, down to the tenth generation. The same applies to eunuchs, who were not competent to receive the honor due to a father, especially among the Jews, where the divine worship was continued through carnal generation: for even among the heathens, those who had many children were marked with special honor, as the Philosopher remarks (*Polit.* ii. 6). Nevertheless, in matters pertaining to the grace of God, eunuchs were not discriminated from others, as neither were strangers, as already stated: for it is written (Isa. lvi. 3): *Let not the son of the stranger that adhereth to the Lord speak, saying: The Lord will divide and separate me from His people. And let not the eunuch say: Behold I am a dry tree.*

Reply Obj. 3. It was not the intention of the Law to sanction the acceptance of usury from strangers, but only to tolerate it on account of the proneness of the Jews to avarice; and in order to promote an amicable feeling towards those out of whom they made a profit.

Reply Obj. 4. A distinction was observed with regard to hostile cities. For some of them were far distant, and were not among those which had been promised to them. When they had taken these cities, they killed all the men who had fought against God's people; whereas the women and children were spared.

But in the neighboring cities which had been promised to them, all were ordered to be slain, on account of their former crimes, to punish which God sent the Israelites as executor of Divine justice: for it is written (Deut. ix. 5): *Because they have done wickedly, they are destroyed at thy coming in.*—The fruit-trees were commanded to be left untouched, for the use of the people themselves, to whom the city with its territory was destined to be subjected.

Reply Obj. 5. The builder of a new house, the planter of a vineyard, the newly married husband, were excluded from fighting, for two reasons. First, because man is wont to give all his affection to those things which he has lately acquired, or is on the point of having, and consequently he is apt to dread the loss of these above ôther things. Wherefore it was likely enough that on account of this affection they would fear death all the more, and be so much the less brave in battle.—Secondly, because, as the Philosopher says (*Phys.* ii. 5), *it is a misfortune for a man if he is prevented from obtaining something good when it is within his grasp.* And so lest the surviving relations should be the more grieved at the death of these men who had not entered into the possession of the good things prepared for them; and also lest the people should be horror-stricken at the sight of their misfortune: these men were taken away from the danger of death by being removed from the battle.

Reply Obj. 6. The timid were sent back home, not that they might be the gainers thereby; but lest the people might be the losers by their presence, since their timidity and flight might cause others to be afraid and run away.

FOURTH ARTICLE

Whether the Old Law Set Forth Suitable Precepts about the Members of the Household?

We proceed thus to the Fourth Article:—

Objection 1. It would seem that the Old Law set forth unsuitable precepts about the members of the household. For a slave *is in every respect his master's property,* as the Philosopher states (*Polit.* i. 2). But that which is a man's property should be his always. Therefore it was unfitting for the Law to command (Exod. xxi. 2) that slaves should *go out free* in the seventh year.

Obj. 2. Further, a slave is his master's property, just as an animal, *e.g.,* an ass or an ox. But it is commanded (Deut. xxii. 1-3) with regard to animals, that they should be brought back to the owner if they be found going astray. Therefore it was unsuitably

commanded (Deut. xxiii. 15): *Thou shalt not deliver to his master the servant that is fled to thee.*

Obj. 3. Further, the Divine Law should encourage mercy more even than the human law. But according to human laws those who ill-treat their servants and maidservants are severely punished: and the worse treatment of all seems to be that which results in death. Therefore it is unfittingly commanded (Exod. xxi. 20, 21) that *he that striketh his bondman or bondwoman with a rod, and they die under his hands . . . if the party remain alive a day . . . he shall not be subject to the punishment, because it is his money.*

Obj. 4. Further, the dominion of a master over his slave differs from that of the father over his son (*Polit.* i., iii). But the dominion of master over slave gives the former the right to sell his slave or maidservant. Therefore it was unfitting for the Law to allow a man to sell his daughter to be a servant or handmaid (Exod. xxi. 7).

Obj. 5. Further, a father has power over his son. But he who has power over the sinner has the right to punish him for his offenses. Therefore it is unfittingly commanded (Deut. xxi. 18 *seqq.*) that a father should bring his son to the ancients of the city for punishment.

Obj. 6. Further, the Lord forbade them (Deut. vii. 3, *seqq.*) to make marriages with strange nations; and commanded the dissolution of such as had been contracted (1 Esdras x). Therefore it was unfitting to allow them to marry captive women from strange nations (Deut. xxi. 10 *seqq.*).

Obj. 7. Further, the Lord forbade them to marry within certain degrees of consanguinity and affinity, according to Levit. xviii. Therefore it was unsuitably commanded (Deut. xxv. 5) that if any man died without issue, his brother should marry his wife.

Obj. 8. Further, as there is the greatest familiarity between man and wife, so should there be the staunchest fidelity. But this is impossible if the marriage bond can be sundered. Therefore it was unfitting for the Lord to allow (Deut. xxiv. 1-4) a man to put his wife away, by writing a bill of divorce; and besides, that he could not take her again to wife.

Obj. 9. Further, just as a wife can be faithless to her husband, so can a slave be to his master, and a son to his father. But the Law did not command any sacrifice to be offered in order to investigate the injury done by a servant to his master, or by a son to his father. Therefore it seems to have been superfluous for the Law to prescribe the *sacrifice of jealousy* in order to investigate a wife's adultery (Num. v. 12 *seqq.*). Consequently it seems that the Law put forth unsuitable judicial precepts about the members of the household.

On the contrary, It is written (Ps. xviii. 10): *The judgments of the Lord are true, justified in themselves.*

I answer that, The mutual relations of the members of a household regard every-day actions directed to the necessities of life, as the Philosopher states (*Polit.* i. 1). Now the preservation of man's life may be considered from two points of view. First, from the point of view of the individual, i.e., in so far as man preserves his individuality: and for the purpose of the preservation of life, considered from this standpoint, man has at his service external goods, by means of which he provides himself with food and clothing and other such necessaries of life: in the handling of which he has need of servants. Secondly, man's life is preserved from the point of view of the species, by means of generation, for which purpose man needs a wife, that she may bear him children. Accordingly the mutual relations of the members of a household admit of a threefold combination: viz., those of master and servant, those of husband and wife, and those of father and son: and in respect of all these relationships the Old Law contained fitting precepts. Thus, with regard to servants, it commanded them to be treated with moderation,—both as to their work, lest, to wit, they should be burdened with excessive labor, wherefore the Lord commanded (Deut. v. 14) that on the Sabbath day *thy manservant and thy maidservant* should *rest even as thyself:* —and also as to the infliction of punishment, for it ordered those who maimed their servants, to set them free (Exod. xxi. 26, 27). Similar provision was made in favor of a maidservant when married to anyone (*ibid.* 7, *seqq.*). Moreover, with regard to those servants in particular who were taken from among the people, the Law prescribed that they should go out free in the seventh year taking whatever they brought with them, even their clothes (*ibid.* 2, *seqq.*): and furthermore it was commanded (Deut. xv. 13) that they should be given provision for the journey.

With regard to wives the Law made certain prescriptions as to those who were to be taken in marriage: for instance, that they should marry a wife from their own tribe (Num. xxxvi. 6): and this lest confusion should ensue in the property of various tribes. Also that a man should marry the wife of his deceased brother when the latter died without issue, as prescribed in Deut. xxv. 5, 6: and this in order that he who could not have successors according to carnal origin, might at least have them by a kind of adoption, and that thus the deceased might not be entirely forgotten.

It also forbade them to marry certain women; to wit, women of strange nations, through fear of their losing their faith; and those of their near kindred, on account of the natural respect due to them.—Furthermore it prescribed in what way wives were to be treated after marriage. To wit, that they should not be slandered without grave reason: wherefore it ordered punishment to be inflicted on the man who falsely accused his wife of a crime (Deut. xxii. 13, *seqq.*). Also that a man's hatred of his wife should not be detrimental to his son (Deut. xxi. 15, *seqq.*). Again, that a man should not ill-use his wife through hatred of her, but rather that he should write a bill of divorce and send her away (Deut. xxiv. 1). Furthermore, in order to foster conjugal love from the very outset, it was prescribed that no public duties should be laid on a recently married man, so that he might be free to rejoice with his wife.

With regard to children, the Law commanded parents to educate them by instructing them in the faith: hence it is written (Exod. xii. 26 *seqq.*): *When your children shall say to you: What is the meaning of this service? you shall say to them: It is the victim of the passage of the Lord.* Moreover, they are commanded to teach them the rules of right conduct: wherefore it is written (Deut. xxi. 20) that the parents had to say: *He slighteth hearing our admonitions, he giveth himself to revelling and to debauchery.*

Reply Obj. 1. As the children of Israel had been delivered by the Lord from slavery, and for this reason were bound to the service of God, He did not wish them to be slaves in perpetuity. Hence it is written (Lev. xxv. 39, seqq.): *If thy brother, constrained by poverty, sell himself to thee, thou shalt not oppress him with the service of bondservants: but he shall be as a hireling and a sojourner . . . for they are My servants, and I brought them out of the land of Egypt: let them not be sold as bondmen:* and consequently, since they were slaves, not absolutely but in a restricted sense, after a lapse of time they were set free.

Reply Obj. 2. This commandment is to be understood as referring to a servant whom his master seeks to kill, or to help him in committing some sin.

Reply Obj. 3. With regard to the ill-treatment of servants, the Law seems to have taken into consideration whether it was certain or not: since if it were certain, the Law fixed a penalty: for maiming, the penalty was forfeiture of the servant, who was ordered to be given his liberty: while for slaying, the punishment was that of a murderer, when the servant died under the blow of his master.— If, however, the hurt were not certain, but only probable, the Law did not impose any penalty as regards a man's own servant: for instance if the servant did not die at once after being struck, but after some days: for it would be uncertain whether he died as a result of the blows he received. For when a man struck a free man, yet so that he did not die at once, but *walked abroad again upon his staff*, he that struck him was quit of murder, even though afterwards he died. Nevertheless he was bound to pay the doctor's fees incurred by the victim of his assault. But this was not the case if a man killed his own servant: because whatever the servant had, even his very person, was the property of his master. Hence the reason for his not being subject to a pecuniary penalty is set down as being *because it is his money*.

Reply Obj. 4. As stated above (*ad* 1), no Jew could own a Jew as a slave absolutely: but only in a restricted sense, as a hireling for a fixed time. And in this way the Law permitted that through stress of poverty a man might sell his son or daughter. This is shown by the very words of the Law, where we read: *If any man sell his daughter to be a servant, she shall not go out as bondwomen are wont to go out.* Moreover, in this way a man might sell not only his son, but even himself, rather as a hireling than as a slave, according to Lev. xxv. 39, 40: *If thy brother, constrained by poverty, sell himself to thee, thou shalt not oppress him with the service of bondservants: but he shall be as a hireling and a sojourner.*

Reply Obj. 5. As the Philosopher says (*Ethic* x. 9), the paternal authority has the power only of admonition; but not that of coercion, whereby rebellious and headstrong persons can be compelled. Hence in this case the Lord commanded the stubborn son to be punished by the rulers of the city.

Reply Obj. 6. The Lord forbade them to marry strange women on account of the danger of seduction, lest they should be led astray into idolatry. And specially did this prohibition apply with respect to those nations who dwelt near them, because it was more probable that they would adopt their religious practices.

When, however, the woman was willing to renounce idolatry and become an adherent of the Law, it was lawful to take her in marriage: as was the case with Ruth whom Booz married. Wherefore she said to her mother-in-law (Ruth i. 16): *Thy people shall be my people, and thy God my God.* Accordingly it was not permitted to marry a captive woman unless she first shaved her hair, and pared her nails, and put off the raiment wherein she was taken, and mourned for her father and mother, in token that she renounced idolatry for ever.

Reply Obj. 7. As Chrysostom says (*Hom.* xlviii. *super Matth.*), *because death was an unmitigated evil for the Jews, who did everything with a view to the present life, it was ordained that children should be born to the dead man through his brother: thus affording a certain mitigation to his death. It was not, however, ordained that any other than his brother or one next of kin should marry the wife of the deceased, because* the offspring of this union *would not be looked upon as that of the deceased: and, moreover, a stranger would not be under the obligation to support the household of the deceased, as his brother would be bound to do from motives of justice on account of his relationship.* Hence it is evident that in marrying the wife of his dead brother, he took his dead brother's place.

Reply Obj. 8. The Law permitted a wife to be divorced, not as though it were just absolutely speaking, but on account of the Jews' hardness of heart, as Our Lord declared (Matth. xix. 8). Of this, however, we must speak more fully in the treatise on Matrimony (Suppl., Q. 67).

Reply Obj. 9. Wives break their conjugal faith by adultery, both easily, for motives of pleasure, and hiddenly, since *the eye of the adulterer observeth darkness* (Job. xxiv. 15). But this does not apply to a son in respect of his father, or to a servant in respect of his master: because the latter infidelity is not the result of the lust of pleasure, but rather of malice: nor can it remain hidden like the infidelity of an adulterous woman.

QUESTION 106

Of the Law of the Gospel, Called the New Law, Considered in Itself

(In Four Articles)

In proper sequence we have to consider now the Law of the Gospel which is called the New Law: and in the first place we must consider it in itself; secondly, in comparison with the Old Law; thirdly, we shall treat of those things that are contained in the New Law.

Under the first head there are four points of inquiry: (1) What kind of law is it? i.e., is it a written law or is it instilled in the heart? (2) Of its efficacy, i.e., does it justify? (3) Of its beginning:—should it have been given at the beginning of the world? (4) Of its end:

i.e., whether it will last until the end, or will another law take its place?

FIRST ARTICLE

Whether the New Law Is a Written Law?

We proceed thus to the First Article:—

Objection 1. It would seem that the New Law is a written law. For the New Law is just the same as the Gospel. But the Gospel is set forth in writing, according to John xx. 31: *But these are written that you may believe.* Therefore the New Law is a written law.

Obj. 2. Further, the law that is instilled in the heart is the natural law, according to Rom. ii. 14, 15: (*The Gentiles*) *do by nature those things that are of the law ... who have* (Vulg., *show*) *the work of the law written in their hearts.* If therefore the law of the Gospel were instilled in our hearts, it would not be distinct from the law of nature.

Obj. 3. Further, the law of the Gospel is proper to those who are in the state of the New Testament. But the law that is instilled in the heart is common to those who are in the New Testament and to those who are in the Old Testament: for it is written (Wis. vii. 27) that Divine Wisdom *through nations conveyeth herself into holy souls, she maketh the friends of God and prophets.* Therefore the New Law is not instilled in our hearts.

On the contrary, The New Law is the law of the New Testament. But the law of the New Testament is instilled in our hearts. For the Apostle, quoting the authority of Jeremias xxxi. 31, 33: *Behold the days shall come, saith the Lord; and I will perfect unto the house of Israel, and unto the house of Juda, a new testament,* says, explaining what this testament is (Heb. viii. 8, 10): *For this is the testament which I will make to the house of Israel ... by giving* (Vulg.,—*I will give*) *My laws into their mind, and in their heart will I write them.* Therefore the New Law is instilled in our hearts.

I answer that, Each thing appears to be that which preponderates in it, as the Philosopher states (*Ethic.* ix. 8). Now that which is preponderant in the law of the New Testament, and whereon all its efficacy is based, is the grace of the Holy Ghost, which is given through faith in Christ. Consequently the New Law is chiefly the grace itself of the Holy Ghost, which is given to those who believe in Christ. This is manifestly stated by the Apostle who says (Rom. iii. 27): *Where is ... thy boasting? It is excluded. By what law? Of works? No, but by the law of faith:* for he calls the grace itself of faith *a law.* And still more clearly it is written (Rom. viii. 2): *The law of the spirit of life, in Christ Jesus, hath*

delivered me from the law of sin and of death. Hence Augustine says (*De Spir. et Lit.* xxiv) that *as the law of deeds was written on tables of stone, so is the law of faith inscribed on the hearts of the faithful:* and elsewhere, in the same book (xxi): *What else are the Divine laws written by God Himself on our hearts, but the very presence of His Holy Spirit?*

Nevertheless the New Law contains certain things that dispose us to receive the grace of the Holy Ghost, and pertaining to the use of that grace: such things are of secondary importance, so to speak, in the New Law; and the faithful needed to be instructed concerning them, both by word and writing, both as to what they should believe and as to what they should do. Consequently we must say that the New Law is in the first place a law that is inscribed on our hearts, but that secondarily it is a written law.

Reply Obj. 1. The Gospel writings contain only such things as pertain to the grace of the Holy Ghost, either by disposing us thereto, or by directing us to the use thereof. Thus with regard to the intellect, the Gospel contains certain matters pertaining to the manifestation of Christ's Godhead or humanity, which dispose us by means of faith through which we receive the grace of the Holy Ghost: and with regard to the affections, it contains matters touching the contempt of the world, whereby man is rendered fit to receive the grace of the Holy Ghost: for *the world,* i.e., worldly men, *cannot receive* the Holy Ghost (Jo. xiv. 17). As to the use of spiritual grace, this consists in works of virtue to which the writings of the New Testament exhort men in divers ways.

Reply Obj. 2. There are two ways in which a thing may be instilled into man. First, through being part of his nature, and thus the natural law is instilled into man. Secondly, a thing is instilled into man by being, as it were, added on to his nature by a gift of grace. In this way the New Law is instilled into man, not only by indicating to him what he should do, but also by helping him to accomplish it.

Reply Obj. 3. No man ever had the grace of the Holy Ghost except through faith in Christ either explicit or implicit: and by faith in Christ man belongs to the New Testament. Consequently whoever had the law of grace instilled into them belonged to the New Testament.

SECOND ARTICLE

Whether the New Law Justifies?

We proceed thus to the Second Article:—

Objection 1. It would seem that the New Law does not justify. For no man is justified unless he obey God's law, according to Heb.

v. 9. *He,* i.e., Christ, *became to all that obey Him the cause of eternal salvation.* But the Gospel does not always cause men to believe in it: for it is written (Rom. x. 16): *All do not obey the Gospel.* Therefore the New Law does not justify.

Obj. 2. Further, the Apostle proves in his epistle to the Romans that the Old Law did not justify, because transgression increased at its advent: for it is stated (Rom. iv. 15): *The Law worketh wrath: for where there is no law, neither is there transgression.* But much more did the New Law increase transgression: since he who sins after the giving of the New Law deserves greater punishment, according to Heb. x. 28, 29: *A man making void the Law of Moses dieth without any mercy under two or three witnesses. How much more, do you think, he deserveth worse punishments, who hath trodden under-foot the Son of God,* etc.? Therefore the New Law, like the Old Law, does not justify.

Obj. 3. Further, justification is an effect proper to God, according to Rom. viii. 33: *God that justifieth.* But the Old Law was from God just as the New Law. Therefore the New Law does not justify any more than the Old Law.

On the contrary, The Apostle says (Rom. i. 16): *I am not ashamed of the Gospel: for it is the power of God unto salvation to everyone that believeth.* But there is no salvation but to those who are justified. Therefore the Law of the Gospel justifies.

I answer that, As stated above (A. 1), there is a twofold element in the Law of the Gospel. There is the chief element, viz., the grace of the Holy Ghost bestowed inwardly. And as to this, the New Law justifies. Hence Augustine says (*De Spir. et Lit.* xvii): *There* i.e., in the Old Testament, *the Law was set forth in an outward fashion, that the ungodly might be afraid; here,* i.e., in the New Testament, *it is given in an inward manner, that they may be justified.*—The other element of the Evangelical Law is secondary: namely, the teachings of faith, and those commandments which direct human affections and human actions. And as to this, the New Law does not justify. Hence the Apostle says (2 Cor. iii. 6): *The letter killeth, but the spirit quickeneth:* and Augustine explains this (*De Spir. et Lit.* xiv, xvii) by saying that the letter denotes any writing that is external to man, even that of the moral precepts such as are contained in the Gospel. Wherefore the letter, even of the Gospel would kill, unless there were the inward presence of the healing grace of faith.

Reply Obj. 1. This argument is true of the New Law, not as to its principal, but as to its secondary element: i.e., as to the dogmas and precepts outwardly put before man either in words or in writing.

Reply Obj. 2. Although the grace of the New Testament helps man to avoid sin, yet it does not so confirm man in good that he cannot sin: for this belongs to the state of glory. Hence if a man sin after receiving the grace of the New Testament, he deserves greater punishment, as being ungrateful for greater benefits, and as not using the help given to him. And this is why the New Law is not said to *work wrath:* because as far as it is concerned it gives man sufficient help to avoid sin.

Reply Obj. 3. The same God gave both the New and the Old Law, but in different ways. For He gave the Old Law written on tables of stone: whereas He gave the New Law written *in the fleshly tables of the heart,* as the Apostle expresses it (2 Cor. iii. 3). Wherefore, as Augustine says (*De Spir. et Lit.* xviii), *the Apostle calls this letter which is written outside man, a ministration of death and a ministration of condemnation: whereas he calls the other letter,* i.e., *the Law of the New Testament, the ministration of the spirit and the ministration of justice: because through the gift of the Spirit we work justice, and are delivered from the condemnation due to transgression.*

THIRD ARTICLE

Whether the New Law Should Have Been Given from the Beginning of the World?

We proceed thus to the Third Article:—

Objection 1. It would seem that the New Law should have been given from the beginning of the world. *For there is no respect of persons with God* (Rom. ii. 11). But *all* men *have sinned and do need the glory of God* (*ibid.* iii. 23). Therefore the Law of the Gospel should have been given from the beginning of the world, in order that it might bring succor to all.

Obj. 2. Further, as men dwell in various places, so do they live in various times. But God, *Who will have all men to be saved* (1 Tim. ii. 4), commanded the Gospel to be preached in all places, as may be seen in the last chapters of Matthew and Mark. Therefore the Law of the Gospel should have been at hand for all times, so as to be given from the beginning of the world.

Obj. 3. Further, man needs to save his soul, which is for all eternity, more than to save his body, which is a temporal matter. But God provided man from the beginning of the world with things that are necessary for the health of his body, by subjecting to his power whatever was created for the sake of man (Gen. i. 26-29). Therefore the New Law also, which is very necessary for the health of the soul, should have been given to man from the beginning of the world.

On the contrary, The Apostle says (1 Cor. xv. 46): *That was not first which is spiritual, but that which is natural.* But the New Law is highly spiritual. Therefore it was not fitting for it to be given from the beginning of the world.

I answer that, Three reasons may be assigned why it was not fitting for the New Law to be given from the beginning of the world. The first is because the New Law, as stated above (A. 1), consists chiefly in the grace of the Holy Ghost: which it behoved not to be given abundantly until sin, which is an obstacle to grace, had been cast out of man through the accomplishment of his redemption by Christ: wherefore it is written (Jo. vii. 39): *As yet the Spirit was not given, because Jesus was not yet glorified.* This reason the Apostle states clearly (Rom. viii. 2, seqq.) where, after speaking of *the Law of the Spirit of life,* he adds: *God sending His own Son, in the likeness of sinful flesh, of sin* hath condemned sin in the flesh, that the justification of the Law might be fulfilled in us.*

A second reason may be taken from the perfection of the New Law. Because a thing is not brought to perfection at once from the outset, but through an orderly succession of time; thus one is at first a boy, and then a man. And this reason is stated by the Apostle (Gal. iii. 24, 25): *The Law was our pedagogue in Christ that we might be justified by faith. But after the faith is come, we are no longer under a pedagogue.*

The third reason is found in the fact that the New Law is the law of grace: wherefore it behoved man first of all to be left to himself under the state of the Old Law, so that through falling into sin, he might realize his weakness, and acknowledge his need of grace. This reason is set down by the Apostle (Rom. v. 20): *The Law entered in, that sin might abound: and when sin abounded grace did more abound.*

Reply Obj. 1. Mankind on account of the sin of our first parents deserved to be deprived of the aid of grace: and so *from whom it is withheld it is justly withheld, and to whom it is given, it is mercifully given,* as Augustine states (*De Perfect. Justit.* iv).† Consequently it does not follow that there is respect of persons with God, from the fact that He did not offer the Law of grace to all from the beginning of the world, which Law was to be published in due course of time, as stated above.

Reply Obj. 2. The state of mankind does not vary according to diversity of place, but according to succession of time. Hence the New Law avails for all places, but not for all times: although at all times there have been some persons belonging to the New Testament, as stated above (A. 1 ad 3).

Reply Obj. 3. Things pertaining to the health of the body are of service to man as regards his nature, which sin does not destroy: whereas things pertaining to the health of the soul are ordained to grace, which is forfeit through sin. Consequently the comparison will not hold.

FOURTH ARTICLE

Whether the New Law Will Last Till the End of the World?

We proceed thus to the Fourth Article:—

Objection 1. It would seem that the New Law will not last till the end of the world. Because, as the Apostle says (1 Cor. xiii. 10), *when that which is perfect is come, that which is in part shall be done away.* But the New Law is *in part,* since the Apostle says (*ibid.* 9): *We know in part and we prophesy in part.* Therefore the New Law is to be done away, and will be succeeded by a more perfect state.

Obj. 2. Further, Our Lord (Jo. xvi. 13) promised His disciples the knowledge of all truth when the Holy Ghost, the Comforter, should come. But the Church knows not yet all truth in the state of the New Testament. Therefore we must look forward to another state, wherein all truth will be revealed by the Holy Ghost.

Obj. 3. Further, just as the Father is distinct from the Son and the Son from the Father, so is the Holy Ghost distinct from the Father and the Son. But there was a state corresponding with the Person of the Father, viz., the state of the Old Law, wherein men were intent on begetting children: and likewise there is a state corresponding to the Person of the Son: viz., the state of the New Law, wherein the clergy who are intent on wisdom (which is appropriated to the Son) hold a prominent place. Therefore there will be a third state corresponding to the Holy Ghost, wherein spiritual men will hold the first place.

Obj. 4. Further, Our Lord said (Matth. xxiv. 14): *This Gospel of the kingdom shall be preached in the whole world . . . and then shall the consummation come.* But the Gospel of Christ is already preached throughout the whole world: and yet the consummation has

---

* S. Thomas, quoting perhaps from memory, omits the *et (and),* after *sinful flesh.* The text quoted should read thus,—*in the likeness of sinful flesh, and a sin offering* (περὶ ἁμαρτίας), *hath,* etc.

† Cf. *Ep.* ccvii; *De Pecc. Mer. et Rem.* ii. 19.

not yet come. Therefore the Gospel of Christ is not the Gospel of the kingdom, but another Gospel, that of the Holy Ghost, is to come yet, like unto another Law.

On the contrary, Our Lord said (Matth. xxiv. 34): *I say to you that this generation shall not pass till all (these) things be done:* which passage Chrysostom (*Hom.* lxxvii) explains as referring to *the generation of those that believe in Christ.* Therefore the state of those who believe in Christ will last until the consummation of the world.

I answer that, The state of the world may change in two ways. In one way, according to a change of law: and thus no other state will succeed this state of the New Law. Because the state of the New Law succeeded the state of the Old Law, as a more perfect law a less perfect one. Now no state of the present life can be more perfect than the state of the New Law: since nothing can approach nearer to the last end than that which is the immediate cause of our being brought to the last end. But the New Law does this: wherefore the Apostle says (Heb. x. 19-22): *Having therefore, brethren, a confidence in the entering into the Holies by the blood of Christ, a new . . . way which He hath dedicated for us . . . let us draw near.* Therefore no state of the present life can be more perfect than that of the New Law, since the nearer a thing is to the last end the more perfect it is.

In another way the state of mankind may change according as man stands in relation to one and the same law more or less perfectly. And thus the state of the Old Law underwent frequent changes, since at times the laws were very well kept, and at other times were altogether unheeded. Thus, too, the state of the New Law is subject to change with regard to various places, times, and persons, according as the grace of the Holy Ghost dwells in man more or less perfectly. Nevertheless we are not to look forward to a state wherein man is to possess the grace of the Holy Ghost more perfectly than he has possessed it hitherto, especially the apostles who *received the firstfruits of the Spirit,* i.e., *sooner and more abundantly than others,* as a gloss expounds on Rom. viii. 23.

Reply Obj. 1. As Dionysius says (*Eccl. Hier.* v), there is a threefold state of mankind; the first was under the Old Law; the second is that of the New Law; the third will take place not in this life, but in heaven. But as the first state is figurative and imperfect in comparison with the state of the Gospel; so is the present state figurative and imperfect in comparison with the heavenly state, with the advent of which the present state will be done away as expressed in that very passage (verse 12): *We see now through a glass in a dark manner; but then face to face.*

Reply Obj. 2. As Augustine says (*Contra Faust.* xix. 31), Montanus and Priscilla pretended that Our Lord's promise to give the Holy Ghost was fulfilled, not in the apostles, but in themselves. In like manner the Manicheans maintained that it was fulfilled in Manes whom they held to be the Paraclete. Hence none of the above received the *Acts of the Apostles,* where it is clearly shown that the aforesaid promise was fulfilled in the apostles: just as Our Lord promised them a second time (Acts i. 5): *You shall be baptized with the Holy Ghost, not many days hence:* which we read as having been fulfilled in Acts ii. However, these foolish notions are refuted by the statement (Jo. vii. 39) that *as yet the Spirit was not given, because Jesus was not yet glorified;* from which we gather that the Holy Ghost was given as soon as Christ was glorified in His Resurrection and Ascension. Moreover, this puts out of court the senseless idea that the Holy Ghost is to be expected to come at some other time.

Now the Holy Ghost taught the apostles all truth in respect of matters necessary for salvation; those things, to wit, that we are bound to believe and to do. But He did not teach them about all future events: for this did not regard them according to Acts i. 7: *It is not for you to know the times or moments which the Father hath put in His own power.*

Reply Obj. 3. The Old Law corresponded not only to the Father, but also to the Son: because Christ was foreshadowed in the Old Law. Hence Our Lord said (Jo. v. 46): *If you did believe Moses, you would perhaps believe me also; for he wrote of Me.* In like manner the New Law corresponds not only to Christ, but also to the Holy Ghost; according to Rom. viii. 2: *The Law of the Spirit of life in Christ Jesus,* etc. Hence we are not to look forward to another law corresponding to the Holy Ghost.

Reply Obj. 4. Since Christ said at the very outset of the preaching of the Gospel: *The kingdom of heaven is at hand* (Matth. iv .17), it is most absurd to say that the Gospel of Christ is not the Gospel of the kingdom. But the preaching of the Gospel of Christ may be understood in two ways. First, as denoting the spreading abroad of the knowledge of Christ: and thus the Gospel was preached throughout the whole world even at the time of the apostles, as Chrysostom states (*Hom.* lxxv. *in Matth.*). And in this sense the words that follow,—*and then shall the consummation come,* refer to the destruction of Jerusalem, of which He was speaking literally.—Secondly, the preaching of the Gospel may be understood as extending throughout the world and producing its full effect, so that, to wit, the Church would be founded in every nation. And in this sense, as Augustine writes to Hesychius (*Epist.* cxcix), the Gospel is not preached to the whole world yet, but, when it is, the consummation of the world will come.

QUESTION 107

Of the New Law As Compared with the Old

(In Four Articles)

WE must now consider the New Law as compared with the Old: under which head there are four points of inquiry: (1) Whether the New Law is distinct from the Old Law? (2) Whether the New Law fulfils the Old? (3) Whether the New Law is contained in the old? (4) Which is the more burdensome, the New or the Old Law?

FIRST ARTICLE

Whether the New Law Is Distinct from the Old Law?

We proceed thus to the First Article:—

Objection 1. It would seem that the New Law is not distinct from the Old. Because both these laws were given to those who believe in God: since *without faith it is impossible to please God,* according to Heb. xi. 6. But the faith of olden times and of nowadays is the same, as the gloss says on Matth. xxi. 9. Therefore the law is the same also.

Obj. 2. Further, Augustine says (*Contra Adamant. Manich. discip.* xvii) that *there is little difference between the Law and Gospel,** —*fear and love.* But the New and Old Laws cannot be differentiated in respect of these two things: since even the Old Law comprised precepts of charity: *Thou shalt love thy neighbor* (Lev. xix. 18), and: *Thou shalt love the Lord thy God* (Deut. vi. 5).—In like manner neither can they differ according to the other difference which Augustine assigns (*Contra Faust.* iv. 2), viz., that *the Old Testament contained temporal promises, whereas the New Testament contains spiritual and eternal promises:* since even the New Testament contains temporal promises, according to Mark x. 30: He shall receive *a hundred times as much . . . in this time, houses and brethren,* etc.: while in the Old Testament they hoped in promises spiritual and eternal, according to Heb. xi. 16: *But now they desire a better, that is to say, a heavenly country,* which is said of the patriarchs. Therefore it seems that the New Law is not distinct from the Old.

Obj. 3. Further, the Apostle seems to distinguish both laws by calling the Old Law *a law of works,* and the New Law *a law of faith*

* See footnote, p. 999.

(Rom. iii. 27). But the Old Law was also a law of faith, according to Heb. xi. 39: *All were* (Vulg.,—*All these being*) *approved by the testimony of faith,* which he says of the fathers of the Old Testament. In like manner the New Law is a law of works: since it is written (Matth. v. 44): *Do good to them that hate you;* and (Luke xxii. 19): *Do this for a commemoration of Me.* Therefore the New Law is not distinct from the Old.

On the contrary, the Apostle says (Heb. vii. 12): *The priesthood being translated it is necessary that a translation also be made of the Law.* But the priesthood of the New Testament is distinct from that of the Old, as the Apostle shows in the same place. Therefore the Law is also distinct.

I answer that, As stated above (Q. 90, A. 2; Q. 91, A. 4), every law ordains human conduct to some end. Now things ordained to an end may be divided in two ways, considered from the point of view of the end. First, through being ordained to different ends: and this difference will be specific, especially if such ends are proximate. Secondly, by reason of being closely or remotely connected with the end. Thus it is clear that movements differ in species through being directed to different terms: while according as one part of a movement is nearer to the term than another part, the difference of perfect and imperfect movement is assessed.

Accordingly then two laws may be distinguished from one another in two ways. First, through being altogether diverse, from the fact that they are ordained to diverse ends: thus a state-law ordained to democratic government, would differ specifically from a law ordained to government by the aristocracy. Secondly, two laws may be distinguished from one another, through one of them being more closely connected with the end, and the other more remotely: thus in one and the same state there is one law enjoined on men of mature age, who can forthwith accomplish that which pertains to the common good; and another law regulating the education of children who need to be taught how they are to achieve manly deeds later on.

We must therefore say that, according to

the first way, the New Law is not distinct from the Old Law: because they both have the same end, namely, man's subjection to God; and there is but one God of the New and of the Old Testament, according to Rom. iii. 30: *It is one God that justifieth circumcision by faith, and uncircumcision through faith.*—According to the second way, the New Law is distinct from the Old Law: because the Old Law is like a pedagogue of children, as the Apostle says (Gal. iii. 24), whereas the New Law is the law of perfection, since it is the law of charity, of which the Apostle says (Coloss. iii. 14) that it is *the bond of perfection.*

Reply Obj. 1. The unity of faith under both Testaments witnesses to the unity of end: for it has been stated above (Q. 62, A. 2) that the object of the theological virtues, among which is faith, is the last end. Yet faith had a different state in the Old and in the New Law: since what they believed as future, we believe as fact.

Reply Obj. 2. All the differences assigned between the Old and New Laws are gathered from their relative perfection and imperfection. For the precepts of every law prescribe acts of virtue. Now the imperfect, who as yet are not possessed of a virtuous habit, are directed in one way to perform virtuous acts, while those who are perfected by the possession of virtuous habits are directed in another way. For those who as yet are not endowed with virtuous habits, are directed to the performance of virtuous acts by reason of some outward cause: for instance, by the threat of punishment, or the promise of some extrinsic rewards, such as honor, riches, or the like. Hence the Old Law, which was given to men who were imperfect, that is, who had not yet received spiritual grace, was called the *law of fear,* inasmuch as it induced men to observe its commandments by threatening them with penalties; and is spoken of as containing temporal promises.—On the other hand, those who are possessed of virtue, are inclined to do virtuous deeds through love of virtue, not on account of some extrinsic punishment or reward. Hence the New Law which derives its pre-eminence from the spiritual grace instilled into our hearts, is called the *Law of love:* and it is described as containing spiritual and eternal promises, which are objects of the virtues, chiefly of charity. Accordingly such persons are inclined of themselves to those objects, not as to something foreign but as to something of their own.—For this reason, too, the Old Law is described as *restraining the hand, not the will;*[*] since when a man refrains from some sins through fear of being punished, his will does not shrink simply from sin, as does

[*] Peter Lombard, *Sent.* iii., D. 40.

the will of a man who refrains from sin through love of righteousness: and hence the New Law, which is the Law of love, is said to restrain the will.

Nevertheless there were some in the state of the Old Testament who, having charity and the grace of the Holy Ghost, looked chiefly to spiritual and eternal promises: and in this respect they belonged to the New Law.—In like manner in the New Testament there are some carnal men who have not yet attained to the perfection of the New Law; and these it was necessary, even under the New Testament, to lead to virtuous action by the fear of punishment and by temporal promises.

But although the Old Law contained precepts of charity, nevertheless it did not confer the Holy Ghost by Whom *charity . . . is spread abroad in our hearts* (Rom. v. 5).

Reply Obj. 3. As stated above (Q. 106, AA. 1, 2). the New Law is called the law of faith, in so far as its pre-eminence is derived from that very grace which is given inwardly to believers, and for this reason is called the grace of faith. Nevertheless it consists secondarily in certain deeds, moral and sacramental: but the New Law does not consist chiefly in these latter things, as did the Old Law. As to those under the Old Testament who through faith were acceptable to God, in this respect they belonged to the New Testament: for they were not justified except through faith in Christ, Who is the Author of the New Testament. Hence of Moses the Apostle says (Heb. xi. 26) that he esteemed *the reproach of Christ greater riches than the treasure of the Egyptians.*

SECOND ARTICLE

Whether the New Law Fulfils the Old?

We proceed thus to the Second Article:—

Objection 1. It would seem that the New Law does not fulfil the Old. Because to fulfil and to void are contrary. But the New Law voids or excludes the observances of the Old Law: for the Apostle says (Gal. v. 2): *If you be circumcised, Christ shall profit you nothing.* Therefore the New Law is not a fulfilment of the Old.

Obj. 2. Further, one contrary is not the fulfilment of another. But Our Lord propounded in the New Law precepts that were contrary to precepts of the Old Law. For we read (Matth. v. 27-32): You have heard that it was said to them of old: . . . *Whosoever shall put away his wife, let him give her a bill of divorce. But I say to you that whosoever shall put away his wife . . . maketh her to commit adultery.* Furthermore, the same evidently applies to the prohibition against swearing, against retaliation, and against hating one's enemies. In like manner Our Lord seems to have done away with the precepts of the Old Law relating to the different kinds of foods (Matth. xv. 11): *Not that which goeth into the mouth defileth a man: but what cometh out of the mouth, this defileth a man.* Therefore the New Law is not a fulfilment of the Old.

Obj. 3. Further, whoever acts against a law does not fulfil the law. But Christ in certain cases acted against the Law. For He touched the leper (Matth. viii. 3), which was contrary to the Law. Likewise He seems to have frequently broken the sabbath; since the Jews used to say of Him (Jo. ix. 16): *This man is not of God, who keepeth not the sabbath.* Therefore Christ did not fulfil the Law: and so the New Law given by Christ is not a fulfilment of the Old.

Obj. 4. Further, the Old Law contained precepts, moral, ceremonial, and judicial, as stated above (Q. 99, A. 4). But Our Lord (Matth. v.) fulfilled the Law in some respects, but without mentioning the judicial and ceremonial precepts. Therefore it seems that the New Law is not a complete fulfilment of the Old.

On the contrary, Our Lord said (Matth. v. 17): *I am not come to destroy, but to fulfil:* and went on to say (*verse* 18): *One jot or one tittle shall not pass of the Law till all be fulfilled.*

I answer that, As stated above (A. 1), the New Law is compared to the Old as the perfect to the imperfect. Now everything perfect fulfils that which is lacking in the imperfect. And accordingly the New Law fulfils the Old by supplying that which was lacking in the Old Law.

Now two things in the Old Law offer themselves to our consideration: viz., the end, and the precepts contained in the Law.

Now the end of every law is to make men righteous and virtuous, as was stated above (Q. 92, A. 1): and consequently the end of the Old Law was the justification of men. The Law, however, could not accomplish this: but foreshadowed it by certain ceremonial actions, and promised it in words. And in this respect, the New Law fulfils the Old by justifying men through the power of Christ's Passion. This is what the Apostle says (Rom. viii. 3, 4): *What the Law could not do . . . God sending His own Son in the likeness of sinful flesh . . . hath condemned sin in the flesh, that the justification of the Law might be fulfilled in us.*—And in this respect, the New Law gives what the Old Law promised,

according to 2 Cor. i. 20: *Whatever are the promises of God, in Him,* i.e., in Christ, *they are "Yea."**—Again, in this respect, it also fulfils what the Old Law foreshadowed. Hence it is written (Coloss. ii. 17) concerning the ceremonial precepts that they were *a shadow of things to come, but the body is of Christ;* in other words, the reality is found in Christ. Wherefore the New Law is called the law of reality; whereas the Old Law is called the law of shadow or of figure.

Now Christ fulfilled the precepts of the Old Law both in His works and in His doctrine. In His works, because He was willing to be circumcised and to fulfil the other legal observances, which were binding for the time being; according to Gal. iv. 4: *Made under the Law.*—In His doctrine He fulfilled the precepts of the Law in three ways. First, by explaining the true sense of the Law. This is clear in the case of murder and adultery, the prohibition of which the Scribes and Pharisees thought to refer only to the exterior act: wherefore Our Lord fulfilled the Law by showing that the prohibition extended also to the interior acts of sins.—Secondly, Our Lord fulfilled the precepts of the Law by prescribing the safest way of complying with the statutes of the Old Law. Thus the Old Law forbade perjury: and this is more safely avoided, by abstaining altogether from swearing, save in cases of urgency.—Thirdly, Our Lord fulfilled the precepts of the Law, by adding some counsels of perfection: this is clearly seen in Matth. xix. 21, where Our Lord said to the man who affirmed that he had kept all the precepts of the Old Law: *One thing is wanting to thee: If thou wilt be perfect, go, sell whatsoever thou hast,* etc.†

Reply Obj. 1. The New Law does not void observance of the Old Law except in the point of ceremonial precepts, as stated above (Q. 103. AA. 3, 4). Now the latter were figurative of something to come. Wherefore from the very fact that the ceremonial precepts were fulfilled when those things were accomplished which they foreshadowed, it follows that they are no longer to be observed: for if they were to be observed, this would mean that something is still to be accomplished and is not yet fulfilled. Thus the promise of a future gift holds no longer when it has been fulfilled by the presentation of the gift. In this way the legal ceremonies are abolished by being fulfilled.

Reply Obj. 2. As Augustine says (*Contra Faust.* xix. 26), those precepts of Our Lord are not contrary to the precepts of the Old Law. For what Our Lord commanded about a man

---

* The Douay version reads thus: *All the promises of God are in Him, "It is."*

† S. Thomas combines Matth. xix. 21 with Mark x. 21.

not putting away his wife, is not contrary to what the Law prescribed. *For the Law did not say: "Let him that wills, put his wife away": the contrary of which would be not to put her away. On the contrary, the Law was unwilling that a man should put away his wife, since it prescribed a delay, so that excessive eagerness for divorce might cease through being weakened during the writing of the bill.* Hence Our Lord, in order to impress the fact that a wife ought not easily to be put away, allowed no exception save in the case of fornication. The same applies to the prohibition about swearing, as stated above.—The same is also clear with respect to the prohibition of retaliation. For the Law fixed a limit to revenge, by forbidding men to seek vengeance unreasonably: whereas Our Lord deprived them of vengeance more completely by commanding them to abstain from it altogether.—With regard to the hatred of one's enemies, He dispelled the false interpretation of the Pharisees, by admonishing us to hate, not the person, but his sin.—As to discriminating between various foods, which was a ceremonial matter, Our Lord did not forbid this to be observed: but He showed that no foods are naturally unclean, but only in token of something else, as stated above (Q. 102, A. 6 *ad* 1).

Reply Obj. 3. It was forbidden by the Law to touch a leper; because by doing so, man incurred a certain uncleanness of irregularity, as also by touching the dead, as stated above (Q. 102, A. 5 *ad* 4). But Our Lord, Who healed the leper, could not contract an uncleanness.—By those things which He did on the sabbath, He did not break the sabbath in reality, as the Master Himself shows in the Gospel: both because He worked miracles by His Divine power, which is ever active among things; and because His works were concerned with the salvation of man, while the Pharisees were concerned for the well-being of animals even on the sabbath; and again because on account of urgency He excused His disciples for gathering the ears of corn on the sabbath. But He did seem to break the sabbath according to the superstitious interpretation of the Pharisees, who thought that man ought to abstain from doing even works of kindness on the sabbath; which was contrary to the intention of the Law.

Reply Obj. 4. The reason why the ceremonial precepts of the Law are not mentioned in Matth. v. is because, as stated above (*ad* 1), their observance was abolished by their fulfilment.—But of the judicial precepts He mentioned that of retaliation: so that what He said about it should refer to all the others. With regard to this precept, He taught that the intention of the Law was that retaliation

should be sought out of love of justice, and not as a punishment out of revengeful spite, which He forbade, admonishing man to be ready to suffer yet greater insults; and this remains still in the New Law.

THIRD ARTICLE
Whether the New Law Is Contained in the Old?

We proceed thus to the Third Article:—

Objection 1. It would seem that the New Law is not contained in the Old. Because the New Law consists chiefly in faith: wherefore it is called the *law of faith* (Rom. iii. 27). But many points of faith are set forth in the New Law, which are not contained in the Old. Therefore the New Law is not contained in the Old.

Obj. 2. Further, a gloss says on Matth. v. 19, *He that shall break one of these least commandments,* that the lesser commandments are those of the Law, and the greater commandments, those contained in the Gospel. Now the greater cannot be contained in the lesser. Therefore the New Law is not contained in the Old.

Obj. 3. Further, who holds the container holds the contents. If, therefore, the New Law is contained in the Old, it follows that whoever had the Old Law had the New: so that it was superfluous to give men a New Law when once they had the Old. Therefore New Law is not contained in the Old.

On the contrary, As expressed in Ezech. i. 16, there was *a wheel in the midst of a wheel,* i.e., *the New Testament within the Old,* according to Gregory's exposition.

I answer that, One thing may be contained in another in two ways. First, actually; as a located thing is in a place, Secondly, virtually; as an effect in its cause, or as the complement in that which is incomplete; thus a genus contains its species, and a seed contains the whole tree, virtually. It is in this way that the New Law is contained in the Old: for it has been stated (A. 1) that the New Law is compared to the Old as perfect to imperfect. Hence Chrysostom, expounding Mark iv. 28, *The earth of itself bringeth forth fruit, first the blade, then the ear, afterwards the full corn in the ear,* expresses himself as follows: *He brought forth first the blade,* i.e., *the Law of Nature; then the ear,* i.e., *the Law of Moses; lastly, the full corn,* i.e., *the Law of the Gospel.* Hence then the New Law is in the Old as the corn in the ear.

Reply Obj. 1. Whatsoever is set down in the New Testament explicitly and openly as a point of faith, is contained in the Old Testament as a matter of belief, but implicitly, under a figure. And accordingly, even as to those things which we are bound to believe, the New Law is contained in the Old.

Reply Obj. 2. The precepts of the New Law are said to be greater than those of the Old Law, in the point of their being set forth explicitly. But as to the substance itself of the precepts of the New Testament, they are all contained in the Old. Hence Augustine says (*Contra Faust.* xix. 23, 28) that *nearly all Our Lord's admonitions or precepts, where He expressed Himself by saying: "But I say unto you," are to be found also in those ancient books. Yet, since they thought that murder was only the slaying of the human body, Our Lord declared to them that every wicked impulse to hurt our brother is to be looked on as a kind of murder.* And it is in the point of declarations of this kind that the precepts of the New Law are said to be greater than those of the Old. Nothing, however, prevents the greater from being contained in the lesser virtually; just as a tree is contained in the seed.

Reply Obj. 3. What is set forth implicitly needs to be declared explicitly. Hence after the publishing of the Old Law, a New Law also had to be given.

FOURTH ARTICLE

Whether the New Law Is More Burdensome Than the Old?

We proceed thus to the Fourth Article:—

Objection 1. It would seem that the New Law is more burdensome than the Old. For Chrysostom (*Opus Imp. in Matth., Hom.* x*) says: *The commandments given to Moses are easy to obey: Thou shalt not kill; Thou shalt not commit adultery: but the commandments of Christ are difficult to accomplish, for instance: Thou shalt not give way to anger, or to lust.* Therefore the New Law is more burdensome than the Old.

Obj. 2. Further, it is easier to make use of earthly prosperity than to suffer tribulations. But in the Old Testament observance of the Law was followed by temporal prosperity, as may be gathered from Deut. xxviii. 1-14; whereas many kinds of trouble ensue to those who observe the New Law, as stated in 2 Cor. vi. 4-10: *Let us exhibit ourselves as the ministers of God, in much patience, in tribulation, in necessities, in distresses,* etc. Therefore the New Law is more burdensome than the Old.

Obj. 3. The more one has to do, the more difficult it is. But the New Law is something added to the Old. For the Old Law forbade perjury, while the New Law proscribed even swearing: the Old Law forbade a man to cast off his wife without a bill of divorce, while the New Law forbade divorce altogether; as is

* The work of an unknown author.

clearly stated in Matth. v. 31 *seqq.,* according to Augustine's expounding. Therefore the New Law is more burdensome than the Old.

On the contrary, It is written (Matth. xi. 28): *Come to Me, all you that labor and are burdened:* which words are expounded by Hilary thus: *He calls to Himself all those that labor under the difficulty of observing the Law, and are burdened with the sins of this world.* And further on He says of the yoke of the Gospel: *For My yoke is sweet and My burden light.* Therefore the New Law is a lighter burden than the Old.

I answer that, A twofold difficult may attach to works of virtue with which the precepts of the Law are concerned. One is on the part of the outward works, which of themselves are, in a way, difficult and burdensome. And in this respect the Old Law is a much heavier burden than the New: since the Old Law by its numerous ceremonies prescribed many more outward acts than the New Law, which, in the teaching of Christ and the apostles, added very few precepts to those of the natural law; although afterwards some were added, through being instituted by the holy Fathers. Even in these Augustine says that moderation should be observed, lest good conduct should become a burden to the faithful. For he says in reply to the queries of Januarius (*Ep.* lv) that, *whereas God in His mercy wished religion to be a free service rendered by the public solemnization of a small number of most manifest sacraments, certain persons make it a slave's burden; so much so that the state of the Jews who were subject to the sacraments of the Law, and not to the presumptuous devices of man, was more tolerable.*

The other difficulty attaches to works of virtue as to interior acts: for instance, that a virtuous deed be done with promptitude and pleasure. It is this difficulty that virtue solves: because to act thus is difficult for a man without virtue: but through virtue it becomes easy to him. In this respect the precepts of the New Law are more burdensome than those of the Old; because the New Law prohibits certain interior movements of the soul, which were not expressly forbidden in the Old Law in all cases, although they were forbidden in some, without, however, any punishment being attached to the prohibition. Now this is very difficult to a man without virtue: thus even the Philosopher states (*Ethic.* v. 9) that it is easy to do what a righteous man does; but that to do it in the same way, viz., with pleasure and promptitude, is difficult to a man who is not righteous. Accordingly we read also (1 Jo. v. 3) that *His commandments are not heavy:* which words Augustine expounds by saying that *they are not heavy to the man that loveth; whereas they are a burden to him that loveth not.*

Reply Obj. 1. The passage quoted speaks expressly of the difficulty of the New Law as to the deliberate curbing of interior movements.

Reply Obj. 2. The tribulations suffered by those who observe the New Law are not imposed by the Law itself. Moreover they are easily borne, on account of the love in which the same Law consists: since, as Augustine says (*De Verb. Dom., Serm.* lxx), *love makes light and nothing of things that seem arduous and beyond our power.*

Reply Obj. 3. The object of these additions to the precepts of the Old Law was to render it easier to do what it prescribed, as Augustine states.* Accordingly this does not prove that the New Law is more burdensome, but rather that it is a lighter burden.

QUESTION 108

Of Those Things That Are Contained in the New Law

(In Four Articles)

WE must now consider those things that are contained in the New Law: under which head there are four points of inquiry: (1) Whether the New Law ought to prescribe or to forbid any outward works? (2) Whether the New Law makes sufficient provision in prescribing and forbidding external acts? (3) Whether in the matter of internal acts it directs man sufficiently? (4) Whether it fittingly adds counsels to precepts?

FIRST ARTICLE

Whether the New Law Ought to Prescribe or Prohibit Any External Acts?

We proceed thus to the First Article:—

Objection 1. It would seem that the New Law should not prescribe or prohibit any external acts. For the New Law is the Gospel of the kingdom, according to Matth. xxiv. 14: *This Gospel of the kingdom shall be preached in the whole world.* But the kingdom of God consists not in exterior, but only in interior acts, according to Luke xvii. 21: *The kingdom of God is within you;* and Rom. xiv. 17: *The kingdom of God is not meat and drink; but justice and peace and joy in the Holy Ghost.* Therefore the New Law should not prescribe or forbid any external acts.

Obj. 2. Further, the New Law is *the law of the Spirit* (Rom. viii. 2). But *where the Spirit of the Lord is, there is liberty* (2 Cor. iii. 17). Now there is no liberty when man is bound to do or avoid certain external acts. Therefore the New Law does not prescribe or forbid any external acts.

Obj. 3. Further, all external acts are understood as referable to the hand, just as interior acts belong to the mind. But this is assigned as the difference between the New and Old Laws that the *Old Law restrains the hand, whereas the New Law curbs the will.*† Therefore the New Law should not contain prohibitions and commands about exterior deeds, but only about interior acts.

On the contrary, Through the New Law, men are made *children of light:* wherefore it is written (Jo. xii. 36): *Believe in the light that you may be the children of light.* Now it is becoming that children of the light should do deeds of light and cast aside deeds of darkness, according to Ephes. v. 8: *You were heretofore darkness, but now light in the Lord. Walk . . . as children of the light.* Therefore the New Law had to forbid certain external acts and prescribe others.

I answer that, As stated above (Q. 106, AA. 1, 2), the New Law consists chiefly in the grace of the Holy Ghost, which is shown forth by faith that worketh through love. Now men become receivers of this grace through God's Son made man, Whose humanity grace filled first, and thence flowed forth to us. Hence it is written (Jo. i. 14): *The Word was made flesh,* and afterwards: *full of grace and truth;* and further on: *Of His fulness we all have received, and grace for grace.* Hence it is added that *grace and truth came by Jesus Christ.* Consequently it was becoming that the grace which flows from the incarnate Word should be given to us by means of certain external sensible objects; and that from this inward grace, whereby the flesh is subjected to the Spirit, certain external works should ensue.

Accordingly external acts may have a twofold connection with grace. In the first place, as leading in some way to grace. Such are the sacramental acts which are instituted in the New Law, *e.g.,* Baptism, the Eucharist, and the like.

In the second place there are those external acts which ensue from the promptings of grace: and herein we must observe a difference. For there are some which are necessarily in keeping with, or in opposition to inward grace consisting in faith that worketh

---

* *De Serm. Dom. in Monte.* i. 17, 21; xix. 23, 26.

† Peter Lombard, *Sent.* iii., D. 40.

through love. Such external works are prescribed or forbidden in the New Law; thus confession of faith is prescribed, and denial of faith is forbidden; for it is written (Matth. x. 32, 33): (*Every one*) *that shall confess Me before men, I will also confess him before My Father.... But he that shall deny Me before men, I will also deny him before My Father.* —On the other hand, there are works which are not necessarily opposed to, or in keeping with faith that worketh through love. Such works are not prescribed or forbidden in the New Law, by virtue of its primitive institution; but have been left by the Lawgiver, i.e., Christ, to the discretion of each individual. And so to each one it is free to decide what he should do or avoid; and to each superior, to direct his subjects in such matters as regards what they must do or avoid. Wherefore also in this respect the Gospel is called the *law of liberty**: since the Old Law decided many points and left few to man to decide as he chose.

Reply Obj. 1. The kingdom of God consists chiefly in internal acts: but as a consequence all things that are essential to internal acts belong also to the kingdom of God. Thus if the kingdom of God is internal righteousness, peace, and spiritual joy, all external acts that are incompatible with righteousness, peace, and spiritual joy, are in opposition to the kingdom of God; and consequently should be forbidden in the Gospel of the kingdom. On the other hand, those things that are indifferent as regards the aforesaid, for instance, to eat of this or that food, are not part of the kingdom of God; wherefore the Apostle says before the words quoted: *The kingdom of God is not meat and drink.*

Reply Obj. 2. According to the Philosopher (*Metaph.* i. 2), what is *free is cause of itself.* Therefore he acts freely, who acts of his own accord. Now man does of his own accord that which he does from a habit that is suitable to his nature: since a habit inclines one as a second nature. If, however, a habit be in opposition to nature, man would not act according to his nature, but according to some corruption affecting that nature. Since then the grace of the Holy Ghost is like an interior habit bestowed on us and inclining us to act aright, it makes us do freely those things that are becoming to grace, and shun what is opposed to it.

Accordingly the New Law is called the law of liberty in two respects. First, because it does not bind us to do or avoid certain things, except such as are of themselves necessary or opposed to salvation, and come under the prescription or prohibition of the law. Secondly,

* *Cf.* Reply Obj. 2.

because it also makes us comply freely with these precepts and prohibitions, inasmuch as we do so through the promptings of grace. It is for these two reasons that the New Law is called *the law of perfect liberty* (James i. 25).

Reply Obj. 3. The New Law, by restraining the mind from inordinate movements, must needs also restrain the hand from inordinate acts, which ensue from inward movements.

SECOND ARTICLE

Whether the New Law Made Sufficient Ordinations about External Acts?

We proceed thus to the Second Article:—

Objection 1. It would seem that the New Law made insufficient ordinations about external acts. Because faith that worketh through charity seems chiefly to belong to the New Law, according to Gal. v. 6: *In Christ Jesus neither circumcision availeth anything, nor uncircumcision: but faith that worketh through charity.* But the New Law declared explicitly certain points of faith which were not set forth explicitly in the Old Law; for instance, belief in the Trinity. Therefore it should also have added certain outward moral deeds, which were not fixed in the Old Law.

Obj. 2. Further, in the Old Law not only were sacraments instituted, but also certain sacred things, as stated above (Q. 101, A. 4; Q. 102, A. 4). But in the New Law, although certain sacraments are instituted, yet no sacred things seem to have been instituted by Our Lord; for instance, pertaining either to the sanctification of a temple or of the vessels, or to the celebration of some particular feast. Therefore the New Law made insufficient ordinations about external matters.

Obj. 3. Further, in the Old Law, just as there were certain observances pertaining to God's ministers, so also were there certain observances pertaining to the people: as was stated above when we were treating of the ceremonial of the Old Law (Q. 101, A. 4; Q. 102, A. 6). Now in the New Law certain observances seem to have been prescribed to the ministers of God; as may be gathered from Matth. x. 9: *Do not possess gold, nor silver, nor money in your purses,* nor other things which are mentioned here and Luke ix, x. Therefore certain observances pertaining to the faithful should also have been instituted in the New Law.

Obj. 4. Further, in the Old Law, besides moral and ceremonial precepts, there were certain judicial precepts. But in the New Law there are no judicial precepts. Therefore the New Law made insufficient ordinations about external works.

On the contrary, Our Lord said (Matth.

vii. 24): *Every one . . . that heareth these My words, and doth them, shall be likened to a wise man that built his house upon a rock.* But a wise builder leaves out nothing that is necessary to the building. Therefore Christ's words contain all things necessary for man's salvation.

I answer that, As stated above (A. 1), the New Law had to make such prescriptions or prohibitions alone as are essential for the reception or right use of grace. And since we cannot of ourselves obtain grace, but through Christ alone, hence Christ of Himself instituted the sacraments whereby we obtain grace: viz., Baptism, Eucharist, Orders of the ministers of the New Law, by the institution of the apostles and seventy-two disciples, Penance, and indissoluble Matrimony. He promised Confirmation through the sending of the Holy Ghost: and we read that by His institution the apostles healed the sick by anointing them with oil (Mark vi. 13). These are the sacraments of the New Law.

The right use of grace is by means of works of charity. These, in so far as they are essential to virtue, pertain to the moral precepts, which also formed part of the Old Law. Hence, in this respect, the New Law had nothing to add as regards external action.—The determination of these works in their relation to the divine worship, belongs to the ceremonial precepts of the Law; and, in relation to our neighbor, to the judicial precepts, as stated above (Q. 99, A. 4). And therefore, since these determinations are not in themselves necessarily connected with inward grace wherein the Law consists, they do not come under a precept of the New Law, but are left to the decision of man; some relating to inferiors,—as when a precept is given to an individual; others, relating to superiors, temporal or spiritual, referring, namely, to the common good.

Accordingly the New Law had no other external works to determine, by prescribing or forbidding, except the sacraments, and those moral precepts which have a necessary connection with virtue, for instance, that one must not kill, or steal, and so forth.

Reply Obj. 1. Matters of faith are above human reason, and so we cannot attain to them except through grace. Consequently, when grace came to be bestowed more abundantly, the result was an increase in the number of explicit points of faith. On the other hand, it is through human reason that we are directed to works of virtue, for it is the rule of human action, as stated above (Q. 19, A. 3; Q. 63, A. 2). Wherefore in such matters as these there was no need for any precepts to be given besides the moral precepts of the

Law, which proceed from the dictate of reason.

Reply Obj. 2. In the sacraments of the New Law grace is bestowed, which cannot be received except through Christ: consequently they had to be instituted by Him. But in the sacred things no grace is given: for instance, in the consecration of a temple, an altar or the like, or, again, in the celebration of feasts. Wherefore Our Lord left the institution of such things to the discretion of the faithful, since they have not of themselves any necessary connection with inward grace.

Reply Obj. 3. Our Lord gave the apostles those precepts not as ceremonial observances, but as moral statutes: and they can be understood in two ways. First, following Augustine (*De Consensu Evang.* 30), as being not commands, but permissions. For He permitted them to set forth to preach without scrip or stick, and so on, since they were empowered to accept their livelihood from those to whom they preached: wherefore He goes on to say: *For the laborer is worthy of his hire.* Nor is it a sin, but a work of supererogation for a preacher to take means of livelihood with him, without accepting supplies from those to whom he preaches; as Paul did (1 Cor. ix. 4, *seqq.*).

Secondly, according to the explanation of other holy men, they may be considered as temporal commands laid upon the apostles for the time during which they were sent to preach in Judea before Christ's Passion. For the disciples, being yet as little children under Christ's care, needed to receive some special commands from Christ, such as all subjects receive from their superiors: and especially so, since they were to be accustomed little by little to renounce the care of temporalities, so as to become fitted for the preaching of the Gospel throughout the whole world. Nor must we wonder if He established certain fixed modes of life, as long as the state of the Old Law endured and the people had not as yet achieved the perfect liberty of the Spirit. These statutes He abolished shortly before His Passion, as though the disciples had by their means become sufficiently practiced. Hence He said (Luke xxii. 35, 26): *When I sent you without purse and shoes, did you want anything? But they said: Nothing. Then said He unto them: But now, he that hath a purse, let him take it, and likewise a scrip.* Because the time of perfect liberty was already at hand, when they would be left entirely to their own judgment in matters not necessarily connected with virtue.

Reply Obj. 4. Judicial precepts also, are not essential to virtue in respect of any particular determination, but only in regard to the common notion of justice. Consequently Our Lord left the judicial precepts to the discretion of those who were to have spiritual or temporal charge of others. But as regards the judicial precepts of the Old Law, some of them He explained, because they were misunderstood by the Pharisees, as we shall state later on (A. 3, *ad* 2).

THIRD ARTICLE

Whether the New Law Directed Man Sufficiently As Regards Interior Actions?

We proceed thus to the Third Article:—

Objection 1. It would seem that the New Law directed man insufficiently as regards interior actions. For there are ten commandments of the decalogue directing man to God and his neighbor. But Our Lord partly fulfilled only three of them: as regards, namely, the prohibition of murder, of adultery, and of perjury. Therefore it seems that, by omitting to fulfil the other precepts, He directed man insufficiently.

Obj. 2. Further, as regards the judicial precepts, Our Lord ordained nothing in the Gospel, except in the matter of divorcing a wife, of punishment by retaliation, and of persecuting one's enemies. But there are many other judicial precepts of the Old Law, as stated above (Q. 104, A. 4; Q. 105). Therefore, in this respect, He directed human life insufficiently.

Obj. 3. Further, in the Old Law, besides moral and judicial, there were ceremonial precepts about which Our Lord made no ordination. Therefore it seems that He ordained insufficiently.

Obj. 4. Further, in order that the mind be inwardly well disposed, man should do no good deed for any temporal end whatever. But there are many other temporal goods besides the favor of man: and there are many other good works besides fasting, alms-deeds, and prayer. Therefore Our Lord unbecomingly taught that only in respect of these three works, and of no other earthly goods ought we to shun the glory of human favor.

Obj. 5. Further, solicitude for the necessary means of livelihood is by nature instilled into man, and this solicitude even other animals share with man: wherefore it is written (Prov. vi. 6, 8): *Go to the ant, O sluggard, and consider her ways . . . she provideth her meat for herself in the summer, and gathereth her food in the harvest.* But every command issued against the inclination of nature is an unjust command, forasmuch as it is contrary to the law of nature. Therefore it seems that Our Lord unbecomingly forbade solicitude about food and raiment.

Obj. 6. Further, no act of virtue should be the subject of a prohibition. Now judgment is an act of justice, according to Ps. xviii. 15: *Until justice be turned into judgment.* Therefore it seems that Our Lord unbecomingly forbade judgment: and consequently that the New Law directed man insufficiently in the matter of interior acts.

On the contrary, Augustine says (*De Serm. Dom. in Monte* i. 1): We should take note that, when He said: *"He that heareth these My words,"* He indicates clearly that this sermon of the Lord is replete with all the precepts whereby a Christian's life is formed.

I answer that, As is evident from Augustine's words just quoted, the sermon, which Our Lord delivered on the mountain, contains the whole process of forming the life of a Christian. Therein man's interior movements are ordered. Because after declaring that his end is Beatitude; and after commending the authority of the apostles, through whom the teaching of the Gospel was to be promulgated, He orders man's interior movements, first in regard to man himself, secondly in regard to his neighbor.

This he does in regard to man himself, in two ways, corresponding to man's two interior movements in respect of any prospective action viz., volition of what has to be done, and intention of the end. Wherefore, in the first place, He directs man's will in respect of the various precepts of the Law: by prescribing that man should refrain not merely from those external works that are evil in themselves, but also from internal acts, and from the occasions of evil deeds. In the second place He directs man's intention, by teaching that in our good works, we should seek neither human praise, nor worldly riches, which is to lay up treasures on earth.

Afterwards He directs man's interior movement in respect of his neighbor, by forbidding us, on the one hand, to judge him rashly, unjustly, or presumptuously; and, on the other, to entrust him too readily with sacred things if he be unworthy.

Lastly, He teaches us how to fulfil the teaching of the Gospel; viz., by imploring the help of God; by striving to enter by the narrow door of perfect virtue; and by being wary lest we be led astray by evil influences. Moreover, He declares that we must observe His commandments, and that it is not enough to make profession of faith, or to work miracles, or merely to hear His words.

Reply Obj. 1. Our Lord explained the manner of fulfilling those precepts which the Scribes and Pharisees did not rightly understand: and this affected chiefly those precepts of the decalogue. For they thought that the prohibition of adultery and murder covered the external act only, and not the internal desire. And they held this opinion about murder and adultery rather than about theft and false witness, because the movement of anger tending to murder, and the movement of desire tending to adultery, seem to be in us from nature somewhat, but not the desire of stealing or of bearing false witness.—They held a false opinion about perjury, for they thought that perjury indeed was a sin; but that oaths were of themselves to be desired and to be taken frequently, since they seem to proceed from reverence to God. Hence Our Lord shows that an oath is not desirable as a good thing; and that it is better to speak without oaths, unless necessity forces us to have recourse to them.

Reply Obj. 2. The Scribes and Pharisees erred about the judicial precepts in two ways. First, because they considered certain matters contained in the Law of Moses by way of permission, to be right in themselves: namely, divorce of a wife, and the taking of usury from strangers. Wherefore Our Lord forbade a man to divorce his wife (Matth. v. 32); and to receive usury (Luke vi. 35), when He said: *Lend, hoping for nothing thereby.*

In another way they erred by thinking that certain things which the Old Law commanded to be done for justice' sake, should be done out of desire for revenge, or out of lust for temporal goods, or out of hatred of one's enemies; and this in respect of three precepts. For they thought that desire for revenge was lawful, on account of the precept concerning punishment by retaliation: whereas this precept was given that justice might be safeguarded, not that man might seek revenge. Wherefore, in order to do away with this, Our Lord teaches that man should be prepared in his mind to suffer yet more if necessary.— They thought that movements of covetousness were lawful, on account of those judicial precepts which prescribed restitution of what had been purloined, together with something added thereto, as stated above (Q. 105, A. 2, *ad* 9); whereas the Law commanded this to be done in order to safeguard justice, not to encourage covetousness. Wherefore Our Lord teaches that we should not demand our goods from motives of cupidity, and that we should be ready to give yet more if necessary.—They thought that the movement of hatred was lawful, on account of the commandments of the Law about the slaying of one's enemies: whereas the Law ordered this for the fulfilment of justice, as stated above (Q. 105, A. 3, *ad* 4), not to satisfy hatred. Wherefore Our Lord teaches us that we ought to love our enemies, and to be ready to do good to them

if necessary. For these precepts are to be taken as binding *the mind to be prepared to fulfil them,* as Augustine says (*De Serm. Dom. in Monte* i. 19).

Reply Obj. 3. The moral precepts necessarily retained their force under the New Law, because they are of themselves essential to virtue: whereas the judicial precepts did not necessarily continue to bind in exactly the same way as had been fixed by the Law: this was left to man to decide in one way or another. Hence Our Lord directed us becomingly with regard to these two kinds of precepts. On the other hand, the observance of the ceremonial precepts was totally abolished by the advent of the reality; wherefore in regard to these precepts He commanded nothing on this occasion when He was giving the general points of His doctrine. Elsewhere, however, He makes it clear that the entire bodily worship which was fixed by the Law, was to be changed into a spiritual worship: as is evident from Jo. iv. 21, 23, where He says: *The hour cometh when you shall neither on this mountain, nor in Jerusalem adore the Father . . . but . . . the true adorers shall adore the Father in spirit and in truth.*

Reply Obj. 4. All worldly goods may be reduced to three,—honors, riches, and pleasures; according to 1 Jo. ii. 16: *All that is in the world is the concupiscence of the flesh,* which refers to pleasures of the flesh, *and the concupiscence of the eyes,* which refers to riches, *and the pride of life,* which refers to ambition for renown and honor. Now the Law did not promise an abundance of carnal pleasures; on the contrary, it forbade them. But it did promise exalted honors and abundant riches; for it is written in reference to the former (Deut. xxviii. 1): *If thou wilt hear the voice of the Lord thy God, . . . He will make thee higher than all the nations;* and in reference to the latter, we read a little further on (*verse* 11): He *will make thee abound with all goods.* But the Jews so distorted the true meaning of these promises, as to think that we ought to serve God, with these things as the end in view. Wherefore Our Lord set this aside by teaching, first of all, that works of virtue should not be done for human glory. And He mentions three works, to which all others may be reduced: since whatever a man does in order to curb his desires, comes under the head of fasting; and whatever a man does for the love of his neighbor, comes under the head of alms-deeds; and whatever a man does for the worship of God, comes under the head of prayer. And He mentions these three specially, as they hold the principal place, and are most often used by men in order to gain glory.—In the second place He taught us that we must not place our end in riches, when He said: *Lay not up to yourselves treasures on earth* (Matth. vi. 19.)

Reply Obj. 5. Our Lord forbade, not necessary, but inordinate solicitude. Now there is a fourfold solicitude to be avoided in temporal matters. First, we must not place our end in them, nor serve God for the sake of the necessities of food and raiment. Wherefore He says: *Lay not up for yourselves*, etc.—Secondly, we must not be so anxious about temporal things, as to despair of God's help: wherefore Our Lord says (*ibid.* 32): *Your Father knoweth that you have need of all these things.*— Thirdly, we must not add presumption to our solicitude; in other words, we must not be confident of getting the necessaries of life by our own efforts without God's help: such solicitude Our Lord sets aside by saying that a man cannot add anything to his stature (*ibid.* 27).—We must not anticipate the time of anxiety; namely, by being solicitous now, for the needs, not of the present, but of a future time: wherefore He says (*ibid.* 34): *Be not . . . solicitous for to-morrow.*

Reply Obj. 6. Our Lord did not forbid the judgment of justice, without which holy things could not be withdrawn from the unworthy. But he forbade inordinate judgment, as stated above.

FOURTH ARTICLE

Whether Certain Definite Counsels Are Fittingly Proposed in the New Law?

We proceed thus to the Fourth Article:—

Objection 1. It would seem that certain definite counsels are not fittingly proposed in the New Law. For counsels are given about that which is expedient for an end, as we stated above, when treating of counsel (Q. 14, A. 2). But the same things are not expedient for all. Therefore certain definite counsels should not be proposed to all.

Obj. 2. Further, counsels regard a greater good. But there are no definite degrees of the greater good. Therefore definite counsels should not be given.

Obj. 3. Further, counsels pertain to the life of perfection. But obedience pertains to the life of perfection. Therefore it was unfitting that no counsel of obedience should be contained in the Gospel.

Obj. 4. Further, many matters pertaining to the life of perfection are found among the commandments, as, for instance, *Love your enemies* (Matth. v. 44), and those precepts which Our Lord gave His Apostles (*ibid* x). Therefore the counsels are unfittingly given in the New Law: both because they are not all mentioned; and because they are not distinguished from the commandments.

On the contrary, The counsels of a wise friend are of great use, according to Prov. xxvii. 9: *Ointment and perfumes rejoice the heart: and the good counsels of a friend rejoice the soul.* But Christ is our wisest and greatest friend. Therefore His counsels are supremely useful and becoming.

I answer that, The difference between a counsel and a commandment is that a commandment implies obligation, whereas a counsel is left to the option of the one to whom it is given. Consequently in the New Law, which is the law of liberty, counsels are added to the commandments, and not in the Old Law, which is the law of bondage. We must therefore understand the commandments of the New Law to have been given about matters that are necessary to gain the end of eternal bliss, to which end the New Law brings us forthwith: but that the counsels are about matters that render the gaining of this end more assured and expeditious.

Now man is placed between the things of this world, and spiritual goods wherein eternal happiness consists: so that the more he cleaves to the one, the more he withdraws from the other, and conversely. Wherefore he that cleaves wholly to the things of this world, so as to make them his end, and to look upon them as the reason and rule of all he does, falls away altogether from spiritual goods. Hence this disorder is removed by the commandments. Nevertheless, for man to gain the end aforesaid, he does not need to renounce the things of the world altogether: since he can, while using the things of this world, attain to eternal happiness, provided he does not place his end in them: but he will attain more speedily thereto by giving up the goods of this world entirely: wherefore the evangelical counsels are given for this purpose.

Now the goods of this world which come into use in human life, consist in three things: viz., in external wealth pertaining to the *concupiscence of the eyes;* carnal pleasures pertaining to the *concupiscence of the flesh;* and honors, which pertain to the *pride of life,* according to 1 John ii. 16: and it is in renouncing these altogether, as far as possible, that the evangelical counsels consist. Moreover, every form of the religious life that professes the state of perfection is based on these three: since riches are renounced by poverty; carnal pleasures by perpetual chastity; and the pride of life by the bondage of obedience.

Now if a man observe these absolutely, this is in accordance with the counsels as they stand. But if a man observe any one of them in a particular case, this is taking that counsel in a restricted sense, namely, as applying to that particular case. For instance, when anyone gives an alms to a poor man, not being bound so to do, he follows the counsels in that particular case. In like manner, when a man for some fixed time refrains from carnal pleasures that he may give himself to prayer, he follows the counsel for that particular time. And again, when a man follows not his will as to some deed which he might do lawfully, he follows the counsel in that particular case: for instance, if he do good to his enemies when he is not bound to, or if he forgive an injury of which he might justly seek to be avenged. In this way, too, all particular counsels may be reduced to these three general and perfect counsels.

Reply Obj. 1. The aforesaid counsels, considered in themselves, are expedient to all; but owing to some people being ill-disposed, it happens that some of them are inexpedient, because their disposition is not inclined to such things. Hence Our Lord, in proposing the evangelical counsels, always makes mention of man's fitness for observing the counsels. For in giving the counsel of perpetual poverty (Matth. xix. 21), He begins with the words: *If thou wilt be perfect,* and then He adds: *Go, sell all* (Vulg.,—*what*) *thou hast.* In like manner when He gave the counsel of perpetual chastity, saying (*ibid.,* 12): *There are eunuchs who have made themselves eunuchs for the kingdom of heaven,* He adds straightway: *He that can take, let him take it.* And, again, the Apostle (1 Cor. vii. 35), after giving the coun-

sel of virginity, says: *And this I speak for your profit; not to cast a snare upon you.*

Reply Obj. 2. The greater goods are not definitely fixed in the individual; but those which are simply and absolutely the greater good in general are fixed: and to these all the above particular goods may be reduced, as stated above.

Reply Obj. 3. Even the counsel of obedience is understood to have been given by Our Lord in the words: *And* (let him) *follow Me.* For we follow Him not only by imitating His works, but also by obeying His commandments, according to Jo. x. 27: *My sheep hear My voice . . . and they follow Me.*

Reply Obj. 4. Those things which Our Lord prescribed about the true love of our enemies, and other similar sayings (Matth. v., Luke vi), may be referred to the preparation of the mind, and then they are necessary for salvation; for instance, that man be prepared to do good to his enemies, and other similar actions, when there is need. Hence these things are placed among the precepts. But that anyone should actually and promptly behave thus towards an enemy when there is no special need, is to be referred to the particular counsels, as stated above.—As to those matters which are set down in Matth. x and Luke ix and x, they were either disciplinary commands for that particular time, or concessions, as stated above (A. 2 *ad* 3). Hence they are not set down among the counsels.

Grace { God assists us by His grace ....
1. Grace itself {
1. The necessity of grace.—Whether without grace man
2. Essence.—Whether it implies anything in the soul.—
3. Division of grace.—Charisms and grace—operating and

2. Its cause—Whether anyone may know he has grace.—Is God alone the

3. Its effects.. {
1. The justification of the ungodly.—Is it miraculous?
2. Merit.—Can man merit anything from God?—Can man

QUESTION 109

Of the Necessity of Grace

(In Ten Articles)

WE must now consider the exterior principle of human acts, i.e., God, in so far as, through grace, we are helped by Him to do right: and, first, we must consider the grace of God; secondly, its cause; thirdly, its effects.

The first point of consideration will be threefold; for we shall consider (1) The necessity of grace; (2) grace itself, as to its essence; (3) its division.

Under the first head there are ten points of inquiry—(1) Whether without grace man can know anything? (2) Whether without God's grace man can do or wish any good? (3) Whether without grace man can love God above all things? (4) Whether without grace man can keep the commandments of the Law? (5) Whether without grace he can merit eternal life? (6) Whether without grace man can prepare himself for grace? (7) Whether without grace he can rise from sin? (8) Whether without grace man can avoid sin? (9) Whether man having received grace can do good and avoid sin without any further Divine help? (10) Whether he can of himself persevere in good?

FIRST ARTICLE

Whether Without Grace Man Can Know Any Truth?

We proceed thus to the First Article:—

Objection 1. It would seem that without grace man can know no truth. For, on 1 Cor. xii. 3: *No man can say, the Lord Jesus, but by the Holy Ghost*, a gloss says: *Every truth, by whomsoever spoken is from the Holy Ghost.* Now the Holy Ghost dwells in us by grace. Therefore we cannot know truth without grace.

Obj. 2. Further, Augustine says (*Solil.* i. 6) that *the most certain sciences are like things lit up by the sun so as to be seen. Now God Himself is He Who sheds the light. And reason is in the mind as sight is in the eye. And the eyes of the mind are the senses of the soul.* Now the bodily senses, however pure, cannot see any visible object, without the sun's light. Therefore the human mind, however perfect, cannot, by reasoning, know any truth without Divine light: and this pertains to the aid of grace.

Obj. 3. Further, the human mind can only understand truth by thinking, as is clear from Augustine (*De Trin.* xiv. 7). But the Apostle says (2 C: .. iii. 5): *Not that we are sufficient to think anything of ourselves, as of ourselves; but our sufficiency is from God.* Therefore man cannot, of himself, know truth without the help of grace.

On the contrary, Augustine says (*Retract.* i. 4): *I do not approve having said in the prayer, O God, Who dost wish the sinless alone to know the truth; for it may be answered that many who are not sinless know many truths.* Now man is cleansed from sin by grace, according to Ps. l. 12: *Create a clean heart in me, O God, and renew a right spirit within my bowels.* Therefore without grace man of himself can know truth.

I answer that, To know truth is a use or act of intellectual light, since, according to the Apostle (Eph. v. 13): *All that is made manifest is light.* Now every use implies movement, taking movement broadly, so as to call thinking and willing movements, as is clear from the Philosopher (*De Anima,* iii. 4). Now in corporeal things we see that for movement there is required not merely the form which is the principle of the movement or action, but there is also required the motion of the first mover. Now the first mover in the order of corporeal things is the heavenly body. Hence no matter how perfectly fire has heat, it would not bring about alteration, except by the motion of the heavenly body. But it is clear that as all corporeal movements are reduced to the motion of the heavenly body as to the first corporeal mover, so all movements, both corporeal and spiritual, are reduced to the simple First Mover, Who is God. And hence no matter how perfect a corporeal or spiritual nature is supposed to be, it cannot proceed to its act unless it be moved by God; but this motion is according to the plan of His providence, and not by a necessity of nature, as the motion of the heavenly body. Now not only is every motion from God as from the First Mover, but all formal perfection is from Him as from the First Act. And thus the act of the intellect or of any created being whatsoever depends upon God in two ways: first, inasmuch as it is from Him that it has the form whereby it acts; secondly, inasmuch as it is moved by Him to act.

Now every form bestowed on created things

by God has power for a determined act, which it can bring about in proportion to its own proper endowment; and beyond which it is powerless, except by a superadded form, as water can only heat when heated by the fire. And thus the human understanding has a form, viz., intelligible light, which of itself is sufficient for knowing certain intelligible things, viz., those we can come to know through the senses. Higher intelligible things the human intellect cannot know, unless it be perfected by a stronger light, viz., the light of faith or prophecy which is called the *light of grace*, inasmuch as it is added to nature. Hence we must say that for the knowledge of any truth whatsoever man needs Divine help, that the intellect may be moved by God to its act. But he does not need a new light added to his natural light, in order to know the truth in all things, but only in some that surpass his natural knowledge. And yet at times God miraculously instructs some by His grace in things that can be known by natural reason, even as He sometimes brings about miraculously what nature can do.

Reply Obj. 1. Every truth by whomsoever spoken is from the Holy Ghost as bestowing the natural light, and moving us to understand and speak the truth, but not as dwelling in us by sanctifying grace, or as bestowing any habitual gift superadded to nature. For this only takes place with regard to certain truths that are known and spoken, and especially in regard to such as pertain to faith, of which the Apostle speaks.

Reply Obj. 2. The material sun sheds its light outside us; but the intelligible Sun, Who is God, shines within us. Hence the natural light bestowed upon the soul is God's enlightenment, whereby we are enlightened to see what pertains to natural knowledge; and for this there is required no further knowledge, but only for such things as surpass natural knowledge.

Reply Obj. 3. We always need God's help for every thought, inasmuch as He moves the understanding to act; for actually to understand anything is to think, as is clear from Augustine (*De Trin.* xiv, *loc. cit.*).

SECOND ARTICLE

Whether Man Can Wish or Do Any Good without Grace?

We proceed thus to the Second Article:—

Objection 1. It would seem that man can wish and do good without grace. For that is in man's power, whereof he is master. Now man is master of his acts, and especially of his willing, as stated above (Q. 1, A. 1; Q. 13,

A. 6). Hence man, of himself, can wish and do good without the help of grace.

Obj. 2. Further, man has more power over what is according to his nature than over what is beyond his nature. Now sin is against his nature, as Damascene says (*De Fide Orthod.* ii. 30); whereas deeds of virtue are according to his nature, as stated above (Q. 71, A. 1). Therefore since man can sin of himself, much more would it seem that of himself he can wish and do good.

Obj. 3. Further, the understanding's good is truth, as the Philosopher says (*Ethic.* vi. 2). Now the intellect can of itself know truth, even as every other thing can work its own operation of itself. Therefore, much more can man, of himself, do and wish good.

On the contrary, The Apostle says (Rom. ix. 16): *It is not of him that willeth,* namely, to will, *nor of him that runneth,* namely, to run, *but of God that showeth mercy.* And Augustine says (*De Corrept. et Gratia,* ii) that *without grace men do nothing good when they either think or wish or love or act.*

I answer that, Man's nature may be looked at in two ways: first, in its integrity, as it was in our first parent before sin; secondly, as it is corrupted in us after the sin of our first parent. Now in both states human nature needs the help of God as First Mover, to do or wish any good whatsoever, as stated above (A. 1). But in the state of integrity, as regards the sufficiency of the operative power, man by his natural endowments could wish and do the good proportionate to his nature, such as the good of acquired virtue; but not surpassing good, as the good of infused virtue. But in the state of corrupt nature, man falls short of what he could do by his nature, so that he is unable to fulfil it by his own natural powers. Yet because human nature is not altogether corrupted by sin, so as to be shorn of every natural good, even in the state of corrupted nature it can, by virtue of its natural endowments, work some particular good, as to build dwellings, plant vineyards, and the like; yet it cannot do all the good natural to it, so as to fall short in nothing; just as a sick man can of himself make some movements, yet he cannot be perfectly moved with the movements of one in health, unless by the help of medicine he be cured.

And thus in the state of perfect nature man needs a gratuitous strength superadded to natural strength for one reason, viz., in order to do and wish supernatural good; but for two reasons, in the state of corrupt nature, viz., in order to be healed, and furthermore in order to carry out works of supernatural virtue, which are meritorious. Beyond this, in both states man needs the Divine help, that he may be moved to act well.

Reply Obj. 1. Man is master of his acts and of his willing or not willing, because of his deliberate reason, which can be bent to one side or another. And although he is master of his deliberating or not deliberating, yet this can only be by a previous deliberation; and since it cannot go on to infinity, we must come at length to this, that man's free-will is moved by an extrinsic principle, which is above the human mind, to wit by God, as the Philosopher proves in the chapter *on Good Fortune* (*Ethic. Eudem.* vii). Hence the mind of man still unweakened is not so much master of its act that it does not need to be moved by God; and much more the free-will of man weakened by sin, whereby it is hindered from good by the corruption of the nature.

Reply Obj. 2. To sin is nothing else than to fail in the good which belongs to any being according to its nature. Now as every created thing has its being from another, and, considered in itself, is nothing, so does it need to be preserved by another in the good which pertains to its nature. For it can of itself fail in good, even as of itself it can fall into non-existence, unless it is upheld by God.

Reply Obj. 3. Man cannot even know truth without Divine help, as stated above (A. 1). And yet human nature is more corrupt by sin in regard to the desire for good, than in regard to the knowledge of truth.

THIRD ARTICLE

Whether by His Own Natural Powers and Without Grace Man Can Love God above All Things?

We proceed thus to the Third Article:—

Objection 1. It would seem that without grace man cannot love God above all things by his own natural powers. For to love God above all things is the proper and principal act of charity. Now man cannot of himself possess charity, since the *charity of God is poured forth in our hearts by the Holy Ghost Who is given to us,* as is said Rom. v. 5. Therefore man by his natural powers alone cannot love God above all things.

Obj. 2. Further, no nature can rise above itself. But to love God above all things is to tend above oneself. Therefore without the help of grace no created nature can love God above itself.

Obj. 3. Further, to God, Who is the Highest Good, is due the best love, which is that He be loved above all things. Now without grace man is not capable of giving God the best love, which is His due; otherwise it would be useless to add grace. Hence man, without grace and with his natural powers alone, cannot love God above all things.

On the contrary, As some maintain, man was first made with only natural endowments; and in this state it is manifest that he loved God to some extent. But he did not love God equally with himself, or less than himself, otherwise he would have sinned. Therefore he loved God above himself. Therefore man, by his natural powers alone, can love God more than himself and above all things.

I answer that, As was said above (P. 1, Q. 60, A. 5), where the various opinions concerning the natural love of the angels were set forth, man in a state of perfect nature, could by his natural power, do the good natural to him without the addition of any gratuitous gift, though not without the help of God moving him. Now to love God above all things is natural to man and to every nature, not only rational but irrational, and even to inanimate nature according to the manner of love which can belong to each creature. And the reason of this is that it is natural to all to seek and love things according as they are naturally fit (to be sought and loved) since *all things act according as they are naturally fit* as stated in Phys. ii. 8. Now it is manifest that the good of the part is for the good of the whole; hence everything, by its natural appetite and love, loves its own proper good on account of the common good of the whole universe, which is God. Hence Dionysius says (*Div. Nom.* iv) that *God leads everything to love of Himself.* Hence in the state of perfect nature man referred the love of himself and of all other things to the love of God as to its end; and thus he loved God more than himself and above all things. But in the state of corrupt nature man falls short of this in the appetite of his rational will, which, unless it is cured by God's grace, follows its private good, on account of the corruption of nature. And hence we must say that in the state of perfect nature man did not need the gift of grace added to his natural endowments, in order to love God above all things naturally, although he needed God's help to move him to it; but in the state of corrupt nature man needs, even for this, the help of grace to heal his nature.

Reply Obj. 1. Charity loves God above all things in a higher way than nature does. For nature loves God above all things inasmuch as He is the beginning and the end of natural good; whereas charity loves Him, as He is the object of beatitude, and inasmuch as man has a spiritual fellowship with God. Moreover charity adds to natural love of God a certain quickness and joy, in the same way that every habit of virtue adds to the good act which is done merely by the natural reason of a man who has not the habit of virtue.

Reply Obj. 2. When it is said that nature

cannot rise above itself, we must not understand this as if it could not be drawn to any object above itself, for it is clear that our intellect by its natural knowledge can know things above itself, as is shown in our natural knowledge of God. But we are to understand that nature cannot rise to an act exceeding the proportion of its strength. Now to love God above all things is not such an act; for it is natural to every creature, as was said above.

Reply Obj. 3. Love is said to be best, both with respect to the degree of love, and with regard to the motive of loving, and the mode of love. And thus the highest degree of love is that whereby charity loves God as the giver of beatitude, as was said above.

FOURTH ARTICLE

Whether Man without Grace and by His Own Natural Powers Can Fulfil the Commandments of the Law?

We proceed thus to the Fourth Article:—

Objection 1. It would seem that man without grace, and by his own natural powers, can fulfil the commandments of the Law. For the Apostle says (Rom. ii. 14) that *the Gentiles who have not the law, do by nature those things that are of the Law.* Now what a man does naturally he can do of himself without grace. Hence a man can fulfil the commandments of the Law without grace.

Obj. 2. Further, Jerome says (*Expos. Cathol. Fid.**) that *they are anathema who say God has laid impossibilities upon man.* Now what a man cannot fulfil by himself is impossible to him. Therefore a man can fulfil all the commandments of himself.

Obj. 3. Further, of all the commandments of the Law, the greatest is this, *Thou shalt love the Lord thy God with thy whole heart* (Matth. xxvii. 37). Now man with his natural endowments can fulfil this command by loving God above all things, as stated above (A. 3). Therefore man can fulfil all the commandments of the Law without grace.

On the contrary, Augustine says (*De Hæres.* lxxxviii) that it is part of the Pelagian heresy that *they believe that without grace man can fulfil all the Divine commandments.*

I answer that, There are two ways of fulfilling the commandments of the Law.—The first regards the substance of the works,—as when a man does works of justice, fortitude, and of other virtues. And in this way man in the state of perfect nature could fulfil all the commandments of the Law; otherwise he would have been unable to sin in that state, since to sin is nothing else than to transgress

the Divine commandments. But in the state of corrupted nature man cannot fulfil all the Divine commandments without healing grace. Secondly, the commandments of the law can be fulfilled, not merely as regards the substance of the act, but also as regards the mode of acting, i.e., their being done out of charity. And in this way, neither in the state of perfect nature, nor in the state of corrupt nature can man fulfil the commandments of the law without grace. Hence, Augustine (*De Corrept. et Grat.* ii) having stated that *without grace men can do no good whatever,* adds: *Not only do they know by its light what to do, but by its help they do lovingly what they know.* Beyond this, in both states they need the help of God's motion in order to fulfil the commandments, as stated above (AA. 2, 3).

Reply Obj. 1. As Augustine says (*De Spir. et Lit.* xxvii), *do not be disturbed at his saying that they do by nature those things that are of the Law; for the Spirit of grace works this, in order to restore in us the image of God, after which we were naturally made.*

Reply Obj. 2. What we can do with the Divine assistance is not altogether impossible to us; according to the Philosopher (*Ethic.* iii. 3): *What we can do through our friends, we can do, in some sense, by ourselves.* Hence Jerome† concedes (*ibid.*) that *our will is in such a way free that we must confess we still require God's help.*

Reply Obj. 3. Man cannot, with his purely natural endowments, fulfil the precept of the love of God, as stated above (A. 3).

FIFTH ARTICLE

Whether Man Can Merit Everlasting Life without Grace?

We proceed thus to the Fifth Article:—

Objection 1. It would seem that man can merit everlasting life without grace. For Our Lord says (Matth. xix. 17): *If thou wilt enter into life, keep the commandments;* from which it would seem that to enter into everlasting life rests with man's will. But what rests with our will, we can do of ourselves. Hence it seems that man can merit everlasting life of himself.

Obj. 2. Further, eternal life is the wage or reward bestowed by God on men, according to Matth. v. 12: *Your reward is very great in heaven.* But wage or reward is meted by God to everyone according to his works, according to Ps. lxi. 12: *Thou wilt render to every man according to his works.* Hence, since man is master of his works, it seems that it is within his power to reach everlasting life.

---

* *Symboli Explanatio ad Damasum,* among the supposititious works of S. Jerome: now ascribed to Pelagius.

† See preceding note.

Obj. 3. Further, everlasting life is the last end of human life. Now every natural thing by its natural endowments can attain its end. Much more, therefore, may man attain to life everlasting by his natural endowments, without grace.

On the contrary, The Apostle says (Rom. vi. 23): *The grace of God is life everlasting.* And as a gloss says, this is said *that we may understand that God, of His own mercy, leads us to everlasting life.*

I answer that, Acts conducing to an end must be proportioned to the end. But no act exceeds the proportion of its active principle; and hence we see in natural things, that nothing can by its operation bring about an effect which exceeds its active force, but only such as is proportionate to its power. Now everlasting life is an end exceeding the proportion of human nature, as is clear from what we have said above (Q. 5, A. 5). Hence man, by his natural endowments, cannot produce meritorious works proportionate to everlasting life; and for this a higher force is needed, viz., the force of grace. And thus without grace man cannot merit everlasting life; yet he can perform works conducing to a good which is natural to man, as *to toil in the fields, to drink, to eat, or to have friends,* and the like, as Augustine says in his third *Reply to the Pelagians.**

Reply Obj. 1. Man, by his will, does works meritorious of everlasting life; but as Augustine says, in the same book, for this it is necessary that the will of man should be prepared with grace by God.

Reply Obj. 2. As the gloss upon Rom. vi. 23, *The grace of God is life everlasting,* says, *It is certain that everlasting life is meted to good works; but the works to which it is meted, belong to God's grace.* And it has been said (A. 4), that to fulfil the commandments of the Law, in their due way, whereby their fulfilment may be meritorious, requires grace.

Reply Obj. 3. This objection has to do with the natural end of man. Now human nature, since it is nobler, can be raised by the help of grace to a higher end, which lower natures can nowise reach; even as a man who can recover his health by the help of medicines is better disposed to health than one who can nowise recover it, as the Philosopher observes (*De Cœlo* ii. 12).

SIXTH ARTICLE

Whether a Man, by Himself and without the External Aid of Grace, Can Prepare Himself for Grace?

We proceed thus to the Sixth Article:—

Objection 1. It would seem that man, by

* *Hypognosticon* iii, among the spurious works of S. Augustine.

himself and without the external help of grace, can prepare himself for grace. For nothing impossible is laid upon man, as stated above (A. 4, *ad* 1). But it is written (Zach. i. 3): *Turn ye to Me . . . and I will turn to you.* Now to prepare for grace is nothing more than to turn to God. Therefore it seems that man of himself, and without the external help of grace, can prepare himself for grace.

Obj. 2. Further, man prepares himself for grace by doing what is in him to do, since if man does what is in him to do God will not deny him grace, for it is written (Matth. vii. 11) that God gives His good Spirit *to them that ask Him.* But what is in our power, is in us to do. Therefore it seems to be in our power to prepare ourselves for grace.

Obj. 3. Further, if a man needs grace in order to prepare for grace, with equal reason will he need grace to prepare himself for the first grace; and thus to infinity, which is impossible. Hence it seems that we must not go beyond what was said first, viz., that man, of himself and without grace, can prepare himself for grace.

Obj. 4. Further, it is written (Prov. xvi. 1) that *it is the part of man to prepare the soul.* Now an action is said to be the part of a man, when he can do it by himself. Hence it seems that man by himself can prepare himself for grace.

On the contrary, It is written (Jo. vi. 44): *No man can come to Me except the Father, Who hath sent Me, draw him.* But if man could prepare himself, he would not need to be drawn by another. Hence man cannot prepare himself without the help of grace.

I answer that, The preparation of the human will for good is twofold:—the first, whereby it is prepared to operate rightly and to enjoy God; and this preparation of the will cannot take place without the habitual gift of grace, which is the principle of meritorious works, as stated above (A. 5). There is a second way in which the human will may be taken to be prepared for the gift of habitual grace itself. Now in order that man prepare himself to receive this gift, it is not necessary to presuppose any further habitual gift in the soul, otherwise we should go on to infinity. But we must presuppose a gratuitous gift of God, Who moves the soul inwardly or inspires the good wish. For in these two ways do we need the Divine assistance, as stated above (AA. 2, 3). Now that we need the help of God to move us, is manifest. For since every agent acts for an end, every cause must direct its effect to its end, and hence since the order of ends is according to the order of agents or movers, man must be directed to the last end by the motion of the first mover, and to the proximate end by the motion of any of the subordinate movers; as the spirit of the soldier is bent towards seeking the victory by the motion of the leader of the army—and towards following the standard of a regiment by the motion of the standard-bearer. And thus since God is the first Mover simply, it is by His motion that everything seeks Him under the common notion of good, whereby everything seeks to be likened to God in its own way. Hence Dionysius says (*Div. Nom.* iv) that *God turns all to Himself.* But He directs righteous men to Himself as to a special end, which they seek, and to which they wish to cling, according to Ps. lxxii. 28, *it is good for Me to adhere to my God.* And that they are *turned* to God can only spring from God's having *turned* them. Now to prepare oneself for grace is, as it were, to be turned to God; just as, whoever has his eyes turned away from the light of the sun, prepares himself to receive the sun's light, by turning his eyes towards the sun. Hence it is clear that man cannot prepare himself to receive the light of grace except by the gratuitous help of God moving him inwardly.

Reply Obj. 1. Man's turning to God is by free-will; and thus man is bidden to turn himself to God. But free-will can only be turned to God when God turns it, according to Jer. xxxi. 18: *Convert me and I shall be converted, for Thou art the Lord, my God;* and Lament. v. 21: *Convert us, O Lord, to Thee, and we shall be converted.*

Reply Obj. 2. Man can do nothing unless moved by God, according to Jo. xv. 5: *Without Me, you can do nothing.* Hence when a man is said to do what is in him to do, this is said to be in his power according as he is moved by God.

Reply Obj. 3. This objection regards habitual grace, for which some preparation is required, since every form requires a disposition in that which is to be its subject. But in order that man should be moved by God, no further motion is presupposed, since God is the First Mover. Hence we need not go to infinity.

Reply Obj. 4. It is the part of man to prepare his soul, since he does this by his free-will. And yet he does not do this without the help of God moving him, and drawing him to Himself, as was said above.

SEVENTH ARTICLE

Whether Man Can Rise from Sin without the Help of Grace?

We proceed thus to the Seventh Article:—
Objection 1. It would seem that man can rise from sin without the help of grace. For

what is presupposed to grace, takes place without grace. But to rise from sin is presupposed to the enlightenment of grace; since it is written (Eph. v. 14): *Arise from the dead and Christ shall enlighten thee.* Therefore man can rise from sin without grace.

Obj. 2. Further, sin is opposed to virtue as illness to health, as stated above (Q. 71, A. 1 *ad* 3). Now, man, by force of his nature, can rise from illness to health, without the external help of medicine, since there still remains in him the principle of life, from which the natural operation proceeds. Hence it seems that, with equal reason, man may be restored by himself, and return from the state of sin to the state of justice without the help of external grace.

Obj. 3. Further, every natural thing can return by itself to the act befitting its nature, as hot water returns by itself to its natural coldness, and a stone cast upwards returns by itself to its natural movement. Now a sin is an act against nature, as is clear from Damascene (*De Fide Orthod.* ii. 30). Hence it seems that man by himself can return from sin to the state of justice.

On the contrary, The Apostle says (Gal. ii. 21; cf. iii. 21): *For if there had been a law given which could give life—then Christ died in vain,* i.e., to no purpose. Hence with equal reason, if man has a nature, whereby he can be justified, *Christ died in vain,* i.e., to no purpose. But this cannot fittingly be said. Therefore by himself he cannot be justified, i.e., he cannot return from a state of sin to a state of justice.

I answer that, Man by himself can no wise rise from sin without the help of grace. For since sin is transient as to the act and abiding in its guilt, as stated above (Q. 87, A. 6), to rise from sin is not the same as to cease the act of sin; but to rise from sin means that man has restored to him what he lost by sinning. Now man incurs a triple loss by sinning, as was clearly shown above (Q. 85, A. 1; Q. 86, A. 1; Q. 87, A. 1), viz., stain, corruption of natural good, and debt of punishment. He incurs a stain, inasmuch as he forfeits the lustre of grace through the deformity of sin. Natural good is corrupted, inasmuch as man's nature is disordered by man's will not being subject to God's; and this order being overthrown, the consequence is that the whole nature of sinful man remains disordered. Lastly, there is the debt of punishment, inasmuch as by sinning man deserves everlasting damnation.

Now it is manifest that none of these three can be restored except by God. For since the lustre of grace springs from the shedding of Divine light, this lustre cannot be brought back, except God sheds His light anew: hence a habitual gift is necessary, and this is the light of grace. Likewise, the order of nature can only be restored, i.e., man's will can only be subject to God when God draws man's will to Himself, as stated above (A. 6). So, too, the guilt of eternal punishment can be remitted by God alone, against Whom the offense was committed and Who is man's Judge. And thus in order that man rise from sin there is required the help of grace, both as regards a habitual gift, and as regards the internal motion of God.

Reply Obj. 1. To man is bidden that which pertains to the act of free-will, as this act is required in order that man should rise from sin. Hence when it is said, *Arise, and Christ shall enlighten thee,* we are not to think that the complete rising from sin precedes the enlightenment of grace; but that when man by his free-will, moved by God, strives to rise from sin, he receives the light of justifying grace.

Reply Obj. 2. The natural reason is not the sufficient principle of the health that is in man by justifying grace. This principle is grace which is taken away by sin. Hence man cannot be restored by himself; but he requires the light of grace to be poured upon him anew, as if the soul were infused into a dead body for its resurrection.

Reply Obj. 3. When nature is perfect, it can be restored by itself to its befitting and proportionate condition; but without exterior help it cannot be restored to what surpasses its measure. And thus human nature undone by reason of the act of sin, remains no longer perfect, but corrupted, as stated above (Q. 85); nor can it be restored, by itself, to its connatural good, much less to the supernatural good of justice.

EIGHTH ARTICLE

Whether Man without Grace Can Avoid Sin?

We proceed thus to the Eighth Article:—

Objection 1. It would seem that without grace man can avoid sin. Because *no one sins in what he cannot avoid,* as Augustine says (*De Duab. Anim.* x, xi; *De Libero Arbit.* iii. 18). Hence if a man in mortal sin cannot avoid sin, it would seem that in sinning he does not sin, which is impossible.

Obj. 2. Further, men are corrected that they may not sin. If therefore a man in mortal sin cannot avoid sin, correction would seem to be given to no purpose; which is absurd.

Obj. 3. Further, it is written (Ecclus. xv. 18): *Before man is life and death, good and evil; that which he shall choose shall be given him.* But by sinning no one ceases to be a man. Hence it is still in his power to choose good or evil; and thus man can avoid sin without grace.

On the contrary, Augustine says (*De Perfect Just.* xxi): *Whoever denies that we ought to say the prayer "Lead us not into temptation"* (*and they deny it who maintain that the help of God's grace is not necessary to man for salvation, but that the gift of the law is enough for the human will*) *ought without doubt to be removed beyond all hearing, and to be anathematized by the tongues of all.*

I answer that, We may speak of man in two ways: first, in the state of perfect nature; secondly, in the state of corrupted nature. Now in the state of perfect nature, man, without habitual grace, could avoid sinning either mortally or venially; since to sin is nothing else than to stray from what is according to our nature,—and in the state of perfect nature man could avoid this. Nevertheless he could not have done it without God's help to uphold him in good, since if this had been withdrawn, even his nature would have fallen back into nothingness.

But in the state of corrupt nature man needs grace to heal his nature in order that he may entirely abstain from sin. And in the present life this healing is wrought in the mind,—the carnal appetite being not yet restored. Hence the Apostle (Rom. vii. 25) says in the person of one who is restored: *I myself, with the mind, serve the law of God, but with the flesh, the law of sin.* And in this state man can abstain from all mortal sin, which takes its stand in his reason, as stated above (Q. 74, A. 5); but man cannot abstain from all venial sin on account of the corruption of his lower appetite of sensuality. For man can, indeed, repress each of its movements (and hence they are sinful and voluntary), but not all, because whilst he is resisting one, another may arise, and also because the reason is not always alert to avoid these movements, as was said above (Q. 74, A. 3, *ad* 2).

So, too, before man's reason, wherein is mortal sin, is restored by justifying grace, he can avoid each mortal sin, and for a time, since it is not necessary that he should be always actually sinning. But it cannot be that he remains for a long time without mortal sin. Hence Gregory says (*Super Ezech. Hom.* xi) that *a sin not at once taken away by repentance, by its weight drags us down to other sins:* and this because, as the lower appetite ought to be subject to the reason, so should the reason be subject to God, and should place in Him the end of its will. Now it is by the end that all human acts ought to be regulated, even as it is by the judgment of the reason that the movements of the lower appetite should be regulated. And thus, even as inordinate movements of the sensitive appetite cannot help occurring since the lower appetite is not subject to reason, so likewise, since man's reason is not entirely subject to God, the consequence is that many disorders occur in the reason. For when man's heart is not so fixed on God as to be unwilling to be parted from Him for the sake of finding any good or avoiding any evil, many things happen for the achieving or avoiding of which a man strays from God and breaks His commandments, and thus sins mortally: especially since, when surprised, a man acts according to his preconceived end and his pre-existing habits, as the Philosopher says (*Ethic.* iii); although with premeditation of his reason a man may do something outside the order of his preconceived end and the inclination of his habit. But because a man cannot always have this premeditation, it cannot help occurring that he acts in accordance with his will turned aside from God, unless, by grace, he is quickly brought back to the due order.

Reply Obj. 1. Man can avoid each but not every act of sin, except by grace, as stated above. Nevertheless, since it is by his own shortcoming that he does not prepare himself to have grace, the fact that he cannot avoid sin without grace does not excuse him from sin.

Reply Obj. 2. Correction is useful *in order that out of the sorrow of correction may spring the wish to be regenerate; if indeed he who is corrected is a son of promise, in such sort that whilst the noise of correction is outwardly resounding and punishing, God by hidden inspirations is inwardly causing him to will,* as Augustine says (*De Corr. et Gratia* vi). Correction is therefore necessary, from the fact that man's will is required in order to abstain from sin; yet it is not sufficient without God's help. Hence it is written (Eccles. vii. 14): *Consider the works of God that no man can correct whom He hath despised.*

Reply Obj. 3. As Augustine says (*Hypognostic.* iii*), this saying is to be understood of man in the state of perfect nature, when as yet he was not a slave of sin. Hence he was able to sin and not to sin. Now, too, whatever a man wills, is given to him; but his willing good, he has by God's assistance.

NINTH ARTICLE

Whether One Who Has Already Obtained Grace, Can, of Himself and without Further Help of Grace, Do Good and Avoid Sin?

We proceed thus to the Ninth Article:—

Objection 1. It would seem that whoever has already obtained grace, can by himself and without further help of grace, do good and avoid sin. For a thing is useless or imper-

* See note on p. 1126.

fect, if it does not fulfil what it was given for. Now grace is given to us that we may do good and keep from sin. Hence if with grace man cannot do this, it seems that grace is either useless or imperfect.

Obj. 2. Further, by grace the Holy Spirit dwells in us, according to 1 Cor. iii. 16: *Know you not that you are the temple of God, and that the Spirit of God dwelleth in you?* Now since the Spirit of God is omnipotent, He is sufficient to ensure our doing good and to keep us from sin. Hence a man who has obtained grace can do the above two things without any further assistance of grace.

Obj. 3. Further, if a man who has obtained grace needs further aid of grace in order to live righteously and to keep free from sin, with equal reason, will he need yet another grace, even though he has obtained this first help of grace. Therefore we must go on to infinity; which is impossible. Hence whoever is in grace needs no further help of grace in order to do righteously and to keep free from sin.

On the contrary, Augustine says (*De Natura et Gratia,* xxvi) that *as the eye of the body though most healthy cannot see unless it is helped by the brightness of light, so, neither can a man, even if he is most righteous, live righteously unless he be helped by the eternal light of justice.* But justification is by grace, according to Rom. iii. 24: *Being justified freely by His grace.* Hence even a man who already possesses grace needs a further assistance of grace in order to live righteously.

I answer that, As stated above (A. 5), in order to live righteously a man needs a twofold help of God—first, a habitual gift whereby corrupted human nature is healed, and after being healed is lifted up so as to work deeds meritorious of everlasting life, which exceed the capability of nature. Secondly, man needs the help of grace in order to be moved by God to act.

Now with regard to the first kind of help, man does not need a further help of grace, e.g., a further infused habit. Yet he needs the help of grace in another way, i.e., in order to be moved by God to act righteously, and this for two reasons: first, for the general reason that no created thing can put forth any act, unless by virtue of the Divine motion. Secondly, for this special reason—the condition of the state of human nature. For although healed by grace as to the mind, yet it remains corrupted and poisoned in the flesh, whereby it serves *the law of sin,* Rom. vii. 25. In the intellect, too, there remains the darkness of ignorance, whereby, as is written (Rom. viii. 26): *We know not what we should pray for as we ought;* since on account of the various turns of circumstances, and because we do not know ourselves perfectly, we cannot fully know what is for our good, according to Wis. ix. 14: *For the thoughts of mortal men are fearful and our counsels uncertain.* Hence we must be guided and guarded by God, Who knows and can do all things. For which reason also it is becoming in those who have been born again as sons of God, to say: *Lead us not into temptation,* and *Thy Will be done on earth as it is in heaven,* and whatever else is contained in the Lord's Prayer pertaining to this.

Reply Obj. 1. The gift of habitual grace is not therefore given to us that we may no longer need the Divine help; for every creature needs to be preserved in the good received from Him. Hence if after having received grace man still needs the Divine help, it cannot be concluded that grace is given to no purpose, or that it is imperfect, since man will need the Divine help even in the state of glory, when grace shall be fully perfected. But here grace is to some extent imperfect, inasmuch as it does not completely heal man, as stated above.

Reply Obj. 2. The operation of the Holy Ghost, which moves and protects, is not circumscribed by the effect of habitual grace which it causes in us; but beyond this effect He, together with the Father and the Son, moves and protects us.

Reply Obj. 3. This argument merely proves that man needs no further habitual grace.

TENTH ARTICLE

Whether Man Possessed of Grace Needs the Help of Grace in Order to Persevere?

We proceed thus to the Tenth Article:—

Objection 1. It would seem that man possessed of grace needs no help to persevere. For perseverance is something less than virtue, even as continence is, as is clear from the Philosopher (*Ethic.* vii. 7, 9). Now since man is justified by grace, he needs no further help of grace in order to have the virtues. Much less, therefore, does he need the help of grace to have perseverance.

Obj. 2. Further, all the virtues are infused at once. But perseverance is put down as a virtue. Hence it seems that, together with grace, perseverance is given to the other infused virtues.

Obj. 3. Further, as the Apostle says (Rom. v. 20) more was restored to man by Christ's gift, than he had lost by Adam's sin. But Adam received what enabled him to persevere; and thus man does not need grace in order to persevere.

* Cf. *De Correp. et Grat.* xii.

On the contrary, Augustine says (*De Persev.* ii): *Why is perseverance besought of God, if it is not bestowed by God? For is it not a mocking request to seek what we know He does not give, and what is in our power without His giving it?* Now perseverance is besought by even those who are hallowed by grace; and this is seen, when we say *Hallowed be Thy name,* which Augustine confirms by the words of Cyprian (*De Correp. et Grat.* xii). Hence man, even when possessed of grace, needs perseverance to be given to him by God.

I answer that, Perseverance is taken in three ways. First, to signify a habit of the mind whereby a man stands steadfastly, lest he be moved by the assault of sadness from what is virtuous. And thus perseverance is to sadness as continence is to concupiscence and pleasure, as the Philosopher says (*Ethic.* vii. 7). Secondly, perseverance may be called a habit, whereby a man has the purpose of persevering in good unto the end. And in both these ways perseverance is infused together with grace, even as continence and the other virtues are. Thirdly, perseverance is called the abiding in good to the end of life. And in order to have this perseverance man does not, indeed, need another habitual grace, but he needs the Divine assistance guiding and guarding him against the attacks of the passions, as appears from the preceding article. And hence after anyone has been justified by grace, he still needs to beseech God for the aforesaid gift of perseverance, that he may be kept from evil till the end of his life. For to many grace is given to whom perseverance in grace is not given.

Reply Obj. 1. This objection regards the first mode of perseverance, as the second objection regards the second.

Hence the solution of the second objection is clear.

Reply Obj. 3. As Augustine says (*De Natura et Gratia,* xliii*); *in the original state man received a gift whereby he could persevere, but to persevere was not given him. But now, by the grace of Christ, many receive both the gift of grace whereby they may persevere, and the further gift of persevering,* and thus Christ's gift is greater than Adam's fault. Nevertheless it was easier for man to persevere, with the gift of grace in the state of innocence in which the flesh was not rebellious against the spirit, than it is now. For the restoration by Christ's grace, although it is already begun in the mind, is not yet completed in the flesh, as it will be in heaven, where man will not merely be able to persevere but will be unable to sin.

QUESTION 110

Of the Grace of God As Regards Its Essence

(In Four Articles)

WE must now consider the grace of God as regards its essence; and under this head there are four points of inquiry: (1) Whether grace implies something in the soul? (2) Whether grace is a quality? (3) Whether grace differs from infused virtue? (4) Of the subject of grace.

FIRST ARTICLE

Whether Grace Implies Anything in the Soul?

We proceed thus to the First Article:—

Objection 1. It would seem that grace does not imply anything in the soul. For man is said to have the grace of God even as the grace of man. Hence it is written (Gen. xxxix. 21) that the Lord gave to Joseph *grace* (Douay,— *favor*) *in the sight of the chief keeper of the prison.* Now when we say that a man has the favor of another, nothing is implied in him who has the favor of the other, but an acceptance is implied in whose favor he has. Hence when we say that a man has the grace of God, nothing is implied in his soul; but we merely signify the Divine acceptance.

Obj. 2. Further, as the soul quickens the body so does God quicken the soul; hence it is written (Deut. xxx. 20): *He is thy life.* Now the soul quickens the body immediately. Therefore nothing can come as a medium between God and the soul. Hence grace implies nothing created in the soul.

Obj. 3. Further, on Rom. i. 7, *Grace to you and peace,* the gloss says: *Grace,* i.e., *the remission of sins.* Now the remission of sin implies nothing in the soul, but only in God, Who does not impute the sin, according to Ps. xxxi. 2: *Blessed is the man to whom the Lord hath not imputed sin.* Hence neither does grace imply anything in the soul.

On the contrary, Light implies something in what is enlightened. But grace is a light of the soul; hence Augustine says (*De Natura et Gratia* xxii): *The light of truth rightly deserts the prevaricator of the law, and those who have been thus deserted become blind.* Therefore grace implies something in the soul.

I answer that, According to the common manner of speech, grace is usually taken in three ways, First, for anyone's love, as we are accustomed to say that the soldier is in the good graces of the king, i.e., the king looks on him with favor. Secondly, it is taken for any gift freely bestowed, as we are accustomed to say: I do you this act of grace. Thirdly, it is taken for the recompense of a gift given *gratis,* inasmuch as we are said to be *grateful* for benefits. Of these three the second depends on the first, since one bestows something on another *gratis* from the love wherewith he receives him into his good *graces.* And from the second proceeds the third, since from benefits bestowed *gratis* arises *gratitude.*

Now as regards the last two, it is clear that grace implies something in him who receives grace: first, the gift given gratis; secondly, the acknowledgment of the gift. But as regards the first, a difference must be noted between the grace of God and the grace of man; for since the creature's good springs from the Divine will, some good in the creature flows from God's love, whereby He wishes the good of the creature. On the other hand, the will of man is moved by the good pre-existing in things; and hence man's love does not wholly cause the good of the thing, but pre-supposes it either in part or wholly. Therefore it is clear that every love of God is followed at some time by a good caused in the creature, but not co-eternal with the eternal love. And according to this difference of good the love of God to the creature is looked at differently. For one is common, whereby He loves *all things that are* (Wis. xi. 25), and thereby gives things their natural being. But the second is a special love, whereby He draws the rational creature above the condition of its nature to a participation of the Divine good; and according to this love He is said to love anyone simply, since it is by this love that God simply wishes the eternal good, which is Himself, for the creature.

Accordingly when a man is said to have the grace of God, there is signified something bestowed on man by God. Nevertheless the grace of God sometimes signifies God's eternal love, as we say the grace of predestination, inasmuch as God gratuitously and not from merits predestines or elects some; for it is written (Eph. i. 5): *He hath predestinated us into the adoption of children . . . unto the praise of the glory of His grace.*

Reply Obj. 1. Even when a man is said to be in another's good graces, it is understood that there is something in him pleasing to the other; even as anyone is said to have God's grace—with this difference, that what is pleasing to a man in another is presupposed to his love, but whatever is pleasing to God in a man is caused by the Divine love, as was said above.

Reply Obj. 2. God is the life of the soul after the manner of an efficient cause; but the soul is the life of the body after the manner of a formal cause. Now there is no medium between form and matter, since the form, of itself, *informs* the matter or subject; whereas the agent *informs* the subject, not by its substance, but by the form, which it causes in the matter.

Reply Obj. 3. Augustine says (*Retract.* i. 25): *When I said that grace was for the remission of sins, and peace for our reconciliation with God, you must not take it to mean that peace and reconciliation do not pertain to general grace, but that the special name of grace signifies the remission of sins.* Not only grace, therefore, but many other of God's gifts pertain to grace. And hence the remission of sins does not take place without some effect divinely caused in us, as will appear later (Q. 113, A. 2).

SECOND ARTICLE

Whether Grace Is a Quality of the Soul?

We proceed thus to the Second Article:—

Objection 1. It would seem that grace is not a quality of the soul. For no quality acts on its subject, since the action of a quality is not without the action of its subject, and thus the subject would necessarily act upon itself. But grace acts upon the soul, by justifying it. Therefore grace is not a quality.

Obj. 2. Furthermore, substance is nobler than quality. But grace is nobler than the nature of the soul, since we can do many things by grace, to which nature is not equal, as stated above (Q. 109, AA. 1, 2, 3). Therefore grace is not a quality.

Obj. 3. Furthermore, no quality remains after it has ceased to be in its subject. But grace remains; since it is not corrupted, for thus it would be reduced to nothing, since it was created from nothing; hence it is called a *new creature* (Gal. vi. 15).

On the contrary, on Ps. ciii. 15, *That he may make the face cheerful with oil;* the gloss says: *Grace is a certain beauty of soul, which wins the Divine love.* But beauty of soul is a quality, even as beauty of body. Therefore grace is a quality.

I answer that, As stated above (A. 1), there is understood to be an effect of God's gratuitous will in whoever is said to have God's grace. Now it was stated (Q. 109, A. 1) that man is aided by God's gratuitous will in two ways:—First, inasmuch as man's soul is

* Pseudo-Bede, *Sent. Phil. ex Artist.*

moved by God to know or will or do something, and in this way the gratuitous effect in man is not a quality, but a movement of the soul; for *motion is the act of the mover in the moved.* Secondly, man is helped by God's gratuitous will, inasmuch as a habitual gift is infused by God into the soul; and for this reason, that it is not fitting that God should provide less for those He loves, that they may acquire supernatural good, than for creatures, whom He loves that they may acquire natural good. Now He so provides for natural creatures, that not merely does He move them to their natural acts, but He bestows upon them certain forms and powers, which are the principles of acts, in order that they may of themselves be inclined to these movements, and thus the movements whereby they are moved by God become natural and easy to creatures, according to Wis. viii. 1: *she . . . ordereth all things sweetly.* Much more therefore does He infuse into such as He moves towards the acquisition of supernatural good, certain forms or supernatural qualities, whereby they may be moved by Him sweetly and promptly to acquire eternal good; and thus the gift of grace is a quality.

Reply Obj. 1. Grace, as a quality, is said to act upon the soul, not after the manner of an efficient cause, but after the manner of a formal cause, as whiteness makes a thing white, and justice, just.

Reply Obj. 2. Every substance is either the nature of the thing whereof it is the substance, or is a part of the nature, even as matter and form are called substance. And because grace is above human nature, it cannot be a substance or a substantial form, but is an accidental form of the soul. Now what is substantially in God, becomes accidental in the soul participating the Divine goodness, as is clear in the case of knowledge. And thus because the soul participates in the Divine goodness imperfectly, the participation of the Divine goodness, which is grace, has its being in the soul in a less perfect way than the soul subsists in itself. Nevertheless, inasmuch as it is the expression or participation of the Divine goodness, it is nobler than the nature of the soul, though not in its mode of being.

Reply Obj. 3. As Boëthius* says, *the being of an accident is to inhere.* Hence no accident is called being as if it had being, but because by it something is; hence it is said to belong to a being rather than to be a being (*Metaph. vii, text. 2*). And because to become and to be corrupted belong to what is, properly speaking no accident comes into being or is corrupted, but is said to come into being and to be corrupted inasmuch as its subject begins or ceases to be in act with this accident. And thus grace is also said to be created inasmuch as men are created with reference to it, i.e., are given a new being out of nothing, i.e., not from merits, according to Eph. ii. 10, *created in Jesus Christ in good works.*

THIRD ARTICLE

Whether Grace Is the Same As Virtue?

We proceed thus to the Third Article:—

Objection 1. It would seem that grace is the same as virtue. For Augustine says (*De Spir. et Litt.* xiv) that *operating grace is faith that worketh by charity.* But faith that worketh by charity is a virtue. Therefore grace is a virtue.

Obj. 2. Further, what fits the definition, fits the defined. But the definitions of virtue given by saints and philosophers fit grace, since *it makes its subject good, and his work good,* and *it is a good quality of the mind, whereby we live righteously,* etc. Therefore grace is virtue.

Obj. 3. Further, grace is a quality. Now it is clearly not in the *fourth* species of quality; viz. *form* which is the *abiding figure of things,* since it does not belong to bodies. Nor is it in the *third,* since it is not a *passion nor a passion-like quality,* which is in the sensitive part of the soul, as is proved in *Physic.* viii; and grace is principally in the mind. Nor is it in the *second* species, which is *natural power* or *impotence;* since grace is above nature and does not regard good and evil, as does natural power. Therefore it must be in the *first* species which is *habit* or *disposition.* Now habits of the mind are virtues; since even knowledge itself is a virtue after a manner, as stated above (Q. 57, AA. 1, 2). Therefore grace is the same as virtue.

On the contrary, If grace is virtue, it would seem before all to be one of the three theological virtues. But grace is neither faith nor hope, for these can be without sanctifying grace. Nor is it charity, since *grace foreruns charity,* as Augustine says in his book on the Predestination of the Saints (*De Dono Persev.* xvi). Therefore grace is not virtue.

I answer that, Some held that grace and virtue were identical in essence, and differed only logically,—in the sense that we speak of grace inasmuch as it makes man pleasing to God, or is given gratuitously;—and of virtue inasmuch as it empowers us to act rightly. And the Master seems to have thought this (*Sent.* ii, D. 27).

But if anyone rightly considers the nature of virtue, this cannot hold, since, as the Philosopher says (*Physic.* vii, text.17), *virtue is a*

* See note on p. 1126.

disposition of what is perfect,—*and I call perfect what is disposed according to its nature.* Now from this it is clear that the virtue of a thing has reference to some pre-existing nature, from the fact that everything is disposed with reference to what befits its nature. But it is manifest that the virtues acquired by human acts of which we spoke above (Q. 55, *seqq.*) are dispositions, whereby a man is fittingly disposed with reference to the nature whereby he is a man; whereas infused virtues dispose man in a higher manner and towards a higher end, and consequently in relation to some higher nature, i.e., in relation to a participation of the Divine Nature, according to 2 Pet. i. 4: *He hath given us most great and most precious promises; that by these you may be made partakers of the Divine Nature.* And it is in respect of receiving this nature that we are said to be born again sons of God.

And thus, even as the natural light of reason is something besides the acquired virtues, which are ordained to this natural light, so also the light of grace which is a participation of the Divine Nature is something besides the infused virtues which are derived from and are ordained to this light, hence the Apostle says (Eph. v. 8): *For you were heretofore darkness, but now light in the Lord. Walk then as children of the light.* For as the acquired virtues enable a man to walk, in accordance with the natural light of reason, so do the infused virtues enable a man to walk as befits the light of grace.

Reply Obj. 1. Augustine calls *faith that worketh by charity* grace, since the act of faith of him that worketh by charity is the first act by which sanctifying grace is manifested.

Reply Obj. 2. Good is placed in the definition of virtue with reference to its fitness with some pre-existing nature essential or participated. Now good is not attributed to grace in this manner, but as to the root of goodness in man, as stated above.

Reply Obj. 3. Grace is reduced to the first species of quality; and yet it is not the same as virtue, but is a certain disposition which is presupposed to the infused virtues, as their principle and root.

FOURTH ARTICLE

Whether Grace Is in the Essence of the Soul As in a Subject, or in One of the Powers?

We proceed thus to the Fourth Article:—

Objection 1. It would seem that grace is not in the essence of the soul, as in a subject, but in one of the powers. For Augustine says (*Hypognost.* iii*) that grace is related to the will or to the free will *as a rider to his horse.*

Now the will or the free will is a power, as stated above (Part I, Q. 83, A. 2). Hence grace is in a power of the soul, as in a subject.

Obj. 2. Further, *Man's merit springs from grace* as Augustine says (*De Gratia et Lib. Arbit.* vi). Now merit consists in acts, which proceed from a power. Hence it seems that grace is a perfection of a power of the soul.

Obj. 3. Further, if the essence of the soul is the proper subject of grace, the soul, inasmuch as it has an essence, must be capable of grace. But this is false; since it would follow that every soul would be capable of grace. Therefore the essence of the soul is not the proper subject of grace.

Obj. 4. Further, the essence of the soul is prior to its powers. Now what is prior may be understood without what is posterior. Hence it follows that grace may be taken to be in the soul, although we suppose no part or power of the soul—viz., neither the will, nor the intellect, nor anything else; which is impossible.

On the contrary, By grace we are born again sons of God. But generation terminates at the essence prior to the powers. Therefore grace is in the soul's essence prior to being in the powers.

I answer that, This question depends on the preceding. For if grace is the same as virtue, it must necessarily be in the powers of the soul as in a subject; since the soul's powers are the proper subject of virtue as stated above (Q. 56, A. 1). But if grace differs from virtue, it cannot be said that a power of the soul is the subject of grace, since every perfection of the soul's powers has the nature of virtue, as stated above (Q. 55, A. 1; Q. 56, A. 1). Hence it remains that grace, as it is prior to virtue, has a subject prior to the powers of the soul, so that it is in the essence of the soul. For as man in his intellective power participates in the Divine knowledge through the virtue of faith, and in his power of will participates in the Divine love through the virtue of charity, so also in the nature of the soul does he participate in the Divine Nature, after the manner of a likeness, through a certain regeneration or re-creation.

Reply Obj. 1. As from the essence of the soul flow its powers, which are the principles of deeds, so likewise the virtues, whereby the powers are moved to act, flow into the powers of the soul from grace. And thus grace is compared to the will as the mover to the moved, which is the same comparison as that of a horseman to the horse—but not as an accident to a subject.

And thereby is made clear the Reply to the second objection. For grace is the principle of meritorious works through the medium of virtues, as the essence of the soul is the principle of vital deeds through the medium of the powers.

Reply Obj. 3. The soul is the subject of grace, as being in the species of intellectual or rational nature. But the soul is not classed in a species by any of its powers, since the powers are natural properties of the soul following upon the species. Hence the soul differs specifically in its essence from other souls, viz., of dumb animals and of plants. Consequently it does not follow that, if the essence of the human soul is the subject of grace, every soul may be the subject of grace; since it belongs to the essence of the soul, inasmuch as it is of such a species.

Reply Obj. 4. Since the powers of the soul are natural properties following upon the species, the soul cannot be without them. Yet, granted that it was without them, the soul would still be called intellectual or rational in its species, not that it would actually have these powers, but on account of the essence of such a species, from which these powers naturally flow.

QUESTION 111

Of the Division of Grace

(In five Articles)

WE must now consider the division of grace; under which head there are five points of inquiry: (1) Whether grace is fittingly divided into gratuitous grace and sanctifying grace? (2) Of the division into operating and co-operating grace; (3) Of the division of it into preventive and subsequent grace; (4) Of the division of gratuitous grace; (5) Of the comparison between sanctifying and gratuitous grace.

FIRST ARTICLE

Whether Grace Is Fittingly Divided into Sanctifying Grace and Gratuitous Grace?

We proceed thus to the First Article:—

Objection 1. It would seem that grace is not fittingly divided into sanctifying grace and gratuitous grace. For grace is a gift of God, as is clear from what has been already stated (Q. 110, A. 1). But man is not therefore pleasing to God because something is given him by God, but rather on the contrary; since something is freely given by God, because man is pleasing to Him. Hence there is no sanctifying grace.

Obj. 2. Further, whatever is not given on account of preceding merits is given gratis. Now even natural good is given to man without preceding merit, since nature is presupposed to merit. Therefore nature itself is given gratuitously by God. But nature is condivided with grace. Therefore to be gratuitously given is not fittingly set down as a difference of grace, since it is found outside the genus of grace.

Obj. 3. Further, members of a division are mutually opposed. But even sanctifying grace, whereby we are justified, is given to us gratuitously, according to Rom. iii. 24: *Being justified freely (gratis) by His grace.* Hence sanctifying grace ought not to be divided against gratuitous grace.

On the contrary, The Apostle attributes both to grace, viz., to sanctify and to be gratuitously given. For with regard to the first he says (Eph. i. 6): *He hath graced us in His beloved Son.* And with regard to the second (Rom. ii 6): *And if by grace, it is not now by works, otherwise grace is no more grace.* Therefore grace can be distinguished by its having one only or both.

I answer that, As the Apostle says (Rom. xiii. 1), *those things that are of God are well ordered* (Vulg.,—*those that are, are ordained by God*). Now the order of things consists in this, that things are led to God by other things, as Dionysius says (*Cœl. Hier.* iv). And hence since grace is ordained to lead men to God, this takes place in a certain order, so that some are led to God by others.

And thus there is a twofold grace;—one whereby man himself is united to God, and this is called *sanctifying grace;*—the other is that whereby one man co-operates with another in leading him to God, and this gift is called *gratuitous grace,* since it is bestowed on a man beyond the capability of nature, and beyond the merit of the person. But whereas it is bestowed on a man, not to justify him, but rather that he may co-operate in the justification of another, it is not called sanctifying grace. And it is of this that the Apostle says (1 Cor. xii. 7): *And the manifestation of the Spirit is given to every man unto utility,* i.e., of others.

Reply Obj. 1. Grace is said to make pleasing, not efficiently, but formally, i.e., because thereby a man is justified, and is made worthy to be called pleasing to God, according to Col. i. 21. He *hath made us worthy to be made partakers of the lot of the saints in light.*

Reply Obj. 2. Grace, inasmuch as it is gratuitously given, excludes the notion of debt. Now debt may be taken in two ways:—first, as arising from merit; and this regards the person whose it is to do meritorious works, according to Rom. iv. 4: *Now to him that worketh, the reward is not reckoned according to grace, but according to* debt. The second debt regards the condition of nature. Thus we say it is due to a man to have reason, and whatever else belongs to human nature. Yet in neither way is debt taken to mean that God is under an obligation to His creature, but rather that the creature ought to be subject to God, that the Divine ordination may be fulfilled in it, which is that a certain nature should have certain conditions or properties, and that by doing certain works it should attain to something further. And hence natural endowments are not a debt in the first sense but in the second. But supernatural gifts are due in neither sense. Hence they especially merit the name of grace.

Reply Obj. 3. Sanctifying grace adds to the notion of gratuitous grace something pertaining to the nature of grace, since it makes man pleasing to God. And hence gratuitous grace which does not do this keeps the common name, as happens in many other cases; and thus the two parts of the division are opposed as sanctifying and non-sanctifying grace.

SECOND ARTICLE

Whether Grace Is Fittingly Divided into Operating and Co-operating Grace?

We proceed thus to the Second Article:—

Objection 1. It would seem that grace is not fittingly divided into operating and co-operating grace. For grace is an accident, as stated above (Q. 110, A. 2). Now no accident can act upon its subject. Therefore no grace can be called operating.

Obj. 2. Further, if grace operates anything in us it assuredly brings about justification. But not only grace works this. For Augustine says, on Jo. xiv. 12, *the works that I do he also shall do,* says (*Serm.* clxix): *He Who created thee without thyself, will not justify thee without thyself.* Therefore no grace ought to be called simply operating.

Obj. 3. Further, to co-operate seems to pertain to the inferior agent, and not to the principal agent. But grace works in us more than free-will, according to Rom. ix. 16: *It is not of him that willeth, nor of him that runneth, but of God that sheweth mercy.* Therefore no grace ought to be called co-operating.

Obj. 4. Further, division ought to rest on opposition. But to operate and to co-operate are not opposed; for one and the same thing can both operate and co-operate. Therefore grace is not fittingly divided into operating and co-operating.

On the contrary, Augustine says (*De Gratia et Lib. Arbit.* xvii): *God by co-operating with us, perfects what He began by operating in us, since He who perfects by co-operation with such as are willing, begins by operating that they may will.* But the operations of God whereby He moves us to good pertain to grace. Therefore grace is fittingly divided into operating and co-operating.

I answer that, As stated above (Q. 110, A. 2) grace may be taken in two ways; first, as a Divine help, whereby God moves us to will and to act; secondly, as a habitual gift divinely bestowed on us.

Now in both these ways grace is fittingly divided into operating and co-operating. For the operation of an effect is not attributed to the thing moved but to the mover. Hence in that effect in which our mind is moved and does not move, but in which God is the sole mover, the operation is attributed to God, and it is with reference to this that we speak of *operating grace.* But in that effect in which our mind both moves and is moved, the operation is not only attributed to God, but also to the soul; and it is with reference to this that we speak of *co-operating grace.* Now there is a double act in us. First, there is the interior act of the will, and with regard to this act the will is a thing moved, and God is the mover; and especially when the will, which hitherto willed evil, begins to will good. And hence, inasmuch as God moves the human mind to this act, we speak of operating grace. But there is another, exterior act; and since it is commanded by the will, as was shown above (Q. 17, A. 9) the operation of this act is attributed to the will. And because God assists us in this act, both by strengthening our will interiorly so as to attain to the act, and by granting outwardly the capability of operating, it is with respect to this that we speak of co-operating grace. Hence after the aforesaid words Augustine subjoins: *He operates that we may will; and when we will, He co-operates that we may perfect.* And thus if grace is taken for God's gratuitous motion whereby He moves us to meritorious good, it is fittingly divided into operating and co-operating grace.

But if grace is taken for the habitual gift, then again there is a double effect of grace, even as of every other form; the first of which is *being,* and the second, *operation;* thus the work of heat is to make its subject hot, and to give heat outwardly. And thus habitual grace, inasmuch as it heals and justifies the soul, or makes it pleasing to God, is called operating grace; but inasmuch as it is the principle of meritorious works, which spring from the free-will, it is called co-operating grace.

Reply Obj. 1. Inasmuch as grace is a certain accidental quality, it does not act upon the soul efficiently, but formally, as whiteness makes a surface white.

Reply Obj. 2. God does not justify us without ourselves, because whilst we are being justified we consent to God's justification (*justitiæ*) by a movement of our free-will. Nevertheless this movement is not the cause of grace, but the effect; hence the whole operation pertains to grace.

Reply Obj. 3. One thing is said to co-operate with another not merely when it is a secondary agent under a principal agent, but when it helps to the end intended. Now man is helped by God to will the good, through the means of operating grace. And hence, the end being already intended, grace co-operates with us.

Reply Obj. 4. Operating and co-operating grace are the same grace; but are distinguished by their different effects, as is plain from what has been said.

THIRD ARTICLE

Whether Grace Is Fittingly Divided into Prevenient and Subsequent Grace?

We proceed thus to the Third Article:—

Objection 1. It would seem that grace is not fittingly divided into prevenient and subsequent. For grace is an effect of the Divine love. But God's love is never subsequent, but always prevenient, according to 1 Jo. iv. 10: *Not as though we had loved God, but because He hath first loved us.* Therefore grace ought not to be divided into prevenient and subsequent.

Obj. 2. Further, there is but one sanctifying grace in man, since it is sufficient, according to 2 Cor. xii. 9: *My grace is sufficient for thee.* But the same thing cannot be before and after. Therefore grace is not fittingly divided into prevenient and subsequent.

Obj. 3. Further, grace is known by its effects. Now there are an infinite number of effects,—one preceding another. Hence if with regard to these, grace must be divided into prevenient and subsequent, it would seem that there are infinite species of grace. Now no art takes note of the infinite in number. Hence grace is not fittingly divided into prevenient and subsequent.

On the contrary, God's grace is the outcome of His mercy. Now both are said in Ps. lviii. 11: *His mercy shall prevent me,* and again, Ps. xxii. 6: *Thy mercy will follow me.* Therefore grace is fittingly divided into prevenient and subsequent.

I answer that, As grace is divided into operating and co-operating, with regard to its diverse effects, so also is it divided into prevenient and subsequent, howsoever we consider grace. Now there are five effects of grace in us: of these, the first is, to heal the soul; the second, to desire good: the third, to carry into effect the good proposed; the fourth, to persevere in good; the fifth, to reach glory. And hence grace, inasmuch as it causes the first effect in us, is called prevenient with respect to the second, and inasmuch as it causes the second, it is called subsequent with respect to the first effect. And as one effect is posterior to this effect, and prior to that, so may grace be called prevenient and subsequent on account of the same effect viewed relatively to divers others. And this is what Augustine says (*De Natura et Gratia* xxxi): *It is prevenient, inasmuch as it heals, and subsequent, inasmuch as, being healed, we are strengthened; it is prevenient, inasmuch as we are called, and subsequent, inasmuch as we are glorified.*

Reply Obj. 1. God's love signifies something eternal; and hence can never be called anything but prevenient. But grace signifies a temporal effect, which can precede and follow another; and thus grace may be both prevenient and subsequent.

Reply Obj. 2. The division into prevenient and subsequent grace does not divide grace in its essence, but only in its effects, as was already said of operating and co-operating grace. For subsequent grace, inasmuch as it pertains to glory, is not numerically distinct from prevenient grace whereby we are at present justified. For even as the charity of earth is not voided in heaven, so must the same be said of the light of grace, since the notion of neither implies imperfection.

Reply Obj. 3. Although the effects of grace may be infinite in number, even as human acts are infinite, nevertheless all are reduced to some of a determinate species, and moreover all coincide in this, — that one precedes another.

FOURTH ARTICLE

Whether Gratuitous Grace Is Rightly Divided by the Apostle?

We proceed thus to the Fourth Article:—

Objection 1. It would seem that gratuitous grace is not rightly divided by the Apostle. For every gift vouchsafed to us by God, may be called a gratuitous grace. Now there are an infinite number of gifts freely bestowed on us by God as regards both the good of the soul and the good of the body—and yet they do not make us pleasing to God. Hence gratuitous graces cannot be contained under any certain division.

Obj. 2. Further, gratuitous grace is distinguished from sanctifying grace. But faith pertains to sanctifying grace, since we are justified by it, according to Rom. v. 1: *Being justified therefore by faith.* Hence it is not right to place faith amongst the gratuitous graces, especially since the other virtues are not so placed, as hope and charity.

Obj. 3. Further, the operation of healing, and speaking divers tongues are miracles. Again, the interpretation of speeches pertains either to wisdom or to knowledge, according to Dan. i. 17: *And to these children God gave knowledge and understanding in every book and wisdom.* Hence it is not correct to divide the grace of healing and kinds of tongues against the working of miracles; and the interpretation of speeches against the word of wisdom and knowledge.

Obj. 4. Further, as wisdom and knowledge are gifts of the Holy Ghost, so also are understanding, counsel, piety, fortitude, and fear, as stated above (Q. 68, A. 4). Therefore these also ought to be placed amongst the gratuitous gifts.

On the contrary, The Apostle says (1 Cor. xii. 8, 9, 10): *To one indeed by the Spirit is given the word of wisdom; and to another the word of knowledge, according to the same Spirit, to another, the working of miracles; to another, prophecy; to another, the discerning of spirits; to another divers kinds of tongues; to another interpretation of speeches.*

I answer that, As was said above (A. 1), gratuitous grace is ordained to this, viz., that a man may help another to be led to God. Now no man can help in this by moving interiorly (for this belongs to God alone), but only exteriorly by teaching or persuading. Hence gratuitous grace embraces whatever a man needs in order to instruct another in Divine things which are above reason. Now for this three things are required: First, a man must possess the fullness of knowledge of Divine things, so as to be capable of teaching others. Secondly, he must be able to confirm or prove what he says, otherwise his words would have no weight. Thirdly, he must be capable of fittingly presenting to his hearers what he knows.

Now as regards the first, three things are necessary, as may be seen in human teaching. For whoever would teach another in any science must first be certain of the principles of the science, and with regard to this there is *faith*, which is certitude of invisible things, the principles of Catholic doctrine. Secondly, it behooves the teacher to know the principal conclusions of the science, and hence we have the word of *wisdom*, which is the knowledge of Divine things. Thirdly, he ought to abound with examples and a knowledge of effects, whereby at times he needs to manifest causes; and thus we have the word of *knowledge,* which is the knowledge of human things, since *the invisible things of Him . . . are clearly seen, being understood by the things that are made* (Rom. i. 20).

Now the confirmation of such things as are within reason rests upon arguments; but the confirmation of what is above reason rests on what is proper to the Divine power, and this in two ways;—first, when the teacher of sacred doctrine does what God alone can do, in miraculous deeds, whether with respect to bodily health—and thus there is the *grace of healing,* or merely for the purpose of manifesting the Divine power; for instance, that the sun should stand still or darken, or that the sea should be divided—and thus there is the *working of miracles.* Secondly, when he can manifest what God alone can know, and these are either future contingents—and thus there is *prophecy,* or also the secrets of hearts, and thus there is the *discerning of spirits.*

But the capability of speaking can regard either the idiom in which a person can be understood, and thus there is *kinds of tongues;* or it can regard the sense of what is said, and thus there is the *interpretation of speeches.*

Reply Obj. 1. As stated above (A. 1), not all the benefits divinely conferred upon us are called gratuitous graces, but only those that surpass the power of nature—*e.g.,* that a fisherman should be replete with the word of wisdom and of knowledge and the like; and such as these are here set down as gratuitous graces.

Reply Obj. 2. Faith is enumerated here under the gratuitous graces, not as a virtue justifying man in himself, but as implying a super-eminent certitude of faith, whereby a man is fittted for instructing others concerning such things as belong to the faith. With regard to hope and charity, they belong to the appetitive power, according as man is ordained thereby to God.

Reply Obj. 3. The grace of healing is distinguished from the general working of miracles because it has a special reason for inducing one to the faith, since a man is all the more ready to believe when he has received the gift of bodily health through the virtue of faith. So, too, to speak with divers tongues and to interpret speeches have special efficacy in bestowing faith. Hence they are set down as special gratuitous graces.

Reply Obj. 4. Wisdom and knowledge are not numbered among the gratuitous graces in the same way as they are reckoned among the gifts of the Holy Ghost, i.e., inasmuch as man's mind is rendered easily movable by the Holy Ghost to the things of wisdom and knowledge; for thus they are gifts of the Holy Ghost, as stated above (Q. 68, AA. 1, 4). But they are numbered amongst the gratuitous graces, inasmuch as they imply such a fullness of knowledge and wisdom that a man may not merely think aright of Divine things, but may instruct others and overpower adversaries. Hence it is significant that it is the *word* of wisdom and the *word* of knowledge that are placed in the gratuitous graces, since, as Augustine says (*De Trin.* xiv. 1), *It is one thing merely to know what a man must believe in order to reach everlasting life, and another thing to know how this may benefit the godly and may be defended against the ungodly.*

FIFTH ARTICLE

Whether Gratuitous Grace Is Nobler Than Sanctifying Grace?

We proceed thus to the Fifth Article:—

Objection 1. It would seem that gratuitous grace is nobler than sanctifying grace. For *the people's good is better than the individual good,* as the Philosopher says (*Ethic.* i. 2). Now sanctifying grace is ordained to the good of one man alone, whereas gratuitous grace is ordained to the common good of the whole Church, as stated above (AA. 1, 4). Hence gratuitous grace is nobler than sanctifying grace.

Obj. 2. Further, it is a greater power that is able to act upon another, than that which is confined to itself, even as greater is the brightness of the body that can illuminate other bodies, than of that which can only shine but cannot illuminate; and hence the Philosopher says (*Ethic.* v. 1) *that justice is the most excellent of the virtues,* since by it a man bears himself rightly towards others. But by sanctifying grace a man is perfected only in himself; whereas by gratuitous grace a man works for the perfection of others. Hence gratuitous grace is nobler than sanctifying grace.

Obj. 3. Further, what is proper to the best is nobler than what is common to all; thus to reason, which is proper to man is nobler than to feel, which is common to all animals. Now sanctifying grace is common to all members of the Church, but gratuitous grace is the proper gift of the more exalted members of the Church. Hence gratuitous grace is nobler than sanctifying grace.

On the contrary, The Apostle (1 Cor. xii. 31), having enumerated the gratuitous graces, adds: *And I shew unto you yet a more excellent way;* and as the sequel proves he is speaking of charity, which pertains to sanctifying grace. Hence sanctifying grace is more noble than gratuitous grace.

I answer that, The higher the good to which a virtue is ordained, the more excellent is the virtue. Now the end is always greater than the means. But sanctifying grace ordains a man immediately to a union with his last end, whereas gratuitous grace ordains a man to what is preparatory to the end; i.e., by prophecy and miracles and so forth, men are induced to unite themselves to their last end. And hence sanctifying grace is nobler than gratuitous grace.

Reply Obj. 1. As the Philosopher says (*Metaph.* xii, text. 52), a multitude, as an army, has a double good; the first is in the multitude itself, viz., the order of the army; the second is separate from the multitude, viz., the good of the leader:—and this is the better good, since the other is ordained to it. Now gratuitous grace is ordained to the common good of the Church, which is ecclesiastical order, whereas sanctifying grace is ordained to the separate common good, which is God. Hence sanctifying grace is the nobler.

Reply Obj. 2. If gratuitous grace could cause a man to have sanctifying grace, it would follow that gratuitous grace was the nobler; even as the brightness of the sun that enlightens is more excellent than that of an object that is lit up. But by gratuitous grace a man cannot cause another to have union with God, which he himself has by sanctifying grace; but he causes certain dispositions towards it. Hence gratuitous grace needs not to be the more excellent, even as in fire, the heat, which manifests its species whereby it produces heat in other things, is not more noble than its substantial form.

Reply Obj. 3. Feeling is ordained to reason, as to an end; and thus, to reason is nobler. But here it is the contrary, for what is proper is ordained to what is common as to an end. Hence there is no comparison.

QUESTION 112

Of the Cause of Grace

(In Five Articles)

WE must now consider the cause of grace; and under this head there are five points of inquiry: (1) Whether God alone is the efficient cause of grace? (2) Whether any disposition towards grace is needed on the part of the recipient, by an act of free-will? (3) Whether such a disposition can make grace follow of necessity? (4) Whether grace is equal in all? (5) Whether anyone may know that he has grace?

FIRST ARTICLE

Whether God Alone Is the Cause of Grace?

We proceed thus to the First Article:—

Objection 1. It would seem that God alone is not the cause of grace. For it is written (Jo. i. 17): *Grace and truth came by Jesus Christ.* Now, by the name Jesus Christ is understood not merely the Divine Nature assuming, but the created nature assumed. Therefore a creature may be the cause of grace.

Obj. 2. Further, there is this difference between the sacraments of the New Law and those of the Old, that the sacraments of the New Law cause grace, whereas the sacraments of the Old Law merely signify it. Now the sacraments of the New Law are certain visible elements. Therefore God is not the only cause of grace.

Obj. 3. Further, according to Dionysius (*Cœl. Hier.* iii, iv, vii, viii), *Angels cleanse, enlighten, and perfect both lesser angels and men.* Now the rational creature is cleansed, enlightened, and perfected by grace. Therefore God is not the only cause of grace.

On the contrary, It is written (Ps. lxxxiii. 12): *The Lord will give grace and glory.*

I answer that, Nothing can act beyond its species, since the cause must always be more powerful than its effect. Now the gift of grace surpasses every capability of created nature, since it is nothing short of a partaking of the Divine Nature, which exceeds every other nature. And thus it is impossible that any creature should cause grace. For it is as necessary that God alone should deify, bestowing a partaking of the Divine Nature by a participated likeness, as it is impossible that anything save fire should enkindle.

Reply Obj. 1. Christ's humanity is an *organ of His Godhead,* as Damascene says (*De Fide Orthod.* iii. 19). Now an instrument does not bring forth the action of the principal agent by its own power, but in virtue of the principal agent. Hence Christ's humanity does not cause grace by its own power, but by virtue of the Divine Nature joined to it, whereby the actions of Christ's humanity are saving actions.

Reply Obj. 2. As in the person of Christ the humanity causes our salvation by grace, the Divine power being the principal agent, so likewise in the sacraments of the New Law, which are derived from Christ, grace is instrumentally caused by the sacraments, and principally by the power of the Holy Ghost working in the sacraments, according to Jo. iii. 5:

Unless a man be born again of water and the Holy Ghost he cannot enter into the kingdom of God.

Reply Obj. 3. Angels cleanse, enlighten, and perfect angels or men, by instruction, and not by justifying them through grace. Hence Dionysius says (*Cœl. Hier.* vii) that *this cleansing and enlightenment and perfecting is nothing else than the assumption of Divine knowledge.*

SECOND ARTICLE

Whether Any Preparation and Disposition for Grace Is Required on Man's Part?

We proceed thus to the Second Article:—

Objection 1. It would seem that no preparation or disposition for grace is required on man's part, since, as the Apostle says (Rom. iv. 4), *To him that worketh, the reward is not reckoned according to grace, but according to debt.* Now a man's preparation by free-will can only be through some operation. Hence it would do away with the notion of grace.

Obj. 2. Further, whoever is going on sinning, is not preparing himself to have grace. But to some who are going on sinning grace is given, as is clear in the case of Paul, who received grace whilst he was *breathing out threatenings and slaughter against the disciples of the Lord* (Act ix. 1). Hence no preparation for grace is required on man's part.

Obj. 3. Further, an agent of infinite power needs no disposition in matter, since it does not even require matter, as appears in creation, to which grace is compared, which is called *a new creature* (Gal. vi .15). But only God, Who has infinite power, causes grace, as stated above (A. 1). Hence no preparation is required on man's part to obtain grace.

On the contrary, It is written (Amos iv. 12): *Be prepared to meet thy God, O Israel,* and (1 Kings vii. 3): *Prepare your hearts unto the Lord.*

I answer that, As stated above (Q. 111, A. 2), grace is taken in two ways:—First, as a habitual gift of God. Secondly, as a help from God, Who moves the soul to good. Now taking grace in the first sense, a certain preparation of grace is required for it, since a form can only be in disposed matter. But if we speak of grace as it signifies a help from God to move us to good, no preparation is required on man's part, that, as it were, anticipates the Divine help, but rather, every preparation in man must be by the help of God moving the soul to good. And thus even the good movement of the free-will, whereby anyone is prepared for receiving the gift of grace is an act of the free-will moved by God. And thus man is said to prepare himself, according to Prov. xvi. 1. *It is the part of man to prepare the soul;* yet it is

principally from God, Who moves the free-will. Hence it is said that man's will is prepared by God, and that man's steps are guided by God.

Reply Obj. 1. A certain preparation of man for grace is simultaneous with the infusion of grace; and this operation is meritorious, not indeed of grace, which is already possessed,—but of glory which is not yet possessed. But there is another imperfect preparation, which sometimes precedes the gift of sanctifying grace, and yet it is from God's motion. But it does not suffice for merit, since man is not yet justified by grace, and merit can only arise from grace, as will be seen farther on (Q. 114, A. 2).

Reply Obj. 2. Since a man cannot prepare himself for grace unless God prevent and move him to good, it is of no account whether anyone arrive at perfect preparation instantaneously, or step by step. For it is written (Ecclus. xi. 23): *It is easy in the eyes of God on a sudden to make the poor man rich.* Now it sometimes happens that God moves a man to good, but not perfect good, and this preparation precedes grace. But He sometimes moves him suddenly and perfectly to good, and man receives grace suddenly, according to Jo. vi. 45: *Every one that hath heard of the Father, and hath learned, cometh to Me.* And thus it happened to Paul, since, suddenly when he was in the midst of sin, his heart was perfectly moved by God to hear, to learn, to come; and hence he received grace suddenly.

Reply Obj. 3. An agent of infinite power needs no matter or disposition of matter, brought about by the action of something else; and yet, looking to the condition of the thing caused, it must cause, in the thing caused, both the matter and the due disposition for the form. So likewise, when God infuses grace into a soul, no preparation is required which He Himself does not bring about.

THIRD ARTICLE

Whether Grace Is Necessarily Given to Whoever Prepares Himself for It, or to Whoever Does What He Can?

We proceed thus to the Third Article:—

Objection 1. It would seem that grace is necessarily given to whoever prepares himself for grace, or to whoever does what he can, because, on Rom. v. 1, *Being justified . . . by faith, let us have peace,* etc., the gloss says: *God welcomes whoever flies to Him, otherwise there would be injustice with Him.* But it is impossible for injustice to be with God. Therefore it is impossible for God not to welcome whoever flies to Him. Hence he receives grace of necessity.

Obj. 2. Further, Anselm says (*De Casu Diaboli*. iii) that the reason why God does not bestow grace on the devil, is that he did not wish, nor was he prepared, to receive it. But if the cause be removed, the effect must needs be removed also. Therefore, if anyone is willing to receive grace it is bestowed on them of necessity.

Obj. 3. Further, good is diffusive of itself, as appears from Dionysius (*Div. Nom.* iv). Now the good of grace is better than the good of nature. Hence, since natural forms necessarily come to disposed matter, much more does it seem that grace is necessarily bestowed on whoever prepares himself for grace.

On the contrary, Man is compared to God as clay to the potter, according to Jer. xviii. 6: *As clay is in the hand of the potter, so are you in My hand.* But however much the clay is prepared, it does not necessarily receive its shape from the potter. Hence, however much a man prepares himself, he does not necessarily receive grace from God.

I answer that, As stated above (A. 2), man's preparation for grace is from God, as Mover, and from the free-will, as moved. Hence the preparation may be looked at in two ways:— First, as it is from free-will, and thus there is no necessity that it should obtain grace, since the gift of grace exceeds every preparation of human power. But it may be considered, secondly, as it is from God the Mover, and thus it has a necessity—not indeed of coercion, but of infallibility—as regards what it is ordained to by God, since God's intention cannot fail, according to the saying of Augustine in his book on the Predestination of the Saints (*De Dono Persev.* xiv) that *by God's good gifts whoever is liberated, is most certainly liberated.* Hence if God intends, while moving, that the one whose heart He moves should attain to grace, he will infallibly attain to it, according to Jo. vi. 45: *Every one that hath heard of the Father, and hath learned, cometh to Me.*

Reply Obj. 1. This gloss is speaking of such as fly to God by a meritorious act of their free-will, already *informed* with grace; for if they did not receive grace, it would be against the justice which He Himself established.— Or if it refers to the movement of free-will before grace, it is speaking in the sense that man's flight to God is by a Divine motion, which ought not, in justice, to fail.

Reply Obj. 2. The first cause of the defect of grace is on our part; but the first cause of the bestowal of grace is on God's according to Osee xiii. 9: *Destruction is thy own, O Israel; thy help is only in Me.*

Reply Obj. 3. Even in natural things, the form does not necessarily ensue the disposition of the matter, except by the power of the agent that causes the disposition.

FOURTH ARTICLE

Whether Grace Is Greater in One Than in Another?

We proceed thus to the Fourth Article:—

Objection 1. It would seem that grace is not greater in one than in another. For grace is caused in us by the Divine love, as stated above (Q. 110, A. 1). Now it is written (Wis. vi. 8): *He made the little and the great and He hath equally care of all.* Therefore all obtain grace from Him equally.

Obj. 2. Further, whatever is the greatest possible, cannot be more or less. But grace is the greatest possible, since it joins us with our last end. Therefore there is no greater or less in it. Hence it is not greater in one than in another.

Obj. 3. Further, grace is the soul's life, as stated above (Q. 110, A. 1, *ad* 2). But there is no greater or less in life. Hence, neither is there in grace.

On the contrary, It is written (Eph. iv. 7): *But to every one of us is given grace according to the measure of the giving of Christ.* Now what is given in measure, is not given to all equally. Hence all have not an equal grace.

I answer that, As stated above (Q. 52, AA. 1, 2; Q. 56, AA. 1, 2), habits can have a double magnitude:—one, as regards the end or object, as when a virtue is said to be more noble through being ordained to a greater good; the other on the part of the subject, which more or less participates in the habit inhering to it.

Now as regards the first magnitude, sanctifying grace cannot be greater or less, since, of its nature, grace joins man to the Highest Good, which is God. But as regards the subject, grace can receive more or less, inasmuch as one may be more perfectly enlightened by grace than another. And a certain reason for this is on the part of him who prepares himself for grace; since he who is better prepared for grace, receives more grace. Yet it is not here that we must seek the first cause of this diversity, since man prepares himself, only inasmuch as his free-will is prepared by God. Hence the first cause of this diversity is to be sought on the part of God, Who dispenses His gifts of grace variously, in order that the beauty and perfection of the Church may result from these various degrees; even as He instituted the various conditions of things, that the universe might be perfect. Hence after the Apostle had said (Eph. iv. 7): *To every one of us is given grace according to the measure of the giving of Christ,* having enumerated the various graces, he adds (*verse* 12): *For the perfecting of the saints . . . for the edifying of the body of Christ.*

Reply Obj. 1. The Divine care may be looked at in two ways:—First, as regards the Divine act, which is simple and uniform; and thus His care looks equally to all, since by one simple act He administers great things and little. But, *secondly*, it may be considered in those things which come to creatures by the Divine care; and thus, inequality is found, inasmuch as God by His care provides greater gifts for some, and lesser gifts for others.

Reply Obj. 2. This objection is based on the first kind of magnitude of grace; since grace cannot be greater by ordaining to a greater good, but inasmuch as it more or less ordains to a greater or less participation of the same good. For there may be diversity of intensity and remissness, both in grace and in final glory as regards the subjects' participation.

Reply Obj. 3. Natural life pertains to man's substance, and hence cannot be more or less; but man partakes of the life of grace accidentally, and hence man may possess it more or less.

FIFTH ARTICLE

Whether Man Can Know That He Has Grace?

We proceed thus to the Fifth Article:—

Objection 1. It would seem that man can know that he has grace. For grace by its physical reality is in the soul. Now the soul has most certain knowledge of those things that are in it by their physical reality, as appears from Augustine (*Gen. ad lit.* xii. 31). Hence grace may be known most certainly by one who has grace.

Obj. 2. Further, as knowledge is a gift of God, so is grace. But whoever receives knowledge from God, knows that he has knowledge, according to Wis. vii. 17: The Lord *hath given me the true knowledge of the things that are.* Hence, with equal reason, whoever receives grace from God, knows that he has grace.

Obj. 3. Further, light is more knowable than darkness, since, according to the Apostle (Eph. v. 13), *all that is made manifest is light.* Now sin, which is spiritual darkness, may be known with certainty by one that is in sin. Much more, therefore, may grace, which is spiritual light, be known.

Obj. 4. Further, the Apostle says (1 Cor. ii. 12): *Now we have received not the Spirit of this world, but the Spirit that is of God; that we may know the things that are given us from God.* Now grace is God's first gift. Hence, the man who receives grace by the Holy Spirit, by the same Holy Spirit knows the grace given to him.

Obj. 5. Further, it was said by the Lord to Abraham (Gen. xxii. 12): *Now I know that thou fearest God.* i.e., *I have made thee know.* Now He is speaking there of chaste fear, which is not apart from grace. Hence a man may know that he has grace.

On the contrary, It is written (Eccles. ix. 1): *Man knoweth not whether he be worthy of love or hatred.* Now sanctifying grace maketh a man worthy of God's love. Therefore no one can know whether he has sanctifying grace.

I answer that, There are three ways of knowing a thing:—First, by revelation, and thus anyone may know that he has grace, for God by a special privilege reveals this at times to some, in order that the joy of safety may begin in them even in this life, and that they may carry on toilsome works with greater trust and greater energy, and may bear the evils of this present life, as when it was said to Paul (2 Cor. xii. 9): *My grace is sufficient for thee.*

Secondly, a man may, of himself, know something, and with certainty; and in this way no one can know that he has grace. For certitude about a thing can only be had when we may judge of it by its proper principle. Thus it is by undemonstrable universal principles that certitude is obtained concerning demonstrative conclusions. Now no one can know he has the knowledge of a conclusion if he does not know its principle. But the principle of grace and its object is God, Who by reason of His very excellence is unknown to us, according to Job xxxvi. 26. *Behold God is great, exceeding our knowledge.* And hence His presence in us and His absence cannot be known with certainty, according to Job ix. 11: *If He come to me, I shall not see Him; if He depart I shall not understand.* And hence man cannot judge with certainty that he has grace, according to 1 Cor. iv. 3, 4: *But neither do I judge my own self . . . but He that judgeth me is the Lord.*

Thirdly, things are known conjecturally by signs; and thus anyone may know he has grace, when he is conscious of delighting in God, and of despising worldly things, and inasmuch as a man is not conscious of any mortal sin. And thus it is written (Apoc. ii. 17): *To him that overcometh I will give the hidden manna . . . which no man knoweth, but he that receiveth it,* because whoever receives it knows, by experiencing a certain sweetness, which he who does not receive it, does not experience. Yet this knowledge is imperfect; hence the Apostle says (1 Cor iv. 4): *I am not conscious to myself of anything, yet am I not hereby justified,* since, according to Ps. xviii 13: *Who can understand sins? From my secret ones cleanse me, O Lord, and from those of others spare Thy servant.*

Reply Obj. 1. Those things which are in the soul by their physical reality, are known through experimental knowledge; in so far as through acts man has experience of their inward principles: thus when we wish, we perceive that we have a will; and when we exercise the functions of life, we observe that there is life in us.

Reply Obj. 2. It is an essential condition of knowledge that a man should have certitude of the objects of knowledge; and again, it is an essential condition of faith that a man should be certain of the things of faith, and this, because certitude belongs to the perfection of the intellect, wherein these gifts exist. Hence, whoever has knowledge or faith is certain that he has them. But it is otherwise with grace and charity and such like, which perfect the appetitive faculty.

Reply Obj. 3. Sin has for its principal object commutable good, which is known to us.

But the object or end of grace is unknown to us on account of the greatness of its light, according to 1 Tim. vi. 16: *Who ... inhabiteth light inaccessible.*

Reply Obj. 4. The Apostle is here speaking of the gifts of glory, which have been given to us in hope, and these we know most certainly by faith, although we do not know for certain that we have grace to enable us to merit them.—Or it may be said that he is speaking of the privileged knowledge, which comes of revelation. Hence he adds (*verse* 10): *But to us God hath revealed them by His Spirit.*

Reply Obj. 5. What was said to Abraham may refer to experimental knowledge which springs from deeds of which we are cognizant. For in the deed that Abraham had just wrought, he could know experimentally that he had the fear of God.—Or it may refer to a revelation.

QUESTION 113

Of the Effects of Grace

(In Ten Articles)

WE have now to consider the effect of grace; (1) the justification of the ungodly, which is the effect of operating grace; and (2) merit, which is the effect of co-operating grace. Under the first head there are ten points of inquiry: (1) What is the justification of the ungodly? (2) Whether grace is required for it? (3) Whether any movement of the free-will is required? (4) Whether a movement of faith is required? (5) Whether a movement of the free-will against sin is required? (6) Whether the remission of sins is to be reckoned with the foregoing? (7) Whether the justification of the ungodly is a work of time or is sudden? (8) Of the natural order of the things concurring to justification. (9) Whether the justification of the ungodly is God's greatest work? (10) Whether the justification of the ungodly is miraculous?

FIRST ARTICLE

Whether the Justification of the Ungodly Is the Remission of Sins?

We proceed thus to the First Article:—

Objection 1. It would seem that the justification of the ungodly is not the remission of sins. For sin is opposed not only to justice, but to all the other virtues, as stated above (Q. 71, A. 1). Now justification signifies a certain movement towards justice. Therefore not even remission of sin is justification, since movement is from one contrary to the other.

Obj. 2. Further, everything ought to be named from what is predominant in it, according to *De Anima* ii, text. 49. Now the remission of sins is brought about chiefly by faith, according to Acts xv. 9: *Purifying their hearts by faith;* and by charity, according to Prov. x. 12: *Charity covereth all sins.* Therefore the remission of sins ought to be named after faith or charity rather than justice.

Obj. 3. Further, the remission of sins seems to be the same as being called, for whoever is called is afar off, and we are afar off from God by sin. But one is called before being justified according to Rom. viii. 30: *And whom He called, them He also justified.* Therefore justification is not the remission of sins.

On the contrary, On Rom. viii. 30, *Whom He called, them He also justified,* the gloss says, i.e., *by the remission of sins.* Therefore the remission of sins is justification.

I answer that, Justification taken passively implies a movement towards justice, as heating implies a movement towards heat. But since justice, by its nature, implies a certain rectitude of order, it may be taken in two ways:—First, inasmuch as it implies a right order in man's act, and thus justice is placed amongst the virtues,—either as particular justice, which directs a man's acts by regulating them in relation to his fellow-man,—or as legal justice, which directs a man's acts by regulating them in their relation to the common good of society, as appears from *Ethic.* v. 1.

Secondly, justice is so-called inasmuch as it implies a certain rectitude of order in the interior disposition of a man, in so far as what is highest in man is subject to God, and the inferior powers of the soul are subject to the superior, i.e., to the reason; and this disposition the Philosopher calls *justice metaphorically speaking* (*Ethic.* v. 11). Now this justice may be in man in two ways:—First, by simple generation, which is from privation to form; and thus justification may belong even to such as are not in sin, when they receive this justice from God, as Adam is said to have received original justice. Secondly, this justice may be brought about in man by a movement from one contrary to the other, and thus justification implies a transmutation from the state of injustice to the aforesaid state of justice. And it is thus we are now speaking of the justification of the ungodly, according to the Apostle (Rom. iv. 5): *But to him that worketh not, yet believeth in Him that justifieth the ungodly,* etc. And because movement is named after its term *whereto* rather than from its term *whence*, the transmutation whereby anyone is changed by the remission of sins from the state of ungodliness to the state of justice, borrows its name from its term *whereto*, and is called *justification of the ungodly*.

Reply Obj. 1. Every sin, inasmuch as it implies the disorder of a mind not subject to God, may be called injustice, as being contrary to the aforesaid justice, according to 1 Jo. iii. 4: *Whosoever committeth sin, committeth also iniquity; and sin is iniquity.* And thus the removal of any sin is called the justification of the ungodly.

Reply Obj. 2. Faith and charity imply a special directing of the human mind to God by the intellect and will; whereas justice implies a general rectitude of order. Hence this transmutation is named after justice rather than after charity or faith.

Reply Obj. 3. Being called refers to God's help moving and exciting our mind to give up sin, and this motion of God is not the remission of sins, but its cause.

SECOND ARTICLE

Whether the Infusion of Grace Is Required for the Remission of Guilt, i.e., for the Justification of the Ungodly?

We proceed thus to the Second Article:—

Objection 1. It would seem that for the remission of guilt, which is the justification of the ungodly, no infusion of grace is required. For anyone may be moved from one contrary without being led to the other, if the contraries are not immediate. Now the state of guilt and the state of grace are not immediate con-

traries; for there is the middle state of innocence wherein a man has neither grace nor guilt. Hence a man may be pardoned his guilt without his being brought to a state of grace.

Obj. 2. Further, the remission of guilt consists in the Divine imputation, according to Ps. xxxi. 2: *Blessed is the man to whom the Lord hath not imputed sin.* Now the infusion of grace puts something into our soul, as stated above (Q. 110, A. 1). Hence the infusion of grace is not required for the remission of guilt.

Obj. 3. Further, no one can be subject to two contraries at once. Now some sins are contraries, as wastefulness and miserliness. Hence whoever is subject to the sin of wastefulness is not simultaneously subject to the sin of miserliness, yet it may happen that he has been subject to it hitherto. Hence by sinning with the vice of wastefulness he is freed from the sin of miserliness. And thus a sin is remitted without grace.

On the contrary, It is written (Rom. iii. 24): *Justified freely by His grace.*

I answer that, by sinning a man offends God as stated above (Q. 71, A. 5). Now an offense is remitted to anyone, only when the soul of the offender is at peace with the offended. Hence sin is remitted to us, when God is at peace with us, and this peace consists in the love whereby God loves us. Now God's love, considered on the part of the Divine act, is eternal and unchangeable; whereas, as regards the effect it imprints on us, it is sometimes interrupted, inasmuch as we sometimes fall short of it and once more require it. Now the effect of the Divine love in us, which is taken away by sin, is grace, whereby a man is made worthy of eternal life, from which sin shuts him out. Hence we could not conceive the remission of guilt, without the infusion of grace.

Reply Obj. 1. More is required for an offender to pardon an offense, than for one who has committed no offense, not to be hated. For it may happen amongst men that one man neither hates nor loves another. But if the other offends him, then the forgiveness of the offense can only spring from a special good-will. Now God's good-will is said to be restored to man by the gift of grace; and hence although a man before sinning may be without grace and without guilt, yet that he is without guilt after sinning can only be because he has grace.

Reply Obj. 2. As God's love consists not merely in the act of the Divine will but also implies a certain effect of grace, as stated above (Q. 110, A. 1), so likewise, when God does not impute sin to a man, there is implied a certain effect in him to whom the sin is not imputed; for it proceeds from the Divine love, that sin is not imputed to a man by God.

Reply Obj. 3. As Augustine says (*De Nup. et Concup.* i. 26), if to leave off sinning was the same as to have no sin, it would be enough if Scripture warned us thus: *"My son, hast thou sinned? do so no more?"* Now this is not enough, but it is added: *"But for thy former sins also pray that they may be forgiven thee."* For the act of sin passes, but the guilt remains, as stated above (Q. 87, A. 6). Hence when anyone passes from the sin of one vice to the sin of a contrary vice, he ceases to have the act of the former sin, but he does not cease to have the guilt, hence he may have the guilt of both sins at once. For sins are not contrary to each other on the part of their turning from God, wherein sin has its guilt.

THIRD ARTICLE

Whether for the Justification of the Ungodly Is Required a Movement of the Free-Will?

We proceed thus to the Third Article:—

Objection 1. It would seem that no movement of the free-will is required for the justification of the ungodly. For we see that by the sacrament of Baptism, infants and sometimes adults are justified without a movement of their free-will: hence Augustine says (*Confess.* iv) that when one of his friends was taken with a fever, *he lay for a long time senseless and in a deadly sweat, and when he was despaired of, he was baptized without his knowing, and was regenerated;* which is effected by sanctifying grace. Now God does not confine His power to the sacraments. Hence He can justify a man without the sacraments, and without any movement of the free-will.

Obj. 2. Further, a man has not the use of reason when asleep, and without it there can be no movement of the free-will. But Solomon received from God the gift of wisdom when asleep, as related in 3 Kings iii and 2 Paral. i. Hence with equal reason the gift of sanctifying grace is sometimes bestowed by God on man without the movement of his free-will.

Obj. 3. Further, grace is preserved by the same cause as brings it into being, for Augustine says (*Gen. ad lit.* viii. 12) that *so ought man to turn to God as he is ever made just by Him.* Now grace is preserved in man without a movement of his free-will. Hence it can be infused in the beginning without a movement of the free-will.

On the contrary, It is written (Jo. vi. 45): *Every one that hath heard of the Father, and hath learned, cometh to Me.* Now to learn cannot be without a movement of the free-will, since the learner assents to the teacher.

Hence no one comes to the Father by justifying grace without a movement of the free-will.

I answer that, The justification of the ungodly is brought about by God moving man to justice. For He it is *that justifieth the ungodly* according to Rom. iv. 5. Now God moves everything in its own manner, just as we see that in natural things, what is heavy and what is light are moved differently, on account of their diverse natures. Hence He moves man to justice according to the condition of his human nature. But it is man's proper nature to have free-will. Hence in him who has the use of reason, God's motion to justice does not take place without a movement of the free-will; but He so infuses the gift of justifying grace that at the same time He moves the free-will to accept the gift of grace, in such as are capable of being moved thus.

Reply Obj. 1. Infants are not capable of the movement of their free-will; hence it is by the mere infusion of their souls that God moves them to justice. Now this cannot be brought about without a sacrament; because as original sin, from which they are justified, does not come to them from their own will, but by carnal generation, so also is grace given them by Christ through spiritual regeneration. And the same reason holds good with madmen and idiots, that have never had the use of their free-will. But in the case of one who has had the use of his free-will and afterwards has lost it either through sickness or sleep, he does not obtain justifying grace by the exterior rite of Baptism, or of any other sacrament, unless he intended to make use of this sacrament, and this can only be by the use of his free-will. And it was in this way that he of whom Augustine speaks was regenerated, because both previously and afterwards he assented to the Baptism.

Reply Obj. 2. Solomon neither merited nor received wisdom whilst asleep; but it was declared to him in his sleep that on account of his previous desire wisdom would be infused into him by God. Hence it is said in his person (Wis. vii. 7): *I wished, and understanding was given unto me.*

Or it may be said that his sleep was not natural, but was the sleep of prophecy, according to Num. xii. 6: *If there be among you a prophet of the Lord, I will appear to him in a vision, or I will speak to him in a dream.* In such cases the use of free-will remains.

And yet it must be observed that the comparison between the gift of wisdom and the gift of justifying grace does not hold. For the gift of justifying grace especially ordains a man to good, which is the object of the will; and hence a man is moved to it by a movement of the will which is a movement of free-will. But wisdom perfects the intellect which precedes the will; hence without any complete movement of the free-will, the intellect can be enlightened with the gift of wisdom, even as we see that things are revealed to men in sleep, according to Job xxxiii. 15, 16: *When deep sleep falleth upon men and they are sleeping in their beds, then He openeth the ears of men, and teaching, instructeth them in what they are to learn.*

Reply Obj. 3. In the infusion of justifying grace there is a certain transmutation of the human soul, and hence a proper movement of the human soul is required in order that the soul may be moved in its own manner. But the conservation of grace is without transmutation: no movement on the part of the soul is required but only a continuation of the Divine influx.

FOURTH ARTICLE

Whether a Movement of Faith Is Required for the Justification of the Ungodly?

We proceed thus to the Fourth Article:—

Objection 1. It would seem that no movement of faith is required for the justification of the ungodly. For as a man is justified by faith, so also by other things, viz., by fear, of which it is written (Ecclus. i. 27): *The fear of the Lord driveth out sin, for he that is without fear cannot be justified;* and again by charity, according to Luke vii. 47: *Many sins are forgiven her because she hath loved much;* and again by humility, according to James iv. 6: *God resisteth the proud and giveth grace to the humble:* and again by mercy, according to Prov. xv. 27: *By mercy and faith sins are purged away.* Hence the movement of faith is no more required for the justification of the ungodly, than the movements of the aforesaid virtues.

Obj. 2. Further, the act of faith is required for justification only inasmuch as a man knows God by faith. But a man may know God in other ways, viz., by natural knowledge, and by the gift of wisdom. Hence no act of faith is required for the justification of the ungodly.

Obj. 3. Further, there are several articles of faith. Therefore if the act of faith is required for the justification of the ungodly, it would seem that a man ought to think on every article of faith when he is first justified. But this seems inconvenient, since such thought would require a long delay of time. Hence it seems that an act of faith is not required for the justification of the ungodly.

On the contrary, It is written (Rom. v. 1): *Being justified therefore by faith, let us have peace with God.*

I answer that, As stated above (A. 3) a movement of free-will is required for the justification of the ungodly, inasmuch as man's mind is moved by God. Now God moves man's soul by turning it to Himself according to Ps. lxxxiv. 7 (Septuagint): *Thou wilt turn us, O God, and bring us to life.* Hence for the justification of the ungodly a movement of the mind is required, by which it is turned to God. Now the first turning to God is by faith, according to Heb. xi. 6: *He that cometh to God must believe that He is.* Hence a movement of faith is required for the justification of the ungodly.

Reply Obj. 1. The movement of faith is not perfect unless it is quickened by charity; hence in the justification of the ungodly, a movement of charity is infused together with the movement of faith. Now free-will is moved to God by being subject to Him; hence an act of filial fear and an act of humility also concur. For it may happen that one and the same act of free-will springs from different virtues, when one commands and another is commanded, inasmuch as the act may be ordained to various ends. But the act of mercy counteracts sin either by way of satisfying for it, and thus it follows justification; or by way of preparation, inasmuch as the merciful obtain mercy; and thus it can either precede justification, or concur with the other virtues towards justification, inasmuch as mercy is included in the love of our neighbor.

Reply Obj. 2. By natural knowledge a man is not turned to God, according as He is the object of beatitude and the cause of justification. Hence such knowledge does not suffice for justification. But the gift of wisdom presupposes the knowledge of faith, as stated above (Q. 68, A. 4, *ad* 3).

Reply Obj. 3. As the Apostle says (Rom. iv. 5), *to him that . . . believeth in Him that justifieth the ungodly his faith is reputed to justice, according to the purpose of the grace of God.* Hence it is clear that in the justification of the ungodly an act of faith is required in order that a man may believe that God justifies man through the mystery of Christ.

FIFTH ARTICLE

Whether for the Justification of the Ungodly There Is Required a Movement of the Free-Will Towards Sin?

We proceed thus to the Fifth Article:—

Objection 1. It would seem that no movement of the free-will towards sin is required for the justification of the ungodly. For charity alone suffices to take away sin, according to Prov. x. 12: *Charity covereth all sins.* Now the object of charity is not sin. Therefore for this justification of the ungodly no movement of the free-will towards sin is required.

Obj. 2. Further, whoever is tending onward, ought not to look back, according to Philip. iii. 13, 14: *Forgetting the things that are behind, and stretching forth myself to those that are before, I press towards the mark, to the prize of the supernal vocation.* But whoever is stretching forth to righteousness has his sins behind him. Hence he ought to forget them, and not stretch forth to them by a movement of his free-will.

Obj. 3. Further, in the justification of the ungodly one sin is not remitted without another, for *it is irreverent to expect half a pardon from God.** Hence, in the justification of the ungodly, if man's free-will must move against sin, he ought to think of all his sins. But this is unseemly, both because a great space of time would be required for such thought, and because a man could not obtain the forgiveness of such sins as he had forgotten. Hence for the justification of the ungodly no movement of the free-will is required.

On the contrary, It is written (Ps. xxxi. 5): *I will confess against myself my injustice to the Lord; and Thou hast forgiven the wickedness of my sin.*

I answer that, As stated above (A. 1), the justification of the ungodly is a certain movement whereby the human mind is moved by God from the state of sin to the state of justice. Hence it is necessary for the human mind to regard both extremes by an act of free-will, as a body in local movement is related to both terms of the movement. Now it is clear that in local movement the moving body leaves the term *whence* and nears the term *whereto.* Hence the human mind whilst it is being justified, must, by a movement of its free-will withdraw from sin and draw near to justice.

Now to withdraw from sin and to draw near to justice, in an act of free-will, means detestation and desire. For Augustine says on the words *the hireling fleeth,* etc. (Jo. x. 12): *Our emotions are the movements of our soul; joy is the soul's outpouring; fear is the soul's flight; your soul goes forward when you seek; your soul flees, when you are afraid.* Hence in the justification of the ungodly there must be two acts of the free-will—one, whereby it tends to God's justice; the other whereby it hates sin.

Reply Obj. 1. It belongs to the same virtue to seek one contrary and to avoid the other; and hence, as it belongs to charity to love God, so likewise, to detest sin whereby the soul is separated from God.

* Cap., *Sunt plures:* Dist. iii., *De Poenit.*

Reply Obj. 2. A man ought not to return to those things that are behind, by loving them; but, for that matter, he ought to forget them, lest he be drawn to them. Yet he ought to recall them to mind, in order to detest them; for this is to fly from them.

Reply Obj. 3. Previous to justification a man must detest each sin he remembers to have committed, and from this remembrance the soul goes on to have a general movement of detestation with regard to all sins committed, in which are included such sins as have been forgotten. For a man is then in such a frame of mind that he would be sorry even for those he does not remember, if they were present to his memory; and this movement co-operates in his justification.

SIXTH ARTICLE

Whether the Remission of Sins Ought to Be Reckoned Amongst the Things Required for Justification?

We proceed thus to the Sixth Article:—

Objection 1. It would seem that the remission of sins ought not to be reckoned amongst the things required for justification. For the substance of a thing is not reckoned together with those that are required for a thing; thus a man is not reckoned together with his body and soul. But the justification of the ungodly is itself the remission of sins, as stated above (A. 1). Therefore the remission of sins ought not to be reckoned among the things required for the justification of the ungodly.

Obj. 2. Further, infusion of grace and remission of sins are the same; as illumination and expulsion of darkness are the same. But a thing ought not to be reckoned together with itself; for unity is opposed to multitude. Therefore the remission of sins ought not to be reckoned with the infusion of grace.

Obj. 3. Further, the remission of sin follows as effect from cause, from the free-will's movement towards God and sin; since it is by faith and contrition that sin is forgiven. But an effect ought not to be reckoned with its cause; since things thus enumerated together, and, as it were, condivided, are by nature simultaneous. Hence the remission of sins ought not to be reckoned with the things required for the justification of the ungodly.

On the contrary, In reckoning what is required for a thing we ought not to pass over the end, which is the chief part of everything. Now the remission of sins is the end of the justification of the ungodly; for it is written (Isa. xxvii. 9): *This is all the fruit, that the sin thereof should be taken away.* Hence the remission of sins ought to be reckoned amongst the things required for justification.

I answer that, There are four things which are accounted to be necessary for the justification of the ungodly, viz., the infusion of grace, the movement of the free-will towards God by faith, the movement of the free-will towards sin, and the remission of sins. The reason for this is that, as stated above (A. 1), the justification of the ungodly is a movement whereby the soul is moved by God from a state of sin to a state of justice. Now in the movement whereby one thing is moved by another, three things are required:—first, the motion of the mover; secondly, the movement of the moved; thirdly, the consummation of the movement, or the attainment of the end. On the part of the Divine motion, there is the infusion of grace; on the part of the free-will which is moved, there are two movements,—of departure from the term *whence,* and of approach to the term *whereto;* but the consummation of the movement or the attainment of the end of the movement is implied in the remission of sins; for in this is the justification of the ungodly completed.

Reply Obj. 1. The justification of the ungodly is called the remission of sins, even as every movement has its species from its term. Nevertheless, many other things are required in order to reach the term, as stated above (A. 5).

Reply Obj. 2. The infusion of grace and the remission of sin may be considered in two ways:—First, with respect to the substance of the act, and thus they are the same; for by the same act God bestows grace and remits sin. Secondly, they may be considered on the part of the objects; and thus they differ by the difference between guilt, which is taken away, and grace, which is infused; just as in natural things generation and corruption differ, although the generation of one thing is the corruption of another.

Reply Obj. 3. This enumeration is not the division of a genus into its species, in which the things enumerated must be simultaneous; but it is a division of the things required for the completion of anything; and in this enumeration we may have what precedes and what follows, since some of the principles and parts of a composite thing may precede and some follow.

SEVENTH ARTICLE

Whether the Justification of the Ungodly Takes Place in an Instant or Successively?

We proceed thus to the Seventh Article:—

Objection 1. It would seem that the justification of the ungodly does not take place in an instant, but successively, since, as already stated (A. 3), for the justification of the ungodly there is required a movement of free-will. Now the act of the free-will is choice, which requires the deliberation of counsel, as stated above (Q. 13, A. 1). Hence, since deliberation implies a certain reasoning process, and this implies succession, the justification of the ungodly would seem to be successive.

Obj. 2. Further, the free-will's movement is not without actual consideration. But it is impossible to understand many things actually and at once, as stated above (P. 1, Q. 85, A. 4). Hence, since for the justification of the ungodly there is required a movement of the free-will towards several things, viz., towards God and towards sin, it would seem impossible for the justification of the ungodly to be in an instant.

Obj. 3. Further, a form that may be greater or less, *e.g.,* blackness or whiteness, is received successively by its subject. Now grace may be greater or less, as stated above (Q. 112, A. 4). Hence it is not received suddenly by its subject. Therefore, seeing that the infusion of grace is required for the justification of the ungodly, it would seem that the justification of the ungodly cannot be in an instant.

Obj. 4. Further, the free-will's movement, which co-operates in justification, is meritorious; and hence it must proceed from grace, without which there is no merit, as we shall state further on (Q. 114, A. 2). Now a thing receives its form before operating by this form. Hence grace is first infused, and then the free-will is moved towards God and to detest sin. Hence justification is not all at once.

Obj. 5. Further, if grace is infused into the soul, there must be an instant when it first dwells in the soul; so, too, if sin is forgiven there must be a last instant that man is in sin. But it cannot be the same instant, otherwise opposites would be in the same simultaneously. Hence they must be two successive instants; between which there must be time, as the Philosopher says (*Phys.* vi. 1). Therefore the justification of the ungodly takes place not all at once, but successively.

On the contrary, The justification of the ungodly is caused by the justifying grace of the Holy Spirit. Now the Holy Spirit comes to men's minds suddenly, according to Acts ii. 2: *And suddenly there came a sound from heaven as of a mighty wind coming,* upon which the gloss says that *the grace of the Holy Ghost knows no tardy efforts.* Hence the justification of the ungodly is not successive, but instantaneous.

I answer that, The entire justification of the ungodly consists as to its origin in the infusion of grace. For it is by grace that free-will is moved and sin is remitted. Now the infusion of grace takes place in an instant and without succession. And the reason of this is that if a form be not suddenly impressed upon its subject, it is either because that subject is not disposed, or because the agent needs time to dispose the subject. Hence we see that immediately the matter is disposed by a preceding alteration, the substantial form accrues to the matter; thus because the atmosphere of itself is disposed to receive light, it is suddenly illuminated by a body actually luminous. Now it was stated (Q. 112, A. 2) that God, in order to infuse grace into the soul, needs no disposition, save what He Himself has made. And sometimes this sufficient disposition for the reception of grace He makes suddenly, sometimes gradually and successively, as stated above (Q. 112, A. 2, *ad* 2). For the reason why a natural agent cannot suddenly dispose matter is that in the matter there is a resistant which has some disproportion with the power of the agent; and hence we see that the stronger the agent, the more speedily is the matter disposed. Therefore, since the Divine power is infinite, it can suddenly dispose any matter whatsoever to its form; and much more man's free-will, whose movement is by nature instantaneous. Therefore the justification of the ungodly by God takes place in an instant.

Reply Obj. 1. The movement of the free-will, which concurs in the justification of the ungodly, is a consent to detest sin, and to draw near to God; and this consent takes place suddenly. Sometimes, indeed, it happens that deliberation precedes, yet this is not of the substance of justification, but a way to justification; as local movement is a way to illumination, and alteration to generation.

Reply Obj. 2. As stated above (P. 1, Q. 85, A. 5), there is nothing to prevent two things being understood at once, in so far as they are somehow one; thus we understand the subject and predicate together, inasmuch as they are united in the order of one affirmation. And in the same manner can the free-will be moved to two things at once in so far as one is ordained to the other. Now the free-will's movement towards sin is ordained to the free-will's movement towards God, since a man detests sin, as contrary to God, to Whom he wishes to cling. Hence in the justification of the ungodly the free-will simultaneously detests sin and turns to God, even as a body approaches one point and withdraws from another simultaneously.

Reply Obj. 3. The reason why a form is not received instantaneously in the matter is

not the fact that it can inhere more or less; for thus the light would not be suddenly received in the air, which can be illumined more and less. But the reason is to be sought on the part of the disposition of the matter or subject, as stated above.

Reply Obj. 4. The same instant the form is acquired, the thing begins to operate with the form; as fire, the instant it is generated moves upwards, and if its movement was instantaneous, it would be terminated in the same instant. Now to will and not to will,— the movements of the free-will,—are not successive, but instantaneous. Hence the justification of the ungodly must not be successive.

Reply Obj. 5. The succession of opposites in the same subject must be looked at differently in the things that are subject to time and in those that are above time. For in those that are in time, there is no last instant in which the previous form inheres in the subject; but there is the last time, and the first instant that the subsequent form inheres in the matter or subject; and this for the reason, that in time we are not to consider one instant as immediately preceding another instant, since neither do instants succeed each other immediately in time, nor points in a line, as is proved in *Physic.* vi. 1. But time is terminated by an instant. Hence in the whole of the previous time wherein anything is moving towards its form, it is under the opposite form; but in the last instant of this time, which is the first instant of the subsequent time, it has the form which is the term of the movement.

But in those that are above time, it is otherwise. For if there be any succession of affections or intellectual conceptions in them (as in the angels), such succession is not measured by continuous time, but by discrete time, even as the things measured are not continuous, as stated above (P. I, Q. 53, AA. 2, 3). In these, therefore, there is a last instant in which the preceding is, and a first instant in which the subsequent is. Nor must there be time in between, since there is no continuity of time, which this would necessitate.

Now the human mind, which is justified, is, in itself, above time, but is subject to time accidentally, inasmuch as it understands with continuity and time, with respect to the phantasms in which it considers the intelligible species, as stated above (P. I, Q. 85, AA. 1, 2). We must, therefore, decide from this about its change as regards the condition of temporal movements, i.e., we must say that there is no last instant that sin inheres, but a last time; whereas there is a first instant that grace inheres; and in all the time previous sin inhered.

EIGHTH ARTICLE

Whether the Infusion of Grace Is Naturally the First of the Things Required for the Justification of the Ungodly?

We proceed thus to the Eighth Article:—

Objection 1. It would seem that the infusion of grace is not what is naturally required first for the justification of the ungodly. For we withdraw from evil before drawing near to good, according to Ps. xxxiii. 15: *Turn away from evil, and do good.* Now the remission of sins regards the turning away from evil, and the infusion of grace regards the turning to good. Hence the remission of sin is naturally before the infusion of grace.

Obj. 2. Further, the disposition naturally precedes the form to which it disposes. Now the free-will's movement is a disposition for the reception of grace. Therefore it naturally precedes the infusion of grace.

Obj. 3. Further, sin hinders the soul from tending freely to God. Now a hindrance to movement must be removed before the movement takes place. Hence the remission of sin and the free-will's movement towards sin are naturally before the infusion of grace.

On the contrary, The cause is naturally prior to its effect. Now the infusion of grace is the cause of whatever is required for the justification of the ungodly, as stated above (A. 7). Therefore it is naturally prior to it.

I answer that, The aforesaid four things required for the justification of the ungodly are simultaneous in time, since the justification of the ungodly is not successive, as stated above (A. 7); but in the order of nature, one is prior to another; and in their natural order the first is the infusion of grace; the second, the free-will's movement towards God; the third, the free-will's movement towards sin; the fourth, the remission of sin.

The reason for this is that in every movement the motion of the mover is naturally first; the disposition of the matter, or the movement of the moved, is second; the end or term of the movement in which the motion of the mover rests, is last. Now the motion of God the Mover is the infusion of grace, as stated above (A. 6); the movement or disposition of the moved is the free-will's double movement; and the term or end of the movement is the remission of sin, as stated above (A. 6). Hence in their natural order the first in the justification of the ungodly is the infusion of grace; the second is the free-will's movement towards God; the third is the free-will's movement towards sin, for he who is being justified detests sin because it is against God, and thus the free-will's movement towards God naturally precedes the free-will's

movement towards sin, since it is its cause and reason; the fourth and last is the remission of sin, to which this transmutation is ordained as to an end, as stated above (AA. 1, 6).

Reply Obj. 1. The withdrawal from one term and approach to another may be looked at in two ways:—first, on the part of the thing moved, and thus the withdrawal from a term naturally precedes the approach to a term, since in the subject of movement the opposite which is put away is prior to the opposite which the subject moved attains to by its movement. But on the part of the agent it is the other way about, since the agent, by the form pre-existing in it, acts for the removal of the opposite form; as the sun by its light acts for the removal of darkness, and hence on the part of the sun, illumination is prior to the removal of darkness; but on the part of the atmosphere to be illuminated, to be freed from darkness is, in the order of nature, prior to being illuminated, although both are simultaneous in time. And since the infusion of grace and the remission of sin regard God Who justifies, hence in the order of nature the infusion of grace is prior to the freeing from sin. But if we look at what is on the part of the man justified, it is the other way about, since in the order of nature the being freed from sin is prior to the obtaining of justifying grace.—Or it may be said that the term *whence* of justification is sin; and the term *whereto* is justice; and that grace is the cause of the forgiveness of sin and of the obtaining of justice.

Reply Obj. 2. The disposition of the subject precedes the reception of the form, in the order of nature; yet it follows the action of the agent, whereby the subject is disposed. And hence the free-will's movement precedes the reception of grace in the order of nature, and follows the infusion of grace.

Reply Obj. 3. As the Philosopher says (*Phys.* ii. 9), in movements of the soul the movement toward the speculative principle or the practical end is the very first, but in exterior movements the removal of the impediment precedes the attainment of the end. And as the free-will's movement is a movement of the soul, in the order of nature it moves towards God as to its end, before removing the impediment of sin.

NINTH ARTICLE

Whether the Justification of the Ungodly Is God's Greatest Work?

We proceed thus to the Ninth Article:—

Objection 1. It would seem that the justification of the ungodly is not God's greatest work. For it is by the justification of the ungodly that we attain the grace of a wayfarer. Now by glorification we receive heavenly grace, which is greater. Hence the glorification of angels and men is a greater work than the justification of the ungodly.

Obj. 2. Further, the justification of the ungodly is ordained to the particular good of one man. But the good of the universe is greater than the good of one man, as is plain from *Ethic.* i. 2. Hence the creation of heaven and earth is a greater work than the justification of the ungodly.

Obj. 3. Further, to make something from nothing, where there is nought to co-operate with the agent, is greater than to make something with the co-operation of the recipient. Now in the work of creation something is made from nothing, and hence nothing can co-operate with the agent; but in the justification of the ungodly God makes something from something, i.e., a just man from a sinner, and there is a co-operation on man's part, since there is a movement of the free-will, as stated above (A. 3). Hence the justification of the ungodly is not God's greatest work.

On the contrary, It is written (Ps. cxliv. 9): *His tender mercies are over all His works,* and in a collect* we say: *O God, Who dost show forth Thine all-mightiness most by pardoning and having mercy,* and Augustine, expounding the words, *greater than these shall he do* (Jo. xiv. 12), says that *for a just man to be made from a sinner, is greater than to create heaven and earth.*

I answer that, A work may be called great in two ways:—first, on the part of the mode of action, and thus the work of creation is the greatest work, wherein something is made from nothing; secondly, a work may be called great on account of what is made, and thus the justification of the ungodly, which terminates at the eternal good of a share in the Godhead, is greater than the creation of heaven and earth, which terminates at the good of mutable nature. Hence, Augustine, after saying that *for a just man to be made from a sinner is greater than to create heaven and earth,* adds, *for heaven and earth shall pass away, but the justification of the ungodly shall endure.*

Again, we must bear in mind that a thing is called great in two ways:—first, in absolute quantity, and thus the gift of glory is greater than the gift of grace that sanctifies the ungodly; and in this respect the glorification of the just is greater than the justification of the ungodly. Secondly, a thing may be said to be great in proportionate quantity, and thus the gift of grace that justifies the ungodly is greater than the gift of glory that beatifies the just, for the gift of grace exceeds

* Tenth Sunday after Pentecost.

the worthiness of the ungodly, who are worthy of punishment, more than the gift of glory exceeds the worthiness of the just, who by the fact of their justification are worthy of glory. Hence Augustine says (*ibid.*): *Let him that can, judge whether it is greater to create the angels just, than to justify the ungodly. Certainly, if they both betoken equal power, one betokens greater mercy.*

And thus the reply to the first is clear.

Reply Obj. 2. The good of the universe is greater than the particular good of one, if we consider both in the same genus. But the good of grace in one is greater than the good of nature in the whole universe.

Reply Obj. 3. This objection rests on the manner of acting, in which way creation is God's greatest work.

TENTH ARTICLE

Whether the Justification of the Ungodly Is a Miraculous Work?

We proceed thus to the Tenth Article:—

Objection 1. It would seem that the justification of the ungodly is a miraculous work. For miraculous works are greater than non-miraculous. Now the justification of the ungodly is greater than the other miraculous works, as is clear from the quotation from Augustine (A. 9). Hence the justification of the ungodly is a miraculous work.

Obj. 2. Further, the movement of the will in the soul is like the natural inclination in natural things. But when God works in natural things against the inclination of their nature, it is a miraculous work, as when He gave sight to the blind or raised the dead. Now the will of the ungodly is bent on evil. Hence, since God in justifying a man moves him to good, it would seem that the justification of the ungodly is miraculous.

Obj. 3. Further, as wisdom is a gift of God, so also is justice. Now it is miraculous that anyone should suddenly obtain wisdom from God without study. Therefore it is miraculous that the ungodly should be justified by God.

On the contrary, Miraculous works are beyond natural power. Now the justification of the ungodly is not beyond natural power; for Augustine says (*De Præd. Sanct.* v) that *to be capable of having faith and to be capable of having charity belongs to man's nature; but to have faith and charity belongs to the grace of the faithful.* Therefore the justification of the ungodly is not miraculous.

I answer that, In miraculous works it is usual to find three things:—the *first* is on the part of the active power, because they can only be performed by Divine power; and they are simply wondrous, since their cause is hidden, as stated above (P. I, Q. 105, A. 7). And thus both the justification of the ungodly and the creation of the world, and, generally speaking, every work that can be done by God alone, is miraculous.

Secondly, in certain miraculous works it is found that the form introduced is beyond the natural power of such matter, as in the resurrection of the dead, life is above the natural power of such a body. And thus the justification of the ungodly is not miraculous, because the soul is naturally capable of grace; since from its having been made to the likeness of God, it is fit to receive God by grace, as Augustine says, in the above quotation.

Thirdly, in miraculous works something is found besides the usual and customary order of causing an effect, as when a sick man suddenly and beyond the wonted course of healing by nature or art, receives perfect health; and thus the justification of the ungodly is sometimes miraculous and sometimes not. For the common and wonted course of justification is that God moves the soul interiorly and that man is converted to God, first by an imperfect conversion, that it may afterwards become perfect; because *charity begun merits increase, and when increased merits perfection,* as Augustine says (*In Epist. Joan., Tract.* v).

Yet God sometimes moves the soul so vehemently that it reaches the perfection of justice at once, as took place in the conversion of Paul, which was accompanied at the same time by a miraculous external prostration. Hence the conversion of Paul is commemorated in the Church as miraculous.

Reply Obj. 1. Certain miraculous works, although they are less than the justification of the ungodly, as regards the good caused, are beyond the wonted order of such effects, and thus have more of the nature of a miracle.

Reply Obj. 2. It is not a miraculous work, whenever a natural thing is moved contrary to its inclination, otherwise it would be miraculous for water to be heated, or for a stone to be thrown upwards; but only whenever this takes place beyond the order of the proper cause, which naturally does this. Now no other cause save God can justify the ungodly, even as nothing save fire can heat water. Hence the justification of the ungodly by God is not miraculous in this respect.

Reply Obj. 3. A man naturally acquires wisdom and knowledge from God by his own talent and study. Hence it is miraculous when a man is made wise or learned outside this order. But a man does not naturally acquire justifying grace by his own action, but by God's. Hence there is no parity.

QUESTION 114

Of Merit

(In Ten Articles)

WE must now consider merit, which is the effect of co-operating grace; and under this head there are ten points of inquiry: (1) Whether a man can merit anything from God? (2) Whether without grace anyone can merit eternal life? (3) Whether anyone with grace may merit eternal life condignly? (4) Whether it is chiefly through the instrumentality of charity that grace is the principle of merit? (5) Whether a man may merit the first grace for himself? (6) Whether he may merit it for someone else? (7) Whether anyone can merit restoration after sin? (8) Whether he can merit for himself an increase of grace or charity? (9) Whether he can merit final perseverance? (10) Whether temporal goods fall under merit?

FIRST ARTICLE

Whether a Man May Merit Anything from God?

We proceed thus to the First Article:—
Objection 1. It would seem that a man can

merit nothing from God. For no one, it would seem, merits by giving another his due. But by all the good we do, we cannot make sufficient return to God, since yet more is His due, as also the Philosopher says (*Ethic.* viii. 14). Hence it is written (Luke xvii. 10): *When you have done all these things that are commanded you, say: We are unprofitable servants; we have done that which we ought to do.* Therefore a man can merit nothing from God.

Obj. 2. Further, it would seem that a man merits nothing from God, by what profits himself only, and profits God nothing. Now by acting well, a man profits himself or another man, but not God, for it is written (Job xxxv. 7): *If thou do justly, what shalt thou give Him, or what shall He receive of thy hand.* Hence a man can merit nothing from God.

Obj. 3. Further, whoever merits anything from another makes him his debtor; for a man's wage is a debt due to him. Now God is no one's debtor; hence it is written (Rom.

xi. 35): *Who hath first given to Him, and recompense shall be made to him?* Hence no one can merit anything from God.

On the contrary, It is written (Jer. xxxi. 16): *There is a reward for thy work.* Now a reward means something bestowed by reason of merit. Hence it would seem that a man may merit from God.

I answer that, Merit and reward refer to the same, for a reward means something given anyone in return for work or toil, as a price for it. Hence, as it is an act of justice to give a just price for anything received from another, so also is it an act of justice to make a return for work or toil. Now justice is a kind of equality, as is clear from the Philosopher (*Ethic.* v. 3), and hence justice is simply between those that are simply equal; but where there is no absolute equality between them, neither is there absolute justice, but there may be a certain manner of justice, as when we speak of a father's or a master's right (*ibid.* 6), as the Philosopher says. And hence where there is justice simply, there is the character of merit and reward simply. But where there is no simple right, but only relative, there is no character of merit simply, but only relatively, in so far as the character of justice is found there, since the child merits something from his father and the slave from his lord.

Now it is clear that between God and man there is the greatest inequality: for they are infinitely apart, and all man's good is from God. Hence there can be no justice of absolute equality between man and God, but only of a certain proportion, inasmuch as both operate after their own manner. Now the manner and measure of human virtue is in man from God. Hence man's merit with God only exists on the presupposition of the Divine ordination, so that man obtains from God, as a reward of his operation, what God gave him the power of operation for, even as natural things by their proper movements and operations obtain that to which they were ordained by God; differently, indeed, since the rational creature moves itself to act by its free-will, hence its action has the character of merit, which is not so in other creatures.

Reply Obj. 1. Man merits, inasmuch as he does what he ought, by his free-will; otherwise the act of justice whereby anyone discharges a debt would not be meritorious.

Reply Obj. 2. God seeks from our goods not profit, but glory, i.e., the manifestation of His goodness; even as He seeks it also in His own works. Now nothing accrues to Him, but only to ourselves, by our worship of Him. Hence we merit from God, not that by our works anything accrues to Him, but inasmuch as we work for His glory.

Reply Obj. 3. Since our action has the character of merit, only on the presupposition of the Divine ordination, it does not follow that God is made our debtor simply, but His own, inasmuch as it is right that His will should be carried out.

SECOND ARTICLE

Whether Anyone Without Grace Can Merit Eternal Life?

We proceed thus to the Second Article:—

Objection 1. It would seem that without grace anyone can merit eternal life. For man merits from God what he is divinely ordained to, as stated above (A. 1). Now man by his nature is ordained to beatitude as his end; hence, too, he naturally wishes to be blessed. Hence man by his natural endowments and without grace can merit beatitude which is eternal life.

Obj. 2. Further, the less a work is due, the more meritorious it is. Now, less due is that work which is done by one who has received fewer benefits. Hence, since he who has only natural endowments has received fewer gifts from God, than he who has gratuitous gifts as well as nature, it would seem that his works are more meritorious with God. And thus if he who has grace can merit eternal life to some extent, much more may he who has no grace.

Obj. 3. Further, God's mercy and liberality infinitely surpass human mercy and liberality. Now a man may merit from another, even though he has not hitherto had his grace. Much more, therefore, would it seem that a man without grace may merit eternal life.

On the contrary, The Apostle says (Rom. vi. 23): *The grace of God, life everlasting.*

I answer that, Man without grace may be looked at in two states, as was said above (Q. 109, A. 2);—the first, a state of perfect nature, in which Adam was before his sin;—the second, a state of corrupt nature, in which we are before being restored by grace. Therefore, if we speak of man in the first state, there is only one reason why man cannot merit eternal life without grace, by his purely natural endowments, viz., because man's merit depends on the Divine pre-ordination. Now no act of anything whatsoever is divinely ordained to anything exceeding the proportion of the powers which are the principles of its act; for it is a law of Divine providence that nothing shall act beyond its powers. Now everlasting life is a good exceeding the proportion of created nature; since it exceeds its knowledge and desire, according to 1 Cor. ii. 9:

Eye hath not seen, nor ear heard, neither hath it entered into the heart of man. And hence it is that no created nature is a sufficient principle of an act meritorious of eternal life, unless there is added a supernatural gift, which we call grace. But if we speak of man as existing in sin, a second reason is added to this, viz., the impediment of sin. For since sin is an offense against God, excluding us from eternal life, as is clear from what has been said above (Q. 71, A. 6; Q. 113, A. 2), no one existing in a state of mortal sin can merit eternal life unless first he be reconciled to God, through his sin being forgiven, which is brought about by grace. For the sinner deserves not life, but death, according to Rom. vi. 23: *The wages of sin is death.*

Reply Obj. 1. God ordained human nature to attain the end of eternal life, not by its own strength, but by the help of grace; and in this way its act can be meritorious of eternal life.

Reply Obj. 2. Without grace a man cannot have a work equal to a work proceeding from grace, since the more perfect the principle, the more perfect the action. But the objection would hold good, if we supposed the operations equal in both cases.

Reply Obj. 3. With regard to the first reason adduced, the case is different in God and in man. For a man receives all his power of well-doing from God, and not from man. Hence a man can merit nothing from God except by His gift, which the Apostle expresses aptly saying (Rom. xi. 35): *Who hath first given to Him, and recompense shall be made to him?* But man may merit from man, before he has received anything from him, by what he has received from God.

But as regards the second proof taken from the impediment of sin, the case is similar with man and God, since one man cannot merit from another whom he has offended, unless he makes satisfaction to him and is reconciled.

THIRD ARTICLE

Whether a Man in Grace Can Merit Eternal Life Condignly?

We proceed thus to the Third Article:—

Objection 1. It would seem that a man in grace cannot merit eternal life condignly, for the Apostle says (Rom. viii. 18): *The sufferings of this time are not worthy (condignae) to be compared with the glory to come, that shall be revealed in us.* But of all meritorious works, the sufferings of the saints would seem the most meritorious. Therefore no works of men are meritorious of eternal life condignly.

Obj. 2. Further, on Rom. vi. 23, *The grace of God, life everlasting,* a gloss says: *He might*

have truly said: *"The wages of justice, life everlasting"*; but He preferred to say *"The grace of God, life everlasting,"* that we may know that God leads us to life everlasting of His own mercy and not by our merits. Now when anyone merits something condignly he receives it not from mercy, but from merit. Hence it would seem that a man with grace cannot merit life everlasting condignly.

Obj. 3. Further, merit that equals the reward, would seem to be condign. Now no act of the present life can equal everlasting life, which surpasses our knowledge and our desire, and, moreover, surpasses the charity or love of the wayfarer, even as it exceeds nature. Therefore with grace a man cannot merit eternal life condignly.

On the contrary, What is granted in accordance with a fair judgment, would seem a condign reward. But life everlasting is granted by God, in accordance with the judgment of justice, according to 2 Tim. iv. 8: *As to the rest, there is laid up for me a crown of justice, which the Lord, the just judge, will render to me in that day.* Therefore man merits everlasting life condignly.

I answer that, Man's meritorious work may be considered in two ways:—first, as it proceeds from free-will; secondly, as it proceeds from the grace of the Holy Ghost. If it is considered as regards the substance of the work, and inasmuch as it springs from free-will, there can be no condignity because of the very great inequality. But there is congruity, on account of an equality of proportion: for it would seem congruous that, if a man does what he can, God should reward him according to the excellence of his power.

If, however, we speak of a meritorious work, inasmuch as it proceeds from the grace of the Holy Ghost moving us to life everlasting, it is meritorious of life everlasting condignly. For thus the value of its merit depends upon the power of the Holy Ghost moving us to life everlasting according to Jo. iv. 14: *Shall become in him a fount of water springing up into life everlasting.* And the worth of the work depends on the dignity of grace, whereby a man, being made a partaker of the Divine Nature, is adopted as a son of God, to whom the inheritance is due by right of adoption, according to Rom. viii. 17: *If sons, heirs also.*

Reply Obj. 1. The Apostle is speaking of the substance of these sufferings.

Reply Obj. 2. This saying is to be understood of the first cause of our reaching everlasting life, viz., God's mercy. But our merit is a subsequent cause.

Reply Obj. 3. The grace of the Holy Ghost which we have at present, although unequal to glory in act, is equal to it virtually as the seed of a tree, wherein the whole tree is virtually. So likewise by grace the Holy Ghost dwells in man; and He is a sufficient cause of life everlasting; hence, 2 Cor. i. 22, He is called the *pledge* of our inheritance.

FOURTH ARTICLE

Whether Grace Is the Principle of Merit Through Charity Rather Than the Other Virtues?

We proceed thus to the Fourth Article:—

Objection 1. It would seem that grace is not the principle of merit through charity rather than the other virtues. For wages are due to work, according to Matth. xx. 8: *Call the laborers and pay them their hire.* Now every virtue is a principle of some operation, since virtue is an operative habit, as stated above (Q. 55, A. 2). Hence every virtue is equally a principle of merit.

Obj. 2. Further, the Apostle says (1 Cor. iii. 8): *Every man shall receive his own reward according to his labor.* Now charity lessens rather than increases the labor, because as Augustine says (*De Verbis Dom., Serm.* lxx), *love makes all hard and repulsive tasks easy and next to nothing.* Hence charity is no greater principle of merit than any other virtue.

Obj. 3. Further, the greatest principle of merit would seem to be the one whose acts are most meritorious. But the acts of faith and patience or fortitude would seem to be the most meritorious, as appears in the martyrs, who strove for the faith patiently and bravely even till death. Hence other virtues are a greater principle of merit than charity.

On the contrary, Our Lord said (Jo. xiv. 21): *He that loveth Me, shall be loved of My Father; and I will love him and will manifest Myself to him.* Now everlasting life consists in the manifest knowledge of God, according to Jo. xvii. 3: *This is eternal life: that they may know Thee, the only true* and living *God.* Hence the merit of eternal life rests chiefly with charity.

I answer that, As we may gather from what has been stated above (A. 1) human acts have the nature of merit from two causes:—first and chiefly from the Divine ordination, inasmuch as acts are said to merit that good to which man is divinely ordained. Secondly, on the part of free-will, inasmuch as man, more than other creatures, has the power of voluntary acts by acting of himself. And in both these ways does merit chiefly rest with charity. For we must first bear in mind that everlasting life consists in the enjoyment of God. Now the human mind's movement to the fruition of the Divine good is the proper act of charity, whereby all the acts of the other virtues are

ordained to this end, since all the other virtues are commanded by charity. Hence the merit of life everlasting pertains first to charity, and secondly, to the other virtues, inasmuch as their acts are commanded by charity. So, likewise, is it manifest that what we do out of love we do most willingly. Hence, even inasmuch as merit depends on voluntariness, merit is chiefly attributed to charity.

Reply Obj. 1. Charity, inasmuch as it has the last end for object, moves the other virtues to act. For the habit to which the end pertains always commands the habits to which the means pertain, as was said above (Q. 9, A. 1).

Reply Obj. 2. A work can be toilsome and difficult in two ways:— first, from the greatness of the work, and thus the greatness of the work pertains to the increase of merit; and thus charity does not lessen the toil— rather, it makes us undertake the greatest toils, *for it does great things, if it exists,* as Gregory says (*Hom. in Evang.* xxx). Secondly, from the defect of the operator; for what is not done with a ready will is hard and difficult to all of us, and this toil lessens merit and is removed by charity.

Reply Obj. 3. The act of faith is not meritorious unless *faith . . . worketh by charity* (Gal. v. 6). So, too, the acts of patience and fortitude are not meritorious unless a man does them out of charity, according to 1 Cor. xiii. 3: *If I should deliver my body to be burned, and have not charity, it profiteth me nothing.*

FIFTH ARTICLE

Whether a Man May Merit for Himself the First Grace?

We proceed thus to the Fifth Article:—

Objection 1. It would seem that a man may merit for himself the first grace, because, as Augustine says (*Ep.* clxxxvi), *faith merits justification.* Now a man is justified by the first grace. Therefore a man may merit the first grace.

Obj. 2. Further, God gives grace only to the worthy. Now, no one is said to be worthy of some good, unless he has merited it condignly. Therefore we may merit the first grace condignly.

Obj. 3. Further, with men we may merit a gift already received. Thus if a man receives a horse from his master, he merits it by a good use of it in his master's service. Now God is much more bountiful than man. Much more, therefore, may a man, by subsequent works, merit the first grace already received from God.

On the contrary, The nature of grace is repugnant to reward of works, according to Rom. iv. 4: *Now to him that worketh, the reward is not reckoned according to grace but according to debt.* Now a man merits what is reckoned to him according to debt, as the reward of his works. Hence a man may not merit the first grace.

I answer that, The gift of grace may be considered in two ways:—first in the nature of a gratuitous gift, and thus it is manifest that all merit is repugnant to grace, since as the Apostle says (Rom. xi. 6), *if by grace, it is not now by works.*—Secondly, it may be considered as regards the nature of the thing given, and thus, also, it cannot come under the merit of him who has not grace, both because it exceeds the proportion of nature, and because previous to grace a man in the state of sin has an obstacle to his meriting grace, viz., sin. But when anyone has grace, the grace already possessed cannot come under merit, since reward is the term of the work, but grace is the principle of all our good works, as stated above (Q. 109). But if anyone merits a further gratuitous gift by virtue of the preceding grace, it would not be the first grace. Hence it is manifest that no one can merit for himself the first grace.

Reply Obj. 1. As Augustine says (*Retract.* i. 23), he was deceived on this point for a time, believing the beginning of faith to be from us, and its consummation to be granted us by God; and this he here retracts. And seemingly it is in this sense that he speaks of faith as meriting justification. But if we suppose, as indeed it is a truth of faith, that the beginning of faith is in us from God, the first act must flow from grace; and thus it cannot be meritorious of the first grace. Therefore man is justified by faith, not as though man, by believing, were to merit justification, but that, he believes, whilst he is being justified; inasmuch as a movement of faith is required for the justification of the ungodly, as stated above (Q. 113, A. 4).

Reply Obj. 2. God gives grace to none but to the worthy, not that they were previously worthy, but that by His grace He makes them worthy, Who alone *can make him clean that is conceived of unclean seed* (Job xiv. 4).

Reply Obj. 3. Man's every good work proceeds from the first grace as from its principle; but not from any gift of man. Consequently, there is no comparison between gifts of grace and gifts of men.

SIXTH ARTICLE

Whether a Man Can Merit the First Grace for Another?

We proceed thus to the Sixth Article:—

Objection 1. It would seem that a man can merit the first grace for another. Because on Matth. ix. 2, *Jesus seeing their faith,* etc., a gloss says: *How much is our personal faith worth with God, Who set such a price on another's faith, as to heal the man both inwardly and outwardly!* Now inward healing is brought about by grace. Hence a man can merit the first grace for another.

Obj. 2. Further, the prayers of the just are not void, but efficacious, according to James v. 16: *The continued prayer of a just man availeth much.* Now he had previously said: *Pray one for another, that you may be saved.* Hence, since man's salvation can only be brought about by grace, it seems that one man may merit for another his first grace.

Obj. 3. Further, it is written (Luke xvi. 9): *Make unto you friends of the mammon of iniquity, that when you shall fail they may receive you into everlasting dwellings.* Now it is through grace alone that anyone is received into everlasting dwellings, for by it alone does anyone merit everlasting life as stated above (A. 2; Q. 109, A. 5). Hence one man may by merit obtain for another his first grace.

On the contrary, It is written (Jer. xv. 1): *If Moses and Samuel shall stand before Me, My soul is not towards this people*—yet they had great merit with God. Hence it seems that no one can merit the first grace for another.

I answer that, As shown above (AA. 1, 3, 4), our works are meritorious from two causes:—first, by virtue of the Divine motion; and thus we merit condignly;—secondly, according as they proceed from free-will in so far as we do them willingly, and thus they have congruous merit, since it is congruous that when a man makes good use of his power, God should by His super-excellent power work still higher things. And therefore it is clear that no one can merit condignly for another his first grace, save Christ alone; since each one of us is moved by God to reach life everlasting through the gift of grace; hence condign merit does not reach beyond this motion. But Christ's soul is moved by God through grace, not only so as to reach the glory of life everlasting, but so as to lead others to it, inasmuch as He is the Head of the Church, and the Author of human salvation, according to Heb. ii. 10: *Who hath brought many children into glory [to perfect] the Author of their salvation.*

But one may merit the first grace for another congruously; because a man in grace fulfils God's will, and it is congruous and in harmony with friendship that God should fulfil man's desire for the salvation of another, although sometimes there may be an impediment on the part of him whose salvation the just man desires. And it is in this sense that the passage from Jeremias speaks.

Reply Obj. 1. A man's faith avails for another's salvation by congruous and not by condign merit.

Reply Obj. 2. The impetration of prayer rests on mercy, whereas condign merit rests on justice; hence a man may impetrate many things from the Divine mercy in prayer, which he does not merit in justice, according to Dan. ix. 18: *For it is not for our justifications that we present our prayers before Thy face, but for the multitude of Thy tender mercies.*

Reply Obj. 3. The poor who receive alms are said to receive others into everlasting dwellings, either by impetrating their forgiveness in prayer, or by meriting congruously by other good works, or materially speaking, inasmuch as by these good works of mercy, exercised towards the poor, we merit to be received into everlasting dwellings.

SEVENTH ARTICLE

Whether a Man May Merit Restoration after a Fall?

We proceed thus to the Seventh Article:—

Objection 1. It would seem that anyone may merit for himself restoration after a fall. For what a man may justly ask of God, he may justly merit. Now nothing may more justly be besought of God than to be restored after a fall, as Augustine says,* according to Ps. lxx. 9: *When my strength shall fail, do not Thou forsake me.* Hence a man may merit to be restored after a fall.

Obj. 2. Further, a man's works benefit himself more than another. Now a man may, to some extent, merit for another his restoration after a fall, even as his first grace. Much more, therefore, may he merit for himself restoration after a fall.

Obj. 3. Further, when a man is once in grace he merits life everlasting by the good works he does, as was shown above (A. 2; Q. 109, A. 5). Now no one can attain life everlasting unless he is restored by grace. Hence it would seem that he merits for himself restoration.

On the contrary, It is written (Ezech. xviii. 24): *If the just man turn himself away from his justice and do iniquity . . . all his justices which he hath done shall not be remembered.* Therefore his previous merits will nowise help him to rise again. Hence no one can merit for himself restoration after a fall.

I answer that, No one can merit for himself restoration after a future fall, either condignly or congruously. He cannot merit for himself

* *Cf. Ennar. i super Ps. lxx.*

condignly, since the reason of this merit depends on the motion of Divine grace, and this motion is interrupted by the subsequent sin; hence all benefits which he afterwards obtains from God, whereby he is restored, do not fall under merit—the motion of the preceding grace not extending to them. Again, congruous merit, whereby one merits the first grace for another, is prevented from having its effect on account of the impediment of sin in the one for whom it is merited. Much more, therefore, is the efficacy of such merit impeded by the obstacle which is in him who merits, and in him for whom it is merited; for both these are in the same person. And therefore a man can nowise merit for himself restoration after a fall.

Reply Obj. 1. The desire whereby we seek for restoration after a fall is called just, and likewise the prayer whereby this restoration is besought is called just, because it tends to justice; and not that it depends on justice by way of merit, but only on mercy.

Reply Obj. 2. Anyone may congruously merit for another his first grace, because there is no impediment (at least, on the part of him who merits), such as is found when anyone recedes from justice after the merit of grace.

Reply Obj. 3. Some have said that no one *absolutely* merits life everlasting except by the act of final grace,—but only *conditionally,* i.e., if he perseveres. But it is unreasonable to say this, for sometimes the act of the last grace is not more, but less meritorious than preceding acts, on account of the prostration of illness. Hence it must be said that every act of charity merits eternal life absolutely; but by subsequent sin, there arises an impediment to the preceding merit, so that it does not obtain its effect; just as natural causes fail of their effects on account of a supervening impediment.

EIGHTH ARTICLE

Whether a Man May Merit the Increase of Grace or Charity?

We proceed thus to the Eighth Article:—

Objection 1. It would seem that a man cannot merit an increase of grace or charity. For when anyone receives the reward he merited, no other reward is due to him; thus it was said of some (Matth. vi. 2): *They have received their reward.* Hence, if anyone were to merit the increase of charity or grace, it would follow that, when his grace has been increased, he could not expect any further reward, which is unfitting.

Obj. 2. Further, nothing acts beyond its species. But the principle of merit is grace or charity, as was shown above (AA. 2, 4)

Therefore no one can merit greater grace or charity than he has.

Obj. 3. Further, what falls under merit a man merits by every act flowing from grace or charity, as by every such act a man merits life everlasting. If, therefore, the increase of grace or charity falls under merit, it would seem that by every act quickened by charity a man would merit an increase of charity. But what a man merits, he infallibly receives from God, unless hindered by subsequent sin; for it is written (2 Tim. i. 12): *I know Whom I have believed, and I am certain that He is able to keep that which I have committed unto Him.* Hence it would follow that grace or charity is increased by every meritorious act; and this would seem impossible since at times meritorious acts are not very fervent, and would not suffice for the increase of charity. Therefore the increase of charity does not come under merit.

On the contrary, Augustine says (super *Ep. Joan.;* cf. *Ep.* clxxxvi) that *charity merits increase, and being increased merits to be perfected.* Hence the increase of grace or charity falls under merit.

I answer that, As stated above (AA. 6, 7), whatever the motion of grace reaches to, falls under condign merit. Now the motion of a mover extends not merely to the last term of the movement, but to the whole progress of the movement. But the term of the movement of grace is eternal life; and progress in this movement is by the increase of charity or grace according to Prov. iv. 18: *But the path of the just as a shining light, goeth forward and increaseth even to perfect day,* which is the day of glory. And thus the increase of grace falls under condign merit.

Reply Obj. 1. Reward is the term of merit. But there is a double term of movement, viz., the last, and the intermediate, which is both beginning and term; and this term is the reward of increase. Now the reward of human favor is as the last end to those who place their end in it; hence such as these receive no other reward.

Reply Obj. 2. The increase of grace is not above the virtuality of the pre-existing grace, although it is above its quantity, even as a tree is not above the virtuality of the seed, although above its quantity.

Reply Obj. 3. By every meritorious act a man merits the increase of grace, equally with the consummation of grace which is eternal life. But just as eternal life is not given at once, but in its own time, so neither is grace increased at once, but in its own time, viz., when a man is sufficiently disposed for the increase of grace.

NINTH ARTICLE

Whether a Man May Merit Perseverance?

We proceed thus to the Ninth Article:—

Objection 1. It would seem that anyone may merit perseverance. For what a man obtains by asking, can come under the merit of anyone that is in grace. Now men obtain perseverance by asking it of God; otherwise it would be useless to ask it of God in the petitions of the Lord's Prayer, as Augustine says (*De Dono Persev.* ii). Therefore perseverance may come under the merit of whoever has grace.

Obj. 2. Further, it is more not to be able to sin, than not to sin. But not to be able to sin comes under merit, for we merit eternal life, of which impeccability is an essential part. Much more, therefore, may we merit not to sin, i.e., to persevere.

Obj. 3. Further, increase of grace is greater than perseverance in the grace we already possess. But a man may merit an increase of grace, as was stated above (A. 8). Much more, therefore, may he merit perseverance in the grace he has already.

On the contrary, What we merit, we obtain from God, unless it is hindered by sin. Now many have meritorious works, who do not obtain perseverance; nor can it be urged that this takes place because of the impediment of sin, since sin itself is opposed to perseverance; and thus if anyone were to merit perseverance, God would not permit him to fall into sin. Hence perseverance does not come under merit.

I answer that, Since man's free-will is naturally flexible towards good and evil, there are two ways of obtaining from God perseverance in good:—first, inasmuch as free-will is determined to good by consummate grace, which will be in glory; secondly, on the part of the Divine motion, which inclines man to good unto the end. Now, as explained above (AA. 6, 7, 8), that which is related as a term to the free-will's movement directed by God the mover, falls under human merit; and not what is related to the aforesaid movement as principle. Hence it is clear that the perseverance of glory which is the term of the aforesaid movement, falls under merit; but perseverance of the wayfarer does not fall under merit, since it depends solely on the Divine motion, which is the principle of all merit. Now God freely bestows the good of perseverance, on whomsoever He bestows it.

Reply Obj. 1. We impetrate in prayer things that we do not merit, since God hears sinners who beseech the pardon of their sins, which they do not merit, as appears from Augustine* on Jo. ix. 31, *Now we know that God doth not hear sinners*, otherwise it would have been useless for the publican to say: *O God, be merciful to me a sinner*, Luke xviii. 13. So too may we impetrate of God in prayer the grace of perseverance either for ourselves or for others, although it does not fall under merit.

Reply Obj. 2. The perseverance which is in heaven is compared as term to the free-will's movement; not so, the perseverance of the wayfarer, for the reason given in the body of the article.

In the same way may we answer the third objection which concerns the increase of grace, as was explained above.

TENTH ARTICLE

Whether Temporal Goods Fall under Merit?

We proceed thus to the Tenth Article:—

Objection 1. It would seem that temporal goods fall under merit. For what is promised to some as a reward of justice, falls under merit. Now, temporal goods were promised in the Old Law as the reward of justice, as appears from Deut. xxviii. Hence it seems that temporal goods fall under merit.

Obj. 2. Further, that would seem to fall under merit, which God bestows on anyone for a service done. But God sometimes bestows temporal goods on men for services done for Him. For it is written (Exod. i. 21): *And because the midwives feared God, He built them houses;* on which a gloss of Gregory (*Moral.* xviii. 4) says that *life everlasting might have been awarded them as the fruit of their good-will, but on account of their sin of falsehood they received an earthly reward.* And it is written (Ezech. xxix. 18): *The King of Babylon hath made his army to undergo hard service against Tyre . . . and there hath been no reward given him,* and further on: *And it shall be wages for his army. . . . I have given him the land of Egypt because he hath labored for me.* Therefore temporal goods fall under merit.

Obj. 3. Further, as good is to merit so is evil to demerit. But on account of the demerit of sin some are punished by God with temporal punishments, as appears from the Sodomites, Gen. xix. Hence temporal goods fall under merit.

Obj. 4. On the contrary, What falls under merit does not come upon all alike. But temporal goods regard the good and the wicked alike; according to Eccles. ix. 2: *All things equally happen to the just and the wicked, to the good and to the evil, to the clean and*

* *Tract.* xliv *in Joan.*

to the unclean, to him that offereth victims and to him that despiseth sacrifices. Therefore temporal goods do not fall under merit.

I answer that, What falls under merit is the reward or wage, which is a kind of good. Now man's good is twofold—the first, simply; the second, relatively. Now man's good simply is his last end, (according to Ps. lxxii. 27: *But it is good for me to adhere to my God*), and consequently what is ordained and leads to this end; and these fall simply under merit. But the relative, not the simple, good of man is what is good to him now, or what is a good to him relatively; and this does not fall under merit simply, but relatively.

Hence we must say that if temporal goods are considered as they are useful for virtuous works, whereby we are led to heaven, they fall directly and simply under merit, even as increase of grace, and everything whereby a man is helped to attain beatitude after the first grace. For God gives men, both just and wicked, enough temporal goods to enable them to attain to everlasting life; and thus these temporal goods are simply good. Hence it is written (Ps. xxxiii. 10): *For there is no want to them that fear Him,* and again, Ps. xxxvi. 25: *I have not seen the just forsaken,* etc.

But if these temporal goods are considered in themselves, they are not man's good simply, but relatively, and thus they do not fall under merit simply, but relatively, inasmuch as men are moved by God to do temporal works, in which with God's help they reach their purpose. And thus as life everlasting is simply the reward of the works of justice in relation to the Divine motion, as stated above (AA. 3, 6), so have temporal goods, considered in themselves, the nature of reward, with respect to the Divine motion, whereby men's wills are moved to undertake these works, even though, sometimes, men have not a right intention in them.

Reply Obj. 1. As Augustine says (*Contra Faust.* iv. 2), *in these temporal promises were figures of spiritual things to come. For the carnal people were adhering to the promises of the present life; and not merely their speech but even their life was prophetic.*

Reply Obj. 2. These rewards are said to have been divinely brought about in relation to the Divine motion, and not in relation to the malice of their wills, especially as regards the King of Babylon, since he did not besiege Tyre as if wishing to serve God, but rather in order to usurp dominion. So, too, although the midwives had a good will with regard to saving the children, yet their will was not right, inasmuch as they framed falsehoods.

Reply Obj. 3. Temporal evils are imposed